WELCOME

Welcome to the seventh edition of the Australian Cricket Digest. There's been a fair bit going on in the last twelve months in Australian cricket, unfortunately headlined by the disappointment of the ball-tampering episode in South Africa. More happily for Australian cricket, there were wins in Ashes series for men's and women's teams amongst many highlights in the season, which I hope are faithfully reported in the following pages.

For starters, I'd like to thank our advertisers throughout the Digest for the financial support. Most notably Gillespie Sports, Morgan's Financial Limited (Peter Chisholm), Kouteris Financial Services (Chris Kouteris), Critchley and Associates (Chris Critchley), ACL Lawyers (Gerard Abood) and NAS Insurance Brokers (Kim Perrin).

I am also most grateful to Ken Piesse for his valuable advertising help and support. He has been working hard in 2018 on more new titles, please go to cricketbooks.com.au to find out about his latest efforts.

Thanks to my friend and cricket historian David Frith for his fine words on the great Stan McCabe. It is now 80 years since the last of McCabe's three great Test innings and I had it in my head that someone needed to pay tribute to such a great name in Australian cricket. David accepted my request for an article (refusing to take any payment) and I hope you enjoy reading about one of our country's Hall of Fame cricketers.

In light of the ball tampering crisis in South Africa, David Jenkins has written a lengthy summary of the events over the period. Thanks to you David for that and also your invaluable proof reading of this year's volume.

Photo-journalist Peter Argent has again come up with a great cover shot for our player of the year and his snaps of events in the Ashes are gratefully received.

Once again, I'd like to thank Greg Lindsay and Murray Hobbs (Digest rookie) at Graphic Print Group for their efforts in the printing of the Digest. They help make the cover look top notch amongst other things and do very well to ensure the whole publishing process goes very smoothly.

Thanks also to Louis Cameron (CA), Richard Boock (New Zealand cricket) and Julian Guyer (Agency France-Presse) for their assistance in gathering attendance figures for Australian matches overseas. Thanks also to all the Media Managers for their help around the country to get all the player profiles in the back of the Digest as correct as possible.

The Digest has increased from 304 pages to 356 this edition. This largely on the back of publishing full WBBL scorecards, which I hope are welcomed by you the reader. We've kept the price at $30 – please spread the word again this year to friends and other cricket fans.

Finally, thanks again to you, the reader for your support. All feedback, good or bad is welcomed at Lawrie.colliver@gmail.com.

Enjoy the read

Lawrie Colliver

Editor Australian Cricket Digest

Australian Cricket Digest 2018-19
CONTENTS
7th Edition

NOTES BY THE EDITOR

Ball-tampering in South Africa – what were they thinking?

It's hard to fathom why members of an Australian cricket team would attempt to change the condition of a cricket ball in the middle of a Test match, with a piece of sandpaper. Sledging and gamesmanship can to be tolerated to a certain level but to actually plan to go out onto the field of play and decide to change the ball with sandpaper is inexcusable.

As I was watching it all unfold on TV, I could scarcely believe what I was seeing and, in due course, cricket fans and former Australians were outraged by what had happened. Steve Smith, David Warner and Cameron Bancroft were all duly suspended and while at times the outrage from the public and media was over the top, it was understandable given the seriousness of what happened.

The administrators acted swiftly, with Iain Roy and James Sutherland doing their best to get to the bottom of what happened very quickly. I support the penalties handed out, and welcome the news that all three players will be giving back to their Grade clubs in the coming season. To find out exactly what happened, experienced author and cricket fan David Jenkins takes up the story in the coming pages, in a piece that covers what happened extensively and offers his own opinion.

The Ashes

Australia were tested at times in the 2017-18 Ashes, by an England side that wasn't as strong as some of the squads they've sent out in recent times. They lacked a genuine pace bowler and their lead spinner could hardly take a wicket. Their batting line up relied heavily on skipper Joe Root, who passed fifty five times but couldn't reach three figures. But there were times in the series, where England had their moments. They were ahead or on level terms for much of the Gabba Test, had a chance in Adelaide leading into the last day, started well in Perth and were the better side in the drawn Melbourne Test. Despite the 4-nil margin, Australia had to fight hard and the cricket played was well worth watching.

Well done to Darren Lehmann

The popular Australian coach decided to quit on the back of the ball tampering events in South Africa. After initially deciding to continue, he saw after a few days that it was perhaps best to finish up. He has plenty to be proud of, top of the list the 2015 ICC Cricket World Cup plus Ashes wins in 2013-14 and last summer. The ball-tampering in South Africa would no doubt top the list of disappointments, even though he was absolved of all blame by the Cricket Australia Integrity Unit.

Darren has been a valuable contributor and friend to the Digest over the years and I'd like to thank him for his support of the publication.

A lot of challenges for new Australian coach Justin Langer

After the sensational happenings in South Africa, Justin Langer took over as coach sooner than he probably expected. He was immediately thrown in the deep end, watching on as Australia was thrashed in England in an ODI series, also losing the one-off Twenty20 game.

Looking ahead, the Australian coach and the team has some big challenges in the next twelve months. The first, to have a successful home summer, as the batting depth will be severely tested with Steve Smith and David Warner both out suspended. The second, to improve the team's ODI form, as Australia's last two years have been poor, winning just six of their last 23 games, including just one in ten in 2018. The last one, and possibly most important, retain the Ashes in England next year. With Australia not having won a series in England since 2001, this could be the hardest of those objectives to fulfil.

Cancelling on Bangladesh – what's more important profit or playing other nations?

So Cricket Australia cancel a home series against Bangladesh, which seems quite odd when they've just signed a record TV rights deal worth over $1 billion. To not play the scheduled series pretty much because it wouldn't make a profit is terrible. Which of the Domestic competitions in Australia make a profit? The JLT Cup? The Sheffield Shield? The WNCL? I doubt if any of them do, in fact I'm almost certain none of them do. But we need them to produce players for the next level. Likewise if we don't support Bangladesh and other less strong nations, one day we'll have no one that we can play against. Sadly our administrators appear to feel profit above all is the most important thing these days.

As Zimbabwe all-rounder Sikander Raza said in the August edition of *Wisden Cricket Magazine,* "Does every series have to make money? Some people might see it as bad business if you can't make a profit on a series, but why can't we run cricket not as a business but as a sport in itself so that it doesn't lose its identity".

Cricket Australia – how well are they running the game?

Good question. As the *The Australian* chief cricket writer Peter Lalor pointed out back in August, it hadn't been a good 18 months for the administrators. The contract dispute dragged on and was a disaster, straining relations from the players down to the fans. It wasn't until the CEO became involved that the dispute even looked like being settled. The ball-tampering in South Africa eroded the trust and goodwill between the Test team and the fans. In my years of following cricket, I've never seen so much outrage from fans. Sponsors jumped off the CA ship very quickly.

Then we have the latest issue where a former CA employee alleges that she was sacked for tweeting about an issue that was of a very personal nature to her. At the time of writing this is under investigation by the Fair Work Commission.

The Chairman has been renewed for three years in his position and another senior member of the administration has had a promotion. From the points raised I'll let you draw your own conclusions.

Australian Cricket Digest 2018-19

The Big Bash League – adding two more weeks, too long or taking the game to the people?

The BBL will expand once again, going from 43 games last summer to 59 in 2018-19. It will effectively run two weeks longer, which means each team will play each other twice, making it a fair draw. It also means that more regional matches will be in the fixture, taking the game to non-city venues around the country. Geelong and Alice Springs hosted matches last season, this year the Gold Coast is locked in for a game and most likely Moe in country Victoria will get to host a match. These are positives – taking the game to the people.

But it also means the Sheffield Shield competition will be put on hold for an extra fortnight this season, meaning there is no interstate four-day cricket between December 11 and February 22 – a break of 73 days. Hardly an ideal situation if you want to try and push for the Test side ahead of the two-Test series against Sri Lanka in late January-early February. Is the BBL going to go too long, will people still flock through the gates? Will the players be keen for such a long tournament? We've already seen a major drawcard in Mitchell Johnson head from Perth to another Twenty20 tournament. Will overseas players be so keen to come out and be part of the tournament, given it lasts an extra two weeks?

Back in January, Dwayne Bravo and Kevin Pietersen have been others to mention that overseas players won't want to commit for so long with any team, the commitment to stay in Australia for an extended period being too great.

The Toss – she was get rid of it?

The more I think about this idea, the more I like it. With more and more Test pitches being prepared to suit the home team, getting rid of the toss might be a way to stop it. Former Australian captains Steve Waugh and Ricky Ponting have said they are open to it. Former Australian coach Darren Lehmann supports it and former West Indies fast-bowler Michael Holding likes the idea and has said it would force home sides to prepare competitive surfaces.

ICC briefing notes from May this year, published on the *ESPN Cricinfo* website say "There is serious concern about the current level of home team interference in Test pitch preparation, and more than one committee member believes that the toss should be automatically awarded to the visiting team in each match, although there are some others on the committee who do not share that view".

As yet, no decision has been. Another decision that has been placed in the "too hard" basket. The MCC World Committee Media notes published in this Digest make no mention of it and the ICC have left it for the time being.

Congrats to the winners in 2017-18, Western Australia, the Adelaide Strikers and Queensland.

All three winners of the domestic titles in the past season were worthy winners. The WA Warriors were the best side in the JLT Cup and went on to win the final against South Australia in Hobart comfortably. Encouragingly they appear to be back producing a quality stable of pace bowlers once more.

In the Big Bash League, the Adelaide Strikers were superbly lead by Travis Head, had a team of solid contributors with Rashid Khan from Afghanistan one of the most exciting players of the competition.

Queensland secured the Sheffield Shield, with Jimmy Peirson doing a splendid job as captain, a rare occurrence for a skipper/keeper. The Bulls are also producing some fine young players who appear capable of higher honours in the years to come.

Another massive year for Women's cricket?

The 2017-18 summer saw more progress being made in women's cricket. With extra pay in their pockets, the standard of the WBBL continued to improve and there was great interest in the Ashes series which was played before the men did battle with England. It was wonderful to see so many people at the Ashes Test at North Sydney Oval, while the TV numbers for WBBL continued to be strong.

With the new TV rights deal, the Seven Network are going to up the amount of matches shown from last summer, starting on AFL Grand Final day, when they will throw straight from the MCG to North Sydney, for the first match of the Women's Twenty20 series with New Zealand.

TV rights – a new ball game in itself

The change in TV rights from the Nine Network/Network Ten combination to Fox Sports/Seven Network is the biggest change in Broadcast rights since 1979-80. Sadly the loser from what happened was the Ten Network, who had done a splendid job of presenting the Big Bash League for five seasons.

In my role as Chief stats man for Fox Sports, I can promise we'll provide the best coverage possible, starting with the JLT Cup on September 18, right through to the Sheffield Shield Final that concludes in early April. Knowing Seven Cricket boss David Barham as I do, I am certain the Seven network will do a brilliant job as well, as they cover the Tests, Women's Internationals and BBL/WBBL.

With strong stables of commentary teams on both broadcast crews, fans have never had it so good. One must also congratulate the Nine Network on their wonderful work since 1977-78 and the Ten Network for their efforts in the past five seasons.

Can Australia win the 2019 Ashes?

Yes they can. But the Australian batsmen will need to be able to play the swinging ball. With James Anderson and Stuart Broad still going strong at the time of writing, making runs against quality swing bowling will be the key to Australia's success. Australia seems to have the strength in bowling, it's the batting that's the concern.

LAWYERS

Agency ▪ Credit Management ▪ Litigation

Making the right decisions on .....
.... and off the field

GERARD ABOOD
National Panel Umpire
Principal Solicitor at ACL Lawyers

We'll help you make the right decisions for the protection and recovery of your debts.

At ACL Lawyers, our focus is on Debt Recovery & Credit Management
Let us help you;

- Manage your debtors and debt recovery work;

- Improve your cash flow;

- Protect your future debts by reviewing & refining your

  Terms and Conditions of Trade;

We provide a professional and reliable service to ensure your debt recovery process is as smooth and efficient as possible…. every time.

☎ 02 8677 9934   ✉ gabood@acllaw.com.au
📱 0414 952 680   🌐 www.acllaw.com.au

Australian Cricket Digest 2018-19
PLAYER OF THE YEAR – PAT CUMMINS

If there was one cricketer that Australian fans could be completely proud of in the 2017-18 season, it was Pat Cummins. His performances alone speak for themselves, as he took 45 wickets in nine Tests across the period, was leading wicket taker for Australia (23) in the five Ashes Tests and the four-Test series (22) in South Africa.

He made crucial lower-order runs in the First (Brisbane) and second (Adelaide) Ashes Tests, batting at number nine, eventually averaging 41 in the series. After his 41 in the Perth Test, he was put up to number eight in the order for the South African series where he made his maiden Test fifty in the fourth Johannesburg Test, a match where Australia had three players suspended due to the ball tampering that occurred in the previous Test.

Having made a spectacular Test debut as a 18 year-old in the Johannesburg Test of 2011-12, where he took 6-79 in the second innings and hit the winning runs, hopes were high that Australia had found its newest fast bowling superstar. Sadly injuries were to take their toll on Cummins, and it was not until he was a key part of Australia's winning ICC World Cup team of 2015, that anyone was convinced he could continue a career that had started so promisingly. He toured with the 2015 Ashes team, only playing the tour games, before being unleashed on England in the ODI series, where he took 12 wickets in the five matches, Australia winning the series 3-2.

Injuries again kept him out of action during 2015-16, but in 2016-17 Cummins made a return to New South Wales in the 50-over competition, taking 15 wickets in six games, with the Blues beating Queensland in the final. Cummins base of fitness was steadily being built, as he was picked for two four-day second XI games for New South Wales. He was then picked for Australia in a three-match ODI series against New Zealand in December 2016, where he took eight wickets, including a best of 4-41 at Manuka Oval in Canberra. Now back fit and firing as a regular member of the ODI and T20 teams for Australia, could he return to the longer forms for his country? In March 2017, he was picked for New South Wales to play against South Australia in a Sheffield Shield match, and took four wickets in each innings, impressing all and sundry with his pace and accuracy.

With Australia locked at one-all in an engrossing Test series in India, it was discovered that Mitchell Starc had succumbed to a stress fracture in his right foot at the conclusion to the loss in the second Test. So came the crunch time for the selectors, who to pick as his replacement? On the back of a base of bowling fitness that had been slowly and steadily built, the selectors opted to go with Cummins, flying him over to India in time for the all-important third Test. Some in the media expressed concern that Cummins hadn't done enough to be picked and that it was major risk to him injury wise if he was sent over there.

The critics were proved wrong as Cummins was superb on a flat pitch in Ranchi, where he bowled wholeheartedly to take 4-106 (39 overs) in the drawn third Test where just 25 wickets fell in the match for 1258 runs, only nine of them to pace bowlers. He took four wickets in the last Test at Dharamsala, where Australia's batsmen failed to fire in both innings and were beaten to lose the series 2-1.

With James Pattinson unfit for the Ashes, it was going to be vital to Australia's chances that Cummins would be fit and able to take his place against England, to compliment the Starc/Hazlewood opening combination. His first day of Ashes cricket was a good one, with England going well at 1-127, he bowled Stoneman from around the wicket and then late in the day trapped Joe Root leg before with an in-ducker, the England skipper possibly done for pace and he fell across his crease. On the second morning he forced Jonny Bairstow to miscue a pull shot, which gave him 3-85 from 30 overs.

Coming into bat at number nine just before lunch on the third day, Australia were 7-209, still 93 behind England's first innings total of 302. With Steve Smith rock solid on 80, albeit batting slowly, Cummins dug in with his skipper providing a vital 41 runs in a 66 run union for the eighth wicket. With the last two wickets adding a further 53, Australia took the lead by 26, which was as much a psychological advantage for the Australia team as it was in terms of actual scoreboard value. Australia went on to win by ten wickets, the team having much to thank Cummins for in his debut Ashes Test.

Cummins carried his excellent work with that bat down to Adelaide, coming in at 7-311 just after tea on the second day, with Shaun Marsh well established on 52. Cummins copped an early barrage of three consecutive bouncers from Stuart Broad but defended his heart out, being scoreless for his 36 balls and 39 minutes as he hung tough with Marsh. The shackles broke with a boundary off Overton to get him off the mark as he showed he could play shots, supporting Shaun Marsh until he reached his ton just before the dinner break. He also saw Australia past 400, an important landmark and ensured England would not get to start their first innings until the floodlights were on. To his first ball after the dinner break, he uppercut Overton straight down third man's throat, but in helping Shaun Marsh add 99, he had again risen to the occasion in his lesser preferred role in the team.

With the ball, he only took three wickets in the match, but they were all key batsmen, as he further enhanced his reputation in the team. In the first innings he had Root edging a drive to third slip and had Malan caught behind off an inside edge. With England 3-169 late on the fourth night, needing a further 185 to win, he knocked over Malan's stumps with a ripping delivery to put the game back in favour of Australia. When Hazlewood dismissed Woakes and Root early on day five, victory was assured for the home side, thanks in no small part to Cummins getting Malan out late the evening before.

In the third Test at the WACA, Cummins dismissed Root for third time in a row in the first innings of a Test, caught gloving one down the leg-side. It was one of four wickets in the Test, his last was Chris Woakes in the second innings, which ended the match and allowed Australia to regain the Ashes.

In the Melbourne Test, Cummins was ill with a stomach bug and spent quite a good deal of time off the field. When he was on, he dismissed Root once again, as he hooked a bouncer straight down the throat of Nathan Lyon at deep square-leg. Sufficiently recovered on the fourth day, he picked up three lower order wickets, the start of his late surge to the top of the wicket-taking tally for the Ashes. Statistically, Cummins saved his best effort until the last Test in Sydney, where he took eight wickets in his home Test and won the Man of the match award. Hauls of 4-80 and 4-39 were the icing on the cake on what was a brilliant first full Test series for him, and put him at the peak of his power as the Test series in South Africa beckoned.

Above: Pat Cummins in full flight during the Adelaide Test – photo Peter Argent (copyright)

In the one-day international series, England were three nil up after three games – Australia facing a whitewash on home soil. In Adelaide for the traditional Australia day clash, this was averted as Cummins and Hazlewood helped reduce England to 5-8 in the opening overs. Alex Hales had his stumps rattled to be his first victim and again he dismissed Root in the summer, as he top-edged a hook to long-leg. Final figures of 4-24 from ten overs saw him given the Man of the Match award.

In South Africa, he was a slow starter in the series, taking just two wickets in the opening Test at Durban, which Australia won. Cummins took 3-79 and 1-13 in the six wicket defeat at Port Elizabeth and then hit his straps in Cape Town, taking 4-78 as he created a middle collapse as South Africa slipped in their first innings from 2-220 to 6-242. Three wickets followed in the second innings which was marred by the ball-tampering episode on the third day.

With Australia under siege in Johannesburg, Cummins was one of the few to fly the flag in a massive 492 run defeat in the last Test. He took 5-83 in the first innings and then made 50 with the bat, helping Australia avoid complete embarrassment in their first innings. In the second dig with the ball, he was the only paceman able to take a wicket, finishing with 4-58, a match haul of 9-141. With 22 wickets in the series and not one of the batsmen able to making a ton with the bat, he was comfortably Australia's top contributor over the four Test matches.

Shortly after the fourth Test, it was announced that Cummins would be unavailable to play in the Indian Premier League, due to the fact he had developed hot spots in his back. He wasn't fit for the ODI/T20 series in England and one hopes he will fit to go for the 2018-19 season, which will be rather more important, now that leading batsman Steve Smith and David Warner are serving bans from the goings on in South Africa.

Over the past twelve months Cummins has shown what a great asset he can be in the longest and best form of the game. With his unfit for the upcoming Pakistan series in the UAS, fingers are tightly crossed he can regain his fitness to help Australia get through the next year, which is going to be a tough one in many respects.

SOME NUMBERS ABOUT PAT CUMMINS IN 2017-18

Cummins 17-18	Tests	Wkts	Avge	Best Figs	Aust Pace 17-18	Tests	Balls	Wkts	Avge
Ashes	5	23	24.65	4-39	Pat Cummins	9	2117	45	23.09
South Africa	4	22	21.45	5-83	Mitchell Starc	7	1631	34	27.38
Total	**9**	**45**	**23.08**	**5-83**	Josh Hazlewood	9	2105	33	30.76

BALL TAMPERING IN SOUTH AFRICA – A REVIEW OF THE SOUTH AFRICA TOUR
WHEN WINNING IS NOT THE ONLY THING
by David Jenkins

It is said that a week is a long time in football. In cricket it can feel like a lifetime. When the Australian cricket team arrived in South Africa in February 2018 they came on the back of demolishing England four-nil during the Australian summer. Suffice to say they were confident and, perhaps, a little cocky. Nathan Lyon had been talking of 'ending careers' when England toured last summer. Quite why a professional cricketer would be thinking and talking in those terms about fellow professionals is best left to Lyon to explain. Perhaps the 'GOAT' tag was true after all.

The Australians have, over recent decades, looked upon each and every Test series as if it's war without guns. Anything and everything has been accepted as a legitimate tactic to upset the opposition and break their concentration. Steve Waugh justified the behaviour with the phrase, 'mental disintegration', which was hyperbole at best and unsportsmanlike bullying at worst. The end, apparently, justified the means.

Australia managed to take it to new levels during the First Test at Durban and a shocked South Africa crumbled under the relentless pressure. They were simply unprepared for this Australian team at this particular time - but they learned very quickly and they scored some points before the match was finished.

Australia got away to a steady start with most of the top order contributing and the end result was an opening score of 351. When Mitchell Starc blew away the back half of South Africa's batting for a final total of 162 the game was over, or so we thought. The visitors got a reasonable start to their second innings then struggled to make headway and the final total of 227 was sufficient only because of the massive first innings lead. South Africa's run chase, an unlikely 417 to win, set the tone for the rest of the series.

While newcomer, Aiden Markram (143), held one end the other end became a revolving door for South Africa's batsmen. Four of them fell for single figures with the best of them, A. B. de Villiers, run out for nought as Markram called him through then sent him back. A fielding highlight rapidly degenerated into an embarrassing lowlight. The fieldsman, David Warner, promptly and loudly sprayed Markram for running out the team's best batsman. It seemed to go on forever as Australian fieldsmen milled around smiling and laughing completely unaware of how terrible it looked to a world-wide television audience. Bowler Nathan Lyon, who removed the bails to facilitate the dismissal, then added his particular brand of brainless behaviour to the mix by deliberately dropping the ball next to the batsman as he lay sprawled on the ground.

Things then went from bad to worse when Quinton de Kock arrived at the crease to finally offer some real resistance, with Markram, to the Australian bowling. He was sledged continually by Warner in the 'Australian way' and, at the tea break, decided enough was enough. A pointed reference to Warner's wife in the hidden safety of the grandstand stairwell inflamed the Australian who then took on the role of 'victim', much to the amusement of the South Africans.

If the Australians had intended 'bad feeling' as part of the game plan they could not have succeeded more. A final victory by 118 runs gave the impression the juggernaut had triumphed once more but the seeds had been sown and South Africa, their hackles raised, were now better prepared.

What happened next is the stuff of South African legend and Australian nightmares. First it got bad, and then it got worse. At Port Elizabeth's St. George's Park, a few days after Durban, the Australian batsmen struggled to 243. The home team's batsmen repeated the struggle until a majestic A. B. de Villiers took the game away from Australia with a magnificent 126 not out while the tail, this time, added important runs. A lead of 139 put pressure back on the visitors and further pressure was applied when the South Africans queried David Warner's use of tape on his hands. The words, 'ball tampering', were heard but...surely not!

Events had earlier been inflamed when Kagiso Rabada, after dismissing Steve Smith, gave him a spirited send-off while also deliberately making shoulder contact with the Australian skipper as he left the wicket. Smith was surprised, the officials were annoyed and the result was a guilty verdict carrying a ban for the rest of the series - given Rabada's already elevated number of demerit points from previous misdemeanours. It was the first obvious sign of South Africa deciding to fight fire with fire.

Rabada had dominated the Australian batting with five first innings wickets and he went one better in the second innings for almost half the number of runs. A series ban, in those circumstances, was a significant penalty given South Africa won the Second Test by six wickets. The questions about Warner's tape, the send-offs and the 'collision' had all combined to create further ill-feeling among the teams and unease among the officials and the fans.

The pressure now on Australia, and the feeling between the teams, was not helped between Tests when South Africa successfully appealed Kagiso Rabada's ban. The locals were cock-a-hoop while the visitors, and the rest of the world, were wondering how on earth the decision could have been reversed - given the clear evidence and Rabada's previous record which carried suspended points.

Steve Smith was furious and the Australians were getting the impression the world, and particularly South Africa, was against them. It appeared to many observers the Rabada reversal had been intended to appease the politics of the home market but only Steve Smith knows if this decision and his subsequent anger influenced what happened next.

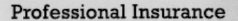

Whatever momentum Australian had gained after Durban, and their home series victory against England, had been seriously dented at Port Elizabeth. When the teams walked onto Newlands in Cape Town for the Third Test the expectations of both teams had changed. South Africa made 311 in their first innings which was not particularly intimidating but Australia could only reach 255 in reply. South Africa then set about grinding down Australia and setting a reasonable target for their bowlers.

The match seemed to be moving along normally until the second session of the third day when the television coverage showed Cameron Bancroft in possession of something which appeared to be surplus to requirement. Unbeknownst to the Australians the television broadcaster, SuperSport, had seven cameras which follow the ball at all times. Head of Production, Alvin Naicker, explained as soon as Bancroft was seen with the foreign object, the footage was shown and cameras immediately trained on the Australian coaching staff for their reaction.

The initial response appeared damning. Coach Darren Lehmann was immediately on the walkie-talkie to non-playing Peter Handscomb, who promptly entered the field of play and approached Bancroft. Words were exchanged, smiles made for the cameras, and Handscomb left the ground. Bancroft knew he'd been sprung because the footage was shown on the ground's 'big screen' and Handscomb's appearance had confirmed that everybody had seen it.

Bancroft was then shown removing the 'object' from his pocket and slipping it down the front of his trousers. The umpires, Nigel Llong and Richard Illingworth, had not seen this but on the evidence of the footage shown at the ground they asked him to empty his pockets. However, all he had there was a cloth sunglasses case. With no further evidence, and no discernable damage to the ball, play resumed with the same ball and no five run penalty against the Australians.

The problem was everybody else had now seen the footage of Bancroft stuffing the 'object' down his trousers and thought, "Why do that if there's nothing to hide?" No doubt there were some heavy discussions at the tea break as to what had actually taken place. The final session was played out in an atmosphere reminiscent of the condemned man knowing his time was running out.

What happened after play both condemned the Australians and highlighted the immense pressure they were now under in this series. An ill-conceived press conference was held by the skipper, Steve Smith, and the man at the centre of the controversy, Cameron Bancroft. The best thing which could be said about the 'presser' was it looked rushed and unprepared.

Smith let Bancroft explain what he was doing but the young Western Australian lied, telling the media and the television audience it was only sticky tape with dirt stuck to it to provide the mechanism to rough up the ball. Smith then compounded the problem by telling everyone the ball-tampering had been discussed at lunch by the team's leadership group and Bancroft had agreed to implement that plan.

This admission by Smith promptly threw the bowlers who would benefit most by Bancroft's action, Starc, Cummins and Hazlewood, under the bus without the immediate mechanism to protest. Smith admitted he knew of and endorsed the plan and added he was 'not proud of it'. This put the skipper on the end of a very long line of Aussies who shared that sentiment but most of them were in the crowd or watching television at home. Smith later added he would continue to be Australia's captain and this event would not change anything. It showed a breathtaking lack of awareness.

It was clear that neither player, nor indeed the team management, had any real understanding of how this event was being viewed by the wider Australian community. The Australian team, or senior members of it, had previously been very quick to lecture the cricket world on ethics and the traditions of the game. The Aussies and the high moral ground had always been close companions when other team's indiscretions were being discussed so it didn't take long for the rest of the world to find considerable humour in the team's hypocrisy and discomfort.

At the end of the conference, there were several viewers, including this author, who wondered what prompted the responsible CA official 'on the ground' to advise the players to say what they said so soon after the event. The lack of a 'game plan' was clearly evident, especially since the bowlers were now heavily implicated while the vision of the coach talking to Handscomb looked suspicious. The phrase, 'rabbit in the headlights' came to mind. Surely it would have been better to simply say, 'CA will be investigating and we will keep you informed when we have the appropriate information'. If the intention was to minimise the damage, and presumably it was, the press conference failed dismally

The immediate upshot was that Bancroft was fined seventy-five percent of his match fee but was free to play the Fourth Test. Steve Smith, as captain and seen as most responsible, was fined one hundred percent of his fee and banned for one game which meant Tim Paine would lead the team in the final Test.

Executive General Manager Team Performance, Pat Howard, CA Senior Legal Counsel and Head of Integrity, Iain Roy and CA CEO James Sutherland, who rushed to Cape Town in the wake of the scandal, conducted the official CA investigation. Previously, the ICC had treated ball-tampering with a virtual slap on the wrist. Indeed, the South African captain, Faf Du Plessis had twice been found guilty of ball-tampering and barely noticed the punishment. ICC's decision in the Smith/Bancroft case confirmed their relatively soft attitude to the offence.

Above: Some of the reaction in Australian newspapers to what happened in South Africa

However, CA was determined to make a statement and the final decision of the panel caught many by surprise, although it was expected to be a more severe penalty than that given by the ICC. The results of the investigation clearly defined where CA thought the responsibility lay.

Vice-captain David Warner, previously not specifically mentioned, was considered to be the mastermind behind the plan and guilty of showing Bancroft what to do and how to do it. In the cold light of day, the offending tape turned out to be a piece of sandpaper. Warner was banned by CA for twelve months and informed he would never again hold a leadership position within the team.

Captain, Steve Smith, was seen as negligent and guilty of bringing the game into disrepute. He knew of the plan, failed to prevent it and was misleading in his comments regarding what happened and who was involved. Smith, too, was banned for twelve months and told any further leadership role would not happen for at least twelve months after the ban was lifted and this would be conditional on several external requisites.

The perpetrator, Cameron Bancroft, was banned for nine months and was seen simply as a young, inexperienced player acting under the influence of senior team members but guilty of attempting to carry out the plan, concealing evidence and making misleading comments to match officials and the public regarding the sandpaper. All three players were immediately sent home from the tour.

Coach Lehmann, and the bowlers implicated by Smith during the press conference, were all found to be innocent bystanders with no case to answer. However, the affair highlighted a team culture which had become toxic in its attitude to the game, the opposition and in its obligation to the Australian cricketing public. The team lived in a bubble of CA's making, highly paid with an inflated sense of entitlement, they looked and behaved like a group who thought they could do as they wished and everybody else had to accept it. It was 'the Australian way'.

The team continually spoke of a 'line in the sand' which they never crossed but it was they who decided where the line was drawn. Quinton de Kock may still be wondering about that line and thinking the Australian team gave themselves a fair margin for error.

Over many years, banter had become abuse and was accepted as not only normal but the only real way to play the game. It was macho rubbish of the first order but it was allowed and encouraged by Lehmann and the team's hierarchy. Only a year or so earlier, Matthew Wade replaced Peter Nevill as wicketkeeper to become the first cricketer to be picked for Australia primarily because of his ability to 'chat'. It said much about what the Australian team hierarchy thought was important.

The Fourth Test was played in a subdued atmosphere with new captain Tim Paine seeking to mend fences with the South Africans in terms of player behaviour. It was a nice gesture but the energy was gone. Chadd Sayers came in for his debut, and perhaps to lift the team's spirit, but South Africa won on the bit by 492 runs as the Aussies just wanted to go home.

The tone was set the day before the match when Darren Lehmann resigned as coach, a move designed to give CA and the new regime clear air. Whether he was guilty of prior knowledge or not, his resignation was the only sensible option as he had helped foster the culture. Given the freedom allowed by CA for the team to behave in the manner it did, it was slightly surprising nobody from the CA administration felt the need to follow Lehmann's example. I guess in corporate life a fall guy can always be found and CA is nothing these days if not corporate.

It took the public response, including that of the media, to give CA an idea of how serious the country viewed this particular indiscretion. If they needed reminding, one of the ruling body's main sponsor's, Magellan Financial Group, got CA's attention by terminating its three year $20 million deal. Perhaps this helped explain the severity of the penalties to the players. It was estimated Smith and Warner lost financial opportunities, including their CA contracts, to the tune of $3-5 million each. It has been a massive price to pay for something for which other players got fined all or part of their match payment and/or the odd match suspension. Finally, perhaps, that famous 'line in the sand' has become slightly more visible.

David Jenkins had recently authored books on Brian Taber and Eric Freeman and is the Glenelg DCC first grade team manager for away matches in the SACA Grade Competition.

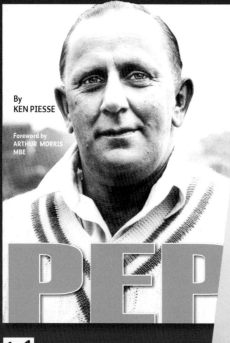

STRIKERS COACH JASON GILLESPIE ON WINNING THE BIG BASH LEAGUE IN 2017-18

What made the Strikers recruit Peter Siddle, with so little Twenty20 cricket behind him?

If you looked at his raw numbers in T20, he'd only played a dozen or so games and being over 30 years of age, people would say, 'why are you doing it?' We felt that Peter was open to learning, looking to try new things, we thought he'd be a ripping bloke to have around our team, especially our young bowlers. With Winter, Grant and Agar and the like, to have a senior bowler around those guys, we thought that give would them a boost, we felt his skills were transferable and that he could adapt his game and have some success in T20. We were delighted that he agreed to join us and he worked hard on a couple of different slower balls, getting his yorker right, put a lot of time and effort into practice and he spent a lot of time with our bowlers. He was brilliant around the team, it was a successful bit of recruiting.

What about Colin Ingram, what was it about him that made you want to get him?

I did my research and was looking for someone who could make an impact. Because we had a lot of young batsmen, we wanted an experienced head and someone who might captain when Travis Head was away. Colin fitted the bill almost perfectly. I was coaching a bit with Kent back in 2017 and we were playing a 50-over game against Glamorgan, Colin was playing and was someone I wanted to watch up close and have a conversation with. He went out and belted 114 off 98 balls. I spoke to a lot of people about him, a few at Glamorgan and South African cricket and they spoke very highly of Colin as a person and there was no question about his skills. The numbers he was producing in Twenty20 cricket were pretty special. It was just a combination of all those things, his batting, leadership qualities, type of bloke and we knew he'd fit in well to our dressing room environment.

What makes Rashid Khan such a special cricketer in Twenty20 Cricket?

He bowls quite quickly and it's difficult to pick his variations. His pace makes it very hard for batsman to get down the wicket to him. He has got a very fast arm action, so he's hard to pick up. Because he is so accurate, he keeps the stumps in play all the time. That's what also makes him very dangerous.

The Strikers weren't the most aggressive team in the Powerplay, was it a deliberate thing, or was it just how things panned out that you didn't lose that many wickets early on?

We encouraged our top order to play the ball as you see it. Be adaptable, and if you felt you could take a calculated risk and take down a bowler, felt it was in your zone, then trust your judgement. Our big thing was, play the ball, play the conditions, adapt and if it meant that that we didn't get off to a flyer then so be it. We talked a lot about communication, if someone ran out a drink or gloves, they would feed back about how the bowling was, the surface was playing and conditions, and we'd adapt that way. There was no set pattern, that we had to have wickets in hand, or score 60 in the Powerplay. We had targets in what we wanted to achieve in the first phase, to get a certain number of runs. In our post-match discussions it was about starting a conversation, did we miss out on some opportunities, could we have scored more runs? Sometimes if we were short of our target, we felt that the pitch might be stopping in the surface and that it wasn't worth the gamble to take a bowler on. It was about trusting the guys out there to know what to do.

Jake Weatherald struggled for runs early on, with just 87 from his first seven digs, what made you keep faith in him?

We knew Jake could do the opening role, we just needed to give him some games to play. We wanted to give him the opportunity to learn from failure. I was very much pick and stick, we'd identified him as a player who could really have some success at the top of the order in Big Bash. We just had to show faith in him and stick with him. It worked with Jake, but another time it may not, I'm not one who likes to chop and change, I like stability, and I think it was great that Jake could play those innings in the back end of the tournament. He made a massive contribution to us winning the title.

With the team qualified for the Semi, there was criticism of changing the batting order in the match you lost against the Scorchers at the WACA. Explain why Jono Dean opened instead of regular opener Alex Carey, who was in the XI?

It was very simple, with the semi-final coming up, we just felt that with Alex Carey unavailable for that match as he would be playing for Australia, we wanted Jono Dean to a least have a game opening the batting beforehand. I understand why we copped it a bit, that you want to keep winning, we felt that it was more important to support Jono and give him the best opportunity to be successful to get a match in. If Jono had come in at six or seven, maybe not batted or only faced a few balls and was then thrown into a semi-final, it would have been a big ask for him. Alex batted down the order and completely understood where we were coming from and what we looking to do from a team point of view. Sure he would have loved to have opened in that game, but being such a good team man he understood the bigger picture. Yes we lost the game, but that one decision didn't cost us the game, we had the trust and belief as a collective group and it was the right decision and it would pay us back, come the semi-final.

What about the future of Alex Carey, he seems well on his way, now he's played a bit for Australia?

I think the world is his oyster, he's a very adaptable and flexible player. He's learning all the time, he is a very respectful young man, has being working incredibly hard and deserves the success that has been coming his way. He understands there is a lot of work to do, he's adding shots to his game off the slow bowlers, how to rotate the strike. He works very hard at that, moving forward I don't expect we'll see him for the full Big Bash. It's exciting times for him and Australian cricket, I am quite optimistic about Australian cricket at the moment, a lot of people are being quite negative about it, but I love seeing young players get opportunities to play in Australian colours.

How were you during the semi against the Renegades, it got pretty tight, did you always have faith you'd win?

Yes it got a bit tight! Young Harry Nielsen did well at the end behind the stumps when Pollard had a big swipe and missed, Ben Laughlin had bowled in those situations before and had a bit of success, it's no surprise he gets his skills right because he practices it. I think that is all you ask as a coach, for the players to put their time and effort working on their skills for those moments. It was close all night, we had good overs and bad overs it was about focussing on the right thing at the right time. As a coach you have to just put faith in the players.

Finally a word on Travis Head, what were the key two or three things that have made him such a terrific skipper?

Some of his great attributes include leading from the front, he likes to get in the contest. What he is very good at is listening to feedback, he listens, ask questions of the coaches, wanting to know how he can improve as a leader. Thing I've noticed is when he talks to the players, be it team meetings or in the team huddle, he knows the message he wants to get across to the team. I've seen a real maturity over the last few years with Trav. The plan three years ago when I arrived at the Strikers was come the third year that Travis would take over the captaincy, he took it over and did very well. For me, he's got a real thirst for getting better and that's a really good attribute that he's got.

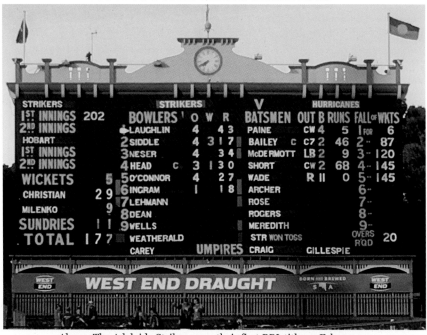

Above: The Adelaide Strikers won their first BBL title on February 4
Below: England amass 6-481 at Trent Bridge in the 3rd ODI against Australia on June 19

Stan McCabe by David Frith

Stan McCabe on the Australian team bus in 1938, McCormick is behind him (Photo: David Frith collection)

Many of today's cricket followers might never have heard of Stan McCabe. He and quite a few other Australian batsmen would be far better known had there never been a Don Bradman (Heaven forbid). Despite the mountains of hectic runs made by the moderns, The Don remains Number One, famous for many innings: the unbeaten 452, the 334, the 304, and even - in dire contrast - for those ducks at Melbourne during the 1932-33 Bodyline series and in his final Test innings at The Oval in 1948. You've got to be pretty good if your scoreless innings are also part of folklore.

But Stan McCabe was famous for *three* Test innings, all of them masterpieces of brave, breathtaking strokeplay. Most renowned was his 187 not out at the SCG against the bounce and shock of Larwood and Voce in the opening Bodyline Test of 1932-33. Sitting in the press-box half-a-century later, I asked Bill O'Reilly where his bosom pal's shots went. "Tiger" stabbed his finger towards the pickets from long leg up to midwicket: "There. And there! And THERE!" he roared. He idolised his late mate.

O'Reilly also revelled in the memory of Stan's other two legendary Test knocks: at the old Johannesburg ground in 1935-36, when McCabe's battering of the South African bowling was so ferocious that the fielding skipper Herby Wade, fearing for his men's safety as a big dark storm dragged towards them, pleaded with the umpires to call it off. Then came the 232 at Trent Bridge in 1938, when Australia were in deep trouble, with hopeless No.11 Fleetwood-Smith at the crease. McCabe masterminded a stand of 77, of which 72 were cracked off his flashing blade against high-class bowling. It was a T20 display many decades before the exhilarating Big Bash was born.

Some batsmen seal their place in history with one great knock. Stanley Joseph McCabe did so with those *three* innings. So why has his name faded?

Perhaps it's because there's little or no room for thoughts about the greats of yesteryear midst today's tumultuous international schedules. Might even Dave Warner's derring-do deeds have faded away 20 years hence, not so much for his Cape Town sandpaper misdemeanours as from the sheer volume of international cricket now staged?

Like Don Bradman, Stan McCabe was a bush product. Born in Grenfell, NSW on July 16, 1910, he was educated at St Joseph's College, Sydney. Soon he was playing grade for Mosman. His NSW debut came in 1928-29. By 1930 he was ready to tour with Australia, one of the exciting young bloods (beside Bradman and the ill-fated Archie Jackson). On their way to England they visited Paris, and when McCabe emerged from a doorway at the Palace of Versailles, one of the players wisecracked that he looked just like Napoleon. So "Napper" he became.

Although he played in all five Tests on that first tour, he averaged only 35. Indeed, he couldn't squeeze a century out of the entire tour (1012 runs at 32; top 96 against Cambridge University). It wasn't until the opening Test of the Bodyline series two years later that he made a Test hundred. And it was absolutely memorable, even if no more than a handful of film clips survive. That brave unbeaten 187 remains very high on the honour roll of greatest innings ever played. "Make sure Mum doesn't run onto the field if I get hit," Stan murmured to his father as he put his baggy green on his balding head, picked up his lightweight bat, and went to battle.

And McCabe secured a sweet little bonus in that match. He dismissed the hated England captain D.R.Jardine with one of his under-estimated medium-pacers.

In England in 1934 he averaged 60.37 in the Tests, with a century at Old Trafford; at Lord's he (192) and Bill Ponsford had a delicious stand of 389 against MCC. In South Africa a year later came his famous "thunderstorm" assault of 189 not out, only a few days after his elegant 149 in the Durban Test. A World Test XI at that time might well have included S.J.McCabe.

Came 1936-37 and the great Australian fightback. He made five half-centuries leading up to the great Ashes climax at Melbourne, where he cracked 112 to go with hundreds by Bradman and Badcock, with young Ross Gregory making 80. It was a truly dramatic Ashes series.

Next summer he captained NSW to the Shield before embarking on his final England tour, when he hit that incredible 232 at Trent Bridge. How would you feel if Don Bradman, of all people, was begging all the other players to come to the balcony and watch you batting?

And how much more eminent would Stan McCabe now be but for the war and for his breakdown in fitness? As war clouds gathered, he stroked a charming century at the MCG in a match to celebrate Melbourne CC's centenary. Next summer, 1939-40, he led NSW to the Shield with a lucrative bat of his own. But by the end of 1941, Stanley Joseph McCabe had played his final first-class match. He was merely 31.

For those who like them, here are the stats: 182 matches, 11,981 runs, average 49.38, with 29 hundreds; 159 wickets with his seamers at 33.72. Six of those hundreds came in Tests, where he averaged 48.21 (55.11 in the Shield, on unprotected pitches, let it be remembered).

Above: McCabe heading out to bat with Don Bradman in the 1930s (Photo: David Frith collection)

The sports shop that Stan McCabe took over in George Street, Sydney flourished for many years. It stood beneath the NSWCA headquarters, and was a place of pilgrimage, alongside shops run by Bert Oldfield (Hunter Street) and Alan Kippax (Martin Place). I found the reserved McCabe not altogether responsive when I tried to get him talking, unlike Oldfield, who would entertain all afternoon. Nor would "Napper" say much when approached by an autograph hunter behind the SCG pavilion. But I'm pleased to reflect that, in the late 1950s, I did see McCabe batting. What's more, Bill O'Reilly was bowling. It was a testimonial match at, I think, North Sydney Oval. And after the snarling "Tiger" stooped and released one of his humdingers, "Napper" swung it to long leg. That's a treasured snippet that still glows brightly in the memory bank.

GILLESPIE SPORTS TEAM TO SOUTH AFRICA, 2018

Back – Michael Parker, Lachlan Hoy, Darcy Herriot, Jack Billing, Jack Bastian, Luca Bernardi, Heath Edey
Front – Charlie Warner, Adam Ward ©, Ollie Blizzard, Jack Ramage (v/capt), Michael Arnold

GILLESPIE SPORTS TOURS TO UK, JULY 2019 (playing)
WATCH THE ASHES 2019 – (for more go to Gillespiesports.com.au)

Books and articles about photography are becoming a feature of modern day cricket writing. Christian Ryan has added to the list with the rather oddly titled *'Feeling is the thing that happens in 1000th of a second.'* As the book's sub title suggests it is a season showcasing the English photographer Patrick Eagar.

The year 1975 was a landmark northern summer for the flowering of some rare cricket talent. The Australians were in England for the Ashes, played after the inaugural World Cup and the names of Jeff Thomson, Dennis Lillee, Clive Lloyd, Andy Roberts, Tony Greig and the Chappell brothers were prominent.

There are some nifty sentences in Feeling but there is also an overwrought nature to the book. Ryan who wrote a terrific biography on Kim Hughes has a habit of stating his opinion as fact. Ryan cites a portrait of Tony Greig that was used on a ghosted book cover as the image that 'came somehow to define him.'

Not for me I'm afraid. I can think of several photos of Greig in commercials that provide much greater insight.

There are some bizarre claims as well in this book. In describing a photo of Ken Wadsworth reaching for an overthrown ball, fifteen months before he died, Ryan suggests there were signs of the New Zealand keeper's imminent doom.

'Wadsworth's death, in the photograph, makes no sound. Maybe it's seeable, or not. 'But a sort of shuddering: that's there.'

Bernard Whimpress is one of the 'old stagers' of the Australian cricket writer's world. A keen observer of cricket history and a strong writer Whimpress is a prolific producer of books but sadly lives in the shadows of more self-promoting authors. *The Official MCC Story of the Ashes* begins in earnest at The Golden Age and travels through to Australia's 2015 loss. Whimpress provides snapshots into players' careers and lives as well as commentators and writers in this well presented book. The slight fawning over Gideon Haigh 'who has never worked on a sports desk' (there I was thinking he covered cricket for Rupert Murdoch) grates a little. There are several other notable modern day Australian cricket writers, Malcolm Knox for one. Haigh is a fine writer but his often acerbic and belittling reviews of fellow contributors is revealing in itself.

Andrew Ramsey's *Under the Southern Cross: The heroics and heartbreak of the Ashes in Australia* is full of beautiful descriptions of play and a cavalcade of black and white and colour photos. The story telling is rich and revealing for any cricket fan, even the well versed.

When I began reading *Tea and No Sympathy*, by Dave Edwards, Sam Perry and Ian Higgins I thought the sequel was a 'step too far' for the creators of that wonderfully humorous yet dark tale of a club cricketer, entitled *The Grade Cricketer*. However, I was pleasantly surprised at the way the key character develops and the story moves beyond the outlandish match fixing narrative. Rarely has the range of masculinity at a cricket club been examined in such a funny and disturbing way. For all its hyperbole it's relatable. It echoes to varying degrees what many young men have thought as they tried in vain to earn a baggy green. Grade cricket is just a few steps from Test cricket as is obliquely revealed in this fine follow up.

English writer Richard Whitehead, like the aforementioned Haigh is another member of the 'bag other cricket writers under the false guise of keeping authors to account society.' I wonder if the former The Times' obituary writer gets out much given how consistently critical is the tone of his reviews in *The Cricketer* edited by Simon Hughes, ironically the author of more average cricket books than most.

Whitehead is the Editor of the rather stuffily titled *The Times on the Ashes: Covering Sport's Greatest Rivalry from 1877 to the Present Day*. It has its moments. For example from Christopher Martin Jenkins take on Steve Waugh. 'If Billy Woodfull was the unbowlable then Steve Waugh is the unbreakable.' The excerpts are largely divided into digestible and easy to read segments, although a dour and self-important tone pervades parts of the book, especially the early history.

Austin Robertson, one of Kerry Packer's foot soldiers during World Series Cricket has written about one of the most tumultuous periods in Australian cricket in *Cricket Outlaws*

It's enjoyable because of its simplicity and for revelations of the author's connections within the community that created WSC. Robertson's story telling style is also straightforward but that is part of book's enchantment.

Former Australian off spinner Ashley Mallett was a late addition to the Kerry Packer troupe and has become an author of significant contributions to cricket literature. *Great Australian Cricket Stories* is a collection of Mallett's writing over several decades and features some engaging stories from cricket's history and the inner sanctum.

Ken Piesse in *Pep the story of Cec Pepper* has brought to life former NSW and Services player who crossed Bradman and because of it was arguably denied the chance to play for Australia. With lines like 'Cec Pepper was the quintessential wild colonial boy. He blued with Bradman. He lived in a 'ménage a trois' and willed his fortune to a woman he's just met' how could you resist? Piesse is in scintillating form with his latest book.

Former ABC journalist Mike Sexton's *Chappell's Last Stand* is a canny observation of Ian Chappell's final Shield winning season for South Australia in 1975/76. It gives insight into Chappell's leadership style and sheds light on some long-forgotten players such as Rick Drewer, Barry Curtin, Geoff Attenborough and Wayne Prior. Freed of the national captaincy and despite unraveling personally, Chappell led his side to an historic win while taking on the increasingly belligerent cricket administrators. Sexton's ability to evoke era and place shines through in what is the best cricket book published in the previous twelve months.

Barry Nicholls is an ABC broadcaster whose latest book is The Pocket History of the Ashes.

MORE BOOK REVIEWS - SOME PERSONAL FAVOURITES OF THE EDTIOR

by Lawrie Colliver

My favourite book of 2017: *CRICKET OUTLAWS – Inside Kerry Packer's Revolution* by Austin Robertson.
Some wonderful stories from those who worked behind the scenes and those who were at the coalface of World Series Cricket. Published to coincide with the 40th Anniversary of WSC, Austin Robertson has put together a gem of a book, with many previously untold stories appearing inside the covers. Barbara-Ann Chappell, wife of Ian, then WSC "Liaison officer" writes one of the best chapters in the book.

As someone who watched this all unfold as a kid, it was an amazing time to be watching cricket. Two Australian teams, plenty of characters in the game plus day/night cricket for the first time.

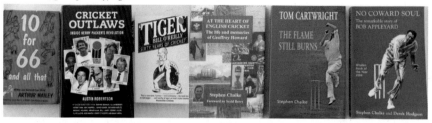

Other great reads

Front Foot! The law that changed cricket by Doug Ackerley
Forensic historical analysis of the no-ball law, how it has effected bowlers over the years, over-rates, captains, injuries and anything else you can think of. Many pace bowlers from over the years have been interviewed by Doug which makes it a fantastic read.

Some old favourites

Arthur Mailey – 10 for 66 an all that plus "Tiger" – Sixty years of cricket by Bill O'Reilly
Classic Autobiographical Stories by two of Australia's great spin bowlers. Mailey was brought up in Sydney's slums and went on to play 21 Tests between 1920 and 1926. His tales of his early days, getting to bowl to Trumper in a Grade game, touring England, getting a deal to have his cartoons published, all marvellous reading.

Tiger's book is also a classic, going through his early days, bowling to a young Bradman, Bodyline, tours to England and South Africa and then his career as a cricket journalist. His four page chapter entitled "Liquid refreshment" is a classic in writing about the benefits of proper hydration.

Recommended reading

Stephen Chalke has been publishing some brilliant books in the last twenty years. My personal favourites are:

At the heart of English Cricket – the life and memories of Geoffrey Howard
Tremendous story of the life of Geoffrey Howard who was the Manager of the MCC tour to Australia in 1954-55. He and scorer/baggage-man George Duckworth were essentially the only off-field members of the England tour party for the 1954-55 Ashes. Some fascinating stories include getting a "depressed" England skipper Len Hutton out of bed to play the Melbourne Test, a low scoring affair which Frank Tyson ended up winning with an amazing spell on the final day.

Micky Stewart – and the changing face of cricket
Played eight Test matches, was a member of the great Surrey teams in the 1950s, managed England and sired son Alec who played over 100 Tests. Stewart was a fine opening batsman, brilliant close catcher and in this book reflects on his life in the game.

No Coward Soul – the remarkable story of Bob Appleyard
Bob Appleyard was a medium paced off-spinner who took 200 wickets for Yorkshire in 1951, then suffered tuberculosis and missed the next two years. Not expected to ever play again, he returned in 1954, found his way back into the Test side and toured Australia on the famous 1954-55 tour. A remarkable story indeed – and that's only the tip of the iceberg.

The Flame still burns – Tom Cartwright
A Wisden book of the year, Cartwright was regarded as one of the finest bowlers in England between the late 1950s and early 1970s. In his time at Somerset he nurtured Ian Botham, Viv Richards and Vic Marks. Regarded as a man of great integrity, he played five Tests for England.

In Sunshine and in shadow – Geoff Cope and Yorkshire Cricket
Geoff Cope was continually under the microscope for his bowling action as an off-spinner. His career was saved by England great Johnny Wardle, so much so he made his Test debut on the 1977-78 tour to Pakistan. Was on a hat-trick in that match, and to read about that other interesting tales, you'll need to buy the book.

MAX KRUGER - STATS MAN EXTROADINAIRE CALLS TIME ON HIS CAREER

How did you get started? It is always interesting to find out how people get started in these terrific jobs in Cricket. How did you get your first gig on the coverage all those years ago?

Max: Nepotism! My eldest brother worked in the Channel Nine news room in Brisbane and he worked in the second season of World Series Cricket, on the games they played in Brisbane. Then the following year he wasn't available, so he nominated me to replace him, and the only question that was asked was 'Does he know anything about Cricket". My brother told the people at David Hill's office yes, he plays it, so that was the start. The first game I ever worked on, I've never forgotten the date, November 28, 1980, the first day of the Australia New Zealand test match, and I thought this would be good, five day's pay, the bloody game only lasted three! It had me thinking at the time, 'Is there a future attached to any of this.'

So you got the first test of the way and it must've gone well, as they wanted you back later on to do some more. Max: That was the following season, at that time I was asked about my availability about doing the whole tour. But as you'd appreciate in the fickle world of television even that far back there was always budgetary constraints, so I got told 'we'd love to have you', but by the following week it was sorry, we've checked with the bean counters and I stayed at home. Then the following season, I got a call up.

That was an exciting season in 1981-82 wasn't it? Max: My first interstate trip was for the Boxing day test in 1981 and to this day nearly 37 years later that remains the best day of cricket that I've seen. I was lucky enough to have been there, my first ever time at the MCG working on the game.

It was a famous day, so your role back then was to make sure the scorecards that appeared on air were accurate and the manual statistics that went up in those days on the Nine coverage were 100% right?

Max: Absolutely, I had the good fortune to work with a lady by the name of Jane Prior, who was the Chyron operator, that was the one and only device that we had to display scorecards batting, bowling figures and all sorts of other stats. That was quite a significant role in its own right, it was all about attention to detail, a great learning curve for me because she gave me total support right from the beginning, we had a great time working together for the next few years before she went on to fame and glory in the US.

You had to sit next to the great Statistician Irving Rosenwater for those years, how would you describe how he went about the Stats job, as I understand he was a very meticulous man himself?

Max: Perfect word, Meticulous. Attention to detail should've been part of his name, I don't think Irving had a second initial but it should've been something along those lines. I learned a great deal from him, which I applied not only working on the cricket but with everything that I did. Research is so important, Irving once brought out a book called "501 memorable quotes", some of the quotes in there were just extraordinary. I asked him one-day about it and he said some of them took a week going through old material and newspaper clipping in libraries to get the information. So that was the sort of standard he set.

His own personal scoresheets were a work of art, is that something you used and how much did the commentators appreciate having that information provided to them?

Max: As you know the linear method, as designed by Bill Ferguson, who was the official scorer for Australia between 1905 to 1953, is very important. Irving always spoke of "Fergy" in reverential terms referring to him as "Fergy, the Prince of scorers". The first game I did I just had an exercise book, ruled up columns and off I went. Later in the summer in Brisbane, New Zealand played India in a one-dayer and Irving said to me 'here Maxy', as he used to call me, 'I'll give you these sheets and see how you go with them'. It helped a lot and the beauty of it was you could compare with each other, because as you know working for a radio station or a TV network there is only yourself normally in the commentary box, it's not like the two official scorers. Since then I've always used those sheets because there's nothing that's going to be better.

Were you nervous meeting Richie Benaud for the first time? Max: I'm one of those people that look at someone and say, 'You've got two arms, two legs, two eyes etc. the same as myself, so not really, but I just thought of him as quite old, Richie was 50 at the time and the last few years I worked for Channel Nine I always referred to that particular episode, so I am over 50 now, so I am old! It was great to meet him and he was a legend then, so his fame only grew over the years. Right from the beginning he was very friendly to me, and in fact all of the commentators were really good.

Now there's a funny story about Richie not having a middle name, can you tell me about that?

Max: Very early on, it may have been on the first trip to Melbourne. David Hill, the Executive Producer, used write out the commentary roster and put it on the notice board. I had a look at it one day and being a bit of a smarty pants at that age, said 'there's a bit of a problem here, you've got IM Chappell, WM Lawry, FH Tyson, but where's Richie's middle initial?' So David said that 'if you're so smart, come up with one'. So I did, it was X for the unknown factor, so from there on his was known as "RX Benaud". From then on he often referred to himself in the third person saying RXB says this or that.

What about David Hill, he's moved on since that time to some massive roles in worldwide TV, what was it like working with him in those days?

Max: He was absolutely unique, there is no one else I that have worked with since that is on the same page as David. So energetic, some days he'd get a bit bored, he'd give something a go, knowing it wouldn't work, but we may learn something else from it. His mind was always ticking and he was fairly demanding, but with Kerry Packer to answer to, and the cricket was Kerry's baby. David was only 34 years old when World Series Cricket started, and was based in Melbourne when it started, I

COUCHMATE®

SAVE SPACE, CREATE COMFORT

COUCH ARM TABLES · BATH CADDIES · LAP TABLES

VISIT WWW.COUCHMATE.COM.AU

think working for Channel Seven. He heard on the radio in his car that this "rebel" cricket was happening, and just said to himself that he wanted to be part of it. He came on board as the first producer, he just ran with the cricket and made it the envy of sports broadcasts, not just in Australia but revered internationally. After that he went on to fame and glory in the US.

A few years later, Irving finished, then Wendy Wimbush did it for a while, then came your chance to be the main Stats man. What year was that? Max: I took over during the World Cup in 1991-92, Irving finished in 1986-87 and then Wendy came in for 1987-88. I was actually the Producer of the cricket that summer, Wendy came in and worked for a couple of years, and then my permanent elevation to that role came in 1992-93, when the West Indies came to Australia.

That was a heck of a series, with West Indies winning by a run in Adelaide, was that a highlight during your career, along with the Ashes series and World Cups?

Max: The disappointing thing about the Ashes was I never really worked on a good series in Australia, they were usually so one-sided that they were dominated by Australia. The 1982-83 Ashes, early days for me when I was still the production scorer, was a pretty good series. But in 1992-93 against the West Indies in Adelaide, I'll never forget it, Greg Chappell was commentating at the time, he was on-air when that last wicket fell, when Craig McDermott caught behind off Courtney Walsh. As soon as it happened, Greg just ripped his ear piece out and threw it out on the ground. Skipper Allan Border was in the rooms and people who were watching at home would remember how he was throwing the ball from hand to hand, back and forward, in what was highly tense time as they edged towards a series win. That was my first summer as the main Stats guy.

The best series I worked on was when Australia was in India in 2001. Australia had towelled them up in Mumbai, had them on the rack well and truly in Calcutta (2nd Test), when they followed on. At the lunch break Tony Greig decided he would stir up the local fans and in response to an Indian who had a sign "Who's going to win Mr Greig?" Tony grabbed some paper and wrote "India" and amazingly they came from behind and won. I had admired VVS Laxman, he got a hundred in Sydney in 2000, when his career was on the line. There he was just over a year later, producing an unbelievable innings.

Stats wise on the various TV broadcasts around the world there is a lot of data shown now, which was previously impossible, do you enjoy what you see nowadays?

Max: Some of it is good, some of it is overkill. I think a lot of it is just shown because you've got access to it, just for the sake of it. I think a bit more analysis of individual players and the right kind of stats is probably the key to it all. I prefer a bit more of the human touch, in my career I tried to stick to things that really mattered. The main thing is you want to work as a team, you're providing a service to people watching, to provide the entertainment, make it all worthwhile.

I had quite a bit to do with getting the first batting wagon wheel on air. We had a programmer trying to get it sorted, but they were having trouble. So I just suggested to base it around a 360 degrees circle, we tried it and it worked. Where it has got to now, is phenomenal. The other classic was the "ticking clock" an idea of David Hill's, where the score updated on the screen. That was part of my job in the early days as I had to call that back to Sydney, where they put it on the screen. The first time we used it at the Gabba it went from 24 to 28, David wasn't pleased saying it was all about a ticking clock, wanting it to go 24, 25, 26, 27, 28 not up to 28 straight away. I said to David the ball had rocketed to the fence and he said "I don't care!" I can go back to those days, whereas now it's all fully computerised.

What made Bill Lawry such a special broadcaster? Max: One day Bill, who was a proud Victorian, was doing a domestic State game. Brad Williams, a Victorian lad had moved to WA and was getting wickets in this game at the MCG. On this day Brad Williams knocked over the top order, playing for WA. When he took his third wicket, Bill jumped up in excitement, and I remember Simon O'Donnell saying later what an object lesson it was, there was never any ho-hum games for Bill, every game is just so important. He'd turn up, so enthused and would always keep me up to the mark, wanting the teams written out for him two hours before play. He was like a little school boy on Christmas Eve, his great slogan was "Just happy to be there". He was a personal favourite and still is.

I had a great relationship with all of them really. Richie put me through the wringer the first time I filled in. We had a double-header domestic weekend and Irving Rosenwater could only be at one place and I got sent to do the other, where Richie was the main commentator. I was only 24 and he was great and very supportive. You have a different relationship with each of them, to know what they like, what areas would really interest them on certain players, teams at the venue whatever.

Bill and Tony were great for me because they relied on stats more than the others. In each case they'd have their "lip-ribbon" microphones poised at their mouth and say something, then pause to allow me to help them fill the rest of the sentence. That was often as much time as you had to provide an answer!

From my early days the other person I'd like to mention is Keith Stackpole. He was the first one to show a lot of interest in me, one day at the Gabba, he came up to me and checked how I was going, introduced himself, asked what I did for a living, asked if I played cricket, all that sort of stuff. He was a very warm, generous man and it was a shame when circumstances changed and he finished with Nine. Stacky still remains a favourite to this day.

Any advice to those eyeing it off as a career? Max: There is no reason why as a start you can't sit at home and score off TV. Have a great appetite for knowledge, perhaps score for a club and then get in touch with various media outlets and get someone to push your cause for you. My sole objective when I started was to earn a bit of money in the University holidays. When I got to travel around the country and somebody was paying for my airfares, the accommodation and paying me to go along to the cricket, I thought well, that is Christmas!

THE 2017-18 ASHES

Any objective cricket fan who watched the 2017-18 Ashes could argue that a margin of four-nil to Australia was not a fair indication of how the 2017-18 Ashes were played out. For many times in the first three Tests, England were in a position where they were either square or slightly in front. In Brisbane, when Australia were 7-209 after England's 302, honours were even. Heading into the last day in Adelaide, England needed 178 to win with six wickets in hand and were given a good chance. Also in Perth, when England were 4-368 during the second day, the visitors were on top and in a position to press on and win. Unfortunately for them at those key moments, Australia responded to regain the ascendency, and not release the pressure when finally on top, which saw them win those Test matches and clinch the series with two matches to play.

In Melbourne, after Australia won the first day, England had a brilliant second day taking seven wickets and went on to dominate the next two as Alistair Cook made an unbeaten double-ton. But rain and an immovable Steve Smith, who batted over seven hours, prevented them winning that Test. By the time the England team reached Sydney they were out of gas, their score of 346 in the first innings totally inadequate on a good batting pitch, where Australia scored in excess of 600 to win by an innings.

As competitive as England were at times, in the end Australia had stronger batting and faster pace bowlers, which saw them to victory. The home batting lineup made nine tons to England's three, and had four bowlers take 20 plus wickets, where James Anderson took the most for the visitors with 17. Australia lower order comfortably made more contributions than England's and looking at individuals, there was one name that dominated proceedings unlike any other – Steve Smith.

Smith's started the series in Brisbane making his slowest, but most certainly one of his most vital Test centuries for Australia. He not only held the first inning together, but guided it through coming in at 2-30 before then batting patiently enough and long enough to gain a first innings lead for his team. After a quiet game with the bat in Adelaide he then made a colossal 239 in Perth, batting all of the third day to bat England completely out of the game. In Melbourne after 76 in the first innings, he batted over seven hours in the second innings to make a match saving ton, having to bat the whole of the last day to do so. He also took ten catches in the field, maintaining his reputation as a fielder of the highest regard. Captaincy wise he was solid, at times though he could have taken a stronger approach on the field in term of the verbals that were going on. He was also lucky that the umpires weren't stricter on their interpretation of what was intimidatory bowling, at times Smith's pace attack were allowed to get away with the overuse of the bouncer to the lower order.

Pat Cummins will be able to look back on his series with pride, having led the wicket taking tally for Australia. Twelve months previously he may well have doubted if he'd have played in the Ashes, but through hard work and persistence, got the rewards he deserved. He played a vital role in ensuring England skipper Joe Root didn't make a century in the series, dismissing him on four occasions at a personal cost of just 71 runs. His batting efforts in the first two Tests were vital, scoring important forties in vital partnerships with his skipper Steve Smith in Brisbane (adding 66) and Shaun Marsh (adding 99) in Adelaide.

Josh Hazlewood and Mitchell Starc were the other vital parts of the pace attack, but often played different roles in the team. Hazlewood was the rock of the attack, good to bowl for his skipper whether the ball was new, middle aged or starting to reverse. Hazlewood also enjoyed bowling the James Vince, knocking him over four times for 41 just runs off his bowling, whilst dismissing Alistair Cook on three occasions in the series. Starc were excellent with the new ball, having the wood over Mark Stoneman and Jonny Bairstow, getting each out four times. As a pace bowling unit they were keen to dominate the England lower order, which they did using either the bouncer or going fuller with the yorker. One could argue they got away with bowling too many bouncers in the series, with the umpires often allowing three or more in an over to the England last three.

Nathan Lyon had a bit too much to say in the lead up to the series, suggesting he was going to end a few careers and other such things, which in the eyes of many in the cricket public, didn't put him in a great light. He did have an excellent series, starting with his brilliant run out from cover of James Vince on the opening day in Brisbane, when the England number three looked set to make a hundred. Seventeen of his 21 wickets were left-handed batsmen, as he completely owned Moeen Ali, dismissing him seven times, which equalled the Ashes record as per below:

HEAD TO HEAD IN ASHES – BOWLERS DISMISSED BATSMEN THE MOST IN A SERIES

Bowler	Batsman	Series	Times out	Runs	Balls faced
NM Lyon	Moeen Ali	2017-18	7	90	218
GD McGrath	MA Atherton	1997	7	84	190
GF Lawson	DI Gower	1989	7	139	201

Thanks to Charles Davis (sportstats.com.au/bloghome.html) for the data on McGrath v Atherton and Lawson v Gower

Shaun Marsh was a surprise pick for many for the first Test at the Gabba, but repaid the faith with important runs, including centuries in Adelaide and Sydney. Brother Mitch returned to the Australian team for the Perth Test and responded with great effect making a century. He also batted for a long time on the last day in Melbourne to help save the match and made his other century of the series in Sydney, a joyous occasion for the Marsh clash as the brothers were batting together when Mitch reached his ton in that Test. David Warner had a largely subdued series, England setting deepish fields for much of the time to

Above: Shaun Marsh repaid the selectors faith in him by making two centuries in the Ashes Series. Here he is pictured celebrating his ton in Adelaide.

Above: In the 2017-18 Ashes, Josh Hazlewood shown again he is the backbone of the Aussie pace-attack

Above: Nathan Lyon had a fine Ashes series, is seen here appealing in the Adelaide Test.

Above: Former England skipper Alistair Cook couldn't get going until Melbourne, where he made 244 not out.

curb his boundary hitting. His one century came in the MCG Test, needing a bit of luck as he was dismissed by Tom Curran at one point, but replays revealed it was a no-ball.

Wicket-keeper Tim Paine was another of the selection surprises at the start of the series, brought back in for Matthew Wade, despite Wade having kept in career best form in the previous series versus Bangladesh. Paine carried out his keeping duties well, especially after a nervous start at the Gabba, when he dropped James Vince off Nathon Lyon on the first day. His only fifty of the series came in Adelaide, when he played an important role in a partnership with Shaun Marsh.

In regards to the rest of the batting, Usman Khawaja had an inconsistent series up until his brilliant 171 in Sydney. Cameron Bancroft made a fine 82 not out to guide Australia home in the first Test in Brisbane, but struggled after that. While Peter Handscomb battled away, playing too much off the back-foot, the selectors making a proactive decision to drop him in favour of Mitch Marsh for the third Test.

For England, some of their less experienced players were the successes of the tour. Dawid Malan stood up against the pace of the Australian attack well, making a fine ton in Perth, to go with three other scores of fifty plus. He seemed to enjoy batting on Australian pitches and appeared to prefer the ball coming onto the bat, as he struggled at times to get Nathan Lyon away, being quite often unable to rotate the strike.

Craig Overton was one of the finds of the tour, unlucky not to play in the first Test in Brisbane, when a not completely fit Jake Ball was preferred to him. Overton showed courage and skill with the bat in Adelaide, bowled his heart out and barring injury would have most likely played in four Tests, instead of just the two.

Joe Root passed fifty on five occasions but couldn't reach a century in what was at times a tough tour for him. He was still England's best batsman on tour and conducted himself well on and off the field. There were a few occasions he wasn't done any favours by members of the touring party, those matters must have been a distraction for him. Also one wondered about some of the on-field tactics and whether his experienced quick bowlers James Anderson and Stuart Broad were having too much say in regards to field placings. But at 27 years of age, one expects he will be at the forefront of Ashes campaigns, none more important than the one that will occur through July-September 2019.

After batting out of the top six for the first two Tests, Jonny Bairstow was at number six for Perth and made a magnificent hundred but couldn't quite repeat that effort for the rest of the series. His dismissal in the second innings at the Gabba, caught upper-cutting to third-man was plain slack batting for someone of his experience. He was steady with the gloves and one hopes from an England point of view he'll retain a spot in the top six, form permitting.

Mark Stoneman showed some qualities as a Test opener, but couldn't get past 56, having made starts in seven of his nine innings. He was also troubled by the pace of Starc, being dismissed by him four times and battled to score against Lyon, out twice for 25 runs off the 99 balls he faced. On his return home he was dropped after one Test in the 2018 English summer and it's unlikely he'll play another Test.

James Vince was the enigma of the England batting line-up, after promising so much with his score of 83 in the first innings at the Gabba. At times he looked like a serious Test player, another example being his superb batting in the second innings in Perth when he was bowled by one from Starc that hit a crack and went sideways. His strength of playing through the off-side was unfortunately also his weakness as he was out caught by either the keeper or in the slips in seven of his nine innings.

Of the players with previous experience in Australia, Alistair Cook struggled up until the third Test and may well have been dropped had he not made his brilliant 244 not out in Melbourne. He battled to get forward to the Aussie quicks, finding the slower Melbourne pitch more to his liking. Stuart Broad was accurate but had a poor tour by his standards, only really coming good in Melbourne, when the series was over. As expected, James Anderson relished the night conditions in Adelaide gaining his first ever five wicket haul in this country but, while very economical for most of the time, didn't have the penetration that he enjoys in the English climate. Chris Woakes was another who found Australian conditions not to his liking, and like Anderson, his one fine moment with the ball was in Adelaide on that third night under the floodlights.

Finally one must come to Moeen Ali who had a poor tour, failing to make fifty while also only taking five wickets at well over 100. He had major troubles against Nathan Lyon, being dismissed by him seven times and looked like a rabbit in the headlights in Melbourne when he aimed to hit his way out of trouble. With the ball he had troubles with his spinning finger and couldn't recover, making little impression with the ball after dismissing Usman Khawaja with his ninth ball bowled in Brisbane. Having previously been an important all-rounder in the team, his lack of output was another factor in why England didn't win a Test in the series.

Of the others to play small parts in the series, Tom Curran showed competitive spirit in the last two Tests with the ball, his overstepping of the front line in Melbourne costing him David Warner's scalp as his first Test wicket. While leg-spinner Mason Crane was brought in as support for the last Test in Sydney and bowled his heart out in terrifyingly hot conditions, despite taking just one wicket in 48 overs.

Overall, Australia were too good when it counted, winning well at home. With a new coach and possibly a new captain for the 2019 series in England, it will be very interesting to see if Australia can retain the Ashes over there, having not won a series in the old dart since 2001.

NON FIRST CLASS TOUR MATCH

At the WACA, Perth. November 4-5, 2017 – Match Drawn. Toss: England.

England XI 6-349 dec (MD Stoneman 85, JM Vince 82, DJ Malan 56, GS Balance 51) **drew with the Western Australia XI 342** (JR Philippe 88, CD Hinchliffe 75; JM Anderson 4-27)

In bright conditions, Alistair Cook (0) was out to the second ball of the tour, off the bowling of Nathan Coulter-Nile. Stoneman (113 balls, 16x4) and Vince (129 balls, 12x4) added 153 for the second wicket and later Malan (88 balls, 8x4) and Ballance (102 balls, 6x4) added 104 before both retired at the same time. Subiaco born Josh Philippe (92 balls, 16x4) played an impressive knock as did Clint Hinchliffe (102 balls, 12x4). Several players batted twice in the WA innings, to given England extra practice on the second day.

FIRST CLASS MATCHES
TOUR MATCH v CRICKET AUSTRALIA XI IN ADELAIDE

In ideal conditions, England's openers looked in good order, until Alistair Cook edged left-arm quick Jackson Coleman to the keeper. Mark Stoneman and James Vince added 61, then Stoneman and Joe Root combined to add 70 to put the tourists in a good position. New South Wales leg-spinner Dan Fallins then played a part, picking up the wickets of Stoneman and Root in the space of half an hour. Bairstow edged behind before the lights took effect and then Malan and Woakes added 76 in good style. In the last half hour Coleman and Sandhu shared three wickets with the second new ball, Malan out to what was the last ball of the day.

England only survived 24 minutes on the second day and when Jake Ball was in the throes of his fourth over, he injured his right ankle in his delivery stride and had to leave the field. England ran through the CA top order, to have them 5-57, WA left-hander Josh Carder the only one to reach double figures. Skipper Tim Paine was joined by Victoria's Matt Short and these two took on the England bowlers, to make it to the Dinner break at 5-128. Paine reached a welcome and polished fifty, then shortly after Short was caught behind, ending an innings saving stand of 86. Paine went not long after and then Simon Milenko went for his shots, at one point hitting Craig Overton for 19 (644·41) in an over. He saw his team past 200 but straight after reaching his fifty, having added 54 with Gurinder Sandhu. Paine declared still 60 behind, wanting to have some overs at England under the lights. The visitors closing on five without loss.

Cook found some needed touch, before being dismissed just before the tea break, with Stoneman making his second fifty of the match. After tea the CA bowlers struck back, reducing England from 1-93 to 7-124 as Milenko started to make the ball talk, taking the wickets of Malan, Woakes and Overton in nine deliveries. Bairstow dug in and was well supported by Mason Crane, the pair adding 70 with some intelligent batting. Bairstow reached his fifty will a six off Fallins, England declaring at 7.39pm local time, setting 268 for victory.

England's bowling then ripped apart the CA XI order, reducing them to 7-25 by 9pm, the game set to be completed inside three days. But Short and Sandhu stuck it out, adding 45, weathering the extra half hour, to ensure a fourth day. Overton knocked over Short in the first over, the match concluding after just half an hour of the final day.

versus Cricket Australia XI at Adelaide Oval (day/night) – November 8-11, 2017
England won by 192 runs

England	First innings	B	M	4	6	Second innings	B	M	4	6
AN Cook	c Paine b Coleman	15	28	27	1	c Paine b Milenko	32	85	119	1
MD Stoneman	c Carder b Fallins	61	130	200	6	b Coleman	51	107	147	5
JM Vince	b Fallins	33	64	84	3	lbw b Sandhu	29	55	75	1	1
JE Root *	c Gibson b Fallins	58	89	119	4	lbw b Sandhu	1	4	5	
DJ Malan	c Short b Coleman	63	128	170	7	c Paine b Milenko	5	22	33	
JM Bairstow+	c Paine b Fallins	9	21	24	1	not out	61	66	108	6	2
CR Woakes	c Gibson b Coleman	33	67	94	1	1	c Paine b Milenko	2	2	5	
C Overton	c Carder b Sandhu	0	9	14		lbw b Milenko	0	3	3	
MS Crane	not out	6	23	27		c Milenko b Fallins	18	53	74	1
JT Ball	b Sandhu	4	3	6		absent injured				
JM Anderson	lbw b Fallins	4	9	17		10	c Pucovski b Milenko	0	9	15	
	6 lb, 1nb	7				8 lb	8			
	95 overs, 395 mins	293				67.4 overs, 296 mins	207			

Fall: 1-24 (Cook), 2-85 (Vince), 3-155 (Stoneman), 4-178 (Root), 5-195 (Bairstow), 6-271 (Woakes), 7-278 (Overton), 8-278 (Malan), 9-283 (Ball), 10-293 (Anderson)

Fall: 1-79 (Cook), 2-93 (Stoneman), 3-94 (Root), 4-121 (Malan), 5-121 (Vince), 6-124 (Woakes), 7-124 (Overton), 8-194 (Crane), 9-207 (Anderson)

CA XI - bowling	O	M	R	W	wd	nb	O	M	R	W	wd	nb
J R Coleman	23	4	72	3			14	3	55	1		
GS Sandhu	23	3	61	2			19	5	47	2		
SA Milenko	19	6	49	0	1		16.4	3	34	5		
DG Fallins	22	1	73	5			13	1	50	1		
MW Short	5	0	19	0			5	0	13	0		
JJ Sangha	3	1	13	0								

Cricket Aust XI First innings			B	M	4	6	Second innings		B	M	4	6
NCR Larkin	lbw b Woakes		6	32	38	1	c Bairstow b Woakes		2	25	22	
JM Carder	c Anderson b Overton		24	65	91	3	b Woakes		0	2	6	
RJ Gibson	c Malan b Ball		4	19	27		c Bairstow b Woakes		9	29	52	1
WJ Pucovski	b Crane		4	30	36		c Vince b Woakes		1	9	8	
TD Paine *+	lbw b Anderson		52	98	153	4	1	b Overton	5	14	19	
JJ Sangha	c Malan b Woakes		3	19	25		c Root b Overton		5	16	18	
MW Short	c Bairstow b Anderson		45	73	96	4	2	b Overton	28	55	73	3
SA Milenko	lbw b Crane		50	58	76	6	1	c Bairstow b Anderson	1	2	3	
GS Sandhu	lbw b Crane		18	48	60	1	lbw b Anderson		17	62	73	1
DG Fallins	not out		15	9	11	2	c Cook b Anderson		1	15	27	
JR Coleman	not out		4	6	8		not out		4	13	13	1
	1 b, 6 lb, 1 nb		8				2 lb		2			
	76 overs, 315 mins		9-233 dec				40.2 overs, 162 mins		75			

Fall: 1-21 (Larkin), 2-32 (Gibson), 3-41 (Carder), 4-47 (Pucovski), 5-57 (Sangha), 6-143 (Short), 7-160 (Paine), 8-214 (Milenko), 9-217 (Sandhu)

Fall: 1-0 (Carder), 2-3 (Larkin), 3-7 (Pucovski), 4-14 (Paine), 5-18 (Gibson), 6-24 (Sangha), 7-25 (Milenko), 8-70 (Short), 9-70 (Sandhu), 10-75 (Fallins)

England - bowling	O	M	R	W	wd	nb	O	M	R	W	wd	nb
JM Anderson	16	7	30	2			10.2	5	12	3		
CR Woakes	14	0	48	2			10	4	17	4		
JT Ball	3.4	2	5	1			11	6	15	3		
C Overton	15	6	40	1			6	0	27	0		
JE Root	4.2	1	11	0			3	1	2	0		
MS Crane	21	2	78	3	1							
JM Vince	2	0	14	0								

Stumps scores:

Day 1	England (1st inns)	8-278	MS Crane 0, JT Ball 0*
Day 2	England (2nd inns)	0-5	AN Cook 1*, MD Stoneman 4*
Day 3	Cricket Aust XI (2nd inns) 7-70		JA Burns 29*, UT Khawaja 12*

Toss: England
Umpires: SD Fry, DJ Shepard
Referee: SJA Taufel
Attendances: 1430, 1245, 1333, free. Total: 4008

TOUR MATCH v CRICKET AUSTRALIA XI IN TOWNSVILLE

With Tim Paine required for Tasmania, Matt Short took over as skipper. South Australian backup keeper Harry Nielsen came into the team, while NSW quick Harry Conway replaced Jackson Coleman. Jake Ball was out through injury, with James Anderson rested, Moeen Ali and Stuart Broad coming into the team.

Nick Larkin and Carder looked the part, adding 66, but either side of lunch, four wickets fell quickly, reducing the CA XI to 4-91. During this period keeper Jonny Bairstow took a nasty blow to his right hand and had to leave the field for n hour, the CA team generously allowing substitute Ben Foakes to take the gloves. Skipper Short put together a solid fifty, but was dropped on 23 by Stoneman and on 36 by Root. Woakes was enjoying the conditions, getting the Kookaburra ball to swing as he took five of the first six wickets to fall, finishing with six for the day. Fallins entertaining the locals taking 16 (44242·) off the last over of the day, bowled by Mason Crane.

After Broad ended the CA XI innings in the second over of the day, Cook and Stoneman enjoyed the excellent batting conditions in dry heat to add 172, although Stoneman had some luck on 41, when Short dropped him in the gully off Milenko. Cook found his land legs before he was caught behind cutting at one, fifty minutes before tea. Vince fell to the leg spin of Fallins caught at short leg, as he looked to work to leg, replays clearly indicating he hadn't hit the ball into the ground. Stoneman was out in the first over after tea but for the rest of the day Root and Malan took advantage of the tired bowlers to add 120 before Stumps, England holding a lead of 87.

On the third day, the fourth wicket stand continued on until it reached 163, when Root was superbly caught down the leg-side by Nielsen, diving to his left. Bairstow mishit a full-toss to mid-on and then Malan brought up his ton with a late cut for three. When he was run out by a clever throw from Carder at backward square-leg, England quickly lost 3-1, but the last two wickets added 76, with Woakes and Crane 58 adding of them as England were all out with a lead of 265.

With Nick Larkin injured, Ryan Gibson joined Jake Carder at the top of the order, and added 80 in good style before Carder was caught at slip edging a drive. Gibson went too far across his stumps aiming a sweep and when Pucovski edged a drive to slip, the CA had lost 3-7. Short joined Sangha and watched as he went for his shots, taking ten from an over off Crane and then spectacularly hooking Overton over deep square-leg for six. The pair added 34 by stumps, their team trailing by 44 with a day to play.

With the pitch showing little signs of wear in the tropical far north Queensland heat, the fourth wicket stand carried on in style, although Sangha had a slice of luck on 43 when he was dropped by Stoneman off Crane at cover. Sangha reached his fifty first, Short having to wait until after lunch to get to his. Short celebrated with a missive six over long-on off Crane, a member of the local groundstaff running several metres to take a terrific catch the other side of the rope. On 98, Sangha was peppered with short balls from Woakes, but calmly worked one off his hip for a boundary to reach his ton from 184 balls. Just before tea, Short forced Moeen Ali off the back foot for three to reach his ton, which took 190 balls, England going wicketless in the first two sessions of play.

After tea, Sangha eventually went, top edging a sweep to short fine-leg, ending a stand of 263. Throughout the heat, Short stuck firm, with Nielsen staying with him until the game was called an hour early – England glad to get off the ground and head for Brisbane to prepare for the first Test.

versus Cricket Australia XI at Riverway Stadium, Townsville on November 15-18, 2017 - Match Drawn

Cricket Aust XI	First innings		B	M	4	6	Second innings			B	M	4	6
NCR Larkin	c Vince b Woakes		30	80	103	1							
JM Carder	c Bairstow b Woakes		39	86	115	6	1 c Root b Moeen			34	69	87	4
RJ Gibson	c sub (BT Foakes) b Woakes		7	20	35	1	2 b Moeen			49	66	101	6
WJ Pucovski	c Bairstow b Overton		20	45	77	3	3 c Root b Crane			1	13	18	
JJ Sangha	lbw b Woakes		0	2	2		4 c Malan b Crane			133	226	302	13	1
MW Short *	c Root b Overton		51	122	138	2	5 not out			134	264	331	11	1
HJ Nielsen +	c Vince b Woakes		20	49	58	3	6 not out			2	22	33	
SA Milenko	b Woakes		19	47	69	1							
GS Sandhu	c Vince b Broad		25	52	64	3							
DG Fallins	not out		29	33	49	5							
HNA Conway	c Stoneman b Broad		1	18	26								
	4 lb, 5 nb		9				2 b, 4 lb, 5 w			11			
	91.3 overs, 372 mins		250				110 overs, 438 mins		4-364				

Fall: 1-66 (Larkin), 2-75 (Carder), 3-91 (Gibson), 4-91 (Sangha), 5-118 (Pucovski), 6-162 (Nielsen), 7-176 (Short), 8-212 (Milenko), 9-230 (Sandhu), 10-250 (Conway)

Fall: 1-80 (Carder), 2-87 (Gibson), 3-87 (Pucovski), 4-350 (Sangha)

England - bowling	O	M	R	W	wd	nb	O	M	R	W	wd	nb
SCJ Broad	16.3	5	33	2		1	14	1	40	0		
CR Woakes	19	3	55	6			11	0	50	0	1	
Moeen Ali	16	4	39	0			32	9	88	2		
C Overton	18	4	32	2			15	3	65	0		
MS Crane	22	3	87	0			30	6	97	2		
JE Root							6	1	12	0		
DJ Malan							2	0	6	0		

England	First innings		B	M	4	6	CA XI - bowling	O	M	R	W	wd	nb
AN Cook	c Nielsen b Short		70	127	176	5	GS Sandhu	25	7	99	0		7
MD Stoneman	c and b Fallins		111	159	229	13	HNA Conway	23	5	77	0		
JM Vince	c Sangha b Fallins		26	38	42	3	SA Milenko	23.5	3	86	2	1	4
JE Root *	c Nielsen b Milenko		83	123	200	8	MW Short	32	2	103	4		
DJ Malan	run out (Carder)		109	210	246	10	DG Fallins	37	2	127	3		
JM Bairstow +	c Gibson b Fallins		19	29	40	1	JJ Sangha	2	0	14	0		
Moeen Ali	b Short		5	22	26								
CR Woakes	c Nielsen b Milenko		36	81	108	3	Fall: 1-172 (Cook), 2-214 (Vince), 3-217 (Stoneman),						
C Overton	c Sangha b Short		0	1	2		4-380 (Root), 5-419 (Bairstow), 6-438 (Malan),						
SCJ Broad	c Pucovski b Short		10	16	22	1	7-439 (Moeen), 8-439 (Overton),						
MS Crane	not out		25	62	78	1	9-457 (Broad), 10-515 (Woakes)						
	5 b, 4 lb, 11 nb, 1 w		21										
	142.5 overs, 583 mins		515										

Stumps scores:

					Toss: England
Day 1	Cricket Aust XI (1st inns)	9-249	DG Fallins 29*, HNA Conway 0*		Umpires: NR Johnstone, P Wilson
Day 2	England (1st inns)	3-337	JE Root 62*, DJ Malan 57*		Referee: RL Parry
Day 3	Cricket Aust XI (2nd inns)	3-121	JJ Sangha 26*, MW Short 8*		Attendances: 1151, 1054, 1562, 1450, Total: 5,217

FIRST TEST – BRISBANE

Australia pulled some surprises in selection ahead of the first Test. Tim Paine was recalled to keep at the expense of Matthew Wade, Matt Renshaw was dropped due to lack of runs in Shield cricket and replaced by Cameron Bancroft, while Glenn Maxwell was dropped to allow Shaun Marsh to come back into the side. Also missing from the team that defeated Bangladesh in the second Test at Chittagong in September were Steve O'Keefe, Ashton Agar and Hilton Cartwright, who were replaced by Josh Hazlewood, Mitchell Starc and Usman Khawaja.

England, whose last Test was against the West Indies at Lord's in September were missing Tom Westley (dropped for tour), Ben Stokes (criminal charges pending) and Toby Roland-Jones, who was injured. James Vince was brought in to bat at three, Chris Woakes returned, having missed much of 2017 and the final spot went to Jake Ball, who despite being injured in Adelaide, was pronounced fit at the toss, and selected ahead of Craig Overton.

Day One - Attendance: 35,144

On a sunny morning England won the toss and elected to bat and lost Cook in the third over, as he edged a full ball to first slip. Against tight bowling the visitors struggle to get the scoreboard moving, until Vince started to crack some impressive drives through mid-off and the covers. Cummins relieved Hazlewood after just three overs and started with a maiden, England a steady 1-39 after 14 overs at drinks, with Stoneman 15 and Vince 22.

It was old fashioned Test cricket in the second hour, with just 20 runs scored, reviving memories of 1958-59 Ashes, where barely 100 runs were scored in each days play. The only boundary for the hour came from an edge by Vince, who went to the break on 32, Stoneman 25, England 1-59 from 29 overs.

Light rain delayed the resumption of play by 91 minutes and thankfully the tempo increased as the England second wicket pair started to find the middle of their bats. While Stoneman continued to struggle to move the score along, Vince grew in confidence, playing some lovely drives through the off-side, to move to his fifty from 106 balls with six fours. This was the signal for Stoneman to get moving as the score passed 100 in the 42nd over. With an edge for two off Cummins, Stoneman reached his fifty (150 balls, 3½ hours, 3x4) and then in the next over, Vince (68) edged Lyon to Paine – the simple catch going down.

In what ended up being the over before tea, Cummins, bowling around the wicket, beat Stoneman's defensive bat with some late in-swing. The partnership had realised 125, and with Root surviving the remaining four balls to tea, England went for a cuppa on 2-128 (Vince 72, Root 1) from 55 overs.

Vince continued to look at the top of his game, but in the fifth over after tea, pushed one to the right of Lyon at cover, took off for a single and was picked off by the spinner just short of his ground. Lyon had got the perfect bounce and made the most of the chance, ending a four hour knock, Vince's best in Test cricket.

The England captain was struggling to score against some tight bowling and had reached 15 when Cummins trapped him in front with a sharp inducker – making England 4-163, Root out for a laboured knock which lasted 50 balls and 76 minutes. Moeen (surprising batting ahead of Bairstow) came to the crease and swept the fourth ball he faced from Lyon for six, while Malan found the boundary on six occasions as the score reached 4-196 after 80 overs. The new ball was taken by Starc, but after three balls, the light was deemed to be too bad and play was called for the day at 6.14pm.

Day Two - Attendance: 34,358

Play started thirty minutes early with Malan and Moeen taking early boundaries against the second new ball. The reins were then tightened, at one point just twelve runs coming in eleven overs, Malan stuck on 36 for 25 balls and 42 minutes. On 38 Malan hooked a Cummins bouncer to deep square leg, where Starc moved around to field, ripping his pants, which caused him to leave the field for a couple of overs. The left-hander reached his fifty from 119 balls, but fell shortly after, hooking Starc straight down the throat of deep square-leg. Next over Moeen was trapped in front by Lyon and in the off-spinner's next, he bowled Woakes for a duck, through the "gate" as he aimed a drive. England lost 3-4 from 18 balls. After a stand of 20 with Broad, Bairstow top edged a pull shot straight up in the air – leaving England 8-270, having lost 4-24.

Jake Ball took three boundaries from a Lyon over, but then Starc returned and had him brilliantly caught at leg slip, as he looked to whip one away off the hip. Broad (10) was dropped at deep square leg by Shaun Marsh, hooking at Starc, and then cracked a bouncer away through square leg to bring up the 300. His luck ran out in the next over when he hooked to deep square leg, England losing their last 6-56 – all out 302.

On debut, Bancroft took strike and got off the mark fourth ball from Anderson, scoring a couple of runs away through point. His maiden innings didn't last long as he edged Broad behind in the fourth over. England had a deep cover point for Warner in the early stages, looking to protect the boundary and potentially keep him away from the strike. Khawaja looked nervous, getting off the mark with an edged boundary, and then Moeen came on in the ninth over to try and expose the left-handed pair apparent weakness against off-spin. The moved worked a treat, as Khawaja was trapped in front from the second ball Moeen bowled to him, leaving Australia 2-30.

Out strode Steve Smith to join Warner with the skipper starting well, on-driving Woakes past mid-on to the rope. Warner was also starting to tick the score over until Ball came on and got the opener caught at shortish mid-wicket, as he miscued a pull shot. Handscomb started well, taking eleven from the over before Tea, Australia 3-76 (24 overs) at the break, Smith 19, Handscomb 14.

Anderson started the final session well, trapping Handscomb in front with the fifth ball, as the Victorian played well back to a full in-swinging ball, England winning the LBW decision after a successful review. Shaun Marsh walked out and played and missed at his first ball, but struck Anderson through mid-off for a boundary to get off the mark. Smith was quietly going about his innings, Australia only able to add 20 runs in 15 overs after the break against some tight bowling. Woakes returned, the Aussie skipper miscued a hook for four to bring up the 100 and then clipped off the pads next ball for another. Marsh had been very patient and eventually the score started to tick over again. The 50 stand was raised and shortly after Smith tapped one behind point for single to reach 50 from 147 minutes off 112 balls. Marsh started to unwind with regular boundaries as the pair reached stumps, having added 89, Australia still trailing by 137.

Day 3 - Attendance: 33,474

Anderson and Broad started for England, with Marsh bringing up his fifty from 133 balls in the third over of the morning. Shortly after the left-hander drove Broad to mid-off, ending a stand of 99. Tim Paine came out to play his first Test knock since October 2010 and got off the mark belting Ball away behind point to the rope. The 200 was raised and immediately after the second new ball was due and duly taken by the visitors. With the fourth ball, Anderson struck, Paine edging a drive to Bairstow, who dived to his right brilliantly to hold the catch. In the second over with the new ball, Starc gloriously drove Broad for six over long-off, but two balls later popped a low catch back to the bowler, which was gratefully held. Thus, the game hung in the balance, Australia 7-209, with Smith 80 not out, as Pat Cummins headed out for his first Test innings on home soil. Just four runs came in the 6.2 overs leading up to the break, Australia 7-213 from 88 overs, Smith 81, Cummins 2, as over 30,000 fans had some lunch and took a breather, wondering what would happen next in this fascinating match.

Having had forty minutes rest, England went with Ball and Woakes to open up after lunch, rather than Anderson and Broad. Smith and Cummins progressed well, with the pair taking ten off the sixth over after the break, bowled by Ball. Smith was content to pick off the singles where he could, while Cummins grew in confidence, glancing Woakes for four and then smacking Moeen for six over long-on. Finally, after the session was 50 minutes old, Broad and Anderson returned to the fray, bowling opening maidens to their spells, as Australia went to drinks on 7-252, Smith 94, Cummins 28 having added 39 in the hour.

Smith reached his ton shortly after the refreshments, with an off-driven boundary off Broad, from 261 balls – the slowest of his 21 Test tons. Cummins celebrated his skipper's milestone taking boundaries in consecutive overs and looked like he was going to bat the session, but ten minutes before the break he drove at Woakes, edging a catch to slip. The Smith/Cummins union had been worth a vital 66, as Australia inched their way closer to the England first innings total. In the two overs before tea, Anderson went for a rare boundary as Smith slashed him away, then the Aussie skipper uppercut Woakes to the rope, Australia heading in for tea on 8-287, Smith 113, Hazlewood 2 – the difference down to just 15.

After 25 minutes of play in the final session, Hazlewood missed a drive at Moeen, ending a handy 23 run stand for the ninth wicket. Lyon came out and watched his skipper clip Ball for four to long-leg to bring up the 300 and put Australia into the lead. Lyon pulled Woakes for four, but when the stand reached 30, Lyon looked to clip Root to leg, only for Cook to take a good catch at leg-slip. With a narrow lead of 26, there were 20 overs left for play in the day.

Things did not start well for England, as Cook hooked Hazlewood hard to long-leg, where Starc took a sharp catch. In his next over Hazlewood struck again, Vince aiming to force away through the off-side, only to edge to second slip. Root came out to face the music and was struck on the helmet by a short one from Starc, which required him to change his helmet after appearing quite unsettled by the incident. He and Stoneman knuckled down, reaching Stumps, having a lead of seven.

Day 4 - Attendance: 21,535

The England skipper looked well recovered from his knock the previous day, taking boundaries off both Starc and Hazlewood in the first three overs. Stoneman was grinding it out at the other end until he edged one from Lyon, Smith taking the catch low and to his left at slip. Cummins and Lyon were bowling very tightly as runs became hard to come by, Malan managing four singles until he took edged Lyon to slip, this time to the right of the Australian skipper, who held the chance. Moeen came out and in one over from Starc, received four short balls in five deliveries, which made one wonder what playing conditions the umpires were using. Five boundaries came in four overs, as Root and Moeen was starting to take control, the England skipper bringing up his fifty with a clip to leg. Sadly for England, Hazlewood trapped him in front the very next ball – the visitors only 87 ahead, with five wickets left. England lunched shortly after on 5-119, Moeen 26, Bairstow, still badly absurdly low at number seven, on a single.

The sixth wicket pair took the attack to the Australians in the half-hour after lunch, adding 36 runs in ten overs, Moeen ripping boundaries off Lyon, with Bairstow lofting the spinner over mid-on for six. When the stand reached 42, Moeen reached forward and missed one from Lyon, replays called to decide a stumping decision. The ruling was in favour of the Australia, Moeen deemed by the TV umpire not to have any of his boot behind the "line" which wasn't all that straight, as it happened. Woakes was an able partner for Bairstow, as the lead crept past 150, but scoring was restricted to just two an over. Starc wound himself up, getting Woakes to edge to second slip, then Bairstow uppercut a bumper straight down the throat of fine third-man, later revealing he wasn't aware the fielder was there. Broad edged Starc behind and then Cummins had Ball caught at short third-man – the last four wickets wickets falling for just nine, leaving England with an inadequate lead of 169, as tea was taken.

England once again set a defensive off-side field to Warner, while Bancroft managed to find the boundary twice, with a clip to leg off Broad and a guide through gully off Anderson. After just 23 came from the first dozen overs, Bancroft smacked Moeen back over his head for six to break the shackles. Warner started to get moving as the fifty was brought up in the 17th over, the left-handed opener smacking a Moeen full-toss to the mid-wicket boundary. England had little they could offer, Warner went past fifty smacking Ball through gully and Bancroft did likewise, when he glanced Anderson to the long-leg rope. Stumps came with Australia needing just 56 to go one–up in the series.

Day 5 - Attendance: 6,154; Match 130,665.

Australia took just over an hour to wrap up a ten wicket win with Bancroft hitting three fours in an over from Woakes. There had been some byplay in the field throughout, with Broad making a real point of talking to Bancroft from his position at mid-off, whilst Woakes was bowling. Post-match it was revealed that Bairstow had "head-butted" Bancroft in a supposed friendly "greeting" earlier in the tour whilst England were in Perth. To his credit, Bancroft made light of it, humorously mentioning at the post-Test press conference, that he had suffered no damage, because he had the "heaviest head" in WA cricket. "I don't know Jonny Bairstow, but he says hello very differently to most others", said Bancroft as Australia immediately enjoyed their one-nil lead.

First Test at the Gabba, Brisbane on November 23-27, 2017 – Australia won by 10 wickets

England	First innings		B	M	4	6	Second innings		B	M	4	6
AN Cook	c Handscomb b Starc	2	10	11			c Starc b Hazlewood	7	13	16	1	
MD Stoneman	b Cummins	53	159	224	3		c Smith b Lyon	27	81	125	4	
JM Vince	run out (Lyon)	83	170	238	12		c Smith b Hazlewood	2	6	10		
JE Root *	lbw b Cummins	15	50	78	1		lbw b Hazlewood	51	104	160	5	
DJ Malan	c Marsh b Starc	56	130	186	11		c Smith b Lyon	4	17	28		
Moeen Ali	lbw b Lyon	38	102	141	2	1	st Paine b Lyon	40	64	84	6	
JM Bairstow +	c Paine b Cummins	9	24	41	1		c Handscomb b Starc	42	75	125	2	1
CR Woakes	b Lyon	0	4	9			c Smith b Starc	17	57	63	2	
SCJ Broad	c Handscomb b Hazlewood	20	32	53	3		c Paine b Starc	2	9	16		
JT Ball	c Warner b Starc	14	11	14	3		c Handscomb b Cummins	1	5	10		
JM Anderson	not out	5	9	14	1		not out	0	1	4		
	5 b, 1nb, 1 w	7					2 nb	2				
	116.4 overs, 509 mins	302					71.4 overs, 325 mins	195				

Fall: 1-2 (Cook), 2-127 (Stoneman), 3-145 (Vince), 4-163 (Root), 5-246 (Malan), 6-249 (Moeen), 7-250 (Woakes), 8-270 (Bairstow), 9-286 (Ball), 10-302 (Broad)

Fall: 1-11 (Cook), 2-17 (Vince), 3-62 (Stoneman), 4-74 (Malan), 5-113 (Root), 6-155 (Ali), 7-185 (Woakes), 8-194 (Bairstow), 9-195 (Broad), 10-195 (Ball)

Australia - bowling	O	M	R	W	wd	nb	O	M	R	W	wd	nb
MA Starc	28	4	77	3	1	1	16	1	51	3		1
JR Hazlewood	22.4	6	57	1			16	3	46	3		
PJ Cummins	30	8	85	3			12.4	4	23	1		
NM Lyon	36	12	78	2			24	4	67	3	1	
SPD Smith							3	0	8	0		

Australia	First innings		B	M	4	6	Second innings		B	M	4	6
CT Bancroft	c Bairstow b Broad	5	19	16			not out	82	182	212	10	1
DA Warner	c Malan b Ball	26	43	84	2		not out	87	119	212	10	
UT Khawaja	lbw b Moeen	11	24	29	2							
SPD Smith *	not out	141	326	514	14							
PSP Handscomb	lbw b Anderson	14	17	23	1							
SE Marsh	c Anderson b Broad	51	141	168	8							
TD Paine +	c Bairstow b Anderson	13	42	62	2							
MA Starc	c and b Broad	6	5	6		1						
PJ Cummins	c Cook b Woakes	42	120	139	5	1						
JR Hazlewood	b Moeen	6	25	36								
NM Lyon	c Cook b Root	9	22	36	1							
	1 lb, 1 nb, 2 w	4					2 lb, 1 nb, 1 w	4				
	130.3 overs, 561 mins	328					50 overs, 212 mins	0-173				

Fall: 1-7 (Bancroft), 2-30 (Khawaja), 3-59 (Warner), 4-76 (Handscomb), 5-175 (Marsh), 6-202 (Paine), 7-209 (Starc), 8-275 (Cummins), 9-298 (Hazlewood), 10-328 (Lyon)

England - bowling	O	M	R	W	wd	nb		O	M	R	W	wd	nb
J M Anderson	29	10	50	2				11	2	27	0		1
S C J Broad	25	10	49	3				10	2	20	0		
Moeen Ali	30	8	74	2				4	0	23	0		
C R Woakes	24	5	67	1				11	1	46	0		
J T Ball	18	3	77	1	2	1		8	1	38	0		1
J E Root	4.3	0	10	1				6	1	17	0		

Stumps scores:

Day 1	England (1st inns)	4-196	DJ Malan 28*, Moeen 13*	Toss: England	
Day 2	Australia (1st inns)	4-165	SPD Smith 64* SE Marsh 44*	Umpires: Aleem Dar, M Erasmus,	
Day 3	England (2nd inns)	2-33	MD Stoneman 19*, JE Root 5*	CB Gaffeney (TV). Ref: RB Richardson	
Day 4	Australia (2nd inns)	0-114	CT Bancroft 51*, DA Warner 60*	Award: SPD Smith (Aus). Attendance: 130,665	

SECOND TEST – ADELAIDE

Australia went in unchanged for the first ever day/night Ashes Test, while Jake Ball was out for Craig Overton, who was to make his debut. A crowd of in excess of 50,962 was expected, which was the ground record for a day of Test cricket at Adelaide Oval, set in the Bodyline series back in 1932-33.

Day One - Attendance: 55,317

On a cool and windy day, England won the toss and fielded, being the first team to do so in what was the 7th day/night Test. Rain caused several delays in the opening session, Australia carefully moving to 33 without loss in 13.5 overs. Off the third ball on resuming, Warner pushed one to cover where Moeen misfielded it, Bancroft took off looking for a single, was sent back but failed to make it back as the ball had rebounded to Woakes at mid-off, who hit the stumps with his throw. As in Brisbane, England kept things tight, with Australia taking 29 overs to reach 64. Warner then opened up against debutant Overton, hitting consecutive fours and Khawaja laid into Moeen, taking ten from an over. As Warner looked set to open up, he edged a forcing shot to the keeper, just as the time struck 6pm, which would normally be the time for Stumps.

As the natural light slowly turned artificial, Smith took his time, needing 22 balls to make his first five and the England side often engaged in some verbals to attempt to distract the Aussie skipper. He and Khawaja helped themselves to 13 in an over from Woakes, where also Khawaja was dropped on the hook at deep backward square-leg by Stoneman on 44. Dinner came at 2-138 (Khawaja 53, Smith 25) and after another rain delay, Khawaja went from the fourth ball on resumption, edging a drive into the gully. Anderson and Broad applied the pressure on Handscomb as he continued to play largely on the back foot and at one point at the non-strikers end, Smith and Anderson, who was fielding at shortish mid-on, were engaged in lengthy verbal discussion, which umpire Dar needed to reign in. Shortly after Smith dragged one on from Overton, to give him his first Test wicket, Australia 4-161, with Smith out for 40.

Shaun Marsh joined Handscomb who was starting to get his innings moving as the pair played carefully under the lights. The new ball was due with an over to go and was duly taken, but caused no concerns, the fifth wicket stand having added 48 by Stumps.

Day Two - Attendance: 52,201

Stuart Broad started the day for England in fine style, trapped Handscomb leg before third ball, with one that swing in sharply beaten his backstroke. Paine came out and looked positive from the word go, but almost lost Marsh on 29 when he was adjudged LBW to Anderson. Marsh reviewed and ball tracking revealed that it was going over the stumps, much to the surprise of many in the Oval. That was at 5-240, then three runs later Paine (24) was trapped in front well forward to an Anderson inducker, but again tracking showed it was going over the top. Nothing was going right for the England attack as the partnership grew with Paine at one stage copping a blow on his right finger, which had troubled him in the past.

Paine passed Marsh on the scoreboard as he struck Moeen over long-on for six, then reached his fifty in the next over, from 91 balls. Paine's luck ran out when he hooked Overton flat and hard to deep square-leg, ending a stand of 85, perhaps like Bairstow in Brisbane, not realising the fielder was there. Australia went to tea on 6-306 (Marsh 49, Starc 4) and immediately after Shaun Marsh reached his fifty, but watched as Starc aimed a hook at Broad, only to miscue the ball to mid-wicket.

Enter Cummins, who hung about defending grimly until getting off the mark from his 37th delivery. Marsh carried on and after initially being on the slow side Cummins opened up, striking three fours in four overs as the pressure eased. Moeen conceded 14 from an over, then the Marsh raised his century with a pull off Woakes to reach his fifth ton in Tests, passing the four by his father Geoff, who was watching on in the stands. By the dinner break, Australia was 7-409, having 1-103 in the session, Marsh 103, Cummins 44, having added 98.

Not for the first in the series, a wicket fell immediately after a break, with Cummins uppercutting the first ball he faced in the final session to third-man. Lyon came in and helped Marsh add 32, with the Australian skipper declaring at 7.22pm local time, leaving England 28 overs to bat under the floodlights. After a positive opening of 29, Stoneham played back and was trapped in front by Starc in the seventh over. Shortly after the rain started again, and at 8.16pm the players were off and didn't return.

Australian Cricket Digest, 2018-19

On another cloudy and cool day, Australia struck in the second over with Vince flashing off the back foot at Hazlewood, only to edge it to the keeper. Twenty minutes later, Root edged a drive to third slip, leaving England 3-50, having lost two wickets in the first half an hour of play. Cook at the other end was looking steady and watched on as Malan was given out leg before off Starc by Umpire Dar – England won the review, otherwise they'd have been 4-66. In the next over from the left-arm quick, Bancroft nearly ran out Malan as he took off for a single that wasn't there. Cook innings came to an end when he pushed hard at Lyon, edging to regulation chance to slip. Moeen, again batting ahead of Bairstow battled away, being dropped by Paine off Lyon on three, before hitting the spinner for consecutive boundaries. Malan's luck finally ran out and he played back and got an inside edge to a diving Paine. Bairstow entered and looked the part, as he and Moeen saw his team to dinner on 5-128 with Moeen 22, Bairstow 18.

In the third over after tea, Moeen popped one up on the on-side and watched as Lyon dived hard to his left, to bring off a remarkable catch, horizontal to the ground. It was to be the session of caught and bowled as Bairstow drove at Starc and was taken right-handed on the second attempt, leaving England in disarray at 7-142. Over the next hour, the England fans were cheered up by the partnership of Woakes and Overton, who got stuck in and added 66, passing the 200 mark with some gritty batting. Eventually it came to an end, as Woakes aimed a pull at Starc, popping a catch back to the bowler, England taking their dinner on 8-219, with Overton 36 and Broad yet to score.

As in Brisbane, England's last two wickets went quickly, with Broad edging behind and Anderson missing a sweep, leaving England 215 behind and Australia the option of making them follow-on, with 29 overs left in the day, to be faced under the lights. Australia elected to bat and England immediately worked themselves back into the match, as Bancroft edged a regulation chance to the keeper in the third over. There were plenty of play and misses as the second wicket added 34 in 16 overs, before Khawaja was trapped in front and then Warner edged to second slip, Australia suddenly 3-41, with still 40 minutes left for play. Smith was given out LBW off Anderson, bowling around the wicket, to make it 4-41, but a review was called for and it showed the ball had pitched outside leg by the smallest of margins. Smith managed to survive further shouts, plus another fifteen minutes, before Woakes trapped him, as the eventful final session continued. Lyon joined Handscomb and was hit on the groin which saw a delay for treatment, which angered the English, as they missed out getting an extra over in. When stumps was called, Australia leading by a comfortable 268, we again saw some heated words between the players as they headed off the field – in what was an unsavoury end to the days play.

The sun shone as the players took the field, England thinking they had Handscomb caught at slip in the first over of the day from Anderson, after being given out by Umpire Dar. Australia reviewed and replays indicated that the ball had taken the shoulder. Lyon meanwhile was struck on the helmet by Broad, but recovered to take ten off the over, before aiming a back foot heave at Anderson to be caught at mid-off. Shortly after Handscomb steered one to gully, leaving Australia 290 ahead with just four wickets left. Paine went hooking for the second time in the match, Overton running in from the scoreboard hill to dive forward to take a good catch.

At 7-90, more runs were needed by Australia to feel comfortable and they came through Marsh and Starc, who added 32, Starc whacking the lightly used Moeen into the crowd over mid-wicket for six. But the bottom end of the tail didn't wag this time, as Marsh was yorked and Starc hit a high catch to mid-off to give Anderson his first five wicket haul in Australia. When Hazlewood fended one to gully, Australia's last three wickets had gone for 18, tea taken with five sessions left and England wanted 354 to win.

England should have been 1-1, with Cook lucky to survive an appeal for LBW off Starc on nought, which had Australia reviewed, would have gone in their favour. The home side lost the plot for the next four overs, as England added 35, with some of their best batting of the series. England passed fifty, but then Cook's innings came to an end when he trapped in front by Lyon, initially given not out while well forward, but in-line and this time the Aussies made sure they reviewed. Stoneman again looked set before edging low to gully, England heading in for dinner on 2-68, Vince 8, Root 7.

Vince didn't last long under the lights, edging a wide half-volley to first slip, but then Root and Malan dug in as they slowly started to dominate the bowling. Australia lost their final reviews and some would argue the plot, in the space of two overs, after a Root (37) caught behind decision off Cummins then a Malan (3) lbw shout off Lyon both went against them. To rub salt into the wound, Smith dropped Malan off Lyon on eight. It was all happening!

Root reached his fifty, but Malan was labouring, having made 11 off 56 balls, before waking from his slumber to hit Starc for 14 (440204) in an over. Just as England looked like getting through to the close three down, Malan was bowled between bat and pad by Cummins with under fifteen minutes to go, much to the relief of the Australians. Root and Woakes survived to Stumps, England fans still with plenty of hope in their hearts, needing a further 178.

It took just under fifteen minutes for England's hopes to evaporate, with Hazlewood knocking over Woakes and Root in his first two overs of the day. Woakes got a fine edge to the keeper from the day's second ball, while in his next over the England skipper was stuck on the crease in edging low to the keepers left. Moeen was out to Lyon aiming a sweep, England having lost 3-12 in first nine overs of the day. Bairstow went for his shots and watched on as Overton ducked into a length ball from from Cummins, copping a blow to the ribs which saw him buckle to his knees. Overton recovered enough to carry on, but when the new ball came, Starc swung his first ball back in, trapping him LBW as he tried to come forward. The finale didn't take long with Broad edging behind and Bairstow chopping on, England having lost six for 57 in 106 minutes play on the final day to go down two-nil in the series.

Second Test at Adelaide Oval on November 23-27, 2017 – Australia won by 120 runs

Australia

Batsman	First innings		B	M	4	6	Second innings		B	M	4	6
CT Bancroft	run out (Woakes)	10	41	59			c Bairstow b Anderson	4	8	12	1	
DA Warner	c Bairstow b Woakes	47	102	133	5		c Root b Woakes	14	60	89	1	
UT Khawaja	c Vince b Anderson	53	112	146	8		lbw b Anderson	20	49	69	3	
SPD Smith *	b Overton	40	90	118	3		lbw b Woakes	6	12	26	1	
PSP Handscomb	lbw b Broad	36	86	126	5		c Malan b Anderson	12	42	76		
SE Marsh	not out	126	231	361	15	1	b Woakes	19	60	83	2	
TD Paine +	c Moeen b Overton	57	102	111	6	1	c Overton b Woakes	11	27	42	1	
MA Starc	c Anderson b Broad	6	29	32			c Moeen b Anderson	20	25	43	1	1
PJ Cummins	c Malan b Overton	44	90	116	7		not out	11	28	32		
NM Lyon	not out	10	11	19	1		c Broad b Anderson	14	30	44	2	
JR Hazlewood							c Malan b Overton	3	7	17		
	6 b, 6 lb, 1 w	13					2 lb, 2 w	4				
	149 overs, 615 mins	8-442 dec					58 overs, 271 mins	138				

Fall: 1-33 (Bancroft), 2-86 (Warner), 3-139 (Khawaja), 4-161 (Smith), 5-209 (Handscomb), 6-294 (Paine), 7-311 (Starc), 8-410 (Cummins)

1-5 (Bancroft), 2-39 (Khawaja), 3-41 (Warner), 4-50 (Smith), 5-71 (Lyon), 6-75 (Handscomb), 7-90 (Paine), 8-122 (Marsh), 9-128 (Starc), 10-138 (Hazlewood)

England - bowling	O	M	R	W	wd	nb	O	M	R	W	wd	nb
JM Anderson	31	5	74	1			22	7	43	5	1	
SCJ Broad	30	11	72	2			13	6	26	0	1	
CR Woakes	27	4	84	1	1		16	3	36	4		
C Overton	33	3	105	3			2	0	11	1		
Moeen Ali	24	3	79	0			5	0	20	0		
JE Root	4	0	16	0								

England

Batsman	First innings		B	M	4	6	Second innings		B	M	4	6
AN Cook	c Smith b Lyon	37	90	127	3		lbw b Lyon	16	66	84	2	
MD Stoneman	lbw b Starc	18	21	32	2		c Khawaja b Starc	36	65	103	6	
JM Vince	c Paine b Hazlewood	2	10	16			c Handscomb b Starc	15	39	60	1	
JE Root *	c Bancroft b Cummins	9	10	22	1		c Paine b Hazlewood	67	123	182	9	
DJ Malan	c Paine b Cummins	19	58	90	1		b Cummins	29	80	114	4	
Moeen Ali	c & b Lyon	25	57	79	2		lbw b Lyon	2	20	42		
JM Bairstow +	c & b Starc	21	50	63	2		b Starc	36	57	92	5	
CR Woakes	c & b Starc	36	62	95	4		c Paine b Hazlewood	5	10	11		
C Overton	not out	41	79	103	5		lbw b Starc	7	34	39	1	
SCJ Broad	c Paine b Lyon	3	17	20			c Paine b Starc	8	12	15		
JM Anderson	lbw b Lyon	0	3	6			not out	0	0	7		
	15 lb, 1 w	16					7 b, 5 lb	12				
	76.1 overs, 331 mins	227					84.2 overs, 379 mins	233				

Fall: 1-29 (Stoneman), 2-31 (Vince), 3-50 (Root), 4-80 (Cook), 5-102 (Malan), 6-132 (Moeen), 7-142 (Bairstow), 8-208 (Woakes), 9-227 (Broad), 10-227 (Anderson)

1-53 (Cook), 2-54 (Stoneman), 3-91 (Vince), 4-169 (Malan), 5-176 (Woakes), 6-177 (Root), 7-188 (Moeen), 8-206 (Overton), 9-224 (Broad), 10-233 (Bairstow)

Australia - bowling	O	M	R	W	wd	nb	O	M	R	W	wd	nb
MA Starc	20	4	49	3			19.2	3	88	5		
JR Hazlewood	16	3	56	1			20	7	49	2		
PJ Cummins	16	3	47	2	1		20	6	39	1		
NM Lyon	24.1	5	60	4			25	6	45	2		

Stumps scores:

Day 1	Australia (1st inns)	4-209	PSP Handscomb 36*, SE Marsh 20*
Day 2	England (1st inns)	1-29	AN Cook 11*, JM Vince 0*
Day 3	Australia (2nd inns)	4-53	PSP Handscomb 3*, NM Lyon 3*
Day 4	England (2nd inns)	4-176	JE Root 67*, CR Woakes 5*

Toss: England
Umpires: Aleem Dar, CB Gaffeney,
M Erasmus (TV). Ref: RB Richardson
Award: SE Marsh (Aus). Attendance: 199,147

Australian Cricket Digest, 2018-19
NON FIRST CLASS TOUR MATCH

At the Richardson Park, Perth. November 4-5, 2017 – Match Drawn. Toss: Cricket Australia XI.

England XI 9-314 dec (KK Jennings 80, TK Curran 77*) **and 3-130 dec drew with the Cricket Australia XI 4-151 dec and 8-269** (WG Bosisto 50, TJ Dean 100; TK Curran 3-28, MJ Leach 4-104)

In what was a twelve a side game, England used six members of the England Lions squads who were also in Australia. Jennings and Curran made half-centuries on the first day and after further declarations, the CA XI needed an unlikely 294 off 37 overs. They had a chance when Travis Dean whacked a 68-ball ton, but Curran and the expensive Leach changed the game, the match ending in a draw.

THIRD TEST – PERTH

Australia decided to bring in home town lad Mitch Marsh, dropping Peter Handscomb after two quiet Tests with the bat. England kept faith in the same team that lost in Adelaide but had changed their batting order, naming Bairstow at six and Moeen dropping down to seven. The match was expected to be the last Ashes Test to be played at the WACA, with the new Perth Stadium within sight of the ground, across the river near the Burswood Casino.

Day One - Attendance: 22,148

England won the toss and after four boundaries off the bat of Stoneman in the first three overs, Cook went in the fifth, trapped plumb in front playing back to Starc. Vince appeared to enjoy the WACA conditions as he and Stoneman got into the grove of Test match batting, adding 63 before Vince went within ten minutes of lunch, edging a drive to the keeper. England lunched on 2-91, with Stoneman 48, Root 1.

Twenty runs came in the two overs after lunch, with Stoneman reached his fifty (82 balls, 9 fours) as England took the early advantage. But the opener's concentration started to waver as he was dropped twice in consecutive overs from Hazlewood on 52, firstly by Mitch Marsh at first slip, then by Lyon at point. But it was his skipper who was next to go, gloving one down the leg side off Cummins, to leave England 3-115. Shortly after, Stoneman's luck ran out as he was given out caught behind off a bouncer from Starc, after the initial decision was not out. Replays appeared to show that the ball took the glove off the bat handle – which means under the laws of cricket he should have been given not out. Thus at 4-131, Bairstow came out at number six for the first time in the series, to the relief of many of their travelling fans. The England keeper and Malan attacked together from the outset of what was to be a long stand. In their first four overs in partnership they added 24, including a hooked six over the head of the keeper by Malan off Starc. Their recovery continued until tea, England 4-175, Malan 42, Bairstow 14.

On what was now a great batting surface, England had their best chance to put Australia under some pressure. Malan reached his fifty as he and Bairstow continued on in fine style. The hundred stand was achieved, with Bairstow eventually getting to his fifty as the new ball loomed. Starc took it in the 82nd over and had Malan (92) dropped first ball by Bancroft at third slip as he dived in front of second. Three overs later, Malan pulled Hazlewood for four to bring up his maiden test ton, England having added 130 in the final session, by far their best in the series.

Day Two - Attendance: 22,179

Australia's opening attack came out with intent on the second day, Hazlewood and Starc bowling two maidens each, with Malan surviving an Australian review for LBW in third over. After that the shackles came off, the stand reached 200 as Bairstow was able to regularly find the boundary. The pair surpassed the fifth wicket record for England against Australia of 206 (Eddie Paynter and Denis Compton at Trent Bridge, 1938) and then Bairstow reached a well-deserved century when pulled Mitch Marsh to long-leg, many pundits again wondering why he wasn't batting at number six instead of seven earlier in the series.

The pair's stand ended on 237, when Malan looked to loft Lyon straight down the ground, only to miscue towards point where twelfth man Handscomb ran around and dived to his left, to bring off a brilliant catch. It was the trigger for an England collapse as Moeen went three balls later, fending a short ball to second slip. Woakes flicked Hazlewood off his hip low to long-leg and then Bairstow played across a full ball from Starc, his fine innings lasting just shy of six and a half hours. Overton popped a catch to short-leg and then after hooking Hazlewood for six, Broad tried to do the same to Cummins, but toed a catch to short-leg. England had lost 6-35 from 51 balls in just 48 minutes to be all out for 403.

After a quiet start, the openers started to get going and added 44 up to drinks before Warner pushed hard at the second ball after the break, edging to the keeper. Bancroft looked set, but was then undone by a sharp in-ducker from Overton as he fell across the crease, the initial decision successfully reviewed by England. Smith hit his third ball for four through mid-off and then embarked on what would be an innings lasting just close to ten hours. He and Khawaja reached tea on 2-88 (Khawaja 14, Smith 24) then Smith hooked Broad for six in the second over after the adjournment. There was little the England attack could do as the pair pressed on, Smith reaching his fifty from just 58 balls, while Khawaja took 122 for his as the pair passed the century mark for the third wicket. Woakes came around the wicket and trapped Khawaja in front, ending the stand on 124. In front of his home crowd, Shaun Marsh took 18 balls to get off the mark and was close to being caught on seven, when he defended a ball into the boot of Stoneman at short-leg, neither he nor Bairstow able to hold onto the rebound. Marsh managed to hold on, with Smith ending the day eight short of his ton, Australia exactly 200 behind when stumps were drawn.

Day Three - Attendance: 20,858

In sunny conditions it took five overs for Smith to reach his ton, working Anderson through mid-wicket for his 16th four. He showed signs that he was set for another long innings and with Shaun Marsh in tow, the pair added 45 in good style. Moeen was brought into the attack and after being hit for consecutive fours, managed to get Marsh to edge to slip, a badly needed breakthrough with just under six overs to the new ball. Mitch Marsh replaced his brother and carefully played himself in before the new ball was taken after 80.3 overs. Anderson, Broad and Woakes all took turns with it in the lead up to Lunch, but couldn't penetrate, at one point Mitch Marsh taking 44304 off consecutive balls, going to the break on 39, Smith 139, Australia 4-314.

The boundaries continued to flow from the fifth wicket pair, with the pitch now at its best for batting. Smith (150) and Marsh (50) both reached milestones, the hundred stand was raised as the England attack began to wilt. On 173 Smith survived a review for LBW because Anderson had overstepped the front line and watched on as Marsh took over the scoring, at one point scoring 26 out of 27 runs in a four over patch. With an over left for Tea, Marsh was on 92, but he managed to get Broad away for a four first ball, then two balls later a square drive reached the rope, bringing up his ton. He walked off for Tea delighted on 100, Smith 182, Australia 4-421 having not lost a wicket in the session.

There was little relief in sight as the pair ground on, Smith reaching 200 (301 balls) content to push the singles, at one stage scoring 17 in a row as the field was now set deep. Marsh dominated the scoring, regularly finding the rope as he reached his 150 from 188 balls, with 25 fours. England toiled as best they could, even trying the leg-spin of Dawid Malan late in the day, to give their main bowlers a rest. A long day came to an end for the visitors, having only gained one wicket, with Smith (having made his Test best) and Marsh putting on 301 – a new record for that stand in Ashes, Australia now 146 ahead and in control.

Day Four - Attendance: 18,688

England had some early joy as Anderson trapped Marsh in front second ball of the day. Smith found the boundary a couple of times before his marathon effort came to end when he was also leg before to Anderson. Starc was run out in a mix up with Paine, as the Aussie keeper thought they could grab a single from a ball off the pad that rebounded to gully. Thus England had three wickets in the opening half-hour and would have been happy for a quick end to proceedings.

But Paine and Cummins settled in and continued to demoralise the England side, as they began to put together a decent partnership. Paine was given out LBW to Anderson on 11, but stayed having won a review, must to the frustration of the visitors. Apart from that moment there was little to bother the pair and with no sign of a declaration, the pair added 83 in the lead in to lunch. Cummins whacked Moeen for six over mid-wicket in the last over before break, Australia heading in on 7-643, Paine 41, Cummins 36, the home sides lead now 240.

In the second over after lunch, Anderson grabbed his third wicket of the day trapping Cummins in front and when Lyon was dismissed, Smith declared, Australia holding a lead of 259. Stoneman didn't last long, caught behind edging Hazlewood's fifth delivery and then Cook drove one back to the same bowler, who dived to his right and brought off a brilliant caught and bowled. Vince was able to get his innings off to a fluent start with regular boundaries (7 fours in his first 29 runs), before he watched his skipper drive at Lyon's first ball, edging to slip via the wicket-keeper's gloves. When some rain hit the ground, an early Tea was taken, England 3-71, Vince 36, Malan 4.

Vince made batting look easy upon resumption, playing some sumptuous drives on the way to a fine fifty (82 balls, 11 fours), which was reminiscent of his first innings effort at the Gabba. Sadly for him it didn't last, with Starc coming wide of the crease from around the wicket, bowling him with a ball that pitched on middle hitting a crack and taking out off and middle, as Vince looked to work to leg. Malan continued to fight the good fight, hitting four fours in five balls in a Cummins over, with Bairstow also looking good until the rain returned at 4.44pm, ending play for the day. Unfortunately for the WACA groundstaff, it took them a bit too long to get the hessian and then the main covers on and it was to cause problems the next day. They weren't helped by the umpires who probably tried to play on too long when the weather radar showed heavy rain was imminent.

Day Five - Attendance: 8,082; Match: 91.955

On a cold and windy morning, well before play, the covers were blown off during a shower in the heavy winds, with water getting on parts of the pitch surface. Head groundsman Matt Page, who was standing next to fourth official Paul Wilson, was knocked over and later needed to go to hospital. Later as the sun emerged, the covers were removed and it was found that there were damp patches on a length at the Lillee/Marsh end of the ground, and quite rightly England didn't want to play. The umpires deemed that the pitch had to be restored into the same state they were at stumps day four, before play could begin.

Blowers were used to try and dry the track, in between further showers, with the covers coming on and off, play got underway at 1pm, some two and a half hours late. After Cummins completed the over from the night before, Hazlewood bowled Bairstow with his first ball of the day, which landed very close to the damp patch. In the same over Moeen appeared to edge a low catch to Smith at second slip, but on the replays shown, the third umpire deemed that he hadn't got his fingers under the ball.

After an hour of resistance, Moeen was trapped in front by Lyon, making it five out of six for Lyon in the battle amongst the off-spinners. Malan brought up a well made fifty (113 balls) but his effort came to an end when he aimed a pull at Hazlewood and got a touch down the leg-side. The tall New South Wales quick grabbed his fifth when Overton edged low to gully and then Cummins got Broad to glove a short one down the leg-side.

Anderson was cleaned up by a bouncer first ball from Starc, which some felt was an overreach of the short stuff from the paceman. Certainly had the Ashes ended at that moment it would have been an anti-climax, but ironic in a series where little observation had been made by the umpires the laws surrounding intimidatory bowling. Four overs later at 3.46pm local time, Woakes went to uppercut Cummins, getting a touch behind and Australia had regained the Ashes. Smith the Man of the match for the second time in the series as Australia eyed a five-nil whitewash.

Australian Cricket Digest, 2018-19

Third Test at the WACA, Perth on December 14-18, 2017 – Australia won by an innings & 41 runs

England

First innings			B	M	4	6	Second innings		B	M	4	6
AN Cook	lbw b Starc		7	16	20	1	c & b Hazlewood		14	20	34	2
MD Stoneman	c Paine b Starc		56	110	177	10	c Paine b Hazlewood		3	8	8	
JM Vince	c Paine b Hazlewood		25	63	92	4	b Starc		55	95	116	12
JE Root *	c Paine b Cummins		20	23	34	4	c Smith b Lyon		14	20	32	3
DJ Malan	c sub (PSP Handscomb) b Lyon		140	227	323	19	1	c Paine b Hazlewood	54	135	208	8
JM Bairstow+	b Starc		119	215	322	18		b Hazlewood	14	26	42	3
Moeen Ali	c Smith b Cummins		0	2	3		lbw b Lyon		11	56	65	2
CR Woakes	c Cummins b Hazlewood		8	12	15	2	c Paine b Cummins		22	48	93	3
C Overton	c Bancroft b Hazlewood		2	7	12		c Khawaja b Hazlewood		12	21	20	2
SCJ Broad	c Bancroft b Starc		12	10	20	1	c Paine b Cummins		0	2	3	
JM Anderson	not out		0	7	10		not out		1	7	25	
	10 b, 2 lb, 1 nb, 1 w		14				6 b, 11 lb, 1 nb		18			
	115.1 overs, 523 mins		403				72.5 overs, 332 mins		218			

Fall: 1-26 (Cook), 2-89 (Vince), 3-115 (Root), 4-131 (Stoneman), 5-368 (Malan), 6-372 (Moeen), 7-389 (Woakes), 8-389 (Bairstow), 9-393 (Overton), 10-403 (Broad)

Fall: 1-4 (Stoneman), 2-29 (Cook), 3-60 (Root), 4-100 (Vince), 5-133 (Bairstow), 6-172 (Moeen), 7-196 (Malan), 8-210 (Overton), 9-211 (Broad), 10-218 (Woakes)

Australia - bowling	O	M	R	W	wd	nb	O	M	R	W	wd	nb
MA Starc	25.1	5	91	4			17	5	44	1		
JR Hazlewood	28	9	92	3		1	18	6	48	5		
PJ Cummins	28	8	84	2	1		19.5	4	53	2	1	
NM Lyon	22	4	73	1			15	4	42	2		
MR Marsh	9	1	43	0			3	1	14	0		
SPD Smith	3	1	8	0								

Australia

First innings			B	M	4	6
CT Bancroft	lbw b Overton		25	55	79	3
DA Warner	c Bairstow b Overton		22	36	61	1
UT Khawaja	lbw b Woakes		50	123	156	8
SPD Smith *	lbw b Anderson		239	399	579	30	1
SE Marsh	c Root b Moeen		28	75	96	4
MR Marsh	lbw b Anderson		181	236	322	29
TD Paine +	not out		49	85	133	6
MA Starc	run out (Vince)		1	3	5	
PJ Cummins	lbw b Anderson		41	63	99	4	1
NM Lyon	c Moeen b Anderson		4	3	6	1
JR Hazlewood						
	4 b, 16 lb, 1 nb, 1 w		22			
	179.3 overs, 776 mins		9-662 dec			

England - bowling	O	M	R	W	wd	nb
JM Anderson	37.3	9	116	4		1
SCJ Broad	35	3	142	0		
CR Woakes	41	8	128	1	1	
C Overton	24	1	110	2		
Moeen Ali	33	4	120	1		
JE Root	3	0	13	0		
DJ Malan	6	1	13	0		

Fall: 1-44 (Warner), 2-55 (Bancroft), 3-179 (Khawaja), 4-248 (S Marsh), 5-549 (M Marsh), 6-560 (Smith), 7-561 (Starc), 8-654 (Cummins), 9-662 (Lyon)

Stumps scores:

Day 1	England (1st inns)	4-305	DJ Malan 110*, JM Bairstow 75*
Day 2	Australia (1st inns)	3-203	SPD Smith 92*, SE Marsh 7*
Day 3	Australia (1st inns)	4-549	SPD Smith 229*, MR Marsh 181*
Day 4	England (2nd inns)	4-132	DJ Malan 28*, JM Bairstow 14*

Toss: England
Umpires: M Erasmus, CB Gaffeney
Aleem Dar (TV). Ref: RB Richardson
Award: SPD Smith (Aus). Attendance: 91,955

Australian Cricket Digest, 2018-19
FOURTH TEST – MELBOURNE

As Australia chased a five-nil result, Mitchell Starc was ruled out of the Australian side due to a bruised heel, with Jackson Bird brought in. England lost Craig Overton to a rib injury with Tom Curran, son of the sadly deceased Kevin who played for Zimbabwe, as his replacement.

Day One - Attendance: 88,172

In front of a typically large Boxing day crowd, on a white, grassless looking surface, Australia took first strike and Warner was out of the blocks in good style. Bancroft was intent on defence, as he ground out just seven runs in the first hour, Australia 0-37 at Drinks with Warner getting 30 of them. Warner put the pedal to the metal after the refreshment, picking off the England bowlers to reach fifty with a pull off Woakes. Bancroft was fighting hard, eventually finding the boundary for the first time, via an edge in Curran's first over. In the last over before Lunch, Warner smacked Moeen back over his head for six to be 83 at the break, Bancroft 19, Australia 0-102 from 28 overs.

Early boundaries came for both batsmen and then Woakes trapped Bancroft in front, as he was stuck on the crease, ending an opening stand of 122. Warner on 99 then played a half-pull at Curran to be caught at mid-on, giving the youngster his first wicket in Tests, but reviews showed he'd overstepped and thus the opener stayed. Next ball Warner reached three figures as he worked one to leg and then sadly overegged his celebration, given the great bit of luck he'd just had. His knock came to an end when Anderson had him feeling for one outside off, giving the paceman his 100th wicket against Australia. Warner scored 76.29% of the runs in the innings while he was at the crease. England's bowlers had really tightened things up, when Steve Smith came in and the pair made it through to tea, with just 42 added in the session, Australia 2-145 at tea, Khawaja 10 off 57 balls, Smith on five.

Khawaja went fifteen minutes post tea, edging Broad behind, giving him first wicket since the Adelaide Test. Shaun Marsh was in and nearly out LBW first ball, surviving an England review, which had the ball clipping the top off middle and leg, but unfortunately for them was deemed "Umpires call", so Marsh stayed. He eventually found his feet and with Smith made careful progress, the skipper reaching another fifty (from 98 balls) in the series. The new ball was taken after 85 overs (Australia 3-242), and survived despite the odd play and miss, the fourth wicket stand making it through to the close worth 84, with a big first innings score on the horizon.

Day Two - Attendance: 67,882

On what was an ideal batting surface, Australia seemed in the box seat once again to bat themselves into a winning position. But the England attack had other ideas and had a tremendous opening session, picking up five wickets. Smith went inside the first half hour, dragging on to Curran, who after the turmoil of the previous day, had a much deserved first Test wicket. Mitch Marsh also chopped on, this time facing Woakes as England scented they had a chance against the Australian lower order. Shaun Marsh brought up his fifty (130 balls, 200 minutes) as he and Paine saw the score past 300. Then in the last half hour before lunch, England's bowlers responded, picking up three wickets. Shaun Marsh was trapped in front by Broad, who had to review the original decision to have him removed, Paine dragged a pull-shot on and then Bird was leg before, Australia slipping from 5-314 to 8-325 in the space of 25 deliveries. After lunch, the innings came to an end quickly, overall England grabbing 7-83 in 30 overs on day two to bowl Australia out for 327 – well below par on this surface.

England started well with Cook moving his feet nicely and Stoneman once more in the groove. Lyon was on in the eighth over and had a wicket in the third of his own, with Stoneman pushing one back to him, Lyon leaping high in the air to bring off a great catch. With Cook driving the ball nicely and Vince looking in fine order, England continued their excellent second day to be 1-72 at tea, Cook 35 and Vince 17.

Alas for Vince, he was leg before in the second over after tea, but had he reviewed he'd have stayed, "Hot spot" revealing there was an inside edge. Root took 14 balls to get off the mark, as Cook reached his fifty (89 balls) with a firm clip off the pads off Cummins. The former England captain had a slice of luck on 66, when Smith dropped one at slip off Mitch Marsh, the Aussie skippers view perhaps affected by Paine standing up to the stumps. Cook didn't let the drop worry him as he and the current skipper took full advantage of the benign batting conditions. With an over to go before stumps, Cook was on 93 and Smith decided to bring himself on to bowl some leg-breaks. Cook enjoyed a full toss first up, which he despatched for four, then two balls later took two runs, before pulling the fourth ball of an ordinary over to the square-leg fence, to bring up his ton, in two minutes over four hours. Stumps were drawn with England trailing by just 135 – arguably having their best day of the series.

Day Three - Attendance: 61,839

In the opening over of the morning, Root reached his fifty and looked set to really cash in on the blameless looking surface. After nearly 50 minutes though, Cummins set a trap and the England skipper fell straight into it. Root hooked at a short one, Lyon was at deep square-leg and calmly took the catch, much to the batsman's dismay. Malan came out and made a brisk start, getting to 13 off 18 balls, before struggling over his next 24 deliveries, managing just a single. The new ball was taken and with his second ball, Hazlewood struck Malan on the pad as he came forward and was adjudged LBW. Like Vince before him, had Malan reviewed, he would have been reprieved, prompting Ian Chappell on Channel Nine to suggest that maybe batsmen aren't hearing their own nicks because of the thickness of the blades. Bairstow came out with just over 20 minutes to lunch and made the most of his blade, reaching 16, while Cook played quietly along to be 134, England 4-264, just 63 behind.

For not the first time in the series, Bairstow looked set, but Lyon came back on and had the Yorkshireman caught behind in his first over, aiming a forcing shot through the off-side. Moeen Ali came out and immediately lofted his opposing off-spinner to the deep, only for the bowler to watch horror as Cummins dropped the ball over the long-off rope, resulting in a six. But in the spinner's next over, Lyon had Moeen caught at cover, Shaun Marsh leaping high to bring off a fine catch and help Lyon maintain his hold over the England offie. Woakes came out and watched Cook hook a four to bring up his 150 (260 balls, 19 fours) with Cook (153) surviving a second chance, Smith again at fault, although it was a tough chance from a pull shot off Cummins. The seventh wicket pair saw their team to a first innings lead for the first time in the series making measured progress in a stand that passed fifty before Tea, England heading in at 6-360, Cook 173, Woakes 26, with a lead of 33.

In the second over of the final session, Woakes gloved a hook shot down the leg side off Cummins, who had been on and off the field with gastro. This brought Curran in on debut, his first runs an edged boundary through slips after several bouncers. They were to be the Surrey all-rounders only runs as he edged Hazlewood behind to leave England 46 ahead, with only Broad and Anderson to come. With Cook on 182, he needed some support if he was to get to his double ton and Broad did this in some style.

Having received his fair share of short stuff in the series, Broad hooked Hazlewood for four and hung in as Cook moved closer to the milestone. Eventually it came with a straight drive for four off Bird, a shot we'd seen frequently throughout his long innings. With his support job done, Broad began to enjoy himself, much as his father Chris did in 1986, when he made his third consecutive century in that summer's Ashes series win. He smacked Lyon for six over long-on and a little later hit a commanding pull off Cummins to reach his fifty from 59 balls before uppercutting to third man, where Khawaja claimed the catch. Replays were checked, but there was no conclusive evidence that the ball had hit the grass, ending a stand of 100 for the ninth wicket. In gloomy light, England batted on rather than declaring, Cook hitting some cracking shots to end up adding 140 for the day, England finishing it with a lead of 164.

Day Four - Attendance: 29,314

With the opening ball of the morning, Anderson gloved a catch to short-leg to end the England innings. With rain predicted for later in the afternoon, Warner and Bancroft set about reducing the deficit with purpose, with Bancroft taking consecutive boundaries off Broad's second over, while Warner added eight runs in Anderson's third. Curran came into the attack, with his fifth ball he and his teammates felt they had Bancroft caught behind, but reviewed and lost, with technology showing no sign of an edge. The runs continued to flow and the deficit continued to reduce, with Bancroft bringing up the fifty, with a nice clip through mid-wicket to the rope. But next ball he was on his way, edging a drive back onto his pad, the ball then rolling onto his stumps. Khawaja came in and went after Moeen, lofting him over long-off for six, then in the same over using his feet nicely to drive a four through the covers. Then Anderson returned and had him caught behind as he played loosely outside off, Australia going to lunch shortly after on 2-70, Warner 28, Smith 4.

The clouds continued to gather, as Australia decided to go into survival mode, scoring just 11 runs in the first eight overs after lunch. England were bowling tightly and Australia's batsmen were defending hard, when the rain came at 1.58, Australia 2-86, Warner 32 and Smith 16. After half an hour, play resumed, with Curran and Woakes drying the scoring right up. Warner was warming to his defensive role, although he was nearly deceived by a Woakes slower-ball, which he played just out of the reach of Anderson and short mid-wicket. As predicted by the forecasters, the rain arrived, ending play for the day at 3.01pm, with Australia 61 behind.

Day Five - Attendance: 14,128; Match: 266,335

With clearer skies, England embarked on picking up early wickets, knowing they it was the only way they could realistically win the match from this point. Australia's third wicket pair continued to take little risks, with Warner bringing up his slowest ever 50 in Tests, from 161 balls, in just over three and a half hours. The surface was offering little, apart from the odd ball keeping low. Once reaching 60, Warner started to play a few more shots, as thoughts gathered as to whether he could reach his second hundred of the match. Smith on the other hand concentrated solely on defence, and when some rain arrived at 11.36am, Australia was 2-159, Warner 83 and Smith 38.

The break was just ten minutes, but it may have caused a problem for Warner's concentration, as he tried to hit Root's second ball of the innings out of the ground, only to give a catch to cover. It was a poor end to one of Warner's most disciplined innings, which lasted right on five hours. Shaun Marsh nervously edged a four to get off the mark and then on the stroke of lunch, edged a catch to the left of Bairstow, who moved quickly to hold the chance. Australia 4-178 - 14 ahead, Smith 50, with still 66 overs left in the match.

England took the new ball four overs after lunch, but only had a miscued hook from Smith that fell safely, to get them excited. It was old fashioned batting for a draw, as the Aussie skipper and Mitch Marsh blocked their hearts out as just 15 runs were added in the 11 overs after lunch. Smith scored the only boundary for the session, when on 59 he pulled Woakes to fine-leg, while Marsh at one point only scored a single in a patch of 35 balls. England stuck to their task but just couldn't get a look in, when tea was taken, Australia were 4-225, Smith 87, Mitch Marsh 10 (97 balls), having added just 47 in their 29 over session.

With 37 overs left in the match and Australia on their way to safety with a lead of 61, England needed six quick wickets in the hour after tea to have a chance of victory. In the early overs of the last session, both Smith and Marsh found the rope, but then resumed their respective defensive games, as they looked to shut England out. The 50 stand was raised and when on 98, Smith reached his 600th run of the series. In the next over Smith calmly hit one through point to bring up his third ton of the series – from 259 balls, just two balls less than the hundred he made in the first innings in Brisbane. Twenty minutes later the match was called off at 4.47pm, with Australia happy to declare with a lead of 99, with 15 overs to go – England content they'd at least avoided a whitewash, but at the same time cursing the weather which cost them half the fourth day and prevented a better chance of victory.

Cook was an obvious choice for Man of the match, with over 261,335 fans attending, well short of the record 350,534 that attended in 1936-37, a number that appears likely to forever stand the test of time.

Fourth Test at the MCG on December 26-30, 2017 – Match Drawn

Australia	First innings	B	M	4	6	Second innings	B	M	4	6
CT Bancroft	lbw b Woakes	26	95	150	2	b Woakes	27	42	71	4
DA Warner	c Bairstow b Anderson	103	151	212	13	1 c Vince b Root	86	227	301	8
UT Khawaja	c Bairstow b Broad	17	65	104	2	c Bairstow b Anderson	11	14	22	1 1
SPD Smith *	b Curran	76	156	209	8	not out	102	275	436	6
SE Marsh	lbw b Broad	61	148	228	8	c Bairstow b Broad	4	22	28	1
MR Marsh	b Woakes	9	18	18	1	not out	29	166	201	3
TD Paine +	b Anderson	24	36	54	4					
PJ Cummins	c Cook b Broad	4	18	27						
JM Bird	lbw b Broad	4	6	8	1					
JR Hazlewood	not out	1	12	23						
NM Lyon	lbw b Anderson	0	10	16						
	1 lb, 1nb	2				4 b	4			
	119 overs, 529 mins	327				124.2 overs, 531 mins	4-263 dec			

Fall: 1-122 (Bancroft), 2-135 (Warner), 3-160 (Khawaja), 4-260 (Smith), 5-278 (M Marsh), 6-314 (S Marsh), 7-318 (Paine), 8-325 (Bird), 9-326 (Cummins), 10-327 (Lyon)

Fall: 1-51 (Bancroft), 2-65 (Khawaja), 3-172 (Warner0, 4-178 (S Marsh)

England - bowling	O	M	R	W	wd	nb	O	M	R	W	wd	nb
JM Anderson	29	11	61	3			30	12	46	1		
SCJ Broad	28	10	51	4			24	11	44	1		
CR Woakes	22	4	72	2			26	7	62	1		
Moeen Ali	12	0	57	0			13.2	2	32	0		
TK Curran	21	5	65	1	1		20	6	53	0		
DJ Malan	7	1	20	0			8	1	21	0		

England	First innings	B	M	4	6
AN Cook	not out	244	409	634	27
MD Stoneman	c & b Lyon	15	37	47	1
JM Vince	lbw b Hazlewood	17	37	52	3
*JE Root	c Lyon b Cummins	61	133	192	7
DJ Malan	lbw b Hazlewood	14	43	47	3
+JM Bairstow	c Paine b Lyon	22	39	43	3
MM Ali	c S Marsh b Lyon	20	14	15	2 1
CR Woakes	c Paine b Cummins	26	62	92	3
TK Curran	c Paine b Hazlewood	4	15	23	1
SCJ Broad	c Khawaja b Cummins	56	63	89	8 1
JM Anderson	c Bancroft b Cummins	0	16	25	
	4 b, 5 lb, 3 nb	12			
	144.1 overs, 634 mins	491			

Australia - bowling	O	M	R	W	wd	nb
JR Hazlewood	30	5	95	3		
JM Bird	30	5	108	0		3
NM Lyon	42	9	109	3		
PJ Cummins	29.1	1	117	4		
MR Marsh	12	1	42	0		
SPD Smith	1	0	11	0		

Fall: 1-35 (Stoneman), 2-80 (Vince), 3-218 (Root), 4-246 (Malan), 5-279 (Bairstow), 6-307 (Moeen), 7-366 (Woakes), 8-373 (Curran), 9-473 (Broad), 10-491 (Anderson)

Stumps scores:

Day 1	Australia (1st inns)	3-244	SPD Smith 65*, SE Marsh 31*
Day 2	England (1st inns)	2-192	AN Cook 104*, JE Root 49*
Day 3	England (1st inns)	9-491	AN Cook 244, JM Anderson 0*
Day 4	Australia (2nd inns)	2-103	DA Warner 40*, SPD Smith 25*

Toss: Australia

Umpires: K Dharmasena, S Ravi

JS Wilson (TV). Ref: RB Richardson

Award: AN Cook (Eng). Attendance: 261,335

FIFTH TEST – SYDNEY

Mitchell Starc returned to the Australia line up from his heel injury, replacing Jackson Bird, who was wicketless in Melbourne. Chris Woakes was out for England which gave young leg-spinner Mason Crane his debut, Crane well familiar with the SCG as he played one Sheffield Shield game there for New South Wales in 2016-17.

Day One - Attendance: 44,874

Rain and a wet outfield delayed the start of play by just over two hours, England happy to bat first after winning the toss. Having missed the Melbourne Test, Starc was right on the money with his first ball, a yorker which was right on line to Cook. The former England skipper was quite circumspect early on while Stoneman got off to a good start, with some nice shots flowing off his bat. Cummins came into the attack in the sixth over, and had Stoneman edging behind in his third over, England 1-28, Stoneman scoring 24 of them. Vince came out and with little in the pitch he and the former skipper found the gaps and developed a strong stand. Vince played some nice drives as he and Cook added fifty, but when the stand reach 60, Vince aimed a cut at a wide one and got a touch behind. Cook was continuing on his form from Melbourne, cutting Lyon for a pair of fours before Hazlewood returned to the crease and trapped Cook in front with the third ball of his spell, the Australians needing a review to get the decision in their favour.

This left England a shaky 3-95, but Root and Malan combined either side of tea (3-122) to put England in a strong position. Root was close to being caught and bowled off Lyon on 16, but found his rhythm, while Malan took 27 balls and 44 minutes to get his first runs at tea. Root reached his fourth fifty (82 balls) of the season, but then Paine missed a run out chase because of a poor throw and Smith dropped Malan (34) off Lyon at slip. The pair saw their stand past 100 and when Malan worked Starc off his pads to reach a three hour fifty, England were 3-213 with just over 20 minutes left for the day.

The new ball was taken and after a drive and edge for four off consecutive balls, Root clipped Starc to leg, only to watch Mitch Marsh diving to his right to bring off a fine catch. The England captain was utterly devastated to get out eight minutes before stumps and would have felt worse watching from the rooms when Bairstow aimed a drive at Hazlewood in the last over of the day and edged behind, England ending the day five down when it could have been as few as three out.

Day Two - Attendance: 43,846

Malan couldn't build on his fine work of the previous day, out in the first half an hour of play, courtesy of a brilliant catch at second slip by Smith diving low to his left. Moeen faced up to his personal "demon" Lyon and was playing him, while Curran looked adept as a batsman, until he was dropped at mid-on on 21 by Cummins off Lyon, in a rare sloppy moment for him in the series. In the next over Cummins had Moeen dropped off his bowling, Hazlewood having to run some distance from mid-on towards square-leg to attempt the catch. Moeen gloved one behind shortly after, but like in Melbourne Broad took up the challenge, pulling Cummins for six over square-leg. The stand reached 41 when Curran fended one to short-leg and then Broad top edged a slog to slip, with Crane run out on debut after hesitating for a single – England all out on lunch for 346.

Jonny Bairstow took the field with a black armband on to mark 20 years since the passing of his father David, who had also played for England. During the Adelaide Test, a man named Andrew Johns presented Jonny's with a pair of keeping gloves signed by his father David, Johns having won them at a shopping centre back on the 1978-79 tour.

Broad started well with the ball, as he bowling Bancroft with his second ball, as the opener went forward to drive. From there success for the England bowlers would be few and far between, as Australia began to build an imposing total. Warner again took his time, but after scoring three fours in an over from Curran, started to score runs without great concern. Khawaja needed a good innings, having averaged just 27 to this point in the series, but he too found his land legs as their stand bear fruit. Just as Warner passed his fifty and looked set, he played back to Anderson and edged behind, giving England another success just before tea, Australia 2-96 at the break, Khawaja 36, Smith 3.

Khawaja scored a brace of boundaries quickly after tea, then lofted Moeen back over his head for six to bring up his third fifty of the series. England were lacking penetration but at least kept the run rate to around three as the third wicket stand continued to look more and more in charge. In the second last over before the pair passed 100 together, Root bowling the last over of the day, Australia 153 behind at stumps, having not lost a wicket in the final session.

Day Three - Attendance: 43,170

Smith continued on from where he left off the previous day, while Khawaja reached his century with a cut for a couple after half an hours play. The pair continued to be methodical in their approach, not worried about the new ball (2-233 after 80) being taken as the score kept ticking over. Khawaja faced quite a bit of pace in the morning session, Khawaja enjoyed the change of pace, scoring regular boundaries off Anderson and Broad. With lunch approaching, and a stand of near 200 within reach, the unexpected happened as Smith was beaten in flight driving at Moeen, providing a low catch back to the bowler. In the over before lunch, Khawaja padded up to one from Crane, England reviewed but the youngster had overstepped and to rub salt into the wound, tracking showed the ball would have hit the stumps. The visitors trudged off for a feed with Australia 3-277, Khawaja 132, Shaun Marsh 2.

Moeen Ali bowled tightly after lunch at the two left handers, at one stage bowling four maidens in a row. Eventually the pair broke the spell, with three fours coming in an over from the offie, two to Khawaja (one lofted over mid-wicket to bring up his 150) and one to Marsh. When the West Aussie reached 22 he was given out caught behind off Root, but reviewed and stayed as there was no evidence that he had hit it. The pitch had now become it's best for batting and the pair were taking full advantage of the conditions. Just before tea Marsh crunched a square drive off Anderson away past point for four to bring up his 50,

Australian Cricket Digest, 2018-19

Australia 3-365 at the break, 19 ahead with Khawaja 166, S Marsh 54.

There was finally some joy for Crane, as he picked up his first test wicket, getting Khawaja stumped as he was deceived by a flatter and slightly wider delivery. Crane then thought he had nervous looking Mitch Marsh caught at slip before he had scored, England went for a review but the umpire had it right. After 18 scoreless deliveries Mitch finally got off the mark as he and his older brother made the most of the ideal batting conditions. Mitch broke the hold the Crane had on him, hitting him for consecutive fours and a little later smacked Moeen over long-off for sixes twice in an over. Not long before stumps he reached his fifty, but on 55 was given out leg before off the bowling of Curran, review replays showing he got an inside edge. The Marsh brothers made it to stumps, with Shaun just two short of his ton – Australia now 133 ahead.

Day Four - Attendance: 33,285

On a stinking hot day, it took Shaun Marsh just five balls to reach his second ton of the series, as he advanced and cracked Moeen through the covers to the rope. The elder Marsh had a moment on 118 when he edged Anderson between first (Cook) and second slip (Root) at ankle height, the ball slightly closer to Cook who was slow to react. Meanwhile Mitch continued to rattle the boundary hoardings and on 99 hit one past cover point to being up his ton, and halfway through the second run quickly embraced his brother – which nearly caused a run out in the emotion of the moment. It was the eight time brothers had made centuries in the same innings, the sixth time by an Aussie brotherly pairing, after the Chappell's (Ian & Greg) who did it three times and the Waugh's (Steve and Mark) who managed it twice.

The emotion of his achievement may have got to him as Curran broke through his back foot defence next ball to rattle his stump, ending a stand of 169. Paine came out and kept his end up in the hot conditions, Australia lunching on 5-578, S Marsh 145, Paine 14, holding a lead of 232.

A declaration was clearly on the agenda when played resumed, in the third over after lunch Paine pushed one to cover point, took off for a quick single which left his partner Shaun Marsh high and dry after a good throw from Stoneman. Starc cracked a six off Moeen and then was caught at mid-off. Cummins came out and cracked Crane over mid-on twice for four, with the declaration coming an hour after lunch, Australia 303 ahead. To give him his due, James Anderson did a great job on a flat pitch and in the worst heat, as figures of 34-14-56-1 would testify.

When England started their second innings, Stoneman's series came to a quick end after being trapped in front in the third over. Cook could have been out to the very next ball, with Shaun Marsh dropping him a first slip off Hazlewood when on five. Lyon came on in the sixth over and had immediate results, bowling Cook with a ball that pitched on middle and spun sharply to hit the off-stump – which left England 2-15. They crept to 2-25 at Tea (Vince 6, Root 8) and battled away after the break, before Vince edged a back foot shot to Smith at slip, who juggled and then held the chance at the second attempt. On still a very hot day, Lyon was wheeling away from the Randwick end, while the quicks rotated from the Paddington end. Root copped a few blows, one on the shoulder from Starc and then later on the right glove from Hazlewood. Sadly Malan was unable to get the score moving and eventually succumbed to Lyon, adjudged LBW playing back to one that touched the pad before his bat.

With just under an hour to stumps, Bairstow joined his skipper and made the most of a fruitless situation by digging in for the long haul, playing some good shots, while his captain struggled along in the heat. Both made it to stumps – England being 210 behind with a day to play.

Day Five - Attendance: 17,174

Due to a virus and gastro, the England skipper was unable to continue his innings as Moeen joined Bairstow for the start of the final day of the series. Thankfully the insane heat from the day before had left Sydney, as the players went through the final throes of the series. Moeen resisted for nearly an hour before Lyon trapped him leg before – taking his wicket for a record equalling seventh time (see table in the Ashes summary) in an innings. Root had sufficiently recovered and stepped out to resume his innings, eventually working Lyon behind square leg for a couple to reach his fifth fifty of the series. Bairstow, who had been sticking hard to the task, made it to Lunch on 38, Root 58, England 5-144 still needing 159 to clear the deficit.

With Root too unwell to resume his innings, he retired ill, with Bairstow out in the third over after the break, leg before looking to work Cummins to leg. Broad edged a four and then gloved a bouncer to the keeper, while Crane got his right thumb in the way of a short ball, to leave Australia needing one more wicket. After half an hour of resistance, Anderson edged Hazlewood behind and the match and series was over, Australia winning the Test midway through day five by an impressive innings margin.

In a Test where three hundreds were made on a good batting wicket, Pat Cummins was rewarded for his two four wicket hauls, being given Man of the match honours. Australian skipper Steve Smith was the obvious Compton-Miller medallist for Man of the series. With 687 runs at 137.40, plus three tons and ten catches it was an easy decision. Given his lengthy ban for involvement in the ball-tampering in South Africa, his next important mission will be the 2019 Ashes in England, where Australia face the tough task of winning their first Ashes series in the old dart since 2001.

Australian Cricket Digest, 2018-19

Fifth Test at the SCG on January 4-8, 2018 – Australia won by an innings & 123 runs

England	First innings		B	M	4	6	Second innings		B	M	4	6
AN Cook	lbw b Hazlewood	39	104	143	3		b Lyon	10	20	27		
MD Stoneman	c Paine b Cummins	24	24	44	4		lbw b Starc	0	9	14		
JM Vince	c Paine b Cummins	25	54	82	4		c Smith b Cummins	18	51	73	1	
JE Root *	c M Marsh b Starc	83	141	225	8		retired ill	58	167	237	1	
DJ Malan	c Smith b Starc	62	180	248	6		lbw b Lyon	5	27	63		
JM Bairstow +	c Paine b Hazlewood	5	7	8	1		lbw b Cummins	38	143	182	4	
Moeen Ali	c Paine b Cummins	30	58	90	2		lbw b Lyon	13	43	60	1	
TK Curran	c Bancroft b Cummins	39	65	91	6		not out	23	40	64	5	
SCJ Broad	c Smith b Lyon	31	32	44	1	2	c Paine b Cummins	4	2	3	1	
MS Crane	run out (M Marsh-Bancroft)	4	7	18			c Paine b Cummins	2	4	15		
JM Anderson	not out	0	3	5			c Paine b Hazlewood	2	23	34		
	2 lb, 2 w	4					2 lb, 5 pen	7				
	112.3 overs, 503 mins	346					88.1 overs, 392 mins	180				

Fall: 1-28 (Stoneman), 2-88 (Vince), 3-95 (Cook), 4-228 (Root), 5-233 (Bairstow), 6-251 (Malan), 7-294 (Moeen), 8-335 (Curran), 9-346 (Broad), 10-346 (Crane)

Fall: 1-5 (Stoneman), 2-15 (Cook), 3-43 (Vince), 4-68 (Malan), 5-121 (Moeen), 6-144 (Bairstow), 7-148 (Broad), 8-156 (Crane), 9-180 (Anderson)

In the second innings, Root retired on 42 at 4-93, returned at 5-121, then retired ill again at 5-144.

Australia - bowling	O	M	R	W	wd	nb	O	M	R	W	wd	nb
MA Starc	21	6	80	2			16	4	38	1		
JR Hazlewood	23	4	65	2			17.1	6	36	1		
PJ Cummins	24.3	5	80	4	2		17	4	39	4		
NM Lyon	37	5	86	1			35	12	54	3		
MR Marsh	7	0	33	0			1	1	0	0		
SPD Smith							2	0	6	0		

Australia	First innings		B	M	4	6	England - bowling	O	M	R	W	wd	nb
CT Bancroft	b Broad	0	7	6			JM Anderson	34	14	56	1		
DA Warner	c Bairstow b Anderson	56	104	122	6		SCJ Broad	30	2	121	1		
UT Khawaja	st Bairstow b Crane	171	381	514	18	1	Moeen Ali	48	10	170	2		
SPD Smith *	c & b Ali	83	158	254	5		TK Curran	25	3	82	1	1	
SE Marsh	run out (Stoneman)	156	291	403	18		MS Crane	48	3	193	1		2
MR Marsh	b Curran	101	141	191	15	2	JE Root	8	3	21	0		
TD Paine +	not out	38	52	105	2								
MA Starc	c Vince b Ali	11	10	15		1							
PJ Cummins	not out	24	16	24	4								
JR Hazlewood													
NM Lyon													
	2 b, 4 lb, 2 nb, 1 w	9											
	193 overs, 820 mins	7-649											

Fall: 1-1 (Bancroft), 2-86 (Warner), 3-274 (Smith), 4-375 (Khawaja), 5-544 (M Marsh), 6-596 (S Marsh), 7-613 (Starc)

Stumps scores:

Day 1	England (1st inns)	5-233	DJ Malan 55*
Day 2	Australia (1st inns)	2-193	UT Khawaja 91*, SPD Smith 44*
Day 3	Australia (1st inns)	4-479	SE Marsh 98*, MR Marsh 63*
Day 4	England (2nd inns)	4-93	JE Root 42*, JM Bairstow 17*

Toss: England
Umpires: K Dharmasena, JS Wilson, S Ravi (TV). Ref: RS Madugalle
Award: PJ Cummins (Aus). Attendance: 182,349

SERIES AVERAGES
AUSTRALIA

Batting & Fielding	M	I	NO	Runs	HS	Avge	100	50	Ct	St
SPD Smith	5	7	2	687	239	137.40	3	2	10	-
MR Marsh	3	4	1	320	181	106.66	2	0	1	-
SE Marsh	5	7	1	445	156	74.16	2	2	2	-
DA Warner	5	8	1	441	103	63.00	1	3	1	-
TD Paine	5	6	2	192	57	48.00	0	1	25	1
UT Khawaja	5	7	0	333	171	47.57	1	2	3	-
PJ Cummins	5	6	2	166	44	41.50	0	0	1	-
CT Bancroft	5	8	1	179	82*	25.57	0	1	5	-
PSP Handscomb	2	3	0	62	36	20.66	0	0	5	-
NM Lyon	5	5	1	37	14	9.25	0	0	3	-
MA Starc	4	5	0	44	20	8.80	0	0	3	-
JR Hazlewood	5	3	1	10	6	5.00	0	0	1	-
JM Bird	1	1	0	4	4	4.00	0	0	0	-

Bowling	Overs	Mdns	Runs	Wkts	Avge	Best	5wI	10wM	Econ
MA Starc	162.3	32	518	22	23.54	5-88	1	0	3.18
PJ Cummins	197.1	43	567	23	24.65	4-39	0	0	2.87
JR Hazlewood	190.5	49	544	21	25.90	5-48	1	0	2.85
NM Lyon	260.1	61	614	21	29.23	4-60	0	0	2.36
JM Bird	30	5	108	0			0	0	3.66
MR Marsh	32	4	132	0			0	0	3.60
SPD Smith	9	1	33	0			0	0	4.12

ENGLAND

Batting & Fielding	M	I	NO	Runs	HS	Avge	100	50	Ct	St
JE Root	5	9	1	378	83	47.25	0	5	2	-
AN Cook	5	9	1	376	244*	47.00	1	0	3	-
DJ Malan	5	9	0	383	140	42.55	1	3	4	-
JM Bairstow	5	9	0	306	119	34.00	1	0	10	1
TK Curran	2	3	1	66	39	33.00	0	0	0	-
JM Vince	5	9	0	242	83	26.88	0	2	3	-
MD Stoneman	5	9	0	232	56	25.77	0	2	0	-
C Overton	2	4	1	62	41*	20.66	0	0	1	-
Moeen Ali	5	9	0	179	40	19.88	0	0	4	-
CR Woakes	4	7	0	114	36	16.28	0	0	0	-
SCJ Broad	5	9	0	136	56	15.11	0	1	2	-
JT Ball	1	2	0	15	14	7.50	0	0	0	-
MS Crane	1	2	0	6	4	3.00	0	0	0	-
JM Anderson	5	9	6	8	5*	2.66	0	0	2	-

Bowling	Overs	Mdns	Runs	Wkts	Avge	Best	5wI	10wM	Econ
JM Anderson	223.3	70	473	17	27.82	5-43	1	0	2.11
C Overton	59	4	226	6	37.66	3-105	0	0	3.83
JE Root	28.3	6	78	2	39.00	1-1	0	0	2.73
SCJ Broad	195	55	525	11	47.72	4-51	0	0	2.69
CR Woakes	167	32	495	10	49.50	4-36	0	0	2.96
TK Curran	66	14	200	2	100.00	1-65	0	0	3.03
Moeen Ali	169.2	27	575	5	115.00	2-74	0	0	3.39
JT Ball	26	4	115	1	115.00	1-77	0	0	4.42
MS Crane	48	3	193	1	193.00	1-193	0	0	4.02
DJ Malan	21	3	54	0		-	0	0	2.57

Australian Cricket Digest, 2018-19

PLAYER V PLAYER

Australia	Anderson			Broad			Woakes			Ball			Overton			Moeen			Root			Curran			Crane			Malan		
	W	R	BB	W	R	BB	W	R	BB	W	R	BB	W	R	BB	W	R	BB	W	R	BB	W	R	BB	W	R	BB	W	R	BB
Warner	2	101	225		73	175	2	83	143	1	24	22	1	12	16		71	127	1	7	18		55	88		10	19		5	11
Bancroft	1	36	135	2	41	111	2	47	108		16	31	1	1	5		11	12		10	19		17	28						
Khawaja	3	34	186	1	59	97	1	39	76					35	62	1	92	172		8	22		15	50	1	51	103			
Smith	1	122	345		110	272	1	148	257		30	55	1	59	79	1	113	187		9	23	1	39	91		26	41		31	66
S Marsh		51	160	3	67	158	1	50	116		8	12	2	35	75	1	121	249		21	56		35	70		46	55		11	17
Handscomb	2	15	42	1	9	47		13	25		14	12		8	11		3	8												
M Marsh	1	31	76		79	124	1	41	70					29	31	1	67	124		9	9	1	27	43		30	52		7	32
Paine	2	43	74		41	57	1	22	66		5	8	1	21	36		36	58		0	4		10	29		14	12			
Cummins	1	21	64	1	22	77	1	35	111		10	12	1	13	21		38	30		13	12					14	8			
Starc	1	3	10	2	10	10		7	10					2	10	1	22	29		0	3									
Hazlewood		4	11		3	9		1	3				1	1	3	1	1	18												
Lyon	3	5	11		10	31		7	17		4	5		10	5		0	2	1	1	5									
Bird		4	4	1	0	2																								

England	Starc			Hazlewood			Cummins			Lyon			M Marsh			Bird			Smith		
	W	R	BB	W	R	BB	W	R	BB	W	R	BB	W	R	BB	W	R	BB	W	R	BB
Cook	2	44	108	3	78	164		89	149	3	73	196		36	48		45	77		11	6
Stoneman	4	80	137	1	82	158	2	41	107	2	25	99					4	13			
Vince	2	59	102	4	41	115	2	62	109		64	169		9	12		7	18			
Root	1	78	155	2	99	185	4	71	171	1	93	199		21	30		15	26		1	5
Malan	2	91	151	2	57	179	2	98	217	3	116	297		16	40					5	13
Moeen		21	63		33	76	2	35	59	7	90	218									
Bairstow	4	60	119	2	64	131	2	58	152	1	67	156		32	47		14	16		11	15
Woakes	2	31	54	2	30	50	2	19	53	1	17	65		2	3		10	15		5	15
Overton	1	9	23	2	27	40		13	45		13	33									
Broad	3	22	30	1	23	26	3	51	58	2	28	56		2	3		10	6			
Ball	1	1	3				1	1	7		13	6									
Anderson		2	14	1	1	12	1	5	25	1	0	12					0	6			
T Curran		16	17	1	8	10	1	14	24		14	54		14	9		0	6			
Crane		1	1				1	5	8		0	2									

FIRST CLASS AVERAGES – ENGLAND

Batting & Fielding	M	I	NO	Runs	HS	Avge	100	50	Ct	St
JE Root	7	12	1	520	83	47.27	0	7	6	-
DJ Malan	7	12	0	560	140	46.66	2	4	7	-
AN Cook	7	12	1	493	244*	44.81	1	1	4	-
MD Stoneman	7	12	0	455	111	37.91	1	4	1	-
JM Bairstow	7	12	1	395	119	35.90	1	1	16	1
TK Curran	2	3	1	66	39	33.00	0	0	0	-
JM Vince	7	12	0	330	83	27.50	0	2	7	-
CR Woakes	6	10	0	185	36	18.50	0	0	0	-
Moeen Ali	6	10	0	184	40	18.40	0	0	4	-
MS Crane	3	5	2	55	25*	18.33	0	0	0	-
SCJ Broad	6	10	0	146	56	14.60	0	1	2	-
C Overton	4	7	1	62	41*	10.33	0	0	1	-
JT Ball	2	3	0	19	14	6.33	0	0	0	-
JM Anderson	6	11	6	12	5*	2.40	0	0	3	-

Bowling	Overs	Mdns	Runs	Wkts	Avge	BB	5wI	10wM	Econ
JM Anderson	249.5	82	515	22	23.40	5-43	1	0	2.06
CR Woakes	221	39	665	22	30.22	6-55	1	0	3.09
C Overton	118	23	378	12	31.50	3-15	0	0	3.20
SCJ Broad	225.3	61	598	13	46.00	4-51	0	0	2.65
JE Root	41.5	9	103	2	51.50	1-1	0	0	2.46
JT Ball	29.4	6	120	2	60.00	1-5	0	0	4.04
MS Crane	127	14	482	6	80.33	3-78	0	0	3.79
TK Curran	66	14	200	2	100.00	1-65	0	0	3.03
Moeen Ali	217.2	40	702	7	100.28	2-74	0	0	3.23
DJ Malan	23	3	60	0			0	0	2.61
JM Vince	2	0	14	0			0	0	7.00

ONE-DAY SERIES, ENGLAND WIN 4-1

England were too strong in the one-dayers, wrapping up the series with two matches in hand. They had a hiccup in Adelaide, when they were 5-8 batting first, but responded well in the final match in Perth to ensure a comprehensive series win.

Australia recalled Cameron White after a four year absence, but he looked out of his depth with the bat and dropped an easy catch in Sydney, which was rare for someone of his standing as a class fielder. Travis Head was another who struggled early on, until he returned to his preferred opening spot later in the series. David Warner and Steve Smith both looked tired from the Ashes as they struggled for form and had little impact.

Aaron Finch played brilliantly in his three games before being forced out with a hamstring injury and Marcus Stoinis made progress as an upper order batsman/all-rounder type, scoring three half-centuries.

For England, Jason Roy played an outstanding hand in Melbourne to get them off to a great start to the series. Joe Root made important runs and bowled very well when called upon. Chris Woakes was outstanding throughout as an all-rounder and Jos Buttler played magnificently in Sydney, when England were under threat batting first. Tom Curran showed class with bat and ball in the last two games, finishing off the match in style in Perth with a five wicket haul. The 4-1 result equalled Australia's worst performance in a series at home, the other occasion being against South Africa in 2008-09

TOUR MATCH – SYDNEY

The CA XI made a good fist of this game, with Travis Dean early on posting an impressive half-century. England's spinners bowled well to restrict things until Mac Harvey and Harry Nielsen both scored freely to ensure the home side passed 250. England weren't greatly troubled in the run chase, helped by skipper Matt Renshaw bowling himself and getting hit for successive sixes by Hales in an over that went for 21. Morgan enjoyed himself as well, getting some good practice in what was a comfortable win with 9.1 overs to spare.

Tour match v Cricket Australia XI at Drummoyne Oval, Sydney on January 11, 2018 (day/night) – Not List A (12 per side)
England won by 5 wickets

Cricket Australia XI			B	M	4	6	England			B	M	4	6
MT Renshaw *	c Buttler b Plunkett		25	39	43	3	JJ Roy	c Renshaw b Pengelley		40	48	60	3	1
TJ Dean	c Morgan b Moeen		62	63	103	2	1	JM Bairstow	c Nielsen b Fallins		36	36	50	3	2
JM Carder	c Ali b Rashid		16	22	24	1	1	AD Hales	c Carder b Fallins		52	35	46	4	3
JR Doran	run out (Morgan)		16	38	43			EJG Morgan *	not out		81	76	102	7	2
JD Dalton	c Billings b Moeen		14	25	34			JC Buttler +	c Nielsen b Bell		28	26	32	1	2
MWG Harvey	st Buttler b Rashid		59	48	52	4	4	Moeen Ali	c Nielsen b Bell		1	2	4		
HJ Nielsen +	b Plunkett		40	35	59	2	2	SW Billings	not out		15	22	34	1	
BJ Pengelley	c Woakes b Rashid		7	16	19	1		CR Woakes							
CJ Sayers	not out		10	11	22	1		LE Plunkett							
DMK Grant	run out (Morgan)		1	2	4			AU Rashid							
GT Bell	not out		0	1	2			MA Wood							
DG Fallins								TK Curran							
	1 lb, 7 w		8						2 lb, 4 w		6				
	50 overs		9-258						40.5 overs		5-259				

Fall: 1-49 (Renshaw), 2-82 (Carder), 3-120 (Dean), 4-123 (Doran), 5-175 (Dalton), 6-202 (Harvey), 7-224 (Pengelley), 8-255 (Nielsen), 9-257 (Grant)

Fall: 1-74 (Bairstow), 2-88 (Roy), 3-154 (Hales), 4-205 (Buttler), 5-207 (Moeen)

England - bowling	O	M	R	W	wd	nb	CA XI - bowling	O	M	R	W	wd	nb
CR Woakes	8	0	46	0	2		CJ Sayers	8	1	48	0		
MA Wood	10	0	68	0	1		GT Bell	7.5	0	35	2	1	
TK Curran	3	0	18	0			DMK Grant	7	0	48	0	3	
LE Plunkett	9	1	52	2			DG Fallins	10	0	56	2		
AU Rashid	10	0	45	3	1		BJ Pengelley	7	0	49	1		
Moeen Ali	10	0	28	2	2		MT Renshaw	1	0	21	0		

Toss: England.   Umpires: GA Abood, CA Polosak, Ref: TM Donahoo.   Award: EJG Morgan (Eng).   Attendance: 1,778

FIRST ONE DAY INTERNATIONAL – MELBOURNE

Australia were at full strength barring paceman Josh Hazlewood, while England were without Ben Stokes. England had a major success in the second over when Warner fended a lifting ball from Wood to gully. Smith was in an attacking mood before he pushed to Rashid and got an inside edge behind. Head dragged on to leave Australia three down after 14, but Mitch Marsh helped add 118 with Finch, who by now was in control. Australia were well placed at 3-162 after 30 overs, Finch reaching his ton in the 33rd, when he lofted Rashid over long-on.

From here Australia lost their way, Finch was caught at deep mid-wicket and then Marsh, after reaching his fifty was bowled between bat and pad. Stoinis played aggressively, scoring 22 off his last ten balls, but with just 19 coming from the last three overs, Australia's score looked to be a par effort only.

England started their reply in a blaze of glory, Bairstow taking 12 off Cummins first over and then Roy went 644 from consecutive balls off Starc in the third. In back to back overs Bairstow edged a half hearted cut and then Hales miscued a pull. This didn't deter Roy, who after some dodgy form with the Thunder in the BBL, reached his fifty from just 32 balls with some powerful strokes, as England reached 2-87 in the powerplay.

With the field set deeper, Roy and Root were content to rotate the strike, while still keeping up the run rate required. Roy was given out leg before by Umpire Fry on 97, the decision reversed after a review, and then pulled his next ball for three to bring up his ton. This was the signal for him to tee off and he again started to find the rope as the England pair upped the ante. All bowlers were tried without luck, the stand reaching 221 before Roy's magnificent innings ended after he hooked a catch to long-leg. Morgan went quickly but Root was there to the bitter end, with Moeen hitting the winning runs with seven balls to go.

First ODI at the MCG on January 14, 2018 (day/night) – England won by 5 wickets

Australia			B	M	4	6	England			B	M	4	6
AJ Finch	c Bairstow b Moeen	107	119	139	10	3	JJ Roy	c sub (JA Richardson)					
DA Warner	c Root b Wood	2	5	7				b Starc	180	151	187	16	5
SPD Smith *	c Buttler b Rashid	23	18	40	3		JM Bairstow	c Paine b Starc	14	11	22	2	
TM Head	b Plunkett	5	8	12	1		AD Hales	c Stoinis b Cummins	4	3	5	1	
MR Marsh	b Rashid	50	68	88	2	2	JE Root	not out	91	110	188	5	
MP Stoinis	c Root b Woakes	60	40	56	5	2	EJG Morgan *	c Smith b Cummins	1	4	9		
TD Paine +	c Moeen b Plunkett	27	31	56	3		JC Buttler +	c Starc b Stoinis	4	10	15		
PJ Cummins	c Roy b Plunkett	12	10	13	1		MM Ali	not out	5	4	3	1	
MA Starc	not out	0	0	4			CR Woakes						
AJ Tye	not out	4	1	1	1		AU Rashid						
A Zampa							LE Plunkett						
							MA Wood						
	7 lb, 7 w	14						5 lb, 4 w	9				
10 overs: 1-52	50 overs, 212 mins	8-304					10 overs: 2-87	48.5 overs, 217 mins	5-308				

Fall: 1-10 (Warner), 2-58 (Smith), 3-78 (Head), 4-196 (Finch), 5-205 (Marsh), 6-285 (Stoinis), 7-296 (Paine), 8-300 (Cummins)

Fall: 1-53 (Bairstow), 2-60 (Hales), 3-281 (Roy), 4-288 (Morgan), 5-302 (Buttler)

England - bowling	O	M	R	W	wd	nb	Australia - bowling	O	M	R	W	wd	nb
CR Woakes	10	0	65	1	1		MA Starc	10	0	71	2	2	
MA Wood	10	0	49	1			PJ Cummins	10	0	63	2	1	
LE Plunkett	10	0	71	3	3		AJ Tye	10	0	43	0		
AU Rashid	10	0	73	2	2		MP Stoinis	6	0	33	1		
Moeen Ali	10	0	39	1			A Zampa	10	0	72	0	1	
							MR Marsh	2	0	15	0		
							TM Head	0.5	0	6	0		

Toss: England. Umpires: SD Fry, CB Gaffeney, K Dharmasena (TV), Ref: RS Madugalle. Award: JJ Roy (Eng). Attendance: 37,171
Finch 50: 65 balls, 7x4; 100: 112 balls, 10x4, 3x6, Marsh 50: 66 balls, 2x4, 2x6, Stonis 50: 37 balls, 5x4,1x6.
Roy 50: 32 balls, 7x4, 2x6; 100: 92 balls, 9x4, 3x6; 150: 126 balls, 15x4, 4x6, Root 50: 59 balls, 3x4

SECOND ONE DAY INTERNATIONAL – BRISBANE

Cameron White came into the side for his first game since 2014, while South Australian keeper Alex Carey and WA speedster Jhye Richardson made their ODI debuts. In the hot Brisbane sun, Australia started well as both Finch and Warner found the rope. Moeen came on in the tenth over, and had results in his second over, when he got Warner to edge a drive to slip. Smith looked scratchy before being trapped in front by Root, then Head failed again, driving a catch back to the bowler. As in Melbourne, Mitch Marsh joined Finch and they kept the score moving along, Finch reaching another fine ton in the 38th over.

When the time came to really motor the score along, Australia lost three wickets in 13 balls, with Marsh stumped, Finch caught at mid-on and Stoinis edging a catch behind. Carey impressed in his first innings for Australia, but only 57 came from the last ten overs, White unable to find the boundary from his 21 balls with Australia well behind with their final score.

Starc had success with the fourth ball of the England chase as Roy chipped to mid-wicket, but Bairstow and Hales went for their shots, with 12 fours coming in the powerplay of 1-60. Australia had no answer to their stroke play as the added 117, with even Finch bowling three overs of his slow left arm stuff. Richardson came back for a second spell and chimed in to take the wicket of Hales as he chopped on and Bairstow, who drove a catch to cover. Morgan started with gusto, hitting two fours and a six from his first nine balls, as England continued to play aggressively. The England skipper chopped on in the 28th over, but then Buttler came out and played a gem of a knock, putting England well ahead of the rate with stand of 68 with Root in 10 overs.

Starc came back and took the wickets of Buttler and Moeen in exciting fashion, but then when under threat Woakes rose to the occasion with some bold shots, England winning with 34 balls to spare.

Second ODI at the Gabba, Brisbane on January 19, 2018 (day/night) – England won by 4 wickets

Australia		B	M	4	6	England		B	M	4	6
DA Warner	c Root b Moeen	35	40	50	5	JJ Roy	c Finch b Starc	2	4	2	
AJ Finch	c Roy b Plunkett	106	114	169	9	JM Bairstow	c Warner b Richardson	60	56	89	9
SPD Smith *	lbw b Root	18	25	32	1	AD Hales	b Richardson	57	60	75	7	1
TM Head	c & b Root	7	18	14		JE Root	not out	46	58	112	1
MR Marsh	st Buttler b Rashid	36	43	64	3	EJG Morgan *	b Starc	21	27	23	2	1
MP Stoinis	c Buttler b Rashid	4	6	11		JC Buttler +	c Carey b Starc	42	32	44	5
CL White	not out	15	21	48		Moeen Ali	b Starc	1	2	2	
AT Carey +	run out (Woakes)	27	24	29	4	CR Woakes	not out	39	27	29	5	1
MA Starc	c Roy b Woakes	3	6	8		AU Rashid					
AJ Tye	run out (Woakes)	8	4	3	1	LE Plunkett					
JA Richardson						MA Wood					
	2 lb, 1 nb, 8 w	11					1 lb, 5 w	6			
10 overs : 0-56	50 overs, 218 mins	270				10 overs : 1-60	44.2 overs, 191 mins	6-274			

Fall: 1-68 (Warner), 2-110 (Smith), 3-124 (Head), 4-209 (Marsh), 5-213 (Finch), 6-216 (Stoinis), 7-255 (Carey), 8-261 (Starc), 9-270 (Tye)

Fall: 1-2 (Roy), 2-119 (Hales), 3-129 (Bairstow), 4-157 (Morgan), 5-225 (Buttler), 6-227 (Moeen)

England - bowling	O	M	R	W	wd	nb	Australia - bowling	O	M	R	W	wd	nb
MA Wood	9	0	55	0			MA Starc	10	0	59	4	1	
CR Woakes	9	0	37	1	1		JA Richardson	10	1	57	2	1	
LE Plunkett	8	0	43	1	5		TM Head	7	0	55	0		
Moeen Ali	7	0	31	1			AJ Tye	9	0	47	0	1	
AU Rashid	10	0	71	2	2		AJ Finch	3	0	17	0	1	
JE Root	7	0	31	2			MP Stoinis	4.2	0	34	0	1	
							MR Marsh	1	0	4	0		

Toss: England. Umpires: K Dharmasena, SJ Nogajski, CB Gaffeney (TV), Ref: RS Madugalle. Award: JE Root (Eng). Attendance: 29,685
Finch 50: 51 balls, 5x4, 1x6; 100: 104 balls, 9x4, 1x6. Bairstow 50: 41 balls, 9x4, Hales 50: 52 balls, 7x4,1x6.

THIRD ONE DAY INTERNATIONAL – SYDNEY

Tim Paine was back for Australia, as was Josh Hazlewood, who had been rested from the first two games of the series. England were sent in and lost Roy in the seventh over driving to cover and Hales went in the tenth, chipping a catch to mid-on. Bairstow had been well contained and fell to Zampa, beaten in the flight aiming to drive at a wrong-un. Morgan started well finding the rope early on but lost Root when he played on to his stumps. With England 4-107 in the 23rd over, Australia were on top but Buttler came out and began what was to be one of his finest knocks. Firstly he and Morgan added 65, and then 113 with Woakes.

England were 6-200 with ten overs left and 6-226 with six to go when the seventh wicket pair launched their final attack. Buttler hit Hazlewood for six over long-off, Woakes pulled Cummins for six as the Australians bowled too short. England scored 76 off their last six overs, with Cummins conceding 44 off his last three. In the last over Woakes pulled Starc for six to reach fifty and off the last ball of the innings, Buttler drove to long-on for a couple to reach his hundred.

It was hoped that Warner could anchor the run chase on his home ground, but it wasn't to be as he was caught at cover point driving in the fourth over. White showed a little more fluency than in the previous game before edging behind, and then Plunkett went off injured in the 12th over, which meant England would need overs from Root's off-spin.

Smith came out and played a laboured knock, looking like a man tired from being overworked. At the other end Finch was making the most of the little strike he was getting (he only faced 20 balls in the first ten overs), reaching his fifty in an over where he hit Root for back to back sixes, the second caught by a policeman. Finch went in the 21st over aiming a sweep, then Mitch Marsh came out and batted well, Australia 3-160 after 30 overs, needing seven an over off the last twenty.

Smith, who took 63 balls to hit his one and only four was controversially given out caught behind, some replays suggesting the ball hit the ground before it went safely into Buttler's right glove. When Marsh miscued a pull to wide long-on it came down to Australia needing 90 off the last ten overs. Stoinis and Paine tried hard, but England restricted them to just one boundary in overs 41-45, with 61 wanted off the last five. Stoinis started to unwind, but it was too big an ask, England winning the match and clinching the five-match series with two games in hand.

Third ODI at the SCG on January 21, 2018 (day/night) – England won by 16 runs

England		B	M	4	6	Australia		B	M	4	6
JJ Roy	c Finch b Cummins	19	24	36	4	AJ Finch	lbw b Rashid	62	53	84	3	3
JM Bairstow	b Zampa	39	57	89	2	DA Warner	c Hales b Woakes	8	10	17	2	
AD Hales	c Zampa b Stoinis	1	8	12		CL White	c Buttler b Wood	17	25	21	3	
JE Root	b Hazlewood	27	31	56	1	SPD Smith *	c Buttler b Wood	45	66	97	1	
EJG Morgan *	c Paine b Hazlewood	41	50	74	2	1	MR Marsh	c Hales b Rashid	55	66	74	4	
JC Buttler +	not out	100	83	131	6	4	MP Stoinis	c sub (SW Billings)					
							b Woakes	56	43	68	3	2
MM Ali	b Marsh	6	12	15		TD Paine +	not out	31	35	53	1	
CR Woakes	not out	53	36	57	5	2	PJ Cummins	not out	1	2	3		
AU Rashid						MA Starc						
LE Plunkett						A Zampa						
MA Wood						JR Hazlewood						
	2 lb, 1 nb, 13 w	16					4 b, 5 lb, 2 w	11				
10 overs : 2-47	50 overs, 238 mins	6-302				10 overs : 2-49	50 overs, 213 mins	6-286				

Fall: 1-38 (Roy), 2-45 (Hales), 3-90 (Bairstow), 4-107 (Root), 5-172 (Morgan), 6-189 (Moeen)

Fall: 1-24 (Warner), 2-44 (White), 3-113 (Finch), 4-181 (Smith), 5-210 (Marsh), 6-284 (Stoinis)

Australia - bowling	O	M	R	W	wd	nb	England - bowling	O	M	R	W	wd	nb
MA Starc	10	0	63	0	3		MA Wood	10	1	46	2	2	
JR Hazlewood	10	0	58	2			CR Woakes	10	0	57	2		
PJ Cummins	10	1	67	1	6	1	LE Plunkett	1.2	0	6	0		
MP Stoinis	8	0	43	1	1		Moeen Ali	10	0	57	0		
A Zampa	9	0	55	1			JE Root	8.4	0	60	0		
MR Marsh	3	0	14	1	2		AU Rashid	10	0	51	2		

Toss: England. Umpires: SD Fry, CB Gaffeney K Dharmasena (TV), Ref: RS Madugalle. Award: JC Buttler (Eng). Attendance: 35,195
Buttler 50: 52 balls, 2x4, 1x6; 100: 83 balls, 6x4, 4x6, Woakes 50: 35 balls, 5x4, 2x6.
Finch 50: 49 balls, 3x4, 2x6, M Marsh 50: 60 balls, 4x4, Stoinis 50: 40 balls, 3x4, 2x6

FOURTH ONE DAY INTERNATIONAL – ADELAIDE

In overcast and cool conditions, Australia's bowlers took full advantage of a pitch that had a reasonable amount of grass on it. Roy drove the second ball of the match to cover point, and in Cummins first over he penetrated the defence of Hales as he played forward. Bairstow edged a drive and when Root top edged a hook to long-leg, England were a remarkable 4-6 in the sixth over. When Buttler wafted a one outside off, they'd slipped to 5-8 and one wondered how long the game was going to last. But Moeen dug in with Morgan adding 53 before Cummins came back and induced the England skipper to glove a hook. Woakes came out and again looked in devastating touch, being severe of Zampa in one over where he conceded 14, including being smacked over long-on for six.

Moeen went to a fine catch by Head right on the deep square-leg rope and then Rashid was caught behind leaving England eight down with 18 overs to go. Curran came out an offered great support, with Woakes going on a Sydney like rampage after reaching fifty. He whacked Stoinis for a couple of sixes and again took Zampa over long-on, but his time ran out when he lifted Tye to long-on. When Curran was last out after an impressive knock, England had almost reached 200, a fighting effort when they were at one point looking like losing before the dinner break.

With Finch out due to an injured hamstring, Head was back at the top of the order and watched as again Warner went early, edging a drive to the keeper. White was trapped in front as he played across his front pad, but with Head batting fluently Australia were progressing well. Smith looked flat again before being edging to slip but then Marsh came out and took the pressure off, in a stand of 42 in eight overs. Head reached his fifty and passed 1,000 ODI runs, but then just as he was getting going, Marsh smacked a low full toss back to a grateful Rashid. Stoinis hit Rashid for consecutive fours, but then misread a wrong-un, hitting a catch to cover point – Australia still wanting 61 with five wickets in hand.

Paine joined Head, the South Aussie still playing his shots and he progressed on towards a ton on his home deck. Sadly for him it wasn't to be as with victory in sight, he flat batted a pull-shot to mid-on to be out for 96. There were some jitters in the final stages as Cummins was run out, Paine refusing his partners call for an easy second run, but the Aussie keeper redeemed himself as he hit two fours in a row off Wood, before Tye finished the game off with 13 overs to spare.

Fourth ODI at Adelaide Oval on January 26, 2018 (day/night) – Australia won by 3 wickets

England			B	M	4	6	Australia			B	M	4	6
JJ Roy	c Smith b Hazlewood	0	2	1			DA Warner	c Buttler b Woakes	13	11	19	2	
JM Bairstow	c Paine b Hazlewood	0	9	20			TM Head	c Morgan b Wood	96	107	146	15	
AD Hales	b Cummins	3	11	13			CL White	lbw b Curran	3	7	13		
JE Root	c Hazlewood b Cummins	0	7	11			SPD Smith *	c Root b Rashid	4	16	23		
EJG Morgan *	c Paine b Cummins	33	61	77	1		MR Marsh	c &b Rashid	32	30	30	3	1
JC Buttler +	c Paine b Hazlewood	0	2	4			MP Stoinis	c Roy b Rashid	14	11	16	3	
MM Ali	c Head b Tye	33	50	102	3		TD Paine +	not out	25	31	57	2	
CR Woakes	c sub (GJ Maxwell)	78	82	88	4	5	PJ Cummins	run out (Curran-Wood)	3	9	10		
	b Tye						AJ Tye	not out	3	1	5		
AU Rashid	c Paine b Cummins	7	8	8	1		A Zampa						
TK Curran	c Marsh b Tye	35	35	40	2	1	JR Hazlewood						
MA Wood	not out	2	2	7									
	1 b, 4 w	5						1 nb, 3 w	4				
10 overs: 5-18	44.5 overs, 195 mins	196					10 overs: 2-61	37 overs, 163 minutes	7-197				

Fall: 1-0 (Roy), 2-4 (Hales), 3-4 (Bairstow), 4-6 (Root), 5-8 (Buttler), 6-61 (Morgan), 7-112 (Ali), 8-120 (Rashid), 9-180 (Woakes), 10-196 (Curran)

Fall: 1-25 (Warner), 2-48 (White), 3-70 (Smith), 4-112 (Marsh), 5-136 (Stoinis), 6-180 (Head), 7-185 (Cummins)

Australia - bowling	O	M	R	W	wd	nb	England - bowling	O	M	R	W	wd	nb
JR Hazlewood	10	0	39	3	1		CR Woakes	7	0	36	1		
PJ Cummins	10	2	24	4	2		MA Wood	9	0	58	1	1	
MR Marsh	5	1	24	0			TK Curran	2	1	10	1	2	
AJ Tye	7.5	0	33	3			Moeen Ali	8	0	41	0		1
TM Head	2	0	9	0			AU Rashid	10	0	49	3		
A Zampa	7	0	42	0	1		JE Root						
MP Stoinis	3	0	24	0									

Toss: England. Umpires: K Dharmasena, SJ Nogajski, CB Gaffeney (TV), Ref: RS Madugalle. Award: PJ Cummins (Aus). Attendance: 24,329. Woakes 50: 62 balls, 4x4, 2x6. Head 50: 55 balls, 9x4

FIFTH ONE DAY INTERNATIONAL – PERTH

It was all systems go in the west for the first cricket match at the new Perth Stadium, with close to 42,000 packed in for the first ball. Roy worked Starc away behind square leg for an all-run four, which will make for a great of trivia question for the locals in the years to come. In the third over Roy belted Starc straight down the ground for six but next ball was brilliantly caught behind, only for replays to show the bowler had overstepped. The pitch had a cracked appearance to it, not unlike the WACA and when Roy faced one that took off from a length, going for four byes over the keepers head, it helped ensured all present would be watching each ball very closely.

Roy was flying along dominating proceedings until quite appropriately, local man Tye took the first wicket, as the opener hit a catch to mid-on. Bairstow then took it upon himself to unleash, belting Maxwell straight in his first over for six and then uppercutting the returning Starc for one as well. Starc had his revenge with Bairstow chopping on and then Hales started to lift the tempo, as he made the most of the short boundary straight, lofting the part-timer for six. Hales was caught when a miscued hook to his helmet on the way to point and another local had a moment in the Perth sun as Marsh had Morgan well caught by a diving Stoinis at deep point.

The pitch seemed to tire a little as the innings wore on, Buttler caught as he mishit a lofted shot to mid-off. Root reached his fifty with an uppercut for four and then Smith fired out Rashid with a wicked throw from point, as he tried for a quick single. Root was second last out in the 48th over, England all out with 14 balls left unused – Tye mopping up the tail to take the first wicket haul at the new venue.

A target of 260 should have been within reach for Australia, but when Warner was yorked in the fourth over, England sensed they had a way in. Stoinis played superbly from the start, as he revelled in the freedom of just two inside the circle in the powerplay. He uppercut Ball in the second deck of the stand and then Head, who had been dropped on four in the second over by Bairstow at slip, was then run out by Morgan. A streaker invaded the field in the 17th over, which caused a delay but it didn't deter Stoinis who reached a 57-ball fifty. Smith again look laboured in his knock, before misreading an arm ball to be stumped. Marsh started well before smacking one hard back at Moeen, the bowler taking a brilliant one handed catch like someone picking a cherry off a tree.

Playing his first match in the series, Maxwell settled in to join Stoinis and looked at ease as he calmly lofted Moeen over long-off for six. Stoinis did likewise to Rashid as they added 66, before Stoinis went to a fine low catch at long-on. Maxwell lost his shape as he aimed a heave to leg and when Starc edged low to Buttler's left, Australia had lost 3-3 in 16 balls. Paine and Zampa added 33 to take Australia to within 24 of a win, before Zampa had his stumps splattered by Curran. After Paine took Ball for 11 in the 48th, including a ramped six to fine-leg, Australia were left wanting 13 off the last two balls.

Curran held his nerve and pitched up to Paine, who missed an in-swinging yorker, which finished the game – England claiming a four-one series win.

Fifth ODI at Perth Stadium on January 28, 2018 – England won by 12 runs

England		B	M	4	6	Australia		B	M	4	6
JJ Roy	c Hazlewood b Tye	49	46	53	8	1	DA Warner	b Curran	15	11	14	2	
JM Bairstow	b Starc	44	48	83	4	2	TM Head	run out (Morgan)	22	30	60	2	
AD Hales	c Maxwell b Marsh	35	47	56	3	1	MP Stoinis	c Curran b Rashid	87	99	130	6	4
JE Root	c Warner b Tye	62	68	126	2		SPD Smith *	st Buttler b Moeen	12	23	31		
EJG Morgan *	c Stoinis b Marsh	3	10	10			MR Marsh	c & b Moeen	13	11	7	2	
JC Buttler +	c Warner b Tye	21	25	31	1	1	GJ Maxwell	lbw b Curran	34	39	54	3	1
Moeen Ali	c Tye b Zampa	6	12	17			TD Paine +	b Curran	34	44	78	2	1
AU Rashid	run out (Smith)	12	16	16	1		MA Starc	c Buttler b Curran	0	2	1		
DJ Willey	c Marsh b Tye	2	6	7			AJ Tye	c Morgan b Moeen	8	11	12	1	
TK Curran	not out	11	7	10		1	A Zampa	b Curran	11	17	37	1	
JT Ball	b Tye	0	2	2			JR Hazlewood	not out	0	3	10		
	4 b, 2 lb, 1 nb, 7 w	14						7 lb, 4 w	11				
10 overs: 0-66	47.4 overs, 214 mins	259					10 overs: 1-63	48.2 overs, 226 mins	247				

Fall: 1-71 (Roy), 2-117 (Bairstow), 3-151 (Hales), 4-157 (Morgan), 5-192 (Buttler), 6-214 (Moeen), 7-238 (Rashid), 8-245 (Willey), 9-258 (Root), 10-259 (Ball)

Fall: 1-24 (Warner), 2-86 (Head), 3-119 (Smith), 4-133 (Marsh), 5-189 (Stoinis), 6-192 (Maxwell), 7-192 (Starc), 8-203 (Tye), 9-236 (Zampa), 10-247 (Paine)

Australia - bowling	O	M	R	W	wd	nb
MA Starc	9	0	63	1	1	1
JR Hazlewood	9	0	51	0	1	
MR Marsh	7	0	24	2		
AJ Tye	9.4	0	46	5	4	
A Zampa	10	0	46	1	1	
GJ Maxwell	3	0	23	0		

England - bowling	O	M	R	W	wd	nb
DJ Willey	9	1	54	0	2	
TK Curran	9.2	0	35	5	1	
Moeen Ali	10	0	55	3		
AU Rashid	10	0	55	1		
JT Ball	10	0	58	0	1	

Toss: England. Umpires: SD Fry, CB Gaffeney, K Dharmasena, (TV), Ref: RS Madugalle. Award: TK Curran (Eng). Attendance: 53,781. Root 50: 57 balls, 2x4. Stoinis 50: 57 balls, 5x4, 2x6

TOUR MATCH – SYDNEY

This match in Canberra was played as a lead in to the Twenty20 tri-series to be started in Australia and completed in New Zealand. Apart from Handscomb, the PM's XI struggled in their innings. Sam Billings took a brilliant catch to dismiss a struggling James Faulkner, as he skipped over and back across the rope at wide long-on – his feet only touching the ground while he was in the field of play, satisfying Law 32.3.

England cruised home in the chase, with David Willey cracking Nathan Lyon for 34 from the sixth over, hitting five sixes from the first five balls until the off-spinner fired in a quicker last ball of the over, which was hit through cover for four.

Tour match v Prime Ministers XI at Manuka Oval, Canberra on February 2, 2018 – England won by 8 wickets

Prime Minister's XI		B	4	6	England		B	4	6
P M Nevill +	b Willey	6	6	1	JM Vince	b Swepson	26	14	3	1
NJ Maddinson	c Rashid b Willey	8	9	1	DJ Willey	c Abbott b Swepson	79	36	6	6
PSP Handscomb	b Dawson	43	29	7	DJ Malan	not out	21	22	1
JP Faulkner	c Billings b Rashid	2	9		EJG Morgan *	not out	8	5	1
KR Patterson	c and b Dawson	11	15		SW Billings				
DP Hughes	st Buttler b Dawson	11	12	1	JC Buttler +				
SE Gotch	c S Curran b Wood	22	22	1	LA Dawson				
GS Sandhu	b Willey	19	14	1	1	SM Curran				
SA Abbott	not out	5	3		AU Rashid				
NM Lyon *	not out	1	1		TK Curran				
MJ Swepson					MA Wood				
	6 lb, 2 w	8				1 nb, 4 w	5		
	20 overs	8-136				12.4 overs	2-139		

Fall: 1-18 (Nevill, 2.1), 2-23 (Maddinson, 2.5), 3-49 (Faulkner, 6.6), 4-74 (Handscomb, 10.4), 5-79 (Patterson, 12.1), 6-90 (Hughes, 14.1), 7-122 (Sandhu, 18.3), 8-135 (Gotch, 19.5)

Fall: 1-87 (Vince, 6.3), 2-127 (Willey, 10.5)

England - bowling	O	M	R	W	wd	nb	Dots	P M's XI - bowling	O	M	R	W	wd	nb	Dots
DJ Willey	4	0	32	3	1		9	GS Sandhu	3	0	27	0	2	1	5
MA Wood	4	0	30	1			8	NM Lyon	2	0	43	0			2
TK Curran	3	0	23	0			9	JP Faulkner	2	0	20	0			4
AU Rashid	3	0	14	1			5	SA Abbott	2	0	16	0			4
SM Curran	2	0	15	0	1		4	MJ Swepson	3.4	0	33	2	1		7
LA Dawson	4	0	16	3			8								

Toss: England. Umpires: DM Koch, DJ Shepard, Ref: SJA Taufel.   Award: DJ Willey (Eng).

Willey 50: 23 balls, 3x4, 4x6

AUSTRALIA GOES UNBEATEN TO WIN TWENTY20 TRI-SERIES

Australia won the first ever Twenty20 tri-series played in both Australia and New Zealand. They were unbeaten across their five matches, winning three straight on home soil, before winning a record high scoring affair in Auckland. The final saw Australia reign in the New Zealand big hitters, restricting them to just 9-150, the win coming despite rain interruptions and the DLS target.

Batting wise, Australia's Glenn Maxwell was one of the outstanding performers in the tournament, making 233 runs (SR 166) for just twice out. Martin Guptill was New Zealand's dominant player, passing fifty three times in five innings. Colin Munro was also a constant danger with that bat for New Zealand, while for England Dawid Malan produced three very good innings.

With the ball, Australia's Billy Stanlake was a dangerous proposition, while AJ Tye did the hack work at the end of the innings to be the leading wicket-taker in the tournament. Ashton Agar was also an important part of the Aussie attack, bowling mostly in the middle overs. For New Zealand, Trent Boult took most wickets but was expensive, while Ish Sodhi impressed with his leg-breaks. England struggled with the ball, with only Adil Rashid and David Willey playing to their ability.

Overall there were some entertaining matches, and the concept of a tri-series played in two countries did work well. On the down side it is fair to say that Eden Park in Auckland is now too small a venue for the shorter forms of International cricket, given the extremely short nature of some of the boundaries at the ground.

MATCH ONE - SYDNEY

Australia were too good for the Blackcaps, blitzing their batting line-up with an impressive bowling display. Stanlake set the ball rolling being on a hat-trick after his first two balls, having Munro caught behind aiming a pull shot, then hitting the top of Guptill's off stump with a peach of a ball. Williamson struggled until getting a leading edge over cover, Warner running back to hold the chance. Taylor also found scoring difficult and it was only de Grandhomme who really fired a shot. He hit Zampa twice for six in the 15th, battling through to the end of what was a disappointing innings.

With rain reducing the target to 95 off 15 overs, Short mistimed a pull in the second over and Warner hooked to deep square-leg in the third, to leave Australia a little stressed. But after that Australia were untroubled, with Lynn and Maxwell dominating proceedings with a stand of 77 – which all but clinched the victory.

Australia v New Zealand at Sydney Cricket Ground on February 3, 2017 (night) – Australia won by 7 wickets (DLS)

New Zealand		B	4	6	Australia	(DLS Target 95 off 15)		B	4	6
MJ Guptill	b Stanlake	5	5	1	DA Warner *	c Bruce b Boult	6	8	1	
C Munro	c Carey b Stanlake	3	3		DJM Short	c Taylor b Southee	4	4	1	
KS Williamson *	c Warner b Tye	8	21		CA Lynn	c Sodhi b Boult	44	33	6	1
TC Bruce	c Richardson b Stanlake	3	3		GJ Maxwell	not out	40	24	5	1
R Taylor	c Carey b Agar	24	35	1	AT Carey +	not out	0	0		
TA Blundell	c Richardson b Zampa	14	16		MP Stoinis					
C de Grandhomme	not out	38	24	1	3	AC Agar					
MJ Santner	c Warner b Tye	1	4		AJ Tye					
TG Southee	c Stoinis b Tye	9	6	1	A Zampa					
IS Sodhi	b Tye	0	3		KW Richardson					
TA Boult					B Stanlake					
	2 b, 4 lb, 6 w	12				2 w	2			
6 overs: 3-29	20 overs	9-117			5 overs: 2-36	11.3 overs	3-96			

Fall: 1-11 (Munro, 1.1), 2-11 (Guptill, 1.2), 3-16 (Bruce, 3.2), 4-34 (Williamson, 7.2), 5-60 (Blundell, 12.1), 6-90 (Taylor, 15.6), 7-92 (Santner, 17.2), 8-114 (Southee, 19.2), 9-117 (Sodhi, 19.6)

Fall: 1-10 (Short, 1.5), 2-10 (Warner, 2.1), 3-87 (Lynn, 10.6)

Australia - bowling	O	Dots	R	W	wd	nb	NZ - bowling	O	Dots	R	W	wd	nb
KW Richardson	4	12	28	0	2		TA Boult	3	11	14	2		
B Stanlake	4	15	15	3			TG Southee	2.3	7	27	1	2	
AC Agar	4	9	22	1	1		MJ Santner	2	6	20	0		
AJ Tye	4	11	23	4	2		IS Sodhi	3	4	24	0		
A Zampa	3	8	21	1	1		C de Grandhomme	1	0	11	0		
MP Stoinis	1	4	2	0									

Toss: Australia. Umpires: CM Brown, SD Fry, GA Abood (TV), Ref: J Srinath   Award: B Stanlake (Aus)   Attendance: 25,621

MATCH TWO – HOBART

Australia fielded first again and were delighted to see the back of Roy in the second over, caught driving to cover. Hales and Malan were at their dangerous best for the rest of the powerplay, until Hales went in the first ball of the seventh, popping back a return catch to the first ball delivered by Agar. Morgan started briskly, being 14 off 6, before he lofted Maxwell's fourth ball of the night to mid-off. Buttler drove a catch to mid-off and then Billings sent Agar another return catch. Malan reached fifty, but went next ball, England's losing 6-33 in the final six overs.

As in Sydney, Australia had early worries, with Warner caught on the pull at deep square-leg, while Lynn was bowled second ball driving hard at a late inducker. Short and Maxwell rose to the occasion adding 78, with Maxwell in consecutive overs taking Jordan for 15 and Rashid for 14 to up the rate. England had a chance to remove Maxwell when he was dropped by Hales at deep square-leg off Curran when he was on 40.

Short went when he drove one hard back to the leg-spinner and when Stoinis was out, Australia was 4-98 still needing 58 off 50 balls. On 59 Maxwell lofted to long-off, with Roy appearing to hold a low catch, but replays were called for and appeared to show that the ball touched the ground. Maxwell stayed and despite losing Head, went on a final blitz to secure the win with a hit over deep square-leg that just carried the fielder, bringing up his ton and the victory.

Australia v England at Bellerive Oval, Hobart on February 7, 2018 (night) - Australia won by 5 wickets

England		B	4	6	Australia		B	4	6
JJ Roy	c Tye b Richardson	9	7	1	DA Warner *	c Hales b Willey	4	2	1
AD Hales	c & b Agar	22	15	4	DJM Short	c & b Rashid	30	20	2	2
DJ Malan	c Tye b Maxwell	50	36	5	2	CA Lynn	b Willey	0	2
EJG Morgan *	c Warner b Maxwell	22	14	2	1	GJ Maxwell	not out	103	58	10	4
JC Buttler +	c Maxwell b Stoinis	5	7		MP Stoinis	c Billings b Wood	6	11	1
SW Billings	c & b Agar	10	9		TM Head	b Willey	6	13
DJ Willey	st Carey b Maxwell	3	6		AT Carey	not out	5	5
CJ Jordan	not out	16	11	1	AC Agar			
AU Rashid	c Stoinis b Stanlake	1	4		AJ Tye			
TK Curran	c Warner b Tye	6	2	1	KW Richardson			
MA Wood	not out	5	9		B Stanlake			
	2 lb, 4 w	6				4 lb, 3 w	7		
6 overs: 1-60	20 overs	9-155			6 overs: 2-59	18.3 overs	5-161		

Fall: 1-16 (Roy, 1.4), 2-60 (Hales, 6.1), 3-94 (Morgan, 9.4), 4-109 (Buttler, 12.2), 5-122 (Billings, 14.1), 6-126 (Malan, 15.3), 7-126 (Willey, 15.4), 8-127 (Rashid, 16.3), 9-137 (Curran, 17.2)

Fall: 1-4 (Warner, 0.2), 2-4 (Lynn, 0.4), 3-82 (Short, 8.4), 4-98 (Stoinis, 11.4) 5-127 (Head, 15.5)

Australia - bowling	O	Dots	R	W	wd	nb	England - bowling	O	Dots	R	W	wd	nb
B Stanlake	4	11	43	1	2		DJ Willey	3	8	28	3	1	
KW Richardson	4	10	27	1			MA Wood	3.3	11	26	1		
AJ Tye	4	6	28	1			CJ Jordan	4	7	34	0		
MP Stoinis	2	4	16	1	2		TK Curran	4	3	39	0		
AC Agar	3	7	15	2			AU Rashid	4	12	30	1	2	
TM Head	1	1	14	0									
GJ Maxwell	2	6	10	3									

Toss: Australia   Umpires: GA Abood, SD Fry, CM Brown (TV), J Srinath (Ref) Award: GJ Maxwell (Aus) Attendance: 9,958
Malan 50: 34 balls, 5x4 2x6. Maxwell 50: 30 balls, 5x4 3x6; 100: 58 balls, 10x4 4x6

MATCH THREE –MELBOURNE

Australia's pace attack again maintained their hold on England with early wickets, Hales caught by a juggling Finch running back at mid-on, while Roy guided one off the edge to the keeper. Warner ran out Malan as the left-hander drove to mid-off and ran with the shot. England were only 3-67 after 10 overs and slipped further when Vince was beaten by a slower ball yorker. After being just two off his first nine balls, Billings played some damaging shots, lifting Agar straight for six, before smacking Stanlake for consecutive fours in the big quicks last over. They managed 32 off the last three overs, with Buttler caught off the last ball of the innings at long-on, despite the late flurry, England were still well short of a par tally.

Warner was beaten first ball by Willey and edged his fourth to the keeper, leaving Australia once again in early bother. But Lynn then dominated proceedings for the rest of the powerplay, bashing 18 off his first six balls to regain the momentum for his team. He and partner Short added 49 before Lynn was out top edging a pull, when Maxwell headed to the crease. After a quiet start (4 off 9) he started to unwind, whacking Dawson over long-on for six before hitting 44641 in an over from Rashid, Australia passing the hundred mark in the 11th over. When Maxwell top edged a pull to the keeper it enabled Finch to come in and finish the job off, as Australia won easily, already qualifying for the final.

Australia v England at the Melbourne Cricket Ground on February 10, 2018 (night) – Australia won by 7 wickets

England		B	4	6	Australia		B	4	6
JJ Roy	c Carey b Richardson	8	7	1	DA Warner *	c Buttler b Willey	2	4	
AD Hales	c Finch b Stanlake	3	3		DJM Short	not out	36	33	3	1
DJ Malan	run out (Warner)	10	10	1	CA Lynn	c Buttler b Jordan	31	19	4	2
JM Vince	b Tye	21	21	2	GJ Maxwell	c Buttler b Jordan	39	26	3	2
JC Buttler *+	c Agar b Richardson	46	49	3	AJ Finch	not out	20	5	2	2
SW Billings	c Warner b Stanlake	29	23	4	1	MP Stoinis			
DJ Willey	c Warner b Richardson	10	6	2	AT Carey			
CJ Jordan	not out	1	1		AC Agar			
LA Dawson					AJ Tye			
AU Rashid					KW Richardson			
TK Curran					B Stanlake			
	2 b, 7 w	9				2 lb, 8 w	10		
6 overs: 3-42	20 overs	7-137			6 overs: 2-52	14.3 overs	3-138		

Fall: 1-12 (Hales, 1.2), 2-16 (Roy, 2.2), 3-34 (Malan, 3.6), 4-70 (Vince, 10.4), 5-113 (Billings, 17.3), 6-133 (Willey, 19.2), 7-137 (Buttler, 19.6)

Fall: 1-2 (Warner, 0.4), 2-51 (Lynn, 5.3), 3-116 (Maxwell, 13.1)

Australia - bowling	O	Dots	R	W	wd	nb
KW Richardson	4	9	33	3	2	
B Stanlake	4	12	28	2	2	
MP Stoinis	4	12	18	0		
AJ Tye	4	9	29	1	3	
AC Agar	4	7	27	0		

England - bowling	O	Dots	R	W	wd	nb
DJ Willey	3.3	15	30	1	1	
TK Curran	2	2	23	0	1	
CJ Jordan	3	8	26	2	1	
AU Rashid	4	7	34	0	1	
LA Dawson	2	3	23	0		

Toss: Australia Umpires: CM Broad, SJ Nogajski, SD Fry (TV), Ref: J Srinath Award: KW Richardson (Aus) Attendance: 42,691

MATCH FOUR – WELLINGTON

With Australia through to the final, New Zealand gained a much needed win over England. Sent in by England, Guptill and Williamson dominated with an 82 run stand, the Kiwis finishing off well with 62 from the last five overs. After losing Roy early, Hales and Malan added 65 from 38 balls, but lost consistent wickets for the rest of the innings to fall 14 runs short.

New Zealand v England at Westpac Stadium, Wellington on February 13, 2018 (night) – New Zealand won by 12 runs

New Zealand		B	4	6
MJ Guptill	c Plunkett b Rashid	65	40	6	3
C Munro	c Billings b Wood	11	13	2	
KS Williamson *	b Jordan	72	46	4	4
C de Grandhomme	c Jordan b Rashid	0	1		
MS Chapman	c Billings b Wood	20	13		2
R Taylor	not out	1	1		
TL Seifert +	not out	14	6		2
MJ Santner				
TG Southee				
IS Sodhi				
TA Boult				
	1 b, 5 lb, 7 w	13		
6 overs: 1-50	20 overs	5-196		

England		B	4	6
JJ Roy	c Boult b Southee	8	8	2
AD Hales	c de Grandhomme b Sodhi	47	24	6	3
DJ Malan	c Boult b Santner	59	40	6	2
JM Vince	run out (Williamson)	10	7	1	
JC Buttler *+	c Southee b Sodhi	2	4		
SW Billings	c Sodhi b Santner	12	11	1	
DJ Willey	run out (Seifert)	21	10		2
CJ Jordan	b Boult	6	6	1	
LE Plunkett	b Boult	0	1		
AU Rashid	not out	8	6	1	
TK Curran	not out	5	3	1	
	2 b, 2 lb, 2 w	6		
6 overs: 1-60	20 overs	9-184		

Fall: 1-39 (Munro, 4.4), 2-121 (Guptill, 13.4), 3-121 (de Grandhomme, 13.5), 4-169 (Williamson, 17.6), 5-189 (Chapman, 18.6)

Fall: 1-14 (Roy, 2.1), 2-79 (Hales, 8.3), 3-95 (Vince, 10.4), 4-109 (Buttler, 11.6), 5-129 (Billings, 14.5), 6-158 (Malan, 16.3), 7-168 (Jordan, 17.5), 8-168 (Plunkett, 17.6), 9-172 (Willey, 18.6)

England - bowling	O	Dots	R	W	wd	nb
DJ Willey	4	9	36	0		
MA Wood	4	9	51	2	3	
CJ Jordan	4	10	34	1	2	
LE Plunkett	4	7	33	0	2	
AU Rashid	4	3	36	2		

NZ - bowling	O	Dots	R	W	wd	nb
TA Boult	4	10	46	2		
MJ Santner	4	11	29	2	1	
TG Southee	4	10	30	1	1	
IS Sodhi	4	7	49	2		
C Munro	2	6	11	0		
C de Grandhomme	2	3	15	0		

Toss: England Umpires: SB Haig, WR Knights, P Wilson (TV), Ref: J Srinath Award: KS Williamson (NZ), Guptill 50: 31 balls, 5x4 2x6, Williamson 50: 34 balls, 3x4 3x6. Malan 50: 36 balls, 6x4 1x6.

MATCH FIVE - AUCKLAND

The teams headed to the historic Eden Park, for what many thought could well be a preview of the final. With over 30,000 present it had the feeling of such a match, as Guptill and Munro headed out to bat. The pair started in brilliant fashion making the most of the short boundaries, adding 67 in the powerplay. Guptill hit Richardson, Stanlake and Tye for sixes down the ground, while Munro was less aerial, having been dropped on 13, a caught and bowled chance to Tye.

Munro started to cut loose in overs 7-11, hitting six sixes in that period, hitting three in a row to start the 11th over, before being caught at long-on off the fourth ball. Seifert started with a six over long-off but went shortly after caught in the deep aiming a swwep. Guptill upped the ante, at one point hitting five sixes in eight balls to bring up his century from just 49 balls. He went in the 17th over hitting a full toss to deep square-leg, a ball that was very close to being a no ball based on height.

New Zealand were 2-206 after 16 overs and looked an outside chance for 300, but with Guptill's dismissal the last four overs went for 37, while four wickets fell. Chapman was hit by a bouncer and fell onto his stumps, de Grandhomme dragged on a slower ball and Williamson was held at long-off. Despite the short boundaries, 243 looked an imposing score, Australia would still have to bat very well to win.

They did bat well, after 11 came from the first over from Boult, Short led the charge hitting 16 off Wheeler's first over as Australia motored to 51 after four overs. Warner then cut loose hitting two sixes in Southee's second over, as Australia reached

91 without loss by the end of the powerplay. Warner reached his fifty and then hit Sodhi straight for six, but fell next ball, bowled aiming a pull shot at a wrong-un. Lynn kept up the momentum hitting a straight six from his fourth ball before he hit one hard and flat to deep point. Short had reached his fifty in the 11th over and then destroyed de Grandhomme in the next, taking him for 6164 as Australia ended the over well on track at 2-162 after 12, Australia needing 82 off the last 48 balls.

Maxwell joined in on the party, hitting three sixes in a 14-ball stint, before he was bowled by Southee. Short's fine knock ended as he edged behind, but Finch took over the chase, clearing the ropes three times, the last of which was a full-toss that went sailing over the boundary to win the game for Australia with seven balls to spare.

New Zealand v Australia at Eden Park, Auckland on February 16, 2018 (night) – Australia won by 5 wickets

New Zealand		B	4	6	Australia		B	4	6
MJ Guptill	c Maxwell b Tye	105	54	6 9	DA Warner *	b Sodhi	59	24	4 5
C Munro	c Maxwell b Tye	76	33	6 6	DJM Short	c Seifert b Boult	76	44	8 3
TL Seifert +	c Finch b Agar	12	6	1 1	CA Lynn	c Guptill b de Grandhomme	18	13	1 1
MS Chapman	hit wkt b Stanlake	16	14	1	GJ Maxwell	b Southee	31	14	3 2
C de Grandhomme	b Richardson	3	4		AJ Finch	not out	36	14	3 3
LRPL Taylor	not out	17	6	2	MP Stoinis	run out (Wheeler-Seifert)	4	5	
KS Williamson *	c Tye b Richardson	1	2		AT Carey +	not out	1	1	
BM Wheeler	not out	1	2		AC Agar				
TG Southee					AJ Tye				
IS Sodhi					KW Richardson				
TA Boult					B Stanlake				
	3 lb, 1nb, 8 w	12				2 nb, 18 w	20		
6 overs: 0-67	20 overs	6-243			6 overs: 0-91	18.5 overs	5-245		

Fall: 1-132 (Munro, 10.4 ov), 2-155 (Seifert, 12.5 ov),
3-212 (Guptill, 16.4 ov), 4-220 (Chapman, 17.6 ov),
5-222 (de Grandhomme, 18.2 ov), 6-224 (Williamson, 18.5 ov)

Fall: 1-121 (Warner, 8.3 ov), 2-143 (Lynn, 11.1 ov), 3-199
(Maxwell, 15.2 ov), 4-217 (Short, 16.4 ov), 5-238 (Stoinis, 18.3 ov)

Australia - bowling	O	M	R	W	wd	nb	Dots	NZ - bowling	O	M	R	W	wd	nb	Dots
KW Richardson	4	0	40	2	2		10	TA Boult	3.5	0	42	1	2		8
B Stanlake	4	0	43	1	1		8	BM Wheeler	3.1	0	64	0	3	2	4
AJ Tye	4	0	64	2	4		5	TG Southee	4	0	48	1	1		5
MP Stoinis	4	0	50	0	1	1	5	IS Sodhi	4	0	35	1	1		6
AC Agar	3	0	24	1			5	C de Grandhomme	3.5	0	56	1	3		2
DJM Short	1	0	19	0			0								

Toss: New Zealand Umpires: SB Haig, P Wilson, WR Knights (TV), Ref: J Srinath Award: DJM Short (Aus). Attendance: 33,692
Guptill 50: 30 balls, 4x4, 4x6: 100: 49 balls, 6x6, 9x6. Munro 50: 27 balls, 5x4, 3x6. Warner 50: 20 balls, 4x4, 4x6;
Short 50: 30 balls, 6x4, 1x6

MATCH SIX - HAMILTON

With New Zealand on one win in the series and England yet to have a victory, the home side could get through to the final with a narrow loss. Malan made things tough with a fifty that included five sixes, while Morgan joined in the fun, hitting six over the rope, including 19 off an over from left-arm spinner Santner. He led the charge to the end of the innings, with 67 coming from the last five overs.

New Zealand only needed to make 175 to reach the final but no one seemed to tell Munro, who unleashed on the England attack to reach his fifty in 18 balls (7 sixes) but the end of the fifth over. When he was dismissed in the seventh the scoring slowed before Guptill and Chapman added 64 from 32 balls. Guptill went nuts just before he was out, hitting four sixes off the last nine balls he faced, dismissed with just 11 needed to make the final. Once NZ passed 175, England clearly looked deflated, but with 12 needed off the last over, Jordan did superbly to concede just nine to give his team a consolation victory.

Australian Cricket Digest, 2018-19

New Zealand v England at Seddon Park, Hamilton on February 18, 2018 (night) – England won by 2 runs

England			B	4	6
JJ Roy	c Williamson b Boult	21	13	3	1
AD Hales	c Williamson b Southee	1	4		
DJ Malan	c Chapman b de Grandhomme	53	36	2	5
EJG Morgan *	not out	80	46	4	6
JC Buttler +	st Seifert b Sodhi	2	5		
SW Billings	b Boult	6	8		
DJ Willey	c Guptill b Southee	10	5	2	
LA Dawson	c Guptill b Boult	10	3	1	1
CJ Jordan	not out	6	1		1
AU Rashid					
TK Curran					
	1 nb, 4 w	5			
6 overs: 2-41	20 overs	7-194			

New Zealand			B	4	6
MJ Guptill	b Malan	62	47	3	4
C Munro	c Willey b Rashid	57	21	3	7
KS Williamson *	b Dawson	8	13		
MS Chapman	not out	37	30	2	2
LRPL Taylor	c Morgan b Curran	7	6	1	
C de Grandhomme	not out	8	5	1	
TL Seifert +					
MJ Santner					
TG Southee					
IS Sodhi					
TA Boult					
	1 b, 8 lb, 2 nb, 2 w	13			
6 overs: 0-77	20 overs	4-192			

Fall: 1-22 (Hales, 2.3 ov), 2-24 (Roy, 3.1 ov), 3-117 (Malan, 12.1 ov), 4-123 (Buttler, 13.6 ov), 5-165 (Billings, 17.5 ov), 6-176 (Willey, 18.6 ov), 7-187 (Dawson, 19.4 ov)

Fall: 1-78 (Munro, 6.3 ov), 2-100 (Williamson, 11.1 ov), 3-164 (Guptill, 16.3 ov), 4-173 (Taylor, 17.5 ov)

NZ - bowling	O	M	R	W	wd	nb	Dots
TA Boult	4	0	50	3			9
MA Santner	2	0	32	0	3		3
TG Southee	4	0	22	2		1	9
C de Grandhomme	4	0	32	1			8
KS Williamson	1	0	16	0			0
IS Sodhi	4	0	31	1	1		12
C Munro	1	0	11	0			0

England - bowling	O	M	R	W	wd	nb	Dots
DJ Willey	3	0	33	0	1		9
TK Curran	3	0	32	1			5
CJ Jordan	4	0	42	0	1	2	8
AU Rashid	4	0	22	1			6
LA Dawson	4	0	27	1			10
DJ Malan	2	0	27	1			2

Toss: New Zealand Umpires: CM Brown, P Wilson, SB Haig (TV), Ref: J Srinath Award: EJG Morgan (Eng)
Malan 50: 32 balls, 2x4, 5x6, Morgan 50: 35 balls, 5x4, 3x6. Munro 50: 18 balls, 2x4, 7x6, Guptill 50: 44 balls, 3x4, 2x6,

THE FINAL - AUCKLAND

The teams were back at Eden Park for the final and most of them felt the game was going the same way as five days before when New Zealand reached 46 off their first four overs. Stanlake having started with the ball, came back to bowl the fifth over and took the vital wicket of Guptill, who toed a drive to mid-off. In the sixth, Munro belted Richardson for six over long-on, but next ball he too toed a catch, finding mid-on. Agar then chipped in with two wickets, Williamson was bowled aiming a slog and Chapman trapped in front, the hosts having lost 4-25 from 22 balls.

A shudder went through the Aussie camp in the ninth over when Lynn dived to stop a ball and suffered an injury to his troublesome right shoulder, forcing him from the field. It didn't affect the teams approach as Agar had de Grandhomme caught at deep mid-wicket and then Tye got Santner to glove a hook to the keeper. When Seifert was yorked off-stump, New Zealand had slipped to 7-101 in the 13th, and then 8-110 in the 14th when Southee was caught at deep mid-wicket. But Taylor kept the innings rolling, as he and Sodhi added 38, Sodhi's six in the last over at least ensured the home side made it to a competitive 150.

With rain in the area, Australia played cooly in the opening four overs, managing 23 before Short took off in the fifth, hitting two fours and a six in an over from Boult. In the next over he pinged Southee for consecutive leg-side sixes, the rains coming at the end of the powerplay with Australia 0-55, Short 41 off just 22 balls.

There was no change to the target after the delay, Short bringing up his fifty with a great pull off Munro. But two balls later the young opener was another to toe one off the bottom of his bat, being caught at long-on. New Zealand had a sniff when Warner was bowled making room against Sodhi while a frustrated Agar was stumped having a swipe at Santner. Finch and Maxwell then pushed the score along, Maxwell clearing the rope against Sodhi, with Finch doing the same against Santner. With 30 needed off 32 balls, the rains returned and after an inspection the outfield was deemed too wet to resume, the match abandoned just after 10.45pm with Australia taking the title having been well ahead on DLS.

Agar was deemed Man of the match for his three wickets in the space of eight balls, while Maxwell was Man of the series for his exciting batting through the tournament.

New Zealand v Australia at Eden Park, Auckland on February 21, 2018 (night) – Australia won by 19 runs (DLS Method)

New Zealand		B	4	6	Australia		B	4	6
MJ Guptill	c Warner b Stanlake	21	15	2	1 DA Warner *	b Sodhi	25	23	2
C Munro	c Agar b Richardson	29	14	3	2 DJM Short	c Chapman b Munro	50	30	6 3
KS Williamson *	b Agar	9	9	1	AC Agar	st Seifert b Santner	2	5	
MS Chapman	lbw b Agar	8	9	1	GJ Maxwell	not out	20	18	1
LRPL Taylor	not out	43	38	2	1 AJ Finch	not out	18	13	1
C de Grandhomme	c Maxwell b Agar	10	6	1	CA Lynn				
MJ Santner	c Carey b Tye	0	1		MP Stoinis				
TL Seifert *	b Stoinis	3	8		AT Carey +				
TG Southee	c Maxwell b Richardson	5	3	1	AJ Tye				
IS Sodhi	b Tye	13	16	1	KW Richardson				
TA Boult	not out	1	1		B Stanlake				
	3 lb, 5 w	8				4 b, 1 lb, 1 nb	6		
6 overs: 2-63	20 overs	9-150			6 overs: 0-55	14.4 overs	3-121		

Fall: 1-48 (Guptill, 4.3 ov), 2-59 (Munro, 5.2 ov), Fall: 1-72 (Short, 7.6 ov), 2-78 (Warner, 9.2 ov),
3-72 (Williamson, 7.4 ov), 4-73 (Chapman, 7.6 ov), 3-84 (Agar, 10.3 ov)
5-91 (de Grandhomme, 9.5 ov), 6-93 (Santner, 10.2 ov),
7-101 (Seifert, 12.4 ov), 8-110 (Southee, 13.4 ov),
9-148 (Sodhi, 19.4 ov)

Australia - bowling	O	M	R	W	wd	nb	Dots	NZ - bowling	O	M	R	W	wd	nb	Dots
B Stanlake	4	0	37	1	3		8	TA Boult	3	0	27	0			7
KW Richardson	4	0	30	2			12	IS Sodhi	4	0	21	1			14
AJ Tye	4	0	30	2			9	TG Southee	2	0	21	0			3
AC Agar	4	0	27	3			7	MA Santner	3.4	0	29	1		1	8
MP Stoinis	4	0	23	1	1		10	C Munro	2	0	18	1			2

Toss: New Zealand   Umpires: CM Brown, WR Knights, SB Haig (TV), Ref: J Srinath   Award: AC Agar (Aus), Series: GJ Maxwell.
Attendance: 20,072. Rain halted play after six overs, Australia 0-55. Short 50: 28 balls, 6x4, 3x6

INDIA TOO STRONG FOR AUSTRALIA IN ODI SERIES

Australia were beaten 4-1 by a very strong Indian line-up who revelled in playing in their home conditions, but they had their chances throughout the series. In the first game, they had India on the rack at 5-97 and couldn't finish them off, while in the third were 1-224 in the 37th over but failed to get past 300, which was a par score on the most of the pitches. Their only win in the series came in the fourth match having posted 334, the bowlers did the job, backed up by some exceptional ground fielding.

Having missed the first two games due to a calf injury, Aaron Finch batted superbly in his three innings, with David Warner making his team's other hundred in the series, in what was his 100th ODI. Nathan Coulter-Nile was comfortably Australia's best bowler, with Kane Richardson and Pat Cummins also performing well. Adam Zampa was dropped after the first game for Ashton Agar, who was omitted after the third, when the selectors opted to go back to Zampa.

Skipper Steve Smith was below par with the bat as was Travis Head, as Australia battled for quick runs in the middle overs. The Twenty20 series was shared after India won a rain affected first match, the second by Australia on the back of some outstanding bowling by Jason Behrendorff. The third game was abandoned without a ball being bowled, after several weeks of rain had rendered the Hyderabad outfield too sodden to play. The team was coached by David Saker, with regular coach Darren Lehmann taking some leave, on the eve of a home Ashes series.

Tour match v Indian Board President's XI at MA Chidambaram Stadium, Chepauk, Chennai on 12th September 2017 – Australia won by 103 runs

Australia 7-347 (50 overs) (DA Warner 64, SPD Smith 55, TM Head 65, MP Stoinis 76, MS Wade 45) **President's XI 244** (48.4 overs) (AC Agar 4-44). *Both teams played 14 a side with 11 batting.*

GAME ONE - CHENNAI

In hot conditions, Australia awarded Hilton Cartwright his first one-day international cap, while paceman Nathan Coulter-Nile played his first international game since June 2016. India won the toss, batted and were in trouble losing three wickets inside six overs, all to Coulter-Nile. Rahane was first, edging a drive to the keeper in the fourth over, while in the sixth, Kohli drove to backward point where Maxwell leapt high to take an excellent catch one-handed. Two balls later in the same over, Pandey was also caught behind aiming a drive, leaving India 3-11. Jadhav joined Rohit, the pair mending the innings to an extent, adding 53, before Rohit top edged a hook to deep square-leg, where Coulter-Nile ran in and took a fine catch diving forward. Jadhav continued to look good until he pulled one to short mid-wicket, which left India 5-87 in the 22nd over.

Dhoni was joined by Pandya, in what would turn out to be an innings changing partnership of 118. Dhoni played the sheet anchor role, with Pandya scoring quicker than his more experienced partner. At 5-148 after 36 overs, Pandya launched an attack on Zampa, belting four, six, six, six from consecutive balls to move the momentum India's way. Zampa eventually had his revenge as Pandya looked to whack him over mid-wicket, top edging the ball to short third-man, ending an excellent knock.

Kumar came out and found the boundary regularly and with Dhoni teeing off in the last three overs, adding 26 off his own bat, the pair added 72 off 54 balls, to see India past 280, a terrific fightback after being in deep trouble at the 22 over mark.

Rain caused a two and a half hour delay, with Australia's new DLS target a difficult 164 off 21 overs. Cartwright on debut was out in the third over, bowled aiming a pull and then Smith went to a similar shot, held low down at long-leg. Head aimed a drive at a wide one and was caught behind and when Warner got a touch behind to an attempted cut, Australia were 4-35 and just about cooked.

Maxwell had other ideas, like Pandya earlier he went four, six, six, six, taking 22 off an over from Kuldeep. But it didn't last long. After a sweep for six off Chahal over deep square leg, next ball he was well held at long-on. India did drop three catches in the last eight overs but had enough runs in the bank to record a convincing victory.

First One Day International MA Chidambaram Stadium, Chepauk, Chennai on September 17, 2017 (day/night)
India won by 26 runs (DLS Method)

India			B	M	4	6	Australia	DLS Target 164 in 21 overs		B	M	4	6
AM Rahane	c Wade b Coulter-Nile	5	15	18			DA Warner	c Dhoni b Yadav	25	28	47	2	
RG Sharma	c Coulter-Nile b Stoinis	28	44	81	3		HWR Cartwright	b Bumrah	1	8	15		
V Kohli *	c Maxwell b Coulter-Nile	0	4	7			SPD Smith *	c Bumrah b Pandya	1	5	8		
MK Pandey	c Wade b Coulter-Nile	0	2	4			TM Head	c Dhoni b Pandya	5	6	6		
KM Jadhav	c Cartwright b Stoinis	40	54	72	5		GJ Maxwell	c Pandey b Chahal	39	18	25	3	4
MS Dhoni +	c Warner b Faulkner	79	88	152	4	2	MP Stoinis	c sub (RA Jadeja) b Yadav	3	10	28		
HH Pandya	c Faulkner b Zampa	83	66	86	5		MS Wade +	st Dhoni b Chahal	9	10	17	1	
B Kumar	not out	32	30	45	5		JP Faulkner	not out	32	25	41	1	1
K Yadav	not out	0	0	2			PJ Cummins	c Bumrah b Chahal	9	7	7	1	
YS Chahal							NM Coulter-Nile	c Jadhav b Kumar	2	5	9		
JJ Bumrah							A Zampa	not out	5	4	9		
	4 b, 2 lb, 3 nb, 5 w	14						1 lb, 5 w	6				
10 overs : 3-34	50 overs, 237 mins	7-281					4 overs : 1-15	21 overs, 103 mins	9-137				

66

Fall: 1-11 (Rahane), 2-11 (Kohli), 3-11 (Pandey), 4-64 (Sharma), 5-87 (Jadhav), 6-205 (Pandya), 7-277 (Dhoni)

Fall: 1-15 (Cartwright), 2-20 (Smith), 3-29 (Head), 4-35 (Warner), 5-76 (Maxwell), 6-76 (Stoinis), 7-93 (Wade), 8-109 (Cummins), 9-129 (Coulter-Nile)

Australia - bowling	O	M	R	W	wd	nb
PJ Cummins	10	1	44	0	2	
NM Coulter-Nile	10	0	44	3	1	1
JP Faulkner	10	1	67	1		2
MP Stoinis	10	1	54	2	2	
A Zampa	10	0	66	1		

India - bowling	O	M	R	W	wd	nb
B Kumar	4	0	25	1	2	
JJ Bumrah	4	0	20	1	1	
HH Pandya	4	0	28	2	1	
K Yadav	4	0	33	2		
YS Chahal	5	0	30	3	1	

Toss: India.   Umpires: AK Chaudhary, M Erasmus, RK Illingworth (TV), Ref: JJ Crowe   Award: HH Pandya (Ind)

Dhoni 50: 75 balls, 1x4. Pandya 50: 48 balls, 3x4 1x6

GAME TWO - KOLKATA

Australia made two changes to the team that lost game one, Agar and Richardson came in for Faulkner and Zampa. India won the toss and batted, the match starting in hot, humid conditions, with many players needing an above average level of fluids to keep them going throughout the afternoon. Rohit Sharma was out in the sixth over, driving one high back to the bowler, who cleverly knocked it up with his right hand before taking it on the second attempt. Rahane then scored a flurry of boundaries as he took charge against some overly full bowling.

The stand of 102 came to an end in the 24th over, when Rahane was run out at the strikers end, attempting a second run to wide long-on, had he run harder, the Indian opener would have made it comfortably. Pandey was knocked over by Agar but then Jadhav and his skipper added 65, with India sitting pretty on 4-185 with 15 overs remaining.

Jadhav went in the 36th over, cutting hard to backward point and then Kohli chopped on, giving Coulter-Nile his third wicket. Dhoni drove one low to cover, where Smith held a fine catch, India had slipped to 6-204, having lost 3-18. Australia maintained control in the next seven overs, when an odd incident occurred in the 48th over. With rain falling, Pandya hit an above waist-high ball to deep cover, where Smith held the catch. Pandya headed off thinking he was out given the umpires hadn't called or signalled no-ball. Smith threw the ball in and the Australians thought they had run out Pandya, but given the umpires eventually deemed it to be a no-ball based on height, Pandya rightly wasn't given run out, based on the Law of the game which state:

Law 27.7 - "An umpire shall intervene if satisfied that a batsman not having been given out, has left his wicket under a misapprehension that he is out. The umpire intervening shall call and signal dead ball to prevent any further action by the fielding side and shall recall the batsman."

After the rain delay, India lost their last four wickets for 15, in all Australia taking 7-67 off the final 15 overs, to restrict India to 252. As in the first game, Australia started poorly, Kumar dominating with the ball, in a spell that could have yielded three wickets. Cartwright was first to go, uncomfortable for 14 balls before being bowled by the 15th, while Warner edged one to second slip to leave Australia 2-9. It should have been 3-27 when Head was dropped on 15 by Rohit Sharma at first slip in the seventh over. Australia then went on the attack, the pair scoring regular boundaries in a stand of 76, before Head clipped a full-toss from Chahal to mid-wicket. Maxwell came out an immediately swept consecutive sixes off Kuldeep, before he got in a tangle advancing at Chahal and was superbly stumped by Dhoni, after the ball clipped the batsman's pad. Smith reached fifty, but Pandya returned and the Aussie skipper pulled one to deep square-leg.

It went from bad to worse, in what was a great moment for Kuldeep, who took a hat-trick. In the 33rd over, Wade dragged on, Agar was plumb missing a full toss and then Cummins edged a wrong-un behind, making the young spinner the third Indian to take a hat-trick in one-day internationals. Australia were on the rack at 8-148, having lost 4-10, but Stoinis and Coulter-Nile dug in to add 34, before Coulter-Nile aimed a pull shot that popped high in the air back to the bowler. With 71 needed, Richardson hung in while Stoinis hit three sixes in consecutive overs, bringing back memories of his 146 versus New Zealand in February. Sadly for Australia, Richardson couldn't last, as Kumar returned and trapped him plumb in front, ending the contest at the iconic Indian cricket venue.

Second One Day International at Eden Gardens, Calcutta on September 21, 2017 (day/night) - India won by 50 runs

India		B	M	4	6	Australia		B	M	4	6
AM Rahane	run out (Cartwright-Wade)	55	64	110	7	HWR Cartwright	b Kumar	1	15	12	
RG Sharma	c and b Coulter-Nile	7	14	24	1	DA Warner	c Rahane b Kumar	1	9	22	
V Kohli *	b Coulter-Nile	92	107	148	8	SPD Smith *	c sub (RA Jadeja) b Pandya	59	76	118	8
MK Pandey	b Agar	3	13	14		TM Head	c Pandey b Chahal	39	39	57	5
KM Jadhav	c Maxwell b Coulter-Nile	24	24	36	2	1	GJ Maxwell	st Dhoni b Chahal	14	18	21		2
MS Dhoni +	c Smith b Richardson	5	10	19	1	MP Stoinis	not out	62	65	97	6	3
HH Pandya	c Warner b Richardson	20	26	56	2	MS Wade +	b Yadav	2	8	16	
B Kumar	c Maxwell b Richardson	20	33	39	1	AC Agar	lbw b Yadav	0	1	1	
K Yadav	c Wade b Cummins	0	2	1		PJ Cummins	c Dhoni b Yadav	0	1	1	
JJ Bumrah	not out	10	6	9	2	NM Coulter-Nile	c and b Pandya	8	20	30	
YS Chahal	run out (Wade)	1	2	3		KW Richardson	lbw b Kumar	0	7	16	
	1b, 1nb, 13 w	15					4 b, 6 lb, 6 w	16			
10 overs: 1-44	50 overs, 234 mins	252				10 overs: 2-47	43.1 overs, 200 mins	202			

Fall: 1-19 (Sharma), 2-121 (Rahane), 3-131 (Pandey), 4-186 (Jadhav), 5-197 (Kohli), 6-204 (Dhoni), 7-239 (Kumar), 8-239 (Yadav), 9-246 (Pandya), 10-252 (Chahal)

Fall: 1-2 (Cartwright), 2-9 (Warner), 3-85 (Head), 4-106 (Maxwell), 5-138 (Smith), 6-148 (Wade), 7-148 (Agar), 8-148 (Cummins), 9-182 (Coulter-Nile), 10-202 (Richardson)

Australia bowling	O	M	R	W	wd	nb	India - bowling	O	M	R	W	wd	nb
P J Cummins	10	1	34	1	1		B Kumar	6.1	2	9	3		
NM Coulter-Nile	10	0	51	3	5		JJ Bumrah	7	1	39	0		
KW Richardson	10	0	55	3	1	1	HH Pandya	10	0	56	2	1	
MP Stoinis	9	0	46	0	2		YS Chahal	10	1	34	2	2	
AC Agar	9	0	54	1	2		K Yadav	10	1	54	3	2	
TM Head	2	0	11	0	1								

Toss: India. Umpires: AK Chaudhary, RK Illingworth, M Erasmus (TV), Ref: JJ Crowe   Award: V Kohli (Ind)
Rain: India 6-237 after 47.3 overs, Pandya 19, Kumar 18. Rahane 50: 62 balls, 6x4, Kohli 50: 60 balls, 5x4. Stoinis 50: 58 balls, 6x4 2x6.

GAME THREE - INDORE

In a must win game for his team, Aaron Finch returned to the Australian side having recovered from a calf injury. He and Warner got the team off to an excellent start, until Warner played inside a length ball, which hit the top of middle stump. Finch took it right up to the Indian bowlers, showing no signs of his calf problems as he regularly found the ground's short boundaries. The Aussie opener reached his 8th ODI ton with a sweep to the boundary off Kuldeep and but in the 38th over, aimed to hit the same bowler over the long-on rope. This was the trigger for the loss of 3-19 in 26 balls, as Smith lofted to long-off and Maxwell advanced to a near wide and was stumped. All up Australia could only manage 39 from their last six overs, as Kumar and Bumrah bowled cleverly, Australia about 30 short of a par score for the small venue.

India's openers started well, although Rohit Sharma had some luck, being dropped by Maxwell on 21. He reached his fifty in the 13th over, with a six over long-on off Agar, India racking up their 100 just two overs later, to be well up with the rate. Finally the breakthrough came for Australia as Rohit Sharma pulled a catch to deep square leg and then Cummins trapped Rahane as he played across the line. Pandya was lifted in the order to number four and immediately laid into Agar, lofting him for sixes over long-on in consecutive overs.

Indian continued to stay well up with the rate and despite losing Kohli (caught at long-off) and Jadhav (caught behind) in consecutive overs, Pandya and Pandey ensured victory with a stand of 79 off 63 balls, to clinch the series with two games to go.

Third One Day International at Holkar Stadium, Indore on September 24, 2017 (day/night) - India won by 5 wickets

Australia		B	M	4	6	India		B	M	4	6
DA Warner	b Pandya	42	44	59	4	AM Rahane	lbw b Cummins	70	76	103	9	
AJ Finch	c Jadhav b Yadav	124	125	154	12	RG Sharma	c sub (HWR Cartwright) b Coulter-Nile	71	62	94	6	4
SPD Smith*	c Bumrah b Yadav	63	71	111	5	*V Kohli	c Finch b Agar	28	35	58	2	
GJ Maxwell	st Dhoni b Chahal	5	13	18		HH Pandya	c Richardson b Cummins	78	72	98	5	4
TM Head	b Bumrah	4	6	18		KM Jadhav	c Handscomb b Richardson	2	4	3		
MP Stoinis	not out	27	28	42	1	MK Pandey	not out	36	32	44	6	
PSP Handscomb+	c Pandey b Bumrah	3	7	13		+MS Dhoni	not out	3	6	9		
AC Agar	not out	9	6	11	1	B Kumar						
PJ Cummins						K Yadav						
NM Coulter-Nile						JJ Bumrah						
KW Richardson						YS Chahal						
	2 lb, 14 w	16					3 lb, 3 w	6			
10 overs : 0-49	50 overs , 216 mins	6-293				10 overs : 0-68	47.5 overs , 212 mins	5-294			

Fall: 1-70 (Warner), 2-224 (Finch), 3-243 (Smith), 4-243 (Maxwell), 5-260 (Head), 6-275 (Handscomb)

Fall: 1-139 (Sharma), 2-147 (Rahane), 3-203 (Kohli), 4-206 (Jadhav), 5-284 (Pandya)

India - bowling	O	M	R	W	wd	nb	Australia - bowling	O	M	R	W	wd	nb
B Kumar	10	0	52	0	4		PJ Cummins	10	0	54	2	1	
JJ Bumrah	10	0	52	2	5		NM Coulter-Nile	10	0	58	1	1	
YS Chahal	10	0	54	1			KW Richardson	8.5	0	45	1		
HH Pandya	10	0	58	1	2		MP Stoinis	8	0	61	0		
K Yadav	10	0	75	2	3		AC Agar	10	0	71	1		
							GJ Maxwell	1	0	2	0		

Toss: Australia   Umpires: M Erasmus, C Shamshuddin, RK Illingworth (TV), Ref: JJ Crowe.   Award: HH Pandya (Ind)
Finch 50: 61 balls, 6x4 1x6, 100: 110 balls, 11x4 3x6. Smith 50: 55 balls, 4x4. Rahane 50: 50 balls, 7x4; Sharma 50: 42 balls, 3x4, 4x6

Australian Cricket Digest, 2018-19
GAME FOUR – BANGALORE

On what proved to be an excellent batting strip, Australia attacked from the outset, with Warner and Finch dominating the Indian attack, minus Kumar and Bumrah, who were replaced by Shami and Umesh Yadav. Warner reached his first fifty of the series in the 15th over, celebrating the fact shortly after with sixes in consecutive overs from Chahal to really put the hammer down. Finch didn't reach his fifty until the 25th over, that being the trigger for him to tee off, as he belted Patel for six over long-off and then whacked Chahal for a straight six.

Warner became the eight player and first Australian to make a ton in his 100th ODI, going in the 35th over, mistiming one to long-on. Finch went in the next over and when Smith fell, Australia had lost 3-5 in 14 balls. Both Head and Handscomb had slow starts, but added 63 off 58 balls, before 28 came off the last two overs, with Handscomb (49th) and Stonis (50th) each hitting sixes.

Australia failed to make an early breakthrough, with Rahane and Rohit Sharma adding 100 plus for the second game in a row, with Stoinis heading off the ground, during the course of his second over. After drinks, Australia found a lease of life as Richardson had Rahane caught at long-on, and then confusion reigned as Rohit and Kohli found themselves at the same end, after a brilliant stop at backward point by Smith saw the Indian opener run out. When Kohli chopped on in the 25th over, Australia were back in the game, Pandya again took the stick to Zampa, hitting him for consecutive sixes, but the leg spinner had his revenge when he had all-rounder caught at long off.

India needed 95 off the last ten overs, with Pandey and Jadhav combining well for a time until Jadhav was caught at long-off and Pandey was bowled having a heave. Australia's pacemen finished the game off, supported by some great work in the field, where Australia saved at least 20 runs – in what was the eventual difference in the sides.

Fourth One Day International at M Chinnaswamy Stadium, Bangalore on September 28, 2017 (day/night)
Australia won by 21 runs

Australia		B	M	4	6	India		B	M	4	6
AJ Finch	c Pandya b Yadav	94	96	140	10	3	AM Rahane	c Finch b Richardson	53	66	75	6	1
DA Warner	c Patel b Jadhav	124	119	134	12	4	RG Sharma	run out	65	55	93	1	5
TM Head	c Rahane b Yadav	29	38	55	1	1		(Smith-Handscomb-Richardson)				
SPD Smith *	c Kohli b Yadav	3	5	5			V Kohli *	b Coulter-Nile	21	21	23	3	
PSP Handscomb	b Yadav	43	30	54	3	1	HH Pandya	c Warner b Zampa	41	40	64	1	3
MP Stoinis	not out	15	9	17	1	1	KM Jadhav	c Finch b Richardson	67	69	95	7	1
MS Wade +	not out	3	3	6			MK Pandey	b Cummins	33	25	40	3	1
PJ Cummins						MS Dhoni +	b Richardson	13	10	12	1	1
NM Coulter-Nile						AR Patel	c sub (GJ Maxwell)	5	6	15	
A Zampa							b Coulter-Nile				
KW Richardson						M Shami	not out	6	6	10	1
						UT Yadav	not out	2	2	3	
						YS Chahal					
	4 b, 7 lb, 12 w	23					4 lb, 3 w	7			
10 overs: 0-63	50 overs, 208 mins	5-334				10 overs: 0-65	50 overs, 219 mins	3 13			

Fall: 1-231 (Warner), 2-231 (Finch), 3-236 (Smith), 46.5), 5-319 (Handscomb)

Fall: 1-106 (Rahane), 2-135 (Sharma), 3-147 (Kohli), 4-299 (Head, 4-225 (Pandya), 5-286 (Jadhav), 6-289 (Pandey), 7-301 (Dhoni), 8-306 (Patel)

India - bowling	O	M	R	W	wd	nb	Australia - bowling	O	M	R	W	wd	nb
M Shami	10	1	62	0	1		Cummins	10	0	59	1	2	
UT Yadav	10	0	71	4	4		Coulter-Nile	10	0	56	2		
AR Patel	10	0	66	0	1		Richardson	10	0	58	3		
HH Pandya	5	0	32	0	2		Stoinis	4.5	0	34	0		
YS Chahal	8	0	54	0	2		Finch	0.1	0	1	0		
KM Jadhav	7	0	38	1	2		Zampa	9	0	63	1		
							Head	6	0	38	0		

Toss: Australia   Umpires: RK Illingworth, C Shamshuddin, M Erasmus (TV), Ref: JJ Crowe.   Award: DA Warner (Aus)
Finch 50: 65 balls, 7x4. Warner 50: 45 balls, 8x4, 1x6; 100: 103 balls, 10x4 3x6. Rahane 50: 58 balls, 6x4, 1x6;
Sharma 50: 42 balls, 1x4, 4x6, Jadhav 50: 54 balls, 6x4, 1x6

GAME FIVE – NAGPUR

Key Indian paceman Kumar and Bumrah returned to the Indian bowling line up for the final match of the series, but it was spin bowling that would set the game up for India, on a turning pitch.

Australia did start well but then Pandya chimed in to take the first wicket, having Finch caught at mid-off, just as he looked like he was going to take control. Australia reached 100 in the 19th over, but the loss of Smith, trapped in front sweeping saw the early impetus evaporate, as Australia lost 3-18 in 30 balls. Warner, perhaps frustrated by a lack of strike, advanced and was caught at long-on, being the first of Patel's three victims. Handscomb struggled to force the pace, watching a top edged sweep caught by slip as he ran behind the keeper to complete the catch. Head and Stoinis did their best to mend things, adding 87 off 110 balls, but just as the final charge was needed, Head was yorked and Stoinis trapped in front. Australia was only able to hit one four and a six as they could only manage 52 in the final ten overs.

For the third game straight, Rahane and Rohit Sharma did as they pleased, adding 124 as the Australian attack could do little to stop them. Coulter-Nile trapped Rahane in the 23rd over, but then Rohit was joined by his skipper Kohli, the pair adding 99 off 100 balls. Rohit brought up his ton with a pull shot off Coulter-Nile, but was eventually dismissed pulling a Zampa long hop to deep square leg with just 20 wanted. Pandey hit back to back boundaries in the 43rd over, to see India easily home with 43 balls to spare.

Fifth One Day International at Vidarbha Cricket Association Stadium, Nagpur on October 1, 2017 (day/night)
India won by 7 wickets

Australia			B	M	4	6	India			B	M	4	6
DA Warner	c Pandey b Patel	53	62	91	5		AM Rahane	lbw b Coulter-Nile	61	74	93	7	
AJ Finch	c Bumrah b Pandya	32	36	46	6		RG Sharma	c Coulter-Nile b Zampa	125	109	165	11	5
SPD Smith *	lbw b Jadhav	16	25	31	1		V Kohli *	c Stoinis b Zampa	39	55	73	2	
PSP Handscomb	c Rahane b Patel	13	17	19			KM Jadhav	not out	5	8	14	1	
TM Head	b Patel	42	59	78	4		MK Pandey	not out	11	11	12	2	
MP Stoinis	lbw b Bumrah	46	63	79	4	1	HH Pandya						
MS Wade +	c Rahane b Bumrah	20	18	29		1	MS Dhoni i						
JP Faulkner	run out (Pandya-Dhoni)	12	17	27			B Kumar						
PJ Cummins	not out	2	2	7			AR Patel						
NM Coulter-Nile	b Kumar	0	1	1			JJ Bumrah						
A Zampa	did not bat						K Yadav						
	1 b, 2 lb, 3 w	6						1 lb, 1 w	2				
10 overs : 0-60	50 overs, 208 mins	242					10 overs : 0-43	42.5 overs, 180 mins	3-243				

Fall: 1-66 (Finch), 2-100 (Smith), 3-112 (Warner), 4-118 (Handscomb), 5-205 (Head), 6-210 (Stoinis), 7-237 (Wade), 8-242 (Faulkner), 9-242 (Coulter-Nile)

Fall: 1-124 (Rahane), 2-223 (Sharma), 3-227 (Kohli)

India bowling	O	M	R	W	wd	nb	Australia - bowling	O	M	R	W	wd	nb
B Kumar	8	0	40	1			PJ Cummins	7	1	29	0		
JJ Bumrah	10	2	51	2			NM Coulter-Nile	9	0	42	1		
HH Pandya	2	0	14	1			MP Stoinis	4	0	20	0		
K Yadav	10	1	48	0			JP Faulkner	5.5	0	37	0	1	
KM Jadhav	10	0	48	1	2		A Zampa	8	0	59	2		
AR Patel	10	0	38	3	1		TM Head	6	0	38	0		
							AJ Finch	3	0	17	0		

Toss: Australia   Umpires: M Erasmus, CK Nandan, RK Illingworth (TV), Ref: JJ Crowe.   Award: RG Sharma (Ind)

Warner 50: 56 balls, 5x4. Rahane: 64 balls, 6x4; Sharma 50: 52 balls, 7x4, 1x6; 100: 94 balls, 10x4, 3x6

FIRST TWENTY20 – RANCHI

In humid conditions, with lightening not far from the ground, Warner took consecutive fours in the first over from Kumar, before chopping one back onto his stumps. Finch and Maxwell found the rope with regularity, as Australia ended the six over powerplay on 1-49. Kohli brought his spinners on and from there Australia struggled. After a two and a four off Chahal, Maxwell pulled a catch to mid-wicket, then Finch was bowled as he appeared to change his mind when initially going for a sweep shot. Henriques was bowled advancing and then Head, who had been struggling, edged a drive back onto his leg stump. Paine took Kumar for four and six in the 17th before being bowled by one that skidded through and shortly after the rain came in the 19th over.

After the weather delay, India needed just 48 off six overs, Rohit clipping Coulter-Nile's first ball for six over long-leg. Coulter-Nile skittled his stumps next ball, but Dhawan and Kohli had things under control, winning with three balls to spare.

Australian Cricket Digest, 2018-19

Australia		B	4	6	India	DLS Target 48 in 6 overs	B	4	6
DA Warner *	b Kumar	8	5	2	RG Sharma	b Coulter-Nile	11	7	1	1
AJ Finch	b Yadav	42	30	4	1	S Dhawan	not out	15	12	3
GJ Maxwell	c Bumrah b Chahal	17	16	2	V Kohli *	not out	22	14	3
TM Head	b Pandya	9	16		MK Pandey				
MC Henriques	b Yadav	8	9	1	KM Jadhav				
DT Christian	run out (Kohli)	9	13		MS Dhoni +				
TD Paine +	b Bumrah	17	16	1	1	HH Pandya				
NM Coulter-Nile	b Bumrah	1	2		B Kumar				
AJ Tye	not out	0	2		YS Chahal				
A Zampa	not out	4	3	1	K Yadav				
JP Behrendorff					JJ Bumrah				
	1 lb, 2 w	3			Extras	(1 lb)	1		
6 overs: 1-49	18.4 overs, 80 mins	118			Total	5.3 overs, 25 mins	1-49		

Fall: 1-8 (Warner, 0.5), 2-55 (Maxwell, 6.3), 3-76 (Finch, 9.5), 4-87 (Henriques, 12.2), 5-89 (Head, 13.3), 6-111 (Paine, 17.1), 7-113 (Coulter-Nile, 17.4), 8-114 (Christian, 18.1)

Fall: 1-11 (Sharma, 1.1)

India - bowling	O	M	R	W	wd	nb	Dots	Australia - bowling	O	M	R	W	wd	nb	Dots
B Kumar	3.4	0	28	1			11	JP Behrendorff	1	0	5	0			4
JJ Bumrah	3	0	17	2	1		7	NM Coulter-Nile	2	0	20	1			4
HH Pandya	4	0	33	1			8	AJ Tye	1	0	10	0			2
YS Chahal	4	0	23	1	1		11	A Zampa	1	0	6	0			3
K Yadav	4	0	16	2			9	DT Christian	0.3	0	7	0			0

Toss: India. Umpires: NM Menon, C Shamshuddin, AK Chaudhary (TV), Ref: RB Richardson. Award: K Yadav (Ind) Rain interrupted play after 18.4 overs, India's target reduced to 48 off six overs.

SECOND TWENTY20 – GUWAHATI

Australia responded brilliantly to the loss in the first game, with Jason Behrendorff dominating with the ball early on. After giving up two fours from his first three balls, he trapped Rohit Sharma in front to one that swung in, then two balls later Kohli edged one onto his pad which rebounded to the bowler. In his next over, Behrendorff had Pandey caught behind as he aimed to guide one to third man and, in his third over, Dhawan was well held as Warner ran back from mid-off to take a fine catch. India ended the powerplay on 4-38, with Behrendorff having figures of 4-16 including 14 dots.

Jadhav and Dhoni added 33 before Zampa chipped in with two wickets, with Dhoni advancing being beaten by spin and bounce, while Jadhav went missing a slog at a wrong-un. At 7-70 in the 13th, Pandya and Kuldeep added 33, but India were all out from the last ball of their innings for just 118.

Australia was in trouble early, when Warner top edged a pull-shot to cover from the first ball he faced from Bumrah and then Finch played back and hit a catch to cover. Head took two boundaries in the fourth over, bowled by Bumrah, and then Henriques, who was just two off nine balls, started to get a move on. At 2-36 after seven overs the game was still in the balance, but with 14 coming from Kuldeep's first over and 11 off the next, bowled by Pandya, the pressure eased. Henriques brought up fifty with a pull off Kuldeep into the crowd, and proceeded to hit the winning runs with 27 balls to spare

Second Twenty20 International at Barsapara Cricket Stadium, Guwahati
on October 10, 2017 (floodlit) – Australia won by 8 wickets

India		B	4	6	Australia		B	4	6
RG Sharma	lbw b Behrendorff	8	4	2	AJ Finch	c Kohli b Kumar	8	8	1
S Dhawan	c Warner b Behrendorff	2	6		DA Warner *	c Kohli b Bumrah	2	5	
V Kohli *	c and b Behrendorff	0	2		MC Henriques	not out	62	46	4 4
MK Pandey	c Paine b Behrendorff	6	7	1	TM Head	not out	48	34	5 1
KM Jadhav	b Zampa	27	27	3 1	GJ Maxwell				
MS Dhoni +	st Paine b Zampa	13	16	1	MP Stoinis				
HH Pandya	c sub (DT Christian) b Stoinis	25	23	1	TD Paine +				
B Kumar	c Henriques b Coulter-Nile	1	6		NM Coulter-Nile				
K Yadav	c Paine b Tye	16	19	1	AJ Tye				
JJ Bumrah	run out (Paine)	7	9	1	A Zampa				
YS Chahal	not out	3	2		JP Behrendorff				
	5 lb, 1 nb, 4 w	10				(2 w)	2		
6 overs: 4-38	20 overs, 104 mins	118			6 overs: 2-34	15.3 overs, 70 mins	2-122		

Fall: 1-8 (Sharma, 0.4), 2-8 (Kohli, 0.6), 3-16 (Pandey, 2.2), 4-27 (Dhawan, 4.3), 5-60 (Dhoni, 9.5), 6-67 (Jadhav, 11.1), 7-70 (Kumar, 12.4), 8-103 (Pandya, 17.3), 9-115 (Bumrah, 19.3), 10-118 (Yadav, 19.6)

Fall: 1-11 (Warner, 1.3), 2-13 (Finch, 2.5)

Australia - bowling	O	M	R	W	wd	nb	Dots	India - bowling	O	M	R	W	wd	nb	Dots
JP Behrendorff	4	0	21	4			17	B Kumar	3	0	9	1	1		13
NM Coulter-Nile	4	0	23	1	2		12	JJ Bumrah	3	0	25	1			8
AJ Tye	4	0	30	1		1	9	HH Pandya	2	0	13	0			6
A Zampa	4	0	19	2	1		11	K Yadav	4	0	46	0			5
MP Stoinis	4	0	20	1	1		10	YS Chahal	3.3	0	29	0	1		7

Toss: Australia. Umpires: NM Menon, CK Nandan, C Shamshuddin (TV), Ref: RB Richardson. Award: JP Behrendorff (Aus)
Henriques 50: 42 balls, 3x4, 4x6

THIRD TWENTY20 – HYDERABAD

With continuous rain for three weeks in the lead up to this game, the match was abandoned due to a water logged outfield, much to the disappointment of the 30,000 in attendance.

Third Twenty20 International at Rajiv Gandhi International Stadium, Uppal, Hyderabad
on October 13, 2017 (floodlit) – Match Abandoned

Australian Cricket Digest, 2018-19
AUSTRALIA IN SOUTH AFRICA, 2017-18
TOUR SUMMARY

In one short irrational moment, the focus of Australia's tour to South Africa went from being about a fine cricketing contest between two good teams, to being about ball tampering and the Australian team's culture. Whatever possessed members of the Australian cricket team to think they could get away with blatant cheating, in using sandpaper to alter the state of the ball, is beyond me. In the earlier part of the Digest, David Jenkins has thoroughly examined who did what and when. But in writing this tour summary, the point has to be repeated that it was a stupid and illogical thing to do, something that has not only hurt the reputation of Australian cricket but also tarnished our other fine men and women in various sports worldwide. No longer can Australia point the finger at other sporting nations for "dodgy" happenings, with the high moral ground now well and truly lost.

As for the cricket in South Africa, the signs for Australia were good early on. Having been hardened in preparation by a strong Ashes win, the Australians won the first Test in convincing fashion, but that in turn was overshadowed by some bad behaviour on the field, most notably by David Warner. His flare up with Quinton de Kock during the tea break on the fourth day was an awful moment for the game in general, being close as anyone has seen to a full blown brawl in a Test match.

In the second Test, Australia were well placed at 98 without loss, but inspired pace-bowling by Kagiso Rabada kept Australia to just 243, with cracks starting to emerge in the batting line-up. At this point AB de Villiers really started to get going, playing a magnificent innings of 126, which gave South Africa a lead of 139 and put them back in the ascendency. Another brittle batting display saw Australia manage just 239 and with just 101 wanted, the hosts levelled the series midway through the fourth day.

South Africa were well ahead deep into the opening day of the third Test, being 2-220, before some inspired bowling from Pat Cummins got Australia back into the match. However, on the second day, with Australia 3-150, they collapsed losing five wickets for just 25 runs with Rabada and Morne Morkel doing much of the damage. Then on the third day, the ball-tampering incident occurred and from there, the tour went completely to pot for Australia.

The final Test in Johannesburg was played with Australia flying in replacement batting talent for the suspended trio of Steve Smith, David Warner and Cameron Bancroft, against a now rampant South Africa, looking to ensure their first home series win over Australia since 1970. New captain Tim Paine did his best to rally his charges but, after losing the toss, the demoralised team faced an uphill battle. In one shining light, Chadd Sayers was awarded his first Test cap, after many seasons of dominating with the ball in the Sheffield Shield competition for South Australia. Australia went on to suffer one of their worst ever defeats anywhere and South Africa completed a much deserved 3-1 victory.

Only two members of the Australian tour party returned home with their reputations enhanced. Pat Cummins was outstanding with the ball, providing great bursts of pace, making breakthroughs when they were really needed. The work he has put into his batting was rewarded when he notched a maiden Test fifty in the final match. As in the Ashes, Tim Paine kept well and was steady with the bat, leading the averages. Having the added responsibility of the captaincy late in the tour was a burden he dealt with extremely well. He seems the man to lead Australia forward in Test cricket, including the Ashes in England next year.

On the downside, David Warner and Steve Smith both had below par tours, with neither registering a century. Warner had his fair share of troubles with Rabada, who dismissed him four out of six innings. Smith averaged just 23, with just one score over fifty. The same can be said for Usman Khawaja, Shaun Marsh and Mitchell Marsh, all of whom disappointed with the bat, and none of whom should expect to be walk up starts for the upcoming Test series against Pakistan in the UAE. Until his ball tampering moment, Cam Bancroft was starting to show he had the makings of a Test batsman, but in one moment of stupidity that has all gone out of the window, until his time as a suspended player comes to an end.

Mitchell Starc and Josh Hazlewood had their moments in the series but, after the first Test, the South African batsmen had their measure. Nathan Lyon took 16 wickets in the four Tests, but went for over 40 apiece, a sign that the South Africans play off-spin bowling better than England.

The South Africans had many players to be proud of in the series. At the top of the order, Aiden Markram showed a touch of class, while fellow opener Dean Elgar played with tremendous grit, his ton in the second Test vital to getting his team back on track after the loss of the first Test. As mentioned earlier, Rabada's extra pace troubled Australia, while Vernon Philander showed that line and length, with a small bit of movement, can be just as hard to face as any other type of bowling. Spinner Keshav Maharaj did a tremendous job and Morne Morkel in his last series bowled as well as ever, finishing his Test career on a well-deserved high.

Finally, one must congratulate and thank AB de Villiers for his contribution to Test cricket over many years. He had a stellar series with the bat, conducted himself in fine fashion and went out on a high, as players of his ilk deserve. It's a shame he's now lost to Test cricket, as he finishes his playing career in many of the Twenty20 tournaments around the cricketing world, which are boosting many players Superannuation.

TOUR MATCH v SOUTH AFRICA A

Under grey skies, Australia went into the match with their expected First Test line up, minus David Warner. Pat Cummins took the first wicket of the tour when Malan jammed at a wide ball, edging to first slip. Hamza and de Bruyn added 82 in good style before de Bruyn appeared unlucky to be given out caught in the gully aiming a pull-shot. Hamza and skipper Zondo were both caught edging cuts to second slip and Bancroft took a sharp catch at short-leg off the face of the bat to dismiss Second. At 5-203 South Africa A looked well placed but Cummins returned to have Mulder edging behind and then bent back von Berg's off-stump, the home side losing their last five for 17 runs.

Bancroft was scratchy early in an opening stand of 33, before Khawaja miscued a pull-shot to mid-on. Then three balls later Handscomb aimed a loose square-drive at a wide ball and was held at point. Smith smacked a couple of boundaries before feathering one to the keeper, Australia closing the day 133 behind. On the second day the fourth wicket stand reached 60, with Bancroft getting a couple of boundaries through the slips, before Shaun Marsh edged a loose drive to slip. Mitch Marsh pulled an impressive six and then saw Bancroft given out caught down the leg side, a decision he wasn't at all happy with. Australia looked like conceding a first innings deficit when Mitch Marsh (yorked) and Paine (aiming a pull) were both leg before, but Cummins and the tail added 151 for the last three wickets, to give Australia a lead of 109.

South Africa A reached the close, 55 without loss, but started the third day poorly, losing at one point 3-9 in 19 balls. Malan was well held low down at third slip, Starc took a sharp caught and bowled from a de Bruyn drive and Hamza was superbly taken behind by Paine diving to his right. The fourth wicket pair made it past lunch and added 60 before Zondo had his leg stump removed, then Muthusamy edged to third slip to give Starc his fourth. Mitch Marsh then chipped in with two wickets, having Mulder lbw to one that appeared to missing leg by some margin, and Second who dragged on. Just when it looked like Australia would need under a hundred to win, the burly von Berg made a 39-ball fifty, taking a liking to Lyon, hitting him for 22 in one over. He and Siboto added 80, before von Berg was caught by Bancroft at short-leg, moving sharply to his right. The last three wickets fell in just ten balls, Smith grabbing two of them, which left Australia needing 140 to win.

Australia started shakily in their chase, Khawaja fending a lifter to second slip, while Handscomb played on, his middle-stump cartwheeling out of the ground. Smith pulled a six from his third ball before falling to the same shot shortly after and then Bancroft was also out pulling, well held low down at deep square-leg. When Mitch Marsh was given out leg before, Australia needed 42 more, but his elder brother and Paine added 42 quickly, Shaun hitting the winning runs with a pull-shot.

Tour match v South Africa A at Willowmoore Park Main Oval, Benoni on February 22-24, 2018

Australia win by 5 wickets

South Africa A	First innings	R	B	M	4	6	Second innings	R	B	M	4	6
MZ Hamza	c Smith b Hazlewood	44	89	125	6		c Paine b Hazlewood	28	68	109	3	
PJ Malan	c Handscomb b Cummins	8	34	53	1		c Bancroft b Starc	34	68	92	6	
TB de Bruyn	c Khawaja b Hazlewood	46	43	66	9		c & b Starc	5	11	13	1	
K Zondo *	c Smith b Hazlewood	3	11	17			b Starc	27	72	96	2	
S Muthusamy	c Paine b M Marsh	36	86	116	6		c Bancroft b Starc	34	76	119	4	
RS Second +	c Bancroft b Starc	21	31	58	5		b M Marsh	20	47	64	3	
PWA Mulder	c Paine b Cummins	29	37	50	5		lbw b M Marsh	5	11	15	1	
S von Berg	b Cummins	4	10	14	1		c Bancroft b Lyon	52	43	64	8	1
MP Siboto	lbw b M Marsh	10	9	18	2		lbw b Smith	32	33	44	1	2
D Olivier	c Smith b Cummins	0	4	3			not out	0	4	6		
BE Hendricks	not out	0	0	4			c Handscomb b Smith	0	4	2		
	6 b, 10 lb, 1nb, 2 w	19					2 b, 6 lb, 3 w	11				
	58.5 overs, 265 mins	220					72.5 overs, 315 mins	248				

Fall: 1-25 (Malan), 2-107 (de Bruyn), 3-108 (Hamza), 4-119 (Zondo), 5-163 (Second), 6-203 (Muthusamy), 7-205 (Mulder), 8-210 (von Berg), 9-210 (Olivier), 10-220 (Siboto)

Fall: 1-62 (Malan), 2-71 (de Bruyn), 3-71 (Hamza), 4-131 (Zondo), 5-144 (Muthusamy), 6-153 (Mulder), 7-167 (Second), 8-248 (von Berg), 9-248 (Siboto), 10-248 (Hendricks, 72.5 ov)

Australia - bowling	O	M	R	W	wd	nb		O	M	R	W	wd	nb
MA Starc	14	4	37	1				15	2	46	4	2	
JR Hazlewood	12	4	40	3	1			12	4	28	1		
PJ Cummins	11	2	32	4	1			12	3	42	0		
MR Marsh	7.5	0	50	2		1		10	3	35	2	1	
NM Lyon	14	3	45	0				18	4	67	1		
SPD Smith								5.5	0	22	2		

Australia	First innings		B	M	4	6	Second innings		B	M	4	6
CT Bancroft	c Second b Hendricks	45	123	188	5		c Muthusamy b Mulder	22	56	91	2	
UT Khawaja	c Zondo b Olivier	22	42	43	4		c von Berg b Olivier	8	19	32		
PSP Handscomb	c Hamza b Olivier	0	3	3			b Olivier	5	9	8	1	
SPD Smith *	c Second b Siboto	23	24	40	4	1	c Siboto b Olivier	25	13	26	3	2
SE Marsh	c de Bruyn b Hendricks	25	59	79	2		not out	39	46	75	5	
MR Marsh	lbw b Hendricks	28	53	84	3	1	lbw b Olivier	14	11	17	3	
TD Paine +	lbw b Siboto	22	50	74	4		not out	17	25	33	3	
PJ Cummins	not out	59	95	141	11							
MA Starc	c de Bruyn b von Berg	18	34	51	3							
NM Lyon	c Hamza b Hendricks	38	34	43	3	2						
JR Hazlewood	b Hendricks	26	32	37	6							
	8 b, 8 lb, 5 nb, 2 w	23					6 lb, 2 nb, 2 w	10				
	90.4 overs, 394 mins	329					29.3 overs, 143 mins	5-140				

Fall: 1-33 (Khawaja), 2-33 (Handscomb), 3-64 (Smith), 4-124 (S Marsh), 5-131 (Bancroft), 6-174 (M Marsh), 7-178 (Paine), 8-225 (Starc), 9-289 (Lyon), 10-329 (Hazlewood)

Fall: 1-16 (Khawaja), 2-22 (Handscomb), 3-61 (Smith), 4-72 (Bancroft), 5-98 (M Marsh)

SAA - bowling	O	M	R	W	wd	nb		O	M	R	W	wd	nb
D Olivier	13	5	37	2		2		12.3	0	74	4	1	2
BE Hendricks	24.4	4	83	5		1		5	3	7	0		
MP Siboto	22	6	56	2	2			5	0	21	0		
P WA Mulder	11	1	52	0		2		5	1	23	1	1	
S von Berg	13	0	55	1				2	0	9	0		
S Muthusamy	7	0	30	0									

Stumps scores:

| Day 1: | Australia (1st inns) | 3-87 | CT Bancroft 24*, SE Marsh 10* | Toss: South Africa A |
| Day 2: | South Africa A (2nd inn) 0-55 | MZ Hamza 25, PJ Malan 27* | Umpires: JD Cloete, PJ Vosloo, Ref: A Barnes |

FIRST TEST – KINGSMEAD, DURBAN

Australia kept the same team that won the Sydney Ashes Test in January, while South Africa made two changes from the team that lost the third Test to India in late January, with Ngidi and Phehlukwayo making way for Maharaj and de Bruyn.

Day One - Attendance: 3,957

Bancroft survived a review (deemed high) for leg before off Morkel in the first over, but went shortly after as he edged Philander behind. Khawaja struck three firm boundaries but failed to see the opening hour out, edged behind to see de Kock dive to his right to bring off a superb catch. Just before drinks, Maharaj was brought into the attack and first ball he had Warner out leg before. A review was called for, showing the ball to be missing and South Africa were out of reviews inside the first hour. After drinks both Warner and Smith looked in control, finding the boundary with regularity. Just before lunch, Warner reached his fifty (72 balls, 6x4) but went off the last ball before the break, edging one to second slip, leaving Australia 3-95 at the break, with skipper Smith on 24.

Shaun Marsh took 12 balls to get off the mark, but once he got going, looked at ease on a slow surface. Smith continued on and reached his fifty off 95 balls (10x4) as the partnership passed 50. The South Africans tightened up with the ball and thought they had Marsh leg before off the bowling of Rabada on 19. There wasn't much they could do, being out of reviews, the replay showing that Marsh would have been on his way. Then unexpectedly, Smith edged a cut to de Kock, the ball rebounding for de Villiers to catch it at slip. Mitch Marsh joined his brother and saw it through to tea, Australia 4-170, Shaun 34, Mitch 8.

Maharaj found the edge of Shaun Marsh's probing bat just after tea, but any thoughts of a middle order collapse were held up by Paine, who added a productive 48 with Mitch Marsh before bad light caused stumps to be drawn early at 3.57pm.

Day 2 - Attendance: 4,865

Day two started quite cloudy, with the floodlights on for the start of play. South Africa found success in the first half-hour, with Paine edging the fourth delivery with the second new ball to the keeper. Starc came in and felt attack was the best form of defence, clubbing Maharaj for three fours in an over, before lofting the same bowler over long-on for six on two separate occasions. The left-arm spinner changed ends and in the last over before lunch, he bowled Starc, beating him in flight as he aimed a drive. Australia heading into the break with Mitch Marsh on 60, with every run after the break being vital.

After lunch, Marsh unleashed his power, moving to 96 very quickly, before hitting a catch to mid-on going for his ton. When Lyon, after sweeping two fours went to a catch at wide mid-off, Australia had added 51 for the last two wickets to end up on 351, a very good score on this slow track.

South Africa were untroubled early with Markram hitting some fine cover drives. Lyon came on in the eighth over and had immediate success, with Elgar getting a leading edge back to the bowler, while Amla went three balls later, edging onto his pad to short-leg. For the third time in the game a wicket was to fall just before a break, as Markram popped a catch to short-leg, South Africa going into tea on 3-55, AB de Villiers not out on 16.

The home side started well after tea, adding 35 in seven overs, before Starc returned and had du Plessis caught behind to a ball delivered from the around the wicket, which reverse swung. de Bruyn fell in similar fashion to leave South Africa 5-108. De Kock came out as he and de Villiers settled in to add 42 for the sixth wicket, but when Lyon penetrated de Kock's defence, it triggered a collapse of 5-12, which saw South Australia all out for 162, 189 behind. The reverse swing of Starc was hard to stop, as he personally took 3-2 off just ten balls. A frustrated de Villiers could only watch from the other end, as he ended up undefeated on 71 after 203 minutes of excellent batting.

Day 3 - Attendance: 6,118.

After his first innings failure, Bancroft would have been a nervous young man as he headed out to open the batting with Warner. He got off the mark in fine fashion with a boundary behind square leg and looked comfortable in the early stages of the third day. Maharaj came on in the ninth over and conceded 20 off his first two overs as the openers continued their positive approach. Having added 56, Warner miscued a pull shot to mid-on and then Khawaja aimed a reckless reverse sweep, gloving a catch behind. Bancroft passed fifty (76 balls, 10x4) with a nice pull shot but shortly after advanced and missed facing Maharaj, in what was the last over before lunch, Australia going in on 3-112, a lead of 301, with Smith 16 and S Marsh 4.

Against tight bowling, Smith survived a very strong appeal for LBW off Maharaj on 30, before being trapped in Elgar's first over, the last before drinks. Mitch Marsh couldn't repeat his first innings efforts, edging a back foot drive to slip and then on the verge of tea, Paine edged one low to slip, where de Villiers took the catch. Australia at tea led by a comfortable 364, with Shaun Marsh unbeaten on 25.

With the clouds gathering, Morkel took his first wickets of the game, as Shaun Marsh was pouched by de Villiers (his fifth catch) at second slip, Starc drove to cover and Lyon edged to Smith. Cummins, who had earlier smacked Maharaj over long-on for six, was there at the close, bad light ending the day, oddly the ball after an off-driven boundary by Hazlewood.

Day 4 - no attendance figure available

After a blow over long-on for six, Cummins was last out, to give Maharaj his ninth wicket of the match, Australia's lead 416. Having just shy of two days to chase the runs, Markram and Elgar were out of the blocks fast adding 29 inside seven overs, before Elgar edged a short one outside off to the keeper. It was the start of a top order collapse as Amla was trapped in front, marginally losing a review for LBW, "umpires call", the decision based on height. Next over, Markram pushed one away behind square-leg, took two paces down for a single and then changed his mind with a charging de Villiers past the point of return, well short of his ground when Warner's throw found Lyon at the bowlers end. Warner's obvious verbal send-off was a poor show for the vice-captain of an Australia team. Ten runs later a breakback from Hazlewood knocked du Plessis' off stumps out of the ground, the hosts having lost 4-20 in 54 balls. De Bruyn (4) Markram (27) survived to tea, South Africa on 4-63.

In the final session, Markram continued to weather the storm well, hitting some lovely off-drives as he reached fifty from 86 balls. De Bruyn found his feet, taking taking three fours in an over from Starc, as he copped a verbal barrage from the frustrated quick who had watched the first of the boundaries edged between the 'keeper and slip. The partnership reached 87 when Hazlewood induced a nick from De Bruyn, Paine this time getting his gloves onto a sharp chance. De Kock started confidently as he and Markram took the score to 5-167 at tea, the opener on 85, while de Kock had reached 21.

It later emerged that Warner and de Kock had a serious verbal stoush as they walk up the stairs into the dressing room, the ICC later issued a level two offence to Warner, and a level one to de Kock. Both players were found guilty

In the final session, the sixth wicket combination took control early on, regularly finding the rope as the Aussie paceman lost patience. De Kock reached his fifty (68 balls) and then in the next over, Markham took a single wide of mid-on off Starc to bring up his hundred from 171 balls with 14 finely struck fours. Cummins returned to the attack and gave the opener a good working over, having a caught at slip shout rejected (it took helmet not glove) and then next ball cracking him on the arm, which required several minutes of treatment.

Markram quickly regained his composure and soldiered on, the partnership reaching 100. Lyon was gaining plenty of turn but the breaks weren't going his way, as the runs continued to flow from both batsman. With the partnership reaching 147, a tired Markram edged Mitch Marsh to the keeper, who had just decided to stand up to the stumps, that very ball. Starc returned to the attack and took three wickets in his second over, as Philander edged behind, with Maharaj and Rabada bowled by reverse swinging deliveries. As the light quickly grew worse, Starc was denied a chance of going for his hat-trick, with Smith and Lyon at the bowling crease, just three singles came from the last nine overs of the day, as South Africa managed to take the game into the final day.

Day 5 - Attendance: not available.

On a sunny final morning, South Africa didn't resist for long, with de Kock trapped in front by Hazlewood in the fourth over of the day. Starc with nine wickets was a deserved Man of the match, but South Africa could take heart from the performances of Markram and de Kock in the second innings as they regrouped ahead of the next Test in Port Elizabeth.

Australian Cricket Digest, 2018-19

First Test at Kingsmead, Durban on March 1-5, 2018 – Australia won by 118 runs

Australia	First innings		B	M	4	6	Second innings		B	M	4	6
CT Bancroft	c de Kock b Philander	5	20	25	1		st de Kock b Maharaj	53	83	115	10	
DA Warner	c de Villiers b Philander	51	79	119	6		c sub (Mulder) b Rabada	28	35	59	4	
UT Khawaja	c de Kock b Rabada	14	19	30	3		c de Kock b Maharaj	6	12	21	1	
SPD Smith *	c de Villiers b Maharaj	56	114	155	11		lbw b Elgar	38	81	97	3	
SE Marsh	c de Villiers b Maharaj	40	96	132	6		c de Villiers b Morkel	33	99	153	5	
MR Marsh	c Morkel b Philander	96	173	265	13	1	c Amla b Rabada	6	12	23	1	
TD Paine +	c de Kock b Rabada	25	72	103	3		c de Villiers b Maharaj	14	29	37	1	
PJ Cummins	b Maharaj	3	38	51			b Maharaj	26	57	95	1	2
MA Starc	b Maharaj	35	25	38	4	2	c Elgar b Morkel	7	16	25	1	
NM Lyon	c de Bruyn b Maharaj	12	24	39	2		c Amla b Morkel	2	11	25		
JR Hazlewood	not out	2	4	6	-		not out	9	13	16	1	
	4 b, 8 lb	12					5 lb	5				
	110.4 overs, 486 mins	351					74.4 overs, 338 mins	227				

Fall: 1-15 (Bancroft), 2-39 (Khawaja), 3-95 (Warner), 4-151 (Smith), 5-177 (S Marsh), 6-237 (Paine), 7-251 (Cummins), 8-300 (Starc), 9-341 (M Marsh), 10-351 (Lyon)

Fall: 1-56 (Warner), 2-71 (Khawaja), 3-108 (Bancroft), 4-146 (Smith), 5-156 (M Marsh), 6-175 (Paine), 7-185 (S Marsh), 8-203 (Starc), 9-209 (Lyon), 10-227 (Cummins)

Sth Africa - bowling	O	M	R	W	wd	nb	O	M	R	W	wd	nb
M Morkel	22	3	75	0			15	4	47	3		
VD Philander	27	12	59	3			14	4	35	0		
KA Maharaj	33.4	5	123	5			29.4	4	102	4		
K Rabada	25	7	74	2			13	5	28	2		
AK Markram	1	0	2	0								
TB de Bruyn	2	0	6	0								
D Elgar							3	1	10	1		

South Africa	First innings		B	M	4	6	Second innings		B	M	4	6
D Elgar	c & b Lyon	7	20	32	1	2	c Paine b Starc	9	20	30	2	
AK Markram	c Bancroft b Cummins	32	59	82	6	1	c Paine b M Marsh	143	218	340	19	
HM Amla	c Bancroft b Lyon	0	3	2			lbw b Hazlewood	8	19	18	1	
AB de Villiers	not out	71	127	202	11		run out (Warner-Lyon)	0	1	5		
F du Plessis *	c Paine b Starc	15	22	35	1	1	b Cummins	4	8	19	1	
TB de Bruyn	c Paine b Starc	6	15	28	1		c Paine b Hazlewood	36	84	111	6	
Q de Kock +	b Lyon	20	33	54	4		lbw b Hazlewood	83	149	218	11	
VD Philander	c Paine b Starc	8	19	20	1		c Paine b Starc	6	16	16		
KA Maharaj	b Hazlewood	0	5	5			b Starc	0	3	3		
K Rabada	lbw b Starc	3	5	6			b Starc	0	1	1		
M Morkel	b Starc	0	2	2			not out	3	38	43		
		0					2 b, 3 lb, 1 nb	6				
	51.4 overs, 239 mins	162					92.4 overs, 408 mins	298				

Fall: 1-27 (Elgar), 2-27 (Amla), 3-55 (Markram), 4-92 (du Plessis), 5-108 (de Bruyn), 6-150 (de Kock), 7-158 (Philander), 8-159 (Maharaj), 9-162 (Rabada), 10-162 (Morkel)

Fall: 1-29 (Elgar), 2-39 (Amla), 3-39 (de Villiers), 4-49 (du Plessis), 5-136 (de Bruyn), 6-283 (Markram), 7-290 (Philander), 8-290 (Maharaj), 9-290 (Rabada), 10-298 (de Kock)

Australia - bowling	O	M	R	W	wd	nb	O	M	R	W	wd	nb
MA Starc	10.4	3	34	5			18	2	75	4		1
JR Hazlewood	13	5	31	1			15.4	2	61	3		
NM Lyon	16	3	50	3			32	7	86	0		
PJ Cummins	12	2	47	1			15	3	47	1		
MR Marsh							7	2	21	1		
SPD Smith							5	3	3	0		

Stumps scores:

Day 1	Australia (1st inns)	5-225 MR Marsh 32*, TD Paine 21*
Day 2	South Africa (1st inns)	162
Day 3	Australia (2nd inns)	9-213 PJ Cummins 17*, JR Hazlewood 4*
Day 4	South Africa (2nd inns)	9-293 Q de Kock 81*, M Morkel 0*

Toss: Australia
Umpires: K Dharmasena, S Ravi
CB Gaffeney (TV), Ref: JJ Crowe
Award: MA Starc (Aus). Attendance: 18,391

SECOND TEST – PORT ELIZABETH

Australia kept the same team that won the first Test, while South Africa made a change to its pace attack with Morne Morkel dropped from the side in favour of Lungi Ngidi. The ICC held a hearing into the de Kock/Warner incident with Warner accepting a fine of 75% of his match fee (approximately $13,000), which also meant he was only a minor infraction away from a ban in the next two years. De Kock was fined 25% of his match fee for his involvement in the stairwell incident, while Nathan Lyon, who intentionally dropped the ball near AB de Villiers when he was run out in the second innings, was fined 15% of his match fee. It all made for a fractious atmosphere as the team headed onto the field for the second Test.

Day One

In front of a small crowd, the South African pace attack kept a tight rein on the scoring early on, with just 23 runs from 14 overs in the opening hour. Philander was impressive in a seven over (0-5) spell with Rabada and Ngidi doing a fine job at the other end. The shackles broke after drinks, when the Aussie openers added 42 in four overs, Warner taking 14 from a Rabada over, which included three fours in four balls. Warner reached his fifty just before lunch and minutes before the break, Bancroft edged a drive, which de Kock swooped on behind, diving to his right – Australia 1-98, Warner 50 not out.

With the shine off the new-ball, Khawaja couldn't take full advantage, edging behind off Philander and then Warner fell to Ngidi, being bowled between bat and pad as he came forward. Shaun Marsh joined his skipper Smith and the pair carefully added 44, with Marsh passing 2,000 runs in Tests. But the dismissal of Smith livened proceedings, as he lbw playing back to Rabada just before tea, the bowler appearing to brush Smith as he headed for the Pavilion. Shaun Marsh was out in the next Rabada over, leg before stuck on the crease and then his brother Mitch, after edging a four, was caught behind off an inside edge aiming a drive. Tea was taken, Australia having slipped from 4-161 to 6-170.

Cummins went first ball after tea, a regulation edge to the keeper, to give Rabada three wickets in the over. When Starc was bowled, playing down the wrong line, Australia had lost 5-21 in 36 balls, Rabada himself taking 4-13 from 14 of them. Paine and Lyon tried to repair the innings, the off-spinner going for his shots before Ngidi bowled him through the "gate" as he aimed a drive. Hazlewood and Paine added 31 for the last wicket, but when Ngidi found a gap between the bat and pad of Paine, Australia were all out for just 243.

With just under an hour to bat, the openers started carefully, with Cummins getting the initial breakthrough with his fourth ball, as trapped Markram in front. Night-watchman Rabada played his shots, hitting four boundaries before the close, South Africa trailing by 204 at stumps.

Day Two

Umpire Gaffeney was ill overnight, being unfit to officiate being replaced on-field by TV official S. Ravi. Hazlewood and Starc couldn't make a breakthrough in the first half hour, as once again Australia had to wait until Cummins came on before getting a wicket. He bowled Rabada as he played back, getting an inside edge onto his thigh, the ball rebounding back onto the stumps. Amla had some nervous moments early, edging his first ball for four, and then on seven he was given out LBW off Cummins, before a review found he had just got his pad outside the line. Both batsmen stuck to the task and reached lunch on 2-110, Elgar 38, Amla 31.

Australia's bowlers gave nothing away in the second session, the third wicket pairing finding every run well earned. Amla on 40 was once more given out LBW, but reviewed, replays showing he had just got himself outside the line. Amla finally reached his fifty (122 balls) while Elgar continued to battle away, he too reaching his fifty (164 balls, 261 mins), South Africa heading in at tea on 2-153, having added just 43 runs in the two hours of play.

The hard work of the Aussie bowlers paid off in the first over of the final session, when Starc yorked Amla from around the wicket, ending a stand of 88. In the next over, Elgar finally went, Hazlewood finding the edge, to end the gritty five hour innings by the opener. de Villiers and du Plessis looked in good touch until the South African skipper was trapped in front by Mitch Marsh. In Marsh's next over de Bruyn went LBW to the same bowler, South Africa were still 60 behind – the match evenly poised. At this point de Villiers was just 18 and it was a signal for him to move up a gear, as he took 14 (including three fours) off a Pat Cummins over. He reached his fifty (62 balls, 10 fours) of a Mitch Starc full toss and then saw de Kock bowled by a ball from Lyon that turned away nicely to hit the off-stump.

With 45 minutes left to stumps, de Villiers found a willing partner in Philander, as the pair pushed past Australia's first innings total, adding 36 before the close of play – to lead by 20 at stumps.

Day Three

The de Villiers/Philander pairing continued where they left off and looked totally composed until just before drinks. Philander (36) was dropped Bancroft at short-leg off Cummins – a tough chance as it came off the full face of the bat. It mattered little as two balls later, the same fielder held onto an almost identical chance as Philander went to work one off his pads. The pair had added 84, South Africa now having a decent advantage of 68 as the small crowd watched de Villiers bring up his ton with a fantastic uppercut for four off Cummins – it was his 22nd in Tests and couldn't have come at a better time.

The ninth wicket pair then went into overdrive with Maharaj hitting Lyon to deep square-leg where Khawaja held a tough catch on the boundary, but gave up six runs as he overstepped the rope. De Villiers pulled Cummins for six and then Maharaj smacked Lyon for six over long-on, 30 runs coming in the space of just three overs. Starc returned to the attack and Maharaj cracked him for three fours in an over, bringing up the fifty stand from just 36 balls. Hazlewood came back on and with his fourth ball, bowled Maharaj as he aimed an ambitious pull shot. Ngidi stepped out, hit a four and then was run out at the bowlers end after de Villiers wanted a tight second run to keep the strike. South Africa led by 139 – de Villiers had played magnificently in an innings which lasted for four and a half hours, undoubtedly one of his finest for South Africa in Tests.

Facing the large deficit, Australia needed to make at least 350 to give themselves any chance in the match. The openers added 27 before Rabada picked up the prize wicket of Warner - bowled between bat and pad in the paceman's fifth over. Rabada's passionate roar in the direction of Warner would have done him no favours, given he was facing a level two charge for his contact with Steve Smith, after the Aussie captains dismissal in the first innings.

Khawaja started impressively with two early fours as he and Bancroft put their heads down in an attempt to put together a big partnership. After batting patiently for over an hour and a half, Bancroft edged a drive into his pad, only to watch in horror as the ball rolled back onto the stumps. This brought Smith in half an hour before tea, he whacked Maharaj over long-off for six before edging a catch behind – Australia going to tea on 3-86, still 53 behind.

Australia's efforts to set a significant target were badly hindered when Shaun Marsh edged a drive to the keeper from the second ball after tea. Khawaja continued to play some elegant shots and perhaps some overly risky ones as he reverse swept Maharaj for four. Mitch Marsh, after struggling over 39 balls for his first five runs, pulled Ngidi for six and when Khawaja moved to 60, Australia had erased the deficit with still six wickets in hand. Rabada came back for one last spell and when the stand reached the dreaded devils number of 87, Khawaja's fine knock came to an end, trapped in front by the paceman bowling wide on the crease. Australia closing the day with a lead of 41.

Day Four

Australia needed a big sixth wicket stand to keep themselves in the match, but it ended in the opening over of the day, when Mitch Marsh had his off-stump spreadeagled by Rabada. Cummins then poked at a wide ball, gully taking a fine catch to his right, giving Rabada his tenth wicket of the match. Starc then gave the quickie his 11th, as he edged a drive through to de Kock and then Ngidi chipped in to get Lyon as he also edged a drive, Australia having lost 4-25.

With Australia just 72 ahead Hazlewood joined Paine, as the pair knuckled down to try and get the lead at least to three figures. They just made it as Hazlewood swept Maharaj for four and then cracked the same bowler for six over mid-wicket. But off the last ball of the same over, Australia's last man went for another slog-sweep was caught at deep mid-wicket, Australia all out for 239 – having lost 5-59 from 16 overs on the fourth day.

With South Africa needing just 101 to win in sunny conditions with the pitch still playing well, it seemed only a matter of time with the homeside red hot favourites to polish off the target. In the second over, Markram (7) was dropped by Mitch Marsh at first slip, a fairly straight forward chance to his right off Hazlewood. Lyon came on to bowl the last over before lunch and with his first ball had Elgar caught and bowled – a low chance to his right, South Africa 1-22 at the break, needing 79 more to win.

Hazlewood had some luck when Markram got a thicker edge, finding the safe hands of Smith at second slip. This brought de Villiers to the crease and he had it in his mind to get the runs needed as quickly as possible as he launched an assault. He pulled Hazlewood for four, reverse swept Lyon to the rope before lifting the off-spinner over mid-wicket for six. In the next over he cut and straight drove Hazlewood for boundaries to move to 25 off his first 14 balls, South Africa 2-60, needing just 41 more. Amla was ticking the score over well and went with 20 needed, edging a wide one, giving Cummins his 50th Test wicket. Still with 20 wanted, de Villiers advanced at Lyon and gloved a catch to short-leg, but then de Bruyn and his skipper du Plessis saw their team home, a classic off-drive by de Bruyn ending the match and levelling the series.

While AB de Villiers played a great knock and was the best batsman on either side in the match, Kagiso Rabada was the one man who continually troubled the Australian batsman and was a fair choice for Man of the match. Post-match it was announced that Rabada would receive at two-match ban, for making inappropriate and deliberate physical conduct with Smith during the first innings. Rabada and South Africa decided to appeal the decision and shortly after the ICC confirmed that Michael Heron QC of New Zealand has been appointed as the Judicial Commissioner for the hearing. At the appeal hearing Judicial Commissioner Heron overturned the suspension, saying he could not find enough evidence to suggest Rabada made deliberate contact with Smith.

"The key issue is whether Mr Rabada made 'inappropriate and deliberate physical contact' with Mr Smith," Heron said.

"I am not 'comfortably satisfied' that Mr Rabada intended to make contact and I therefore find him not guilty of the charge under 2.2.7.

"I am entitled, however, to consider whether the conduct involved constitutes a lower level offence. I consider the conduct was inappropriate, lacked respect for his fellow player and involved non-deliberate and minor contact. The actions contravened the principle that a dismissed batsman should be left alone.

"I consider a penalty of the imposition of a fine of 25 per cent of the applicable match fee to be the appropriate penalty for the breach of Article 2.1.1. As a consequence, 1 demerit point accrues.

"Mr. Rabada will be well aware of the consequences of any further breaches of the code."

The hearing lasted six hours, Rabada enlisting the services of high-profile barrister Dali Mpofu who argued the 22-year-old's innocence. There was also some suggestions that there were people behind the scenes, perhaps of a political persuasion away from cricket, pushing hard to ensure the suspension was overturned. Either way Rabada was free to play as the teams had a nine-day gap to gather their thoughts ahead of the third Test in Cape Town.

Second Test at St Georges Park, Port Elizabeth on March 9-12, 2018 - South Africa won 6 wickets

Australia

Batsman	First innings	R	B	M	4	6	Second innings	R	B	M	4	6
CT Bancroft	c de Kock b Philander	38	91	117	6		b Ngidi	24	70	97	2	
DA Warner	b Ngidi	63	100	156	9		b Rabada	13	21	43	3	
UT Khawaja	c de Kock b Philander	4	15	14			lbw b Rabada	75	136	225	14	
SPD Smith *	lbw b Rabada	25	58	93	3		c de Kock b Maharaj	11	18	20	1	1
SE Marsh	lbw b Rabada	24	52	76	4		c de Kock b Rabada	1	5	12		
TD Paine +	b Ngidi	36	68	99	5		not out	28	50	92	2	
MR Marsh	c de Kock b Rabada	4	3	3	1		b Rabada	45	125	155	4	1
PJ Cummins	c de Kock b Rabada	0	1	1			c de Bruyn b Rabada	5	14	17	1	
MA Starc	b Rabada	8	11	18	1		c de Kock b Rabada	1	10	11		
NM Lyon	b Ngidi	17	20	27	4		c de Kock b Ngidi	5	8	14	1	
JR Hazlewood	not out	10	10	39	2		c Ngidi b Maharaj	17	17	32	2	1
	14 lb	14					2 b, 10 lb, 2 w	14				
	71.3 overs, 325 mins	243					79 overs, 362 mins	239				

Fall: 1-98 (Bancroft), 2-104 (Khawaja), 3-117 (Warner), 4-161 (Smith), 5-166 (S Marsh), 6-170 (M Marsh), 7-170 (Cummins), 8-182 (Starc), 9-212 (Lyon), 10-243 (Paine)

Fall: 1-27 (Warner), 2-62 (Bancroft), 3-77 (Smith, 4-86 (S Marsh), 5-173 (Khawaja), 6-186 (M Marsh), 7-202 (Cummins), 8-204 (Starc), 9-211 (Lyon), 10-239 (Hazlewood)

Sth Africa - bowling	O	M	R	W	wd	nb	O	M	R	W	wd	nb
VD Philander	18	7	25	2			18	5	56	0		
K Rabada	21	2	96	5			22	9	54	6	1	
LT Ngidi	13.3	3	51	3			13	5	24	2		
KA Maharaj	18	1	51	0			23	2	90	2		
D Elgar	1	0	6	0								
AK Markram							3	1	3	0		

South Africa

Batsman	First innings	R	B	M	4	6		Second innings	R	B	M	4	6
D Elgar	c Paine b Hazlewood	57	197	306	6		2	c & b Lyon	5	17	24		
AK Markram	lbw b Cummins	11	21	33	1		1	c Smith b Hazlewood	21	28	37	3	
K Rabada	b Cummins	29	40	58	6								
HM Amla	b Starc	56	148	203	6		3	c Paine b Cummins	27	42	54	3	
AB de Villiers	not out	126	146	261	20	1	4	c Bancroft b Lyon	28	26	44	4	1
F du Plessis *	lbw b M Marsh	9	16	40	1		5	not out	2	10	19		
TB de Bruyn	lbw b M Marsh	1	8	10			6	not out	15	14	15	2	
Q de Kock +	b Lyon	9	20	31									
VD Philander	c Bancroft b Cummins	36	85	104	5								
KA Maharaj	b Hazlewood	30	24	38	3	2							
LT Ngidi	run out (Smith)	5	7	15	1								
	9 b, 2 lb, 2 w	13						4 b	4				
	118.4 overs, 558 mins	382						22.5 overs, 98 mins	4-102				

Fall: 1-22 (Markram), 2-67 (Rabada), 3-155 (Amla), 4-155 (Elgar), 5-179 (du Plessis), 6-183 (de Bruyn), 7-227 (de Kock), 8-311 (Philander), 9-369 (Maharaj), 10-382 (Ngidi)

Fall: 1-22 (Elgar), 2-32 (Markram), 3-81 (Amla), 4-81 (de Villiers)

Australia - bowling	O	M	R	W	wd	nb	O	M	R	W	wd	nb
MA Starc	33.4	5	110	1			3	0	15	0		
JR Hazlewood	30	5	98	2			6	0	26	1		
PJ Cummins	24	6	79	3	2		4.5	0	13	1		
NM Lyon	22	5	58	1			9	0	44	2		
MR Marsh	9	1	26	2								

Stumps scores:

Day 1	South Africa (1st inns)	1-39	D Elgar 11*, K Rabada 17*
Day 2	South Africa (1st inns)	7-263	AB deVilliers 74*, VD Philander 14*
Day 3	Australia (2nd inns)	5-180	PJ Cummins 17*, JR Hazlewood 4*

Toss: Australia
Umpires: K Dharmasena, CB Gaffeney
S Ravi (TV), Ref: JJ Crowe
Award: K Rabada (SA). Attendance: 13,305

Australian Cricket Digest, 2018-19
THIRD TEST – CAPE TOWN

After a decent gap following the Port Elizabeth Test, the teams knuckled down to the task of winning in Cape Town. Australia kept the same team for the fourth test in a row, while South Africa made two changes, Morkel was back for Ngidi while Temba Bavuma was back from injury replacing de Bruyn.

Day One

On a bright day South Africa batted first and lost Markram in the fourth over, edged a drive low to second slip where Smith swooped on it, moving to his left. The Australian attack gave little away early, as Elgar and Amla dug in, much as they had during the first innings in Port Elizabeth. Amla started to get his feet moving, hitting Cummins for two fours in an over, Elgar playing his favourite cut shot to bring up the fifty stand. Mitch Marsh was on fifteen minutes before lunch, and was twice hit for boundaries by Elgar, in an over which went for 11. Lunch was taken with the left handed opener on 40, Amla 31, South Africa 1-75.

The pitch had carry, but not great pace as Elgar pulled Cummins for four to bring up a solid fifty. He lost Amla in the next over to Hazlewood, top edging a hook to long-leg, the paceman claiming the South Africa veteran for the seventh time in Test cricket. AB de Villiers got off the mark with a clip wide of mid-on for four as the boundaries flowed early in his innings. Elgar was given a life on 53, when Lyon dropped one he should have taken a point, the plucky opener making the most of his luck, punching some nice drives back down the ground. Elgar also attacked the off-spinner when his chance came, smacking an on-drive for four and then cracking him back over his head for six. In the second last over before tea, Elgar on 87 edged Mitch Marsh just wide of second slip, South Africa going in at tea on top at 2-185, Elgar 91, de Villiers 41 – their stand worth 93.

Three overs after the adjournment, the hundred stand was raised and then Elgar on-drove Starc in fine style for four to bring up his own hundred. In the next over de Villiers worked one off his hip for four to reach his fifty and raise the South Africa 200 – giving the home side a strong base to build a large first innings total. But the Aussie attack fought back, with the previously expensive Cummins (1-52 off 13 overs) picking up four quick wickets, as the ball started to swing late in the afternoon sunshine. The first was de Villiers, caught at mid-off which ended a third wicket stand of 128. Then du Plessis fended at a wide ball, edging to second slip, with Bavuma in his return Test also held there by the Australian skipper, after he played back. When de Kock edged a pull to Paine, South Africa had lost 4-22 in just under an hour, Cummins taking 4-7 from 38 balls. Mitch Marsh returned to the crease and had Maharaj driving to cover to make it 8-257 in the 84th over, with Australia yet to take the new ball. They finally did so in the 87th over, with bad light intervening shortly after at 5.55pm, with Elgar still unbeaten after just under six and a half hours defiant and patient batting.

Day Two

In the previous Test Kagiso Rabada showed skill when batting in the night-watchman role, and again proved hard to move in the early stages of the second day. He hooked Cummins for four and stuck to the task with Elgar, who continued on from where he left off the previous day. The fifty stand was raised and then immediately after Rabada drove at Lyon's first ball of the day, edging it to first slip. Morkel cracked a four but then went also edging to slip, to give Smith his fifth catch of the innings, joining 11 other fielders who had taken a handful of catches in an innings.

FIVE CATCHES IN A TEST INNINGS

Vic Richardson Australia v South Africa, Durban 1935-36	Darren Sammy West Indies v India, Bombay 2013-14
Yujurvindra Singh India v England, Bangalore 1976-77	Darren Bravo West Indies v Bangladesh, Arnos Vale 2014
Mohammad Azharuddin India v Pakistan, Karachi 1989-90	Ajinkya Rahane India v Sri Lanka, Galle 2015
Kris Srikkanth India v Australia, Perth 1991-92	Jermaine Blackwood West Indies v Sri Lanka, Colombo (P Sara Oval) 2015-16
Stephen Fleming New Zealand v Zimbabwe 1997-98	
Graeme Smith South Africa v Australia, Perth 2012-13	Steve Smith Australia v South Africa, Cape Town 2017-18

Elgar had carried his bat for the third time in his career, lasting just shy of seven and a half hours. The Australian first innings got underway with an hour to go to lunch, and Rabada came hard at Warner, cracking him on the left forearm with his second delivery. Warner responded as he only can, hitting the paceman for three consecutive fours in the next over. In the following over, a hook for six was followed by an edged four and then Rabada had his revenge, sending the opener's off stump cartwheeling out of the ground. The delivery so excited one fan at the ground that as Warner headed up the race to the rooms, he copped an earful from him. With lunch approaching, Khawaja top-edged a pull from Morkel's third ball and was nicely held at long-leg. Smith came out and copped a nasty ball in the armpit, Australia lunching on 2-67, Bancroft steady on 22, Smith 4.

Morkel put South Africa on top when he had the Aussie skipper fending a catch to gully, but then Bancroft and Shaun Marsh steadied things, the Aussie opener cutting the tall paceman for four to bring up his second fifty of the series. Both players found the pitch and bowling to their liking, until Australia suffered a mid-innings collapse, much like South Africa the previous day. Shaun Marsh edged a wild drive at a wide ball, giving de Kock the catch and Morkel his 300th Test wicket. Then on the stroke of tea, Bancroft, who was playing his most composed Test innings to date, was beaten on the forward stroke by one from Philander that cut back in. The opener unsuccessfully reviewed – as he headed into tea with Australia a precarious 5-150 still 161 in arrears.

Philander found Mitch Marsh's edge after tea and then Rabada returned to the attack, having both Cummins and Starc caught at second slip in a spell of six deliveries as Australia subsided to 8-175, a loss of 5-25. Just when Australia looked to be facing a large deficit, Lyon came to the rescue hitting some forceful shots. He had plenty of luck, firstly being dropped by Amla at first slip on 13 off Rabada and then on 32 by the normally reliable de Villiers off Morkel. When the stand reached fifty, Lyon had 38 of them as Paine was playing a secondary role in the ninth wicket union. A hook for four off Morkel saw Lyon reach his Test best but the tall quick had his revenge when the off-spinner went for another drive over the off-side, only to be caught by cover running back to take a fine catch. When bad light ended play at 5.46pm, Paine was still there on 34, having batted the whole of the final session, with Australia trailing by 66.

Day three

After two fours in the first over of the day by Hazlewood off Rabada, the Aussie number eleven edged the paceman to first slip, ending the innings with the visitors still 56 runs behind. South Africa could well have been one down in the opening over, as Markram was dropped by Khawaja in the gully, the chance not sticking in his left-hand. After 28 had been added Elgar was dismissed for the first time in the match, as he edged a loose looking drive to second slip. With a few clouds gathering, many South Africans were hoping for a spot of rain in the city, which had been suffering from a drought and dangerously low water supplies. Markram and Amla dug in against some tight bowling moving the score at lunch to 1-65, a lead of 120.

In the second over after lunch, Amla was given out caught on 24 off Starc, but called for review which revealed the ball had taken his shoulder rather than glove or bat. Markram pushed one through mid-on to reach fifty, but then lost Amla who drove a catch to short-cover. De Villiers announced his arrival in a positive fashion, by smashing a bouncer from Cummins over cover for six. Markram continued to find the gap in the field and then within half an hour of tea, came an event which was to turn the cricket world upside down.

During the 43rd over, with South Africa two down and leading by 194, TV coverage showed Cameron Bancroft shine the ball intensely before placing the something in his pocket. At the end of the over, the umpires are seen to be consulting each other and then a replay showed Bancroft placing what appears to be some yellow paper, down the front of his trousers. The umpires head over to speak to Bancroft and with Australia skipper Steve Smith joining in on the conversation, question Bancroft about what was going on. Bancroft then pulls out a sunglasses storage bag, with no sign of the yellow piece of paper. The umpires decide not to replace the ball, apparently deeming that no damage has been caused to it.

In what ends up being the over before tea, Markram hit a catch to mid-on and was out after a solid knock of 84, South Africa 3-151 at the break, de Villiers 18, the lead by now 217.

At tea, on the TV coverage, Mark Nicholas had a discussion with former South African skipper Graeme Smith and Aussie leg-spinner Shane Warne. All are concerned and suspect that the Australian have tried to change the state of the ball.

After tea, the game resumed in poor light, de Villiers continued to bat well, with du Plessis finding some much needed form. Just as the South African skipper looked set to get a decent score, he was trapped in front by Lyon, an Aussie review needed to overturn the original decision of not out. Bavuma didn't last long, edging low to second slip, leaving South Africa 257 ahead with five wickets still in hand. De Kock joined de Villiers, starting quietly before taking twelve off an over from Lyon, which included a lofted six over long-on. With a reverse sweep boundary off Lyon, de Villiers moved to 50 (92 balls), the players trudging off for bad light shortly after at 5.17pm – South Africa 294 ahead

After play Bancroft admitted to ball tampering, and was charged by match referee Andy Pycroft with a Level 2 offence of attempting to alter the condition of the ball. He later said at a press conference after play that "We had a discussion during the break, on myself I saw an opportunity to potentially use some tape, granules from the rough patches on the wicket and try and change the ball condition".

Captain Steve Smith, who was sitting alongside Bancroft at the Press conference said "I'm not naming names but the leadership group talked about it and 'Bangers' (Bancroft) was around at the time. "We spoke about it and thought it was a possible way to get an advantage.

"Obviously it didn't work, the umpires didn't see it change the way the ball was behaving or how it looked or anything like that, so it was a poor choice and deeply regrettable."

Despite what had happened, Smith also said he wouldn't be standing down, ""Obviously, today was a big mistake on my behalf and on the leadership group's behalf as well, but I take responsibility as the captain, I need to take control of the ship, but this is certainly something I'm not proud of and something that I hope I can learn from and come back strong from.

"I am embarrassed to be sitting here talking about this.

"We're in the middle of such a great series and for something like this to overshadow the great cricket that's been played and not have a single cricket question (in this press conference), that's not what I'm about and not what the team's about.

"We'll move past this. It's a big error in judgement but we'll learn from it and move past it."

While the players slept overnight, Cricket Australia CEO James Sutherland addressed the media in Melbourne the next morning to explain action will be taken against the players involved in due course and that a full investigation had been launched led by Head of Integrity, Iain Roy.

Day four

Unfortunately for Smith – by the start of play the next day, he had been stood down as captain for the rest of the match, with Warner being demoted as vice-captain, for his alleged role in what had happened. So Tim Paine led the Australians out on the ground for the start of play, to a certain amount of booing from the locals. The "Wavingtheflag.com" Australian troop of supporters decided to not wave their flags for the day, as a sign of disappointment and disgust at what had happened.

In the subdued atmosphere, play started with Mitch Marsh conceding two boundaries to de Kock in his opening over. Lyon took up the attack from the other end, with South Africa quietly adding to their lead in the first half an hour. 31 runs were added in the first 40 minutes before de Villiers played back and edged one to first slip, giving Hazlewood his 150th Test wicket.

De Kock brought up his fifty (67 balls) in the next over as he and Philander pressed home the advantage. Philander top edged a hook off Starc for six, the left-arm quick's over going for 15 all up, then hit him for three fours in a row off his next, as South Africa passed 300. De Kock eventually went, edging one to the keeper as he advanced at Cummins – South Africa heading to lunch on 7-333, Philander 39, Rabada 4, holding a lead of 389.

Starc continued to have a poor day, with Rabada cracking him for three fours in an over, before Lyon had him stumped, having a slog, which gave the off-spinner his 300th Test wicket. In normal circumstances this would have been well celebrated, but on this occasion the congratulations were quite subdued. After Maharaj was caught at deep mid-on, Philander brought up his fifty (78 balls) with a nice cut, Morkel out shortly after, South Africa all out 373, a lead of 429.

The Australia opening pair headed out, to a less than friendly welcome, knowing they were both unlikely to be playing the next Test. They were cautious early, with Bancroft playing confidently, despite copping a whack on the right elbow from a ball bowled by Rabada. Just before tea the South African skipper and Umpire Llong had a lengthy chat – Australia walking in to the break on 0-47, Bancroft 22, Warner 25.

The fifty was raised just after tea, courtesy of inside edge by Bancroft to fine-leg for four off Rabada. Shortly after Warner drove one to cover and shouted for a single, with a slow out of the blocks Bancroft caught short by a superb direct hit by du Plessis at cover. One wondered given how well they were going, as to whether such a single was worth the risk. What the run out did do was trigger an epic collapse, which saw Australia lose 9-50 and fall to one of their most humiliating defeats ever.

Warner was caught at fine gully, aiming a cut at Rabada, it being the fourth time he'd been dismissed by him in the series. Then Smith headed out to bat, with security guards holding back vocal supporters as the Australian skipper walked down the players race. The next over saw Maharaj grab two wickets, with Khawaja not offering the full face of the bat as he edged to slip, while next ball Shaun Marsh, gloved a turning ball to short-leg – where a fine diving catch was taken. Australia had lost 4-2 from 26 deliveries, and it was only to get worse against a charged up South Africa attack.

Smith top-edged a bouncer from Rabada that went for six, but then was caught in the gully off Morkel as he aimed to slash a ball away with a straight bat. Mitch Marsh showed some fight, before toeing a pull shot to gully, with Cummins out the very next ball gloving a bouncer to the same area. Starc copped a crack on the helmet from a Morkel bouncer, then two balls later fended a chest high ball to give short-leg an easy catch. Paine was there still, but then pushed one to cover, with Bavuma too quick with the throw for a scrambling Lyon. Then it all came to an end when Hazlewood was caught uppercutting to fine third man – Australia all out in 39.4 overs, with South Africa winning by 332 runs to go two-one up in the series.

After the match, Smith was suspended for the fourth Test by the ICC after he was charged with "conduct contrary to the spirit of the game". In addition to the suspension he was fined 100 per cent of his match fee. For his involvement, Bancroft was fined 75 per cent of his match fee and at that point it meant he was cleared to play in the fourth Test.

After the match, Cricket Australia officials arrived and prior to the fourth Test it was announced by CA CEO James Sutherland that Smith, Bancroft and Warner were going to be sent home – all of them to miss the last Test. It had been established by the CA investigations team that they were the only three that had prior knowledge of the ball tampering incident.

"No other players or support staff had prior knowledge. This includes Darren Lehmann," Sutherland said. "He will continue to coach the Australian men's team under his current contract (which runs until the end of the 2019 Ashes)."

Well that changed the next day, when a tearful and emotional Lehmann announced his resignation as coach. Having seen the press conferences given by Smith and Bancroft back in Australia, Lehmann decided it was time to call it quits.

""I just want to let you know this will be by my last Test as head coach of the Australian cricket team as I'm stepping down," said Lehmann, reading from a prepared statement.

"After seeing events in the media today with Steve Smith and Cameron Bancroft, the feeling is that Australian cricket needs to move forward and this is the right thing to do. "I really felt for Steve, as I saw him crying in front of the media, and all the players are really hurting. "As I stated before I had no prior knowledge of the incident and do not condone what happened. But good people can make mistakes.

"My family and I have copped a lot of abuse over the last week and it's taken its toll on them. "As many who sit in this room will know life on the road means a long time away from our loved ones and after speaking to my family at length over the last few days it's the right time to step away.

"I'm ultimately responsible for the culture of the team and I've been thinking about my position for a while. "Despite telling media yesterday that I'm not resigning, after viewing Steve and Cameron hurting it's only fair that I make this decision. Lehmann went on to say that his decision to resign would allow Cricket Australia to make a full review into the culture of the team and allow changes to be made to regain the trust of the Australian public.

"The players involved have been handed down very serious sanctions and they know they must face the consequences. They have made a grave mistake but they are not bad people." Lehmann said.

Australian Cricket Digest, 2018-19

Tim Paine was appointed captain for the final Test, with Joe Burns, Matt Renshaw and Glenn Maxwell all flown in as possible replacements for the last game of the series.

Third Test at Newlands, Cape Town on March 22-25, 2018 - South Africa won by 322 runs

South Africa	First innings		B	M	4	6	Second innings		B	M	4	6
D Elgar	not out		141	284	434	20	1	2 c Smith b Cummins	14	23	43	2
AK Markram	c Smith b Hazlewood		0	11	17		1	c Cummins b Starc	84	145	216	10
HM Amla	c Cummins b Hazlewood		31	87	128	3		c Bancroft b Cummins	31	80	106	5
AB de Villiers	c Warner b Cummins		64	95	136	10		c S Marsh b Hazlewood	63	136	221	7	1
F du Plessis *	c Smith b Cummins		5	14	19	1		lbw b Lyon	20	44	58	3
T Bavuma	c Smith b Cummins		1	12	14			c sub (PSP Handscomb) b Hazlewood	5	4	5	1
Q de Kock +	c Paine b Cummins		3	11	20			c Paine b Cummins	65	97	145	8	1
VD Philander	c Paine b M Marsh		8	23	27	1		not out	52	79	127	6	1
KA Maharaj	c Bancroft b Starc		3	7	7		10	c Cummins b Lyon	5	14	17	1
K Rabada	c Smith b Lyon		22	42	62	3	9	st Paine b Lyon	20	46	43	3
M Morkel	c Smith b Lyon		4	4	3	1		c Khawaja b Hazlewood	6	7	10		1
	13 b, 11 lb, 3 nb, 2 w		29					4 b, 1 lb, 1 nb, 2 w	8			
	97.5 overs, 434 mins		311					112.2 overs, 492 mins	373			

Fall: 1-6 (Markram), 2-92 (de Villiers), 3-220 (de Villiers), 4-234 (du Plessis), 5-236 (Bavuma), 6-242 (de Kock), 7-254 (Philander), 8-257 (Maharaj), 9-307 (Rabada), 10-311 (Morkel)

Fall: 1-28 (Elgar), 2-104 (Amla), 3-151 (Markram), 4-196 (du Plessis), 5-201 (Bavuma), 6-269 (de Villiers), 7-324 (de Kock), 8-354 (Rabada), 9-362 (Maharaj), 10-373 (Morkel, 112.2 ov)

Australia - bowling	O	M	R	W	wd	nb	O	M	R	W	wd	nb
MA Starc	21	3	81	1		2	23	5	98	1	1	
JR Hazlewood	23	4	59	2			25.2	5	69	3		
NM Lyon	19.5	6	43	2			31	2	102	3		
PJ Cummins	26	6	78	4	1		27	5	67	3	2	
MR Marsh	7	2	26	1	1	1	5	0	26	0		
SPD Smith	1	1	0	0			1	0	6	0		

Australia	First innings		B	M	4	6	Second innings		B	M	4	6
CT Bancroft	lbw b Philander		77	103	178	14		run out (du Plessis)	26	64	88	3
DA Warner	b Rabada		30	14	28	5	1	c de Villiers b Rabada	32	67	100	4
UT Khawaja	c Rabada b Morkel		5	22	25			c de Villiers b Maharaj	1	9	18	
SPD Smith *	c Elgar b Morkel		5	18	19	1		c Elgar b Morkel	7	21	29		1
SE Marsh	c de Kock b Morkel		26	63	88	3		c Markram b Maharaj	0	1	3	
MR Marsh	c de Kock b Philander		5	22	34	1		c de Villiers b Morkel	16	28	39	3
TD Paine +	not out		34	84	148	3		not out	9	27	58	2
PJ Cummins	c de Villiers b Rabada		4	40	38			c Elgar b Morkel	0	1	5	
MA Starc	c de Villiers b Rabada		2	5	9			c Markram b Morkel	7	14	18	1
NM Lyon	c Elgar b Morkel		47	38	58	8		run out (Bavuma-de Kock)	0	0	4	
JR Hazlewood	c Amla b Rabada		10	14	26	2		c Philander b Morkel	5	6	13	1
	1 b, 5 lb, 4 nb		10					4 b	4			
	69.5 overs, 328 minutes		255					39.4 overs, 187 minutes	107			

Fall: 1-43 (Warner), 2-61 (Khawaja), 3-72 (Smith), 4-150 (S Marsh), 5-150 (Bancroft), 6-156 (M Marsh), 7-173 (Cummins), 8-175 (Starc), 9-241 (Lyon), 10-255 (Hazlewood)

Fall: 1-57 (Bancroft), 2-59 (Warner), 3-59 (Khawaja), 4-59 (S Marsh), 5-75 (Smith), 6-86 (M Marsh), 7-86 (Cummins), 8-94 (Starc), 9-94 (Lyon), 10-107 (Hazlewood)

Sth Africa - bowling	O	M	R	W	wd	nb	O	M	R	W	wd	nb
VD Philander	15	5	26	2		1	6	2	17	0		
K Rabada	20.5	1	91	4		3	12	6	31	1		
M Morkel	21	7	87	4			9.4	3	23	5		
KA Maharaj	12	3	35	0			12	2	32	2		
T Bavuma	1	0	10	0								

Stumps scores:

Day 1	South Africa (1st inns)	8-266 D Elgar 121*, K Rabada 6*
Day 2	Australia (1st inns)	9-245 TD Paine 33*, JR Hazlewood 1*
Day 3	South Africa (2nd inns)	5-238 AB de Villiers 51*, Q de Kock 29*

Toss: South Africa
Umpires: RK Illingworth, NJ Llong
IJ Gould (TV), Ref: AJ Pycroft
Award: M Morkel (SA). Attendance: 44,170

Australian Cricket Digest, 2018-19
FOURTH TEST – JOHANNESBERG

After the dramas of the third Test, Australia made four changes from the previous match with Smith, Warner and Bancroft all sent home, while Mitchell Starc was left out due to a with tibia bone stress injury in his right leg. This meant good news for Chadd Sayers who was given a much awaited Test debut. Matt Renshaw and Joe Burns came straight from Queensland's winning Shield final team, while Peter Handscomb was brought in for his first Test of the series.

Day One – Attendance 16,500

South Africa won the toss and batted with Dean Elgar glancing the first ball of the match to long leg for a boundary. Aiden Markram also looked in good touch early, taking two boundaries in the Hazlewood's second over. Hazlewood managed to beat the bat on the odd occasion but Sayers, while accurate, wasn't getting the ball to swing. Pat Cummins came on in the eleventh over, but couldn't break through, South Africa hitting the drinks break on 35 without loss from 14 overs.

Nathan Lyon came on in the 16th over and had success in his second over, with Elgar aiming an on-drive, only to get a leading edge to mid-off, where Sayers held onto the chance above his head. Markram continued to bat nicely, lofting Lyon for six over long-on, the off-spinner quite expensive in his first spell with figures of 4-0-22-1. In the last over before lunch, Markram reached his fifty (90 balls, 7 fours, 1 six) with a straight drive off Sayers, the homeside lunching on 1-88, Markram 53, Amla 13.

Cummins and Sayers bowled in tandem after the break, as Markram and Amla continued to bat well. Hazlewood returned after a four-over spell from Cummins, conceding 11 runs in his first over, with both batsmen scoring boundaries. South Africa reached drinks on 1-135 (Markam 83, Amla 25) and looked set for a long stand, but it came to an end shortly after, when Amla edged a drive at Cummins, with Handscomb able to dive to his right at second slip and swoop onto the ball. Markram continued towards his ton, bringing it up off Lyon, working a ball behind square leg, having faced 152 balls, hitting 11 fours and a six. At tea South Africa were 2-177 from 55 overs, with Markram 111 and de Villiers 8.

Markram went for his shots in the early part of the final session, while de Villiers laid into Lyon, hitting him for two fours and a pulled six over square leg in the one over. Markram reached his 150 (214 balls, 17 fours, 1 six) with a fine off-drive off Cummins, but went two balls later, edging one low to the left of gully, where Mitch Marsh held a fine catch. Drinks were taken (70.5 overs, de Villiers 37*) and immediately after, Faf du Plessis padded up to one that ducked back in sharply, to be leg before. De Villiers survived the hat-trick ball in Cummins next over and passed fifty (93 balls, 5 fours, 1 six) as the South African batsmen reasserted themselves. Renshaw bowled the 79th over and then the new ball was taken after 80, with the score on 4-294, de Villiers 64, Bavuma 20.

Chadd Sayers, who had been accurate all day, finally took his first Test wicket, in the fourth over with the new ball, de Villiers getting a fine inside edge to the keeper as he aimed a drive. It had been a fine knock, during the course of which he had passed 2,000 runs against Australia. Two balls later Sayers had his second wicket as Kagiso Rabada, who came out as night-watchman, popped a catch to mid-off leaving South Africa 6-299, with fifteen minutes left for the day. Quinton de Kock and Bavuma negotiated the time remaining, with two overs left unbowled.

Day two

Cummins and Sayers started with the ball, and after a single to Bavuma in the second over of the morning, he went scoreless for an hour. At the other end, de Kock kept the score moving but started to find batting more difficult, with Lyon regularly passing his outside edge. Just 37 runs came in the opening hour, South Africa at drinks being 6-350, De Kock on 30 having already caught up with Bavuma, who was on 26.

South Africa picked up the tempo, with Bavuma hitting three boundaries in the space of two Cummins overs, before reaching his fifty with a square drive for three off Lyon, completed 120 balls, with six blows. The off-spinner was continually beating the bat of de Kock and finally took his wicket, as he miscued a pull-shot, Mitch Marsh running from mid-on behind the bowler to take the catch. Lunch came with South Africa 7-400, Bavuma 61, Philander 6.

Twenty-five minutes after lunch, Philander looked to loft Lyon into the stands, but fell short of that, providing a catch to Usman Khawaja at deep square leg. Keshav Maharaj was slow to start but then took on Lyon hitting him for a six and two fours in his 38th over, before hitting a four and six in his 40th, as South Africa charged towards 500. Bavuma reverse swept Lyon to move from 90 to 94 but after taking a single in the next over from Cummins, watched on as Maharaj went for a big drive, only to get a fine edge behind. Morkel then edged his first ball towards first slip, where Handscomb dived to his right from second to bring off a fine catch, giving Cummins a well deserved fifth wicket, whilst leaving Bavuma stranded on 95.

With 41 overs left in the day, Australia's new opening pair of Renshaw and Burns headed out to face the music. Burns didn't last long, edging Rabada's eighth ball to second slip. Renshaw stuck at the task for close to an hour, before edging a drive at a wide one and then Handscomb went to his first ball, unable to get his bat out of the way of a length ball he was trying to leave. At the other end, Khawaja was showing some fluency as he tried to recover the situation for Australia. Shaun Marsh was a willing ally, as the pair added 52, to reach 3-90 with 35 minutes left in the day.

Khawaja, having reached his fifty (77 balls, 9 fours) went in the following over, caught down the leg-side glancing at one from Philander, de Kock holding onto a fine catch, standing up to the stumps. Morkel returned to the attack and in the first over of his spell, had Mitch Marsh bowled, playing on having aimed a drive at a wide ball. With shadows lengthening, Shaun Marsh went three balls later, edging Maharaj to slip, Australia having lost 3-6 from 26 balls to slip to 6-96. Paine and Cummins saw Australia through to Stumps, with three overs lost for the day, still 378 behind.

Australian Cricket Digest, 2018-19

Day three

Overcast conditions greeted the players on the third morning, with the floodlights on from the start of play. Paine and Cummins played confidently, although Paine was given out LBW off Philander by Umpire Gould when on 10, but was able to continue as he won a review thanks to getting an inside edge. Maharaj came on for his first bowl of the day, Paine taking him for two fours before cracking him over mid-wicket for six in his next. Morkel returned to the crease, but was unable to finish the fourth over of his spell, going down with a side-strain, which prevented him bowling again for the rest of the innings.

Cummins continued to grow in confidence, cutting Morkel for two boundaries in an over and then later hitting consecutive fours off Maharaj before carting him away for six over long-on. He reached his fifty (91 balls, 6 fours, 1 six) straight driving Rabada for three, but in the next over was leg before as he aimed a paddle sweep at Maharaj, a decision won on review by South Africa. A Lyon edged four brought up the 200, Australia going in at lunch on 7-201 with Paine 47 and Lyon 4.

The Australian innings came to a quick end after lunch, as the last three wickets fell for 20 runs in just 21 mintes. Lyon aimed a lofted drive at Rabada only to hole out to mid-off and then in the next over, Sayers cut Maharaj to backward point. Paine reached a well-deserved 50 (89 balls, 6 fours, 2 sixes) after lofting Maharaj over long-on for a second six. But in the next over he ill-advisedly advanced at Rabada, driving in the air over mid-off, only to see Elgar run back and dive with the flight of the ball, to bring off one of the catches of the series. Australia were all out for 221, 267 behind, but with Morkel unfit, the hosts elected to bat again, with 56 over left in the day.

Markram and Elgar got straight into Sayers, taking 11 from his opening and only over of his first spell. Lyon was on in the fourth over and immediately troubled Elgar, getting the ball to spin away. Just before tea, Markram edged one to second slip, South Africa heading in on 1-58 (Elgar 16, Amla 4) with a lead of 325.

Australia had a good hour after tea, having Amla well caught at leg-slip and then de Villiers gloved a lifter off a length from Cummins to Paine. Elgar went close to an hour without scoring a run, while du Plessis copped a nasty blow on the hand, which required treatment. There were little other worries, the pair adding 40 before the close, South Africa 401 ahead at the day's end.

Day four

Play started a quarter of an hour late, then from 10.37 to 10.53 bad light (SA 3-143) brought about a delay. Upon resumption, du Plessis copped one on the right index finger from Cummins. The South Africa skipper carried on, reaching his fifty (103 balls, 6 fours) ashe and a patient Elgar continued to add more to the already imposing lead. Elgar reached his fifty after 306 minutes of batting, as he played an out of character lofted on-drive off Mitch Marsh to reach the milestone. In the over before lunch, du Plessis whacked Lyon over deep backward square-leg for six, going into the break on 81, Elgar 59, South Africa 3-202, a lead of 469.

Both batsmen unwound after lunch, du Plessis eventually bringing up his ton with an edge for four off Hazlewood. He celebrated shortly after with a cut over third-man for six off Cummins, before edging the same bowler to second slip, for Handscomb to take a fine diving catch. In the next over Elgar finally went, caught having a slog sweep with de Kock not far behind him being trapped in front by Cummins. There was no declaration in sight, as Philander joined Bavuma, clubbing Lyon for two sixes over mid-wicket. At tea South Africa led by 612 and finally took pity on the Australians, by declaring.

Facing the daunting task of batting four sessions to salvage a draw, Renshaw was given out caught behind, but reviewed and stayed as the replay showed it had hit his arm, not glove or bat. He was dropped in the gully on two off Philander, and continued to look uncomfortable until he was trapped by a reduced paced Morkel, who swung one in at him from around the wicket. Khawaja was next to go, deemed to be leg before not offering a shot to Maharaj – his review unsuccessful. Burns continued to fight on, having a little luck here and there, until he was LBW to Morkel as he looked to work a yorker to the leg side. Handscomb looked susceptible while continuing to play almost solely off the back foot, but he and Shaun Marsh made it through to stumps – Australia needing an impossible 524 to win on the last day.

Day five

It was clear early on the final day that any fight the Australians had left in them had evaporated, as two wickets fell in the Philander's opening over. First ball, Shaun Marsh inside edged one onto his pad that rebounded to gully and then three balls later, his brother Mitch edged one behind to de Kock's right side – giving Philander his 200th Test wicket.

In the fifth over of the day, Handscomb intended to leave one, only to keep his bat hanging in the way, playing onto the stumps much as he had in the first innings. Paine also edged Philander behind and when Cummins shouldered arms and was bowled, it summed up the situation perfectly. Sayers was caught at 3rd slip to complete his pair and then Lyon was run out attempting a second run – Australia losing 7-31 in 16.4 overs on the last day to be all out for 119, South Africa winners by 492 runs.

It was their first home series win over Australia since 1969-70, a series they won 4-0 back then, before being isolated out of cricket for over 20 years, due to the Apartheid policies of the South Africa Nationlist Government.

Vernon Philander was Man of the match for his nine wickets in the game, plus a second innings fifty, while Kagiso Rabada was Man of the series, for taking 23 wickets at 19.26. For Australia, it was a shocking end to a series in every sense of the word. For South Africa it was a great moment in their cricketing history, their first win at home over Australia, since re-entry and by a record margin to boot.

Australian Cricket Digest, 2018-19

Fourth Test at the New Wanderer's, Johannesburg on March 30-April 3, 2018 - South Africa won by 492 runs

South Africa	First innings		B	M	4	6		Second innings		B	M	4	6
D Elgar	c Sayers b Lyon	19	47	79	2		2	c S Marsh b Lyon	81	250	378	10	1
AK Markram	c M Marsh b Cummins	152	216	309	17	1	1	c Handscomb b Cummins	37	56	76	4	
HM Amla	c Handscomb b Cummins	27	81	112	3			c M Marsh b Lyon	16	48	51	1	
AB de Villiers	c Paine b Sayers	69	119	173	7	1		c Paine b Cummins	6	5	14	1	
F du Plessis *	lbw b Cummins	0	1	4				c Handscomb b Cummins	120	178	227	18	2
T Bavuma	not out	95	194	285	13			not out	35	40	80	4	
K Rabada	c Renshaw b Sayers	0	2	3									
Q de Kock +	c M Marsh b Lyon	39	74	117	4		7	lbw b Cummins	4	4	8		
VD Philander	c Khawaja b Lyon	12	35	43	1		8	not out	33	49	64	1	2
KA Maharaj	c Paine b Cummins	45	51	65	4	2							
M Morkel	c Handscomb b Cummins	0	1	2									
	13 b, 12 lb, 5 w	30						4 b, 8 lb	12				
	136.5 overs, 599 minutes	488						105 overs, 452 minutes	6-344 dec				

Fall: 1-53 (Elgar), 2-142 (Amla), 3-247 (Markram), 4-247 (du Plessis), 5-299 (de Villiers), 6-299 (Rabada), 7-384 (de Kock), 8-412 (Philander), 9-488 (Maharaj), 10-488 (Morkel)

Fall: 1-54 (Markram), 2-79 (Amla), 3-94 (de Villiers), 4-264 (du Plessis), 5-266 (Elgar), 6-273 (de Kock)

Australia - bowling	O	M	R	W	wd	nb	O	M	R	W	wd	nb
JR Hazlewood	26	3	86	0			21	6	41	0		
CJ Sayers	35	9	78	2			14	2	68	0		
PJ Cummins	28.5	5	83	5	1		18	5	58	4		
NM Lyon	40	3	182	3			41	13	116	2		
MR Marsh	6	1	30	0			8	0	40	0		
MT Renshaw	1	0	4	0			3	0	9	0		

Australia	First innings		B	M	4	6	Second innings		B	M	4	6
MT Renshaw	c de Kock b Philander	8	32	47	1		lbw b Morkel	5	42	55		
JA Burns	c du Plessis b Rabada	4	8	14			lbw b Morkel	42	80	108	5	1
UT Khawaja	c de Kock b Philander	53	84	124	9		lbw b Maharaj	7	12	20	1	
PSP Handscomb	b Philander	0	1	6			b Philander	24	44	77	4	
SE Marsh	c de Villiers b Maharaj	16	74	104	1		c Bavuma b Philander	7	20	21	1	
MR Marsh	b Morkel	4	10	17	1		c de Kock b Philander	0	3	2		
TD Paine *+	c Elgar b Rabada	62	96	161	7	2	c de Kock b Philander	7	28	40		
PJ Cummins	lbw b Maharaj	50	92	127	6	1	b Philander	1	12	25		
NM Lyon	c Elgar b Rabada	8	18	13	2		run out (Markram-de Kock)	9	23	37	1	
CJ Sayers	c Amla b Maharaj	0	4	5			c Elgar b Philander	0	1	2		
JR Hazlewood	not out	1	4	15			not out	9	22	28	2	
	3 b, 9 lb, 3 nb	15					1 lb, 7 nb	8				
	70 overs, 321 minutes	221					46.4 overs, 210 mins	119				

Fall: 1-10 (Burns), 2-34 (Renshaw), 3-38 (Handscomb), 4-90 (Khawaja), 5-96 (M Marsh), 6-96 (S Marsh), 7-195 (Cummins), 8-206 (Lyon), 9-207 (Sayers), 10-221 (Paine)

Fall: 1-21 (Renshaw), 2-34 (Khawaja), 3-68 (Burns), 4-88 (S Marsh), 5-88 (M Marsh), 6-95 (Handscomb), 7-99 (Paine), 8-100 (Cummins), 9-100 (Sayers), 10-119 (Lyon)

Sth Africa - bowling	O	M	R	W	wd	nb	O	M	R	W	wd	nb
VD Philander	18	8	30	3			13	5	21	6		1
K Rabada	19	7	53	3		1	8	3	16	0		4
M Morkel	12.2	3	34	1		2	10.4	5	28	2		1
KA Maharaj	20	3	92	3			13	2	47	1		1
AK Markram	0.4	0	0	0			2	0	6	0		

Stumps scores:

Day 1	South Africa (1st inns)	6-313	T Bavuma 25*, Q de Kock 7*
Day 2	Australia (1st inns)	6-110	TD Paine 5*, PJ Cummins 7*
Day 3	South Africa (2nd inns)	3-134	D Elgar 39*, F du Plessis 34*
Day 4	Australia (2nd inns)	3-88	PSP Handscomb 23*, SE Marsh 7*

Toss: South Africa
Umpires: IJ Gould, NJ Llong, RK Illingworth (TV).
Ref: AJ Pycroft. Award: VD Philander (SA),
Series: K Rabada (SA). Attendance: 43,390

TEST SERIES AVERAGES

AUSTRALIA

Batting & Fielding	M	I	NO	Runs	HS	Avge	100	50	Ct	St
TD Paine	4	8	3	215	62	43.00	0	1	15	1
CT Bancroft	3	6	0	223	77	37.16	0	2	6	-
DA Warner	3	6	0	217	63	36.16	0	2	1	-
SPD Smith	3	6	0	142	56	23.66	0	1	7	-
JA Burns	1	2	0	46	42	23.00	0	0	0	-
MR Marsh	4	8	0	176	96	22.00	0	1	3	-
JR Hazlewood	4	8	5	63	17	21.00	0	0	0	-
UT Khawaja	4	8	0	165	75	20.62	0	2	2	-
SE Marsh	4	8	0	147	40	18.37	0	0	2	-
NM Lyon	4	8	0	100	47	12.50	0	0	2	-
PSP Handscomb	1	2	0	24	24	12.00	0	0	4	-
PJ Cummins	4	8	0	89	50	11.12	0	1	3	-
MA Starc	3	6	0	60	35	10.00	0	0	0	-
MT Renshaw	1	2	0	13	8	6.50	0	0	1	-
CJ Sayers	1	2	0	0	0	0.00	0	0	1	-

Bowling	Overs	Mdns	Runs	Wkts	Avge	Best	5wI	10wM	Econ
PJ Cummins	155.4	32	472	22	21.45	5-83	1	0	3.03
MA Starc	109.2	18	413	12	34.41	5-34	1	0	3.77
JR Hazlewood	160	30	471	12	39.25	3-61	0	0	2.94
MR Marsh	42	6	169	4	42.25	2-26	0	0	4.02
NM Lyon	210.5	39	681	16	42.56	3-50	0	0	3.23
CJ Sayers	49	11	146	2	73.00	2-78	0	0	2.97
SPD Smith	7	4	9	0	-	-	0	0	1.28
MT Renshaw	4	0	13	0	-	-	0	0	3.25

SOUTH AFRICA

Batting & Fielding	M	I	NO	Runs	HS	Avge	100	50	Ct	St
AB de Villiers	4	8	2	427	126*	71.16	1	4	11	-
T Bavuma	2	4	2	136	95*	68.00	0	1	1	-
AK Markram	4	8	0	480	152	60.00	2	1	2	-
D Elgar	4	8	1	333	141*	47.57	1	2	8	-
Q de Kock	4	7	0	223	83	31.85	0	2	18	1
VD Philander	4	7	2	155	52*	31.00	0	1	1	-
F du Plessis	4	8	1	175	120	25.00	1	0	1	-
HM Amla	4	8	0	196	56	24.50	0	1	4	-
TB de Bruyn	2	4	1	58	36	19.33	0	0	2	-
KA Maharaj	4	6	0	83	45	13.83	0	0	0	-
K Rabada	4	6	0	74	29	12.33	0	0	1	-
L Ngidi	1	1	0	5	5	5.00	0	0	1	-
M Morkel	3	5	1	13	6	3.25	0	0	1	-

Bowling	Overs	Mdns	Runs	Wkts	Avge	Best	5wI	10wM	Econ
L Ngidi	26.3	8	75	5	15.00	3-51	-	-	2.83
D Elgar	4	1	16	1	16.00	1-10	-	-	4.00
VD Philander	129	48	269	16	16.81	6-21	1	-	2.08
K Rabada	140.5	40	443	23	19.26	6-54	2	1	3.14
M Morkel	90.4	25	294	15	19.60	5-23	1	-	3.24
KA Maharaj	161.2	22	572	17	33.64	5-123	1	-	3.54

Also bowled: T Bavuma 1-0-10-0, TB de Bruyn 2-0-6-0, AK Markram 6.4-1-11-0

Australia	Philander			Morkel			Rabada			Ngidi			Maharaj			Markram			Elgar			Bavuma			De Bruyn		
	W	R	BB	W	R	BB	W	R	BB	W	R	BB	W	R	BB	W	R	BB	W	R	BB	W	R	BB	W	R	BB
Warner	1	53	109	0	18	25	4	99	83	1	9	17	0	38	82												
Bancroft	3	31	125	0	63	84	0	59	135	1	19	18	1	51	69												
Renshaw	1	10	40	1	0	10	0	3	24																		
Burns	0	8	19	1	11	25	1	7	18					20	26												
Khawaja	2	36	69	1	20	36	2	46	91	0	11	44	3	50	63	0	2	6									
Smith	0	9	42	2	22	47	1	31	74	0	14	18	2	64	122							1	2	7			
Handscomb	2	0	10	0	4	5	0	1	6				0	13	19	0	6	5									
S Marsh	1	25	108	2	13	49	2	40	94	0	0	10	3	59	134	0	1	8				0	9	7			
M Marsh	3	28	66	2	23	69	3	31	67	0	6	7	0	80	139	0	2	17	0	5	10				0	1	1
Paine	1	40	82	0	24	64	2	52	127	1	7	26	1	86	142							0	1	2	0	5	11
Cummins	1	9	62	1	17	46	3	16	54				3	47	89	0	0	4									
Starc	0	4	7	2	25	29	3	7	23				1	24	22												
Hazlewood	0	11	20	1	13	14	1	11	17	0	9	13	1	19	26												
Lyon	0	3	16	2	38	44	1	30	39	2	0	6	1	20	33							0	9	4			
Sayers	1	0	1				0	0	1																		

South Africa	Starc			Hazlewood			Cummins			Lyon			M Marsh			Sayers			Smith			Renshaw		
	W	R	BB	W	R	BB	W	R	BB	W	R	BB	W	R	BB	W	R	BB	W	R	BB	W	R	BB
Markram	1	82	112	2	100	191	4	90	123	0	115	207	1	25	36	0	61	74	0	7	11			
Elgar	1	82	167	0	62	170	1	54	133	4	67	267	0	37	62	0	26	49				0	5	10
Amla	1	22	61	2	45	141	3	52	146	2	64	123	0	7	12	0	6	25						
de Villiers	0	85	113	1	77	123	2	120	195	1	113	161	0	23	25	1	7	30	0	0	6	0	2	2
du Plessis	1	7	18	0	34	72	4	41	78	1	54	67	1	9	6	0	26	44				0	4	8
de Bruyn	1	19	29	1	8	13	0	9	35	0	22	33	1	0	11									
Bavuma				1	12	34	1	23	49	0	69	96	0	22	31	0	8	36				0	2	4
de Kock	0	34	49	1	55	77	3	39	80	3	62	108	0	21	28	0	10	23	0	2	23			
Philander	2	41	56	0	28	44	1	17	58	1	52	110	1	17	32	0	0	6						
Maharaj	2	15	17	2	11	32	1	2	4	1	47	36	0	6	10	0	2	5						
Rabada	2	22	33	0	31	47	1	15	32	2	6	22				1	0	2						
Morkel	1	0	5	1	3	9	1	0	1	1	10	35							0	0	2			
Ngidi				0	5	7																		

TOUR AVERAGES

Batting & Fielding	M	I	NO	Runs	HS	Avge	100	50	Ct	St
TD Paine	5	10	4	254	62	42.33	0	1	18	1
CT Bancroft	4	8	0	290	77	36.25	0	2	10	-
DA Warner	3	6	0	217	63	36.16	0	2	1	-
SPD Smith	4	8	0	190	56	23.75	0	1	10	-
SE Marsh	5	10	1	211	40	23.44	0	0	2	-
JA Burns	1	2	0	46	42	23.00	0	0	0	-
JR Hazlewood	5	9	5	89	26	22.25	0	0	0	-
MR Marsh	5	10	0	218	96	21.80	0	1	3	-
UT Khawaja	5	10	0	195	75	19.50	0	2	3	-
PJ Cummins	5	9	1	148	59*	18.50	0	2	3	-
NM Lyon	5	9	0	138	47	15.33	0	0	2	-
MA Starc	4	7	0	78	35	11.14	0	0	1	-
PSP Handscomb	2	4	0	29	24	7.25	0	0	6	-
MT Renshaw	1	2	0	13	8	6.50	0	0	1	-
CJ Sayers	1	2	0	0	0	0.00	0	0	1	-

Bowling	Overs	Mdns	Runs	Wkts	Avge	Best	5wI	10wM	Econ
SPD Smith	12.5	4	31	2	15.50	2-22	0	0	2.41
PJ Cummins	178.4	37	546	26	21.00	5-83	1	0	3.05
MA Starc	138.2	24	496	17	29.17	5-34	1	0	3.58
MR Marsh	59.5	9	254	8	31.75	2-26	0	0	4.24
JR Hazlewood	184	38	539	16	33.68	3-40	0	0	2.92
NM Lyon	242.5	46	793	17	46.64	3-50	0	0	3.26
CJ Sayers	49	11	146	2	73.00	2-78	0	0	2.97

Also bowled: MT Renshaw 4-0-13-0.

ENGLAND WHITEWASH AUSTRALIA IN SHORT FORM SERIES

The number one ranked ODI team England were too good for Australia in five matches played in June, inflicting the first five-nil defeat on Australia in over 140 years of battle in all formats between the two nations. Australia were competitive in three of the first four games, and should have won the last match when they had England 8-114 chasing Australia's 205.

While England were well and truly the stronger team, Australia didn't do themselves any favours in selection. Nathan Lyon, the teams most experienced International bowler didn't play the first three games, and was only selected after the Australia bowlers were embarrassed by England making a record 6-481 at Trent Bridge. To try bolster a perceived weakness in the middle order against spin, they weakened the top two by batting Aaron Finch at number five, scores of nought and twenty soon saw him return to the top for the fourth ODI, where he made an even 100.

Despite the whitewash there were some positives. Shaun Marsh made the most of Steve Smith's enforced absence, making fine hundreds at Cardiff and Chester-le-Street. Travis Head showed himself to be worthy of a spot as opener, making fifties in the last three matches, although he would have been annoyed to have not turned one of those efforts into a century. While paceman Billy Stanlake made progress, his peak performance coming in the final game, where he dismantled the England top order, taking 3-35.

Of the others to do well, Ashton Agar progressed as an all-rounder, while Darcy Short transferred some of his fine Twenty20 play into the International 50-over format. On the downside, Marcus Stoinis was disappointing, often caught playing back to full pitched balls when he could have come forward. Skipper Tim Paine did his best as captain, but made too few runs, despite being a quality keeper. One would hope the selectors took note of the batting of Alex Carey (44) in the final match, who proved to many that he is ready to take over the role in the team, with the 2019 ICC World Cup only twelve months away.

TOUR MATCH v SUSSEX AT HOVE

In front of a packed ground, Australia started well with Finch and Short looking in good touch until Short was trapped in front by left-arm spinner Briggs with his third ball. Stoinis joined Finch and the pair took control, as Stoinis lifted Briggs twice for sixes. They added 93 before Finch aimed a hook at Archer and edged it behind in the 31st over, a wicket that triggered the sudden loss of four wickets for 13. Maxwell then hit a catch off leg-spinner Wells to mid-off, Head was trapped in front looking to work to leg and Paine drove an easy catch to the bowler. Agar joined Stoinis, as they recovered the innings with a stand of 48, Stoinis eventually out in the 47th over, caught at long-off.

Sussex lost Wells to a bad mix up with his partner in the 3rd over and then Salt was dropped twice whilst on nought, both times by Short at square-leg. Salt made the most of his luck, reached a 33-ball fifty, with two sixes in consecutive balls from Agar. After three expensive overs for 25, Kane Richardson responded better in his fourth, yorking Salt to end a partnership of 91. Finch looked good for the home side until he popped back a return catch to Agar, and at 3-180 in the 34th over, the homeside looked set for an upset, needing just 98 off 99 balls. Brown was then trapped in front by Agar and when Evans was stumped, the innings fell away, Sussex losing their last seven wickets for just 40 runs.

Australia v Sussex at the County Ground, Hove on June 7, 2018 (day/night) - Australia won by 57 runs

Australia		R	B	M	4	6
AJ Finch	c Brown b Archer	78	97	121	9	
DJM Short	lbw b Briggs	21	27	43	4	
MP Stoinis	c Evans b Archer	110	112	145	9	4
GJ Maxwell	c Evans b Wells	1	2	6		
TM Head	lbw b Briggs	2	6	5		
TD Paine *+	c &b Wells	2	6	9		
AC Agar	run out (Archer)	21	24	35	2	
MG Neser	c Brown b Jordan	2	4	8		
JA Richardson	c Wells b Archer	11	10	13	2	
AJ Tye	not out	13	10	16	1	
KW Richardson	not out	2	2	5		
	7 lb, 7 w	14				
10 overs: 0-74	50 overs	9-277				

Sussex		R	B	M	4	6
LWP Wells	run out (K Richardson)	1	9	10		
PD Salt	b K Richardson	62	49	57	7	4
HZ Finch	c &b Agar	45	57	80	5	1
JL Evans	st Paine b Agar	57	63	90	4	2
MGK Burgess	b Stoinis	6	10	10		
BC Brown *+	lbw b Agar	17	23	31	1	
D Wiese	c Paine b Neser	3	10	10		
CJ Jordan	run out (Stoinis)	5	12	18		
JC Archer	b Tye	10	13	20	1	
DR Briggs	not out	3	5	12		
A Sakande	b J Richardson	0	4	4		
	8 lb, 3 w	11				
10 overs: 1-74	42.3 overs	220				

Fall: 1-74 (Short), 2-167 (Finch), 3-170 (Maxwell), 4-173 (Head), 5-180 (Paine), 6-238 (Agar), 7-250 (Neser), 8-250 (Stoinis), 9-264 (JA Richardson)

Fall: 1-1 (Wells), 2-92 (Salt), 3-130 (Finch), 4-139 (Burgess), 5-180 (Brown), 6-192 (Wiese), 7-202 (Evans), 8-210 (Jordan), 9-219 (Archer), 10-220 (Sakande)

Australian Cricket Digest, 2018-19

Sussex - bowling	O	M	R	W	wd	nb		Australia - bowling	O	M	R	W	wd	nb
JC Archer	10	0	62	3	4			MG Neser	8	1	36	1	1	
CJ Jordan	10	0	64	1				JA Richardson	7.3	1	35	1		
D Wiese	5	1	27	0				AC Agar	10	0	64	3		
DR Briggs	10	2	42	2				KW Richardson	6	0	37	1		
A Sakande	5	0	31	0	2			AJ Tye	8	0	28	1	2	
LWP Wells	10	0	44	2	1			MP Stoinis	3	0	12	1	-	

Toss: Sussex.   Umpires: ID Blackwell, GD Lloyd.   Attendance: 6,000 (approx.)

Finch 50: 58 balls, 8x4. Stoinis 50: 57 balls, 4x4, 2x6; 100: 103 balls, 8x4, 4x6. Salt 50: 33 balls, 5x4, 2x6. Evans 50: 58 balls, 3x4 2x6

TOUR MATCH v MIDDLESEX AT LORD'S

On a sunny day at Lord's, Australia put the pressure on early until Short was superbly caught at mid-wicket, aiming a pull shot in the fourth over. Shaun Marsh looked in control from the word go, as he and Head kept the score ticking over nicely. The spinners then bowled tightly, Australia unable to put the foot down as they would have liked. Marsh went one short of his fifty, clipping a low catch to mid-wicket, then Maxwell had another failure, missing an attempted sweep shot. Finch coming in at number four, went for his shots as he helped see Head to his hundred, brought up in the 43rd over. The centurion went shortly after, Australia adding 45 off their last five overs.

Middlesex started well, with Holden finding the rope while Gubbins cracked Neser for six over mid-wicket. Two balls later Neser had his revenge, with a sharp one-handed caught and bowled from a firm drive. Eskinazi swept a catch to deep square-leg off Agar's first over and then Stanlake removed the middle stump of Scott as he looked to whip to leg. Cartwright, who had earlier dropped Finch, looked in good order, as he and Holden combined to add 61, before the West Aussie miscued a pull-shot at Short's first ball, to hole out at long-on. Holden popped a catch to forward square-leg on their way to Middlesex losing their last six wickets for 43, with Kane Richardson taking the last three wickets, in a boost to his confidence ahead of the first ODI.

Australia v Middlesex at the Lord's on June 9, 2018 - Australia won by 101 runs

Australia		B	M	4	6		Middlesex		B	M	4	6
DJM Short	c Sowter b Barber	18	12	18	2	1	MDE Holden	c S Marsh b Stanlake	71	71	118	8
TM Head	c White b Sowter	106	141	169	9		NRT Gubbins	c &b Neser	18	24	37	1	1
SE Marsh	c Finn b Holden	49	64	91	6		SS Eskinazi	c J Richardson b Agar	2	5	6	
GJ Maxwell	lbw b Patel	3	7	6			GFB Scott	b Stanlake	2	10	11	
AJ Finch	c Franklin b Barber	54	52	60	2	3	HWR Cartwright	c Head b Short	31	44	47	5
AC Agar	not out	20	15	26	2		JEC Franklin	c Agar b K Richardson	31	45	61	3
TD Paine *+	c Franklin b Barber	9	6	14	1		RG White+	c Short b J Richardson	12	17	23	1
MG Neser	not out	4	6	4	1		NA Sowter	c Finch b Neser	1	10	13	
JA Richardson							ST Finn *	not out	11	13	21	2
B Stanlake							RH Patel	c Paine b Richardson	0	2	2	
KW Richardson							TE Barber	c Paine b Richardson	0	5	10	
	1 b, 7 lb, 1 nb, 11 w	20						3 w	3			
10 over: 1-64	50 overs	6-283					10 overs : 2-55	41 overs	182			

Fall: 1-31 (Short), 2-145 (Marsh), 3-150 (Maxwell), 4-239 (Head), 5-251 (Finch), 6-275 (Paine)

Fall: 1-48 (Gubbins), 2-55 (Eskinazi), 3-60 (Scott), 4-121 (Cartwright), 5-139 (Holden), 6-160 (White), 7-170 (Sowter), 8-172 (Franklin), 9-172 (Patel), 10-182 (Barber)

Middlesex - bowling	O	M	R	W	wd	nb		Australia - bowling	O	M	R	W	wd	nb
ST Finn	7	0	50	0				B Stanlake	9	1	45	2	2	
TE Barber	9	0	62	3	6			KW Richardson	9	1	31	3		
RH Patel	10	0	56	1				MG Neser	7	2	33	2	1	
MDE Holden	10	1	29	1	2			AC Agar	5	0	27	1		
HWR Cartwright	4	0	31	0		1		JA Richardson	8	0	30	1		
NA Sowter	10	0	47	1	3			DJM Short	3	0	16	1		

Toss: Australia.   Umpires: JH Evans, M Newell.

Head 50: 68 balls, 6x4; 100: 133 balls, 9x4. Finch 50: 51 balls, 2x4, 3x6. Holden 50: 52 balls, 5x4

THE ONE-DAY INTERNATIONALS
GAME ONE - THE OVAL, LONDON

Missing up to six first choice players, Australia won the toss and batted but lost Head in the second over as he aimed a drive at a wide away swinger from Wood to slip. Shaun Marsh joined Finch and the pair found the rope and were pushing the score along nicely. Moeen Ali came on in the ninth over and struck with his fourth ball, as Finch made room to drive and was held at short third man. In Moeen's next over, Marsh played down the wrong line and was bowled and when Paine reverse swept Moeen to short third man, Australia had lost 3-23 in the space of 46 deliveries.

Stoinis couldn't rescue the situation, as he top edged a cut, leaving Australia 5-90 in the 20th over. Maxwell turned things back Australia's way a little, belting Moeen for 14 off his last over, he and Agar adding 84 from 103 balls. Just as he was about to really hit his straps, Maxwell clipped one off the pads in the air to deep square leg. When Agar was trapped in front for 40, Australia lost 4-21 to be all out with three overs still to face.

Stanlake knocked over Roy second ball and when debutant Neser trapped Hales, England were two down inside four overs. Bairstow looked a man in career best form, as he effortlessly hit six fours, before a hard flat pull shot was well held at deep backward square-leg. Then came the decisive stand of the match, as Root and Morgan added 115, with neither batsman looking troubled against any of the Australian bowlers. The stand came to an end when Morgan edged a cut, and when Buttler and Root went in the space of four balls, Australia had a hope. But Willey played calmly, adding 34 with Moeen and then 21 with Plunkett as England got home with six overs up their sleeve.

First ODI at the Oval, London on June 13, 2018 (day/night) – England won by 3 wickets

Australia		B	M	4	6	England		B	M	4	6
AJ Finch	c Wood b Moeen	19	24	36	2	JJ Roy	b Stanlake	0	2	1	
TM Head	c Bairstow b Willey	5	4	5		JM Bairstow	c Head b Richardson	28	23	30	6
SE Marsh	b Moeen	24	30	39	4	AD Hales	lbw b Neser	5	10	12	1
MP Stoinis	c Buttler b Rashid	22	32	42		1	JE Root	c Paine b Stanlake	50	71	112	4
TD Paine *+	c Wood b Moeen	12	19	19	1	EJG Morgan *	c Paine b Tye	69	74	81	11
GJ Maxwell	c Bairstow b Plunkett	62	64	76	4	2	JC Buttler +	c Richardson b Iye	9	11	9	2
AC Agar	lbw b Rashid	40	62	81	4	MM Ali	c sub (DJM Short) b Neser	17	17	34	3
MG Neser	c Root b Plunkett	6	14	24		DJ Willey	not out	35	41	49	5	1
AJ Tye	c Buttler b Plunkett	19	20	27	2	1	LE Plunkett	not out	3	15	19	
KW Richardson	c Root b Wood	1	10	12		AU Rashid					
B Stanlake	not out	0	3	8		MA Wood					
	4 w	4					2 w	2			
10 overs: 2-51	47 overs, 189 mins	214				10 overs: 3-48	44 overs, 177 mins	7-218			

Fall: 1-7 (Head), 2-47 (Finch), 3-52 (Marsh), 4-70 (Paine), 5-90 (Stoinis), 6-174 (Maxwell), 7-193 (Agar), 8-197 (Neser), 9-208 (Richardson), 10-214 (Tye)

Fall: 1-0 (Roy), 2-23 (Hales), 3-38 (Bairstow), 4-153 (Morgan), 5-163 (Buttler), 6-163 (Root), 7-197 (Moeen)

England - bowling	O	M	R	W	wd	nb	Australia - bowling	O	M	R	W	wd	nb
MA Wood	8	1	32	1	1		B Stanlake	10	1	44	2		
DJ Willey	8	0	41	1			MG Neser	8	1	46	2		
Moeen Ali	10	1	43	3			KW Richardson	9	1	49	1		
AU Rashid	10	0	36	2	1		AJ Tye	10	1	42	2	2	
JE Root	3	0	20	0	1		AC Agar	5	0	28	0		
LE Plunkett	8	0	42	3	1		GJ Maxwell	2	0	9	0		

Toss: Australia. Umpires: RJ Bailey, K Dharmasena, M Erasmus (TV), Ref: RS Madugalle. Attendance: 22,317

Maxwell 50: 52 balls, 3x4, 2x6. Root 50: 65 balls, 4x4; Morgan 50: 58 balls, 9x4

GAME TWO - CARDIFF

Australia had to replace Stanlake (injured big toe) with Jhye Richardson and elected to omit Michael Neser giving D'Arcy Short his ODI debut. For England Eoin Morgan injured his back in the warm up, with Jos Buttler taking on the captaincy, Sam Billings the man to come in.

With rain in the air, Australia decided to field first and watched as Bairstow started in a blaze of glory, hitting eight fours and a six in 42 before under-edging a cut to the keeper in the ninth over. Roy and Hales continued on in a positive vain until Jhye Richardson managed to get the England number three to drag one back onto his stumps. Roy reached his fifty in the 20th over and continued to score rapidly, before rain interrupted play with the score on 2-149 after 23.3 overs, Roy 66, Root 15.

In the 28th over, Root pulled a catch to deep square-leg, then the rain delayed play again with England 3-184 after 30 overs, with Roy 91 and Buttler 2. After a 45 minute delay, Roy brought up his fifth ODI ton and then watched Aussie keeper Tim Paine cop one in the face behind the stumps, Paine needing immediate dentistry to get rid of a tooth. After a brief stoppage for rain (Eng 3-233 after 35.2, Roy 116, Buttler 27), Roy's great knock came to an end as he was caught behind but the scoring rate didn't slow at all, as Buttler started to get going, taking 19 off an over from Jhye Richardson. Despite wickets falling at the other end, Buttler ensured England made 89 in their last ten overs, scoring 58 of them himself.

Australia needed a quick start and got it thanks to early boundaries from Head, including an uppercut over the keepers head for six off Wood. But his brief knock came to an end in the fourth over, as he clipped one to mid-wicket and was brilliantly held one-handed by Hales. Shaun Marsh joined Short and pair scored steadily until Short played back to one, edging to slip. Stoinis couldn't get going, being bowled playing back to one when he could have been forward and then Finch was leg before, sweeping at the first ball he faced from Moeen. By then Marsh was past fifty and well settled, with he and Maxwell adding 54 in ten overs, before he skied a catch to mid-on. Needing nine an over, Agar played well in a stand of 96 in just 10 overs, watching Shaun Marsh bringing up a fine hundred from 95 balls. With 84 wanted off the last nine overs, Agar went down the wicket to Rashid and was stumped and after adding 32 from 18 balls with Marsh, Paine was caught at long-leg. Australia's challenge ended next ball when Marsh was bowled by a slower ball, Australia losing their last four wickets for 12 runs from 12 deliveries.

Second ODI at the Sophia Gardens, Cardiff on June 16, 2018 – England won by 38 runs

England			B	M	4	6	Australia			B	M	4	6
JJ Roy	c Paine b Tye	120	108	194	12	2	TM Head	c Hales b Wood	19	15	16	3	1
JM Bairstow	c Paine b K Richardson	42	24	35	8	1	DJM Short	c Root b Ali	21	33	60	2	
AD Hales	b J Richardson	26	38	39	3		SE Marsh	b Plunkett	131	116	179	10	3
JE Root	c Short b Stoinis	22	24	38	2		MP Stoinis	b Plunkett	9	18	21		
JC Buttler *+	not out	91	70	98	8	2	AJ Finch	lbw b Rashid	0	4	6		
SW Billings	b Tye	11	18	31			GJ Maxwell	c Willey b Ali	31	34	37	4	
MM Ali	c Agar b J Richardson	8	6	10	1		AC Agar	st Buttler b Rashid	46	42	50	7	
DJ Willey	c and b K Richardson	11	10	16	2		TD Paine *+	c Rashid b Plunkett	15	11	14	1	
LE Plunkett	run out (Short-Tye)	1	2	6			AJ Tye	c Billings b Rashid	10	6	9	1	
AU Rashid	not out	0	0	2			JA Richardson	c Roy b Plunkett	2	3	9		
MA Wood	did not bat						KW Richardson	not out	0	1	2		
	5 lb, 5 w	10						13 lb, 7 w	20				
10 overs: 1-71	50 overs, 213 mins	342					10 overs: 1-60	47.1 overs, 206 mins	304				

Fall: 1-63 (Bairstow), 2-113 (Hales), 3-179 (Root), 4-239 (Roy), 5-289 (Billings), 6-300 (Moeen), 7-325 (Willey), 8-332 (Plunkett)

Fall: 1-24 (Head), 2-77 (Short), 3-99 (Stoinis), 4-110 (Finch), 5-164 (Maxwell), 6-260 (Agar), 7-292 (Paine), 8-293 (Marsh), 9-303 (Tye), 10-304 (J Richardson)

Australia - bowling	O	M	R	W	wd	nb	England - bowling	O	M	R	W	wd	nb
JA Richardson	10	0	64	2	1		DJ Willey	7	0	40	0	1	
KW Richardson	8	0	56	2	1		MA Wood	9	1	57	1	4	
AC Agar	9	0	52	0			LE Plunkett	9.1	1	53	4	1	
MP Stoinis	10	0	60	1			Moeen Ali	10	0	47	2		
AJ Tye	9	0	81	2	3		JE Root	4	0	24	0		
MP Stoinis	4	0	24	0			AU Rashid	8	0	70	3	1	

Toss: Australia. Umpires: M Erasmus, AG Wharf, K Dharmasena (TV), Ref: RS Madugalle. Attendance: 15,010

Roy 50: 52 balls, 6x4; 100: 97 balls, 9x4, 2x6, Buttler 50: 38 balls, 3x4, 2x6. S Marsh 50: 54 balls, 3x4, 1x6: 100: 95 balls, 10x4, 1x6

GAME THREE - NOTTINGHAM

With Morgan back for England, they were once again at near full-strength, while Australia brought Stanlake back in for Kane Richardson. What happened for the best part of the next four hours was absolute carnage, as England made a record tally for a one-day international. On the best batting wicket in the country, Australia send England in and Bairstow got started early, taking 14 off the second over bowled by Jhye Richardson, including three fours. Roy joined in, hitting 14 off Stanlake's third over, the sixth of the innings. In the ninth over, Bairstow (27) was given out leg before after sweeping at Agar, but reviewed and got a reprieve as technology showed the ball to be going over the stumps. In the next over, Bairstow (30) looked to loft Tye over mid-off, Stoinis ran back but couldn't hold onto the chance. From there England hardly put a foot wrong, until the 20th over, when Roy attempted a second run to backward square-leg, to be run out by a fast throw from Short.

New bat Hales hardly missed a beat, taking three fours in an over from Stoinis, and watched as Bairstow reached his ton in the 26th over, with a slog sweep off Short that carried the ropes at mid-wicket. At the 30 over mark England had reached 1-253 and added 57 off the next four before Bairstow finally departed, caught hitting a hard flat pull-shot to deep square leg. Buttler missed out on the party, hitting a slower ball to long-on and then Hales brought up his ton from 62 balls, with a pull-shot that ran away to fine leg.

Skipper Morgan started quietly with five off his first seven balls, before exploding into action, at one stage scoring 4, 1, 6, 4, 3, 6, 4, 6, 1, 6, 6, 1 off consecutive balls, (48 off 11 balls, to save you adding it up) as he reached his fifty from 21 balls, a record for England. With England an amazing 3-450 from 46 overs, they looked poised to reach 500, but with Hales miscuing to mid-wicket and Morgan out next ball to a top edged slog, the homeside could only manage 31 off their last four overs, as the shattered Australian attack slowly made their way off the ground.

Australian Cricket Digest, 2018-19

In reply Short started impressively, cracking Willey's first ball for six over point, but went in the left-arm quicks next over driving a low catch to mid-on. Head took up the impossible chase, playing fluently to reach a 36-ball fifty, before playing back to Moeen and popping him back the simplest of catches. Marsh looked good until lofting to long-on and Finch, again batting absurdly low at number five, was bowled aiming to loft Moeen for six, trying to repeat his shot from the previous ball. Stoinis found some form until attempting a risky second run to the leg-side and when Maxwell was caught at long-on it was time for the mercy rule, on a day where England could consider that they had played the perfect game.

Third ODI at Trent Bridge, Nottingham on June 19, 2018 (day/night) – England won by 242 runs

England		B	M	4	6	Australia		B	M	4	6
JJ Roy	run out (Short-Paine)	82	61	87 7	4	DJM Short	c Moeen b Willey	15	12	13 1	1
JM Bairstow	c Richardson b Agar	139	92	150 15	5	TM Head	c & b Moeen	51	39	50 7	
AD Hales	c Agar b Richardson	147	92	125 16	5	SE Marsh	c Plunkett b Moeen	24	30	44	1
JC Buttler +	c Finch b Richardson	11	12	15	1	MP Stoinis	run out (Bairstow-Buttler)	44	37	49 4	1
EJG Morgan *	c Paine b Richardson	67	30	48 3	6	AJ Finch	b Rashid	20	19	27	2
Moeen Ali	run out (Paine)	11	9	13		GJ Maxwell	c Plunkett b Willey	19	19	28 1	1
JE Root	not out	4	6	13		TD Paine *+	c Hales b Rashid	5	9	10	
DJ Willey	not out	1	1	1		AC Agar	c & b Rashid	25	23	30 2	1
LE Plunkett						JA Richardson	st Buttler b Moeen	14	25	33	
AU Rashid						AJ Tye	not out	5	5	10	
MA Wood						B Stanlake	st Buttler b Rashid	1	4	3	
	1 b, 8 lb, 3 nb, 7 w	19					10 lb, 6 w	16			
10 overs: 0-79	50 overs, 229 mins	6-481				10 overs: 1-83	37 overs, 163 mins	239			

Fall: 1-159 (Roy), 2-310 (Bairstow), 3-335 (Buttler), 4-459 (Hales), 5-459 (Morgan), 6-480 (Moeen)

Fall: 1-27 (Short), 2-95 (Head), 3-100 (Marsh), 4-152 (Finch), 5-173 (Stoinis), 6-190 (Paine), 7-194 (Maxwell), 8-230 (Agar), 9-236 (Richardson), 10-239 (Stanlake)

Australia - bowling	O	M	R	W	wd	nb	England - bowling	O	M	R	W	wd	nb
B Stanlake	8	0	74	0	1		MA Wood	7	0	38	0	2	
JA Richardson	10	1	92	3			DJ Willey	7	0	56	2	4	
AC Agar	10	0	70	1	2		JE Root	2	0	19	0		
AJ Tye	9	0	100	0	1	2	Moeen Ali	5	0	28	3		
GJ Maxwell	2	0	21	0			LE Plunkett	6	0	41	0		
MP Stoinis	8	0	85	0	2	1	AU Rashid	10	0	47	4		
AJ Finch	1	0	7	0									
DJM Short	2	0	23	0									

Toss: Australia. Umpires: K Dharmansena, RT Robinson, M Erasmus (TV), Ref: RS Madugalle. Award: AD Hales (Eng).
Roy 50: 41 balls, 4x4, 3x6; Bairstow 50: 39 balls, 9x4, 100: 69 balls, 11x4, 4x6. Hales 50: 38 balls, 7x4, 2x6; 100: 62 balls, 14x4, 3x6. Morgan 50: 21 balls, 3x4, 4x4 (fastest ever for England). Head 50: 36 balls, 7x4. Attendance: 17,007

GAME FOUR – CHESTER LE STREET

On one of the longest days of sunlight for the year, Australia won the toss and skipper Paine couldn't say quickly enough that his team would like to bat first. With Australia's bowlers sent to all parts in the previous game, Nathan Lyon was picked for his first game of the series, Short making way, Tye had a spell for Neser, while the injured Maxwell was replaced by Alex Carey. Head and Finch, the middle-order experiment having ended, opened up quietly, adding 19 off the first five overs before Head started to launch, whacking eight fours over the course of the next five. Having reached a polished fifty he threw his innings away, pulling a Rashid long-hop straight into the hands of square-leg. Finch started to open up, cracking Rashid for two sixes over long-on as he and Marsh pushed on past the hundred mark with their stand. Marsh smashed Moeen for six over long-on and then saw Finch reach his ton in the same over, the 39th, six of his 11 tons now having been against England.

Wood halted the momentum in the 40th, when he trapped Finch plumb in front and skittled Stoinis, who played back when again he may well have gone forward. Several quiet overs occurred until Marsh started to cut loose, taking 24 (642426) off Rashid's last over, the last stroke a slog sweep over mid-wicket which brought up his second ton of the series. But with his dismissal in the next over, Australia could only manage to score 14 off their last three, 8-310 considered well under par in the conditions against England's strong batting line-up.

Roy dominated from ball one, which he hit to long-leg for four off Neser, for once over shadowing Bairstow at the crease. He reached his 50 in the tenth over and powered on, with the Australian bowlers unable to gain any assistance early in the air or off the pitch as the sun sank ever so slowly in the west. No bowler could stem the pair, with Roy smacking Lyon for six over long-on in the 25th over to reach his second ton of the series. Lyon had his revenge later in the same over, with Roy edging a drive to short third-man, ending a stand of 174 for the first wicket. When Bairstow was caught behind two overs later, aiming to guide to third man, Australia pushed hard, but Paine dropped Hales on 17 at 2-208 in the 32nd over to take the wind out of their sails. Root missed a sweep off Agar and then after a brisk 15 from Morgan, Buttler came out to join Hales with 67 needed off 13 overs. Almost immediately the England keeper took control and blazed the ball to all parts, adding 70 with Hales from just 47 balls, as England walted to victory with 31 balls in hand, still in daylight at 8.58pm – fifty minutes before the official time for the sunset in the floodlit fixture.

Fourth ODI at Riverside Ground, Chester-le-Street on June 21, 2018 (day/night) – England won by 6 wickets

Australia		B	M	4	6	England			B	M	4	6
AJ Finch	lbw b Wood	100	106	131	6	3	JJ Roy	c Marsh b Lyon	101	83	95	12	2
TM Head	c Willey b Rashid	63	64	66	9		JM Bairstow	c Paine b Stanlake	79	66	103	10	
SE Marsh	c Overton b Willey	101	92	107	5	4	AD Hales	not out	34	45	87	3	
MP Stoinis	b Wood	1	2	3			JE Root	b Agar	27	35	37	2	1
AC Agar	c Buttler b Rashid	19	15	21	3		*EJG Morgan	c Paine b Agar	15	11	9	2	
AT Carey	c Overton b Willey	6	5	14	1		+JC Buttler	not out	54	29	29	9	1
TD Paine *+	lbw b Willey	3	5	14			Moeen Ali						
MG Neser	c Buttler b Willey	2	2	3			DJ Willey						
JA Richardson	not out	5	6	12			AU Rashid						
NM Lyon	not out	3	3	4			MA Wood						
B Stanlake							C Overton						
	3 lb, 4 w	7						1 b, 1 nb, 2 w	4				
10 overs : 0-61	50 overs, 191 mins	8-310					10 overs : 0-76	44.4 overs, 183 mins	4-314				

Fall: 1-101 (Head), 2-225 (Finch), 3-227 (Stoinis), 4-256 (Agar), 5-296 (Carey), 6-296 (Marsh), 7-299 (Neser), 8-305 (Paine)

Fall: 1-174 (Roy), 2-183 (Bairstow), 3-228 (Root), 4-244 (Morgan)

England bowling	O	M	R	W	wd	nb	Australia - bowling	O	M	R	W	wd	nb
Wood	9	1	49	2	2	-	MG Neser	8.4	0	74	0	1	1
Willey	7	0	43	4	-	-	B Stanlake	8	0	54	1	-	-
Root	10	0	44	0	1	-	NM Lyon	7	0	38	1	-	-
Overton	7	0	55	0	-	-	JA Richardson	7	0	58	0	-	-
Rashid	10	0	73	2	1	-	AC Agar	8	0	48	2	-	-
Moeen Ali	7	0	43	0	-	-	MP Stoinis	6	0	41	0	1	-

Toss: Australia. Umpires: M Erasmus, MA Gough, K Dharmasena (TV), Ref: RS Madugalle. Award: JJ Roy (Eng). Attendance: 13,912
Finch 50: 65 balls, 3x4, 1x6; 100: 105 balls, 6x4, 3x6. Head 50: 43 balls, 9x4. S Marsh 50: 62 balls, 2x4, 1x6; 100: 91 balls, 5x4, 4x6. Roy 50: 36 balls, 8x4, 1x6; 100: 81 balls, 12x4, 2x6. Bairstow 50: 40 balls, 8x4, Buttler 50: 28 balls, 8x4, 1x6

GAME FIVE – MANCHESTER

Australia recalled Short for Jhye Richardson for the final match, with England resting their first choice opening attack, with Willey and Wood having games off. Australia won the toss again and with Head and Finch both in glorious touch, adding 58 from the first six overs. Moeen was introduced for the seventh with Finch edging on to his third ball and then Stoinis playing an inglorious sweep that went straight down the throat of backward square-leg. Head continued his streak of good form, racing to his third fifty on the trot before again giving up his wicket too easily as he hit a catch to mid-wicket. In the next over Marsh missed a wrong-un from Rashid and then Paine took a risky single towards square-leg, being brilliantly run out at the bowlers end by a throw from the keeper.

Carey, who opened his scoring with a reverse sweep for four, was joined by Short, the pair adding 59 in good style in ten overs before Carey went, caught behind as he aimed a to guide one to third man. Agar had a brain fade two balls later, shouldering arms and losing his off-stump and then Richardson, who had just hit Rashid for six over long-on, was run out by short fine-leg after being sent back by his partner. Lyon and Stanlake held on for seven overs between them, as Australia passed 200, Short stranded on 47 not out, with over 15 overs unbowled.

Paine started the bowling with Agar and this paid off as he bowled Roy with his fourth ball. On the bouncy track Stanlake appeared to be enjoying the Gabba like conditions, as he got Bairstow to drag on and Root to edge behind in the sixth over, to reduce England to 3-23. The tall quicks next, Morgan dragged on to make it 4-27, giving the Stanlake 3-4 in a spell of just ten balls.

Hales and Buttler steadied things, until just before the scheduled lunch break, Hales aimed a cut at Kane Richardson, edging to the keeper, leaving England 5-50, before they moved to 5-66 at the break off 16 overs, Buttler 27 and Moeen 3.

After lunch, Buttler and Moeen progressed well adding 36 before Moeen drove at one from Stoinis and was held by Lyon at backward point. Curran started slowly, before hitting Short over long-on for six, but then drove at and edged Richardson behind and from the next ball, Plunkett did much the same, Paine diving hard to his right which left England 8-114 in the 30th over, with Buttler on 47.

With an edged four off Richardson, Buttler reached his fifty as he and a very composed Rashid began to build a partnership. Stanlake returned to bowl his last couple of overs without success, with Rashid content to push the singles, while Buttler was still able to regularly find the rope, as England moved to 8-194 after 44 overs. Agar bowled a maiden to Rashid and then in the

46th, Rashid looked to flick Stoinis to leg, getting a top edge towards long-leg, where Stanlake ran in and dived forward to bring off a brilliant catch. With 11 now wanted and just a wicket in hand, Buttler smashed the last ball of the over from Stoinis back over his head for six, to bring up his ton, leaving just five runs to win. Ball managed to play out a maiden from Agar and eventually the winning runs came in the 49th over, with Buttler smacking Stoinis through the covers to win the match and clinch the series five-nil.

Fifth ODI at Old Trafford, Manchester on June 24, 2018 – England won by 1 wicket

Australia		B	M	4	6	England		B	M	4	6
AJ Finch	b Moeen	22	17	27	3 1	JJ Roy	b Agar	1	3	2	
TM Head	c Morgan b Plunkett	56	42	50	9	JM Bairstow	b Stanlake	12	20	19 1	
MP Stoinis	c Ball b Moeen	0	2	2		AD Hales	c Paine b Richardson	20	29	50 3	
SE Marsh	st Buttler b Moeen	8	12	24		JE Root	c Marsh b Stanlake	1	3	4	
AT Carey	c Buttler b Curran	44	40	47	5 1	EJG Morgan *	b Stanlake	0	4	6	
TD Paine *+	run out (Buttler)	1	2	6		JC Buttler +	not out	110	122	170 12 1	
DJM Short	not out	47	52	76	4	Moeen Ali	c Lyon b Stoinis	16	31	34	
AC Agar	b Curran	0	2	2		SM Curran	c Paine b Richardson	15	21	27 1 1	
KW Richardson	run out (Ali-Buttler)	14	16	13	1	LE Plunkett	c Paine b Richardson	0	1	2	
NM Lyon	lbw b Rashid	1	10	14		AU Rashid	c Stanlake b Stoinis	20	47	67	
B Stanlake	b Moeen	2	13	8		JT Ball	not out	1	10	14	
	3 lb, 7 w	10					7 lb, 5 w	12			
10 overs: 2-79	34.4 overs, 139 mins	205				10 overs: 4-34	48.3 overs, 202 mins	208			

Fall: 1-60 (Finch), 2-60 (Stoinis), 3-90 (Head), 4-97 (Marsh), 5-100 (Paine), 6-159 (Carey), 7-159 (Agar), 8-181 (Richardson), 9-193 (Lyon), 10-205 (Stanlake)

Fall: 1-2 (Roy), 2-19 (Bairstow), 3-23 (Root), 4-27 (Morgan), 5-50 (Hales), 6-86 (Moeen), 7-114 (Curran), 8-114 (Plunkett), 9-195 (Rashid)

England bowling	O	M	R	W	wd	nb	Australia - bowling	O	M	R	W	wd	nb
JT Ball	5	0	29	0	1		AC Agar	10	2	34	1	1	
SM Curran	6	0	44	2	2		B Stanlake	10	1	35	3		
JE Root	3	0	32	0			NM Lyon	10	0	32	0		
Moeen Ali	8.4	0	46	4	1		KW Richardson	9	0	51	3	1	
LE Plunkett	4	0	19	1	2		MP Stoinis	8.3	0	37	2	2	
AU Rashid	8	0	32	1	1		DJM Short	1	0	12	0		

Toss: Australia   Umpires: RJ Bailey, K Dharmasena, M Erasmus (TV), Ref: RS Madugalle.   Award: JC Buttler (Eng)
Head 50: 36 balls, 8x4. Buttler 50: 74 balls, 5x4; 100: 117 balls, 11x4, 1x6. Attendance: 23,500 (sell-out)

ONLY TWENTY20 INTERNATIONAL – BIRMINGHAM

On a glorious evening at a packed venue, Australia sent England in and watched as Roy took 13 off the first over from Stanlake. Agar conceded just four singles in the second over, but after that England dominated proceedings. On debut, Mitch Swepson bowled the third over, going for 16 and then Kane Richardson was belted for 23 off the fourth, with Buttler very severe, going 6444 off consecutive balls, England 56 without loss after just four overs. Richardson's day got worse when fielding at long-off in the sixth over, as he dropped an easy catch off the bat of Roy when he was 27, facing Agar.

Buttler continued to blaze away reaching his fifty from just 22 balls, the fastest in Twenty20s for England before he pulled one to deep square-leg, to give Swepson his first wicket. After whacking Stanlake for six, Roy mistimed a pull high to mid-wicket and when Morgan hit a reverse sweep to third man, England were charging along at 3-132 in the 12th over. Hales and Root added 72 off 39 balls, with Hales dominating, before he hooked a slower ball back to bowler Stoinis, who brought off a remarkable caught and bowled one handed. Bairstow hit two sixes in an eight-ball stay, the second off the last ball of innings seeing England past 220.

After a tight opening over from Willey, which conceded just four, Australia began their charge, as Short laid into Jordan, hitting him for three fours in a row in the second. But he went in the next over, clipping one to short fine-leg and then Maxwell was brilliantly deceived by an excellent slower ball from Jordan. Finch was struggling to get the strike, having only faced seven balls in the first five overs, and watched on as Head was caught at long-on, Carey was bowled by a skidder and Stoinis hit hard and flat straight to long-off, Australia losing 3-8 to be 5-72 in the ninth.

With more than 13 an over needed, Finch started to take control, with Agar providing great support, as the pair added 86 from 39 balls. At one point Finch hit six sixes in 17 balls, five of them off Moeen, mainly massive blows over deep mid-wicket. With 69 needed off the last 30 balls, Rashid changed ends, and after a straight-hit four to Finch, the Aussie was caught at long-on, ending the charge, England in the end comfortable winners.

Australian Cricket Digest, 2018-19

Only Twenty20 at Edgbaston, Birmingham on June 27th, 2018 – England won by 28 runs

England		B	4	6		Australia		B	4	6
JJ Roy	c Finch b Stanlake	44	26	6	1	DJM Short	c Moeen b Plunkett	16	12	3
JC Buttler+	c Short b Swepson	61	30	6	5	AJ Finch *	c Jordan b Rashid	84	41	7	6
EJG Morgan *	c Tye b Swepson	15	8	1	1	GJ Maxwell	b Jordan	10	7	1
AD Hales	c and b Stoinis	49	24	5	2	TM Head	c Hales b Moeen	15	10	1
JE Root	run out (Carey-Tye)	35	24	4		AT Carey+	b Rashid	3	3
JM Bairstow	not out	14	8		2	MP Stoinis	c Roy b Rashid	0	2
MM Ali	not out	0	0			AC Agar	b Jordan	29	23	3	1
DJ Willey						AJ Tye	c Plunkett b Willey	20	11		2
LE Plunkett						KW Richardson	c Hales b Jordan	0	1
CJ Jordan						MJ Swepson	not out	3	4
AU Rashid						B Stanlake	c Morgan b Plunkett	7	5		1
	1 lb, 2 w	3					1 b, 1 nb, 4 w	6
6 overs:0-70	20 overs	5-221				6 overs:2-59	19.4 overs	193

Fall: 1-95 (Buttler, 8.5 ov), 2-108 (Roy, 9.3 ov), 3-132 (Morgan, 11.4 ov), 4-204 (Hales, 18.1 ov), 5-215 (Root, 19.5 ov)

Fall: 1-17 (Short, 2.2 ov), 2-33 (Maxwell, 3.4 ov), 3-64 (Head, 7.2 ov), 4-72 (Carey, 8.2 ov), 5-72 (Stoinis, 8.4 ov), 6-158 (Finch, 15.2 ov), 7-174 (Agar, 17.2 ov), 8-174 (Richardson), 9-184 (Tye, 18.4 ov), 10-193 (Stanlake, 19.4 ov)

Australia - bowling	O	M	R	W	wd	nb	Dots
B Stanlake	3	0	44	1			5
AC Agar	4	0	34	0			8
MJ Swepson	4	0	37	2	1		6
KW Richardson	4	0	59	0	1		3
AJ Tye	4	0	37	0			8
MP Stoinis	1	0	9	1			2

England - bowling	O	M	R	W	wd	nb	Dots
DJ Willey	4	0	31	1	3		8
CJ Jordan	4	0	42	3		1	6
LE Plunkett	3.4	0	34	2	1		8
AU Rashid	4	0	27	3			11
Moeen Ali	4	0	58	1			3

Toss: Australia   Umpires: MA Gough, AG Wharf, RJ Bailey (TV), Ref: RS Madugalle.   Award: AU Rashid (Eng).   Attendance: 24,227
Buttler 50: 22 balls, 6x4, 4x6. Finch 50: 27 balls, 5x4, 3x6

PAKISTAN WIN TRI-SERIES IN ZIMBABWE

On the way home from the England ODI/Twenty20 series, Australia stopped off in Zimbabwe for an eight day tri-series. The Australians started the series well with wins over Pakistan and Zimbabwe on consecutive days, before losing to Pakistan when the teams met the second time around. Having already qualified for the final, Australia met a much improved Zimbabwe team in the final group match, only managing to win with a ball to spare. In the final against Pakistan they posted a competitive 8-183, and when Pakistan were 2-2 in the first over, looked in a good place to win the tournament. But Fakhar Zaman proved a force to be reckoned with as he led Pakistan to a fine win with four balls to go.

For Australia, Aaron Finch had a strong series as the team's leading run getter, making a Twenty20 International record score of 172 against Zimbabwe. D'Arcy Short at times struggled to score quickly on the slow pitches, but showed he had learned from the previous matches and played a very good hand of 76 in the final. Others chipped in here and there with the bat, while bowling wise, AJ Tye was leading wicket-taker, doing well bowling in the late overs. Billy Stanlake started the series on fire taking 4-8 in the first game and was Australia's most economical performer. Jhye Richardson impressed at times, while Ashton Agar bowled some tight spells in the middle overs, but couldn't perform when needed in the final.

MATCH ONE - ZIMBABWE V PAKISTAN

Zimbabwe v Pakistan at Harare Sports Club on July 1, 2018 - Pakistan won by 74 runs.

Toss: Zimbabwe. **Pakistan 4-182** (Fakhar Zaman 61, Asif Ali 41*) **def Zimbabwe 108** (17.5 overs) (TK Musakanda 43) **by 74 runs.** Award: Asif Ali who faced 21 balls, hit 1x4, 4x6)

MATCH TWO - AUSTRALIA v PAKISTAN

With the game starting at 10am, Billy Stanlake ripped the heart out of the Pakistan top order, as Australia stormed to a nine wicket win. Pakistan's woes started from the third ball of the match, where Hafeez edged a catch to slip, then in the third over, Talat gloved a short one, Finch running from slip to dive to his left to bring off a brilliant catch. In the fifth over, Fakhar gloved a hook and in the seventh, Sarfraz edged to the right of Finch at slip, where he dived and took his third catch. Stanlake bowled his four overs straight, leaving the crease with Pakistan 4-26 after seven overs.

Pakistan's innings occasionally threatened to get going, with Asif hitting two sixes before he was bowled aiming a pull-shot at a full ball, while Raheem hit Tye for 644 off consecutive balls, before top-edging a hook to long-leg. Shadab top scored and was eighth out, Tye mopping up the tail.

Australian Cricket Digest, 2018-19

Australia didn't mess about in reply, Finch hitting consecutive sixes off Nawaz in the second over, with Short three fours in a row off Usman in the third. Short was out playing a pull-shot to mid-wicket in the fourth, but Finch plundered away hitting all up six sixes, with Head content to feed him the strike, Australia cruised home with 55 balls to spare.

Australia v Pakistan at Harare Sports Club on July 2, 2018 – Australia won by 9 wickets

Pakistan			B	4	6	Australia			B	4	6
Moh Hafeez	c Finch b Stanlake		0	3		DJM Short	c Talat b Hasan Ali	15	14	3	
Fakhar Zaman	c Carey b Stanlake		6	11	1	AJ Finch *	not out	68	33	4	6
Hussain Talat	c Finch b Stanlake		10	10	2	TM Head	not out	20	18	1	
Sarfraz Ahmed *+	c Finch b Stanlake		4	5		GJ Maxwell					
Shoaib Malik	run out (Maddinson-Carey)		13	16	1	NJ Maddinson					
Asif Ali	b Stoinis		22	20		2	MP Stoinis					
Shadab Khan	c Head b Tye		29	25	1	1	AT Carey +					
Fahim Ashraf	c Tye b Richardson		21	17	2	1	AC Agar					
Moh Nawaz	c Agar b Tye		6	11		AJ Tye					
Hasan Ali	c Agar b Tye		0	1		JA Richardson					
Usman Khan	not out		0	0		B Stanlake					
	1 lb, 4 w		5				5 lb, 9 w	14			
6 overs : 3-23	19.5 overs		116			6 overs : 1-60	10.5 overs	1-117			

Fall: 1-0 (Hafeez, 0.3 ov), 2-12 (Talat, 2.5 ov), 3-19 (Fakhar, 4.3 ov), Fall: 1-35 (Short, 3.2)
4-24 (Sarfraz, 6.2 ov), 5-47 (Malik, 9.4 ov), 6-61 (Asif, 11.3 ov),
7-92 (Ashraf, 16.3 ov), 8-114 (Shadab, 19.2 ov), 9-116 (Hasan, 19.4 ov),
10-116 (Nawaz, 19.5 ov)

Australia - bowling	O	M	R	W	wd	nb	Dots	Pakistan - bowling	O	M	R	W	wd	nb	Dots
B Stanlake	4	0	8	4	1		18	Usman Khan	3	0	31	0	1		6
JA Richardson	4	0	22	1	1		13	Mohammad Nawaz	2	0	22	0	2		3
MP Stoinis	3	0	17	1	1		9	Hasan Ali	2	0	18	1	1		7
AJ Tye	3.5	0	38	3	1		6	Shadab Khan	3.5	0	41	0			4
AC Agar	4	0	27	0			7								
GJ Maxwell	1	0	3	0			3								

Toss: Australia. Umpires: TJ Matibiri, RB Tiffin, I Chabi (TV), Ref: JJ Crowe. Award: B Stanlake (Aus). Finch 50: 27 balls, 2x4, 5x6.

MATCH THREE - AUSTRALIA v ZIMBABWE

Australia dominated this game from start to finish as Aaron Finch made the highest ever score in a Twenty20 International. He dominated a record partnership with D'Arcy Short, where they became the first pair to ever add over 200 for any wicket. Finch was brutal in the powerplay, making 56 off 24 balls, Australia 0-75 after the first six overs. While Short was having trouble finding the rope, Finch was brutal in every sense of the word, clubbing ten sixes and 16 fours, before chopping down his stumps, aiming to cut an extremely wide ball in the final over. Finch reached his ton in the 14th over and his 150 in the 19th as all the bowlers bar slow-armer Chisoro were hit to all parts.

Zimbabwe started well enough to peel of 30 in the first three overs, Mire looking the best of the batsman, until he hit a catch to mid-on in the sixth over. Moor cracked Short for 446 in consecutive balls in the ninth over, but when he was caught and bowled in the tenth, the innings fell away so badly, that Zimbabwe could only score 36 in the final ten overs.

Zimbabwe v Australia at Harare Sports Club on July 3, 2018 – Australia won by 100 runs

Australia			B	4	6	Zimbabwe			B	4	6
AJ Finch *	hit wkt b Muzarabani	172	76	16	10	CJ Chibhabha	c Carey b Richardson	18	10	1	1
DJM Short	c Moor b Muzarabani	46	42	3	2	SF Mire	c Stoinis b Stanlake	28	19	5	1
GJ Maxwell	not out	0	1			H Masakadza *	st Carey b Agar	12	14	1	
MP Stoinis	not out	1	1			TK Musakanda	lbw b Agar	10	7		1
TM Head						PJ Moor +	c & b Tye	19	11	2	1
NJ Maddinson						E Chigumbura	c Short b Tye	7	10	1	
AT Carey +						RP Burl	c Richardson b Tye	10	15	1	
AC Agar						TS Chisoro	c Agar b Maxwell	6	7		1
AJ Tye						CB Mpofu	c Short b Stoinis	3	16		
JA Richardson						B Muzarabani	not out	1	2		
B Stanlake						JC Nyumbu	not out	6	9	1	
	5 lb, 5 w	10					1 lb, 8 w	9			
6 overs : 0-75	20 overs	2-229				6 overs : 2-63	20 overs	9-129			

Fall: 1-223 (Short, 19.2 ov), 2-228 (Finch, 19.4 ov)   Fall: 1-42 (Chibhabha, 3.3 ov), 2-57 (Mire, 5.5 ov), 3-71
(Musakanda, 7.5 ov), 4-90 (Masakadza, 9.3 ov), 5-98
(Moor, 10.5 ov), 6-101 (Chigumbura, 12.4 ov), 7-108
(Chisoro, 13.6 ov), 8-121 (Burl, 17.1 ov), 9-122 (Mpofu, 18.1 ov)

Zimbabwe bowling	O	M	R	W	wd	nb	Dots	Australia - bowling	O	M	R	W	wd	nb	Dots
J C Nyumbu	3	0	44	0			2	B Stanlake	3	0	39	1	3		8
B Muzarabani	4	0	38	2	3		8	J A Richardson	4	0	23	1	2		14
C B Mpofu	4	0	53	0	1		7	AC Agar	4	1	16	2			12
TS Chisoro	4	0	19	0			11	DJM Short	2	0	20	0			3
RP Burl	2	0	30	0			1	AJ Tye	4	1	12	3			18
CJ Chibhabha	2	0	19	0			2	GJ Maxwell	1	0	7	1			4
SF Mire	1	0	21	0				MP Stoinis	2	0	11	1	3		7

Toss: Zimbabwe.   Umpires: TJ Matibiri, L Rusere, RB Tiffin (TV), Ref: JJ Crowe.   Award: AJ Finch (Aus)

Finch 50: 22 balls, 6x4, 3x6; 100: 50 balls, 10x4, 5x6; 150: 69 balls, 15x4, 8x6

MATCH FOUR - ZIMBABWE V PAKISTAN

Zimbabwe v Pakistan at Harare Sports Club on July 4, 2018 - Pakistan won by 7 wickets

Toss: Pakistan. **Zimbabwe 4-162** (20 overs) (SF Mire 94) **lost to Pakistan 3-163** (19.1 overs) (Farkar Zaman 47, Hussain Talat 44). Man of the Match was Solomon Mire, who faced 63 balls, hit 6x4 and 6x6.

MATCH FIVE - AUSTRALIA v PAKISTAN

Australia sent Pakistan in on a very cold morning, the temperature not much above 12 degrees. Sohail popped a catch to square-leg from Richardson's first ball, but Pakistan were a healthy 1-40 after four overs, as Fakhar took Stanlake for three fours in a row, with 17 coming from the fourth. Talat smacked Maxwell for six over long-off, before being bowled two balls later as he aimed a cut. Farkhar dominated the innings, before being fourth out, after mistiming a pull shot. Malik played his shots and Asif Ali gave the innings some final impetus as Pakistan added 60 off their last five overs.

Finch got an inside edge to the keeper in the fifth over and with Short struggling to get bat on ball, Australia fell well behind the rate early on. Head was bowled between bat and pad and when Maxwell was trapped in front by Shaheen, Australia were 3-49 in the seventh. Maddinson walked past a googly and then Short, who'd battled along until the 13th over, was finally out bowled by Shaheen. With around 15 per over needed, Carey started in a flurry scoring 18 off his first nine, but it was way too much to ask, Pakistan winning comfortably.

Australia v Pakistan at Harare Sports Club on July 5, 2018 – Pakistan won by 49 runs

Pakistan		B	4	6	Australia		B	4	6
Fakhar Zaman	c Maxwell b Stoinis	73	42	9	3	DJM Short	b Shaheen	28	34	1	
Haris Sohail	c Short b Richardson	0	1			AJ Finch *	c Sarfraz b Shaheen	16	11	3	
Hussain Talat	b Maxwell	30	25	3	1	TM Head	b Ashraf	7	4	1	
Sarfraz Ahmed *+	c Carey b Tye	14	13	1	1	GJ Maxwell	lbw b Shaheen	10	8	2	
Shoaib Malik	c Finch b Tye	27	15	3	1	NJ Maddinson	st Sarfraz b Shadab	5	8		
Asif Ali	not out	37	18	3	2	MP Stoinis	c Asif b Usman	16	15	2	
Faheem Ashraf	c Maxwell b Richardson	0	3			AT Carey +	not out	37	24	2	2
Shabab Khan	c Stoinis b Tye	7	3		1	AC Agar	b Amir	11	8		1
Mohammed Amir	not out	0	0			AJ Tye	not out	12	8		1
Usman Khan						J A Richardson					
Shaheen Afridi						B Stanlake					
	6 w	6					5 lb, 2 w	7			
6 overs: 1-51	20 overs	7-194				6 overs: 2-44	20 overs	7-149			

Fall: 1-8 (Sohail, 1.1 ov), 2-80 (Talat, 8.6 ov), 3-107 (Sarfraz, 12.4 ov), 4-132 (Fakhar, 14.2 ov), 5-158 (Malik, 17.3 ov), 6-176 (Ashraf, 18.6 ov), 7-190 (Shadab, 19.5 ov)

Fall: 1-29 (Finch, 4.2), 2-38 (Head, 5.2), 3-49 (Maxwell, 6.5), 4-67 (Maddinson, 9.6), 5-75 (Short, 12.2), 6-106 (Stoinis, 14.6), 7-131 (Agar, 17.5)

Australia - bowling	O	M	R	W	wd	nb	Dots	Pakistan - bowling	O	M	R	W	wd	nb	Dots
B Stanlake	4	0	30	0			15	Mohammad Amir	4	0	25	1			8
J A Richardson	4	0	43	2	3		7	Fahim Ashraf	4	0	30	1			10
AJ Tye	4	0	35	3	1		9	Shaheen Afridi	4	0	37	3	1		7
MP Stoinis	3	0	29	1	1		6	Shadab Khan	4	0	26	1			10
GJ Maxwell	3	0	30	1			5	Usman Khan	4	0	26	1	1		8
AC Agar	2	0	27	0			3								

Toss: Australia.   Umpires: L Rusere, RB Tiffin, TJ Matibiri (TV), Ref: JJ Crowe.   Award: Fakhar Zaman (Pak)

Fakhar 50: 33 balls, 7x4, 3x6.

Australian Cricket Digest, 2018-19
MATCH SIX – ZIMBABWE v AUSTRALIA

With Pakistan v Australia already confirmed as the final, an improved Zimbabwe side pushed Australia to the limit in the final group game, the visitors getting home with just one ball to spare. Jack Wildermuth came in for his debut, with D'Arcy Short omitted, which saw Alex Carey pushed up to the top of the order to open the batting.

After Stanlake had Zhuwao caught behind driving at the first ball of the match, Mire played a fine hand reaching his fifty in the 17th over. He gained good support from Moor, the pair adding 68 off 58 balls for the fourth wicket, with Moor hitting Stoinis for 644 in consecutive balls during the 14th over. Mire was eighth out in the 19th over, with ninth wicket pair Mavuta and Wellington Masakadze adding nine from the last over to take the hosts past 150.

Finch went in the third over, pulling a long-hop to deep mid-wicket, and when Carey guided a catch to the keeper, Australia were under a little bit of pressure. Head and Maxwell took control, with Maxwell clearing the rope five times on his way to a vital fifty. The pair added 103 from 71 balls to put Australia on top, but then three wickets fell for ten runs, with Maxwell caught at cover, Maddinson out to a miscued pull-shot and Head holing out at long-on. Seven were needed off the last over, Stoinis pulling a four off the second last ball to get Australia home.

Zimbabwe v Australia at Harare Sports Club on July 6, 2018 – Australia won by 5 wickets

Zimbabwe		B	4	6	Australia		B	4	6
C Zhuwao	c Carey b Stanlake	0	1		AJ Finch *	c Musakanda b W Masakadza	3	5	
SF Mire	b Tye	63	52	5	2	AT Carey +	c +sub (RC Murray) b Muzarabani	16	17	2
H Masakadza *	b Richardson	13	12	1	1	TM Head	c W Masakadza b Muzarabani	48	42	3
TK Musakanda	c Wildermuth b Stanlake	12	10	1	1	GJ Maxwell	c Chigumbura b Muzarabani	56	38	1	5
PJ Moor +	c Maddinson b Richardson	30	29	2	1	NJ Maddinson	c Muzarabani b Tiripano	2	5	
E Chigumbura	c Richardson b Tye	2	4		MP Stoinis	not out	12	7	1
MN Waller	c Richardson b Tye	13	6	1	1	AC Agar	not out	5	5	
DT Tiripano	run out (Agar-Tye)	0	0		JD Wildermuth			
BA Mavuta	not out	6	3	1	AJ Tye			
WP Masakadza	c Stoinis b Wildermuth	3	3		JA Richardson			
B Muzarabani					B Stanlake			
	1 lb, 8 w	9				4 lb, 8 w	12		
6 overs: 3-44	20 overs	9-151			6 overs: 2-35	19.5 overs	5-154		

Fall: 1-0 (Zhuwao, 0.1 ov), 2-21 (H Masakadza, 3.3 ov), 3-44 (Musakanda, 5.5 ov), 4-112 (Moor, 15.3 ov), 5-116 (Chigumbura, 16.4 ov), 6-141 (Waller, 18.3 ov), 7-142 (Tiripano, 18.5 ov), 8-142 (Mire, 18.6 ov), 9-151 (W Masakadza, 20 ov)

Fall: 1-15 (Finch, 2.1 ov), 2-26 (Carey, 4.3 ov), 3-129 (Maxwell, 16.2 ov), 4-134 (Maddinson, 17.3), 5-139 (Head, 18.2)

Australia - bowling	O	M	R	W	wd	nb	Dots
B Stanlake	4	1	21	2			17
JA Richardson	4	0	32	2	2		11
MP Stoinis	3	0	31	0	1		5
AC Agar	3	0	22	0			6
AJ Tye	4	0	28	3	1		9
JD Wildermuth	2	0	16	1			2

Zimbabwe - bowling	O	M	R	W	wd	nb	Dots
WP Masakadza	4	0	32	1	-	-	10
B Muzarabani	4	0	21	3	2	-	8
DT Tiripano	3.5	0	27	1	3	-	10
SF Mire	2	0	17	0	-	-	2
BA Mavuta	4	0	33	0	2	-	7
MN Waller	2	0	20	0	-	-	3

Toss: Zimbabwe.   Umpires: TJ Matibiri, RB Tiffin, L Rusere (TV), Ref: JJ Crowe.   Award: AJ Tye (Aus)
Mire 50: 44 balls, 4x4, 1x6. Maxwell 50: 34 balls, 1x4, 4x6

POINTS TABLE

	P	W	L	POINTS	NET RUN RATE
AUSTRALIA	4	3	1	12	+1.809
PAKISTAN	4	3	1	12	+0.707
Zimbabwe	4	0	4	0	-2.340

Australian Cricket Digest, 2018-19
THE FINAL - AUSTRALIA v PAKISTAN

D'Arcy Short returned to the team for the final, with Nic Maddinson dropped and Alex Carey moved back down to the middle order. Short finally found his mojo at the top of the order, hitting two sixes off Faheem in the sixth over, as Australia dominated early on. Finch then started to lift the tempo further, clearing the rope three times in the next four overs before he smashed one off the back foot to be caught at cover, ending an opening stand of 95. Short reached his fifty in the 12th over, but then lost Maxwell caught at long-on. Interestingly Stoinis came in ahead of Head, hit Amir for six over long-on in the 16th over before smacking a low full-toss to deep point. Head scored 18 off his first seven balls, including a six over long-on off Faheem before he was also caught at long-on. Australia lost 6-46 off the last five overs to end up on 8-183, when they might have got closer to 200.

Maxwell took the new-ball for Australia, having Farhan stumped down leg-side off a wide, then in the same over Talat was caught driving off an edge to short third-man. After Stanlake's tight first over (just two singles), Finch gave Maxwell a second over, which went for 21, with Sarfraz whacking him for six over square-leg and four through point.

Sarfraz continued his assault until he was run out by Richardson attempting a third run. Malik took his time, scoring just a single off his first seven balls, as Fakhar played the role of senior batsman. With 105 wanted off the last ten overs, the game was in the balance, but Wildermuth went for 16 in the 11th, including three wides in a row, which saw the game start to head Pakistan's way. Agar who had been held back, went for 16 off the 12th and when Tye was pummelled for 15 in 13th, Pakistan had reduced the target to 57 off the last seven overs. Fakhar smacked Stanlake for six over wide third-man and within sight of a century, uppercut a catch to deep point. By then Malik was started to get going, belting Richardson for six over long-on in the 18th over, while Asif did likewise to put their side within touching distance.

With just 11 needed off the last 12 balls, Tye forced the game into the last over conceding nine, but it mattered little as Asif belted Stoinis for four to wrap the match with four balls to spare.

The Final - Australia v Pakistan at Harare Sports Club on July 8, 2018 – Pakistan won by 6 wickets

Pakistan		B	4	6	Australia		B	4	6
DJM Short	c Farhan b Shaheen	76	53	7	4	Fakhar Zaman	c sub (NJ Maddinson)	91	46	12	3
						b Richardson			
AJ Finch *	c Farhan b Shadab	47	27	2	3	Sahibzada Farhan	st Carey b Maxwell	0	0		
GJ Maxwell	c Asif b Shadab	5	5			Hussain Talat	c Richardson b Maxwell	0	3		
MP Stoinis	c Fakhar b Amir	12	10		1	Sarfraz Ahmed *+	run out (Richardson-Tye)	28	19	4	1
TM Head	c Hasan b Amir	19	11	2	1	Shoaib Malik	not out	43	37	3	1
AT Carey +	c Shadab b Ashraf	2	3			Asif Ali	not out	17	11	1	1
AC Agar	b Hasan	7	7	1		Faheem Ashraf				
JD Wildermuth	not out	1	1			Shadab Khan				
AJ Tye	b Amir	0	2			Moh Amir				
JA Richardson	not out	6	2	1		Hasan Ali				
B Stanlake						Shaheen Afridi				
	4 lb, 1nb, 3 w	8					1 b, 1 lb, 6 w	8		
6 overs : 0-54	20 overs	8-183				6 overs : 3-48	19.2 overs	4-187		

Fall: 1-95 (Finch, 9.5 ov), 2-109 (Maxwell, 11.6 ov), 3-146 (Stoinis, 15.4 ov), 4-148 (Short, 16.2 ov), 5-166 (Carey, 17.4 ov), 6-176 (Agar, 18.6 ov), 7-176 (Head, 19.1 ov), 8-177 (Tye, 19.4 ov)

Fall: 1-2 (Farhan, 0.1 ov), 2-2 (Talat, 0.4 ov), 3-47 (Sarfraz, 5.2), 4-154 (Farkar, 15.6)

Pakistan - bowling	O	M	R	W	wd	nb	Dots	Australia - bowling	O	M	R	W	wd	nb	Dots
Mohammad Amir	4	0	33	3	1		12	GJ Maxwell	3	0	35	2	1		4
Faheem Ashraf	4	0	38	1	2		10	B Stanlake	4	0	25	0			11
Hasan Ali	4	0	38	1		1	8	JA Richardson	4	0	29	1	1		11
Shaheen Afridi	4	0	32	1			7	AJ Tye	4	0	33	0			8
Shadab Khan	4	0	38	2			9	MP Stoinis	2.2	0	31	0			1
								JD Wildermuth	1	0	16	0	4		1
								AC Agar	1	0	16	0			1

Toss: Australia.   Umpires: L Rusere, RB Tiffin, TJ Matibiri (TV), Ref: JJ Crowe.   Award: Fakhar Zaman (Pak)
Short 50: 39 balls, 6x4, 2x6. Fakhar 50: 30 balls, 6x4, 2x6.

JLT CUP 2017-18
WARRIORS TOO STRONG AND WIN
SECOND TITLE IN FOUR SEASONS

Western Australia won their 13th limited overs title, their second in four seasons and first for new skipper Mitchell Marsh. Marsh like many of his teammates was superb with the bat. The win in the final also gave coach Justin Langer his fifth domestic title as coach, this being his second one-day title, to go with three BBL championships. They were the best side in the competition, despite a hiccup in their narrow loss to South Australia. Shaun Marsh dominated with the bat from outset, being later named as man of the series, welcoming the fact the Warriors early games were played at the WACA. The experience of Michael Klinger once again was apparent, while Cam Bancroft combined his batting and keeping duties with style.

They also had ample supply of quick bowling, with Jhye Richardson bowling with plenty of pace, Andrew Tye with good skill and variations and newcomer Matt Kelly impressing in his first season. Darcy Short chipped in with handy wickets and made a fine 119* with the bat later in the tournament.

South Australia were runners-up for the second time in three seasons as they continue to play very good 50-over cricket under coach Jamie Siddons. Experienced campaigner Callum Ferguson captained the side well and played one of the innings of the tournament, 169 v WA at Drummoyne Oval. The innings set up the only defeat for the eventual title winner. The rest of the batting was strong, with Tom Cooper, Jake Weatherald and Alex Carey all consistent performers, as they were the only team to pass 300 on four occasions. Cam Valente contines to develop as an all-rounder, while the bowlers played their part, Dan Worrall being excellent with the new ball and Joe Mennie continues to make strides playing in this format.

Victoria improved on last season, but despite regaining their international players, were absolutely outplayed in the Elimination final by South Australia. They were a bit light on for runs, with no one passing 300 in total, but Travis Dean showed his skill, with Matt Short taking his chances when they came, while Seb Gotch chipped in with two half centuries. Cameron White made a magnificent 165 against Tasmania, but was quiet in his other three knocks. With the ball, Peter Siddle was miserly, conceding just 3.95 per over after his first two deliveries of the tournament went for five wides. Fawad Ahmed bowled well in the middle overs, while Chris Tremain continues to be a consistent performer in these matches.

New South Wales, who won the previous two titles, missed the top three largely on the back of a poor batting performance versus Victoria at North Sydney, in a match that was later abandoned because of a "dangerous" pitch. The Cricket NSW CEO was very critical on Twitter about what had happened and was later given a suspended fine from Cricket Australia. On the field Nic Maddinson and Dan Hughes each made two tons and Kurtis Patterson was consistent to make a strong top three in the order. Sean Abbott led the wicket takers but Aussie pair Mitch Starc and Nathan Lyon were the pick of their bowlers.

Queensland didn't have the tournament they hoped for. Michael Neser as an all-rounder was very good, making a brilliant ton v WA and later bowling well in their win over Tasmania at Bellerive. Usman Khawaja was a dominant figure averaging over 60 and Marnus Labuschagne almost always good for a fifty, making four in six knocks. Their bowling was lacking, no one took more than Neser's eight wickets.

Tasmania struggled losing their first three games, then found form in the next two, before being thrashed at home by Queensland, to comfortably miss the top three. George Bailey led the batting, which at times was thin, the skipper being the only batsman to make a century. Matthew Wade made useful runs but didn't keep as well as he would have liked, dropping two catches versus Queensland.

Rookie paceman Riley Meredith impressed with the ball. Ben Dunk not only kept wicket for the Tigers, but took wickets against South Australia, sadly his batting form was well down on his efforts for the Adelaide Strikers in BBL06. Ben McDermott and Jordan Silk each showed what they were capable of, but didn't do it enough. The bowling was thin, but in part could be blamed on the loss of Andrew Fekete and Jackson Bird to injury. Cameron Boyce was dependable with ten wickets, while Riley Meredith was unearthed and how he progresses in 2018-19 will be of interest.

The Cricket Australia XI started the competition well with a surprise win over South Australia and were more than competitive. Harry Nielsen impressed with the gloves and led the averages, skipper Beau Webster and Jake Carder each made centuries in the win over the Redbacks and both had a good series. Max Bryant hit the ball hard and looks an exciting prospect, while Clint Hinchliffe chipped in with that bat and was the leading wicket taker with his spinners Jackson Coleman impressed early, taking 4-46 in the win over SA. In 2018-19 they won't be part of the competition, which will start very early, on September 16 in Townsville.

THE LADDER

Final standings in brackets	Matches	Won	Lost	Bonus Points	Points	Net Run Rate	300+ Totals
Western Australia (1)	6	5	1	2	22	+0.886	2
South Australia (2)	6	4	2	1	17	-0.017	4
Victoria (3)	6	3	3	3	15	+0.556	2
New South Wales (4)	6	3	3	2	14	+0.412	3
Queensland (5)	6	3	3	1	13	+0.013	2
Tasmania (6)	6	2	4	2	10	-0.427	2
Cricket Australia XI (7)	6	1	5	0	4	-1.312	0

Most Runs

	M	Inn	NO	Runs	HS	Avge	S/Rate	100s	50s	6s
SE Marsh (WA)	7	6	1	412	132*	82.40	87.47	1	3	1
NJ Maddinson (NSW)	6	6	0	398	137	66.33	96.13	2	1	9
UT Khawaja (Qld)	6	6	0	380	138	63.33	94.52	1	2	6
DP Hughes (NSW)	6	6	0	379	122	63.16	90.45	2	2	8
GJ Bailey (Tas)	6	6	0	373	126	62.16	105.96	1	3	15
CJ Ferguson (SA)	8	8	0	358	169	44.75	98.62	1	1	2
TLW Cooper (SA)	8	8	1	344	115*	49.14	103.92	1	2	11
MR Marsh (WA)	7	6	4	338	124	169.00	111.55	1	2	9
M Klinger (WA)	7	6	0	337	143	56.16	85.96	2	0	8
JB Weatherald (SA)	8	8	0	337	116	42.12	96.01	2	1	4

Highest Scores (23 hundreds in all)

		BF	4s	6s		Venue
CJ Ferguson	169	138	23	2	SA v WA	Drummoyne Oval
CL White	165	154	16	6	Vic v Tas	WACA
M Klinger	143	138	10	2	WA v SA	Drummoyne Oval
UT Khawaja	138	139	15	2	Qld v NSW	Drummoyne Oval
NJ Maddinson	137	119	23	1	NSW v Tas	WACA

Most Wickets

Bowling	M	Overs	Mdns	Runs	Wkts	Avge	Econ	Best	4w	SR
JM Mennie (SA)	7	62.5	3	293	13	22.53	4.66	5-36	2	29.0
JA Richardson (WA)	7	69	3	356	13	27.38	5.15	3-60	0	31.8
SA Abbott (NSW)	6	49.2	1	297	12	24.75	6.02	3-29	0	24.6
Fawad Ahmed (Vic)	7	59	1	322	12	26.83	5.45	3-24	0	29.5
DJ Worrall (SA)	8	70.4	8	394	12	32.83	5.57	5-62	1	35.3
CP Tremain (Vic)	7	66	3	398	12	33.16	6.03	3-50	0	33.0
CJ Boyce (Tas)	6	55	2	297	10	29.70	5.40	3-27	0	33.0
AJ Tye (WA)	4	37.5	3	156	9	17.33	4.12	3-37	0	25.2
SP Mackin (WA)	4	37	2	193	9	21.44	5.22	5-33	1	24.6
NM Lyon (NSW)	5	49	4	245	9	27.22	5.00	3-58	0	32.6
PM Siddle (Vic)	7	70	8	277	9	30.78	3.96	3-27	0	46.6
DJM Short (WA)	7	57	2	305	9	33.89	5.35	3-53	0	38.0

Five wickets in an innings

	Figures		Venue
SP Mackin	5-33	WA v CA XI	North Sydney
JM Mennie	5-36	SA v Qld	Allan Border Field
DJ Worrall	5-62	SA v Vic	Bellerive Oval

Most Dismissals in a match by keeper

	Total	Ct/St		Venue
PM Nevill	8	6ct/2st	NSW v CA XI	Hurstville Oval
PM Nevill	4	4ct	NSW v Tas	WACA
PSP Handscomb	4	3ct/1st	Vic v CA XI	Hurstville Oval

Australian Cricket Digest, 2018-19

Match 1 – South Australia v Cricket Australia XI at Allan Border Field, Brisbane on September 27, 2017
CA XI won by 7 wickets

With a 9.00am start time, the Redbacks were under pressure early from pumped up left-arm quickie Jackson Coleman. Cam Valente's second domestic one-day hundred kept SA in the game. Despite losing Bryant early, Carder and Webster dominated the bowlers in a stand 229, which helped see the CA XI to their second ever win in the competition.

South Australia		B	M	4	6	CA XI		B	M	4	6
AT Carey +	c Nielsen b Grant	6	4	11	1	JM Carder	c Lehmann b Worrall	102	129	184	12	1
JB Weatherald	c Nielsen b Coleman	0	2	3		MA Bryant	c Carey b Winter	1	6	9		
CJ Ferguson *	c Webster b Colemar	5	10	13	1	BJ Webster *	c Lehmann b Andrews	121	133	189	17	2
TLW Cooper	run out (Carder)	17	25	36	3	CD Hinchliffe	not out	13	9	17	1	1
AI Ross	c Bryant b Pengelley	12	16	23	3	P Uppal	not out	4	4	2	1	
JS Lehmann	c Nielsen b Coleman	37	50	97	3	1	JA Merlo					
CT Valente	b Merlo	100	138	145	10	4	BJ Pengelley					
JM Mennie	not out	43	50	68	3	2	HJ Nielsen +					
TD Andrews	c Grant b Coleman	7	7	7	1		GT Hankins					
NP Winter	c Pengelley b Merlo	0	2	5			JL Coleman					
DJ Worrall						DMK Grant					
	4 b, 4 lb, 4 nb, 15 w	27					3 lb, 12 w	15			
10 overs: 5-51	50 overs, 208 mins	9-254				10 overs: 1-47	46.5 overs, 202 mins	3-256			

Fall: 1-1 (Weatherald), 2-11 (Carey), 3-17 (Ferguson), 4-46 (Ross), 5-51 (Cooper), 6-145 (Lehmann), 7-229 (Valente), 8-238 (Andrews), 9-254 (Winter)

Fall: 1-3 (Bryant), 2-232 (Carder), 3-252 (Webster)

CA XI - bowling	O	M	R	W	wd	nb	SA - bowling	O	M	R	W	wd	nb
JR Coleman	10	1	46	4	2		DJ Worrall	10	1	40	1	2	
DMK Grant	10	0	63	1	9	2	NP Winter	7	0	66	1	6	
BJ Pengelley	6	0	36	1			JM Mennie	10	1	44	0	2	
BJ Webster	10	2	25	0			CT Valente	9	0	42	0	1	
GT Hankins	3	0	23	0		1	TD Andrews	9.5	0	51	1	1	
JA Merlo	7	1	38	2		1	TLW Cooper	1	0	10	0		
P Uppal	4	0	15	0									

Toss: Cricket Australia XI Umpires: MW Graham-Smith, GC Joshua, Ref: PL Marshall. Award: BJ Webster (CA XI) Crowd: 130

Match 2 – Queensland v CA XI at Allan Border Field, Brisbane on September 29, 2017 – Queensland won by 4 wickets

The new "Mock fielding" playing condition was invoked by umpire Paul Wilson, with Marnus Labuschagne and Queensland receiving a five run penalty. Bryant and Pengelley made rapid fifties as the CA backed up their good batting performance from two days previously. Half-centuries to Renshaw and Labuschagne set up the chase, with Cutting finishing off the game in the 49th over. Steketee bowled well against his home state.

CA XI		B	M	4	6	Queensland		B	M	4	6
JM Carder	c Peirson b Neser	12	19	22	3	*UT Khawaja	c Nielsen b Pengelley	27	29	33	2	1
MA Bryant	lbw b Floros	60	48	59	8	2	MT Renshaw	run out (Grant-Hinchliffe)	67	97	132	6	1
BJ Webster *	lbw b Swepson	29	52	64	2	JA Burns	c Merlo b Steketee	49	40	68	6	2
CD Hinchliffe	run out (Neser)	41	62	83			M Labuschagne	c Bryant b Merlo	61	62	88	5	
P Uppal	c Wildermuth b Gannon	32	50	64	3	+JJ Peirson	c Nielsen b Steketee	17	17	31	2	
JA Merlo	c &b Gannon	20	27	47	1	JD Wildermuth	b Steketee	4	12	10		
BJ Pengelley	c Cutting b Neser	53	36	44	4	3	BCJ Cutting	not out	39	25	30	5	1
MT Steketee	not out	2	3	10			MG Neser	not out	5	9	14		
HJ Nielsen +	not out	0	4	4			JS Floros					
DMK Grant						CJ Gannon					
JR Coleman						MJ Swepson					
	3 b, 5 lb, 16 w, 1 nb, 5 p	30					4 lb, 9 w	13			
10 overs: 1-57	50 overs, 202 mins	7-279				10 overs: 1-47	48.3 overs, 206 mins	6-282			

Fall: 1-33 (Carder), 2-89 (Bryant), 3-117 (Webster), 4-187 (Hinchliffe), 5-192 (Uppal), 6-267 (Merlo), 7-274 (Pengelley)

Fall: 1-47 (Khawaja), 2-134 (Burns), 3-169 (Renshaw), 4-226 (Peirson), 5-233 (Wildermuth), 6-252 (Labuschagne)

Qld - bowling	O	M	R	W	wd	nb	CA XI - bowling	O	M	R	W	wd	nb
MG Neser	9	0	58	2	4		MT Steketee	10	0	48	3	4	
CJ Gannon	9	1	54	2	2		JR Coleman	8	1	30	0	1	
MJ Swepson	10	0	31	1	2		DMK Grant	8	0	45	0		
BCJ Cutting	4	0	34	0	2		BJ Pengelley	3	0	27	1	2	
JS Floros	10	0	44	1			BJ Webster	3	0	29	0		
JD Wildermuth	8	0	45	0	4	1	JA Merlo	8.3	0	53	1	1	
							CD Hinchliffe	8	0	46	0		

Toss: Queensland Umpires: DM Koch, P Wilson, Ref: PL Marshall. Award: MJ Swepson (Qld) Crowd: 507

Match 3 – Western Australia v New South Wales at the WACA, Perth (day/night) on September 29, 2017
Western Australia won by 3 runs

Shaun Marsh held the innings together in making his eighth ton for WA in this format. He and Jono Wells added 119 for the fifth wicket which was a WA record v NSW. NSW looked in control until Henriques was caught at long-off, losing their last five wickets for 28.

Western Australia		B	M	4	6
M Klinger	c Maddinson b Sandhu	0	9	10	
SE Marsh	not out	132	136	216	17
CT Bancroft +	c Nevill b Abbott	28	33	46	3
MR Marsh *	c Hughes b Lyon	13	18	22	2
AJ Turner	lbw b Abbott	0	3	3	
JW Wells	lbw b Abbott	57	75	87	7
DJM Short	c Hughes b Conway	10	9	8	1
JA Richardson	c & b Sandhu	17	14	21	1
AJ Tye	c Conway b Sandhu	0	1	1	
JP Behrendorff	c Henriques b Sandhu	0	1	2	
DJM Moody	not out	1	1	1	
8 lb, 3 w		11			
10 overs 1-42	50 overs, 216 mins	9-269			

Fall: 1-8 (Klinger), 2-65 (Bancroft), 3-86 (M Marsh), 4-91 (Turner), 5-210 (Wells), 6-226 (Short), 7-267 (Richardson), 8-267 (Tye), 9-268 (Behrendorff)

New South Wales		B	M	4	6
DP Hughes	lbw b Behrendorff	25	30	37	4
NJ Maddinson	c Turner b Behrendorff	19	38	45	2
KR Patterson	c & b Tye	51	48	56	6
MC Henriques *	c Richardson b Short	72	70	102	7	1
EJM Cowan	c Short b Tye	53	67	105	3
P M Nevill +	c Bancroft b Richardson	15	16	20	2
SA Abbott	lbw b Richardson	0	1	1	
GS Sandhu	run out (Richardson)	0	5	4	
NM Lyon	c Klinger b Short	2	7	8	
MW Edwards	b Behrendorff	10	13	16	1
HNA Conway	not out	0	1	2	
9 lb, 4 w		13			
10 overs: 1-39	49.2 overs, 206 mins	260			

Fall: 1-39 (Hughes), 2-52 (Maddinson), 3-133 (Patterson), 4-202 (Henriques), 5-232 (Nevill), 6-232 (Abbott), 7-233 (Sandhu), 8-240 (Lyon), 9-259 (Cowan), 10-260 (Edwards)

NSW - bowling	O	M	R	W	wd	nb
GS Sandhu	9	1	57	4	1	
HNA Conway	9	0	49	2		
SA Abbott	10	0	54	2	1	
MW Edwards	10	1	50	0	1	
NM Lyon	10	0	38	1		
MC Henriques	2	0	13	0		

WA - bowling	O	M	R	W	wd	nb
JA Richardson	10	0	54	2	2	
JP Behrendorff	9.2	0	34	3		
AJ Tye	10	0	55	2	1	
DJM Moody	8	0	51	0	1	
AJ Turner	6	0	31	0		
DJM Short	6	0	26	2		

Toss: New South Wales. Umpires: GJ Davidson, PJ Gillespie, Ref: D Talalla. Award: SE Marsh (WA). Crowd: 1,529

Match 4 – Queensland v South Australia at Allan Border Field, Brisbane on October 1, 2017
South Australia won by 83 runs (BP)

Struggling at 3-44, Tom Cooper made his fifth hundred for SA in Australian domestic one-day cricket. After early breakthrough from Worrall and Winter. Mennie destroyed the Queensland middle order, taking his first five wicket haul.

South Australia		B	M	4	6
JB Weatherald	c Neser b Doggett	22	22	19	5
AT Carey +	c Swepson b Wildermuth	9	28	57	1
CJ Ferguson *	c Burns b Cutting	7	28	33	
TLW Cooper	not out	115	107	160	12	3
AI Ross	c Peirson b Wildermuth	25	35	41	3	1
JS Lehmann	c Doggett b Wildermuth	0	5	7	
CT Valente	c Burns b Doggett	24	50	58	1
JM Mennie	c Doggett b Wildermuth	14	9	7	2
MJA Cormack	c Renshaw b Cutting	3	10	23	
NP Winter	not out	7	7	15	1
DJ Worrall					
1 b, 6 lb, 1 nb, 6 w		14			
10 overs: 1-30	50 overs, 214 mins	8-240			

Fall: 1-29 (Weatherald), 2-43 (Ferguson), 3-44 (Carey), 4-87 (Ross), 5-99 (Lehmann), 6-157 (Valente), 7-172 (Mennie), 8-206 (Cormack)

Queensland		B	M	4	6
UT Khawaja *	c Carey b Winter	8	8	6	2
MT Renshaw	c Carey b Worrall	1	3	10	
JA Burns	c Carey b Valente	24	43	86	2
M Labuschagne	c Lehmann b Mennie	21	29	28	4
JD Wildermuth	c Cooper b Mennie	0	1	1	
JJ Peirson +	lbw b Mennie	60	69	91	9
BCJ Cutting	c Ferguson b Worrall	0	7	10	
MG Neser	c Worrall b Cormack	21	31	43	1
JS Floros	c Lehmann b Mennie	10	16	19	1
MJ Swepson	c Lehmann b Mennie	2	9	10	
BJ Doggett	not out	0	5	5	
1 lb, 9 w		10			
10 overs: 4-49	36.5 overs, 159 mins	157			

Fall: 1-10 (Khawaja), 2-16 (Renshaw), 3-44 (Labuschagne), 4-44 (Wildermuth), 5-87 (Burns), 6-94 (Cutting), 7-139 (Peirson), 8-153 (Neser), 9-156 (Floros), 10-157 (Swepson)

Qld - bowling	O	M	R	W	wd	nb
BJ Doggett	10	3	46	2	2	1
MG Neser	10	1	59	0		
BCJ Cutting	10	2	41	2	3	
JD Wildermuth	10	0	39	4	1	
MJ Swepson	8	0	41	0		
JS Floros	2	0	7	0		

SA - bowling	O	M	R	W	wd	nb
DJ Worrall	7	1	34	2	1	
NP Winter	6	1	30	1	5	
JM Mennie	9.5	0	36	5		
CT Valente	4	1	12	1		
MJA Cormack	10	0	44	1	3	

Toss: Queensland. Umpires: MW Graham-Smith, P Wilson, Ref: PL Marshall. Award: TLW Cooper (SA) Crowd: 439

Match 5 – Western Australia v Victoria at the WACA, Perth on October 1, 2017– Western Australia won by 38 runs

Shaun Marsh continued his fine form, having faced Peter Siddle's first two balls, which each went for five wides. Cam Bancroft also played for well for his half-century, while Mitch Marsh and Jono Wells both hit out well in the later overs. White went in the third over and while most batsmen got started, only Gotch could pass fifty. WA ended up winning comfortably, with only late order runs from Siddle preventing a bonus point being conceded.

Western Australia		B	M	4	6
SE Marsh	b Boland	88	112	159	8
M Klinger	c Tremain b Siddle	20	37	59	2
CT Bancroft +	c Harper b Siddle	59	61	77	8
MR Marsh *	not out	47	52	75	2
AJ Turner	c Harris b Tremain	7	14	13	
J W Wells	not out	34	25	39	5
DJM Short					
J A Richardson					
AJ Tye					
JP Behrendorff					
DJM Moody					
	4 b, 5 lb, 1 nb, 18 w	28			
10 overs : 0-52	50 overs, 215 mins	4-283			

Fall: 1-60 (Klinger), 2-175 (Bancroft), 3-191 (S Marsh), 4-200 (Turner, 40.4)

Victoria		B	M	4	6
MS Harris	c Bancroft b Tye	47	46	56	3	3
CL White *	b Richardson	5	11	11	1
TJ Dean	b Short	30	51	70	1
WJ Pucovski	c Behrendorff b Short	15	20	35	2
SE Gotch	b Behrendorff	61	61	93	5
DT Christian	c Bancroft b Moody	14	18	18	1
SB Harper +	c Klinger b Moody	11	11	16	1
CP Tremain	lbw b Short	7	21	25	
PM Siddle	c Richardson b Tye	32	29	42	3	1
SM Boland	c Klinger b Tye	4	13	19	
Fawad Ahmed	not out	0	0	1	
	5 lb, 14 w	19			
10 overs : 1-50	46.5 overs, 202 mins	245			

Fall: 1-9 (White), 2-72 (Harris), 3-96 (Dean), 4-112 (Pucovski), 5-145 (Christian), 6-170 (Harper), 7-195 (Tremain), 8-227 (Gotch), 9-245 (Boland), 10-245 (Siddle)

Victoria - bowling	O	M	R	W	wd	nb
P M Siddle	10	0	48	2	2	
CP Tremain	9	1	34	1	2	
SM Boland	10	2	56	1	3	1
Fawad Ahmed	10	0	64	0		
DT Christian	10	0	63	0		
CL White	1	0	9	0	1	

WA - bowling	O	M	R	W	wd	nb
J A Richardson	10	1	46	1	4	
JP Behrendorff	8	0	43	1		
AJ Tye	8.5	0	37	3	2	
DJM Short	10	0	53	3	2	
DJM Moody	9	0	48	2	2	
AJ Turner	1	0	13	0		

Toss: Victoria. Umpires: SAJ Craig, AK Wilds, Ref: D Talalla. Award: SE Marsh (WA). Crowd: 1,435

Match 6 – New South Wales v Tasmania at the WACA, Perth on October 2, 2017
New South Wales won by 102 runs (BP)

Dan Hughes and Nic Maddinson started in fine style, although the bowling of debutant paceman Riley Meredith did cause a few uncertain moments. Maddinson scored his fourth domestic one-day ton and with Ed Cowan scoring fifty, New South Wales raced past 300.

Tasmania started well before Ben Dunk went in the ninth over, which saw them lose 4-27. Jordan Silk batted positively for his fifty but had little other support as the Blues comfortably gained a bonus point win.

New South Wales		B	M	4	6
DP Hughes	st Dunk b Boyce	56	63	86	11
NJ Maddinson	c Doolan b Bird	137	119	155	23	1
KR Patterson	b Bird	26	36	49	3
RJ Gibson	st Dunk b Boyce	13	19	27	1
EJM Cowan	not out	51	32	53	5	1
P M Nevill *+	b Milenko	21	20	22	2
SA Abbott	b Fekete	1	6	4	
GS Sandhu	not out	4	5	12	
NM Lyon					
MW Edwards					
HNA Conway					
	1 lb, 6 w	7			
10 overs : 0-68	50 overs, 210 mins	6-316			

Fall: 1-136 (Hughes), 2-207 (Patterson), 3-230 (Maddinson), 4-247 (Gibson), 5-282 (Nevill), 6-284 (Abbott)

Tasmania		B	M	4	6
BR Dunk +	c Nevill b Lyon	38	30	38	7
BR McDermott	c Nevill b Edwards	31	34	53	2	2
AJ Doolan	c Hughes b Abbott	4	21	22	
GJ Bailey *	b Abbott	11	18	25	1
JC Silk	c sub (JS Lenton) b Edwards	55	52	87	6
CA Wakim	c Cowan b Edwards	5	11	12	
SA Milenko	c Abbott b Lyon	30	40	36	3
CJ Boyce	b Lyon	24	15	23	2	1
JM Bird	c Nevill b Edwards	5	7	9	1
AL Fekete	c Nevill b Abbott	1	4	9	
RP Meredith	not out	0	4	4	
	(3 lb, 7 w)	10			
10 overs : 1-69	39.2 overs, 168 mins	214			

Fall: 1-69 (Dunk), 2-75 (McDermott), 3-80 (Doolan), 4-96 (Bailey), 5-117 (Wakim), 6-168 (Milenko), 7-197 (Silk), 8-211 (Boyce), 9-213 (Bird), 10-214 (Fekete)

Tasmania - bowling	O	M	R	W	wd	nb
JM Bird	10	0	62	2		
AL Fekete	10	1	65	1	3	
SA Milenko	10	0	84	1	1	
RP Meredith	10	0	54	0	1	
CJ Boyce	10	0	50	2	1	

NSW - bowling	O	M	R	W	wd	nb
HNA Conway	7	1	47	0	1	
GS Sandhu	7	1	46	0		
NM Lyon	10	1	58	3	1	
SA Abbott	6.2	0	29	3	3	
MW Edwards	9	1	31	4	2	

Toss: Tasmania. Umpires: GJ Davidson, PJ Gillespie, Ref: RW Stratford. Award: NJ Maddinson (NSW). Crowd: 287

Match 7 – Victoria v Tasmania at the WACA, Perth on October 4, 2017 – Victoria won by 111 runs (BP)

Cameron White played an exceptional knock, the highest by a Victoria in this format of the game. Harris and White powered the Bushrangers to a great start, before Harris went in the 23rd over. Dean helped White add 87, with White leading the final onslaught, as Victoria added 98 from the last ten overs. In reply Tasmania were quickly two down, before McDermott and Bailey added 103 in 22 overs. When Bailey went, the middle and lower order offered little, McDermott out three short of ton, pulling a catch to deep square-leg, as the Tigers lost their last seven wickets for 55.

Victoria		B	M	4	6	Tasmania		B	M	4	6
MS Harris	c Wakim b Fekete	75	66	96	9	2	BR Dunk +	c White b Siddle	1	10	13	
CL White *	c Bailey b Fekete	165	154	217	16	6	BR McDermott	c Gotch b Tremain	97	124	54	8	3
TJ Dean	c Dunk b Meredith	40	43	59	4		AJ Doolan	b Siddle	2	6	15	
WJ Pucovski	b Bird	0	3	3		GJ Bailey *	c Short b Boland	52	56	78	7	
SE Gotch	c Wakim b Fekete	15	21	31	1		JC Silk	b Short	8	14	24	
MW Short	c Silk b Fekete	14	8	12	1	1	CA Wakim	lbw b Fawad	6	9	9	
SB Harper +	not out	6	5	8		SA Milenko	b Siddle	5	11	11	
CP Tremain	not out	0	0	1		CJ Boyce	c & b Tremain	6	9	16	
PM Siddle						JM Bird	c Dean b Tremain	16	16	20	2	
SM Boland						AL Fekete	not out	9	12	16	1
Fawad Ahmed						RP Meredith	b White	2	9	8	
	1 lb, 9 w	10					2 lb, 8 w	10			
10 overs : 0-46	50 overs, 219 mins	6-325				10 overs : 2-34	46 overs, 189 mins	214			

Fall: 1-130 (Harris), 2-217 (Dean), 3-218 (Pucovski), 4-275 (Gotch), 5-307 (Short), 6-323 (White)

Fall: 1-10 (Dunk), 2-21 (Doolan), 3-124 (Bailey), 4-159 (Silk), 5-174 (Wakim), 6-178 (McDermott), 7-181 (Milenko), 8-199 (Boyce), 9-207 (Bird), 10-214 (Meredith)

Tasmania - bowling	O	M	R	W	wd	nb	Victoria - bowling	O	M	R	W	wd	nb
JM Bird	10	0	49	1			PM Siddle	10	3	27	3		
AL Fekete	10	2	48	4			CP Tremain	10	0	50	3	8	
RP Meredith	10	0	65	1	3		SM Boland	7	0	32	1		
SA Milenko	10	0	77	0	1		MW Short	7	0	35	1		
CJ Boyce	10	0	85	0	1		Fawad Ahmed	9	0	52	1		
							CL White	3	0	16	1		

Toss: Victoria. Umpires: SAJ Craig, AK Wilds, Ref: RW Stratford   Award: CL White (Vic).   Crowd: 281

Match 8 – New South Wales v South Australia at the Hurstville Oval, Sydney on October 6, 2017
South Australia won by 45 runs

In a high scoring game, Alex Carey and Jake Weatherald set the tone adding 100 from 93 balls for the first wicket. When Nathan Lyon took two wickets in as many balls, SA had slipped to 3-149 after 24 overs. But Alex Ross took over, adding 138 with Weatherald, including 32 (466466) off the 40th over bowled by Lyon. New South Wales lost Maddinson, but were well on track for a win, with Dan Hughes and Kurtis Patterson adding 189 in 30 overs. In the 34th over, the Redbacks picked up wickets from consecutive balls, with Hughes caught at third man and Patterson brilliant run out by Ferguson at mid-off. The innings fell away after that, SA recording a comfortable win.

South Australia		B	M	4	6	New South Wales		B	M	4	6
AT Carey +	b Abbott	60	55	68	7	3	DP Hughes	c Valente b Worrall	105	104	126	8	4
JB Weatherald	c Nevill b Starc	103	114	191	14	2	NJ Maddinson	c Carey b Winter	5	8	10	
CJ Ferguson *	lbw b Lyon	19	25	37	3		KR Patterson	run out (Ferguson)	84	88	117	8	
TLW Cooper	lbw b Lyon	0	1	1		RJ Gibson	c Worrall b Mennie	5	13	23	
AI Ross	c Nevill b Abbott	110	85	114	7	7	EJM Cowan	b Valente	23	21	32	3	
JS Lehmann	c Conway b Starc	24	19	29	2	1	PM Nevill *+	lbw b Mennie	16	10	19		2
CT Valente	not out	0	1	4		SA Abbott	c Weatherald b Mennie	5	7	6	1	
JM Mennie	not out	1	1	1		MA Starc	c Worrall b Cooper	23	21	38	2	
MJA Cormack						NM Lyon	c Cooper b Mennie	4	4	8	1	
NP Winter						MW Edwards	b Worrall	11	14	17		1
DJ Worrall						HNA Conway	not out	10	8	9	2	
	14 lb, 13 w, 2 nb	29					2 lb, 8 w	10			
10 overs : 0-70	50 overs, 226 mins	6-346				10 overs : 1-50	49.4 overs, 207 mins	301			

Fall: 1-100 (Carey), 2-149 (Ferguson), 3-149 (Cooper), 4-287 (Weatherald), 5-341 (Lehmann), 6-345 (Ross)

Fall: 1-13 (Maddinson), 2-202 (Hughes), 3-202 (Patterson), 4-226 (Gibson), 5-241 (Cowan), 6-252 (Abbott), 7-252 (Nevill), 8-264 (Lyon), 9-283 (Edwards), 10-301 (Starc)

NSW - bowling	O	M	R	W	wd	nb	SA - bowling	O	M	R	W	wd	nb
MA Starc	10	0	55	1	3	1	NP Winter	7	0	40	1	5	
HNA Conway	10	0	77	0	2	1	DJ Worrall	10	1	53	2	2	
SA Abbott	10	1	59	3	3		JM Mennie	10	0	53	4		
NM Lyon	9	0	88	2	1		MJA Cormack	8	0	61	0	1	
MW Edwards	10	1	48	0	1		CT Valente	10	0	62	1		
NJ Maddinson	1	0	5	0			TLW Cooper	4.4	0	30	1		

Toss: Victoria. Umpires: GJ Davidson, MW Graham-Smith, Ref: D Talalla   Award: AI Ross (SA)   Crowd: 1,106

Australian Cricket Digest, 2018-19

Match 9 – Queensland v Victoria at North Sydney Oval on October 7, 2017 (day/night) – Queensland won by 11 runs

Renshaw and Khawaja added 149 in 29 overs, before Labuschagne and Peirson cracked 76 in under seven overs to ensure they passed 300. Siddle and Fawad did well to prevent a much larger chase. In reply, Victoria were off to a bad start, but were encouraged by a stand of 68 in 13 overs between Dean and Handscomb. But, after their efforts, the chase appeared doomed until Short and Tremain added 57 and then Siddle and Tremain put on 67 to put them back in the hunt. 16 were needed off the last, Gannon finishing the game off.

Queensland		B	M	4	6	Victoria		B	M	4	6
MT Renshaw	c White b Fawad	74	91	111	8	MS Harris	c Labuschagne b Doggett	0	3	2	
UT Khawaja *	c Dean b Fawad	85	97	133	7	1	CL White	c Peirson b Gannon	2	4	8	
JA Burns	st Handscomb b Fawad	29	36	48	1	2	TJ Dean	b Cutting	40	48	60	7
M Labuschagne	c Short b Tremain	52	40	57	4	3	PSP Handscomb *+	c Doggett b Swepson	48	44	81	2	3
JJ Peirson +	c Gotch b Tremain	46	27	40	4	2	WJ Pucovski	b Swepson	5	17	21	
BCJ Cutting	c Handscomb b Boland	7	4	8		1	SE Gotch	c Peirson b Neser	17	28	34	2
JD Wildermuth	not out	1	2	4			MW Short	c Labuschagne				
MG Neser	not out	4	3	3	1			b Wildermuth	51	49	63	2	3
MJ Swepson						CP Tremain	c Doggett b Neser	50	45	72	3	3
CJ Gannon						PM Siddle	b Gannon	62	45	69	10	1
BJ Doggett						SM Boland	c Neser b Doggett	12	12	15		1
						Fawad Ahmed	not out	0	4	13	
	9 lb, 2 w	11					2 lb, 1 nb, 8 w	11			
10 overs: 0-34	50 overs, 205 mins	6-309				10 overs: 2-36	49.4 overs, 224 mins	298			

Fall: 1-149 (Renshaw), 2-168 (Khawaja), 3-206 (Burns), 4-282 (Labuschagne), 5-303 (Cutting), 6-303 (Peirson)

Fall: 1-1 (Harris), 2-7 (White), 3-75 (Dean), 4-99 (Handscomb), 5-130 (Gotch), 6-135 (Pucovski), 7-192 (Short), 8-259 (Tremain), 9-283 (Boland), 10-298 (Siddle).

Pucovski retired hurt on 3 (3-87) and returned at 5-130

Victoria - bowling	O	M	R	W	wd	nb	Queensland - bowling	O	M	R	W	wd	nb
MW Short	6	0	26	0	1		BJ Doggett	10	1	63	2	2	
PM Siddle	10	0	33	0			CJ Gannon	8.4	0	43	2	2	
CP Tremain	10	0	84	2			MG Neser	10	0	47	2		
SM Boland	10	0	88	1			MJ Swepson	10	1	74	2	1	
Fawad Ahmed	10	0	44	3	1		BCJ Cutting	8	0	49	1	3	1
CL White	4	0	25	0			JD Wildermuth	2	0	12	1		
							M Labuschagne	1	0	8	0		

Toss: Victoria.   Umpires: GC Joshua, SA Lightbody, Ref: PL Marshall   Award: UT Khawaja (Qld).   Crowd: 679

Match 10 – Western Australia v Tasmania at the WACA, Perth on October 7, 2017 (part floodlight)
WA won by 8 wickets (BP)

Tasmania again struggled, reduced to 3-44 in the 11th over. Bailey and Silk attempted a recovery but at 6-99, WA looked headed for bonus point territory. On debut, Tom Rogers showed fight, as he and Silk helped push the visitors close to 200. In reply Shaun Marsh and Klinger were only troubled by Meredith, who continued to bowl with good pace. Mitch Marsh ensured a double point, smashing Rainbird to all parts of the WACA.

Tasmania		B	M	4	6	Western Australia		B	M	4	6
BR Dunk +	c M Marsh b Richardson	0	5	2		M Klinger	c Boyce b Faulkner	45	76	103	3	2
BR McDermott	lbw b Moody	18	34	46	1	1	SE Marsh	c Rogers b Boyce	62	68	95	6	1
AJ Doolan	b Kelly	8	10	19	2		CT Bancroft +	not out	29	28	57	2	
GJ Bailey *	st Bancroft b Short	36	39	52	5		MR Marsh *	not out	67	49	49	7	3
JC Silk	c Moody b Richardson	80	86	145	9		HWR Cartwright					
CA Wakim	b Mackin	1	8	6			AJ Turner					
JP Faulkner	c Bancroft b Cartwright	5	42	31			DJM Short					
TS Rogers	c Kelly b Moody	38	54	69	4		JA Richardson					
CJ Boyce	run out (Short)	6	11	16			ML Kelly					
SL Rainbird	c Bancroft b Moody	4	5	4			DJM Moody					
RP Meredith	not out	2	5	6			SP Mackin					
	(3 lb, 6 w)	9					2 lb, 1nb, 2 w	5			
10 overs: 2-39	49.5 overs, 207 mins	207				10 overs: 0-43	36.4 overs, 154 mins	2-208			

Fall: 1-0 (Dunk), 2-20 (Doolan), 3-44 (McDermott), 4-78 (Bailey), 5-83 (Wakim), 6-99 (Faulkner), 7-192 (Rogers), 8-196 (Silk), 9-201 (Rainbird), 10-207 (Boyce)

Fall: 1-108 (S Marsh), 2-114 (Klinger)

WA - bowling	O	M	R	W	wd	nb	Tasmania - bowling	O	M	R	W	wd	nb
JA Richardson	10	1	40	2	1		RP Meredith	7	0	26	0	1	
ML Kelly	9	1	39	1	3		TS Rogers	6	1	43	0		1
DJM Moody	7.5	0	47	3			JP Faulkner	8	1	42	1		
SP Mackin	10	2	30	1			SL Rainbird	5.4	0	59	0	1	
DJM Short	10	1	35	1	2		CJ Boyce	10	0	36	1		
HWR Cartwright	3	0	13	1									

Toss: Tasmania.   Umpires: SAJ Craig, PJ Gillespie, Ref: RW Stratford   Award: SE Marsh (WA)   Crowd: 1,452

Australian Cricket Digest, 2018-19

Match 11 – New South Wales v CA XI at Hurstville Oval, Sydney on October 8, 2017 - NSW won by 93 runs (BP)

NSW powered away to a stand of 132 for the first wicket in 21 overs, with Maddinson flying to fifty from just 31 balls, on his way to a 90 ball ton, his fifth in Australian Domestic one day cricket and second of the season. Bryant showed his class as the CA XI chased hard, his fifty took 31 balls, with 5x4 and 3x6. He and his skipper Webster added 96 in 11 overs, whereupon the middle order struggled. Nielsen showed nine was too low for him in the order. The match ended weirdly, with Maddinson having Kuhneman stumped off a wide.

New South Wales		B	M	4	6	CA XI		B	M	4	6
DP Hughes *	c Nielsen b Hinchliffe	68	72	79	10	JM Carder	c Nevill b Sandhu	6	15	18	
NJ Maddinson	b Hinchliffe	123	113	170	10	3	MA Bryant	c Nevill b Lyon	89	61	88	10	4
KR Patterson	st Nielsen b Kuhnemann	30	28	26	4	BJ Webster *	c Nevill b Bollinger	29	34	48	2	1
RJ Gibson	c Steketee b Hinchliffe	51	45	47	6	2	CD Hinchliffe	c Edwards b Bollinger	7	7	6		1
EJM Cowan	run out (Carder-Nielsen)	2	3	5		P Uppal	c Nevill b Bollinger	7	8	18	1
PM Nevill +	c Kuhnemann b Merlo	24	16	22	2	1	JA Merlo	st Nevill b Lyon	18	26	37	2
SA Abbott	c Nielsen b Merlo	0	1	3		BJ Pengelley	c Nevill b Abbott	3	15	18	
GS Sandhu	c Bryant b Hinchliffe	15	13	13		1	HTRY Thornton	c Maddinson b Abbott	10	18	17	2
NM Lyon	not out	8	5	11		1	HJ Nielsen +	not out	38	36	50	4	1
DE Bollinger	not out	4	5	6		MT Steketee	c Nevill b Edwards	10	13	15	1
MW Edwards	did not bat					MP Kuhnemann	st Nevill b Maddinson	14	13	28	2
	1 b, 2 lb, 1 nb, 3 w	7					2 lb, 6 w	8			
10 overs: 0-72	50 overs, 195 mins	8-332				10 overs: 1-74	41 overs, 177 mins	239			

Fall: 1-132 (Hughes), 2-184 (Patterson), 3-269 (Gibson), 4-275 (Cowan), 5-294 (Maddinson), 6-295 (Abbott), 7-311 (Nevill), 8-318 (Sandhu)

Fall: 1-21 (Carder), 2-117 (Webster), 3-127 (Hinchliffe), 4-143 (Bryant), 5-145 (Uppal), 6-165 (Pengelley), 7-171 (Merlo), 8-175 (Thornton), 9-192 (Steketee), 10-239 (Kuhnemann)

CA XI - bowling	O	M	R	W	wd	nb	NSW - bowling	O	M	R	W	wd	nb
MT Steketee	7	0	58	0			GA Sandhu	6	0	32	1	1	
HTRY Thornton	8	0	40	0	2		SA Abbott	10	0	69	2	2	
BJ Webster	4	0	35	0			DE Bollinger	10	0	62	3		
BJ Pengelley	5	0	30	0			MW Edwards	5	0	48	1	2	
JA Merlo	10	0	53	2	1	1	NM Lyon	10	2	25	2		
CD Hinchliffe	10	0	71	4			NJ Maddinson	0	0	1	1	1	
MP Kuhnemann	5	0	33	1									
P Uppal	1	0	9	0									

Toss: New South Wales   Umpires: CA Polosak, P Wilson, Ref: D Talalla   Award: NJ Maddinson (NSW)   Crowd: 648

Match 12 – Cricket Australia XI v Victoria at Hurstville Oval, Sydney on October 10, 2017 – Victoria won by 7 wickets

Victoria's pace attack were too good in the early stage of this match, reducing the CA XI to 6-45 in the 15th over. From there Nielsen showed class, combining with Wright, Steketee and Stobo to add consecutive fifty stands, as they reached a respectable 232. After being 3-74 in the 17th over, Handscomb and Gotch took control, Handscomb hitting a boundary to win the game and bring up his ton.

CA XI		B	M	4	6	Victoria		B	M	4	6
JM Carder	c Dean b Tremain	8	9	6	2	MS Harris	run out (Carder)	37	35	48	4	2
MA Bryant	c Short b Siddle	9	21	29			CL White	c Hinchliffe b Steketee	27	53	70	4
BJ Webster *	c Handscomb b Boland	12	24	51			TJ Dean	c Nielsen b Steketee	4	13	24	
CD Hinchliffe	c White b Siddle	0	12	14			PSP Handscomb *+	not out	103	73	91	10	6
P Uppal	c Handscomb b Tremain	12	19	22	2		SE Gotch	not out	51	59	90	2	3
HJ Nielsen +	c Tremain b Short	94	93	135	5	6	MW Short					
BJ Pengelley	c Handscomb b Tremain	0	1	2			BR Thomson					
MB Wright	st Handscomb b Short	30	48	53	2	2	CP Tremain					
MT Steketee	b Fawad	28	38	40	4		PM Siddle					
CH Stobo	not out	25	27	38	1	1	SM Boland					
JR Coleman	not out	5	8	9			Fawad Ahmed					
	3 lb, 6 w	9					(3 lb, 1nb, 7 w)	11			
10 overs: 2-28	50 overs, 204 mins	9-232				10 overs: 0-60	38.4 overs, 164 mins	3-233			

Fall: 1-9 (Carder), 2-25 (Bryant), 3-28 (Hinchliffe), 4-36 (Webster), 5-45 (Uppal), 6-45 (Pengelley), 7-104 (Wright), 8-157 (Steketee), 9-216 (Nielsen)

Fall: 1-62 (Harris), 2-74 (White), 3-74 (Dean)

Victoria - bowling	O	M	R	W	wd	nb	CA XI - bowling	O	M	R	W	wd	nb
PM Siddle	10	2	20	2			JR Coleman	10	1	32	0	1	
CP Tremain	10	1	51	3	2		CH Stobo	7	0	57	0	1	
SM Boland	10	0	45	1	1		MT Steketee	9.4	1	57	2	3	
Fawad Ahmed	10	0	47	1			CD Hinchiffe	3	0	21	0		1
MW Short	9	1	59	2	3		BJ Pengelley	5	0	26	0	2	
CL White	0.4	0	7	0			MB Wright	4	0	37	0		
BR Thomson	0.2	0	0	0									

Toss: Victoria   Umpires: SA Lightbody, P Wilson (TV)   Ref: RL Parry   Award: PSP Handscomb (Vic)   Crowd: 163

Match 13 – South Australia v Tasmania at North Sydney Oval, on October 10, 2017 – Tasmania won by 129 runs (BP)

Oddly, South Australia having made 346 batting first in their win over NSW, bowled first and paid big time for it as Tasmania reeled off an imposing total. Skipper Bailey crunched the bowlers to all parts, the Tigers hitting 12 sixes in their innings, Winter conceded the most runs ever by an SA bowler in a ten over spell, and the third worst overall. SA were well placed at 1-84 in the 16th over, but then collapsed badly with Meredith impressive. Ben Dunk took his first ever wickets, his off-spinners dismissing three batsmen in the space of 17 balls.

Tasmania		B	M	4	6	South Australia		B	M	4	6
BR McDermott	lbw b Winter	0	7	10		JB Weatherald	c Dunk b Buchanan	10	23	33	1
BR Dunk	b Cormack	45	61	86	6	AT Carey+	c Boyce b Rogers	41	49	67	8
AJ Doolan	lbw b Cormack	62	90	111	8	CJ Ferguson*	c Rogers b Dunk	43	45	72	7
GJ Bailey*	c Ferguson b Winter	86	62	96	6	TLW Cooper	c McDermott b Meredith	7	12	11	1
MS Wade+	c Cooper b Mennie	46	45	64	1	AI Ross	c Buchanan b Meredith	6	8	10	1
JC Silk	c Lehmann b Valente	10	7	13	1	JS Lehmann	b Dunk	9	15	21	1
JP Faulkner	not out	34	19	26	3	CT Valente	lbw b Boyce	16	21	32	2
TS Rogers	not out	9	10	16	-	JM Mennie	b Boyce	7	7	7	1
CJ Boyce						MJA Cormack	c Rogers b Boyce	15	22	25	3
ND Buchanan						DJ Worrall	c Meredith b Dunk	16	19	24	3
RP Meredith						NP Winter	not out	3	15	15	
	8 lb, 1 nb, 14 w	23					2 b, 4 lb, 7 w	13			
10 overs: 1-47	50 overs, 214 mins	315				10 overs: 1-55	39.2 overs, 154 mins	186			

Fall: 1-8 (McDermott), 2-85 (Dunk), 3-134 (Doolan), 4-259 (Bailey), 5-261 (Wade), 6-285 (Silk)

Fall: 1-46 (Weatherald), 2-84 (Carey), 3-98 (Cooper), 4-108 (Ross), 5-124 (Ferguson), 6-128 (Lehmann), 7-141 (Mennie), 8-158 (Valente), 9-167 (Cormack), 10-186 (Worrall)

SA - bowling	O	M	R	W	wd	nb
DJ Worrall	10	1	65	0	3	1
NP Winter	10	0	94	2	10	
JM Mennie	10	1	37	1	1	
CT Valente	10	0	51	1		
MJA Cormack	9	0	52	2		
TLW Cooper	1	0	8	0		

Tasmania - bowling	O	M	R	W	wd	nb
RP Meredith	7	0	31	2	1	
TS Rogers	6	0	35	1	2	
BR Dunk	4.2	0	14	3		
JP Faulkner	6	0	30	0	1	
ND Buchanan	7	0	43	1	3	
CJ Boyce	9	2	27	3		

Toss: Tasmania.   Umpires: GA Abood, SD Fry, Ref: PL Marshall   Award: GJ Bailey (Tas)   Crowd: 316

Match 14 –Queensland v Western Australia at Drummoyne Oval on October 11, 2017 – WA won by 11 runs (DLS)

A small crowd witnessed a high scoring clash, which was reduced to 41 overs per side after a 90 minute rain delay early in the WA innings. Shaun Marsh continued his fine form in the competition, adding 128 in 25 overs with Klinger, who later added 144 in just 15 overs with Bancroft. DLS decided Queensland needed 304, and at 3-10 and later 5-63 little hope was held out for a close game, Matt Kelly doing most of the damage. Coming in during the 16th over, Neser took 20 balls over his first eight runs before bringing up his fifty from 49 balls, taking just a further 24 to reach his ton off 73, with 8 fours and 5 sixes. 70 were needed off the last four, which was too hard.

Western Australia		B	M	4	6	Queensland	DLS Target 304	B	M	4	6
SE Marsh	c Peirson b Neser	69	72	106	11	UT Khawaja*	c Klinger b Short	81	78	118	9	2
M Klinger	c Peirson b Cutting	128	120	176	9	4	MT Renshaw	c M Marsh b Richardson	0	1	3	
CT Bancroft+	c Burns b Cutting	73	47	66	7	3	JA Burns	c M Marsh b Kelly	0	1	2	
MR Marsh*	not out	7	3	5	1	M Labuschagne	c Bancroft b Kelly	2	7	8	
AJ Turner	not out	9	4	4	2	JJ Peirson+	c Bancroft b Kelly	13	35	41	1
HWR Cartwright						JD Wildermuth	c M Marsh b Kelly	4	10	8	
DJM Short						MG Neser	run out (Short-Bancroft)	122	81	104	8	7
JA Richardson						BCJ Cutting	c Kelly b Moody	4	4	11	1
DJM Moody						CJ Gannon	c Turner b Mackin	27	17	19	1	2
ML Kelly						MJ Swepson	not out	23	13	24	4
SP Mackin						BJ Doggett	not out	1	1	3	
	1 b, 4 lb, 10 w	15					8 lb, 2 nb, 5 w	15			
	41 overs, 181 mins	3-301					41 overs, 175 mins	292			

Fall: 1-141 (S Marsh), 2-285 (Bancroft), 3-285 (Klinger)

Fall: 1-3 (Renshaw), 2-4 (Burns), 3-10 (Labuschagne), 4-53 (Peirson), 5-63 (Wildermuth), 6-146 (Khawaja), 7-169 (Cutting), 8-227 (Gannon), 9-285 (Neser)

Queensland - bowling	O	M	R	W	wd	nb
BJ Doggett	8	0	56	0	3	
CJ Gannon	7	0	48	0	1	
MG Neser	7	0	45	1		
BCJ Cutting	8	0	64	2	5	
JD Wildermuth	5	0	34	0		
MJ Swepson	4	0	38	0	1	
MT Renshaw	2	0	11	0		

WA - bowling	O	M	R	W	wd	nb
JA Richardson	9	0	80	1	3	
ML Kelly	8	2	25	4	1	
SP Mackin	8	0	61	1	1	2
DJM Short	8	0	56	1		
DJM Moody	5	0	33	1		
HWR Cartwright	3	0	29	0		

Toss: Queensland.   Umpires: PJ Gillespie, DM Koch, Ref: RW Stratford.   Award: MG Neser (Qld)   Crowd: 140

Match 15 – South Australia v Victoria at North Sydney Oval, on October 12, 2017 - South Australia won by 11 runs

Both teams scored freely on a flat surface which saw over 700 runs scored for just the sixth time in the competition. Weatherald was first out in the 18th over after a breezy innings, with skipper Ferguson keeping the momentum going. Late in the innings, Lehmann reached his fifty from 22 balls, the third fastest ever, and just one ball less than the record 21-ball fifty for SA, scored by David Hookes at the WACA in 1990-91. Lehmann's knock help propel SA to 118 off the final ten overs, including 78 off the last five. Victoria were well on their way at 1-160 in the 24th over, when Worrall knocked over Short in the 25th. Dean made his first ton in this format (77 balls, 16x4, 1x6) but when he was out in the 45th over, the target became too tough, despite a couple of late blows by Tremain and Siddle.

South Australia		B	M	4	6	Victoria		B	M	4	6
AT Carey +	c Thomson b Fawad	33	66	80	4	1	MW Short	b Worrall	81	83	94	10	1
JB Weatherald	c Handscomb b Fawad	71	51	64	13	1	MS Harris	c Carey b Valente	22	20	28	4	
CJ Ferguson *	c Tremain b Fawad	73	72	104	11		TJ Dean	b Valente	119	98	159	16	2
TLW Cooper	c Handscomb b Siddle	37	32	48	3	2	PSP Handscomb *+	c and b Cooper	21	18	24	3	
AI Ross	b Sutherland	33	37	53	5	1	SE Gotch	lbw b Johnson	32	31	39	1	2
JS Lehmann	not out	63	25	44	8	3	BR Thomson	c Sayers b Valente	24	27	43	2	
CT Valente	c Thomson b Tremain	36	17	28	1	4	CP Tremain	c Ferguson b Sayers	14	7	7		
MJA Cormack	not out	0	0	1			WJ Sutherland	run out (Worrall-Valente)	4				
SH Johnson							PM Siddle	not out	20	10	11	1	2
CJ Sayers							SM Boland	not out	5	5	9		
DJ Worrall							Fawad Ahmed						
	6 lb, 4 w	10						1 lb, 5 w	6				
10 overs : 0-55	50 overs, 214 mins	6-356					10 overs : 1-58	50 overs, 213 mins	8-345				

Fall: 1-107 (Weatherald), 2-112 (Carey), 3-188 (Cooper), 4-249 (Ferguson), 5-271 (Ross), 6-355 (Valente)

Fall: 1-45 (Harris), 2-160 (Short), 3-203 (Handscomb), 4-263 (Gotch), 5-295 (Dean), 6-311 (Tremain), 7-317 (Sutherland), 8-319 (Thomson)

Victoria - bowling	O	M	R	W	wd	nb	SA - bowling	O	M	R	W	wd	nb
PM Siddle	10	0	59	1	1		SH Johnson	10	0	72	1		
CP Tremain	10	1	66	1	1		DJ Worrall	10	0	72	1		
MW Short	6	1	32	0	1		CJ Sayers	10	0	74	1	4	
SM Boland	6	0	75	0	1		CT Valente	10	0	54	3		
Fawad Ahmed	10	0	62	3			MJA Cormack	8	0	54	0	1	
WJ Sutherland	8	1	56	1			TLW Cooper	2	0	18	1		

Toss: Victoria.   Umpires: GJ Davidson, AK Wilds, Ref: RW Stratford   Award: TJ Dean (Vic)   Crowd: 323

Match 16 –Cricket Australia XI v Tasmania at Hurstville Oval, Sydney on October 13, 2017
Tasmania won by 114 runs (BP)

Tasmanian skipper George Bailey dominated proceedings making his fifth Australian one-day ton and first since 2012-13, in what was a comfortable win. Doolan and Bailey added 182 from 149 as Tasmania passed 300 for the second time in four days. Meredith knocked over the first two CA XI wickets and even though Carder batted well to pass fifty, it was always going to be a hopeless task for the CA XI.

Tasmania		B	M	4	6	CA XI		B	M	4	6
BR McDermott	c Webster b Stobo	27	38	46	4	1	JM Carder	c Silk b Dunk	54	68	82	8	1
BR Dunk	b Fallins	34	43	76	4	1	MA Bryant	c Wade b Meredith	0	4	10		
AJ Doolan	b Thornton	83	95	113	8	1	BJ Webster *	c Wade b Meredith	4	6	7	1	
GJ Bailey *	c Webster b Hinchliffe	126	100	116	9	9	CD Hinchliffe	b Dunk	40	63	72	4	1
MS Wade +	c Webster b Thornton	39	16	18	1	5	P Uppal	c Doolan b Milenko	26	42	59	2	
JC Silk	c & b Coleman	11	5	6	1	1	HJ Nielsen +	c sub b Boyce	15	19	25	2	
JP Faulkner	c Coleman b Hinchliffe	7	3	5		1	BJ Pengelley	c Milenko b Boyce	15	19	19	1	1
SA Milenko	not out	0	0	1			HTRY Thornton	c Silk b Boyce	2	7	9		
CJ Boyce							CH Stobo	not out	24	24	36	1	1
TS Rogers							DG Fallins	c Rogers b Faulkner	17	14	14	1	2
RP Meredith							JR Coleman	c Rogers b Faulkner	17	12	14	1	1
	1 lb, 6 w	7						1 b, 2 lb, 3 w	6				
10 overs : 0-42	50 overs, 193 mins	7-334					10 overs : 2-36	46.2 overs, 179 mins	220				

Fall: 1-48 (McDermott), 2-86 (Dunk), 3-248 (Doolan), 4-301 (Wade), 5-315 (Silk), 6-334 (Faulkner), 7-334 (Bailey)

Fall: 1-5 (Bryant), 2-13 (Webster), 3-91 (Carder), 4-104 (Hinchliffe), 5-126 (Nielsen), 6-156 (Pengelley), 7-156 (Uppal), 8-160 (Thornton), 9-185 (Fallins), 10-220 (Coleman)

CA XI - bowling	O	M	R	W	wd	nb	Tasmania - bowling	O	M	R	W	wd	nb
JR Coleman	10	1	67	1	1		RP Meredith	6	1	26	2		
CH Stobo	8	0	32	1			TS Rogers	8	0	43	0		
HTRY Thornton	10	0	79	2	2		JP Faulkner	9.2	2	42	2	2	
BJ Pengelley	4	0	32	0			SA Milenko	8	0	26	1	1	
DG Fallins	7	0	51	1			CJ Boyce	10	0	61	3		
CD Hinchliffe	8	1	51	2	1		BR Dunk	5	0	19	2		
BJ Webster	3	0	21	0									

Toss: Tasmania   Umpires: SD Fry, GC Joshua, Ref: RW Stratford   Award: GJ Bailey (Tas)   Crowd: 240

Match 17 – New South Wales v Queensland at Drummoyne Oval, Sydney on October 16, 2016 (day/night)
NSW won by 6 wickets

After a poor start, Khawaja and Labuschagne added 217 from 225 balls which was a record for the third wicket for Queensland. In reply the Bulls bowlers were powerless in stopping the Hughes/Maddinson union, as they added 192 in 33 overs to set up a comfortable win.

Queensland			B	M	4	6	New South Wales			B	M	4	6
MT Renshaw	c Gibson b Lyon		4	13	15		DP Hughes	c Swepson b Neser		122	137	165	8	4
UT Khawaja *	c Abbott b Starc	138	139	196	15	2	NJ Maddinson	c Peirson b Doggett		86	89	122	3	5
JA Burns	hit wkt b Starc		4	11	14		KR Patterson	run out (Neser)		43	54	64	3
M Labuschagne	b Starc		91	111	156	7	RJ Gibson	c Neser b Gannon		14	12	19	3
SD Heazlett	c Nevill b Abbott		3	9	12		EJM Cowan	not out		4	2	3	1
BCJ Cutting	not out		23	10	19	3	1	PM Nevill *+	not out		0	0	1
JJ Peirson +	c Nevill b Abbott		7	5	10		AJ Nair						
MG Neser	run out (Abbott)		1	3	2		MA Starc						
CJ Gannon	not out		0	0	1		SA Abbott						
MJ Swepson							NM Lyon						
BJ Doggett							DE Bollinger						
	5 lb, 1 nb, 5 w		11					6 lb, 1 nb, 7 w		14			
10 overs : 2-32	50 overs, 216 mins	282					10 overs : 0-61	48.5 overs, 189 mins	4-283			

Fall: 1-8 (Renshaw), 2-20 (Burns), 3-237 (Labuschagne), 4-248 (Khawaja), 5-251 (Heazlett,), 6-274 (Peirson), 7-276 (Neser)

Fall: 1-192 (Maddinson), 2-250 (Hughes), 3-279 (Gibson), 4-279 (Patterson)

NSW - bowling	O	M	R	W	wd	nb	Queensland - bowling	O	M	R	W	wd	nb
NM Lyon	10	1	36	1			BJ Doggett	8	0	58	1	2	
MA Starc	10	1	48	3	1		CJ Gannon	8.5	1	39	1	2	
DE Bollinger	10	0	49	0		1	MG Neser	9	0	48	1	1	1
SA Abbott	10	0	73	2	3		MJ Swepson	10	0	69	0		
AJ Nair	10	0	71	0	1		BCJ Cutting	3	0	20	0		
							MT Renshaw	10	0	43	0	2	

Toss: New South Wales   Umpires: GA Abood, JD Ward, Ref: DJ Harper.   Award: DP Hughes (NSW)   Crowd: 1,022

Match 18 – South Australia v Western Australia at Drummoyne Oval, Sydney on October 15, 2017 - SA won by 5 runs

Another high scoring affair, with three centuries made, South Australia's bowlers held their nerve to hang on for the win. Ferguson's 169 was his best score and South Australia's second best ever, behind Travis Head's 202 back in 2015-16 at Hurstville. At 2-60 in the 15th over, Klinger and Mitch Marsh combined to add 241 in 33 overs, leaving WA needing 30 off the last three overs. Klinger went to the first ball of the 48th, caught at deep square-leg, then next ball, Mitch Marsh was caught at long off, to put SA back on top. WA needed 18 off the last over and when Richardson hit Valente for six they got it down to 11 off three, but Valente keep his cool with three yorkers and SA got home by a handful of runs.

South Australia			B	M	4	6	Western Australia			B	M	4	6
JB Weatherald	c S Marsh b Richardson	11	11	13	2		M Klinger	c Weatherald b Sayers	143	138	191	10	2
AT Carey +	c Moody b Kelly	8	15	23	1		SE Marsh	c Ross b Mennie	29	42	50	4
CJ Ferguson *	c Cartwright b Richardson	169	138	177	23	2	CT Bancroft +	c Carey b Mennie	0	3	7
TLW Cooper	c M Marsh b Mackin	46	46	60	4	2	MR Marsh *	c Cooper b Sayers	124	101	133	8	5
AI Ross	b Kelly	6	22	28			AJ Turner	c Lehmann b Cooper	4	4	6
JS Lehmann	c Turner b Richardson	46	48	76	3	1	DJM Short	b Cooper	3	3	7
CT Valente	b Mackin	5	9	14			HWR Cartwright	not out	5	4	11
JM Mennie	not out	21	10	14	1	2	JA Richardson	not out	9	5	9	1
DJ Worrall	not out	1	2	3			ML Kelly					
TD Andrews							SP Mackin					
CJ Sayers							DJM Moody					
	(4 b, 2 lb, 1nb, 10 w)	17						1 b, 3 lb, 4 w	8			
10 overs : 2-48	50 overs, 210 mins	7-330					10 overs : 0-46	50 overs, 210 mins	6-325			

Fall: 1-13 (Weatherald), 2-31 (Carey), 3-138 (Cooper), 4-169 (Ross), 5-300 (Ferguson), 6-302 (Lehmann), 7-317 (Valente)

Fall: 1-56 (S Marsh), 2-60 (Bancroft), 3-301 (Klinger), 4-301 (M Marsh), 5-306 (Turner), 6-308 (Short)

WA - bowling	O	M	R	W	wd	nb	SA - bowling	O	M	R	W	wd	nb
ML Kelly	10	0	52	2	1		DJ Worrall	3.4	1	10	0		
JA Richardson	10	0	60	3	2		CJ Sayers	10	0	58	2		
SP Mackin	9	0	69	2	2		TD Andrews	10	0	70	0	1	
DJM Moody	4	0	36	0	2	1	TLW Cooper	6.2	0	40	2	1	
DJM Short	8	0	61	0			JM Mennie	10	1	58	2	1	
AJ Turner	4	0	20	0			CT Valente	10	0	85	0	1	
HWR Cartwright	5	0	26	0	2								

Toss: South Australia.   Umpires: SA Lightbody, P Wilson, Ref: RW Stratford   Award: CJ Ferguson (SA)   Crowd: 474

Australian Cricket Digest, 2018-19

Match 19 – New South Wales v Victoria at North Sydney Oval on October 15, 2017 (day/night)
Victoria won by 35 runs (BP) (DLS)

Under the lights, the match came to an early conclusion with the match officials and captains deciding the pitch conditions were too dangerous to continue under playing condition 2.7.2. Victoria needed 37 to win in 24 overs and were awarded the game on DLS, also gaining a bonus point in the process. The Cricket Australia website reported that the umpires had "raised concerns on the unevenness of the pitch throughout the first innings, and noted this at the interval". In what turned out to be the last three overs of the match, four or five balls jumped dangerously, including the last two balls of the 26th. NSW CEO Andrew Jones was less than impressed by what had happened and took to twitter to vent his displeasure. Days later he was reprimanded and handed a suspended fine by Cricket Australia.

New South Wales		B	M	4	6
DP Hughes	c Thomson b Boland	3	13	1	
NJ Maddinson	c Gotch b Tremain	28	47	62	5
KR Patterson	c Short b Tremain	14	35	44	2
RJ Gibson	b Sutherland	10	20	32	2
EJM Cowan	c Handscomb b Sutherland	13	13	17	3
PM Nevill +	lbw b Fawad	18	39	57	2
MA Starc	b Sutherland	6	12	22	1
PJ Cummins	b Fawad	8	16	16	1
SA Abbott	c Harris b Fawad	0	3	1	
WER Somerville	not out	9	22	42	1
DE Bollinger	b Sutherland	30	34	35	6
	5 w	5			
10 overs: 1-31	42.2 overs, 174 mins	144			

Victoria		B	M	4	6
MW Short	lbw b Bollinger	43	50	75	6	1
MS Harris	c Abbott b Starc	2	2	2	
TJ Dean	c Nevill b Starc	6	17	28	1
PSP Handscomb *+	c Cowan b Starc	0	7	10	
SE Gotch	not out	25	44	94	3
BR Thomson	not out	17	36	61	3
WJ Sutherland					
CP Tremain					
PM Siddle					
SM Boland					
Fawad Ahmed					
	4 b, 5 lb, 6 w	15			
10 overs: 3-41	26 overs, 137 mins	108			

Fall: 1-7 (Hughes), 2-47 (Patterson), 3-48 (Maddinson), 4-65 (Cowan), 5-73 (Gibson), 6-87 (Starc), 7-99 (Cummins), 8-99 (Abbott), 9-104 (Nevill), 10-144 (Bollinger)

Fall: 1-3 (Harris), 2-22 (Dean), 3-28 (Handscomb), 4-66 (Short)

Victoria - bowling	O	M	R	W	wd	nb
MW Short	5	0	13	0	1	
SM Boland	8	1	34	1	3	
PM Siddle	10	3	14	0		
CP Tremain	8	0	48	2		
WJ Sutherland	5.2	2	11	4		
Fawad Ahmed	6	1	24	3	1	

NSW - bowling	O	M	R	W	wd	nb
MA Starc	8	0	35	3	1	
PJ Cummins	8	2	24	0	1	
DE Bollinger	6	0	24	1		
SA Abbott	3	0	13	0		
WER Somerville	1	0	3	0		

Toss: New South Wales   Umpires: PJ Gillespie, JD Ward, Ref: DJ Harper   Award: WJ Sutherland (Vic)   Crowd: 2,084

Match 20 – Cricket Australia XI v Western Australia at North Sydney Oval on October 17, 2017
WA won by 9 wickets (BP)

Western Australia had a comfortable win to finish atop the JLT Cup ladder and qualify for the Final. Webster and Hinchliffe, who added 95 for the wicket, were the only batsmen to show their wares against the quality WA attack, with Mackin taking a maiden five wicket haul. WA altered their batting order and Darcy Short took full advantage to peel off a maiden List A ton, his fifty from just 39 balls and hundred off 79 as WA cruised home.

CA XI		B	M	4	6
JM Carder	c S Marsh b Tye	18	29	32	4
MA Bryant	c Bancroft b Richardson	9	17	25	1
BJ Webster *	c Klinger b Richardson	52	106	129	6
CD Hinchliffe	b Mackin	49	70	88	3	2
JA Merlo	lbw b Mackin	0	3	2	
HJ Nielsen +	b Mackin	0	2	6	
P Uppal	b Mackin	2	8	10	
HTRY Thornton	c Turner b Mackin	3	14	18	
MB Wright	c Richardson b Tye	12	21	32	1
MT Steketee	c Short b Kelly	22	21	29	1	1
DG Fallins	not out	1	2	4	
	7 lb, 1 nb, 3 w	11			
10 overs: 1-31	48.4 overs, 193 mins	179			

Western Australia		B	M	4	6
DJM Short	not out	119	92	115	13	6
HWR Cartwright	c Bryant b Webster	34	66	81	1
AJ Turner	not out	13	26	33	1
CT Bancroft +					
M Klinger					
MR Marsh *					
SE Marsh					
JA Richardson					
AJ Tye					
ML Kelly					
SP Mackin					
	4 lb, 2 nb, 10 w	16			
10 overs: 0-40	30.2 overs, 115 mins	1-182			

Fall: 1-25 (Bryant), 2-31 (Carder), 3-126 (Hinchliffe), 4-126 (Merlo), 5-128 (Nielsen), 6-139 (Uppal), 7-141 (Webster), 8-144 (Thornton), 9-177 (Wright), 10-179 (Steketee)

Fall: 1-109 (Cartwright)

WA - bowling	O	M	R	W	wd	nb
JA Richardson	10	0	29	2	2	
ML Kelly	9.4	1	42	1		
AJ Turner	4	0	20	0	1	
AJ Tye	9	2	21	2		
SP Mackin	10	0	33	5		1
DJM Short	6	0	27	0		

CA XI - bowling	O	M	R	W	wd	nb
MT Steketee	5	0	29	0	2	
HTRY Thornton	10	1	39	0	1	
JA Merlo	5	0	33	0	1	1
DG Fallins	4	0	32	0		
BJ Webster	4	0	17	1	1	
MB Wright	2.2	0	28	0		1

Toss: CA XI   Umpires: SAJ Craig, GC Joshua, Ref: DJ Harper   Award: SP Mackin (WA).   Crowd: 327

Match 21 – Tasmania v Queensland at Bellerive Oval, Hobart on October 17, 2017 (day/night)
Queensland won by 83 runs (BP)

After the early loss of Renshaw, consistent batting saw Queensland to a large total. It was also a tough day for Tasmanian keeper Matthew Wade, who put down two chances, and was later out aiming a pull-shot which took the back of his bat and was caught at short third man. Coming in at 7-171, Boyce rattled off Tasmania's fastest ever fifty (24 balls) which enabled them to push past 250.

Queensland		B	M	4	6
UT Khawaja *	c Silk b Boyce	41	51	77	4
MT Renshaw	c Wade b Fekete	5	9	18	1
M Labuschagne	b Milenko	64	79	106	6
SD Heazlett	c Faulkner b Milenko	72	65	101	4	3
JA Burns	b Faulkner	79	62	85	6	3
JJ Peirson +	c Dunk b Milenko	43	26	46	5
BCJ Cutting	c Boyce b Faulkner	8	4	26	1
JD Wildermuth	c Silk b Milenko	13	4	8	2
MG Neser	not out	0	1	6
CJ Gannon	not out	0	0	4
MJ Swepson					
	4 b, 1 lb, 1 nb, 8 w	14			
10 overs: 1-46	50 overs, 218 mins	8-339			

Fall: 1-21 (Renshaw), 2-80 (Khawaja), 3-145 (Labuschagne), 4-234 (Heazlett), 5-292 (Burns), 6-313 (Cutting), 7-326 (Peirson), 8-338 (Wildermuth)

Tasmania		B	M	4	6
TD Paine	c Peirson b Gannon	12	13	20	2
BR Dunk	c Peirson b Neser	0	3	1
AJ Doolan	b Neser	13	24	34	3
GJ Bailey *	b Swepson	62	77	112	8
MS Wade +	c Gannon b Swepson	38	46	74	2	2
JC Silk	c Peirson b Wildermuth	24	40	52	1
JP Faulkner	c sub (J Floros) b Swepson	15	19	23	1
SA Milenko	c sub (B Doggett) b Cutting	17	14	22	2
CJ Boyce	b Gannon	52	31	51	2	4
AL Fekete	lbw b Cutting	15	18	20	1	1
RP Meredith	not out	3	8	14
	5 w	5			
10 overs: 2-39	48.5 overs, 215 mins	256			

Fall: 1-3 (Dunk), 2-17 (Paine), 3-34 (Doolan), 4-110 (Wade), 5-137 (Bailey), 6-146 (Faulkner), 7-171 (Silk), 8-200 (Milenko), 9-246 (Fekete), 10-256 (Boyce)

Tasmania - bowling	O	M	R	W	wd	nb
AL Fekete	10	0	59	1	2	
RP Meredith	10	0	65	0	3	
BR Dunk	4	0	21	0		
JP Faulkner	10	0	71	2	1	1
CJ Boyce	6	0	38	1		
SA Milenko	10	0	80	4	2	

Queensland - bowling	O	M	R	W	wd	nb
MG Neser	10	3	27	2	1	
BCJ Cutting	10	0	81	2	1	
CJ Gannon	8.5	1	32	2	1	
JD Wildermuth	10	0	64	1	2	
MJ Swepson	10	0	52	3		

Toss: Queensland.   Umpires: GA Abood, SJ Nogajski, Ref: SR Bernard.   Award: MG Neser (Qld).   Crowd: 849

Preliminary Final – South Australia v Victoria at Bellerive Oval, Hobart on October 19, 2017 (day/night)
South Australia won by 176 runs (DLS)

With a dominant batting display, South Australia powered into the JLT Cup final with their biggest ever win in terms of a runs margin against Victoria. After being sent in, Carey and Weatherald reached 100 in the 21st over before really upping the ante, taking just 14 more overs to get to 200. Weatherald reached his ton (103 balls, 14x4, 1x6) in the 34th over and watched Carey edge behind in the 37th, with the pair just short of the SA first wicket record of 217 set by Darren Lehmann and Paul Nobes versus Tasmania at Adelaide Oval in 1994-95.

Rain came at 4.46pm, with SA 1-215 after 37.3 overs, a delay of 23 minutes reduced the game to 48 overs each. Ferguson went in the 41st over, but for the last seven overs, SA added an incredible 112, as Cooper blasted a 22-ball fifty, with Head and Ross doing their fair share of big hitting.

Victoria needed a good start, but lost Finch in the first over, bowled through the gate. From there it was one way traffic as SA progressed to the final.

South Australia		B	M	4	6
AT Carey +	c Handscomb b Boland	92	107	161	9	1
JB Weatherald	c Handscomb b Christian	116	121	174	15	1
CJ Ferguson	c Christian b Fawad	5	11	20
TM Head *	c Short b Siddle	29	16	34	2	2
TLW Cooper	c Tremain b Christian	59	24	33	8	2
AI Ross	not out	18	6	14	2
CT Valente	not out	5	4	7
DJ Worrall					
JM Mennie					
A Zampa					
KW Richardson					
	3 lb, 1 nb, 11 w	15			
10 overs: 0-39	48 overs, 196 mins	5-339			

Fall: 1-212 (Carey), 2-218 (Weatherald), 3-224 (Ferguson), 4-292 (Head), 5-313 (Cooper)

Victoria		B	M	4	6
MS Harris	c Carey b Worrall	11	19	23	1
AJ Finch	b Worrall	0	1	3
TJ Dean	b Valente	31	36	51	4
PSP Handscomb *+	c Cooper b Valente	12	14	25	2
GJ Maxwell	lbw b Zampa	12	24	36
MW Short	b Zampa	30	39	52	2	1
DT Christian	c Ross b Worrall	26	24	29	3
CP Tremain	b Worrall	27	31	37	2	1
PM Siddle	c Ross b Worrall	10	10	13	1
SM Boland	not out	3	11	21
Fawad Ahmed	b Zampa	0	6	4
	1 lb, 5 w	6			
10 overs: 2-51	35.5 overs, 152 mins	168			

Fall: 1-6 (Finch), 2-22 (Harris), 3-54 (Handscomb), 4-59 (Dean), 5-85 (Maxwell), 6-118 (Short), 7-128 (Christian), 8-145 (Siddle), 9-167 (Tremain), 10-168 (Fawad)

Victoria - bowling	O	M	R	W	wd	nb
MW Short	3	0	26	0	2	
SM Boland	10	0	51	1	1	
PM Siddle	10	0	76	1	2	1
CP Tremain	9	0	65	0	1	
DT Christian	10	0	69	2	2	
GJ Maxwell	2	0	20	0		
Fawad Ahmed	4	0	29	1		

SA - bowling	O	M	R	W	wd	nb
DJ Worrall	10	0	62	5	2	
KW Richardson	6	0	37	0	3	
JM Mennie	5	0	14	0		
CT Valente	5	0	23	2		
A Zampa	9.5	0	31	3		

Toss: Victoria. Umpires: GA Abood, SJ Nogajski, P Wilson (TV). Ref: SR Bernard Award: JB Weatherald (SA) Crowd: 222

THE FINAL – WESTERN AUSTRALIA v SOUTH AUSTRALIA

Having added a near record 212 for the first wicket two days ago, South Australia were two down inside five overs, as Weatherald edged a drive to the keeper and Carey was trapped in front. Ferguson put the foot down, hitting seven fours in a hurry before he was brilliantly caught behind, as Bancroft dived hard to his right. Head continued the aggressive approach from SA, and when Cooper whacked Short for a six over mid wicket in his first over, SA were well placed at 3-126 after 22 overs.

Richardson returned to the attack and splattered Head's stumps as he aimed a drive and when Ross gave a low catch to mid-wicket, SA were 5-154 in the 28th over. Cooper continued to fight the good fight, reaching his fifty (60 balls, 2x6 4x4) and with nine overs to go SA were 5-203 and hoping to reach at least 270. It wasn't to be as Cooper lofted one to deep square leg and Mennie was yorked in the next over. Valente lobbed a catch to mid-off and sadly for them SA could only manage 50 from the last ten overs, all WA bowlers playing their part, sharing the wickets, as well as bowling six maidens in the innings.

SA had a much needed early wicket, when Klinger cut a catch to backward point in the fifth over, but from there Shaun Marsh and Bancroft steadied things with a stand of 48 in nine overs. Marsh edged a drive to slip in the 14th over, but was replaced by his brother Mitch as he brilliantly off-drove his first ball to the rope. Bancroft survived a tough caught and bowled off Mennie on 23, then should have been caught by a diving Valente off Zampa on 27, which would have made WA 3-88 in the 18th over.

After that the pair dominated proceedings adding 126 in 20 overs, before Bancroft pulled a catch to forward square-leg. Turner took the pressure off his skipper, taking two fours and two sixes off the 38th over, and despite being out in the next over, WA cruised home, with Mitch Marsh on-driving for four to clinch the match and title for his team.

The Final – Western Australia v South Australia on October 21, 2017 – Western Australia won by 6 wickets

South Australia		B	M	4	6
AT Carey +	lbw b Behrendorff	16	18	21	3
JB Weatherald	c Bancroft b Coulter-Nile	4	7	15	1
CJ Ferguson	c Bancroft b Coulter-Nile	37	34	42	7
TM Head *	b Richardson	34	40	75	5
TLW Cooper	c Richardson b Short	63	84	117	5	2
AI Ross	c M Marsh b Short	14	17	24	1
CT Valente	c sub (J W Wells) b Tye	38	62	70	5
JM Mennie	b Richardson	0	4	3
A Zampa	c Cartwright b Tye	26	23	22	2	2
KW Richardson	not out	8	8	15	1
DJ Worrall	not out	2	3	6
	1 lb, 5 w	6			
10 overs: 2-55	50 overs, 209 mins	248			

Western Australia		B	M	4	6
SE Marsh	c Cooper b Mennie	32	41	53	5
M Klinger	c Weatherald b Worrall	1	12	15
CT Bancroft +	c Cooper b Richardson	76	83	121	7	1
MR Marsh *	not out	80	80	128	9	1
AJ Turner	b Zampa	35	24	21	5	2
HWR Cartwright	not out	15	23	21	3
DJM Short					
NM Coulter-Nile					
JA Richardson					
AJ Tye					
JP Behrendorff					
	4 lb, 1 nb, 6 w	11			
10 overs: 1-43	43.4 overs, 182 mins	4-250			

Fall: 1-17 (Weatherald), 2-21 (Carey), 3-72 (Ferguson), 4-127 (Head), 5-154 (Ross), 6-209 (Cooper), 7-209 (Mennie), 8-216 (Valente), 9-238 (Zampa)

Fall: 1-9 (Klinger), 2-57 (SE Marsh), 3-183 (Bancroft), 4-225 (Turner)

WA - bowling	O	M	R	W	wd	nb
JP Behrendorff	10	2	49	1	1	
NM Coulter-Nile	10	1	54	2	2	
JA Richardson	10	1	47	2	2	
AJ Tye	10	1	43	2		
DJM Short	9	1	47	2		
HWR Cartwright	1	0	7	0		

SA - bowling	O	M	R	W	wd	nb
DJ Worrall	10	3	58	1		1
KW Richardson	8.4	0	47	1	1	
JM Mennie	8	0	51	1	1	
CT Valente	7	0	31	0	1	
A Zampa	10	0	59	1	3	

Toss: South Australia Umpires: SJ Nogajski, P Wilson, GA Abood (TV), Ref: PL Marshall Award: MR Marsh (WA) Crowd: 767

2017-18 AVERAGES
Cricket Australia XI

Batting & Fielding	M	Inn	NO	Runs	HS	Avge	S/Rate	100s	50s	6s	Ct	St
HJ Nielsen	6	5	2	147	94	49.00	95.45	0	1	7	8	1
BJ Webster	6	6	0	247	121	41.16	69.57	1	1	3	4	-
JM Carder	6	6	0	200	102	33.33	74.34	1	1	2	0	-
CD Hinchliffe	6	6	1	150	49	30.00	67.26	0	0	7	1	-
M Bryant	6	6	0	168	89	28.00	107.00	0	2	6	4	-
JR Coleman	4	2	1	22	17	22.00	110.00	0	0	1	2	-
M Wright	3	2	0	42	30	21.00	60.86	0	0	2	0	-
MT Steketee	4	4	1	62	28	20.66	82.66	0	0	1	1	-
D Fallins	2	2	1	18	17	18.00	112.50	0	0	2	0	-
B Pengelley	5	4	0	71	53	17.75	100.00	0	1	4	1	-
P Uppal	6	6	1	83	32	16.60	63.35	0	0	0	0	-
J Merlo	4	3	0	38	20	12.66	67.85	0	0	1	1	-
HTRY Thornton	3	3	0	15	10	5.00	38.46	0	0	0	0	-
CH Stobo	2	2	2	49	25*	-	96.07	0	0	2	0	-

Also played: MP Kuhnemann (1 match) 14 (1 catch); DMK Grant (2 matches) did not bat, 1 catch.

Bowling	M	Overs	Mdns	Runs	Wkts	Avge	Econ	Best	4w	SR
CD Hinchliffe	6	29	1	189	6	31.50	6.51	4-71	1	29.0
JR Coleman	4	38	4	175	5	35.00	4.60	4-46	1	45.6
J Merlo	4	30.3	1	177	5	35.40	5.80	2-38	-	36.6
MT Steketee	4	31.4	1	192	5	38.40	6.06	3-48	-	38.0
B Pengelley	5	23	0	151	2	75.50	6.56	1-27	-	69.0
HTRY Thornton	3	20	1	158	2	79.00	5.64	2-79	-	79.0
D Fallins	2	11	0	83	1	83.00	7.54	1-51	-	66.0
CH Stobo	2	15	0	89	1	89.00	5.93	1-32	-	90.0
DMK Grant	2	18	0	108	1	108.00	6.00	1-63	-	108.0
BJ Webster	6	24	2	127	1	127.00	5.29	1-17	-	144.0
M Wright	3	9.2	0	88	0	-	9.42	-	-	-

Also bowled: MP Kuhnemann (1 match) 5-0-33-1; P Uppal (6 matches) 5-0-24-0.

New South Wales

Batting & Fielding	M	Inn	NO	Runs	HS	Avge	S/Rate	100s	50s	6s	Ct	St
NJ Maddison	6	6	0	398	137	66.33	96.13	2	1	9	2	-
DP Hughes	6	6	0	379	122	63.16	90.45	2	2	9	3	-
KR Patterson	6	6	0	248	84	41.33	85.81	0	2	8	1	-
EJM Cowan	6	6	2	146	53	36.50	105.79	0	2	0	2	-
DE Bollinger	3	2	1	34	30	34.00	87.17	0	0	1	0	-
PM Nevill	6	6	1	94	24	18.80	93.06	0	0	0	17	2
RJ Gibson	5	5	0	93	51	18.60	85.32	0	1	3	1	-
MA Starc	3	2	0	29	23	14.50	87.87	0	0	2	0	-
MW Edwards	4	2	0	21	11	10.50	77.77	0	0	1	1	-
GS Sandhu	3	3	1	19	15	9.50	82.60	0	0	1	1	-
NM Lyon	5	3	1	14	8*	7.00	87.50	0	0	1	0	-
SA Abbott	6	5	0	6	5	1.20	33.33	0	0	0	3	-
HNA Conway	3	2	2	10	10*	-	111.11	0	0	0	2	-

Also played: PJ Cummins (1 match) 8; MC Henriques (1 match) 72 (1 catch), AJ Nair (1 match) did not bat, WER Somerville (1 match) 9*.

Bowling	M	Overs	Mdns	Runs	Wkts	Avge	Econ	Best	4w	SR
MA Starc	3	28	1	138	7	19.71	4.92	3-35	0	24.0
SA Abbott	6	49.2	1	297	12	24.75	6.02	3-29	0	24.6
GS Sandhu	3	22	2	135	5	27.00	6.13	4-57	1	26.4
NM Lyon	5	49	4	245	9	27.22	5.00	3-58	0	32.6
DE Bollinger	3	26	0	135	4	33.75	5.19	3-62	0	39.0
MW Edwards	4	34	3	177	5	35.40	5.20	4-31	0	40.8
HNA Conway	3	26	1	172	2	86.50	6.65	2-49	0	86.5

Also bowled: PJ Cummins (1 match) 8-2-24-0, MC Henriques (1 match) 2-0-13-0, NJ Maddison (6 matches) 1-0-6-1 (Best 1-1), AJ Nair (1 match) 10-0-71-0, WER Somerville (1 match) 1-0-3-0.

Australian Cricket Digest, 2018-19

Queensland

Batting & Fielding	M	Inn	NO	Runs	HS	Avge	S/Rate	100s	50s	6s	Ct	St
UT Khawaja	6	6	0	380	138	63.33	94.52	1	2	6	0	-
MG Neser	6	6	3	153	122	51.00	119.53	1	0	7	3	-
M Labuschagne	6	6	0	291	91	48.50	88.71	0	4	3	2	-
SD Heazlett	2	2	0	75	72	37.50	101.35	0	1	3	0	-
JJ Peirson	6	6	0	186	60	31.00	103.91	0	1	2	10	0
JA Burns	6	6	0	185	79	30.83	95.85	0	1	7	3	-
CJ Gannon	5	3	2	27	27	27.00	158.82	0	0	2	2	-
MT Renshaw	6	6	0	151	74	25.16	70.56	0	2	1	1	-
MJ Swepson	6	2	1	25	23*	25.00	113.63	0	0	0	2	-
BCJ Cutting	6	6	2	81	39*	20.25	150.00	0	0	4	2	-
JS Floros	2	1	0	10	10	10.00	62.50	0	0	0	0	-
JD Wildermuth	5	5	1	22	13	5.50	75.86	0	0	2	1	-
B Doggett	4	2	2	1	1*	-	16.66	0	0	0	3	-

Bowling	M	Overs	Mdns	Runs	Wkts	Avge	Econ	Best	4w	SR
CJ Gannon	5	42.2	3	216	7	30.85	5.10	2-32	0	36.2
JD Wildermuth	5	35	0	194	6	32.33	5.54	4-39	1	35.0
MG Neser	6	55	4	284	8	35.50	5.16	2-27	0	41.2
B Doggett	4	36	4	223	5	44.60	6.19	2-46	0	43.2
BCJ Cutting	6	43	2	289	7	41.28	6.72	2-41	0	36.8
MJ Swepson	6	52	1	305	6	50.83	5.86	3-52	0	52.0
JS Floros	2	12	0	51	1	51.00	4.25	1-44	0	72.0

Also bowled: M Labuschagne (6 matches) 1-0-8-0, MT Renshaw (2 matches) 12-0-54-0.

South Australia

Batting & Fielding	M	Inn	NO	Runs	HS	Avge	S/Rate	100s	50s	6s	Ct	St
TLW Cooper	8	8	1	344	115*	49.14	103.92	1	2	11	8	-
CJ Ferguson	8	8	0	358	169	44.75	98.62	1	1	2	3	-
JB Weatherald	8	8	0	337	116	42.12	96.01	2	1	4	3	-
CT Valente	8	8	2	224	100	37.33	74.17	1	0	8	1	-
JS Lehmann	6	6	1	179	63*	35.80	110.49	0	1	6	7	-
AT Carey	8	8	0	265	92	33.12	77.48	0	2	6	8	0
AI Ross	8	8	1	224	110	32.00	99.11	1	0	11	3	-
TM Head	2	2	0	63	34	31.50	112.50	0	0	2	0	-
JM Mennie	7	6	3	86	43*	28.66	106.17	0	0	4	0	-
DJ Worrall	8	3	2	19	16	19.00	79.16	0	0	0	3	-
NP Winter	4	3	2	10	7*	10.00	41.66	0	0	0	0	-
MJA Cormack	4	3	1	18	15	9.00	56.25	0	0	0	0	-

Also played: TJ Andrews (2 matches) 7, SH Johnson (1 match) did not bat, KW Richardson (2 matches) 8*, CJ Sayers (2 matches) did not bat; 1 catch, A Zampa (2 matches) 26.

Bowling	M	Overs	Mdns	Runs	Wkts	Avge	Econ	Best	4w	SR
A Zampa	2	19.5	0	90	4	22.50	4.53	3-31	0	29.7
JM Mennie	7	62.5	3	293	13	22.53	4.66	5-36	2	29.0
TLW Cooper	8	15	0	106	4	26.50	7.06	2-40	0	22.5
DJ Worrall	8	70.4	8	394	12	32.83	5.57	5-62	1	35.3
CJ Sayers	2	20	0	132	3	44.00	6.60	2-58	0	40.0
CT Valente	8	65	1	360	8	45.00	5.53	3-54	0	48.7
NP Winter	4	30	1	230	5	46.00	7.66	2-94	0	36.0
MJA Cormack	4	35	0	211	3	70.33	6.02	2-52	0	70.0
KW Richardson	2	14.4	0	84	1	84.00	5.72	1-47	0	88.0
TD Andrews	2	19.5	0	121	1	121.00	6.10	1-51	0	119.0

Also bowled: SH Johnson (1 match) 10-0-72-1

Australian Cricket Digest, 2018-19

Tasmania

Batting & Fielding	M	Inn	NO	Runs	HS	Avge	S/Rate	100s	50s	6s	Ct	St
GJ Bailey	6	6	0	373	126	62.16	105.96	1	3	15	1	-
T Rogers	3	2	1	47	38	47.00	73.43	0	0	0	5	-
MS Wade	3	3	0	123	46	41.00	114.95	0	0	10	3	0
BR McDermott	5	5	0	173	97	34.60	72.99	0	1	7	1	-
JC Silk	6	6	0	188	80	31.33	92.15	0	2	2	5	-
AJ Doolan	6	6	0	172	83	28.66	69.91	0	2	1	2	-
CJ Boyce	6	4	0	88	52	22.00	133.33	0	1	5	3	-
JP Faulkner	4	4	1	61	34*	20.33	73.49	0	0	2	1	-
BR Dunk	6	6	0	118	45	19.66	77.63	0	0	2	3	2
ST Milenko	4	4	1	52	30	17.33	80.00	0	0	0	1	-
AL Fekete	3	3	1	25	15	12.50	73.52	0	0	1	0	-
JM Bird	2	2	0	21	16	10.50	91.30	0	0	0	0	-
RP Meredith	6	4	3	7	3*	7.00	26.92	0	0	0	1	-
CA Wakim	3	3	0	12	6	4.00	42.85	0	0	0	2	-

Also played: ND Buchanan (1 match) did not bat, 1 catch, TD Paine (1 match) 12, SL Rainbird (1 match) 4.

Tasmania bowling

Bowling	M	Overs	Mdns	Runs	Wkts	Ave	Econ	Best	4w	SR
BR Dunk	6	13.2	0	54	5	10.80	4.05	3-14	0	16.0
AL Fekete	3	30	3	172	6	28.66	5.73	4-48	1	30.0
CJ Boyce	6	55	2	297	10	29.70	5.40	3-27	0	33.0
JP Faulkner	4	33.2	3	185	5	37.00	5.55	2-42	0	40.0
JM Bird	2	20	0	111	3	37.00	5.55	2-62	0	40.0
ST Milenko	4	38	0	267	6	44.50	7.02	4-80	1	38.0
RP Meredith	6	50	1	267	5	53.40	5.34	2-26	0	60.0
T Rogers	1	20	1	121	1	121.00	6.05	1-35	0	120.0

Also bowled: ND Buchanan (1 match) 7-0-43-1. SL Rainbird (1 match) 5.4-0-59-0

Victoria

Batting & Fielding	M	Inn	NO	Runs	HS	Avge	S/Rate	100s	50s	6s	Ct	St
SE Gotch	6	6	2	201	61	50.25	82.37	0	2	5	3	-
CL White	4	4	0	199	165	49.75	89.63	1	0	6	3	-
PSP Handscomb	5	5	1	184	103*	46.00	117.94	1	0	9	9	2
MW Short	6	5	0	219	81	43.80	95.63	0	2	7	5	-
PM Siddle	7	4	1	124	62	41.33	131.91	0	1	4	0	-
BR Thomson	3	2	1	41	24	41.00	65.07	0	0	0	3	-
TJ Dean	7	7	0	270	119	38.57	88.23	1	0	2	3	-
MS Harris	7	7	0	194	75	27.71	101.57	0	1	7	2	-
CP Tremain	7	5	1	98	50	24.50	94.23	0	1	6	5	-
DT Christian	2	2	0	40	26	20.00	95.23	0	0	1	1	-
SB Harper	2	2	1	17	11	17.00	106.25	0	0	0	1	-
SM Boland	7	4	2	24	12	12.00	58.53	0	0	1	0	-
WJ Pucovski	3	3	0	20	15	6.66	50.00	0	0	0	0	-
W Sutherland	2	1	0	1	1	1.00	100.00	0	0	0	0	-
Fawad Ahmed	7	3	2	0	0*	-	0.00	0	0	0	0	-

Also batted: AJ Finch (1 match) 0, GJ Maxwell (1 match) 12.

Bowling	M	Overs	Mdns	Runs	Wkts	Avge	Econ	Best	4w	SR
W Sutherland	2	13.2	3	67	5	13.40	5.02	4-11	1	16.0
Fawad Ahmed	7	59	1	322	12	26.83	5.45	3-24	0	29.5
PM Siddle	7	70	8	277	9	30.77	3.95	3-27	0	46.6
CP Tremain	7	66	3	398	12	33.16	6.03	3-50	0	33.0
CL White	4	8.4	0	57	1	57.00	6.57	1-16	0	52.0
SM Boland	7	61	3	381	6	63.50	6.24	1-32	0	61.0
MW Short	6	36	2	191	3	63.66	5.30	2-59	0	72.0
DT Christian	2	20	0	132	2	66.00	6.60	2-69	0	60.0

Also bowled: BR Thomson (1 match) 0.2-0-0-0, GJ Maxwell (1 match) 2-0-20-0,

Australian Cricket Digest, 2018-19
Western Australia

Batting & Fielding	M	Inn	NO	Runs	HS	Avge	S/Rate	100s	50s	6s	Ct	St
MR Marsh	7	6	4	338	124	169.00	111.55	1	2	9	6	-
JW Wells	2	2	1	91	57	91.00	91.00	0	1	0	0	-
SE Marsh	7	6	1	412	132*	82.40	87.47	1	3	1	2	-
DJM Short	7	3	1	132	119*	66.00	126.92	1	0	6	2	-
M Klinger	7	6	0	337	143	56.16	85.96	2	0	8	5	-
HWR Cartwright	5	3	2	54	34	54.00	58.06	0	0	0	2	-
CT Bancroft	7	6	1	265	76	53.00	103.92	0	3	4	10	1
JA Richardson	7	2	1	26	17	26.00	136.84	0	0	1	4	-
AJ Turner	7	6	2	68	35	17.00	90.66	0	0	2	4	-

Also played: JP Behrendorff (3 matches) 0, 1 catch; NM Coulter-Nile (1 match) did not bat, DJM Moody (5 matches), 1*, 2 catches; M Kelly (4 matches) did not bat, 2 catches, SP Mackin (4 matches) did not bat.

Bowling	M	Overs	Mdns	Runs	Wkts	Avge	Econ	Best	4w	SR
AJ Tye	4	37.5	3	156	9	17.33	4.12	3-37	0	25.2
M Kelly	4	36.4	4	158	8	19.75	4.30	4-25	1	27.5
SP Mackin	4	37	2	193	9	21.44	5.21	5-33	1	24.6
JP Behrendorff	3	27.2	2	126	5	25.20	4.60	3-34	0	32.8
JA Richardson	7	69	3	356	13	27.38	5.15	3-60	0	31.8
DJM Short	7	57	2	305	9	33.88	5.35	3-53	0	38.0
DJM Moody	5	33.5	0	215	6	35.83	6.35	3-47	0	33.8
HWR Cartwright	5	12	0	75	1	75.00	6.25	1-13	0	72.0
AJ Turner	7	15	0	84	0	-	5.60	-	0	-

Also Bowled: NM Coulter-Nile (1 match) 10-1-54-2,

CAREER RECORDS FOR PLAYERS IN DOMESTIC ONE DAY CRICKET (TO END OF 2017-18 SEASON)

	M	Runs	HS	Avge	S/R	H/F	C/S	Wkt	Avge	Eco	Best	4w
SA Abbott	36	343	50	15.5	96.8	0/1	17	55	25.0	5.52	3-29	-
AC Agar	20	283	64	25.7	102.5	0/1	10	20	38.8	5.11	3-8	-
WA Agar	5	2	1*	-	25.0	0/0	1	8	32.1	5.84	3-38	-
TD Andrews	15	57	9	6.3	64.0	0/0	7	16	42.6	5.42	4-41	1
GJ Bailey	116	3488	126	35.5	83.8	5/21	45	1	40.0	4.62	1-19	-
CT Bancroft	30	911	176	36.4	82.7	1/7	20					
JP Behrendorff	33	110	24*	10.0	51.6	0/0	8	38	31.4	4.72	5-27	1
JM Bird	20	40	16	8.0	108.1	0/0	8	20	44.5	5.00	3-39	-
SM Boland	35	86	19	7.8	65.6	0/0	4	41	41.2	5.60	5-63	2
DE Bollinger	72	97	30	13.8	65.9	0/0	11	100	30.3	4.77	4-24	5
WG Bosisto	13	386	86	29.6	73.5	0/3	5	1	63.0	7.00	1-19	-
CJ Boyce	28	174	52	17.4	122.5	0/1	14	33	35.0	5.62	4-55	1
M Bryant	6	168	89	28.0	107.0	0/2	4					
ND Buchanan	1	0	-	-	-	0/0	1	1	43.0	6.14	1-43	-
JA Burns	42	1281	115	33.7	79.8	1/8	18					
JM Carder	11	367	102	33.3	89.2	1/2	1					
AT Carey	15	456	92	30.4	73.6	0/3	16/1					
HWR Cartwright	27	491	99	24.5	79.7	0/2	9	9	46.33	6.00	2-14	-
DT Christian	84	1988	117	31.5	98.5	2/7	28	71	36.51	5.62	6-48	2
JR Coleman	6	25	17	25.0	86.2	0/0	2	8	30.0	5.14	4-46	1
HNA Conway	4	10	10*	-	111.1	0/0	3	3	71.6	6.17	2-49	-
TLW Cooper	73	2541	115*	39.0	85.0	5/18	38	4	38.5	6.16	2-40	-
TA Copeland	21	75	23	9.3	79.7	0/0	5	25	39.0	5.22	5-44	1
MJA Cormack	6	18	15	9.0	56.2	0/0	0	5	64.8	6.11	2-52	-
NM Coulter-Nile	28	292	53*	20.8	89.3	0/1	13	56	22.8	4.90	5-26	4
EJM Cowan	87	2804	131*	40.0	72.6	4/22	26					
PJ Cummins	14	99	38	19.8	79.8	0/0	7	25	24.3	5.13	4-26	2
BCJ Cutting	57	704	98*	19.5	119.5	0/2	14	79	32.6	5.40	4-50	4
TJ Dean	7	270	119	38.5	88.2	1/0	3					
B Doggett	8	22	11	7.3	43.1	0/0	4	11	41.2	6.47	2-36	-
AJ Doolan	27	908	93	41.2	76.8	0/7	8					
JR Doran	10	126	34*	25.2	67.7	0/0	6					
BR Dunk	44	1347	229*	33.6	87.4	3/6	28/3	5	15.4	4.44	3-14	-
BJ Dwarshuis	1	-	-	-	-	0/0	0	1	44.0	8.25	1-44	-
MW Edwards	4	21	11	10.5	77.7	0/0	1	5	35.4	5.21	4-31	1
D Fallins	2	18	17	18.0	112.5	0/0	0	1	83.0	7.55	1-51	-
JP Faulkner	45	810	76	27.9	84.9	0/6	12	64	29.6	5.17	4-20	4
Fawad Ahmed	19	5	4*	2.5	23.8	0/0	3	29	27.5	5.04	4-38	2
AL Fekete	21	50	15	16.6	67.5	0/0	2	31	29.1	5.15	4-30	3
LW Feldman	28	145	33	24.1	140.7	0/0	4	27	39.3	5.07	5-57	2
CJ Ferguson	97	3268	169	38.9	85.7	7/19	26	1	8.0	2.67	1-8	-

Australian Cricket Digest, 2018-19

Career records	M	Runs	HS	Avge	S/R	H/F	C/S	Wkt	Avge	Econ	Best	4w
AJ Finch	56	1944	154	38.1	87.4	2/14	20	1	38.0	5.85	1-2	-
JS Floros	27	376	68*	25.0	85.0	0/2	16	17	34.8	5.03	3-37	-
PJ Forrest	44	986	98	26.6	68.1	0/6	24	0		4.50	-	-
CJ Gannon	19	108	28	18.0	75.0	0/0	8	30	26.5	4.54	5-38	2
PR George	22	11	4*	5.5	33.3	0/0	7	25	37.7	4.87	5-39	1
RJ Gibson	11	386	106	35.5	86.9	1/3	0					
SE Gotch	11	270	61	30.0	74.3	0/2	5					
DMK Grant	3	0	-	-	-	-	1	3	50.6	5.43	2-44	-
CJ Green	4	40	15	20.0	61.5	0/0	1	1	103.0	4.51	1-11	-
AJ Gregory	9	95	42*	19.0	63.3	0/0	4	4	46.5	6.00	2-39	-
EP Gulbis	33	636	63	27.6	86.7	0/4	11	36	25.7	4.91	4-8	4
PSP Handscomb	44	1020	103*	30.9	80.4	1/3	42/4					
SB Harper	8	111	48	15.8	130.5	0/0	5					
MS Harris	30	813	84	28.0	83.6	0/4	8					
JR Hazlewood	37	50	17	4.5	52.6	0/0	8	56	29.8	4.79	7-36	2
TM Head	20	604	202	31.7	109.8	1/1	8	4	48.0	5.82	2-9	-
SD Heazlett	2	75	72	37.5	101.3	0/1	0					
CR Hemphrey	6	97	26	16.1	58.7	0/0	1	1	67.0	3.94	1-18	-
MC Henriques	68	1907	164*	36.6	88.0	2/7	28	54	44.8	5.08	4-17	1
CD Hinchliffe	6	150	49	30.0	67.2	0/0	1	6	31.5	6.52	4-71	1
JM Holland	47	136	14	9.0	59.1	0/0	13	60	31.7	4.77	6-29	2
DP Hughes	14	782	122	65.1	88.0	3/4	6					
JP Inglis	6	187	68	31.1	119.1	0/2	1/1					
SH Johnson	1	0	-	-	-	0/0	0	1	72.0	7.20	1-72	-
UT Khawaja	42	2246	166	53.3	87.8	7/12	16					
M Klinger	129	5124	143	43.7	73.8	12/30	44					
MP Kuhnemann	1	14	14	14.0	107.6	0/0	1	1	33.0	6.60	1-33	-
M Labuschagnex	16	591	91	39.4	86.4	0/7	6	0		8.00		-
JS Lehmann	20	425	63*	25.0	79.5	0/2	9					
CA Lynn	28	771	98	32.1	88.9	0/6	13	1	45.0	3.91	1-3	-
NM Lyon	36	121	37*	11.0	108.0	0/0	16	42	37.6	4.78	4-10	2
BR McDermott	7	225	97	32.1	70.3	0/0	3					
SP Mackin	6			-	-	0	0	10	28.5	5.48	5-33	1
NJ Maddinson	56	1949	137	38.0	89.4	5/9	26	2	141.0	5.04	1-36	-
MR Marsh	37	1190	124	44.0	95.2	2/7	21	19	30.4	5.21	4-40	1
SE Marsh	76	2960	186	42.9	78.8	8/15	29	1	31.0	5.17	1-14	-
GJ Maxwell	32	659	67	26.3	110.0	0/5	19	21	30.2	4.91	3-30	-
JM Mennie	29	257	43*	16.0	87.1	0/0	4	34	36.8	5.06	5-36	3
RP Meredith	6	7	3*	7.0	26.9	0/0	1	5	53.4	5.34	2-26	-
J Merlo	4	38	20	12.6	67.8	0/0	1					
S Milenko	17	264	54	24.0	79.5	0/1	5	19	38.8	6.41	4-80	1
DJM Moody	8	2	1*	-	50.0	0/0	3	8	41.2	6.25	3-47	-
AJ Nair	6	77	67	25.6	77.0	0/1	1	11	29.1	6.29	3-15	-
MG Neser	34	480	122	30.0	86.3	1/1	11	37	37.2	5.24	4-41	2
PM Nevill	61	993	74	22.5	76.5	0/5	87/9					
HJ Nielsen	6	147	94	49.0	85.4	0/1	8/1					
SNJ O'Keefe	43	563	70*	26.8	85.4	0/1	19	25	58.0	4.92	3-65	-
TD Paine	76	2437	125	37.4	70.4	6/10	89/12					
JS Paris	13	39	16*	39.0	51.3	0/0	6	24	17.7	4.38	4-13	1
KR Patterson	29	877	84	36.5	77.1	0/5	12					
JL Pattinson	22	181	44	13.9	75.7	0/0	3	44	22.5	4.86	6-48	3
JJ Peirson	22	540	85	24.5	84.1	0/3	15/3					
WJ Pucovski	3	20	15	6.6	50.0	0/0	0					
SL Rainbird	15	28	9*	4.0	59.5	0/0	3	17	36.4	5.32	5-29	1
MT Renshaw	8	277	88	39.5	75.4	0/3	2					
JA Richardson	8	30	17	15.0	130.4	0/0	5	13	30.0	5.20	3-60	-
KW Richardson	39	250	36	10.8	85.6	0/0	6	64	28.6	5.15	6-48	5
TS Rogers	3	47	38	47.0	73.4	0/0	5	1	121.0	6.05	1-35	-
AI Ross	36	871	110	31.1	83.4	1/5	16					
GS Sandhu	30	114	16	12.6	60.3	0/0	7	58	22.5	5.04	5-35	3
JJS Sangha	1	8	8	8.0	53.3	0/0	1	0		7.00		-
CJ Sayers	12	23	14	5.7	50.0	0/0	2	9	65.0	5.22	2-41	-
DJM Short	12	228	119*	32.5	107.0	1/1	4	12	33.7	5.19	3-53	-
MW Short	20	447	81	27.9	92.1	0/2	8	8	71.7	5.63	2-48	-
PM Siddle	33	206	62	13.7	108.4	0/1	5	40	33.0	4.51	4-27	1
JC Silk	20	484	80	28.4	80.9	0/5	8	0		6.25		-
SPD Smith	43	1726	143*	55.6	87.9	2/13	27	19	42.4	5.41	3-43	-
WER Somerville	1	9	9*	-	40.9	0/0	0	0		3.00		-
B Stanlake	4	1	1	0.5	5.8	0/0	2	7	25.4	5.09	4-37	1
MA Starc	19	112	34*	22.4	90.3	0/0	4	58	14.5	4.64	6-25	7
MT Steketee	15	118	30*	19.6	88.0	0/0	5	23	24.4	5.34	4-29	2
CH Stobo	2	49	25*	-	96.0	0/0	0	1	89.0	5.93	1-32	-

Australian Cricket Digest, 2018-19

Career Stats	M	Runs	HS	Avge	S/R	H/F	C/S	Wkt	Avge	Econ	Best	4w
MP Stoinis	27	687	109	27.4	70.9	1/6	7	16	40.0	5.33	4-43	1
W Sutherland	2	1	1	1.0	100.0	0/0	0	5	13.4	5.03	4-11	1
MJ Swepson	18	52	23*	10.4	92.8	0/0	9	14	53.5	5.50	3-52	-
BR Thomson	3	41	24	41.0	65.0	0/0	3	0		0.00		
HTRY Thornton	3	15	10	5.0	38.4	0/0	0	2	79.0	5.64	2-79	-
CP Tremain	12	140	50	20.0	83.3	0/1	5	14	43.4	5.68	3-50	-
AJ Turner	17	284	51	28.4	97.5	0/1	7	4	64.2	5.71	2-26	-
AJ Tye	24	135	28*	15.0	108.8	0/0	8	50	21.3	5.37	5-46	3
P Uppal	6	83	32	16.6	63.3	0/0	0	0		4.80		-
CT Valente	14	386	100	35.0	80.7	2/0	4	23	26.5	5.32	4-49	1
MS Wade	57	1848	120	37.7	85.3	4/9	61/9					
DA Warner	35	1416	197	42.9	106.3	4/4	11	3	39.3	5.90	1-11	-
JB Weatherald	14	621	141	44.3	101.4	3/1	5					
BJ Webster	12	334	121	33.4	69.5	1/1	5	2	107.5	5.24	1-17	-
JW Wells	30	678	121*	30.8	77.5	2/2	9	1	36.0	5.14	1-6	-
CL White	113	3311	165	36.7	80.7	6/20	50	57	39.0	5.32	4-15	3
SM Whiteman	33	518	74	20.7	66.3	0/2	29/3					
JD Wildermuth	10	46	13	5.1	59.7	0/0	2	12	35.1	5.40	4-39	1
NP Winter	6	11	7*	11.0	44.0	0/0	0	5	70.8	7.70	2-94	-
DJ Worrall	16	34	16	17.0	68.0	0/0	5	20	36.2	5.17	5-62	1
M Wright	2	42	30	21.0	60.8	0/0	0	0		10.26		-
A Zampa	25	329	66	20.5	110.0	0/2	5	36	31.7	5.07	4-18	2

DOMESTIC ONE DAY FINALISTS

Season	Winner	Runner-up	Season	Winner	Runner-up
1969-70	New Zealand	Victoria	1994-95	Victoria	South Australia
1970-71	Western Australia	Queensland	1995-96	Queensland	Western Australia
1971-72	Victoria	South Australia	1996-97	Western Australia	Queensland
1972-73	New Zealand	Queensland	1997-98	Queensland	New South Wales
1973-74	Western Australia	New Zealand	1998-99	Victoria	New South Wales
1974-75	New Zealand	Western Australia	1999-2000	Western Australia	Queensland
1975-76	Queensland	Western Australia	2000-01	New South Wales	Western Australia
1976-77	Western Australia	Victoria	2001-02	New South Wales	Queensland
1977-78	Western Australia	Tasmania	2002-03	New South Wales	Western Australia
1978-79	Tasmania	Western Australia	2003-04	Western Australia	Queensland
1979-80	Victoria	New South Wales	2004-05	Tasmania	Queensland
1980-81	Queensland	Western Australia	2005-06	New South Wales	South Australia
1981-82	Queensland	New South Wales	2006-07	Queensland	Victoria
1982-83	Western Australia	New South Wales	2007-08	Tasmania	Victoria
1983-84	South Australia	Western Australia	2008-09	Queensland	Victoria
1984-85	New South Wales	South Australia	2009-10	Tasmania	Victoria
1985-86	Western Australia	Victoria	2010-11	Victoria	Tasmania
1986-87	South Australia	Tasmania	2011-12	South Australia	Tasmania
1987-88	New South Wales	South Australia	2012-13	Queensland	Victoria
1988-89	Queensland	Victoria	2013-14	Queensland	New South Wales
1989-90	Western Australia	South Australia	2014-15	Western Australia	New South Wales
1990-91	Western Australia	New South Wales	2015-16	New South Wales	South Australia
1991-92	New South Wales	Western Australia	2016-17	New South Wales	Queensland
1992-93	New South Wales	Victoria	2017-18	Western Australia	South Australia
1993-94	New South Wales	Western Australia			

Titles won: Western Australia 13, New South Wales 11, Queensland 10, Victoria 5, Tasmania 4, South Australia 3, New Zealand 3, Cricket Australia 0

How teams have finished in the recent seasons

State	17/18	16/17	15/16	14/15	13/14	12/13	11/12	10/11	09/10	08/09
New South Wales	4	1	1	2	2	4	3	3	4	6
Queensland	5	2	6	3	1	1	4	6	3	1
South Australia	2	6	2	6	6	3	1	5	6	3
Tasmania	6	5	4	4	4	5	2	2	1	4
Victoria	3	3	3	5	3	2	5	1	2	2
W Australia	1	4	5	1	5	6	6	4	5	5
Cricket Aust XI	7	7	7							

Australian Cricket Digest, 2018-19

OVERALL RECORDS

	M	W	L	T	NR	Titles	R-up
A.C.T	18	3	15	0	0	0	0
Cricket Aust XI	18	2	16	0	0	0	0
New South Wales	272	150	116	4	2	11	8
New Zealand	10	7	3	0	0	3	1
Queensland	272	151	116	0	5	10	8
South Australia	265	112	148	4	1	3	8
Tasmania	249	94	146	4	5	4	4
Victoria	274	132	134	2	6	5	10
Western Australia	286	161	118	2	5	13	10

Highest Team Totals

Total	for	v..	Season	Venue
7-420	SA	CA XI	2016-17	Hurstville
4-405	Qld	WA	2003-04	Gabba
3-402	Qld	Tas	2014-15	Nth Sydney
1-398	Tas	Qld	2014-15	Nth Sydney
4-397	NSW	Tas	2001-02	Bankstown
2-379	Vic	Qld	2012-13	Gabba
5-372	Qld	Vic	2014-15	Nth Sydney
6-356	**SA**	**Vic**	**2017-18**	**Nth Sydney**
4-354	SA	WA	2015-16	Hurstville
4-352	Vic	NSW	2012-13	Nth Sydney
8-352	Vic	NSW	2007-08	SCG

Lowest Team Totals

Total	for	v..	Season	Venue
51	SA	Tas	2002-03	Bellerive
59	CA	NSW	2015-16	Bankstown
59	WA	NZ	1969-70	MCG
62	Qld	WA	1976-77	WACA
62	Tas	WA	2014-15	Gabba
65	Vic	Qld	2002-03	Ballarat
76	WA	NZ	1974-75	MCG
77	WA	Qld	1976-77	WACA
78	Vic	Qld	1989-90	Gabba
79	CA XI	Vic	2015-16	Hurstville

Leading Run Scorers

	for	M	Inn	NO	Runs	HS	Ave	SR	100	50s	0s	Sixes
BJ Hodge	Vic	139	137	18	5597	144	47.03	81.0	20	25	8	64
M Klinger	**Vic/SA/WA**	**129**	**128**	**11**	**5124**	**140***	**43.79**	**73.8**	**12**	**30**	**7**	**57**
JP Maher	Qld	112	112	10	4589	187	44.99	75.0	10	25	0	34
DS Lehmann	SA/Vic	98	96	15	4155	142*	51.30	87.5	7	31	6	30
MTG Elliott	Vic/SA	103	101	10	3804	146	41.80	74.2	10	22	8	34
DJ Hussey	Vic	101	96	15	3546	140*	43.78	93.9	6	25	3	87
GS Blewett	SA	100	98	9	3544	125	39.82	68.5	6	19	5	26
GJ Bailey	**Tas**	**116**	**109**	**11**	**3546**	**126**	**35.59**	**83.8**	**5**	**21**	**3**	**76**
JL Langer	NSW/Tas	100	96	9	3374	146	38.78	70.5	7	23	8	32
CL White	**Vic**	**113**	**103**	**13**	**3311**	**165**	**36.79**	**80.7**	**6**	**20**	**9**	**95**

Highest Scores

		BF	4s	6s	for	v..	Season	Venue
BR Dunk	229*	157	15	13	Tas	Qld	2014-15	North Sydney
TM Head	202	120	20	12	SA	WA	2015-16	Hurstville
DA Warner	197	141	20	10	NSW	Vic	2013-14	North Sydney
JP Maher	187	129	26	3	Qld	WA	2003-04	Gabba
SE Marsh	186	148	23	6	WA	CA	2015-16	North Sydney
DLR Smith	179*	122	13	11	NSW	Vic	2011-12	North Sydney
CT Bancroft	176	155	14	8	WA	SA	2015-16	Hurstville
PA Jaques	171*	143	20	2	NSW	Qld	2009-10	SCG
CJ Ferguson	**169**	**138**	**23**	**2**	**SA**	**WA**	**2017-18**	**Drummoyne**
MW Goodwin	167	138	21	0	WA	NSW	2000-01	Perth

Record Partnerships

Wkt				for	v..	Season	Venue
1	280	UT Khawaja	CD Hartley	Qld	Tas	2014-15	North Sydney
2	263*	MG Dighton	RT Ponting	Tas	NSW	2007-08	North Sydney
3	278	TM Head	CJ Ferguson	SA	WA	2015-16	Hurstville
4	205	DJ Hussey	CL White	Vic	Qld	2005-06	Gabba
5	180	JP Maher	CT Perren	Qld	SA	2003-04	Gabba
6	173*	MEK Hussey	GB Hogg	WA	Vic	1999-00	MCG
7	124	GT Cunningham	CM Smart	ACT	Vic	1999-00	Punt Rd, Richmond
8	110*	L Ronchi	NJ Rimmington	WA	SA	2011-12	Adelaide
9	96	TIF Triffitt	XJ Doherty	Tas	Vic	2011-12	MCG
9	96*	SM Thompson	SD Bradstreet	NSW	Qld	1998-99	North Sydney
10	61	CD Hartley	NJ Rimmington	Qld	Tas	2010-11	Gabba

Australian Cricket Digest, 2018-19

Highest Partnerships

	Wkt			for	v..	Season	Venue
280	1st	UT Khawaja	CH Hartley	Qld	Tas	2014-15	North Sydney
278	3rd	TM Head	CJ Ferguson	SA	WA	2015-16	Hurstville
277	1st	BR Dunk	TD Paine	Tas	Qld	2014-15	North Sydney
263*	2nd	MG Dighton	RT Ponting	Tas	NSW	2007-08	North Sydney
260	2nd	ML Hayden	SG Law	Qld	Tas	1993-94	Brisbane
257	3rd	MW Goodwin	MEK Hussey	WA	NSW	2000-01	Perth
253	1st	RB McCosker	J Dyson	NSW	SA	1981-82	Sydney
250	1st	ML Hayden	JP Maher	Qld	ACT	1999-00	Canberra
241	**3rd**	**M Klinger**	**MR Marsh**	**WA**	**SA**	**2017-18**	**Drummoyne**
240	3rd	SR Waugh	ME Waugh	NSW	Vic	1991-92	North Sydney

Quickest Innings

Fastest 50s	BF		Season	Venue	Fastest 100s	BF		Season	Venue
GJ Maxwell	19	Vic v Tas	2011-12	Bellerive	L Ronchi	56	WA v NSW	2006-07	Perth
DW Hookes	21	SA v WA	1990-91	Perth	DJ Hussey	60	Vic v NSW	2007-08	SCG
JS Lehmann	22	SA v Vic	2017-18	Nth Sydney	AC Voges	62	WA v NSW	2004-05	Nth Sydney
TLW Cooper	22	SA v Vic	2017-18	Bellerive	AC Gilchrist	63	WA v Qld	2006-07	Perth
DT Christian	23	SA v NSW	2010-11	Nth Sydney	DJ Hussey	63	Vic v NSW	2012-13	Nth Sydney
DA Nash	24	NSW v WA	2000-01	Nth Sydney	RJ Quiney	64	Vic v SA	2010-11	Adelaide
MR Marsh	24	WA v NSW	2009-10	Perth	JB Weatherald	66	SA v CA XI	2016-17	Hurstville
TLW Cooper	24	SA v Tas	2009-10	Bellerive	SG Law	69	Qld v Tas	2003-04	Bellerive
L Ronchi	24	WA v Tas	2010-11	Bunbury	UT Khawaja	70	Qld v Tas	2014-15	Nth Sydney
JP Inglis	24	CA XI v SA	2016-17	HUrstville	DT Christian	71	Vic v NSW	2013-14	Nth Syd
CJ Boyce	**24**	**Tas v Qld**	**2017-18**	**Bellerive**					

Leading Wicket Takers

	for	Wkts	M	Balls	Mdns	Runs	Ave	Best	4i	SR	Econ
JR Hopes	Qld	155	114	5594	51	4236	27.33	5-29	9	36.09	4.54
SCG MacGill	NSW	124	62	3173	24	2773	22.36	5-40	11	25.59	5.24
NM Hauritz	Qld/NSW	120	100	4938	24	3759	31.33	4-39	4	41.15	4.57
XJ Doherty	Tas	120	106	5059	40	3865	32.21	4-18	5	42.16	4.58
SR Clark	NSW	104	84	4500	57	3153	30.32	4-24	5	43.27	4.20
SW Tait	SA	103	53	2733	21	2361	22.92	8-43	7	26.53	5.18
KM Harvey	WA	103	80	3488	33	2794	27.13	4-8	6	33.86	4.81
MS Kasprowicz	Qld	101	83	4207	51	2941	29.12	4-19	3	41.65	4.19
DE Bollinger	**NSW**	**100**	**72**	**3816**	**37**	**3034**	**30.34**	**4-24**	**5**	**38.16**	**4.77**
J Angel	WA	94	74	3686	52	2524	26.85	5-16	2	39.21	4.11

Best Bowling

	for	v..	Season	Venue
SW Tait	8-43	SA	Tas	2003-04	Adelaide
CG Rackemann	7-34	Qld	SA	1988-89	Adelaide
JR Hazlewood	7-36	NSW	SA	2014-15	AB Field
JR Thomson	6-18	Qld	SA	1978-79	Gabba
B Laughlin	6-23	Qld	NSW	2008-09	Cairns
MA Starc	6-25	NSW	CA XI	2015-16	Bankstown
BE McNamara	6-25	NSW	Tas	1996-97	SCG
JM Holland	6-29	Vic	SA	2011-12	Adelaide
SW Tait	6-41	SA	NSW	2005-06	Adelaide
SM Harwood	6-46	Vic	WA	2010-11	WACA

Hat Tricks

	for	v..	Season	Venue
AG Hurst	Vic	WA	1978-79	Perth
RM Baker	WA	ACT	1999-2000	Perth
NW Bracken	NSW	Vic	2001-02	MCG
DE Bollinger	NSW	SA	2004-05	Canberra
KM Harvey	WA	Tas	2004-05	Devonport
NJ Rimmington	WA	Tas	2009-10	Gabba
MA Beer	Vic	SA	2016-17	Perth

Leading Wicket-keepers

	for	Total	M	Ct	St	b/Inn	Runs	Ave	100s
BJ Haddin	ACT/NSW	164	94	128	36	0.78	3010	34.60	6
GA Manou	SA	159	109	144	15	0.58	1554	22.20	0
DS Berry	SA/Vic	134	87	105	29	0.72	812	18.04	0
WA Seccombe	Qld	126	77	104	22	0.35	794	19.85	0
L Ronchi	WA	122	71	107	15	0.61	1803	29.56	4
CD Hartley	Qld	121	90	107	14	0.76	2033	33.33	1
TD Paine	**Tas**	**98**	**70**	**86**	**12**	**0.54**	**2268**	**37.80**	**6**

Australian Cricket Digest, 2018-19

Captaincy Records – most games as Skipper

	Team	M	W	L	T	NR	%W
CL White	Vic	71	38	32	1	0	53.52
JP Maher	Qld	54	30	23	0	1	55.56
GJ Bailey	**Tas**	**54**	**27**	**25**	**1**	**1**	**50.00**
DS Lehmann	SA	51	25	25	1	0	49.02
DJ Marsh	Tas	49	23	24	1	1	46.94
SG Law	Qld	42	23	17	0	2	54.76
AC Voges	WA	42	19	22	1	0	45.24

Leading Fielders

	for	Ct	M
DJ Hussey	Vic	54	101
DJ Marsh	SA/Tas	54	115
JP Maher	Qld	50	112
CL White	**Vic**	**50**	**113**
MJ Di Venuto	Tas	50	103
JL Langer	WA	49	100
MEK Hussey	WA	45	84

NEW SOUTH WALES RECORDS

Results

	M	W	L	NR	T
A.C.T	3	3	0	0	0
Cricket Aust XI	2	2	0	0	0
New Zealand	1	0	1	0	0
Queensland	59	31	27	1	0
South Australia	47	26	21	0	0
Tasmania	45	29	14	0	2
Victoria	56	26	28	1	1
Western Australia	58	32	25	0	1
	272	150	116	2	4

Highest team scores

Total	v..	Season	Venue
4-397	Tas	2001-02	Bankstown
350	Vic	2012-13	Nth Sydney
3-338	CA XI	2015-16	Bankstown

Lowest team scores

Total	v..	Season	Venue
92	Qld	1972-73	Gabba
112	SA	2008-09	SCG
116	WA	1994-95	SCG

Leading Run Scorers

	M	Inn	NO	Runs	HS	Ave	SR	100	50s	0s	Sixes
BJ Haddin	87	86	6	2724	138*	34.05	93.8	5	16	8	56
MG Bevan	58	58	19	2400	135*	61.54	73.1	1	21	3	6
PA Jaques	65	64	5	2341	171*	39.68	88.0	5	9	3	32
SR Waugh	55	54	10	2269	131	51.57	84.2	5	13	2	25
ME Waugh	64	60	6	1984	123	36.74	80.6	3	10	3	20

Highest Scores

	BF	4s	6s	v..	Season	venue
DA Warner	197*	141	20	10	Vic	2013-14	North Sydney
DLR Smith	179*	122	13	11	Vic	2011-12	North Sydney
PA Jaques	171*	143	20	2	Qld	2009-10	Sydney
DA Warner	165*	112	19	9	Tas	2008-09	Hurstville
MC Henriques	164	135	17	4	CA XI	2016-17	Hurstville
RB McCosker	164	144	15	5	SA	1981-82	Sydney

Record Partnerships

Wkt				v..	Season	Venue
1	253	RB McCosker	J Dyson	SA	1981-82	Sydney
2	190	R Chee Quee	MG Bevan	WA	1993-94	Sydney
3	240	SR Waugh	ME Waugh	Vic	1991-92	North Sydney
4	181	SPD Smith	MC Henriques	Qld	2015-16	Drummoyne
5	171*	PA Jaques	DJ Thorneley	SA	2005-06	Adelaide
6	105*	SR Waugh	MA Higgs	Qld	2001-02	Sydney
6	105*	PJ Forrest	SNJ O'Keefe	WA	2010-11	Hurstville
6	105	MG Bevan	GRJ Matthews	WA	1990-91	Perth
7	116	CJ Richards	BJ Haddin	SA	2000-01	North Sydney
8	93	SNJ O'Keefe	NM Hauritz	Vic	2010-11	Sydney
9	96*	SM Thompson	SD Bradstreet	Qld	1998-99	North Sydney
10	54	BE McNamara	GR Robertson	SA	1996-97	Adelaide

Leading Wicket takers

	M	Balls	Mdns	Runs	Wkts	Ave	Best	4w	SR	Econ
SCG MacGill	62	3173	24	2773	124	22.36	5-40	11	25.59	5.24
SR Clark	84	4500	57	3153	104	30.32	4-24	5	43.27	4.20
DE Bollinger	72	3816	37	3034	100	30.34	4-24	5	38.16	4.77
NW Bracken	68	3622	57	2588	87	29.75	5-38	3	41.63	4.29
GS Sandhu	**30**	**1557**	**15**	**1308**	**58**	**22.55**	**5-35**	**1**	**26.84**	**5.04**

Best Bowling

		v	Season	Venue
JR Hazlewood	7-36	SA	2014-15	AB Field
MA Starc	6-25	CA XI	2015-16	Bankstown
BE McNamara	6-25	Tas	1996-97	Sydney
SJ Coyte	6-60	Tas	2011-12	Hobart
AC Bird	5-26	Qld	2008-09	Sydney

Wicket keeping

Total		M	Ct	St
155	BJ Haddin	85	119	36
94	**PM Nevill**	**57**	**85**	**9**
81	PA Emery	58	69	12

Fielders

Ct		M
37	ME Waugh	64
31	S Lee	59
28	**MC Henriques**	**68**
28	**NJ Maddinson**	**56**

QUEENSLAND RECORDS

Results

v..	M	W	L	NR
A.C.T	3	3	0	0
Cricket Australia	2	2	0	0
New South Wales	59	27	31	1
New Zealand	1	0	1	0
South Australia	47	31	16	0
Tasmania	51	31	19	1
Victoria	53	30	22	1
Western Australia	55	26	27	2
	272	151	116	5

Highest team scores

Total	v..	Season	Venue
4-405	WA	2003-04	Gabba
3-402	Tas	2014-15	Nth Sydney
5-372	Vic	2014-05	Nth Sydney

Lowest team scores

Total	v..	Season	Venue
62	WA	1976-77	WACA
79	WA	1970-71	MCG
99	NSW	2005-06	Gabba

Leading Run Scorers

	M	Inn	NO	Runs	HS	Ave	SR	100	50s	0s	Sixes
JP Maher	112	112	10	4589	187	44.99	75.0	10	25	0	34
CT Perren	98	90	14	2844	117	37.42	68.0	2	21	7	28
ML Hayden	61	61	9	2616	152*	50.31	73.7	8	15	1	25
SG Law	85	78	7	2534	159	35.69	93.1	6	10	3	17
NJ Reardon	87	85	8	2466	116	32.03	81.4	2	20	5	65
ML Love	82	79	11	2412	127*	35.47	76.8	4	9	6	13

Highest Scores

	BF	4s	6s	v..	Season	venue
JP Maher	187	129	26	3	WA	2003-04	Gabba
UT Khawaja	166	110	18	7	Tas	2014-15	North Sydney
SG Law	159	136	18	0	Tas	1993-94	Gabba
ML Hayden	152*	167	15	1	Vic	1998-99	MCG
CD Hartley	142	120	13	4	Tas	2014-15	North Sydney

Record Partnerships

Wkt				v..	Season	Venue
1	280	UT Khawaja	CD Hartley	Tas	2014-15	North Sydney
2	260	ML Hayden	SG Law	Tas	1993-94	Gabba
3	217	UT Khawaja	M Labuschagne	NSW	2017-18	Drummoyne
4	173	ML Love	CT Perren	NSW	2001-02	Gabba
5	180	JP Maher	CT Perren	SA	2003-04	Gabba
6	123*	CA Philipson	CP Simpson	Vic	2009-10	MCG
7	112	JR Hopes	BCJ Cutting	NSW	2014-15	Blacktown
8	58	MG Neser	CJ Gannon	WA	2017-18	Drummoyne
9	84*	BCJ Cutting	MG Gale	Vic	2013-14	North Sydney
10	61	CD Hartley	NJ Rimmington	Tas	2010-11	Gabba

Leading Wicket Takers

	M	Balls	Mdns	Runs	Wkts	Ave	Best	4w	SR	Econ
JR Hopes	114	5594	51	4236	155	27.33	5-29	9	36.09	4.54
MS Kasprowicz	83	4207	51	2941	101	29.12	4-19	3	41.65	4.19
AJ Bichel	78	4001	45	2941	87	33.80	4-45	1	45.99	4.41
NM Hauritz	66	3140	11	2432	80	30.40	4-39	4	39.25	4.65
BCJ Cutting	57	2868	27	2868	79	32.68	4-50	4	36.30	5.40

Best Bowling

	v	Season	Venue
CG Rackemann	7-34	SA	1988-89	Adelaide
JR Thomson	6-18	SA	1978-79	Brisbane
B Laughlin	6-23	NSW	2008-09	Cairns
G Dymock	5-27	NSW	1981-82	Sydney
JR Hopes	5-29	SA	2000-01	Adelaide

Wicket keeping

Total		M	Ct	St
126	WA Seccombe	77	104	22
121	CD Hartley	90	107	14
54	IA Healy	29	47	7
33	JA MacLean	19	32	1

Fielders

Ct		M
50	JP Maher	112
40	A Symonds	77
35	SG Law	85
34	CT Perren	98

Australian Cricket Digest, 2018-19
SOUTH AUSTRALIA RECORDS

Results

v..	M	W	L	NR	T
A.C.T	3	3	0	0	0
Cricket Aust XI	2	2	0	0	0
New South Wales	47	21	26	0	0
New Zealand	2	0	2	0	0
Queensland	46	16	31	0	0
Tasmania	49	24	22	1	2
Victoria	55	21	33	0	1
Western Australia	58	24	33	0	1
	265	112	148	1	4

Highest team scores

Total	v..	Season	Venue
7-420	CA XI	2016-17	Hurstville
6-356	Vic	2017-18	Nth Syd
6-346	NSW	2017-18	Hurstville

Lowest team scores

Total	v..	Season	Venue
51	Tas	2002-03	Bellerive
83	Qld	2002-03	Gabba
87	WA	1989-90	WACA

Leading Run Scorers

	M	Inn	NO	HS	Ave	SR	100	50s	0s	Sixes
DS Lehmann	87	86	14	142*	55.04	88.6	7	30	2	29
GS Blewett	100	98	9	125	39.82	68.5	6	19	5	26
CJ Ferguson	97	94	10	169	38.90	85.7	7	19	5	25
TLW Cooper	73	71	6	115*	39.09	85.0	5	18	4	46
M Klinger	51	51	3	140*	52.58	76.5	7	16	1	26
MJ Cosgrove	64	64	3	121	32.43	83.5	3	12	4	30

Highest Scores

	BF	4s	6s	v..	Season	venue
TM Head	202	120	20	12	WA	2015-16	Hurstville
CJ Ferguson	169	138	23	2	WA	2017-18	Drummoyne
CJ Ferguson	154	113	17	3	CA XI	2016-17	Hurstville
MTG Elliott	146	141	14	3	WA	2007-08	Perth
DS Lehmann	142*	119	14	2	Tas	1994-95	Adelaide
JB Weatherald	141	104	17	6	CA XI	2016-17	Hurstville

Record Partnerships

Wkt			v..		Season	Venue
1	217	DS Lehmann	PC Nobes	Tas	1994-95	Adelaide
2	225	JB Weatherald	CJ Ferguson	CA XI	2016-17	Hurstville
3	278	TM Head	CJ Ferguson	WA	2015-16	Hurstville
4	138	JB Weatherald	AI Ross	NSW	2017-18	Hurstville
5	150	M Klinger	DT Christian	NSW	2009-10	Wollongong
6	130	DS Lehmann	MC Miller	NSW	2003-04	Adelaide
7	111	GA Manou	MF Cleary	NSW	2003-04	Adelaide
8	70	CJ Borgas	AW O'Brien	WA	2010-11	Perth
9	65*	CJ Ferguson	NM Lyon	WA	2011-12	Adelaide
10	57	A Zampa	PR George	Qld	2013-14	North Sydney

Leading Wicket Takers

	M	Balls	Mdns	Runs	Wkts	Ave	Best	4w	SR	Econ
SW Tait	53	2733	21	2361	103	22.92	8-43	7	26.53	5.18
P Wilson	46	2540	42	1676	70	23.94	4-23	2	36.29	3.96
MF Cleary	49	2440	23	2072	67	30.93	4-55	1	36.42	5.10
JN Gillespie	52	2906	35	2001	65	30.78	4-46	2	44.71	4.13
KW Richardson	39	2135	19	1831	64	28.61	6-48	5	33.36	5.15
GS Blewett	100	2394	15	2051	62	33.08	4-16	2	38.61	5.14

Best Bowling

	Wkts	v	Season	Venue
SW Tait	8-43	Tas	2003-04	Adelaide
SW Tait	6-41	NSW	2005-06	Adelaide
DT Christian	6-48	Vic	2010-11	Geelong
KW Richardson	6-48	Qld	2012-13	Adelaide
KW Richardson	6-51	NSW	2012-13	Sydney

Wicket keeping

	M	Total	Ct	St
GA Manou	109	159	144	15
TJ Nielsen	45	58	55	3
TP Ludeman	33	31	28	3
WB Phillips	13	18	18	0

Fielders

	Ct	M
TLW Cooper	38	73
GS Blewett	32	100
DS Lehmann	27	87
BE Young	27	42
CJ Ferguson	26	97

TASMANIA RECORDS

Results

v..	M	W	L	NR	T
A.C.T	3	2	1	0	0
Cricket Aust XI	2	1	1	0	0
New South Wales	45	14	29	0	2
New Zealand	1	0	1	0	0
Queensland	50	19	31	1	0
South Australia	49	22	24	1	2
Victoria	47	18	27	2	0
Western Australia	50	17	32	1	0
	249	94	146	5	4

Highest team scores

Total	v..	Season	Venue
1-398	Qld	2014-15	North Sydney
5-340	SA	2004-05	Bellerive
7-334	**CA XI**	**2017-18**	**Hurstville**

Lowest team scores

Total	v..	Season	Venue
62	WA	2014-15	Gabba
80	NSW	1984-85	Devonport
89	Qld	1976-77	Gabba

Leading Run Scorers

	M	Inn	NO	Runs	HS	Ave	SR	100	50s	0s	Sixes
GJ Bailey	116	109	11	3448	126	35.59	83.8	5	21	3	76
MJ Di Venuto	103	101	7	2891	129*	30.76	79.3	5	12	7	10
DJ Marsh	104	96	18	2575	106*	33.01	76.6	4	13	4	32
MG Dighton	73	72	1	2476	146*	34.87	78.1	3	17	3	32
TD Paine	76	74	9	2437	125	37.49	70.4	6	10	3	20

Highest Scores

		BF	4s	6s	v..	Season	Venue
BR Dunk	229*	157	15	13	NSW	2007-08	North Sydney
MG Dighton	146*	138	13	7	NSW	2007-08	North Sydney
TR Birt	145	143	13	6	SA	2004-05	Hobart
EJM Cowan	131*	120	9	2	NSW	2010-11	Sydney
MJ Di Venuto	129*	150	10	0	SA	1996-97	Hobart

Record Partnerships

Wkt				v..	Season	Venue
1	277	BR Dunk	TD Paine	Qld	2014-15	North Sydney
2	263*	MG Dighton	RT Ponting	NSW	2007-08	North Sydney
3	221	MJ Cosgrove	GJ Bailey	Vic	2010-11	Bellerive
4	174	GJ Bailey	RT Ponting	SA	2011-12	Adelaide
5	172	EJM Cowan	TR Birt	NSW	2010-11	Sydney
6	129	JW Wells	EP Gulbis	Vic	2014-15	AB Field
7	114	JP Faulkner	EP Gulbis	WA	2012-13	Burnie
8	82*	XJ Doherty	AJ Doolan	Vic	2016-17	North Sydney
9	96	TIF Triffitt	XJ Doherty	Vic	2011-12	MCG
10	42	CJ Duval	BW Hilfenhaus	Qld	2008-09	Bellerive

Leading Wicket Takers

	M	Balls	Mdns	Runs	Wkts	Ave	Best	4w	SR	Econ
XJ Doherty	106	5059	40	3865	120	32.21	4-18	5	42.16	4.58
B Geeves	64	3144	34	2671	89	30.01	5-45	1	35.33	5.10
BG Drew	46	2139	13	1983	70	28.33	4-38	2	30.56	5.56
DG Wright	55	2939	44	1895	65	29.15	4-23	2	45.22	3.87
JP Faulkner	45	2204	14	1899	64	29.67	4-20	4	29.67	5.17
BW Hilfenhaus	51	2875	36	2070	58	35.69	4-24	1	49.57	4.32

Best Bowling

		v..	Season	Venue
B Laughlin	6-53	NSW	2011-12	Canberra
JJ Krejza	6-55	NSW	2011-12	Bellerive
JP Marquet	5-23	Qld	1995-96	Bellerive
PJ Hutchison	5-27	SA	1996-97	Bellerive
SL Rainbird	5-29	Vic	2014-15	AB Field

Wicket keeping

	M	Total	Ct	St
TD Paine	70	98	86	12
MN Atkinson	35	50	43	7
SG Clingeleffer	40	42	39	3
RD Woolley	17	17	16	1

Fielders

	Ct	M
MJ Di Venuto	50	103
DJ Marsh	50	104
GJ Bailey	45	116
XJ Doherty	33	106

Australian Cricket Digest, 2018-19
VICTORIA RECORDS

Results

v..	M	W	L	NR	T
A.C.T	3	1	2	0	0
Cricket Aust XI	2	2	0	0	0
New South Wales	56	28	26	1	1
New Zealand	2	1	1	0	0
Queensland	53	22	30	1	0
South Australia	55	33	21	0	1
Tasmania	47	27	18	2	0
Western Australia	55	17	36	2	0
	274	132	134	6	2

Highest team scores

Total	v..	Season	Venue
2-379	Qld	2012-13	Gabba
4-352	NSW	2012-13	Nth Sydney
8-352	NSW	2007-08	SCG

Lowest team scores

Total	v..	Season	Venue
65	Qld	2002-03	Ballarat
78	Qld	1989-90	Gabba
90	Qld	1988-89	MCG

Leading Run Scorers

	M	Inn	NO	Runs	HS	Ave	SR	100	50s	0s	Sixes
BJ Hodge	139	137	18	5597	144	47.03	81.0	20	25	8	64
DJ Hussey	101	96	15	3546	140*	43.78	93.9	6	25	3	87
CL White	113	103	13	3311	165	36.79	80.7	6	20	9	95
MTG Elliott	78	76	6	2640	118*	37.71	71.5	6	17	5	17
RJ Quiney	74	69	5	2361	119	36.89	90.7	2	20	1	48

Highest Scores

		BF	4s	6s	v..	Season	Venue
CL White	165	154	16	6	Tas	2017-18	Perth
AJ Finch	154	141	14	5	Qld	2012-13	Brisbane
CL White	145	130	12	4	SA	2016-17	Perth
BJ Hodge	144	123	14	6	NSW	2011-12	North Sydney
BJ Hodge	140*	121	11	8	Qld	2010-11	Brisbane
DJ Hussey	140*	84	15	4	NSW	2012-13	North Sydney
CJL Rogers	140	116	14	3	SA	2009-10	Melbourne
AJ Finch	140	121	8	10	NSW	2012-13	North Sydney

Record Partnerships

Wkt				v..	Season	Venue
1	226	RJ Quiney	AJ Finch	Qld	2012-13	Gabba
2	222	MTG Elliott	BJ Hodge	Qld	2003-04	Gabba
3	227	BJ Hodge	DJ Hussey	SA	2003-04	Adelaide
4	205	DJ Hussey	CL White	Qld	2005-06	Brisbane
5	171	CL White	RJ Quiney	SA	2010-11	Adelaide
6	149	BJ Hodge	RJ Quiney	NSW	2011-12	North Sydney
7	106	CJL Rogers	JW Hastings	SA	2009-10	MCG
8	73*	AM Smith	AIC Dodemaide	Qld	1996-97	MCG
9	77	DJ Hussey	CJ McKay	Tas	2014-15	AB Field
10	30	DW Fleming	DJ Saker	WA	1995-96	MCG

Leading Wicket Takers

	M	Balls	Mdns	Runs	Wkts	Ave	Best	4w	SR	Econ
SM Harwood	54	2786	28	2088	88	23.73	6-46	5	31.66	4.50
ML Lewis	62	3063	42	2365	83	28.49	4-41	1	36.90	4.63
IJ Harvey	69	3007	30	2220	81	27.41	5-34	3	37.12	4.43
JW Hastings	48	2644	22	2271	78	29.12	4-30	4	33.90	5.15
AB McDonald	84	3292	20	2753	72	38.24	5-38	2	45.72	5.02

Best Bowling

		v..	Season	Venue
JM Holland	6-29	SA	2011-12	Adelaide
SM Harwood	6-46	WA	2010-11	Perth
JL Pattinson	6-48	NSW	2009-10	Sydney
GD Watson	5-20	WA	1969-70	Melbourne
DJ Hickey	5-26	WA	1985-86	Melbourne

Wicket keeping

	M	Total	Ct	St
DS Berry	83	127	100	27
AJ Crosthwaite	54	78	69	9
MS Wade	49	65	56	9
PSP Handscomb	19	37	33	4

Fielders

	Ct	M
DJ Hussey	54	101
CL White	50	113
BJ Hodge	45	139
RJ Quiney	36	74

Australian Cricket Digest, 2018-19

WESTERN AUSTRALIA RECORDS

Results

v..	M	W	L	NR	T
A.C.T	3	3	0	0	0
Cricket Aust XI	2	2	0	0	0
New South Wales	58	25	32	0	1
New Zealand	3	2	1	0	0
Queensland	55	27	26	2	0
South Australia	59	33	25	0	1
Tasmania	50	32	17	1	0
Victoria	55	36	17	2	0
	286	161	118	5	2

Highest team scores

Total	v..	Season	Venue
4-350	SA	2015-16	Hurstville
5-347	CA XI	2015-16	Nth Sydney
6-340	Qld	2006-07	WACA

Lowest team scores

Total	v..	Season	Venue
59	Vic	1969-70	MCG
76	NZ	1974-75	MCG
77	Qld	1976-77	WACA

Leading Run Scorers

	M	Inn	NO	Runs	HS	Ave	SR	100	50s	0s	Sixes
JL Langer	100	96	9	3374	146	38.78	70.5	7	23	8	32
AC Voges	91	90	17	3133	112	42.92	75.7	3	26	5	27
SE Marsh	**76**	**73**	**4**	**2960**	**186**	**42.90**	**78.8**	**8**	**15**	**4**	**48**
MJ North	86	82	12	2935	134*	41.93	78.9	5	20	4	37
MEK Hussey	84	80	10	2720	106	38.86	75.2	3	21	5	18

Highest Scores

		BF	4s	6s	v..	Season	Venue
SE Marsh	186	148	23	6	SA	2015-16	Hurstville
CT Bancroft	176	155	14	8	SA	2015-16	Hurstville
MW Goodwin	167	138	21	0	NSW	2000-01	Perth
SEMarsh	155*	147	12	6	Qld	2012-13	Brisbane
JL Langer	146	148	13	2	SA	1999-00	Perth

Record Partnerships

Wkt				v..	Season	Venue
1	216	CT Bancroft	SE Marsh	SA	2015-16	Hurstville
2	188*	JL Langer	DR Martyn	Vic	1997-98	MCG
3	257	MW Goodwin	MEK Hussey	NSW	2000-01	Perth
4	167	SM Katich	MEK Hussey	Vic	2001-02	Perth
5	141	AC Voges	TM Beaton	Qld	2010-11	Perth
6	173*	MEK Hussey	GB Hogg	Vic	1999-00	MCG
7	111*	RW Marsh	B Yardley	NSW	1973-74	SCG
8	110*	L Ronchi	NJ Rimmington	SA	2011-12	Adelaide
9	87	MJ North	BR Dorey	NSW	2008-09	Perth
10	43	PC Worthington	MW Clark	NSW	2002-03	Perth

Leading Wicket Takers

	M	Balls	Mdns	Runs	Wkts	Ave	Best	4w	SR	Econ
KM Harvey	80	3488	33	2794	103	27.13	4-8	6	33.86	4.81
J Angel	74	3686	52	2524	94	26.85	5-16	2	39.21	4.11
TM Moody	75	3205	42	2131	70	30.44	4-30	1	45.79	3.99
GB Hogg	77	2338	7	1953	60	32.55	4-37	2	38.97	5.01
BA Williams	35	1761	18	1298	59	22.00	4-29	5	29.85	4.42
BP Julian	54	2318	19	1779	59	30.15	4-41	2	39.29	4.60

Best Bowling

		v..	Season	Venue
DL Boyd	5-15	Vic	1982-83	Perth
J Angel	5-16	Vic	2001-02	Perth
NM Coulter-Nile	5-26	Vic	2014-15	Blacktown
JP Behrendorff	5-27	NSW	2014-15	SCG
KH MacLeay	5-30	Tas	1984-85	Perth

Wicket keeping

	M	Total	Ct	St
L Ronchi	71	122	107	15
RJ Campbell	47	88	82	6
AC Gilchrist	42	81	74	7
RW Marsh	33	51	50	1

Fielders

	Ct	M
JL Langer	49	100
MEK Hussey	45	84
AC Voges	39	86
MJ North	32	86

Australian Cricket Digest, 2018-19
SOME AUSTRALIAN LIST A RECORDS

Most runs

	Years	M	Inn	NO	Runs	HS	Ave	100	50s
RT Ponting	1992-2013	456	455	53	16363	164	41.74	34	99
MG Bevan	1989-2006	427	385	124	15103	157*	57.86	13	116
ME Waugh	1985-2004	434	417	42	14663	173	39.10	27	85
DS Lehmann	1998-2007	367	341	61	13122	191	46.86	19	94
MEK Hussey	1996-2013	381	346	71	12123	123	44.08	12	90
ML Hayden	1991-2008	308	299	29	12051	181*	44.63	27	67
SG Law	1998-2009	392	371	28	11812	163	34.43	20	64
SR Waugh	1984-2004	436	393	81	11764	140*	37.70	13	67
MW Goodwin	1994-2014	383	364	42	11477	167	35.64	14	71
AC Gilchrist	1992-2010	356	343	19	11326	172	34.95	18	63

Highest Scores

		BF	4s	6s		Venue	Season
BR Dunk	229	157	15	13	Tasmania v Queensland	North Sydney	2014-15
PJ Hughes	202*	151	18	6	Australia A v South Africa A	Darwin	2014
TM Head	202	120	20	12	South Australia v Western Australia	Hurstville	2015-16
DA Warner	197	141	20	10	New South Wales v Victoria	North Sydney	2013-14
CJ Ferguson	192	143	21	5	Worcestershire v Leicestershire	Worcester	2018
DS Lehmann	191	103	20	11	Yorkshire v Nottinghamshire	Scarborough	2001
JP Maher	187	129	26	3	Queensland v Western Australia	Gabba	2003-04
SE Marsh	186	148	23	6	Western Australia v Cricket Aust XI	North Sydney	2015-16
SR Watson	185*	96	15	15	Australia v Bangladesh	Dhaka	2010-11
ML Hayden	181*	166	11	10	Australia v New Zealand	Hamilton	2006-07

Highest team scores

	versus	Venue	Season
Australia	4-434	South Africa	Johannesburg	2005-06
Australia	6-417	Afghanistan	WACA	2014-15
Queensland	4-405	Western Australia	Gabba	2003-04
Queensland	3-402	Tasmania	North Sydney	2014-15
Tasmania	1-398	Queensland	North Sydney	2014-15
New South Wales	4-397	Tasmania	Bankstown	2001-02

Most Wickets

		M	Balls	Runs	Wkts	Ave	Best	Econ
SK Warne	1991-2007	311	16419	11642	473	24.61	6-42	4.25
GD McGrath	1992-2007	305	15808	10004	463	21.60	7-15	3.79
IJ Harvey	1993-2010	305	13607	9952	445	22.36	5-19	4.38
B Lee	1997-2012	262	13475	10524	438	24.05	5-22	4.69
AJ Bichel	1992-2007	235	11433	8362	320	26.13	7-20	4.38
MS Kasprowicz	1990-2008	226	11037	7977	298	26.76	5-45	4.33
NW Bracken	1998-2010	205	10339	7520	286	26.29	5-38	4.36
MG Johnson	2003-2015	184	9228	7386	284	26.00	6-31	4.80
A Symonds	1994-2009	424	11713	9379	282	33.25	6-14	4.80
GB Hogg	1994-2008	233	9297	7213	257	28.06	5-23	4.65
SR Waugh	1984-2004	436	11233	8610	257	33.50	4-32	4.59

Best Bowling

			Venue	Season
SW Tait	8-43	South Australia v Tasmania	Adelaide	2003-04
GD McGrath	7-15	Australia v Namibia	Potchefstroom	2002-03
AJ Bichel	7-20	Australia v England	Port Elizabeth	2002-03
JR Thomson	7-22	Middlesex v Hampshire	Lord's	1981
CG Rackemann	7-34	Queensland v South Australia	Adelaide	1998-99
JR Hazlewood	7-36	New South Wales v South Australia	Allan Border Field	2014-15

STRIKERS GRAB FIRST EVER BBL TITLE

LADDER	M	W	L	NR	Pts	Net Run Rate
Perth Scorchers (3)	10	8	2	-	16	+0.154
Adelaide Strikers (1)	**10**	**7**	**3**	**-**	**14**	**+0.801**
Melbourne Renegades (4)	10	6	4	-	12	+0.297
Hobart Hurricanes (2)	10	5	5	-	10	-0.291
Sydney Sixers (5)	10	4	6	-	8	+0.331
Sydney Thunder (6)	10	4	6	-	8	-0.039
Brisbane Heat (7)	10	4	6	-	8	-0.437
Melbourne Stars (8)	10	2	8	-	4	-0.926

Most Runs

	Team	M	Inn	NO	Runs	HS	Avge	S/Rate	100s	50s	6s
DJM Short	HH	11	11	1	572	122*	57.20	148.5	1	4	26
AT Carey	AS	11	11	2	443	100	49.22	141.5	1	2	13
JB Weatherald	AS	12	12	0	383	115	31.92	126.8	1	3	19
TM Head	AS	9	9	2	374	85*	53.43	133.1	0	3	12
SR Watson	ST	10	10	1	331	77	36.78	139.0	0	2	15
BR McDermott	HH	12	12	3	325	67*	36.11	138.3	0	1	15
MS Harris	MR	11	11	0	324	64	29.45	129.0	0	2	10
CL White	MR	8	8	4	304	79*	76.00	111.3	0	3	8
GJ Maxwell	MS	9	9	1	299	84	37.38	154.1	0	3	12
TLW Cooper	MR	11	9	3	298	65*	49.67	141.2	0	3	12

Highest Scores

		BF	4s	6s		Venue
DJM Short	122*	69	8	8	HH v BH	Gabba
JB Weatherald	115	70	9	8	AS v HH	Adelaide Oval
AT Carey	100	56	12	4	AS v HH	Adelaide Oval
MP Stoinis	99*	51	6	6	MS v BH	Gabba
DJM Short	97	63	9	4	HH v ST	Syd Showground

Most Wickets

Bowling	Team	M	Overs	Mdns	Runs	Wkts	Avge	Econ	Best
Rashid Khan	AS	11	44	0	249	18	13.83	5.66	3-20
DJ Bravo	MR	11	42.5	0	363	18	20.17	8.47	5-28
AJ Tye	PS	6	23.4	0	192	16	12.00	8.11	5-23
B Laughlin	AS	12	44	0	368	16	23.00	8.36	4-26
JC Archer	HH	12	46.2	1	371	16	23.19	8.01	3-15
SA Abbott	SS	10	33.2	0	283	13	21.77	8.49	4-11
MG Neser	AS	11	40.5	0	372	13	28.62	9.11	3-29
Fawad Ahmed	ST	10	40	1	245	12	20.42	6.13	3-31
KW Richardson	MR	10	39	1	314	12	26.17	8.05	4-22
PM Siddle	AS	11	37	2	220	11	20.00	5.95	3-17
B Stanlake	AS	10	38	0	246	11	22.36	6.47	2-22
DT Christian	HH	12	33	0	293	11	26.64	8.88	4-17
MJ McClenaghan	ST	10	39.2	0	361	11	32.82	9.18	2-19

Five wickets in an innings

	Figures		Venue
AJ Tye	5-23	PS v MS	WACA
DJ Bravo	5-28	MR v HH	Bellerive
BJ Doggett	5-35	BH v PS	Gabba

Hat-trick

		Venue
AJ Tye	PS v SS	SCG

Australian Cricket Digest, 2018-19

MATCHES PLAYED (all matches played under floodlights unless otherwise stated)

Match 1 –Thunder v Sixers at the Showgrounds, Homebush on December 19, 2017 - Thunder won by 5 wickets

Sixers		B	4	6	Thunder		B	4	6
J J Roy	c Gibson b McClenaghan	2	5		KR Patterson	b Sams	29	37	2
DP Hughes	c sub (NJ McAndrew)	29	27	1	2	JC Buttler +	c &b Sams	0	3	
	b Fawad					SR Watson *	c Henriques b Sams	77	46	6	6
NJ Maddinson	lbw b Fawad Ahmed	31	21	4	2	BJ Rohrer	c Henriques b Botha	7	6	1
MC Henriques *	c Watson b Nair	13	11		1	RJ Gibson	c O'Keefe b Sams	8	17	
S W Billings	run out	32	21	2	1	AJ Nair	not out	12	6	2
	(McClenaghan-Buttler)					AC Blizzard	not out	11	7	2
J Botha	lbw b Nair	0	3			CJ Green				
P M Nevill +	c Buttler b Fekete	13	15	1		AL Fekete				
SNJ O'Keefe	c Green b McClenaghan	19	14	3		MJ McClenaghan				
SA Abbott	run out (Green-Buttler)	7	4	1		Fawad Ahmed				
DR Sams	not out	0	0							
DE Bollinger										
	1 nb, 2 w	3					1 lb, 2 nb, 3 w	6		
6 overs: 1-55	20 overs	9-149				6 overs: 1-37	20 overs	5-150		

Fall: 1-16 (Roy, 2.2), 2-55 (Maddinson, 6.3), 3-74 (Henriques, 9.3), 4-77 (Hughes, 10.5), 5-79 (Botha, 11.4), 6-116 (Nevill, 16.1), 7-139 (Billings, 18.2), 8-144 (O'Keefe, 19.4), 9-149 (Abbott, 20)

Fall: 1-1 (Buttler, 0.6), 2-76 (Patterson, 11.1), 3-85 (Rohrer, 12.4), 4-126 (Gibson, 17.4), 5-126 (Watson, 17.5)

Thunder - bowling	O	M	R	W	wd	nb	Dots	Sixers - bowling	O	M	R	W	wd	nb	Dots
CJ Green	3	0	32	0			5	DR Sams	4	0	14	4	1		17
AL Fekete	4	0	37	1	1	1	8	SNJ O'Keefe	4	0	29	0		1	8
MJ McClenaghan	4	0	25	2	1		12	DE Bollinger	4	0	35	0	1	1	9
SR Watson	1	0	15	0			2	SA Abbott	4	0	39	0	1		6
Fawad Ahmed	4	1	11	2			13	J Botha	4	0	32	1			9
AJ Nair	4	0	29	2			10								

Toss: Thunder. Umpires: GA Abood, PJ Gillespie, AK Wilds (TV) Ref: SR Bernard. Award: SR Watson (ST) Crowd: 21,589
Watson 50 off 34 balls, 4x4, 4x4.

Match 2 – Heat v Stars at the Gabba, Brisbane on December 20, 2017 – Heat won by 15 runs

Heat		B	4	6	Stars		B	4	6
J J Peirson +	c Hastings b Beer	1	5		BR Dunk +	c Swepson b Lalor	0	2	
BB McCullum *	c Maxwell b Stoinis	40	22	4	2	LJ Wright	b Shadab Khan	19	15	2	
SD Heazlett	c Hastings b Beer	14	11	1		KP Pietersen	c McCullum b Doggett	10	9		1
J A Burns	c Dunk b Stoinis	50	28	4	3	GJ Maxwell	c Doggett b Shadab	8	5		1
AIRoss	c Pietersen b Boland	51	36	1	2	MP Stoinis	run out	99	51	6	6
BCJ Cutting	run out (Maxwell-Dunk)	35	18	3	2		(sub [M Labuschagne]-Peirson)			
MT Steketee	c Gulbis b Stoinis	0	2			JP Faulkner	not out	47	38	1	2
Shadab Khan	not out	0	0			EP Gulbis	c Doggett b Steketee	0	1	
J K Lalor	not out	6	2	1		J W Hastings *	not out	0	0	
BJ Doggett					A Zampa				
MJ Swepson					SM Boland				
					MA Beer				
	3 lb, 4 nb, 2 w	9				2 lb, 1 nb, 5 w	8		
6 overs: 2-57	20 overs	7-206			6 overs: 3-51	20 overs	6-191		

Fall: 1-8 (Peirson, 1.3), 2-57 (Heazlett, 5.6), 3-61 (McCullum, 6.3), 4-143 (Burns, 14.2), 5-194 (Ross, 18.5), 6-199 (Steketee, 19.3), 7-200 (Cutting, 19.4)

Fall: 1-0 (Dunk, 0.2), 2-16 (Pietersen, 2.4), 3-38 (Maxwell, 4.3), 4-53 (Wright, 6.5), 5-190 (Stoinis, 19.4), 6-190 (Gulbis, 19.5)

Stars - bowling	O	M	R	W	wd	nb	Dots	Sixers - bowling	O	M	R	W	wd	nb	Dots
J P Faulker	1	0	7	0		1	4	J K Lalor	4	0	34	1			7
MA Beer	4	0	21	2			7	MT Steketee	4	0	39	1	4		6
SM Boland	3	0	48	1	1		3	BJ Doggett	3	0	27	1			6
J W Hastings	3	0	48	0	1	1	6	Shadab Khan	4	0	41	2			8
MP Stoinis	4	0	38	3		1	9	MJ Swepson	4	0	26	0	1	1	7
A Zampa	3	0	24	0		1	2	BCJ Cutting	1	0	22	0			6
EP Gulbis	1	0	9	0			3								
GJ Maxwell	1	0	8	0											

Toss: Stars. Umpires: SAJ Craig, JD Ward, DM Koch (TV). Ref: RW Stratford   Award: MP Stoinis (MS)   Crowd: 27,433
Burns 50: 27 balls, 4x4, 3x6; Ross 50: 34 balls, 1x4, 2x6; Stoinis 50: 26 balls, 4x4, 3x6

Match 3 – Hurricanes v Renegades at Bellerive Oval, Hobart on December 21, 2017 - Renegades won by 7 wickets

Hurricanes

			B	4	6
AJ Doolan	c Hogg b Bravo	26	21	5	
DJM Short	lbw b Hogg	34	19	4	1
BR McDermott	c Finch b Bravo	34	24	2	2
GJ Bailey *	st Ludeman b Nabi	25	24	2	
DT Christian	c Cooper b Richardson	23	18		1
MS Wade +	c Ludeman b Bravo	15	10		1
JC Archer	c Richardson b Bravo	1	2		
CJ Boyce	c Nabi b Bravo	4	2	1	
CA Rose	not out	0	0		
TS Mills					
A Summers					
	2 w	2			
6 overs: 1-53	20 overs	8-164			

Renegades

			B	4	6
AJ Finch *	c Wade b Rose	4	2	1	
MS Harris	c Boyce b Archer	50	34	6	1
CL White	not out	79	59	8	2
TLW Cooper	c Wade b Archer	0	4		
BJ Hodge	not out	22	14	1	2
DJ Bravo					
TP Ludeman +					
JD Wildermuth					
M Nabi					
KW Richardson					
GB Hogg					
	1 lb, 2 nb, 7 w	10			
6 overs: 1-52	18.3 overs	3-165			

Fall: 1-53 (Doolan, 5.6), 2-62 (Short, 7.2), 3-114 (McDermott, 13.4), 4-126 (Bailey, 15.4), 5-149 (Christian, 18.3), 6-153 (Archer, 19.1), 7-158 (Boyce, 19.4), 8-164 (Wade, 19.6)

Fall: 1-4 (Finch, 0.2), 2-117 (Harris, 13.2), 3-117 (Cooper, 13.6)

Renegades - bowling	O	M	R	W	wd	nb	Dots
TLW Cooper	1	0	9	0			3
KW Richardson	4	0	36	1			9
JD Wildermuth	4	0	32	0	1		6
M Nabi	4	0	25	1			8
DJ Bravo	4	0	28	5	1		10
GB Hogg	3	0	34	1			4

Hurricanes - bowling	O	M	R	W	wd	nb	Dots
CA Rose	3	0	30	1			5
TS Mills	4	0	36	0	2	1	7
JC Archer	4	1	17	2	1		14
A Summers	3	0	31	0	3	1	5
CJ Boyce	1.3	0	17	0			2
DT Christian	2	0	23	0	1		2
MW Short	1	0	10	0			2

Toss: Renegades. Umpires: MW Graham-Smith, SJ Nogajski, GC Joshua (TV), Ref: D Talalla. Award: DJ Bravo (MR)   Crowd: 11,010
Harris 50: 32 balls, 6x4, 1x6; White 50: 45 balls, 4x4, 2x6.

Match 4 – Strikers v Thunder at Adelaide Oval on December 22, 2016 - Strikers won by 53 runs

Strikers

			B	4	6
AT Carey +	c Rohrer b Nair	44	26	5	2
JB Weatherald	lbw b McClenaghan	8	6	2	
TM Head *	c Buttler b Nair	36	29	4	1
CA Ingram	c Fawad Ahmed b Nair	15	15		1
JW Wells	run out (McClenaghan	13	17		
	-Buttler)				
JS Lehmann	c Patterson b McClenaghan	23	22	3	
JR Dean	not out	12	6	1	1
Rashid Khan	not out	0	0		
PM Siddle					
B Laughlin					
B Stanlake					
	5 b, 3 lb, 1 nb, 3 w	12			
6 overs: 1-54	20 overs	6-163			

Thunder

			B	4	6
JC Buttler +	c Stanlake b Siddle	10	9	2	
KR Patterson	c Siddle b Stanlake	48	37	4	1
SR Watson *	c Wells b Head	12	12	2	
RJ Gibson	c Carey b Rashid	4	8		
BJ Rohrer	b Rashid	0	2		
AJ Nair	not out	23	22		1
AC Blizzard	c Head b Laughlin	2	2		
CJ Green	lbw b Laughlin	0	1		
MJ McClenagha	c Head b Laughlin	0	1		
Fawad Ahmed	c Carey b Siddle	0	5		
AL Fekete	c Ingram b Laughlin	1	7		
	4 b, 1 lb, 5 w	10			
6 overs: 1-35	17.4 overs	110			

Fall: 1-10 (Weatherald, 1.4), 2-89 (Head, 9.5), 3-96 (Carey, 11.2), 4-111 (Ingram, 13.3), 5-141 (Wells, 18.1), 6-162 (Lehmann, 19.5)

Fall: 1-17 (Buttler, 2.5), 2-46 (Watson, 7.1), 3-69 (Gibson, 10.1), 4-69 (Rohrer, 10.3), 5-83 (Patterson, 12.3), 6-87 (Blizzard, 13.2), 7-88 (Green, 13.4), 8-88 (McClenaghan, 13.5), 9-107 (Fawad, 16.1), 10-110 (Fekete, 17.4)

Thunder - bowling	O	M	R	W	wd	nb	Dots
CJ Green	4	0	23	0			12
MJ McClenaghan	4	0	37	2	3	1	10
AL Fekete	4	0	35	0			9
Fawad Ahmed	4	0	24	0			9
AJ Nair	4	0	36	3			4

Strikers - bowling	O	M	R	W	wd	nb	Dots
CA Ingram	1	0	9	0			3
B Stanlake	3	0	14	1	2		11
PM Siddle	3	0	6	2			12
B Laughlin	3.4	0	26	4			10
Rashid Khan	4	0	22	2	2		12
TM Head	3	0	28	1			4

Toss: Strikers. Umpires: GJ Davidson, SA Lightbody, SD Fry (TV), Ref: DJ Harper. Award: Rashid Khan (AS). Crowd: 36,278

Match 5 – Sixers v Scorchers at the SCG on December 23, 2017 (day) – Scorchers won by 6 wickets

Sixers		B	4	6	Scorchers		B	4	6
JJ Roy	c Voges b Richardson	19	11	3	WG Bosisto	c Nevill b Abbott	21	20	4
DP Hughes	b Richardson	7	7	1	JR Philippe	c Bollinger b Abbott	7	10	
NJ Maddinson	c Tye b Johnson	31	33	2	DJ Willey	c Maddinson b Abbott	13	16	1
MC Henriques*	c Inglis b Willey	1	3		HWR Cartwright	c and b Bollinger	20	19	1	1
SW Billings	c Turner b Tye	0	1		AJ Turner	not out	52	27	2	5
J Botha	b Willey	4	6		AC Voges *	not out	19	17	1
PM Nevill+	b Johnson	18	20	2	AC Agar				
SNJ O'Keefe	c Richardson b Tye	23	18	1	JA Richardson				
SA Abbott	c Johnson b Tye	23	13	3	AJ Tye				
DR Sams	lbw b Tye	0	1		MG Johnson				
DE Bollinger	not out	0	0			3 lb, 1 w	4		
	1 nb, 5 w	6							
6 overs:4-42	18.4 overs	132			6 overs:2-33	18.1 overs	4-136		

Fall: 1-13 (Hughes, 1.6), 2-28 (Roy, 3.2), 3-40 (Henriques, 4.6), 4-41 (Billings), 5-46 (Botha, 6.5), 6-83 (Maddinson, 13.2), 7-84 (Nevill, 13.4), 8-132 (Abbott, 18.2), 9-132 (O'Keefe, 18.3), 10-132 (Sams, 18.4)

Fall: 1-31 (Bosisto, 4.5), 2-31 (Philippe, 4.6), 3-52 (Willey, 9.3), 4-66 (Cartwright, 11.5)

Scorchers - bowling	O	M	R	W	wd	nb	Dots	Sixers - bowling	O	M	R	W	wd	nb	Dots
MG Johnson	4	0	27	2	2		11	DR Sams	4	0	34	0	1		13
JA Richardson	3	0	28	2	1		6	DE Bollinger	3	0	30	1			8
DJ Willey	4	0	35	2	1	1	8	SNJ O'Keefe	4	0	23	0			9
AJ Tye	3.4	0	21	4	1		8	SA Abbott	3.1	0	28	3			6
AC Agar	4	0	21	0			4	J Botha	4	0	18	0			9

Toss: Scorchers. Umpires: GC Joshua, RJ Tucker, MW Graham-Smith (TV), Ref: D Talalla. Award: AJ Turner (PS) Crowd: 22,017
Hat trick for AJ Tye (Abbott, O'Keefe and Sams). Turner 50: 27 balls, 2x4 5x6

Match 6 – Renegades v Heat at Etihad Stadium, Melbourne on December 23, 2017 - Renegades won by 7 wickets

Heat		B	4	6	Renegades		B	4	6
JJ Peirson+	b Wildermuth	12	13	1	AJ Finch *	c Peirson b Shadab	8	9	1
BB McCullum *	b Cooper	5	6	1	MS Harris	b Shadab Khan	9	13	1
SD Heazlett	c Finch b Wildermuth	11	11	2	CL White	c Steketee b Cutting	51	43	4	2
M Labuschagne	b Wildermuth	20	19	2	TLW Cooper	not out	52	44	2	2
AI Ross	b Bravo	48	44	3	1	BJ Hodge	not out	9	4	1
BCJ Cutting	c Richardson b Hogg	18	13	2	DJ Bravo				
Shadab Khan	c Finch b Hogg	0	1		TP Ludeman +				
JK Lalor	c White b Bravo	10	9	1	M Nabi				
MT Steketee	not out	4	1	1	GB Hogg				
BJ Doggett	not out	1	3		KW Richardson				
MJ Swepson					JD Wildermuth				
	2 lb, 1 w	3				4 lb, 1 nb, 3 w	8		
6 overs:3-29	20 overs	8-132			6 overs:2-40	18.4 overs	3-137		

Fall: 1-6 (McCullum, 1.2), 2-24 (Heazlett, 3.5), 3-28 (Peirson, 5.2), 4-67 (Labuschagne, 11.5), 5-108 (Cutting, 16.3), 6-109 (Shadab, 16.5), 7-127 (Lalor, 19.1), 8-127 (Ross, 19.2)

Fall: 1-18 (Finch, 2.5), 2-29 (Harris, 4.3), 3-118 (White, 16.6)

Renegades - bowling	O	M	R	W	wd	nb	Dots	Heat - bowling	O	M	R	W	wd	nb	Dots
M Nabi	2	0	14	0			5	Shadab Khan	4	0	17	2	1		14
TLW Cooper	1	0	6	1			4	MT Steketee	3.4	0	35	0	1		6
JD Wildermuth	4	0	16	3			14	BJ Doggett	2	0	22	0		1	5
KW Richardson	4	0	37	0	1		9	MJ Swepson	4	0	25	0			12
GB Hogg	4	0	25	2			9	JK Lalor	3	0	17	0			5
AJ Finch	1	0	5	0			2	M Labuschagne	1	0	5	0			3
DJ Bravo	4	0	27	2			6	BCJ Cutting	1	0	12	1	1		1

Toss: Renegades. Umpires: JD Ward, P Wilson, SAJ Craig (TV), Ref: RW Stratford. Award: JD Wildermuth (MR). Crowd: 22,017
White 50: 40 balls, 4x4, 2x6; Cooper 50: 44 balls 2x4, 2x6 2x4.

Match 7 – Scorchers v Stars at the WACA, Perth on December 26, 2017 (day) – Scorchers won by 13 runs

Scorchers		B	4	6
WG Bosisto	c Dunk b Faulkner	4	4	1
M Klinger	c Quiney b Faulkner	1	4	
HWR Cartwright	c Quiney b Zampa	58	53	5	2
AJ Turner	b Beer	0	3	
AC Voges *	c Handscomb b Hastings	35	31	2	
AC Agar	not out	33	21	1	2
DJ Willey	c Handscomb b Stoinis	2	2	
JP Inglis +	not out	2	2	
AJ Tye				
MG Johnson				
JA Richardson				
	1 b, 2 lb, 4 w	7		
6 overs: 3-29	20 overs	6-142		

Stars		B	4	6
BR Dunk	c Turner b Johnson	6	8	1
LJ Wright	c Agar b Tye	21	14	3	1
PSP Handscomb+	c Bosisto b Tye	8	8	2
GJ Maxwell	b Richardson	4	6	1
MP Stoinis	c Cartwright b Tye	13	15	1
RJ Quiney	run out (Voges)	25	27	2
JP Faulkner	not out	35	31	2	1
JW Hastings*	c Inglis b Tye	5	10	
A Zampa	b Tye	0	1	
MA Beer				
SM Boland				
	6 b, 2 lb, 4 w	12		
6 overs: 4-40	20 overs	8-129		

Fall: 1-5 (Bosisto, 0.4), 2-9 (Klinger, 2.6), 3-10 (Turner, 3.5), 4-93 (Voges, 14.4), 5-111 (Cartwright, 17.2), 6-125 (Willey, 18.3)

Fall: 1-14 (Dunk, 2.1), 2-30 (Handscomb, 4.2) 3-36 (Wright, 4.6), 4-40 (Maxwell, 5.6), 5-59 (Stoinis, 9.5), 6-97 (Quiney, 15.4), 7-128 (Hastings, 19.3), 8-129 (Zampa, 19.6)

Stars - bowling	O	M	R	W	wd	nb	Dots
JP Faulkner	3	0	19	2	2		12
MA Beer	4	0	14	1	1		15
MP Stoinis	3	0	27	1			6
A Zampa	4	0	36	1			5
JW Hastings	3	0	25	1	1		4
SM Boland	3	0	18	0			5

Scorchers - bowling	O	M	R	W	wd	nb	Dots
MG Johnson	4	0	24	1	1		11
DJ Willey	4	0	30	0	1		10
JA Richardson	4	0	26	1			11
AJ Tye	4	0	23	5	2		14
AC Agar	4	0	18	0			7

Toss: Stars. Umpires: SD Fry, SA Lightbody, GJ Davidson (TV), Ref: SR Bernard. Award: HWR Cartwright (PS)   Crowd: 19,444.
Cartwright 50: 46 balls, 4x4, 2x6.

Match 8 – Heat v Thunder at the Gabba, Brisbane on December 27, 2017 – Heat won by 6 wickets

Thunder		B	4	6
JC Buttler +	b Shadab Khan	23	24	1
KR Patterson	c Cutting b Lalor	11	10	1
SR Watson *	c Burns b Shadab	56	34	6	2
CJ Ferguson	c Lynn b Lalor	37	26	4
BJ Rohrer	not out	16	9	2
AJ Nair	not out	0	0	
CJ Green				
RJ Gibson				
Fawad Ahmed				
MJ McClenaghan				
ALFekete				
	1 lb, 1 nb, 4 w	6		
	17 overs	4-149		

Heat		B	4	6
JJ Peirson +	c Green b Nair	43	39	4	1
BB McCullum*	b McClenaghan	5	4	1
CA Lynn	c Green b Watson	25	9	4	1
JA Burns	not out	45	35	1	1
BCJ Cutting	c Watson b McClenag	3	5	
AI Ross	not out	25	9	2	2
Shadab Khan				
MT Steketee				
JK Lalor				
BJ Doggett				
MJ Swepson				
	2 lb, 5 w	7		
	16.5 overs	4-153		

Fall: 1-23 (Patterson, 4.1), 2-47 (Buttler, 6.6), 3-107 (Watson, 13.3), 4-141 (Ferguson, 16.3)

Fall: 1-9 (McCullum, 1.6), 2-48 (Lynn, 5.1), 3-92 (Peirson, 10.2), 4-112 (Cutting, 13.1)

Heat - bowling	O	M	R	W	wd	nb	Dots
Shadab Khan	4	0	27	2			7
MT Steketee	3	0	14	0			10
JK Lalor	4	0	42	2	3	1	8
MJ Swepson	3	0	38	0			1
BJ Doggett	3	0	27	0			4

Thunder - bowling	O	M	R	W	wd	nb	Dots
CJ Green	2	0	11	0			5
MJ McClenaghan	4	0	45	2	5		9
ALFekete	1.5	0	22	0			4
SR Watson	2	0	13	1			4
Fawad Ahmed	4	0	41	0			3
AJ Nair	3	0	19	1			8

Toss: Thunder. Umpires: GA Abood, AK Wilds, PJ Gillespie (TV), Ref: SR Bernard.   Award: AI Ross (BH)   Crowd: 34,343.
Watson 50: 25 balls, 6x4, 2x6.

FOR ALL YOUR COACHING NEEDS RING THEM ON 08 8293 3400

Australian Cricket Digest, 2018-19

Match 9 – Sixers v Strikers at the SCG on December 28, 2017 - Strikers won by 6 runs

Strikers			B	4	6
AT Carey+	not out	83	59	8	2
JB Weatherald	c Hughes b Dwarshuis	0	3		
TM Head *	st Billings b Botha	29	24	3	1
CA Ingram	c Roy b Dwarshuis	15	15	1	
JW Wells	not out	33	19	3	1
MG Neser					
JS Lehmann					
Rashid Khan					
PM Siddle					
B Laughlin					
B Stanlake					
1 b, 1 lb, 5 w		7			
6 overs: 1-47	20 overs	3-167			

Sixers			B	4	6
JJ Roy	c Lehmann b Laughlin	21	18	2	1
DP Hughes	c Wells b Stanlake	4	4		
NJ Maddinson	c Carey b Neser	0	2		
JC Silk	b Rashid Khan	50	32	7	
SW Billings +	b Rashid Khan	8	10		
J Botha *	c Head b Laughlin	25	26	1	
SNJ O'Keefe	b Neser	28	15	2	2
SA Abbott	b Stanlake	0	2		
BJ Dwarshuis	not out	21	11	1	2
DR Sams					
WER Somerville					
4 w		4			
6 overs: 3-42	20 overs	8-161			

Fall: 1-4 (Weatherald, 0.6), 2-58 (Head, 7.6), 3-93 (Ingram, 12.5)

Fall: 1-20 (Hughes, 2.4), 2-24 (Maddinson, 3.2), 3-33 (Roy, 5.1), 4-58 (Billings, 8.2), 5-104 (Silk, 14.1), 6-127 (Botha, 16.6), 7-127 (Abbott, 17.2), 8-161 (O'Keefe, 19.6)

Sixers - bowling	O	M	R	W	wd	nb	Dots
BJ Dwarshuis	4	0	41	2	3	-	10
J Botha	4	0	30	1	-	-	7
WER Somerville	4	0	31	0	-	-	7
DR Sams	4	0	29	0	-	-	7
SA Abbott	4	0	34	0	2	-	6

Strikers - bowling	O	M	R	W	wd	nb	Dots
B Stanlake	4	0	31	2	1		11
MG Neser	4	0	42	2			8
PM Siddle	3	0	17	0	1		7
B Laughlin	4	0	39	2	2		7
Rashid Khan	4	0	22	2			9
TM Head	1	0	10	0			0

Toss: Sixers. Umpires: SA Craig, P Wilson, JD Ward (TV), Ref: PL Marshall. Award: AT Carey (AS). Crowd: 25,879
Carey 50: 39 balls, 4x4 2x6. Silk 50: 31 balls, 7x4

Match 10 – Renegades v Scorchers at Etihad Stadium on December 29, 2017 - Scorchers won by 3 wickets

Renegades			B	4	6
MS Harris	lbw b Agar	32	25	1	2
AJ Finch *	c Inglis b Johnson	0	5		
CL White	c Richardson b Johnson	3	8		
TLW Cooper	b Tye	34	24	4	1
BJ Hodge	b Johnson	3	10		
DJ Bravo	c and b Willey	16	10	1	1
JD Wildermuth	c Agar b Richardson	5	10		
M Nabi	c Voges b Tye	13	16		
TP Ludeman +	b Tye	1	3		
KW Richardson	not out	12	8	1	
GB Hogg	not out	1	1		
9 lb, 1 w		10			
6 overs: 2-41	20 overs	9-130			

Scorchers			B	4	6
DJ Willey	b Hogg	31	21	27	2
M Klinger	c Ludeman b Nabi	37	37	54	2
AC Agar	st Ludeman b Hogg	13	11	15	
AC Voges*	run out (Bravo--Ludeman)	24	18	27	2
HWR Cartwright	c Cooper b Wildermuth	4	9	12	
AJ Turner	not out	11	7	17	
JP Inglis+	b Bravo	7	7	6	1
JA Richardson	run out	2	4	4	
	(Hodge-Richardson)				
AJ Tye	not out	0	0	1	
JM Muirhead					
MG Johnson					
(1b, 3 w)		4			
6 overs: 0-49	19 overs	7-133			

Fall: 1-3 (Finch, 0.6), 2-14 (White, 2.5), 3-77 (Cooper, 9.6), 4-79 (Harris, 10.4), 5-92 (Hodge, 12.4), 6-102 (Wildermuth, 14.6), 7-106 (Bravo, 16.2), 8-111 (Ludeman, 17.2), 9-122 (Nabi, 19.2)

Fall: 1-58 (Willey, 6.6), 2-78 (Agar, 10.3), 3-90 (Klinger, 12.4), 4-109 (Cartwright, 15.5), 5-113 (Voges, 16.2), 6-122 (Inglis, 17.5), 7-125 (Richardson, 18.4)

Scorchers - bowling	O	M	R	W	wd	nb	Dots
Johnson	4	1	13	3			17
Richardson	4	0	23	1	1		12
Tye	4	0	37	3			6
Agar	4	0	20	1			13
Willey	2	0	12	1			4
Muirhead	2	0	16	0			3

Strikers - bowling	O	M	R	W	wd	nb	Dots
M Nabi	4	0	16	1	1		12
TLW Cooper	2	0	22	0			3
JD Wildermuth	2	0	26	1			5
KW Richardson	4	0	30	0			11
GB Hogg	4	0	16	2	1		14
DJ Bravo	3	0	22	1	1		7

Toss: Scorchers. Umpires: PJ Gillespie, AK Wilds, GA Abood (TV), Ref: RW Stratford. Award: MG Johnson (PS). Crowd: 30,018

Match 11 – Hurricanes v Thunder at York Park, Launceston on December 30, 2017
Hurricanes won by 57 runs

Thunder			B	4	6	Hurricanes			B	4	6
KR Patterson	c Bailey b Archer	15	10	3		AJ Doolan	c Green b Nair	34	32	2	
JC Buttler +	b Rose	67	41	5	4	DJM Short	b McClenaghan	15	9	2	1
SR Watson *	run out (Boyce-Wade)	41	35	4	1	BR McDermott	c Buttler b Sandhu	4	7		
CJ Ferguson	not out	24	21	1		GJ Bailey *	c Gibson b Fawad	3	6		
BJ Rohrer	lbw b Rose	2	5			MS Wade +	c and b Nair	2	6		
RJ Gibson	run out (Archer)	14	10		1	CJ Boyce	c Green b Fawad	0	2		
CJ Green						DT Christian	b Green	10	13		
AJ Nair						CA Rose	c sub (AL Fekete) b Green	13	17		
Fawad Ahmed						JC Archer	not out	25	16	1	1
GS Sandhu						TS Rogers	b McClenaghan	0	2		
MJ McClenaghan						TS Mills	b Sandhu	1	7		
	2 nb, 1 w	3					2 w	2			
6 overs: 1-49	20 overs	5-166				6 overs: 2-44	19.3 overs	109			

Fall: 1-24 (Patterson, 2.3), 2-119 (Buttler, 13.2),
3-138 (Watson, 15.3), 4-141 (Rohrer, 16.4),
5-166 (Gibson, 19.6)

Fall: 1-23 (Short, 2.3), 2-35 (McDermott, 3.5), 3-52 (Bailey, 4.3), 4-56 (Wade, 8.5),
5-57 (Boyce, 9.4), 6-62 (Doolan, 10.5), 7-75 (Christian, 14.1), 8-102
(Rose, 17.3), 9-108 (Rogers, 18.2), 10-109 (Mills, 19.3)

Hurricanes - bowling	O	M	R	W	wd	nb	Dots	Thunder - bowling	O	M	R	W	wd	nb	Dots
CA Rose	4	0	20	2			10	CJ Green	4	0	30	2			8
TS Rogers	3	0	50	0		1	4	GS Sandhu	3.3	0	29	2	1		9
JC Archer	4	0	22	1			11	MJ McClenaghan	4	0	19	2	1		10
TS Mills	4	0	32	0		1	11	AJ Nair	4	0	17	2			10
CJ Boyce	4	0	32	0	1		7	Fawad Ahmed	4	0	14	2			12
DT Christian	1	0	10	0			-								

Toss: Hurricanes. Umpires: GJ Davidson, SD Fry, SA Lightbody (TV), Ref: RL Parry. Award: JC Buttler (ST). Crowd: 16,734
Buttler 50: 35 balls, 4x4, 3x6

Match 12 – Strikers v Heat at Adelaide Oval on December 31, 2017 – Strikers won by 56 runs

Strikers			B	4	6	Heat			B	4	6
AT Carey +	b Lalor	2	6			JJ Peirson +	c Lehmann b Head	7	5	1	
JB Weatherald	b Lalor	20	15	2	1	BB McCullum *	c Lehmann b Neser	15	21	1	
TM Head *	b Yasir	13	18			CA Lynn	c Carey b Rashid	0	3		
CA Ingram	c Gannon b Yasir	23	22	2		JA Burns	c Rashid b Stanlake	1	2		
JW Wells	c McCullum b Gannon	12	13	1		AI Ross	b Neser	1	2		
JS Lehmann	c Burns b Steketee	22	17	3		BCJ Cutting	c Ingram b Laughlin	14	13	2	
MG Neser	not out	40	26	3	2	CJ Gannon	b Rashid	23	28	3	
Rashid Khan	c Lynn b Lalor	6	2		1	JK Lalor	run out (Siddle)	9	10	1	
PM Siddle	not out	1	1			MT Steketee	b Laughlin	2	5		
B Laughlin						Yasir Shah	not out	6	8		
B Stanlake						MJ Swepson	c Weatherald b Laughlin	0	1		
	5 lb, 3 w	8					4 b, 2 lb, 7 w	13			
6 overs: 2-38	20 overs	7-147				6 overs: 4-37	16.2 overs	91			

Fall: 1-14 (Carey, 2.2), 2-29 (Weatherald, 4.3), 3-43 (Head, 7.4),
4-70 (Wells, 11.3), 5-76 (Ingram, 12.6), 6-121 (Lehmann, 17.5),
7-139 (Rashid, 18.6)

Fall: 1-8 (Peirson, 0.6), 2-8 (Lynn, 1.3), 3-11 (Burns, 2.2), 4-15
(Ross, 3.1), 5-38 (Cutting, 6.2), 6-56 (McCullum, 10.2), 7-71
(Lalor, 12.6), 8-77 (Steketee, 13.5), 9-90 (Gannon, 15.6),
10-91 (Swepson, 16.2)

Heat - bowling	O	M	R	W	wd	nb	Dots	Strikers - bowling	O	M	R	W	wd	nb	Dots
JA Burns	1	0	5	0			4	TM Head	1	0	8	1			2
MT Steketee	4	0	26	1			10	Rashid Khan	4	0	19	2	1		13
JK Lalor	4	0	40	3	2		9	B Stanlake	4	0	26	1	3		12
Yasir Shah	4	0	18	2			11	MG Neser	2	0	7	2			6
MJ Swepson	4	0	27	0	1		8	B Laughlin	2.2	0	11	3	1		9
CJ Gannon	3	0	26	1			4	PM Siddle	2	0	10	0			6
								CA Ingram	1	0	4	0	1		3

Toss: Strikers. Umpires: MW Graham-Smith, GC Joshua, DJ Shepard (TV), Ref: SR Bernard. Award: MG Neser (AD). Crowd: 46,594

Australian Cricket Digest, 2018-19

Match 13 –Thunder v Hurricanes at the Sydney Showgrounds, Homebush on January 1, 2018 (day)
Thunder won by 9 runs

Hurricanes		B	4	6
AJ Doolan	c Patterson b Sandhu	5	11	
DJM Short	c Green b Watson	97	63	9	4
MS Wade +	c McClenaghan b Fawad	27	23	2
BR McDermott	not out	49	25	6	2
DT Christian	not out	0	0
GJ Bailey *				
CJ Boyce				
CA Rose				
JC Archer				
TS Mills				
SA Milenko				
	4 lb, 2 nb, 5 w	11		
6 overs: 1-34	20 overs	3-189		

Fall: 1-26 (Doolan, 4.2), 2-84 (Wade, 11.3), 3-188 (Short, 19.5)

Thunder		B	4	6
KR Patterson	run out (Short)	36	26	3
JC Buttler +	run out (Wade)	81	43	7	5
SR Watson *	c Doolan b Boyce	36	31	4	1
CJ Ferguson	c Archer b Boyce	0	1
BJ Rohrer	c Rose b Christian	5	4
AJ Nair	b Archer	0	1
RJ Gibson	b Mills	2	5
CJ Green	c Bailey b Archer	5	3	1
GS Sandhu	not out	11	4	1	1
MJ McClenaghan	not out	1	2
Fawad Ahmed				
	(2 lb, 1 w)	3		
6 overs: 0-65	20 overs	8-180		

Fall: 1-69 (Patterson, 7.1), 2-125 (Watson, 14.3), 3-125
(Ferguson, 14.4), 4-137 (Rohrer, 15.5), 5-149 (Nair, 16.4), 6-156
(Gibson, 17.5), 7-167 (Green, 18.6), 8-167 (Buttler, 19.1)

Thunder - bowling	O	M	R	W	wd	nb	Dots
CJ Green	3	0	19	0			6
Fawad Ahmed	4	0	27	1			10
MJ McClenaghan	3.2	0	32	0	1	2	6
GS Sandhu	4	1	48	1	2		8
AJ Nair	2	0	24	0	2		3
SR Watson	3.4	0	35	1			5

Hurricanes - bowling	O	M	R	W	wd	nb	Dots
CA Rose	4	0	32	0			10
TS Mills	4	0	46	1	1		5
JC Archer	4	0	42	2			6
CJ Boyce	3	0	14	2			10
DJM Short	1	0	6	0			3
DT Christian	4	0	38	1			6

Toss: Thunder. Umpires: GA Abood, PJ Gillespie, AK Wilds (TV), Ref: RW Stratford. Award: DJM Short (HH). Crowd: 16,496
Short 50: 36 balls, 4x4, 2x6. Buttler 50: 29 balls, 4x4, 3x6.

Match 14 – Scorchers v Sixers at the WACA, Perth on January 1, 2018 – Scorchers won by 6 wickets

Sixers		B	4	6
JJ Roy	lbw b Willey	6	7	1
PM Nevill +	st Inglis b Muirhead	33	30	5
NJ Maddinson	c Tye b Willey	30	22	4
JC Silk	not out	45	33	3	1
SW Billings	c Willey b Tye	33	21	2	2
BJ Dwarshuis	not out	15	8	1	1
J Botha *				
SA Abbott				
SNJ O'Keefe				
WER Somerville				
DR Sams				
	1 b, 1 lb, 1 nb, 2 w	5		
6 overs: 1-47	20 overs	4-167		

Scorchers		B	4	6
DJ Willey	c Nevill b Dwarshuis	1	5
M Klinger	c Maddinson b Sams	83	61	9	4
HWR Cartwright	run out (Botha-Nevill)	10	6	2
AJ Turner	c Silk b Sams	45	32	2	3
TH David	not out	17	10		2
AC Voges *	not out	6	1	1
JP Inglis +				
AJ Tye				
JM Muirhead				
MG Johnson				
JA Richardson				
	2 lb, 6 w	8		
6 overs: 2-35	19.1 overs	4-170		

Fall: 1-27 (Roy, 3.1), 2-61 (Nevill, 8.1), 3-81 (Maddinson, 11.2),
4-137 (Billings, 17.5 ov)

Fall: 1-4 (Willey, 1.3), 2-17 (Cartwright, 2.6), 3-113 (Turner, 14.5),
4-153 (Klinger, 18.4)

Scorchers - bowling	O	M	R	W	wd	nb	Dots
MG Johnson	4	0	25	0	1		11
JA Richardson	4	0	45	0	1		8
DJ Willey	4	0	30	2			9
AJ Tye	4	0	28	1	1		10
AC Voges	2	0	23	0			2
JM Muirhead	2	0	14	1			1

Sixers - bowling	O	M	R	W	wd	nb	Dots
SNJ O'Keefe	3	0	20	0			6
BJ Dwarshuis	4	0	26	1	1		8
WER Somerville	4	0	32	0			7
DR Sams	3	0	25	2			9
SA Abbott	3.1	0	42	0	1		7
J Botha	1	0	9	0			2
NJ Maddinson	1	0	14	0			0

Toss: Scorchers. Umpires: DM Koch, JD Ward, SAJ Craig (TV), Ref: PL Marshall. Award: M Klinger (PS) Crowd: 20,892
Klinger 50: 42 balls, 5x4, 1x6.

Australian Cricket Digest, 2018-19

Match 15 – Stars v Heat at the MCG on January 2, 2018 – Heat won by 9 wickets

Stars		B	4	6		Heat		B	4	6
BR Dunk +	lbw b Yasir	5	5			CA Lynn	not out	63	46	7	3
LJ Wright	st Peirson b Swepson	19	21	2		BB McCullum *	c Quiney b Bowe	61	30	7	3
KP Pietersen	c Doggett b Swepson	30	25	3		JA Burns	not out	18	12	3
GJ Maxwell	c Doggett b Steketee	50	39	5	1	JJ Peirson +				
MP Stoinis	run out (Doggett-Yasir)	4	5			AI Ross				
RJ Quiney	c and b Swepson	0	2			BCJ Cutting				
JP Faulkner	not out	20	20	1		BJ Doggett				
JW Hastings *	c McCullum b Cutting	0	2			Yasir Shah				
A Zampa	not out	4	3			CJ Gannon				
LP Bowe						MJ Swepson				
MA Beer						MT Steketee				
	2 lb, 2 nb, 5 w	9					1 b, 1 w	2		
6 overs: 1-45	20 overs	7-141				6 overs: 0-50	14.4 overs	1-144		

Fall: 1-12 (Dunk, 2.1), 2-55 (Wright, 7.5), 3-63 (Pietersen, 9.3), 4-80 (Stoinis, 12.4), 5-82 (Quiney, 13.2), 6-124 (Maxwell, 17.6), 7-125 (Hastings, 18.3 ov)

Fall: 1-101 (McCullum, 10.4)

Heat - bowling	O	M	R	W	wd	nb	Dots		Stars - bowling	O	M	R	W	wd	nb	Dots
Yasir Shah	4	0	16	1	1		10		Faulkner	2	0	14	0			4
Steketee	4	0	36	1	2		7		Beer	2.4	0	28	0			5
Doggett	4	0	35	0	1		6		Zampa	4	0	28	0			11
Gannon	2	0	24	0		1	2		Hastings	2	0	22	0			3
Swepson	4	0	14	3	1		11		Stoinis	2	0	30	0	1		3
Cutting	2	0	14	1	1		4		Bowe	2	0	21	1			5

Toss: Heat. Umpires: MW Graham-Smith, GC Joshua, DJ Shepard (TV), Ref: SR Bernard. Award: MJ Swepson (BH). Crowd: 38,834
Maxwell 50: 38 balls, 5x4, 1x6. Lynn 50: 40 balls, 5x4, 3x6; McCullum 50: 27 balls, 5x4, 3x6

Match 16 – Renegades v Sixers at Kardinia Park, Geelong on January 3, 2018 – Renegades won by 8 wickets

Sixers		B	4	6		Renegades		B	4	6
JJ Roy	c Finch b Bravo	5	13			MS Harris	b Dwarshuis	1	4	
PM Nevill +	c Ludeman b Nabi	0	1			AJ Finch *	run out (Roy)	51	38	6	2
NJ Maddinson	run out (Bravo)	24	28	1		CL White	not out	49	44	5	1
JC Silk	c White b Hogg	16	18	1		DJ Bravo	not out	6	7	1
SW Billings	c White b Bravo	22	26	2		TLW Cooper				
SA Abbott	c Bravo b Wildermuth	6	5	1		BJ Hodge				
DR Sams	c Cooper b Nabi	1	2			M Nabi				
J Botha *	not out	32	23	3	1	GB Hogg				
BJ Dwarshuis	c Richardson b Bravo	3	4			TP Ludeman +				
MW Edwards	not out	0	0			JD Wildermuth				
WER Somerville						KW Richardson				
	1 lb, 1 w	2					2 lb, 3 w	5		
6 overs: 2-20	20 overs	8-111				6 overs: 1-39	15.3 overs	2-112		

Fall: 1-1 (Nevill, 0.4), 2-11 (Roy, 3.2), 3-34 (Silk, 8.2), 4-56 (Maddinson, 12.1), 5-64 (Abbott, 13.3), 6-65 (Sams, 14.1), 7-88 (Billings, 17.1), 8-109 (Dwarshuis, 19.5)

Fall: 1-2 (Harris, 0.5) 2-93 (Finch, 13.2)

Renegades - bowling	O	M	R	W	wd	nb	Dots		Sixers - bowling	O	M	R	W	wd	nb	Dots
M Nabi	4	0	22	2			11		BJ Dwarshuis	4	0	19	1	1		14
KW Richardson	4	1	13	0			12		MW Edwards	3	0	31	0			7
DJ Bravo	4	0	29	3	1		10		DR Sams	3.3	0	27	0	2		9
JD Wildermuth	4	0	20	1			11		WER Somerville	2	0	13	0			7
GB Hogg	4	0	26	1			6		SA Abbott	2	0	13	0			5
									J Botha	1	0	7	0			1

Toss: Renegades. Umpires: GJ Davidson, SD Fry, SA Lightbody (TV), Ref: RL Parry. Award: AJ Finch (MR) Crowd: 23,586
Finch 50: 38 balls, 5x4, 3x6

Match 17 –Hurricanes v Strikers at the Bellerive Oval, Hobart on January 4, 2018 – Hurricanes won by 7 runs

Hurricanes		B	4	6
AJ Doolan	c Carey b Rashid Khan	29	23	3
DJM Short	c Siddle b Stanlake	96	58	9
BR McDermott	c Weatherald b Rashid	18	18	
GJ Bailey*	c Neser b Stanlake	1	3	
DT Christian	run out (Carey-Neser)	7	3	
MS Wade +	not out	20	13	1
SA Milenko	not out	7	3	1
JC Archer				
CA Rose				
CJ Boyce				
TS Mills				
	1 lb, 1nb, 3 w	5		
6 overs: 0-51	20 overs	5-183		

Strikers		B	4	6
AT Carey+	c Mills b Archer	2	4	
JB Weatherald	c Bailey b Rose	7	10	1
TM Head*	c Milenko b Archer	44	32	1	3
CA Ingram	c Short b Mills	66	44	9	2
JW Wells	run out (Wade)	28	18		2
JS Lehmann	lbw b Archer	16	8	1	1
MG Neser	not out	1	2	
Rashid Khan	not out	4	3	
PM Siddle				
B Laughlin				
B Stanlake				
	1 lb, 1nb, 6 w	8		
6 overs: 2-30	20 overs	6-176		

Fall: 1-60 (Doolan, 8.1), 2-111 (McDermott, 13.6), 3-143 (Bailey, 16.3), 4-148 (Short, 16.5), 5-172 (Christian, 19.1)

Fall: 1-9 (Carey, 1.5), 2-10 (Weatherald, 2.3), 3-112 (Head, 13.1), 4-142 (Ingram, 16.5), 5-171 (Lehmann, 19.1), 6-171 (Wells, 19.2)

Strikers - bowling	O	M	R	W	wd	nb	Dots
TM Head	1	0	13	0			1
B Stanlake	4	0	27	2	1		10
Rashid Khan	4	0	18	2			12
MG Neser	4	0	47	0			3
B Laughlin	3	0	42	0	1		5
PM Siddle	4	0	35	0	2		6

Hurricanes - bowling	O	M	R	W	wd	nb	Dots
CA Rose	4	0	32	1	1		9
JC Archer	4	0	15	3			13
TS Mills	4	0	41	1	2	1	10
CJ Boyce	4	0	34	0			4
DT Christian	3	0	33	0	3		4
SA Milenko	1	0	20	0			1

Toss: Hurricanes. Umpires: GC Joshua, SJ Nogajski, MW Graham-Smith (TV), Ref: PL Marshall. Award: DJM Short (HH). Crowd: 12,167. Short 50: 37 balls, 4x4, 2x6. Ingram 50: 33 balls, 7x4, 2x6.

Match 18 – Heat v Scorchers at the Gabba, Brisbane on January 5, 2018 – Heat won by 49 runs

Heat		B	4	6
CA Lynn	c Klinger b Willey	39	20	5	2
BB McCullum*	c Voges b Paris	32	27	4	
SD Heazlett	c David b Agar	11	11	1	
JA Burns	lbw b Tye	36	26	1	3
AI Ross	b Richardson	3	7		
BCJ Cutting	c Richardson b Willey	46	20	1	5
JJ Peirson+	not out	16	9	3	
MT Steketee	not out	0	0		
Yasir Shah				
BJ Doggett				
MJ Swepson				
	2 lb, 6 w	8		
6 overs: 1-66	20 overs	6-191		

Scorchers		B	4	6
DJ Willey	c Burns b Swepson	25	27	1	1
M Klinger	c Cutting b Steketee	15	13	2	
HWR Cartwright	c Burns b Steketee	0	1		
AJ Turner	c Swepson b Doggett	18	15	1	
AC Voges *	c Doggett b Yasir	13	12		
AC Agar	c sub (CJ Gannon) b Steketee	31	18	1	2
TH David	b Doggett	16	13	2	
JP Inglis +	c Heazlett b Doggett	2	4		
JA Richardson	not out	8	6	1	
AJ Tye	lbw b Doggett	7	4	1	
JS Paris	c sub (CJ Gannon) b Doggett	1	2		
	1 nb, 5 w	6		
6 over: 2-38	19 overs	142		

Fall: 1-59 (Lynn, 5.3), 2-84 (Heazlett, 9.1), 3-88 (McCullum), 4-94 (Ross, 12.4), 5-156 (Burns, 17.3), 6-189 (Cutting, 19.5)

Fall: 1-23 (Klinger, 4.1), 2-23 (Cartwright, 4.2), 3-53 (Willey, 8.2), 4-62 (Turner), 5-102 (Voges, 13.3), 6-113 (Agar, 14.6), 7-120 (Inglis, 16.3), 8-126 (David 16.8), 9-136 (Tye, 18.2), 10-142 (Paris, 18.6)

Scorchers - bowling	O	M	R	W	wd	nb	Dots
JA Richardson	4	0	44	1	1		8
DJ Willey	4	0	40	2	3		11
AJ Tye	4	0	47	1			7
AC Agar	4	0	22	1	1		7
JS Paris	4	0	36	1	1		8

Heat - bowling	O	M	R	W	wd	nb	Dots
JA Burns	1	0	4	0	2		4
Yasir Shah	4	0	27	1			6
MT Steketee	4	0	28	3			11
BJ Doggett	4	0	35	5	1	1	9
MJ Swepson	4	0	34	1			5
BCJ Cutting	2	0	14	0	2		3

Toss: Scorchers. Umpires: PJ Gillespie, AK Wilds, NR Johnstone (TV), Ref: DJ Harper. Award: BJ Doggett (BH) Crowd: 35,564

Match 19 – Stars v Renegades at the MCG on January 6, 2018 – Renegades won by 6 wickets

Stars		B	4	6	Renegades		B	4	6
LJ Wright	c Cooper b Bravo	12	13	2	MS Harris	c Hastings b Coleman	8	13	1
BR Dunk	c Ludeman b Wildermuth	47	30	5 1	AJ Finch *	b Zampa	43	22	7 1
KP Pietersen	c Cooper b Nabi	40	30	6	CL White	not out	35	37	2
GJ Maxwell	b Richardson	33	23	3	M Nabi	c Dunk b Hastings	52	30	2 3
MP Stoinis	not out	24	24	1	BJ Hodge	c Dunk b Hastings	4	5	
PSP Handscomb+					DJ Bravo	not out	6	2	1
JP Faulkner					TLW Cooper				
JW Hastings *					TP Ludeman +				
A Zampa					GB Hogg				
MA Beer					JD Wildermuth				
JR Coleman					KW Richardson				
	1 w		1			5 lb, 2 nb, 4 w		11	
6 overs: 1-50	20 overs		4-157		6 overs: 1-58	17.5 overs		4-159	

Fall: 1-18 (Wright, 2.6), 2-89 (Pietersen, 10.6), 3-106 (Dunk, 13.1), 4-157 (Maxwell, 19.6)

Fall: 1-43 (Harris, 4.1), 2-72 (Finch, 7.6), 3-144 (Nabi, 15.5 ov), 4-152 (Hodge, 17.2)

Renegades - bowling	O	M	R	W	wd	nb	Dots
M Nabi	4	0	27	1			10
KW Richardson	4	0	39	1			4
DJ Bravo	4	0	31	1			9
JD Wildermuth	4	0	28	1	1		10
GB Hogg	4	0	32	0			5

Stars - bowling	O	M	R	W	wd	nb	Dots
JR Coleman	4	0	22	1	1		13
MA Beer	1	0	23	0			0
MP Stoinis	3	0	28	0	1	1	5
JW Hastings	3.5	0	24	2	2		9
A Zampa	3	0	26	1			3
JP Faulkner	2	0	21	0		1	3
GJ Maxwell	1	0	10	0			1

Toss: Renegades. Umpires: SAJ Craig, JD Ward, DM Koch (TV), Ref: RL Parry. Award: M Nabi (MR) Crowd: 48,086
Nabi 50: 27 balls, 2x4 3x6

Match 20 – Thunder v Strikers at the Showgrounds, Homebush on January 7, 2018 – Strikers won by 25 runs

Strikers		B	4	6	Thunder		B	4	6
AT Carey+	b Fawad	34	28	4 1	KR Patterson	c Wells b Stanlake	29	36	3
JB Weatherald	c Buttler b Sandhu	15	13	2	JC Buttler+	b Rashid Khan	21	21	3 1
TM Head *	c Patterson b Fawad	12	13	1	SR Watson *	c Lehmann b Neser	14	16	1
CA Ingram	c Buttler b Sandhu	48	31	2 4	CJ Ferguson	c Neser b Laughlin	9	13	
JW Wells	b Fawad Ahmed	10	13		AJ Nair	c Weatherald b Rashid	10	9	1
MG Neser	c Rohrer b Green	12	13	1	BJ Rohrer	c Laughlin b Neser	29	13	1 3
JS Lehmann	run out	4	3		CJ Green	c Rashid b Neser	8	5	1
	(Buttler-McClenaghan)				RJ Gibson	not out	2	2	
Rashid Khan	not out	16	6	2	GS Sandhu	c Carey b Siddle	0	1	
PM Siddle	not out	0	0	-	MJ McClenaghan	lbw b Siddle	0	2	
B Laughlin					Fawad Ahmed	not out	0	2	
B Stanlake									
	3 lb, 4 w		7			4 b, 4 lb, 3 w		11	
6 overs: 1-38	20 overs		7-158		6 overs: 0-42	20 overs		9-133	

Fall: 1-29 (Weatherald, 3.5), 2-54 (Head, 8.1), 3-64 (Carey, 8.6), 4-98 (Wells, 14.1), 5-127 (Neser, 17.4), 6-140 (Ingram, 18.5), 7-141 (Lehmann, 19.1)

Fall: 1-45 (Buttler, 6.5), 2-61 (Patterson, 10.6), 3-75 (Watson, 13.1), 4-87 (Ferguson, 15.1), 5-97 (Nair, 16.2), 6-125 (Rohrer, 18.3), 7-131 (Green, 18.5), 8-133 (Sandhu, 19.2), 9-133 (McClenaghan, 19.4)

Thunder - bowling	O	M	R	W	wd	nb	Dots
SR Watson	1	0	8	0	1		2
MJ McClenaghan	4	0	38	0	1		8
CJ Green	4	0	22	1			13
GS Sandhu	3	0	28	2	2		8
Fawad Ahmed	4	0	31	3			11
AJ Nair	4	0	28	0			5

Strikers - bowling	O	M	R	W	wd	nb	Dots
MG Neser	4	0	29	3	1		11
B Stanlake	4	0	24	1	1		14
Rashid Khan	4	0	21	2			10
PM Siddle	4	1	13	2			14
B Laughlin	4	0	38	1	1		8

Toss: Strikers. Umpires: SD Fry, SA Lightbody, GJ Davidson (TV), Ref: RW Stratford. Award: Rashid Khan (AS). Crowd: 13,052

Australian Cricket Digest, 2018-19

Match 21 – Hurricanes v Sixers at Bellerive Oval on January 8, 2018 – Hurricanes 5 runs

Hurricanes		B	4	6
DJM Short	c Botha b Abbott	42	36	3	2
AJ Doolan	c Maddinson b Dwarshuis	3	4	
MS Wade +	c Billings b Bird	41	30	5	1
BR McDermott	c Maddinson b Abbott	19	19		1
GJ Bailey *	c Botha b Abbott	11	7	2
DT Christian	not out	28	14	5
SA Milenko	c Maddinson b Sams	22	10	3	1
JC Archer	not out	0	0	
CA Rose				
CJ Boyce				
TS Mills				
	4 lb	4		
6 overs: 1-46	20 overs	6-170		

Sixers		B	4	6
JJ Roy	c Bailey b Rose	9	6		1
DP Hughes	c Boyce b Christian	33	35	3
NJ Maddinson	c McDermott b Mills	7	6	1
JC Silk	c Doolan b Mills	45	37	2	2
SW Billings	not out	61	31	6	3
BJ Dwarshuis	not out	3	6	
J Botha *				
PM Nevill +				
DR Sams				
JM Bird				
SA Abbott				
	(3 b, 1 nb, 3 w)	7		
6 overs: 2-45	20 overs	4-165		

Fall: 1-4 (Doolan, 1.1), 2-81 (Wade, 10.4), 3-88 (Short, 11.4), 4-106 (Bailey, 14.1), 5-128 (McDermott, 16.4), 6-166 (Milenko, 19.5)

Fall: 1-15 (Roy, 1.3), 2-31 (Maddinson, 4.3), 3-64 (Hughes, 9.3), 4-124 (Silk, 16.3)

Sixers - bowling	O	M	R	W	wd	nb	Dots
JM Bird	4	0	31	1			11
BJ Dwarshuis	4	0	30	1			10
J Botha	4	0	29	0			5
DR Sams	4	0	49	1			4
SA Abbott	4	0	27	3			14

Hurricanes - bowling	O	M	R	W	wd	nb	Dots
SA Milenko	1	0	14	0	1	1	1
CA Rose	3	0	22	1	1		8
JC Archer	4	0	35	0			8
TS Mills	4	0	42	2	1		6
CJ Boyce	4	0	22	0			5
DT Christian	4	0	27	1			10

Toss: Hurricanes. Umpires: SAJ Craig, DM Koch, JD Ward (TV), Ref: RL Parry. Award: SW Billings (SS) Crowd: 12,896
Billings 50: 29 balls, 6x4, 1x6

Match 22 – Scorchers v Renegades at the WACA on January 8, 2018 – Scorchers won by 2 wickets

Renegades		B	4	6
MS Harris	c Turner b Tye	48	28	6	2
AJ Finch *	c Inglis b Johnson	2	3	
CL White	not out	68	55	4	3
TLW Cooper	c Johnson b Tye	57	34	5	4
DJ Bravo	not out	0	1	
BJ Hodge				
M Nabi				
TP Ludeman +				
GB Hogg				
JD Wildermuth				
KW Richardson				
	1 b, 2 lb, 1 nb, 6 w	10		
6 overs: 1-51	20 overs	3-185		

Scorchers		B	4	6
DJ Willey	c Harris b Richardson	55	41	5	2
M Klinger	c Ludeman b Nabi	0	1	
HWR Cartwright	st Ludeman b Hogg	22	23	3
AJ Turner	run out (Bravo)	70	32	3	5
AC Agar	not out	26	17	1	2
AC Voges *	run out (Cooper-Bravo)	1	1	
TH David	not out	3	5	
JP Inglis +				
AJ Tye				
MG Johnson				
JA Richardson				
	4 b, 1 lb, 1 nb, 3 w	9		
6 overs: 1-40	19.5 overs	5-186		

Fall: 1-19 (Finch, 2.1), 2-84 (Harris, 9.4), 3-182 (Cooper, 19.5)

Fall: 1-2 (Klinger, 0.1), 2-46 (Cartwright, 6.5), 3-133 (Willey, 14.3), 4-167 (Turner, 17.2), 5-169 (Voges, 17.4)

Scorchers - bowling	O	M	R	W	wd	nb	Dots
MG Johnson	4	0	23	1	4		12
DJ Willey	4	0	34	0			8
JA Richardson	4	0	55	0			6
AC Agar	3	0	26	0			4
AJ Tye	4	0	36	2	1	1	11
HWR Cartwright	1	0	8	0			1

Renegades - bowling	O	M	R	W	wd	nb	Dots
M Nabi	3.5	0	30	1	1		9
KW Richardson	4	0	32	1			10
JD Wildermuth	4	0	38	0			7
DJ Bravo	4	0	43	0			3
GB Hogg	4	0	38	1		1	9

Toss: Scorchers. Umpires: MW Graham-Smith, SJ Nogajski, GC Joshua (TV), Ref: PL Marshall. Award: AJ Turner (PS). Crowd: 22,475
White 50: 44 balls, 3x4, 2x6; Cooper 50: 32 balls, 4x4, 4x6; Willey 50: 38 balls, 5x4 2x6; Turner 50: 23 balls, 3x4, 3x6

Australian Cricket Digest, 2018-19

Match 23 – Strikers v Stars on January 9, 2018 – Strikers won by 8 wickets

Stars		B	4	6
MP Stoinis	c Laughlin b Rashid	39	29 6	1
BR Dunk	c Laughlin b Neser	1	4	
KP Pietersen	b Stanlake	5	6	1
PSP Handscomb+	c Carey b Laughlin	1	5	
GJ Maxwell	c Head b Siddle	60	39 7	1
SE Gotch	run out (Ingram-Laughlin)	14	18	
JP Faulkner	not out	6	9	
JW Hastings *	not out	17	10	1
A Zampa				
SM Boland				
JR Coleman				
	3 lb, 5 w	8		
6 overs: 3-34	20 overs	6-151		

Strikers		B	4	6
AT Carey+	not out	59	52 4	1
JB Weatherald	st Handscomb b Maxwell	18	17 1	1
TM Head *	c Faulkner b Stoinis	53	32 5	3
CA Ingram	not out	15	11 1	1
JW Wells				
JS Lehmann				
MG Neser				
Rashid Khan				
PM Siddle				
B Laughlin				
B Stanlake				
	2 lb, 5 w	7		
6 overs: 0-40	18.4 overs	2-152		

Fall: 1-2 (Dunk, 1.3), 2-11 (Pietersen, 2.5), 3-34 (Handscomb, 5.6), 4-51 (Stoinis, 7.4), 5-112 (Gotch, 15.4), 6-132 (Maxwell, 17.6)

Fall: 1-50 (Weatherald, 6.5), 2-124 (Head, 15.4)

Strikers - bowling	O	M	R	W	wd	nb	Dots
B Stanlake	4	0	31	1	2		14
MG Neser	4	0	29	1			10
PM Siddle	4	0	33	1	2		10
B Laughlin	4	0	32	1	1		5
Rashid Khan	4	0	23	1			8

Stars - bowling	O	M	R	W	wd	nb	Dots
JP Faulkner	2	0	6	0			6
JR Coleman	2	0	10	0			5
SM Boland	2	0	26	0			3
JW Hastings	2	0	13	0			7
GJ Maxwell	3	0	24	1	1		3
MP Stoinis	4	0	47	1	3		8
A Zampa	3.4	0	24	0	1		8

Toss: Stars. Umpires: PJ Gillespie, AK Wilds, NR Johnstone (TV), Ref: DJ Harper. Award: TM Head (AS) Crowd: 42,624
Maxwell 50: 34 balls 5x4, 1x6. Carey 50: 47 balls, 4x4; Head 50: 30 balls, 5x4, 3x6

Match 24 – Heat v Hurricanes at the Gabba, Brisbane on January 10, 2018 - Hurricanes won by 3 runs

Hurricanes		B	4	6
AJ Doolan	b Steketee	9	10	1
DJM Short	not out	122	69 8	8
MS Wade +	c Swepson b Cutting	16	19	1
BR McDermott	c Ross b Cutting	19	15	1
GJ Bailey *	c McCullum b Steketee	4	7	
DT Christian				
JC Archer				
CA Rose				
CJ Boyce				
TS Mills				
SA Milenko				
	4 lb, 5 w	9		
6 overs: 1-56	20 overs	4-179		

Heat		B	4	6
SD Heazlett	lbw b Short	45	33 4	2
BB McCullum *	c Bailey b Boyce	33	22 6	
JA Burns	c Archer b Boyce	13	14	
AI Ross	obstructing the field	27	19 2	1
BCJ Cutting	c and b Archer	4	7	
M Labuschagne	run out (Wade-Boyce)	1	5	
JJ Pierson +	not out	26	13 2	1
MT Steketee	run out (Wade-Archer)	13	4	2
BJ Doggett	c Archer b Christian	3	3	
Yasir Shah				
MJ Swepson				
	5 b, 1 lb, 5 w	11		
6 overs: 0-62	20 overs	8-176		

Fall: 1-14 (Doolan, 2.1), 2-78 (Wade, 9.4), 3-133 (McDermott, 15.6), 4-179 (Bailey, 20 ov)

Fall: 1-64 (McCullum, 6.3), 2-91 (Burns, 10.4), 3-95 (Heazlett, 11.5), 4-113 (Cutting, 14.3), 5-118 (Labuschagne, 15.3), 6-132 (Ross, 16.6), 7-156 (Steketee, 18.3), 8-176 (Doggett, 19.6)

Heat - bowling	O	M	R	W	wd	nb	Dots
JA Burns	1	0	5	0			1
Yasir Shah	4	0	29	0	1		5
MT Steketee	4	0	51	2	2		10
BJ Doggett	4	0	39	2			4
MJ Swepson	3	0	24	0			3
BCJ Cutting	4	0	27	2			6

Hurricanes - bowling	O	M	R	W	wd	nb	Dots
SA Milenko	1	0	16	0			2
CA Rose	2	0	29	0			2
JC Archer	4	0	39	1	2		10
TS Mills	4	0	35	0			8
CJ Boyce	4	0	23	2			8
DJM Short	4	0	20	1	1		8
DT Christian	1	0	8	1	1		2

Toss: Hurricanes. Umpires: GJ Davidson, SD Fry, SA Lightbody (TV), Ref: RW Stratford. Award: DJM Short (HH). Crowd: 33,017
Short 50: 29 balls, 5x4, 2x6; 100: 63 balls, 8x4, 5x6.

Australian Cricket Digest, 2018-19

Match 25 – Thunder v Scorchers at the Showgrounds, Homebush on January 11, 2018 – Thunder won by 3 runs

Thunder		B	4	6
UT Khawaja	c Klinger b Agar	85	51	8 4
KR Patterson	c Bancroft b Kelly	14	12	2
SR Watson *	c Kelly b Bresnan	21	15	3
CJ Ferguson	c Cartwright b Bresnan	25	23	2
BJ Rohrer	not out	22	16	1 1
AJ Nair	not out	4	3	
JS Lenton +				
CJ Green				
Fawad Ahmed				
GS Sandhu				
MJ McClenaghan				
	2 lb, 2 w	4		
6 overs: 1-55	20 overs	4-175		

Fall: 1-45 (Patterson, 4.5), 2-84 (Watson, 9.3), 3-138 (Khawaja, 15.3), 4-157 (Ferguson, 17.5)

Scorchers		B	4	6
WG Bosisto	c Fawad b McClenaghan	9	7	1
M Klinger	c Sandhu b Green	4	9	
CT Bancroft +	not out	75	56	5 3
AJ Turner	lbw b Sandhu	3	5	
AC Voges *	b Fawad Ahmed	1	3	
HWR Cartwright	not out	65	41	4 3
AC Agar				
JS Paris				
TT Bresnan				
ML Kelly				
MG Johnson				
	1 b, 9 lb, 1 nb, 4 w	15		
6 overs: 3-34	20 overs	4-172		

Fall: 1-11 (Bosisto, 1.4), 2-25 (Klinger, 4.2), 3-32 (Turner, 5.3), 4-35 (Voges, 6.2)

Scorchers - bowling	O	M	R	W	wd	nb	Dots
MG Johnson	4	0	25	0	1		12
JS Paris	4	0	28	0	1		8
WG Bosisto	1	0	19	0			1
ML Kelly	4	0	32	1			6
TT Bresnan	3	0	38	2			4
AC Agar	4	0	31	1			6

Thunder - bowling	O	M	R	W	wd	nb	Dots
GS Sandhu	4	0	21	1			10
MJ McClenaghan	4	0	53	1	4	1	5
CJ Green	4	0	43	1			10
Fawad Ahmed	4	0	19	1			10
AJ Nair	4	0	26	0			6

Toss: Thunder. Umpires: PJ Gillespie, AK Wilds, NR Johnstone (TV), Ref: D Talalla. Award: UT Khawaja (ST).   Crowd: 14,703

Match 26 – Renegades v Stars at Etihad Stadium, Melbourne on January 12, 2018 – Stars won by 23 runs

Stars		B	4	6
PSP Handscomb+	c Webster b Nabi	41	37	4
BR Dunk	lbw b Nabi	0	1	
KP Pietersen	c Short b Wildermuth	74	46	4 5
GJ Maxwell	not out	31	16	2 2
SE Gotch	c Ludeman b Richardson	9	8	1
JP Faulkner	not out	10	12	
JW Hastings *				
EP Gulbis				
DG Fallins				
DJ Worrall				
JR Coleman				
	2 w	2		
6 overs: 1-46	20 overs	4-167		

Fall: 1-2 (Dunk, 0.3), 2-112 (Handscomb, 13.1), 3-119 (Pietersen, 14.3), 4-132 (Gotch, 16.3)

Renegades		B	4	6
TP Ludeman +	c Maxwell b Coleman	13	14	1
MS Harris	c Gulbis b Coleman	0	3	
MW Short	c Gotch b Hastings	16	15	1 1
DJ Bravo *	c Maxwell b Gulbis	26	18	2 1
TLW Cooper	c Pietersen b Coleman	19	19	1
M Nabi	c Maxwell b Faulkner	23	17	3
BJ Webster	b Worrall	9	10	
JD Wildermuth	c Maxwell b Hastings	23	11	1 2
KW Richardson	not out	9	8	
JM Holland	b Worrall	1	3	
GB Hogg	not out	1	2	
	2 lb, 2 w	4		
6 overs: 3-36	20 overs	9-144		

Fall: 1-2 (Harris, 1.4), 2-24 (Ludeman, 3.6), 3-33 (Short, 5.4), 4-56 (Cooper, 9.3), 5-91 (Bravo, 13.1), 6-102 (Nabi, 14.4), 7-125 (Webster, 17.1), 8-138 (Wildermuth, 18.3), 9-142 (Holland, 19.3)

Renegades - bowling	O	M	R	W	wd	nb	Dots
M Nabi	4	0	15	2	1		10
JM Holland	2	0	21	0			4
KW Richardson	4	0	36	1			7
DJ Bravo	4	0	38	0	1		6
JD Wildermuth	4	0	27	1			5
GB Hogg	2	0	30	0			0

Stars - bowling	O	M	R	W	wd	nb	Dots
DJ Worrall	4	0	25	2	1		11
JR Coleman	4	0	27	3			10
DG Fallins	3	0	19	0			5
JW Hastings	4	0	28	2	1		10
JP Faulkner	3	0	25	1			6
EP Gulbis	2	0	18	1			2

Toss: Renegades. Umpires: MW Graham-Smith, GC Joshua, DJ Shepard (TV), Ref: DJ Harper. Award: KP Pietersen (MS). Crowd: 44,316. Pietersen 50: 28 balls, 4x4, 3x6

144

Match 27 – Strikers v Scorchers at Traeger Park, Alice Springs on January 13, 2018 (day)
Scorchers won by 6 wickets

Strikers			B	4	6
AT Carey +	c Paris b Kelly		44	32	2	2
J B Weatherald	lbw b Bosisto		19	21	2
CA Ingram *	c Bosisto b Agar		3	5
J W Wells	run out (Klinger-Bancroft)		10	10
J S Lehmann	c Johnson b Agar		1	5
J R Dean	c Cartwright b Agar		13	17	1
M G Neser	c Cartwright b Kelly		5	7
Rashid Khan	b Bresnan		5	6
P M Siddle	c sub (HJ Morton) b Bres		2	5
B Laughlin	b Paris		1	3
B Stanlake	not out		4	5
	(2 lb, 3 w)		5
6 overs: 0-47	(all out, 19.2 overs)		112

Scorchers			B	4	6
WG Bosisto	c Siddle b Neser		3	9
M Klinger	c Laughlin b Neser		17	14	3
CT Bancroft +	c Weatherald b Siddle		15	14		1
HWR Cartwright	not out		47	44	2	2
AJ Turner *	b Rashid Khan		1	2
AC Agar	not out		26	29	1
TH David					
J S Paris					
TT Bresnan					
M L Kelly					
M G Johnson					
	1 lb, 2 nb, 2 w		5
6 overs: 2-28	18.2 overs		4-114

Fall: 1-49 (Weatherald, 6.2), 2-56 (Ingram, 7.6), 3-79 (Wells, 11.1), 4-80 (Carey, 11.5), 5-81 (Lehmann, 12.3), 6-92 (Neser, 15.1), 7-105 (Dean, 16.6), 8-105 (Rashid, 17.1), 9-108 (Laughlin, 18.2), 10-112 (Siddle, 19.2)

Fall: 1-11 (Bosisto, 2.3), 2-26 (Klinger, 4.5), 3-412 (Bancroft, 7.5), 4-43 (Turner, 8.1)

Scorchers - bowling	O	M	R	W	wd	nb	Dots
M G Johnson	4	0	22	0	1		10
J S Paris	4	0	33	1	1		10
WG Bosisto	2	0	9	1			4
AC Agar	4	0	19	3			8
TT Bresnan	2.2	0	14	2			5
M L Kelly	3	0	13	2	1		11

Stars - bowling	O	M	R	W	wd	nb	Dots
M G Neser	3.2	0	18	2	1		13
B Stanlake	3	0	23	0			6
Rashid Khan	4	0	15	1			11
CA Ingram	1	0	11	0			1
P M Siddle	4	0	25	1		1	11
B Laughlin	3	0	21	0		1	5

Toss: Scorchers. Umpires: DM Koch, JD Ward, SAJ Craig (TV), Ref: SR Bernard. Award: AC Agar (PS)   Crowd: 3,906

Match 28 – Sixers v Thunder at the SCG on January 13, 2018 – Sixers won by 8 wickets

Thunder			B	4	6
UT Khawaja	lbw b Brathwaite		8	17		1
J M Vince	c Maddinson b Lyon		34	25	2	2
SR Watson *	b Abbott		3	5
CJ Ferguson	c Denly b Henriques		7	14
CJ Green	run out (Henriques-Nevill)		49	27	2	3
AJ Nair	c Silk b Henriques		17	17
BJ Rohrer	not out		7	8	1
J S Lenton +	not out		18	7	2	1
Fawad Ahmed					
GS Sandhu					
MJ McClenaghan					
	4 b, 4 lb, 5 w		13
6 overs: 1-45	20 overs		6-156

Sixers			B	4	6
J L Denly	b Fawad Ahmed		43	29	4	3
DP Hughes	not out		66	55	4	1
NJ Maddinson	c Rohrer b Nair		28	23		2
MC Henriques	not out		18	13	1
JC Silk					
CR Brathwaite					
J Botha *					
P M Nevill +					
NM Lyon					
BJ Dwarshuis					
S A Abbott					
	1 lb, 1 w		2
6 overs: 0-54	20 overs		2-157

Fall: 1-39 (Khawaja, 5.2), 2-48 (Watson, 6.5), 3-58 (Vince, 9.2), 4-63 (Ferguson, 10.4), 5-122 (Nair, 17.1), 6-129 (Green, 17.3)

Fall: 1-69 (Denly, 8.6), 2-127 (Maddinson, 16.1)

Sixers - bowling	O	M	R	W	wd	nb	Dots
BJ Dwarshuis	3	0	21	0	4		12
CR Brathwaite	4	0	31	1			9
NM Lyon	4	0	24	1			12
S A Abbott	3	0	25	1	1		5
J Botha	3	0	22	0			4
MC Henriques	3	0	25	2			8

Thunder - bowling	O	M	R	W	wd	nb	Dots
GS Sandhu	2	0	26	0	1		6
MJ McClenaghan	4	0	34	0			9
CJ Green	4	0	22	0			8
SR Watson	2	0	26	0			1
Fawad Ahmed	4	0	22	1			8
AJ Nair	4	0	26	1			7

Toss: Sixers. Umpires: GJ Davidson, SA Lightbody, CA Polosak (TV), Ref: PL Marshall. Award: DP Hughes (SS)   Crowd: 36,458
Hughes 50: 43 balls, 4x4, 1x6

Match 29 – Hurricanes v Heat at Bellerive Oval, Hobart on January 15, 2018 – Hurricanes won by 6 wickets

Heat		B	4	6
SD Heazlett	c Wade b Rose	5	3	1
BB McCullum *	c Bailey b Mills	51	38	5	1
JA Burns	c Doolan b Short	38	24	3	3
AI Ross	b Boyce	4	7	
BCJ Cutting	run out (Bailey)	30	26	2	1
JJ Peirson +	c Short b Christian	16	12	2	1
CJ Gannon	c Bailey b Archer	9	7	1
MT Steketee	b Archer	5	3	1
BJ Doggett	not out	0	0	
Yasir Shah				
MJ Swepson				
	2 lb, 5 w	7		
6 overs: 1-62	20 overs	8-165		

Hurricanes		B	4	6
AJ Doolan	c Gannon b Burns	10	5	2
DJM Short	c Burns b Steketee	59	49	8
GJ Bailey *	c Gannon b Cutting	19	21	1
DT Christian	c Ross b Doggett	23	9		3
BR McDermott	not out	32	19	3	1
MS Wade +	not out	11	9	1
JC Archer				
CA Rose				
CJ Boyce				
TS Mills				
SA Milenko				
	2 lb, 2 nb, 8 w	12		
6 overs: 1-56	18.2 overs	4-166		

Fall: 1-6 (Heazlett, 0.4), 2-65 (Burns, 6.6), 3-85 (Ross, 9.6), 4-112 (McCullum, 13.2), 5-137 (Cutting, 17.2), 6-152 (Peirson, 18.3), 7-161 (Gannon, 19.4), 8-165 (Steketee, 19.6)

Fall: 1-10 (Doolan, 0.5), 2-83 (Bailey, 10.2), 3-121 (Christian, 12.5), 4-125 (Short, 14.2)

Hurricanes - bowling	O	M	R	W	wd	nb	Dots
CA Rose	3	0	26	1	2		6
JC Archer	4	0	32	2			11
TS Mills	4	0	41	1	2		9
DJM Short	3	0	24	1			7
CJ Boyce	4	0	28	1	1		9
DT Christian	2	0	12	1			6

Heat - bowling	O	M	R	W	wd	nb	Dots
JA Burns	1	0	10	1			3
Yasir Shah	4	0	28	0			6
MT Steketee	4	0	38	1			8
BJ Doggett	4	0	43	1	2	1	9
MJ Swepson	4	0	31	0	2		5
BCJ Cutting	1.2	0	14	1		1	1

Toss: Heat. Umpires: GA Abood, AK Wilds, PJ Gillespie (TV), Ref: D Talalla. Award: DT Christian (HH) Crowd: 14,873
McCullum 50: 35 balls, 5x4 1x6. Short 50: 35 balls, 7x4

Match 30 – Stars v Sixers at the MCG on January 16, 2018 – Sixers won by 8 wickets

Stars		B	4	6
LJ Wright	c Dwarshuis b Abbott	11	13	1
BR Dunk	c Nevill b Lyon	7	12	1
KP Pietersen	c Abbott b Lyon	9	8	2
GJ Maxwell	c Nevill b Abbott	28	16	1	3
PSP Handscomb+	c Silk b Lyon	14	16	1
JP Faulkner	c Abbott b Brathwaite	28	30	3
EP Gulbis	run out (Brathwaite)	24	25	1	1
JW Hastings *	not out	0	0	
DJ Worrall				
DG Fallins				
JR Coleman				
	5 lb, 2 w	7		
6 overs: 3-31	20 overs	7-128		

Sixers		B	4	6
JL Denly	c Maxwell b Faulkner	12	13	1
DP Hughes	not out	49	46	6
NJ Maddinson	c Dunk b Coleman	62	31	6	6
MC Henriques	not out	1	1	
JC Silk				
J Botha *				
CR Brathwaite				
PM Nevill +				
NM Lyon				
SA Abbott				
BJ Dwarshuis				
	5 w	5		
6 overs: 1-49	15.1 overs	2-129		

Fall: 1-20 (Wright, 3.6), 2-31 (Pietersen, 5.2), 3-31 (Dunk, 5.3), 4-76 (Maxwell, 10.4), 5-78 (Handscomb, 11.2), 6-128 (Faulkner, 19.5), 7-128 (Gulbis, 19.6)

Fall: 1-29 (Denly, 3.6), 2-121 (Maddinson, 13.2)

Sixers - bowling	O	M	R	W	wd	nb	Dots
BJ Dwarshuis	4	0	20	0	1		16
J Botha	3	0	20	0			8
SA Abbott	4	0	35	2			8
CR Brathwaite	4	0	26	1	1		12
NM Lyon	4	0	18	3			14
JL Denly	1	0	4	0			2

Stars - bowling	O	M	R	W	wd	nb	Dots
DJ Worrall	3	0	21	0			11
JR Coleman	2.1	0	14	1	2		7
JP Faulkner	2	0	20	1			5
JW Hastings	3	0	27	0	1		10
GJ Maxwell	1	0	11	0			1
DG Fallins	2	0	25	0	1		3
EP Gulbis	2	0	11	0			5

Toss: Sixers. Umpires: SAJ Craig, JD Ward, DM Koch (TV), Ref: SR Bernard. Award: NM Lyon (SS) Crowd: 26,134
Maddinson 50 off 23 balls, 5x4 4x6

Australian Cricket Digest, 2018-19

Match 31 – Strikers v Hurricanes at Adelaide Oval on January 17, 2018 – Strikers won by 11 runs

Strikers		R	B	4	6
AT Carey+	b Archer	100	56	12	4
JB Weatherald	run out (Archer)	65	52	5	4
CA Ingram *	not out	4	4		
JW Wells	lbw b Archer	8	7	1	
JS Lehmann	b Archer	4	2	1	
JR Dean					
MG Neser					
Rashid Khan					
PM Siddle					
B Laughlin					
B Stanlake					
	4 lb, 1 nb, 1 w	6			
6 overs: 0-45	20 overs	4-187			

Hurricanes		R	B	4	6
AJ Doolan	not out	70	55	4	3
DJM Short	c Carey b Neser	28	24	2	2
GJ Bailey*	b Siddle	7	7	1	
BR McDermott	c Wells b Laughlin	45	29	4	1
DT Christian	run out (Wells-Carey)	2	4		
JC Archer	not out	4	4		
MS Wade +					
CA Rose					
CJ Boyce					
NJ Reardon					
TS Mills					
	5 b, 7 lb, 3 nb, 5 w	20			
6 overs: 0-42	20 overs	4-176			

Fall: 1-171 (Weatherald, 17.4), 2-171 (Carey, 17.5), 3-183 (Wells), 4-187 (Lehmann, 19.6)

Fall: 1-45 (Short, 6.6), 2-57 (Bailey, 8.6), 3-159 (McDermott, 17.6), 4-167 (Christian, 19.1)

Hurricanes - bowling	O	M	R	W	wd	nb	Dots
CA Rose	3	0	22	0			7
DJM Short	3	0	25	0	1		8
JC Archer	4	0	27	3		1	13
TS Mills	4	0	35	0			7
CJ Boyce	3	0	32	0			4
DT Christian	3	0	42	0			4

Strikers - bowling	O	M	R	W	wd	nb	Dots
CA Ingram	1	0	6	0			2
B Stanlake	4	0	25	0			11
MG Neser	4	0	40	1		1	7
Rashid Khan	4	0	35	0	2		10
B Laughlin	4	0	40	1	1	1	10
PM Siddle	3	0	18	1	1	1	5

Toss: Strikers. Umpires: GJ Davidson, SA Lightbody, CA Polosak (TV), Ref: PL Marshall. Award: AT Carey (AS) Crowd: 40,335

Carey 50: 32 balls, 5x4, 2x6; 100: 54 balls, 12x4, 4x6. Weatherald 50: 41 balls, 4x4, 3x6. Doolan 50: 41 balls, 4x4, 3x6.

Match 32 – Sixers v Heat at the SCG on January 18, 2018 - Sixers won by 9 wickets

Heat		R	B	4	6
SD Heazlett	c Silk b Lyon	10	11	2	
BB McCullum *	c Brathwaite b Botha	1	4		
M Labuschagne	c Henriques b Dwarshuis	0	5		
AI Ross	c Nevill b Abbott	15	21	1	
JJ Peirson +	c Nevill b Abbott	14	12	1	
BCJ Cutting	c Denly b Lyon	5	5		
JS Floros	c Lyon b Abbott	3	10		
JK Lalor	c Silk b Brathwaite	14	18	2	
MT Steketee	c Brathwaite b Abbott	5	12		
Yasir Shah	b Brathwaite	0	1		
MJ Swepson	not out	1	1		
	2 b, 1 lb, 2 w	5			
6 overs: 3-27	16.4 overs	73			

Sixers		R	B	4	6
JL Denly	not out	19	24	2	1
DP Hughes	lbw b Yasir	37	28	4	1
NJ Maddinson	not out	17	8		2
MC Henriques					
JC Silk					
J Botha *					
CR Brathwaite					
PM Nevill +					
NM Lyon					
SA Abbott					
BJ Dwarshuis					
	1 w	1			
6 overs: 0-46	10 overs	1-74			

Fall: 1-10 (McCullum, 1.6), 2-10 (Labuschagne, 2.5), 3-11 (Heazlett, 3.2), 4-42 (Peirson, 8.2), 5-43 (Ross, 8.6), 6-47 (Cutting, 9.4), 7-53 (Floros, 12.3), 8-67 (Steketee, 15.6), 9-67 (Yasir, 16.1), 10-73 (Lalor, 16.4)

Fall: 1-49 (Hughes, 7.1)

Sixers - bowling	O	M	R	W	wd	nb	Dots
BJ Dwarshuis	2	0	9	1			9
J Botha	4	0	13	1			15
NM Lyon	4	0	17	2			13
SA Abbott	4	0	11	4	1		15
CR Brathwaite	2.4	0	20	2	1		5

Heat - bowling	O	M	R	W	wd	nb	Dots
JK Lalor	3	0	20	0			10
Yasir Shah	4	0	37	1	1		9
MT Steketee	1	0	7	0			2
MJ Swepson	1	0	3	0			3
JS Floros	1	0	7	0			4

Toss: Sixers. Umpires: MW Graham-Smith, GC Joshua, DJ Shepard (TV), Ref: DJ Harper. Award: SA Abbott (SS) Crowd: 22,900

Australian Cricket Digest, 2018-19

Match 33 – Stars v Thunder at the MCG on January 20, 2018 – Thunder won by 7 wickets

Stars			B	4	6
PSP Handscomb+	c & b McClenaghan	57	44	7	
BR Dunk	c Green b Watson	12	10	2	
KP Pietersen	c Lenton b Green	12	11	2	
GJ Maxwell	b Fawad Ahmed	1	3		
SE Gotch	c Khawaja b Sandhu	31	25	2	1
JP Faulkner	b Green	5	9		
JW Hastings *	not out	9	10	1	
EP Gulbis	not out	13	8	1	
LP Bowe					
DJ Worrall					
JR Coleman					
	1 lb, 6 w	7			
6 overs: 1-50	20 overs	6-147			

Fall: 1-29 (Dunk, 3.1), 2-52 (Pietersen, 6.3), 3-55 (Maxwell, 7.2), 4-104 (Handscomb, 14.3), 5-123 (Gotch, 16.4), 6-124 (Faulkner, 17.2)

Thunder - bowling	O	M	R	W	wd	nb	Dots
MJ McClenaghan	4	0	30	1	1		6
GS Sandhu	4	0	26	1	3		11
CJ Green	4	0	27	2	1		8
SR Watson	4	0	34	1			8
Fawad Ahmed	4	0	29	1	1		8

Thunder			B	4	6
UT Khawaja	c Pietersen b Bowe	44	26	9	
JM Vince	st Handscomb b Bowe	40	29	4	2
SR Watson *	not out	49	28	5	2
CJ Green	c Dunk b Hastings	4	13		
BJ Rohrer	not out	0	1		
CJ Ferguson					
JS Lenton +					
AJ Nair					
Fawad Ahmed					
GS Sandhu					
MJ McClenaghan					
	9 lb, 3 w	12			
6 overs: 0-64	16.1 overs	3-149			

Fall: 1-85 (Khawaja, 8.2), 2-102 (Vince, 10.3), 3-135 (Green, 15.2)

Stars - bowling	O	M	R	W	wd	nb	Dots
DJ Worrall	3	0	32	0	2		8
JR Coleman	2.1	0	22	0	1		5
JP Faulkner	2	0	14	0			4
JW Hastings	4	0	32	1			9
LP Bowe	4	0	30	2			12
EP Gulbis	1	0	10	0			0

Toss: Thunder. Umpires: GJ Davidson, SA Lightbody, CA Polosak (TV), Ref: D Talalla. Award: SR Watson (ST) Crowd: 27,421
Handscomb 50: 39 balls, 6x4

Match 34 – Scorchers v Hurricanes at the WACA, Hobart on January 20, 2018 - Scorchers won by 5 wickets

Hurricanes			B	4	6
MS Wade +	c Whiteman b Paris	31	17	5	1
DJM Short	c Agar b Kelly	11	13	2	
GJ Bailey *	b Kelly	37	33	5	
BR McDermott	st Bancroft b Agar	8	15	1	
DT Christian	b Agar	1	2		
SA Milenko	not out	66	37	4	5
JC Archer	not out	3	4		
TS Rogers					
CA Rose					
CJ Boyce					
TS Mills					
	5 lb, 1 nb, 4 w	10			
6 overs: 2-51	20 overs	5-167			

Fall: 1-41 (Wade, 4.1), 2-51 (Short, 5.3), 3-66 (McDermott, 10.1), 4-68 (Christian, 10.4), 5-138 (Bailey, 17.1)

Scorchers - bowling	O	M	R	W	wd	nb	Dots
MG Johnson	4	0	35	0	2		10
JS Paris	4	0	46	1			9
ML Kelly	4	0	23	2	1		12
AC Agar	4	1	14	2			16
TT Bresnan	4	0	44	0	1	1	7

Scorchers			B	4	6
SM Whiteman	c Short b Rogers	1	3		
M Klinger	b Archer	17	18	2	
CT Bancroft +	c Wade b Mills	54	36	5	2
HWR Cartwright	b Christian	17	13	1	1
AJ Turner	not out	50	27	4	2
AC Voges *	run out (Archer)	11	8	1	
AC Agar	not out	13	11	1	
JS Paris					
ML Kelly					
TT Bresnan					
MG Johnson					
	2 lb, 3 w	5			
6 overs: 2-43	19.2 overs	5-168			

Fall: 1-2 (Whiteman, 0.4), 2-34 (Klinger, 4.6), 3-78 (Cartwright, 10.2), 4-114 (Bancroft, 13.3), 5-127 (Voges, 15.3)

Hurricanes - bowling	O	M	R	W	wd	nb	Dots
TS Rogers	4	0	29	1			11
CA Rose	2	0	15	0			2
JC Archer	3.2	0	31	1			6
TS Mills	4	0	25	1	1		7
CJ Boyce	2	0	30	0			1
DJM Short	1	0	8	0	1		2
DT Christian	3	0	28	1			4

Toss: Scorchers. Umpires: SAJ Craig, DM Koch, JD Ward (TV), Ref: RW Stratford. Award: AC Agar (PS) Crowd: 22,236

Australian Cricket Digest, 2018-19

Match 35 – Renegades v Strikers at Etihad Stadium, Melbourne on January 22, 2018 – Strikers won by 26 runs

Strikers		B	4	6	Renegades		B	4	6
AT Carey+	c Harris b Wildermuth	32	24	4	MS Harris	c Carey b Stanlake	25	31	2
JB Weatherald	b Tremain	3	9		TP Ludeman+	c Carey b Siddle	14	11	2
TM Head *	b Pollard	58	47	4 2	CL White *	b Rashid	17	23	
CA Ingram	c White b Bravo	68	36	4 5	TLW Cooper	c Carey b Stanlake	24	16	2 1
JW Wells	not out	5	4		KA Pollard	c Lehmann b Laughlin	14	12	1
JS Lehmann	c Hogg b Bravo	0	1		DJ Bravo	c Weatherald b Rashid	4	3	1
MG Neser					BJ Hodge	not out	30	18	1 3
Rashid Khan					JD Wildermuth	c Weatherald b Laughlin	3	5	
PM Siddle					CP Tremain	not out	2	3	
B Laughlin					GB Hogg				
B Stanlake					KW Richardson				
	1 lb, 1 nb, 5 w	7				4 b, 7 lb, 2 nb, 1 w	14		
6 overs: 1-33	20 overs	5-173			6 overs: 1-37	20 overs	7-147		

Fall: 1-11 (Weatherald, 2.5), 2-59 (Carey, 9.3), 3-147 (Head, 18.2), 4-173 (Ingram, 19.5), 5-173 (Lehmann, 19.6)

Fall: 1-33 (Ludeman, 4.3), 2-51 (Harris, 9.1), 3-70 (White, 12.1), 4-92 (Cooper, 14.1), 5-100 (Bravo, 15.2), 6-111 (Pollard, 16.1), 7-121 (Wildermuth, 18.1)

Renegades - bowling	O	M	R	W	wd	nb	Dots	Strikers - bowling	O	M	R	W	wd	nb	Dots
TLW Cooper	2	0	8	0			6	MG Neser	4	0	46	0			5
KW Richardson	3	0	34	0			5	B Stanlake	4	0	22	2			13
CP Tremain	3	0	21	1			8	PM Siddle	4	0	24	1		1	10
DJ Bravo	4	0	30	2	1		8	B Laughlin	4	0	18	2	1	1	10
GB Hogg	3	0	30	0			5	Rashid Khan	4	0	26	2			8
JD Wildermuth	3	0	29	1	3		4								
KA Pollard	2	0	20	1	1	1	4								

Toss: Renegades. Umpires: MW Graham-Smith, GC Joshua, DJ Shepard (TV), Ref: SR Bernard. Award: CA Ingram (AS). Crowd: 23,809
Head 50: 39 balls, 4x4, 2x6; Ingram 50: 31 balls, 4x4, 2x6

Match 36 – Sixers v Stars at the SCG on January 23, 2018 - Sixers won by 5 wickets

Stars		B	4	6	Sixers		B	4	6
PSP Handscomb+	c Henriques b Brathwaite	8	11	1	JL Denly	not out	72	45	6 3
BR Dunk	b Dwarshuis	7	10	1	DP Hughes	c Gulbis b Faulkner	2	4	
GJ Maxwell	c Abbott b Brathwaite	84	47	7 4	NJ Maddinson	lbw b Hastings	61	26	9 3
RJ Quiney	st Nevill b Lyon	36	23	3 2	MC Henriques	c Faulkner b Gulbis	21	13	1 1
SE Gotch	c Silk b Denly	2	3		J Botha *	b Gulbis	14	10	1 1
JP Faulkner	not out	21	17	1	CR Brathwaite	c Maxwell b Hastings	9	6	2
EP Gulbis	not out	14	9	2	PM Nevill+	not out	4	1	1
JW Hastings *					JC Silk				
MA Beer					NM Lyon				
DJ Worrall					BJ Dwarshuis				
LP Bowe					SA Abbott				
	6 b, 4 lb, 7 w	17				2 lb, 5 w	7		
6 overs: 2-51	20 overs	5-189			6 overs: 1-71	17.3 overs	5-190		

Fall: 1-18 (Dunk, 2.6), 2-18 (Handscomb, 3.3), 3-137 (Quiney, 13.2), 4-142 (Gotch, 14.1), 5-161 (Maxwell, 16.6)

Fall: 1-7 (Hughes, 0.6), 2-115 (Maddinson, 9.4), 3-154 (Henriques, 13.5), 4-176 (Botha, 16.2), 5-186 (Brathwaite, 17.2)

Sixers - bowling	O	M	R	W	wd	nb	Dots	Stars - bowling	O	M	R	W	wd	nb	Dots
BJ Dwarshuis	4	0	36	1	3		11	JP Faulkner	3	0	35	1			7
J Botha	2	0	15	0			4	DJ Worrall	3	0	39	0	2		6
CR Brathwaite	4	0	31	2	2		8	MA Beer	3	0	29	0	1		6
SA Abbott	2	0	29	0	1		3	JW Hastings	3.3	0	27	2	1		9
JL Denly	3	0	19	1			6	EP Gulbis	3	0	22	2	1		6
NM Lyon	4	0	35	1			6	LP Bowe	2	0	36	0			6
MC Henriques	1	0	14	0			3								

Toss: Sixers. Umpires: PJ Gillespie, AK Wilds, GA Abood (TV), Ref: RL Parry. Award: JL Denly (SS) Crowd: 16,925
Maxwell 50: 23 balls, 3x4, 4x6. Denly 50: 32 balls, 4x4, 3x6; Maddinson 50: 22 balls, 9x4, 2x6

Australian Cricket Digest, 2018-19

Match 37 – Thunder v Renegades at Manuka Oval, Canberra on January 24, 2018 – Renegades won by 9 runs

Renegades		R	B	4	6
MS Harris	b Green	64	41	7	2
MW Short	st Lenton b Fawad	28	24	3	
TLW Cooper	run out (Rohrer-Fawad)	11	5		1
DJ Bravo *	c and b McClenaghan	16	18		1
KA Pollard	c Green b Sandhu	23	19	2	1
JD Wildermuth	c Blizzard b Sandhu	14	8	1	1
TP Ludeman +	not out	5	2	1	
BJ Webster	not out	18	4	1	2
JM Holland					
CP Tremain					
KW Richardson					
	4 lb, 1 nb, 5 w	10			
6 overs: 0-59	20 overs	6-189			

Fall: 1-77 (Short, 8.2), 2-100 (Cooper, 10.2), 3-112 (Harris, 12.6), 4-134 (Bravo, 15.5), 5-164 (Pollard, 18.5), 6-164 (Wildermuth, 18.6 ov)

Thunder		R	B	4	6
JM Vince	c Holland b Tremain	1	6		
KR Patterson	c Webster b Tremain	3	6		
SR Watson *	c Pollard b Wildermuth	22	16		3
JS Lenton +	c Webster b Holland	23	17	1	2
AJ Nair	c Pollard b Richardson	45	25	1	3
BJ Rohrer	c Wildermuth b Richardson	48	21	6	2
CJ Green	c Wildermuth b Pollard	22	14		2
AC Blizzard	c Short b Richardson	2	4		
GS Sandhu	c Webster b Richardson	0	2		
MJ McClenaghan	lbw b Pollard	9	8		
Fawad Ahmed	not out	1	2		
	3 lb, 1 nb	4			
6 overs: 2-45	20 overs	180			

Fall: 1-1 (Vince, 1.2), 2-13 (Patterson, 3.2), 3-46 (Watson, 6.4), 4-51 (Lenton, 7.5), 5-135 (Nair, 14.1), 6-143 (Rohrer, 14.6) 7-148 (Blizzard, 16.1), 8-149 (Sandhu, 6.5), 9-76 (Green, 19.1), 10-180 (McClenaghan, 19.6)

Thunder - bowling	O	M	R	W	wd	nb	Dots
GS Sandhu	4	0	37	2			9
MJ McClenaghan	4	0	48	1	3	1	9
CJ Green	4	0	36	1			8
SR Watson	4	0	37	0	1		6
Fawad Ahmed	4	0	27	1	1		10

Renegades - bowling	O	M	R	W	wd	nb	Dots
TLW Cooper	1	0	1	0			5
CP Tremain	4	0	33	2			9
KW Richardson	4	0	22	4			16
DJ Bravo	4	0	43	0			6
JD Wildermuth	3	0	43	1			6
JM Holland	2	0	16	1			
KA Pollard	2	0	19	2		1	3

Toss: Thunder. Umpires: SAJ Craig, JD Ward, DM Koch (TV), Ref: RW Stratford. Award: KW Richardson (MR). Crowd: 11,319
Harris 50: 31 balls, 6x4, 1x6

Match 38 – Scorchers v Strikers at the WACA, Perth on January 25, 2018 – Scorchers won by 4 wickets

Strikers		R	B	4	6
JR Dean	c Johnson b Kelly	7	15	1	
JB Weatherald	b Kelly	56	43	4	4
CA Ingram *	c Bancroft b Bresnan	5	8		
JW Wells	c Johnson b Bresnan	15	23	1	
JS Lehmann	not out	21	17	2	
AT Carey +	b Richardson	25	10	4	1
MG Neser	b Richardson	0	1		
Rashid Khan	not out	5	3	1	
WA Agar					
B Stanlake					
B Laughlin					
	2 lb, 1 w	3			
6 overs: 1-35	20 overs	137			

Fall: 1-22 (Dean, 4.1), 2-42 (Ingram, 7.2), 3-68 (Wells, 13.2), 4-94 (Weatherald, 15.5), 5-126 (Carey, 18.5), 6-126 (Neser, 18.6)

Scorchers		R	B	4	6
SM Whiteman	c Stanlake b Neser	8	5	2	
M Klinger	c Ingram b Stanlake	5	10	1	
CT Bancroft +	b Rashid Khan	49	39	6	
HWR Cartwright	c Neser b Rashid	2	5		
AJ Turner	lbw b Rashid	0	1		
AC Voges *	not out	56	45	6	1
AC Agar	c Carey b Laughlin	7	9		
TT Bresnan	not out	7	3	1	
ML Kelly					
JA Richardson					
MG Johnson					
	1 lb, 6 w	7			
6 overs: 4-35	19.3 overs	6-141			

Fall: 1-8 (Whiteman, 0.5), 2-25 (Klinger, 3.3), 3-28 (Cartwright, 4.5), 4-28 (Turner, 4.6), 5-105 (Bancroft, 15.4), 6-124 (Agar, 18.2)

Scorchers - bowling	O	M	R	W	wd	nb	Dots
MG Johnson	4	0	17	0	1		14
ML Kelly	4	0	31	2			11
JA Richardson	4	0	23	2			13
AC Agar	4	0	30	0			7
TT Bresnan	4	0	34	2			9

Strikers - bowling	O	M	R	W	wd	nb	Dots
MG Neser	3.3	0	35	1	2		8
B Stanlake	4	0	23	1	3		14
Rashid Khan	4	0	20	3			11
AC Agar	3	0	26	0	1		2
B Laughlin	4	0	27	1			7
CA Ingram	1	0	9	0			0

Toss: Scorchers.   Umpires: GJ Davidson, SA Lightbody, CA Polosak (TV), Ref: D Talalla. Award: AC Voges (PS)   Crowd: 22,355
Weatherald 50: 38 balls, 4x4, 3x6. Voges 50: 44 balls, 5x4, 1x6

Match 39 – Stars v Hurricanes at the MCG on January 27, 2018 (day) – Stars won by 3 wickets

Hurricanes			B	4	6	Stars			B	4	6
MS Wade +	c Gotch b Hastings	17	11	3		PSP Handscomb+	c Milenko b Christian	7	9		
DJM Short	lbw b Dunk	0	1			BR Dunk	c Rose b Short	30	20	2	2
GJ Bailey*	c Worrall b Gulbis	32	20	3	1	JP Faulkner	c Milenko b Boyce	16	13	1	1
BR McDermott	lbw b Bowe	21	21	2		RJ Quiney	run out (Bailey-Wade)	11	9		1
DT Christian	c Handscomb b Hasting	56	37	4	2	KP Pietersen	c and b Mills	46	23	6	2
SA Milenko	c Hastings b Faulkner	4	6			JW Hastings *	c Wade b Mills	20	6	2	2
NJ Reardon	run out (Hastings)	32	22	2	2	SE Gotch	lbw b Rose	16	16	2	
JC Archer	not out	7	3		1	EP Gulbis	not out	19	13		2
CJ Boyce	not out	0	0			DJ Worrall	not out	13	8	2	
CA Rose						JR Coleman					
TS Mills						LP Bowe					
	1 b, 4 lb, 1 nb, 10 w	16					1 b, 1 lb, 2 nb, 4 w	8			
6 overs: 3-57	20 overs	7-185				6 overs: 1-46	19.1 overs	7-186			

Fall: 1-2 (Short, 0.4), 2-53 (Bailey, 4.6), 3-57 (Wade, 5.2), 4-101 (McDermott, 11.4), 5-107 (Milenko, 13.1), 6-177 (Christian, 19.2), 7-184 (Reardon, 19.5)

Fall: 1-25 (Handscomb, 3.1), 2-46 (Dunk, 6.1), 3-56 (Faulkner, 7.2), 4-71 (Quiney, 9.2), 5-104 (Hastings, 10.6), 6-151 (Pietersen, 15.5), 7-153 (Gotch, 16.2)

Stars - bowling	O	M	R	W	wd	nb	Dots	Hurricanes - bowling	O	M	R	W	wd	nb	Dots
BR Dunk	2	0	19	1	1		5	CA Rose	3	0	23	1			3
DJ Worrall	2	0	18	0	1		4	JC Archer	4	0	35	0	2	2	9
JR Coleman	1	0	16	0	3		2	DT Christian	2.1	0	17	1			5
EP Gulbis	4	0	36	1	1		5	TS Mills	4	0	56	2	2		8
JW Hastings	4	0	41	2	2	1	10	DJM Short	2	0	21	1			5
LP Bowe	4	0	28	1	1		9	CJ Boyce	4	0	32	1			8
JP Faulkner	3	0	22	1	1		6								

Toss: Stars Umpires: MW Graham-Smith, GC Joshua, DJ Shepard (TV), Ref: RL Parry. Award: KP Pietersen (MS). Crowd: 19,671
Christian 50: 34 balls, 3x4, 2x6

Match 40 – Heat v Renegades at the Gabba, Brisbane on January 27, 2018 – Renegades won by 26 runs

Renegades			B	4	6	Heat			B	4	6
MS Harris	c McCullum b Swepson	42	30	6	1	CA Lynn	c Harris b Richardson	21	13	2	2
MW Short	c &b Lalor	62	48	7	1	SD Heazlett	c Richardson b Tremain	3	9		
TLW Cooper	c Swepson b Steketee	65	36	8	2	BB McCullum *	c Bravo b Richardson	5	9		
KA Pollard	c Swepson b Steketee	1	2			MT Renshaw	c Cooper b Bravo	22	19	2	
BJ Webster	not out	8	4			AI Ross	c Holland b Tremain	36	27	2	1
JD Wildermuth						BCJ Cutting	c Harris b Bravo	35	18	1	4
+TP Ludeman						JJ Peirson+	not out	25	13	2	1
*DJ Bravo						MT Steketee	c Webster b Tremain	8	5	1	
JM Holland						JK Lalor	c Bravo b Richardson	1	2		
CP Tremain						Yasir Shah	c Ludeman b Richardson	0	1		
KW Richardson						MJ Swepson	b Bravo	2	3		
	5 lb, 4 w	9					1 lb, 2 w	3			
6 overs: 0-46	20 overs	3-187				6 overs: 3-34	19.5 overs	161			

Fall: 1-75 (Harris, 9.4), 2-158 (Short, 17.4), 3-163 (Pollard, 18.1)

Fall: 1-22 (Lynn, 2.4), 2-29 (Heazlett, 4.6), 3-29 (McCullum, 5.1), 4-76 (Renshaw, 11.1), 5-124 (Cutting, 15.4), 6-126 (Ross, 16.1), 7-134 (Steketee, 16.6), 8-151 (Lalor, 18.1), 9-152 (Yasir, 18.3), 10-161 (Swepson, 19.5)

Heat - bowling	O	M	R	W	wd	nb	Dots	Renegades - bowling	O	M	R	W	wd	nb	Dots
JK Lalor	4	0	32	1	3		11	TLW Cooper	2	0	15	0			6
MT Steketee	4	0	48	1	1		7	CP Tremain	4	0	29	3			13
Yasir Shah	4	0	25	0			12	KW Richardson	4	0	35	4			13
BCJ Cutting	4	0	50	0			0	JD Wildermuth	2	0	15	0			3
MJ Swepson	4	0	27	1			11	JM Holland	2	0	18	0			2
								DJ Bravo	3.5	0	25	3	1		7
								KA Pollard	2	0	23	0	1		3

Toss: Heat. Umpires: GA Abood, PJ Gillespie, AK Wilds (TV), Ref: PL Marshall. Award: TLW Cooper (MR). Crowd: 34,543
Short 50: 42 balls, 5x4, 1x6; Cooper 50: 30 balls, 7x4, 1x6

Australian Cricket Digest, 2018-19

First Semi Final – Scorchers v Hurricanes at Perth Stadium on February 1, 2018 – Hurricanes won by 71 runs

Hurricanes		B	4	6	Scorchers		B	4	6
MS Wade	c Kelly b Bresnan	71	45	10	M Klinger	c Reardon b Rogers	15	11	1
TD Paine +	c M Marsh b Kelly	4	7		SE Marsh	c Meredith b Rogers	30	18	6
GJ Bailey *	c Johnson b Bresnan	17	15	1	1	CT Bancroft +	c Milenko b Rogers	1	6
BR McDermott	not out	67	30	4	6	MR Marsh	c Archer b Christian	3	5
DT Christian	run out (Bancroft)	37	22	4	2	AJ Turner	run out (Bailey)	2	4
SA Milenko	not out	2	1		HWR Cartwright	b Rose	4	8
NJ Reardon					AC Voges *	c Paine b Meredith	3	5
JC Archer					TT Bresnan	lbw b Christian	43	26	4	1
CA Rose					JA Richardson	c Paine b Christian	16	12		2
TS Rogers					ML Kelly	c Milenko b Christian	7	7	1
RP Meredith					MG Johnson	not out	4	6
	3 lb, 9 w	12				2 lb, 1 nb, 8 w	11
6 overs: 1-48	20 overs	4-210			6 overs: 3-51	17.5 overs	139

Fall: 1-44 (Paine, 4.5), 2-80 (Bailey, 9.4), 3-120 (Wade, 13.2), 4-208 (Christian, 19.5 ov)

Fall: 1-21 (Klinger, 2.5), 2-41 (Bancroft, 5.1), 3-51 (SE Marsh, 5.6), 4-56 (MR Marsh, 7.1), 5-57 (Turner, 7.2), 6-65 (Voges, 8.6), 7-68 (Cartwright, 9.5), 8-104 (Richardson, 13.4), 9-116 (Kelly, 15.3), 10-139 (Bresnan, 17.5)

Scorchers - bowling	O	M	R	W	wd	nb	Dots	Hurricanes - bowling	O	M	R	W	wd	nb	Dots
MR Marsh	4	0	53	0	2	-	6	TS Rogers	4	0	31	3	1	1	9
MG Johnson	4	0	43	0	-	-	9	RP Meredith	3	0	29	1	2		6
JA Richardson	4	0	37	0	5	-	13	JC Archer	3	0	28	0	3		9
ML Kelly	4	0	34	1	-	-	6	CA Rose	3	0	22	1			7
TT Bresnan	4	0	40	2	2	-	6	DT Christian	3.5	0	17	4	2		14
								SA Milenko	1	0	10	0			0

Toss: Scorchers. Umpires: GA Abood, SJ Nogajski, SD Fry (TV), Ref: SR Bernard. Award: MS Wade (HH) Crowd: 52,960
Wade 50: 31 balls, 9x4; McDermott 50: 25 balls, 4x4, 4x6

Second Semi Final – Strikers v Renegades on Adelaide Oval on February 2, 2018 – Strikers won by 1 run

Strikers		B	4	6	Renegades		B	4	6
JR Dean	c Pollard b Tremain	19	8	1	2	CL White *	c Siddle b Neser	2	4
JB Weatherald	c Holland b Pollard	57	43	7	1	MS Harris	c Weatherald b Head	45	29	4	2
TM Head *	not out	85	57	8	1	TP Ludeman +	c Lehmann b Rashid	28	20	3	1
CA Ingram	c Ludeman b Mennie	1	2		TLW Cooper	not out	36	29	3
JW Wells	b Bravo	5	6		DJ Bravo	c Dean b Laughlin	26	17	1	1
JS Lehmann	c Mennie b Wildermuth	2	3		KA Pollard	not out	29	21	1	1
MG Neser	not out	4	2	1	JD Wildermuth				
HJ Nielsen +					BJ Webster				
Rashid Khan					CP Tremain				
PM Siddle					JM Mennie				
B Laughlin					JM Holland				
	1 b, 1 nb, 3 w	5				2 b, 3 lb, 6 w	11
6 overs: 1-54	20 overs	5-178			6 overs: 1-64	20 overs	4-177

Fall: 1-19 (Dean, 1.2), 2-123 (Weatherald, 13.6), 3-135 (Ingram, 15.2), 4-149 (Wells, 17.4), 5-159 (Lehmann, 18.4)

Fall: 1-10 (White, 1.1), 2-81 (Harris, 8.2), 3-87 (Ludeman, 9.1), 4-139 (Bravo, 15.2)

Renegades - bowling	O	M	R	W	wd	nb	Dots	Strikers - bowling	O	M	R	W	wd	nb	Dots
TLW Cooper	3	0	28	0			8	TM Head	4	0	27	1	1		7
CP Tremain	4	0	36	1	2		7	MG Neser	4	0	45	1	2		4
JM Mennie	4	0	21	1			9	PM Siddle	2	0	22	0			3
DJ Bravo	4	0	47	1		1	3	Rashid Khan	4	0	28	1			8
JD Wildermuth	4	0	37	1	1		7	B Laughlin	4	0	31	1	1		8
KA Pollard	1	0	8	1			1	CA Ingram	2	0	19	0			2

Toss: Strikers. Umpires: SAJ Craig, PJ Gillespie, GJ Davidson (TV), Ref: RW Stratford Award: TM Head (AS) Crowd: 36,310
Weatherald 50: 38 balls, 6x4, 1x6, Head 50: 37 balls, 7x4

Australian Cricket Digest, 2018-19
THE FINAL

The Hurricanes headed into the final with plenty of confidence, having pumped the Scorchers in the semi in Perth, while also welcoming back D'Arcy Short from the Aussie Twenty20 team. The Strikers were just glad to be there, having hung on to win by one run in their semi against the Renegades. Both sides were keen to bat first and Adelaide skipper Travis Head had no hesistation in batting first when he won the toss.

Left-arm Clive Rose bowled the first over, which only went for seven, but from there the Strikers steadily lifted the scoring rate. Carey hit Archer's first ball for four, then three overs later, Weatherald uppercut the same bowler for six to increase the momentum. Carey cut one onto his stumps in the fifth over, but then Weatherald really got going, at one point scoring 28 off eight consecutive deliveries, including 646 off Dan Christian's first three balls, as the Strikers reached 1-74 after eight.

Weatherald smashed Short for six over square-leg to reach a 29-ball fifty and whacked him over cover point in the same over for another six – 16 coming off the ninth over. Rogers dropped a tough caught and bowled when Head was five, and in the next over off Rose, Head (10) miscued to deep mid-wicket, where Short misjudged and dropped a high catch. Weatherald was still smashing it to all parts, reaching 82 off just 44 balls, the Strikers 1-120 after a dozen overs.

Head found the rope in the 13th and 14th overs, before Rose returned to bowl the 15th over, with both Weatherald and Head clearing the fence in an over that conceded 15. The left-handed opener reached his ton in the next over from just 58 balls, and was finally dismissed in the 19th over, miscuing a pull to cover. Ingram came out and put icing on the cake, hitting an unfit looking Archer for a six and a four in the final over to raise the 200 and put the Strikers in the box seat for their first title.

Despite his blazing knock 71 in the semi-final three days ago, Wade found himself down the order instead of Paine as the run chase commenced. Head bowled himself in the opening over and had Paine caught behind aiming a pull-shot. Bailey came out with fire in his belly, hitting the Strikers skipper for two sixes over long-on in the third over, the Hurricanes ahead of the required rate early on. Short after four early boundaries, found the Strikers bowlers hard to get away as they angled into his pads. At 1-68 after seven, a nervous looking O'Connor came on to bowl to his leg-breaks, and after getting away with two long-hop dot balls, he kept the over to just four singles. Neser then conceded six off the ninth and when O'Connor went for just seven off the tenth over, the Hurricanes were 1-85 after ten, needing 118 off the last ten to win.

Siddle, whose first over went for just seven, returned to dismiss Bailey in the 11th over – well held at long-on in an over that conceded just five. A calm O'Connor went for just five in the 12th before Short then smashed Laughlin over long-on for six in the 13th and O'Connor over square-leg for six in the 14th to reach his fifty off 36 balls. McDermott battled to score more than singles before Siddle won a dubious LBW and with 82 needed off 30 balls, the engravers of the trophy were making a start.

Ingram came on to bowl the fourth over from the "fifth" bowler and was sent packing by Short for 466, as 19 came from the over. Siddle bowled the 17th and conceded just five, getting Short caught behind off the last ball of his spell, to finish with three wickets and end the match as a contest. Wade was run out without facing a ball at the top of the 18th over and understandably reacted with anger and frustration when he returned back to the team bench. Tactically the Hurricanes had made a bad tactical error by not opening with him. In the end it mattered little, as the Strikers cruised home to win their first title.

BBL07 FINAL – Strikers v Hurricanes at Adelaide Oval on February 4, 2018 – Strikers won by 25 runs

Strikers		B	4	6	Hurricanes		B	4	6
AT Carey +	b Archer	18	16	3	TD Paine +	c Carey b Head	5	4	1
JB Weatherald	c Bailey b Christian	115	70	9	8	DJM Short	c Carey b Siddle	68	44	6	4
TM Head *	not out	44	29	2	1	GJ Bailey *	c Lehmann b Siddle	46	33	2	2
CA Ingram	not out	14	6	1	1	BR McDermott	lbw b Siddle	9	13		
JR Dean					DT Christian	not out	29	19	3	1
JW Wells					MS Wade	run out (Carey)	0	0		
JS Lehmann					SA Milenko	not out	9	7	1	
MG Neser					JC Archer					
LN O'Connor					CA Rose					
PM Siddle					TS Rogers					
B Laughlin					RP Meredith					
	4 lb, 1 nb, 6	11				8 lb, 3 w	11		
6 overs: 1-53	20 overs	2-202			6 overs: 1-60	20 overs	5-177		

Fall: 1-41 (Carey, 4.6), 2-181 (Weatherald, 18.2)

Fall: 1-6 (Paine, 0.5), 2-87 (Bailey, 10.2), 3-120 (McDermott, 14.5), 4-145 (Short, 16.6), 5-145 (Wade, 17.1)

Hurricanes - bowling	O	M	R	W	wd	nb	Dots	Strikers - bowling	O	M	R	W	wd	nb	Dots
CA Rose	3	0	30	0			3	TM Head	3	0	30	1	1		5
JC Archer	4	0	46	1	2	1	8	MG Neser	4	0	34	0			6
TS Rogers	4	0	30	0			8	B Laughlin	4	0	43	0	1		7
RP Meredith	3	0	34	0	2		8	PM Siddle	4	1	17	3	1		15
DJM Short	2	0	20	0	1		4	LN O'Connor	4	0	27	0			6
DT Christian	4	0	38	1	1		7	CA Ingram	1	0	18	0			1

Toss: Strikers. Umpires: SAJ Craig, PJ Gillespie, GC Joshua (TV), Ref: PL Marshall   Award: JB Weatherald (AS)   Crowd: 40,732

Weatherald 50: 29 balls, 4x4, 5x6; 100: 58 balls, 7x4, 8x6. Short 50: 36 balls, 5x4, 2x6

Australian Cricket Digest, 2018-19
ADELAIDE STRIKERS – BBL07 Champions

The Strikers first BBL title was a great triumph for their skipper Travis Head and coach Jason Gillespie. The process towards their maiden title started early, with key recruiting of Afghanistan's Rashid Khan, one of the world's most exciting Twenty20 spinners. Other key recruits were South African hard hitter Colin Ingram, who had been dominating around the Twenty20 circuit, namely at the England T20 Blast for Glamorgan. The riskiest pickup was Australian and Victorian pace bowler Peter Siddle, who in racing parlance, had little form to go on, but proved as important a player as any in the team. All three players repaid in kind the team with excellent performances at various stages.

Gillespie showed patience in keeping opening bat Jake Weatherald in the team, after a slow start, being fully repaid in the latter stages of the BBL, where the left-hander made an exhilarating century in the final. Alex Carey was an outstanding opening partner, with wickets in hand rather than rash stroke play the key to their opening partnerships.

With the ball, Rashid Khan and Siddle were backed up the experienced Ben Laughlin and youthful Billy Stanlake. Stanlake was the key bowler in the powerplay while Laughlin was a vital bowler at the death. Michael Neser made up a fine pace quartet, one of the few bowlers in the competition who could bowl a yorker at will.

Finally another word or two on the skipper Travis Head. Just 24 years of age, this lad has not only made critical runs, but bowled at key times and captained the team with calmness beyond his years. He rarely missed a beat in the field, kept his head at all times, especially in the one run win in the semi versus the Renegades, where he could have easily lost the plot. The team worked out early in the series that they were better when batting first, with eight of their nine wins coming that way. To emulate a team like the Scorchers, and win back to back will be a big task in BBL08, but with talented all-rounder Matt Short coming across from the Melbourne Renegades – they have every chance of doing so again in 2018-19.

STATISTICS

Batting & Fielding	M	Inn	NO	Runs	HS	Avge	100s	50s	6s	S/Rate	Ct	St
TM Head	9	9	2	374	85*	53.42	0	3	12	133.09	4	-
AT Carey	11	11	2	443	100	49.22	1	2	13	141.53	14	0
JB Weatherald	12	12	0	383	115	31.91	1	3	19	126.82	7	-
CA Ingram	12	12	3	277	68	30.77	0	2	14	139.19	3	-
MG Neser	11	6	3	62	40*	20.66	0	0	3	121.56	3	-
Rashid Khan	11	6	4	36	16*	18.00	0	0	3	180.00	2	-
JW Wells	12	10	2	139	33*	17.37	0	0	3	106.92	4	-
JR Dean	6	4	1	51	19	17.00	0	0	4	110.86	1	-
JS Lehmann	12	9	1	93	23	11.62	0	0	1	119.23	7	-
PM Siddle	11	3	2	3	2	3.00	0	0	0	50.00	4	-
B Laughlin	12	1	0	1	1	1.00	0	0	0	33.33	4	-
B Stanlake	10	1	1	4	4*	-	0	0	0	80.00	2	-

Also played: WA Agar, HJ Nielsen & LN O'Connor all played one game, did not bat nor take a catch

Bowling	M	Overs	Mdns	Runs	Wkts	Avge	Best	Econ	SR	4w	Dot %
Rashid Khan	11	44	0	249	18	13.83	3-20	5.65	14.6	0	42
PM Siddle	11	37	2	220	11	20.00	2-17	5.94	20.1	0	47
B Stanlake	10	38	0	246	11	22.36	2-22	6.47	20.7	0	50
B Laughlin	12	44	0	368	16	23.00	4-26	8.36	16.5	1	35
TM Head	9	13	0	116	4	29.00	1-8	8.92	19.5	0	24
MG Neser	11	40.5	0	372	13	28.61	3-29	9.11	18.8	0	33
CA Ingram	12	8	0	76	0	-	-	9.50	-	0	25

Also bowled: WA Agar (1 match) 3-0-26-0, LN O'Connor (1 match) 4-0-27-0

Best BBL07 Powerplay batting & bowling

Batting	Runs/Balls	SR	Sixes	Bowling	Ov	Figs	Econ	Dot %
AT Carey	182/146	125	5	PM Siddle	8	2-39	4.88	60
JR Dean	26/23	113	2	B Stanlake	21	4-113	5.38	59
JB Weatherald	177/161	110	7	Rashid Khan	8	3-47	5.88	52
TM Head	87/80	109	1	MG Neser	20	5-160	8.00	48
CA Ingram	20/22	90	0	B Laughlin	7	2-60	8.57	43

ADELAIDE STRIKERS - HONOUR ROLL

Season	Finished	Captain	Coach	MVP	Minor Rd W/L
2011-12	6th	M Klinger	DS Berry	M Klinger	2/5
2012-13	5th	J Botha	DS Berry	J Botha	4/4
2013-14	7th	J Botha/PJ Hughes	DS Berry	MG Neser	2/5
2014-15	Lost Semi	J Botha	DS Berry	A Zampa	6/1 NR 1
2015-16	Lost Semi	BJ Hodge	JN Gillespie	AU Rashid	7/1
2016-17	6th	BJ Hodge	JN Gillespie	BR Dunk	3/5
2017-18	Won title	TM Head/CA Ingram	JN Gillespie	Rashid Khan	7/3

Leading team records

Most Runs	M	Runs	HS	Avge	SR	Most Wickets	M	W	Avge	Best	Econ
TM Head	**35**	**988**	**101***	**34.0**	**138**	**B Laughlin**	**37**	**50**	**19.8**	**4-26**	**7.95**
TP Ludeman	37	846	92*	30.2	123	KW Richardson	36	37	26.0	3-9	7.95
M Klinger	22	663	86*	34.8	119	**MG Neser**	**35**	**37**	**26.1**	**3-24**	**8.73**
BJ Hodge	20	593	56*	42.3	128	SW Tait	18	28	17.9	3-22	7.86
J Weatherald	**19**	**500**	**115**	**26.3**	**127**	J Botha	27	20	31.3	2-11	6.79

Highest Individual scores

	Runs	Bls	4s	6s	Versus	Venue	Season
JB Weatherald	**115**	**70**	**9**	**8**	**Hurricanes**	**Adelaide**	**2017-18**
TM Head	101*	53	4	9	Sixers	Adelaide	2015-16
AT Carey	**100**	**56**	**12**	**4**	**Hurricanes**	**Adelaide**	**2017-18**
TP Ludeman	92*	44	9	5	Stars	Adelaide	2014-15

Best score away from Adelaide Oval by a Striker: AT Carey 83* (59) v Sydney Sixers at the SCG, 2017-18

Fastest Fifties

	Balls	Versus	Venue	Season
TP Ludeman	18	Stars	Adelaide	2014-15
TM Head	24	Heat	Gabba	2015-16
BR Dunk	24	Heat	Adelaide	2016-17

Highest Team totals

	Versus	Venue	Season
2-202	**Hurricanes**	**Adelaide**	**2017-18**
6-198	Scorchers	WACA	2013-14
6-196	Heat	Adelaide	2016-17
5-189	Renegades	Adelaide	2011-12

Highest total against: 5-206 by Heat at the Adelaide Oval, 2016-17

Lowest Team totals

	Versus	Venue	Season
87	Sixers	Adelaide	2011-12
9-90	Stars	MCG	2013-14
91	Scorchers	Adelaide	2012-13

Best Bowling

		Overs	Dots	Versus	Venue	Season
HS Sodhi	6-11	3.3	12	Thunder	Syd Showground	2016-17
B Laughlin	**4-26**	**3.4**	**10**	**Thunder**	**Adelaide**	**2017-18**
KW Richardson	3-9	3.4	15	Thunder	Stadium Australia	2012-13
TM Head	3-16	2	8	Renegades	Docklands	2015-16

Most Economical Bowling (Min 4 overs)

		Dots	Versus	Venue	Season
B Laughlin	2-10	13	Sixers	Adelaide	2016-17
J Botha	2-11	14	Heat	Adelaide	2013-14
AW O'Brien	0-12	14	Stars	MCG	2011-12
PM Siddle	**2-13**	**14**	**Thunder**	**Syd Showground**	**2017-18**

BRISBANE HEAT - 7th

The Heat were well placed after six games, having won four of them, but floundered in the later stages of the BBL, losing their last four games to miss out on the finals. Once again skipper Brendon McCullum applied an aggressive approach to his captaincy and batting, some wondering at times whether he went a little too hard, as batting collapses against the Strikers (91) and Sixers (73) would suggest.

When available, Chris Lynn proved his star quality, while Joe Burns was strong performer until injuring his upper leg quite badly, in the lead up to the clash against the Sixers. Alex Ross and James Peirson made contributions but only passed fifty once, the Heat batting overall only passing fifty on five occasions.

As in past years, the bowling for the Heat was a concern, with wickets very light on in the powerplay. Young spinner Shadab Khan was excellent in his three games, while the experienced Yasir Shah did well as his replacement, despite taking only five wickets. Josh Lalor was serviceable, while Brendan Doggett is an exciting prospect.

Ben Cutting, who has the ability to be one of the best all-rounders in the competition, only rarely showed what he is capable of and leg-spinner Mitch Swepson, while economical, did not take quite as many wickets as he would have hoped for.

STATISTICS

Batting & Fielding	M	Inn	NO	Runs	HS	Avge	100s	50s	6s	S/Rate	Ct	St
JA Burns	7	7	2	201	50	40.20	0	1	10	142.55	5	-
CA Lynn	5	5	1	148	63*	37.00	0	1	8	162.63	2	-
JJ Peirson	10	9	3	160	43	26.66	0	0	4	132.23	1	1
AI Ross	10	9	1	210	51	26.25	0	1	7	122.09	2	-
BB McCullum	10	10	0	248	61	24.80	0	2	6	135.51	5	-
MT Renshaw	1	1	0	22	22	22.00	0	0	0	115.78	0	-
BCJ Cutting	10	9	0	190	46	21.11	0	0	14	152.00	2	-
CJ Gannon	3	2	0	32	23	16.00	0	0	0	91.42	3	-
SD Heazlett	7	7	0	99	45	14.14	0	0	2	111.23	1	-
JK Lalor	6	5	1	40	14	10.00	0	0	0	97.56	1	-
M Labuschagne	3	3	0	21	20	7.00	0	0	0	72.41	0	-
MT Steketee	10	8	2	37	13	6.16	0	0	3	115.62	1	-
B Doggett	7	3	2	4	3	4.00	0	0	0	66.66	5	-
Yasir Shah	7	3	1	6	6*	3.00	0	0	0	60.00	0	-
JS Floros	1	1	0	3	3	3.00	0	0	0	30.00	0	-
MJ Swepson	10	3	1	3	2	1.50	0	0	0	60.00	5	-

Bowling	M	Overs	Mdns	Runs	Wkts	Avge	Best	Econ	SR	4w	Dot %
JA Burns	7	4	0	24	1	24.00	1-10	6.00	24.0	-	50
Yasir Shah	7	28	0	180	5	36.00	2-18	6.42	33.6	-	35
Shadab Khan	3	12	0	85	6	14.16	2-17	7.08	12.0	-	40
MJ Swepson	10	35	0	249	5	49.80	3-14	7.11	42.0	-	31
JK Lalor	6	22	0	185	7	26.42	3-40	8.40	18.8	-	38
MT Steketee	10	35	0	322	10	32.20	3-28	9.02	21.4	-	37
B Doggett	7	24	0	228	7	32.57	5-35	9.50	20.5	1	30
BCJ Cutting	10	15.2	0	153	5	30.60	2-27	9.97	18.4	-	18
CJ Gannon	3	5	0	50	1	50.00	1-26	10.00	30.0	-	20

Also bowled: M Labuschagne (3 matches) 1-0-5-0, JS Floros (1 match) 1-0-7-0,

Best BBL07 Powerplay batting & bowling

Batting	Runs/Balls	SR	Sixes	Bowling	Ov	Figs	Econ	Dot %
JA Burns	38/23	165	3	JA Burns	4	1-24	6.00	50
CA Lynn	97/63	154	5	JK Lalor	10	3-64	6.40	48
BB McCullum	174/121	144	4	Yasir Shah	12	1-80	6.67	38
SD Heazlett	71/61	116	1	Shadab Khan	5	3-34	6.80	50
JJ Peirson	44/49	89	0	MT Steketee	19	3-147	7.74	44

Australian Cricket Digest, 2018-19
BRISBANE HEAT - HONOUR ROLL

Season	Finished	Captain	Coach	MVP	Minor Rd W/L
2011-12	5th	JR Hopes/PJ Forrest	DS Lehmann	A McDermott	3/4
2012-13	Won Title	JR Hopes/CD Hartley	DS Lehmann	LA Pomersbach	4/4
2013-14	5th	JR Hopes/DL Vettori	SG Law	DL Vettori	3/5
2014-15	Last	JR Hopes	SG Law	PJ Forrest	2/6
2015-16	6th	CA Lynn	DL Vettori	CA Lynn	3/5
2016-17	3rd	BB McCullum/JA Burns	DL Vettori	BB McCullum	5/3
2017-18	7th	BB McCullum	DL Vettori	Yasir Shah	4/6

Leading team records

Most Runs	M	Runs	HS	Avge	SR	Most Wickets	M	W	Avge	Best	Econ
CA Lynn	49	1560	101	41.0	157	**BCJ Cutting**	51	40	31.7	3-25	8.78
JA Burns	37	898	69	30.9	128	**MT Steketee**	32	37	25.3	3-28	8.59
BCJ Cutting	51	733	46	20.3	151	DT Christian	30	25	28.2	5-26	8.42
DT Christian	30	622	75*	24.8	131	JR Hopes	30	24	29.7	3-23	7.12

Highest Individual scores

	Runs	Bls	4s	6s	Versus	Venue	Season
LA Pomersbach	112*	70	15	2	Renegades	Docklands	2012-13
CA Lynn	101	51	5	7	Hurricanes	Brisbane	2015-16
CA Lynn	98*	49	3	11	Scorchers	Perth	2016-17

Fastest Fifties

	Balls	Versus	Venue	Season
BB McCullum	18	Renegades	Gabba	2016-17
CA Lynn	18	Hurricanes	Gabba	2014-15
CA Lynn	19	Stars	MCG	2015-16
CA Lynn	21	Thunder	Gabba	2015-16

Highest Team totals

	Versus	Venue	Season
3-209	Hurricanes	Gabba	2013-14
6-208	Hurricanes	Hobart	2014-15
5-206	Strikers	Adelaide	2016-17
7-206	**Stars**	**Gabba**	**2017-18**

Highest total against: 7-210 by Hurricanes at the Gabba, 2013-14 and 3-210 by Renegades at Docklands, 2013-14

Lowest Team totals

	Versus	Venue	Season
73	**Sixers**	**SCG**	**2017-18**
80	Renegades	Docklands	2014-15
91	**Strikers**	**Adelaide**	**2017-18**

Best Bowling

	Overs	Dots	Versus	Venue	Season
S Badree	5-22	4	12	Stars	MCG	2015-16
BJ Doggett	**5-35**	**4**	**9**	**Scorchers**	**Gabba**	**2017-18**
DT Christian	5-26	4	9	Thunder	Stadium Australia	2012-13
CJ Gannon	4-10	2.2	14	Thunder	Stadium Australia	2013-14

Most Economical Bowling (Min 4 overs)

	Dots	Versus	Venue	Season
JR Hopes	1-8	17	Renegades	Docklands	2014-15
DL Vettori	2-10	15	Strikers	Adelaide	2013-14
BCJ Cutting	2-12	14	Renegades	Docklands	2012-13

Australian Cricket Digest, 2018-19
HOBART HURRICANES – Runner Up

The Hurricanes played to the best of their ability in BBL07 to make the final, their success underpinned largely by the batting efforts of Darcy Short at the top of the order. Having shown his potential at times in 2016-17, he took his game to another level in 2017-18, with some outstanding innings, which saw him awarded the player of the tournament. He also bowled some important overs with his left arm chinaman, in particular a spell of 1-20 from four overs in an important win at the 'Gabba.

Vying for recruit of the tournament was the exciting Barbadian born/Sussex all-rounder, Jofra Archer. He was an excitement machine with the ball and in the field and his fine efforts in the BBL saw him propelled into the IPL, when initially he was reluctant to be part of it.

Ben McDermott continued to be a key batsman, while Matthew Wade got better as the tournament wore on, his brilliant 71 off 45 in the semi-final one the best Twenty20 innings you'd wish to see. Tactically it was hard to work out why he didn't open in the final against the Strikers, especially once they were chasing over 200 to win. The experienced all-rounder Dan Christian continued to hit hard and take his share of wickets, but conversely England recruit Tymal Mills was poor with the ball and was dropped for the last two matches of the tournament.

As always, George Bailey led the team with enthusiasm and, like the Strikers, were keen to bat first, having recorded five of their six wins in such a fashion. With Mills out of sorts, Tom Rogers was brilliant with the ball when selected for the semi-final. Conversly one had to feel for leg-spinner Cameron Boyce late in the tournament, being dropped for the finals, having played the previous 40 games in a row. Given the onslaught they copped in the final at Adelaide Oval, an experienced spinner may have helped them.

STATISTICS

Batting & Fielding	M	Inn	NO	Runs	HS	Avge	100s	50s	6s	S/Rate	Ct	St
DJM Short	11	11	1	572	122*	57.20	1	4	26	148.57	3	-
S Milenko	9	6	4	110	66*	55.00	0	1	6	171.87	5	-
JC Archer	12	6	5	40	25*	40.00	0	0	1	137.93	5	-
BR McDermott	12	12	3	325	67*	36.11	0	1	15	138.29	1	-
NJ Reardon	3	1	0	32	32	32.00	0	0	2	145.45	1	-
MS Wade	12	11	2	251	71	27.88	0	1	6	137.15	5	0
DT Christian	12	11	3	216	56	27.00	0	1	10	153.19	0	-
AJ Doolan	8	8	1	186	70*	26.57	0	1	4	115.52	3	-
GJ Bailey	12	11	0	202	46	18.36	0	0	4	114.77	8	-
CA Rose	12	2	1	13	13	13.00	0	0	0	76.47	2	-
TD Paine	2	2	0	9	5	4.50	0	0	0	81.81	2	-
CJ Boyce	10	3	1	4	4	2.00	0	0	0	100.00	2	-
TS Mills	10	1	0	1	1	1.00	0	0	0	14.28	2	-
TS Rogers	4	1	0	0	0	0.00	0	0	0	0.00	0	-

Also played: RP Meredith (2 matches) did not bat, 1 catch, A Summers (1 match) did not bat

Bowling	M	Overs	Mdns	Runs	Wkts	Avge	Best	Econ	SR	4w	Dot %
CJ Boyce	10	33.3	0	264	6	44.00	2-14	7.88	33.5	0	29
DJM Short	11	17	0	134	3	44.66	1-20	7.88	34.0	0	33
JC Archer	12	46.2	1	369	16	23.06	3-15	7.96	17.3	0	42
CA Rose	12	37	0	303	8	37.87	2-20	8.18	27.7	0	32
DT Christian	12	33	0	293	11	26.63	4-17	8.87	18.0	1	33
TS Rogers	4	15	0	140	4	35.00	3-31	9.33	22.5	0	36
TS Mills	10	40	0	389	8	48.62	2-42	9.72	30.0	0	33
RP Meredith	2	6	0	63	1	63.00	1-29	10.50	36.0	0	39
S Milenko	9	4	0	60	0	-	-	15.00	-	0	17

Also bowled: A Summers (1 match) 3-0-31-0

Best BBL07 Powerplay batting & bowling

Batting	Runs/Balls	SR	Sixes	Bowling	Ov	Figs	Econ	Dot %
DJM Short	242/161	150	8	JC Archer	21	4-150	7.14	50
MS Wade	115/84	37	2	TS Rogers	7	4-51	7.29	43
GJ Bailey	84/62	135	3	CA Rose	22	4-169	7.68	36
AJ Doolan	113/101	112	1	RP Meredith	4	0-41	10.25	38
				TS Mills	13	1-138	10.61	36

Australian Cricket Digest, 2018-19
HOBART HURRICANES - HONOUR ROLL

Season	Finished	Captain	Coach	MVP	Minor Rd W/L
2011-12	Lost Semi	XJ Doherty	AS de Winter	TR Birt	5/2
2012-13	6th	GJ Bailey/TD Paine	TC Coyle	B Laughlin	4/4
2013-14	Lost Final	GJ Bailey/TD Paine	DG Wright	BR Dunk	3/4 NR1
2014-15	5th	GJ Bailey/TD Paine	DG Wright	BW Hilfenhaus	3/5
2015-16	7th	GJ Bailey/TD Paine	DG Wright	DT Christian	3/5
2016-17	7th	TD Paine	DG Wright	SCJ Broad	3/5
2017-18	R-up	GJ Bailey	G Kirsten	DJM Short	5/5

Leading team records

Most Runs	M	Runs	HS	Avge	SR	Most Wickets	M	W	Avge	Best	Econ
TD Paine	42	1119	91	27.9	122	CJ Boyce	40	43	25.7	3-11	8.23
GJ Bailey	43	1023	74*	35.2	132	B Laughlin	25	35	19.7	4-31	7.52
JW Wells	41	814	72	30.1	120	XJ Doherty	26	24	26.2	4-17	7.15
DJM Short	19	770	122*	42.7	152	DT Christian	28	22	26.8	5-14	8.31

Highest Individual scores

	Runs	Bls	4s	6s	Versus	Venue	Season
DJM Short	122*	69	8	8	Heat	Gabba	2017-18
BR McDermott	114	52	8	9	Renegades	Docklands	2016-17
DJM Short	97	63	9	4	Thunder	Syd Showground	2017-18
BR Dunk	96	54	8	5	Thunder	Hobart	2013-14
DJM Short	96	58	9	4	Strikers	Hobart	2017-18

Fastest Fifties

	Balls	Versus	Venue	Season
BR Dunk	20	Heat	Gabba	2013-14
DJM Short	21	Sixers	SCG	2016-17
DT Christian	21	Heat	Gabba	2015-16
TR Birt	22	Stars	Bellerive	2011-12

Highest Team totals

	Versus	Venue	Season
8-223	Renegades	Docklands	2016-17
7-210	Heat	Gabba	2013-14
4-210	Scorchers	Perth Stadium	2017-18
4-209	Heat	Hobart	2014-15

Highest total against: 4-222 by Renegades at the Docklands, 2016-17

Lowest Team totals

	Versus	Venue	Season
91	Sixers	SCG	2015-16
9-102	Renegades	Docklands	2012-13
109	Thunder	Launceston	2017-18
111	Renegades	Hobart	2013-14

Best Bowling

	Overs	Dots	Versus	Venue	Season
DT Christian	5-14	4	15	Strikers	Hobart	2016-17
JK Reed	4-11	4	18	Thunder	Syd Showgrounds	2014-15
DT Christian	4-17	3.5	14	Scorchers	Perth Stadium	2017-18
XJ Doherty	4-17	4	12	Strikers	Adelaide	2011-12

Most Economical Bowling (Min 4 overs)

	Dots	Versus	Venue	Season
BW Hilfenhaus	2-10	18	Scorchers	WACA	2011-12
JK Reed	4-11	18	Thunder	Syd Showgrounds	2014-15

Three bowlers have conceded 14 runs in a four over spell

MELBOURNE RENEGADES – Lost Semi

The Renegades had a fine BBL07 and could argue they should have made the final, having lost the semi to the Strikers in Adelaide by just one run. They, like the Strikers recruited well, with Kane Richardson and Jack Wildermuth both taking important wickets that had been lacking in previous seasons. At the top of the order Marcus Harris made up for a rare run of poor form from skipper Aaron Finch, while Cameron White was the rock of the batting order, despite as strike rate of just over 110. Tom Cooper was the side's most valuable player, scoring with power to all parts of the ground, while bowling handy overs in the powerplay. Ignored for the first part of the tournament, Chris Tremain came into in the latter stages, swinging the ball to pick up crucial breakthroughs with the new ball. Matt Short also came into the team late in the campaign, impressed with 62 in the last minor round game at the Gabba and then was was dropped for the semi. He has been snapped by the Strikers for BBL08.

Largely their overseas players were very good and played a positive part in the side making the semis. Off-spinning all-rounder Mohammad Nabi was excellent with the ball in the powerplay, until International duties with Afghanistan took him away. Dwayne Bravo was fit throughout and had one of the best slower balls around, as he led the wicket taking tally for his team. Kieron Pollard replaced Nabi and again couldn't quite live up to his IPL reputation, especially when he was unable to make contact with the final ball of the semi final in Adelaide, when even just a single would have ensured a superover and given them a second chance of a spot in the final. Brad Hogg was omitted towards the end of BBL07, and at 47, one doubts whether he'll get another chance. Finally one must congratulate Brad Hodge on a fine career, appendicitis causing him to miss the later stages of BBL07. Hodge deserves many plaudits for his fine on-field efforts and will no doubt find plenty on offer post career.

Batting & Fielding	M	Inn	NO	Runs	HS	Avge	100s	50s	6s	S/Rate	Ct	St
CL White	8	8	4	304	79*	76.00	0	3	8	111.35	4	-
TLW Cooper	11	9	3	298	65*	49.66	0	3	12	141.23	6	-
MW Short	3	3	0	106	62	35.33	0	1	2	121.83	2	-
BJ Webster	4	3	2	35	18*	35.00	0	0	2	194.44	5	-
BJ Hodge	7	5	3	68	30*	34.00	0	0	6	133.33	0	-
MS Harris	11	11	0	324	64	29.45	0	2	10	129.08	4	-
Mohammad Nabi	7	3	0	88	52	29.33	0	1	2	139.68	1	-
KA Pollard	4	4	1	67	29*	22.33	0	0	2	124.07	3	-
DJ Bravo	11	8	3	100	26	20.00	0	0	5	131.57	3	-
AJ Finch	6	6	0	108	51	18.00	0	1	3	136.70	4	-
TP Ludeman	11	5	1	61	28	15.25	0	0	2	122.00	8	3
JD Wildermuth	11	4	0	45	23	11.25	0	0	3	132.35	2	-
JM Holland	4	1	0	1	1	1.00	0	0	0	33.33	3	-
KW Richardson	10	2	2	21	12*	-	0	0	1	131.25	4	-
GB Hogg	8	2	2	2	1*	-	0	0	0	66.66	2	-
CP Tremain	4	1	1	2	2*	-	0	0	0	66.66	0	-

Also played: JM Mennie (1 match) did not bat, 1 catch.

Bowling	M	Overs	Mdns	Runs	Wkts	Avge	Best	SR	Econ	4w	Dot %
Mohammad Nabi	7	25.5	0	149	8	18.62	2-15	5.76	19.3	0	42
TLW Cooper	11	12	0	89	1	89.00	1-6	7.41	72.0	0	49
CP Tremain	4	15	0	119	7	17.00	3-29	7.93	12.8	0	41
KW Richardson	10	39	1	314	12	26.16	4-22	8.05	19.5	2	41
JD Wildermuth	11	38	0	311	10	31.10	3-16	8.18	22.8	0	34
GB Hogg	8	28	0	231	7	33.00	2-16	8.25	24.0	0	31
DJ Bravo	11	42.5	0	363	18	20.16	5-28	8.47	14.2	0	29
JM Holland	4	6	0	55	1	55.00	1-16	9.16	36.0	0	22
KA Pollard	4	7	0	70	4	17.50	2-19	10.00	10.5	0	26

Also bowled: AJ Finch (6 matches) 1-0-5-0, JM Mennie (1 match) 4-0-21-1 (38% Dots).

Best BBL07 Powerplay batting & bowling

Batting	Runs/Balls	SR	Sixes	Bowling	Ov	Figs	Econ	Dot %
AJ Finch	79/53	149	4	M Nabi	12	3-63	5.25	47
TP Ludeman	52/37	141	1	JD Wildermuth	9	2-59	6.56	52
MS Harris	202/156	129	3	CP Tremain	8	5-53	6.63	50
TLW Cooper	21/18	117	0	KW Richardson	17	1-115	6.76	53
CL White	70/80	88	1	DJ Bravo	8	3-62	7.75	44

Australian Cricket Digest, 2018-19
MELBOURNE RENEGADES - HONOUR ROLL

Season	Finished	Captain	Coach	MVP	Minor Rd W/L
2011-12	7th	AB McDonald	S Helmot	AJ Finch	2/5
2012-13	Lost Semi	AJ Finch/BJ Rohrer	S Helmot	AJ Finch	7/1
2013-14	6th	AJ Finch/BJ Rohrer	S Helmot	AJ Finch	3/5
2014-15	6th	AJ Finch/BJ Rohrer	S Helmot	JL Pattinson	3/5
2015/16	5th	AJ Finch/CL White	DJ Saker	DJ Bravo	3/5
2016-17	5th	AJ Finch	AB McDonald	AJ Finch	4/4
2017-18	Lost Semi	AJ Finch/DJ Bravo/CL White	AB McDonald	TLW Cooper	6/4

Leading team records

Most Runs	M	Runs	HS	Avge	SR	Most Wickets	M	W	Avge	Best	Econ
AJ Finch	46	1669	111*	39.7	139	NJ Rimmington	35	34	25.8	4-26	8.14
TLW Cooper	46	789	65*	26.3	131	DJ Bravo	27	33	24.6	5-28	8.08
CL White	24	766	79*	42.5	119	JL Pattinson	14	19	23.8	4-24	9.20
MS Harris	18	544	85	30.2	130	M Muralitharan	16	19	18.3	3-18	5.70

Highest Individual scores

	Runs	Bls	4s	6s	Versus	Venue	Season
AJ Finch	111*	65	12	4	Stars	Docklands	2012-13
AD Hales	89	52	5	8	Sixers	SCG	2012-13
MS Harris	85	53	6	4	Strikers	Adelaide	2016-17
AJ Finch	84*	55	3	6	Stars	Docklands	2013-14

Fastest Fifties

	Balls	Versus	Venue	Season
CH Gayle	12	Strikers	Docklands	2015-16
AJ Finch	20	Heat	Gabba	2016-17
TLW Cooper	22	Hurricanes	Docklands	2016-17
BA Stokes	26	Hurricanes	Hobart	2014-15

Highest Team totals

	Versus	Venue	Season
4-222	Hurricanes	Docklands	2016-17
3-210	Heat	Docklands	2013-14
5-199	Heat	Gabba	2016-17
6-189	**Thunder**	**Canberra**	**2017-18**

Highest total against: 8-223 by Hurricanes at Docklands, 2016-17

Lowest Team totals

	Versus	Venue	Season
57	Stars	Docklands	2014-15
104	Thunder	Docklands	2013-14
8-111	Scorchers	WACA	2013-14

Best Bowling

	Overs	Dots	Versus	Venue	Season
DJ Bravo	**5-28**	4	10	**Hurricanes**	**Hobart**	**2017-18**
Shakib-al-Hasan	4-13	4	15	Heat	Docklands	2014-15
KW Richardson	**4-22**	4	16	**Thunder**	**Canberra**	**2017-18**
JL Pattinson	4-24	4	15	Hurricanes	Hobart	2013-14

Most Economical Bowling (Min 4 overs)

	Dots	Versus	Venue	Season
Fawad Ahmed	1-7	18	Heat	Docklands	2014-15
DP Nannes	0-10	14	Thunder	Homebush	2011-12
CP Tremain	1-11	16	Hurricanes	Hobart	2015-16

MELBOURNE STARS - Last

The Stars run of seven consecutive finals appearances came to an end, as their aging list finally caught up with them. Long term batsmen Rob Quiney, Luke Wright and Kevin Pietersen have all played their final games with the team, with only Pietersen playing anywhere to his potential in BBL07. One could also argue that the pressure of captaincy for first time skipper John Hastings was too big an ask, despite his prowess as an all-rounder. Not a lot went right for Hastings, with Ben Dunk, fresh from an outstanding BBL06 with the Strikers, unable to replicate his form in any shape or form. Previous mainstays of the bowling attack Michael Beer and Scott Boland were well below form and James Faulkner, despite an impressive average, struggled to reach or clear the boundary with the bat enough in the middle or latter overs.

On the positive side, Glenn Maxwell was a class act in the games he could play before he was called up for Australian duties. Marcus Stoinis made a brilliant 99 in the opening game at the 'Gabba and shortly after was selected in the Aussie ODI and Twenty20 teams. With the ball left-arm quick Jackson Coleman looks like someone who can be a part of the Stars line-up going forward.

With Quiney, Wright, Pietersen gone and Hastings (Sixers) plus Faulkner (Hurricanes) heading elsewhere, it will be an interesting time ahead for the team. The recruitment of the enigmatic Nic Maddison (Sixers) is a start, the ability to get good overseas recruits and an improved output from those on already on the list, the key to improved results in BBL08.

Batting & Fielding	M	Inn	NO	Runs	HS	Avge	100	50s	6s	S/Rate	Ct	St
JP Faulkner	10	9	6	188	47*	62.66	0	0	4	105.02	2	-
MP Stoinis	5	5	1	179	99	44.75	0	1	7	144.35	0	-
GJ Maxwell	9	9	1	299	84	37.37	0	3	12	154.12	7	-
EP Gulbis	6	5	3	70	24	35.00	0	0	3	125.00	3	-
KP Pietersen	8	8	0	226	74	28.25	0	1	8	143.03	3	-
PSP Handscomb	8	7	0	136	57	19.42	0	1	0	104.61	3	2
RJ Quiney	4	4	0	72	36	18.00	0	0	3	118.03	3	-
JW Hastings	10	7	4	51	20	17.00	0	0	3	134.21	4	-
LJ Wright	5	5	0	82	21	16.40	0	0	1	107.89	2	-
SE Gotch	5	5	0	72	31	14.40	0	0	1	102.85	2	-
BR Dunk	10	10	0	115	47	11.50	0	0	3	112.74	6	-
A Zampa	5	2	1	4	4*	4.00	0	0	0	100.00	0	-
DJ Worrall	5	1	1	13	13*	-	0	0	0	162.50	1	-

Also played but did not bat: MA Beer (5 matches), SM Boland (3 matches), LP Bowe (4 matches), JR Coleman (6 matches), DG Fallins (2 matches).

Bowling	M	Overs	Mdns	Runs	Wkts	Avge	Best	Econ	4w	SR	Dot %
JR Coleman	6	15.2	0	111	5	22.20	3-27	7.23	0	18.4	46
A Zampa	5	17.4	0	138	2	69.00	1-26	7.81	0	53.0	28
MA Beer	5	14.4	0	115	3	38.33	2-21	7.84	0	29.3	38
JP Faulkner	10	23	0	183	6	30.50	2-19	7.95	0	23.0	41
EP Gulbis	6	13	0	106	4	26.50	2-22	8.15	0	19.5	27
D Fallins	2	5	0	44	0	-	-	8.80	0	-	27
GJ Maxwell	9	6	0	53	1	53.00	1-24	8.83	0	36.0	14
JW Hastings	10	32.2	0	287	10	28.70	2-24	8.87	0	19.4	40
DJ Worrall	5	15	0	135	2	67.50	2-25	9.00	0	45.0	46
BR Dunk	10	2	0	19	1	19.00	1-19	9.50	0	12.0	42
LP Bowe	4	12	0	115	4	28.75	2-30	9.58	0	18.0	38
MP Stoinis	5	16	0	170	5	34.00	3-38	10.62	0	19.2	32
SM Boland	3	8	0	92	1	92.00	1-48	11.50	0	48.0	23

Best BBL07 Powerplay batting & bowling

Batting	Runs/Balls	SR	Sixes	Bowling	Ov	Figs	Econ	Dot %
GJ Maxwell	36/20	180	3	JR Coleman	10	3-70	7.00	50
KP Pietersen	103/77	134	2	JP Faulkner	12	4-91	7.58	49
MP Stoinis	36/29	124	1	MA Beer	10	3-81	8.10	38
LJ Wright	76/67	113	1	DJ Worrall	10	0-85	8.50	50
BR Dunk	85/83	102	2	JW Hastings	8	2-71	8.88	52

Australian Cricket Digest, 2018-19
MELBOURNE STARS - HONOUR ROLL

Season	Finished	Captain	Coach	MVP	Minor Rd W/L
2011-12	Lost Semi	CL White	GRJ Shipperd	DJ Hussey	4/3
2012-13	Lost Semi	SK Warne/CL White	GRJ Shipperd	LS Malinga	5/3
2013-14	Lost Semi	CL White/BJ Hodge	GRJ Shipperd	LJ Wright	8/-
2014-15	Lost Semi	CL White	GRJ Shipperd	JW Hastings	5/3
2015-16	Lost Final	DJ Hussey	SP Fleming	KP Pietersen	5/3
2016-17	Lost Semi	DJ Hussey	SP Fleming	LJ Wright	4/4
2017-18	Last	JW Hastings	SP Fleming	GJ Maxwell	2/8

Leading team records

Most Runs	M	Runs	HS	Avge	SR	Most Wickets	M	W	Avge	Best	Econ
LJ Wright	57	1479	117	29.0	131	JW Hastings	38	50	21.2	4-29	7.88
KP Pietersen	33	1110	76	37.0	137	JP Faulkner	45	44	23.8	4-46	7.61
GJ Maxwell	37	973	84	32.4	156	SM Boland	25	31	24.6	4-30	8.47
DJ Hussey	48	855	52	26.7	129.1	JM Bird	24	28	22.6	4-31	7.15

Highest Individual scores

	Runs	Bls	4s	6s	Versus	Venue	Season
LJ Wright	117	60	8	9	Hurricanes	Hobart	2011-12
LJ Wright	109*	63	11	4	Renegades	MCG	2015-16
PSP Handscomb	103*	64	6	5	Scorchers	MCG	2014-15

Fastest Fifties

	Balls	Versus	Venue	Season
GJ Maxwell	23	Renegades	Docklands	2013-14
LJ Wright	23	Hurricanes	Hobart	2011-12
GJ Maxwell	23	Sixers	SCG	2017-18
DJ Hussey	25	Thunder	MCG	2011-12
KP Pietersen	25	Thinder	MCG	2015-16

Highest Team totals

	Versus	Venue	Season
7-208	Renegades	MCG	2013-14
3-203	Hurricanes	Hobart	2011-12
5-200	Sixers	SCG	2013-14
7-200	Renegades	Docklands	2016-17

Highest total against: 7-206 by Heat at the Gabba, 2017-18

Lowest Team totals

	Versus	Venue	Season
126	Scorchers	WACA	2014-15
5-128	Scorchers	WACA	2011-12
7-128	Sixers	MCG	2017-18

Best Bowling

	Overs	Dots	Versus	Venue	Season
SL Malinga	6-7	4	19	Scorchers	WACA	2012-13
JW Hastings	4-29	4	10	Renegades	MCG	2015-16
SM Boland	4-30	4	9	Strikers	MCG	2016-17
JM Bird	4-31	4	11	Renegades	MCG	2013-14

Most Economical Bowling (Min 4 overs)

		Dots	Versus	Venue	Season
SL Malinga	6-7	19	Scorchers	WACA	2012-13
SL Malinga	2-8	16	Strikers	MCG	2013-14
JP Faulkner	3-9	17	Strikers	MCG	2013-14

Australian Cricket Digest, 2018-19
PERTH SCORCHERS – Lost Semi

It was another fine season for the most successful team in the BBL, which came to an unexpected end in a home semi-final at the new and impressive Perth Stadium. One could ask the question whether playing at the new venue, rather than at the WACA, which had become somewhat of a fortress, caused them to miss making the final.

With national commitments robbing them of two Marsh's and Cameron Bancroft, plus a shoulder injury to Sam Whiteman, the Scorchers won their first four games against the odds. From there their confidence grew and with the Test stars back for the semi-final, they bowed out in an unexpected result.

The Scorchers preferred to be set targets, winning seven of their minor round games in such a fashion, with Ashton Turner a key batsman, all of his three fifties coming in those successful run chases. Ashton Agar was elevated in his role as an all-rounder, bowling far more than in previous years, in doing so ending up as the MVP for the season. Michael Klinger's output was less than past years, most likely he was distracted by his wife's serious illness.

As we've come to expect from the Scorchers, they once again had a high quality pace attack, led by Mitchell Johnson, who was economical in the powerplay. AJ Tye did brilliantly once more at the back end of the innings and when he was called up to Australian ODI duties, Matt Kelly ably filled the breach in what was an impressive first season.

Batting & Fielding	M	Inn	NO	Runs	HS	Avge	100s	50s	6s	S/Rate	Ct	St
TT Bresnan	5	2	1	50	43	50.00	0	0	2	172.41	0	-
AC Agar	9	7	4	149	33*	49.66	0	0	8	128.44	3	-
CT Bancroft	5	5	1	194	75*	48.50	0	2	6	128.47	2	1
TH David	4	3	2	36	17*	36.00	0	0	2	128.57	1	-
AJ Turner	11	11	3	252	70	31.50	0	3	16	162.58	3	-
SE Marsh	1	1	0	30	30	30.00	0	0	0	166.66	0	-
HWR Cartwright	11	11	2	249	65*	27.66	0	2	9	112.16	4	-
AC Voges	10	10	3	169	56*	24.14	0	1	3	119.85	3	-
DJ Willey	6	6	0	127	55	21.16	0	1	5	113.39	2	-
M Klinger	10	10	0	194	83	19.40	0	1	4	108.98	2	-
JA Richardson	8	3	1	26	16	13.00	0	0	2	118.18	3	-
WG Bosisto	4	4	0	37	21	9.25	0	0	0	92.50	2	-
ML Kelly	5	1	0	7	7	7.00	0	0	0	100.00	2	-
JR Philippe	1	1	0	7	7	7.00	0	0	0	70.00	0	-
AJ Tye	6	2	1	7	7	7.00	0	0	0	175.00	2	-
JP Inglis	6	3	1	11	7	5.50	0	0	0	84.61	4	1
SM Whiteman	2	2	0	9	8	4.50	0	0	0	112.50	1	-
MR Marsh	1	1	0	3	3	3.00	0	0	0	60.00	1	-
JS Paris	4	1	0	1	1	1.00	0	0	0	50.00	1	-
MG Johnson	10	1	1	4	4*	-	0	0	0	66.66	6	-

Also played: JM Muirhead (2 matches)

Bowling	M	Overs	Mdns	Runs	Wkts	Avge	Best	Econ	SR	4w	Dot %
AC Agar	9	35	1	201	8	25.12	3-19	5.74	26.2	0	34
MG Johnson	10	40	1	254	7	36.28	3-13	6.35	34.2	0	49
ML Kelly	5	19	0	133	8	16.62	2-13	7.00	14.2	0	40
JM Muirhead	2	4	0	30	1	30.00	1-14	7.50	24.0	0	17
AJ Tye	6	23.4	0	192	16	12.00	5-23	8.11	8.8	1	40
DJ Willey	6	22	0	181	7	25.85	2-30	8.22	18.8	0	38
JS Paris	4	16	0	143	3	47.66	1-33	8.93	32.0	0	36
JA Richardson	8	31	0	281	7	40.14	2-23	9.06	26.5	0	40
WG Bosisto	4	3	0	28	1	28.00	1-9	9.33	18.0	0	28
TT Bresnan	5	17.2	0	170	8	21.25	2-14	9.80	13.0	0	32
MR Marsh	1	4	0	53	0	-	-	13.25	-	0	25

Also bowled: HWR Cartwright (11 matches) 1-0-8-0,

Best BBL07 Powerplay batting & bowling

Batting	Runs/Balls	SR	Sixes	Bowling	Ov	Figs	Econ	Dot %
SE Marsh	30/18	167	0	MG Johnson	23	4-133	5.78	54
CT Bancroft	60/51	118	1	ML Kelly	6	4-36	6.00	61
DJ Willey	57/55	104	1	AJ Tye	5	3-39	7.80	47
M Klinger	120/121	99	2	JA Richardson	16	3-137	8.56	50
WG Bosisto	38/40	95	0	DJ Willey	6	3-57	9.50	53

Australian Cricket Digest, 2018-19
PERTH SCORCHERS - HONOUR ROLL

Season	Finished	Captain	Coach	MVP (Katich Medal)	Minor Rd W/L
2011-12	R-up	MJ North	LM Stevens	HH Gibbs	5/2
2012-13	R-up	SM Katich	JL Langer	SE Marsh	5/3
2013-14	Champions	SM Katich	JL Langer	CJ Simmons	5/3
2014-15	Champions	AC Voges	JL Langer	JP Behrendorff	5/3
2015-16	Lost Semi	M Klinger/ AC Voges	JL Langer	DJ Willey	5/3
2016-17	Champions	AC Voges/M Klinger	JL Langer	AJ Tye	5/3
2017-18	Lost Semi	AC Voges/AJ Turner	JL Langer	AC Agar	8/2

Leading team records

Most Runs	M	Runs	HS	Avge	SR	Most Wickets	M	W	Avge	Best	Econ
SE Marsh	34	1337	99*	49.5	128	AJ Tye	35	53	18.0	5-23	7.21
M Klinger	39	1139	105*	32.5	123	GB Hogg	44	46	21.8	4-29	6.24
AC Voges	48	961	58	30.0	125	JP Behrendorff	32	45	19.0	4-22	6.96
MR Marsh	26	738	77*	38.8	129	NM Coulter-Nile	25	32	20.5	3-9	7.62

Highest Individual scores

	Runs	Bls	4s	6s	Versus	Venue	Season
CJ Simmons	112	58	4	11	Sixers	SCG	2013-14
M Klinger	105*	60	7	4	Renegades	WACA	2014-15
CJ Simmons	102	41	8	8	Strikers	WACA	2013-14

Fastest Fifties

	Balls	Versus	Venue	Season
AJ Turner	23	Renegades	WACA	2017-18
CJ Simmons	24	Strikers	WACA	2013-14
MA Carberry	24	Heat	WACA	2014-15

Highest Team totals

	Versus	Venue	Season
7-203	Strikers	WACA	2013-14
7-197	Strikers	WACA	2016-17
5-193	Sixers	SCG	2013-14

Highest total against: 4-210 by Hurricanes at Perth Stadium, 2017-18

Lowest Team totals

	Versus	Venue	Season
69	Stars	Perth	2012-13
94	Stars	Perth	2015-16
109	Hurricanes	Perth	2011-12

Best Bowling

		Overs	Dots	Versus	Venue	Season
AJ Tye	5-23	4	14	Stars	WACA	2017-18
AC Thomas	4-8	3.1	12	Renegades	WACA	2012-13
AJ Tye	4-18	4	13	Stars	WACA	2014-15
AJ Tye	4-21	3.4	8	Sixers	SCG	2017-18

Most Economical Bowling (Min 4 overs)

		Dots	Versus	Venue	Season
MG Johnson	3-3	21	Stars	WACA	2016-17
GB Hogg	2-8	16	Thunder	Stadium Australia	2011-12
NM Coulter-Nile	1-9	16	Sixers	SCG	2012-13
GB Hogg	2-11	16	Strikers	Adelaide	2014-15

SYDNEY SIXERS – 5th

The Sixers were the most enigmatic team in BBL07, lost their first six then winning their last four (all chasing) to show what they were capable of. Losing appointed skipper Moises Henriques after the second match, due to personal reason didn't help matters. It was a relief to the cricket community that he was back after missing four games, with Johan Botha continuing as skipper.

In those six games, Jason Roy could barely make a run, while Nic Maddison made 24 or more on five occasions, without passing 31. The Sixers started to hit their straps after a win over the Thunder, with Joe Denly, in to replace Roy, showing great form, while Maddison made two blistering knocks in the 60s which contributed to wins. The fact they won their last four games can always be traced to the return of Nathan Lyon, from Test duties, who showed he is a fine bowler in this format.

Sam Billings made useful runs but it was sign of a team who had a poor season, when your MVP made just 156 runs. Dan Hughes was a consistent run getter if not a destroyer of attack, while Jordan Silk played nicely in his four knocks before getting injured against the Stars in the final game of the season, after making a diving save on the rope.

With the ball, Sean Abbott retained his happy knack of taking wickets, while Ben Dwarshuis was a good honest performer, doing best with the ball in the powerplay. Daniel Sams, who took four wickets on debut looks a good prospect, with Botha was always hard to get away, making up for his lack of being able to take wickets.

Batting & Fielding	M	Inn	NO	Runs	HS	Avge	100s	50s	6s	S/Rate	Ct	St
JL Denly	4	4	2	146	72*	73.00	0	1	7	131.53	2	-
JC Silk	8	4	1	156	50	52.00	0	1	3	130.00	6	-
BJ Dwarshuis	8	4	3	42	21*	42.00	0	0	3	144.82	1	-
DP Hughes	8	8	2	227	66*	37.83	0	1	4	110.19	1	-
NJ Maddinson	10	10	1	291	62	32.33	0	2	14	145.50	6	-
SW Billings	6	6	1	156	61*	31.20	0	1	6	141.81	1	1
SNJ O'Keefe	4	3	0	70	28	23.33	0	0	2	148.93	1	-
J Botha	10	5	1	75	32*	18.75	0	0	2	110.29	2	-
MC Henriques	6	5	2	54	21	18.00	0	0	2	131.70	4	-
PM Nevill	9	5	1	68	33	17.00	0	0	0	101.49	6	1
JJ Roy	6	6	0	62	21	10.33	0	0	2	103.33	1	-
SA Abbott	10	4	0	36	23	9.00	0	0	0	150.00	3	-
CR Brathwaite	4	1	0	9	9	9.00	0	0	0	150.00	2	-
DR Sams	6	3	1	1	1	0.50	0	0	0	33.33	1	-
DE Bollinger	2	1	1	0	0*	-	0	0	0	-	2	-
MW Edwards	1	1	1	0	0*	-	0	0	0	-	0	-

Also played: JM Bird (1 match), NM Lyon 4 (matches) 1 catch, WER Somerville (3 matches)

Bowling	M	Overs	Mdns	Runs	Wkts	Avge	Best	Econ	SR	4w	Dot Ball%
JL Denly	4	4	0	23	1	23.00	1-19	5.75	24.0	0	33
NM Lyon	4	16	0	94	7	13.42	3-18	5.87	13.7	0	46
J Botha	10	30	0	195	3	65.00	1-13	6.50	60.0	0	34
SNJ O'Keefe	4	11	0	72	0	-	-	6.54	-	0	35
BJ Dwarshuis	8	29	0	202	7	28.85	2-41	6.96	24.8	0	52
CR Brathwaite	4	14.4	0	108	6	18.00	2-20	7.36	14.6	0	39
WER Somerville	3	10	0	76	0	-	-	7.60	-	0	35
JM Bird	1	4	0	31	1	31.00	1-31	7.75	24.0	0	46
DR Sams	6	22.3	0	178	7	25.42	4-14	7.91	19.2	1	44
SA Abbott	10	33.2	0	283	13	21.76	4-11	8.49	15.3	1	38
DE Bollinger	2	7	0	65	1	65.00	1-30	9.28	42.0	0	40
MC Henriques	6	4	0	39	2	19.50	2-25	9.75	12.0	0	46

Also bowled: MW Edwards (1 match) 3-0-31-0, NJ Maddinson (10 matches) 1-0-14-0

Best BBL07 Powerplay batting & bowling

Batting	Runs/Balls	SR	Sixes	Bowling	Ov	Figs	Econ	Dot %
NJ Maddinson	123/78	158	5	BJ Dwarshuis	16	5-67	4.18	69
JL Denly	85/62	137	4	J Botha	5	1-24	4.80	50
DP Hughes	130/106	123	3	DR Sams	7	1-40	5.71	67
PM Nevill	28/25	112	0	NM Lyon	4	3-25	6.25	67
JJ Roy	62/60	103	2	SNJ O'Keefe	5	0-35	7.00	33

Australian Cricket Digest, 2018-19
SYDNEY SIXERS - HONOUR ROLL

Season	Finished	Captain	Coach	MVP	Minor Rd W/L
2011-12	Champions	BJ Haddin/SPD Smith	TH Bayliss	MC Henriques	5/2
2012-13	7th	BJ Haddin/MC Henriques	TH Bayliss	JR Hazlewood	3/5
2013-14	Lost Semi	SPD Smith/MC Henriques/ MJ North	TH Bayliss	NJ Maddinson	6/2
2014-15	R-up	MC Henriques/NJ Maddison	TH Bayliss	MC Henriques	5/3
2015-16	Last	MC Henriques/NJ Maddison/ BJ Haddin	GRJ Shipperd	MJ Lumb	2/6
2016-17	R-up	MC Henriques	GRJ Shipperd	SA Abbott/DP Hughes	5/3
2017-18	5th	MC Henriques/J Botha	GRJ Shipperd	SW Billings	4/6

Leading team records

Most Runs	M	Runs	HS	Avge	SR	Most Wickets	M	W	Avge	Best	Econ
NJ Maddinson	**56**	**1349**	**85**	**25.4**	**133**	**SA Abbott**	**40**	**53**	**21.4**	**5-16**	**8.73**
MC Henriques	**53**	**1189**	**77**	**28.3**	**126**	B Lee	36	35	28.3	4-28	7.08
MJ Lumb	42	986	80	24.0	124	**NM Lyon**	**21**	**34**	**15.5**	**5-23**	**6.63**
JC Silk	**37**	**670**	**69***	**27.9**	**122**	**BJ Dwarshuis**	**25**	**29**	**24.7**	**3-25**	**8.11**

Highest Individual scores

	Runs	Bls	4s	6s	Versus	Venue	Season
DP Hughes	85	55	7	4	Heat	Gabba	2016-17
NJ Maddinson	85	48	7	5	Strikers	Adelaide	2014-15
NJ Maddinson	84*	54	4	6	Renegades	SCG	2014-15
MJ Lumb	80	61	6	3	Stars	MCG	2014-15

Fastest Fifties

	Balls	Versus	Venue	Season
NJ Maddinson	22	Thunder	SCG	2015-16
NJ Maddinson	**22**	**Stars**	**SCG**	**2017-18**
NJ Maddinson	**23**	**Stars**	**MCG**	**2017-18**
MC Henriques	24	Heat	Gabba	2016-17
SPD Smith	24	Scorchers	SCG	2011-12

Highest Team totals

	Versus	Venue	Season
7-191	Heat	Gabba	2016-17
5-190	**Stars**	**SCG**	**2017-18**
7-186	Hurricanes	SCG	2015-16
4-181	Strikers	Adelaide	2014-15

Highest total against: 5-202 by Thunder at the SCG, 2015-16

Lowest Team totals

	Versus	Venue	Season
99	Scorchers	SCG	2014-15
9-99	Thunder	SCG	2016-17
104	Strikers	Adelaide	2016-17

Best Bowling

		Overs	Dots	Versus	Venue	Season
SA Abbott	5-16	4	12	Strikers	Adelaide	2016-17
NM Lyon	5-23	3.5	12	Hurricanes	SCG	2015-16
SA Abbott	**4-11**	**4**	**15**	**Heat**	**SCG**	**2017-18**
DR Sams	**4-14**	**4**	**17**	**Thunder**	**Sydney Showground**	**2017-18**
NM Lyon	4-23	4	11	Heat	Gabba	2016-17

Most Economical Bowling (Min 4 overs)

		Dots	Versus	Venue	Season
SA Abbott	**4-11**	**15**	**Heat**	**SCG**	**2017-18**
SCG MacGill	2-12	15	Strikers	Adelaide	2011-12
J Botha	**1-13**	**13**	**Heat**	**SCG**	**2017-18**

SYDNEY THUNDER – 6th

The Thunder started the season full of promise after a win in the Sydney derby, but couldn't string back to back wins at any stage in BBL07. Shane Watson was their best performer, passing twenty in seven games, while Jos Buttler played two brilliant knocks in his six games, until selected for England against Australia in the ODI series. Usman Khawaja showed his class in his three knocks, with Kurtis Patterson making a few scores, before being dropped, perhaps because his strike rate was down. Callum Ferguson didn't have the impact that he or the team would have hoped for, injuries curtailing the top and tail of his tournament.

Fawad Ahmed was the team's best bowler, in terms of wicket haul and economy rate, bowling in the middle overs. Overseas quick Mitch McClenaghan was an interesting character, who took regular wickets early in the piece, while at times being wildly inaccurate, particularly at the end of innings when he trying different variations. Always handy with the ball, Chris Green bowled tightly once again in the powerplay, and when given the chance up the batting order, showed he has the knowhow succeed at this level. Shunned for the first three games, Gurinder Sandhu had his moments, underlying the potential he has as a bowler.

After doing well with the ball in the first eight games, spinner Arjun Nair was banned from bowling for three months, his action deemed suspect. He is fortunate he does have another string to his bow, as his batting does look to have potential.

At the end of BBL07, Paddy Upton decided to move on as coach, with former New Zealand pace bowler Shane Bond taking over, having previously been an assistant to Dan Vettori at the Heat.

STATISTICS

Batting & Fielding	M	Inn	NO	Runs	HS	Avge	100s	50s	6s	S/Rate	Ct	St
UT Khawaja	3	3	0	137	85	45.66	0	1	5	145.74	1	-
JS Lenton	4	2	1	41	23	41.00	0	0	3	170.83	1	1
SR Watson	10	10	1	331	77	36.77	0	2	15	139.07	2	-
JC Buttler	6	6	0	202	81	33.66	0	2	10	143.26	5	-
AJ Nair	10	8	4	111	45	27.75	0	0	4	133.73	1	-
JM Vince	3	3	0	75	40	25.00	0	0	4	125.00	0	-
KR Patterson	8	8	0	185	48	23.12	0	0	1	106.32	3	-
BJ Rohrer	10	10	4	136	48	22.66	0	0	6	160.00	3	-
CJ Ferguson	7	6	1	102	37	20.40	0	0	6	104.08	1	-
CJ Green	10	6	0	88	49	14.66	0	0	6	139.68	8	-
RJ Gibson	6	5	1	30	14	7.50	0	0	1	71.42	2	-
AC Blizzard	3	3	1	15	11*	7.50	0	0	0	115.38	1	-
GS Sandhu	7	3	1	11	11*	5.50	0	0	1	157.14	1	-
MJ McClenaghan	10	4	1	10	9	3.33	0	0	0	76.92	3	-
Fawad Ahmed	10	3	2	1	1*	1.00	0	0	0	11.11	2	-
AL Fekete	3	1	0	1	1	1.00	0	0	0	14.28	0	-

Bowling	M	Overs	Mdns	Runs	Wkts	Avge	Best	Econ	SR	4w	Dot Ball%
Fawad Ahmed	10	40	1	245	12	20.41	3-31	6.12	20.0	0	39
AJ Nair	10	29	0	205	9	22.77	3-36	7.06	19.3	0	30
CJ Green	10	36	0	265	7	37.85	2-27	7.36	30.8	0	38
GS Sandhu	7	24.3	1	215	9	23.88	2-28	8.77	16.3	0	42
MJ McClenaghan	10	39.2	0	361	11	32.81	2-19	9.17	21.4	0	36
SR Watson	10	17.4	0	168	3	56.00	1-13	9.50	35.3	0	27
AL Fekete	3	9.5	0	94	1	94.00	1-37	9.55	59.0	0	37

Best BBL07 Powerplay batting & bowling

Batting	Runs/Balls	SR	Sixes	Bowling	Ov	Figs	Econ	Dot %
UT Khawaja	84/60	140	2	CJ Green	19	1-129	6.79	43
JC Buttler	94/73	129	3	GS Sandhu	12	4-90	7.50	53
JM Vince	49/38	129	3	MJ McClenaghan	17	5-129	7.59	51
SR Watson	70/55	127	5	AL Fekete	4	0-41	10.25	46
KR Patterson	130/115	113	0	SR Watson	6	1-62	10.33	33

Australian Cricket Digest, 2018-19
SYDNEY THUNDER
HONOUR ROLL

Season	Finished	Captain	Coach	MVP	Minor Rd W/L
2011-12	Last	DA Warner/DLR Smith	S Duff	CH Gayle	2/5
2012-13	Last	CJR Rogers/CH Gayle	S Duff	DP Nannes	0/8
2013-14	Last	MEK Hussey	C Hathurusinghe	GS Sandhu	1/7
2014-15	7th	MEK Hussey/CD Hartley	P Upton	JH Kallis	2/5 NR 1
2015-16	Champions	MEK Hussey/SR Watson	P Upton	SR Watson/UT Khawaja	4/4
2016-17	Last	BJ Rohrer/SR Watson	P Upton	PJ Cummins	3/5
2017-18	6th	SR Watson	P Upton	SR Watson	4/6

Leading team records

Most Runs	M	Runs	HS	Avge	SR	Most Wickets	M	W	Avge	Best	Econ
UT Khawaja	21	819	109*	51.1	127.9	GS Sandhu	32	31	28.6	3-19	7.97
MEK Hussey	23	741	96	39.0	133.7	Fawad Ahmed	28	27	25.4	4-14	6.95
CH Gayle	14	389	100*	29.9	125.4	DP Nannes	20	23	22.4	4-17	7.15
AC Blizzard	18	375	97*	28.8	118.6	CJ Green	27	22	28.1	3-27	7.05

Highest Individual scores

	Runs	Bls	4s	6s	Versus	Venue	Season
UT Khawaja	109*	70	12	3	Stars	MCG	2015-16
UT Khawaja	104*	59	13	3	Strikers	Adelaide	2015-16
DA Warner	102*	51	6	6	Stars	MCG	2011-12
CH Gayle	100*	54	3	11	Strikers	Stadium Australia	2011-12

Fastest Fifties

	Balls	Versus	Venue	Season
UT Khawaja	24	Strikers	Adelaide Oval	2015-16
CH Gayle	25	Stars	MCG	2012-13
DA Warner	25	Stars	MCG	2011-12
SR Watson	25	Heat	Gabba	2017-18

Highest Team totals

	Versus	Venue	Season
1-208	Heat	Stadium Australia	2014-15
5-202	Sixers	SCG	2015-16
5-186	Heat	Gabba	2015-16

Highest total against: 4-195 by Heat at the Gabba, 2011-12

Lowest Team totals

	Versus	Venue	Season
94	Hurricanes	Hobart	2013-14
99	Scorchers	Stadium Australia	2011-12
101	Strikers	Syd Showground	2016-17

Best Bowling

	Overs	Dots	Versus	Venue	Season
Fawad Ahmed	4-14	4	13	Sixers	SCG	2016-17
DP Nannes	4-17	4	12	Strikers	Stadium Australia	2012-13
CJ McKay	4-28	3	8	Hurricanes	Hobart	2015-16

Most Economical Bowling (Min 4 overs)

	Dots	Versus	Venue	Season
Fawad Ahmed	2-11	13	Sixers	Syd Showground	2017-18
AD Russell	3-13	18	Sixers	Syd Showground	2015-16
SJ Coyte	2-14	15	Hurricanes	Hobart	2011-12
CJ Green	0-14	12	Sixers	SCG	2014-15
Fawad Ahmed	2-14	12	Hurricanes	Launceston	2017-18

Australian Cricket Digest, 2018-19
OVERALL RECORDS

Season	PREVIOUS FINALS	Margin	Venue	Attendance	Man of Match
2011-12	Sixers 3-158 d Scorchers 5-156	Sixers 7 wkts	WACA	16,255	MC Henriques (SS)
2012-13	Heat 5-167 d Scorchers 9-133	Heat 34 runs	WACA	18,517	NM Hauritz (BH)
2013-14	Scorchers 4-191 d Hurricanes 7-152	Scorchers 39 runs	Perth	18,517	GB Hogg (PS)
2014-15	Sixers 5-147 lost to Scorchers 6-148	Scorchers 4 wkts	Manuka	11,741	SE Marsh (PS)
2015-16	Stars 9-176 lost to Thunder 7-181	Thunder 3 wkts	MCG	47,672	UT Khawaja (ST)
2016-17	Sixers 9-141 lost to Scorchers 1-144	Scorchers 9 wkts	WACA	21,832	JA Richardson (PS)
2017-18	Strikers 2-202 d Hurricanes 5-177	Strikers 25 runs	Adel Oval	40,732	JB Weatherald (AS)

WIN/LOSS RECORD OF EACH TEAM

	Matches	Wins	Losses	No Result	Titles	Runners-up
Adelaide Strikers	61	33	26	2	1	0
Brisbane Heat	60	26	34	0	1	0
Hobart Hurricanes	62	28	33	1	0	2
Melbourne Renegades	59	28	31	0	0	0
Melbourne Stars	64	34	30	0	0	1
Perth Scorchers	69	46	23	0	3	2
Sydney Sixers	64	34	30	0	1	2
Sydney Thunder	59	18	40	1	1	0

MOST RUNS – THE TOP TEN

	M	Inn	NO	Runs	HS	Avge	SR	100s	50s	0s	Sixes
Michael Klinger	61	61	7	1802	105*	33.37	121.6	1	12	5	37
Aaron Finch	46	46	4	1669	111*	39.74	139.0	1	14	2	59
Chris Lynn	49	48	10	1560	101	41.05	157.8	1	12	3	102
Luke Wright	57	57	6	1479	117	29.00	131.4	2	6	3	42
Brad Hodge	50	45	12	1412	88	42.79	134.4	0	11	1	54
Cameron White	58	57	8	1381	88	28.18	116.1	0	11	1	47
Nic Maddinson	56	56	3	1349	85	25.45	133.3	0	8	3	57
Shaun Marsh	34	34	7	1337	99*	49.52	128.5	0	13	0	43
Ben Dunk	51	50	2	1221	96	25.44	131.2	0	7	5	39
Moises Henriques	53	52	10	1189	77	28.31	126.3	0	6	4	31

FASTEST FIFTIES (Balls faced)

Chris Gayle	12	Renegades v Strikers	Docklands	2015-16
Brendon McCullum	18	Heat v Renegades	Gabba	2016-17
Tim Ludeman	18	Strikers v Stars	Adelaide	2014-15
Chris Lynn	18	Heat v Hurricanes	Gabba	2014-15
Chris Lynn	19	Heat v Stars	MCG	2015-16

FASTEST HUNDREDS (Balls Faced)

Craig Simmons	39	Scorchers v Strikers	WACA	2013-14
Luke Wright	44	Stars v Hurricanes	Hobart	2011-12

HUNDREDS (15)

Darcy Short	**122* (69)**	**Hurricanes v Heat**	**Gabba**	**2017-18**
Luke Wright	117 (60)	Stars v Hurricanes	Hobart	2011-12
Jake Weatherald	**115 (70)**	**Strikers v Hurricanes**	**Adelaide**	**2017-18**
Ben McDermott	114 (52)	Hurricanes v Renegades	Docklands	2016-17
Luke Pomersbach	112* (70)	Heat v Renegades	Docklands	2012-13
Craig Simmons	112 (58)	Scorchers v Sixers	SCG	2013-14
Aaron Finch	111* (65)	Renegades v Stars	Docklands	2012-13
Usman Khawaja	109* (70)	Thunder v Stars	MCG	2015-16
Luke Wright	109* (63)	Stars v Renegades	MCG	2015-16
Michael Klinger	105* (60)	Scorchers v Renegades	WACA	2014-15
Usman Khawaja	104* (59)	Thunder v Strikers	Adelaide	2015-16
Peter Handscomb	103* (64)	Stars v Scorchers	MCG	2014-15
David Warner	102* (51)	Thunder v Stars	MCG	2011-12
Craig Simmons	102 (41)	Scorchers v Strikers	WACA	2013-14
Travis Head	101* (53)	Strikers v Sixers	Adelaide	2015-16
Chris Lynn	101 (51)	Heat v Hurricanes	Gabba	2015-16
Chris Gayle	100* (54)	Thunders v Strikers	Stadium Australia	2011-12
Alex Carey	**100 (56)**	**Strikers v Hurricanes**	**Adelaide**	**2017-18**

SCORES OF 99

Shaun Marsh	99* (52)	Scorchers v Renegades	Docklands	2011-12
Marcus Stonis	**99 (51)**	**Stars v Heat**	**Gabba**	**2017-18**

Australian Cricket Digest, 2018-19

RECORD PARTNERSHIPS

Wkt				for	v..	Season	venue
1	172	RJ Quiney	LJ Wright	Stars	Hurricanes	2011-12	Hobart
2	148*	BB McCullum	CA Lynn	Heat	Scorchers	2016-17	WACA
3	151	BR McDermott	GJ Bailey	Hurricanes	Renegades	2016-17	Docklands
4	145	TD Paine	GJ Bailey	Hurricanes	Stars	2016-17	Hobart
5	**137***	**CT Bancroft**	**HWR Cartwright**	**Scorchers**	**Thunder**	**2017-18**	**Syd Showg**
6	89	JW Wells	BJ Webster	Hurricanes	Strikers	2016-17	Adelaide
7	59	J Botha	SA Abbott	Sixers	Stars	2016-17	MCG
8	56*	RGL Carters	CP Tremain	Thunder	Renegades	2012-13	Homebush
9	48	JC Silk	NM Lyon	Sixers	Strikers	2014-15	SCG
10	27	CP Tremain	GB Hogg	Renegades	Stars	2016-17	Docklands

HIGHEST SCORES BY TEAM

8-223	Hurricanes v Renegades	Docklands	2016-17
4-222	Renegades v Hurricanes	Docklands	2016-17
3-210	Renegades v Heat	Docklands	2013-14
4-210	**Hurricanes v Scorchers**	**Perth Stadium**	**2017-18**
7-210	Hurricanes v Heat	Brisbane	2013-14
3-209	Heat v Hurricanes	Brisbane	2013-14

LOWEST COMPLETED SCORES BY TEAM

57	Renegades v Stars	Docklands	2014-15
69	Scorchers v Stars	Perth	2012-13
80	Heat v Renegades	Docklands	2014-15
87	Strikers v Sixers	Adelaide	2011-12
9-90	Strikers v Stars	MCG	2013-14
91	Strikers v Scorchers	Adelaide	2012-13
91	Hurricanes v Sixers	SCG	2015-16

MOST RUNS OFF AN OVER

30	CA Lynn (066666) v BW Hilfenhaus	Heat v Stars, MCG	2015-16
29	EP Gulbis (1) DJG Sammy (wide, 6646, wide 4) v DJ Worrall	Hurricanes v Stars, MCG	2014-15
28	TR Birt (0446 6nb 6nb wkt) OA Shah (0) v CJ McKay	Hurricanes v Stars, Hob	2014-15
27	SE Marsh (664461) v AR Keath	Scorchers v Stars, WACA	2012-13

MOST WICKETS

	M	Balls	Mdns	Runs	Wkts	Ave	Best	4i	Econ
Ben Laughlin	62	1300	1	1683	85	19.80	4-26	2	7.77
Sean Abbott	54	1005	0	1467	63	23.29	5-16	3	8.76
Brad Hogg	60	1326	1	1466	61	24.03	4-29	1	6.63
Andrew Tye	38	862	0	1036	55	15.67	5-23	4	7.21
John Hastings	38	809	1	1062	50	21.24	4-29	1	7.88
Kane Richardson	46	962	4	1278	49	26.08	4-22	2	7.97
Cameron Boyce	46	897	0	1228	49	25.06	3-11	0	8.21
Daniel Christian	58	930	0	1297	47	27.60	5-14	3	8.37
Shaun Tait	35	740	0	1068	46	23.22	3-16	0	8.66
Clint McKay	40	825	2	1127	46	24.50	4-28	1	8.20

BEST BOWLING

		Dots			
Lasith Malinga	6-7	19	Stars v Scorchers	WACA	2012-13
Ish Sodhi	6-11	12	Strikers v Thunder	Syd Showground	2016-17
Daniel Christian	5-14	15	Hurricanes v Strikers	Hobart	2016-17
Sean Abbott	5-16	12	Sixers v Strikers	Adelaide	2016-17
Samuel Badree	5-22	12	Heat v Stars	MCG	2015-16

BEST ECONOMY IN A FOUR OVER SPELL

		Dots			
Mitchell Johnson	3-3	21	Scorchers v Sixers	WACA	2016-17
Lasith Malinga	6-7	19	Stars v Scorchers	WACA	2012-13
Fawad Ahmed	1-7	18	Renegades v Heat	Docklands	2014-15
Lasith Malinga	2-8	16	Stars v Strikers	MCG	2013-14
Brad Hogg	2-8	16	Scorchers v Thunder	Stadium Australia	2011-12
James Hopes	1-8	17	Heat v Renegades	Docklands	2014-15

HAT TRICKS (3)

Xavier Doherty	Hurricanes v Thunder	Hobart	2012-13
Andrew Tye	Scorchers v Heat	Gabba	2016-17
Andrew Tye	**Scorchers v Sixers**	**SCG**	**2017-18**

BIG BASH LEAGUE & AUSTRALIAN PLAYERS INVOLVED WITH IPL

	Team	M	R	HS	Avg	SR	H/F	6s	W	Avg	BB	Eco
JC Archer (HH)	Rajasthan	10	15	8	3.0	71	0	0	15	21.6	3-22	8.3
JC Buttler (ST)	Rajasthan	13	548	95*	54.8	155	5	21	-			
DT Christian (MR)	Delhi	4	26	13	13.0	78	0	1	4	25.2	2-35	8.5
BCJ Cutting (BH)	Mumbai	9	96	37	24.0	165	0	8	2	84.0	1-12	9.8
AJ Finch (MR)	Kings XI	10	34	46	16.7	134	0	8	-			
B Laughlin (AS)	Rajasthan	7	1	1	1.0	25	0	0	9	23.4	2-15	10
BB McCullum (BH)	RC Bang	6	127	43	21.1	144	0	6	-			
MG Johnson (PS)	Kolkata	6	16	12*	-	145	5	0	2	108.0	1-30	10
CA Lynn (BH)	Kolkata	16	491	74	32.7	130	3	18	-			
MJ McClenaghan (ST)	Mumbai	11	11	11*	5.5	110	0	1	14	23.7	2-2	8.3
GJ Maxwell (MS)	Delhi	12	169	47	14.0	140	0	9	5	26.4	2-22	8.2
KA Pollard (MR)	Mumbai	9	133	50	19.0	133	1	7	-			
Rashid Khan (AS)	Sunr Hyd	17	59	34*	11.8	190	0	6	21	21.8	3-19	6.7
DJM Short (HH)	Rajasthan	7	115	44	16.4	116	0	5	1	19.0	1-10	6.3
B Stanlake (AS)	Sunr Hyd	4	5	5*	-	250	0	0	5	26.0	2-21	8.1
MP Stoinis (MS)	Kings XI	7	99	29*	24.7	130	0	4	3	40.0	1-15	10
AJ Tye (PS)	Kings XI	14	32	14	5.3	84	0	1	24	18.6	4-16	8.0
SR Watson (ST)	Chennai	15	555	117	39.6	154	2/2	35	6	41.8	2-29	8.9
DJ Willey (PS)	Chennai	3	-	-	-	-	-	-	2	47.5	1-24	9.5

Guide to team names: Chennai Superkings, Delhi Daredevils, Kings XI Punjab, Kolkata Knight Riders, Mumbai Indians, Rajasthan Royals, Royal Challengers Bangalore, Sunrisers Hyderbad

The Final on May 27, 2018 – Chennai Super Kings won by 8 wickets

Sunrisers Hyderabad 6-178 cc (KS Williamson 47off 36, YK Pathan 45* off 25) **lost to Chennai Super Kings 2-181** (18.3 overs) (SR Watson 117* off 57 balls, 8x6 11x4)

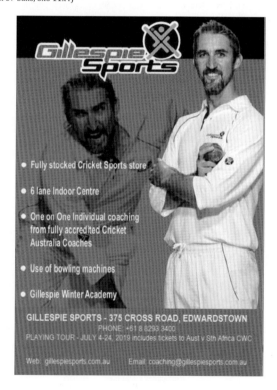

QUEENSLAND WIN FIRST SHIELD SINCE 2011-12

	Won	Lost	Drawn	Match Points	Bat Pts	Bowl Pts	Total
Queensland	6	1	3	39	7.40	8.60	55.00
Tasmania	5	3	2	32	5.85	9.70	47.55
Victoria	3	2	5	23	8.11	8.80	39.91
Western Australia	3	5	2	20	8.19	8.90	37.09
New South Wales	3	5	2	20	6.47	7.90	34.37
South Australia	2	6	2	14	7.04	8.00	29.04

Queensland which won their first Sheffield Shield in six seasons are, at the moment producing some of the best young players in the competition. Matt Renshaw, omitted from the Ashes side at the start of the summer, made most runs for them, after having a horrific first half of the season. Sam Heazlett had a solid season, while paceman Brendon Doggett emerged, taking 28 wickets in his first season. Jack Wildermuth, also in the early stages of his career, showed he is one of the leading all-rounders in the competition. Of the more experienced players, Joe Burns batted superbly when fit, Marnus Labuschange was consistent with six scores over fifty in eleven games, while Michael Neser and Luke Feldman enabled the Bulls to be the most potent attack of the six teams. Throw in Mitch Swepson, who took 32 wickets and wicket-keeper/skipper Jimmy Peirson and you have a very consistent reliable outfit.

Tasmania were the big improvers in 2017-18, making the final for the first time in five seasons. Jake Doran led the batting in terms of runs and average, while Matt Wade made three centuries and was good with the gloves, having returned from Victoria to his native Tasmania. Tom Rogers emerged as an all-rounder, while Jack Bird on occasion was a class above those that he bowled to. Jordan Silk was steady with the bat, while Sam Rainbird was a vital part of the Tigers attack. Gabe Bell backed up well in his second season with the ball and one must not forget skipper George Bailey, who while down a little on runs, made up for it as a skipper.

After winning the last three titles, Victoria finally came unstuck, largely because they could not win any of their four matches at the MCG, being all drawn. The experienced Cameron White was reliable, with Glenn Maxwell and Marcus Harris having very good seasons. Chris Tremain was again an outstanding bowler, with he and Scott Boland the chief workhorses, both getting through more than 340 overs each. Despite two tons, Travis Dean was down on overall output, with Aaron Finch making a ton but only averaging 35. Despite reasonable seasons, the careers of Shield winning players Daniel Christian and Fawad Ahmed appear at an end, with neither being offered a contract for 2018-19, although both will still be busy on BBL duties. Peter Siddle took 29 wickets at nearly 40, but did well in County Cricket for Essex so who knows whether he might be looked at for the 2019 Ashes.

Western Australia came fourth and, having lost players to International commitments and injuries, used 24 players in 2017-18. Injuries saw Nathan Coulter-Nile and Joel Paris play just one game each, while Jason Behrendorff managed only two matches, having taken 37 at 17.59 in seven games last season. Cameron Bancroft when available, was far and away their best bat, his 228 not out coming against South Australia at the WACA, in a match that they lost, after a poor second innings. Ashton Turner played every game and still managed 650 runs, but at only 36, well down from 2017-18.

Paceman Matt Kelly had a fine first season, while Simon Mackin led the wicket-taking tally, but they came at 35.35, which would have been more expensive than he would have liked. Of the players to be blooded, left-arm quick Liam Guthrie has the ability to swing the ball, much like Peter Capes, while Andrew Holder, who was Man of the match in last season's Grade final, also impressed. In the end runs were too hard to come by, with just four centuries scored, with Hilton Cartwright, Darcy Short and Will Bosisto well down on what would have been hoped for.

New South Wales came fifth, they too like Western Australia light on for runs, with just two tons all season. Apart from Steve Smith in his three games, Daniel Hughes was the only batsman to average over forty. Kurtis Patterson slipped a bit, neither Moises Henriques nor Nic Maddinson doing enough as both averaged under 25. With the ball, Trent Copeland carried the attack, taking 34 wickets in 344 overs, the next most bowled was by spinner Steve O'Keefe who managed 19 in his 196.1 overs. Mitchell Starc and Nathan Lyon (both four games) were brilliant when available, but unfortunately Sean Abbott's wickets came at a rather expensive 51, whilst only averaging 20 with the bat. On a slightly sad note, Doug Bollinger and Ed Cowan announced their retirements having both been tremendous servants of the game, with Cowan also quite prominent in sharing his thoughts on the game via the media.

After making the last two finals, South Australia went back to the bottom of the ladder, winning just one and losing four games after Christmas. They struggled their first innings runs in the second half of the season, with only three tons, of nine in the season, over coming after the break. One man who enjoyed the post-Christmas break was Nick Winter who took four five wicket hauls, enjoying the English Duke ball with his pacey left-arm swingers. Dan Worrall also showed his skills and at a slightly fast pace and Joe Mennie was consistent once again. South Australia could only fit in Kane Richardson for four games, while Chadd Sayers only managed five games, having been picked to tour South Africa, where he was finally rewarded with a Test cap. Callum Ferguson was reliable with the bat, skipper Travis Head dynamic when the runs flowed, but could often be scratchy in technique early in his innings. Hopefully his stint with Worcestershire will help, his work as captain still highly regarded. Of the rest of the batting Jake Weatherald and Alex Carey had their moments, but after Christmas Jake Lehmann could only average 20, while Tom Cooper was dropped for the last game. Sadly after a promising start to his career in 2016-17, John Dalton struggled and was omitted for the last two games while Alex Ross failed to deliver a fifty in his three matches.

Australian Cricket Digest, 2018-19

Match 1 – Queensland v Victoria at the Gabba on October 26-28, 2017 (day/night)
Queensland won by 110 runs. Qld 7.00 points, Vic 1.00

Queensland	First innings		B	M	4	6	Second innings		B	M	4	6
MT Renshaw	c Finch b Boland		17	42	74	2	c Fawad b Christian	16	70	93	2	
JA Burns	c Handscomb b Tremain		3	12	15		lbw b Tremain	38	67	106	6	
UT Khawaja *	c Handscomb b Fawad		40	70	97	7	c Handscomb b Fawad	122	195	316	16	
M Labuschagne	lbw b Fawad		19	72	97	2	c Christian b Tremain	39	83	107	6	
SJ Truloff	c Harper b Boland		10	19	24	1	c Harper b Boland	45	75	89	6	
JD Wildermuth	c Harper b Boland		0	1	1		b Siddle	7	9	14	1	
JJ Peirson +	c Harper b Tremain		16	32	48	2	b Tremain	9	26	22	2	
MG Neser	c Harper b Tremain		0	5	6		c Christian b Siddle	8	4	11	1	
MJ Swepson	b Boland		29	36	43	3	1	b Boland	19	28	49	2	
BJ Doggett	c Harper b Tremain		9	46	63		b Boland	0	1	1		
LW Feldman	not out		16	23	29	3	not out	2	3	3		
	5 lb, 2 w		7				(2 b, 1 lb, 1 nb, 2 w)	6				
	59.4 overs, 253 minutes		166				93.2 overs, 410 mins	311				

Fall: 1-5 (Burns), 2-43 (Renshaw), 3-80 (Khawaja), 4-92 (Truloff), 5-92 (Wildermuth), 6-105 (Labuschagne), 7-106 (Neser), 8-113 (Peirson), 9-148 (Swepson), 10-166 (Doggett)

Fall: 1-47 (Renshaw), 2-60 (Burns), 3-144 (Labuschagne), 4-229 (Truloff), 5-244 (Wildermuth) 6-259 (Peirson), 7-270 (Neser), 8-309 (Swepson), 9-309 (Doggett), 10-311 (Khawaja)

Victoria - bowling	O	M	R	W	wd	nb	O	M	R	W	wd	nb
PM Siddle	15	5	30	0			22	5	64	2	1	1
CP Tremain	14.4	2	36	4	1		21	5	81	3		
SM Boland	16	3	43	4	1		21	5	57	3		
Fawad Ahmed	14	1	52	2			12.2	1	51	1		
DT Christian							15	1	42	1		
GJ Maxwell							2	0	13	0		

Victoria	First innings		B	M	4	6	Second innings		B	M	4	6
TJ Dean	c Peirson b Doggett		13	32	38	2	b Neser	28	52	75	2	
MS Harris	lbw b Doggett		10	31	51	1	c Renshaw b Wildermuth	14	35	50	3	
PM Siddle	c Neser b Wildermuth		3	5	6		9 c Swepson b Wildermuth	13	13	11	3	
GJ Maxwell	b Doggett		7	17	27	1	3 c Neser b Wildermuth	20	17	28	4	
PSP Handscomb *	lbw b Feldman		9	9	14	1	4 lbw b Neser	34	108	149	3	
AJ Finch	c Doggett b Neser		41	52	75	4	5 c Feldman b Neser	0	1	4		
SB Harper +	lbw b Feldman		0	1	3		6 c Burns b Feldman	9	18	32	2	
DT Christian	c Neser b Swepson		27	46	59	3	7 lbw b Wildermuth	39	97	154	4	
CP Tremain	lbw b Doggett		20	17	25	2	1 8 c Feldman b Doggett	47	46	62	6	
SM Boland	not out		7	17	27	1	10 c Burns b Swepson	8	23	30	1	
Fawad Ahmed	b Swepson		1	4	6		11 not out	1	22	26		
	1 b, 9 lb		10				1 lb, 3 nb, 2 w	6				
	38.3 overs, 170 mins		148				71.3 overs, 315 mins	219				

Fall: 1-27 (Dean), 2-30 (Siddle), 3-30 (Harris), 4-45 (Handscomb), 5-47 (Maxwell), 6-52 (Harper), 7-111 (Christian), 8-116 (Finch), 9-143 (Tremain), 10-148 (Fawad)

Fall: 1-27 (Harris), 2-60 (Dean), 3-64 (Maxwell), 4-64 (Finch), 5-77 (Harper), 6-43 (Handscomb), 7-195 (Christian), 8-209 (Siddle), 9-211 (Tremain), 10-219 (Boland)

Qld - bowling	O	M	R	W	wd	nb	O	M	R	W	wd	nb
MG Neser	11	2	39	1			15	4	47	3		
LW Feldman	7	2	19	2			15	6	28	1	1	
BJ Doggett	9	0	33	4			19	4	62	0		1
JD Wildermuth	8	0	26	1			15	5	41	4	1	1
MJ Swepson	3.3	0	21	2			7.3	0	40	1		1

Stumps scores:
Day 1   Victoria (1st inns)   3-43   GJ Maxwell 6*, PSP Handscomb 7*
Day 2   Queensland (2nd inns) 5-254   UT Khawaja 99*, JJ Peirson 5*

Toss: Queensland
Umpires: GC Joshua, SA Lightbody
Referee: D Talalla. Award: UT Khawaja (Qld)

174

Australian Cricket Digest, 2018-19

Match 2 –Western Australia v Tasmania at the WACA, Perth on October 26-29, 2017 (day/night)
Western Australia won by 301 runs. WA 8.23 points, Tas 1.31

Western Australia	First innings		B	M	4	6	Second innings		B	M	4	6
CT Bancroft	b Bell	18	29	40	4		c Doolan b Rainbird	17	38	48	2	
SE Marsh	c Rainbird b Fekete	63	138	200	9		c Webster b Rainbird	11	25	39	2	
HWR Cartwright	lbw b Rainbird	61	128	181	10	1	lbw b Bell	38	84	129	6	
MR Marsh *	c Wade b Bird	36	37	34	7		lbw b Rainbird	4	3	6	1	
MP Stoinis	c Doran b Bird	9	21	38	2		c Webster b Fekete	32	65	99	5	
AJ Turner	lbw b Rainbird	32	62	77	4		c Doolan b Bird	18	18	30	4	
JP Inglis +	b Bell	0	6	4			c Bell b Bird	16	19	25	2	
NM Coulter-Nile	c Bird b Bell	42	76	119	5		run out (Paine-Webster)	52	79	107	4	
JA Richardson	c Wade b Bird	19	41	42	3		c Wade b Fekete	71	80	95	8	
M Kelly	not out	15	17	52	1		not out	7	5	2	1	
SP Mackin	b Bird	4	17	21								
	4 b, 16 lb, 1 nb, 3 w	24					5 lb, 1 nb	6				
	97.3 overs, 413 mins	323					69.2 overs, 298 mins	9-272 dec				

Fall: 1-35 (Bancroft), 2-146 (S Marsh), 3-170 (Cartwright), 4-194 (M Marsh), 5-216 (Stoinis), 6-217 (Inglis), 7-258 (Turner), 8-298 (Richardson), 9-310 (Coulter-Nile), 10-323 (Mackin)

Fall: 1-28 (S Marsh), 2-31 (Bancroft), 3-39 (M Marsh), 4-99 (Stoinis), 5-121 (Cartwright), 6-142 (Turner), 7-145 (Inglis), 8-265 (Richardson), 9-272 (Coulter-Nile)

Tasmania - bowling	O	M	R	W	wd	nb	O	M	R	W	wd	nb
JM Bird	28.3	9	61	4	2	1	20	2	85	2	1	
AL Fekete	24	5	90	1			19	3	80	2		
GT Bell	22	5	73	3	1		8	1	32	1		
SL Rainbird	23	2	79	2			18	3	47	3		
BJ Webster							4.2	0	23	0		

Tasmania	First innings		B	M	4	6	Second innings		B	M	4	6
JC Silk	c Inglis b Kelly	3	21	22		2	lbw b Kelly	4	6	9	1	
JR Doran	run out (Cartwright)	54	159	202	7	1	lbw b Coulter-Nile	4	5	3	1	
AJ Doolan	b Richardson	11	18	20	2		lbw b Coulter-Nile	0	5	8		
GJ Bailey*	b Richardson	37	56	102	4		c & b Coulter-Nile	3	17	21		
MS Wade +	c Inglis b Mackin	1	3	2			c Inglis b Mackin	6	18	28	1	
BJ Webster	c Stoinis b Coulter-Nile	19	30	35	4		not out	33	49	71	7	
BR McDermott	not out	45	63	119	8		lbw b Mackin	0	4	6		
SL Rainbird	c Inglis b Richardson	9	16	17	1		run out (Stoinis)	4	5	4	1	
GT Bell	lbw b Kelly	7	38	45			c Inglis b Mackin	0	8	5		
JM Bird	b Kelly	19	26	26	3		b Richardson	1	10	11		
AL Fekete	lbw b Kelly	12	9	12	2		run out (Richardson)	6	13	26	1	
	4 lb, 7 nb, 3 w	14					1 lb, 1 nb	2				
	72 overs, 311 mins	231					23.1 overs, 105 mins	62				

Fall: 1-15 (Silk), 2-30 (Doolan), 3-94 (Bailey), 4-95 (Wade), 5-126 (Webster), 6-134 (Doran), 7-148 (Rainbird), 8-186 (Bell), 9-213 (Bird), 10-231 (Fekete)

Fall: 1-4 (Doran), 2-8 (Silk), 3-8 (Doolan), 4-13 (Bailey), 5-25 (Wade), 6-25 (McDermott) 7-29 (Rainbird), 8-30 (Bell), 9-35 (Bird), 10-63 (Fekete)

WA - bowling	O	M	R	W	wd	nb	O	M	R	W	wd	nb
NM Coulter-Nile	9	2	23	1			6	2	18	3		
M Kelly	17	5	58	4			3.1	0	7	1		
SP Mackin	20	4	62	1		3	8	1	20	3		
JA Richardson	17	4	64	3			6	2	17	0		1
MP Stoinis	9	2	20	0	3	4						

Stumps scores:

Day 1	Western Australia (1st inn)	7-285	NM Coulter-Nile 36*, JA Richardson 9*
Day 2	Tasmania (1st inn)	6-134	BR McDermott 3*, SL Rainbird 0*
Day 3	Western Australia (2nd inn)	7-202	NM Coulter-Nile 26*, JA Richardson 34*

Toss: Tasmania
Umpires: GA Abood, P Wilson
Referee: SR Bernard
Award: NM Coulter-Nile (WA)

Match 3 –South Australia v New South Wales at Adelaide Oval on October 27-29, 2017 (day/night)
New South Wales won by 6 wickets. SA 1.00 points, NSW 7.42

South Australia

First innings		R	B	M	4	6	Second innings	R	B	M	4	6
JD Dalton	b Cummins	15	32	46	2		c Nevill b Starc	64	148	220	4	
JB Weatherald	c Lyon b Cummins	30	51	73	5		c Smith b Lyon	71	178	217	5	
CJ Ferguson	c Maddinson b Copeland	0	4	5			lbw b Lyon	36	61	105	5	
TM Head *	c Cummins b Copeland	8	29	52			b Starc	0	1	1		
JS Lehmann	lbw b Copeland	10	16	21	2		b Starc	6	13	18	1	
TLW Cooper	b Copeland	0	1	1		7	c Smith b Starc	3	10	17		
AT Carey +	c Maddinson b Copeland	12	33	54	1	8	lbw b Starc	4	13	12	1	
JM Mennie	c Warner b Starc	3	16	13		6	c Patterson b Starc	2	13	18		
A Zampa	b Copeland	10	7	87	1	1	b Starc	5	6	5	1	
CJ Sayers	c Hughes b Starc	2	4	6			b Starc	7	15	29		
DJ Worrall	not out	2	8	18			not out	3	2	3		
		0					1 b, 2 lb, 2 w	5				
	33.3 overs, 152 mins	92					76.4 overs, 327 mins	206				

Fall: 1-32 (Dalton), 2-35 (Ferguson), 3-47 (Weatherald), 4-62 (Lehmann), 5-62 (Cooper), 6-63 (Head), 7-66 (Mennie), 8-77 (Zampa), 9-84 (Sayers), 10-92 (Carey)

Fall: 1-137 (Weatherald), 2-139 (Dalton), 3-139 (Head), 4-145 (Lehmann), 5-155 (Mennie), 6-164 (Cooper), 7-176 (Carey), 8-182 (Zampa), 9-200 (Ferguson), 10-206 (Sayers)

NSW - bowling	O	M	R	W	wd	nb	O	M	R	W	wd	nb
MA Starc	13	0	46	2			24.4	3	73	8	1	
PJ Cummins	7	1	22	2			24	8	71	0	1	
TA Copeland	13.3	3	24	6			14	3	33	0		
NM Lyon							14	2	26	2		

New South Wales

First innings		R	B	M	4	6	Second innings	R	B	M	4	6
DA Warner	c Carey b Mennie	83	139	191	8		b Worrall	32	73	87	2	
NJ Maddinson	b Worrall	5	12	16	1		lbw b Sayers	0	3	9		
SPD Smith *	lbw b Sayers	3	13	12			c Carey b Worrall	9	17	22	1	
KR Patterson	b Sayers	14	47	62	1		lbw b Sayers	0	19	30		
MC Henriques	lbw b Zampa	11	40	62			not out	4	11	30		
DP Hughes	c Ferguson b Head	57	101	150	3		not out	7	9	6	1	
PM Nevill +	lbw b Mennie	20	67	89	2							
MA Starc	b Sayers	23	51	53	1							
PJ Cummins	b Sayers	9	34	45								
TA Copeland	not out	7	15	24	1							
NM Lyon	b Worrall	6	8	7								
	2 lb, 2 w	4					3 lb, 1 nb, 1 w	5				
	87.5 overs, 360 mins	242					21.5 overs, 94 mins	4-57				

Fall: 1-14 (Maddinson), 2-19 (Smith), 3-47 (Patterson), 4-95 (Henriques), 5-132 (Warner), 6-183 (Nevill), 7-206 (Hughes), 8-224 (Starc), 9-235 (Cummins), 10-242 (Lyon)

Fall: 1-2 (Maddinson), 2-26 (Smith), 3-31 (Patterson), 4-50 (Warner)

SA - bowling	O	M	R	W	wd	nb	O	M	R	W	wd	nb
CJ Sayers	27	3	82	4			10	3	22	2		
DJ Worrall	21.5	4	64	2	2		7	1	19	2	1	1
JM Mennie	20	9	42	2			4.5	1	13	0		
A Zampa	15	2	49	1								
TM Head	4	2	3	1								

Stumps scores:

Day 1 New South Wales (1st inn)   5-153   DP Hughes 30*, PM Nevill 5*
Day 2 South Australia (2nd inn)   4-145   CJ Ferguson 0*, JM Mennie 0*

Toss: South Australia
Umpires: SJ Nogaski, JD Ward
Referee: DJ Harper. Award: MA Starc (NSW)

Australian Cricket Digest, 2018-19

Match 4 –Tasmania v Queensland at Bellerive Oval on November 4-6, 2017
Queensland won by 7 wickets. Tas 1.00 point, Qld 7.00.

Tasmania — First innings

Batsman	Dismissal	R	B	M	4	6
JC Silk	b Neser	16	31	45	2	
JR Doran	b Neser	0	3	4		
AL Doolan	c &b Neser	2	11	12		
GJ Bailey*	b Wildermuth	20	39	58	4	
MS Wade+	b Feldman	9	41	63	1	
BR McDermott	c Feldman b Neser	37	114	161	4	1
BJ Webster	c Khawaja b Steketee	11	37	51	2	
TS Rogers	b Neser	36	55	69	5	
SL Rainbird	c Feldman b Neser	24	30	45	4	
GT Bell	b Feldman	5	17	21		
JM Bird	not out	19	11	15	3	
	7 lb	7				
	64.5 overs, 285 mins	186				

Tasmania — Second innings

Batsman	Dismissal	R	B	M	4	6
	c Labuschagne b Neser	44	108	134	6	
	b Feldman	0	4	12		
	lbw b Feldman	58	112	143	10	
	b Wildermuth	0	3	6		
	c Neser b Steketee	17	44	58	4	
	lbw b Steketee	0	15	30		
	b Neser	1	2	4		
	b Feldman	0	31	43		
	c Peirson b Feldman	16	48	67	3	
	c Peirson b Feldman	0	1	1		
	not out	11	19	29	1	
	3 lb	3				
	64.3 overs, 268 mins	150				

Fall: 1-1 (Doran), 2-5 (Doolan), 3-24 (Silk), 4-48 (Bailey), 5-55 (Wade), 6-68 (Webster), 7-128 (Rogers), 8-135 (McDermott), 9-152 (Bell), 10-186 (Rainbird)

Fall: 1-12 (Doran), 2-92 (Silk), 3-100 (Bailey), 4-106 (Doolan), 5-115 (McDermott), 6-120 (Webster), 7-120 (Wade), 8-122 (Rogers), 9-122 (Bell), 10-150 (Rainbird)

Queensland - bowling

Bowler	O	M	R	W	wd	nb		O	M	R	W	wd	nb
MG Neser	17.5	5	57	6				16	9	19	2		
LW Feldman	20	7	45	2				15.3	7	31	5		
JD Wildermuth	11	3	35	1				10	4	26	1		
MT Steketee	13	5	30	1				16	6	42	2		
MJ Swepson	3	0	12	0				7	0	29	0		

Queensland — First innings

Batsman	Dismissal	R	B	M	4	6
MT Renshaw	c Doolan b Bird	1	16	25		
JA Burns	lbw b Bird	11	33	37	1	
UT Khawaja*	c Wade b Rainbird	27	49	67	5	
M Labuschagne	run out (McDermott)	2	9	19		
SJ Truloff	lbw b Bell	23	27	40	5	
JD Wildermuth	c Bailey b Rainbird	35	57	72	5	
JJ Peirson+	b Rainbird	14	39	57	1	
MG Neser	lbw b Bird	2	11	16		
MT Steketee	c Bailey b Rogers	27	42	50	4	
MJ Swepson	not out	19	42	59	3	
LW Feldman	c Doolan b Bird	9	12	13	1	
	5 lb, 6 nb	11				
	55.1 overs, 233 mins	181				

Queensland — Second innings

Batsman	Dismissal	R	B	M	4	6
	c Wade b Bell	19	109	160	2	
	b Bell	70	120	181	8	1
	not out	28	48	92	5	
	lbw b Bird	6	26	29		
	not out	24	38	41	3	
	5 b, 3 lb, 3 nb	11				
	56.2 overs, 253 mins	3-158				

Fall: 1-12 (Renshaw), 2-17 (Burns), 3-43 (Labuschagne), 4-64 (Khawaja), 5-72 (Truloff), 6-119 (Peirson), 7-126 (Wildermuth), 8-126 (Neser), 9-165 (Steketee), 10-186 (Feldman)

Fall: 1-82 (Renshaw), 2-101 (Burns), 3-127 (Labuschagne)

Tasmania - bowling

Bowler	O	M	R	W	wd	nb		O	M	R	W	wd	nb
JM Bird	17	5	41	3		4		16	4	42	1		3
GT Bell	13	5	37	1				13	4	31	2		
SL Rainbird	14	3	51	3		2		14	3	43	0		
TS Rogers	8.1	2	39	2				12.2	1	29	0		
BJ Webster	3	1	8	0				1	0	5	0		

Stumps scores:

Day 1:	Queensland (1st inns)	5-79	JD Wildermuth 4, JJ Peirson 3
Day 2:	Tasmania (2nd inns)	9-150	SL Rainbird 16*, JM Bird 11*

Toss: Tasmania
Umpires: MW Graham-Smith, JD Ward.
Ref: RL Parry. Award: MG Neser (Qld)

Match 5 – New South Wales v Western Australia at the Hurstville Oval, Sydney on November 4-7, 2017
New South Wales won by 171 runs. NSW 7.70 points, WA 1.00

New South Wales	First innings		B	M	4	6	Second innings		B	M	4	6
DA Warner	c S Marsh b Behrendorff	5	17	16			2 c Bancroft b Richardson	5	11	15	1	
NJ Maddinson	b Mackin	16	33	49	2		1 c Mackin b Moody	22	35	44	4	
SPD Smith *	c Wells b Cartwright	76	130	174	14		c Richardson b Mackin	127	167	237	17	1
KR Patterson	c Mackin b Richardson	36	65	84	5		c Behrendorff	66	126	151	7	
							b Richardson					
MC Henriques	lbw b Mackin	0	5	7			c Behrendorff b Mackin	45	54	70	5	1
DP Hughes	c Moody b Richardson	25	51	80	5		c Moody b Short	1	3	3		
PM Nevill +	c Bancroft b Richardson	32	90	140	5		not out	11	14	19		
MA Starc	c Wells b Mackin	43	61	66	7	1	not out	14	12	9	1	1
PJ Cummins	not out	27	62	74	3							
JR Hazlewood	c S Marsh b Behrendorff	6	12	20	1							
NM Lyon	c Bancroft b Richardson	2	10	11								
	2 w	2					3 lb, 4 w, 2 nb	9				
	89.2 overs, 365 mins	270					70 overs, 279 mins	6-300 dec				

Fall: 1-6 (Warner), 2-35 (Maddinson), 3-101 (Patterson), 4-105 (Henriques), 5-146 (Smith), 6-166 (Hughes), 7-225 (Starc), 8-254 (Nevill), 9-263 (Hazlewood), 10-270 (Lyon)

Fall: 1-14 (Warner), 2-42 (Maddinson), 3-182 (Patterson), 4-267 (Smith), 5-270 (Hughes), 6-281 (Henriques)

WA - bowling	O	M	R	W	wd	nb	O	M	R	W	wd	nb
JP Behrendorff	21	3	56	2			13	1	58	0	1	
JA Richardson	21.2	4	47	4	1		20	0	77	2		
SP Mackin	19	5	60	3			17	0	75	2	1	2
DJM Moody	16	3	68	0			8	0	32	1	2	
HWR Cartwright	7	1	20	1	1							
DJM Short	5	0	19	0			12	1	55	1		

Western Australia	First innings		B	M	4	6	Second innings		B	M	4	6
CT Bancroft +	not out	76	186	286	8		lbw b Cummins	86	168	219	8	2
SE Marsh	c Nevill b Hazlewood	2	11	17			c Nevill b Hazlewood	91	130	195	13	2
HWR Cartwright	lbw b Hazlewoo	0	5	8			c Patterson b Cummins	0	6	5		
MR Marsh *	b Hazlewood	0	5	8			c Nevill b Hazlewood	6	14	23	1	
AJ Turner	c Smith b Cummins	52	89	115	7		lbw b Lyon	5	31	50		
JW Wells	c Nevill b Hazlewood	1	14	21			c Smith b Starc	16	73	104	1	
DJM Short	c Nevill b Lyon	14	30	43	2		c Patterson b Lyon	3	14	14		
JA Richardson	c Hughes b Cummins	2	22	21			b Hazlewood	9	13	14	1	
JP Behrendorff	b Starc	20	39	41	2		c Nevill b Starc	0	13	19		
DJM Moody	lbw b Starc	0	1	2			b Starc	0	1	2		
SP Mackin	b Starc	0	1	1			not out	0	1	5		
	1 b, 5 lb, 2 w, 1 nb	9					2 b, 4 lb, 1 nb	7				
	67 overs, 286 mins	176					77.1 overs, 329 mins	223				

Fall: 1-8 (S Marsh), 2-8 (Cartwright), 3-8 (M Marsh), 4-97 (Turner), 5-104 (Wells), 6-134 (Short), 7-145 (Richardson), 8-176 (Behrendorff), 9-176 (Moody), 10-176 (Mackin)

Fall: 1-179 (S Marsh), 2-180 (Cartwright), 3-185 (Bancroft), 4-191 (M Marsh), 5-203 (Turner), 6-207 (Short), 7-218 (Richardson), 8-222 (Behrendorff), 9-222 (Moody), 10-223 (Wells)

NSW - bowling	O	M	R	W	wd	nb	O	M	R	W	wd	nb
MA Starc	20	6	56	4	2	1	15.1	5	41	3		
JR Hazlewood	13	3	24	3			20	6	49	3		
MC Henriques	4	0	20	0			8	1	19	0		
PJ Cummins	17	6	31	2			17	3	52	2		1
NM Lyon	13	1	39	1			17	5	56	2		

Stumps Scores

Day 1	New South Wales (1st inn)	7-254	PM Nevill 32*, PJ Cummins 19*
Day 2	Western Australia (2nd inn)	4-102	CT Bancroft 41*, JW Wells 1*
Day 3	New South Wales (2nd inn)	2-166	SPD Smith 74*, KR Patterson 60*

Toss: Western Australia
Umpires: SAJ Craig, MR Marsh,
Referee: D Talalla
Award: MA Starc (NSW)

Australian Cricket Digest, 2018-19

Match 6 – Victoria v South Australia at the MCG on November 4-7, 2017

Match Drawn – Vic 3.05 points, SA 3.09

South Australia	First innings	R	B	M	4	6	Second innings	R	B	M	4	6
JD Dalton	lbw b Tremain	12	21	24			c Harper b Tremain	10	53	74		
JB Weatherald	c Harper b Tremain	2	5	9			c Tremain b Boland	21	72	108	2	
CJ Ferguson	c Christian b Siddle	4	9	20	1		not out	182	213	320	20	1
TM Head *	c Dean b Boland	67	136	179	9		c Harper b Fawad	4	10	18		
JS Lehmann	c Finch b Boland	103	115	152	14		c Finch b Fawad	93	143	178	9	
TLW Cooper	not out	70	185	244	9	1	run out (Maxwell-Fawad)	12	28	24	1	
AT Carey +	c Maxwell b Boland	36	104	139	4		b Tremain	20	43	46	3	
JM Mennie	b Boland	18	38	62	3		st Harper b Fawad	11	9	6		1
A Zampa	c Harper b Fawad	7	15	11	1		c Boland b Tremain	0	2	2		
CJ Sayers	b Fawad	0	2	1			not out	4	6	6		
DJ Worrall	lbw b Fawad	0	2	6								
	2 b, 1 w	3					2 b, 7 lb, 3 nb, 1 w	13				
	100 overs: 6-309 105.2 overs, 428 mins	322					96 overs, 395 mins 8-370 dec					

Fall: 1-9 (Weatherald), 2-18 (Dalton), 3-18 (Ferguson), 4-182 (Lehmann), 5-193 (Carey), 6-273 (Head), 7-310 (Mennie), 8-319 (Zampa), 9-319 (Sayers), 10-322 (Worrall)

Fall: 1-27 (Dalton), 2-51 (Weatherald), 3-59 (Head), 4-271 (Lehmann), 5-289 (Cooper), 6-344 (Carey), 7-355 (Mennie), 8-356 (Zampa)

Victoria - bowling	O	M	R	W	wd	nb	O	M	R	W	wd	nb
PM Siddle	19	8	58	1			19	3	71	0		
CP Tremain	21	6	68	2			17	4	60	3	1	1
SM Boland	24	8	71	4		1	16	3	42	1		1
Fawad Ahmed	28.2	5	82	3			24	1	122	3		
GJ Maxwell	2	1	2	0			5	0	16	0		
DT Christian	11	1	39	0			12	0	39	0		1
AJ Finch							3	0	11	0		

Victoria	First innings	R	B	M	4	6	Second innings	R	B	M	4	6
TJ Dean	b Zampa	34	47	54	6		c Cooper b Mennie	15	42	64	1	
MS Harris	run out (Mennie-Zampa)	103	139	242	12	2	c Carey b Mennie	12	33	38	1	
GJ Maxwell	b Worrall	60	113	132	8	1	lbw b Mennie	64	82	112	5	2
PSP Handscomb*	c and b Lehmann	43	81	107	4		c Sayers b Zampa	58	73	124	6	
AJ Finch	c Carey b Sayers	62	75	92	6	2	c Weatherald b Head	54	80	91	5	1
SB Harper +	lbw b Worrall	11	21	26	1	7	b Mennie	8	35	53		
DT Christian	c Carey b Worrall	8	9	8		6	b Sayers	38	59	72	4	1
CP Tremain	not out	10	38	51	1		c Weatherald b Zampa	3	50	55		
PM Siddle	lbw b Sayers	0	4	3			not out	14	37	43	1	
SM Boland	c Cooper b Sayers	0	1	1			not out	6	14	22	1	
Fawad Ahmed	b Mennie	1	25	41								
	4 b, 7 lb, 2 nb	13					1 nb	1				
	91.5 overs, 382 mins	345					84 overs, 341 mins 8-273					

Fall: 1-58 (Dean), 2-178 (Maxwell), 3-225 (Harris), 4-296 (Handscomb), 5-325 (Harper), 6-333 (Christian), 7-337 (Finch), 8-337 (Siddle), 9-337 (Boland), 10-345 (Fawad)

Fall: 1-24 (Harris), 2-35 (Dean), 3-139 (Maxwell), 4-166 (Handscomb), 5-242 (Finch), 6-248 (Christian), 7-252 (Harper), 8-262 (Tremain)

SA - bowling	O	M	R	W	wd	nb	O	M	R	W	wd	nb
CJ Sayers	21	5	62	3			17	4	39	1		
DJ Worrall	20	5	62	3			20	4	74	0		1
JM Mennie	15.5	3	35	1		2	18	5	39	4		
A Zampa	22	2	123	1			24	2	112	2		
TM Head	8	0	34	0			5	2	9	1		
JS Lehmann	5	0	18	1								

Stumps scores:

Day 1	South Australia (1st inn)	6-291	TLW Cooper 55*, JM Mennie 10*	
Day 2	Victoria (1st inns)	9-337	CP Tremain 4*	
Day 3	South Australia (2nd inn)	5-298	CJ Ferguson 140*, AT Carey 8*	

Toss: South Australia

Umpires: PJ Gillespie, AK Wilds

Ref: RW Stratford. Award: JS Lehmann (SA)

Australian Cricket Digest, 2018-19

Match 7 – Queensland v New South Wales at Allan Border Field, Brisbane on November 13-15, 2017

New South Wales won by 6 wickets. Qld 1.00 points, NSW 7.71

Queensland

Batsman	First innings	R	B	M	4	6	Second innings	R	B	M	4	6
MT Renshaw	c Nevill b Copeland	16	38	46	2		c Nevill b Bollinger	1	3	10		
JA Burns	c Nevill b Bollinger	2	16	20			lbw b Bolllinger	0	1	1		
UT Khawaja *	not out	78	192	261	8	1	c Hughes b Lyon	52	87	124	9	
M Labuschagne	c Nevill b Copeland	6	18	29	1		b Abbott	88	169	286	11	
SJ Truloff	c Smith b Bollinger	13	27	28	3		c Smith b Henriques	10	12	18	1	
JD Wildermuth	c Henriques b Copeland	27	69	69	4		lbw b Abbott	7	20	25	1	
JJ Pierson +	c Nevill b Bollinger	1	8	15			c Nevill b Abbott	2	9	7		
MG Neser	c Smith b Abbott	0	4	11			c Nevill b Copeland	31	60	66	5	
MJ Swepson	b Lyon	16	27	46	3		c Patterson b Abbott	5	12	13		
BJ Doggett	c Henriques b Lyon	4	16	14	1		b Bollinger	2	21	18		
LW Feldman	c Bollinger b Lyon	8	15	16	1		not out	1	10	17		
	10 b, 1 lb, 1 nb	12					9 b, 4 lb, 2 nb, 1 w	16				
	71.3 overs, 282 mins	183					67 overs, 297 mins	215				

Fall: 1-11 (Burns), 2-21 (Renshaw), 3-51 (Labuschagne), 4-68 (Truloff), 5-118 (Wildermuth), 6-122 (Peirson), 7-123 (Neser), 8-152 (Swepson), 9-164 (Doggett), 10-183 (Feldman)

Fall: 1-0 (Burns), 2-5 (Renshaw), 3-91 (Khawaja), 4-114 (Truloff), 5-128 (Wildermuth), 6-140 (Peirson), 7-193 (Neser), 8-200 (Swepson), 9-205 (Doggett), 10-205 (Labuschagne)

NSW - bowling	O	M	R	W	wd	nb		O	M	R	W	wd	nb
DE Bollinger	15	3	38	3				22	4	66	3		
TA Copeland	23	8	33	3				14	6	25	1		
NM Lyon	22.3	5	59	3				7	0	29	1		
SA Abbott	11	1	42	1		1		19	3	65	4	1	2
MC Henriques								5	0	17	1		

New South Wales

Batsman	First innings	R	B	M	4	6	Second innings	R	B	M	4	6
DA Warner	c Swepson b Wildermuth	26	51	66	5		c Doggett b Feldman	37	41	56	7	
NJ Maddinson	c Peirson b Neser	8	11	16	2		c Truloff b Feldman	24	49	83	5	
SPD Smith *	c Truloff b Wildermuth	44	57	72	9		b Doggett	9	15	20	2	
KR Patterson	c Peirson b Neser	12	31	61	2		not out	16	35	61	3	
MC Henriques	c Peirson b Feldman	36	68	82	5		lbw b Feldman	5	9	8	1	
DP Hughes	not out	98	125	164	17		not out	23	36	46	5	
PM Nevill +	c Khawaja b Swepson	17	22	33	3							
TA Copeland	c Swepson b Doggett	8	13	22	2							
SA Abbott	run out (Labuschagne-Peirson)	15	31	36	2							
NM Lyon	c & b Neser	1	15	20								
DE Bollinger	run out (Swepson-Neser)	0	3	6								
	1 lb, 5 nb	6					6 lb, 10 w	16				
	70.2 overs, 293 mins	271					30.5 overs, 139 mins	4-130				

Fall: 1-21 (Maddinson), 2-68 (Warner), 3-83 (Smith), 4-111 (Patterson), 5-150 (Henriques), 6-183 (Nevill), 7-205 (Copeland), 8-248 (Abbott), 9-263 (Lyon), 10-271 (Bollinger)

Fall: 1-72 (Warner), 2-81 (Smith), 3-81 (Maddinson), 4-87 (Henriques)

Qld - bowling	O	M	R	W	wd	nb		O	M	R	W	wd	nb
MG Neser	16.2	3	58	3				9.2	0	35	0		
LW Feldman	14	2	56	1				12	1	45	3	1	
JD Wildermuth	13	3	53	2		1							
BJ Doggett	14	3	53	1		4		9	3	44	1		
MJ Swepson	13	1	50	1									

Stumps Scores

Day 1	New South Wales (1st inn) 3-83	KR Patterson 4*
Day 2	Queensland (2nd inn) 5-129	M Labuschagne 56*, JJ Peirson 0*

Toss: Queensland
Umpires: PJ Gillespie, SA Lightbody
Referee: DJ Harper. Award: DP Hughes (NSW)

Match 8 –Victoria v Tasmania at the MCG on November 13-16, 2017
Match Drawn. Vic 2 points, Tas 2.

Tasmania	First innings		B	M	4	6	Second innings		B	M	4	6
JC Silk	b Fawad	36	54	82	4		subbed out (concussion)					
JR Doran							c Gotch b Siddle	35	147	184	3	
AJ Doolan	b Tremain	0	3	7			not out	247	380	538	30	1
GJ Bailey*	c Gotch b Boland	106	178	250	13	1	c Dean b Tremain	59	129	166	4	1
TD Paine	lbw b Tremain	0	3	3			not out	71	156	185	7	
MS Wade +	b Siddle	5	42	44								
BR McDermott	c Finch b Boland	3	20	30								
JP Faulkner	c Handscomb b Fawa	1	6	5								
TS Rogers	c Gotch b Boland	10	16	13	1							
SL Rainbird	c Handscomb b Fawa	8	15	19	1							
GT Bell	b Fawad	2	40	59								
RP Meredith	not out	0	2	3								
	1 w	1					2 b, 5 lb, 2 nb, 3 w	12				
	63.1 overs, 262 mins	172					135 overs, 538 mins	2-424 dec				

Fall: 1-1 (Doolan), 2-62 (Silk), 3-63 (Paine), 4-83 (Wade),
5-91 (McDermott), 6-92 (Faulkner), 7-105 (Rogers), 8-124 (Rainbird),
9-172 (Bailey), 10-172 (Bell)

Fall: 1-101 (Doran), 2-233 (Bailey)

Victoria - bowling	O	M	R	W	wd	nb		O	M	R	W	wd	nb
PM Siddle	11	5	20	1	1			20	6	41	1		2
CP Tremain	12	3	27	2				20	6	42	1	2	
SM Boland	14	3	43	3				20	8	33	0	1	
Fawad Ahmed	23.1	4	68	4				29	2	121	0		
AJ Finch	1	0	5	0				6	0	29	0		
DT Christian	2	0	9	0				24	2	95	0		
GJ Maxwell								14	0	52	0		
TJ Dean								2	0	4	0		

Victoria	First innings		B	M	4	6	Second innings		B	M	4	6
TJ Dean	b Bell	3	7	4			lbw b Rainbird	12	27	30	2	
MS Harris	c Bailey b Rogers	86	96	167	15		c Wade b Faulkner	28	54	76	3	
GJ Maxwell	c Wade b Bell	4	9	10			not out	45	115	171	4	
PSP Handscomb*	c Paine b Bell	0	5	8			b Bell	13	49	67		
AJ Finch	lbw b Bell	0	2	2			c Wade b Rainbird	3	17	19		
DT Christian	c Silk b Rogers	35	115	146	3		c Wade b Meredith	0	7	14		
SE Gotch +	c Wade b Rainbird	0	7	24			not out	1	14	22		
CP Tremain	c Wade b Rogers	2	19	24								
PM Siddle	c Wade b Faulkner	3	9	21								
SM Boland	c Paine b Rogers	3	7	7								
Fawad Ahmed	not out	0	3	6								
	4 b, 3 lb, 1 w	8					2 lb, 1 nb, 1 w	4				
	46.3 overs, 214 mins	144					47 overs, 202 mins	5-106				

Fall: 1-3 (Dean), 2-13 (Maxwell), 3-25 (Handscomb), 4-25 (Finch),
5-134 (Harris), 6-135 (Christian), 7-138 (Gotch), 8-138 (Tremain),
9-142 (Boland), 10-144 (Siddle)

Fall: 1-21 (Dean), 2-58 (Harris), 3-81 (Handscomb),
4-86 (Finch), 5-99 (Christian)

Tasmania - bowling	O	M	R	W	wd	nb		O	M	R	W	wd	nb
RP Meredith	8	1	31	0				10	2	27	1	1	1
GT Bell	13	2	38	4				12	3	20	1		
JP Faulkner	4.3	0	13	1				6	2	9	1		
SL Rainbird	12	3	34	1				14	4	33	2		
TS Rogers	9	3	21	4	1			5	1	15	0		

Stumps Scores

Day 1	Victoria (1st inn)	4-103	MS Harris 61* DT Christian 28*	
Day 2	Tasmania (2nd inn)	1-180	AJ Doolan 107*, GJ Bailey 30*	
Day 3	Victoria (2nd inn)	2-67	GJ Maxwell 20*, PSP Handscomb 5*	

Toss: Tasmania
Umpires: DM Koch, SJ Nogajski
Referee: D Talalla
Award: AJ Doolan (Tas)

HIGHEST SCORES BY FOR TASMANIA IN A SHEFFIELD SHIELD MATCH
DF Hills 265 Tas v SA, Bellerive, 1997-98   **AJ Doolan 247* Tas v Vic, MCG, 2017-18**

Match 9 –Western Australia v South Australia at the WACA, Perth on November 13-16, 2017
South Australia won by 5 wickets. WA 2.89 points, SA 8.13

Western Australia

Batsman	First innings		B	M	4	6	Second innings		B	M	4	6
CT Bancroft +	not out	228	351	513	22	3	c Carey b Mennie	17	44	47	3	
SE Marsh	b Mennie	17	24	30	2		lbw b Sayers	52	77	114	10	
HWR Cartwright	b Sayers	35	76	102	5		lbw b Richardson	18	30	40	4	
MR Marsh *	c Carey b Worrall	95	110	132	14	2	lbw b Mennie	28	35	54	6	
MP Stoinis	c Carey b Richardson	22	18	22	4		absent					
AJ Turner	c Ferguson b Mennie	36	46	64	6		5 lbw b Sayers	0	5	7		
WG Bosisto	c Carey b Mennie	36	86	103	5		6 b Richardson	11	33	48	2	
JA Richardson	c Mennie b Worrall	17	13	12	3		7 c Lehmann b Worrall	13	28	40	2	
AB Holder	not out	20	26	33	1	1	8 not out	10	36	56		
DJM Moody							9 b Mennie	10	20	27	1	
SP Mackin							10 c Dalton b Sayers	4	10	13		

7 lb, 1 w — 8   8 lb, 1 nb, 1 w — 10

100 overs: 5-389   125 overs, 513 mins   7-514 dec   52.5 overs, 237 mins — 173

Fall: 1-32 (SE Marsh), 2-112 (Cartwright), 3-251 (MR Marsh), 4-277 (Stoinis), 5-362 (Turner), 6-422 (Bosisto), 7-445 (Richardson)

Fall: 1-42 (Bancroft), 2-78 (Cartwright), 3-100 (S Marsh), 4-108 (Turner), 5-124 (M Marsh), 6-142 (Bosisto), 7-146 (Richardson), 8-166 (Moody), 9-173 (Mackin)

SA - bowling	O	M	R	W	wd	nb	O	M	R	W	wd	nb
CJ Sayers	30	4	101	1			15.5	5	45	3		
DJ Worrall	27	3	122	2	1		12	1	48	1	1	
JM Mennie	25	3	127	3			12	3	28	3		1
KW Richardson	26	5	77	1			13	2	44	2		
TM Head	15	1	74	0								
TLW Cooper	2	0	6	0								

South Australia

Batsman	First innings		B	M	4	6	Second innings		B	M	4	6
JD Dalton	c Turner b Moody	15	34	40	3		b Holder	29	46	52	6	
JB Weatherald	c S Marsh b Moody	152	160	202	27	1	b Holder	143	281	381	20	1
CJ Ferguson	run out (Turner-Bancroft)	33	32	51	7		lbw b Holder	88	151	213	17	
TM Head *	c Bancroft b Moody	18	25	35	3		5 c Moody b Richardson	16	21	29	4	
JS Lehmann	c S Marsh b Richardson	13	16	22	3		6 not out	24	21	32	3	
TLW Cooper	c Richardson b Holder	34	52	83	4		7 not out	0	2	4		
AT Carey +	not out	46	99	140	6							
JM Mennie	b Mackin	24	31	42	4		3 c S Marsh b Moody	11	42	53	2	
KW Richardson	b Richardson	6	11	12	1							
CJ Sayers	c Bancroft b Richardson	10	36	42	1							
DJ Worrall	c M Marsh b Richardson	0	2	1								

10 lb, 1 nb, 1 w — 12   5 b, 6 lb, 1 nb, 2 w — 14

82.5 overs, 344 mins — 363   93.4 overs, 387 mins — 5-325

Fall: 1-40 (Dalton), 2-98 (Ferguson), 3-159 (Head), 4-197 (Lehmann), 5-257 (Weatherald), 6-290 (Cooper), 7-334 (Mennie), 8-341 (Richardson), 9-363 (Sayers), 10-363 (Worrall)

Fall: 1-45 (Dalton), 2-75 (Mennie), 3-255 (Ferguson), 4-280 (Head), 5-318 (Weatherald)

WA - bowling	O	M	R	W	wd	nb	O	M	R	W	wd	nb
JA Richardson	20.5	1	90	4			23	6	77	1		
SP Mackin	18	3	65	1			21.4	6	90	0		
DJM Moody	19	3	95	3	1		15	4	58	1	2	1
AB Holder	15	2	51	1			16	7	45	3		
WG Bososito	8	0	32	0			12	2	27	0		
HWR Cartwright	2	0	20	0		1	6	1	17	0		

Stumps Scores

Day 1	Western Australia (1st inn)	5-381	CT Bancroft 161*, WG Bososito 8*	
Day 2	South Australia (1st inn)	6-322	AT Carey 26*, JM Mennie 21*	
Day 3	South Australia (2nd inn)	1-54	JB Weatherald 17*, JM Mennie 8*	

Toss: Tasmania
Umpires: MW Graham-Smith, AK Wilds
Referee: RW Stratford
Award: JB Weatherald (SA)

HIGHEST SCORES BY A WICKET-KEEPER IN A SHEFFIELD SHIELD MATCH

PM Nevill	235* NSW v Tas, Bellerive Oval, 2014-15	
WB Phillips	213* SA v Tas, Adelaide Oval, 1986-87	**CT Bancroft 228* WA v SA, WACA, 2017-18**
BN Jarman	196 SA v NSW, Adelaide Oval, 1965-66	AC Gilchrist 203* WA v SA, WACA, 1997-98

Australian Cricket Digest, 2018-19
Match 10 – South Australia v Tasmania at Adelaide Oval, on November 23-26, 2017
Tasmania won by 142 runs – SA 0.90 points, Tas 7.43

Tasmania	First innings		B	M	4	6	Second innings		B	M	4	6
JC Silk	c Cooper b Valente	23	44	56	1		c Head b Zampa	29	90	107	3	
AJ Doolan	c Carey b Richardson	1	7	5			c Zampa b Richardson	14	26	41	1	
GJ Bailey *	lbw b Mennie	3	12	19			c Carey b Valente	86	138	187	11	
JR Doran	c &b Zampa	114	294	349	9		lbw b Valente	23	86	107	3	
MS Wade +	c Weatherald b Zampa	30	66	100	3		c Weatherald b Mennie	14	29	39	1	1
BR McDermott	c Mennie b Zampa	18	57	49	2		c Cooper b Zampa	7	63	74		
BJ Webster	c Cooper b Zampa	4	13	16			lbw b Zampa	12	36	62		
TS Rogers	c Head b Richardson	33	68	74	4		c Dalton b Richardson	19	46	59	1	1
SL Rainbird	b Mennie	6	6	12			c Mennie b Richardson	21	30	35	4	
GT Bell	not out	16	75	108	2	11	not out	0	0	2		
JM Bird	c Carey b Zampa	26	27	45	3	10	c Lehmann b Richardson	6	7	12	1	
	6 lb, 2 nb	8					8 b, 2 lb, 2 nb, 1 w	13				
100 overs: 9-243	111.1 overs, 421 mins	282					91.3 overs, 367 mins	244				

JM Bird substituted for RP Meredith after day one, when Bird was released for Australian duties.

Fall: 1-2 (Doolan), 2-11 (Bailey), 3-31 (Silk), 4-97 (Wade), 5-125 (McDermott), 6-140 (Webster), 7-202 (Rogers), 8-217 (Rainbird), 9-240 (Doran), 10-282 (Bird)

Fall: 1-30 (Doolan), 2-74 (Silk), 3-144 (Doran), 4-161 (Bailey), 5-177 (Wade), 6-192 (McDermott), 7-197 (Webster), 8-238 (Rainbird), 9-244 (Rogers), 10-244 (Bird)

SA - bowling	O	M	R	W	wd	nb	O	M	R	W	wd	nb
JM Mennie	26	5	58	2		2	16	3	44	1		1
KW Richardson	27	4	86	2			13.3	3	30	4	1	
CT Valente	16	5	41	1			23	9	40	2		1
TM head	13	2	32	0			12	3	35	0		
A Zampa	29.1	6	59	5			27	3	85	3		

South Australia	First innings		B	M	4	6	Second innings		B	M	4	6
JD Dalton	c Wade b Bird	0	1	1			c Webster b Bell	12	22	31		
JB Weatherald	c Doran b Rogers	23	45	72	4		lbw b Bell	11	26	40	1	
CJ Ferguson	c Doran b Bird	0	2	2			c Webster b Rainbird	94	192	278	12	
TM Head *	c Bird b Rainbird	80	91	134	12		c Webster b Rainbird	31	40	70	2	
JS Lehmann	c Wade b Bell	1	4	3			b Bird	17	23	44	2	
TLW Cooper	c Wade b Bird	3	16	17		7	c Wade b Bird	4	15	23	1	
AT Carey +	lbw b Bird	0	4	14		8	c Wade b Rogers	24	63	87	2	
CT Valente	c Wade b Bird	5	15	22		9	b Rainbird	11	28	30	1	
JM Mennie	c Doolan b Rogers	8	11	19		6	b Bird	0	3	3		
A Zampa	c Bell b Rogers	6	18	29			not out	9	19	24		
KW Richardson	not out	9	14	16	1		c Silk b Webster	21	21	17	3	
	5 lb, 1 nb	6					2 b, 2 lb, 5 nb	9				
	36.4 overs, 169 mins	141					74.3 overs, 328 mins	243				

Fall: 1-0 (Dalton), 2-0 (Ferguson), 3-76 (Weatherald), 4-77 (Lehmann), 5-86 (Cooper), 6-100 (Carey), 7-108 (Valente), 8-122 (Head), 9-128 (Mennie), 10-141 (Zampa)

Fall: 1-19 (Dalton), 2-24 (Weatherald), 3-84 (Head), 4-119 (Lehmann), 5-119 (Mennie), 6-128 (Cooper), 7-190 (Carey), 8-213 (Valente), 9-216 (Ferguson), 10-243 (Richardson)

Tasmania - bowling	O	M	R	W	wd	nb	O	M	R	W	wd	nb
JM Bird	12	1	30	5		1	21	5	51	3		
GT Bell	9	1	45	1			16	3	36	2		
SL Rainbird	8	1	37	1			18	1	56	3		4
BJ Webster	1	0	2	0			9.3	1	41	1		
TS Rogers	6.4	1	22	3			9	1	45	1		
JC Silk							1	0	10	0		

Stumps Scores

Day 1	Tasmania (1st inn)	8-228 JR Doran 103, GT Bell 0*
Day 2	Tasmania (2nd inn)	2-79 GJ Bailey 32*, JR Doran 1*
Day 3	South Australia (2nd inn)	5-124 CJ Ferguson 46*, TLW Cooper 4*

Toss: Tasmania
Umpires: PJ Gillespie, MW Graham-Smith
Referee: PL Marshall
Award: JM Bird (Tas)

Australian Cricket Digest, 2018-19
Match 11 –New South Wales v Victoria at North Sydney Oval on November 24-27, 2017
Match Drawn – NSW 1.73 points, Vic 4.00

Victoria	First innings		B	M	4	6	Second innings		B	M	4	6
TJ Dean	c Nevill b Bollinger	36	143	206	7		lbw b Bollinger	0	1	1		
MS Harris	c Hughes b Bollinger	9	20	26	2		not out	62	62	97	4	2
GJ Maxwell	b O'Keefe	278	318	468	36	4	c Henriques b Copeland	16	20	30		
AJ Finch *	c Nevill b Henriques	76	99	122	10	2	c Larkin b Copeland	43	28	37	4	2
CL White	run out (Cowan-Copeland)	66	129	170	11		not out	19	15	27	1	1
MW Short	c Maddinson b O'Keefe	22	46	56	1							
SE Gotch +	c Cowan b O'Keefe	0	7	6								
CP Tremain	not out	45	61	86	4	2						
PM Siddle	c Nevill b Abbott	5	19	32								
JM Holland	b Abbott	9	6	7		1						
SM Boland												
	5 b, 7 lb, 3 nb, 1 w	16					2 lb, 6 w	8				
100 overs : 3-400	140.5 overs, 593 mins	9-562 dec					21 overs, 97 mins	3-148 dec				

Fall: 1-17 (Harris), 2-162 (Dean), 3-310 (Finch), 4-478 (Maxwell), 5-478 (White), 6-480 (Gotch), 7-531 (Short), 8-550 (Siddle), 9-562 (Holland)

Fall: 1-0 (Dean), 2-37 (Maxwell), 3-106 (Finch)

NSW - bowling	O	M	R	W	wd	nb	O	M	R	W	wd	nb
DE Bollinger	30	4	146	2	1	3	6	0	38	1		
TA Copeland	34	8	116	0			9	1	52	2		
SNJ O'Keefe	35	6	128	3			2	0	25	0	1	
SA Abbott	28.5	3	112	2			3	0	24	0	3	
MC Henriques	13	1	48	1			1	0	7	0		

New South Wales	First innings		B	M	4	6	Second innings		B	M	4	6
DP Hughes	c Maxwell b Tremain	44	64	87	7		b Holland	21	26	32	5	
NJ Maddinson	c Gotch b Tremain	31	76	97	3		c Dean b Boland	32	116	160	5	
NCR Larkin	c and b Holland	11	26	41	1		b Tremain	8	23	32		
KR Patterson	c White b Holland	16	34	38	2	5	c Boland b Tremain	61	135	147	15	
MC Henriques *	b Holland	5	15	31		6	c Dean b Holland	0	24	19		
EJM Cowan	c Finch b Holland	32	84	105	4	9	not out	40	99	128	5	
PM Nevill +	run out (Siddle)	25	86	122	3		c Gotch b Boland	8	19	25	2	
SNJ O'Keefe	not out	50	96	124	7		c Gotch b Maxwell	22	40	57	5	
TA Copeland	lbw b Holland	8	39	38		10	not out	5	62	73	1	
SA Abbott	c Dean b Boland	9	30	37	1	4	lbw b Finch	47	175	195	9	1
DE Bollinger	c Dean b Boland	0	8	8								
	5 b, 5 lb, 2 nb	12					8 b, 4 lb	12				
	92.5 overs, 370 mins	243					119.5 overs, 438 mins 8-256					

Fall: 1-75 (Hughes), 2-80 (Maddinson), 3-101 (Larkin), 4-110 (Patterson), 5-115 (Henriques), 6-162 (Cowan), 7-184 (Nevill), 8-218 (Copeland), 9-243 (Abbott), 10-243 (Bollinger)

Fall: 1-31 (Hughes), 2-46 (Larkin), 3-87 (Maddinson), 4-161 (Abbott), 5-161 (Henriques), 6-181 (Nevill), 7-181 (Patterson), 8-215 (O'Keefe)

Victoria - bowling	O	M	R	W	wd	nb	O	M	R	W	wd	nb
PM Siddle	19	7	47	0			15	6	45	0		
CP Tremain	11	3	30	2	2		18	9	47	2		
JM Holland	33	13	67	5			34	19	36	2		
SM Boland	16.5	5	52	2			23.5	9	66	2		
MW Short	5	0	17	0			1	1	0	0		
CL White	5	0	14	0			4	3	4	0		
TJ Dean	2	1	2	0								
GJ Maxwell	1	0	4	0			18	9	42	1		

Stumps Scores

Day 1	Victoria (1st inn)	3-365	GJ Maxwell 213* CL White 24*
Day 2	New South Wales (1st inn)	5-125	EJM Cowan 13*, PM Nevill 1
Day 3	New South Wales (2nd inn)	2-46	NJ Maddinson 17*, SA Aboott 0*

Toss: Victoria
Umpires: SD Fry, GC Joshua
Referee: RL Parry
Award: GJ Maxwell (Vic)

Australian Cricket Digest, 2018-19

Match 12 – Western Australia v Queensland at the WACA, Perth on November 24-27, 2018
Match Drawn – WA 3.51 points, Qld 3.81

Western Australia

Batsman	First innings	R	B	M	4	6	Second innings	R	B	M	4	6
WG Bosisto	lbw b Swepson	60	131	200	12		c Wildermuth b Swepson	27	83	130	5	
JW Wells	c Peirson b Feldman	0	2	6			c Labuschagne b Doggett	45	131	170	3	
HWR Cartwright	b Doggett	42	45	65	8	1	b Swepson	9	19	21	2	
MR Marsh *	c Peirson b Feldman	141	209	253	23	1	b Swepson	11	15	11	2	
AJ Turner	lbw b Wildermuth	22	35	45	3		not out	101	160	254	13	
DJM Short	c Labuschagne b Wildermuth	59	88	125	11		c Truloff b Doggett	1	13	16		
JP Inglis +	b Doggett	53	74	112	8	2	lbw b Wildermuth	54	95	114	8	
AB Holder	c Peirson b Wildermuth	6	15	18	1		c Peirson b Wildermuth	2	6	9		
ML Kelly	b Doggett	0	1	4			c sub (CJ Gannon) b Swepson	0	5	3		
JP Behrendorff	c Peirson b Feldman	10	22	28	1		not out	39	83	101	5	
SP Mackin	not out	12	10	13	2							

Extras: 4 b, 3 lb, 2 w = 9 ; Second: 8 b, 8 lb, 1 nb = 17
100 overs: 8-381, 105.2 overs, 443 mins = 414 ; 101.2 overs, 422 mins = 8-306 dec

Fall: 1-0 (Wells), 2-73 (Cartwright), 3-165 (Bosisto), 4-221 (Turner), 5-319 (Marsh), 6-347 (Short), 7-355 (Holder), 8-363 (Kelly), 9-388 (Behrendorff), 10-414 (Inglis)

Fall: 1-67 (Bosisto), 2-81 (Cartwright), 3-93 (Marsh), 4-93 (Wells), 5-99 (Short), 6-191 (Inglis), 7-195 (Holder), 8-196 (Kelly)

Queensland - bowling

Bowler	O	M	R	W	wd	nb		O	M	R	W	wd	nb
MG Neser	19	6	55	0				22	4	49	0		
LW Feldman	27	8	104	3	1								
BJ Doggett	19.2	2	89	3				21	5	57	2	1	
MJ Swepson	16	1	74	1				37	1	131	4		
JD Wildermuth	18	4	69	3				21.2	7	53	2		
CR Hemphrey	6	1	16	0									

Queensland

Batsman	First innings	R	B	M	4	6	No.	Second innings	R	B	M	4	6
MT Renshaw	c Bosisto b Behrendorff	18	35	43	4			c Inglis b Kelly	7	22	24	1	
JA Burns	lbw b Mackin	81	142	201	9	1		b Kelly	103	142	201	10	2
CR Hemphrey	c Inglis b Kelly	21	40	58	3		4	lbw b Marsh	72	94	98	12	
SJ Truloff	c Inglis b Short	24	23	43	5		7	not out	8	10	24		
JD Wildermuth	c Turner b Kelly	95	151	187	17		5	c Turner b Marsh	24	21	29	3	1
M Labuschagne	c Inglis b Mackin	92	107	138	17		3	lbw b Kelly	72	94	139	12	
JJ Peirson *+	b Holder	26	49	79	2	1	6	c Inglis b Kelly	6	7	16		
MJ Swepson	b Mackin	0	6	9				c Wells b Kelly	1	5	7		
BJ Doggett	not out	43	68	79	9								
LW Feldman	lbw b Holder	12	14	13	1	1	9	not out	0	1	1		
MG Neser	absent hurt												

Extras: 4 b, 7 lb, 1 w = 12 ; Second: 6 b, 2 lb, 1 w = 9
100 overs: 7-401, 105.5 overs, 433 mins = 424 ; 59 overs, 276 mins = 7-290

Fall: 1-34 (Renshaw), 2-84 (Hemphrey), 3-132 (Truloff), 4-198 (Burns), 5-343 (Wildermuth), 6-343 (Labuschagne), 7-343 (Swepson), 8-404 (Peirson), 9-424 (Feldman)

Fall: 1-11 (Renshaw), 2-165 (Labuschagne), 3-203 (Burns), 4-243 (Wildermuth), 5-269 (Peirson), 6-281 (Hemphrey), 7-286 (Swepson)

WA - bowling

Bowler	O	M	R	W	wd	nb		O	M	R	W	wd	nb
JP Behrendorff	20	5	72	1									
ML Kelly	22	6	91	2	1			17	2	60	5		
AB Holder	16.5	1	74	2				7	1	28	0		
SP Mackin	29	2	106	3				17	0	86	0		
HWR Cartwright	1	0	7	0				6	0	36	0		1
DJM Short	14	3	42	1				3	0	23	0		
WG Bosisto	3	0	21	0									
MR Marsh								9	0	49	2		

Stumps Scores

Day 1	Western Australia (1st inn)	7-355	JP Inglis 16*
Day 2	Queensland (1st inn)	4-343	JD Wildermuth 95* M Labuschagne 92*
Day 3	Western Australia (2nd inn)	5-165	AJ Turner 30*, JP Inglis 38*

Toss: Western Australia
Umpires: GJ Davidson, AK Wilds
Referee: D Talalla
Award: JD Wildermuth (Qld)

Match 13 – Tasmania v New South Wales at Bellerive Oval, Hobart on December 3-6, 2017

Tasmania won by 10 wickets - NSW 0.38 points, Tasmania 7.90

Tasmania	First innings		B	M	4	6	Second innings		B	M	4	6
J C Silk	lbw b Bollinger	104	248	319	14		not out	4	2	1	1	
AJ Doolan	c Nevill b Conway	42	140	187	4		not out	0	0	1		
GJ Bailey*	c Nevill b Bollinger	71	126	158	7	1						
J R Doran	b O'Keefe	75	85	118	8	1						
MS Wade +	not out	72	68	100	9	1						
BR McDermott	not out	16	10	8	2	1						
BJ Webster												
TS Rogers												
J M Bird												
SL Rainbird												
GT Bell												
	7 lb, 5 nb		12									
100 overs: 3-290	112 overs, 446 mins		4-392	dec			0.2 overs, 1 min		0-4			

Fall: 1-92 (Doolan), 2-216 (Silk), 3-232 (Bailey), 4-373 (Doran)

NSW - bowling	O	M	R	W	wd	nb		O	M	R	W	wd	nb
DE Bollinger	22	6	82	2		2							
TA Copeland	31	12	58	0				0.2	0	4	0		
HNA Conway	22	4	68	1									
SA Abbott	21	4	100	0		3							
SNJ O'Keefe	16	1	77	1									

New South Wales	First innings		B	M	4	6	Second innings		B	M	4	6
DP Hughes	lbw b Bird	2	9	10			lbw b Bird	9	11	12	2	
NJ Maddinson	lbw b Bell	0	2	5			c Webster b Bird	39	72	95	6	
NCR Larkin	c Doolan b Bell	0	9	10			c Doran b Bird	0	1	1		
KR Patterson	c Bird b Rainbird	22	57	73	3		c Doolan b Rainbird	17	67	105	3	
EJM Cowan	b Bird	67	141	225	9	1	c Webster b Bird	0	4	8		
P M Nevill *+	c Bailey b Webster	38	141	162	4		c &b Silk	70	160	206	5	
SNJ O'Keefe	not out	52	103	126	4	1	c &b Rogers	8	33	54		
TA Copeland	c Bailey b Rogers	9	28	45	1		c Doran b Rogers	4	15	28		
SA Abbott	c Silk b Bird	13	39	52			c Bell b Rainbird	0	15	15		
DE Bollinger	b Bell	0	3	10			not out	26	76	114	2	1
HNA Conway	b Rogers	0	10	11			lbw b Rogers	1	19	23		
	2 b, 3 nb		5				9 lb, 1 w		10			
	89.5 overs, 369 mins		208				78.5 overs, 333 mins		184			

Fall: 1-2 (Maddinson), 2-2 (Hughes), 3-4 (Larkin), 4-51 (Patterson), 5-134 (Cowan), 6-134 (Nevill), 7-161 (Copeland), 8-195 (Abbott), 9-208 (Bollinger), 10-208 (Conway)

Fall: 1-14 (Hughes), 2-14 (Larkin), 3-62 (Maddinson), 4-66 (Cowan), 5-72 (Patterson), 6-101 (O'Keefe), 7-119 (Copeland) 8-120 (Abbott), 9-162 (Nevill), 10-184 (Conway)

Tasmania - bowling	O	M	R	W	wd	nb		O	M	R	W	wd	nb
J M Bird	20	3	65	3		1		19	7	40	4		
GT Bell	17	6	36	3				14	4	42	0		
SL Rainbird	18	8	33	1		2		16	6	30	2		
TS Rogers	17.5	6	37	2				18.5	6	32	3	1	
BJ Webster	17	5	35	1				10	1	27	0		
J C Silk								1	0	4	1		

Stumps Scores

Day 1	No play
Day 2	Tasmania (1st inn) 4-392 MS Wade 72*, BR McDermott 16*
Day 3	New South Wales (2nd inn) 2-50 NJ Maddinson 36*, KR Patterson 4*

Toss: New South Wales
Umpires: SA Lightbody, P Wilson
Referee: SR Bernard
Award: JM Bird (Tas)

Match 14 – Queensland v South Australia at Cazaly's Stadium, Cairns on December 3-6, 2017
Match Drawn – Qld 2.61 points, SA 2.94

South Australia	First innings	B	M	4	6	Second innings	B	M	4	6
JD Dalton	c Heazlett b Hemphrey	53	120	168	6	b Rimmington	10	14	26	2
JB Weatherald	c Heazlett b Gannon	4	9	15	1	c Peirson b Rimmington	0	10	17	
CJ Ferguson	b Swepson	45	94	124	4	b Labuschagne	59	103	182	6
TM Head *	lbw b Swepson	132	162	210	19 1	c Renshaw b Steketee	65	105	135	9
JS Lehmann	b Labuschagne	43	91	132	4	c Burns b Labuschagne	26	29	53	3
TLW Cooper	lbw b Swepson	0	5	4		c Peirson b Swepson	17	29	49	2
AT Carey+	c Renshaw b Labuschagne	139	209	254	12 2	not out	20	61	77	3
JM Mennie	c Peirson b Swepson	0	6	8		b Swepson	23	27	35	4
A Zampa	c Peirson b Swepson	2	24	19		not out	0	2	7	
CJ Sayers	c Burns b Labuschagne	46	92	145	7					
DMK Grant	not out	8	16	34	1					
	6 b, 3 lb, 2 nb, 2 w	13				7 b, 5 lb, 2 nb	14			
100 overs: 8-344	137.4 overs, 561 mins	485				63 overs, 294 mins	7-234 dec			

Fall: 1-10 (Weatherald), 2-99 (Ferguson), 3-114 (Dalton), 4-250 (Lehmann), 5-251 (Cooper), 6-307 (Head), 7-313 (Mennie), 8-323 (Zampa), 9-440 (Sayers), 10-485 (Carey)

Fall: 1-12 (Weatherald), 2-23 (Dalton), 3-121 (Head), 4-165 (Ferguson), 5-172 (Lehmann), 6-199 (Cooper), 7-233 (Mennie)

Queensland - bowling	O	M	R	W	wd	nb	O	M	R	W	wd	nb
MT Steketee	16	6	55	0			14	4	32	1		
CJ Gannon	22	9	48	1			7	2	19	0		
NJ Rimmington	15	3	39	0	2		13	4	35	2		1
JD Wildermuth	12	1	32	0		1	6	1	16	0		1
MJ Swepson	36	4	142	5			17	1	87	2		
M Labuschagne	19.4	1	85	3		1	6	1	33	2		
CR Hamphrey	17	2	75	1								

Queensland	First innings	B	M	4	6	Second innings	B	M	4	6
MT Renshaw	lbw b Sayers	4	11	12	1	not out	51	133	175	4
JA Burns	not out	202	332	498	15 4	c Ferguson b Sayers	4	12	21	
M Labuschagne	c Sayers b Grant	6	54	63		b Head	26	57	79	2
CR Hemphrey	lbw b Zampa	24	50	52	1	c Weatherald b Sayers	8	14	14	1
SD Heazlett	c Ferguson b Mennie	10	15	19	2	not out	22	39	58	1
JD Wildermuth	b Zampa	56	118	171	5					
JJ Peirson *+	not out	82	155	176	8					
MT Steketee										
CJ Gannon										
MJ Swepson										
NJ Rimmington										
	1 b, 3 nb, 1 w	5				9 b, 1 lb, 3 nb, 1 w	14			
100 overs: 5-281	122 overs, 498 mins	5-389 dec				42 overs, 175 mins	3-125			

Fall: 1-12 (Renshaw), 2-40 (Labuschagne), 3-84 (Hemphrey), 4-99 (Heazlett), 5-203 (Wildermuth)

Fall: 1-9 (Burns), 2-66 (Labuschagne), 3-82 (Hemphrey)

SA - bowling	O	M	R	W	wd	nb	O	M	R	W	wd	nb
CJ Sayers	20	5	59	1			9	3	13	2	1	1
JM Mennie	19	4	51	1	2		7	0	16	0		2
DMK Grant	17	6	38	1	1		3	1	4	0		
A Zampa	43	7	138	2	1		16	2	49	0		
TM Head	19	2	82	0			5	0	23	1		
JS Lehmann	3	1	12	0			1	0	7	0		
TLW Cooper	1	0	8	0								
JD Dalton							1	0	3	0		

Stumps Scores
Day 1	South Australia (1st inn)	8-328	AT Carey 39*, CJ Sayers 3*
Day 2	Queensland (1st inn)	4-123	JA Burns 67*, JD Wildermuth 10*
Day 3	South Australia	2-59	CJ Ferguson 25*, TM Head 21*)

Toss: South Australia
Umpires: GC Joshua, DM Koch
Referee: DJ Harper
Award: JA Burns (Qld)

Australian Cricket Digest, 2018-19

Match 15 – Victoria v Western Australia at the MCG on December 3-6, 2017

Match Drawn – Vic 3.06 points, WA 1.93

Western Australia	First innings	B	M	4	6	Second innings	B	M	4	6
WG Bosisto	c White b Fawad	57	161	211	5	c Gotch b Tremain	98	300	371	11
JW Wells	c Finch b Tremain	0	5	10		c White b Holland	107	198	278	12
HWR Cartwright	b Boland	0	7	5		c Gotch b Christian	13	37	34	
MR Marsh *	b Fawad	43	60	79	6	not out	38	71	102	5
MP Stoinis	c White b Holland	24	50	48	1	1	not out	16	39	44	1
AJ Turner	st Gotch b Holland	25	73	87						
JP Inglis +	lbw b Tremain	46	84	88	3					
AC Agar	b Holland	0	3	5						
DJM Short	st Gotch b Fawad	29	59	91	1					
JA Richardson	c & b Boland	5	5	12	1					
ML Kelly	not out	7	16	17	1					
	1 b, 4 lb, 2 nb	7				5 b, 1 lb, 3 nb	9			
	86.5 overs, 331 mins	243				107 overs, 416 mins	3-281	dec		

Fall: 1-7 (Wells), 2-8 (Cartwright), 3-73 (Marsh), 4-106 (Stoinis), 5-147 (Bosisto), 6-167 (Turner), 7-167 (Agar), 8-218 (Inglis), 9-231 (Richardson), 10-243 (Short)

Fall: 1-195 (Wells), 2-214 (Cartwright), 3-244 (Bosisto)

Victoria - bowling	O	M	R	W	wd	nb	O	M	R	W	wd	nb
CP Tremain	15	7	35	2		1	16	4	57	1		2
SM Boland	17	5	49	2			19	4	56	0		
JM Holland	22	6	60	3			30	11	42	1		
DT Christian	5	1	14	0		1	10	3	18	1		1
Fawad Ahmed	19.5	4	58	3			19	5	60	0		
GJ Maxwell	8	1	22	0			6	2	9	0		
CL White							4	0	18	0		
MS Harris							1	0	5	0		
AJ Finch							1	0	4	0		
TJ Dean							1	0	6	0		

Victoria	First innings	B	M	4	6	WA - bowling	O	M	R	W	w	nb
TJ Dean	b Richardson	3	18	28		JA Richardson	28	6	75	2		3
MS Harris	c Richardson b Agar	43	86	121	4	ML Kelly	21	9	50	1	1	
GJ Maxwell	lbw b Richardson	96	152	222	9	1	AC Agar	50	13	119	4		2
AJ Finch *	b Kelly	21	32	44	2	MR Marsh	13	1	47	0	1	2
CL White	lbw b Short	82	187	257	8	1	DJM Short	21.5	2	78	3		
DT Christian	c Kelly b Agar	34	108	134	3	1	MP Stoinis	16	1	66	0		10
SE Gotch +	c Stoinis b Agar	98	200	224	8	HWR Cartwright	4	0	10	0		
CP Tremain	c Cartwright b Agar	9	15	17	1							
JM Holland	lbw b Short	0	2	2								
SM Boland	not out	29	130	175	3	1						
Fawad Ahmed	b Short	11	10	10	1							
	3 b, 2 lb, 17 nb, 2 w	24										
100 overs: 5-306	153.5 overs, 621 mins	450										

Fall: 1-20 (Dean), 2-91 (Harris), 3-128 (Finch), 4-202 (Maxwell), 5-279 (Christian), 6-310 (White), 7-331 (Tremain), 8-331 (Holland), 9-429 (Gotch), 10-450 (Fawad)

Stumps Scores

Day 1	Victoria (1st inn)	1-20	MS Harris 17*
Day 2	Victoria (1st inn)	4-247	CL White 53, DT Christian 17*
Day 3	Western Australia (2nd inn)	0-86	WG Bosisto 38*, JW Wells 46*

Toss: Western Australia
Umpires: SAJ Craig, SB Haig
Referee: RW Stratford
Award: WG Bosisto (WA)

Australian Cricket Digest, 2018-19

Match 16 – Queensland v Tasmania at the Gabba on February 8-11, 2018
Queensland won by 206 runs - Qld 7.55 points, Tasmania 1.00

Queensland	First innings	B	M	4	6	Second innings		B	M	4	6
LD Pfeffer	c Doran b Rainbird	36	119	164	4	b Bird	2	6	4		
MT Renshaw	c Wade b Rogers	56	91	116	6	c Webster b Rainbird	32	49	68	6	
M Labuschagne	c Webster b Bell	11	39	51	1	c Webster b Rogers	26	65	100	3	
CR Hemphrey	b Rainbird	0	2	6		lbw b Bell	52	154	212	4	
SD Heazlett	lbw b Rainbird	1	11	14		c Wade b Bell	39	76	95	7	
JD Wildermuth	c Webster b Bell	8	24	34		c Wade b Bell	0	3	2		
JJ Peirson *+	c Doran b Milenko	15	57	74	1	c Doolan b Wade	61	128	175	9	
MG Neser	c Webster b Rogers	29	34	47	4	c Bailey b Milenko	34	56	78	6	
MJ Swepson	not out	25	39	63	3	c Rogers b Wade	0	2	10		
BJ Doggett	c Webster b Milenko	0	1	1		lbw b Wade	10	16	20	2	
LW Feldman	c Wade b Bell	47	41	57	5	1	not out	9	7	11	1	
	4 b, 4 lb, 7 nb, 12 w	27				5 lb, 13 nb, 2 w	20				
	75.1 overs, 318 mins	255				91.4 overs, 392 mins	285				

Fall: 1-90 (Renshaw), 2-119 (Pfeffer), 3-119 (Labuschagne), 4-119 (Hemphrey), 5-124 (Heazlett), 6-143 (Wildermuth), 7-183 (Neser), 8-183 (Peirson), 9-183 (Doggett), 10-255 (Feldman)

Fall: 1-2 (Pfeffer), 2-56 (Renshaw), 3-74 (Labuschagne), 4-136 (Heazlett), 5-136 (Wildermuth), 6-191 (Hemphrey), 7-259 (Neser), 8-264 (Swepson), 9-270 (Peirson), 10-285 (Doggett)

Tasmania - bowling	O	M	R	W	wd	nb		O	M	R	W	wd	nb
JM Bird	16	4	44	0				15.1	4	41	1		2
GT Bell	14.1	3	43	3	2	1		15.5	3	42	3	1	
SL Rainbird	15	5	50	3		5		24	5	76	1	1	10
BJ Webster	3	1	11	0				3	0	8	0		
SA Milenko	12	4	64	2		1		15	4	49	1		
TS Rogers	15	3	35	2	2			14.5	2	51	1		
GJ Bailey								0.1	0	0	0		
MS Wade								3.4	0	13	3		

Tasmania	First innings	B	M	4	6	Second innings		B	M	4	6
BJ Webster	c Peirson b Neser	18	26	26	3	b Neser	4	4	1	1	
AJ Doolan	b Feldman	13	27	45	2	c Hemphrey b Neser	28	68	80	5	
GJ Bailey *	lbw b Neser	25	42	75	4	c Hemphrey b Feldman	6	10	21		
JR Doran	c Renshaw b Feldman	7	32	37	1	c Labuschagne b Swepson	95	182	249	15	
MS Wade +	c Peirson b Feldman	0	1	2		c Pfeffer b Wildermuth	26	40	72	3	
BR McDermott	c Peirson b Feldman	4	10	8		lbw b Neser	28	60	83	6	
SA Milenko	c Renshaw b Doggett	21	18	29	3	1	c Peirson b Feldman	23	39	57	2	
TS Rogers	c Pfeffer b Feldman	4	10	14	1	c Heazlett b Feldman	1	5	8		
JM Bird	b Feldman	0	3	10		10	absent hurt					
SL Rainbird	not out	6	19	27	1	not out	3	7	12		
GT Bell	b Doggett	5	16	24		11	absent hurt					
	4 b, 5 lb, 3 w	12				3 lb, 1 nb, 1 w	5				
	34 overs, 153 mins	115				69 overs, 295 mins	219				

Fall: 1-30 (Webster), 2-44 (Doolan), 3-72 (Doran), 4-72 (Wade), 5-76 (McDermott), 6-80 (Bailey), 7-101 (Rogers), 8-102 (Milenko), 9-102 (Bird), 10-115 (Bell)

Fall: 1-4 (Webster), 2-19 (Bailey), 3-55 (Doolan), 4-116 (Wade), 5-175 (McDermott), 6-205 (Doran), 7-209 (Rogers), 8-219 (Milenko)

Queensland - bowling	O	M	R	W	wd	nb		O	M	R	W	wd	nb
MG Neser	12	2	43	2				15	3	47	3		
BJ Doggett	7	1	19	2	2			15	5	34	0		1
JD Wildermuth	4	1	12	0				13	5	32	1		
LW Feldman	11	2	32	6				14	2	53	3	1	
MJ Swepson								12	2	50	1		

Close of Play Scores

Day 1	Tasmania (1st inn)	2-60	GJ Bailey 19*, JR Doran 6*
Day 2	Queensland (2nd inn)	6-195	JJ Peirson 24*, MG Neser 4*
Day 3	Tasmania (2nd inns)	6-208	SA Milenko 16*, TS Rogers 1*

Toss: Queensland
Umpires: SAJ Craig, BM White
Referee: PL Marshall
Award: LW Feldman (Qld)

Match 17 – South Australia v Victoria at Adelaide Oval on February 8-11, 2018
Victoria won by 6 wickets - SA 2.39 points, Vic 8.10

South Australia	First innings		B	M	4	6	Second innings		B	M	4	6
KR Smith	c Handscomb b Tremain	8	35	54	1		c Handscomb b Tremain	10	13	24	1	
JB Weatherald	c Gotch b Tremain	0	1	4			c Handscomb b Boland	62	101	145	7	1
JD Dalton	c Handscomb b Siddle	1	6	8			lbw b Boland	11	33	50	1	
JS Lehmann	c Short b Boland	83	149	227	7		c White b Holland	19	21	19	3	
TLW Cooper *	c Handscomb b Boland	35	44	50	5	1	run out (Siddle)	4	14	25	-	
AI Ross	c Dean b Siddle	21	24	39	3		b Siddle	49	86	140	6	
HJ Nielsen +	b Boland	105	182	240	11		lbw b Boland	24	94	106	1	
JM Mennie	c Harris b Tremain	75	96	136	6	2	c Short b Tremain	11	18	30	1	
CJ Sayers	b Tremain	1	4	9			c Handscomb b Boland	8	20	25	2	
DJ Worrall	c Handscomb b Boland	12	17	27	1	1	not out	3	13	25		
NP Winter	not out	10	17	27	1		c Gotch b Siddle	7	13	20		
	7 b, 7 lb, 5 nb, 9 w	28					16 b, 13 lb, 1 nb, 5 w	35				
	95 overs, 416 mins	379					70.5 overs, 309 mins	243				

Fall: 1-0 (Weatherald), 2-1 (Dalton), 3-34 (Smith), 4-92 (Cooper), 5-126 (Ross), 6-212 (Lehmann), 7-355 (Mennie), 8-356 (Nielsen), 9-356 (Sayers), 10-379 (Worrall)

Fall: 1-40 (Smith), 2-73 (Dalton), 3-98 (Lehmann), 4-120 (Cooper), 5-134 (Weatherald), 6-214 (Nielsen), 7-216 (Ross), 8-233 (Mennie), 9-233 (Sayers), 10-243 (Winter)

Victoria - bowling	O	M	R	W	wd	nb	O	M	R	W	wd	nb
PM Siddle	24	5	75	2	2	3	16.5	4	63	2	1	1
CP Tremain	25	6	86	4			16	0	53	2		
SM Boland	23	4	88	4	3		21	6	41	4		
JM Holland	15	1	78	0			17	1	57	1		
MW Short	3	0	9	0								
TJ Dean	5	1	29	0		2						

Victoria	First innings		B	M	4	6	Second innings		B	M	4	6
TJ Dean	c Smith b Winter	42	108	167	4		c Cooper b Mennie	11	35	45	1	
MS Harris	lbw b Winter	66	109	148	10		c Dalton b Mennie	30	53	70	5	
EM Vines	lbw b Cooper	27	108	129	1		c Nielsen b Worrall	23	56	76	4	
PSP Handscomb *	b Winter	0	7	10			not out	114	127	195	8	2
CL White	c Ross b Mennie	149	218	331	10	4	c Nielsen b Lehmann	50	99	115	3	
MW Short	c Worrall b Mennie	3	19	35			not out	14	23	27	1	
SE Gotch +	b Worrall	22	38	46	2							
CP Tremain	c Nielsen b Winter	23	54	81	2							
PM Siddle	b Worrall	9	20	21	2							
JM Holland	lbw b Winter	0	8	21								
SM Boland	not out	4	7	22	1							
	9 b, 8 lb, 3 nb, 6 w	26					5 lb, 3 nb, 3 w	11				
	100 overs: 6-310											
	115.3 overs, 510 mins	371					65 overs, 266 mins	4-253				

Fall: 1-114 (Harris), 2-121 (Dean), 3-121 (Handscomb), 4-188 (Vines), 5-213 (Short), 6-248 (Gotch), 7-311 (Tremain), 8-326 (Siddle), 9-352 (Holland), 10-371 (White)

Fall: 1-31 (Dean), 2-52 (Harris), 3-84 (Vines), 4-222 (White)

SA - bowling	O	M	R	W	wd	nb	O	M	R	W	wd	nb
CJ Sayers	27	5	85	0	1	2	15	3	50	0		1
DJ Worrall	28	9	78	3	1		15	4	63	1	1	2
JM Mennie	23.3	3	66	2			13	5	40	2	1	
NP Winter	27	5	85	5	2		11	0	42	0		1
TLW Cooper	9	0	40	1			5	0	24	0		
JS Lehmann	1	1	0	0			6	0	29	1		

Stumps Scores

Day 1	South Australia (1st inn)	9-357	DJ Worrall 0*, NP Winter 1*
Day 2	Victoria (1st inn)	5-248	CL White 68*, SE Gotch 22*
Day 3	South Australia (2nd inn)	5-208	AI Ross 48, HJ Nielsen 20*

Toss: Victoria
Umpires: AD Deshmukh, JD Ward
Referee: RW Stratford
Award: CL White (Vic)

Match 18 –Western Australia v New South Wales at the WACA on February 8-11, 2018
Western Australia won by 4 wickets - WA 7.15 points, NSW 1.04

New South Wales	First innings		B	M	4	6	Second innings		B	M	4	6
NCR Larkin	c Turner b M Marsh	13	38	60	1		c Inglis b Mackin	19	55	74	2	
DP Hughes	c Turner b M Marsh	49	112	154	9		c Richardson b Mackin	25	50	71	3	
KR Patterson	c Kelly b M Marsh	24	90	124	2		c Turner b Kelly	16	40	50	2	
MC Henriques	c Mackin b M Marsh	5	11	26	1		lbw b Mackin	0	2	1		
EJM Cowan	c Bancroft b Kelly	46	73	108	5	1	c Bevilaqua b Kelly	55	110	194	6	
PM Nevill *+	c Inglis b Mackin	16	74	83	1		c Bancroft b Kelly	4	19	26		
TA Copeland	c & b Kelly	11	29	50	1		not out	1	6	11		
GS Sandhu	c Cartwright b Bosisto	6	30	47			c Bevilaqua b Mackin	14	47	60	1	
CH Stobo	c Inglis b Bevilaqua	2	15	19			c S Marsh b Kelly	8	28	30		
NM Lyon	not out	6	15	17			lbw b Mackin	4	7	5	1	
MW Edwards	c Bancroft b Richardson	4	9	14	1		c Inglis b Mackin	8	10	16	2	
	6 b, 10 lb, 2 nb, 4 w	22					16 b, 2 lb, 7 w	25				
	82.2 overs, 360 mins	204					62.2 overs, 278 mins	179				

Fall: 1-40 (Larkin), 2-89 (Hughes), 3-104 (Henriques), 4-105 (Patterson), 5-157 (Nevill), 6-174 (Cowan), 7-188 (Copeland), 8-193 (Sandhu), 9-194 (Stobo), 10-204 (Edwards)

Fall: 1-45 (Hughes), 2-45 (Larkin), 3-45 (Henriques), 4-81 (Patterson), 5-89 (Nevill), 6-136 (Sandhu, 7-162 (Stobo), 8-167 (Lyon), 9-175 (Cowan), 10-179 (Edwards)

WA - bowling	O	M	R	W	wd	nb	O	M	R	W	wd	nb
JA Richardson	18.2	6	30	1		1	18	3	55	0	2	
ML Kelly	16	4	34	2			15	6	25	4		
SP Mackin	18	5	42	1			17.2	5	43	6	1	
MR Marsh	16	3	50	4	1	1	10	2	34	0		
AA Bevilaqua	10	3	21	1	1		2	0	4	0		
WG Bosisto	4	1	11	1								

Western Australia	First innings		B	M	4	6	Second innings		B	M	4	6
CT Bancroft	c Cowan b Stobo	38	83	120	4		c Cowan b Stobo	13	20	24	2	
WG Bosisto	c Stobo b Copeland	0	3	2			lbw b Copeland	22	30	43	4	
ML Kelly	c Nevill b Copeland	1	3	5								
HWR Cartwright	c Nevill b Edwards	78	172	216	11	1	3 c Copeland b Sandhu	32	32	47	7	
SE Marsh	c Nevill b Lyon	29	87	88	4		4 c Copeland b Sandhu	39	51	64	7	
MR Marsh *	c Edwards b Stobo	8	22	42			5 c Copeland b Edwards	14	10	12	2	1
AJ Turner	c Nevill b Copeland	6	15	18	1		6 st Nevill b Lyon	22	36	58	3	
JP Inglis +	st Nevill b Lyon	4	8	22			7 not out	10	27	39	2	
JA Richardson	c Larkin b Stobo	0	1	1								
AA Bevilaqua	b Lyon	36	23	23	2	3	8 not out	0	1	3		
SP Mackin	not out	0	3	9								
	9 b, 4 lb, 2 w	15					15 b, 2 lb, 3 w	20				
	70 overs, 281 mins	215					34.3 overs, 151 mins	6-172				

Fall: 1-1-3 (Bosisto), 2-5 (Kelly), 3-98 (Bancroft), 4-147 (SE Marsh), 5-163 (Cartwright), 6-173 (Turner), 7-174 (M Marsh), 8-174 (Richardson), 9-194 (Inglis), 10-215 (Bevilaqua)

Fall: 1-25 (Bancroft), 2-59 (Bosisto), 3-93 (Cartwright), 4-120 (M Marsh), 5-136 (S Marsh), 6-160 (Turner)

NSW - bowling	O	M	R	W	wd	nb	O	M	R	W	wd	nb
TA Copeland	19	7	42	3	1		9.3	1	44	1		
GA Sandhu	11	2	30	0			8	1	22	2		
CH Stobo	10	3	32	3			8	1	48	1	1	
MW Edwards	10	3	39	1	1		4	0	26	1	2	
NM Lyon	20	5	59	3			5	1	15	1		

Stumps Scores
Day 1   Western Australia (1st inn)   2-17   CT Bancroft 7*, HWR Cartwright 8*
Day 2   New South Wales (2nd inn)   3-77   KR Patterson 12*, EJM Cowan 11*

Toss: New South Wales
Umpires: SA Lightbody, AK Wilds
Referee: RL Parry. Award: SP Mackin (WA)

Match 19 – New South Wales v South Australia at the Sydney Cricket Ground on February 16-19, 2018
South Australia won by 7 wickets - NSW 1.56 points, SA 7.81

New South Wales	First innings		B	M	4	6	Second innings		B	M	4	6
NCR Larkin	c Nielsen b Worrall		19	47	85	2	lbw b Winter		3	22	23	
DP Hughes	c Ferguson b Cooper		93	214	256	11	c Nielsen b Worrall		41	68	95	6
EJM Cowan	lbw b Winter		1	20	23		c Ross b Worrall		27	57	81	3
KR Patterson	b Winter		89	150	206	10	c Cooper b Winter		41	69	88	7
MC Henriques	lbw b Winter		1	15	18		c and b Worrall		26	71	100	1
PM Nevill *+	c Nielsen b Worrall		1	10	11		c Nielsen b Winter		13	29	51	1
WER Somerville	c Ferguson b Mennie		0	7	9		b Winter		3	5	11	
TA Copeland	b Winter		10	39	48	1	lbw b Andrews		23	39	51	2	1
DG Fallins	not out		6	23	38		b Winter		10	32	42	2
CH Stobo	b Mennie		5	16	20	1	not out		1	13	22	
MW Edwards	b Winter		1	7	7		c Dalton b Worrall		0	9	12	
	5 b, 9 lb, 4 nb, 12 w		30				7 b, 6 lb, 2 nb, 10 w		25			
	90.4 overs, 385 mins		256				68.4 overs, 293 mins		213			

Fall: 1-59 (Larkin), 2-66 (Cowan), 3-183 (Hughes), 4-194 (Henriques), 5-203 (Nevill), 6-205 (Somerville), 7-240 (Copeland), 8-241 (Patterson), 9-251 (Stobo), 10-256 (Edwards)

Fall: 1-11 (Larkin), 2-87 (Hughes), 3-90 (Cowan), 4-145 (Patterson), 5-159 (Henriques), 6-168 (Somerville), 7-179 (Nevill), 8-202 (Copeland), 9-207 (Fallins), 10-213 (Edwards)

SA - bowling	O	M	R	W	wd	nb		O	M	R	W	wd	nb
DJ Worrall	23	7	59	2	1			20.4	4	55	4	3	
JM Mennie	22	3	74	2	5	3		13	2	44	0	2	2
NP Winter	25.4	9	48	5	2	1		24	5	61	5	1	
TLW Cooper	5	3	12	1				1	0	5	0		
TD Andrews	15	0	49	0				10	2	35	1		

South Australia	First innings		B	M	4	6	Second innings		B	M	4	6
JD Dalton	b Copeland		20	43	55	3	st Nevill b Fallins		29	47	70	2	1
JB Weatherald	lbw b Stobo		37	71	118	4	c Stobo b Edwards		56	93	130	7	1
CJ Ferguson *	c Larkin b Copeland		1	5	10		not out		49	85	137	6	
JS Lehmann	c Hughes b Edwards		22	38	37	3	c Somerville b Stobo		10	16	17	2	
TLW Cooper	not out		105	135	216	11	4						
AI Ross	c Stobo b Copeland		17	30	41	4							
HJ Nielsen +	c Nevill b Copeland		1	11	10								
JM Mennie	c & b Fallins		5	17	21		5	not out		26	58	59	3
TD Andrews	b Fallins		50	72	84	8							
DJ Worrall	st Nevill b Fallins		0	4	2								
NP Winter	c Nevill b Edwards		1	20	40								
	18 lb, 1 nb, 3 w		22				11 b, 1 lb, 1 nb, 9 w		22			
	74.1 overs, 321 mins		281				49.4 overs, 208 mins		192			

Fall: 1-42 (Dalton), 2-46 (Ferguson), 3-78 (Lehmann), 4-88 (Weatherald), 5-128 (Ross), 6-130 (Nielsen), 7-141 (Mennie), 8-237 (Andrews), 9-237 (Worrall), 10-281 (Winter)

Fall: 1-63 (Dalton), 2-122 (Weatherald), 3-141 (Lehmann)

NSW - bowling	O	M	R	W	wd	nb		O	M	R	W	wd	nb
TA Copeland	25	8	63	4				16	3	39	0	1	
CH Stobo	17	1	74	1	1	1		8	1	39	1	3	1
WER Somerville	10	0	27	0				6	1	11	0		
MW Edwards	13.1	3	48	2	2			12	2	40	1	1	
DG Fallins	9	1	51	3				7.4	1	51	1		

Stumps Scores

Day 1   New South Wales (1st inn)   256
Day 2   New South Wales (2nd inn)   1-61   DP Hughes 32* EJM Cowan 16*
Day 3   South Australia (2nd inns)   3-146   CJ Ferguson 35*, JM Mennie 2*

Toss: New South Wales
Umpires: GC Joshua, BM White
Ref: SR Bernard
Award: NP Winter (SA)

Australian Cricket Digest, 2018-19

Match 20 – Tasmania v Western Australia at Bellerive Oval, Hobart on February 16-18, 2018

Tasmania won by an innings & 87 runs – Tasmania 8.50 points, WA 0.70

Tasmania	First innings		B	M	4	6
BJ Webster	b Holder	8	35	45	1	
AJ Doolan	c Wells b Holder	12	56	64	1	
GJ Bailey *	lbw b Mackin	10	22	28	2	
JR Doran	b Bosisto	37	120	151	6	
MS Wade +	b Guthrie	139	242	314	19	1
BR McDermott	c Turner b Bevilaqua	14	44	46	1	
SA Milenko	b Guthrie	78	82	118	12	1
TS Rogers	c Bosisto b Guthrie	48	57	70	5	2
SL Rainbird	c Guthrie b Hinchliffe	40	42	52	6	
AL Fekete	not out	1	5	10		
RP Meredith						
	7 b, 18 lb, 11 nb, 8 w	44				
100 overs : 7-350	115.4 overs, 453 mins	431				

WA - bowling	O	M	R	W	w	nb
SP Mackin	30	10	65	1	1	2
LCJ Guthrie	22.4	3	104	3	1	1
AA Bevilaqua	20	5	67	1	2	1
AB Holder	22	6	74	2		3
HWR Cartwright	11	2	56	0		4
WG Bosisto	4	1	26	1		
CD Hinchcliff	6	0	14	1		

Fall: 1-32 (Webster), 2-45 (Doolan), 3-51 (Bailey),
4-133 (Doran), 5-159 (McDermott), 6-339 (Milenko),
7-344 (Wade), 8-425 (Rainbird), 9-431 (Rogers)

Western Australia	First innings		B	M	4	6
WG Bosisto	lbw b Fekete	1	4	8		
JR Philippe	lbw b Fekete	11	21	30	1	
HWR Cartwright	c Doolan b Rainbird	11	20	22	2	
AJ Turner *	c Webster b Meredith	19	42	47	2	
JW Wells	c Wade b Rogers	13	43	62	2	
CD Hinchliffe	c Wade b Rainbird	1	6	10		
JP Inglis +	c Webster b Rogers	0	9	14		
AB Holder	not out	2	13	24		
AA Bevilaqua	b Rogers	4	4	7	1	
LCJ Guthrie	c Wade b Rogers	4	5	3	1	
SP Mackin	c McDermott b Milenko	0	1	3		
	1 nb	1				
	27.5 overs, 119 mins	67				

Second innings		B	M	4	6
b Rogers	21	51	72	2	
c Webster b Fekete	74	82	113	15	
c McDermott b Rainbird	19	29	37	3	
c Wade b Milenko	81	94	124	15	
c Wade b Fekete	6	11	12	1	
lbw b Rainbird	0	3	3		
lbw b Milenko	30	64	96	3	
c Wade b Milenko	8	22	35	1	
c Milenko b Rogers	17	14	12	2	
c Bailey b Rogers	0	4	3		
not out	0	0	9		
4 b, 10 lb, 7 nb	21				
61.1 overs, 264 mins	277				

Fall: 1-8 (Bosisto), 2-23 (Philippe), 3-23 (Cartwright), 4-50 (Turner),
5-57 (Hinchliffe), 6-57 (Wells), 7-58 (Inglis), 8-62 (Bevilaqua),
9-66 (Guthrie), 10-67 (Mackin)

Fall: 1-82 (Bosisto), 2-129 (Cartwright), 3-129
(Philippe), 4-141 (Wells), 5-142 (Hinchliffe), 6-251
(Inglis), 7-252 (Turner), 8-269 (Bevilaqua), 9-269
(Guthrie), 10-277 (Holder)

Tasmania - bowling	O	M	R	W	wd	nb
AL Fekete	7	2	20	2		
RP Meredith	7	2	25	1	1	
SL Rainbird	8	3	12	2		
TS Rogers	3	1	9	4		
SA Milenko	2.5	2	1	1		

O	M	R	W	wd	nb
14	2	57	2		
9	0	54	0		
17	4	57	3		4
13	3	46	3		
8.1	0	49	3		3

Stumps Scores

Day 1   Tasmania (1st inn)   5-327   MS Wade 138*, SA Milenko 66*
Day 2   Western Australia (2nd inn) 5-176   AJ Turner 33*, JP Inglis 4*

Toss: Western Australia
Umpires: GJ Davidson, AD Deshmukh
Ref: DJ Harper, Award: MS Wade

INNINGS VICTORIES BY TASMANIA OVER WESTERN AUSTRALIA

2001-02	Bellerive	Tas 347	WA 137 & 134	Tas won by an innings & 81 runs
2010-11	WACA	WA 160 & 137	Tas 426	Tas won by an innings & 129 runs
2012-13	Bellerive	WA 67 & 277	Tas 448	Tas won by an innings & 118 runs
2017-18	Bellerive	Tas 9-431 declared	WA 67 & 277	Tas won by an innings & 87 runs

* WA won the toss in all four matches

Australian Cricket Digest, 2018-19

Match 21 – Victoria v Queensland at the MCG on February 16-19, 2018

Match Drawn - Vic 1.98 points, Qld 2.95

Queensland	First innings		B	M	4	6	Second innings		B	M	4	6
LD Pfeffer	c Gotch b Boland		16	63	91	2	lbw b Siddle		11	27	36	
MT Renshaw	c White b Fawad		170	218	297	12	4	c Gotch b Siddle		0	8	12
M Labuschagne	c Vines b Tremain		24	63	86	2	not out		100	161	208	8
CR Hemphrey	c Vines b Short		8	43	41	1	c White b Siddle		49	91	104	5
SD Heazlett	not out		124	220	285	11	b Fawad		20	54	76	1
JD Wildermuth	b Siddle		94	135	172	10						
JJ Peirson *+	not out		6	26	35							
MG Neser												
MT Steketee												
MJ Swepson												
LW Feldman												
	7 b, 3 lb		10				2 b, 1 lb, 1 nb		4			
100 overs : 4-355	128 overs, 506 mins		5-452	dec			57 overs, 221 mins		4-184			

Fall: 1-64 (Pfeffer), 2-140 (Labuschagne), 3-169 (Hemphrey), 4-258 (Renshaw), 5-413 (Wildermuth)

Fall: 1-7 (Renshaw), 2-26 (Pfeffer), 3-26 (Hemphrey), 4-125 (Heazlett)

Victoria - bowling	O	M	R	W	wd	nb	O	M	R	W	wd	nb
PM Siddle	26	8	82	1			10	3	21	3		
CP Tremain	26	7	54	1			10	3	21	0		
Fawad Ahmed	34	2	138	1			24	3	72	1		1
SM Boland	24	6	94	1			5	1	24	0		
MW Short	16	0	73	1			6	0	36	0		
TJ Dean	2	1	1	0								
CL White							2	0	7	0		

Victoria	First innings		B	M	4	6	Queensland - bowling	O	M	R	W	w	nb
TJ Dean	lbw b Feldman		5	8	14		MG Neser	20	9	39	1		
MS Harris	c Peirson b Neser		4	3	3	1	LW Feldman	23	7	58	2		
EM Vines	c Peirson b Steketee		34	61	76	6	MT Steketee	27	12	50	2		
WJ Pucovski	c and b Swepson		188	414	524	25	MJ Swepson	49	6	151	3		
CL White *	b Steketee		62	182	254	5	JD Wildermuth	13	4	25	0	1	
MW Short	c Hemphrey b Feldman		16	49	59	1	1	M Labuschagne	9	0	43	0		
SE Gotch +	b Swepson		63	137	134	6	CR Hemphrey	8	0	37	0		
CP Tremain	lbw b Swepson		16	41	45	1	MT Renshaw	5	1	12	1		
PM Siddle	c Pfeffer b Renshaw		23	22	31	2							
SM Boland	not out		0	6	8		Fall: 1-5 (Harris), 2-13 (Dean), 3-59 (Vines),						
Fawad Ahmed	not out		3	1	3		4-234 (White), 5-263 (Short), 6-387 (Gotch),						
	7 b, 14 lb, 1 w		22				7-396 (Pucovski), 8-433 (Siddle), 9-433 (Tremain)						
100 overs : 4-259	154 overs, 580 mins		9-436	dec									

Stumps Scores

Day 1	Queensland (1st inn)	4-333	SD Hezalett 63*, JD Wildermuth 42*	Toss: Victoria
Day 2	Victoria (1st inn)	3-153	WJ Pucovski 64*, CL White 36*	Umpires: PJ Gillespie, MW Graham-Smith
Day 3	Queensland (2nd inn)	0-7	(LD Pfeffer 6*, MT Renshaw 0*)	Referee: RL Parry. Award: WJ Pucovski (Vic)

YOUNGEST VICTORIAN BATSMEN TO MAKE THE MAIDEN SHIELD TON

	Yr Days	
LR Joslin	18 341	126 v Western Australia, MCG, 1966-67
BJ Hodge	18 348	106 v Tasmania, Bellerive, 1993-94
AP Sheahan	19 149	106* v South Australia, MCG, 1965-66
J Potter	19 265	115 v South Australia, MCG, 1957-58
WJ Pucovski	**20 16**	**188 v Queensland, MCG, 2017-18**

Australian Cricket Digest, 2018-19

Match 22 –New South Wales v Tasmania at the SCG on February 24-27, 2018

Match Drawn - New South Wales 3.25 points, Tasmania 2.30

New South Wales	First innings		B	M	4	6
NCR Larkin	c Webster b Rogers	85	156	187	9	
DP Hughes	c Wade b Milenko	22	42	74	3	
EJM Cowan	c Bailey b Freeman	68	89	133	11	
KR Patterson	b Rogers	72	105	152	8	
MC Henriques	not out	131	183	233	14	1
NJ Maddinson	c Doolan b Rogers	9	21	28	1	
P M Nevill *+	b Rainbird	5	14	22	1	
SNJ O'Keefe	c Doran b Fekete	0	5	6		
TA Copeland	c McDermott b Rogers	41	33	42	6	1
GS Sandhu						
HNA Conway						
	4 b, 3 lb, 7 nb, 2 w	16				
100 overs: 6-395	106.5 overs, 442 mins	8-449 dec				

Tasmania - bowling	O	M	R	W	w	nb
AL Fekete	21	2	77	1		1
TS Rogers	20.5	3	88	4		
SL Rainbird	24	3	118	1	2	6
SA Milenko	15	2	49	1		
JA Freeman	22	1	92	1		
BJ Webster	4	0	18	0		

Fall: 1-52 (Hughes), 2-167 (Larkin), 3-185 (Cowan), 4-341 (Patterson), 5-363 (Maddinson), 6-392 (Nevill), 7-393 (O'Keefe), 8-449 (Copeland)

Tasmania	First innings		B	M	4	6
BJ Webster	c Copeland b Sandhu	136	354	477	12	
AJ Doolan	c Larkin b Sandhu	9	11	22	1	
GJ Bailey *	b O'Keefe	34	67	81	7	
JR Doran	c Nevill b O'Keefe	97	236	274	11	
MS Wade +	not out	108	166	230	7	3
BR McDermott	not out	75	117	132	7	3
SA Milenko						
TS Rogers						
SL Rainbird						
AL Fekete						
JA Freeman						
	14 b, 11 lb, 3 nb, 2 w	30				
100 overs: 3-260	158 overs, 610 mins	4-489 dec				

NSW - bowling	O	M	R	W	w	nb
Copeland	32	4	85	0		
Sandhu	40	7	121	2		2
Conway	26	4	81	0	1	1
O'Keefe	40	10	80	2		
Cowan	14	0	62	0		
Maddinson	6	1	35	0	1	

Fall: 1-18 (Doolan), 2-80 (Bailey), 3-259 (Doran), 4-337 (Webster)

Close of Play Scores

Day 1	New South Wales (1st inn)	5-392	MC Henriques 116*, PM Nevill 5*
Day 2	Tasmania (1st inn)	1-79	BJ Webster 31*, GJ Bailey 34*
Day 3:	Tasmania (1st inn)	2-240	BJ Webster 102*, JR Doran 86*

Toss: New South Wales
Umpires: SJ Nogajski, JD Ward
Referee: PL Marshall.
Award: BJ Webster (Tas)

Australian Cricket Digest, 2018-19

Match 23 – Western Australia v Victoria at the WACA on February 24-27, 2018

Victoria won by 255 runs - WA 2.02 pts, Vic 8.92

Victoria	First innings		B	M	4	6	Second innings		B	M	4	6
TJ Dean	c Mackin b Tye	111	195	265	18	1	c Inglis b Tye	28	34	47	4	
MS Harris	c Short b Kelly	46	84	139	5		c Mackin b Agar	55	79	107	10	
GJ Maxwell	c Stoinis b Kelly	47	52	75	8		4 b Stoinis	12	32	42	1	
WJ Pucovski	c Inglis b Stoinis	16	36	33	3		5 lbw b Stoinis	13	22	28	3	
AJ Finch *	lbw b Agar	14	38	57	1		6 not out	151	122	161	16	7
CL White	c Inglis b Mackin	57	74	79	8	1	7 b Stoinis	41	74	85	5	1
DT Christian	b Stoinis	18	35	54	3		8 b Stoinis	12	13	27	2	
SB Harper +	c Philippe b Tye	38	49	62	4		9 c Wells b Tye	12	26	39	1	
CP Tremain	c Kelly b Tye	8	12	12	1							
PM Siddle	c Inglis b Stoinis	0	6	10	-		3 st Inglis b Agar	21	31	50	2	
SM Boland	not out	6	7	16	1							
	12 lb, 1 nb, 18 w	31					4 b, 16 lb, 4 nb, 9 w	33				
	97.5 overs, 410 mins	392					71.3 overs, 300 mins	8-378				

Fall: 1-113 (Harris), 2-193 (Maxwell), 3-229 (Pucovski), 4-240 (Dean), 5-282 (Finch), 6-321 (White), 7-355 (Christian), 8-366 (Tremain), 9-371 (Siddle), 10-392 (Harper)

Fall: 1-61 (Dean), 2-120 (Siddle,), 3-127 (Harris), 4-146 (Pucovski), 5-153 (Maxwell), 6-260 (White), 7-302 (Christian), 8-378 (Harper)

WA - bowling	O	M	R	W	wd	nb		O	M	R	W	wd	nb
ML Kelly	20	5	75	2				9	3	42	0		
SP Mackin	16	4	68	1		10		4	1	17	0	3	3
MP Stoinis	20	4	63	3	1			20	1	85	4	2	
AC Agar	12	1	50	1				22	1	115	2		
AJ Tye	21.5	3	90	3				15.3	2	91	2		1
DJM Short	6	0	28	0				1	0	11	0		
HWR Cartwright	2	0	6	0									

Western Australia	First innings		B	M	4	6	Second innings		B	M	4	6
JR Philippe	c Christian b Tremain	62	79	106	10		c Pucovski b Boland	19	28	40	3	
DJM Short	c Harris b Tremain	10	12	14	2		c Harper b Siddle	1	3	9	-	
HWR Cartwright	c Christian b Tremain	17	24	33	4		c Harper b Tremain	16	41	51	3	
MP Stoinis	c Harper b Christian	33	38	60	5		b Tremain	9	23	32	1	
AJ Turner *	c Harper b Tremain	44	73	90	9		lbw b Siddle	19	31	65	1	
JW Wells	c Siddle b Boland	28	76	133	2		c Christian b Tremain	9	12	16	2	
AC Agar	c Harper b Tremain	32	50	70	5		b Boland	4	21	23	1	
JP Inglis +	c Harper b Tremain	20	21	36	3		lbw b Christian	87	63	88	12	1
AJ Tye	b Tremain	10	11	19	2		b Boland	3	6	4		
ML Kelly	not out	4	9	11			c Maxwell b Christian	41	75	75	7	
SP Mackin	c Christian b Maxwell	11	7	4	1	1	not out	2	6	4		
	6 b, 12 lb, 5 nb, 8 w	31					2 lb, 1 nb	3				
	65.5 overs, 297 mins	302					51.3 overs, 213 mins	213				

Fall: 1-18 (Short), 2-61 (Cartwright), 3-125 (Philippe), 4-127 (Stoinis), 5-199 (Turner), 6-241 (Wells), 7-254 (Agar), 8-281 (Inglis), 9-291 (Tye), 10-302 (Mackin)

Fall: 1-15 (Short), 2-31 (Philippe), 3-41 (Cartwright), 4-48 (Stoinis), 5-62 (Wells), 6-77 (Agar), 7-94 (Turner), 8-99 (Tye), 9-208 (Inglis), 10-213 (Kelly)

Victoria - bowling	O	M	R	W	wd	nb		O	M	R	W	wd	nb
PM Siddle	15	0	61	0		3		10	2	39	2		1
CP Tremain	18	3	82	7	2			15	1	61	3		
SM Boland	15	4	67	1				14	1	44	3		
DT Christian	13	0	51	1	1	2		5.3	0	27	2		
GJ Maxwell	4.5	1	23	1				5	0	31	0		
CL White								2	0	9	0		

Stumps Scores

Day 1	Victoria (1st inn)	9-375	SB Harper 27*, SM Boland 0*
Day 2	Victoria (2nd inn)	1-70	MS Harris 31*, PM Siddle 0*
Day 3	Western Australia (2nd inn) 8-161		JP Inglis 54*, ML Kelly 24*

Toss: Victoria
Umpires: GC Joshua, AK Wilds
Referee: RW Stratford
Award: CP Tremain (Vic)

Match 24 – South Australia v Queensland at the Adelaide Oval on February 25-28, 2017
Queensland won by 118 runs. SA 0.90 points, Qld 8.42

Queensland – First innings

Batsman		Runs	B	M	4	6
LD Pfeffer	b Worrall	15	21	28	3	
MT Renshaw	c Carey b Winter	112	148	215	9	
M Labuschagne	b Mennie	3	12	19		
CR Hemphrey	c Lehmann b Mennie	9	24	30		
SD Heazlett	b Winter	59	126	145	5	2
JD Wildermuth	c Carey b Winter	39	77	117	5	
JJ Peirson *+	c Ferguson b Worrall	40	74	73	4	
MG Neser	lbw b Zampa	29	58	75	4	
MJ Swepson	c Head b Worrall	22	50	61	3	
BJ Doggett	b Worrall	0	4	5	-	
LW Feldman	not out	6	8	14	1	
	6 lb, 2 w	8				
100 overs: 9-342	100.2 overs, 395 mins	342				

Second innings

Batsman		Runs	B	M	4	6
LD Pfeffer	lbw b Winter	17	41	51	3	
MT Renshaw	c Weatherald b Winter	12	38	59	-	
M Labuschagne	c Head b Zampa	62	144	189	4	
CR Hemphrey	lbw b Mennie	24	90	147	2	
SD Heazlett	c Cooper b Winter	16	20	23	3	
JD Wildermuth	c Ferguson b Zampa	17	22	25	2	
JJ Peirson	not out	51	87	130	3	
MG Neser	c Cooper b Head	24	55	80	1	
MJ Swepson	c Weatherald b Head	35	25	32	5	1
	13 b, 9 lb, 4 nb, 1 w	27				
	86.2 overs, 371 mins	8-285 dec				

Fall: 1-28 (Pfeffer), 2-39 (Labuschagne), 3-59 (Hemphrey), 4-201 (Renshaw), 5-205 (Heazlett), 6-268 (Peirson), 7-292 (Wildermuth), 8-326 (Neser), 9-327 (Doggett), 10-342 (Swepson)

Fall: 1-33 (Pfeffer), 2-40 (Renshaw), 3-122 (Hemphrey), 4-142 (Heazlett), 5-154 (Labuschagne), 6-172 (Wildermuth), 7-233 (Neser), 8-285 (Swepson)

SA - bowling

Bowler	O	M	R	W	wd	nb		O	M	R	W	wd	nb
DJ Worrall	23.2	2	75	4				18	5	46	0	1	3
NP Winter	26	4	85	3	2			18	3	55	3	1	
JM Mennie	21	4	65	2				17	3	40	1		
A Zampa	22	2	75	1				27	4	99	2		
TM Head	7	0	36	0				6.2	0	23	2		
JS Lehmann	1	1	0	0									

South Australia – First innings

Batsman		Runs	B	M	4	6
JD Dalton	b Wildermuth	8	51	70		
JB Weatherald	c Hemphrey b Doggett	17	41	62	3	
CJ Ferguson	c Peirson b Neser	19	44	66	3	
TM Head *	lbw b Doggett	5	8	13	1	
JS Lehmann	b Neser	30	36	62	7	
TLW Cooper	c Peirson b Neser	3	21	30		7
AT Carey +	b Neser	0	2	3		8
JM Mennie	c &b Swepson	16	23	40	1	6
A Zampa	c Peirson b Swepson	57	57	68	6	1
DJ Worrall	c Neser b Swepson	1	24	28		
NP Winter	not out	0	4	7		
	4 b, 2 nb	6				
	51.3 overs, 229 mins	162				

Second innings

Batsman		Runs	B	M	4	6
JD Dalton	c Pfeffer b Feldman	23	55	65	3	
JB Weatherald	b Doggett	28	51	81	2	
CJ Ferguson	c Hemphrey b Neser	6	9	18	1	
TM Head	b Wildermuth	85	89	149	14	
JS Lehmann	c Peirson b Doggett	9	22	26	1	
TLW Cooper	c Peirson b Wildermuth	15	50	60	2	
AT Carey	c Swepson b Doggett	98	107	132	15	
JM Mennie	lbw b Doggett	38	80	94	5	1
A Zampa	c Pfeffer b Feldman	33	76	104		
DJ Worrall	c Heazlett b Doggett	0	4	4		
NP Winter	not out	0	0	2		
	1 b, 4 lb, 6 nb, 1 w	12				
	89.3 overs, 372 mins	347				

Fall: 1-29 (Weatherald), 2-29 (Dalton), 3-38 (Head), 4-81 (Ferguson), 5-86 (Lehmann), 6-86 (Carey), 7-89 (Cooper), 8-141 (Mennie), 9-153 (Worrall), 10-162 (Zampa)

Fall: 1-51 (Dalton), 2-57 (Weatherald), 3-57 (Ferguson), 4-78 (Lehmann), 5-177 (Mennie), 6-200 (Head), 7-238 (Cooper), 8-346 (Carey), 9-347 (Worrall), 10-347 (Zampa)

Queensland - bowling

Bowler	O	M	R	W	wd	nb		O	M	R	W	wd	nb
MG Neser	15	6	32	4				17	1	68	1		1
LW Feldman	13	2	38	0				16.3	0	60	2		
BJ Doggett	11	4	30	2				22	6	77	5	1	1
JD Wildermuth	6	2	34	1		2		12	4	49	2		4
MJ Swepson	6.3	0	24	3				21	0	80	0		
MT Renshaw								1	0	8	0		

Stumps Scores

Day 1	Queensland (1st inn)	8-326	MJ Swepson 13*
Day 2	Queensland (2nd inn)	2-75	M Labuschagne 25, CR Hemphrey 9*
Day 3	South Australia (2nd inn)	4-82	TM Head 14*, JM Mennie 2*

Toss: South Australia
Umpires: SAJ Craig, SA Lightbody
Referee: SR Bernard
Award: MT Renshaw (Qld)

Match 25 – Victoria v New South Wales at the Junction Oval, Melbourne on March 3-6, 2018
Victoria won by 23 runs - Victoria 7.00 points, NSW 1.00

Victoria	First innings		B	M	4	6	Second innings		B	M	4	6
TJ Dean	c Nevill b O'Keefe		6	40	54	1	c Larkin b Abbott		106	270	364	7
MS Harris	c Nevill b Conway		109	161	179	14	2	c Larkin b Copeland		4	11	11	
GJ Maxwell	c Patterson b O'Keefe		8	4	9	1	lbw b Abbott		33	43	55	5
WJ Pucovski	c Abbott b O'Keefe		2	28	23		retired hurt		4	7	10	1
DT Christian							9	b Henriques		22	35	33	5
AJ Finch *	c Henriques b O'Keefe		0	1	3		5	lbw b Copeland		14	22	31	1
CL White	lbw b O'Keefe		23	41	45	3	6	b Copeland		0	3	5	
SE Gotch +	c Nevill b Abbott		28	100	120	2	7	b Copeland		25	99	106	2
CP Tremain	c Conway b O'Keefe		7	28	27		10	c O'Keefe b Copeland		9	16	39	1
PM Siddle	c Uppal b O'Keefe		4	7	14		8	b O'Keefe		28	80	102	2
SM Boland	c Nevill b O'Keefe		4	39	93		11	b O'Keefe		13	31	31	3
Fawad Ahmed	not out		1	5	6		12	not out		2	2	3	
	5 b, 1 lb, 1 w		7					16 lb, 2 nb, 2 w		20			
	75.4 overs, 266 mins		199					103.1 overs, 400 mins		280			

Fall: 1-37 (Dean), 2-53 (Maxwell), 3-71 (Pucovski), 4-75 (Finch), 5-125 (White), 6-161 (Harris), 7-176 (Tremain), 8-184 (Siddle), 9-197 (Gotch), 10-199 (Boland)

Fall: 1-4 (Harris), 2-58 (Maxwell), 3-93 (Finch), 4-97 (White), 5-156 (Gotch), 6-211 (Siddle), 7-252 (Christian), 8-256 (Dean), 9-278 (Boland), 10-280 (Tremain). Pucovski retired hurt at 2-68

NSW - bowling	O	M	R	W	wd	nb	O	M	R	W	wd	nb
TA Copeland	11	4	18	0			24.1	9	59	5		
HNA Conway	10	2	28	1			11	1	32	0		
SNJ O'Keefe	32.4	7	77	8			32	4	75	2		
P Uppal	14	4	40	0			5	0	13	0		
SA Abbott	8	1	30	1	1		20	3	59	2	2	2
MC Henriques							11	2	26	1		

New South Wales	First innings		B	M	4	6	Second innings		B	M	4	6
NCR Larkin	lbw b Siddle		2	7	11		c White b Fawad		45	53	83	5
DP Hughes	b Tremain		30	55	63	5	hit wkt b Siddle		59	162	215	7
EJM Cowan	c White b Maxwell		5	16	24		st Gotch b Fawad		6	6	8	1
KR Patterson	c Maxwell b Tremain		43	73	96	6	run out (Maxwell)		53	143	173	3
SA Abbott	c Harris b Fawad		0	8	12		10	b Fawad Ahmed		4	4	2	1
MC Henriques	lbw b Boland		24	34	31	4	5	lbw b Siddle		49	95	127	5
P Uppal	lbw b Siddle		24	76	102	3	1	6	b Tremain		5	15	23	1
PM Nevill *+	c Dean b Fawad		0	1	3		7	st Gotch b Fawad		26	90	124	1
TA Copeland	lbw b Boland		29	47	62	6		c Gotch b Fawad		3	7	12	
SNJ O'Keefe	c Maxwell b Fawad		8	12	17	1	8	c Siddle b Tremain		23	33	45	2
HNA Conway	not out		0	2	3		not out		0	3	9	
	4 b, 2 lb		6					4 b, 8 lb		12			
	55.1 overs, 215 mins		171					101.5 overs, 415 mins		285			

Fall: 1-8 (Larkin), 2-29 (Cowan), 3-51 (Hughes), 4-54 (Abbott), 5-85 (Henriques), 6-111 (Patterson), 7-112 (Nevill), 8-154 (Copeland), 9-171 (Uppal), 10-171 (O'Keefe)

Fall: 1-83 (Larkin), 2-89 (Cowan), 3-157 (Hughes), 4-180 (Patterson), 5-199 (Uppal), 6-241 (Henriques), 7-274 (O'Keefe), 8-280 (Copeland), 9-284 (Abbott), 10-285 (Nevill)

Victoria - bowling	O	M	R	W	wd	nb	O	M	R	W	wd	nb
PM Siddle	11	3	39	2			21	3	56	2		
CP Tremain	10	3	37	2			21	3	54	2		
GJ Maxwell	11	1	39	1			10	1	32	0		
Fawad Ahmed	13.1	4	32	3			24.5	0	94	5		
SM Boland	10	4	18	2			24	6	34	0		
CL White							1	0	3	0		

Stumps Scores
Day 1 New South Wales (1st inn)   4-65 KR Patterson 22*, MC Henriques 5*
Day 2 Victoria (2nd inn)   5-156 TJ Dean 64*, PM Siddle 0*
Day 3 New South Wales (2nd inn) 2-150 DP Hughes 59* KR Patterson 34*

Toss: Victoria
Umpires: GA Abood, SA Lightbody
Referee: D Talalla.
Award: SNJ O'Keefe

Match 26 – Tasmania v South Australia at the Bellerive Oval, Hobart on March 5-8, 2018
Tasmania by 16 runs – Tas 7.85 points, SA 0.87

Tasmania	First innings	B	M	4	6	Second innings	B	M	4	6
JC Silk	c Ferguson b Richardson	19	48	74	1		b Mennie	53	80	90	9
AJ Doolan	c Carey b Worrall	7	26	32	1		lbw b Mennie	17	35	45	3
BJ Webster	c Carey b Richardson	42	100	133	3		c Carey b Worrall	18	42	73	2
JR Doran	c Carey b Winter	74	204	254	10		lbw b Winter	2	15	33	
GJ Bailey*	b Winter	55	119	182	8	1	b Worrall	0	6	10	
MS Wade +	c Weatherald b Richardson	68	111	140	11	1	c Weatherald b Worrall	0	12	14	
SA Milenko	c Weatherald b Winter	0	1	6			c Winter b Richardson	33	42	69	4
TS Rogers	c Cooper b Richardson	41	86	130	7		b Winter	0	5	6	
SL Rainbird	b Winter	10	22	43	2		not out	12	53	75	
JM Bird	c McInerney b Winter	32	36	36	4		b Richardson	4	4	8	1
AL Fekete	not out	0	1	9			c Carey b Worrall	8	9	12	2
	9 b, 21 lb, 15 w	45					6 b, 9 lb, 1 nb, 1 w	17			
100 overs : 6-285	125.5 overs, 524 mins	393					50.2 overs, 222 mins	164			

Fall: 1-15 (Doolan), 2-43 (Silk), 3-108 (Webster), 4-219 (Doran), 5-242 (Bailey), 6-249 (Milenko), 7-343 (Wade), 8-352 (Rogers), 9-383 (Rainbird), 10-393 (Bird)

Fall: 1-41 (Doolan), 2-83 (Silk), 3-94 (Webster), 4-94 (Doran), 5-94 (Bailey), 6-99 (Wade), 7-100 (Rogers), 8-145 (Milenko), 9-151 (Bird), 10-164 (Fekete)

SA - bowling	O	M	R	W	wd	nb	O	M	R	W	wd	nb
DJ Worrall	29	12	77	1	1		12.2	5	17	4		
NP Winter	31.5	9	81	5	1		12	3	42	2		
JM Mennie	28	6	79	0	2		13	4	35	2	1	
KW Richardson	30	8	99	4	3		13	1	55	2	1	
TM Head	6	1	20	0								
CJW McInerney	1	0	7	0								

South Australia	First innings	B	M	4	6	Second innings	B	M	4	6
CJW McInerney	lbw b Fekete	12	26	32	2		c Webster b Rainbird	19	38	51	3
JB Weatherald	b Rogers	22	43	69	2		c Webster b Rainbird	17	70	99	3
CJ Ferguson	c Doran b Milenko	51	119	202	11		lbw b Fekete	11	35	42	1
TM Head *	b Rogers	4	9	15	1		c Webster b Rainbird	145	167	273	23	1
JS Lehmann	b Rogers	15	43	48	1		lbw b Fekete	7	6	8	1
TLW Cooper	c Wade b Bird	33	52	73	6		c Milenko b Bird	38	97	131	6	1
AT Carey +	c Wade b Milenko	8	18	18	2		b Milenko	6	19	24	1
JM Mennie	c Doran b Bird	6	26	35	1		b Bird	29	42	56	2	1
KW Richardson	c Doran b Rainbird	32	43	58	6		c Doolan b Bird	0	3	2	
NP Winter	c Silk b Rogers	18	28	42	4		b Bird	25	41	54	3
DJ Worrall	not out	1	8	10			not out	0	10	11	
	12 b, 4 lb, 4 nb, 5 w	25					1 b, 11 lb, 5 nb	17			
	68.3 overs, 305 mins	227					87.1 overs, 380 mins	314			

Fall: 1-19 (McInerney), 2-51 (Weatherald), 3-59 (Head), 4-90 (Lehmann), 5-151 (Cooper), 6-165 (Carey), 7-166 (Ferguson), 8-180 (Mennie), 9-221 (Richardson), 10-227 (Winter)

Fall: 1-35 (McInerney), 2-50 (Ferguson), 3-54 (Weatherald), 4-69 (Lehmann), 5-184 (Cooper), 6-200 (Carey), 7-255 (Mennie), 8-255 (Richardson), 9-312 (Head), 10-314 (Winter)

Tasmania - bowling	O	M	R	W	wd	nb	O	M	R	W	wd	nb
JM Bird	19	4	58	2		4	24.1	7	64	4		1
AL Fekete	14	3	48	1	1		20	5	75	2		
SL Rainbird	17	3	38	1	1		23	3	86	3		4
TS Rogers	14.3	3	58	4			9	2	43	0		
SA Milenko	4	2	9	2			10	4	29	1		
BJ Webster							1	0	5	0		

Stumps Scores
Day 1 Tasmania (1st inn) 6-281 MA Wade 34*, TS Rogers 11*
Day 2 South Australia (1st inn) 7-170 JM Mennie 4*, KW Richardson 0*
Day 3 South Australia (2nd inn) 1-49 JB Weatherald 16*, CJ Ferguson 11*

Toss: Tasmania
Umpires: MW Graham-Smith, AK Wilds
Referee: RL Parry
Award: TM Head (SA)

CLOSE RESULTS BETWEEN SOUTH AUSTRALIA AND TASMANIA

2012-13	Hobart	SA 112 & 237	Tas 138 & 196	South Australia won by 15 runs
2017-18	**Hobart**	**Tas 393 & 164**	**SA 227 & 314**	**Tasmania won by 16 runs**
1995-96	Adelaide	SA 7-507 dec & 9-182 dec	Tas 320 & 348	South Australia won by 21 runs

Australian Cricket Digest, 2018-19

Match 27 – Queensland v Western Australia at the Gabba, Brisbane on March 6-9, 2018
Queensland won by 211 runs - Qld 7.53 points, WA 1.11

Queensland	First innings	B	M	4	6	Second innings	B	M	4	6
LD Pfeffer	c Inglis b Guthrie	5	11	13		c Short b Kelly	25	58	89	3	1
MT Renshaw	c Mackin b Kelly	3	24	34		not out	143	196	272	15
M Labuschagne	c Wells b Agar	23	84	123	2	lbw b Stoinis	2	19	25	
CR Hemphrey	not out	103	219	306	8	not out	68	118	156	8
SD Heazlett	c Inglis b Agar	18	22	24	2					
JJ Peirson *+	c Guthrie b Mackin	8	39	37						
MG Neser	b Mackin	9	17	18						
MT Steketee	c Stoinis b Mackin	4	18	15	1					
JD Wildermuth	b Short	4	9	11	1					
MJ Swepson	c Turner b Kelly	15	33	32						
LW Feldman	c Agar b Short	52	38	61	4	3				
	10 lb, 6 nb, 3 w	19				3 b, 3 lb, 7 nb, 1 w	14			
	84.4 overs, 341 minx	263				64 overs, 272 mins	2-252 dec			

Fall: 1-5 (Pfeffer), 2-16 (Renshaw), 3-63 (Labuschagne), 4-91 (Heazlett), 5-110 (Peirson), 6-127 (Neser), 7-138 (Steketee), 8-146 (Wildermuth), 9-176 (Swepson), 10-263 (Feldman)

Fall: 1-64 (Pfeffer), 2-77 (Labuschagne)

WA - bowling	O	M	R	W	wd	nb	O	M	R	W	wd	nb
ML Kelly	22	7	57	2			16	4	31	1		
LCJ Guthrie	7	1	30	1	1		16	2	73	0		
SP Mackin	16	1	61	3	2	3	9	0	53	0	1	3
MP Stoinis	10	5	20	0		3	9	1	26	1		4
AC Agar	26	4	70	2			13	0	58	0		
DJM Short	3.4	1	15	2			1	0	5	0		

Western Australia	First innings	B	M	4	6	Second innings	B	M	4	6
JR Philippe	c Labuschagne b Feldman	1	3	5		c Labuschagne b Neser	6	10	9	1
DJM Short	c sub (BJ Doggett) b Neser	38	56	75	4	c Peirson b Neser	7	12	19	
JW Wells	c Peirson b Wildermuth	15	55	75		c Peirson b Feldman	2	4	6	
MP Stoinis	lbw b Neser	13	27	41	2	c Hemphrey b Neser	0	1	6	
AJ Turner *	c Peirson b Steketee	29	57	76	2	lbw b Wildermuth	19	43	49	2
HWR Cartwright	c Renshaw b Swepson	22	28	34	2	c Peirson b Wildermuth	12	41	65	2
AC Agar	c Heazlett b Wildermuth	11	10	18		c Labuschagne b Swepson	18	89	98	2
JP Inglis +	not out	39	50	65	5	c Peirson b Wildermuth	0	3	6	
ML Kelly	st Peirson b Swepson	24	38	40	2	c Labuschagne b Wildermuth	1	2	3	
LCJ Guthrie	c Hemphrey b Swepson	12	8	10	2	c Hemphrey b Feldman	16	22	37	3
SP Mackin						not out	2	8	29	
	1 b, 1 lb, 4 nb, 1 w	7				4 nb, 1 w, 5 pen	10			
	54.4 overs, 223 mins	9-211 dec				38.2 overs, 168 mins	93			

Fall: 1-5 (Philippe), 2-58 (Short), 3-58 (Wells), 4-88 (Stoinis), 5-123 (Cartwright), 6-125 (Turner), 7-142 (Agar), 8-189 (Kelly), 9-211 (Guthrie)

Fall: 1-12 (Philippe), 2-15 (Wells), 3-15 (Short), 4-16 (Stoinis), 5-43 (Turner), 6-50 (Cartwright), 7-50 (Inglis), 8-52 (Kelly), 9-81 (Guthrie), 10-93 (Agar)

Queensland - bowling	O	M	R	W	wd	nb	O	M	R	W	wd	nb
MG Neser	13	1	61	2			12	1	41	3		
LW Feldman	9	2	30	1		3	9	2	13	2	1	1
MT Steketee	9	2	41	1			4	1	7	0		
JD Wildermuth	10	2	23	2	1	1	12	3	25	4		3
MJ Swepson	13.4	0	54	3			1.2	0	2	1		

Stumps Scores

Day 1	Queensland (1st inn)	0-3	LD Pfeffer 3*, MT Renshaw 0*
Day 2	Queensland (1st inn)	8-146	CR Hemphrey 60*
Day 3	Queensland (2nd inn)	0-58	LD Pfeffer 22*, MT Renshaw 34*

Toss: Western Australia
Umpires: PJ Gillespie, JD Ward
Referee: DJ Harper
Award: CR Hemphrey (Qld)

Australian Cricket Digest, 2018-19

Match 28 – New South Wales v Queensland at North Dalton Park, Wollongong on March 14-17, 2018

Queensland won by 36 runs – NSW 2.58 points, Qld 7.13

Queensland	First innings		B	M	4	6	Second innings		B	M	4	6
MT Renshaw	b Copeland	8	12	19	1							
LD Pfeffer							1 b Copeland	9	22	27	1	
JA Burns	c Hughes b Conway	97	171	259	10		2 lbw b Copeland	24	34	52	4	
M Labuschagne	b Copeland	17	36	47	2		3 b Copeland	134	218	287	12	
CR Hemphrey	c Copeland b Conway	13	46	58	3		4 lbw b Conway	101	240	289	12	
SD Heazlett	lbw b Copeland	11	22	23	2		5 b O'Keefe	13	53	70	1	
JD Wildermuth	b Copeland	0	2	2			6 not out	45	98	146	3	
JJ Peirson *+	c Maddinson b Copeland	1	4	5			7 b Copeland	0	8	11		
MG Neser	c O'Keefe b Abbott	55	118	151	7		8 c Copeland b Henriques	15	53	46	1	
MT Steketee	c Copeland b O'Keefe	16	40	56	1		9 b Henriques	28	40	38	6	
MJ Swepson	not out	4	4	12			10 run out (Maddinson)	8	4	4	2	
BJ Doggett	c Larkin b O'Keefe	0	7	7								
	14 lb, 3 nb, 4 w	21					28 b, 15 lb, 10 nb, 3 w, 5 pen	61				
	76.3 overs, 324 mins	243					126.4 overs, 489 mins	9-438 dec				

Fall: 1-10 (Renshaw), 2-50 (Labuschagne), 3-87 (Hemphrey), 4-115 (Heazlett), 5-115 (Wildermuth), 6-117 (Peirson), 7-191 (Burns), 8-238 (Steketee), 9-239 (Steketee), 10-243 (Doggett)

Fall: 1-32 (Pfeffer), 2-53 (Burns), 3-299 (Labuschagne), 4-325 (Hemphrey), 5-348 (Heazlett), 6-354 (Peirson), 7-388 (Neser), 8-429 (Steketee), 9-438 (Swepson)

Pfeffer was subbed in for Renshaw at the start of Day 3

NSW - bowling	O	M	R	W	wd	nb	O	M	R	W	wd	nb
TA Copeland	29	3	74	5			39.3	9	94	4		
HNA Conway	15	0	49	2	2		24	5	80	1	1	
SNJ O'Keefe	10.3	1	30	2			28	2	88	1		1
SA Abbott	16	1	55	1	2	3	20.1	3	81	0	2	9
MC Henriques	6	1	21	0			4	0	20	2		
P Uppal							11	1	27	0		

New South Wales	First innings		B	M	4	6	Second innings		B	M	4	6
NCR Larkin	b Steketee	34	69	118	2		lbw b Neser	0	2	1		
DP Hughes	c Peirson b Steketee	28	95	109	3		b Neser	27	23	30	5	
KR Patterson	c Burns b Swepson	45	99	140	4		b Steketee	29	31	51	4	
MC Henriques	c Hemphrey b Neser	17	51	71	3		lbw b Wildermuth	15	12	15	3	
NJ Maddinson	b Wildermuth	87	63	94	11	2	c Wildermuth b Doggett	34	30	58	3	2
P Uppal	lbw b Swepson	23	23	24	4		c Labuschagne b Neser	20	35	39	3	
PM Nevill *+	b Steketee	57	162	196	2		c Burns b Doggett	53	55	114	6	
TA Copeland	lbw b Swepson	1	9	8			c Hemphrey b Wildermuth	12	15	16	2	
SA Abbott	lbw b Neser	79	122	155	7	2	c Peirson b Swepson	20	19	20	2	1
SNJ O'Keefe	b Neser	3	4	6			lbw b Swepson	18	40	41	1	1
HNA Conway	not out	2	10	12			not out	5	22	22		
	15 b, 7 lb, 3 nb, 1 w	26					3 b, 13 lb, 3 nb, 1 w	10				
100 overs: 7-358	117.2 overs, 472 mins	402					46.5 overs, 208 mins	243				

Fall: 1-71 (Hughes), 2-74 (Larkin), 3-111 (Henriques), 4-191 (Patterson), 5-235 (Uppal), 6-251 (Maddinson), 7-252 (Copeland), 8-384 (Abbott), 9-392 (O'Keefe), 10-402 (Nevill)

Fall: 1-0 (Larkin), 2-40 (Hughes), 3-64 (Henriques), 4-72 (Patterson), 5-125 (Uppal), 6-131 (Maddinson), 7-156 (Copeland), 8-191 (Abbott), 9-226 (O'Keefe), 10-243 (Nevill)

Queensland - bowling	O	M	R	W	wd	nb	O	M	R	W	wd	nb
MG Neser	25	7	45	3			9	0	43	3		
BJ Doggett	25	4	92	0	2		9.5	1	51	2		2
JD Wildermuth	17	5	50	1			8	0	54	0		
MT Steketee	27.2	5	79	3	1	1	9	1	39	1		1
MJ Swepson	18	3	97	3			11	1	50	2		1
M Labuschagne	5	0	17	0								

Stumps Scores

Day 1	New South Wales (1st inn)	0-41	NCR Larkin 19*, DP Hughes 17*
Day 2	New South Wales (1st inn)	7-382	PM Nevill 52*, SA Abbott 79*
Day 3	Queensland (2nd inns)	3-315	CR Hemphrey 95*, SD Heazlett 4*

Toss: New South Wales

Umpires: PJ Gillespie, SJ Nogajski

Ref: PL Marshall. Award: M Labuschagne (Qld)

Australian Cricket Digest, 2018-19

Match 29 –Tasmania v Victoria at Bellerive Oval, Hobart on March 14-16, 2018
Tasmania won by 156 runs – Tas 8.26 points, Vic 0.80

Tasmania

First innings		B	M	4	6	Second innings		B	M	4	6
JC Silk	lbw b Tremain	55	122	155	8	b Tremain	26	43	79	4	
AJ Doolan	lbw b Siddle	6	19	24	1	lbw b Siddle	4	10	11	1	
BJ Webster	c Finch b Christian	40	81	109	7	c Gotch b Siddle	4	12	14		
JR Doran	b Tremain	57	102	125	9	lbw b Christian	48	137	194	7	
GJ Bailey *	c Gotch b Christian	29	53	91	5	lbw b Boland	7	17	28		
MS Wade +	c Dean b Tremain	49	90	120	4	c Gotch b Boland	2	20	29		
SA Milenko	c Maxwell b Tremain	37	57	79	6	c White b Tremain	3	5	13		
TS Rogers	c Siddle b Tremain	24	51	77	2	b Fawad	80	104	129	13	
SL Rainbird	c Christian b Tremain	10	18	25	1	c Dean b Siddle	8	28	38		
JM Bird	not out	9	18	31	1	run out (Dean)	19	12	23	3	
AL Fekete	c White b Siddle	8	20	17		not out	0	2	1		
	5 b, 10 lb, 2 nb, 3 w	20				4 b, 7 lb, 3 nb	14				
100 overs : 8-326	104.5 overs, 436 mins	344				64.3 overs, 284 mins	215				

Fall: 1-15 (Doolan), 2-97 (Webster), 3-115 (Silk), 4-193 (Bailey), 5-193 (Doran), 6-272 (Milenko), 7-297 (Wade), 8-313 (Rainbird), 9-326 (Rogers), 10-344 (Fekete)

Fall: 1-9 (Doolan), 2-17 (Webster), 3-47 (Silk), 4-62 (Bailey), 5-74 (Wade), 6-87 (Milenko), 7-138 (Doran), 8-176 (Rainbird), 9-215 (Rogers), 10-215 (Bird)

Victoria - bowling	O	M	R	W	wd	nb	O	M	R	W	wd	nb
PM Siddle	23.5	6	64	2	1		20	5	76	3		2
CP Tremain	27	5	81	6			16	3	63	2		1
SM Boland	24	7	55	0		1	20	7	46	2		
Fawad Ahmed	14	1	62	0			3.3	0	7	1		
DT Christian	15	0	66	2	2	1	5	1	12	1		
GJ Maxwell	1	0	1	0								

Victoria

First innings		B	M	4	6	Second innings		B	M	4	6
TJ Dean	c Bird b Fekete	1	5	5		lbw b Fekete	46	72	120	8	
MS Harris	c Webster b Fekete	16	18	32	3	c Wade b Fekete	9	11	12	1	
GJ Maxwell	b Fekete	17	30	45	3	c Doolan b Fekete	0	1	1		
AJ Finch *	c Doran b Bird	11	11	14	2	lbw b Bird	4	19	20		
CL White	c Webster b Rainbird	21	44	59	3	c & b Rainbird	4	15	19	1	
DT Christian	b Rogers	69	87	128	10	2	c Doolan b Fekete	35	54	74	6	
SE Gotch +	c Wade b Fekete	13	38	45	3	c Doolan b Rainbird	31	45	66	5	
CP Tremain	c Webster b Fekete	0	4	3		c Bird b Rainbird	45	47	64	6	
PM Siddle	c Doolan b Fekete	0	1	8		c Rainbird b Bird	18	15	20	1	1
SM Boland	not out	9	17	36	2	not out	7	11	22	1	
Fawad Ahmed	c Bailey b Rogers	12	18	22	2	c Silk b Milenko	15	9	9		2
	7 lb, 5 nb, 1 w	13				5 lb, 1 nb, 1 w	7				
	44.4 overs, 203 mins	182				49.4 overs, 218 mins	221				

Fall: 1-5 (Dean), 2-29 (Harris), 3-46 (Finch), 4-46 (Maxwell), 5-96 (White), 6-131 (Gotch), 7-131 (Tremain), 8-139 (Siddle), 9-164 (Christian), 10-182 (Fawad)

Fall: 1-14 (Harris), 2-14 (Maxwell), 3-21 (Finch), 4-37 (White), 5-98 (Dean), 6-101 (Christian), 7-176 (Gotch), 8-185 (Tremain), 9-204 (Siddle), 10-221 (Fawad)

Tasmania - bowling	O	M	R	W	wd	nb	O	M	R	W	wd	nb
JM Bird	11	2	33	1	1	2	14	2	54	2		
AL Fekete	12	3	67	6			11	3	43	4	1	
SL Rainbird	9	3	28	1		2	14	0	69	3		1
TS Rogers	6.4	0	24	2			4	1	11	0		
SA Milenko	6	2	23	0		1	5.4	0	24	1		
BJ Webster							1	0	15	0		

Stumps Scores

Day 1	Tasmania (1st inn)	7-304	TS Rogers 15*, SL Rainbird 4*
Day 2	Victoria (2nd inn)	4-73	JR Doran 23*, MS Wade 2*

Toss: Victoria
Umpires: GC Joshua, JD Ward
Referee: SR Bernard, Award: AL Fekete (Tas)

WINS by TASMANIA in THREE DAYS versus VICTORIA

1981-82	MCG	Tas 215 & 155	Vic 191 & 83	Tas won by 96 runs
1983-84	TCA Hobart	Vic 89 & 232	Tas 323	Tas won by an innings and 2 runs
2017-18	**Bellerive Oval**	**Tas 344 & 215**	**Vic 182 & 221**	**Tas won by 156 runs**

Match 30 –South Australia v Western Australia at Glenelg Oval, on March 14-17, 2018
Western Australia won by 241 runs - SA 1.01 points, WA 8.55

Western Australia

First innings		B	M	4	6	Second innings		B	M	4	6
JR Philippe	c Carey b Worrall	0	6	3		lbw b Winter	7	14	13	1	
DJM Short	c McInerney b Mennie	35	41	64	7	c Carey b Winter	66	131	188	9	
WG Bosisto	c Lehmann b Worrall	0	4	7		c Ferguson b Worrall	4	8	6	1	
MP Stoinis	c Richardson b Worrall	13	23	35	2	c McInerney b Richardson	2	8	14		
AJ Turner*	c Richardson b Worrall	79	89	115	11	c Carey b Winter	41	113	134	4	
HWR Cartwright	c Head b Mennie	83	117	192	14	not out	111	181	270	8	1
AC Agar	c Ross b Richardson	20	35	44	3	c Carey b Winter	86	134	139	10	
JP Inglis+	c McInerney b Worrall	86	110	166	9	2	c Ferguson b Head	20	39	39	3	
JS Paris	c Mennie b Winter	23	96	91	2	not out	14	86	72	1	
LCJ Guthrie	c Ferguson b Winter	0	6	6							
SP Mackin	not out	1	5	18							
	4 b, 9 lb, 2 w	15				7 b, 10 lb, 2 w	19				
	88.4 overs, 375 mins	355				119 overs, 441 mins	7-370 dec				

Fall: 1-0 (Philippe), 2-2 (Bosisto), 3-44 (Stoinis), 4-63 (Short), 5-164 (Turner), 6-207 (Agar), 7-255 (Cartwright), 8-341 (Paris), 9-347 (Guthrie), 10-355 (Inglis)

Fall: 1-13 (Guthrie), 2-18 (Bosisto), 3-30 (Stoinis), 4-121 (Turner), 5-137 (Short), 6-273 (Agar), 7-311 (Inglis)

SA - bowling	O	M	R	W	wd	nb	O	M	R	W	wd	nb
DJ Worrall	22.4	4	72	5			17	2	42	1	1	
NP Winter	24	1	81	2			21	2	90	4	1	
JM Mennie	17	1	76	2	1		12	2	42	0		
KW Richardson	16	0	83	1	1		16	3	49	1		
TM Head	7	2	22	0			41	10	100	1		
CJW McInerney	2	0	8	0								
JS Lehmann							11	2	24	0		
AI Ross							1	0	6	0		

South Australia

First innings		B	M	4	6	Second innings		B	M	4	6
CJW McInerney	b Guthrie	51	90	146	4	2	c Turner b Paris	0	2	1		
JB Weatherald	c Short b Paris	7	19	34	1	c Turner b Stoinis	62	111	180	7	
CJ Ferguson	c Guthrie b Mackin	10	16	23	2	c Inglis b Paris	92	228	313	14	
TM Head*	c Stoinis b Guthrie	31	39	47	5	c and b Agar	47	59	81	5	1
JS Lehmann	c Inglis b Guthrie	4	6	9	1	c Bosisto b Paris	1	15	20		
AI Ross	c Mackin b Guthrie	4	12	18		c Turner b Mackin	10	19	20	2	
AT Carey+	c Cartwright b Short	25	36	44	4	c Short b Agar	17	41	51	2	
JM Mennie	c Philippe b Mackin	12	14	20	2	not out	7	83	103		
KW Richardson	c Cartwright b Paris	16	18	32	2	1	c Short b Agar	3	12	11		
NP Winter	c Bosisto b Short	15	51	56	2	c Stoinis b Short	15	35	36	3	
DJ Worrall	not out	14	24	36	3	c Stoinis b Short	0	2	2		
	8 b, 2 nb, 2 w	12				15 b, 8 lb, 1 nb, 5 w	29				
	53.5 overs, 237 mins	201				101 overs, 408 mins	283				

Fall: 1-24 (Weatherald), 2-40 (Ferguson), 3-103 (Head), 4-107 (Lehmann), 5-115 (Ross), 6-120 (McInerney), 7-143 (Mennie), 8-154 (Carey), 9-174 (Richardson), 10-201 (Winter)

Fall: 1-0 (McInerney), 2-123 (Weatherald), 3-210 (Head), 4-216 (Lehmann), 5-229 (Ross), 6-239 (Ferguson), 7-262 (Carey), 8-266 (Richardson), 9-283 (Winter), 10-283 (Worrall)

WA - bowling	O	M	R	W	wd	nb	O	M	R	W	wd	nb
JS Paris	16	6	31	2	1		23	7	52	3	2	
LCJ Guthrie	18	3	59	4		1	14	3	50	0		1
SP Mackin	8	0	46	2	1		11	3	31	1	2	1
MP Stoinis	4	0	37	0			14	1	44	1		
DJM Short	7.5	3	20	2			5	1	23	2		
AC Agar							25	10	41	3		
WG Bosisto							9	3	19	0		

Stumps Scores

Day 1	South Australia (1st inn)	0-4	CJW McInerney 3*, JB Weatherald 0*
Day 2	Western Australia (2nd inn)	3-115	DJM Short 56*, AJ Turner 39*
Day 3	South Australia (2nd inn)	1-7	JB Weatherald 2*, CJ Ferguson 1*

Toss: South Australia
Umpires: GA Abood, GJ Davidson
Referee: RW Stratford
Award: HWR Cartwright (WA)

The Final – Queensland v Tasmania at Allan Border Field, Brisbane on March 23-27, 2018.

There had been quite a bit of rain about in the lead up to the final, which due to the unavailability of the Gabba (because of a potential AFLW Grand Final, would you believe!) the match was set down to be played at Allan Border Field.

Day One: March 23, 2018
Not known for its good drainage, play was unable to start at Allan Border Field on the opening day due to a wet outfield.

Day Two: March 24, 2018
Played started at 9am on what was to become the opening day of the final. Tasmania lost Doolan early, as he edged to first slip. Doggett came on in the ninth over and saw Silk cover drive him for four, before he inside edged just past his stumps for back to back boundaries. Silk looked in good touch and brought up his fifty then saw Webster get an inside edge to the keeper. Lunch was taken after two and a half hours play with Tasmania 2-99 (35 overs) Silk 68, Doran 12.

Twenty minutes after lunch, Silk's fine knock ended when he hooked to long-leg, where Feldman took a brilliant catch. When Doran pulled at Doggett and was caught behind, Tasmania were a nervous 4-141. But Bailey and Wade, who pulled a six off Neser, combined to add 80 before tea, Tasmania 4-221 (73 overs) with the skipper 51, Wade 39.

Bailey pushed the second ball after tea wide of mid-on, took off and was superbly run out by Michael Neser who moved quickly to his left. Milenko joined Wade, slog sweeping Swepson for six over deep square-leg. The new ball was taken (5-240 after 80 overs) and shortly after Wade passed his fifty with a straight drive for four off Feldman. Milenko lifted Feldman over cover for six, reaching his fifty from just 54 balls, before pulling Doggett straight down the throat of deep square leg. Short hit Wildermuth for six over point as he and Wade added 55 in positive fashion before the close.

Day Three – March 25, 2018
Rogers was caught in the slip from the fourth ball of the day, while Wade reached his ton with an edge off Neser that went to the ropes. Wade didn't last much longer as he gloved a hook off Doggett, then Rainbird hit three fours in an over off Wildermuth to raise the 400. Bird was caught at point and then Fekete and Rainbird added 57 for the last wicket, both lower order batsmen clearing the ropes. Tasmania were all out 20 minutes before lunch which left Queensland a tricky period to bat before the break.

After the Bulls reached six from the first two overs, Renshaw clipped Bird for two sixes off the last three balls before lunch, the break taken with Queensland 0-23, Renshaw 21, Burns 1. Renshaw continued to look in fine touch when he aimed a drive at Bird, edging behind. Burns then cut loose on Rainbird, hitting 6444 off consecutive deliveries, as the pitch continued to play very well. The pair batted nicely, until rain brought about an early tea at 2.16, Queensland 1-128, Burns 49, Labuschagne 27.

Rogers trapped Burns lbw first ball after tea and then in his next over bowled Labuschagne with a fuller ball. Heazlett started confidently with three fours in an over from Bird, as he and Hemphrey took little risk and knuckled down to some old fashioned Shield Final batting. The visitors toiled hard but couldn't get a breakthrough, Queensland ending the day 244 behind.

Day Four: March 26, 2018
Hemphrey edged his third ball of the day for four, to bring up a hard fought fifty from 116 balls. Three overs later, Heazlett was caught behind, the promising youngster having helped add a valuable 116 for the fourth wicket. Wildermuth came in and was untroubled on the still plumb pitch, and just when he looked set for a ton, Hemphrey edged Bird behind, Queensland still 20 short of the follow-on. Wildermuth off-drove Fekete to reach his fifty (60 balls, 8 fours) and made it through to lunch on 67, Peirson 7, Queensland 5-351.

Wildermuth's fine knock came to an end when he drove hard back at Milenko, who took a sharp catch off his own bowling. Neser joined Peirson and the pair kept the score ticking over in between two rain interruptions, reaching tea on 6-424, just 53 behind.

Neser opened up after the break, cracking Webster over long-on for six before the 100 stand was raised. Neser and Peirson went in consecutive overs, before Swepson and Doggett added to the Tigers frustration, adding 33 for the ninth wicket. When Swepson was caught behind, Queensland led by 39, with five overs left in the day. Silk and Doolan played carefully, still 29 behind with 105 overs left to try and manufacture and outright result on the final day.

Day Five: March 27, 2018
With rain in the air, Tasmania went out to bat with purpose to set some sort of target to force an unlikely win. Doolan hit Neser for 6444 in an over and the pair played their shots with abandon, to raise the hundred stand in the 20th over. As the rain clouds got closer, Doolan lofted Doggett for a couple of sixes, then Silk went 6464 before he was out to Wildermuth, after a stand of 160. Shortly after with rain imminent, the umpires went off for bad light at 10.45, the rain started at 11.00, Tasmania holding a lead of 127.

Due to run-ups that were unfit for play and again the poor drainage, play didn't resume until 3.14, by which time Tasmania had declared, setting Queensland 128 in 32 overs. Burns played with freedom and with Renshaw in good touch, the fifty was raised in 11 overs. Renshaw then found his range to move the score on quickly, as the crowd grew to see the final moments. Renshaw edged a four to reach his fifty and shortly after Burns was caught at deep mid-off with 22 to win. With Labuschagne partnering him, Renshaw made short work off the task, hitting the winning runs through point with 9.1 overs to spare, to claim their first Shield since 2011-12. Wade was an interesting choice for Man of the match, given rookie quick Doggett took five wickets.

The Final – Queensland v Tasmania at Allan Border Field, Brisbane on March 23-27, 2018
Queensland won by 9 wickets

Tasmania	First innings		B	M	4	6	Second innings		B	M	4	6
JC Silk	c Feldman b Doggett	76	135	174	11		c Swepson b Wildermuth	74	78	113	9	2
AJ Doolan	c Renshaw b Neser	2	12	18			not out	82	74	123	8	4
BJ Webster	c Peirson b Wildermuth	10	53	86			not out	3	4	9		
JR Doran	c Peirson b Doggett	34	65	98	6							
GJ Bailey*	run out (Neser)	51	90	128	5	1						
MS Wade+	c Peirson b Doggett	108	190	279	14	1						
SA Milenko	c Swepson b Doggett	50	58	69	5	2						
TS Rogers	c Heazlett b Neser	28	55	65	2	1						
SL Rainbird	b Feldman	57	105	127	7	2						
JM Bird	c Neser b Doggett	13	21	27	2							
AL Fekete	not out	25	49	54	3	1						
	4 b, 14 lb, 3 nb, 2 w	23					4 b, 3 lb	7				
	138.2 overs, 567 mins	477					26 overs, 123 mins	1-166 dec				

Fall: 1-7 (Doolan), 2-65 (Webster), 3-120 (Silk), 4-141 (Doran), 5-221 (Bailey), 6-305 (Milenko), 7-360 (Rogers), 8-384 (Wade), 9-420 (Bird), 10-477 (Rainbird)

Fall: 1-106 (Burns)

Queensland - bowling	O	M	R	W	wd	nb		O	M	R	W	wd	nb
MG Neser	28	6	89	2				7	2	34	0		
LW Feldman	26.2	9	78	1				8	1	31	0		
BJ Doggett	31	4	101	5	2	3		4	0	34	0		
JD Wildermuth	23	5	99	1				6	0	54	1		
MJ Swepson	23	1	83	0				1	0	6	0		
MT Renshaw	3	0	4	0									
M Labuschagne	3	1	2	0									
SD Heazlett	1	0	3	0									

Queensland	First innings		B	M	4	6	Second innings		B	M	4	6
MT Renshaw	c Wade b Bird	37	63	66	4	2	not out	81	83	104	12	2
JA Burns	lbw b Rogers	49	76	136	6	1	c Bailey b Webster	41	50	92	6	1
M Labuschagne	b Rogers	32	48	77	6		not out	5	4	11	1	
CR Hemphrey	c Wade b Bird	77	194	254	8							
SD Heazlett	c Wade b Fekete	43	105	157	4							
JD Wildermuth	c &b Milenko	73	107	156	12							
JJ Peirson*+	b Milenko	48	131	179	6							
MG Neser	c Milenko b Webster	58	77	105	9	1						
MJ Swepson	c Wade b Webster	27	44	66	3							
BJ Doggett	b Webster	15	37	42	3							
LW Feldman	not out	11	24	17	1							
	15 b, 13 lb, 15 nb, 3 w	46					1 lb	1				
	148.3 overs, 632 mins	516					22.5 overs, 104 mins	1-128				

Fall: 1-59 (Renshaw), 2-128 (Burns), 3-133 (Labuschagne), 4-247 (Heazlett), 5-308 (Hemphrey), 6-362 (Wildermuth), 7-462 (Neser), 8-466 (Peirson), 9-499 (Doggett,), 10-516 (Swepson,)

Fall: 1-106 (Burns)

Tasmania - bowling	O	M	R	W	wd	nb		O	M	R	W	wd	nb
JM Bird	25	7	77	2	1	2		4	0	22	0		
AL Fekete	27	2	81	1		2		6	0	21	0		
SL Rainbird	27	3	117	0	2	6		4.5	0	37	0		
TS Rogers	23	3	61	2				3	0	13	0		
SA Milenko	21	4	69	2		5		3	0	27	0		
BJ Webster	25.3	4	83	3				2	0	7	1		

Toss: Tasmania. Umpires: GA Abood, SJ Nogajski, PJ Gillespie (TV), Ref: PL Marshall. Award: MS Wade (Tas)

Session by session Scores: Day 1 No play due to a saturated outfield.

Day 2 Lunch: Tas (1) 2-99 (35 overs) Silk 68, Doran 12, 35 overs, Tea: Tas (1) 4-221 (73) Bailey 51, Wade 39, Stumps: Tas (1) 6-360 (105) Wade 92, Rogers 28.

Day 3 Lunch: Qld (1) 0-23 (3) Renshaw 21, Burns 1, Tea: Qld (1) 1-128 (28.4) Burns 49, Labuschagne 27, Stumps: Qld (1): 3-233 (64) Hemphrey 48 Heazlett 37

Day 4 Lunch: Qld (1) 5-351 (97) Wildermuth 67, Peirson 7, Tea: Qld (1) 6-424 (121) Peirson 37, Neser 31, Stumps: Tas (2) 0-10 (5) Silk 5, Doran 5

Day 5 Lunch: Tas 1-166 (26) Doolan 82, Webster 3, Rain prevented play 10.45 – 3.15, Queensland won at 4.59pm

Australian Cricket Digest, 2018-19
NEW SOUTH WALES AVERAGES

Batting & Fielding	M	Inn	NO	Runs	HS	Avge	100	50	0	S/Rate	Ct	St
SPD Smith	3	6	0	268	127	44.66	1	1	0	67.16	7	-
DP Hughes	10	19	3	661	98*	41.31	0	4	0	52.62	7	-
MA Starc	2	3	1	80	43	40.00	0	0	0	64.51	0	-
KR Patterson	10	19	1	672	89	37.33	0	5	1	47.45	5	-
PJ Cummins	2	2	1	36	27*	36.00	0	0	0	37.50	1	-
EJM Cowan	6	11	1	347	68	34.70	0	3	1	49.64	3	-
DA Warner	3	6	0	188	83	31.33	0	1	0	56.62	1	-
SNJ O'Keefe	5	9	2	184	52*	26.28	0	2	1	50.27	2	-
MC Henriques	9	17	2	374	131*	24.93	1	0	3	53.42	4	-
PM Nevill	10	17	1	396	70	24.75	0	3	1	37.60	30	4
NJ Maddinson	7	13	0	307	87	23.61	0	1	2	58.69	4	-
SA Abbott	5	9	0	187	79	20.77	0	1	2	42.21	1	-
NCR Larkin	7	13	0	239	85	18.38	0	1	3	47.04	7	-
P Uppal	2	4	0	72	24	18.00	0	0	0	48.32	1	-
D Fallins	1	2	1	16	10	16.00	0	0	0	29.09	1	-
TA Copeland	9	15	3	172	41	14.33	0	0	0	43.43	7	-
GS Sandhu	2	2	0	20	14	10.00	0	0	0	25.97	0	-
DE Bollinger	3	4	1	26	26*	8.66	0	0	3	28.88	1	-
CH Stobo	2	4	1	16	8	5.33	0	0	0	22.22	3	-
NM Lyon	4	5	1	19	6*	4.75	0	0	0	34.54	1	-
HNA Conway	4	6	4	8	5*	4.00	0	0	1	12.12	1	-
MW Edwards	2	4	0	13	8	3.25	0	0	0	37.14	1	-
WER Somerville	1	2	0	3	3	1.50	0	0	1	25.00	1	-

Also batted: JR Hazlewood (1 matches) 6.

Bowling	M	Overs	Mdns	Runs	Wkts	Avge	Best	5i	10m	SR	Econ
JR Hazlewood	1	33	9	73	6	12.16	3-24	0	0	33.0	2.21
MA Starc	4	72.5	14	216	17	12.70	8-73	1	1	25.7	2.96
NM Lyon	4	98.3	18	283	13	21.76	3-59	0	0	45.4	2.87
TA Copeland	9	344	89	863	34	25.38	6-24	3	0	60.7	2.50
D Fallins	1	16.4	2	102	4	25.50	3-51	0	0	25.0	6.12
PJ Cummins	2	65	18	176	6	29.33	2-22	0	0	65.0	2.70
SNJ O'Keefe	8	196.1	31	580	19	30.52	8-77	1	1	61.9	2.95
MW Edwards	2	39.1	8	153	5	30.60	2-48	0	0	47.0	3.90
CH Stobo	2	43	6	193	6	32.16	3-32	0	0	43.0	4.48
DE Bollinger	3	95	17	370	11	33.63	3-38	0	0	51.8	3.89
MC Henriques	9	52	5	178	5	35.60	2-41	0	0	62.4	3.42
GS Sandhu	2	59	10	173	4	43.25	2-52	0	0	88.5	2.93
SA Abbott	5	147	19	568	11	51.63	4-65	0	0	80.1	3.86
HNA Conway	4	108	16	338	5	67.60	2-49	0	0	129.6	3.12

Also bowled: EJM Cowan (6 matches) 14-0-62-0, NJ Maddinson (7 matches) 6-1-35-0, WER Somerville (1 match) 16-1-38-0, P Uppal (2 matches) 30-5-80-0.

NEW SOUTH WALES SHEFFIELD SHIELD RECORDS
Results

versus	M	W	L	D	T	%W	%L	Toss	%toss
Queensland	178	71	47	60	0	39.89	26.40	83	46.63
South Australia	227	126	59	42	0	55.51	25.99	111	48.90
Tasmania	80	29	23	28	0	36.25	28.75	31	38.75
Victoria	234	80	73	80	1	34.19	31.20	115	49.15
Western Australia	135	56	39	40	0	41.48	28.89	70	51.85
	854	**362**	**241**	**250**	**1**	**42.39**	**28.22**	**29.39**	**48.01**

Highest Team Totals

Total	v..	Season	Venue
918	SA	1900-01	Sydney
815	Vic	1908-09	Sydney
807	SA	1899-00	Adelaide
805	Vic	1905-06	Melbourne
802	SA	1920-21	Sydney

Lowest Completed Team Totals

Total	v..	Season	Venue
53	Tas	2006-07	Hobart
56	WA	1998-99	Perth
66	Vic	1894-95	Melbourne
71	Qld	1976-77	Brisbane
73	WA	1993-94	Perth

Australian Cricket Digest, 2018-19

Leading Run Scorers

	M	Inn	NO	HS	Runs	Ave	100s	50s	0s
MG Bevan	93	163	31	216	8174	61.92	32	33	7
ME Waugh	93	158	18	229*	7232	51.66	23	30	14
SR Waugh	85	147	14	216*	6609	49.69	22	24	10
AF Kippax	61	95	9	315*	6096	70.88	23	14	2
MA Taylor	85	147	3	199	6090	42.29	15	34	3

Highest Individual scores

		v..	Season	Venue
452*	DG Bradman	Qld	1929-30	Sydney
359	RB Simpson	Qld	1963-64	Brisbane
340*	DG Bradman	Vic	1928-29	Sydney
315*	AF Kippax	Qld	1927-28	Sydney
306	SM Katich	Qld	2007-08	Sydney

Most Catches (Fielders)

	M	Ct
MA Taylor	85	120
ME Waugh	92	112
GRJ Matthews	116	102
R Benaud	73	92
RB McCosker	70	91

Most Appearances

M		Start	Start
116	GRJ Matthews	12 Nov 1982	25 Oct 1997
109	PA Emery	22 Jan 1988	14 Mar 1999
103	GF Lawson	18 Feb 1978	1 April 1992
94	SJ Rixon	25 Oct 1974	4 Jan 1988
94	BJ Haddin	19 Oct 1999	28 Nov 2014
93	MG Bevan	16 Nov 1990	7 Mar 2004
93	ME Waugh	25 Oct 1985	7 Mar 2004

Most Dismissals (Keepers)

	M	Ct	St	Total
PA Emery	109	298	41	339
BJ Haddin	93	282	24	306
SJ Rixon	93	218	43	261
PM Nevill	63	212	17	229
HB Taber	64	179	32	211
WAS Oldfield	51	109	70	179
DA Ford	56	107	51	158

Record Partnerships

Wkt	Runs			v..	Season	Venue
1	319	RB McCosker	J Dyson	WA	1980-81	Sydney
2	378	LA Marks	KD Walters	SA	1964-65	Adelaide
3	363	DG Bradman	AF Kippax	Qld	1933-34	Sydney
4	325	NC O'Neill	BC Booth	Vic	1957-58	Sydney
5	464*	ME Waugh	SR Waugh	WA	1990-91	Perth
6	332	NG Marks	G Thomas	SA	1958-59	Sydney
7	255	G Thomas	R Benaud	Vic	1961-62	Melbourne
8	270	VT Trumper	EP Barbour	Vic	1912-13	Sydney
9	226	C Kelleway	WAS Oldfield	Vic	1925-26	Melbourne
10	307	AF Kippax	JEH Hooker	Vic	1928-29	Melbourne

Leading Wicket takers

	M	Balls	Mdns	Runs	Wkts	Ave	Best	5wI	10M	SR	Econ
GF Lawson	103	20933	870	8673	367	23.63	6-31	12	0	57.04	2.49
GRJ Matthews	116	26764	1375	10518	363	28.98	8-52	19	4	73.73	2.36
SCG MacGill	86	19189	549	11239	328	34.27	6-64	17	0	58.50	3.51
DE Bollinger	89	15668	589	8166	290	28.16	6-47	10	2	54.03	3.13
R Benaud	73	18106	474	7172	266	26.96	7-32	12	3	68.07	2.38
JW Martin	70	15890	239	7949	263	30.22	8-97	12	0	60.42	3.00

Best Bowling in an innings

		v..	Season	Venue
WJ O'Reilly	9-41	SA	1937-38	Adelaide
WJ O'Reilly	9-50	Vic	1933-34	Melbourne
WP Howell	9-52	Vic	1902-03	Melbourne
DW Hourn	9-77	Vic	1978-79	Sydney
RG Holland	9-83	SA	1984-85	Sydney

Best Bowling in a Match

		v..	Season	Venue
TR McKibbin	15-125	SA	1896-97	Adelaide
WJ O'Reilly	14-45	Qld	1939-40	Sydney
WJ O'Reilly	14-98	SA	1937-38	Adelaide
TR McKibbin	14-189	SA	1894-95	Sydney
HV Hordern	13-87	Vic	1910-11	Sydney

QUEENSLAND AVERAGES

Batting & Fielding	M	Inn	NO	Runs	HS	Avge	100	50	0	S/Rate	Ct	St
UT Khawaja	3	6	2	347	122	86.75	1	2	0	54.13	2	-
JA Burns	7	14	1	725	202*	55.76	2	3	1	60.01	6	-
MT Renshaw	11	21	3	804	170	44.66	3	3	1	57.06	7	-
CR Hemphrey	8	15	2	568	103*	43.69	2	4	2	44.09	10	-
SD Heazlett	7	12	2	405	124*	40.50	1	1	0	50.62	6	-
M Labuschagne	11	22	2	795	134	39.75	2	4	0	50.25	9	-
LW Feldman	9	12	7	173	52	34.60	0	1	0	88.26	5	-
JD Wildermuth	11	18	2	551	95	34.43	0	4	3	56.39	2	-
JJ Peirson	11	17	3	386	82*	27.57	0	3	1	43.91	38	1
SJ Truloff	4	8	2	157	45	26.16	0	0	0	67.96	3	-
MG Neser	10	13	0	294	58	22.61	0	2	2	53.26	8	-
MJ Swepson	11	15	3	225	35	18.75	0	0	2	62.15	8	-
MT Steketee	5	4	0	75	28	18.75	0	0	0	55.55	0	-
LD Pfeffer	5	9	0	136	36	15.11	0	0	0	36.95	4	-
B Doggett	7	10	1	83	43*	9.22	0	0	4	38.24	2	-

Also played: CJ Gannon (1 match) and NJ Rimmington (1 match) both did not bat.

Bowling	M	Overs	Mdns	Runs	Wkts	Avge	Best	5i	10m	SR	Econ
MG Neser	10	278	69	852	39	21.84	6-57	1	0	42.7	3.06
LW Feldman	9	262.2	64	770	34	22.64	6-32	2	0	46.2	2.93
B Doggett	7	216.1	42	776	28	27.71	5-77	2	0	46.3	3.58
JD Wildermuth	11	238.2	59	808	29	27.86	4-25	0	0	49.3	3.39
MT Steketee	5	135.2	42	375	11	34.09	3-79	0	0	73.8	2.77
M Labuschagne	11	42.4	3	180	5	36.00	3-85	0	0	51.2	4.21
MJ Swepson	11	296.3	21	1183	32	36.96	5-142	1	0	55.5	3.98
NJ Rimmington	1	28	7	74	2	37.00	2-35	0	0	84.0	2.64
CJ Gannon	1	29	11	67	1	67.00	1-67	0	0	174.0	2.31
CR Hemphrey	8	31	3	128	1	128.00	1-75	0	0	186.0	4.12

Also bowled: SD Heazlett (7 matches) 1-0-3-0, MT Renshaw (11 matches) 9-1-24-1 (Best: 1-12).

QUEENSLAND SHEFFIELD SHIELD RECORDS
Results

versus	M	W	L	D	T	%W	%L	Toss	%toss
New South Wales	178	47	71	60	0	26.40	39.89	95	53.37
South Australia	171	63	56	51	1	36.84	32.75	70	40.94
Tasmania	81	34	16	31	0	41.98	19.75	38	46.91
Victoria	174	55	63	56	0	31.61	36.21	87	50.00
Western Australia	136	34	49	53	0	25.00	36.03	62	45.59
	740	**233**	**255**	**251**	**1**	**31.49**	**34.46**	**352**	**47.57**

Highest Team Totals

	v..	Season	Venue
6-900	Vic	2005-06	Brisbane
687	NSW	1930-31	Brisbane (Ex)
664	SA	1994-95	Brisbane
5-650	NSW	1997-98	Brisbane
613	NSW	1963-64	Brisbane
7-605	Vic	2003-04	St. Kilda

Lowest Completed Team Totals

	v..	Season	venue
49	Vic	1936-37	Melbourne
52	WA	1982-83	Perth
54	Vic	1932-33	Brisbane
61	Vic	2016-17	AB Field
62	Tas	2008-09	Brisbane
65	Vic	1957-58	Melbourne
65	Vic	1970-71	Melbourne

Australian Cricket Digest, 2018-19
Leading Run Scorers

	M	Inn	NO	HS	Runs	Ave	100s	50s	0s
ML Love	139	244	20	300*	10132	45.23	27	43	22
JP Maher	141	253	22	223	9086	39.33	17	44	15
SG Law	142	234	28	216	9034	43.85	24	47	20
SC Trimble	123	230	13	252*	8647	39.85	22	40	16
ML Hayden	89	161	17	234	7913	54.95	25	33	6
PJP Burge	83	138	12	283	7084	56.22	22	31	9

Highest Individual Scores

		v..	Season	Venue
300*	ML Love	Vic	2003-04	St. Kilda
283	PJP Burge	NSW	1963-64	Brisbane (Gab)
275*	FC Thompson	NSW	1930-31	Brisbane (Ex)
253	WC Andrews	NSW	1934-35	Sydney
252*	SC Trimble	NSW	1963-64	Sydney

Most Catches (Fielders)

Ct		M
158	ML Love	139
153	JP Maher	141
126	SG Law	142
99	AR Border	87
86	ML Hayden	89

Most Appearances

M		Start	End
142	SG Law	28 Oct 1988	16 Mar 2004
141	JP Maher	25 Nov 1993	3 Mar 2008
139	ML Love	26 Mar 1993	17 Mar 2009
128	CD Hartley	19 Dec 2003	18 Mar 2017
123	SC Trimble	11 Dec 1959	19 Jan 1976
105	TV Hohns	02 Feb 1973	17 Mar 1991

Most Dismissals (Keepers)

	M	Ct	St	Total
CD Hartley	128	535	15	550
WA Seccombe	101	474	14	488
JA MacLean	86	289	24	313
ATW Grout	84	213	63	276
R Phillips	68	214	12	226
D Tallon	67	145	61	206

Record Wicket Partnerships

Wkt				v..	Season	Venue
1	388	KC Wessels	RB Kerr	Vic	1982-83	St. Kilda
2	369	CT Perren	SG Law	WA	2003-04	Brisbane
3	326	ML Love	SG Law	Tas	1994-95	Brisbane
4	329*	SR Watson	CT Perren	Vic	2005-06	Brisbane
5	273	CA Lynn	CD Hartley	Vic	2014-15	Brisbane
6	233	ML Love	CD Hartley	NSW	2008-09	Brisbane
7	335	WC Andrews	EC Bensted	NSW	1934-35	Sydney
8	146	TV Hohns	G Dymock	Vic	1978-79	Melbourne
9	152*	ATW Grout	WT Walmsley	NSW	1956-57	Sydney
10	105*	WT Walmsley	JE Freeman	NSW	1957-58	Brisbane

Leading Wicket takers

	M	Balls	Mdns	Runs	Wkts	Ave	Best	5w	10m	SR	Econ
MS Kasprowicz	101	22216	927	10833	441	24.56	8-44	26	2	50.38	2.93
AJ Bichel	89	19654	785	9994	430	23.24	7-54	22	4	45.71	3.05
CG Rackemann	102	22400	921	10079	383	26.32	7-43	12	1	58.49	2.70
JR Thomson	77	15172	403	7927	328	24.17	7-27	17	3	46.26	3.13
CJ McDermott	67	14974	541	7605	303	25.10	8-44	22	2	49.42	3.05

Best Bowling in an Innings

		v..	Season	Venue
PJ Allan	10-61	Vic	1965-66	Melbourne
CJ McDermott	8-44	Tas	1989-90	Brisbane
MS Kasprowicz	8-44	Vic	2005-06	Brisbane
MA Polzin	8-51	Vic	1989-90	Melbourne
JRF Duncan	8-55	Vic	1970-71	Melbourne

Best Bowling in a Match

		v..	Season	Venue
PJ Allan	13-110	NSW	1968-69	Sydney
JRF Duncan	13-125	Vic	1970-71	Melbourne
CR Swan	13-144	SA	2010-11	AB Field
PJ Allan	12-56	Vic	1968-69	Brisbane
JR Thomson	12-112	NSW	1976-77	Brisbane

Australian Cricket Digest, 2018-19
SOUTH AUSTRALIA AVERAGES

Batting & Fielding	M	Inn	NO	Runs	HS	Avge	100	50	0	S/Rate	Ct	St
CJ Ferguson	9	18	2	780	182*	48.75	1	5	2	55.63	12	-
TM Head	8	16	0	738	145	46.12	2	4	1	74.62	5	-
HJ Nielsen	2	3	0	130	105	43.33	1	0	0	45.29	7	0
JB Weatherald	10	20	0	765	152	38.25	2	4	2	53.19	10	-
AT Carey	8	15	2	455	139	35.00	1	1	2	53.40	23	0
JS Lehmann	10	20	1	536	103	28.21	1	2	0	64.96	5	-
TLW Cooper	9	17	3	376	105*	26.85	1	1	2	49.73	10	-
CJ McInerney	2	4	0	82	51	20.50	0	1	1	52.56	4	-
AI Ross	3	5	0	101	49	20.20	0	0	0	59.06	3	-
JD Dalton	8	16	0	312	64	19.50	0	2	1	42.97	4	-
JM Mennie	10	2	2	325	75	18.05	0	1	2	49.77	4	-
A Zampa	5	10	2	129	57	16.12	0	1	1	57.07	2	-
NP Winter	5	9	3	91	25	15.16	0	0	0	43.54	1	-
KW Richardson	4	7	1	87	32	14.50	0	0	1	71.31	2	-
CJ Sayers	5	8	1	78	46	11.14	0	0	1	43.57	2	-
KR Smith	1	2	0	18	10	9.00	0	0	0	37.50	1	-
C Valente	1	2	0	16	11	8.00	0	0	0	37.20	0	-
DJ Worrall	8	13	6	36	14*	5.14	0	0	5	30.00	2	-

Also batted: TD Andrews (1 match) 50, DMK Grant (1 match) 8*

Bowling	M	Overs	Mdns	Runs	Wkts	Avge	Best	5i	10m	S/Rate	Econ
NP Winter	5	220.3	41	670	34	19.70	5-48	4	1	38.9	3.03
C Valente	1	39	14	81	3	27.00	2-40	0	0	78.0	2.07
DJ Worrall	8	316.5	72	973	34	28.61	5-72	1	0	55.9	3.07
KW Richardson	4	154.3	27	523	17	30.76	4-30	0	0	54.5	3.38
CJ Sayers	5	191.5	40	558	17	32.82	4-82	0	0	67.7	2.90
JM Mennie	10	343.1	69	1015	30	33.83	4-39	0	0	68.6	2.95
DMK Grant	1	20	7	42	1	42.00	1-38	0	0	120.0	2.10
JS Lehmann	10	28	5	89	2	44.50	1-18	0	0	84.0	3.17
A Zampa	5	225.1	30	789	17	46.41	5-59	1	0	79.4	3.50
TLW Cooper	9	23	3	95	2	47.50	1-12	0	0	69.0	4.13
TM Head	8	148.2	25	493	6	82.16	2-23	0	0	148.3	3.32
TD Andrews	1	25	2	84	1	84.00	1-35	0	0	150.0	3.36

Also bowled: JD Dalton (8 matches) 1-0-3-0, CJ McInerney (2 matches) 3-0-15-0, AI Ross (3 matches) 1-0-6-0.

SOUTH AUSTRALIA SHEFFIELD SHIELD RECORDS
Results

versus	M	W	L	D	T	%W	%L	toss	%toss
New South Wales	227	59	126	42	0	25.99	55.51	116	51.10
Queensland	171	56	63	51	1	32.75	36.84	101	59.06
Tasmania	77	28	21	28	0	36.36	27.27	42	54.55
Victoria	230	53	119	58	0	23.04	51.74	116	50.43
Western Australia	136	40	57	39	0	29.41	41.91	86	63.24
	841	**236**	**386**	**218**	**1**	**28.06**	**45.90**	**461**	**54.82**

Highest Team Totals

	v..	Season	venue
7-821	Qld	1939-40	Adelaide
673	Tas	1987-88	Adelaide
7-644	Qld	1934-35	Adelaide
3-643	Tas	1986-87	Adelaide
8-642	Qld	1935-36	Adelaide
638	Tas	2005-06	Hobart

Lowest Completed Team Totals

	v..	Season	venue
27	NSW	1955-56	Sydney
29	NSW	2004-05	Sydney
45	Tas	2014-15	Hobart
55	Tas	2010-11	Hobart
56	WA	1959-60	Perth
61	NSW	1906-07	Adelaide

Australian Cricket Digest, 2018-19

Leading Run Scorers

	M	Inn	NO	HS	Runs	Ave	100s	50s	0s
DS Lehmann	119	218	14	301*	11622	56.97	39	41	14
GS Blewett	117	223	13	268	9682	46.10	23	48	15
DW Hookes	120	205	9	306*	9364	47.78	26	44	14
LE Favell	121	220	4	164	8269	38.28	20	43	18
IM Chappell	89	157	13	205*	7665	53.23	22	45	9

Highest Individual Scores

		v..	Season	venue
365*	C Hill	NSW	1900-01	Adelaide
357	DG Bradman,	Vic	1935-36	Melbourne
356	BA Richards	WA	1970-71	Perth
325	CL Badcock	Vic	1935-36	Adelaide
306*	DW Hookes	Tas	1986-87	Adelaide

Most Catches (Fielders)

Ct		M
128	DW Hookes	120
113	JD Siddons	82
113	IM Chappell	89
99	VY Richardson	77
84	PR Sleep	127

Most Appearances

M		Start	End
127	PR Sleep	4 Feb 1977	21 Mar 1993
121	LE Favell	30 Nov 1951	16 Feb 1970
120	DW Hookes	7 Nov 1975	2 Mar 1992
119	DS Lehmann	11 Dec 1987	25 Nov 2007
117	GS Blewett	1 Nov 1991	21 Feb 2006
107	HN Dansie	27 Jan 1950	31 Jan 1967

Most Dismissals (Keepers)

	M	Ct	St	Total
GA Manou	96	307	21	328
TJ Nielsen	92	255	29	284
BN Jarman	77	193	57	250
CW Walker	57	103	87	190
TP Ludeman	47	158	7	165
GRA Langley	46	111	24	135

Record Wicket Partnerships

Wkt				v..	Season	venue
1	281	LE Favell	JP Causby	NSW	1967-68	Adelaide
2	386	GS Blewett	DS Lehmann	Tas	2001-02	Hobart
3	286	GS Blewett	DS Lehmann	Tas	1993-94	Adelaide
4	462*	DW Hookes	WB Phillips	Tas	1986-87	Adelaide
5	281	CL Badcock	MG Waite	Qld	1939-40	Adelaide
6	260	DS Lehmann	TJ Nielsen	Qld	1996-97	Adelaide
7	198	TLW Cooper	AT Carey	WA	2016-17	WACA
7	198	GA Bishop	TBA May	Tas	1990-91	Adelaide
8	250	GA Manou	JN Gillespie	Tas	2007-08	Hobart
9	232	C Hill	E Walkley	NSW	1900-01	Adelaide
10	104	L Michael	EI Pynor	Vic	1949-50	Adelaide

Leading Wicket takers

	M	Balls	Mdns	Runs	Wkts	Ave	Best	5i	10m	SR	Econ
CV Grimmett	78	28144	442	12878	504	25.55	9-180	47	13	55.84	2.75
AA Mallett	77	20988	674	8171	344	23.75	7-57	19	2	61.01	2.34
TBA May	80	22575	930	9943	270	36.83	7-93	15	2	83.61	2.64
PE Sleep	127	19482	671	9883	254	38.91	8-133	7	0	76.70	3.04
PE McIntyre	61	17431	576	8974	215	41.74	6-64	8	2	81.07	3.09

Best Bowling in an Innings

		v..	Season	venue
TW Wall	10-36	NSW	1932-33	Sydney
JPF Travers	9-30	Vic	1900-01	Melbourne
G Giffen	9-147	Vic	1892-93	Adelaide
CV Grimmett	9-180	Qld	1934-35	Adelaide
JN Gillespie	8-50	NSW	2001-02	Sydney

Best Bowling in a Match

	Runs	v..	Season	venue
G Giffen	16-186	NSW	1894-95	Adelaide
CV Grimmett	16-289	Qld	1934-35	Adelaide
G Giffen	15-185	Vic	1902-03	Adelaide
EW Freeman	13-105	NSW	1970-71	Adelaide
PC Rofe	13-112	NSW	2001-02	Adelaide

Australian Cricket Digest, 2018-19
TASMANIA AVERAGES

Batting & Fielding	M	Inn	NO	Runs	HS	Avge	100	50	0	S/Rate	Ct	St
JR Doran	11	17	0	756	114	44.47	1	6	2	40.29	12	-
MS Wade	11	17	2	654	139	43.60	3	2	2	55.28	37	0
JC Silk	8	15	1	566	104	40.42	1	4	0	50.99	6	-
GJ Bailey	11	18	0	602	106	33.44	1	5	2	53.55	10	-
AJ Doolan	11	20	3	555	247*	32.64	1	2	2	53.36	15	-
SA Milenko	6	8	0	245	78	30.62	0	2	1	81.12	4	-
BR McDermott	8	12	3	247	75*	27.44	0	1	2	42.80	3	-
BJ Webster	10	16	2	363	136	25.92	1	0	0	41.34	23	-
TS Rogers	10	13	0	324	80	24.92	0	1	2	55.00	2	-
SL Rainbird	11	15	3	234	57	19.50	0	1	0	52.70	3	-
JM Bird	8	12	3	159	32	17.66	0	0	1	81.95	5	-
AL Fekete	6	8	4	60	25*	15.00	0	0	0	55.55	0	-
GT Bell	6	8	2	35	16*	5.83	0	0	2	17.94	3	-

Also played: JP Faulkner (1 match) 1, JA Freeman (1 match) did not bat, RP Meredith (2 matches) 0*, TD Paine (1 match) 0, 71* (2 ct)

Bowling	M	Overs	Mdns	Runs	Wkts	Avge	Best	5i	10m	SR	Econ
TS Rogers	10	213.4	42	680	37	18.37	4-9	0	0	34.6	3.18
GT Bell	6	167	40	475	24	19.79	4-38	0	0	41.7	2.84
JM Bird	8	281.5	67	807	37	21.81	5-30	1	0	45.7	2.86
SA Milenko	6	102.4	24	393	14	28.07	3-49	0	0	44.0	3.82
AL Fekete	6	175	30	659	22	29.95	6-67	1	1	47.7	3.76
SL Rainbird	11	337.5	66	1131	35	32.31	3-47	0	0	57.9	3.34
BJ Webster	10	85.2	13	288	6	48.00	3-83	0	0	85.3	3.37
RP Meredith	2	34	5	137	2	68.50	1-25	0	0	102.0	4.02

Also bowled: GJ Bailey (11 matches) 0.1-0-0-0, JP Faulkner (1 match) 10.3-2-22-2 (Best 1-9), JA Freeman (1 match) 22-1-92-1, JC Silk (8 matches) 2-0-14-1 (Best 1-4), MS Wade (11 matches) 3.4-0-13-3

TASMANIA SHEFFIELD SHIELD RECORDS
Results

versus	M	W	L	D	%W	%L	toss	%toss
New South Wales	80	23	29	28	28.75	36.25	49	61.25
Queensland	81	16	34	31	19.75	41.98	43	53.09
South Australia	77	21	28	28	27.27	36.36	35	45.45
Victoria	77	19	26	32	24.68	33.77	39	50.65
Western Australia	78	17	36	25	21.79	46.15	46	58.97
	393	96	153	144	24.43	38.93	36.64	53.94

Highest Team Totals

	v..	Season	venue
651	SA	2013-14	Hobart
592	SA	1987-88	Adelaide
6-569	SA	1997-98	Hobart
8-566	Vic	2015-16	Hobart
7-553	WA	2006-07	Perth
550	NSW	1990-91	Hobart

Lowest Team Totals

	v..	Season	Venue
76	NSW	1991-92	Hobart
82*	Qld	2001-02	Brisbane
86	WA	2005-06	Hobart
91	SA	2015-16	Glenelg
94	WA	2006-07	Hobart
95	Qld	2012-13	Hobart

includes one batsman retired hurt

Leading Run Scorers

	M	Inn	NO	HS	Runs	Ave	100s	50s	0s
J Cox	161	295	17	245	10821	38.92	30	47	26
MJ Di Venuto	140	250	11	189	9974	41.73	19	67	23
DC Boon	119	204	8	227	8029	40.96	20	43	7
GJ Bailey	**117**	**212**	**17**	**200***	**7698**	**39.48**	**19**	**39**	**22**
DJ Marsh	133	230	33	134	7134	36.21	13	38	23
DF Hills	100	187	8	265	6887	38.47	18	36	20

Australian Cricket Digest, 2018-19

Highest Individual Scores

		v..	Season	Venue
265	DF Hills	SA	1997-98	Hobart
245	J Cox	NSW	1999-00	Hobart
233	RT Ponting	Qld	2000-01	Brisbane (ABF)
229	EP Gulbis	SA	2013-14	Hobart
227	DC Boon	Vic	1983-84	Melbourne

Most Catches (Fielders)

Ct		M
171	DJ Marsh	133
151	MJ Di Venuto	140
98	**GJ Bailey**	**117**
93	DC Boon	119
78	J Cox	161

Most Appearances

M		Start	End
161	J Cox	20 Nov 1987	20 Nov 2005
140	MJ Di Venuto	13 Mar 1992	10 Mar 2008
133	DJ Marsh	07 Nov 1996	12 Mar 2010
119	DC Boon	15 Dec 1978	14 Mar 1999
104	S Young	29 Nov 1991	14 Dec 2001
100	DF Hills	29 Nov 1991	14 Dec 2001

Most Catches (Keepers)

Dis		M	Ct	St
262	MN Atkinson	84	237	25
231	SG Clingeleffer	74	219	12
181	**TD Paine**	**55**	**176**	**5**
110	RD Woolley	43	97	13
107	RE Soule	51	103	4
70	TIF Triffitt	16	70	2

Record Wicket Partnerships

Wkt				v..	Season	Venue
1	297	DF Hills	J Cox	Vic	1997-98	Hobart
2	294	J Cox	MJ Di Venuto	NSW	1999-00	Hobart
3	294	BR Dunk	AJ Doolan	Vic	2015-16	Hobart
4	319	MG Bevan	DJ Marsh	WA	2004-05	Hobart
5	319	RT Ponting	RJ Tucker	WA	1994-95	Hobart
6	213	BF Davison	RD Woolley	SA	1980-81	Adelaide
7	293*	RT Ponting	JJ Krejza	NSW	2012-13	Hobart
8	148	BF Davison	PI Faulkner	SA	1983-84	Adelaide
9	119	MJ Di Venuto	XJ Doherty	SA	2004-05	Hobart
10	120	SL Saunders	PM Clough	WA	1981-82	Perth

Leading Wicket Takers

	M	Balls	Mdns	Runs	Wkts	Avg	Best	5i	10m	SR	Econ
BW Hilfenhaus	68	15341	604	7742	262	29.55	7-58	9	1	58.55	3.03
LR Butterworth	69	11919	573	5440	221	24.62	6-49	8	1	53.93	2.74
CR Miller	54	13846	546	6657	210	31.70	7-49	8	2	65.93	2.88
S Young	104	16399	744	7884	201	39.22	5-26	5	1	81.59	2.88
JM Bird	**42**	**8513**	**344**	**4151**	**199**	**20.86**	**7-45**	**11**	**3**	**42.78**	**2.93**
DG Wright	64	13541	655	6330	197	32.13	6-25	6	0	68.74	2.80

Best Bowling in an Innings

		v..	Season	venue
PM Clough	8-95	WA	1983-84	Launceston
JM Bird	7-45	NSW	2015-16	Hobart
CR Miller	7-49	Vic	1997-98	Melbourne
AR Griffith	7-54	Vic	2004-05	Hobart
DJ Marsh	7-57	NSW	1997-98	Sydney

Best Bowling in a Match

		v..	Season	Venue
CR Miller	12-119	SA	1997-98	Bellerive
SR Watson	11-78	Qld	2001-02	Bellerive
JM Bird	11-95	WA	2011-12	Bellerive
SJ Jurgensen	11-103	NSW	2001-02	Bellerive
SJ Jurgensen	11-172	Qld	2001-02	Gabba

Australian Cricket Digest, 2018-19
VICTORIA AVERAGES

Batting & Fielding	M	Inn	NO	Runs	HS	Avge	100	50	0	S/Rate	Ct	St
WJ Pucovski	3	5	1	223	188	55.75	1	0	0	43.98	1	-
CL White	7	12	1	574	149	52.18	1	5	1	53.09	11	-
GJ Maxwell	8	15	1	707	278	50.50	1	3	1	70.34	6	-
MS Harris	10	18	1	706	109	41.52	2	4	0	65.06	3	-
PSP Handscomb	4	8	1	271	114*	38.71	1	1	2	59.04	12	-
AJ Finch	8	15	1	494	151*	35.28	1	3	3	82.47	7	-
SE Gotch	7	10	1	281	98	31.22	0	2	2	41.02	16	4
DT Christian	7	12	0	337	69	28.08	0	1	1	50.67	8	-
EM Vines	2	3	0	84	34	28.00	0	0	0	37.33	2	-
TJ Dean	10	18	0	500	111	27.77	2	0	1	44.01	10	-
CP Tremain	10	14	2	244	47	20.33	0	0	1	54.45	1	-
SM Boland	10	13	8	96	29*	19.20	0	0	1	30.76	3	-
MW Short	3	4	1	55	22	18.33	0	0	0	40.14	2	-
SB Harper	3	6	0	78	38	13.00	0	0	1	52.00	16	1
PM Siddle	9	14	1	141	28	10.84	0	0	3	52.41	3	-
Fawad Ahmed	7	10	5	47	15	9.40	0	0	0	47.47	1	-
JM Holland	3	3	0	9	9	3.00	0	0	2	56.25	1	-

Bowling	M	Overs	Mdns	Runs	Wkts	Avge	Best	5i	10m	SR	Econ
CP Tremain	10	349.4	83	1075	51	21.07	7-82	2	1	41.1	3.07
SM Boland	10	367.4	99	1023	38	26.92	4-41	0	0	58.0	2.78
JM Holland	3	151	51	340	12	28.33	5-67	1	0	75.5	2.25
Fawad Ahmed	7	283.1	33	1019	27	37.74	5-94	1	0	62.9	3.59
PM Siddle	9	317.4	81	952	24	39.66	3-21	0	0	79.4	2.99
DT Christian	7	117.3	9	412	8	51.50	2-27	0	0	88.1	3.50
AJ Finch	8	17	5	53	1	53.00	1-4	0	0	102.0	3.11
GJ Maxwell	8	87.5	16	286	3	95.33	1-23	0	0	175.6	3.25
MW Short	3	31	1	135	1	135.00	1-73	0	0	186.0	4.35

Also bowled: TJ Dean (10 matches) 12-3-42-0, MS Harris (10 matches) 1-0-5-0, CL White (7 matches) 18-3-55-0.

VICTORIA SHEFFIELD SHIELD RECORDS
Results

versus	M	W	L	D	T	%W	%L	toss	%toss
New South Wales	234	73	80	80	1	31.20	34.19	119	50.85
Queensland	174	63	55	56	0	36.21	31.61	87	50.00
South Australia	230	119	53	58	0	51.74	23.04	114	49.57
Tasmania	77	26	19	32	0	33.77	24.68	38	49.35
Western Australia	134	47	37	50	0	35.07	27.61	71	52.99
	849	328	244	276	1	38.63	28.74	429	50.53

Highest Team Totals

Total	v..	Season	venue
1107	NSW	1926-27	Melbourne
8-806	Qld	2008-09	Melbourne
793	Qld	1927-28	Melbourne
724	SA	1920-21	Melbourne
710	Qld	2003-04	Melbourne

Lowest Completed Team Totals

Total	v..	Season	venue
31	NSW	1906-07	Sydney
35	NSW	1926-27	Sydney
43	SA	1895-96	Melbourne
73	WA	1971-72	Melbourne
76	Qld	1974-75	Brisbane

Australian Cricket Digest, 2018-19

Leading Run Scorers

	M	Inn	NO	HS	Runs	Ave	100s	50s	0s
BJ Hodge	140	254	23	286*	10474	45.34	29	49	19
DM Jones	110	194	16	324*	9622	54.06	31	40	15
MTG Elliott,	103	197	16	203	9470	52.32	32	43	7
DJ Hussey	105	179	15	212*	7476	45.59	19	43	10
CL White	**126**	**215**	**23**	**150***	**7003**	**36.47**	**10**	**43**	**14**
WM Lawry	85	139	14	266	6615	52.92	17	41	6

Highest Individual scores

		for	Season	Venue
437	WH Ponsford	Vic	1927-28	Melbourne
352	WH Ponsford	Vic	1926-27	Melbourne
336	WH Ponsford	Vic	1927-28	Melbourne
324*	DM Jones	Vic	1994-95	Melbourne
295	J Ryder	Vic	1926-27	Melbourne

Most Catches (Fielders)

Ct		M
167	CL White	126
138	DJ Hussey	105
125	MTG Elliott	103
109	DF Whatmore	85
96	DM Jones	110

Most Appearances

M		Start	end
140	BJ Hodge	27 Oct 1993	13 Dec 2009
129	DS Berry	9 Nov 1990	16 Mar 2004
126	**CL White**	**9 Mar 2001**	**16 Mar 2018**
110	DM Jones	29 Jan 1982	15 Mar 1998
105	DJ Hussey	5 Feb 2003	25 Mar 2015
103	MTG Elliott	3 Feb 1993	13 Mar 2005
103	RJ Bright	29 Dec 1972	1 Feb 1988

Most Dismissals (Keepers)

Dis		M	Ct	St
512	DS Berry	129	468	44
278	MS Wade	74	271	7
238	RD Robinson	68	212	26
230	RC Jordon	70	199	31
168	MGD Dimattina	60	149	19
156	JL Ellis	49	111	45

Record Partnerships

Wkt				V..	Season	venue
1	375	WM Woodfull	WH Ponsford	NSW	1926-27	Melbourne
2	314	WH Ponsford	HSTL Hendry	Qld	1927-28	Melbourne
3	390*	JM Wiener	JK Moss	WA	1981-82	St. Kilda
4	309*	J Moss	DJ Hussey	WA	2003-04	Perth
5	316*	LD Harper	GB Gardiner	SA	1997-98	Carlton
6	290	MTG Elliott	DS Berry	NSW	1996-97	Sydney
7	205	CL White	IJ Harvey	Qld	2004-05	Brisbane
8	215	RL Park	WW Armstrong	SA	1919-20	Melbourne
9	143	GR Hazlitt	A Kenny	SA	1910-11	Melbourne
10	211	M Ellis	TJ Hastings	SA	1902-03	Melbourne

Leading Wicket takers

Wkts		M	Balls	Mdns	Runs	Ave	Best	5i	10m	SR	Econ
318	PR Reiffel	86	19137	843	8242	25.92	6-57	7	2	60.18	2.58
297	AN Connolly	71	17973	367	7745	26.08	9-67	12	4	60.52	2.59
281	AIC Dodemaide	94	19880	824	8884	31.62	6-67	12	0	70.75	2.68
267	MG Hughes	76	16762	582	8169	30.60	7-81	10	2	62.78	2.92
252	RJ Bright	101	22899	1013	8821	35.00	6-61	10	0	90.87	2.31

Best Bowling in an innings

		v..	Season	Venue
EL McCormick	9-40	SA	1936-37	Adelaide
AN Connolly	9-67	Qld	1964-65	Brisbane
L Fleetwood-Smith	8-135	SA	1937-38	MCG
DJ Pattinson	8-35	WA	2010-11	Perth
H Trumble	8-39	SA	1898-99	MCG

Best Bowling in a Match

		v..	Season	Venue
LOB Fleetwood-Smith	15-96	Qld	1936-37	MCG
LOB Fleetwood-Smith	15-226	NSW	1934-35	Sydney
AL Thomson	13-141	NSW	1969-70	MCG
GE Tribe	13-153	SA	1946-47	Adel
J Ryder	13-155	SA	1912-13	MCG

Australian Cricket Digest, 2018-19
WESTERN AUSTRALIA AVERAGES

Batting & Fielding	M	Inn	NO	Runs	HS	Avge	100	50	0	S/Rate	Ct	St
CT Bancroft	4	8	2	493	228*	82.16	1	2	0	53.64	8	0
NM Coulter-Nile	1	2	0	94	52	47.00	0	1	0	60.64	1	-
MR Marsh	6	12	1	424	141	38.54	1	1	1	71.74	1	-
SE Marsh	4	8	0	304	91	38.00	0	3	0	55.98	6	-
JS Paris	1	2	1	37	23	37.00	0	0	0	20.32	0	-
AJ Turner	10	19	1	650	101*	36.11	1	3	1	58.45	11	-
JP Inglis	8	15	2	465	87	35.76	0	4	3	69.19	22	1
HWR Cartwright	10	20	1	617	111*	32.47	1	3	3	54.99	4	-
WG Bosisto	6	12	0	337	98	28.08	0	3	2	37.69	4	-
AC Agar	4	7	0	171	86	24.42	0	1	1	50.14	2	-
DJM Short	6	11	0	263	66	23.90	0	2	0	57.29	5	-
JP Behrendorff	2	4	1	69	39*	23.00	0	0	1	43.94	2	-
JR Philippe	4	8	0	180	74	22.50	0	2	1	74.07	2	-
JW Wells	6	12	0	242	107	20.16	1	0	2	38.78	6	-
AA Bevilaqua	2	4	1	57	36	19.00	0	0	0	135.71	2	-
MP Stoinis	6	11	1	173	33	17.30	0	0	1	55.27	7	-
JA Richardson	5	8	0	136	71	17.00	0	1	1	70.10	4	-
M Kelly	6	10	4	100	41	16.66	0	0	2	51.28	4	-
AB Holder	3	6	3	48	20*	16.00	0	0	0	40.67	0	-
SP Mackin	9	12	7	36	12*	7.20	0	0	2	52.17	7	-
AJ Tye	1	2	0	13	10	6.50	0	0	0	76.47	0	-
L Guthrie	3	5	0	32	16	6.40	0	0	2	71.11	3	-
DJM Moody	2	3	0	10	10	3.33	0	0	2	45.45	3	-
CD Hinchliffe	1	2	0	1	1	0.50	0	0	1	11.11	0	-

Bowling	M	Overs	Mdns	Runs	Wkts	Avge	Best	5i	10m	SR	Econ
NM Coulter-Nile	1	15	4	41	4	10.25	3-18	0	0	22.5	2.73
JS Paris	1	39	13	83	5	16.60	3-52	0	0	46.8	2.12
M Kelly	6	178.1	51	530	24	22.08	5-60	1	0	44.5	2.97
DJM Short	6	80.2	11	319	11	29.00	3-78	0	0	43.8	3.97
JA Richardson	5	172.3	32	532	18	29.55	4-47	0	0	57.5	3.08
MR Marsh	6	48	6	180	6	30.00	4-50	0	0	48.0	3.75
AB Holder	3	76.5	17	272	8	34.00	3-45	0	0	57.6	3.54
SP Mackin	9	279	50	990	28	35.35	6-43	1	0	59.7	3.54
AJ Tye	1	37.2	5	181	5	36.20	3-90	0	0	44.8	4.84
AC Agar	4	148	29	453	12	37.75	4-119	0	0	74.0	3.06
L Guthrie	3	77.4	12	316	8	39.50	4-59	0	0	58.2	4.06
MP Stoinis	6	102	15	358	9	39.77	4-82	0	0	68.0	3.50
AA Bevilaqua	2	32	8	92	2	46.00	1-21	0	0	96.0	2.87
DJM Moody	2	58	10	253	5	50.60	3-95	0	0	69.6	4.36
JP Behrendorff	2	54	9	186	3	62.00	2-56	0	0	108.0	3.44
WG Bosisto	6	40	7	136	2	68.00	1-11	0	0	120.0	3.40
HWR Cartwright	10	39	4	172	1	172.00	1-20	0	0	234.0	4.41

Also bowled: CD Hinchliffe (1 match) 6-0-14-1.

WESTERN AUSTRALIA SHEFFIELD SHIELD RECORDS
Results

versus	M	W	L	D	%W	%L	toss	%toss
New South Wales	135	39	56	40	28.89	41.48	65	48.15
Queensland	136	49	34	53	36.03	25.00	74	54.41
South Australia	136	57	40	39	41.91	29.41	50	36.76
Tasmania	78	36	17	25	46.15	21.79	32	41.03
Victoria	134	37	47	50	27.61	35.07	63	47.01
	619	**218**	**194**	**207**	**35.22**	**31.34**	**284**	**45.88**

Australian Cricket Digest, 2018-19

Highest Team Totals

	v..	Season	venue
654	Vic	1986-87	Perth
633	SA	2014-15	Glenelg
5-615	Qld	1968-69	Brisbane
3-608	Vic	2006-07	Perth
8-607	Qld	1989-90	Perth
8-607	NSW	2004-05	Perth

Lowest Team Totals

	v..	Season	venue
41	SA	1989-90	Adelaide
50	NSW	1951-52	Sydney
51	NSW	1950-51	Perth
54	Qld	1972-73	Brisbane
58	NSW	1998-99	Sydney
67	Tas	2012-13	Hobart

Leading Run Scorers

	M	Inn	NO	HS	Runs	Ave	100s	50s	0s
JL Langer	108	195	15	274*	9406	52.26	29	35	10
TM Moody	132	228	22	272	8853	42.98	20	46	17
MEK Hussey	112	207	12	223*	8007	41.06	16	41	14
AC Voges	112	200	32	249	7522	44.77	19	35	20
MRJ Veletta	114	198	20	262	7306	41.04	18	40	17

Highest Individual Scores

		v..	Season	venue
355*	GR Marsh	SA	1989-90	Perth
303*	LM Davis	NSW	2011-12	Perth
279	CJL Rogers	Vic	2006-07	Perth
274*	JL Langer	SA	1996-97	Perth
272	TM Moody	Tas	1994-95	Hobart

Most Catches (Fielders)

Ct		M
170	AC Voges	112
138	RJ Inverarity	108
114	TM Moody	132
105	JL Langer	108
104	MEK Hussey	112
104	MRJ Veletta	114

Most Appearances

M		Start	End
132	TM Moody	10 Jan 1986	5 Mar 2001
114	MRJ Veletta	21 Oct 1983	19 Mar 1995
112	AC Voges	8 Dec 2002	19 Mar 2017
112	MEK Hussey	4 Nov 1994	17 Mar 2013
111	MJ North	15 Oct 1999	24 Mar 2014
109	GM Wood	29 Oct 1977	23 Dec 1991

Most Dismissals (Keepers)

Dis		M	Ct	St
348	TJ Zoehrer	105	320	28
344	RW Marsh	81	311	33
265	AC Gilchrist	53	257	8
218	L Ronchi	55	208	10
198	RJ Campbell	52	187	11
149	BL Buggins	57	131	18

Record Wicket Partnerships

Wkt	Runs			v..	Season	Venue
1	431	MRJ Veletta	GR Marsh	SA	1989-90	Perth
2	324	CT Bancroft	M Klinger	NSW	2014-15	Perth
3	459	CJL Rogers	MJ North	Vic	2006-07	Perth
4	369	CJL Rogers	MJ North	NSW	2002-03	Perth
5	301*	RB Simpson	KD Meuleman	NSW	1959-60	Perth
6	244	JT Irvine	R Edwards	NSW	1968-69	Sydney
7	214	M Klinger	AC Agar	Tas	2015-16	Hobart
8	242*	TJ Zoehrer	KH MacLeay	NSW	1990-91	Perth
9	168*	KH MacLeay	VJ Marks	NSW	1986-87	Perth
10	94	AC Agar	MG Hogan	Qld	2012-13	Brisbane

Leading Wicket Takers

Wkts		M	Balls	Mdns	Runs	Ave	Best	5i	10m	SR	Econ
419	J Angel	105	22351	1030	10418	24.86	6-35	13	0	53.34	2.80
384	TM Alderman	97	20482	778	9299	24.22	7-28	17	3	53.34	2.72
323	DK Lillee	70	16617	440	7544	23.36	7-36	18	4	51.45	2.72
302	GAR Lock	66	20107	555	7210	23.87	7-53	16	2	66.58	2.15
292	BP Julian	87	16149	614	8573	29.36	7-39	15	1	55.30	3.19

Best Bowling in an Innings

		v..	Season	venue
IJ Brayshaw	10-44	Vic	1967-68	Perth
JP Behrendorff	9-37	WA	2016-17	Perth
SJ Magoffin	8-47	SA	2005-06	Perth
HR Gorringe	8-56	Qld	1952-53	Perth
DE Hoare	8-98	NSW	1964-65	Perth
CD Matthews	8-101	Qld	1987-88	Perth

Best Bowling in a Match

		v..	Season	venue
TM Alderman	14-87	NSW	1981-82	Perth
JP Behrendorff	14-89	Vic	2016-17	Perth
IJ Brayshaw	12-90	Vic	1967-68	Perth
DK Lillee	12-113	SA	1975-76	Adelaide
B Mulder	11-67	NSW	1996-97	Perth
BR Dorey	11-88	Qld	2008-09	Brisbane
B Yardley	11-98	Tas	1980-81	Devonport
GAR Lock	11-131	Qld	1968-69	Brisbane
HR Gorringe	11-138	Qld	1952-53	Perth
BA Reid	11-143	SA	1990-91	Adelaide

Australian Cricket Digest, 2018-19
SHEFFIELD SHIELD RECORDS
RECENT WINNERS

1990-91	Victoria	2000-01	Queensland	2010-11	Tasmania
1991-92	Western Australia	2001-02	Queensland	2011-12	Queensland
1992-93	New South Wales	2002-03	New South Wales	2012-13	Tasmania
1993-94	New South Wales	2003-04	Victoria	2013-14	New South Wales
1994-95	Queensland	2004-05	New South Wales	2014-15	Victoria
1995-96	South Australia	2005-06	Queensland	2015-16	Victoria
1996-97	Queensland	2006-07	Tasmania	2016-17	Victoria
1997-98	Western Australia	2007-08	New South Wales	2017-18	Queensland
1998-99	Western Australia	2008-09	Victoria		
1999-2000	Queensland	2009-10	Victoria		

Overall results

Team	M	W	L	D	T	%W	%L	toss	%toss
New South Wales	854	362	241	250	1	42.39	28.22	410	48.01
Queensland	740	233	255	251	1	31.49	34.46	352	47.57
South Australia	841	236	386	218	1	28.06	45.90	461	54.82
Tasmania	393	96	153	144	0	24.43	38.93	212	53.94
Victoria	849	328	244	276	1	38.63	28.74	429	50.53
Western Australia	619	218	194	207	0	35.22	31.34	284	45.88

Highest Team Totals

Total	for	v..	Season	Venue
1107	Vic	NSW	1926-27	Melbourne
918	NSW	SA	1900-01	Sydney
6-900	Qld	Vic	2005-06	Brisbane
7-821	SA	Qld	1939-40	Adelaide
815	NSW	Vic	1908-09	Sydney
807	NSW	SA	1899-00	Adelaide
8-806	Vic	Qld	2008-09	Melbourne
805	NSW	Vic	1905-06	Melbourne
802	NSW	SA	1920-21	Sydney

Lowest Team Totals

Total	for	v..	Season	Venue
27	SA	NSW	1955-56	Sydney
29	SA	NSW	2004-05	Sydney
31	Vic	NSW	1906-07	Sydney
35	Vic	NSW	1926-27	Sydney
41	WA	SA	1989-90	Adelaide
43	Vic	SA	1895-96	Melbourne
45	SA	Tas	2014-15	Adelaide
49	Qld	Vic	1936-37	Melbourne
50	WA	NSW	1951-52	Sydney
51	WA	NSW	1950-51	Perth

Leading Run scorers

	for	M	Inn	NO	HS	Runs	Avge	100s	50s	0s
DS Lehmann	SA/Vic	147	266	18	301*	13635	54.98	45	51	15
J Cox	Tas	161	295	17	245	10821	38.92	30	47	26
JD Siddons	Vic/SA	146	259	21	245	10643	44.72	30	50	17
MG Bevan	SA/NSW/Tas	118	211	36	216	10621	60.69	42	41	9
BJ Hodge	Vic	140	254	23	286*	10474	45.34	29	49	19
MTG Elliott	SA/Vic	122	235	18	203	10263	47.29	32	48	12
ML Love	Qld	139	244	20	300*	10132	45.23	27	43	22
MJ Di Venuto	Tas	140	250	11	189	9974	41.73	19	67	23
CJL Rogers	WA/Vic	120	214	13	279	9917	49.34	33	42	10
GS Blewett	SA	117	223	13	268	9682	46.10	23	48	15

Australian Cricket Digest, 2018-19

Highest Individual Scores

		for	v..	Season	Venue
DG Bradman	452*	NSW	Qld	1929-30	Sydney
WH Ponsford	437	Vic	Qld	1927-28	Melbourne
C Hill	365*	SA	NSW	1900-01	Adelaide
RB Simpson	359	NSW	Qld	1963-64	Brisbane
DG Bradman	357	SA	Vic	1935-36	Melbourne
BA Richards	356	SA	WA	1970-71	Perth
GR Marsh	355*	WA	SA	1989-90	Perth
WH Ponsford	352	Vic	NSW	1926-27	Melbourne
DG Bradman	340*	NSW	Vic	1928-29	Sydney
WH Ponsford	336	Vic	SA	1927-28	Melbourne

Most Appearances

	M	Period
J Cox	161	1987/88-2004/05
RJ Inverarity	159	1962/63-1984/85
DS Lehmann	147	1987/88-2007/08
JD Siddons	146	1984/85-1999/00
SG Law	142	1988/89-2003/04
JP Maher	141	1993/94-2007/08
MJ Di Venuto	140	1991/92-2007/08
BJ Hodge	140	1993/94-2009/10
DS Berry	139	1989/90-2003/04
ML Love	139	1992/93-2008/09

Record Partnerships

Wkt				for	v..	Season	venue
1	431	MRJ Veletta	GR Marsh	WA	SA	1989-90	Perth
2	386	GS Blewett	DS Lehmann	SA	Tas	2001-02	Hobart
3	459	CJL Rogers	MJ North	WA	Vic	2006-07	Perth
4	462*	DW Hookes	WB Phillips	SA	Tas	1986-87	Adelaide
5	464*	ME Waugh	SR Waugh	NSW	WA	1990-91	Perth
6	332	NG Marks	G Thomas	NSW	SA	1958-59	Sydney
7	335	WC Andrews	EC Bensted	Qld	NSW	1934-35	Sydney
8	270	VT Trumper	EP Barbour	NSW	Vic	1912-13	Sydney
9	232	C Hill	E Walkley	SA	NSW	1900-01	Adelaide
10	307	AF Kippax	JEH Hooker	NSW	Vic	1928-29	Melbourne

Highest Partnerships

	Wkt			for	v..	Season	Venue
464*	5th	ME Waugh	SR Waugh	NSW	WA	1990-91	Perth
462*	4th	DW Hookes	WB Phillips	SA	Tas	1986-87	Adelaide
459	3rd	CJL Rogers	MJ North	WA	Vic	2006-07	Perth
431	1st	MRJ Veletta	GR Marsh	WA	SA	1989-90	Perth
397	5th	W Bardsley	C Kelleway	NSW	SA	1920-21	Sydney
391	5th	MC Henriques	PM Nevill	NSW	Qld	2016-17	Sydney
390*	3rd	JM Wiener	JK Moss	Vic	WA	1981-82	St. Kilda
388	1st	KC Wessels	RB Kerr	Qld	Vic	1982-83	St. Kilda
386	2nd	GS Blewett	DS Lehmann	SA	Tas	2001-02	Hobart
379	3rd	N Jewell	BJ Hodge	Vic	Qld	2007-08	Brisbane
379	3rd	LM Davis	AC Voges	WA	NSW	2011-12	Perth
378	2nd	LA Marks	KD Walters	NSW	SA	1964-65	Adelaide
378	4th	CJ Ferguson	JS Lehmann	SA	Tas	2015-16	Hobart
375	1st	WM Woodfull	WH Ponsford	Vic	NSW	1926-27	Melbourne

Leading Wicket Takers

	for	M	Balls	Mdns	Runs	Wkt	Ave	Best	5i	10	SR	Econ
CV Grimmett	Vic/SA	79	28321	443	12976	513	25.29	9-180	48	13	55.21	2.75
MS Kasprowicz	Qld	101	22216	927	10833	441	24.56	8-44	26	2	50.38	2.93
AJ Bichel	Qld	89	19654	785	9994	430	23.24	7-54	22	4	45.71	3.05
J Angel	WA	105	22351	1030	10418	419	24.86	6-35	13	0	53.34	2.80
TM Alderman	WA	97	20482	778	9299	384	24.22	7-28	17	3	53.34	2.72
CG Rackemann	Qld	102	22400	921	10079	383	26.32	7-43	12	1	58.49	2.70
GF Lawson	NSW	103	20933	870	8673	367	23.63	6-31	12	0	57.04	2.49
GRJ Matthews	NSW	116	26764	1375	10518	363	28.98	8-52	19	4	73.73	2.36
JR Thomson	NSW/Q	84	16545	428	8591	355	24.20	7-27	18	3	46.61	3.12
AA Mallett	SA	77	20988	674	8171	344	23.75	7-57	19	2	61.01	2.34
DK Lillee	WA/Tas	75	17813	476	8086	338	23.92	7-36	18	4	52.70	2.72

Best Bowling in an Innings

		for	v..	Season	Venue
TW Wall	10-36	SA	NSW	1932-33	Sydney
IJ Brayshaw	10-44	WA	Vic	1967-68	Perth
PJ Allan	10-61	Qld	Vic	1965-66	Melbourne
JPF Travers	9-30	SA	Vic	1900-01	Melbourne
JP Behrendorff	9-37	WA	Vic	2016-17	Perth
EL McCormick	9-40	Vic	SA	1936-37	Adelaide
WJ O'Reilly	9-41	NSW	SA	1937-38	Adelaide
WJ O'Reilly	9-50	NSW	Vic	1933-34	Melbourne
WP Howell	9-52	NSW	Vic	1902-03	Melbourne
AN Connolly	9-67	Vic	Qld	1964-65	Brisbane

Best Bowling in a Match

		for	v..	Season	Venue
G Giffen	16-186	SA	NSW	1894-95	Adelaide
CV Grimmett	16-289	SA	Qld	1934-35	Adelaide
LO'B Fleetwood-Smith	15-96	Vic	Qld	1936-37	Melbourne
TR McKibbin	15-125	NSW	SA	1896-97	Adelaide
G Giffen	15-185	SA	Vic	1902-03	Adelaide
LO'B Fleetwood-Smith	15-226	Vic	NSW	1934-35	Sydney
WJ O'Reilly	14-45	NSW	Qld	1939-40	Sydney
TM Alderman	14-87	WA	NSW	1981-82	Perth
WJ O'Reilly	14-98	NSW	SA	1937-38	Adelaide
JP Behrendorff	14-89	WA	Vic	2016-17	Perth
TR McKibbin	14-189	NSW	SA	1894-95	Sydney

Leading Wicket-Keepers

	for	M	Total	Ct	St	byes/Inn	Runs	Avge	100
CD Hartley	Qld	128	550	535	15	1.33	6038	34.70	10
DS Berry	SA/Vic	139	546	499	47	2.73	3963	21.77	4
WA Seccombe	Qld	101	488	474	14	1.91	3207	25.05	4
TJ Zoehrer	WA	105	348	320	28	1.89	4177	30.71	6
RW Marsh	WA	81	344	311	33	1.72	4306	35.01	6
PA Emery	NSW	109	339	298	41	3.02	3081	25.67	1
GA Manou	SA	96	328	307	21	3.49	3827	25.68	6
MS Wade	**Vic/Tas**	**85**	**315**	**308**	**7**	**3.11**	**4559**	**41.45**	**9**
JA MacLean	Qld	86	313	289	24	2.42	3277	25.21	2
BJ Haddin	NSW	93	306	282	24	3.93	5629	42.01	11
TJ Nielsen	SA	92	284	255	29	2.49	3531	26.16	4
ATW Grout	Qld	84	276	213	63	3.21	3016	24.13	2

Leading Fielders

	For	Ct	M
JD Siddons	Vic/SA	189	146
RJ Inverarity	WA/SA	188	159
DJ Marsh	SA/Tas	172	137
AC Voges	WA	170	112
CL White	**Vic**	**167**	**126**
ML Love	Qld	158	139
JP Maher	Qld	153	141
MJ Di Venuto	Tas	151	140
MTG Elliott	Vic/SA	143	122
DJ Hussey	Vic	138	105

Captains Records – most games as skipper

	For	M	W	L	D	%W
LE Favell	SA	80	30	29	21	37.50
DM Wellham	NSW/Tas/Qld	78	19	16	43	24.36
DW Hookes	SA	78	20	22	36	25.64
CL White	Vic	76	38	22	16	50.00
JD Siddons	SA	74	20	27	27	27.03
GJ Bailey	**Tas**	**73**	**27**	**31**	**15**	**36.99**
PL Ridings	SA	70	11	28	31	15.71
SG Law	Qld	69	35	10	24	50.72
VY Richardson	SA	64	23	37	4	35.94
DC Boon	Tas	58	13	25	20	22.41
WM Lawry	Vic	56	18	13	25	32.14

Australian Cricket Digest, 2018-19
CAREER RECORDS to the end of 2017-18

	M	Runs	HS	Avge	100	50	Ct	St	W	Avg	Best	5/10
SA Abbott	39	814	79	15.07	0	2	17	0	91	38.11	6-14	1/-
AC Agar	39	1373	106	25.43	2	7	16	0	108	39.46	6-110	5/2
TD Andrews	3	83	50	41.50	0	1	0	0	8	49.13	3-106	-/-
GJ Bailey	117	7698	200*	39.48	19	39	98	0	0			
CT Bancroft	46	3107	228*	38.84	9	9	63	1	0			
JP Behrendorff	30	389	39*	12.16	0	0	12	0	126	23.29	9-37	6/2
GT Bell	7	37	16*	6.17	0	0	3	0	31	20.48	4-38	-/-
AA Bevilaqua	2	57	36	19.00	0	0	2	0	2	46.00	1-21	-/-
JM Bird	42	476	39	12.21	0	0	21	0	199	20.86	7-45	11/3
SM Boland	51	620	51	14.42	0	2	17	0	159	28.33	7-31	3/-
DE Bollinger	89	480	41*	8.28	0	0	34	0	290	28.16	6-47	10/2
WG Bosisto	16	636	108	21.93	1	3	13	0	9	52.89	2-28	-/-
CJ Boyce	44	821	66	16.10	0	4	29	0	84	49.86	7-68	3/-
JA Burns	63	4567	202*	42.68	12	24	62	0	1	34.00	1-0	-/-
AT Carey	26	1249	139	28.39	1	7	98	2				
HWR Cartwright	29	1921	170*	42.69	4	10	9	0	18	51.00	3-61	-/-
DT Christian	78	3576	131*	30.83	5	16	86	0	158	34.30	5-24	3/-
HNA Conway	11	41	11	5.13	0	0	4	0	24	34.67	5-45	1/-
TLW Cooper	69	4096	203*	34.71	8	23	87	0	9	56.44	1-6	-/-
TA Copeland	62	1325	106	17.91	1	4	56	0	231	27.29	8-92	11/2
NM Coulter-Nile	32	904	64	18.83	0	3	23	0	116	27.59	6-84	2/-
EJM Cowan	97	6886	225	41.48	19	30	58	0	0			
PJ Cummins	6	88	42	22.00	0	0	3	0	23	30.30	4-47	-/-
BCJ Cutting	47	1434	109	22.76	1	6	14	0	158	27.54	6-37	6/-
JD Dalton	10	455	71	22.75	0	3	4	0	0			
TJ Dean	32	1971	154*	35.84	6	7	26	0	0			
BJ Doggett	7	83	43*	9.22	0	0	2	0	28	27.71	5-77	2/-
AJ Doolan	82	4573	247*	32.43	8	23	60	0				
JR Doran	25	1345	114	31.28	1	9	37	1				
BR Dunk	43	2303	190	30.30	4	11	43	0	4	42.25	1-4	-/-
MW Edwards	2	13	8	3.25	0	0	1	0	5	30.60	2-48	-/-
DG Fallins	1	16	10	16.00	0	0	1	0	4	25.50	3-51	-/-
JP Faulkner	50	2034	100*	29.48	1	12	21	0	156	24.71	5-5	4/-
Fawad Ahmed	41	229	21	11.45	0	0	6	0	147	30.61	8-89	8/-
AL Fekete	31	267	30	9.54	0	0	8	0	108	30.31	6-67	4/1
LW Feldman	54	655	52	17.24	0	1	21	0	199	26.07	6-37	7/-
CJ Ferguson	107	7351	213	39.74	17	38	59	0	2	49.50	2-32	-/-
AJ Finch	53	2840	151*	31.21	3	20	48	0	4	48.00	1-0	-/-
JA Freeman	1	0		-	0	0	0	0	1	92.00	1-92	-/-
CJ Gannon	30	258	27	11.73	0	0	16	0	61	27.25	6-53	2/-
PR George	57	148	22	3.79	0	0	10	0	184	31.08	8-84	4/1
RJ Gibson	3	75	65*	18.75	0	1	0	0				
SE Gotch	11	452	98	32.29	0	3	27	5				
DMK Grant	4	23	8*	11.50	0	0	0	0	6	49.83	2-55	-/-
CD Green	3	47	45	15.67	0	0	0	0	12	18.50	5-24	1/-
LCJ Guthrie	3	32	16	6.40	0	0	3	0	8	39.50	4-59	-/-
JC Hancock	5	75	28	8.33	0	0	3	0				
PSP Handscomb	54	3372	215	39.67	9	19	86	4				
SB Harper	9	262	80	17.47	0	1	43	1				
MS Harris	62	3561	158*	32.97	8	13	26	0	0			
JR Hazlewood	37	261	43*	11.35	0	0	11	0	96	24.73	6-50	1/-
TM Head	60	3909	192	36.19	7	24	25	0	31	62.26	3-42	-/-
SD Heazlett	24	1337	129	33.42	2	8	18	0				
CR Hemphrey	22	1260	118	33.16	4	6	15	0	6	66.00	2-56	-/-
MC Henriques	60	3121	265	36.29	7	12	27	0	70	33.51	5-17	1/-
CD Hinchliffe	1	1	1	0.50	0	0	0	0	1	14.00	1-14	-/-
AB Holder	3	48	20*	16.00	0	0	0	0	8	34.00	3-45	-/-
JM Holland	46	580	55	15.68	0	1	12	0	149	32.17	7-82	5/-

Australian Cricket Digest, 2018-19

	M	Runs	HS	Avge	100	50	Ct	St	W	Avg	Best	5/10
DP Hughes	27	1725	124	38.33	3	10	28	0				
JP Inglis	13	694	55	36.53	0	6	47	1				
CP Jewell	3	29	12	4.83	0	0	1	0				
UT Khawaja	52	4048	214	50.60	12	19	25	0	1	68.00	1-21	-/-
HP Kingston	15	195	29	15.00	0	0	5	0	30	38.87	4-61	-/-
M Klinger	117	7565	255	39.61	18	35	117	0	0			
M Labuschagne	33	2050	134	34.75	4	12	29	0	12	55.25	3-85	-/-
NCR Larkin	15	627	130	24.12	1	3	14	0				
JS Lehmann	31	1996	205	36.96	5	8	25	0	2	75.00	1-18	-/-
JS Lenton	3	22	16	7.33	0	0	3	1				
CA Lynn	38	2546	250	42.43	5	11	23	0	0			
NM Lyon	34	519	75	13.66	0	2	9	0	92	38.57	4-63	-/-
ML Kelly	6	100	41	16.67	0	0	4	0	24	22.08	5-60	1/-
SP Mackin	28	81	12	4.50	0	0	16	0	97	28.63	7-81	5/2
NJ Maddinson	62	3492	154	32.94	6	17	45	0	4	57.75	2-10	-/-
MR Marsh	42	1894	141	27.06	2	11	21	0	64	27.30	6-84	1/-
SE Marsh	94	6046	166*	40.04	13	32	98	0	4	52.50	2-20	-/-
GJ Maxwell	39	2656	278	44.27	4	17	34	0	40	42.75	4-42	-/-
BR McDermott	19	794	104	28.36	1	4	14	0				
CJW McInerney	2	82	51	20.50	0	1	4	0				
JM Mennie	55	1358	79*	16.98	0	5	23	0	200	27.82	7-96	4/-
RP Meredith	2	0	0*	-	0	0	0	0	2	68.50	1-25	-/-
SA Milenko	19	839	87	29.96	0	8	9	0	47	30.74	5-15	1/-
DJM Moody	20	100	22	7.14	0	0	10	0	61	37.15	5-59	1/-
AJ Nair	3	64	37	16.00	0	0	2	0	3	69.67	2-71	-/-
MG Neser	30	950	77	23.17	0	6	17	0	90	29.59	6-57	1/-
PM Nevill	71	3870	235*	42.07	9	18	216	17	0			
HJ Nielsen	2	130	105	43.33	1	0	7	0				
SNJ O'Keefe	59	1710	99	26.72	0	8	26	0	188	24.94	8-77	5/2
EK Opie	2	19	15	19.00	0	0	0	0	4	38.75	2-92	-/-
TD Paine	69	3089	215	27.83	1	19	188	5	0			
JS Paris	7	135	31	16.33	0	0	4	0	40	19.20	6-23	2/-
KR Patterson	45	3015	157	40.74	5	20	27	0				
JL Pattinson	24	559	80	20.70	0	2	6	0	93	23.29	6-32	3/-
JJ Peirson	14	595	82*	31.32	0	5	43	1				
LD Pfeffer	5	136	36	15.11	0	0	5	0				
JR Philippe	4	180	74	22.50	0	2	2	0				
WJ Pucovski	4	251	188	50.20	1	0	1	0				
SL Rainbird	40	770	57	16.38	0	1	10	0	120	32.82	6-68	1/-
MT Renshaw	23	1746	170	42.59	6	5	22	0	1	24.00	1-12	-/-
JA Richardson	6	158	71	17.56	0	1	5	0	22	28.41	4-47	-/-
KW Richardson	29	622	49	14.47	0	0	9	0	94	32.49	5-69	1/-
NJ Rimmington	37	649	102*	16.64	1	0	11	0	99	30.78	5-27	3/-
TS Rogers	10	324	80	24.92	0	1	2	0	37	18.35	4-9	-/-
AI Ross	18	868	92*	28.00	0	6	22	0				
GS Sandhu	24	481	97*	18.50	0	2	11	0	49	39.69	5-31	1/-
CJ Sayers	51	834	46	13.03	0	0	12	0	218	23.89	7-46	11/2
DJM Short	9	401	66	23.59	0	2	7	0	16	34.06	3-78	-/-
MW Short	3	55	22	18.33	0	0	2	0	1	135.0	1-73	-/-
PM Siddle	46	872	87	16.45	0	2	14	0	175	24.85	8-54	9/-
JC Silk	37	2235	127	32.39	5	13	25	0	1	61.00	1-4	-/-
KR Smith	17	680	75	21.94	0	4	4	0	0			
SPD Smith	38	3159	177	51.79	10	14	56	0	40	50.92	7-64	1/-
WER Somerville	12	140	26	10.77	0	0	5	0	48	25.29	8-136	4/-
B Stanlake	2	1	1*	-	0	0	0	0	7	21.57	3-50	-/-
MA Starc	24	326	54*	21.73	0	1	14	0	84	25.11	8-73	4/1
MT Steketee	19	291	53	18.19	0	1	5	0	51	32.69	4-33	-/-
CH Stobo	3	24	8*	6.00	0	0	3	0	13	23.69	4-46	-/-
MP Stoinis	42	2273	170	32.94	3	15	17	0	33	49.33	4-82	-/-
MJ Swepson	21	357	35	14.88	0	0	15	0	59	38.27	5-142	1/-

Australian Cricket Digest, 2018-19

	M	Runs	HS	Avge	100	50	Ct	St	W	Avg	Best	5/10
CP Tremain	41	656	111	15.26	1	0	4	0	161	23.16	7-82	4/1
SJ Truloff	9	267	45	19.07	0	0	6	0				
AJ Turner	30	1769	110	36.85	3	7	32	0	10	43.60	6-111	1/-
AJ Tye	9	52	10	5.20	0	0	1	0	27	36.70	3-47	-/-
P Uppal	2	72	24	18.00	0	0	1	0	0			
CT Valente	4	92	43	13.14	0	0	0	0	8	54.38	2-40	-/-
EM Vines	2	84	34	28.00	0	0	2	0				
MS Wade	86	4559	152	41.45	10	27	309	7	4	9.50	3-13	-/-
DA Warner	19	1331	148	42.94	4	5	7	0	1	125.0	1-0	-/-
JB Weatherald	25	1669	152	35.51	3	10	21	0	1	14.00	1-14	-/-
BJ Webster	34	1521	136	27.16	4	6	52	0	32	48.06	3-18	-/-
JW Wells	51	2265	120	24.35	3	8	34	0	1	203.0	1-28	-/-
CL White	126	7003	150*	36.47	10	43	167	0	141	41.08	6-66	2/1
SM Whiteman	44	2102	120	33.90	2	14	139	5				
JD Wildermuth	30	1444	110	29.47	2	7	8	0	79	28.80	5-40	1/-
NP Winter	5	91	25	15.17	0	0	1	0	34	19.71	5-48	4/1
DJ Worrall	33	260	26	9.29	0	0	11	0	129	29.61	6-96	5/-
A Zampa	35	1111	74	21.78	0	6	9	0	100	46.29	6-62	2/1

SHEFFIELD SHIELD CRICKETERS OF THE SEASON

Season		Season	
1975-76	Ian Chappell (SA) & Greg Chappell (Qld)	1997-98	Dene Hills (Tas)
1976-77	Richie Robinson (Vic)	1998-99	Matthew Elliott (Vic)
1977-78	David Ogilvie (Qld)	1999-2000	Darren Lehmann (SA)
1978-79	Peter Sleep (SA)	2000-01	Jamie Cox (Tas)
1979-80	Ian Chappell (SA)	2001-02	Brad Hodge (Vic) & Jimmy Maher (Qld)
1980-81	Greg Chappell (Qld)	2002-03	Clinton Perren (Qld)
1981-82	Kepler Wessels (Qld)	2003-04	Matthew Elliott (Vic)
1982-83	Kim Hughes (WA)	2004-05	Michael Bevan (Tas)
1983-84	Brian Davison (Tas) & John Dyson (NSW)	2005-06	Andy Bichel (Qld)
1984-85	David Boon (Tas)	2006-07	Chris Rogers (WA)
1985-86	Allan Border (Qld)	2007-08	Simon Katich (NSW)
1986-87	Craig McDermott (Qld)	2008-09	Phillip Hughes (NSW)
1987-88	Dirk Tazelaar (Qld) & Mark Waugh (NSW)	2009-10	Chris Hartley (Qld)
1988-89	Tim May (SA)	2010-11	James Hopes (Qld)
1989-90	Mark Waugh (NSW)	2011-12	Jackson Bird (Tas)
1990-91	Stuart Law (Qld)	2012-13	Ricky Ponting (Tas)
1991-92	Tony Dodemaide (Vic)	2013-14	Marcus North (WA)
1992-93	Jamie Siddons (SA)	2014-15	Adam Voges (WA)
1993-94	Matthew Hayden (Qld)	2015-16	Travis Head (SA)
1994-95	Dean Jones (Vic)	2016-17	Chadd Sayers (SA)
1995-96	Matthew Elliott (Vic)	2017-18	Chris Tremain (Vic)
1996-97	Andy Bichel (Qld)		

PLAYER OF THE TOURNAMENT IN DOMESTIC ONE DAY CRICKET

Season		Season	
1998-99	Matthew Hayden (Qld)	2008-09	Shane Harwood (Vic)
1999-2000	Matthew Hayden (Qld)	2009-10	Brad Hodge (Vic)
2000-01	Shaun Young (Tas) & Darren Lehmann (SA)	2010-11	Brad Hodge (Vic)
2001-02	Darren Lehmann (SA)	2011-12	Tom Cooper (SA)
2002-03	Justin Langer (WA)	2012-13	Aaron Finch (Vic)
2003-04	Not awarded	2013-14	Cameron White (Vic)
2004-05	Not awarded	2014-15	Cameron White (Vic)
2005-06	Not awarded	2015-16	Mitchell Starc (NSW)
2006-07	Matthew Elliott (SA)	2016-17	Marnus Labuschagne (Qld)
2007-08	Matthew Elliott (SA)	2017-18	Shaun Marsh (WA)

SOUTH AUSTRALIA TOP THE FUTURES LEAGUE

Table	M	W	L	D	Points
South Australia	6	4	2	-	32.16
Victoria	6	3	3	-	29.30
Queensland	6	3	3	-	28.43
Western Australia	6	3	3	-	28.04
NSW Metro	6	3	2	1	27.20
ACT/NSW Country	6	2	3	1	21.50
Tasmania	6	2	4	-	20.36

Best Batting	M	Inns	NO	Runs	HS	Avge	100s	50s
Peter Forrest (Qld)	6	11	1	759	158	75.90	3	3
Jay Lenton (ACT C/NSW)	6	11	1	538	109	53.80	2	3
Josh Philippe (WA)	5	10	0	462	93	46.20	0	5
Eammon Vines (Vic)	4	7	0	437	178	62.43	2	0
Justin Avendano (ACT C/NSW)	5	10	1	425	205	47.22	1	2
Will Bosisto (WA)	3	6	0	422	200	70.33	2	0
Daniel Solway (NSW M)	5	10	0	416	139	41.60	1	2
Tim David (WA)	5	10	1	411	126	45.66	2	2
Kelvin Smith (SA)	4	8	0	397	138	49.62	2	0
Charlie Hemphrey (Qld)	4	7	1	388	135*	64.66	1	2

Best Bowling	M	Overs	Mdns	Runs	Wkts	Avge	Best	5/10
Luke Robins (SA)	5	152.4	26	529	31	17.06	6-31	2/1
Cameron Green (WA)	3	129.5	50	302	23	13.13	6-41	3/-
Sam Grimwade (Vic)	5	183.1	42	514	20	25.70	4-30	-/-
Nathan McAndrew (ACT/NSW C)	4	126	23	462	19	24.32	5-30	2/-
Xavier Crone (Vic)	6	173.4	41	566	19	29.79	5-47	1/-
Joe Kershaw (ACT/NSW C)	6	111.4	16	435	18	24.16	5-79	1/-
Mac Wright (Tas)	5	102.1	10	445	16	27.81	5-82	1/-
Elliott Opie (SA)	5	159	37	500	16	31.25	3-43	-/-
Kyle Gardiner (WA)	6	145.3	19	501	16	31.31	4-57	-/-

Matches played

Round One – October 16-19, 2017

ACT/NSW Country v New South Wales Metro at Manuka Oval, Canberra – Match Drawn.
ACT/NSW Country 9-461 dec (NCR Larkin 189, JS Lenton 101, AG Harriott 50*) **and 3-244 dec** (NCR Larkin 129*, BD Macdonald 55*) **drew with NSW Metro 9-416 dec** (DL Solway 139, NL Bertus 128*, DJP Mortimer 61; HD Medhurst 5-84) **and 7-242** (DL Solway 90, JA Clarke 55, DJP Mortimer 49; ST Devoy 4-76)

South Australia v Queensland at Adelaide Oval No. 2 – South Australia won by 84 runs.
South Australia 438 (BR Davis 81, NJ Benton 67*, PC Page 54; NJ Rimmington 4-103) **and 3-280 dec** (JL Winter 116*, BP Wakim 64) **def Queensland 306** (PJ Forrest 89) **and 328** (PJ Forrest 78, LD Pfeffer 65*; LJ Robins 5-59)

Western Australia v Tasmania at Lilac Hill, Perth – Western Australia won by 5 wickets.
Tasmania 201 (AB Holder 4-41) **and 257** (JC Hancock 79; LCJ Guthrie 4-35) **lost to Western Australia 348** (WG Bosisto 1-8. JR Philippe 92, TH David 58; JA Freeman 5-98) **and 5-111** (JR Philippe 64)

Round Two – November 6-9, 2017

Queensland v Tasmania at Kerrydale, Robina – Queensland won by 15 runs.
Queensland 332 (LD Pfeffer 117, BCJ Cutting 65; RP Meredith 5-30) **and 6-328 dec** (CR Hemphrey 135*, NA McSweeney 106) **def Tasmania 367** (CA Wakim 104, JR White 77, ND Buchanan 50*; CJ Gannon 5-67) **and 278** (CP Jewell 69, BR Dunk 68, JC Hancock 52)

Victoria v South Australia at Shepley Oval, Melbourne – South Australia won by 6 wickets.
Victoria 8-398 dec (EM Vines 178, TF Rogers 54) **and 9-172 dec** (SE Gotch 70) **lost to South Australia 192** (JL Winter 56; JE Koop 6-40, SEJ Grimwade 4-30) **and 4-380** (KR Smith 137, AI Ross 111*, JL Winter 72,)

Western Australia v ACT/NSW Country at Richardson Park, Perth – Western Australia won by 252 runs.
Western Australia 6-416 dec (WG Bosisto 200, CD Hinchliffe 121) **and 6-309 dec** (TH David 119*, AB Holder 81*) **def ACT/NSW Country 260** (JS Lenton 76, JJ Avendano 73; AB Holder 4-49) **and 213**

Round Three - November 20-23, 2017

NSW Metro v Western Australia at Olympic Park, Blacktown – NSW Metro won by 8 wickets.
Western Australia 188 (JR Philippe 54) **and 281** (TH David 70, JR Philippe 60) **lost to NSW Metro 334** (NL Bertus 99, P Uppal 55) **and 2-138** (JA Clarke 62*)

Australian Cricket Digest, 2018-19

South Australia v ACT/NSW Country at Woodville Oval, Adelaide – South Australia won by 1 wicket.
ACT/NSW Country 198 (JJ Avandano 57) and 7-495 dec (JJ Avendano 205, JS Lenton 96, MR Gilkes 77*) lost to South Australia 303 (JL Barrett 77, AI Ross 53; JT Kershaw 5-79) and 9-391 (KR Smith 138, LJ Robins 54*)

Victoria v Tasmania at Casey Fields, Melbourne – Tasmania won by 3 wickets.
Victoria 9-265 dec (EM Vines 129; AL Fekete 5-57) and 297 (JM Muirhead 52; MB Wright 5-82) lost to Tasmania 353 (BJ Webster 150, SA Milenko 73, CA Wakim 51) and 7-210 (CA Wakim 60)

Round Four - January 22-25, 2018

Queensland v Victoria at Allan Border Field, Brisbane – Victoria won by 150 runs.
Victoria 5-429 dec (TJ Dean 230, BR Thomson 85, EJ Newman 59) and 6-276 dec (WJ Pucovski 57, TJ Dean 53) def Queensland 266 (BE Street 67, AJ Gode 59) and 289 (CR Hemphrey 81, NJ Rimmington 65*; SEJ Grimwade 4-91)

Tasmania v NSW Metro at University Oval, Hobart – NSW Metro won by 58 runs.
NSW Metro 193 (WER Somerville 51; GT Bell 5-35) and 112 def Tasmania 116 and 131

Western Australia v South Australia at Stevens Reserve, Fremantle – Western Australia won by 44 runs.
Western Australia 232 (CD Hinchliffe 87; NP Winter 4-41) and 207 (TD Andrews 4-67) def South Australia 89 (MA Hanna 5-25, AA Bevilaqua 4-17) and 306 (CJW McInerney 80, TD Andrews 62, PC Page 58)

Round Five – February 5-8, 2018

NSW Metro v Queensland at Olympic Park, Blacktown – Queensland won by 37 runs.
Queensland 7-429 dec (PJ Forrest 147*, CR Hamphrey 98, AD Day 86) and 2-152 (BE Street 71) def NSW Metro 145 (CJ Gannon 5-39) and 399 (AJ Adlam 95, NL Bertus 81, SA Abbott 62, DR Sams 52; JS Floros 4-104)

Tasmania v ACT/NSW Country at Lindisfarne Oval, Hobart – Tasmania won by 6 wickets.
ACT/NSW Country 177 (HJ Hunt 82) and 225 (BD Macdonald 86) lost to Tasmania 87 (NJ McAndrew 5-30) and 4-316 (JC Hancock 80, BR Dunk 75, CP Jewell 59)

Victoria v Western Australia at the Junction Oval, Melbourne – Victoria won by 156 runs.
Victoria 9-445 dec (WJ Pucovski 207*) and 191 (WJ Pucovski 65; KJ Gardiner 4-57) def Western Australia 246 (JM Carder 78, JR Philippe 54) and 234 (XA Crone 5-47)

Round Six – February 19-22, 2018

ACT/NSW Country v Victoria at Chisholm No 1, Canberra – ACT/NSW Country won by 10 wickets.
Victoria 172 and 235 (MWG Harvey 67; ST Devoy 4-36) lost to ACT/NSW Country 401 (TP Engelbrecht 80, JS Lenton 77, MR Gilkes 65, NJ Maddinson 51) and 0-7

Queensland v Western Australia at the Gabba, Brisbane – Queensland won by 229 runs.
Queensland 8-291 dec and 9-385 dec (PJ Forrest 158, JS Floros 61; BM Hope 5-54) def Western Australia 310 (TH David 126, SM Whiteman 78; CJ Gannon 6-41) and 137 (SM Whiteman 53; JS Floros 5-46)

South Australia v NSW Metro at Adelaide Oval No 2 – NSW Metro won by 102 runs.
NSW Metro 8-442 (P Uppal 133, RJ Gibson 88, AD Adlam 64, AJ Nair 53; NJ Benton 4-61) and 5-237 dec (DL Solway 93, JR Edwards 80) def South Australia 234 (CJW McInerney 68; HNA Conway 6-30) and 343 (CJW McInerney 72, PC Page 69, LJ Robins 68; SA Abbott 4-65, P Uppal 4-70)

Round Seven – March 5-8, 2018

ACT/NSW Country v Queensland at Chisholm No 1 Oval, Canberra – ACT/NSW Country won by 146 runs.
ACT/NSW Country 306 (JD Cook 56, TP Engelbrecht 51) and 8-383 (JS Lenton 109; X Bartlett 4-59) def Queensland 250 (PJ Forrest 106; NJ McAndrew 5-50) and 293 (PJ Forrest 72, SJ Truloff 71; JD Cook 4-54)

NSW Metro v Victoria at Olympic Park, Blacktown – Victoria won by 5 wickets.
NSW Metro 158 (AC Agar 4-39) and 332 (AJ Nair 95, JAS Gauci 69; JR Coleman 5-84)

Tasmania v South Australia at Kingston Twin Ovals, Hobart – South Australia won by 96 runs.
South Australia 179 (BJ Pengelley 57; AB Perrin 6-29) and 379 (AI Ross 100, CT Valente 68*; CAH Stevenson 6-91) def Tasmania 211 (BR McDermott 70; LJ Robins 6-31) and 251 (BR Dunk 114, CA Wakim 50; LJ Robins 4-57)

UNDER 19 ODI SERIES – PAKISTAN TOO GOOD FOR AUSTRALIA

Match 1 at the Albert Ground, Melbourne on December 27, 2017 – Pakistan won by 6 wickets

Mac Harvey peeled off a brilliant ton, but apart from Aaron Hardie had very little support in the Australian innings. Pakistan comfortably won with 34 balls to spare.

Australia		B	M	4	6	Pakistan		B	M	4	6
R Hackney	b Arshad	5	11	18		Zaid Alam	c Rowe b Neil-Smith	35	29	37	3	2
M Spoors	c Nazir b Arshad	1	7	8		Imran Shah	lbw b Macoun	35	41	68	5	
H Wood	c Nazir b Musa	21	35	74	1	Rohail Nazir +	run out (Spoors)	34	40	66	2	1
MWG Harvey	c Zaryab b Musa	136	130	181	13	3	Ali Zaryab	not out	63	92	123	3	1
WJ Sutherland *	c Alam b Zaryab	4	12	21		Mohammad Taha	c Rowe b Hardie	6	5	8	1	
AM Hardie	c Alam b Arshad	46	48	59	6	1	Saad Khan	not out	53	62	78	6	
P J Rowe +	c Nazir b Shafqat	0	4	4		Hasan Khan *						
BM Hope	c Zaryab b Shafqat	0	1	1		Musa Khan						
L Neil-Smith	lbw b Musa	3	10	20		Shaheen Shah Afridi						
H Macoun	c Nazir b Musa	7	9	16		Suleman Shafqat						
IJ Carlisle	not out	4	8	9	1	Arshad Iqbal						
	4 lb, 4 nb, 6 w	14					2 lb, 3 nb, 12 w	17			
10 overs : 2-44	45. 1 overs , 2 10 mins	241				10 overs : 1-63	44.2 overs , 192 mins	4-243			

Fall: 1-4 (Spoors), 2-9 (Hackney), 3-74 (Wood), 4-96 (Sutherland), 5-190 (Hardie), 6-190 (Rowe), 7-190 (Hope), 8-223 (Neil-Smith), 9-236 (Harvey), 10-241 (Macoun)

Fall: 1-52 (Alam), 2-94 (Shah), 3-134 (Nazir), 4-145 (Taha)

Pakistan - bowling	O	M	R	W	wd	nb	Australia - bowling	O	M	R	W	wd	nb
Shaheen Shah Afridi	8	1	38	0	3		L Neil-Smith	7	1	39	1	2	1
Arshad Iqbal	9	1	53	3	1		IJ Carlisle	7	0	47	0	5	
Hasan Khan	8	0	53	0			H Wood	1	0	12	0		1
Musa Khan	7.1	0	33	4	1	1	WJ Sutherland	7	0	25	0		
Suleman Shafqat	10	2	34	2			H Macoun	8	0	52	1	1	
Ali Zaryab	3	0	26	1	1	3	AM Hardie	4	0	18	1		
							MWG Harvey	1	0	5	0		

Toss: Pakistan Under 19s. Umpires: S Brne, TM Penman, Ref: K Hannam. Award: MWG Harvey (Aus U19)

Match 2 at the Albert Ground, Melbourne on December 29, 2017 – No Result (rain)

Again the top order struggled for Australia, until Aaron Hardie and Patrick Rowe added 87 for the seventh wicket in 13 overs. When the rains came, Pakistan were up with the run rate, but not enough overs had been bowled to declare a result. Despite the washout, a Man of the match was named, Aaron Hardie to recipient.

Australia		B	M	4	6	Pakistan		B	M	4	6
CD Green	b Shaheen	12	37	73		Zaid Alam	c Sutherland b Edwards	28	21	35	5	
M Spoors	c Shafqat b Musa	0	4	9		Imran Shah	b Sutherland	13	39	53		
J R White	run out (Taha)	27	34	46	4	Rohail Nazir +	not out	8	12	25		
MWG Harvey	lbw b Zaryab	22	27	48	3	Ali Zaryab	not out	1	2	7		
O Davies	lbw b Hasan	3	14	18		Saad Khan						
AM Hardie	b Hasan	85	94	105	3	3	Mohammad Taha						
WJ Sutherland *	b Arshad	26	29	44	3	Suleman Shafqat						
P J Rowe +	c Hasan b Arshad	39	41	59	4	Musa Khan						
H Macoun	b Arshad	7	13	17		Shaheen Shah Afridi						
BL Edwards	b Shaheen	1	2	2		Arshad Iqbal						
IJ Carlisle	not out	1	1	2		Hasan Khan *						
	5 lb, 1 nb, 6 w	12					10 w	10			
10 overs : 1-40	49. 1 overs , 2 16 mins	235				10 overs : 1-51	12.2 overs , 61 mins	2-60			

Fall: 1-0 (Spoors), 2-43 (White), 3-55 (Green), 4-61 (Davies), 5-81 (Harvey), 6-144 (Sutherland), 7-221 (Hardie), 8-230 (Rowe), 9-233 (Edwards), 10-235 (Macoun)

Fall: 1-44 (Alam), 2-54 (Shah)

Pakistan - bowling	O	M	R	W	wd	nb
Arshad Iqbal	8.1	1	39	3	1	
Musa Khan	4	1	12	1	1	
Shaheen Shah Afridi	10	0	43	2	1	
Zaid Alam	4	0	14	0		1
Hasan Khan	10	1	49	2		
Ali Zaryab	4	0	15	1		
Suleman Shafqat	7	0	37	0		
Mohammad Taha	2	0	21	0	3	

Australia - bowling	O	M	R	W	wd	nb
IJ Carlisle	5	0	18	0	3	
BL Edwards	6	0	38	1	5	
WJ Sutherland	1.2	0	4	1		

Toss: Pakistan Under 19s. Umpires: TM Penman, D Taylor, Ref: K Hannam. Award: AM Hardie (Aus U19)

Match 3 at the Albert Ground, Melbourne on December 31, 2017 – Pakistan won by 49 runs

Lahore born right-hander Zaid Alam dominated the Pakistan innings before being dismissed in the 43rd over. Ali Zayrab provided a late boost which helped Pakistan past 300. In reply Ryan Hackney and Jack White passed the hundred mark, with White dismissed in the 22nd over. Regular wickets fell after that, including that of Hackney, in the 36th over. By then, the run rate required was over eight and Australia were unable to maintain that rate, to be beaten comfortably.

Pakistan			B	M	4	6
Zaid Alam	run out (Hope)	128	134	166	10	4
Rohail Nazir +	c Edwards b Davies	33	40	65	3	
Ammad Alam	c Hackney b Davies	39	54	44	2	1
Ali Zaryab	run out (Neil-Smith)	56	46	86	3	1
Mohammad Taha	c Wood b Neil-Smith	11	11	11		
Hasan Khan*	c Davies b Edwards	21	11	13	1	1
Saad Khan	not out	12	5	8		1
Shaheen Shah Afridi	c Green b Neil-Smith	0	1	1		
Suleman Shafqat	not out	0	0	1		
Mohammad Ali Khan						
Arshad Iqbal						
	1 lb, 2 nb, 6 w	9				
10 overs : 0-43	50 overs, 209 mins	7-309				

Fall: 1-90 (Nazir), 2-160 (Ammad), 3-239 (Alam, 42.6 ov), 4-258 (Taha), 5-292 (Hasan), 6-301 (Zaryab), 7-301 (Shaheen)

Australia			B	M	4	6
R Hackney	c Ammad b Shafqat	109	110	134	10	2
JR White	lbw b Shafqat	39	63	86	4	
H Wood	b Shafqat	5	8	7		
MWG Harvey	run out (Nazir)	8	13	19		
O Davies	c & b Zaryab	0	1	3		
CD Green	c Saad b Hasan	47	53	62	2	2
BM Hope	run out (Shafqat)	7	21	39		
AM Hardie *	not out	28	16	25	1	1
PJ Rowe +	b Shaheen	1	4	3		
BL Edwards	b Shaheen	0	1	1		
L Neil-Smith	not out	9	10	12		
	5 lb, 2 w	7				
10 overs : 0-48	50 overs, 200 mins	9-260				

Fall: 1-103 (White), 2-115 (Wood), 3-145 (Harvey), 4-147 (Davies), 5-179 (Hackney), 6-216 (Hope), 7-228 (Green), 8-229 (Rowe), 9-229 (Edwards)

Australia - bowling	O	M	R	W	wd	nb
BL Edwards	10	1	63	1	1	1
L Neil-Smith	10	0	75	2	2	
BM Hope	9	0	71	0		1
AM Hardie	1	0	19	0		
O Davies	10	0	40	2		
JR White	10	0	40	0	2	

Pakistan - bowling	O	M	R	W	wd	nb
Arshad Iqbal	8	0	25	0	2	
Mohammad Ali Khan	5	0	30	0		
Shaheen Shah Afridi	7	0	38	2		
Hasan Khan	10	0	59	1		
Ali Zaryab	10	0	50	1		
Suleman Shafqat	10	0	53	3		

Toss: Pakistan Under 19s. Umpires: D Taylor, P Wilson, Ref: K Hannam. Award: Zaid Alam (Pak)

UNDER 19'S - NEW SOUTH WALES METRO WIN TITLE IN TASMANIA

Matches Played (all 50 overs per side) - for full scores go to nationalchamps.com.au (all matches in Hobart unless stated)

Round One on December 4, 2017

NSW Metro 4-269 cc (R Hackney 133*, BJ Holt 55, A Bariol 50*) **tied with Tasmania 9-269 cc** (D Hay 70, JA Freeman 53) at Kingston Twin Ovals

Other matches – Vic Metro v CA XI, ACT/NSW Country v South Australia, Northern Territory v Vic Country and Western Australia v Queensland were all abandoned without a ball being bowled.

Round Two on December 5, 2017

Western Australia 205 (50 overs) (B Hope 75; L Neil-Smith 3-30) **lost to NSW Metro 5-206** (47 overs) (P Uppal 72*, JW Foster 54*) at Queenborough Oval

Vic Country 9-158 cc (B Melville 51; NA McSweeney 3-21, H Macoun 3-37) **lost to Queensland 5-159** (31.2 overs) (A Lovell 73*) and Uni of Hobart Oval

Northern Territory 139 (47.5 overs) (JT Ralston 4-14) **lost to ACT/NSW Country 6-141** (38.3 overs) at Ferguson Park

Cricket Australia XI 195 (47.4 overs) (MW Harvey 78; S Redman 4-34) **lost to Tasmania 4-197** (44.2 overs) (J White 69*, K Oates 62) at Kingston Twin Ovals

South Australia 194 (43.1 overs) (JA Merlo 4-20) **def Vic Metro 9-183 cc** (JA Merlo 62; J Pengelley 3-33) at King George V Oval

Round Three on December 7, 2017

NSW Metro 7-250 cc (R Hackney 98, P Uppal 62; W McGillivray 3-33, L Gandy 3-54) **def Vic Country 244** (49.2 overs) (T Rogers 84, B Melville 54; J Edwards 3-35) at Windsor Park, Launceston

Vic Metro 169 (42 overs) (J Kight 62; R Meppem 3-32) **lost to ACT/NSW Country 4-173** (46 overs) (JJ Sangha 87*) at Invermay Park, Mowbray

Queensland 205 (47.2 overs) (HA Martin 4-36, D Curran 3-25) **lost to Northern Territory 9-208** (49.1 overs) (DR Fry 53; NA McSweeney 3-50) at NTCA No 1, Launceston

Cricket Australia XI 6-246 cc (T Kelly 73, O Davies 57) **tied with Western Australia 9-246 cc** (CD Green 76; DA Burrage 3-45) at York Park, Launceston

Tasmania 129 (38,5 overs) (LAJ Pope 4-23) **lost to South Australia 1-130** (22.5 overs) (HT Dall 60*, BT Capel 57) at NTCA No 2, Launceston

Round Four on December 8, 2017

Vic Country 212 (48.1 overs) (AH France 3-32) **lost to Western Australia 3-215** (49.3 overs) (A Hardie 68, CD Green 56*) at Windsor Park, Launceston

Northern Territory 127 (39 overs) (ST Fanning 67; R McElduff 3-34) **lost to NSW Metro 1-128** (32.1 overs) (P Uppal 61*) at NTCA No 2, Launceston

South Australia 202 (44.5 overs) **lost to Queensland 0-203** (30.1 overs) (MA Bryant 125*, A Lovell 63*) at Invermay Park, Launceston

ACT/NSW Country 9-171 cc (T Engelbrecht 71; DA Burrage 3-24) **def Cricket Australia 142** (30.1 overs) (O Davies 58; T Engelbrecht 5-54, JT Ralston 3-31) at NTCA No 1, Launceston

Vic Metro 8-192 cc (AP Young 78; JA Freeman 4-23) **lost to Tasmania 4-193** (47.1 overs) (K Oates 68, J White 51' MC Edwards 3-39) at York Park, Launceston

Round Five on December 10, 2017

Vic Country 6-196 cc def Vic Metro 9-194 cc at NTCA No 1, Launceston

Tasmania 221 (50 overs) (JA Freeman 87; IJ Carlisle 6-29) **lost to ACT/NSW Country 4-224** (47.1 overs) (JJ Sangha 62) at Windsor Park, Launceston

Northern Territory 9-252 cc (L Hearne 64: A Hardie 6-49) **def Western Australia 9-246 cc** (H McKenzie 100; AA Naqvi 3-36) at Invermay Park, Launceston

South Australia 67 (28.1 overs) (O Davies 4-19) **lost to Cricket Australia 4-68** (12.2 overs) (LAJ Pope 4-13) at NTCA No 2, Launceston

NSW Metro 191 (overs) (J Edwards 51; DM Whyte 4-26) **lost to Queensland 7-194** (39.3 overs) (MA Bryant 78, B Maynard 53) at York Park, Launceston

STANDINGS

POOL A	W	NR/T	L	Pts	NRR	POOL B	W	NR/T	L	Pts	NRR
Queensland	3	1	1	16	+1.22	ACT/NSW C	4	1	-	18	+0.54
NSW Metro	3	1	1	15	+0.21	South Australia	2	1	2	11	-0.66
North Territory	2	1	2	9	-0.57	Tasmania	2	1	2	10	-0.41
Western Australia	1	2	2	7	-0.07	CA XI	1	2	2	9	+0.50
Vic Country	1	1	3	5	-0.47	Vic Metro	-	1	4	1	-0.22

Australian Cricket Digest, 2018-19

Quarter Finals on December 12, 2017

NSW Metro 7-251 cc (P Uppal 71, A Waugh 67; S Redman 3-26) **def Tasmania 111** (32.5 overs) (L Neil-Smith 5-17) at New Town Oval

ACT/NSW Country 8-208 cc (B Nikitaris 76) **lost to Western Australia 5-210** (44.3 overs) (M Spoors 75) at Lindisfarne Oval

Queensland 6-289 cc (L Prince 75, H Wood 63, NA McSweeney 55) **lost to Cricket Australia XI 7-291** (45.4 overs) (MW Harvey 119, DA Burrage 66*, J Hoffman 61) at Bellerive Oval

South Australia 155 (45 overs) (LA Scott 3-14) **def Northern Territory 119** (40 overs) (LAJ Pope 4-16) at Kangaroo Bay Oval

Bottom of Pool A v Bottom of Pool B

Vic Country 9-226 cc (B Melville 75; JA Merlo 4-44, B Parsons 3-41) **lost to Vic Metro 2-232** (45.2 overs) (AN Heldt 111*, EJ Newman 78) at Ferguson Park

Semi Finals on December 13, 2017

NSW Metro 6-288 cc (P Uppal 91, BJ Holt 61, A Bariol 50) **def Western Australia 179** (38.2 overs) (A Hardie 77; A Waugh 5-27) at New Town Oval

South Australia 9-245 cc (C Dudley 51: D O'Shannessy 4-53) **lost to Cricket Australia XI 6-249** (47 overs) (O Davies 77*, P Rowe 56) at Kingston Twin Ovals

Position 5 to 10 Playoffs

ACT/NSW Country 283 (50 overs) (MR Gilkes 83, T Engelbrecht 50; M Connolly 4-54) **def Queensland 252** (45.2 overs) (A Lovell 65, MA Bryant 57; JJ Sangha 3-47) at Queenborough Oval

Vic Metro 172 (49.4 overs) (HA Martin 3-39) **lost to Northern Territory 7-173** (44.2 overs) at King George V Oval

Vic Country 3-288 cc (T Rogers 127*, J Lalor 79) **def Tasmania 180** (48.3 overs) (D Hay 52*; W McGillivray 4-19 (inc Hat-trick), R Lane 3-44) at University of Hobart Oval

Finals Day Playoffs on December 15, 2017

The Final – NSW Metro 6-296 cc (J Edwards 147) **def Cricket Australia XI 176** (37.3 overs) (P Uppal 3-26) at Bellerive Oval

3rd v 4th playoff – Western Australia 3-291 cc (M Spoors 115, H McKenzie 66, A Hardie 60*) **def South Australia 230** (44.4 overs) (E Fletcher 79; B Jackson 3-62) at Kingston Twin Ovals

Other playoff matches

ACT/NSW Country 9-260 cc (C Drummer 111, JJ Sangha 68; W McGillivray 5-48, inc Hat-trick) **lost to Vic Country 6-261** (48 overs) (T Rogers 75, J Mitchell 75) at Queenborough Oval

Tasmania 6-247 cc (L Devlin 84) **lost to Northern Territory 8-251** (42.5 overs) (S Dick 60, DR Fry 52) at New Town Oval

Vic Metro 6-227 cc (EJ Newman 78) **lost to Queensland 8-228** (48.1 overs) (S Bhargave 3-37) at Lindisfarne Oval

Final Positions: 1. NSW Metro, 2. Cricket Australia XI, 3. Western Australia, 4. South Australia, 5. ACT/NSW Country, 6. Queensland, 7. Northern Territory, 8. Vic Country, 9. Tasmania, 10. Vic Metro.

LEADING BATTING	M	Runs	Avge	HS	100s	50s	LEADING BOWLING	M	Wkts	Avge	Best
Tom Rogers (Vic C)	7	410	68.33	127*	1	2	Wilson McGillivray (Vic C)	7	16	12.13	5-48
Ryan Hackney (NSW M)	8	382	63.67	133*	1	1	Lawrence Neil-Smith (NSW M)	8	15	14.87	5-17
Param Uppal (NSW M)	8	370	61.67	91	0	5	Lloyd Pope (SA)	7	15	17.13	4-13
Max Bryant (Qld)	7	342	68.40	125*	1	2	Jonathan Merlo (Vic M)	7	12	14.00	4-20
Jack White (Tas)	8	309	44.14	69	0	2	Aaron Hardie (WA)	7	12	17.08	6-49

RECENT WINNERS

Season	Won by	Player of Tournament	Season	Won by	Player of Tournament
2017-18	NSW M	Param Uppal (NSW M)	2006-07	NSW	Matthew Wade (Vic)
2016-17	WA	Will Pucovski (Vic M)	2005-06	NSW	Usman Khawaja (NSW)
2015-16	NSW M	Clint Hinchliffe (WA)	2004-05	NSW	John Hastings (NSW)
2014-15	NSW M	Luke Bartier (NSW M)	2003-04	NSW	Callum Ferguson (SA)
2013-14	NSW	Billy Stanlake (Qld)	2002-03	Vic	Mark Cosgrove (SA)
2012-13	SA	Travis Head (SA)	2001-02	NSW	Adam Crosthwaite (Vic)
2011-12	Qld	Travis Head (SA)	2000-01	Qld	Beau Casson (WA)
2010-11	Vic	Matt Dixon (WA)	1999-00	Qld-Vic	Liam Buchanan (vic)
2009-10	NSW	Jason Floros (Qld)	1998-99	NSW	Michael Klinger (Vic)
2008-09	NSW	DIE Tormey (Vic)	1997-98	SA	Graham Manou (SA)
2007-08	Vic	Michael Hill (Vic)	1996-97	NSW	DJ McLauchlan (NSW)

UNDER 17'S – NSW METRO GO BACK TO BACK IN QUEENSLAND

Matches Played - all 50 over matches. Round One on September 25, 2017

ACT/NSW Country 8-279 cc (W Fort 70, K Phillips 43) **lost to South Australia 9-280** (49.5 overs) (W Montgomery 88, J Hoffman 53, C Kelly 42; D O'Shannessy 3-28) at Landsborough

Queensland 6-273 cc (M Conder 70, H Burdon 54) **def Northern Territory 99** (38.2 overs) (B Haylett 3-27) at John Blanck Oval

Tasmania 9-170 (L Drury 46; H Manenti 3-22) **lost NSW Metro 4-171** (36.2 overs) O Davies 66*, Y Sharma 48) at Ron McMullen Oval

Australian Cricket Digest, 2018-19

Western Australia 7-282 cc (C Smith 53*, K Prashanth 51, D Burrage 50) **def Vic Country 8-224 cc** (L Field 45, T Jackson 42; C Smith 4-27) at Kerry Emery Oval

Cricket Australia XI 270 (48.1 overs) (J Fraser-McGurk 97, K Brazell 58; W Lovell 6-51, M Watt 3-44) **def Vic Metro 267** (46.1 overs) (K Novacek 58, M Harvey 56; M Pascoe 4-66, M Jenkins 3-47) at Kev Hackney Oval

Round Two on September 26, 2017

Cricket Australia XI 271 (49.5 overs) (K Brazell 85, B Larance 60, Y Pedneker 55; C Kuepper 4-37) **def Tasmania 135** (36.3 overs) (M Jenkins 3-27, K Brazell 3-30) at John Blanck Oval

Northern Territory 179 (46.3 overs) (Z Ahmed 48; K Phillips 4-35) **lost to ACT/NSW Country 5-180** (30.4 overs) (W Fort 70) at Ron McMullen Oval

Vic Metro 5-311 cc (D Brasher 112, N Severin 84, M Harvey 49; J Size 3-65) **def South Australia 151** (33.5 overs) (B Clarke 3-38, M Sellenger 3-5) at Kerry Emery Oval

Western Australia 199 (48.5 overs) (C Smith 55; A Singh 3-28) **lost to NSW Metro 7-201** (45.2 overs) (H Manenti 75, L Scott 48) at Kev Hackney Oval

Queensland 9-255 cc (H Burdon 43; L Fitzsimmons 3-47) **def Vic Country 212** (46.2 overs) (R Hammel 57, L Field 55; B Haylett 3-34) at Landsborough

Round Three on September 28, 2017

Western Australia 7-233 cc (J Goodwin 91*, B Foster 43; M Pascoe 3-21) **lost to Cricket Australia XI 4-237** (39.2 overs) (B Larance 83, J Fraser-McGurk 62, Y Pednekar 53*) at Landsborough Oval

Victoria Metro 9-221 cc (M Harvey 66, J Woinarski 48*; K Phillips 3-30) **lost to ACT/NSW Country 7-223** (47.5 overs) (J Claridge 46, K Phillips 46, J Low-McMahon 43; M Watt 5-41) at John Blanck Oval

Tasmania 9-232 cc (S Lewis-Johnson 83*; W Bowering 3-26) **lost to South Australia 6-235** (46.1 overs) (W Montgomery 93*, T Kelly 41) at Caloundra No 1

Vic Country 9-309 cc (T Jackson 75, T Murphy 63; N Sathyajith 4-35) **def Northern Territory 5-219 cc** (N Sathyajith 47*, A Dave 43; Z Worden 41) at Kev Hackney Oval

NSW Metro 6-235 cc (T Reynolds 63, L Hearne 48, L Scott 42) **def Queensland 185** (45.2 overs) (J Cooper 45, M Clayton 40; L Hearne 4-37, R Singh 3-25) at Kerry Emery Oval

Round Four on September 29, 2017

Western Australia 8-270 cc (K Prashanth 62, C Smith 50) **def Northern Territory 186** (47.4 overs) (N Sathyajith 68; J Pike 3-16) at John Blanck Oval

NSW Metro 243 (47.3 overs) (T Reynolds 103, S Fanning 56; L Field 5-45) **def Vic Country 159** (41.3 overs) (P Rowe 64) at Caloundra No 1

Cricket Australia XI 255 (49.3 overs) (J Fraser-McGurk 71, K Brazell 42; L Hextell 3-49) **def ACT/NSW Country 241** (49.4 overs) (G Winsor 85, B Hardy 59; M Jenkins 3-25) at Kerry Emery Oval

Vic Metro 137 (45 overs) (B Clarke 51*; F Keeling 4-35, S Lewis-Johnson 3-21) **def Tasmania 120** (33.2 overs) (B Clarke 4-40, W Lovell 3-25) at Landsborough Oval

Queensland 212 (45.4 overs) (T Olsen 61, H Walker 41*; W Bowering 4-41) **lost to South Australia 3-214** (46.4 overs) (T Kelly 108*, R King 57*) at Kev Hackney Oval

Round Five on October 1, 2017

Northern Territory 205 (49.2 overs) (Z Ahmed 72; H Manenti 3-18) **lost to NSW 4-165** (42 overs) (T Reynolds 48, O Davies 45*) by DLS Method at Peter Burge Oval

Vic Country 8-226 cc (T Murphy 52, T Jackson 44) **def Vic Metro 9-223 cc** (K Novacek 51) at Trevor Barsby Oval

Western Australia 9-270 cc (D Burrage 115, B Foster 76; T Nicholson 3-35) **lost to Queensland 6-208** (38.1 overs) (H Walker 51 no) by DLS Method at Bill Albury Oval

Tasmania 9-264 cc (L Drury 79, M Owen 47; NG Clarke 3-39, M Harper 3-49) **def ACT/NSW Country 197** (38.3 overs) (W Fort 63; K Applebee 3-2, S Lewis-Johnson 3-0) by DLS Method at Ian Healy Oval

Cricket Australia XI 9-269 cc (K Brazell 90, B Larance 49) **def South Australia 255** (49.1 overs) (J Hoffman 85, R King 47; B Larance 3-56) at Trevor Hohns Oval

STANDINGS

POOL A	W	L	Pts	NRR	POOL B	W	L	Pts	NRR
NSW Metro	5	0	23	+0.9595	Cricket Aust XI	5	0	23	+0.9161
Queensland	3	2	14	+0.6607	South Australia	3	2	12	-0.5348
Western Australia	2	3	10	+0.2407	Vic Metro	2	3	10	+0.6414
Vic Country	2	3	9	-0.3680	ACT/NSW Country	2	3	9	+0.1023
Northern Territory	0	5	0	-1.9212	Tasmania	1	4	5	-0.6644

Australian Cricket Digest, 2018-19

Quarter Finals on October 2, 2017

NSW Metro 233 (46.2 overs) (O Davies 60, S Fanning 48; D O'Shannessy 4-41) **v ACT/NSW Country 4-51** (10 overs) **was rained out** at Ian Healy Oval. *NSW Metro went through to Semis.*

Victoria 7-302 (49 overs) (P Rowe 101, T Murphy 82, R Hammel 70; W Prestwidge 4-53) **v Cricket Australia XI was rained out** at Trevor Hohns Oval. *Cricket Australia XI went through to Semis.*

Queensland 5-280 (41 overs) (W Kettleton 108, M Clayton 48, J Cooper 41; W Lovell 3-48) **v Vic Metro was rained out** at Bill Albury Oval. *Queensland went through to Semis.*

South Australia 207 (49.4 overs) (R King 48, A Sareen 44, W Montgomery 40; J Goodwin 4-36) **tied with Western Australia 5-105** (22 overs) (L Hardy 40, J Goodwin 40) **by DLS Method at Peter Burge Oval.** *South Australia went through to Semis.*

Plate match - Bottom Pool A v Bottom Pool B

Tasmania 9-199 (41.4 overs) (K Applebee 68; W Ryan 3-37) **v Northern Territory was washed out** at Trevor Barsby Oval

Semi Finals on October 4, 2017

South Australia 152 (44 overs) (T Kelly 35) **lost to NSW Metro 6-153** (29.3 overs) (T Reynolds 36) at Marist College Oval

Cricket Australia XI 87 (41 overs) (T Nicholson 6-20) **lost to Queensland 4-90** (12.4 overs) (J Cooper 59*) at Churchie

Plate matches

ACT/NSW Country 9-303 cc (J Claridge 81, W Fort 59, G Winsor 41; J Withers 3-44) **def Northern Territory 158** (29.4 overs) (J Withers 68, J Varatharajan 34; G Winsor 4-30, D O'Shannessy 3-28) at Fred Kratzman Oval

Tasmania 217 (49 overs) (S Lewis-Johnson 56, J Henley 41, L Drury 35; D Billington 3-31, J Pike 3-39) **lost to Western Australia 6-220** (39.2 overs) (J Goodwin 83, L Berry 46*, S Lewis-Johnson 3-38) at Trevor Hohns Oval

Vic Country 9-221 cc (M Davey 75*, P Keogh 48; J Woinarski 4-52, B Aggelis 3-44) **def Vic Metro 175** (42.3 overs) (D Hendawitharana 31) at Trevor Barsby Oval

The Final on October 5, 2017 - NSW Metro 6-272 cc (O Davies 58, L Scott 57, Y Sharma 48) **def Queensland 131** (28.2 overs) at Allan Border Field

3rd v 4th Playoff - South Australia 272 (50 overs) (C Kelly 85, T Kelly 68, R Boschma 41; C Griffiths 6-57) **lost to Cricket Australia XI 3-273** (38.5 overs) (K Brazell 103, J Fraser-McGurk 80) at Marist College Oval

Other Playoffs

ACT/NSW Country 9-247 cc (J Low-McMahon 48, G Winsor 37, H Railz 32) **lost to Western Australia 9-248** (50 overs) (D Burrage 76, J Goodwin 64; B Hardy 5-33) at Churchie

Northern Territory 190 (46 overs) (Z Worden 84; C Stow 3-28, T Murphy 3-28) **lost to Vic Country 3-191** (33.3 overs) (Z Keighran 50, T Murphy 42, P Keogh 36, P Rowe 33*) at Fred Kratzman Oval

Tasmania 122 (42.5 overs) (S Lewis-Johnson 38; B Clarke 4-22) **lost to Vic Metro 8-123** (42.5 overs) (Z Sleeman 36; J Curran 4-23) at Ian Healy Oval

Final Positions: 1. NSW Metro, 2. Queensland, 3. CA XI, 4. South Australia, 5. Western Australia, 6. Vic Country, 7. Vic Metro, 8. ACT/NSW Country, 9. Tasmania, 10. Northern Territory.

Team of the Championships: Kyle Brazell (CA XI), Damien Burrage (WA), Oliver Davies (NSW Metro), Will Fort (ACT/NSW Country), Mackenzie Harvey (VIC Metro), Josh Hoffmann (SA), Thomas Kelly (SA), Liam Marshall (NSW Metro), Todd Murphy (VIC Country), Dominic O'Shannessy (ACT/NSW Country), Patrick Rowe (Vic Country), Ajay Singh (NSW Metro), Matthew Willans (QLD), Glenn Winsor (ACT/NSW Country)

LEADING BATTING	M	Runs	Avge	HS	100s	50s
Kyle Brazell (CA XI)	7	417	59.57	103	1	3
Jayden Goodwin (WA)	8	347	57.83	91*	0	3
Jake Fraser McGurk (CA XI)	8	321	45.86	97	0	4
William Fort (ACT/NSW C)	8	318	39.75	70	0	4
Tom Kelly (SA)	8	313	44.71	108*	1	1

LEADING BOWLING	M	Wkts	Avge	Best
Dominc O'Shannessy (ACT/NSW)	8	16	13.63	4-41
Tom Nicholson (Qld)	8	15	17.80	6-20
Samuel Lewis-Johnson (Tas)	8	13	11.92	3-2
Todd Murphy (Vic C)	8	13	17.62	3-28
Will Bowering (SA)	8	13	22.62	4-41

RECENT WINNERS

Season	Won by	Player of Tournament	Season	Won by	Player of Tournament
2017-18	NSW M	Kyle Brazell (CA XI from SA)	2006-07	SA	James Pattinson (Vic)
2016-17	NSW M	Angus Lovell (Qld)	2005-06	NSW	Michael Hill
2015-16	Qld	Ryan Hackney (NSW Metro)	2004-05	NSW	Jono Wells (Tas)
2014-15	SA	Patrick Page (SA)	2003-04	Vic	Tom Cooper (NSW)
2013-14	SA	Jake Winter (SA)	2002-03	NSW	Drew Porter (WA)
2012-13	Vic	Guy Walker (Vic)	2001-02	NSW	Callum Ferguson (SA)
2011-12	NSW	Kelvin Smith (SA)	2000-01	SA	Cameron Borgas (SA)
2010-11	WA	Tom Rogers (ACT)	1999-00	Vic	PM Boraston (Vic)
2009-10	WA	Harry Allanby (Tas)	1998-99	NSW	Ed Cowan (NSW)
2008-09	NSW	Travis Dean (Vic)	1997-98	Vic	Andrew Kent (Vic)
2007-08	SA	Tom Brinsley (SA)	1996-97	NSW	Luke Williams (SA)

GRADE/DISTRICT/PREMIER LEAGUE CRICKET REVIEW

In Adelaide, Tea Tree Gully were the team of the season, taking out their third first-grade Premiership, as well as the Twenty 20 title. The Gullies have now won a remarkable 11 titles in the various competitions since 2007-08. Port Adelaide won the 50-over final with a tight win over University. The Bradman Medal was won in a tie between Conor McInerney (Woodville) and Kelvin Smith (West Torrens).

In Brisbane, Norths won their first flag since 1986-87 winning on first innings over Sandgate Redcliffe, with Tom Healy Man of the match thanks to his 124 in the first innings. Sandgate Redcliffe won the 50-over Final and Twenty20 Finals. **Alecz Day from Sunshine Coast won the Peter Burge Medal** with Nathan Rimmington (Sandgate-Redcliffe) the runner-up.

In Canberra, Western Creek Molonglo won the Premiership, making 4-430 in reply to Eastlake's 290 in the Grand Final. Western Creek Molonglo won the 50-over Final, with Western District/Uni of Canberra chasing down 196 to win the Twenty Final. There was a tie for the DB Robin Medal with Tom Engelbrecht (Western Districts/Uni of Canberra) and Tim Floros (Tuggeranong Valley) tied on 19 votes

Darwin cricket saw the return of the suspended David Warner and Cameron Bancroft in the newly formed Mens Strike League. The combined Twenty20/50-over series in July, was won by the City Cyclones.

In Perth, Claremont-Nedlands won their first WACA District Cricket flag since 2005-06. They also won the 50-over Final, while the Olly Cooley Medal was won by Dane Ugle from Rockingham-Mandurah, the first Indigenous player to do so.

Paramatta won their first title since 1964-65, when they beat Sydney University in the final at Bankstown Oval. It was their fourth title, having previously been known at Central Cumberland when it won titles in 1964/65, 1932/33 and 1899/1900. Scott Copperfield took 6-69 and won the Benaud Medal as Man of the match.

Sydney University won a high scoring 50-over Final against Paramatta, while Sydney won its second Twenty 20 title, beating Penrith in the Final at the SCG. Western Suburbs leg-spinner Jonathan Cook (53 wickets) won the Bill O'Reilly Medal.

In Tasmanian Premier League Cricket, Clarence won outright by two wickets, in a low scoring final. Caleb Jewell (North Hobart) made 107 in the first innings, in a match where neither side passed 200. **Jewell also tied for the Emerson Rodwell Medal with Harry Allenby (Clarence) who both polled 16 votes.** University won the 50-over final, with South Hobart/Sandy Bay winning the Premier League and Statewide Twenty20 Finals.

Dandenong won the Victorian Premier League title, their first since 2010-11, beating Fitzroy-Doncaster who were going for their third flag in a row. Peter Siddle was the star of the show, taking eight wickets in the match, his only one for the club in the season. Dandenong did the double as they bowled out Carlton for an embarrassing 49 in the "White-ball 50 over final" with Darren Pattinson taking 4-12 from his ten overs. Experienced all-rounder Trent Lawford of Fitzroy-Doncaster won the Jack Ryder Medal.

Due to tight deadlines – Darwin club cricket for 2018 will be held over to Volume Eight.

ADELAIDE GRADE CRICKET
LADDER (13 sides, 12 matches, top four)

	Won Out	Won 1st inns	Drawn	Lost 1st inns	Lost Out	Points	Quotient
Tea Tree Gully	1	7	1	2	1	195	1.4978
Sturt	1	7	2	2	-	185	1.1818
Adelaide University	2	5	1	3	1	170	1.1401
Glenelg	1	6	-	5	-	150	1.1660
Woodville	-	7	1	4	-	145	1.3805
Adelaide	1	5	1	5	-	140	1.1136
East Torrens	2	4	1	3	2	130	1.1213
Kensington	1	5	-	6	-	130	1.0567
Port Adelaide	1	3	1	5	2	115	0.8351
West Torrens	-	4	1	7	-	90	0.9539
Southern District	-	4	-	5	3	80	0.5916
Northern Districts	-	3	1	7	1	65	0.6751
Prospect	-	2	2	8	-	55	0.8169

Leading Batting

	M	Inns	NO	HS	Runs	Avge	100/50
Patrick Page (Tea Tree Gully)	14	18	3	148	894	59.60	2/6
Ben Wakim (Port Adelaide)	13	19	4	150*	755	50.33	3/2
Sam Raphael (Adelaide)	12	12	0	165	747	62.25	2/3
Conor McInerney (Woodville)	12	14	1	150	744	57.23	3/4
Ben Dougall (East Torrens)	10	13	1	178	734	61.17	3/3

Leading Bowling

	M	Overs	Wkts	Avge	Best	5/10
Tom O'Connell (Sturt)	13	255	47	19.43	6-34	2/1
Alex Gregory (Sturt)	14	222.3	33	21.79	5-49	1/-
Nick Patterson (Adelaide)	12	223.4	33	24.24	5-68	1/-
Adam Somerfield (Tea Tree Gully)	14	196.4	32	17.56	6-44	2/-
Ben Turley (Woodville)	12	247	32	25.19	6-55	2/-

AWARDS

Bradman Medal: Co-winners Kelvin Smith (West Torrens) and Conor McInerney (Woodville) with 22 votes, equal third was Patrick Page (Tea Tree Gully) and Sam Raphael (Adelaide) both on 21, tied for fifth were Nick Benton (Port Adelaide) and Tom Andrews (Woodville) on 20.

Grade Cricket Team of the Year - voted by captains and coaches in batting order:
Sam Raphael (Adelaide – captain), Conor McInerney (Woodville), Harry Nielsen (Woodville – keeper), Ben Dougall (East Torrens), Patrick Page (Tea Tree Gully), Tom Plant (Glenelg), Kelvin Smith (West Torrens), Tom Andrews (Woodville), Luke Robins (East Torrens), Tom O'Connell (Sturt), Ben Turley (Woodville), Nick Patterson (Adelaide).

Coach of the Year – Ben Cameron (Sturt).   **Grade Cricket Umpire of the Year** – Craig Thomas.
Grade Cricket Volunteer of the Year – Mick Weatherald (Sturt).   **C W Walker Memorial (First Grade keeper)** – Josh Barrett from Southern Districts

Fred Godson Medal (West End One Day Cup) – Conor McInerney of Woodville
The Darren Lehmann Medal (West End Twenty 20 Cup Player of the series) – Tied between Daniel Drew (West Torrens) and Dilshan de Soysa (Adelaide University)
Jason Gillespie Medal, for Premier Cricket's rising star, won by Tom O'Connell of Sturt
Talbot Smith (Fielding) Trophy was won by Sam Kerber of Adelaide University

WEST END TWENTY 20 FINAL

Sunday February 18, 2018 at Adelaide Oval – Tea Tree Gully won by seven wickets
Adelaide University 3-106 (16 overs) (BP Wakim 61*, SL Kerber 32) **lost to Tea Tree Gully 3-111** (13 overs) (MK Weaver 46)
Rain delayed the start of play, reducing it to 16 overs per side. After being 2-6, Ben Wakim and Sam Kerber added 90 for the third wicket. Further rain came, ending the Uni innings, but with no DLS in the playing conditions, TTG still only needed 107 from 16 overs. Matt Weaver led the early onslaught, facing just 30 balls, whilst hitting 2x6 4x4. Veteran Tim Evans hit the winning runs over long-on, giving Tea Tree Gully their sixth Twenty20 title in 11 seasons.

WEST END ONE DAY CUP FINAL

Sunday February 25, 2018 at University No 1 – Port Adelaide won by 16 runs
Port Adelaide 8-222 (50 overs) (AD Sayers 49, NJ Benton 75; HA Martin 3-34) **defeated Adelaide Unversity 206** (46.4 overs) (P Salt 41, PJ Wilson 55; NJ Benton 3-33)
Port skipper Nick Benton won the Bob Zadow Medal, faced 89 balls, hit 4x6 and 4x as he and Sayers added 104 for the second wicket. With Uni nine down needing 15 off 21 deliveries, Matthew Weeks took a brilliant catch off Benton to win the match.

A Grade Final: Tea Tree Gully v Sturt at Glenelg Oval on March 24 & 25, 2018 – Tea Tree Gully won on first innings.

Sturt	First innings	B	M	4	6
JP Dick	c Holliday b Atkinson	0	2	1	
C Dudley	c B Evans b Hutchinson	4	3	7	1
BR Davis *+	c Somerfield b Atkinson	4	15	21	1
AJ Gregory	c Davey b Somerfield	26	94	138	2
T Kelly	c Holliday b T Evans	17	34	47	2
E Woods	c Davey b Somerfield	7	29	37	
TA Watson	run out (T Evans)	0	0	1	
C Kelly	c Atkinson b Somerfield	5	6	5	1
U van Duyker	c Weaver b Hutchinson	26	71	75	4
T O'Connell	c Davey b Atkinson	12	28	49	2
KC Sinodinos	not out	0	0	3	
	1 nb, 1 w	2			
	46.5 overs	103			

	Second innings	B	M	4	6
2	c Gatting b Hutchinson	21	16	25	3
1	c &b Hutchinson	9	6	5	1
	c Head b Atkinson	9	7	14	1
4	b Hutchinson	21	14	14	2	1
5	c Head b Evans	7	13	20	
6	not out	5	6	11	
7	not out	0	0	0	
	1 lb	1			
	10.2 overs	5-73			

Fall: 1-0 (Dick), 2-4 (Dudley), 3-11 (Davis), 4-36 (Kelly), 5-52 (Woods), 6-52 (Watson), 7-57 (Kelly), 8-80 (Gregory), 9-99 (van Duyker) 10-103 (O'Connell)

Fall: 1-11 (Dudley), 2-39 (Davis), 3-52 (Dick), 4-61 (Kelly), 5-73 (Wood)

TTG - bowling	O	M	R	W	wd	nb
B Atkinson	13.5	6	26	3		
BJ Hutchinson	11	2	33	2		1
TJ Evans	6	3	10	1	1	
AJ Somerfield	10	2	16	3		
TM Head	6	0	18	0		

	O	M	R	W	wd	nb
	5	0	39	1		
	5	0	32	3		
	0.2	0	1	1		

Tea Tree Gully	First innings	B	M	4	6
TJ Evans	c Davis b Kelly	15	43	66	3	
JS Holliday	c Dudley b Sinodinos	0	2	5		
P Page	c van Duyker b Kelly	40	47	46	5	
TM Head	b O'Connell	35	65	76	6	
JS Gatting	c Davis b O'Connell	7	10	16		
TJ Davey +	c Davis b Gregory	76	57	70	7	7
MK Weaver *	c Davis b Gregory	18	69	87	2	
AJ Somerfield	st Davis b O'Connell	33	67	77	5	
BJ Hutchinson	c Watson b O'Connell	19	66	68	1	1
BD Evans	not out	66	83	88	10	2
B Atkinson	c sub b Sinodinos	0	21	36		
	2 b, 4 lb, 1 nb	7				
	88.2 overs	316				

Sturt - bowling	O	M	R	W	w	nb
AJ Gregory	18	6	56	2		
KC Sinodinos	6.2	0	48	2		
T O'Connell	29	6	117	4		1
C Kelly	16	5	49	2		
E Woods	6	3	10	0		
U van Duyker	13	5	30	0		

Fall: 1-4 (Holliday), 2-49 (Page), 3-60 (Evans), 4-73 (Gatting), 5-134 (Head), 6-184 (Davey), 7-220 (Weaver), 8-236 (Somerfield), 9-280 (Hutchinson), 10-316 (Atkinson)

Toss: Sturt   Umpires: C Thomas, L Uthenwoldt   David Hookes Medal: Ben Atkinson (TTG)

TEA TREE GULLY WINS THEIR THIRD FIRST GRADE PREMIERSHIP

ADELAIDE GRADE STATISTICS

Recent First Grade Premierships

1998-99	Adelaide	2008-09	Woodville
1999-2000	Kensington	2009-10	Sturt
2000-01	Prospect	2010-11	Kensington
2001-02	Kensington	2011-12	Woodville
2002-03	Kensington	2012-13	Glenelg
2003-04	Adelaide	2013-14	Port Adelaide
2004-05	Northern Districts	2014-15	Tea Tree Gully
2005-06	Sturt	2015-16	Southern Districts
2006-07	West Torrens	2016-17	West Torrens
2007-08	Woodville	2017-18	Tea Tree Gully

Recent Limited-overs Titles

2006-07	Kensington	2012-13	Tea Tree Gully
2007-08	Sturt	2013-14	Tea Tree Gully
2008-09	Glenelg	2014-15	East Torrens
2009-10	Kensington	2015-16	Glenelg
2010-11	Glenelg	2016-17	West Torrens
2011-12	Tea Tree Gully	2017-18	Port Adelaide

Twenty20 Titles

2004-05	Northern Districts	2011-12	Tea Tree Gully
2005-06	Sturt	2012-13	Tea Tree Gully
2006-07	Kensington	2013-14	Tea Tree Gully
2007-08	Tea Tree Gully	2014-15	Glenelg
2008-09	Port Adelaide	2015-16	Tea Tree Gully
2009-10	Nortern Districts	2016-17	West Torrens
2010-11	Sturt	2017-18	Tea Tree Gully

Recent Bradman Medalists

1996-97	Shane Martin (Glenelg)	2007-08	Luke Williams (Adelaide)
1997-98	Ben Hook (Adelaide)	2008-09	Matthew Weeks (Port Adel)
1998-99	Anthony Heidrich (ND) tied w Adam Polkinghorne (ET)	2009-10	Luke Williams (Adelaide)
1999-2000	John Lee (Kensington)	2010-11	Chadd Sayers (Woodville)
2000-01	Mike Smith (University)	2011-12	Sam Raphael (Adelaide)
2001-02	Tim Haysman (Sturt)	2012-13	Sam Miller (Prospect)
2002-03	Ryan Harris (Northern Dists)	2013-14	Jake Brown (Kensington)
2003-04	Shane Deitz (Southern Dists)	2014-15	Jake Brown (Kensington)
2004-05	Ben Johnson (Adelaide)	2015-16	Simon Roberts (Sturt)
2005-06	Luke Williams (Adelaide)	2016-17	Daniel Drew (West Torrens)
2006-07	Ben Hook (Glenelg)	2017-18	Kelvin Smith (West Torrens) Conor McInerney (Woodville)

Most runs ever in A Grade

	Career	Inns	NO	HS	Runs	Avge	100s
CW Bradbrook	1971-1997	325	24	169	9509	31.59	17
RJ Zadow	1971-1996	326	47	166	9505	34.06	16
MP Faull	1983-2003	278	24	208*	9094	35.80	20
DE Pritchard	1910-1936	249	27	327*	8817	39.71	25
GW Harris	1915-1940	234	24	205*	8744	41.63	27

Most wickets

	Career Span	Wickets	Avge	Best	5 w I
NL Williams	1918-1942	894	18.85	9-22	84
JPF Travers	1890-1922	819	17.11	9-86	74
AT Sincock	1966-1995	762	20.66	9-50	30
G Giffen	1874-1911	744	12.69	10-67	74
GC Clarke	1955-1979	724	16.57	10-21	43

Australian Cricket Digest, 2018-19
CANBERRA GRADE CRICKET
LADDER (8 sides, 7 matches, top four)

	Won Out	Won 1st inns	Drawn	Lost 1st inns	Lost Out	Points	Quotient
Eastlake	1	3	1	2	-	30	1.24
Western Creek Molonglo	1	3	1	2	-	30	0.95
Queanbeyan	1	3	1	2	-	26	1.32
North Canberra-Gungahlin	-	3	2	1	1	26	1.11
Western Dist/Uni of Canberra	1	2	1	2	1	24	0.93
Tuggeranong	-	3	2	2	-	22	1.16
Ginninderra	1	1	1	4	-	18	0.92
ANU	-	-	1	3	3	2	0.62

Leading Batting	M	Inns	NO	HS	Runs	Avge	100/50
John Rogers (WCM)	7	7	2	179*	515	103.00	2/1
Tom Henry (Eastlake)	9	10	1	96	429	47.67	-/4
Mark Bennett (WCM)	9	11	1	167*	392	39.20	1/1
Jono Dean (WCM)	3	3	0	205	390	130.00	2/1
Vele Dukoski (Queanbeyan)	8	9	1	135	386	48.25	2/1

Leading Bowling	M	Overs	Wkts	Avge	Best	5/10
Hayden Page (Eastlake)	9	178	27	16.67	5-24	1/-
Harry Medhurst (WCM)	9	140	22	23.05	5-61	1/-
Tom Engelbrecht (WD/Uni of Canb)	5	124	21	19.10	7-79	1/1
Djali Bloomfield (WD/Uni of Canb)	9	142.5	20	23.05	5-66	1/-
Praveen Mathai (Eastlake)	8	150	20	26.75	4/68	-/-

GRADE FINAL (Douglas Cup) on March 16-18, 2018 at Chisholm No 1 Oval – Western Creek Molonglo won on first innings.
Eastlake 290 (NT Mathai 64, R Bartley 86; H Medhurst 4-63) **lost to Western Creek Molonglo 4-430** (MD Bennett 167, JR Dean 66, SR Taylor 82*) *Match conceded by Eastlake with a day to play. Mark Bennett (216 balls, 17x4) won Greg Irvine Medal for Man of the match. Stumps Day one: Eastlake all out 290.*

McDonald's 50 OVER FINAL (John Gallup Cup Final) at Stirling Oval on Sunday December 17, 2018 - Weston Creek Molonglo won by 4 wickets.
ANU 9-225 (50 overs) (D Leerdam 98, SW Murn 42; H Medhurst 3-57) **lost to Weston Creek Molonglo 6-226** (49.1 overs) (MD Bennett 70, H Medhurst 52*; C Herath 3-30). *On a very hot day, ANU skipper Dan Leerdam (158 balls, 6x4) was struck early in his innings and later collapsed whilst in the field. He had suffered delayed concussion and later recovered.*

KONICA MINOLTA REGIONAL TWENTY 20 FINAL at Manuka Oval on Sunday October 22, 2017 (floodlit) – Western District UC won by 8 wickets.
Weston Creek Molonglo 3-196 (20 overs) (JW Rogers 72, SR Taylor 42, MD Bennett 37; A Ritchard 3-30) **lost to Western District UC 2-197** (17.2 overs) (EJ Bartlett 72, M Condon 65)

AWARDS
DB Robin Medal: Tied between Tom Engelbrecht (Western Districts/Uni of Canberra) and Tim Floros (Tuggeranong Valley) both on 19 votes, there was a three-way tie for third between Queanbeyan's Michael Spaseski while Ethan Bartlett (Western Districts UC) and Shane Devoy (Tuggeranong Valley), on 18 votes
Grade team of the year: Tim Floros (Tuggeranong Valley), Matt Condon (Western Districts UC), John Rogers (Weston Creek Molonglo), Rhys Healy (Ginninderra), Michael Spaseski (Queanbeyan), Ethan Bartlett (Western Districts UC), Mark Bennett (Weston Creek Molonglo), Tom Engelbrecht (Western District-UC), Scott Murn (ANU), Harry Medhurst (Weston Creek Molonglo), Ben Mitchell (ANU), Hayden Page (Eastlake)
Club Championship: Tuggeranong Valley. **Greg Lord Administrator of the Year:** Adelaide Jones (North Canberra-Gungahlin).
Paul Egan Volunteer award: Gary Molineux (Eastlake). **Lord's Taverners Spirit of Cricket Award:** Weston Creek Molonglo

Recent Titles and Awards

Season	First Grade	50 over	Twenty 20	DB Robin Medalist
2017-18	Weston Creek Molonglo	Weston Creek Molonglo	Western District UC	Tied – Tom Engelbrecht (WDUC) & Tim Floros (TV)
2016-17	Tuggeranong Valley	Tuggeranong Valley	West Creek Molonglo	Shane Devoy (TV)
2015-16	Western District UC	Queanbeyan	Queanbeyan	Mark Bennett (WCM)
2014-15	West Creek Molonglo	Western District UC	Nth Canb/Gungaahlin	Blake Dean (WCM)

Australian Cricket Digest, 2018-19
DARWIN CRICKET
MENS STRIKE LEAGUE

Round One – July 1, 2018 (Twenty20 matches)
Northern Tide 95 (19.1 overs) **lost to City Cyclone 5-96** (15.1 overs) (H Hunt 43, J Connelly 4-12)
Southern Storm 142 (19.4 overs) (JS Neill 64) **lost to Desert Blaze 3-143** (15.5 overs) (G Beghin 54, MR Gilkes 51*)
Cameron Bancroft was playing his first game since his ban for ball-tampering in South Africa, made 1 off 3 balls.
Northern Tide 9-101 cc **lost to Southern Storm 4-102** (16 overs) (WG Bosisto 61*)
City Cyclones 5-155 cc (J Doyle 72*, H Hunt 42) **lost to Desert Blaze 4-159** (18.4 overs) (AI Ross 101*, A Summers 3-32)

Round Two – July 8, 2018 (Twenty20 matches)
Desert Blaze 6-163 cc (G Beghin 105 off 55 balls, 13x4 3x6) **def Northern Tide 105** (18 overs) (C Kelly 3-16)
Southern Storms 1-164 cc (WG Bosisto 78*, D Mortimer 45*) **lost to City Cyclones 4-168** (19.5 overs) (H Hunt 82)
Desert Blaze 2-187 cc (CT Bancroft 78, G Beghin 43) **def Southern Storm 143** (184 overs) (C Kelly 3-23)
City Cyclones 8-162 cc (CK Leopard 52, J Dickman 44; H Martin 4-25) **def Northern Tide 8-136 cc** (CA Wakim 45; S Hook 3-29)

Round Three – July 15, 2018 (Twenty20 matches)
Desert Blaze 7-88 cc **lost to Northern Tide 2-94** (14 overs) (JR Doran 55*)
City Cyclones 8-151 cc (JJ Logan 4-24) **lost to Southern Storm 4-155** (overs) (N Burtus 100* off 53 balls, 7x4 7x6; J Doyle 3-16)
Southern Storm 7-162 cc (RJ van der Meulen 40; HA Martin 3-29) **def Northern Tide 4-131 cc** (SP Underhill 44*)
Desert Blaze 9-125 cc (CT Bancroft 55) **lost to City Cyclones 6-130** (191 overs)

Round Four – 50 over matches on July 21, 2018
Northern Tide 9-197 cc (CJ Sabburg 91, A Summers 3-48) **lost to City Cyclones 3-201** (31.2 overs) (JD Dalton 93*, H Hunt 42)
David Warner made 36 off 32 balls in his first game since his ban for his involvement in the ball tampering in South Africa.
Southern Storm 7-290 cc (KR Smith 131, JS Neill 49) **lost to Desert Blaze 4-291** (43.4 overs) (B Abbott 147, CT Bancroft 62)
July 22, 2018
City Cyclones 5-248 cc (DA Warner 93, JD Dalton 42, BD Schmulian 42) **def Desert Blaze 230** (48,1 overs) (G Beghin 84, MM Hammond 42; J Lennox 3-34, L Zanchetta 3-38). *David Warner took his time in his second hit of the weekend, facing 139 balls, hitting 5x4, 2x6.*
Northern Tide 254 (48 overs) (SJ Truloff 114, JR Doran 56; JJ Logan 3-32, M Bacon 3-53) **def Southern Storm 187** (40 overs) (KR Smith 49, BE Baxter 48; T Pinson 3-32, CJ Sabburg 3-39)

Round Five – July 28, 2018 (50 over matches)
City Cyclones 7-282 cc (BD Schmulian 126*, CK Leopard 66, H Hunt 41; BE Baxter 3-67) **def Southern Storm 214** (43 overs) (U van Duyker 51*, KR Smith 48; J Lennox 3-43). *Brad Schmulian faced 107 balls, hit 13x4, 1x6*
Northern Tide 4-325 (overs) (JR Doran 168*, CJ Sabburg 101) **def Desert Blaze 8-323 cc** (B Abbott 133, DC Mullen 64, MM Hammond; HA Martin 3-32, JK Reed 3-61).
Chris Sabburg (121 balls, 11x4, 2x6) and Jake Doran (126 balls, 14x4, 4x6) added 164 for the third wicket. Ben Abbott faced 96 balls, hit 12x4, 10x6

LADDER	W	L	Points
City Cyclones	7	2	28
Desert Blaze	5	4	22
Northern Tide	3	6	16
Southern Storm	3	6	12

The Final – July 29, 2018 (50 overs per side)
City Cyclones 9-261 cc (J Doyle 125; DD Enniss 3-36, C Kelly 3-65) **def Desert Blaze 232** (overs) MR Gilkes 48; J Doyle 4-62)

Leading Batting (notables)	Inns	NO	HS	Runs	Avge	100/50
Jake Doran (Northern Tide)	5	2	168*	312	104.00	1/2
Alex Ross (Desert Blaze)	4	2	101*	184	92.00	1/-
David Warner (City Cyclones)	2	0	93	129	64.50	-/1
Cameron Bancroft (Desert Blaze)	7	0	78	217	31.00	-/3

Leading Bowling	Overs	Wkts	Avge	Best	Econ
Corey Kelly (Desert Blaze)	45.4	17	15.76	3-16	5.87
Hamish Martin (Northern Tide)	45	15	16.67	4-25	5.56
Joel Logan (Southern Storm)	45	14	17.21	4-17	5.36

Due to tight deadlines – Darwin club cricket for 2018 will be held over to Volume Eight. Apologies.

Australian Cricket Digest, 2018-19
QUEENSLAND PREMIER LEAGUE CRICKET
LADDER (12 sides, 11 matches, top four)

	Won Out	Won 1st inn	Drawn	Lost 1st inn	Lost Out	Points	Quotient
Northern Suburbs	-	5	5	1	-	80	1.1203
Sandgate-Redcliffe	-	5	4	2	-	75	1.4328
University of Queensland	-	4	5	2	-	73	1.5348
Toombul	-	3	6	2	-	66	1.0544
Valley	1	3	4	3	-	59.5	1.1566
Western Suburbs	-	4	3	4	-	58	1.0233
Redlands	-	3	4	4	-	56	0.9812
Ipswich/Logan	-	3	4	4	-	56	0.7880
Wynnum/Manly	-	3	4	4	-	56	0.6691
Sunshine Coast	-	3	4	3	1	45	0.8939
Gold Coast	-	3	3	5	-	45	0.7606
South Brisbane	-	1	4	6	-	32	0.9022

Leading Batting

	M	Inns	NO	HS	Runs	Avge	100/50
Lachy Pfeffer (Valley)	10	10	1	158	692	76.89	4/1
Lachlan Thompson (Sandgate-Redcliffe)	13	11	1	113	620	62.00	1/7
Peter Forrest (Uni of Qld)	12	12	4	154	608	76.00	1/5
Tom Rowley (Toombul)	12	11	0	191	544	49.45	3/1
Preston White (Toombul)	12	11	1	155	509	50.90	1/2

Leading Bowling

	M	Overs	Wkts	Avge	Best	5/10
Nathan Rimmington (Sandgate-Redcliffe)	13	267	52	14.79	7-33	6/2
Scott Walter (Uni of Qld)	12	164.4	36	10.33	7-56	4/-
Jack Prestwidge (Norths)	11	120.5	30	12.77	5-24	2/-
Alecz Day (Sunshine Coast)	11	233	28	21.21	6-79	3/-
Chris Knight (Valley)	11	137.2	23	22.70	4-47	-/-

AWARDS
Peter Burge Medal: Alecz Day (Sunshine Coast) 62 points, then Nathan Rimmington (Sandgate-Redcliffe) 60 points, Chris Sabburg (Wests) 48, Scott Walter (Uni of Qld) 47, Andrew Gode (Valley) 45.

Bob Spence (Umpires) Medal: Steve Farley. Ken Mackay Trophy for most improved Under 21: Max Bryant (Gold Coast). Groundsman's award: Jonathon Walker (Sandgate-Redcliffe). Clem Jones Perpetual trophy (Volunteer of the season): Graham Mapri (President of Wynnum-Manly)

Team of the season: Lachy Pfeffer (keeper, Valley), Chris Sabburg (Wests), Tom Rowley (Toombul), Peter Forrest (Uni of Qld), Sam Truloff (Wests), Charlie Hemphrey (Sandgate-Redcliffe), Alecz Day (Sunshine Coast), Lachlan Thompson (Captain, Sandgate-Redcliffe), Andrew Gode (Valley), Jack Prestwidge (Norths), Nathan Rimmington (Sandgate-Redcliffe), Scott Walter (Uni of Qld),

TOM VEIVERS CUP/KFC T20 State Premier League on Sunday January 14, 2018 at Allan Border Field – Sandgate-Redcliffe won by 19 runs.
Sandgate-Redcliffe 177 (19.1 overs) (MR Dolan 41, ZJ Keune 65) **def Western Suburbs 8-158** (20 overs) (CJ Sabburg 36, SJ Truloff 45; JJ Connolly 3-30).

KOOKABURRA/JOHN McKNOULTY ONE DAY CUP FINAL on Sunday February 4, 2018 at Allan Border Field – Sandgate-Redcliffe won by 6 wickets
Western Suburbs 60 (19 overs) (NJ Rimmington 3-27, MJ Swepson 6-11) **lost to Sandgate-Redcliffe 4-63** (16.3 overs)

Australian Cricket Digest, 2018-19

My FootDr First Grade Final – Northern Suburbs v Sandgate-Redcliffe

at Ian Healy Oval on March 17, 18, 24 & 25, 2018 – Northern Suburbs won on first innings

Sandgate-Redcliffe – First innings

Batsman	Dismissal	Runs	B	M	4	6
BE Street	b Prestwidge	0	3	1		
MR Dolan	c Bester b Prestwidge	0	10	12		
MJ Simmers	c Prestwidge b Sully	24	48	60	2	
LA Thompson*	c Healy b Bester	28	49	83	5	
ZJ Keune	b Sully	2	12	16		
LJ Aspin	b McSweeney	118	116	175	18	3
NJ Rimmington	c McPherson b Prestwidge	8	24	38	1	
JJ Connolly	lbw b Gannon	2	6	13		
SP Underhill+	c McPherson b Bester	27	51	60	5	
AJ Mabb	not out	13	43	47	2	
BJ Powell	b Prestwidge	1	8	5		
Extras	2 b, 2 lb, 4 nb, 1 w	9				
Total	61 overs	232				

Sandgate-Redcliffe – Second innings

Batsman	Dismissal	Runs	B	M	4	6
BE Street	c Gannon b Prestwidge	43	113	119	4	
MR Dolan	c Wright b Bester	8	6	7	2	
MJ Simmers	c Sully b McSweeney	103	162	221	8	
LA Thompson	c Healy b McSweeney	55	56	67	4	1
ZJ Keune	c Healy b Prestwidge	10	18	27	2	
LJ Aspin	b Prestwidge	7	8	9	1	
NJ Rimmington	c Dawson b Bester (8)	62	49	63	4	2
JJ Connolly	lbw b McSweeney (7)	0	3	5		
SP Underhill	c Sully b Prestwidge	29	49	73	2	
AJ Mabb	b McSweeney	17	16	17	2	1
BJ Powell	not out	0	1	4		
Extras	10 b, 3 lb, 9 nb	22				
Total	79.1 overs	356				

Fall: 1-0 (Street), 2-5 (Dolan), 3-41 (Simmers), 4-50 (Keune), 5-63 (Thompson), 6-83 (Rimmington), 7-94 (Connolly), 8-171 (Underhill), 9-231 (Aspin), 10-232 (Powell)

Fall: 1-9 (Dolan), 2-103 (Street) 3-204 (Thompson), 4-230 (Keune), 5-240 (Aspin), 6-240 (Simmers), 7-240 (Connolly), 8-330 (Rimmington), 9-355 (Underhill), 10-356 (Mabb)

Norths - bowling

Bowler	O	M	R	W	wd	nb		O	M	R	W	wd	nb
JA Prestwidge	16	3	45	4	1			20	2	88	4		2
CJ Gannon	13	3	54	1									
C Sully	9	1	29	2				7	1	44	0		1
BB Bester	8	0	39	2		4		10	0	68	2		6
M Connolly	10	1	28	0				10	0	50	0		
NA McSweeney	5	1	33	1				32.1	4	93	4		

Norths – First innings

Batsman	Dismissal	Runs	B	M	4	6
T Healy+	lbw b Street	124	287	365	17	1
M Dawson	b Rimmington	24	65	86	4	
NA McSweeney	lbw b Connolly	68	147	217	9	
KS Fleming	lbw b Rimmington	54	125	151	7	
J McPherson*	b Rimmington	18	80	108	2	
JA Prestwidge	b Rimmington	2	12	19		
CJ Gannon	lbw b Mabb	0	8	15		
WG Wright	not out	22	53	69	2	
BB Bester	b Mabb	7	25	37	1	
M Connolly	c Underhill b Rimmington	13	17	22	3	
C Sully	c Underhill b Mabb	0	1	1		
Extras	1 b, 5 lb, 2 nb, 7 w	15				
Total	136.2 overs	347				

Norths – Second innings

Batsman	Dismissal	Runs	B	M	4	6
	b Connolly	58	90	115	6	2
	st Underhill b Connolly	54	126	155	7	
	not out	5	49	53		
	c Mabb b Connolly	0	3	2		
	not out	1	3	11		
Extras	2 lb, 1 w	3				
Total	45 overs	3-121				

Fall: 1-49 (Dawson), 2-214 (McSweeney), 3-230 (Healy), 4-299 (Fleming), 5-302 (McPherson), 6-303 (Prestwidge), 7-307 (Gannon), 8-329 (Bester), 9-346 (Connolly), 10-347 (Sully)

Fall: 1-104 (Healy), 2-118 (Dawson), 3-118 (Fleming)

Sandg-Red - bowling

Bowler	O	M	R	W	wd	nb		O	M	R	W	wd	nb
NJ Rimmington	43.4	7	116	5	7	1		9	1	35	0		
BJ Powell	17	4	62	0		1		7	2	19	0		1
AJ Mabb	26.2	13	23	2				6	4	10	0		
JJ Connolly	33	6	107	1				18	6	35	3		
BE Street	15	8	25	1				5	2	20	0		
MJ Simmers	1	0	8	0									

Toss: Sandgate-Redcliffe.   Umpires: D Taylor, S Farrell.   Andy Bichel Award: Tom Healy (Norths)

Stumps scores: Day 1: Norths (1) 1-88 (T Healy 51, NA McSweeney 11), Day 2: Norths 7-327 (BB Bester 5, WB Wright 17)
Day 3: Sandgate-Redcliffe 7-240 (NJ Rimmington 0, SP Underhill 0)

NORTHS - PREMIERS IN 2017-18 (Courtesy: Queensland Cricket)

QUEENSLAND GRADE STATISTICS

Recent Premierships

1996-97	Valley	2007-08	Western Suburbs
1997-98	Sandgate-Redcliffe	2008-09	Gold Coast
1998-99	Sandgate-Redcliffe	2009-10	Toombul
1999-2000	Sandgate-Redcliffe	2010-11	Wynnum-Manly
2000-01	South Brisbane	2011-12	University of Queensland
2001-02	Sandgate-Redcliffe	2012-13	Toombul
2002-03	Gold Coast	2013-14	Valley
2003-04	Sandgate-Redcliffe	2014-15	University of Queensland
2004-05	Western Suburbs	2015-16	Redlands
2005-06	Sunshine Coast	2016-17	Western Suburbs
2006-07	University of Queensland	2017-18	Northern Suburbs

Recent One-Day Premiers

2006-07	University of Queensland	2012-13	Toombul
2007-08	University of Queensland	2013-14	University of Queensland
2008-09	University of Queensland	2014-15	Wynnum-Manly
2009-10	Gold Coast	2015-16	University of Queensland
2010-11	University of Queensland	2016-17	University of Queensland
2011-12	University of Queensland	2017-18	Sandgate-Redcliffe

Recent Twenty20 Premiers (First title: 2005/06 – University of Queensland)

2006-07	Norths	2012-13	Valley
2007-08	University of Queensland	2013-14	Valley
2008-09	Wynnum-Manly	2014-15	University of Queensland
2009-10	Toombul	2015-16	Sandgate-Redcliffe
2010-11	University of Queensland	2016-17	Sandgate-Redcliffe
2011-12	University of Queensland	2017-18	Sandgate-Redcliffe

Recent Peter Burge Medalists

1996-97	Jeff Pfaff (Gold Coast)	2007-08	Glen Batticciotto (Sand-Red)
1997-98	Paul Argent (South Brisbane)	2008-09	Craig Philipson (Uni of Qld)
1998-99	Mick Miller (Norths)	2009-10	Chris Lynn (Toombul)
1999-2000	Brendan Creevey (Sand-Red)	2010-11	Nick Fitzpatrick (Sunshine Coast)
2000-01	Dale Turner (Souths)	2011-12	Brian May (South Bris)
2001-02	Greg Rowell (Wests)	2012-13	Brad Ipson (Gold Coast)
2002-03	Aaron Nye (Wests)	2013-14	Simon Milenko (Redlands)
2003-04	Nathan Rimmington (Sand-Red)	2014-15	Scott Walter (Uni of Qld)
2004-05	Derek Tate (Toombul)	2015-16	Sam Truloff (Wests)
2005-06	Ben Laughlin (Wynnum-Manly)	2016-17	Michael Philipson (Uni of Qld)
2006-07	Aaron Nye (Wests)	2017-18	Alecz Day (Sunshine Coast)

Australian Cricket Digest, 2018-19
WACA FIRST GRADE CRICKET
LADDER (16 sides, 15 matches, top six)

	Won Out	Won 1st inn	Drawn	Lost 1st inn	Lost Out	Points	Quotient
Claremont-Nedlands	-	11	-	4	-	86	1.7011
Willeton	2	8	-	5	-	86	1.2981
South Perth	2	6	-	7	-	78	1.3180
Perth	-	9	1	5	-	75	1.1814
Melville	-	10	1	3	1	75	1.0810
University	-	8	-	7	-	72	1.0167
Bayswater-Morley	1	7	-	7	-	65	1.1392
Subiaco Floreat	-	8	-	7	-	64	1.0212
Joondalup	-	6	-	7	-	60	1.0526
Rockingham-Mandurah	-	7	-	6	2	58	0.7862
Fremantle	-	8	-	7	-	56	0.9477
Gosnells	-	5	-	10	-	42	0.8286
Mount Lawley	-	6	-	9	-	40	0.8323
Scarborough	-	4	-	11	-	40	0.7027
Wanneroo	-	5	-	10	-	38	0.8275
Midland-Guildford	-	5	-	8	2	34	0.7266

Leading Batting

	M	Inns	NO	HS	Runs	Avge	100/50
Nick Maiolo (Scarborough)	15	18	1	104*	901	53.00	2/7
Jacob Whiteaker (Claremont-Nedlands)	20	20	3	122*	826	48.59	2/4
Nick Hobson (Claremont-Nedlands)	19	18	4	124*	770	55.00	3/3
Luke Jury (Perth)	16	17	2	122	711	47.40	2/5
Viv Paver (University)	18	19	1	119	697	38.72	1/5

Leading Bowling

	M	Overs	Wkts	Avge	Best	5/10
Matthew Hanna (Mt Lawley)	17	244.4	52	15.00	7-44	2/1
Chris Chellew (South Perth)	14	247.2	46	15.00	6-68	2/-
Josh Dallimore (University)	18	261.3	44	18.20	5-13	2/-
Mark Turner (Melville)	17	231.5	41	17.34	4-37	-/-
Haydan Morton (Claremont-Nedlands)	18	213.5	38	16.47	5-38	1/-

AWARDS

Olly Cooley Medal: Dane Ugle of Rockingham Mandurah became the first Indigenous player to win the medal. Runner-up was Darius D'Silva from South Perth.

Team of the Year: Jacob Whiteaker (Claremont-Nedlands), Garrick Morgan (Joondalup), Luke Towers (Melville), Luke Jury (Perth), Nicholas Maiolo (Scarborough), Darius D'Silva (South Perth), Brooke Guest (South Perth), Chris Hansberry (Subiaco Floreat), Chris Chellew (Sputh Perth), Mark Turner (Melville), Matthew Hanna (Willetton), Josh Dallimore (University)

Coach of the Year: James Allenby (Claremont-Nedlands)   Best First Grade Umpire: Trent Steenholdt
Male Spirit of Cricket Award: Claremont-Nedlands. Best Pitch (Ry Abbott) Award: Floreat Park Oval (Subiaco Floreat). Most Improved Pitch Award: Hillcrest Lower.   Club Championship: Willetton

50 OVER FINAL on Sunday March 4, 2018 at the WACA – Claremont-Nedlands won by 7 wickets
Willetton 170 (42.3 overs) (A Hardie 53; HJ Morton 5-38) **lost to Claremont-Nedlands 3-174** (32.2 overs) (N Hobson 83*)
Hobson faced 78 balls, hit 14x4

STATEWIDE TWENTY 20 FINAL on Sunday February 18, 2018 at the WACA (floodlit) – Wanneroo Districts won by 43 runs
Wanneroo Districts 5-186 (20 overs) (M Holden 91, J Johnston 51) **def Country XI 7-143** (20 overs) (C Yeates 44, ML Ardagh 3-20)

Australian Cricket Digest, 2018-19
First Grade Final

Claremont-Nedlands v University at the WACA on March 24-25, 2018 – Claremont-Nedlands won on first innings

University		B	4	6
J O'Brien	c Whiteaker b May	25	82	3
S Stuart	c Whiteaker b Allenby	39	114	7
WG Bosisto *	lbw b Allenby	23	53	4
V Paver	c Hobson b Hope	10	35	1
AC Agar	c Steel b Paris	64	109	7 1
MD Birrell	c Whiteaker b May	18	62	3
JW Mason	c Whiteaker b Paris	10	25	2
R Honeybul +	c Morton b Allenby	5	12	1
B Richards	not out	7	21	
M Drennan	c Turkich b Paris	1	6	
J Dallimore	not out	0	0	
7 lb, 1 w		8		
86.3 overs	9-210 dec			

Claremont-Nedlands		B	4	6
C Steel	c Honeybul b Dallimore	27	50	4
J Whiteaker +	c Mason b Bosisto	65	130	7
B Hope	c & b Bosisto	12	80	
C Brabazon *	b Richards	25	72	3
N Hobson	not out	42	98	9
TH David	not out	38	40	7
DJ Turkich				
J Allenby				
JS Paris				
HJ Morton				
C Simpson				
2 lb, 1 nb		3		
78.1 overs	4-212			

Fall: 1-65 (O'Brien), 2-88 (Stuart), 3-99 (Bosisto), 4-109 (Paver), 5-175 (Birrell), 6-192 (Mason), 7-202 (Agar), 8-202 (Honeybul), 9-210 (Drennan)

Fall: 1-53 (Steel), 2-96 (Hope), 3-109 (Whiteaker), 4-165 (Brabazon)

Clare-Ned - bowling	O	M	R	W	wd	nb
JS Paris	23	7	51	3		
J Allenby	22	6	56	3		1
DJ Turkich	5	2	6	0		
B Hope	9	3	33	1		
TH David	13	6	25	0		
HJ Morton	1	0	6	0		
T May	13	2	26	2		

Uni - bowling	O	M	R	W	wd	nb
J Dallimore	19	6	52	1		1
M Drennan	8.1	1	39	0		
V Paver	2	0	7	0		
B Richards	15	5	31	1		
AC Agar	21	6	41	0		
S Stuart	4	0	17	0		
W Bosisto	9	1	23	2		

Toss: Claremont-Nedlands.   Umpires: N Johnstone, T Rann   Award: Jacob Whiteaker (Claremont-Nedlands)

Stumps Day 1: University 5-175

Recent Premierships

1996-97	South Perth	2007-08	Scarborough
1997-98	Scarborough	2008-09	Scarborough
1998-99	Bayswater-Morley	2009-10	Scarborough
1999-2000	Scarborough	2010-11	Subiaco-Floreat
2000-01	Subiaco-Floreat	2011-12	Wanneroo
2001-02	Subiaco-Floreat	2012-13	Joondalup
2002-03	Subiaco-Floreat	2013-14	Wanneroo
2003-04	Melville	2014-15	Joondalup
2004-05	Melville	2015-16	Rockingham-Mandurah
2005-06	Claremont-Nedlands	2016-17	Subiaco-Floreat
2006-07	Scarborough	2017-18	Claremont-Nedlands

Recent One-day League Premierships

2010-11	Subiaco-Floreat	2014-15	Joondalup
2011-12	Melville	2015-16	Claremont-Nedlands
2012-13	Melville	2016-17	Claremont-Nedlands
2013-14	Subiaco-Floreat	2017-18	Claremont-Nedlands

Statewide Twenty20 Titles (First played in 2005/06 – won by Willeton)

2006-07	Willeton	2012-13	Melville
2007-08	Fremantle	2013-14	Melville
2008-09	Melville	2014-15	Claremont-Nedlands
2009-10	Rockingham-Mandurah	2015-16	Joondalup
2010-11	Melville	2016-17	Fremantle
2011-12	Scarborough	2017-18	Wanneroo Districts

Recent Cooley Medalists

1996-97	MP Atkinson (Perth)	2007-08	Wes Robinson (Claremont-Nedlands)
1997-98	T Canning (Fremantle)	2008-09	G Dixon (Wanneroo)
1998-99	Kade Harvey (Scarborough)	2009-10	P Davis (Mt Lawley)
	Darren Wates (Sth Perth)		M Johnston (Willeton)
1999-2000	Kade Harvey (Scarborough)	2010-11	David Bandy (Subiaco-Floreat)
			Matt Johnston (Willeton)
2000-01	Peter Worthington	2011-12	T Hopes (Scarborough)
	(Midland-Guildford)		

2001-02	Adam Voges (Melville)	2012-13	Craig Simmons (Rock-Mand)
2002-03	CG Mason (Baysw-Morley)	2013-14	Tim Armstrong (Fremantle)
		2014-15	Justin Coetzee (Scarborough)
2003-04	Jim Allenby (Claremont-Nedlands)	2015-16	Stewart Walters (Midland-Guildford)
	David Bandy (Scarborough)		
2004-05	PM Kennan (Perth)		Brendon Diamanti (Rock-Mandurah)
2005-06	S Howman (Subiaco-Floreat)	2016-17	Tim David (Claremont-Nedlands)
2006-07	Stewart Walters (Mid-Guildford)	2017-18	Dane Ugle (Rockingham-Mandurah)

SYDNEY GRADE CRICKET
LADDER (20 sides, 15 matches, top six)

The Belvidere Cup	Won Out	Won 1st inns	Drawn	Lost 1st inn	Lost Out	Points	Quotient
Campbelltown- Camden	-	9	4	2	-	58	1.4008
Paramatta	-	9	2	4	-	58	1.3485
Sydney University	-	9	2	4	-	57	1.5101
Sutherland	-	9	1	5	-	55	1.0277
Gordon	-	8	3	4	-	52	1.1770
Sydney	-	8	3	4	-	52	1.1657
Bankstown	-	8	2	5	-	52	1.0182
Manly-Warringah	-	8	1	6	-	51	13342
Randwick-Petersham	-	8	2	5	-	51	0.9958
St George	-	8	1	6	-	49	1.0124
Eastern Suburbs	-	7	2	6	-	44	1.0792
Western Suburbs	-	7	1	7	-	43	1.0514
Penrith	-	6	2	7	-	38	0.9611
Hawkesbury	-	6	1	8	-	38	0.9089
Fairfield-Liverpool	-	5	-	10	-	30	0.8451
Northern District	-	4	3	8	-	27	0.7924
Mosman	-	4	2	9	-	26	0.9567
Uni of NSW	-	3	4	8	-	22	0.7616
North Sydney	-	2	3	10	-	15	0.6806
Blacktown	-	2	1	12	-	13	0.5451

Leading Batting	M	Inns	NO	HS	Runs	Avge	100/50
Nick Larkin (Syd Uni)	11	11	1	246	1033	103.30	5/2
Josh Clarke (Hawkesbury)	15	15	1	188*	894	63.86	3/4
Daniel Solway (Bankstown)	15	15	3	177	880	73.33	4/2
Jake Fawcett (Blacktown)	15	19	1	116	877	48.72	2/7
Jamie Brown (Sutherland)	16	17	1	126	852	53.25	4/3

Leading Bowling	M	Overs	Wkts	Avge	Best	5/10
Jonathan Cook (Western Suburbs)	15	304.5	53	15.62	6-90	5/-
Ben Manenti (Sydney)	17	407	45	25.82	5-25	3/-
Jarrad Burke (Camp-Camden)	17	371.5	44	21.11	6-16	1/-
Tim Ley (Sydney Uni)	17	267	43	19.21	6-18	1/-
Nic Bills (Sydney)	17	284.1	38	26.82	6-37	2/-

50 OVER FINAL, Sunday March 4, 2018 at Old Kings Oval – Sydney University won by 5 runs
Sydney University 7-277 (50 overs) (D Mortimer 71, TP Cummins 121*; J White 4-58) **def Paramatta 8-272** (50 overs) (N Bertus 68, B Cherry 75; T Ley 3-48). *Man of the Match (Michael Bevan Medal): Tim Cummins (100 balls, 7x4 2x6)*

TWENTY 20 FINAL, Sunday December 17, 2017 (floodlit) at the SCG – Sydney won by 36 runs
Sydney 7-158 (20 overs) (DM Rawlins 57, BR McClintock 41) **def Penrith 122** (19.1 overs)
Man of the match: Delray Rawlins (42 balls, 4x4, 4x6 1-26 off 4 overs)

AWARDS

Bill O'Reilly Medal: Won by Jonathan Cook of Western Suburbs. The leg-spinner was the clubs first winner for 45 seasons, polling 19 votes, with Nick Stapledon (St George) runner-up on 17. Veteran allrounder and Campbelltown-Camden captain Jarrad Burke finished in outright third on 16.

The Kingsgrove Sports Merit XII: Jonathon Cook (Captain, Western Suburbs), Daniel Solway (Bankstown), Josh Clarke (Hawkesbury), Scott Rodgie (Mosman), Jamie Brown (Sutherland), Nick Selman (UNSW), Jake Fawcett (Blacktown), Beau McClintock, Blacktown, keeper), Jarrad Burke (Campbelltown-Camden), Ben Manenti (Sydney), Tim Ley (Sydney Uni), Nick Stapledon (St George)

Club Championship: Northern District. Spirit of cricket: Northern District.

Coach (Bob Simpson award) of the Year: Jason Coleman (Parramatta), Ground of the year: Joe McAleer Reserve (Blacktown)

Australian Cricket Digest, 2018-19
First Grade Grand Final
Parramatta v Sydney University at Bankstown Oval on March 31 - April 1, 2018
Parramatta won on first innings

Parramatta	First innings	B	M	4	6		Syd Uni - bowling	O	M	R	W	w	nb
WJ Affleck	c Cummins b Kerr	20	66	89	2		T Ley	27	5	66	0		4
T Ward	b Neil-Smith	1	15	19			L Neil-Smith	27	10	49	4		
N Bertus *+	c Cummins b Kerr	85	222	361	6		B Joy	31	7	88	2		6
B Cherry	c Cummins b Neil-Smith	25	42	48	3		LS Robertson	10	2	22	0		2
SA Abbott	c Malone b Cowan	62	77	94	6	2	H Kerr	17	3	57	3	2	
B Abbott	c Mortimer b Kerr	9	40	49	2		D Malone	19	3	44	0		
L Dempsey	c Cummins b Joy	25	41	48	4		EJM Cowan	1	0	3	1		
A Turrell	c Robertson b Neil-Smith	55	153	213	7								
S Copperfield	c Trevor-Jones b Neil-Smith	15	97	117	1		Fall: 1-3 (Ward), 2-36 (Affleck), 3-68 (Cherry), 4-160						
J White	c Cummins b Neil-Smith	15	48	54	2		(S Abbott), 5-186 (B Abbott), 6-226 (Dempsey)						
B Martin	not out	3	2	7			7-252 (Bertus), 8-301 (Copperfield), 9-323 (Turrell),						
	5 lb, 12 nb, 2 w	19					10-334 (White)						
	132 overs	334											

Syd Uni	First innings	B	M	4	6		Parramatta - bowling	O	M	R	W	w	nb
NCR Larkin *	c Cherry b Martin	6	32				SA Abbott	20	4	47	3	1	
B Trevor-Jones	c B Abbott b Copperfield	7	39				B Martin	19	7	50	1		
D Mortimer	c B Abbott b Copperfield	14	43	1			S Copperfield	22.1	5	69	6	5	1
LS Robertson	b S Abbott	31	59	5			J White	20	5	47	0		
EJM Cowan	lbw b S Abbott	35	37	5									
H Kerr	c Bertus b Copperfield	39	40	4	2		Fall: 1-9 (Larkin), 2-23 (Trevor-Jones), 3-30 (Mortimer)						
TP Cummins +	c Bertus b Copperfield	11	19	2			4-86 (Cowan), 5-105 (Robertson), 6-137 (Cummins),						
T Ley	c Bertus b Copperfield	38	82	6			7-153 (Kerr), 8-203 (Ley), 9-214 (Joy),						
L Neil-Smith	b Copperfield	21	110	3			10-216 (Neil-Smith)						
B Joy	b S Abbott	4	20										
D Malone	not out	0	7										
	3 lb, 1 nb, 6 w	10											
	81.1 overs	216											

Toss: Parramatta   Umpires: GA Abood, GJ Davidson   Benaud Medal: Scott Copperfield (Paramatta)

Stumps Day 1: Parramatta 7-268   Day 2: Syd Uni 7-167 (T Ley 15, L Neil-Smith 4)

Recent Premierships

1996-97	St George		2007-08	St George
1997-98	Sutherland		2008-09	St George
1998-99	Balmain		2009-10	St George
1999-2000	Bankstown-Canterbury		2010-11	Sydney University
2000-01	St George		2011-12	Sydney University
2001-02	Fairfield-Liverpool		2012-13	St George
2002-03	Sydney University		2013-14	Sydney University
2003-04	Eastern Suburbs		2014-15	Manly-Warringah
2004-05	Sydney University		2015-16	Bankstown
2005-06	Fairfield-Liverpool		2016-17	Sydney University
2006-07	Bankstown		2017-18	Paramatta

Recent One-day Titles

2006-07	Bankstown		2012-13	North Sydney
2007-08	Northern District		2013-14	Northern District
	and Eastern Suburbs (joint)			
2008-09	Mosman		2014-15	Bankstown
2009-10	Sutherland		2015-16	Bankstown
2010-11	Sydney University		2016-17	Penrith
2011-12	Randwick Petersham		2017-18	Sydney University

Australian Cricket Digest, 2018-19

Twenty20 Cup Winners

2008-09	Northern District	2013-14	Randwick Petersham
2009-10	Manly-Warringah	2014-15	St George
2010-11	Sydney	2015-16	Randwick Petersham
2011-12	Randwick Petersham	2016-17	Northern District
2012-13	Fairfield-Liverpool	2017-18	Sydney

Recent Bill O'Reilly Medalists

1996-97	Gavin Robertson (Balmain)	2007-08	Anthony Clark (Fairf-Liverpool)
1997-98	Grant Lambert (Fairf-Liverpool)	2008-09	Jonathan Moss (Sydney)
1998-99	Scott Thompson (Banks-Cant)	2009-10	Greg Mail (Syd U) & Trent Copeland (St G)
1999-2000	Ian Salisbury (Uni of NSW)	2010-11	Dominic Thornely (Sydney)
2000-01	Robert Aitken (Parramatta)	2011-12	Greg Mail (Sydney Uni)
2001-02	Richard Chee Quee (Rand-Peter)	2012-13	Harry Evans (Gordon)
2002-03	Grant Lambert (Fairf-Liverpool)	2013-14	Patrick Jackson (Penrith)
2003-04	Trent Johnston (Mosman)	2014-15	Ahillen Beadle (Manly-Warringah)
2004-05	Jarrad Burke (Campb-Camden)	2015-16	Charlie Stobo (Gordon)
2005-06	Ian Moran (Sydney Univ)	2016-17	Mason Crane & Elliot Richtor (both Gordon)
2006-07	Grant Lambert (Fairf-Liverpool)	2017-18	Jonathan Cook (Western Suburbs)

Most runs ever in Competition

	Clubs	Career	Inns	NO	HS	Runs	Avge	100s
GJ Mail	Parramatta, Hawkesbury, Balmain, Sydney Uni	1995-2017	382	54	214*	15230	46.43	44
GJ Hayne	UTS-Balmain, Gordon	1987-2007	365	30	161	12354	36.87	26
W Bardsley	Glebe, Western Suburbs	1898-1933	291	49	217*	12116	50.06	36
R Chee Quee	Randwick, Randwick-Petersham	1987-2006	346	24	182	11886	36.91	20
RJ Bower	Bankstown-Canterbury, Penrith, Balmain	1977-1998	322	40	200	11841	41.98	24

Most wickets

	Clubs	Career Span	Wickets	Avge	Best	5 w I
HC Chilvers	Northern District	1925-52	1153	15.99	9/46	105
KC Gulliver	Mosman	1930-63	1029	18.26	8/92	70
WJ O'Reilly	North Sydney, St George	1926-1949	962	9.44	9/27	104
OP Asher	Sydney, Paddington	1910-1933	861	17.30	9/46	65
AA Mailey	Redfern, Balmain, Middle Harbour, Manly, Waverley	1906-1935	828	18.84	9/53	79

TASMANIA PREMIER LEAGUE CRICKET

LADDER (8 sides, 19 matches, top four)

	Won Out	Won 1st inns	Drawn	Tied	Lost 1st inns	Lost Out	Pts	Quot
Clarence	1	11	2	-	5	-	72	1.63
North Hobart	1	8	3	1	6	-	60	1.09
South Hobart/Sandy Bay	-	10	4	-	5	-	56	1.72
Lindisfarne	-	8	4	1	6	-	53	1.13
University of Tasmania	-	8	2	-	9	-	46	0.90
Kingborough	-	7	3	-	9	-	37	0.79
New Town	-	5	3	-	11	-	29	0.75
Glenorchy	-	4	3	-	10	2	23	0.59

Leading Batting

	M	Inns	NO	HS	Runs	Avge	100/50
Caleb Jewell (North Hobart)	19	21	2	119	935	49.21	3/5
Ben Rohrer (Clarence)	11	12	2	103	759	75.90	2/6
Harry Allanby (Clarence)	21	23	2	142	739	35.19	2/1
Sean Willis (South Hob/Sandy)	20	17	5	125	709	59.08	3/1
Nathan Freitag (Kingborough)	15	17	2	223*	591	39.40	1/2

Australian Cricket Digest, 2018-19

Leading Bowling	M	Overs	Wkts	Avge	Best	5/10
Cameron Stevenson (Clarence)	20	233	49	17.06	5-31	4/-
Alex Pyecroft (North Hobart)	18	224.2	45	15.07	6-17	3/1
Hamish Kingston (SH/SB)	19	179.3	38	13.45	5-55	2/-
Tim Spotswood (Glenorchy)	16	155.3	36	16.81	6-22	1/1
Andrew Perrin (Uni of Tas)	18	142.1	35	15.66	4-22	-/-

KOOKABURRA CUP - 50 OVER FINAL, Monday February 12, 2018 at Kangaroo Bay Oval – University of Tasmania won by 8 wickets.
Clarence 157 (44.3 overs) (J Dinnie 42; JJ Logan 3-25, J Laraman 5-37) **lost to University of Tasmania 2-158** (34.3 overs) (J Laraman 67, RJG Lockyear 72*)
Man of the match: Jack Laraman (118 balls, 7x4), he and Rhett Lockyear (80 balls, 9x4) added 138 for the second wicket

PREMIER LEAGUE TWENTY 20 FINAL, Friday December 22, 2017 (floodlit) at Bellerive Oval – South Hobart/Sandy Bay won by 37 runs.
South Hobart/Sandy Bay 8-134 (20 overs) (AJ Doolan 48) **def Kingborough 97** (19.4 overs) (HP Kingston 4-18, SA Milenko 4-19). *Award: Simon Milenko (20 off 14 balls, 2x6) hit Alex Vincent out of the ground. Highlights are available on youtube.*

STATEWIDE TWENTY 20 FINAL on Sunday March 11, 2018 at NTCA No 2 Ground, Launceston – South Hobart/Sandy Bay won by 70 runs.
South Hobart/Sandy Bay 3-209 (20 overs) (M Clark 36, BR Dunk 68, S Willis 59*) **def Longford 9-139** (20 overs) (D Blair 33, JD Arnol 38; D Hughes-Churchett 3-20). *Man of the match (Danny Buckingham Medal): Ben Dunk (34 balls, 6x4, 2x6), Sean Willis faced 38 balls, hit 5x4 2x4*

AWARDS: Emerson Rodwell Medal had dual winners, Harry Allanby (Clarence) and Caleb Jewell (North Hobart) both on 16 votes.
Team of the Year: Harry Allanby (Captain, Clarence), Caleb Jewell (North Hobart), Sean Willis (South Hobart/Sandy Bay), Ben Rohrer (Clarence), Nathan Freitag (Kingborough), Clive Rose (Kingborough), Mac Wright (Lindisfarne), Hamish Kingston (South Hobart/Sandy Bay), Alex Pyecroft (North Hobart), Andrew Perrin (Uni of Tasmania). Coach – Daniel Salpietro (Clarence)
Umpires: Muhammad Qureshi & Jamie Mitchell.
Wicket Keeping Award: Michael Jones (Clarence).   Curator of the year: Steven Thompson (Kangaroo Bay Oval)

Premier League Grand Final
Clarence v North Hobart at Bellerive Oval on March 23-25, 2018 – Clarence won by 2 wickets

North Hobart	First innings		B	M	4	6	Second innings		B	M	4	6
CP Jewell	c Irvine b Stevenson	107	210	271	13	1	st Jones b Salpietro	27	32	50	3	
LD Williams	b Stevenson	6	23	36			c Absolom b Stevenson	7	5	10	1	
J White	b Salpietro	6	44	60	1		c Rohrer b Allanby	53	59	78	7	1
A Pyecroft *	c Absolom b Stevenson	0	10	11			c Jones b Stevenson	1	2			
CJ Murfet	lbw b Stevenson	10	16	20	1		c Jones b Salpietro	1	4	4		
KG Scrimegour	lbw b Allanby	30	49	67	4	1	not out	16	82	106	1	
CJ Boyce	c Allanby b Seymour	0	7	6			c Jones b Salpietro	11	20	14	1	
L Drury +	c Rohrer b Seymour	0	1	1			c Irvine b Salpietro	0	2	1		
R Macmillan	c Rohrer b Seymour	21	25	35	3		c Seymour b Stevenson	5	25	31	1	
S Lewis-Johnson	not out	9	25	37	1		c Jones b Salpietro	1	6	10		
B Fraser	c Rohrer b Stevenson	1	13	12			c Absolom b Salpietro	11	13	17	2	
	3 lb, 2 w	5					7 b, 1 nb	8				
	70.3 overs	195					41.3 overs	141				

Fall: 1-19 (Williams), 2-40 (White), 3-45 (Pyecroft), 4-63 (Murfet), 5-115 (Scrimegour), 6-116 (Boyce), 7-116 (Drury), 8-154 (Macmillan), 9-190 (Jewell), 10-195 (Fraser)

Fall: 1-19 (Williams), 2-68 (Jewell), 3-69 (Pyecroft), 4-74 (Murfet), 5-102 (White), 6-115 (Boyce), 7-115 (Drury), 8-128 (Macmillan), 9-129 (Lewis-Johnson), 10-141 (Fraser)

Clarence - bowling	O	M	R	W	wd	nb	O	M	R	W	wd	nb
CA Stevenson	22.3	5	91	5	2		14	1	71	3	1	
D Meredith	14	5	27	0			4	0	18	0		
DR Salpietro	9	8	25	1			16.3	6	32	6		
HJ Allanby	6	1	20	1			6	2	7	1		
F Seymour	6	0	29	3			1	0	6	0		

Australian Cricket Digest, 2018-19

Clarence

Batsman	First innings	B	M	4	6	Second innings	B	M	4	6
HJ Allanby *	c &b Pyecroft	33	44	56	5	lbw b Pyecroft	38	53	68	5
J Dinnie	c Lewis-Johnson b Pyecroft	2	6	7		c Drury b Fraser	6	21	25	
L Devlin	c Scrigemour b Pyecroft	3	6	7		c Macmillan b Pyecroft	2	18	19	
M Jones +	c Jewell b Pyecroft	6	19	23	1	c Boyce b Fraser	38	104	114	2
BJ Rohrer	c White b Fraser	50	93	117	4	st Drury b Boyce	34	40	47	3	2
DR Salpietro	b Murfet	28	73	85	3	not out	26	51	77	2
W Irvine	c Drury b Pyecroft	23	60	79	2	lbw b Pyecroft	4	4	5	1
N Absolom	c Drury b Boyce	2	25	40	2	b Pyecroft	1	18	15	
CA Stevenson	lbw b Pyecroft	0	6			b Pyecroft	0	1	4	
F Seymour	not out	5	11	20		not out	4	2	4	
D Meredith	lbw b Boyce	0	2	3						
	1 b, 7 lb, 4 nb, 1 w	13				4 b, 4 lb, 1 nb	9			
	56.5 overs	175				51.5 overs	8-162			

Fall: 1-9 (Dinnie), 2-21 (Devlin), 3-44 (Jones), 4-53 (Allanby), 5-121 (Salpietro), 6-129 (Rohrer), 7-160 (Absolom), 8-161 (Stevenson), 9-174 (Irvine), 10-175 (Meredith)

Fall: 1-29 (Dinnie), 2-42 (Devlin), 3-57 (Allanby), 4-107 (Rohrer), 5-141 (Jones), 6-149 (Irvine), 7-153 (Absolom), 8-155 (Stevenson)

North Hobart - bowling	O	M	R	W	wd	nb	O	M	R	W	wd	nb
B Fraser	12	2	57	1		2	7	0	35	2		1
A Pyecroft	22	6	42	6			20.5	3	55	5		
CJ Murfet	9	1	22	1	1	2	3	0	16	0		
KG Scrimegour	2	0	12	0								
CJ Boyce	11.5	2	34	2			17	3	39	1		
R Macmillan							4	2	9	0		

Toss: Clarence. Umpires: M Graham-Smith, D Close   Roger Woolley Medalist – Daniel Salpietro (Clarence)

Stumps scores - Day 1: Clarence 4-84 (BJ Rohrer 16*, D Salpietro 18*), Day 2: North Hobart (2nd inns) 7-128

Dual winners of the Emerson Rodwell Medal – Caleb Jewell and Harry Allenby
(Photo – courtesy Cricket Tasmania)

Recent Premierships

1996-97	Kingborough	2007-08	Kingborough
1997-98	Kingborough	2008-09	University
1998-99	North Hobart	2009-10	North Hobart
1999-2000	University	2010-11	Lindisfarne
2000-01	Lindisfarne	2011-12	Clarence
2001-02	North Hobart	2012-13	Glenorchy
2002-03	Clarence	2013-14	Glenorchy
2003-04	Clarence	2014-15	Kingborough
2004-05	North Hobart	2015-16	South Hobart/Sandy Bay
2005-06	North Hobart	2016-17	South Hobart/Sandy Bay
2006-07	Kingborough	2017-18	Clarence

Australian Cricket Digest, 2018-19

Recent One-day Titles

2006-07	South Hobart/Sandy Bay	2012-13	University of Tasmania
2007-08	South Hobart/Sandy Bay	2013-14	Lindisfarne
2008-09	South Hobart/Sandy Bay	2014-15	Glenorchy
2009-10	North Hobart	2015-16	South Hobart/Sandy Bay
2010-11	Kingborough	2016-17	Clarence
2011-12	Clarence	2017-18	University of Tasmania

Twenty20 Winners

2005-06	University	2012-13	Lindisfarne
2006-07	South Hobart/Sandy Bay	2013-14	Glenorchy
2007-08	South Hobart/Sandy Bay	2014-15	South Hobart/Sandy Bay
2008-09	Clarence	2015-16	Lindisfarne
2009-10	North Hobart	2016-17	New Town
2010-11	University	2017-18	South Hobart/Sandy Bay
2011-12	Kingborough		

Recent Emerson Rodwell Medalists

1996-97	Andrew Dykes (Clarence)	2007-08	Alex Doolan (SH/SB)
1997-98	Mark Colgrave (Clarence)	2008-09	Adam Polkinghorne (SH/SB)
1998-99	Brad Thomas (University)	2009-10	Andrew Kealy (Uni)
1999-2000	Josh Marquet (Uni) & Shane Jurgensen (Lindisfarne)	2010-11	Mark Divin (Kingborough)
2000-01	Adam Polkinghorne (SH/SB)	2011-12	Mark Divin (Kingborough)
2001-02	Adam Polkinghorne (SH/SB)	2012-13	Brett Geeves (Glenorchy)
2002-03	Adam Polkinghorne (SH/SB)	2013-14	Jonathon Wells (Clarence)
2003-04	Mark Colgrave (Clarence) & Graeme Cunningham (Uni)	2014-15	Luke Butterworth (Glenorchy)
2004-05	Adam Polkinghorne (SH/SB)	2015-16	Daniel Salpietro (Clarence)
2005-06	Jamie Cox (Lindisfarne)	2016-17	Harry Evans (Kingborough)
2006-07	Stuart H Clark (Kingborough)	2017-18	Harry Allanby (Clarence) & Caleb Jewell (North Hobart)

VICTORIAN PREMIER LEAGUE CRICKET
LADDER (18 sides, 17 matches, top eight)

	Won Out	Won 1st Inn	Drawn	Lost 1st Inn	Lost Out	Pts	Quotient
Fitzroy-Doncaster	2	11	2	3	-	75	1.9388
Carlton	1	12	2	3	-	67	1.6917
Dandenong	-	11	2	3	1	58	1.4349
Monash Tigers	3	6	1	8	-	56	1.1973
Footscray	1	9	3	4	-	55	1.1675
St Kilda	1	8	4	5	-	53	1.4452
Essendon	-	10	2	6	-	51	1.0898
Geelong	-	9	2	7	-	45	1.1067
Melbourne University	-	9	2	5	2	45	0.9680
Melbourne	-	8	2	8	-	44	1.0254
Ringwood	1	6	3	8	-	39	1.0251
Camberwell Magpies	-	8	2	7	1	38	0.8674
Prahran	-	7	2	8	1	35	0.9571
Frankston Peninsula	-	6	4	8	-	28	0.7898
Kingston Hawthorn	1	4	1	12	-	28	0.7407
Northcote	-	4	2	12	1	17	0.6957
Casey-South Melbourne	1	2	1	13	2	9	0.5493
Greenvale Kangaroos	-	2	1	12	3	9	0.4857

Leading Batting

	M	Inns	NO	HS	Runs	Avge	100/50
Brett Forsyth (Dandenong)	22	22	5	144	825	48.53	1/8
Harrison Smyth (Carlton)	21	18	2	147	814	50.88	2/5
Eamonn Vines (Geelong)	16	14	3	121*	804	73.09	2/6
Tom Donnell (Dandenong)	22	22	4	90	752	41.78	-/7
David King (Ringwood)	18	18	2	155*	736	46.00	2/4

Australian Cricket Digest, 2018-19

Leading Bowling	M	Overs	Wkts	Avge	Best	5/10
Trent Lawford (Fitzroy-Doncaster)	21	265.1	62	13.24	6-24	4/1
Ejaaz Alavi (Fitzroy-Doncaster)	21	199.5	44	11.82	3-10	-/-
Matthew Doric (Essendon)	19	234.3	42	17.69	6-66	2/-
James Nanopoulos (Dandenong)	21	254.4	40	16.63	4-15	-/-
Josh Barlett (St Kilda)	19	212.4	38	14.24	6-54	1/-

AWARDS:

Jack Ryder Medal: Won by Trent Lawford (Fitzroy-Doncaster) with 35 votes, who finished four votes clear of Ringwood skipper David King on 31.

Team of the year: David King (Ringwood), Brett Forsythe (Dandenong), Eamonn Vines (Captain, Geelong), Harrison Smyth (Carlton), Liam Tonkin (Frankston Peninsula), Tom Smyth (Carlton), Dylan Kight (Keeper, Footscray), Trent Lawford (Fitzroy-Doncaster), James Nanopoulos (Dandenong), Ejaaz Alavi (Fitzroy-Doncaster), Matthew Doric (Essendon), Will Walker (Camberwell Magpies) **Club Championship: Fitzroy-Doncaster.** Spirit of cricket - Fitzroy-Doncaster.

WHITE BALL 50 OVER FINAL, Sunday 21 January 2018 at the Princes Park No 1 Oval – Dandenong won by 10 wickets.
Carlton 49 (36.2 overs) (JD Jowett 3-18, DJ Pattinson 4-12) **lost to Dandenong 0-53** (16 overs)
Man of the Match – Darren Pattinson 10-3-12-4. Jacques Augustin took 6 catches as keeper.

Premier League Grand Final

Fitzroy Doncaster v Dandenong at the Junction Oval on March 31 to April 2, 2018 - Dandenong won by 10 wickets.

Fitzroy-Doncaster First innings			B	4	6	Second innings		B	4	6
J Blyth	c Newman b Siddle	29	93	4		2 b Buch	41	123	5	
J Rudd	b Siddle	2	5			1 c C Forsyth b Cassidy	32	71	4	
N Vardi	c C Forsyth b Siddle	4	9	1		c C Forsyth b Buch	13	44	2	
MP Firth	c C Forsyth b Siddle	12	19	2		lbw b Pattinson	24	53	1	
PJ Dickson *	c Augustin b Pattinson	14	32	3		lbw b Cassidy	4	6	1	
L Banthorpe +	b Pattinson	0	1			c Augustin b Pattinson	15	39		
LR Mash	c C Forsyth b Cassidy	25	50	5		c Augustin b Pattinson	14	21	1	
TL Lawford	c C Forsyth b Cassidy	3	3			c Augustin b Pattinson	2	4		
E Alavi	c Augustin b Siddle	7	24			c B Forsyth b Siddle	5	23		
CA Moore	c Edwards b Siddle	5	16			c Augustin b Siddle	2	6		
T Law	not out	1	1			not out	0	11		
	2 lb, 1 nb	3				2 b, 7 lb	9			
	42 overs	105				67 overs	161			

Fall: 1-4 (Rudd), 2-8 (Vardi), 3-24 (Frith), 4-51 (Dickson),
5-51 (Banthorpe), 6-74 (Blyth), 7-81 (Lawford), 8-95 (Mash),
9-104 (Moore), 10-105 (Alavi)

Fall: 1-70 (Rudd), 2-91 (Vardi), 3-92 (Blyth), 4-103
(Dickson), 5-131 (Frith), 6-142 (Banthorpe), 7-150
(Lawford), 8-155 (Mash), 9-158 (Moore), 10-161 (Alavi)

Dandenong - bowling	O	M	R	W	wd	nb	O	M	R	W	wd	nb
DJ Pattinson	9	4	19	2			13	3	29	4		
PM Siddle	16	3	45	6			18	4	45	2		
J Nanopoulos	9	2	18	0	1		8	2	15	0		
PE Cassidy	8	2	21	2			15	7	29	2		
AB Buch							13	3	34	2		

Dandenong	First innings		B	4	6	Second innings		B	4	6
B Forsyth	c Blyth b Lawford	13	69	1		2 not out	10	10	1	
T Donnell *	c Alavi b Frith	32	54	5		1 not out	28	21	5	
CP Forsyth	b Frith	2	5							
EJ Newman	c Banthorpe b Moore	40	113	6						
LJ Edwards	c &b Alavi	56	127	8						
J Nanopoulos	c Dickson b Lawford	16	38	2						
J Augustin +	c Banthorpe b Moore	29	44	4						
PM Siddle	not out	24	65	4						
PE Cassidy	c Banthorpe b Lawford	1	7							
DJ Pattinson	c Banthorpe b Lawford	3	16							
AB Buch	b Moore	1	16							
	4 b, 3 lb, 3 nb, 2 w	12					0			
	92 overs	229				5.1 overs	0-38			

Fall: 1-46 (Donnell), 2-48 (C Forsyth), 3-68 (B Forsyth),
4-122 (Newman), 5-146 (Nanopoulos), 6-174 (Edwards),
7-211 (Augustin), 8-212 (Cassidy), 9-218 (Pattinson), 10-229 (Buch)

Australian Cricket Digest, 2018-19

Fitz-Do nc - bo wling	O	M	R	W	wd	nb		O	M	R	W	wd	nb
TL Lawfo rd	23	4	84	4	2			3	0	16	0		
CA Mo o re	27	7	66	3				2	0	21	0		
MP Frith	20	5	30	2		3							
E Alavi	17	8	24	1				0.1	0	1	0		
T Law	3	0	17	0									
PJ Dickson	2	1	1	0									

Toss: Dandenong.   Umpires: PJ Gillespie, D Shepard   John Scholes Medal: Peter Siddle (Dandenong)
Stumps Day 1: Dandenong 3-119 (Newman 40*, Edwards 24*), Day 2: Fitzroy/Doncaster 4-128 (M Frith 22*, L Banthorpe 11*)

Recent Premierships

1998-99	Hawthorn/Waverley		2008-09	Ringwood
1999-2000	Richmond		2009-10	Melbourne
2000-01	St Kilda		2010-11	Dandenong
2001-02	Fitzroy-Doncaster		2011-12	Richmond
2002-03	St Kilda		2012-13	Melbourne
2003-04	St Kilda		2013-14	Footscray-Edgewater
2004-05	St Kilda		2014-15	Ringwood
2005-06	St Kilda		2015-16	Fitzroy-Doncaster
2006-07	Dandenong		2016-17	Fitzroy-Doncaster
2007-08	Ringwood		2017-18	Dandenong

Recent One-day/White-ball Titles

2005-06	St Kilda		2011-12	Prahran
2006-07	St Kilda		2012-13	Melbourne
2007-08	Carlton		2013-14	Melbourne
2008-09	Melbourne		2014-15	Monash Tigers
2009-10	St Kilda		2015-16	Fitzroy Doncaster
2010-11	Carlton		2016-17	Melbourne

Recent Twenty20 Titles

2005-06	Richmond		2010-11	No Final Played
2006-07	Dandenong		2011-12	Prahran
2007-08	Melbourne		2012-13	Melbourne
2008-09	St Kilda		2013-14	Footscray Edgewater
2009-10	Geelong		2014-15	to 2017-18 No Final contested

Recent Jack Ryder Medalists

1995-96	BA Joyce (Fitzroy-Doncaster)		2006-07	Graeme Rummans (St Kilda)
1996-97	Ian Wrigglesworth (Carlton)		2007-08	S Spoljaric (Hawthorn-Monash Uni)
1997-98	PQ Harper (University)		2008-09	GD Cross (St Kilda)
1998-99	Abdul Qadir (Carlton)		2009-10	GC Rummans (St Kilda)
1999-2000	Carl Hooper (Carlton)		2010-11	Theo Doropoulos (Northcote)
2000-01	Paul Collingwood (Richmond)		2011-12	Clive Rose (Casey/Sth Melbourne)
	Darren Dempsey (Ringwood)		2012-13	Brenton McDonald (Melbourne)
2001-02	Warren Ayres (Melbourne)		2013-14	James Miller (Prahran)
2002-03	CBD Street (Fitzroy-Doncaster)		2014-15	Ian Holland (Ringwood)
2003-04	RA Bartlett (Northcote) tied		2015-16	Steven Taylor (Northcote)
	with Adam Dale (Nth Melbourne)		2016-17	Brendan Drew (Camberwell Magpies)
2004-05	Simon Dart (Hawthorn-Mon Uni)		2017-18	Trent Lawford (Fitzroy-Doncaster)
2005-06	MD Allen (Carl) &			
	Graeme Rummans (St Kilda)			

Most runs ever in Competition

	Clubs	Career	Inns	NO	HS	Runs	Avge	100s
WG Ayres	Melbourne, Dandenong	1983-2008	396	36	218	15277	42.43	41
GM Watts	Fitzroy-Doncaster	1975-2001	344	38	260*	12933	42.26	25
WJ Scholes	Carlton, Fitzroy-Doncaster	1965-1996	400	47	156	12693	35.96	26
J Ryder	Collingwood, Northcote,	1906-1943	364	61	267	12677	41.83	37
PA McAlister	E Melb, Hawthorne E Melb	1889-1927	331	45	265*	11893	41.58	31

Most wickets

	Clubs	Career Span	Wickets	Avge	Best	5 wI	10wM
H Ironmonger	Melbourne, St Kilda	1913-1935	862	13.03	9-30	80	11
DD Blackie	St Kilda, Prahran	1905-1935	803	15.09	10-64	70	8
JL Keating	Collingwood, Richmond	1910-1942	636	18.49	9-13	35	-
TA Carlton	North Melbourne, Essendon	1908-1941	632	16.14	9-58	46	3
KW Kirby	Essendon	1959-1982	623	19.67	9-34	39	2

Australian Cricket Digest, 2018-19
QUEENSLAND MEN/SOUTH AUSTRALIAN WOMEN
WIN NATIONAL COUNTRY CHAMPIONSHIPS IN GERALDTON, WA.

Overall champions: New South Wales. One-day title: Victoria. Twenty20 title: New South Wales.
Final points: NSW 22 (NRR +1.18), Vic 22 (+1.07), Queensland 19, East Asia Pacific 18, Western Australia 11, South Australia 10
Player of the Championships: Joe Price (NSW) 29 points, Caleb Ziebell (NSW) 18, Ben Boyd (Vic) 17
Don Bradman batting award: Mitchell English (Qld)
Bill O'Reilly bowling award: Ben Boyd (Vic) & Cameron Suidgeest (NSW)
Doug Walters fielding award: SESE Bau (EAP). Ian Healy wicket-keeping award: Tom Groth (NSW)
Spirit of Cricket: Western Australia

Matches played
Round 1 on January 5, 2018 (20 overs) – **Qld 6-124 lost to East Asia Pacific 6-127** (W Nalisa 51), **Vic 9-105 lost to SA 5-106, NSW 3-172** (JL Price 88) **def WA 97**

Round 2 on January 5, 2018 (20 overs) – **Qld 113** (TJ Hutchinson 4-22) **def WA 5-112, Vic 8-101 lost to NSW 9-105, SA 6-158** (B Parish 54) **def EAP 9-132**

Round 3 on January 6, 2018 (20 overs) – **NSW 8-102 def EAP 67, SA 9-113** (PJ Wilson 50) **lost to Qld 1-115** (MJ English 83), **WA 6-109 def Vic 8-103**

Round 4 on January 6, 2018 (20 overs) – **Vic 5-157** (L McCann 62) **lost to Qld 6-158** (JT Spargo 71*), **NSW 5-166** (C Ziebell 56) **d SA 96** (C Suidgeest 4-14), **WA 9-83 lost to EAP 5-84**

Round 5 on January 7, 2018 (20 overs) – **NSW 8-151 d Qld 102, SA 8-128 d WA 4-125** (R O'Connell 50), **Vic 7-129 lost to EAP 5-130**

T20 Grand Final (Jan 7) – NSW Country 3-190 cc (C Ziebell 110 off 60 balls, 5x4, 6x6, J Moran 50) **d Qld 151** (S Keen 4-19)

Round 6 on January 9, 2018 (50 overs) – **Qld 9-143 lost to SA 9-145, WA 196 lost to Vic 6-197, EAP 250 d NSW 192**

Round 7 on January 10, 2018 (50 overs) – **NSW 138 lost to Vic 9-141, WA 9-180 lost to Qld 0-184** (MJ English 116*), **SA 9-229 lost to EAP 6-230**

Round 8 on January 11, 2018 (50 overs) – **NSW 8-196 lost to Qld 8-199, EAP 87** (BD Boyd 5-32) **lost to Vic 3-88, WA 8-186 d SA 185**

Round 9 on January 12, 2018 (50 overs) – **Vic 7-240 def SA 87, WA 9-213 lost to NSW 7-216, EAP 9-252 def Qld 225**

Round 10 on January 13, 2018 (50 overs) – **Vic 9-263** (MS Salerno 5-50) **lost to Qld 2-266** (JT Spargo 134*), **SA 95 lost to NSW 4-96, WA 162 def EAP 87**

Australian Country XII: Mitchell English (Qld), Joseph Price (NSW), Caleb Ziebell (NSW), Tom Buchanan (WA), Sam Lowry (Qld), James Spargo (Qld), Chris Stanger (Qld), Tom Groth (wk), Jelany Chilla (EAP), Jason Seng (Qld), Cameron Suidgest (NSW), Ben Boyd (VIC). Coach: Jeff Cook (NSW). Manager: Robbie Jackson (NSW)

Previous winners on the Mens title

1984-85	NSW	Beenleigh, Qld		2001-02	Qld	Warrnambool, Vic
1985-86	NSW	Riverland, SA		2002-03	WA	Bundaberg, Qld
1986-87	ACT	Dubbo, NSW		2003-04	Vic	Mt Gambier, SA
1987-88	Qld	Canberra, ACT		2004-05	Qld	Far North Coast, NSW
1988-89	NSW	Bunbury, WA		2005-06	Qld	Mandurah, WA
1989-90	NSW	Bendigo, Vic		2006-07	Vic	Sunraysia District, Vic
1990-91	Vic	Townsville, Qld		2007-08	NSW	Harrup Park, Mackay, Qld
1991-92	NSW	Riverland, SA		2008-09	Qld	Barossa Valley, SA
1992-93	NSW	Newcastle, NSW		2009-10	NT	Albury-Wadonga, NSW
1993-94	ACT	Canberra, ACT		2010-11	WA	Bunbury Region, WA
1994-95	Qld	Albany/Mt Barker, WA		2011-12	NSW	Geelong, Vic
1995-96	NSW	Sale/Maffra, Qld		2012-13	NSW	Bundaberg, Qld
1996-97	Qld	Toowoomba, Qld		2013-14	WA	Canberra, ACT
1997-98	WA	Mt Gambier, SA		2014-15	Qld	Bendigo, Vic
1998-99	Qld	Barooga, NSW		2015-16	SA	Mt Gambier, SA
1999-2000	Qld	Canberra, ACT		2016-17	Qld	Wollongong, NSW
2000-01	NSW	Albany/Mt Barker, WA		2017-18	NSW	Geraldton, WA

South Australia won the women's title played January 7-13, 2018. Ladder: Vic 12, SA 10, NSW 8, Qld 6, EAP 4, WA 2, NT 0.
Semi-Finals: Qld 8-136 (LJ Randall 63) **def Vic 7-125** (A Yates 64), **SA 5-118** (BA Perry 74*) **def NSW 6-110**
Grand Final: SA 6-107 (C Fiebig 27) **def Qld 7-94** (M Dixon 33; S Tansell 3-19)
Player of the Championships: Brittany Perry (SA) 29 points, Rebecca Cady (NSW) 20, Amy Yates (Vic) 17
Batting award: Brittany Perry (SA) – 372 runs at 62.00, Strike Rate 111.0
Bowling award: Chelsea Moscript (Vic) – 15 wickets at 7.67, Economy 4.86
Fielding award: Brittany Perry (SA). Wicket-keeping award: Teagan Parker (Vic). Spirit of Cricket: Queensland
Australian Country XII: Brittany Perry (SA), Naomi McDonald (NSW), Rebecca Cady (NSW), Stephanie Baldwin (Qld), Brenda Tau (EAP), Amy Yates (Vic), Kelly Armstrong (SA), Chelsea Moscript (Vic), Teagan Parker (Vic), Georgie Middleton (WA), Stephanie Townsend (Vic), Amy Edgar (WA). Coaches: Kevin Frick (SA). Manager: Amy Wiseman (SA)

Australian Cricket Digest, 2018-19
AUSTRALIAN ABORGINAL TEAMS IN ENGLAND
Mens tour: June 5 – 12, 2018

Squad: Dan Christian (c) Nick Boland, Scott Boland, Brendan Doggett, Sam Doggett, Damon Egan, Brock Larance, Tyran Liddiard, Ben Patterson, Jonte Pattison, Nathan Price, D'arcy Short, Brendan Smith, Rex Strickland, Dane Ugle. Coach: Jeffrey Cook

Matches Played

At Arundle Castle on June 5, 2018 (Twenty 20 match) – Australian XI won by 21 runs
Australian XI 8-150 cc (BL Patterson 49*; MRJ Watt 3-14, JA Letchford 3-38) **def Marylebone Cricket Club 129** (19.3 overs) (DE Budge 52; SM Boland 3-29). *Ben Patterson faced 23 balls, hit 4x4 3x6.*

At Arundle Castle on June 5, 2018 (Twenty 20 match) – Australian XI won by 6 wickets
Marylebone Cricket Club 3-147 cc (SJW Lambert 78*, DE Budge 43*) **lost to Australian XI 4-148** (19.2 overs) (DT Christian 78*) *Daniel Christian faced 23 balls, hit 8x4 1x6.*

At the Oval, London on June 7, 2018 (Twenty 20 match) – Australian XI won by 5 runs
Australian XI 8-176 cc (BA Smith 61) **def Surrey Championship XI 5-171 cc** (BR McDermott 67) *Brendan Smith faced 24 balls, hit 8x4 4x6.*

At the County Ground, Hove on June 8, 2018 (Twenty 20 match) – Sussex won by 99 runs
Sussex 5-188 cc (D Wiese 49*, LJ Evans 44, MGK Burgess 44) **def Australian XI 89** (15.4 overs) (DR Briggs 3-28)

At the County Ground, Derby on June 10, 2018 (Twenty 20 match) – Australian XI won by 7 wickets
Derbyshire XI 6-156 cc (TA Wood 65) **lost to Australian XI 3-160** (17.2 overs) (BA Smith 57, DT Christian 44*) *Smith faced 28 balls, hit 5x4, 4x4; Christian faced 23 balls, hit 2x4 4x6.*

At Trent Bridge, Nottingham on June 12, 2018 (Twenty 20 match) – Australian XI won by 61 runs
Australian XI 6-182 cc (DT Christian 61, BA Smith 43) **def Nottinghamshire XI 121** (17.3 overs) (L Wood 41; SK Doggett 3-34, BL Larance 3-27) *Christian faced 25 balls, hit 3x4 4x6.*

Womens tour: June 7 – 12, 2018

Squad: Ashleigh Gardner (c), Jemma Astley, Dharmini Chauhan, Christina Coulson, Hannah Darlington, Sara Darney, Zoe Fleming, Haylee Hoffmeister, Emma Manix-Geeves, Sally Moylan, Natalie Plane, Roxanne Van Veen, Naomi Woods. Coach: Shelley Nitschke

At the Oval, London on June 7, 2018 (Twenty 20 match) – Surrey won by 36 runs
Surrey 6-149 cc (BF Smith 58) **def Australian XI 113** (20 overs) (HJ Darlington 32; HV Jones 5-18, BF Smith 3-15)

At the County Ground, Hove on June 8, 2018 (Twenty 20 match) – Sussex won by 79 runs
Sussex 4-182 cc (PJ Schofield 58, FC Wilson 53) **def Australian XI 8-103 cc** (CR Coulson 33, R Van-Veen 31)

At the County Ground, Derby on June 10, 2018 (Twenty 20 match) – Australian XI won by 137 runs
Australian XI 4-199 cc (AK Gardner 129*) **def National Cricket Conference 5-62 cc.** *Gardner faced 71 balls, hit 15x4 4x6.*

At Trent Bridge, Nottingham on June 12, 2018 (Twenty 20 match) – England Academy won by 116 runa
England Academy 5-228 cc (LCN Smith 82, FC Wilson 76; AK Gardner 3-38) **def Australian XI 9-112 cc** (AK Gardner 33; S Glenn 3-12)

ENGLAND LIONS IN AUSTRALIA

At Allan Border Field, Brisbane (non first-class) on November 27-29, 2017 – Match Drawn
Queensland XI 8-396 dec (SD Heazlett 79, NA McSweeney 77, BE Street 69, PJ Forrest 62; GS Virdi 4-71) **drew with England Lions 5-250 dec** (KK Jennings 89, BT Foakes 67)

At Perth Stadium (Twenty20) on December 11, 2017 (floodlit) – England Lions won by 12 runs
England Lions 6-160 cc (LS Livingstone 36; DJ Willey 3-32) **def Perth Scorchers 9-148 cc** (HWR Cartwright 56; S Mahmood 4-14). *The first ever cricket match at Perth Stadium, an "invite" only game as far as the public was concerned, which annoyed many English fans who were around for the Perth Ashes Test.*

At Perth Stadium (Twenty20) on December 13, 2017 (floodlit) – Perth Scorchers won by 6 runs
Perth Scorchers 5-148 cc (M Klinger 39) **def England Lions 142** (19.3 overs) (NRT Gubbins 68; JM Muirhead 3-21)

At Murdoch University, Perth (Twenty20) on December 15, 2017 – Perth Scorchers won by 6 wickets
England Lions 7-163 cc (KK Jennings 45) **lost to Perth Scorchers 4-164** (16.2 overs) (WG Bosisto 66, JR Philippe 38)

WOMENS CRICKET

AUSSIES RETAIN ASHES, NEW SOUTH WALES AND SIXERS WIN DOMESTIC TITLES

In another action packed summer, Australia retained the Ashes, despite a late run by England, which saw the series tied at eight points each. After winning the ODI series 2-1 and having the better of the Test, Australia wrapped up the series with a win in the first Twenty20 match under lights at North Sydney Oval. England fought back well to win the last two Twenty20 Internationals.

The highlights of the series for Australia were the consistently fine bowling of Megan Schutt, and the double ton made in the day/night Test by Ellyse Perry. Good crowds attended the matches, with the Nine Network showing LIVE the ODIs and Twenty20s, the Test was live-streamed on the Cricket Australia website, and treated with a full blown TV coverage, that was picked up by the BT Pay network in the UK.

In March Australia headed for India and won the three ODI's there comfortably, Nicole Bolton batting superbly in the first two matches. Following that Australia took out the Twenty20 Tri-series over the hosts and England. The series there saw the return of Meg Lanning from injury, the Aussie skipper started slowly, but in the Final of the T20 tri-series made a brilliant 88 not out to show she was back to her best form.

At the time of publication Australia are in second spot on the ICC Womens World Championship table, two points behind New Zealand, but are effectively number one, having won 83% of their games compared to New Zealand's 66%. Individual rankings wise, Australia have three of the top five ODI batters and three of the top ODI bowlers, with Ellyse Perry ranked as the leading all-rounder. In the Twenty20 rankings, Australia have two of the top four batters, with Megan Schutt regarded as the leading bowler.

Domestically, New South Wales showed their class to go through the WNCL tournament undefeated, with Western Australia the runner-up, making their first final since 2009-10.

Sydney Sixers won back to back WBBL titles, smashing Perth Scorchers in the final in Adelaide.

ICC WOMENS WORLD CHAMPIONSHIP (2017-2021) STANDINGS (as at July 31, 2018)

TEAM	M	W	L	T	P	NRR
New Zealand	9	6	3	0	12	0.401
Australia	**6**	**5**	**1**	**0**	**10**	**1.105**
England	9	5	4	0	10	0.571
Pakistan	6	4	2	0	8	0.581
West Indies	6	3	3	0	6	-0.616
India	6	2	4	0	4	0.066
South Africa	6	2	4	0	4	-1.147
Sri Lanka	6	0	6	0	0	-1.350

CURRENT RANKINGS in WOMENS INTERNATIONAL CRICKET AS AT AUGUST 16, 2018

ODI Team	M	Rank	Batting		Bowling	
Australia	55	132	Ellyse Perry (Aus)	744	Jess Jonassen (Aus)	676
England	60	126	Lizelle Lee (SA)	724	Megan Schutt (Aus)	667
New Zealand	69	120	Meg Lanning (Aus)	684	Shibnam Ismail (SA)	641
India	66	112	Smriti Mandhana (Ind)	678	Marizanne Kapp (SA)	630
West Indies	48	98	Nicole Bolton (Aus)	666	Sana Mir (Pak)	620
South Africa	76	95	Tammy Beaumont (Eng)	657	Jhulan Goswami (Ind)	609
Pakistan	55	74	Suzie Bates (NZ)	656	Katherine Brunt (Eng)	599
Sri Lanka	55	62	Mithali Raj (Ind)	656	Ayabonga Khaka (SA)	597
Bangladesh	35	43	Stafanie Taylor (WI)	653	Stafanie Taylor (WI)	591
Ireland	25	26	Sophie Devine (NZ)	613	Ellyse Perry (Aus)	567

All rounders: Ellyse Perry (Aus) 421, Stafanie Taylor (WI) 385, Dane van Niekerk (SA) 323, Deepti Sharma (Ind) 298

Twenty20 batting		Twenty20 bowling	
Stafanie Taylor (WI)	676	Megan Schutt (Aus)	669
Suzie Bates (NZ)	674	Poonam Yadav (Ind)	621
Meg Lanning (Aus)	631	Hayley Matthews (WI)	610
Beth Mooney (Aus)	631	Anam Amin (Pak)	602
Deandra Dottin (WI)	617	Nahida Akter (Ban)	599
Mithali Raj (Ind)	591	Dani Hazell (Eng)	593
Harmanpreet Kaur (Ind)	587	Jess Jonassen (Aus)	587
Sophie Devine (NZ)	558	Leigh Kasperek (NZ)	583
Dane van Niekerk (SA)	550	Nida Dar (Pak)	570
Natalie Sciver (Eng)	548	Anya Shrubsole (Eng)	568

All rounders: **Hayley Matthews (WI) 311,** Deandra Dottin (WI) 289, Stafanie Taylor (WI) 285, Dane van Niekerk (SA) 274

Australian Cricket Digest, 2018-19
2017-18 WOMENS ASHES
FIRST ONE-DAY INTERNATIONAL - BRISBANE

After a week of rain in Brisbane, Allan Border Field was ready to go on-time, thanks to the magnificent work of the groundstaff, who spent all night getting the ground ready. In the sunny conditions, England started well, until Beaumont lofted one low to mid-off where Schutt took a great catch diving forward. Winfield was starting to dominate proceedings, lofting Jonassen and later Gardner for sixes over long-on, before she was run out wanting a risky run to short third man. Taylor was also going well before being trapped in front, and with Sciver and Wilson scoring freely, England were well placed at 4-188 with eight overs left. The Australian bowling and fielders rallied, restricting England just 40 more runs, with Gardner and Schutt maintaining control.

In reply, Healy whacked three fours in the first over, before Bolton nicked one behind in the second. Healy was caught at mid-off in the fifth over and then Perry and Villani steadied, adding 54. Perry lost concentration first ball after drinks and was stumped and then Haynes wanted a risky single to short cover, which saw Villani picked off by Sciver. The experienced Blackwell came out looked assured from the word go as she and Haynes added 63 for the fifth wicket. After Haynes went to good diving catch at mid-wicket, McGrath struggled to find the gaps as the run rate required increased. Her dismissal saw Gardner come out and score 15 off her first five balls, including a six off Sciver over deep square-leg. In the 47th over, Gardner top-edged a ball from Brunt into her helmet, but continued on, her rapid-fire innings taking the pressure off Blackwell. Despite two late wickets, Jonassen, batting absurdly low at ten, cracked one through the covers, to see Australia home with five balls to spare.

First One-day International at Allan Border Field, Brisbane on October 22, 2017 - Australia won by 2 wickets

England		B	M	4	6	Australia		B	M	4	6
L Winfield	run out (Jonassen)	48	63	82	2	2	AJ Healy +	c Shrubsole b Brunt	18	15	16	4
TT Beaumont	c Schutt b Perry	24	35	40	3	1	NE Bolton	c Taylor b Shrubsole	2	5	6	
SJ Taylor +	lbw b Gardner	34	44	56	2		EA Perry	st Taylor b Hartley	20	44	57	1	1
HC Knight *	c Schutt b Jonassen	15	33	34			EJ Villani	run out (Sciver)	38	38	59	7
NR Sciver	c Villani b Gardner	36	52	55	2		RL Haynes *	c Sciver b Hartley	30	56	66	1
FC Wilson	c Perry b Gardner	26	31	43	1	1	AJ Blackwell	not out	67	86	117	7
KH Brunt	b Perry	11	12	13	2		TM McGrath	c Winfield b Brunt	7	26	30	
JL Gunn	c Wellington b Schutt	9	15	20			AK Gardner	c Marsh b Gunn	27	18	21	2	2
LA Marsh	c Healy b Schutt	2	5	6			A Wellington	run out (Sciver)	3	6	7	
A Shrubsole	not out	11	9	10	2		JL Jonassen	not out	4	1	1	1
A Hartley	not out	2	1	2			M Schutt					
	4 lb, 6 w	10						4 b, 3 lb, 8 w	15			
10 overs: 1-47	50 overs, 195 mins	9-228					10 overs: 2-36	49.1 overs, 194 mins	8-231			

Fall: 1-47 (Beaumont), 2-103 (Winfield), 3-122 (Taylor), 4-140 (Knight), 5-190 (Sciver), 6-198 (Wilson), 7-205 (Brunt), 8-211 (Marsh), 9-221 (Gunn)

Fall: 1-14 (Bolton), 2-20 (Healy), 3-74 (Perry), 4-87 (Villani), 5-150 (Haynes), 6-181 (McGrath), 7-220 (Gardner), 8-227 (Wellington)

Australia - bowling	O	M	R	W	wd	nb	England - bowling	O	M	R	W	wd	nb
ML Schutt	10	2	44	2	1		KH Brunt	10	3	47	2	2	
EA Perry	10	2	50	2	3		A Shrubsole	9.1	0	31	1	1	
JL Jonassen	10	0	38	1			NR Sciver	7	0	32	0	1	
AJ Wellington	10	1	39	0			JL Gunn	4	0	26	1		
AK Gardner	9	0	47	3	2		A Hartley	10	1	40	2		
TM McGrath	1	0	6	0			LA Marsh	7	1	34	0		
							HC Knight	2	0	14	0		

Toss: Australia. Umpires: SAJ Craig, GJ Davidson, CA Polosak (TV). Ref: RW Stratford. Award: AJ Blackwell (Aus). Points: Aus 2, Eng 0

SECOND ONE-DAY INTERNATIONAL - COFFS HARBOUR

Both teams made one change for this game, for England Laura Marsh made way for Sophie Ecclestone while Ash Gardner was reported to have suffered concussion after her knock to the head in the first match, and was replaced by experienced leg-spinner, Kristen Beams. Healy got Australia off to a great start, her and Bolton adding 98 including an over where she took 17 off Nat Sciver. Off the last ball of the 20th over Healy was bowled aiming a cut at an arm ball. Bolton went in the 33rd over, then Villani in the 34th as England tried to fight back. Any collapse was averted when skipper Rachel Haynes joined Perry, the pair adding 86 off 70 balls, with Haynes hitting 21 (244641) herself off the 47th over, bowled by Katherine Brunt. Australia added 94 in the final ten overs.

Needing 297, England lost Winfield in the first over, then the rain came with England 1-10 (2.4 overs, Beaumont 1*, Taylor 5*), the 21 minute delay changing England's target to 285 off 46 overs. Shortly after the players returned, Schutt trapped Beaumont in front and then in the sixth over, Perry was removed from the attack by the umpires for bowling two head-high full tosses in a row. Taylor and Knight added over 50, before Taylor edged McGrath behind to gain her first ODI wicket. When Sciver drove to mid-on and then Knight was unlucky to be given leg before, England had slipped to 5-91 in the 21st over.

254

Australian Cricket Digest, 2018-19

Wilson and Brunt knuckled down to add 68, to try and keep England in it, but when Wilson was well caught at deep mid-wicket and Brunt, after reaching her maiden ODI fifty, was bowled sweeping, by then the game was done and dusted.

Second One-day International at International Sports Stadium, Coffs Harbour – October 26, 2017 (day/night)
Australia won by 75 runs (DLS Method)

Australia		B	M	4	6	England	DLS Target 285 off 46	B	M	4	6
NE Bolton	b Hartley	66	100	125	7	L Winfield	lbw b Schutt	2	3	1	
AJ Healy +	b Ecclestone	56	55	80	6	1	TT Beaumont	lbw b Schutt	8	17	22	1
EA Perry	st Taylor b Gunn	67	75	96	4	2	SJ Taylor +	c Healy b McGrath	26	41	68	1
EJ Villani	c Knight b Gunn	1	6	5		HC Knight *	lbw b Wellington	36	53	60	2
RL Haynes *	not out	89	56	65	9	3	NR Sciver	c Villani b Jonassen	5	9	7	1
AJ Blackwell	c Brunt b Gunn	8	8	15	1	FC Wilson	c Perry b Schutt	37	43	55	2
TM McGrath	c Hartley b Gunn	1	2	1		KH Brunt	b Schutt	52	54	64	5	1
A Wellington	not out	0	0	1		JL Gunn	b Beams	9	14	21	1
JL Jonassen						A Shrubsole	c Villani b Jonassen	21	14	14	4
M Schutt						S Ecclestone	c Blackwell b Beams	3	8	7	
KM Beams						A Hartley	not out	0	0	2	
	2 nb, 6 w	8					3 lb, 2 nb, 5 w	10			
10 overs : 0-33	50 overs, 197 mins	6-296				10 overs : 2-42	42.2 overs, 166 mins	209			

Fall: 1-98 (Healy), 2-161 (Bolton), 3-164 (Villani), 4-250 (Perry), 5-291 (Blackwell), 6-294 (McGrath)

Fall: 1-2 (Winfield), 2-20 (Beaumont), 3-77 (Taylor), 4-85 (Sciver), 5-91 (Knight), 6-159 (Wilson), 7-182 (Brunt), 8-198 (Gunn), 9-208 (Shrubsole), 10-209 (Ecclestone)

England - bowling	O	M	R	W	wd	nb	Australia - bowling	O	M	R	W	wd	nb
A Shrubsole	10	0	57	0	1	1	ML Schutt	8	0	26	4	2	
KH Brunt	8	0	55	0	1		EA Perry	2.4	0	15	0	1	2
JL Gunn	10	0	55	4	1	1	TM McGrath	8.2	0	35	1		
NR Sciver	5	0	40	0			KM Beams	7.2	0	38	2		
S Ecclestone	10	0	49	1			A Wellington	7	0	42	1	1	
A Hartley	7	0	40	1	2		JL Jonassen	9	0	50	2	1	

Toss: England. Umpires: SAJ Craig, CA Polosak, GJ Davidson (TV), Ref: RW Stratford. Award: RL Haynes (Aus). Points: Aus 2, Eng 0

THIRD ONE-DAY INTERNATIONAL - COFFS HARBOUR

Leading the Ashes series four points to nil, Australia replaced Kristen Beams with Ash Gardner who had recovered from concussion. England were unchanged and lost Winfield, plumb in front to the last ball of the second over. Beaumont and Taylor took control adding 122, with Taylor playing some crisp shots on the way to a 55-ball fifty. After cutting one point, Taylor was replaced by skipper Sciver, who helped Beaumont add 68 to keep the early momentum going. England slipped to 5-201 in the 39th over, but Knight batted to the end, England adding 72 off the last ten overs, to reach their best ever score against Australia.

Australia started well to add 39 in 6.1 overs, before the rains came, taking two overs off the match. At 1-118 in the 22nd over, Australia were well on track, when Healy was caught at deep mid-wicket, aiming a slog-sweep. Perry joined Bolton to add 41, but the loss of Bolton, driving to long-on, saw Australia lose 3-15 to slip to 4-174 in the 34th over. Blackwell batted well, but with wickets falling regularly at the other end, England gained a comfortable win and a much needed two points.

Third One-day International at International Sports Stadium, Coffs Harbour on October 29, 2017
England won by 20 runs (DLS Method)

England		B	M	4	6	Australia	DLS Target 278 off 48	B	M	4	6
L Winfield	lbw b Perry	0	10	7		AJ Healy +	c Brunt b Hartley	71	72	83	12
TT Beaumont	st Healy b Schutt	74	98	136	10	NE Bolton	c Winfield b Ecclestone	62	80	111	7
SJ Taylor +	c Jonassen b Schutt	69	66	81	12	EA Perry	c Gunn b Shrubsole	23	33	39	2
HC Knight *	not out	88	80	104	5	1	EJ Villani	c Winfield b Hartley	8	12	15	1
NR Sciver	b Schutt	7	8	7	1	RL Haynes *	c Brunt b Sciver	9	15	24	1
FC Wilson	lbw b Perry	0	4	4		AJ Blackwell	c Sciver b Gunn	37	44	54	2
KH Brunt	c Perry b Gardner	12	17	20	1	AK Gardner	c Ecclestone b Sciver	3	9	9	
JL Gunn	c Healy b Schutt	15	14	14	1	JL Jonassen	c and b Hartley	6	4	6	1
A Shrubsole	c Schutt b Jonassen	1	3	5		TM McGrath	not out	17	17	25	1
S Ecclestone	not out	1	1	2		A Wellington	st Taylor b Gunn	0	0	3	
A Hartley						M Schutt	not out	6	2	1	1
	3 b, 6 lb, 1 nb, 7 w	17					7 lb, 8 w	15			
10 overs : 1-45	50 overs, 192 mins	284				10 overs : 0-55	48 overs, 191 mins	9-257			

Fall: 1-2 (Winfield), 2-124 (Taylor), 3-192 (Beaumont), 4-200 (Sciver), 5-201 (Wilson), 6-235 (Brunt), 7-269 (Gunn), 8-275 (Shrubsole)

Fall: 1-118 (Healy), 2-159 (Bolton), 3-172 (Perry), 4-174 (Villani), 5-194 (Haynes), 6-206 (Gardner), 7-216 (Jonassen), 8-249 (Blackwell), 9-251 (Wellington)

Australian Cricket Digest, 2018-19

Australia - bowling	O	M	R	W	wd	nb	England - bowling	O	M	R	W	wd	nb
ML Schutt	10	1	44	4	1		KH Brunt	6	0	44	0	2	
EA Perry	10	0	51	2	3	1	A Shrubsole	10	0	40	1		
TM McGrath	4	0	27	0			JL Gunn	10	0	59	2	3	
A Wellington	10	0	50	0	1		S Ecclestone	5	0	38	1		
JL Jonassen	7	0	53	1	1		A Hartley	9	1	45	3		
AK Gardner	9	0	50	1			NR Sciver	8	1	24	2	1	

Toss: England. Umpires: GJ Davidson, CA Polosak, SAJ Craig (TV), Ref: RW Stratford. Award: HC Knight (Eng). Points: Eng 2, Aus 0

TOUR MATCH at Blacktown International Sports Park on November 3-5, 2017 - Match Drawn

England 231 (L Winfield 82; SG Molineux 3-27, LG Smith 3-18) **and 7-305 dec** (SJ Taylor 85) **drew with Cricket Australia XI 271** (NE Stalenberg 114; KH Brunt 4-37) **and 7-182** (NJ Carey 52; HC Knight 3-12).

Lauren Winfield (161 balls, 189 mins, 15x4) had some excellent batting practice on the opening day, as the CA finished on 4-82 at the close. Naomi Stalenberg (165 balls, 202 mins, 18x4, 1x6) played a brilliant hand as the home side grabbed a first innings lead of 40, seven of the wickets to fall in the innings to LBW decisions. Katherine Brunt showed some good pre-Test form taking four wickets, as England batted under lights to close the second day on 3-87. Sarah Taylor (145 balls, 208 mins, 13x4) showed her class as she helped England to a lead of 265. The CA XI batted out time with Nicola Carey (62 balls, 66 mins, 6x4) passing fifty, in what was a great work out against competitive opponents under lights.

TEST MATCH - NORTH SYDNEY OVAL

The much awaited day/night Test at North Sydney Oval saw Australia give Test debuts to opener Beth Mooney, all-rounder Tahlia McGrath and leg-spinner Amanda Wellington. England had two themselves with batter Fran Wilson and 18 year-old slow-arm spinner Sophie Ecclestone playing their first ever Tests. Conditions were excellent, with the visitors set to bat first on winning the toss. Against tight bowling, the scoring was a laborious early, with 13 runs coming from the first 14 overs. Thankfully the action livened up after that, when Winfield drove to short cover and Bolton dived to her left to bring off a brilliant catch. Knight found some fluency, taking ten runs (including two fours) off Wellington's first over in Test cricket. The second hour yielding a more spectator friendly scoring rate, England going to Tea on 1-63 from 33 overs, with Beaumont 36 and Knight 21.

In the hour after the break, Beaumont brought up her fifty (136 balls) and then the 100 stand was raised, with England starting to get on top. Knight reached her fifty (87 balls) but then lost Beaumont as she edged a catch to slip. Knight's fine innings came to an end when she was trapped in front aiming a sweep, England going in at Tea on 3-157.

In front of an enthusiastic home crowd, Australia got back into the match in the final session, taking four wickets. Sciver was trapped in front playing back to give Jonassen her second wicket, while Elwiss top edged a pull shot behind square leg. Taylor was caught and bowled on the second attempt by Perry and when Brunt drove a catch to point, England slumped from 4-214 to 7-227. Wilson saw the day out with Shrubsole to be 7-235, Australia's bowlers having got through 100 overs, Jonassen (2-52) having bowled 31 of them.

On the second day, Schutt used the short ball to good effect getting Wilson and Shrubsole out to miscued pull shots, England losing their last three wickets from 45, to be all out for 280, a few short of what they'd hoped for after being 1-129. Like England's openers, Australia's took their time also, reaching 22 without loss at Tea from 19 overs, with Bolton 15 and Mooney 7. After the break Australia tried to lift the rate, but lost Bolton and Mooney both to pull shots to mid-wicket, while Blackwell was trapped in front on the forward stroke. Perry (16) and Villani (9) saw Australia to the dinner break on 3-84 from 49 overs, England having won the session.

Under the floodlights, Villani aimed a wild drive and edged behind, but then Perry and Haynes stuck together in an important stand of 73. Perry reached her 50 from 137 balls but Haynes, who was dropped in the slips on 29 off Brunt, went the very next ball, trapped in front by one that swung back in the first over with the second new ball. Australia ended the day 103 in arrears.

With the game evenly poised, Healy started day three well with a boundary off the second ball and she and Perry looked to get close to the England total. Perry made the most of a few full tosses and brought up her century from 225 balls, with a back foot sweep off Marsh to fine-leg. Healy played positively in a stand of 102 before advancing on Marsh, being well held at deep mid-off. McGrath drove her first ball to cover, only to be dropped but grew in confidence and made it to tea on 13, Perry 125, Australia 6-292 from 120 overs.

Perry continued to look untroubled, reaching her 150 from 358 balls as she and McGrath pushed on with their partnership. Having added 103, McGrath, needing three for a maiden fifty, mistimed a full toss to mid-wicket, Australia going in at dinner on 7-374 (151 overs) with Perry 167 and Jonassen 0. In the final session, Jonassen and Wellington both fell, leaving Perry on 193 when she was joined by number eleven Megan Schutt. Perry thought she'd reached her double-ton with a six, only to be denied by the third umpire. In the next over she got there (off her 371th ball) with an elegant straight drive back past spinner Sophie Ecclestone, Australia declaring shortly after, with a lead of 168, Perry's triumphant on an unbeaten 213, the highest ever score in a women's Test match.

With 17 overs to bat, England had a few close calls, with Winfield nearly being run out and Beaumont almost playing on facing Wellington. On the final day with the pitch having not broken up, Wellington found some turn, pitching one on leg which hit the top of off stump, as Beaumont played back. When Winfield was hit on the toe aiming a drive, Australia had high hopes, given England were still 79 behind with eight wickets in hand. But the experienced Knight found a willing ally in Elwiss, as they made it to tea (2-98, Knight 13, Elwiss 5) and after the break they got stuck into the task of saving the game.

They were resolute in the middle session, adding 54 (Dinner: 2-152, Knight 45, Elwiss 24) before batting out the last session to force a draw, Knight reaching her fifty from 162 balls, as the stand lasted 380 balls, when Knight and Haynes shook hands without playing the final hour. Perry was the obvious player of the match, the points shared with Australia leading 6-4 heading into Twenty20 matches, needing to only win one of the three games to retain the Ashes.

Only Test at North Sydney Oval on November 9-12, 2017 (day/night) – Match Drawn

England	First innings		B	M	4	6	Second innings		B	M	4	6
L Winfield	c Bolton b McGrath		4	56	70		lbw b McGrath	34	145	155	3	
TT Beaumont	c Blackwell b Wellington		70	173	193	9	b Wellington	37	81	114	5	
HC Knight *	lbw b Jonassen		62	111	141	7	not out	79	220	245	11	
GA Elwiss	c Schutt b Perry		27	95	120	2	not out	41	190	204	3	
NR Sciver	lbw b Jonassen		18	52	52	3						
SJ Taylor +	c & b Perry		29	58	62	4						
FC Wilson	c Perry b Schutt		13	53	66							
KH Brunt	c Jonassen b McGrath		1	4	11							
A Shrubsole	c Villani b Schutt		20	47	49	4						
LA Marsh	c Healy b Perry		13	32	37	2						
S Ecclestone	not out		8	19	28	1						
	3 b, 8 lb, 4 nb		15				7 b, 2 lb, 6 nb	15				
	116 overs, 419 mins		280				105 overs, 360 mins	2-206				

Fall: 1-25 (Winfield), 2-129 (Beaumont), 3-145 (Knight), 4-177 (Sciver), 5-214 (Elwiss), 6-226 (Taylor), 7-227 (Brunt), 8-249 (Wilson), 9-262 (Shrubsole), 10-280 (Marsh)

Fall: 1-71 (Beaumont), 2-89 (Winfield)

Australia - bowling	O	M	R	W	wd	nb	O	M	R	W	wd	nb
ML Schutt	24	7	52	2		2	13	4	28	0		1
EA Perry	21	2	59	3		2	14	3	26	0		5
TM McGrath	19	8	45	2			11	4	12	1		
JL Jonassen	31	7	52	2			23	10	40	0		
A Wellington	21	1	61	1			36	8	69	1		
NE Bolton							5	1	10	0		
RL Haynes							2	0	8	0		
EJ Villani							1	0	4	0		

Australia	First innings		B	M	4	6	England - bowling	O	M	R	W	w	nb
NE Bolton	c Shrubsole b Marsh		24	70	90	4	KH Brunt	22	9	44	1		
BL Mooney	c Sciver b Ecclestone		27	102	114	2	A Shrubsole	22	7	57	1		
AJ Blackwell	lbw b Ecclestone		6	35	41	1	LA Marsh	44	11	109	3		
EA Perry	not out		213	374	472	27	1	S Ecclestone	37	7	107	3		
EJ Villani	c Taylor b Shrubsole		14	48	55	2	NR Sciver	20	2	59	0	1	
RL Haynes *	lbw b Brunt		33	74	86	6	HC Knight	8	1	21	0		
AJ Healy +	c Shrubsole b Marsh		45	104	116	5	2	GA Elwiss	13	2	40	1		
TM McGrath	c Sciver b Elwiss		47	131	133	7							
JL Jonassen	c Winfield b Marsh		24	39	37	3							
A Wellington	lbw b Ecclestone		2	12	10								
M Schutt	not out		1	6	11								
	1 b, 10 lb, 1 w		12										
	166 overs, 587 mins		9-448 dec										

Fall: 1-48 (Bolton), 2-54 (Mooney), 3-61 (Blackwell), 4-95 (Villani), 5-168 (Haynes), 6-270 (Healy), 7-373 (McGrath), 8-420 (Jonassen), 9-427 (Wellington)

Stumps scores:

Day 1	England (1st inn)	7-235	FC Wilson 11, A Shrubsole 0*	
Day 2	Australia (1st inn)	5-177	EA Perry 70*, AJ Healy 1*	
Day 3	England (2nd inn)	0-40	L Winfield 12, TT Beaumont 25*	

Toss: England
Umpires: GA Abood, GC Joshua, GJ Davidson (TV)
Referee: SR Bernard. Award: EA Perry (Aus)
Attendance: 12,674. Points: Aus 2, Eng 2

GAME ONE - SYDNEY

Needing to win to stay in the hunt for the Ashes, England made an appalling start, losing their first four wickets inside the first five overs. Knight was out second ball of the game, edging Jonassen behind and then Schutt, with her first ball of the match trapped Taylor in front. In the fifth over, Healy held two catches in consecutive balls, the first a brilliant effort, diving to her right to catch Beaumont, the second a more regulation chance. Wyatt survived the hat-trick ball but was put down by Healy on 11, a tough chance to her left, which would have left England 5-31 in the seventh over. England got back into the match as the pair added 64 in eight overs, Sciver aimed a sweep at Kimmince and was adjudged leg before. Wyatt reached her maiden Twenty20 fifty, before being run out by Gardner off her own bowling. Fran Wilson played some clever strokes as England reached their final total of 9-132.

Mooney started the chase in a blaze of glorious drives, dominating a first wicket stand until Healy was out to a good running catch at deep square-leg. Mooney continued to dominate proceedings, as she and Villani careered towards the target with a stand of 47 in five overs. Villani was caught at cover, but Mooney was undeterred, doing as she pleased, until a powerful square drive ended the match and retained the Ashes for Australia.

First Twenty20 at North Sydney Oval on November 17, 2017 (Floodlit) – Australia won by 6 wickets

England		B	4	6	Australia			B	4	6
HC Knight *	c Healy b Jonassen	0	2		AJ Healy +	c Wyatt b Brunt	5	11		
TT Beaumont	c Healy b Perry	4	9		BL Mooney	not out	86	56	11	2
SJ Taylor +	lbw b Schutt	2	5		EJ Villani	c Knight b Ecclestone	17	10	2	1
NR Sciver	lbw b Kimmince	26	32	3	AK Gardner	b Hartley	10	7	2	
KH Brunt	c Healy b Perry	0	1		EA Perry	c & b Hazell	1	2		
DN Wyatt	run out (Gardner-Healy)	50	36	6	RL Haynes *	not out	12	10		1
FC Wilson	not out	23	22	2	DM Kimmince					
JL Gunn	c Haynes b Schutt	4	5		A Wellington					
D Hazell	c Mooney b Schutt	5	6	1	JL Jonassen					
S Ecclestone	st Healy b Schutt	6	2	1	SE Aley					
A Hartley	did not bat				M Schutt					
	1 lb, 11 w	12				1 nb, 2 w	3			
6 overs : 4-28	20 overs, 83 mins	9-132			6 overs: 1-45	15.5 overs, 67 mins	4-134			

Fall: 1-0 (Knight, 0.2), 2-4 (Taylor, 1.1), 3-16 (Beaumont, 4.2), 4-16 (Brunt, 4.3), 5-80 (Sciver, 12.4), 6-100 (Wyatt, 15.5), 7-108 (Gunn, 17.2), 8-125 (Hazell, 19.3), 9-132 (Ecclestone, 19.6)

Fall: 1-30 (Healy, 4.2), 2-77 (Villani, 9.2), 3-93 (Gardner, 11.2), 4-104 (Perry, 12.2)

Australia - bowling	O	M	R	W	wd	nb	Dots	England - bowling	O	M	R	W	wd	nb	Dots
JL Jonassen	3	0	14	1			11	KH Brunt	3	0	33	1	2	1	6
ML Schutt	4	0	22	4	3		15	S Ecclestone	3.5	0	26	1			9
EA Perry	4	0	26	2	3		10	D Hazell	3	0	14	1			10
AJ Wellington	2	0	15	0			3	JL Gunn	2	0	20	0			3
SE Aley	2	0	16	0			1	A Hartley	2	0	24	1			3
AK Gardner	3	0	23	0			4	NR Sciver	2	0	17	0			3
DM Kimmince	2	0	15	1			3								

Toss: Australia.　　　Umpires: SAJ Craig, GC Joshua, JD Ward (TV), Ref: SR Bernard.　　　Award: BL Mooney (Aus)
Wyatt 50: 35 balls, 6x4. Mooney 50: 34 balls, 6x4, 2x6

GAME TWO - CANBERRA

With the Ashes decided, England started well with the bat, as Wyatt struck four early boundaries, before being caught at cover. A sluggish Beaumont was trapped in front before Taylor played some craft sweeps, both reverse and paddle style, until she took on Kimmince at backward point, who picked her off with a direct hit at the bowler's end. Sciver was joined by Brunt who cleared the ropes twice, the pair keeping the momentum going by adding 44 in just over four overs, as England passed 150 to set up a competitive target.

Australia again got off to a flyer, but progressed was halted once Mooney was run out by a direct hit from Gunn at mid-off. The dismissal triggered the loss of 4-7 in 23 balls, with Villani stumped, Healy caught at long-on and Perry dragging on a pull shot. After her brilliant run out earlier, Gunn mopped up the tail to helped England to a comfortable win.

Second Twenty20 International at Manuka Oval, Canberra on November 19, 2017 – England won by 40 runs

England		B	4	6
DN Wyatt	c Haynes b Schutt	19	16	4
TT Beaumont	lbw b Jonassen	9	16	
SJ Taylor +	run out (Kimmince)	30	23	4
NR Sciver	c Haynes b Perry	40	32	3
KH Brunt	not out	32	24	2 2
HC Knight *	b Kimmince	4	3	
FC Wilson	b Schutt	6	5	1
JL Gunn	not out	3	2	
S Ecclestone				
A Shrubsole				
D Hazell				
	2 b, 2 lb, 1 nb, 4 w	9		
6 overs: 1-38	20 overs, 77 mins	6-152		

Australia		B	4	6
BL Mooney	run out (Gunn)	17	16	2
AJ Healy +	c Shrubsole b Gunn	24	21	5
EJ Villani	st Taylor b Brunt	1	6	
EA Perry	b Brunt	5	7	
RL Haynes *	c Sciver b Ecclestone	14	12	2
AK Gardner	c Brunt b Hazell	8	8	1
DM Kimmince	b Ecclestone	17	14	1
JL Jonassen	c Sciver b Gunn	11	11	1
SE Aley	lbw b Gunn	1	3	
MR Strano	b Gunn	3	9	
M Schutt	not out	1	2	
	5 lb, 4 w	10		
6 overs: 1-47	18 overs, 73 mins	112		

Fall: 1-26 (Wyatt, 3.5), 2-40 (Beaumont, 6.3), 3-85 (Taylor, 12.1), 4-119 (Sciver, 16.4), 5-128 (Knight, 17.3), 6-148 (Wilson, 19.1)

Fall: 1-45 (Mooney, 5.3), 2-47 (Villani, 6.4), 3-49 (Healy, 7.3), 4-52 (Perry, 8.1), 5-65 (Gardner, 9.6), 6-90 (Haynes, 13.2), 7-93 (Kimmince), 8-104 (Aley, 15.3), 9-110 (Jonassen, 17.1), 10-112 (Strano)

Australia - bowling	O	M	R	W	wd	nb	Dots
MR Strano	4	0	30	0			7
ML Schutt	4	0	16	2			15
EA Perry	2	0	21	1	1		4
JL Jonassen	4	0	18	1			8
AK Gardner	2	0	17	0			2
DM Kimmince	2	0	24	1	1		2
SE Aley	2	0	22	0	1	1	3

England - bowling	O	M	R	W	wd	nb	Dots
A Shrubsole	3	0	23	0	1		9
S Ecclestone	4	0	24	2			12
D Hazell	3	0	24	1		1	7
KH Brunt	4	0	10	2	1		16
JL Gunn	3	0	13	4	1		10
MR Sciver	1	0	13	0	1		1

Toss: England.   Umpires: GC Joshua, JD Ward, SAJ Craig (TV), Ref: SR Bernard.   Award: KH Brunt (Eng)
Wyatt 50: 35 balls, 6x4. Mooney 50: 34 balls, 6x4, 2x6

GAME THREE - CANBERRA

In what ended up being the highest aggregate of runs in a Twenty20 International ever, England chased down an imposing target with an over to spare, thanks to a magnificent knock by Dani Wyatt. Needing 179 to win, England were up against it at 3-30 in the fifth over, whereupon Wyatt and skipper Heather Knight added 139 from 75 balls, to take control of the match. Earlier, Australia scored at will, before Knight took a great catch at cover, diving forward. Mooney continued her superb form from the first match, hitting the attack to all parts, before dabbing one into the covers to bring up her ton from just 65 balls, in the 19th over. Wyatt responded with a 56-ball hundred bringing an end to an outstanding Ashes series – which was tied on eight points each.

Third Twenty20 International at Manuka Oval, Canberra on November 21, 2017 (floodlit) – England won by 4 wickets

Australia		B	4	6
BL Mooney	not out	117	70	19 1
AJ Healy +	c Knight b Brunt	19	17	3
EJ Villani	b Ecclestone	16	13	1 1
EA Perry	not out	22	20	2
RL Haynes *				
AK Gardner				
DM Kimmince				
JL Jonassen				
A Wellington				
MR Strano				
M Schutt				
	1 lb, 3 w	4		
6 overs: 0-47	20 overs, 74 mins	2-178		

England		B	4	6
DN Wyatt	b Kimmince	100	57	13 2
TT Beaumont	c Gardner b Jonassen	1	2	
SJ Taylor +	c Haynes b Jonassen	5	3	1
NR Sciver	run out (Villani)	7	8	
HC Knight *	run out (Healy)	51	37	3 1
KH Brunt	c Perry b Kimmince	5	4	1
FC Wilson	not out	5	3	1
JL Gunn	not out	0	0	
S Ecclestone				
A Shrubsole				
D Hazell				
	1 lb, 6 w	7		
6 overs: 3-36	19 overs, 75 mins	6-181		

Fall: 1-59 (Healy, 7.4), 2-93 (Villani, 11.5)

Fall: 1-3 (Beaumont, 0.5), 2-16 (Taylor, 2.1), 3-30 (Sciver, 4.6), 4-169 (Knight, 17.3), 5-171 (Wyatt, 18.1), 6-177 (Brunt, 18.5)

Australian Cricket Digest, 2018-19

England - bowling	O	M	R	W	wd	nb	Dots	Australia - bowling	O	M	R	W	wd	nb	Dots
A Shrubsole	3	0	36	0	1		6	Jonassen	4	0	25	2			10
S Ecclestone	4	0	34	1			8	Schutt	3	0	41	0	1		2
D Hazell	4	0	31	0	1		7	Strano	3	0	27	0			1
KH Brunt	4	0	25	1	1		11	Perry	2	0	11	0			5
JL Gunn	3	0	31	0			3	Gardner	2	0	21	0			3
HC Knight	2	0	20	0			2	Wellington	2	0	25	0			0
								Kimmince	3	0	30	2	1		4

Toss: Australia.   Umpires: SAJ Craig, JD Ward, GC Joshua, (TV), Ref: SR Bernard.   Award: DN Wyatt (Aus)
Mooney 50: 38 balls, 9x4; 100: 65 balls, 15x4, 1x6. Wyatt 50: 37 balls, 5x4, 1x6; 100: 56 balls, 13x4, 2x6. Knight 50: 35 balls, 3x4, 1x6

LEADING AVERAGES
2017-18 ASHES
ACROSS THE THREE FORMATS
Batting

	M	Inn	NO	Runs	HS	Avge	100S	50s
EA Perry (Aus)	7	7	2	351	213*	70.20	1	1
HC Knight (Eng)	7	8	2	335	88*	55.83	0	4
BL Mooney (Aus)	4	4	2	247	117*	123.50	1	1
AJ Healy (Aus)	7	7	0	238	71	34.00	0	2
TT Beaumont (Eng)	7	8	0	227	74	28.37	0	2
SJ Taylor (Eng)	7	7	0	195	69	27.85	0	1
RL Haynes (Aus)	7	6	2	187	89*	46.75	0	1
DN Wyatt (Eng)	3	3	0	169	100	56.33	1	1
NE Bolton (Aus)	4	4	0	154	66	38.50	0	2

Bowling

	M	Overs	Mdns	Runs	Wkts	Avge	Best
ML Schutt (Aus)	7	76	14	273	18	15.16	4-22
JL Gunn (Eng)	6	32	0	204	11	18.54	4-13
EA Perry (Aus)	7	65.4	5	259	10	25.90	3-59
JL Jonassen (Aus)	7	91	17	290	10	29.00	2-25
S Ecclestone (Eng)	6	63.5	7	278	9	30.88	3-107
A Hartley (Eng)	4	28	2	149	7	21.28	3-45
KH Brunt (Eng)	7	57	11	258	7	36.85	2-10

Wicket-keeping: AJ Healy (Aus) 9 dismissals (7 ct, 2 st), SJ Taylor (Eng) 6 (2 ct, 4 st)
Fielding: 6 - NR Sciver (Eng), EA Perry (Aus)
4 - L Winfield (Eng), A Shrubsole (Eng), KH Brunt (Eng), RL Haynes (Aus), ML Schutt (Aus), EJ Villani (Aus)

ASHES SERIES 1934-35 TO 2017-18

Year	Host	M	Winner	Result	Holder	Year	Host	M	Winner	Result	Holder
1934-35	Aus	3	Eng	2-0	Eng	1987	Eng	3	Aus	1-0	Aus
1937	Eng	3		1-1	Eng	1991-92	Aus	1	Aus	1-0	Aus
1948-49	Aus	3	Aus	1-0	Aus	1998	Eng	3		0-0	Aus
1951	Eng	3		1-1	Aus	2001	Eng	2	Aus	2-0	Aus
1957-58	Aus	3		0-0	Aus	2002-03	Aus	2	Aus	1-0	Aus
1963	Eng	3	Eng	1-0	Eng	2005	Eng	2	Eng	1-0	Eng
1968-69	Aus	3		0-0	Eng	2007-08	Aus	1	Eng	1-0	Eng
1976	Eng	3		0-0	Eng	2009	Eng	1		0-0	Eng
1984-85	Aus	5	Aus	2-1	Aus	2010-11	Aus	1	Aus	1-0	Aus

In 2013 a points system came in combining points for the Test, ODIs and Twenty20s to decide the winner

Year	Host	Test	Result	ODIs	T20s	Winner	Result	Holder
2013	Eng	1	Drawn	Eng 3-0	Eng 2-1	Eng	12-4	Eng
2013-14	Aus	1	Eng	Aus 2-1	Aus 2-1	Eng	10-8	Eng
2015	Eng	1	Aus	Aus 2-1	Eng 2-1	Aus	10-6	Aus
2017-18	Aus	1	Drawn	Aus 2-1	Eng 2-1	Drawn	8-8	Aus

AUSTRALIA'S SUCCESSFUL TOUR TO INDIA

Australia had a very successful time in India in February, winning three One-day internationals very comfortably against India before taking out the Twenty20 tri-series that followed. Nicole Bolton dominated with the bat in the first two Odis with Ellyse Perry consistent with bat and ball. The bowling was strong, with Megan Schutt excellent with the new ball, while spinners Jess Jonassen, Amanda Wellington and Ash Gardner were all amongst the wickets.

Skipper Meg Lanning was also back, finding her feet somewhat in the ODIs, before finishing the tour brilliantly, with 88 not out in the final of Twenty20 tri-series. Alyssa Healy made a brilliant ton in the third ODI and Elyse Villani was a consistent run getter in the Twenty20 matches. Schutt took most wickets in the tri-series and a hat-trick against England, with Delissa Kimmince also a regular wicket taker in the Twenty20 matches.

Tour match v India A at Bandra Kurla Complex, Mumbai on March 6, 2018 – Australia won by 321 runs
Australia 8-413 (50 overs) (NE Bolton 58, BL Mooney 115, EA Perry 65, AK Gardner 90; S Koli 3-67) **def India A 92** (29.5 overs) (ML Schutt 3-24). *The visitors were too strong, Mooney facing 83 balls, hitting 18 fours, while Gardner faced 44 balls, hit 9x4, 6x6*

Tour match v India A at Bandra Kurla Complex, Mumbai on March 8, 2018 – Australia won by 7 wickets
India A 170 (46.2 overs) (AJ Wellington 3-30) **lost to Australia 3-171** (26 overs) (MM Lanning 63 retired out)

ONE-DAY INTERNATIONALS v INDIA
GAME ONE - VADODARA

Australia, who welcomed back Meg Lanning after over seven months out with a shoulder injury, were too good for India in the opening match of the series. At 7-113, Verma was joined by Vastraker, who added 78 for the eight wicket, to give the home side's innings some respectability, Jonassen taking three of the last four wickets to fall. In reply Australia made short work of the target, Bolton scoring her fourth ODI ton and first against India.

First ODI v India at Reliance Cricket Stadium, Vadodara on March 12, 2018 – Australia won by 8 wickets

India			B	4	6	Australia			B	4	6
P G Raut	lbw b Wellington	37	50	6	1	NE Bolton	not out	100	101	12	
SS Mandhana	c Lanning b Gardner	12	25	2		AJ Healy+	c Krishnamurthy b Pandey	38	29	6	1
J I Rodriques	c Healy b Wellington	1	8			MM Lanning *	run out (Krishnamurthy)	33	38	5	
H Kaur *	c Healy b Schutt	9	29	1		EA Perry	not out	25	26	1	
DB Sharma	c Carey b Jonassen	18	25	1	1	BL Mooney					
V Krishnamurthy	c Mooney b Wellington	16	19	2		RL Haynes					
S Verma +	c Bolton b Jonassen	41	71	3		AK Gardner					
SS Pandey	c Perry b Jonassen	2	6			NJ Carey					
P Vastrakar	c Haynes b Jonassen	51	56	7	1	J L Jonassen					
P Yadav	run out (Perry-Jonassen)	5	11			A Wellington					
RS Gayakwad	not out	0	0			M Schutt					
	1 lb, 7 w	8					3 lb, 1nb, 2 w	6			
10 overs: 1-44	50 overs	200				10 overs: 1-67	32.1 overs	2-202			

Fall: 1-38 (Mandhana), 2-45 (Rodriques), 3-60 (Raut), 4-83 (Sharma), 5-87 (Kaur), 6-110 (Krishnamurthy), 7-113 (Pandey), 8-189 (Verma), 9-199 (Vastrakar), 10-200 (Yadav)

Fall: 1-60 (Healy), 2-128 (Lanning)

Australia - bowling	O	M	R	W	wd	nb	India - bowling	O	M	R	W	wd	nb
ML Schutt	10	1	37	1	4		SS Pandey	7	1	38	1		
EA Perry	7	0	46	0			P Vastrakar	3	0	16	0		
AK Gardner	7	0	34	1			DB Sharma	6	0	47	0		
NJ Carey	10	2	28	0			RS Gayakwad	5	0	24	0		
AJ Wellington	6	0	24	3	2		P Yadav	8	0	49	0	2	1
J L Jonassen	10	1	30	4			H Kaur	3.1	0	25	0		

GAME TWO - VADODARA
Bolton top scored for Australia but was dropped three times before reaching fifty. Perry also had luck, dropped on 37, while Mooney should have been given out caught behind on 37 off Poonam. Australia scored 84 off the last ten overs as they made the most of the dropped chances. Mandhana dominated an opening stand which ended with her dismissal in the 18th over. From there Australia took control and made it back to back wins.

261

Australian Cricket Digest, 2018-19

Second ODI v India at Reliance Cricket Stadium, Vadodara on March 15, 2018 – Australia won by 60 runs

Australia		R	B	4	6
NE Bolton	lbw b Bisht	84	88	12	
AJ Healy+	c Krishnamurthy b Yadav	19	37	3	
MM Lanning *	c Raut b Pandey	24	43	2	
EA Perry	not out	70	70	6	2
RL Haynes	b Kaur	0	3		
BL Mooney	c & b Pandey	56	40	9	
AK Gardner	st Verma b Yadav	6	6	1	
NJ Carey	c Krishnamurthy b Pandey	16	11	3	
JL Jonassen	run out (Raj)	1	2		
A Wellington	run out (Vastrakar-Sharma)	0	0		
M Schutt	not out	0	0		
	1b, 2 lb, 8 w	11			
10 overs: 0-47	50 overs	9-287			

India		R	B	4	6
PG Raut	c Wellington b Gardner	27	61	2	
SS Mandhana	c Schutt b Jonassen	67	53	12	1
DB Sharma	c Lanning b Jonassen	26	45	1	
MD Raj *	c Healy b Perry	15	14	2	
H Kaur	c Healy b Wellington	17	26	2	
V Krishnamurthy	st Healy b Wellington	2	5		
S Verma +	c & b Jonassen	8	12	1	
SS Pandey	c Jonassen b Carey	15	19	2	
P Vastrakar	c Healy b Schutt	30	33	2	1
EK Bisht	not out	8	20		
P Yadav	lbw b Perry	3	9		
	3 lb, 1nb, 5 w	9			
10 overs: 0-44	49.2 overs	227			

Fall: 1-54 (Healy), 2-130 (Lanning), 3-143 (Bolton), 4-144 (Haynes), 5-240 (Mooney), 6-248 (Gardner), 7-273 (Carey), 8-285 (Jonassen), 9-286 (Wellington)

Fall: 1-88 (Mandhana), 2-99 (Raut), 3-123 (Raj), 4-155 (Kaur), 5-159 (Krishnamurthy), 6-168 (Verma), 7-170 (Verma), 8-197 (Pandey), 9-223 (Vastrakar), 10-227 (Yadav)

India - bowling	O	M	R	W	wd	nb
SS Pandey	10	0	61	3	3	
P Vastrakar	7	0	42	0	2	
DB Sharma	8	0	51	0		
EK Bisht	10	1	55	1		
P Yadav	10	0	52	2	1	
H Kaur	5	0	23	1	1	

Australia - bowling	O	M	R	W	wd	nb
ML Schutt	10	3	24	1	1	
AK Gardner	10	0	44	1	1	
EA Perry	8.2	0	41	2	1	
NJ Carey	7	0	44	1	1	1
JL Jonassen	10	0	51	3		
AJ Wellington	4	0	20	2		

Toss: India. Umpires: AY Dandekar, A Nand Kishore, J Madanagopal (TV), Ref: M Nayyar. Award: NE Bolton (Aus)
Bolton 50: 50 balls, 9x4, Perry 50: 58 balls, 5x4, 5x6, Mooney 50: 36 balls, 8x4. Mandhana 50: 41 balls, 9x4, 1x6

GAME THREE – VADODARA

Alyssa Healy's maiden hundred was the backbone of the Aussie innings, where India missed at least half a dozen chances. India's openers got off to a brilliant start, but then went in consecutive balls in the 14th over. When Kaur went in the 22nd, caught behind edging a cut, the Aussies took control and ensured a comfortable win.

Third ODI v India at Reliance Cricket Stadium, Vadodara on March 18, 2018 – Australia won by 97 runs

Australia		R	B	4	6
NE Bolton	c & b Bisht	11	18	1	
AJ Healy+	c sub b Yadav	133	115	17	2
MM Lanning *	c Raj b Sharma	18	14	4	
EA Perry	c Verma b Pandey	32	60	2	
RL Haynes	run out	43	39	5	
BL Mooney	not out	34	19	5	
AK Gardner	c Yadav b Kaur	35	20	6	
NJ Carey	b Kaur	17	15	3	
JL Jonassen					
A Wellington					
M Schutt					
	1b, 3 lb, 5 w	9			
10 overs: 1-63	50 overs	7-332			

India		R	B	4	6
J IRodriques	c Haynes b Gardner	42	41	7	
SS Mandhana	lbw b Gardner	52	42	10	
MD Raj *	c Haynes b Jonassen	21	38	1	
H Kaur	c Healy b Carey	25	26	4	
DB Sharma	b Perry	37	47	4	
MR Meshram	c Carey b Gardner	1	5		
S Verma +	c Lanning b Schutt	29	37	3	1
P Vastrakar	c Carey b Schutt	6	17	1	
SS Pandey	c Healy b Perry	0	1		
P Yadav	not out	7	14	1	
EK Bisht	absent hurt				
	1b, 2 lb, 12 w	15			
10 overs: 0-68	44.4 overs	235			

Fall: 1-19 (Bolton), 2-64 (Lanning), 3-143 (Perry), 4-239 (Healy), 5-242 (Haynes), 6-285 (Gardner), 7-332 (Carey)

Fall: 1-101 (Rodriques), 2-101 (Mandhana), 3-147 (Kaur), 4-179 (Raj), 5-182 (Meshram), 6-221 (Verma), 7-221 (Sharma), 8-221 (Pandey, 39.4 ov), 9-235 (Vastrakar, 44.4 ov)

Australian Cricket Digest, 2018-19

India - bowling	O	M	R	W	wd	nb		Australia - bowling	O	M	R	W	wd	nb
SS Pandey	9	0	61	1				ML Schutt	9.4	0	54	2	1	
DB Sharma	10	1	50	1				AK Gardner	8	0	40	3		
EK Bisht	7.3	0	38	1				JL Jonassen	10	0	40	1		
P Vastrakar	5	0	44	0	1			EA Perry	9	1	40	2	1	
P Yadav	10	0	54	1	1			NJ Carey	5	0	34	1	1	
H Kaur	5.3	0	51	2	2			AJ Wellington	3	0	24	0	1	
MR Meshram	2	0	25	0										
JI Rodriques	1	0	5	0										

Toss: Australia.   Umpires: AY Dandekar, A Nand Kishore, J Madanagopal (TV), Ref: M Nayyar.   Award: AJ Healy (Aus)

Healy 50: 47 balls, 8x4, 1x6, 100: 94 balls, 12x4, 2x6. Mandhana 50: 41 balls, 10x4

AUSTRALIA WIN TWENTY20 TRI SERIES

MATCH ONE – INDIA v AUSTRALIA

India started in fine style adding 72 with Mandhana scoring a 30-ball fifty (fastest for India), reaching it in the ninth over when she pulled Perry for six. Mandhana went in the 14th over and despite losing 3-1 from seven balls, India scored 48 off the last five overs to go past 152.

After the early loss of Healy and Gardner, both to Goswami in the powerplay, Mooney and Villani prospered adding 79 from 57 balls, before skipper Lanning finished the game off with 11 balls to spare.

Match 1 – India v Australia at Brabourne Stadium, Mumbai on March 22, 2018 – Australia won by 6 wickets

India		B	4	6		Australia		B	4	6	
MD Raj	st Healy b Gardner	18	27	2		BL Mooney	c Pandey b Goswami	45	32	8	
SS Mandhana	c Molineux b Gardner	67	41	11	2	+AJ Healy	b Goswami	4	2	1	
H Kaur*	c Molineux b Perry	13	16	2		AK Gardner	b Goswami	15	8	3	
JI Rodriques	c Gardner b Perry	1	3			EJ Villani	c &b Yadav	39	33	4	
V Krishnamurthy	not out	15	10	1	1	*MM Lanning	not out	35	25	4	1
AA Patil	c Molineux b Kimmince	35	21	6	1	RL Haynes	not out	12	9	1	
SS Pandey	not out	1	2			EA Perry					
RA Dhar						SG Molineux					
T Bhatia +						DM Kimmince					
JN Goswami						JL Jonassen					
P Yadav						M Schutt					
	1 b, 1w	2					4 lb, 2 w	6			
6 overs: 0-47	20 overs	5-152				6 overs: 2-57	18.1 overs	4-156			

Fall: 1-72 (Raj, 9.3), 2-99 (Mandhana, 13.3), 3-100 (Rodriques, 14.1), 4-100 (Kaur, 14.3), 5-141 (Patil, 18.6)

Fall: 1-9 (Healy, 0.5), 2-29 (Gardner, 2.4), 3-108 (Mooney, 12.1), 4-112 (Villani, 13.1)

Australia - bowling	O	M	R	W	wd	nb	Dots		India - bowling	O	M	R	W	wd	nb	Dots
ML Schutt	4	1	23	0			18		JN Goswami	4	0	30	3	1		12
AK Gardner	4	1	22	2	1		13		SS Pandey	2	0	24	0			3
JL Jonassen	2	0	22	0			4		AA Patil	4	0	25	0			8
DM Kimmince	4	0	38	1			8		P Yadav	4	0	22	1			9
WA Perry	4	0	31	2			13		RA Dhar	2.1	0	28	0	1		2
SG Molineux	2	0	15	0			3		H Kaur	1	0	12	0			2
									JI Rodriques	1	0	11	0			2

Toss: Australia. Umpires: KN Ananthapadmanabhan, HAS Khalid, RR Pandit (TV), Ref: M Nayyar   Award: AK Gardner (Aus)

Mandhana 50: 30 balls, 9x4, 2x6

MATCH TWO – AUSTRALIA v ENGLAND

After losing Mooney in the fourth over, Australia were well placed at 1-49 at the end of the Powerplay, but then lost Healy and Gardner in the same over from Sciver. Haynes played well but couldn't get much help from the other end, before she was dismissed in the final over, as Hazell and Gunn bowled well in the middle and late overs.

Australia had a hope when Smith and Wyatt were both out inside the first five overs, but then Beaumont and Sciver dominated proceedings in a stand worth 116 off 73 balls, giving Australia their first taste of defeat on the tour.

Australian Cricket Digest, 2018-19

Match 2 – Australia v England at Brabourne Stadium, Mumbai on March 23, 2018 – England won by 8 wickets

Australia		B	4	6
AJ Healy +	c Wyatt b Sciver	31 23	2	2
BL Mooney	run out (George)	4	9	
AK Gardner	c Beaumont b Sciver	28 16	3	2
EJ Villani	c Davidson-Richards b Gunn	5	7	
RL Haynes *	c Sciver b Gunn	65 45	8	1
EA Perry	c Knight b Hazell	2	3	
SG Molineux	c Sciver b Gunn	6	12	
DM Kimmince	run out (Gunn-Sciver)	1	2	
NJ Carey	not out	1	2	
JL Jonassen	not out	1	1	
M Schutt				
	1 b, 4 w	5		
6 overs: 1-49	20 overs	8-149		

England		B	4	6
DN Wyatt	b Kimmince	18 10	2	1
BF Smith	st Healy b Schutt	1	5	
TT Beaumont +	not out	58 44	8	
NR Sciver	not out	68 43	10	2
HC Knight *				
FC Wilson				
AN Davidson-Richards				
JL Gunn				
D Hazell				
S Ecclestone				
KL George				
	3 b, 1 lb, 1w	5		
6 overs: 2-51	17 overs	2-150		

Fall: 1-26 (Mooney, 3.5), 2-54 (Healy, 7.1), 3-66 (Gardner, 7.6), 4-86 (Villani, 10.5), 5-97 (Perry, 12.4), 6-131 (Molineux, 17.6), 7-134 (Kimmince, 18.4), 8-147 (Haynes, 19.4)

Fall: 1-2 (Smith, 1.1), 2-34 (Wyatt, 4.5)

England - bowling	O	M	R	W	wd	nb	Dots
NR Sciver	3	0	29	2			6
KL George	3	0	22	0	2		7
S Ecclestone	3	0	26	0	1		7
D Hazell	4	0	24	1			10
JL Gunn	4	0	26	3	1		7
HC Knight	3	0	21	0			6

Australia - bowling	O	M	R	W	wd	nb	Dots
JL Jonassen	4	0	25	0			11
ML Schutt	3	0	30	1			6
EA Perry	3	0	28	0			7
DM Kimmince	1	0	12	1			3
NJ Carey	2	0	19	0			2
SG Molineux	3	0	23	0	1		8
AK Gardner	1	0	9	0			1

Toss: England. Umpires: RR Pandit, RR Pandit, KN Ananthapadmanabhan (TV), Ref: M Nayyar   Award: NR Sciver (Eng)
Haynes 50: 37 balls, 7x4. Beaumont 50: 37 balls, 8x4, Sciver 50: 34 balls, 7x4, 2x6

MATCH THREE – INDIA v ENGLAND

India would have been well pleased with their total of just under 200, with Raj passing fifty and Mandhana taking just 40 balls over her 76. England were out of the blocks at pace, 0-13 after the first over, 0-26 after two, 0-44 after four and 1-67 after six. Wyatt reached her fifty before the Powerplay had ended, from just 24 balls (8x4, 2x6) as the Indian attack could do very little to stop her.

In the ninth over Wyatt struck Poonam for consecutive sixes and reached her ton in the 15th, when she lofted Sharma back over her head to the boundary. Interestingly her second fifty was four balls slower than her first, as she reached three figures from 52 balls (13x4, 1x6) before being dismissed in the 17th over with just 16 wanted from the last three overs. Sciver and Knight ensured England won, getting there with eight balls to spare, in what was the biggest ever run chase in Women's T20 Internationals.

Match 3 – India v England at Brabourne Stadium, Mumbai on March 25, 2018 – England won by 7 wickets

Toss: England. **India 4-198** (20 overs) (MD Raj 53, SS Mandhana 76, H Kaur 30*; NE Farrant 2-32) **lost to England 3-199** (18.4 overs) (DN Wyatt 124, TT Beaumont 35; DB Sharma 2-36). *Player of the match Wyatt in all faced 64 balls, hit 15x4, 5x6*

MATCH FOUR – INDIA v AUSTRALIA

Australia were under the pump early with Vastrakar taking two early wickets, but then Mooney and Villani joined forces in a stand of 114 from just 72 balls as the Indian attack wilted. Megan Schutt took the valuable wickets of Mandhana and Raj in the second over of the innings, before completing the hat-trick when she returned to bowl the fifth over, with Sharma hitting a catch to mid-off. India fought back with a stand of 54 for the fourth wicket and despite good knocks from 17 year-old Rodriques, Kaur and Patil, Australia always had the match firmly under control.

Australian Cricket Digest, 2018-19

Match 4 – India v Australia at Brabourne Stadium, Mumbai on March 26, 2018 – Australia won by 36 runs

Australia		R	B	4	6
BL Mooney	c Rodriques b Goswami	71	46	8	
AJ Healy+	c Rodriques b Vastrakar	9	8	2	
AK Gardner	b Vastrakar	17	10	4	
EJ Villani	c Rodriques b P Yadav	61	42	10	
MM Lanning*	not out	11	10	1	
EA Perry	c Mandhana b R Yadav	1	2	-	
RL Haynes	not out	10	4	1	
DM Kimmince					
JL Jonassen					
M Schutt					
A Wellington					
	1 lb, 2 nb, 3 w	6			
6 overs: 2-46	20 overs	5-186			

India		R	B	4	6
JI Rodriques	c Schutt b Kimmince	50	41	8	
SS Mandhana	b Schutt	3	4		
MD Raj	b Schutt	0	1		
DB Sharma	c Wellington b Schutt	2	4		
H Kaur*	c Kimmince b Gardner	33	30	2	1
AA Patil	not out	38	26	6	
P Vastrakar	not out	19	14	1	
T Bhatia+					
RP Yadav					
JN Goswami					
P Yadav					
	1 b, 4 w	5			
6 overs: 3-35	20 overs	5-150			

Fall: 1-12 (Healy, 1.5), 2-29 (Gardner, 3.5), 3-143 (Villani, 15.3), 4-173 (Mooney, 18.4), 5-175 (Perry, 19.1)

Fall: 1-15 (Mandhana, 1.5), 2-15 (Raj, 1.6), 3-26 (Sharma, 4.1), 4-80 (Rodriques, 12.3), 5-97 (Kaur, 13.5)

India - bowling	O	M	R	W	wd	nb	Dots
JN Goswami	4	0	35	1		1	9
P Vastrakar	3	0	28	2			9
AA Patil	4	0	35	0			6
DB Sharma	1	0	14	0			1
P Yadav	4	0	34	1		1	6
RP Yadav	4	0	39	1	2		5

Australia - bowling	O	M	R	W	wd	nb	Dots
JL Jonassen	4	0	31	0	1		6
ML Schutt	4	0	31	3	1		9
EA Perry	4	0	24	0			9
DM Kimmince	4	0	27	1	2		7
AJ Wellington	2	0	12	0			6
AK Gardner	2	0	24	1			2

Toss: India. Umpires: KN Ananthapadmanabhan, RR Pandit, UV Gandhe (TV), Ref: M Nayyar.   Award: ML Schutt (Aus)
Mooney 50: 35 balls, 5x4, Villani 50: 35 balls, 8x4. Rodriques 50: 37 balls, 8x4.
M Schutt took a hat-trick - S Mandhana, M Raj, DB Sharma

MATCH FIVE – AUSTRALIA v ENGLAND

Australia got their revenge in this game, after being hammered by England in the previous encounter. The in-form Wyatt started with a boundary first ball, was dropped second ball before being caught at mid-on from her fourth. England steadied to be 1-20 after three overs, before losing three wickets in their next three, to be 4-40 at the end of the Powerplay. When Knight was out LBW missing an attempted paddle in the seventh over, England were all but cooked.

Australia started poorly in reply, being two down in the third over, but Lanning started to take control, hitting Hazell for five consecutive fours in the sixth over. The skipper and Perry, restored back to the top of the order added 85 from 54 balls to complete the most comfortable of victories.

Match 5 – Australia v England at Brabourne Stadium, Mumbai on March 28, 2018 – Australia won by 8 wickets

England		R	B	4	6
DN Wyatt	c Wellington b Jonassen	6	4	1	
AE Jones+	c Villani b Perry	4	8		
TT Beaumont	c Healy b Kimmince	17	12	3	
NR Sciver	c Lanning b Schutt	10	9	2	
HC Knight*	lbw b Wellington	0	3		
FC Wilson	c Perry b Gardner	11	15	1	
AN Davidson-Richards	c Haynes b Jonassen	24	24	2	
JL Gunn	b Kimmince	12	12	2	
D Hazell	b Kimmince	0	3		
S Eccleston	b Schutt	5	11		
NE Farrant	not out	3	5		
	2 lb, 2 w	4			
6 overs: 4-40	17.4 overs	96			

Australia		R	B	4	6
AJ Healy+	c Gunn b Sciver	6	4	1	
EA Perry	not out	47	32	9	
EJ Villani	c Sciver b Eccleston	1	5		
MM Lanning*	not out	41	28	8	
AK Gardner					
RL Haynes					
SG Molineux					
DM Kimmince					
JL Jonassen					
ML Schutt					
AJ Wellington					
	2 w	2			
6 overs: 2-42	11.3 overs	2-97			

Fall: 1-6 (Wyatt, 0.4), 2-28 (Beaumont, 3.4), 3-31 (Jones, 4.4), 4-40 (Sciver, 5.3), 5-40 (Knight, 6.3), 6-61 (Wilson, 10.5), 7-88 (Gunn, 14.2), 8-88 (Hazell, 14.5), 9-90 (Davidson-Richards, 15.4), 10-96 (Ecclestone, 17.4 ov)

Fall: 1-9 (Healy, 0.6), 2-12 (Villani, 2.3)

Australia - bowling	O	M	R	W	wd	nb	Dots	Australia - bowling	O	M	R	W	wd	nb	Dots
JL Jonassen	4	0	21	2			11	NR Sciver	1	0	9	1	1		1
ML Schutt	2.4	0	13	2			9	NE Farrant	2	0	7	0			8
EA Perry	3	0	25	1	1		9	S Ecclestone	3	0	15	1			10
DM Kimmince	4	0	20	3	1		10	DN Hazell	1.3	0	30	0			0
AJ Wellington	1	0	2	1			4	JL Gunn	2	0	19	0	1		6
SG Molineux	2	0	9	0			6	AN Davidson							
AK Gardner	1	0	4	1			2	-Richards	2	0	17	0			5

Toss: Australia. Umpires: KN Ananthapadmanabhan, UV Gandhe, HAS Khalid (TV), Ref: M Nayyar   Award: EA Perry (Aus)

MATCH SIX – INDIA v ENGLAND

India salvaged some pride from the series with a convincing win in their final game. England started well to be 1-59 in the seventh over, before India's bowlers took control, taking the last nine wickets for just 48. The consistent Mandhana batted throught the chase, India winning easily with 26 balls in hand.

Match 6 – India v England at Brabourne Stadium, Mumbai on March 29, 2018 – India won by 8 wickets
Toss: England. **England 107** (18.5 overs) (DN Wyatt 31; AA Patil 3-21) **lost to India 2-108** (15.4 overs) (SS Mandhana 62*) *Mandhana faced 41 balls, hit 8x4, 1x6. Off-spinner Anuja Patil was player of the match.*

THE FINAL – AUSTRALIA v ENGLAND

Australia rose to the occasion in the final, making the highest ever score in a Women's T20 International. After losing Mooney off the fourth ball, Healy and Gardner took their team past the Powerplay adding 61, before both went in the space of three balls in the eighth over. Lanning and Villani then dominated proceedings to add 139, as Australia piled on 129 off the last ten overs and 60 off the last five.
After hitting her first ball for four, Wyatt's partner was run out from mid-on as she slipped trying to regain her ground. 13 came from the over but then Perry had Beaumont caught behind with her first ball in the second to put England in early bother. Wyatt was looking very dangerous until she gave a catch to cover off the last ball of the fifth over. Sciver and Jones added 51 for the fourth wicket, but they slipped way behind the rate as Australia pulled off an easy win. Schutt cleaned up the middle and lower order, taking out the player of the series, with her skipper Lanning a clear choice of the player of the match.

The Final – Australia v England at Brabourne Stadium, Mumbai on March 31, 2018 – Australia won by 57 runs

Australia			B	4	6	England			B	4	6
AJ Healy+	b Gunn	33	24	5	1	DN Wyatt	c Lanning b Kimmince	34	17	7	
BL Mooney	lbw b Farrant	0	1			BF Smith	run out				
							(Wellington-Jonassen)	0	0		
AK Gardner	c Jones b Gunn	33	20	3	3	TT Beaumont	c Healy b Perry	0	1		
MM Lanning*	not out	88	45	16	1	NR Sciver	c &b Gardner	50	42	5	
EJ Villani	run out (Smith-Gunn)	51	30	8		AE Jones+	c Villani b Gardner	30	28	2	
RL Haynes	not out	1	1			FC Wilson	c Perry b Schutt	14	15	1	
EA Perry						AN Davidson-Richards	b Schutt	1	4		
DM Kimmince						JL Gunn	b Schutt	5	6		
JL Jonassen						S Ecclestone	c Mooney b Kimmince	2	1		
A Wellington						D Hazell*	not out	4	4		
M Schutt						NE Farrant	not out	1	1		
	1 nb, 2 w	3					5 lb, 1nb, 5 w	11			
6 overs: 1-52	20 overs	4-209				6 overs: 3-49	20 overs	9-152			

Fall: 1-1 (Mooney, 0.4), 2-62 (Gardner, 7.1),   Fall: 1-4 (Smith, 0.2), 2-14 (Beaumont, 1.1), 3-47 (Wyatt, 4.6), 4-98
3-66 (Healy, 7.3), 4-205 (Villani, 19.3)   (Jones, 12.1), 5-138 (Sciver, 16.4), 6-140 (Wilson, 17.1), 7-140
            (Davidson-Richards, 17.4), 8-143 (Ecclestone, 18.3), 9-151 (Gunn, 19.5)

England - bowling	O	M	R	W	wd	nb	Dots	Australia - bowling	O	M	R	W	wd	nb	Dots
NE Farrant	4	0	44	1			10	JL Jonassen	4	0	38	0			3
S Ecclestone	4	0	41	0			12	EA Perry	4	0	35	1	1	1	10
NR Sciver	4	0	39	0			6	ML Schutt	4	0	14	3			13
DN Hazell	3	0	30	0			3	DM Kimmince	4	0	35	2	2		8
JL Gunn	4	0	38	2	2	1	7	AJ Wellington	1	0	5	0			4
AN Davidson								AK Gardner	3	0	20	2			2
-Richards	1	0	17	0			1								

Toss: England. Umpires: KN Ananthapadmanabhan, RR Pandit, HAS Khalid (TV), Ref: M Nayyar. Award: EA Perry (Aus).
Series: ML Schutt (Aus). Lanning 50: 28 balls, 8x4, Villani 50: 27 balls, 11x4. Sciver 50: 41 balls, 5x4.

Australian Cricket Digest, 2018-19

AUSTRALIAN ODI AVERAGES in 2017-18

Batting & Fielding	M	Inn	NO	Runs	HS	Avge	S/Rate	100S	50s	Ct	St
BL Mooney	3	2	1	90	56	90.00	152.5	0	1	1	-
NE Bolton	6	6	1	325	100*	65.00	82.9	1	3	1	-
EA Perry	6	6	2	237	70*	59.25	76.9	0	2	4	-
AJ Blackwell	3	3	1	112	67*	56.00	81.1	0	1	1	-
AJ Healy	6	6	0	335	133	55.83	103.7	1	2	10	2
RL Haynes	6	5	1	171	89*	42.75	101.1	0	1	3	-
MM Lanning	3	3	0	75	33	25.00	78.9	0	0	3	-
AK Gardner	5	4	0	71	35	17.75	133.9	0	0	0	-
NJ Carey	3	2	0	33	17	16.50	126.9	0	0	3	-
EJ Villani	3	3	0	47	38	15.67	83.9	0	0	3	-
TM McGrath	3	3	1	25	17*	12.50	55.5	0	0	0	-
JL Jonassen	6	3	1	11	6	5.50	157.1	0	0	3	-
AJ Wellington	6	4	1	3	3	1.00	50.0	0	0	2	-
ML Schutt	6	2	2	6	6*	-	300.0	0	0	4	-

Also played: KM Beams (1 match) did not bat.

Bowling	M	Overs	Mdns	Runs	Wkts	Avge	Best	4wI	5wI	Econ
ML Schutt	6	57.4	7	229	14	16.36	4-26	2	0	3.97
KM Beams	1	7.2	0	38	2	19.00	2-38	0	0	5.18
JL Jonassen	6	56	1	262	12	21.83	4-30	1	0	4.68
AK Gardner	5	43	0	215	9	23.89	3-40	0	0	5.00
EA Perry	6	47	1	243	8	30.38	2-40	0	0	5.17
AJ Wellington	6	40	1	199	6	33.17	3-24	0	0	4.97
NJ Carey	3	22	2	106	2	53.00	1-34	0	0	4.82
TM McGrath	3	13.2	0	68	1	68.00	1-35	0	0	5.10

AUSTRALIAN TWENTY20 AVERAGES in 2017-18

Batting & Fielding	M	Inn	NO	Runs	HS	Avge	S/Rate	100S	50s	Ct	St
MM Lanning	4	4	4	175	88*	-	162.0	0	1	2	-
BL Mooney	7	7	2	340	117*	68.00	147.8	1	2	1	-
RL Haynes	8	6	4	114	65	57.00	140.7	0	1	5	-
EJ Villani	8	8	0	191	61	23.88	130.8	0	2	2	-
EA Perry	5	6	2	78	47*	19.50	118.1	0	0	3	-
AK Gardner	8	6	0	111	33	18.50	160.8	0	0	4	-
AJ Healy	8	8	0	131	33	16.38	119.0	0	0	5	3
JL Jonassen	8	2	1	12	11	12.00	100.0	0	0	0	-
DM Kimmince	8	2	0	18	17	9.00	112.5	0	0	1	-
SG Molineux	3	6	1	6	6	6.00	50.0	0	0	3	-
MR Strano	2	1	0	3	3	3.00	33.3	0	0	0	-
SE Aley	2	1	0	1	1	1.00	33.3	0	0	0	-
NJ Carey	1	1	1	1	1*	-	50.0	0	0	0	-
ML Schutt	8	1	1	1	1*	-	50.0	0	0	1	-

Also played: AJ Wellington (5 matches) did not bat, 2 catches.

Bowling	M	Overs	Mdns	Runs	Wkts	Avge	Best	4wI	5wI	Econ
ML Schutt	8	28.4	1	190	15	12.67	4-22	1	0	6.63
JL Jonassen	8	29	0	194	6	32.33	2-21	0	0	6.69
SG Molineux	3	7	0	47	0	-	-	0	0	6.71
AJ Wellington	5	8	0	59	1	59.00	1-2	0	0	7.38
EA Perry	8	26	0	201	7	28.71	2-26	0	0	7.73
AK Gardner	8	18	1	140	6	23.33	2-20	0	0	7.78
MR Strano	2	7	0	57	0	-	-	0	0	8.14
DM Kimmince	8	24	0	201	12	16.75	3-20	0	0	8.38
SE Aley	2	4	0	38	0	-	-	0	0	9.50
NJ Carey	1	2	0	19	0	-	-	0	0	9.50

Australian Cricket Digest, 2018-19
CAREER RECORDS
up to August 16, 2018 – **bold** indicates Test debut in 2017-18 Ashes

TESTS

	Batting M	Inn	NO	Runs	HS	Avg	100	50	C	Bowling Wkts	Avg	BB	5/10
KM Beams	1	1	1	26	26*	-	0	0	0	0	-		-
AJ Blackwell	12	22	2	444	74	22.20	0	4	6	0	-		-
NE Bolton	2	3	0	85	36	28.33	0	0	1	0	-		-
JE Cameron	3	5	0	109	50	21.80	0	1	5				-
RM Farrell	3	5	1	31	11	7.75	0	0	0	17	9.88	5-23	1/-
HL Ferling	3	3	3	5	5*	-	0	0	0	3	64.33	2-59	-
RL Haynes	4	7	0	205	98	29.29	0	1	0	2	27.00	1-0	-
AJ Healy	3	4	0	130	45	32.50	0	0	7				-
JL Jonassen	2	3	0	177	99	59.00	0	2	0	3	47.67	2-52	-
MM Lanning	3	6	0	107	48	17.83	0	0	2	0	-		-
TM McGrath	1	1	0	47	47	47.00	0	0	0	3	19.00	2-45	-
BL Mooney	1	1	0	27	27	27.00	0	0	0				
EA Osborne	2	4	2	78	40	39.00	0	0	2	5	27.40	4-67	-
EA Perry	7	11	4	432	213*	61.71	1	1	5	30	17.33	6-32	2/-
ML Schutt	3	2	1	12	11	12.00	0	0	2	9	19.44	4-26	-
EJ Villani	3	5	0	72	33	14.40	0	0	2	0	-		-
A Wellington	1	1	0	2	2	2.00	0	0	2	2	65.00	1-61	-

ONE-DAY INTERNATIONALS

	M	I	NO	R	HS	Av	SR	H	50	C	Wkt	Avg	BB	Ec
SE Aley	1	1	1	15	15*	-	187	0	0	1	2	14.5	2-29	2.9
KM Beams	30	9	4	34	11*	6.8	61	0	0	10	42	22.4	4-15	3.8
AJ Blackwell	144	124	27	3493	114	36.0	66	3	25	55	6	10.5	2-8	2.8
NE Bolton	44	44	4	1849	124	46.2	73	4	12	13	2	9.0	2-18	6.0
LR Cheatle	2	1	0	7	7	7.0	116	0	0	1	2	53.0	1-42	6.2
RM Farrell	44	20	10	182	39*	18.2	70	0	0	9	42	30.8	3-17	4.1
HL Ferling	22	6	3	9	4	3.0	33	0	0	9	24	22.0	3-4	4.3
AK Gardner	15	9	1	121	35	15.1	128	0	0	3	20	30.8	3-17	4.1
RL Haynes	42	36	4	1031	89*	32.2	75	0	8	9	7	13.4	3-10	5.2
AJ Healy	58	47	10	830	133	22.4	96	1	4	42	17	Stps		
JL Jonassen	56	34	10	405	39	16.8	82	0	0	14	78	23.1	5-50	4.1
DM Kimmince	11	1	0	42	42	42.0	79	0	0	7	7	45.2	2-46	3.8
MM Lanning	66	66	8	3074	152*	53.0	95	11	11	38	1	114	1-30	5.1
TM McGrath	4	4	1	29	17*	9.6	58	0	0	1	1	96.0	1-35	5.2
BL Mooney	20	18	1	656	100	38.5	78	1	6	8				
EA Osborne	60	33	17	359	47*	22.4	78	0	0	18	68	25.5	3-9	4.0
EA Perry	97	75	26	2540	95*	51.8	77	0	25	30	130	25.6	5-19	4.4
ML Schutt	46	19	6	85	18	6.5	63	0	0	15	66	24.2	4-18	4.4
B Vakarewa	1	0						0	0	1	0	-	-	5.5
EJ Villani	31	28	2	585	75	22.5	78	0	3	16	7	35.7	3-42	5.9
A Wellington	12	7	2	16	11	3.2	61	0	0	3	15	31.8	3-24	4.8

TWENTY20 INTERNATIONALS

	M	I	NO	Runs	HS	Avg	SR	50	C	Wkt	Avg	BB	Ec
SE Aley	2	1	0	1	1	1.0	33	0	0	0			9.5
KM Beams	18	2	1	6	4*	6.0	85	0	4	20	16.6	3-16	5.2
AJ Blackwell	95	81	19	1315	61*	21.0	92	1	34	0	-		14
NE Bolton	2	1	0	6	6	6.0	50	0	3				
LR Cheatle	7	1	1	4	4*	-	50	0	1	5	24.4	2-13	6.4
NJ Carey	1	1	1	1	1*	-	50	0	0	0	-		9.5
RM Farrell	54	14	6	95	31*	11.8	131	0	9	55	20.9	4-15	6.2
A Gardner	11	9	0	116	33	12.8	29	0	1	7	22.2	2-20	7.4
AJ Healy	80	66	12	942	90	17.4	112	2	22	31	Stps		
JL Jonassen	58	32	7	396	47	15.8	91	0	18	41	24.1	3-25	5.4
MM Lanning	74	73	12	2105	126	34.5	118	11	25	4	9.7	2-17	6.5
SG Molineux	3	1	0	6	6	6.0		0	3	0			6.7
BL Mooney	20	17	5	479	117*	39.9	125	2	4	0			
EA Osborne	59	18	9	78	17*	8.6	96	0	25	48	22.5	4-19	5.8
EA Perry	90	52	18	875	55*	25.7	104	3	22	84	20.4	4-12	5.8
ML Schutt	35	6	1	12	6	2.4	63	0	3	38	17.6	4-22	6.1
NE Stalenberg	1	0						0	1				
MR Strano	5	3	0	4	3	1.3	30	0	3	7	17.1	5-10	6.3
EJ Villani	50	50	7	1240	90*	28.8	117	11	3				
A Wellington	8	2	1	9	8	9.0	90	0	3	10	11.2	4-16	5.6

Lanning and Mooney both have scored one century.

WOMENS CRICKET RECORDS SECTION (up to September 1, 2017)
Australia in Test cricket

Versus	Tests	Won	Lost	Drawn	Tied
England	49	12	9	28	0
India	9	4	0	5	0
New Zealand	13	4	1	8	0
West Indies	2	0	0	2	0
Total	**73**	**20**	**10**	**43**	**0**

HIGHEST TEAM SCORES

	Versus	Season	Venue
6-569	England	1998	Guildford
525	India	1983-84	Ahmedabad
9-448	**England**	**2017-18**	**North Sydney**
4-427	England	1998	Worcester
4-383	England	2001	Headingley

LOWEST TEAM SCORES

	Versus	Season	Venue
38	England	1957-58	Junction Oval
47	England	1934-35	Gabba
78	England	2002-03	Gabba
83	England	1951	The Oval

MOST RUNS

	M	Inn	NO	HS	Runs	Avge	100s	50s	0s
KL Rolton	14	22	4	209*	1002	55.66	2	5	3
BJ Clark	15	25	5	136	919	45.95	2	6	2
ER Wilson	11	16	1	127	862	57.46	3	3	0
DA Annetts	10	13	3	193	819	81.90	2	6	0

HIGHEST SCORES

		Balls	versus	Season	Venue
EA Perry	**213**	374	**England**	**2017-18**	**Nth Sydney**
KL Rolton	209*	313	England	2001	Headingley
MAJ Goszko	204	345	England	2001	Shenley
J Broadbent	200	476	England	1998	Guildford
DA Annetts	193	365	England	1987	Collingham

MOST WICKETS

	M	Balls	Runs	Wkts	Avge	Best	5i	10m	SR
ER Wilson	11	2885	803	68	11.80	7/7	4	2	42.4
CL Fitzpatrick	13	303	1147	60	19.11	5/29	2	0	60.0
R Thompson	16	4304	1040	57	18.24	5/33	1	0	75.5
DL Wilson	11	2812	880	48	18.33	5/27	2	0	58.5

BEST BOWLING

		versus	Season	Venue
ER Wilson	7-7	England	1957-58	St Kilda
A Palmer	7-18	England	1934-35	Brisbane
L Johnston	7-24	New Zealand	1971-72	Junction Oval
ER Wilson	6-23	England	1948-49	Adelaide Oval

WICKET KEEPING

	M	Total	Ct/St	Byes/Inns
C Matthews	20	60	46/14	3.49
MJ Jennings	8	24	14/10	4.64
JC Price	10	22	20/2	3.89

FIELDING

	M	Total
LA Fullston	12	20
DA Annetts	10	12

Australian Cricket Digest, 2018-19
Australian results in One-day Internationals

Team	ODIs	Won	Lost	NR	Tied
Denmark	2	2	0	0	0
England	75	49	22	3	1
India	46	37	9	0	0
International XI	4	3	0	1	0
Ireland	15	15	0	0	0
Jamaica	1	1	0	0	0
Netherlands	5	5	0	0	0
New Zealand	123	90	31	2	0
Pakistan	9	9	0	0	0
South Africa	14	13	0	1	0
Sri Lanka	8	8	0	0	0
Trinidad & Tobago	1	1	0	0	0
West Indies	10	9	1	0	0
Young England	1	1	0	0	0
Total	**314**	**243**	**63**	**6**	**2**

HIGHEST TEAM SCORES

	Versus	Season	Venue
3-412	Denmark	1997-98	Mumbai
4-397	Pakistan	1996-97	Wesley Coll, Melb
7-332	India	2017-18	Vadodara
4-307	New Zealand	2008-09	Hamilton
7-300	India	2011-12	Wand Stad, Mum

LOWEST TEAM SCORES

	Versus	Season	Venue
77	New Zealand	1993	Beckenham
77	India	2004-05	St Peters College, Chennai
86	New Zealand	1995-96	Adelaide

LEADING RUN SCORERS

	M	Inn	NO	Runs	HS	Avge	S/Rate	100s	50s	0s
BJ Clark	118	114	12	4844	229*	47.49	66.2	5	30	3
KL Rolton	141	132	32	4814	154*	74.1		8	33	4
AJ Blackwell	144	124	27	3493	114	36.01	66.2	3	25	8
MM Lanning	66	66	8	3074	152*	53.00	95.1	11	11	5
LC Sthalekar	125	111	22	2728	104*	30.65	68.7	2	16	9
LM Keightley	82	78	12	2630	156*	39.84	57.4	4	21	5
EA Perry	97	75	26	2540	95*	51.84	77.5	0	25	4

HIGHEST SCORES

	Balls	versus	Season	Venue
BJ Clark	229*	155	Denmark	1997-98	Mumbai
LM Keightley	156*	147	Pakistan	1996-97	Wesley Coll, Melbourne
KL Rolton	154*	118	Sri Lanka	2000-01	Hagley Oval, Christchurch
MM Lanning	152*	135	Sri Lanka	2017	Bristol
KL Rolton	151	114	Ireland	2005	Dublin

LEADING WICKET TAKERS

	M	Balls	Runs	Wkts	Avge	Best	4i	5i	Econ
CL Fitzpatrick	109	6017	3023	180	16.79	5-14	11	4	3.01
LC Sthalekar	125	5965	3646	146	24.97	5-35	2	1	3.67
EA Perry	97	4528	3331	130	25.62	5-19	3	2	4.41
S Nitschke	80	3626	2159	98	22.03	7-24	3	1	3.57
KL Rolton	141	3267	1769	85	20.81	4-29	1	0	3.25
CL Mason	46	2366	1150	83	13.85	5-9	6	2	2.92
JL Jonassen	56	2592	1808	78	23.18	5-50	4	1	4.19
LA Fullston	41	2366	968	73	13.26	5-27	6	2	2.45

BEST BOWLING

		versus	Season	Venue
S Nitschke	7-24	England	2005	Kidderminster
CL Mason	5-9	England	1999-2000	Newcastle
J Broadbent	5-10	New Zealand	1992-93	Lismore

WICKET KEEPING

	M	Total	Ct/St	Byes/Inns
JC Price	83	99	69/30	1.05
JM Fields	60	74	55/19	0.85

FIELDING

	M	Total
AJ Blackwell	144	55
LC Sthalekar	125	49

Australian Cricket Digest, 2018-19

Australian results in Twenty20 Internationals

Team	T20s	Won	Lost	NR	Tied
England	31	13	17	0	1
India	14	11	2	1	0
Ireland	5	5	0	0	0
New Zealand	35	15	19	0	1
Pakistan	6	6	0	0	0
South Africa	4	4	0	0	0
Sri Lanka	2	2	0	0	0
West Indies	9	8	1	0	0
Total	**106**	**64**	**39**	**1**	**2**

HIGHEST TEAM SCORES

	Versus	Season	Venue
4-209	**England**	**2017-18**	**Brab Stadium**
4-191	Ireland	2013-14	Sylhet
1-186	Ireland	2015	Dublin
5-186	India	2017-18	Brab Stadium
2-185	Pakistan	2013-14	Sylhet

LOWEST TEAM SCORES

	Versus	Season	Venue
66	New Zealand	2016-17	Adelaide Oval
73	New Zealand	2009-10	WTS, Wellington
9-80	New Zealand	2007-08	Lincoln
89	India	2011-12	Visag

LEADING RUN SCORERS

	M	Inn	NO	Runs	HS	Avge	S/Rate	100s	50s	0s
MM Lanning	**74**	**73**	**12**	**2105**	**126**	**34.51**	**118.6**	**1**	**11**	**1**
AJ Blackwell	95	81	19	1314	61	21.19	92.9	0	1	5
EJ Villani	**50**	**50**	**7**	**1240**	**90***	**28.84**	**117.9**	**0**	**11**	**4**
AJ Healy	**80**	**66**	**12**	**942**	**90**	**17.44**	**112.8**	**0**	**2**	**8**
JE Cameron	64	55	10	941	68*	20.91	107.5	0	3	4
EA Perry	**90**	**52**	**18**	**875**	**55***	**25.74**	**104.0**	**0**	**3**	**3**

HIGHEST SCORES

	Balls	versus	Season	Venue
MM Lanning	126	65	Ireland	2013-14	Sylhet
BL Mooney	**117***	**70**	**England**	**2017-18**	**Canberra**
KL Rolton	96*	53	England	2005	Taunton
EJ Villani	90*	54	Pakistan	2013-14	Sylhet
AJ Healy	90	61	India	2011-12	Visag

LEADING WICKET TAKERS

	M	Balls	Mdns	Runs	Wkts	Avge	Best	4i	5i	Econ
EA Perry	**90**	**1714**	**4**	**1714**	**84**	**20.40**	**4-12**	**2**	**0**	**5.87**
LC Sthalekar	54	1196	1	1161	60	19.35	4-18	1	0	5.82
RM Farrell	54	1113	5	1150	55	20.91	4-15	1	0	6.20
EA Osborne	59	1124	0	1080	48	22.50	4-19	1	0	5.77
SJ Coyte	47	962	1	979	47	20.83	4-5	1	0	6.11

BEST BOWLING

		versus	Season	Venue
MR Strano	5-10	New Zealand	2016-17	Geelong
JL Hunter	5-22	West Indies	2012-13	Colombo (RPS)
SJ Coyte	4-5	India	2011	Billericay

WICKET KEEPING

	M	Total	Ct/St	Byes/Inns
AJ Healy	65	51	20/31	0.89
JM Fields	37	40	25/15	0.51

FIELDING

	M	Total
AJ Blackwell	95	34
JE Cameron	64	33

Australian Cricket Digest, 2018-19
INTERSTATE 50 OVER COMPETITION – UNBEATEN NEW SOUTH WALES TAKE THE TITLE

LADDER (all teams 6 games)	W	L	Bonus	Pts	Net Run Rate
New South Wales	6	-	6	30	+1.864
Western Australia	5	1	2	22	+0.622
South Australia	3	3	3	15	+0.021
Australian Capital Territory	3	3	2	14	+0.053
Queensland	2	4	3	11	+0.080
Victoria	2	4	-	8	-0.867
Tasmania	-	6	-	0	-1.753

Matches Played

October 6, 2017

Australian Capital Territory 203 cc (D van Niekerk 63; MR Strano 3-39, AM King 3-22) **def Victoria 7-173** (SG Molineux 50, MR Strano 36; D van Niekerk 3-31) **by 30 runs at Manuka Oval, Canberra.** *Coming in at 5-85 in the 23rd over, van Niekerk (Award) faced 74 balls, hit 6x4 & 1x6. Victoria, who were missing Meg Lanning who was recovering from shoulder surgery, struggled with only Sophie Molineux (54 balls, 7x4) doing much with the bat. Van Niekerk and Sam Bates (ACT) (10-2-20-1) gave little away with the ball*

Queensland 225 (49.4 overs) (BL Mooney 73, KLH Short 53; EA Perry 3-37) **lost to New South Wales 4-226** (38.1 overs) (RL Haynes 103*) **by 6 wickets (BP) at Blacktown International Sportspark No 2.** *Queensland got off to fine start, with Mooney (88 balls, 9x4, 1x6) and Short (63 balls, 7x4 1x6) adding 112 for the first wicket. Short went in the 22nd over and Mooney in the 28th, the rest of the batting unable to build from the fine start. In reply Haynes (Award, 93 balls, 13x4 1x6) scored her 6th WNCL ton and Naomi Stalenburg (41*) added 100 for the 5th wicket to get NSW home with 11.5 overs to spare, thus gaining a bonus point win.*

Western Australia 4-323 cc (NE Bolton 125*, EJ Villani 139) **def South Australia 302** (48.4 overs) (A Wellington 116, TMS Saville 53; PM Cleary 4-57) **by 21 runs at Adelaide Oval No 2.** *A stand of 204 in 29 overs for the second wicket between Nicole Bolton (130 balls, 13x4) and skipper Elyse Villani (Award, 103 balls, 19x4, 4x6) set up a massive chase for SA. It was Bolton's 8th WNCL ton (6th for WA, after two with Vic) and Villani's 4th (2nd for WA, also two with Vic), while Megan Schutt (10-1-76-0) had her most expensive ever figures for SA. The Scorpions came out hard in the run chase, and when Sophie Devine (36 off 38) went with the score at 4-97 in the 16th over, SA looked set for a heavy defeat. But Amanda Wellington (125 balls, 11x4, 2x6) made her maiden ton (her previous best was 37) and shared in stands of 71 for the 5th wicket with Ash Gardner (34) and 117 for the sixth with Tabatha Saville (52 balls, 5x4, 2x6), to give SA a chance. When Saville was dismissed at the end of the 46th over, SA were 6-285 and lost their last five wickets for 17 runs.*

October 7, 2017

Tasmania 222 (49.3 overs) (GP Redmayne 89; KL Cross 3-26, HL Graham 4-52) **lost to Western Australia 3-225** (38.5 overs) (NE Bolton 93*, CL Piparo 56, AE Jones 48*) **by 7 wickets (BP) at Adelaide Oval No 2.** *Georgia Redmayne (124 balls, 8x4) who was eighth out in the 45th over, saw her side to a respectable tally. For the second day in a row, Nicole Bolton (Award, 104 balls, 11x4) dominated with the bat as she and Chloe Piparo (74 balls, 9x4) added 111 in 21.1 overs for the first wicket. Piparo's demise started a mini-collapse of 3-24, before Amy Jones (39 balls, 9x4) added 90 with Bolton to see WA home to a bonus point victory.*

October 8, 2017

Australian Capital Territory 6-285 cc (KM Mack 113*, D van Niekerk 61) **def Queensland 219** (45.3 overs) (DM Kimmince 61; HNK Jensen 5-33) **by 66 runs (BP) at Manuka Oval, Canberra.** *Opener Katie Mack (Award, 125 balls, 13x4) scored her second WNCL ton, batting through the innings, as she and Dane van Niekerk (57 balls, 6x4, 2x6) added 110 for the third wicket. Beth Mooney (1) went in the second over to Sam Bates (7-2-15-2) as only Delissa Kimmince (63 balls, 5x4, 1x6) could master the ACT bowling attack. Hayley Jenson, in her tenth game took a career best, having only taken four wickets in the previous nine.*

New South Wales 9-302 cc (RL Haynes 83, AJ Healy 68, AJ Blackwell 77; MR Strano 3-39, KM Beams 5-52) **def Victoria 7-212 cc** (SG Molineux 62, EJ Inglis 63; NJ Carey 3-26) **by 90 runs (BP) at Blacktown International Sportspark No 2.** *Rachel Haynes (Award, 79 balls, 13x4, 1x6) and Alyssa Healy (66 balls, 12x4, 1x6) added 123 in 20 overs for the first wicket, with Alex Blackwell (73 balls, 7x4, 3x6) dominating the middle stages of the innings. Looking set a for a score well over 300, Ellyse Perry (30 off 39) was out at 3-273 in the 43rd overs, which started a collapse, with NSW losing 7-29 in the last 7.3 overs. Victoria reached their fifty in the 12th over, but couldn't accelerate, despite fifties to Sophie Molineux (70 balls, 10x4) and Emma Inglis (82 balls, 8x4) surrendering a bonus point to the reigning title holders.*

Tasmania 216 (49.4 overs) (SM Betts 3-21) **lost to South Australia 4-217** (35.4 overs) (TM McGrath 80, SFM Devine 117) **by 6 wickets (BP) at Adelaide Oval No 2.** *Tight bowling and a partnership of 192 for the third wicket between Tahlia McGrath (110 balls, 8x4) and NZ import Sophie Devine (Award, 85 balls, 13x4, 4x6), who made her maiden WNCL ton, saw the home team to a comfortable win.*

November 25, 2017

Queensland 163 (45.1 overs) **def South Australia 104** (29.5 overs) (SJ Johnson 3-14, JL Barsby 4-7) **by 59 runs (BP) at Russell Lucas Oval, Melbourne.** *In a low scoring game Sammy-Jo Johnson (Award, 42 off 78 balls) ensured that Queensland at least had something on the board to bowl to. South Australia collapse to be 5-22 in the 11th over, with Johnson (3-14 off 6 overs) starring with the ball. Jemmy Barsby mopped up the tail as Queensland grabbed an unlikely bonus point victory.*

Tasmania 9-186 cc (LE Wright 104*; SG Molineux 4-27) **lost to Victoria 6-187** (46 overs) (MA Blows 91*, BL Hepburn 3-32) **by 4 wickets at the**

Australian Cricket Digest, 2018-19

MCG. *In her 45th WNCL game, Laura Wright (142 balls, 9x4) made her maiden ton, batting through the innings, having faced the first ball of the day. Sadly, not one of her teammates could pass 20. Makinley Blows (Award, 136 balls, 13x4) ensured a comfortable four wicket win.*

Western Australia 239 (50 overs) (AR Jason-Jones 67, MP Banting 50; LG Smith 3-52) **lost to New South Wales 3-241** (39.2 overs) (AJ Healy 99, AJ Blackwell 68) **by 7 wickets (BP) at Murdoch University, Perth.** *Set 240 win to, Alyssa Healy (Award, 89 balls, 14x4) and Alex Blackwell (82 balls, 10x4) added 165 for the first wicket in 26.1 overs, as NSW scored another bonus point victory.*

November 26, 2017
New South Wales 7-246 cc (EA Perry 127*; M Kapp 4-24) **def Australian Capital Territory 149** (42.5 overs) (RM Farrell 4-35, SE Aley 3-26, NJ Carey 3-28) **by 97 runs (BP) at Murdoch University, Perth.** *Ellyse Perry (Award, 120 balls, 13x4, 3x6) came in with the score at 2-24 in the eighth over. Rene Farrell (35 off 31) joined her at the start of the 40th over (score 7-160) and the pair added 86 in the last ten overs. When Marizanne Kapp (1) was dismissed, ACT were 5-42 in the 12th over and never were in the hunt, Farrell completed a fine all-round match, taking four wickets.*

November 27, 2017
Tasmania 137 (47.3 overs) (JL Jonassen 3-22, DM Kimmince 3-17) **lost to Queensland 2-140** (23.2 overs) (BL Mooney 47, KLH Short 54) **by 8 wickets (BP) at Russell Lucas Oval, Melbourne.** *Tasmania started the game well with Laura Wright (24 off 44) and Georgia Redmayne (18 off 43) adding 51 for the first wicket in 13.2 overs, but they soon slipped to 3-56 in the 18th. Beth Mooney (51 balls, 6x4) and Kirby Short (54 off 58) added 110 for the first wicket in 17.2 overs. Award: Delissa Kimmince (5-0-17-3 & 13 not out)*

Victoria 83 (36.1 overs) (ML Schutt 3-16) **lost to South Australia 7-84** (32.2 overs) (AM King 4-33) **by 3 wickets (BP) at the MCG.** *Victoria recorded their fourth lowest ever total and second worst v South Australia, as no one in the top five reached double figures. In reply SA were going well at 1-32 in the 13th over, but slipped to 7-70 when Alex Price (9) was dismissed in the 27th over. Tahlia McGrath (20* off 65) and Sarah Lowe (9* off 21) steering their team home to a win and a bonus point. Award: Alana King completed her third "four for" in her 10th match.*

Western Australia 237 (50 overs) (CL Piparo 88, MG Carmichael 96) **def Australian Capital Territory 214** (47.5 overs) (EA Osborne 52; KL Cross 3-22) **by 23 runs at Murdoch University, Perth.** *Coming together at 3-15 in the fifth over, Chloe Piparo (113 balls, 4x4, 1x6) and Mathilda Carmichael (Award, 139 balls, 10x4) added a record 194 for the fourth wicket. When Carmichael was dismissed in the 44th over, WA lost their last 7-28. Erin Osborne (83 balls, 3x4) and Erin Burns (37 off 41) added 80 for the third wicket and at 5-192 in the 40th over, the visitors looked set to win. But then Marizanne Kapp (29 off 36) became Kat Cross' third victim, triggering a collapse of 5-22.*

February 16, 2018
Queensland 183 (47.2 overs) (GM Harris 56 retired ill; KM Beams 5-13) **lost to Victoria 8-184** (49.5 overs) (KM Beams 59*) **by 2 wickets at Allan Border Field, Brisbane.** *Grace Harris (41 balls, 8x4, 2x6) was batting well until she had to retire due to illness. Kristen Beams (10-1-13-5) took her 5th ever five wicket haul in WNCL and had her best ever economy rate in a ten over spell. Victoria slumped from 2-55 in the 19th over to 8-104 in the 40th, before Beams (Award, 48 balls, 6x4, 1x6) scored her first ever fifty and Nicole Faltum (23 off 29) added 80 for the ninth wicket getting Victoria home with a ball to spare.*

Australian Capital Territory 5-268 cc (KM Mack 52, CJ Koski 132*) **lost to South Australia 5-269** (40 overs) (BE Patterson 56, TM McGrath 75, SFM Devine 88) **by 5 wickets (BP) at Kingston Twin Ovals, Hobart.** *In her 39th WNCL game, Claire Koski (Award, 153 balls, 8x4, 1x6) batted through the innings, having added 125 for the first wicket with Katie Mack (70 balls, 6x4) in 25.1 overs. Bridget Patterson (60 balls, 5x4) and Tahlia McGrath (99 balls, 2x4) added 98 for the second wicket and then Sophie Devine (53 balls, 8x4, 4x6) added 124 with McGrath, SA hitting the runs off the last ball of the 40th over to gain a bonus point.*

Tasmania 175 (49.3 overs) (SG Daffara 63; RM Farrell 3-24) **lost to New South Wales 3-179** (27 overs) (RL Haynes 92*) **lost by 7 wickets (BP) at Lindisfarne Oval, Hobart.** *Georgia Redmayne (44 off 84) and Stef Daffara (91 balls, 7x4, 1x6) added 98 for the second wicket, but then Tasmania went from 2-102 in the 31st over, to lose their last 8-73. Opener Rachel Haynes (Award, 71 balls, 10x4, 3x6) ensured a bonus point for NSW.*

February 17, 2018
Victoria 109 (39.5 overs) (EL King 4-17) **lost to Western Australia 2-112** (30.3 overs) **by 8 wickets (BP) at Allan Border Field, Brisbane.** *Subiaco born off-spinner Emma King took her first ever four wicket haul in her 42nd WNCL game, to help reduce Victoria from 1-37 to 5-54. WA were untroubled in gaining a bonus point, Heather Graham (43* off 66) gained the player of the match after also taking 2-15 off 6.5 overs.*

February 18, 2018
New South Wales 9-272 cc (RL Haynes 76, AJ Blackwell 76) **def South Australia 169** (37.5 overs) (TM McGrath 48, SFM Devine 73) **by 103 runs (BP) at Lindisfarne Oval, Hobart.** *NSW batters dominated with Rachel Haynes (67 balls, 10x4, 1x6) and Alex Blackwell (78 balls, 9x4) adding 90 for the second wicket. Coming together at 2-17 in the sixth over, Tahlia McGrath (60 balls, 6x4) and Sophie Devine (52 balls, 6x4x 4x6) added 92 for the second wicket in 15 overs, but the wicket of McGrath in the 21st over, triggered a collapse of 3-5. All hopes died when Devine was the sixth wicket to fall on 133, in the 25th over.*

Western Australia 222 (48.3 overs) (EJ Villani 91; SJ Johnson 3-44, GM Harris 3-31) **defeated Queensland 191** (46.3 overs) (HL Graham 4-31) **by 31 runs at Allan Border Field, Brisbane.** *Elyse Villani (Award, 108 balls, 13x4) played a fine hand and was dismissed in the 41st over. In reply, Beth Mooney (1) fell to Piepa Cleary's first delivery and when Fire skipper Kirby Short (40 off 55) went in the 25th over, Queensland were 5-118 and unable to threaten to the target.*

Australian Cricket Digest, 2018-19

Australian Capital Territory 246 (49.4 overs) (EA Burns 57, AR Reakes 46; IMHC Joyce 5-24) **beat Tasmania 160** (41.4 overs) (CL Hall 60) **by 86 runs (BP) at Kingston Twin Ovals, Hobart.** *Former Tasmanian player Erin Burns (57 balls, 6x4) scored her first fifty for ACT, while Irish International Isobel Joyce (Award) took her first five wicket haul for Tasmania. Batting at number four, Corinne Hall (80 balls, 4x4) scored her first fifty of the season, but apart from opener Georgia Redmayne (34 off 37) no one passed 20, Tasmania ending up winless in 2017-18.*

The Final - New South Wales v Western Australia at Blacktown ISP on February 24, 2018 - NSW won by 51 runs

Alyssa Healy dominated proceedings, making her 4th WNCL ton, as she and Ellyse Perry added 147 for the third wicket in 22 overs. Kate Cross was the pick of the bowlers, as the rest of the WA attack went for six per over. WA made a decent start and were on track after 30 overs (3-158), with Villani and then later Jones scoring freely. Farrell dismissed Villani in the 31st over and then when Jones went in the 38th, the rate was up to eight per over, which was too much for the WA lower order.

New South Wales		B	M	4	6	Western Australia		B	M	4	6
RL Haynes	c Jones b Cleary	5	6	5	1	NE Bolton	c Healy b Farrell	15	19	27	2
AJ Healy +	c Cross b Graham	122	109	132	18	CL Piparo	c Smith b Carey	29	56	77	3
AJ Blackwell *	lbw b Bolton	24	43	54	3	EJ Villani *	c Perry b Farrell	74	67	92	11
EA Perry	c King b Graham	96	96	135	11	HL Graham	b Carey	5	3	6	1
NE Stalenberg	c Banting b Cross	28	33	37	2	AE Jones +	c Healy b Perry	59	64	67	10
NJ Carey	c Carmichael b Cross	7	7	13	1	MG Carmichael	c and b Perry	8	17	23	
RM Farrell	not out	8	6	6	1	MP Banting	not out	22	26	46	2
SE Aley						KL Cross	c Blackwell b Aley	12	11	16	1
LG Smith						PM Cleary	c &b Aley	14	14	11	1
ML Gibson						TCJ Peschel	run out (Aley)	2	5	5	
BW Vakarewa						EL King	c Stalenberg b Aley	0	2	3	
	4 lb, 8 w	12					3 b, 4 lb, 4 w	11			
10 overs: 1-37	50 overs, 204 mins	6-302				10 overs: 2-36	47.2 overs, 191 mins	251			

Fall: 1-5 (Haynes, 1.3), 2-67 (Blackwell, 15.2), 3-214 (Healy, 37.2), 4-278 (Stalenberg, 47.1), 5-288 (Perry, 48.2), 6-302 (Carey, 49.6)

Fall: 1-23 (Bolton, 6.6), 2-82 (Piparo, 18.2), 3-93 (Graham, 20.3), 4-158 (Villani, 30.2), 5-184 (Carmichael, 35.6), 6-201 (Jones, 37.5), 7-218 (Cross, 41.6), 8-239 (Cleary, 45.2), 9-245 (Peschel. 46.3), 10-251 (King)

WA - bowling	O	M	R	W	wd	nb	NSW - bowling	O	M	R	W	wd	nb
KL Cross	10	3	35	2	1		RM Farrell	9	0	31	2	1	
PM Cleary	10	0	62	1	1		EA Perry	8	1	38	2		
TCJ Peschel	5	0	42	0	1		SE Aley	7.2	0	37	3	1	
HL Graham	10	1	58	2			BW Vakarewa	3	0	21	0		
NE Bolton	3	0	26	1	1		ML Gibson	9	1	41	0	2	
EL King	10	0	60	0	2		NJ Carey	8	0	49	2		
EJ Villani	2	0	15	0			LG Smith	3	0	27	0		

Toss: Western Australia. Umpires: DR Close, NR Johnstone, Ref: RL Parry. Award: AJ Healy (NSW)

2017-18 WNCL AVERAGES

	M	I	NO	Run	HS	Avge	SR	H	F	Ct/S	W	Avg	BB	Eco
SE Aley (NSW)	7	3	0	8	8	2.7	44	0	0	4	8	34.6	3-26	4.5
MP Banting (WA)	7	4	1	82	50	27.3	88	0	1	2/1				
JL Barsby (Qld)	6	5	1	45	16	11.3	50	0	0	2	9	26.2	4-7	4.0
SL Bates (ACT)	6	4	0	16	6	4.0	41	0	0	3	10	32.2	2-15	3.2
KM Beams (Vic)	6	6	4	95	59*	47.5	63	0	1	4	11	26.2	5-13	3.2
SM Betts (SA)	6	3	1	4	2*	2.0	17	0	0	2	9	23.8	3-21	5.2
HP Birkett (Qld)	4	3	0	44	19	14.7	75	0	0	3	1	108	1-46	4.9
AJ Blackwell (NSW)	7	7	0	281	77	40.1	83	0	3	3				
M Blows (Vic)	6	6	1	168	91*	33.6	45	0	1	1	1	48.0	1-24	7.1
NE Bolton (WA)	7	7	2	281	125*	56.2	85	1	1	8	4	45.0	1-12	5.1
HM Brennan (Vic)	4	1	0	0	0	0.0	0	0	0	2	2	63.0	1-21	4.5
MJ Brown (ACT)	2	1	0	1	1	1.0	20	0	0	1	1	54.0	1-19	5.3
EA Burns (Tas)	6	6	0	148	57	24.7	85	0	1	4	2	63.0	2-16	5.3
NJ Carey (NSW)	7	6	0	45	25	7.5	60	0	0	5	12	26.4	3-26	4.4
MG Carmichael (WA)	7	5	1	157	96	39.3	68	0	1	3				
LR Cheatle (NSW)	1	0						0	0	0	0			4.4
PM Cleary (WA)	7	4	0	24	14	6.0	65	0	0	3	9	36.0	4-57	5.5
TM Cooper (Qld)	3	3	0	62	35	20.7	52	0	0	1				
KL Cross (WA)	7	4	0	24	12	6.0	55	0	0	4	13	29.2	3-22	3.9
SG Daffara (Tas)	6	6	0	138	63	23.0	63	0	1	1				
SFM Devine (SA)	6	6	0	342	117	57.0	137	1	2	4	4	42.0	1-11	4.7
JE Dooley (Qld)	1	1	0	29	29	29.0	48	0	0	0				
NM Faltum (Vic)	6	6	1	30	23*	6.0	39	0	0	2				
RM Farrell (NSW)	7	4	2	68	35*	34.0	103	0	0	2	16	24.3	4-35	3.6
EG Fazackerley (Tas)	5	5	0	101	41	20.2	73	0	0	3	3	46.0	1-20	5.9
HL Ferling (Qld)	7	5	2	14	10	4.7	40	0	0	4	4	42.0	2-19	4.5
KR Fryett (Tas)	4	4	1	20	8	6.7	36	0	0	1	1	162.	1-33	5.0

Australian Cricket Digest, 2018-19

	M	I	NO	Run	HS	Avge	SR	H	F	C/S	W	Avge	BB	Eco
AK Gardner (SA)	6	6	1	69	34	13.8	92	0	0	3	4	73.5	1-24	3.9
ML Gibson (NSW)	5	1	1	2	2*		33	0	0	1	3	63.0	2-24	4.5
NM Goodwin (ACT)	2	1	1	2	2*		50	0	0	0	0			6.6
HL Graham (WA)	7	7	1	84	43*	14.0	59	0	0	2	14	26.6	4-31	4.8
CL Hall (Tas)	6	6	1	116	60*	23.2	61	0	1	0	0			10
NM Hancock (Vic)	6	4	0	22	13	5.5	39	0	0	1	4	48.0	2-30	5.7
GM Harris (Qld)	4	4	1	91	56*	30.3	117	0	1	0	3	38.0	3-31	4.5
LM Harris (Qld)	4	4	1	60	25	20.0	66	0	0	4				
KJ Hartshorn (WA)	1	1	1	2	2*		50	0	0	1	0			4.7
RL Haynes (NSW)	7	6	2	363	103*	90.8	113	1	3	3				
AJ Healy (NSW)	7	7	0	342	122	48.9	99	1	2	8/2				
BL Hepburn (Tas)	5	5	1	38	18	9.5	67	0	0	1	4	28.5	3-32	5.2
C Hill (Qld)	4	3	1	9	8	4.5	60	0	0	0	1	108	1-28	5.2
MC Hinkley (NSW)	4	2	0	31	24	15.5	52	0	0	0	1	12.0	1-6	3.0
CM Iemma (ACT)	1	1	1	5	5*		83	0	0	0				
EJ Inglis (Vic)	6	6	0	89	63	14.8	62	0	1	5/4				
AR Jason-Jones (WA)	2	1	0	29	29	29.0	48	0	0	0				
HNK Jensen (ACT)	6	6	1	30	23*	6.0	39	0	0	2	7	44.1	5-33	4.6
SJ Johnson (Qld)	6	4	2	68	35*	34.0	103	0	0	2	9	27.2	3-14	3.6
JL Jonassen (Qld)	6	5	0	101	41	20.2	73	0	0	3	9	33.8	3-22	3.9
AE Jones (WA)	4	5	2	14	10	4.7	40	0	0	0				
IMHC Joyce (Tas)	6	4	1	20	8	6.7	36	0	0	0	8	16.5	5-24	6.1
M Kapp (ACT)	4	6	1	69	34	13.8	92	0	0	3	7	30.0	4-24	3.5
E Kershaw (ACT)	6	1	1	2	2*		33	0	0	1				
DM Kimmince (Qld)	6	1	1	2	2*		50	0	0	0				
AM King (Vic)	6	7	1	84	43*	14.0	59	0	0	2	7	31.7	3-17	4.9
EL King (WA)	7	6	1	116	60*	23.2	61	0	1	0	10	24.8	4-33	3.7
CJ Koski (ACT)	6	4	0	22	13	5.5	39	0	0	1	7	54.9	4-17	4.4
AJ Lanning (Vic)	6	4	1	91	56*	30.3	117	0	1	0				
EA Leys (ACT)	1	4	1	60	25	20.0	66	0	0	4				
SJ Lowe (SA)	4	1	1	2	2*		50	0	0	1	2	48.0	1-25	5.1
TM McGrath (SA)	6	6	1	243	80	48.6	68	0	2	0	3	54.0	2-10	4.8
TJ McPharlin (SA)	6	6	0	33	13	5.5	48	0	0	7/2				
KM Mack (ACT)	6	6	1	230	113*	46.00	75	1	1	0				
SG Molineux (Vic)	6	6	0	170	62	28.3	90	0	2	3	8	37.5	4-27	3.5
BL Mooney (Qld)	6	6	0	150	73	25.0	81	0	1	9/1				
EA Osborne (ACT)	6	6	0	159	52	26.5	62	0	1	2	4	54.0	2-27	4.7
BE Patterson (SA)	6	6	0	89	56	14.8	60	0	1	2				
BA Perry (SA)	1	1	0	10	10	10.0	42	0	0	0				
EA Perry (NSW)	7	7	2	372	127*	74.4	97	1	1	3	9	34.7	3-37	3.9
TCJ Peschel (WA)	7	4	0	17	8	4.3	74	0	0	2	7	37.0	2-28	5.5
M Phillips (Tas)	3	3	0	34	16	11.3	45	0	0	1	2	45.0	2-42	5.2
C Piparo (WA)	7	7	1	262	88	43.7	62	0	2	2				
KL Pope (SA)	2	1	1	3	3*		100	0	0	0	0			9.0
GK Prestwidge (Qld)	2	2	1	1	1	1.0	14	0	0	0	1	48.0	1-12	4.8
AE Price (SA)	5	3	0	18	9	6.0	38	0	0	1	2	63.0	1-15	5.9
V Pyke (Tas)	6	6	0	46	17	7.7	46	0	0	0	2	150	1-29	4.5
C Raack (Tas)	5	5	3	4	3*	2.0	14	0	0	1	4	45.0	2-38	5.9
AR Reakes (ACT)	6	6	0	100	46	16.7	81	0	0	4	1	54.0	1-16	6.8
GP Redmayne (Qld)	6	6	0	213	89	35.5	59	0	1	4/1				
TMS Saville (SA)	6	4	1	107	53	35.7	85	0	1	2	2	18.5	2-8	4.4
ML Schutt (SAus)	6	4	1	12	6	4.0	48	0	0	3	8	38.3	3-16	3.8
KLH Short (SA)	6	6	0	187	54	31.2	79	0	2	6				
LG Smith (NSW)	7	2	1	3	2	3.0	100	0	0	4	10	29.4	3-52	4.7
NE Stalenburg(NSW)	7	7	3	150	41*	37.5	70	0	0	5	1	12.0	1-5	2.5
MR Strano (Vic)	6	6	1	81	36*	16.2	46	0	0	3	8	34.8	3-39	3.5
AJ Sutherland (Vic)	2	2	0	14	9	7.0	25	0	0	1	1	30.0	1-33	9.0
K Sutherland (Qld)	2	1	0	2	2	2.0	40	0	0	1	1	30.0	1-8	3.6
EE Thompson (Tas)	4	4	0	14	9	3.5	40	0	0	3	1	72.0	1-18	6.9
BW Vakarewa (NSW)	4	1	1	0	0*		0	0	0	2	3	39.7	1-7	4.4
D van Niekerk (ACT)	2	2	0	124	63	62.0	95	0	2	1	5	21.6	3-31	4.3
EJ Villani (WA)	7	7	0	362	139	51.7	101	1	2	3	0			7.5
TJ Vlaeminck (Vic)	6	2	1	0	0*	0.0	0	0	0	6	4	46.0	2-34	5.3
GL Wareham (Vic)	6	6	1	76	32	15.2	36	0	0	2	1	59.0	1-12	5.2
CA Webb (Tas)	4	4	0	17	13	4.3	28	0	0	1	3	43.0	2-28	4.8
AJ Wellington (SA)	6	6	2	130	116	32.5	85	1	0	1	9	30.8	2-2	4.7
LE Wright (Tas)	6	6	1	144	104*	28.8	62	1	0	3	10	29.4	3-52	4.7

WNCL RECORDS
RECENT WINNERS
(The modern WNCL came into being in 1996-97)

1991-92	South Australia	2003-04	New South Wales
1992-93	South Australia	2004-05	Victoria
1993-94	New South Wales	2005-06 to 2014-15	New South Wales
1994-95	South Australia	2015-16	South Australia
1995-96	Victoria	2016-17	New South Wales
1996-97 to 2001-02	New South Wales	2017-18	New South Wales
2002-03	Victoria		

RESULTS

Team	Matches	Won	Lost	Tied	NR
Australian Capital Territory	54	24	28	0	0
New South Wales	192	154	36	1	1
Queensland	159	61	91	2	5
South Australia	159	69	85	1	3
Tasmania	41	5	36	0	0
Victoria	178	109	65	1	3
Western Australia	158	37	118	1	2

LEADING RUN SCORERS

	M	Inn	NO	Runs	HS	Avge	S/Rate	100s	50s	0s
KL Rolton	114	111	14	5521	173	56.92	73.97	14	41	5
AJ Blackwell	**132**	**122**	**27**	**4507**	**157**	**47.44**	**70.85**	**11**	**27**	**6**
BJ Clark	89	89	13	4059	122*	53.41	66.55	7	35	3
MJ Bulow	122	120	1	3617	130	30.39	60.13	7	16	10
KL Britt	**114**	**111**	**17**	**3471**	**145***	**36.93**	**66.83**	**2**	**21**	**7**
LC Sthalekar	145	128	28	3393	108*	33.93	69.80	2	17	5
M Jones	122	120	10	3338	95	30.35	58.82	0	21	7

HIGHEST SCORES

MM Lanning	190 (153)	Vic v Tas at Bellerive, 2016-17
MM Lanning	175 (143)	Vic v ACT at Manuka Oval, 2012-13
KL Rolton	173 (136)	SA v WA at Adel Oval No 2, 1998-99
EJ Villani	173 (129)	Vic v SA at Camberwell, 2012-13
NE Bolton	170* (156)	Vic v Tas at Bellerive, 2014-15

LEADING WICKET TAKERS

	Wkts	M	Balls	Runs	Avge	Best	4i	5i	Econ
LC Sthalekar	167	145	7194	3628	21.72	4-7	4	0	3.03
CL Fitzpatrick	148	103	5487	2614	17.66	6-22	2	1	2.86
CR Smith	128	117	6006	3065	23.95	5-10	5	2	3.06
J Hayes	114	111	5731	3026	26.54	4-12	3	0	3.17
KL Rolton	106	114	3969	1946	18.36	5-7	6	2	2.94
KE Pike	102	86	4069	2228	21.84	4-15	4	0	3.29

BEST BOWLING

SR Theodore	7-14	Vic v WA at Kingsway, Perth, 1998-99
KM Beams	6-20	Vic v ACT at Central Reserve, Melb, 2011-12
CL Fitzpatrick	6-22	Vic v NSW at Central Reserve, Melb, 2006-07
AJ Wellington	6-25	SA v Tas, Adel Oval No 2, 2014-15
MR Strano	6-46	Vic v NSW, at Junction Oval, St Kilda, 2014-15

Australian Cricket Digest, 2018-19
WBBL03 – SIXERS GO BACK TO BACK
TABLE

	W	L	NR	Points	Net Run Rate
Sydney Sixers (1)	10	4	-	20	+0.89
Sydney Thunder (3)	10	4	-	20	+0.68
Perth Scorchers (2)	8	6	-	16	+0.26
Adelaide Strikers (4)	8	6	-	16	+0.25
Brisbane Heat (5)	7	7	-	14	+0.14
Melbourne Renegades (6)	6	8	-	12	+0.09
Melbourne Stars (7)	5	9	-	10	-0.634
Hobart Hurricanes (8)	2	12	-	4	-1.73

MOST RUNS

	Team	M	Inn	NO	Runs	HS	Avge	S/Rate	100s	50s	6s
EA Perry	SS	16	16	4	552	91*	46.00	98.5	0	3	10
EL Villani	PS	16	16	3	535	84*	41.15	125.8	0	5	7
NE Bolton	PS	16	16	1	482	71	32.13	101.2	0	3	10
BL Mooney	BH	14	14	3	465	86*	42.27	143.5	0	5	5
SW Bates	AS	15	15	1	434	102	31.00	109.6	1	1	2
RL Haynes	ST	15	15	1	426	78*	30.43	120.6	0	4	7
AJ Healy	SS	16	16	0	421	106	26.31	136.6	1	2	5
AE Satterthwaite	MR	14	12	1	368	65	33.45	108.5	0	2	2
SFM Devine	AS	15	15	1	355	70	25.36	117.5	0	1	17
L Lee	MS	12	12	0	349	76	29.08	111.1	0	3	17
AK Gardner	SS	14	14	1	347	114	26.69	138.8	1	1	21

HIGHEST SCORES

	BF	4s	6s		Venue
AK Gardner	114	52	9	10	Sixers v Stars	North Sydney No 1
AJ Healy	106	66	13	3	Sixers v Strikers	Hurstville Oval
SW Bates	102	65	15	0	Strikers v Hurricanes	Glenelg
EA Perry	91*	49	9	4	Sixers v Stars	North Sydney No 1

MOST WICKETS

Bowling	Team	M	Overs	Mdns	Runs	Wkts	Avge	Econ	Best
KH Brunt	PS	14	54	1	261	23	11.35	4.83	3-11
SE Aley	SS	16	58.5	3	361	23	15.70	6.14	4-18
D van Niekerk	SS	12	42	0	234	20	11.70	5.57	4-13
SFM Devine	AS	15	48	0	298	17	17.53	6.21	2-10
RM Farrell	ST	15	58.4	1	354	17	20.82	6.03	3-19
LM Tahuhu	MR	13	44.5	1	280	17	15.82	6.25	3-25
NJ Carey	ST	15	52.1	0	350	17	20.59	6.71	3-10
AJ Wellington	AS	15	54.2	0	355	17	20.88	6.53	3-9
SL Bates	ST	14	48.4	1	286	16	17.88	5.88	3-12
SR Taylor	ST	15	37.4	0	234	15	15.60	6.21	4-15
MJ Brown	MR	14	44.5	0	284	15	18.93	6.33	3-28
EA Osborne	MS	14	53.3	0	339	15	22.60	6.34	4-20
EL King	PS	16	56.5	1	341	15	22.73	6.00	3-17

BEST BOWLING

	Figures		Venue
JL Barsby	4-2	BH v ST	Allan Border Field
D van Niekerk	4-13	SS v MR	Camberwell
SR Taylor	4-15	ST v HH	York Park, Launceston
V Pyke	4-17	HH v AS	Glenelg Oval
SE Aley	4-18	SS v AS	Adelaide Oval

HAT-TRICK

		Venue
D van Niekerk	Sixers v Hurricanes	Bellerive Oval, Hobart

277

Australian Cricket Digest, 2018-19

Match 1 - Renegades v Thunder at North Sydney Oval No 2 on December 9, 2017 - Thunder won by 11 runs

Thunder		B	4	6	Renegades		B	4	6
RL Haynes	b Atapattu	55	41	7	SG Molineux	c Stalenberg b Taylor	25	14	4	1
RH Priest +	c Brown b Strano	5	5	1	C Atapattu	c Stalenberg b Carey	42	30	5	1
AJ Blackwell *	c Duffin b Jensen	8	6	1	JE Duffin	c Griffith b Bates	81	47	12	1
SR Taylor	c Molineux b Tahuhu	1	2		EJ Inglis +	c Blackwell b Farrell	20	12	4
H Kaur	run out (Strano-Inglis)	8	11	1	AE Satterthwaite *	c Kaur b Taylor	5	9
NE Stalenberg	st Inglis b Brown	38	25	6	1	CJ Koski	b Farrell	9	5	1
NJ Carey	not out	47	17	9	1	KL Britt	not out	3	3
RM Farrell	not out	25	13	4	HNK Jensen				
L Griffith					MJ Brown				
ML Gibson					LM Tahuhu				
SL Bates					MR Strano				
	(4 b, 9 w)	13				(2 b, 2 w)	4		
6 overs: 3-38	20 overs	6-200			6 overs: 1-49	20 overs	6-189		

Fall: 1-12 (Priest, 1.3 ov), 2-29 (Blackwell, 3.4 ov), 3-30 (Taylor, 4.1 ov), 4-41 (Kaur, 6.6 ov), 5-117 (Stalenberg, 14.5 ov), 6-117 (Haynes, 15.1 ov)

Fall: 1-30 (Molineux, 2.4 ov), 2-117 (Atapattu, 12.2 ov), 3-163 (Inglis, 16.3 ov), 4-173 (Duffin, 17.2 ov), 5-185 (Koski, 18.5 ov), 6-189 (Satterthwaite, 20 ov)

Renegades - bowling	O	M	R	W	wd	nb	Dots
LMM Tahuhu	4	0	43	1	1		9
MR Strano	4	0	37	1	1		10
HNK Jensen	3	0	34	1			4
MJ Brown	4	0	29	1	1		13
C Atapattu	4	0	35	1	2		5
AE Satterthwaite	2	0	18	0			4

Thunder - bowling	O	Dots	R	W	wd	nb	Dots
SL Bates	3	0	33	1			5
RM Farrell	4	0	44	2			5
SR Taylor	4	0	30	2	1		5
L Griffith	4	0	35	0	1		8
NJ Carey	4	0	29	1			9
H Kaur	1	0	16	0			1

Toss – Renegades. Award: JE Duffin (MR) Umpires: RM Nelson, DJ Shepard, AK Wilds (TV), Ref: IS Thomas.

Haynes 50: 37 balls, 6x4 1x6. Duffin 50: 32 balls, 8x4 1x6

Match 2 - Strikers v Hurricanes at Glenelg Oval, Adelaide on December 9, 2017 - Strikers won by 45 runs

Strikers		B	4	6	Hurricanes		B	4	6
SW Bates *	c Hall b Hepburn	31	24	6	L Winfield	lbw b Schutt	7	9	1
TT Beaumont	c Matthews b Hepburn	43	39	4	1	GP Redmayne +	run out (Betts)	17	14	3
TM McGrath	lbw b Raack	22	21	3	HK Matthews	c Betts b Dick	35	27	6
SFM Devine	not out	46	21	4	2	V Krishnamurthy	c Bates b Devine	6	12
BE Patterson	not out	26	18	2	CL Hall *	c Bates b McGrath	11	9	1
SM Betts					NM Hancock	st McPharlin b Wellington	0	2
TJ McPharlin +					EE Thompson	c Bates b McGrath	9	14
RS Dick					VP yke	not out	26	20	3
TMS Saville					BL Hepburn	b Schutt	11	8	2
M Schutt					KR Fryett	c Dick b Devine	3	4
A Wellington					C Raack	not out	5	2	1
	4 b, 3 lb, 3 nb, 5 w	15				(2 lb, 1 nb, 5 w)	8		
6 overs: 0-47	20 overs	3-183			6 overs: 2-47	20 overs	9-138		

Fall: 1-48 (Bates, 6.2 ov), 2-96 (Beaumont, 12.3 ov), 3-114 (McGrath, 14.2 ov), 11.2 ov),

Fall: 1-14 (Winfield, 2.1 ov), 2-46 (Redmayne, 5.3 ov), 3-57 (Krishnamurthy, 8.4 ov), 4-74 (Matthews, 10.5 ov), 5-74 (Hancock, 11.2 ov), 6-85 (Hall, 12.5 ov), 7-106 (Thompson, 16.1 ov), 8-126 (Hepburn, 18.2 ov), 9-131 (Fryett, 19.3 ov)

Hurricanes - bowling	O	M	R	W	wd	nb	Dots
HK Matthews	4	0	47	0	1		7
KR Fryett	3	0	29	0	1		5
VP yke	2	0	14	0	1		5
NM Hancock	3	0	20	0		3	7
BL Hepburn	4	0	35	2	1		9
V Krishnamurthy	1	0	9	0			2
C Raack	3	0	22	0			6

Strikers - bowling	O	M	R	W	wd	nb	Dots
ML Schutt	4	0	26	2			11
SM Betts	2	0	23	0			2
SW Bates	3	0	20	0			7
SFM Devine	3	0	20	2	3		7
AJ Wellington	4	0	20	1	1		9
RS Dick	1	0	12	1		1	7
TM McGrath	3	0	15	2			7

Toss – Hurricanes. Award – SFM Devine (AS). Umpires - SJ Farrell, L Uthernwoldt, Ref: JP Biddiss

Australian Cricket Digest, 2018-19
Match 3 – Sixers v Stars on December 9, 2017 (floodlit) - Sixers won by 86 runs

Sixers		B	4	6
AJ Healy +	c Mack b Osborne	4	6	
EA Perry *	not out	91	49	9	4
AK Gardner	c King b Kearney	114	52	9	10
EA Burns	b Osborne	18	11	3
SJ McGlashan	run out (Osborne)	4	4	
D van Niekerk	not out	0	0	
M Kapp				
AR Reakes				
SE Aley				
LG Smith				
JC Hicks				
	4 lb, 2 nb, 5 w	11		
6 overs: 0-64	20 overs	4-242		

Stars		B	4	6
L Lee +	lbw b Smith	64	36	8	4
AM King	c Smith b Aley	10	15	2
M du Preez	run out (Perry)	4	3	1
AJ Lanning	lbw b van Niekerk	8	13	1
KM Mack	b Kapp	25	24	1	1
EA Osborne	c Burns b Aley	19	20	2
EM Kearney	b Kapp	11	7	1
HM Brennan	not out	1	2	
MA Blows				
KM Beams *				
GL Triscari				
	1 lb, 13 w	14		
6 overs: 1-66	20 overs	7-156		

Fall: 1-10 (Healy, 1.3 ov), 2-160 (Gardner, 13.6 ov), 3-211 (Burns, 17.5 ov), 4-221 (McGlashan, 18.6 ov)

Fall: 1-61 (King, 5.3 ov), 2-71 (du Preez, 6.5 ov), 3-89 (Lanning, 10.5 ov), 4-93 (Lee, 11.2 ov), 5-124 (Osborne, 16.4 ov), 6-147 (Mack, 19.1 ov), 7-156 (Kearney, 20 ov)

Stars - bowling	O	M	R	W	wd	nb	Dots
EM Kearney	4	0	40	1	1	1	7
EA Osborne	4	0	33	2	1		9
HM Brennan	2	0	36	0			2
KM Beams	4	0	51	0	1		7
AM King	3	0	41	0		1	6
GL Triscari	3	0	37	0			3

Sixers - bowling	O	M	R	W	wd	nb	Dots
AK Gardner	1	0	20	0			2
M Kapp	4	0	31	2	3		14
EA Perry	2	0	21	0	4		7
SE Aley	4	0	30	2	5		9
D van Niekerk	4	0	20	1			13
LG Smith	4	0	20	1	1		9
EA Burns	1	0	13	0			1

Toss: Stars. Award: AK Gardner (SS). Umpires: MAW Nickl, BC Treloar, SA Lightbody (TV), Ref: TM Donahoo
Perry 50: 32 balls, 3x6 3x4; Gardner 50: 22 balls, 7x4 3x6, 100: 47 balls, 9x4 8x6. Lee 50: 22 balls, 6x4 4x6. Attendance: 3,909

Match 4 - Scorchers v Heat at North Sydney Oval on December 10, 2017 - Scorchers won by 18 runs

Scorchers		B	4	6
EJ Villani *	lbw b Johnson	16	12	3
NE Bolton	run out (Harris)	0	3	
HL Graham	b Jonassen	8	7	2
NR Sciver	c and b Birkett	84	46	11
KH Brunt	c Mooney b Johnson	22	24	1	1
LK Ebsary	not out	37	20	6
MG Carmichael	run out (Mooney)	12	11	1
TMM Newton	not out	0	0	
EL King				
EJ Smith +				
PM Cleary				
	3 b, 3 nb, 3 w	9		
6 overs: 3-43	20 overs	6-188		

Heat		B	4	6
BL Mooney +	c Sciver b Brunt	23	12	3	1
KLH Short *	b Brunt	5	9	
L Wolvaardt	run out (Sciver)	0	0	
DJS Dottin	b Graham	10	8	1
DM Kimmince	not out	87	54	9	3
LM Harris	b Newton	6	10	
JL Jonassen	c Sciver b Newton	3	6	
SJ Johnson	lbw b King	8	7	1
HP Birkett	c Graham b Brunt	6	7	1
JL Barsby	c Brunt b Graham	13	7	2
HL Ferling	not out	1	1	
	2 lb, 1 nb, 5 w	8		
6 overs: 3-53	20 overs	9-170		

Fall: 1-16 (Villani, 2.1 ov), 2-18 (Bolton, 2.5 ov), 3-27 (Graham, 3.5 ov), 4-111 (Brunt, 12.1 ov), 5-146 (Sciver, 15.5 ov), 6-186 (Carmichael, 19.5 ov)

Fall: 1-27 (Mooney, 2.4 ov), 2-29 (Wolvaardt, 3.1 ov), 3-38 (Short, 4.1 ov), 4-61 (Dottin, 7.4 ov), 5-82 (Harris, 10.5 ov), 6-90 (Jonassen, 14.2 ov), 7-118 (Johnson, 15.2 ov), 8-127 (Birkett, 16.5 ov), 9-167 (Barsby, 19.3 ov)

Heat - bowling	O	M	R	W	wd	nb	Dots
SJ Johnson	4	0	24	2	1		15
JlJonassen	3	0	32	1		1	6
DM Kimmince	4	0	36	0	2	1	8
JL Barsby	2	0	20	0			3
DJS Dottin	4	0	34	0		1	7
HL Ferling	1	0	17	0			2
HP Birkett	2	0	22	1			2

Scorchers - bowling	O	M	R	W	wd	nb	Dots
KH Brunt	4	1	23	3	3		13
NE Bolton	1	0	10	0			2
NR Sciver	3	0	39	0	2	1	5
PM Cleary	2	0	13	0			3
HL Graham	4	0	37	2			5
TMM Newton	3	0	27	2			5
EL King	3	0	19	1			6

Toss: Scorchers. Award: NR Sciver (PS). Umpires: RM Nelson, DJ Shepard, AK Wilds (TV), Ref: TM Donahoo.
Sciver 50: 28 balls, 6x4 2x6. Kimmince 50: 37 balls, 5x4 2x6.

Australian Cricket Digest, 2018-19

Match 5 - Strikers v Hurricanes at Glenelg Oval, Adelaide on December 10, 2017 - Strikers won by 83 runs

Strikers		B	4	6
SW Bates *	c Hepburn b Pyke	102	65	15
TT Beaumont	b Pyke	3	5	
TM McGrath	c Fryett b Hancock	8	8	1
SFM Devine	c Fryett b Pyke	43	29	1 4
BE Patterson	not out	5	4	
A Wellington	c Raack b Pyke	9	7	1
TMS Saville	run out (Matthews)	1	3	
SM Betts				
TJ McPharlin +				
M Schutt				
RS Dick				
	1b, 1nb, 3 w	5		
6 overs: 2-38	20 overs	6-176		

Fall: 1-18 (Beaumont, 3.4 ov), 2-38 (McGrath, 5.6 ov), 3-155 (Devine, 17.1 ov), 4-163 (Bates, 17.6 ov), 5-175 (Wellington, 19.3 ov), 6-176 (Saville, 20 ov)

Hurricanes		B	4	6
L Winfield	c Wellington b McGrath	15	14	3
GP Redmayne +	run out (Patterson)	2	7	
HK Matthews	c Bates b McGrath	4	8	1
V Krishnamurthy	c McPharlin b Betts	21	24	2
CL Hall *	c McPharlin b Devine	1	3	
EE Thompson	st McPharlin b Wellington	7	11	
VPyke	st McPharlin b Wellington	2	9	
NM Hancock	lbw b Wellington	0	3	
BL Hepburn	lbw b Schutt	9	13	1
KR Fryett	c and b Betts	19	15	2
C Raack	not out	5	6	
	1b, 1lb, 6 w	8		
6 overs: 3-29	18.5 overs	93		

Fall: 1-19 (Redmayne, 3.2 ov), 2-20 (Winfield, 3.5 ov), 3-28 (Matthews, 5.2), 4-29 (Hall, 6.1 ov), 5-43 (Thompson, 9.2 ov), 6-48 (Pyke, 11.1 ov), 7-48 (Hancock, 11.4 ov), 8-65 (Krishnamurthy, 14.4 ov), 9-73 (Hepburn, 16.2 ov), 10-93 (Fryett, 18.5 ov)

Hurricanes - bowling	O	M	R	W	wd	nb	Dots
KR Fryett	2	0	17	0			4
VPyke	4	0	17	4			12
HK Matthews	3	0	28	0			4
NM Hancock	3	0	28	1		1	7
BL Hepburn	3	0	32	0	2		3
C Raack	3	0	35	0	-		5
EE Thompson	2	0	18	0	1		3

Strikers - bowling	O	M	R	W	wd	nb	Dots
ML Schutt	4	0	25	1	2		13
TM McGrath	3	0	9	2			12
SFM Devine	3	0	14	1			7
AJ Wellington	4	0	9	3	2		18
SM Betts	2.5	0	22	2	2		8
RS Dick	2	0	12	0			1

Toss: Strikers. Award: SW Bates (AS). Umpires: C Thomas, L Uthenwoldt, Ref: JP Biddiss.
Bates 50: 39 balls, 5x4; 100: 64 balls, 15x4

Match 6 - Thunder v Sixers on December 10, 2018 - Sixers won by 6 wickets

Thunder		B	4	6
RH Priest +	lbw b Kapp	4	2	1
RL Haynes	c van Niekerk b Perry	17	18	2
AJ Blackwell *	c Burns b van Niekerk	58	52	9
SR Taylor	st Healy b Aley	1	3	
H Kaur	c Smith b Perry	29	21	3 1
NE Stalenberg	run out (Kapp)	23	17	4
NJ Carey	not out	5	7	
ML Gibson				
SL Bates				
L Griffith				
RM Farrell				
	3 lb, 2 w	5		
6 overs: 1-41	20 overs	6-142		

Fall: 1-4 (Priest, 0.2 ov), 2-57 (Haynes, 8.1 ov), 3-66 (Taylor, 9.3 ov), 4-111 (Blackwell, 15.2 ov), 5-114 (Kaur, 16.3 ov), 6-142 (Stalenberg, 20 ov)

Sixers		B	4	6
AJ Healy `+	c Farrell b Carey	49	27	11
EA Perry *	run out (Blackwell)	12	18	2
AK Gardner	c Priest b Taylor	47	35	7
EA Burns	b Gibson	10	8	1
SJ McGlashan	not out	13	13	1
D van Niekerk	not out	11	11	2
M Kapp				
AR Reakes				
SE Aley				
LG Smith				
JC Hicks				
	4 w	4		
6 overs: 0-57	18.4 overs	4-146		

Fall: 1-57 (Perry, 6.3 ov), 2-82 (Healy, 10.1 ov), 3-106 (Burns, 13.1 ov), 4-124 (Gardner, 15.3 ov)

Sixers - bowling	O	M	R	W	wd	nb	Dots
M Kapp	4	0	23	1			12
EA Perry	4	0	15	2	1		16
AK Gardner	2	0	21	0			4
LG Smith	3	0	26	0			4
SE Aley	4	0	34	1	1		6
D van Niekerk	3	0	20	0			7

Thunder - bowling	O	M	R	W	wd	nb	Dots
SR Taylor	3	0	27	1	1		8
L Griffith	2	0	21	0			6
SL Bates	2	0	15	0			6
RM Farrell	3.4	0	26	0	3		11
ML Gibson	4	0	29	1			10
NJ Carey	4	0	28	1			7

Toss: Thunder. Award: AJ Healty (SS). Umpires: MAW Nickl, BC Treloar, SA Lightbody (TV), Ref: IS Thomas
Blackwell 50: 46 balls, 8x4. Attendance 4,812.

Australian Cricket Digest, 2018-19

Match 7 - Sixers v Scorchers at North Dalton Park, Wollongong on December 12, 2017
Scorchers won by 9 wickets

Sixers		B	4	6	Scorchers		B	4	6
AJ Healy +	c Ebsary b Brunt	15	9	3	EJ Villani *	not out	74	61	11	2
EA Perry *	c Sciver b King	15	30	1	NE Bolton	c Kapp b Aley	42	46	2	2
AK Gardner	c Ebsary b King	7	12	1	NR Sciver	not out	3	5	
EA Burns	c King b Graham	33	25	3	1	HL Graham			
SJ McGlashan	c Carmichael b Graham	13	15		1	KH Brunt			
D van Niekerk	run out (Newton)	7	10			LK Ebsary			
M Kapp	run out (Brunt)	3	3			MG Carmichael			
SE Aley	lbw b Brunt	2	3			TMM Newton			
LG Smith	not out	13	9	2		PM Cleary			
KJ Garth	not out	3	6			EL King			
JC Hicks	did not bat					EJ Smith +			
	2 lb, 2 nb, 7 w	11					2 nb, 2 w	4	
6 overs: 1-38	20 overs	8-122				6 overs: 0-38	18.2 overs	1-123	

Fall: 1-16 (Healy, 1.3 ov), 2-38 (Gardner, 6.2 ov), 3-47
(Perry, 8.6 ov), 4-89 (McGlashan, 14.1 ov), 5-100
(Burns, 16.2 ov), 6-102 (van Niekerk, 16.4 ov), 7-106
(Kapp, 17.2 ov), 8-107 (Aley, 17.4 ov)

Fall: 1-106 (Bolton, 15.3 ov)

Scorchers - bowling	O	M	R	W	wd	nb	Dots	Sixers - bowling	O	M	R	W	wd	nb	Dots
NR Sciver	3	0	28	0	1		5	M Kapp	4	0	16	0	1		18
KH Brunt	4	0	19	2	2	1	16	EA Perry	2.2	0	22	0	1		7
HL Graham	4	0	20	2			12	SE Aley	4	0	22	1		1	13
PM Cleary	4	0	25	0			10	KJ Garth	3	0	14	0			10
EL King	4	0	19	2	1		11	LG Smith	3	0	33	0		1	5
TMM Newton	1	0	9	0	3	1	1	D van Niekerk	2	0	16	0			3

Toss: Scorchers.   Award: EJ Villani (PS).   Umpires: RM Nelson, MAW Nickl,   Ref: N Findlay.
Villani 50: 46 balls, 9x4

Match 8 - Stars v Thunder at Lavington Sports Club, Albury on December 12, 2017 - Thunder won by 8 wickets

Stars		B	4	6	Thunder		B	4	6
L Lee +	c Kaur b Vakarewa	31	25	5	1	RL Haynes	c Lee b Kearney	54	33	8	1
AJ Lanning	run out (Gibson)	25	31	3		RH Priest +	c Osborne b Triscari	38	35	4	1
M du Preez	c Taylor b Carey	3	4			AJ Blackwell *	not out	3	3	
GA Elwiss	b Carey	3	7			SR Taylor	not out	17	16	1
KM Mack	lbw b Kaur	1	3			H Kaur			
EA Osborne	b Kaur	25	31	1		NE Stalenberg			
EM Kearney	lbw b Gibson	0	1			NJ Carey			
AM King	c Farrell b Kaur	21	19	1	1	RM Farrell			
*KM Beams	not out	0	0			L Griffith			
MA Blows						ML Gibson			
GL Triscari						BW Vakarewa			
	2 lb, 1 nb, 2 w	5					3 w	3	
6 overs: 1-45	20 overs	8-114				6 overs: 0-46	14.3 overs	2-115	

Fall: 1-40 (Lee, 5.3 ov), 2-51 (du Preez, 7.4 ov), 3-61 (Elwiss),
9.4 ov), 4-62 (Mack, 10.2 ov), 5-71 (Lanning, 12.3 ov),
6-73 (Kearney, 13.1 ov), 7-114 (King, 19.5 ov),
8-114 (Osborne, 20 ov)

Fall: 1-86 (Priest, 10.3 ov), 2-95 (Haynes, 11.2 ov)

Thunder - bowling	O	M	R	W	wd	nb	Dots	Stars - bowling	O	M	R	W	wd	nb	Dots
RM Farrell	4	1	19	0			15	EM Kearney	3	0	25	1			7
BW Vakarewa	3	0	24	1		1	10	EA Osborne	2.3	0	19	0	2		7
L Griffith	1	0	14	0			2	GA Elwiss	3	0	25	0			5
ML Gibson	4	0	20	1			11	KM Beams	3	0	17	0			9
NJ Carey	4	0	17	2			11	AM King	2	0	19	0	1		5
H Kaur	4	0	18	3	1		14	GL Triscari	1	0	10	1			2

Toss: Thunder. Award: RL Haynes (ST). Umpires: PRDS Bandara, AR Crozier, Ref: K Hannam.
Haynes 50: 31 balls, 7x4 1x6

Match 9 - Heat v Scorchers at Allan Border Field, Brisbane on December 15, 2017 – Heat won by 6 wickets

Scorchers		B	4	6	Heat		B	4	6
EJ Villani *	c Johnson b Kimmince	15	16	3	BL Mooney +	c Newton b Brunt	10	10	2
NE Bolton	c Birkett b Jonassen	14	14	3	KLH Short *	not out	50	48	5
HL Graham	lbw b Barsby	7	16	1	L Wolvaardt	b Brunt	2	2	
NR Sciver	b Dottin	4	5	1	DJS Dottin	c Bolton b Newton	45	48	4 1
KH Brunt	st Mooney b Kimmince	29	32	3	DM Kimmince	c Sciver b Newton	1	2	
LK Ebsary	c Wolvaardt b Ferling	6	8	1	LM Harris	not out	7	4	1
MG Carmichael	b Jonassen	22	25		JL Jonassen				
TMM Newton	not out	7	4	1	SJ Johnson				
PM Cleary	not out	1	1		HP Birkett				
EL King					JL Barsby				
EJ Smith +					HL Ferling				
	2 b, 1 nb, 4 w	7				1 nb	1		
6 overs: 2-33	20 overs	7-112			6 overs: 2-24	18.5 overs	4-116		

Fall: 1-23 (Bolton, 3.3 ov), 2-33 (Villani, 5.5 ov), 3-38 (Sciver, 6.4 ov), 4-48 (Graham, 9.5 ov), 5-54 (Ebsary, 11.1 ov), 6-103 (Brunt, 18.5 ov), 7-111 (Carmichael, 19.4 ov)

Fall: 1-13 (Mooney, 2.1 ov), 2-15 (Wolvaardt, 2.3 ov), 3-93 (Dottin, 16.2 ov), 4-95 (Kimmince, 16.5 ov)

Heat - bowling	O	M	R	W	wd	nb	Dots	Scorchers - bowling	O	M	R	W	wd	nb	Dots
SJ Johnson	2	0	14	0			7	KH Brunt	4	0	17	2			14
JL Jonassen	4	0	31	2	1		9	PM Cleary	4	0	14	0		1	16
DJS Dottin	3	0	22	1	1	1	8	HL Graham	3	0	24	0			5
DM Kimmince	4	1	17	2			14	EL King	4	0	27	0			6
JL Barsby	2	0	4	1			8	NR Sciver	1	0	12	0			2
HP Birkett	3	0	14	0			9	NE Bolton	1	0	7	0			
HL Ferling	2	0	8	1			3	TMM Newton	1.5	0	15	2			5

Toss: Scorchers. Award: SW Bates (AS). Umpires: MS Branch, SJ Farrell, Ref: N Findlay.
Short 50: 48 balls, 5x4

Match 10 – Thunder v Stars at Howell Oval, Sydney on December 16, 2017 – Thunder won by 9 wickets

Stars		B	4	6	Thunder		B	4	6
L Lee +	c Haynes b Farrell	0	1		RH Priest +	b Osborne	42	35	7 1
AJ Lanning	c Vakarewa b Bates	35	41	2 1	RL Haynes	not out	78	49	4 3
M du Preez	c Carey b Gibson	58	49	6 1	AJ Blackwell *	not out	6	8	
GA Elwiss	not out	23	20		SR Taylor				
KM Mack	b Carey	5	7		H Kaur				
EA Osborne	not out	5	4		NE Stalenberg				
EM Kearney					NJ Carey				
AM King					RM Farrell				
KM Beams *					ML Gibson				
MA Blows					BW Vakarewa				
GL Triscari					SL Bates				
	2 b, 1 lb, 2 nb, 1 w	6				2 b, 1 lb, 1 nb, 5 w	9		
6 overs: 1-31	20 overs	4-132			6 overs: 0-53	15.1 overs	1-135		

Fall: 1-0 (Lee, 0.1 ov), 2-82 (Lanning, 13.2 ov), 3-106 (du Preez, 16.3 ov), 4-115 (Mack, 18.2 ov)

Fall: 1-95 (Priest, 10.5 ov)

Thunder - bowling	O	M	R	W	wd	nb	Dots	Stars - bowling	O	M	R	W	wd	nb	Dots
RM Farrell	4	0	27	1			8	EM Kearney	2.1	0	21	0	1		6
SL Bates	4	0	16	1			13	EA Osborne	4	0	26	1			9
BW Vakarewa	2	0	17	0			6	KM Beams	3	0	25	0			6
ML Gibson	4	0	26	1	1		6	GA Elwiss	2	0	18	0		1	2
NJ Carey	4	0	27	1		2	7	AM King	4	0	42	0			5
H Kaur	1	0	8	0			1								
SR Taylor	1	0	8	0			0								

Toss: Thunder. Award: RL Haynes (ST). Umpires: RM Nelson, GS Stubbings, Ref: IS Thomas.
du Preez 50: 41 balls, 5x4, 1x6. Haynes 50: 32 balls, 4x4 2x6

Australian Cricket Digest, 2018-19

Match 11 – Strikers v Renegades at Glenelg Oval, Adelaide on December 16, 2017 – Strikers won by 1 run

Strikers		B	4	6
SW Bates *	c Duffin b Brown	24	18	3	1
TT Beaumont	c Duffin b Atpattu	45	53	5	1
TM McGrath	b Jensen	9	19	1
SFM Devine	c Brown b Tahuhu	15	16	2
BE Patterson	run out (Jensen-Satterthwaite)	14	22	1
A Wellington	c Duffin b Strano	8	13
M Schutt	not out	20	8	1	1
TJ McPharlin +	not out	1	1
AE Price				
TMS Saville				
SM Betts				
	1b, 1 nb, 1w	3		
6 overs: 1-46	20 overs	6-139		

Fall: 1-34 (Bates, 4.5 ov), 2-65 (McGrath, 10.1 ov), 3-95 (Beaumont, 13.6 ov), 4-95 (Devine, 14.1 ov), 5-115 (Wellington, 17.5 ov), 6-128 (Patterson, 19.1 ov)

Renegades		B	4	6
SG Molineux	c Bates b McGrath	3	5
C Attapattu	c Saville b Devine	7	10	1
JE Duffin	c Saville b McGrath	8	9	2
AE Satterthwaite *	c Bates b Devine	56	40	6
KL Britt	c Devine b Wellington	9	10	1
EJ Inglis +	c Bates b Wellington	18	22	1
CJ Koski	run out (McPharlin)	16	10		2
HNK Jensen	not out	10	10
LM Tahuhu	c &b Bates	4	5
MR Strano				
MJ Brown				
	1 b, 3 lb, 3 w	7		
6 overs: 3-29	20 overs	8-138		

Fall: 1-3 (Molineux, 1.3), 2-18 (Duffin, 3.5), 3-18 (Atapattu, 4.1), 4-38 (Britt, 7.4), 5-90 (Inglis, 14.3), 6-122 (Satterthwaite, 17.1), 7-127 (Koski, 18.1 ov), 8-138 (Tahuhu, 20 ov)

Renegades - bowling	O	M	R	W	wd	nb	Dots
LM Tahuhu	4	0	32	1	1	1	13
MR Strano	4	0	22	1			9
MJ Brown	3	0	19	1			8
AE Satterthwaite	3	0	23	0			7
HNK Jensen	2	0	17	1			4
C Atapattu	4	0	25	1			7

Strikers - bowling	O	M	R	W	wd	nb	Dots
ML Schutt	4	0	14	0			14
TM McGrath	4	0	27	2			10
SFM Devine	4	0	28	2	2		10
AJ Wellington	4	0	33	2	1		6
SW Bates	4	0	32	1			6

Toss: Renegades. Award: TM McGrath (AS). Umpires: C Thomas, LA Uthenwoldt, Ref: JP Biddiss
Sattherthwaite 50: 37 balls, 6x4

Match 12 – Hurricanes v Sixers at Bellerive Oval, Hobart on December 17, 2017 – Sixers won by 33 runs

Sixers		B	4	6
AJ Healy +	c Matthews b Fryett	11	9	2
EA Perry *	run out (Matthews)	65	49	8	1
EA Burns	st Redmayne b Pyke	0	5
M Kapp	b Matthews	11	14	1
SJ McGlashan	run out (Daffara)	44	33	5
D van Niekerk	c Winfield b Hancock	5	6	1
AR Reakes	c Winfield b Matthews	4	4	1
SE Aley	run out (Matthews)	0	0
LG Smith	not out	6	2	1
KJ Garth	not out	0	0
JC Hicks				
	2 nb, 4 w	6		
6 overs: 2-37	20 overs	8-152		

Fall: 1-23 (Healy, 2.3), 2-25 (Burns, 3.5), 3-54 (Kapp, 8.3), 4-120 (McGlashan, 16.4), 5-132 (van Niekerk, 18.3), 6-142 (Perry, 19.1), 7-142 (Aley, 19.2), 8-146 (Reakes, 19.4)

Hurricanes		B	4	6
L Winfield	b Aley	13	15	2
GP Redmayne +	c Burns b Smith	22	29	2
HK Matthews	c Healy b Garth	11	13	2
V Krishnamurthy	b van Niekerk	13	16	1
NM Hancock	b van Niekerk	4	10
CL Hall *	b van Niekerk	0	1
SG Daffara	b van Niekerk	0	1
VP yke	not out	35	26	5
EG Fazackerley	c Kapp b Smith	12	9	2
BL Hepburn	not out	0	0
KR Fryett				
	1 b, 5 lb, 3 w	9		
6 overs: 1-25	20 overs	8-119		

Fall: 1-18 (Winfield, 3.3 ov), 2-36 (Matthews, 7.2 ov), 3-64 (Redmayne, 11.5 ov), 4-65 (Krishnamurthy, 12.2 ov), 5-65 (Hall, 12.3 ov), 6-65 (Daffara, 12.4 ov), 7-72 (Hancock, 14.6 ov), 8-110 (Fazackerley, 19.3 ov)

Hurricanes - bowling	O	M	R	W	wd	nb	Dots
NM Hancock	3	0	26	1			7
VP yke	4	0	27	1	1		11
KR Fryett	3	0	24	1	3	1	8
BL Hepburn	4	0	25	0	1		10
HK Matthews	4	0	29	2			9
EG Fazackerley	2	0	21	0			2

Sixers - bowling	O	M	R	W	wd	nb	Dots
M Kapp	4	0	10	0			15
EA Perry	2	0	9	0	1		8
SE Aley	3	0	23	1			10
KJ Garth	2	0	8	1	1		5
D van Niekerk	4	0	20	4	1		11
LG Smith	4	0	32	2			9
AR Reakes	1	0	11	0			0

Toss: Sixers. Award: EA Perry (SS). Umpires: M Qureshi, H Wolff, Ref: JM Mitchell
Perry 50: 44 balls, 7x4. Hat-trick taken by D van Niekerk (V Krishnamurthy, CL Hall, SG Daffara)

Australian Cricket Digest, 2018-19

Match 13 – Strikers v Renegades at Glenelg Oval, Adelaide on December 17, 2017 – Renegades won by 9 runs

Renegades		R	B	4	6
SG Molineux	c Price b Bates	28	23	5	
KL Britt	lbw b Schutt	8	9	1	
JE Duffin	c Schutt b Devine	30	28	3	1
AE Satterthwaite *	c &b Wellington	49	37	6	
C Atapattu	c Price b Devine	8	8		
EJ Inglis +	not out	18	13	1	
CJ Koski	not out	7	4		
MR Strano					
GL Wareham					
MJ Brown					
LM Tahuhu					
	5 b, 4 lb, 2 nb, 1 w	12			
6 overs: 1-42	20 overs	5-160			

Fall: 1-12 (Britt, 2.2), 2-52 (Molineux, 7.2), 3-100 (Duffin, 13.2), 4-120 (Atapattu, 15.4), 5-147 (Satterthwaite, 18.5)

Strikers		R	B	4	6
SW Bates *	b Wareham	63	42	9	1
TT Beaumont	c Duffin b Tahuhu	9	11	1	
TM McGrath	c Inglis b Tahuhu	13	12	2	
SFM Devine	st Inglis b Wareham	12	11	1	
BE Patterson	c Strano b Brown	9	14		
TMS Saville	not out	16	15	1	
A Wellington	c Duffin b Satterthwaite	2	3		
TJ McPharlin +	c Atapattu b Strano	5	7		
M Schutt	c Koski b Satterthwaite	7	4	1	
AE Price	run out (Tahuhu)	2	3		
SM Betts	not out	5	3		
	2 lb, 6 w	8			
6 overs: 1-46	20 overs	9-151			

Fall: 1-18 (Beaumont, 2.4), 2-47 (McGrath, 3.3), 3-79 (Devine, 9.5), 4-92 (Patterson, 12.5), 5-116 (Bates, 14.6), 6-119 (Wellington, 15.4), 7-126 (McPharlin, 17.2), 8-135 (Schutt, 18.2), 9-145 (Price, 19.2)

Strikers - bowling	O	M	R	W	wd	nb	Dots
ML Schutt	4	0	25	1			10
TM McGrath	3	0	23	0	1		8
AE Price	3	0	26	0		1	6
SW Bates	2	0	17	1			4
A Wellington	3	0	22	1			6
SFM Devine	4	0	25	2			8
SM Betts	1	0	13	0	1		2

Renegades - bowling	O	M	R	W	wd	nb	Dots
LM Tahuhu	4	0	20	2	1		9
MR Strano	4	0	29	1			8
AE Satterthwaite	4	0	33	2	1		8
MJ Brown	3	0	21	1			8
C Atapattu	1	0	9	0	1		1
CJ Koski	1	0	13	0	3		2
GL Wareham	3	0	24	2			6

Toss: Renegades.   Award: TM McGrath (AS).   Umpires: C Thomas, LA Uthenwoldt, Ref: JP Biddiss
Bates 50: 34 balls, 7x4, 1x6

Match 14 – Renegades v Heat at Camberwell Sports Ground on December 22, 2017 – Renegades won by 8 runs

Renegades		R	B	4	6
SG Molineux	c Jonassen b Kimmince	40	32	3	2
C Atapattu	c Wolvaardt b Birkett	15	18	2	
JE Duffin	st Mooney b Jonassen	17	18		
AE Satterthwaite *	c Harris b Kimmince	38	33	5	1
EJ Inglis +	run out (Ferling)	11	10	1	
CJ Koski	c Short b Jonassen	0	1		
HNK Jensen	not out	4	5		
MJ Brown	not out	2	3		
GL Wareham					
LM Tahuhu					
MR Strano					
	2 lb, 4 w	6			
6 overs: 0-42	20 overs	6-133			

Fall: 1-43 (Atapattu, 6.2), 2-65 (Molineux, 10.2), 3-85 (Duffin, 12.6), 4-120 (Inglis, 17.3), 5-... (Koski, 17.6), 6-130 (Satterthwaite, 19.2)

Heat		R	B	4	6
BL Mooney +	c Molineux b Jensen	39	28	4	2
KLH Short *	b Tahuhu	20	21	3	
L Wolvaardt	c Satterthwaite b Strano	13	21	1	
DJS Dottin	c Duffin b Wareham	1	4		
DM Kimmince	b Strano	1	2		
LM Harris	c Duffin b Brown	17	17	1	
JL Jonassen	c Inglis b Satterthwaite	6	4	1	
SJ Johnson	c Satterthwaite b Brown	10	10		1
HP Birkett	c Jensen b Strano	5	4		
JL Barsby	c Jensen b Tahuhu	5	5	1	
HL Ferling	not out	4	3		
	4 w	4			
6 overs: 1-39	19.5 overs	125			

Fall: 1-38 (Short, 5.4), 2-71 (Mooney, 10.5), 3-75 (Dottin, 11.5), 4-77 (Kimmince, 12.1), 5-80 (Wolvaardt, 12.6), 6-94 5-121 (Jonassen, 14.6), 7-104 (Harris, 17.1), 8-112 (Johnson, 17.6), 9-116 (Birkett, 18.3 ov), 10-125 (Barsby, 19.5 ov)

Heat - bowling	O	M	R	W	wd	nb	Dots
JL Jonassen	4	0	27	2			12
SJ Johnson	2	0	12	0			8
DM Kimmince	4	0	26	2	1		10
DJS Dottin	2	0	12	0	1		7
HP Birkett	4	0	26	1			7
JL Barsby	4	0	28	0	2		8

Renegades - bowling	O	M	R	W	wd	nb	Dots
MR Strano	4	0	16	3			13
LM Tahuhu	3.5	0	28	2			12
MJ Brown	3	0	22	2			7
AE Satterthwaite	4	0	25	1	1		8
HNK Jensen	2	0	14	1			6
GL Wareham	3	0	20	1	3		7

Toss: Heat.   Award: AE Satterthwaite (MR).   Umpires: DJ Brigham, D Ireland, Ref: DP Herft

Match 15 – Sixers v Hurricanes at the SCG on December 23, 2017 – Sixers won by 9 wickets

Hurricanes		B	4	6	Sixers		B	4	6
L Winfield	c Hicks b Aley	6	10		AJ Healy +	c Hall b Hancock	6	3	1
HK Matthews	run out (Perry-Aley)	5	11		EA Perry *	not out	41	43	5
V Krishnamurthy	c Hicks b Smith	16	17	2	EA Burns	not out	48	38	4	1
GP Redmayne +	lbw b Garth	15	20	2	M Kapp				
V Pyke	c Reakes b van Niekerk	8	8	1	SJ McGlashan				
CL Hall *	lbw b Aley	14	16	1	D van Niekerk				
SG Daffara	b Kapp	13	16	1	AR Reakes				
NM Hancock	c Burns b van Niekerk	12	11	2	SE Aley				
BL Hepburn	run out (Healy)	0	0		LG Smith				
KR Fryett	b Perry	2	8		KJ Garth				
C Raack	not out	1	1		JC Hicks				
	2 lb, 4 w	6				1 lb, 1 nb, 2 w	4		
6 overs: 2-25	19.4 overs	98			6 overs: 1-49	13.5 overs	1-99		

Fall: 1-12 (Winfield, 3.3), 2-12 (Matthews, 3.5),
3-40 (Krishnamurthy, 8.5), 4-50 (Redmayne, 10.3),
5-54 (Pyke, 11.2), 6-72 (Hall, 15.1), 7-91 (Hancock, 17.3),
8-91 (Hepburn, 17.4), 9-95 (Daffara, 18.6), 10-98 (Fryett, 19.4)

Fall: 1-6 (Healy, 0.3)

Sixers - bowling	O	M	R	W	wd	nb	Dots	Hurricanes - bowling	O	M	R	W	wd	nb	Dots
M Kapp	4	0	11	1			14	NM Hancock	2	0	14	1	1	1	6
EA Perry	2.4	0	18	1	3		6	V Pyke	3	0	18	0			9
SE Aley	3	0	18	2			7	HK Matthews	3.5	0	29	0			6
LG Smith	3	0	15	1			7	BL Hepburn	2	0	18	0			2
D van Niekerk	4	0	18	2			15	C Raack	2	0	11	0	1		5
KJ Garth	3	0	16	1	1		8	V Krishnamurthy	1	0	8	0	-		1

Toss: Hurricanes. Award: M Kapp (SA). Umpires: RM Nelson, CA Polosak, BC Treloar (TV), Ref: TM Donahoo

Match 16 – Renegades v Heat at Etihad Stadium on December 23, 2017 – Renegades won by 10 wickets

Heat		B	4	6	Renegades		B	4	6
BL Mooney +	b Brown	11	12	2	SG Molineux	not out	45	37	5	1
KLH Short *	b Tahuhu	0	1		C Atapattu	not out	20	28	1
L Wolvaardt	c &b Strano	4	5	1	JE Duffin				
DJS Dottin	c Strano b Tahuhu	14	20	1	AE Satterthwaite *				
DM Kimmince	b Wareham	3	7		EJ Inglis +				
LM Harris	c &b Satterthwaite	4	7		CJ Koski				
JL Jonassen	c Tahuhu b Satterthwaite	5	9		HNK Jensen				
SJ Johnson	b Wareham	5	10		MR Strano				
HP Birkett	b Jensen	4	8		MJ Brown				
JL Barsby	b Strano	4	12		GL Wareham				
HL Ferling	not out	4	6		LM Tahuhu				
	1 b, 1 lb, 6 w	8				1 lb, 1 w	2		
6 overs: 3-33	16.1 overs	66			6 overs: 0-28	10.5 overs	0-67		

Fall: 1-2 (Short, 0.3), 2-9 (Wolvaardt, 1.2), 3-26 (Mooney, 4.2),
4-36 (Kimmince, 6.6), 5-39 (Dottin, 7.4), 6-47 (Jonassen, 9.6),
7-51 (Harris, 11.1), 8-55 (Johnson, 12.4), 9-59 (Birkett, 13.6),
10-66 (Barsby, 16.1)

Renegades - bowling	O	M	R	W	wd	nb	Dots	Heat - bowling	O	M	R	W	wd	nb	Dots
LM Tahuhu	2	0	10	2	4		7	SJ Johnson	1	0	10	0			1
MR Strano	3.1	0	13	2	1		10	JL Jonassen	2.5	0	19	0			8
MJ Brown	3	0	19	1	1		10	DM Kimmince	2	0	9	0	1		6
SG Molineux	1	0	2	0			4	DJS Dottin	2	0	9	0			4
GL Wareham	3	0	11	2			8	JL Barsby	2	0	8	0			5
AE Satterthwaite	2	0	5	2			6	HL Ferling	1	0	11	0			1
HNK Jensen	2	0	4	1			8								

Toss: Heat. Award: SG Molineux (MR). Umpires: DJ Brigham, D Ireland, Ref: K Hannam

Australian Cricket Digest, 2018-19

Match 17 – Scorchers v Stars at the WACA on December 26, 2017 – Scorchers won by 9 wickets

Stars		B	4	6
L Lee +	c Newton b King	76	62	8 3
AJ Lanning	c Villani b Brunt	4	4	1
M du Preez	c Hinkley b King	40	35	5
GA Elwiss	run out (Villani)	5	4	
KM Mack	not out	29	14	5
EA Osborne	not out	1	1	
EM Kearney				
AM King				
KM Beams *				
MA Blows				
GL Triscari				
	2 lb, 6 w	8		
6 overs: 1-45	20 overs	4-163		

Scorchers		B	4	6
EJ Villani *	not out	84	53	12 2
NE Bolton	c & b Osborne	67	52	11
NR Sciver	not out	6	6	1
MC Hinkley				
KH Brunt				
LK Ebsary				
MG Carmichael				
TMM Newton				
PM Cleary				
EL King				
EJ Smith +				
	1 lb, 6 w	7		
6 overs: 0-46	18.3 overs	1-164		

Fall: 1-28 (Lanning, 2.2), 2-124 (Lee, 16.4), 3-124 (du Preez, 16.5), 4-157 (Elwiss, 19.3 ov)

Fall: 1-140 (Bolton, 16.5)

Scorchers - bowling	O	M	R	W	wd	nb	Dots
KH Brunt	4	0	25	1	1		15
PM Cleary	4	0	33	0	1		9
NR Sciver	4	0	37	0	2		8
TMM Newton	3	0	31	0	2		5
EL King	4	0	24	2			8
NE Bolton	1	0	11	0			2

Stars - bowling	O	M	R	W	wd	nb	Dots
KM Beams	4	0	17	0			12
EA Osborne	4	0	24	1			15
AM King	3	0	40	0			5
GA Elwiss	2.3	0	37	0	1		1
EM Kearney	3	0	28	0	1		5
GL Triscari	2	0	17	0			4

Toss: Scorchers.   Award: NE Bolton (PS)   Umpires: A Kovalevs, JW Taylor, Ref: IS Thomas
Lee 50: 48 balls, 6x4, 2x6, Villani 50: 36 balls, 9x4, Bolton 50: 38 balls, 9x4

Match 18 – Scorchers v Stars at the WACA on December 27, 2017 – Stars won by 12 runs

Stars		B	4	6
L Lee +	c Cleary b Brunt	9	9	2
AJ Lanning	c Graham b Brunt	19	22	2
M du Preez	c Ebsary b Cleary	23	17	2
GA Elwiss	run out (Graham)	25	24	2
KM Mack	b Sciver	20	17	2 1
EA Osborne	not out	17	14	1
AM King	run out (Sciver-Smith)	23	19	2
EM Kearney				
KM Beams *				
MA Blows				
GL Triscari				
	3 lb, 2 nb, 8 w	13		
6 overs: 2-41	20 overs	6-149		

Scorchers		B	4	6
EJ Villani *	c Triscari b King	72	44	10 1
NE Bolton	c Osborne b Kearney	9	28	
NR Sciver	b Triscari	9	14	
MC Hinkley	run out (Lanning)	9	13	
LK Ebsary	not out	18	16	1
HL Graham	not out	5	5	1
KH Brunt				
PM Cleary				
EL King				
EJ Smith +				
KJ Hartshorn				
	5 b, 1 lb, 9 w	15		
6 overs: 0-40	20 overs	4-137		

Fall: 1-20 (Lee, 3.4), 2-38 (Lanning, 5.3), 3-72 (du Preez, 10.1), 4-88 (Elwiss, 13.2), 5-105 (Mack, 14.6), 6-149 (King, 19.6)

Fall: 1-59 (Bolton, 9.2), 2-98 (Sciver, 13.4), 3-107 (Villani, 15.6) 4-113 (Hinkley, 17.3)

Scorchers - bowling	O	M	R	W	wd	nb	Dots
EL King	4	0	26	0	1		10
KH Brunt	3	0	13	2	1		11
PM Cleary	4	0	28	1	2	1	10
KJ Hartshorn	4	0	39	0	1	1	5
HL Graham	4	0	26	0	1		6
NR Sciver	1	0	14	1			3

Stars - bowling	O	M	R	W	wd	nb	Dots
EA Osborne	4	0	28	0			10
KM Beams	4	0	24	0			9
EM Kearney	4	0	21	1	1		12
GA Elwiss	4	0	26	0	2		11
GL Triscari	2	0	21	1	2		3
AM King	2	0	11	1			3

Toss: Stars.   Award: EJ Villani (PS)   Umpires: J Hewitt, JW Taylor, Ref: IS Thomas
Villani 50: 30 balls, 6x4, 1x6.

Match 19 – Strikers v Heat at Adelaide Oval on December 29, 2017 – Heat won by 9 wickets

Strikers			B	4	6
SW Bates *	c Barsby b Jonassen	1	3		
TT Beaumont	c Mooney b Johnson	5	9		
TM McGrath	b Dottin	15	17	2	
SFM Devine	b Dottin	13	17		
RS Dick	c Dottin b Ferling	6	10		
BE Patterson	c Short b Jonassen	32	30	3	
TMS Saville	not out	31	34	1	
A Wellington					
TJ McPharlin +					
AE Price					
M Schutt					
	1 b, 2 lb, 7 w	10			
6 overs: 2-30	20 overs	6-113			

Heat			B	4	6
BL Mooney +	not out	86	57	10	1
KLH Short *	st McPharlin b Wellington	18	23	2	
L Wolvaardt	not out	9	16		
DJS Dottin					
DM Kimmince					
JL Jonassen					
LM Harris					
SJ Johnson					
HP Birkett					
JL Barsby					
HL Ferling					
	1 w	1			
6 overs: 0-42	16 overs	1-114			

Fall: 1-5 (Bates, 1.2), 2-7 (Beaumont, 2.3), 3-34 (McGrath, 6.5), 4-39 (Devine, 8.1), 5-49 (Dick, 10.4), 6-113 (Patterson, 19.6)

Fall: 1-56 (Short, 8.1)

Heat - bowling	O	M	R	W	wd	nb	Dots
SJ Johnson	3	0	14	1	1		11
JL Jonassen	4	0	20	2	1		10
DM Kimmince	4	0	24	0	1		9
DJS Dottin	3	0	13	2	1		9
JL Barsby	2	0	12	0			3
HL Ferling	2	0	16	1			3
HP Birkett	2	0	11	0	1		2

Strikers - bowling	O	M	R	W	wd	nb	Dots
ML Schutt	3	0	23	0			5
TM McGrath	2	0	13	0	1		7
SW Bates	3	0	23	0			6
SFM Devine	1	0	8	0			2
AJ Wellington	4	0	24	1			9
AE Price	2	0	14	0			4
RS Dick	1	0	9	0			2

Toss: Heat.　　　Award: BL Mooney (BH).　　　Umpires: SJ Farrell, LA Uthenwoldt, Ref: JP Biddiss
Mooney 50: 37 balls, 7x4.

Match 20 – Scorchers v Sixers at the Lilac Hill, Perth on December 30, 2017 – Scorchers won by 6 wickets

Sixers			B	4	6
AJ Healy +	c Carmichael b Bolton	0	1		
EA Perry *	c Villani b King	45	47	4	
AK Gardner	c Smith b Sciver	14	12	2	
EA Burns	c Hinkley b Newton	25	17	3	1
SJ McGlashan	c King b Bolton	0	3		
D van Niekerk	c Graham b King	29	20	3	1
M Kapp	run out (Graham)	1	4		
AR Reakes	c Newton b Graham	11	7	1	
LG Smith	b Graham	4	6		
SE Aley	run out (Sciver-Smith)	2	3		
KJ Garth	not out	0	0		
	1 nb, 6 w	7			
6 overs: 2-39	19.5 overs	138			

Scorchers			B	4	6
EJ Villani *	c Perry b Kapp	63	43	10	1
NE Bolton	lbw b van Niekerk	42	49	2	1
NR Sciver	c Garth b van Niekerk	16	11	2	
HL Graham	b Aley	13	8	2	
LK Ebsary	not out	1	1		
MG Carmichael	not out	2	1		
MC Hinkley					
TMM Newton					
TCJ Peschel					
EL King					
EJ Smith +					
	2 w	2			
6 overs: 0-42	18.5 overs	4-139			

Fall: 1-0 (Healy, 0.1), 2-15 (Gardner, 3.2), 3-71 (Burns, 9.5), 4-73 (McGlashan, 10.4), 5-115 (Perry, 16.1), 6-116 (van Niekerk), 7-126 (Kapp, 17.3), 8-136 (Smith, 19.1), 9-137 (Reakes, 19.4), 10-138 (Aley, 19.5)

Fall: 1-103 (Villani, 14.3), 2-108 (Bolton, 15.4), 3-128 (Sciver, 17.5), 4-137 (Graham, 18.4)

Scorchers - bowling	O	M	R	W	wd	nb	Dots
NE Bolton	3	0	15	2			10
NR Sciver	4	0	29	1	1		9
HL Graham	3.5	1	27	2	1	1	15
EL King	4	0	23	2			8
TCJ Peschel	3	0	27	0			3
TMM Newton	2	0	17	1			0

Sixers - bowling	O	M	R	W	wd	nb	Dots
M Kapp	4	1	24	1			13
EA Perry	3	0	29	0	2		6
AK Gardner	2	0	17	0			4
SE Aley	2.5	0	18	1			7
KJ Garth	2	0	16	0			3
D van Niekerk	4	0	24	2			9
LG Smith	1	0	11	0			2

Toss: Sixers.　　　Award: NE Bolton (PS).　　　Umpires: T Steenholdt, JW Taylor, Ref: IS Thomas
Villani 50: 33 balls, 8x4, 1x6.

Australian Cricket Digest, 2018-19

Match 21 – Hurricanes v Thunder at York Park, Launceston on December 30, 2017 – Thunder won by 7 wickets

Hurricanes		B	4	6	Thunder		B	4	6
L Winfield	c Carey b Farrell	5	9		RL Haynes	c Matthews b Hepburn	64	49	9
HK Matthews	b Taylor	39	40	3	RH Priest +	c Krishnamurthy b Hepburn	13	18	1
V Krishnamurthy	c Blackwell b Vakarewa	2	7		AJ Blackwell *	run out (Hancock)	13	14	2
GP Redmayne +	lbw b Taylor	13	17	1	SR Taylor	not out	10	8	2
V Pyke	c Haynes b Taylor	14	18	1	H Kaur	not out	4	10	1
NM Hancock	run out (Taylor)	0	1		SL Bates				
CL Hall *	c Haynes b Carey	14	13	1	ML Gibson				
SG Daffara	not out	13	14	1	NJ Carey				
BL Hepburn	c Blackwell b Taylor	0	1		NE Stalenberg				
KR Fryett	not out	1	1		RM Farrell				
C Raack					BW Vakarewa				
	1 b, 5 lb, 1 nb, 4 w	11				4 lb, 1 nb, 7 w	12		
6 overs: 2-23	20 overs	8-112			6 overs: 0-50	16.2 overs	3-116		

Fall: 1-5 (Winfield, 1.5), 2-11 (Krishnamurthy, 3.5), 3-46 (Redmayne, 9.2), 4-77 (Pyke, 14.2), 5-79 (Matthews, 14.6), 6-81 (Hancock, 15.4), 7-105 (Hall, 18.5), 8-107 (Hepburn, 19.2)

Fall: 1-56 (Priest, 7.5), 2-94 (Blackwell, 12.3), 3-106 (Haynes, 13.6)

Thunder - bowling	O	M	R	W	wd	nb	Dots	Hurricanes - bowling	O	M	R	W	wd	nb	Dots
SL Bates	4	0	21	0			14	KR Fryett	3	0	25	0		1	5
RM Farrell	4	0	14	1	1		15	V Pyke	1	0	13	0	1		2
BW Vakarewa	2	0	12	1		1	5	HK Matthews	3	0	27	0			6
ML Gibson	2	0	18	0	3		4	NM Hancock	3.2	0	20	0	2		12
SR Taylor	4	0	15	4			14	BL Hepburn	3	0	14	2	1		10
NJ Carey	4	0	26	1			6	C Raack	3	0	13	0	1		10

Toss: Hurricanes.   Award: SR Taylor (ST).   Umpires: G Beechey, M Qureshi, Ref: DA Johnston

Haynes 50: 37 balls, 7x4.

Match 22 – Hurricanes v Thunder at York Park, Launceston on December 31, 2017 – Thunder won by 8 wickets

Hurricanes		B	4	6	Thunder		B	4	6
HK Matthews	c Kaur b Bates	8	12	1	RL Haynes	b Raack	22	18	3
SG Daffara	st Priest b Gibson	30	32	3	SR Taylor	c Hall b Matthews	5	8	1
CL Hall *	c Haynes b Taylor	11	20		AJ Blackwell *	not out	43	34	6
GP Redmayne +	run out (Kaur)	3	8		H Kaur	not out	24	31	2
L Winfield	b Farrell	7	13		RH Priest +				
V Pyke	not out	16	14	1	NE Stalenberg				
SK Moloney	run out (Blackwell)	5	6		NJ Carey				
NM Hancock	b Bates	0	2		RM Farrell				
M Phillips	lbw b Bates	0	1		ML Gibson				
BL Hepburn	run out (Vakarewa)	7	9		SL Bates				
C Raack	st Priest b Taylor	0	1		BW Vakarewa				
	1 b, 7 lb, 2 w	10				1 nb, 4 w	5		
6 overs: 1-34	19.4 overs	97			6 overs: 2-35	15 overs	2-99		

Fall: 1-11 (Matthews, 2.2), 2-49 (Hall, 9.4), 3-59 (Daffara, 11.3), 4-64 (Redmayne, 12.6), 5-73 (Winfield, 14.6), 6-87 (Moloney, 16.6), 7-87 (Hancock, 17.2), 8-87 (Phillips, 17.3), 9-97 (Hepburn, 19.3), 10-97 (Raack, 19.4)

Fall: 1-13 (Taylor), 2-34 (Haynes, 5.3)

Thunder - bowling	O	M	R	W	wd	nb	Dots	Hurricanes - bowling	O	M	R	W	wd	nb	Dots
SL Bates	4	0	12	3	2		19	V Pyke	3	0	26	0			8
BW Vakarewa	2	0	11	0			7	NM Hancock	3	0	15	0	2		10
RM Farrell	4	0	19	1			9	HK Matthews	3	0	16	1	1		8
NJ Carey	4	0	17	0			9	C Raack	3	0	14	1			9
SR Taylor	2.4	0	13	2			6	BL Hepburn	1	0	9	0	1	1	4
ML Gibson	3	0	17	1			6	M Phillips	2	0	19	0			4

Toss: Hurricanes.   Award: SL Bates (ST).   Umpires: DR Close, M Qureshi, Ref: DA Johnston

Match 23 – Strikers v Heat at Adelaide Oval on December 31, 2017 – Heat won by 8 wickets

Strikers		B	4	6	Heat		B	4	6
SW Bates *	c Short b Birkett	32	34	3	BL Mooney +	not out	81	48	10
TT Beaumont	run out (Johnson)	17	21	2	KLH Short *	c Patterson b Price	27	39	1	1
TM McGrath	c Mooney b Barsby	1	2		L Wolvaardt	c Saville b Wellington	4	10
SFM Devine	c Mooney b Barsby	10	11		DJS Dottin	not out	4	1	1
BE Patterson	c and b Birkett	37	29	3	1	DM Kimmince			
TMS Saville	c Jonassen b Birkett	12	20		JL Jonassen			
M Schutt	not out	1	1		LM Harris			
A Wellington	run out (Dottin)	1	1		SJ Johnson			
TJ McPharlin +	not out	1	2		HP Birkett			
AE Price					JL Barsby			
SM Betts					HL Ferling			
	5 b, 1 nb, 1 w	7				2 b, 4 w	6		
6 overs: 0-31	20 overs	7-119			6 overs: 0-54	16.2 overs	2-122		

Fall: 1-33 (Beaumont, 6.5), 2-34 (McGrath, 7.1), 3-57 (Bates, 10.2), 4-64 (Devine, 11.5), 5-116 (Saville, 19.1), 6-117 (Patterson, 19.3), 7-118 (Wellington, 19.4)

Fall: 1-88 (Short, 11.6), 2-118 (Woolvaardt, 16.1)

Heat - bowling	O	M	R	W	wd	nb	Dots	Strikers - bowling	O	M	R	W	wd	nb	Dots
SJ Johnson	3	0	7	0			11	ML Schutt	4	0	29	0	2		11
JL Jonassen	3	0	17	0			7	SM Betts	1	0	12	0			1
DJS Dottin	4	0	31	0		1	10	SFM Devine	2	0	19	0	2		3
DM Kimmince	1	0	11	0			2	AE Price	4	0	28	1			8
JL Barsby	4	0	25	2			6	TM McGrath	2	0	15	0			3
HP Birkett	3	0	15	3	1		11	AJ Wellington	3.2	0	17	1			11
HL Ferling	2	0	8	0			6								

Toss: Heat.   Award: BL Mooney (BH).   Umpires: NR Johnstone, C Thomas, CA Polosak (TV), Ref: JP Biddiss

Mooney 50: 31 balls, 5x4.

Match 24 – Renegades v Sixers at Camberwell Sports Ground on January 2, 2018 – Sixers won by 36 runs

Sixers		B	4	6	Renegades		B	4	6
AJ Healy +	c Jensen b Molineux	7	15	1	SG Molineux	lbw b Gardner	8	5	2
EA Perry *	c Strano b Jensen	64	56	4	3	C Atapattu	c Healy b Kapp	0	3
AK Gardner	c Jensen b Satterthwaite	16	16	2	JE Duffin	c Burns b Kapp	35	42	2	1
EA Burns	c Atapattu b Jensen	2	4		AE Satterthwaite	c Kapp b Aley	11	13	2
SJ McGlashan	lbw b Brown	1	2		EJ Inglis +	c Gardner b Aley	3	8
D van Niekerk	run out (Wareham-Inglis)	10	9	1	CJ Koski	b van Niekerk	1	4
M Kapp	run out (Brown)	14	15	1	HNK Jensen	c & b Smith	14	16	2
AR Reakes	not out	5	3	1	MJ Brown	c Burns b van Niekerk	11	12	2
LG Smith					MR Strano	lbw b van Niekerk	3	6
SE Aley					LM Tahuhu	c McGlashan b van Niekerk	2	4
KJ Garth					GL Wareham	not out	1	1
	3 b, 3 lb, 3 w	9				2 lb, 1 w	3		
6 overs: 1-36	20 overs	7-128			6 overs: 2-30	19 overs	92		

Fall: 1-23 (Healy, 4.6), 2-44 (Gardner, 8.2), 3-53 (Burns, 10.4), 4-54 (McGlashan, 11.1), 5-72 (van Niekerk, 14.1), 6-115 (Perry, 18.5), 7-128 (Kapp, 19.6)

Fall: 1-8 (Molineux, 0.5), 2-8 (Atapattu, 1.3), 3-31 (Satterthwaite, 6.3), 4-37 (Inglis, 8.3), 5-44 (Koski, 9.4), 6-63 (Jensen, 13.2), 7-75 (Brown, 15.3), 8-81 (Strano, 17.1), 9-83 (Tahuhu, 17.5), 10-92 (Duffin)

Renegades - bowling	O	M	R	W	wd	nb	Dots	Sixers - bowling	O	M	R	W	wd	nb	Dots
MR Strano	4	0	24	0			10	AK Gardner	2	0	15	1			8
SG Molineux	2	0	12	1			8	M Kapp	4	0	13	2			16
LM Tahuhu	3	0	26	0	2		10	EA Perry	1	0	10	0			3
AE Satterthwaite	3	0	23	1	1		6	SE Aley	4	0	12	2			13
MJ Brown	3	0	11	1			10	D van Niekerk	4	0	13	4			15
GL Wareham	2	0	13	0			5	LG Smith	2	0	11	1	1		6
HNK Jensen	3	0	13	2			10	KJ Garth	2	0	10	0			5

Toss: Renegades.   Award: EA Perry (SS)   Umpires: DJ Brigham, D Ireland, Ref: DP Herft

Perry 50: 46 balls, 4x4, 2x6.

Australian Cricket Digest, 2018-19

Match 25 – Renegades v Sixers at Kardinia Park, Geelong on January 3, 2018 – Renegades won in a Superover

Renegades		B	4	6
SG Molineux	c van Niekerk b Perry	14	19	1
C Atapattu	run out (Kapp)	0	6	
JE Duffin	b Gardner	2	5	
AE Satterthwaite *	c Garth b van Niekerk	44	44	4
KL Britt	c Perry b Garth	19	21	1
EJ Inglis +	c Burns b van Niekerk	31	17	3	1
CJ Koski	not out	4	5	
MJ Brown	run out (Burns)	4	3	
HNK Jensen				
MR Strano				
GL Wareham				
	2 w	2		
6 overs: 2-17	20 overs	7-120		

Sixers		B	4	6
AJ Healy +	c Strano b Molineux	25	17	5
EA Perry *	c Brown b Atapattu	37	41	3	1
AK Gardner	c Satterthwaite b Strano	3	2	
EA Burns	c Koski b Atapattu	20	23	1
SJ McGlashan	run out (Wareham)	2	4	
D van Niekerk	b Jensen	10	11	
M Kapp	c Jensen b Satterthwaite	13	15	
AR Reakes	not out	4	5	
SE Aley	not out	3	2	
LG Smith				
KJ Garth				
	3 w	3		
6 overs: 2-40	20 overs	7-120		

Fall: 1-8 (Atapattu, 2.4), 2-11 (Duffin, 3.6), 3-17 (Molineux, 6.1), 4-61 (Britt, 13.4), 5-109 (Satterthwaite, 18.1), 6-113 (Inglis, 18.5),

Fall: 1-33 (Healy, 4.4), 2-38 (Gardner, 5.3), 3-81 (Perry, 12.4), 4-90 (McGlashan, 14.2), 5-90 (Burns, 14.3), 7-120 (Brown, 19.6) 6-111 (van Niekerk, 18.2), 7-115 (Kapp, 19.2)

Sixers - bowling	O	M	R	W	wd	nb	Dots
M Kapp	4	0	15	0			13
AK Gardner	3	0	9	1	1		13
EA Perry	2	0	7	1			6
SE Aley	4	0	39	0			6
LG Smith	1	0	9	0			1
D van Niekerk	4	0	25	2			6
KJ Garth	1	0	9	1	1		7
EA Burns	1	0	7	0			1

Renegades - bowling	O	M	R	W	wd	nb	Dots
MR Strano	4	0	20	1			10
MJ Brown	3	0	20	0	2		8
SG Molineux	3	0	19	1			9
HNK Jensen	3	0	22	1	1		6
AE Satterthwaite	4	0	21	1			8
GL Wareham	1	0	12	0			2
C Atapattu	2	0	6	2			6

Toss: Renegades. Award: AE Satterthwaite (MR) Umpires: S Brne, D Ireland, Ref: K Hannam

Superover: SS 2-8 bowled by Jensen, then MR 0-9 off 1 bowled by Kapp

Match 26 – Stars v Strikers at Casey Fields, Melbourne on January 5, 2018 – Strikers won by 22 runs

Strikers		B	4	6
SW Bates *	hit wkt b Osborne	2	8	
TT Beaumont	run out (King)	46	48	4
SFM Devine	c Lee b Triscari	44	33	4	2
BE Patterson	not out	22	17	1
M Schutt	b Elwiss	8	7	
TM McGrath	c du Preez b Elwiss	11	7	2
TMS Saville	not out	1	1	
A Wellington				
TJ McPharlin +				
AE Price				
KL Pope				
	5 b, 2 lb, 1 nb, 2 w	10		
6 overs: 1-39	20 overs	5-144		

Stars		B	4	6
L Lee +	c Beaumont b Price	44	42	5	2
AJ Lanning	c and b Devine	24	34	3
M du Preez	st McPharlin b Price	16	9	2
GA Elwiss	b Wellington	3	6	
KM Mack	run out (Price-McPharlin)	16	12	1
EA Osborne *	c Devine b Schutt	5	7	
AM King	run out (Schutt)	0	1	
EM Kearney	c Saville b Schutt	0	3	
NM Faltum	b Devine	0	2	
MA Blows	not out	3	3	
GL Triscari	not out	0	2	
	(1b, 1nb, 9 w)	11		
6 overs: 0-39	20 overs	9-122		

Fall: 1-17 (Bates, 2.5), 2-95 (Devine, 13.6), 3-105 (Beaumont, 15.2), 4-126 (Schutt, 17.4), 5-142 (McGrath, 19.4)

Fall: 1-73 (Lee, 11.2), 2-92 (du Preez, 13.5), 3-92 (Lanning, 14.2), 4-96 (Elwiss, 15.3), 5-115 (Mack, 17.5), 6-115 (King, 18.1), 7-119 (Osborne, 18.4), 8-119 (Kearney, 18.5), 9-122 (Faltum, 19.4)

Stars - bowling	O	M	R	W	wd	nb	Dots
EA Osborne	4	0	21	1	1		9
EM Kearney	4	0	33	0	1		11
GA Elwiss	4	0	22	2			9
EL King	3	0	25	0			3
MA Blows	3	0	19	0	1		5
GL Triscari	2	0	17	1			2

Strikers - bowling	O	M	R	W	wd	nb	Dots
ML Schutt	4	0	23	2	3	1	18
AJ Wellington	4	0	25	1	3		13
SW Bates	2	0	18	0	1		3
TM McGrath	3	0	24	0	2		10
AE Price	4	0	21	2			10
SFM Devine	3	0	10	2			10

Toss: Stars. Award: AE Price (AS) Umpires: S Brne, D Ireland, Ref: DP Herft

Match 27 – Renegades v Stars at the MCG on January 6, 2018 – Stars won by 7 wickets

Renegades		B	4	6	Stars		B	4	6
SG Molineux	c du Preez b Osborne	11	11	2	L Lee	c Britt b Molineux	16	12	3
C Atapattu	c Lee b Osborne	8	15	1	KM Mack	c Britt b Tahuhu	4	11	
JE Duffin	b Kearney	40	34	6	M du Preez	st Inglis b Brown	45	34	5
AE Satterthwaite*	c du Preez b King	12	13	1	GA Elwiss	not out	58	51	5
KL Britt	st Faltum b King	10	8	1	EA Osborne*	not out	11	7	1
EJ Inglis +	c & b Blows	4	5	1	AJ Lanning				
CJ Koski	not out	33	25	3	AM King				
MJ Brown	not out	16	9	1	EM Kearney				
HNK Jensen					NM Faltum +				
MR Strano					MA Blows				
LM Tahuhu					GL Triscari				
	3 lb, 5 w	8				1 b, 2 lb, 2 nb, 6 w	11		
6 overs: 2-27	20 overs	6-142			6 overs: 2-35	19 overs	3-145		

Fall: 1-18 (Molineux, 2.6), 2-19 (Atapattu, 4.2), 3-51 (Satterthwaite, 8.5), 4-64 (Britt, 10.5), 5-69 (Inglis, 11.5), 6-112 (Duffin, 16.2 ov)

Fall: 1-15 (Mack, 2.6), 2-23 (Lee, 3.6), 3-120 (du Preez, 16.6)

Stars - bowling	O	M	R	W	wd	nb	Dots	Renegades - bowling	O	M	R	W	wd	nb	Dots
EA Osborne	4	0	14	2	1		14	LM Tahuhu	3	0	21	1	2		10
EM Kearney	4	0	32	1			10	MR Strano	3	0	27	0			7
GA Elwiss	4	0	27	0			8	SG Molineux	4	0	26	1			6
GL Triscari	1	0	14	0	1		1	HNK Jensen	3	0	19	0	2	1	8
AM King	4	0	30	2			11	MJ Brown	4	0	27	1	1	1	6
MA Blows	3	0	22	1	1		6	AE Satterthwaite	2	0	22	0			1

Toss: Renegades.   Award: GA Elwiss (MS)   Umpires: DJ Brigham, D Ireland, Ref: K Hannam
Elwiss 50: 47 balls, 4x4

Match 28 – Hurricanes v Heat at Bellerive Oval on January 7, 2018 – Heat won by 8 wickets

Hurricanes		B	4	6	Heat		B	4	6
HK Matthews	c Ferling b Barsby	34	40	3	BL Mooney+	not out	62	43	8
SG Daffara	b Jonassen	11	15	1	KLH Short *	run out (Hancock)	19	18	3
GP Redmayne +	b Jonassen	20	29		DJS Dottin	c Winfield b Krishnamurthy	15	16	2
L Winfield	run out (Short)	15	16		DM Kimmince	not out	13	11	2
V Pyke	not out	14	15	1	JL Jonassen				
V Krishnamurthy	not out	9	5	1	LM Harris				
CL Hall*					SJ Johnson				
SK Moloney					HP Birkett				
NM Hancock					JL Barsby				
BL Hepburn					HL Ferling				
C Raack					GK Prestwidge				
	4 lb, 4 w	8				1 lb, 4 w	5		
6 overs: 1-27	20 overs	4-111			6 overs: 1-51	14.4 overs	2-114		

Fall: 1-18 (Daffara, 3.4), 2-59 (Matthews, 11.4), 3-77 (Redmayne, 15.5), 4-100 (Winfield, 18.5)

Fall: 1-41 (Short, 5.1), 2-80 (Dottin, 10.2)

Heat - bowling	O	M	R	W	wd	nb	Dots	Hurricanes - bowling	O	M	R	W	wd	nb	Dots
SJ Johnson	3	0	18	0			9	V Pyke	2	0	19	0			6
JL Jonassen	4	0	17	2			12	CA Raack	4	0	29	0			9
DJS Dottin	2	0	16	0	4		5	HK Matthews	3.4	0	21	0			9
DM Kimmince	3	0	12	0			9	NM Hancock	3	0	26	0	3		6
HL Ferling	2	0	13	0			6	V Krishnamurthy	2	0	18	1	1		5
JL Barsby	4	0	21	1			11								
HP Birkett	2	0	10	0			4								

Toss: Heat.   Award: BL Mooney (BH)   Umpires: DR Close, M Qureshi, Ref: JM Mitchell
Mooney 50: 32 balls, 7x4

Australian Cricket Digest, 2018-19

Match 29 – Scorchers v Thunder at Lilac Hill, Perth on January 7, 2018 – Thunder won by 1 run

Thunder			B	4	6	Scorchers			B	4	6
RH Priest +	c Graham b Bolton	42	32	6	1	EJ Villani *	c Griffith b Farrell	22	13	3	
RL Haynes	c Villani b Bolton	1	6			NE Bolton	c Griffith b Farrell	71	58	7	1
AJ Blackwell *	c Bolton b Peschel	26	28	2		HL Graham	c Gibson b Taylor	14	20		
SR Taylor	c Sciver b Cleary	6	8			NR Sciver	run out (Farrell)	13	13		
H Kaur	c Hinkley b Cleary	14	15	1		LK Ebsary	b Carey	13	10	1	
NE Stalenberg	c Bolton b Cleary	24	21	3		MG Carmichael	run out (Griffith-Priest)	4	5		
NJ Carey	not out	15	7	3		MC Hinkley	not out	2	2		
RM Farrell	not out	5	5			PM Cleary					
L Griffith						TCJ Peschel					
ML Gibson						EL King					
SL Bates						EJ Smith +					
	6 lb, 2 nb, 4 w	12					(1 b, 2 lb, 2 w)	5			
6 overs: 1-37	20 overs	6-145				6 overs: 1-41	20 overs	5-144			

Fall: 1-3 (Haynes, 2.3), 2-56 (Priest, 8.4), 3-74 (Taylor, 10.6), 4-82 (Blackwell, 12.5), 5-121 (Kaur, 17.4), 6-121 (Stalenberg, 17.6)

Fall: 1-40 (Villani, 5.1), 2-86 (Graham, 11.6), 3-111 (Sciver, 15.5), 4-126 (Bolton, 17.4), 5-140 (Ebsary, 19.2), 6-144 (Carmichael, 19.6)

Scorchers - bowling	O	M	R	W	wd	nb	Dots	Thunder - bowling	O	M	R	W	wd	nb	Dots
NE Bolton	4	0	14	2			15	SL Bates	4	0	26	0			10
NR Sciver	4	0	30	0			12	RM Farrell	4	0	19	2			11
HL Graham	3	0	25	0			6	L Griffith	2	0	26	0			1
EL King	4	0	32	0			4	SR Taylor	4	0	30	1	1		5
PM Cleary	3	0	19	3	2	2	12	ML Gibson	2	0	13	0			4
TCJ Peschel	2	0	19	1	2		1	NJ Carey	4	0	27	1			6

Toss: Thunder.   Award: RM Farrell (ST)   Umpires: A Kovalevs, T Steenholdt, Ref: IS Thomas

Bolton 50: 42 balls, 4x4, 1x6

Match 30 – Hurricanes v Heat at Bellerive Oval on January 8, 2018 – Heat won by 42 runs

Heat			B	4	6	Hurricanes			B	4	6
BL Mooney +	c Krishnamurthy b Hancock	7	8	1		HK Matthews	c Short b Johnson	8	10	1	
KLH Short *	c Hall b Thompson	79	55	11		SG Daffara	c Jonassen b Ferling	19	28	1	
DJS Dottin	c & b Matthews	17	15	3		GP Redmayne +	run out (Kimmince)	28	26	2	
DM Kimmince	b Thompson	43	36	3	1	V Krishnamurthy	c Short b Kimmince	33	20	4	1
JL Jonassen	not out	15	7	2	1	NM Hancock	c Short b Kimmince	8	9		
LM Harris	not out	1	1			L Winfield	c Kimmince b Barsby	4	4		
SJ Johnson						V Pyke	b Kimmince	1	3		
HP Birkett						CL Hall *	b Jonassen	1	3		
JL Barsby						SK Moloney	not out	7	4	1	
HL Ferling						EE Thompson	c Jonassen b Birkett	4	5		
GK Prestwidge						C Raack	run out (Short)	0	1		
	2 nb, 4 w	6					13 w	13			
6 overs: 1-51	20 overs	4-168				6 overs: 1-33	18.5 overs	126			

Fall: 1-10 (Mooney, 1.4), 2-44 (Dottin, 6.6), 3-143 (Short, 17.3), 4-161 (Kimmince, 19.4)

Fall: 1-16 (Matthews, 3.2), 2-40 (Daffara, 7.6), 3-88 (Redmayne, 12.4), 4-104 (Krishnamurthy, 14.5), 5-109 (Winfield, 15.4), 6-112 (Pyke, 16.2), 7-115 (Hancock, 16.6), 8-116 (Hall, 17.2), 9-121 (Thompson, 18.2), 10-126 (Raack)

Hurricanes - bowling	O	M	R	W	wd	nb	Dots	Heat - bowling	O	M	R	W	wd	nb	Dots
HK Matthews	4	0	26	1	1		9	JL Jonassen	3	0	11	1			11
NM Hancock	4	0	31	1	2	1	11	SJ Johnson	3	0	29	1	2		6
V Pyke	4	0	40	0			7	DM Kimmince	4	0	21	2	1		9
CA Raack	3	0	29	0	1		4	DJS Dottin	1	0	10	0	2		
EE Thompson	4	0	26	2			9	HL Ferling	2	0	13	1	2		6
V Krishnamurthy	1	0	16	0	1		0	JL Barsby	3	0	24	1			1
								HP Birkett	2.5	0	18	2			7

Toss: Hurricanes.   Award: KLH Short (BH)   Umpires: DR Close, WA Stewart, Ref: DA Johnston

Short 50: 32 balls, 7x4

Match 31 – Scorchers v Thunder at the WACA, Perth on January 8, 2018 – Scorchers won by 8 wickets

Thunder			B	4	6	Scorchers			B	4	6
RL Haynes	c Ebsary b Bolton		8	13	1	EJ Villani *	run out (Stalenberg)		9	9	1
RH Priest +	b Brunt		0	2		NE Bolton	c Kaur b Gibson		28	22	5
AJ Blackwell *	not out		81	58	10	1	NR Sciver	not out		61	50	9
SR Taylor	b Cleary		31	45	3	KH Brunt	not out		17	28	2
H Kaur	run out (Sciver-Smith)		1	1		LK Ebsary					
NE Stalenberg	not out		1	1		HL Graham					
NJ Carey						MC Hinkley					
RM Farrell						EJ Smith +					
ML Gibson						EL King					
SL Bates						TMM Newton					
L Griffith						PM Cleary					
	1 b, 4 lb, 7 w	12					1 lb, 20 w	21			
6 overs: 2-29	20 overs	4-134				6 overs: 1-64	18. 1 overs	2-136			

Fall: 1-1 (Priest, 0.4), 2-15 (Haynes, 3.3), 3-128 (Taylor, 19.3), 4-129 (Kaur, 19.4)

Fall: 1-17 (Villani, 2.6), 2-86 (Bolton, 8.2)

Scorchers - bowling	O	M	R	W	wd	nb	Dots	Thunder - bowling	O	M	R	W	wd	nb	Dots
KH Brunt	4	0	13	1			17	RM Farrell	4	0	21	0	1		14
NE Bolton	4	0	20	1			12	SL Bates	4	0	22	0	1		10
EL King	4	0	26	0			8	NE Stalenberg	1	0	14	0	1		2
NR Sciver	2	0	19	0	1		3	NJ Carey	1	0	27	0	4		2
HL Graham	2	0	21	0	1		3	L Griffith	2.1	0	25	0	2		3
TMM Newton	1	0	10	0			2	ML Gibson	4	0	18	1			9
PM Cleary	3	0	20	1	1		4	SR Taylor	2	0	8	0			7

Toss: Scorchers   Award: AJ Blackwell (ST)   Umpires: J Hewitt, A Kovalevs, Ref: IS Thomas

Blackwell 50: 39 balls, 6x4, 1x6, Sciver 50: 39 balls, 7x4

Match 32 – Strikers v Stars at Adelaide Oval on January 9, 2018 – Strikers won by 1 wicket

Stars			B	4	6	Strikers			B	4	6
L Lee	c McGrath b Devine		52	52	1	4	SW Bates *	b Beams		10	13	1
KM Mack	c Beaumont b Devine		42	34	6	TT Beaumont	lbw b King		27	23	4	1
M du Preez	c &b Price		9	13		SFM Devine	b Sutherland		17	20		1
EA Osborne	run out (Devine)		10	11		TM McGrath	c Lanning b Sutherland		13	13	1
AJ Lanning	run out (Schutt-Price)		3	2		BE Patterson	c Osborne b Sutherland		1	4	
EM Kearney	not out		9	8	1	TMS Saville	not out		28	27	2
AM King	not out		0	0		A Wellington	run out (Lee-Faltum)		0	0	
MA Blows						M Schutt	c Beams b Blows		18	13	2
KM Beams *						TJ McPharlin+	lbw b Sutherland		1	2	
NM Faltum+						AE Price	run out (Beams)		11	6	2
AJ Sutherland						KL Pope	not out		0	0	
	1 b, 1 lb, 5 w	7					1 b, 2 lb, 1 nb, 4 w	8			
6 overs: 0-36	20 overs	5-132				6 overs: 1-36	20 overs	9-134			

Fall: 1-69 (Mack, 10.6), 2-94 (du Preez, 15.2), 3-108 (Lee, 16.4), 4-114 (Lanning, 17.3), 5-130 (Osborne, 19.5)

Fall: 1-33 (Bates, 5.1), 2-43 (Beaumont, 6.6), 3-70 (McGrath, 11.1), 4-71 (Devine, 11.3), 5-75 (Patterson, 13.1), 6-77 (Wellington, 13.5), 7-102 (Schutt, 16.5), 8-110 (McPharlin, 17.4), 9-129 (Price, 19.4)

Strikers - bowling	O	M	R	W	wd	nb	Dots	Stars - bowling	O	M	R	W	wd	nb	Dots
ML Schutt	4	0	28	0	1		11	EA Osborne	4	0	24	0			12
AJ Wellington	4	0	35	0	2		6	EM Kearney	3	0	28	0	2		6
TM McGrath	2	0	11	0			2	KM Beams	4	0	25	1		1	9
SW Bates	2	0	9	0	1		4	AM King	2	0	15	1			4
AE Price	4	0	19	1			6	MA Blows	3	0	19	1	1		8
SFM Devine	4	0	28	2	1		10	AJ Sutherland	4	0	20	4	1		13

Toss: Stars   Award: TMS Saville (AS)   Umpires: DJ Shepard, C Thomas, Ref: JP Biddiss

Lee 50: 51 balls, 1x4, 4x6

Australian Cricket Digest, 2018-19

Match 33 – Heat v Stars at Harrup Park, Mackay (floodlit) on January 12, 2018 – Heat won by 5 wickets

Stars		B	4	6	Heat		B	4	6
L Lee	c Mooney b Dottin	15	19	1	BL Mooney +	st Faltum b King	57	38	7
KM Mack	st Mooney b Birkett	57	48	4	KLH Short *	c Sutherland b Beams	13	14	1
M du Preez	lbw b Dottin	30	35	2	DJS Dottin	lbw b King	2	11	
EA Osborne	not out	14	13		DM Kimmince	c Beams b Blows	16	16	1
AJ Lanning	not out	9	6	1	JL Jonassen	not out	23	21	1	1
EM Kearney					LM Harris	c du Preez b Sutherland	9	5	1
AM King					SJ Johnson	not out	4	4	
MA Blows					HP Birkett				
KM Beams *					JL Barsby				
NM Faltum +					HL Ferling				
AJ Sutherland					GK Prestwidge				
	4 lb, 1 nb, 3 w	8				(3 lb, 7 w)	10		
6 overs 1-32	20 overs	3-133			6 overs: 1-49	18.1 overs	5-134		

Fall: 1-32 (Lee, 5.6), 2-109 (Mack, 16.3), 3-113 (du Preez, 17.2)

Fall: 1-49 (Short, 5.3), 2-68 (Dottin, 9.2), 3-80 (Mooney, 11.2), 4-101 (Kimmince, 14.4 ov), 5-119 (Harris, 16.3 ov)

Heat - bowling	O	M	R	W	wd	nb	Dots
JL Jonassen	4	0	25	0	3		11
SJ Johnson	2	0	11	0			6
DM Kimmince	2	0	17	0			4
DJS Dottin	3	0	13	2			8
JL Barsby	3	0	20	0			7
HP Birkett	4	0	31	1	1		6
HL Ferling	2	0	12	0			4

Stars - bowling	O	M	R	W	wd	nb	Dots
EA Osborne	4	0	35	0			6
EM Kearney	1	0	16	0	1		2
KM Beams	4	0	16	1			10
MA Blows	3	0	19	1	2		5
AM King	4	0	22	2			11
M du Preez	1	0	6	0	1		5
AJ Sutherland	1.1	0	17	1	2		4

Toss: Stars   Award: BL Mooney (BH)   Umpires: SE Dionysius, D Taylor, Ref: K Hannam

Mack 50: 43 balls, 3x4, Mooney 50: 35 balls, 6x4

Match 34 – Strikers v Scorchers at Traeger Park, Alice Springs on January 13, 2018 – Strikers won by 6 wickets

Scorchers		B	4	6	Strikers		B	4	6
EJ Villani *	b Schutt	2	6		SW Bates *	not out	49	47	2
NE Bolton	c McGrath b Bates	10	12		TT Beaumont	lbw b Brunt	0	1	
NR Sciver	b Devine	12	12	2	SFM Devine	run out (Smith)	18	25	2
LK Ebsary	c & b McGrath	16	22	2	TM McGrath	b Brunt	14	18	1
HL Graham	st McPharlin b McGrath	19	17	1	1	BE Patterson	b King	0	3	
KH Brunt	run out (McGrath)	4	4	1	M Schutt	not out	1	1	
CL Piparo	st McPharlin b McGrath	2	4		KL Pope				
TMM Newton	b Wellington	5	8		AE Price				
PM Cleary	run out (Bates)	4	5		TMS Saville				
EL King	not out	2	3		TJ McPharlin +				
EJ Smith +	not out	0	3		A Wellington				
	2 lb, 9 w	11				3 lb, 3 w	6		
4 overs : 2-22	16 overs	9-87			4 overs : 1-17	15.5 overs	4-88		

Fall: 1-2 (Villani, 0.6), 2-22 (Sciver, 3.5), 3-35 (Bolton, 7.4), 4-46 (Ebsary, 9.1), 5-50 (Brunt, 9.5), 6-65 (Piparo, 11.5), 7-74 (Graham, 13.4), 8-79 (Newton, 14.4), 9-87 (Cleary, 15.3)

Fall: 1-7 (Beaumont, 0.4), 2-51 (Devine, 8.6), 3-82 (McGrath, 14.4), 4-87 (Patterson, 15.4)

Strikers - bowling	O	M	R	W	wd	nb	Dots
ML Schutt	4	0	18	1			14
SFM Devine	2	0	11	1	1		7
SW Bates	2	0	9	1			4
AJ Wellington	3	0	23	1	2		5
TM McGrath	3	0	17	3	2		9
AE Price	2	0	7	0			5

Scorchers - bowling	O	M	R	W	wd	nb	Dots
KH Brunt	4	0	17	2	1		13
NE Bolton	3	0	14	0			9
PM Cleary	2	0	17	0	2		3
HL Graham	3	0	15	0			7
EL King	2.5	0	13	1			6
NR Sciver	1	0	9	0			1

Toss: Strikers.   Award: TM McGrath (AS)   Umpires: DR Close, C Thomas, BC Treloar (TV), Ref: DP Herft.

Rain reduced to 16 overs each.

Match 35 – Heat v Stars at Harrup Park, Mackay (floodlit) on January 13, 2018 – Stars won by 6 wickets

Heat		B	4	6	Stars		B	4	6
BL Mooney+	b Osborne	2	4		L Lee	b Dottin	9	20	1
KLH Short *	b Osborne	5	7	1	KM Mack	c Mooney b Jonassen	20	24	1
DJS Dottin	c Sutherland b King	9	18		M du Preez	not out	36	34	4
DM Kimmince	lbw b Beams	0	6		EA Osborne	lbw b Johnson	15	14	2
JL Jonassen	c Lanning b Osborne	46	46	1	1	AJ Lanning	c Jonassen b Johnson	1	4	
LM Harris	c Mack b King	2	4		AM King	not out	6	8	1
SJ Johnson	c & b Osborne	4	12		EM Kearney				
HP Birkett	c Osborne b Blows	15	17	1	AJ Sutherland				
HL Ferling	not out	10	6		MA Blows				
GK Prestwidge	not out	0	0		NM Faltum +				
C Hill					KM Beams *				
		0				2 lb, 5 w	7		
6 overs: 3-14	20 overs	8-93			6 overs: 1-26	17.2 overs	4-94		

Fall: 1-2 (Mooney, 0.4), 2-7 (Short, 2.5), 3-8 (Kimmince, 3.6), 4-23 (Dottin, 7.6), 5-29 (Harris, 9.1), 6-40 (Johnson, 12.4), 7-81 (Jonassen, 18.3), 8-87 (Birkett, 19.3)

Fall: 1-25 (Lee, 5.5), 2-43 (Mack, 8.4), 3-71 (Osborne, 13.4), 4-79 (Lanning, 15.2)

Stars - bowling	O	M	R	W	wd	nb	Dots	Heat - bowling	O	M	R	W	wd	nb	Dots
EA Osborne	4	0	20	4			15	JL Jonassen	3	1	6	1			13
KM Beams	4	0	7	1			17	SJ Johnson	3.2	0	26	2	1		8
EM Kearney	3	0	22	0			3	DJS Dottin	3	0	18	1	1		9
AM King	4	0	12	2			12	DM Kimmince	3	0	12	0			7
AJ Sutherland	2	0	11	0			2	HP Birkett	4	0	23	0			9
MA Blows	3	0	21	1			5	HL Ferling	1	0	7	0	1		2

Toss: Heat   Award: EA Osborne (MS)   Umpires: SE Dionysius, D Taylor, Ref: K Hannam

Match 36 – Sixers v Thunder at the SCG on January 13, 2018 – Thunder won by 4 wickets

Sixers		B	4	6	Thunder		B	4	6
AJ Healy+	c Kaur b Bates	1	3		RL Haynes	c Gardner b Aley	17	18	3
EA Perry*	lbw b Gibson	25	25	5	RH Priest +	b Kapp	0	1	
AK Gardner	c Stalenberg b Vakarewa	11	16	2	AJ Blackwell *	c Healy b Aley	0	7	
EA Burns	c Taylor b Vakarewa	2	6		H Kaur	c van Niekerk b Gardner	27	23	2	2
SJ McGlashan	b Farrell	23	23	3	NE Stalenberg	b Aley	48	41	5	2
D van Niekerk	c Farrell b Carey	17	19	2	SR Taylor	not out	9	16	
M Kapp	run out (Blackwell)	0	2		NJ Carey	b Garth	3	6	
AR Reakes	not out	13	12	1	RM Farrell	not out	5	2	1
SE Aley	run out (Taylor-Priest)	9	8	1	ML Gibson				
LG Smith	b Bates	3	4		SL Bates				
KJ Garth	lbw b Bates	0	2		BW Vakarewa				
		7 lb, 2 w	9			4 lb, 1 w	5		
6 overs: 1-35	20 overs	113			6 overs: 3-21	19 overs	6-114		

Fall: 1-7 (Healy, 1.6), 2-35 (Gardner, 6.2), 3-40 (Perry, 7.5), 4-44 (Burns, 8.3), 5-82 (van Niekerk, 14.4), 6-82 (Kapp, 14.6), 7-87 (McGlashan, 15.5), 8-104 (Aley, 18.2), 9-113 (Smith, 19.4), 10-113 (Garth, 20 ov)

Fall: 1-1 (Priest, 0.2), 2-20 (Blackwell, 3.2), 3-21 (Haynes, 5.4), 4-64 (Kaur, 10.6), 5-104 (Stalenberg, 17.2), 6-109 (Carey, 18.4)

Thunder - bowling	O	M	R	W	wd	nb	Dots	Sixers - bowling	O	M	R	W	wd	nb	Dots
RM Farrell	4	0	20	1			14	M Kapp	4	0	26	1			13
SL Bates	4	0	21	3			10	EA Perry	2	0	12	0	1		8
SR Taylor	1	0	12	0			3	SE Aley	4	2	11	3			17
BW Vakarewa	3	0	10	2	1		13	AK Gardner	3	0	16	1			10
ML Gibson	4	0	26	1	1		12	D van Niekerk	2	0	15	0			7
NJ Carey	4	0	17	1			14	KJ Garth	3	0	20	1			8
								LG Smith	1	0	10	0			1

Toss: Sixers   Award: NE Stalenberg (ST)   Umpires: A Hobson, GS Stubbings, Ref: IS Thomas

Australian Cricket Digest, 2018-19

Match 37 – Hurricanes v Renegades at Bellerive Oval, Hobart on January 14, 2018 – Renegades won by 10 wickets

Hurricanes			B	4	6
HK Matthews	c Molineux b Tahuhu	40	40	6	
SG Daffara	run out (Strano)	27	28	3	
GP Redmayne +	run out (Tahuhu)	1	7		
V Krishnamurthy	b Satterthwaite	4	6		
IMHC Joyce	lbw b Satterthwaite	1	2		
V Pyke	b Brown	6	9		
CL Hall *	lbw b Tahuhu	1	2		
EE Thompson	lbw b Strano	2	6		
NM Hancock	b Brown	4	4		
BL Hepburn	b Brown	0	2		
C Raack	not out	6	7	1	
	1 lb, 1 nb, 6 w	8			
6 overs: 0-30	18.5 overs	100			

Renegades			B	4	6
SG Molineux	not out	53	39	10	
EJ Inglis +	not out	42	32	5	1
KL Britt					
AE Satterthwaite *					
C Atapattu					
GL Wareham					
CJ Koski					
MR Strano					
HNK Jensen					
MR Strano					
LM Tahuhu					
	2 nb, 5 w	7			
6 overs: 0-50	11.3 overs	0-102			

Fall: 1-62 (Matthews, 10.2), 2-68 (Redmayne, 11.4), 3-75 (Daffara),
4-76 (Krishnamurthy, 13.3), 5-77 (Joyce, 13.5), 6-78 (Hall, 14.1),
7-83 (Thompson, 15.5), 8-88 (Hancock, 16.4), 9-88 (Hepburn, 16.5),
10-100 (Pyke, 18.5)

Renegades - bowling	O	M	R	W	wd	nb	Dots
LM Tahuhu	4	0	14	2			12
SG Molineux	1	0	6	0			3
MR Strano	3	0	11	1			10
MJ Brown	3.5	0	28	3	1	1	11
GL Wareham	2	0	13	0	1		4
HNK Jensen	2	0	17	0			5
AE Satterthwaite	3	0	10	2			9

Hurricanes - bowling	O	M	R	W	wd	nb	Dots
HK Matthews	4	0	25	0	2		11
NM Hancock	1	0	7	0	1	1	1
C Raack	3	0	28	0			5
V Pyke	1	0	15	0	1		2
BL Hepburn	1.3	0	18	0		1	4
EE Thompson	1	0	9	0			3

Toss: Renegades   Award: SG Molineux (MR)   Umpires: M Qureshi, W Stewart, Ref: JM Mitchell
Molineux 50: 35 balls, 10x4

Match 38 – Strikers v Scorchers at Traeger Park, Alice Springs on January 14, 2018 – Strikers won by 31 runs

Strikers			B	4	6
SW Bates *	b Brunt	27	38	4	
TT Beaumont	run out (Ebsary)	2	4		
SFM Devine	c Sciver b King	29	33	2	2
TM McGrath	c Sciver b Graham	34	28	5	
BE Patterson	b Sciver	4	5		
M Schutt	c Ebsary b Graham	3	4		
TMS Saville	not out	2	3		
AE Price	b Brunt	3	5		
TJ McPharlin +					
A Wellington					
KL Pope					
	3 lb	3			
6 overs: 1-25	20 overs	7-107			

Scorchers			B	4	6
NE Bolton	lbw b Price	30	38	4	
EJ Villani *	lbw b Bates	5	12		
NR Sciver	b Bates	0	2		
LK Ebsary	run out (Patterson)	1	7		
KH Brunt	c Saville b Wellington	4	8		
TMM Newton	st McPharlin b McGrath	16	15	1	1
HL Graham	lbw b Schutt	2	6		
CL Piparo	c McPharlin b Schutt	0	1		
PM Cleary	not out	8	6	1	
EL King	c Price b McGrath	5	9		
EJ Smith +	b Price	0	2		
	1 lb, 1nb, 3 w	5			
6 overs: 1-23	17.3 overs	76			

Fall: 1-9 (Beaumont, 2.1), 2-54 (Devine, 10.6), 3-81 (Bates, 15.1),
4-99 (Patterson, 17.5), 5-101 (McGrath, 18.2), 6-103 (Schutt, 18.5),
7-107 (Price, 20)

Fall: 1-19 (Villani, 4.5), 2-23 (Sciver, 6.1), 3-26 (Ebsary, 7.4),
4-36 (Brunt, 10.2), 5-47 (Bolton, 11.3), 6-61 (Graham, 13.5),
7-61 (Piparo, 13.6), 8-63 (Newton, 14.5), 9-75 (King, 16.6),
10-76 (Smith, 17.3 ov)

Scorchers - bowling	O	M	R	W	wd	nb	Dots
KH Brunt	4	0	15	2			
NE Bolton	4	0	22	0			
NR Sciver	3	0	7	1			
HL Graham	4	0	23	2			
PM Cleary	2	0	10	0			
EL King	3	0	27	1			

Strikers - bowling	O	M	R	W	wd	nb	Dots
ML Schutt	4	0	14	2	1		
SFM Devine	3	0	11	0			
SW Bates	3	1	6	2	1		
TM McGrath	4	0	17	2	1		
AJ Wellington	2	0	23	1		1	
AE Price	1.3	0	4	2			

Toss: Scorchers.   Award: SW Bates (AS).   Umpires: C Thomas, BC Treloar, Ref: DP Herft.

Match 39 – Hurricanes v Renegades at Bellerive Oval, Hobart on January 15, 2018 – Hurricanes won by 4 runs

Hurricanes		B	4	6
HK Matthews	c Molineux b Tahuhu	11	12	2
SG Daffara	st Inglis b Wareham	28	23	4
V Krishnamurthy	run out (Molineux)	40	35	6
GP Redmayne +	c Satterthwaite b Jensen	20	26	1
EG Fazackerley	b Wareham	0	1	
IMHC Joyce *	c Britt b Tahuhu	9	8	2
VP yke	c Inglis b Tahuhu	0	4	
SK Moloney	c Satterthwaite b Jensen	2	5	
NM Hancock	c Brown b Satterthwaite	0	1	
BL Hepburn	not out	5	5	
C Raack	not out	0	0	
	1 b, 4 w	5		
6 overs: 1-42	20 overs	9-120		

Renegades		B	4	6
SG Molineux	c Moloney b Hancock	2	6	
EJ Inglis +	c Fazackerley b Hepburn	14	20	1
AE Satterthwaite *	run out (Matthews)	65	58	9
KL Britt	c Redmayne b Hepburn	0	4	
C Atapattu	c Pyke b Hepburn	19	25	1
CJ Koski	c Moloney b Joyce	12	7	2
MJ Brown	not out	0	0	
HNK Jensen				
LM Tahuhu				
MR Strano				
GL Wareham				
	2 lb, 2 w	4		
6 overs: 1-21	20 overs	6-116		

Fall: 1-20 (Matthews, 2.6), 2-58 (Daffara, 8.6), 3-96 (Krishnamurthy, 13.6), 4-97 (Fazackerley, 14.2), 5-109 (Joyce, 16.2), 6-109 (Pyke, 16.6), 7-115 (Moloney, 18.5), 8-115 (Redmayne, 18.6), 9-118 (Hancock, 19.5)

Fall: 1-5 (Molineux, 1.1), 2-34 (Inglis, 8.1), 3-34 (Britt, 8.5), 4-84 (Atapattu, 16.5), 5-108 (Koski, 19.3), 6-116 (Satterthwaite, 19.6)

Renegades - bowling	O	M	R	W	wd	nb	Dots
LM Tahuhu	4	1	25	3	2		13
MR Strano	4	0	23	0	1		12
MJ Brown	1	0	8	0	1		2
SG Molineux	1	0	4	0			5
HNK Jensen	2	0	11	2			6
AE Satterthwaite	4	0	15	1			12
GL Wareham	3	0	22	2			5
C Atapattu	1	0	11	0			2

Hurricanes - bowling	O	M	R	W	wd	nb	Dots
HK Matthews	4	0	16	0	1		13
NM Hancock	3	1	9	1	1		14
C Raack	2	0	16	0			3
BL Hepburn	4	1	24	3			11
VP yke	3	0	23	0			4
IMHC Joyce	4	0	26	1			10

Toss: Renegades   Award: BL Hepburn (HH)   Umpires: G Beechey, DR Close, Ref: DA Johnston
Satterthwaite 50: 49 balls, 8x4

Match 40 – Sixers v Heat at the SCG on January 18, 2018 – Sixers won by 9 runs

Sixers		B	4	6	
AJ Healy +	c Jonassen b Barsby	70	43	9	1
EA Perry *	c Barsby b G Harris	25	30	3	
AK Gardner	c GM Harris b Dottin	1	6		
EA Burns	c Kimmince b Barsby	4	4	1	
SJ McGlashan	c Kimmince b G Harris	8	10		
D van Niekerk	not out	44	23	4	3
AR Reakes	not out	4	5		
M Kapp					
SE Aley					
LG Smith					
KJ Garth					
	1 nb, 3 w	4			
6 overs: 0-61	20 overs	5-160			

Heat		B	4	6	
BL Mooney +	c Reakes b van Niekerk	60	42	8	1
KLH Short *	c van Niekerk b Garth	35	36	5	
DJS Dottin	b van Niekerk	18	14	2	1
DM Kimmince	st Healy b Aley	1	1		
JL Jonassen	c van Niekerk b Gardner	9	8	1	
GM Harris	b Aley	9	5		1
LM Harris	not out	6	6		
SJ Johnson	c van Niekerk b Aley	0	1		
HP Birkett	run out (Burns)	1	1		
JL Barsby	c Healy b Kapp	5	5	1	
HL Ferling	run out (Healy)	1	2		
	(1 b, 2 lb, 1 nb, 2 w)	6			
6 overs: 0-48	20 overs (all out)	151			

Fall: 1-84 (Perry, 10.3), 2-95 (Gardner, 12.4), 3-103 (Burns, 13.4), 4-104 (Healy, 13.6), 5-129 (McGlashan, 17.6)

Fall: 1-94 (Short, 12.1), 2-101 (Mooney, 13.1), 3-108 (Kimmince, 14.2), 4-126 (Dottin, 15.6), 5-130 (Jonassen, 16.5), 6-139 (G Harris, 17.4), 7-139 (Johnson, 17.5), 8-140 (Birkett, 17.6), 9-148 (Barsby, 19.2), 10-151 (Ferling, 19.6)

Heat - bowling	O	M	R	W	wd	nb	Dots
JL Jonassen	3	0	26	0			7
SJ Johnson	2	0	19	0			5
DJS Dottin	2	0	14	1	2		6
DM Kimmince	3	0	29	0	1		6
GM Harris	4	0	22	2			10
HP Birkett	3	0	31	0	1		6
JL Barsby	3	0	19	2			7

Sixers - bowling	O	M	R	W	wd	nb	Dots
M Kapp	4	0	28	1			7
AK Gardner	4	0	30	1			10
SE Aley	4	0	31	3	1		8
D van Niekerk	4	0	28	2		1	10
LG Smith	1	0	9	0			3
KJ Garth	3	0	22	1	1		7

Toss: Sixers   Award: D van Niekerk (SS)   Umpires: A Hobson, MAW Nickl, Ref: TM Donahoo
Healy 50: 26 balls, 8x4 1x6, Mooney 50: 35 balls, 6x4 1x6

Match 41 – Sixers v Heat at Hurstville Oval on January 19, 2018 – Sixers won by 18 runs

Sixers			B	4	6
AJ Healy+	lbw b G Harris	0	1		
EA Perry*	lbw b Ferling	18	17	3	
AK Gardner	c Mooney b Johnson	26	21	2	2
EA Burns	not out	54	39	2	3
SJ McGlashan	lbw b Kimmince	10	10	1	
D van Niekerk	b Kimmince	3	7		
M Kapp	c Ferling b Birkett	8	12		
AR Reakes	b Kimmince	9	4		1
SE Aley	not out	13	9	1	
LG Smith					
KJ Garth					
	1 lb, 2 w	3			
6 overs: 2-44	20 overs	7-144			

Fall: 1-0 (Healy, 0.1), 2-32 (Gardner, 4.2), 3-58 (Perry, 8.3), 4-81 (McGlashan, 11.4), 5-93 (van Niekerk, 13.3), 6-114 (Kapp, 16.4), 7-125 (Reakes, 17.4)

Heat			B	4	6
BL Mooney+	c Burns b Kapp	0	4		
KLH Short*	c van Niekerk b Garth	17	21	1	
DJS Dottin	lbw b van Niekerk	20	23	4	
DM Kimmince	b Smith	20	19	1	1
JL Jonassen	not out	55	38	2	3
GM Harris	not out	12	16		
LM Harris					
SJ Johnson					
HP Birkett					
JL Barsby					
HL Ferling					
	1 nb, 1 w	2			
6 overs: 1-30	20 overs	4-126			

Fall: 1-0 (Mooney, 0.4), 2-35 (Dottin, 7.4), 3-39 (Short, 8.4), 4-97 (Kimmince, 15.2)

Heat - bowling	O	M	R	W	wd	nb	Dots
GM Harris	3	0	29	1			5
DJS Dottin	2	0	12	0			8
JL Jonassen	3	0	21	0	1		7
SJ Johnson	2	0	15	1			6
JL Barsby	3	0	16	0			9
HL Ferling	1	0	11	1			3
DM Kimmince	4	0	23	3	1		8
HP Birkett	2	0	16	1			3

Sixers - bowling	O	M	R	W	wd	nb	Dots
M Kapp	4	0	17	1			12
AK Gardner	4	0	33	0			9
SE Aley	3	0	17	0			10
KJ Garth	3	0	27	1			5
D van Niekerk	3	0	19	1		1	9
LG Smith	3	0	13	1		1	6

Toss: Sixers Award: EA Burns (SS) Umpires: A Hobson, TM Penman, Ref: TM Donahoo
Burns 50: 35 balls, 2x4 3x6, Jonassen 50: 35 balls, 2x4 3x6

Match 42 – Stars v Renegades at the MCG on January 20, 2018 – Stars won in a Superover

Stars			B	4	6
L Lee	lbw b Strano	31	26	2	2
KM Mack	c Koski b Tahuhu	11	15		
M du Preez	c Molineux b Brown	1	2		
GA Elwiss	run out (Koski)	18	21		
EA Osborne	lbw b Jensen	7	18	1	
AJ Lanning	not out	21	21	1	
AM King	run out (Wareham)	22	17	2	1
AJ Sutherland	not out	1	1		
MA Blows					
KM Beams*					
NM Faltum+					
	1b, 1 lb, 1 nb, 3 w	6			
6 overs: 1-32	20 overs	6-118			

Fall: 1-30 (Mack, 5.4), 2-43 (Lee, 6.6), 3-44 (du Preez, 7.1), 4-68 (Osborne, 12.4), 5-78 (Elwiss, 14.4), 6-116 (King, 19.4)

Renegades			B	4	6
SG Molineux	c Lee b Sutherland	25	31	2	
EJ Inglis+	run out (King)	4	6		
CJ Koski	c du Preez b King	19	16	1	1
AE Satterthwaite*	not out	31	27	1	1
KL Britt	c Osborne b Sutherland	1	3		
HNK Jensen	b Elwiss	19	25	1	
MJ Brown	c King b Elwiss	5	3	1	
AMC Jayangani	not out	10	9		
MR Strano					
LM Tahuhu					
GL Wareham					
	4 w	4			
6 overs: 1-39	20 overs	6-118			

Fall: 1-9 (Inglis, 1.4), 2-49 (Koski, 8.1), 3-57 (Molineux, 9.2), 4-59 (Britt, 9.6), 5-89 (Jensen, 16.2), 6-95 (Brown, 16.6)

Renegades - bowling	O	M	R	W	wd	nb	Dots
SG Molineux	3	0	18	0			9
LM Tahuhu	4	0	19	1	1		14
MR Strano	2	0	17	1			6
MJ Brown	4	0	17	1	2		12
GL Wareham	1	0	6	0	1		2
HNK Jensen	4	0	21	1			9
AE Satterthwaite	2	0	18	0			2

Stars - bowling	O	M	R	W	wd	nb	Dots
EA Osborne	4	0	23	0	1		11
KM Beams	4	0	21	0			9
GA Elwiss	4	0	34	2			7
AM King	4	0	29	1	1		6
AJ Sutherland	4	0	11	2			14

Toss: Stars Award: AM King (MS) Umpires: S Brne, DJ Shepard, DR Close (TV), Ref: K Hannam
Superover: Renegades 4-10 lost to Stars 0-10, Stars won based on the boundary countback playing condition.

Match 43 – Thunder v Strikers at Robertson Oval, Wagga Wagga on January 20, 2018 – Thunder won by 37 runs

Thunder			B	4	6	Strikers			B	4	6
RH Priest +	c Schutt b McGrath	51	27	5	3	SFM Devine	st Priest b Bates	8	8	1	
RL Haynes	c Bates b Devine	1	4			SW Bates *	c Bates b Gibson	18	21	2	
AJ Blackwell *	lbw b McGrath	7	19			TM McGrath	c Farrell b Taylor	11	8	2	
NE Stalenberg	c Patterson b Devine	41	30	4	2	TT Beaumont	st Priest b Taylor	13	21	1	
SR Taylor	not out	33	29	2	1	BE Patterson	c Stalenberg b Bates	30	20	5	
NJ Carey	not out	10	11			TMS Saville	b Vakarewa	6	14		
RM Farrell						M Schutt	b Bates	2	3		
SL Bates						AJ Wellington	c Stalenberg b Carey	16	13	1	1
ML Gibson						AE Price	c Carey b Farrell	2	6		
BW Vakarewa						TJ McPharlin +	st Priest b Carey	1	2		
FC Wilson						KL Pope	not out	0	0		
	5 w	5					2 b, 2 w	4			
6 overs: 1-41	20 overs	4-148				6 overs: 2-37	19.2 overs	111			

Fall: 1-6 (Haynes, 1.6), 2-59 (Blackwell, 8.1), 3-64 (Priest, 8.6), 4-123 (Stalenberg, 16.5)

Fall: 1-11 (Devine, 1.5), 2-28 (McGrath, 4.2), 3-47 (Bates, 8.4), 4-69 (Beaumont, 11.4), 5-89 (Saville, 14.6), 6-89 (Patterson, 15.2), 7-91 (Schutt, 15.5), 8-109 (Price, 18.2), 9-111 (Wellington, 19.1), 10-111 (McPharlin, 19.2)

Strikers - bowling	O	M	R	W	wd	nb	Dots	Thunder - bowling	O	M	R	W	wd	nb	Dots
ML Schutt	4	1	27	0	1		12	RM Farrell	4	0	27	1	1		10
SFM Devine	4	0	35	2			9	SL Bates	4	0	21	3			13
TM McGrath	4	0	16	2			14	SR Taylor	4	0	20	2			10
SW Bates	1	0	20	0			1	ML Gibson	3	0	15	1			8
AJ Wellington	3	0	28	0			6	AJ Carey	2.2	0	14	2			7
AE Price	4	0	22	0			8	BW Vakarewa	2	0	12	1	1		8

Toss: Thunder   Award: RH Priest (ST)   Umpires: AI Scotford, D Young, Ref: IS Thomas

Priest 50: 26 balls, 5x4 3x6

Match 44 – Scorchers v Hurricanes at the WACA, Perth on January 20, 2018 – Scorchers won by 9 wickets

Hurricanes			B	4	6	Scorchers			B	4	6
HK Matthews	c Villani b Brunt	10	13	1		EJ Villani *	not out	70	48	11	
SG Daffara	lbw b Brunt	4	5			NE Bolton	c Hall b Hancock	34	25	5	1
GP Redmayne +	c and b Cleary	43	51	4		NR Sciver	not out	18	23	1	
IMHC Joyce *	not out	52	47	5		HL Graham					
VP yke	c Villani b Cleary	0	2			KH Brunt					
CL Hall	not out	0	2			LK Ebsary					
SK Moloney						MP Banting					
NM Hancock						TMM Newton					
BL Hepburn						PM Cleary					
KR Fryett						EL King					
C Raack						EJ Smith +					
	2 b, 2 lb, 9 w	13					2 lb, 2 w	4			
6 overs: 2-28	20 overs	4-122				6 overs: 0-55	16 overs	1-126			

Fall: 1-21 (Matthews, 2.5), 2-21 (Daffara, 2.6), 3-119 (Redmayne, 19.1), 4-119 (Pyke, 19.3)

Fall: 1-79 (Bolton, 9.3)

Scorchers - bowling	O	M	R	W	wd	nb	Dots	Hurricanes - bowling	O	M	R	W	wd	nb	Dots
KH Brunt	4	0	22	2	3		14	HK Matthews	4	0	24	0			13
NE Bolton	2	0	16	0	1		4	NM Hancock	4	0	25	1			9
NR Sciver	4	0	16	0			13	KR Fryett	3	0	29	0	1		5
EL King	2	0	16	0			3	BL Hepburn	1	0	11	0			2
HL Graham	4	0	30	0	1		6	C Raack	1	0	11	0			2
PM Cleary	3	0	11	2			8	VP yke	2	0	13	0	1		3
TMM Newton	1	0	7	0			2	IMHC Joyce	1	0	11	0			1

Toss: Scorchers   Award: EJ Villani (PS)   Umpires: J Paterson, T Steenholdt, Ref: TA Prue

Joyce 50: 45 balls, 5x4, Villani 50: 39 balls, 6x4

Match 45 – Scorchers v Hurricanes at Lilac Hill, Perth on January 21, 2018 – Scorchers won by 6 wickets

Hurricanes			B	4	6
HK Matthews	c Sciver b Cleary	14	15	2	
SG Daffara	b Sciver	10	9	1	
GP Redmayne +	c &b Brunt	53	49	7	
IMHC Joyce *	c Bolton b Newton	20	23	3	
V Pyke	c Villani b Graham	7	8		
CL Hall	c Sciver b Bolton	4	4	1	
SK Moloney	not out	15	8	2	
EG Fazackerley	run out (Sciver-Smith)	5	4		
BL Hepburn					
KR Fryett					
NM Hancock					
	2 w	2			
6 overs:2-35	20 overs	7-130			

Scorchers			B	4	6
EJ Villani *	c Hepburn b Fryett	21	14	4	
NE Bolton	not out	60	61	5	2
MP Banting	c Fazackerley b Fryett	0	2		
NR Sciver	c Moloney b Fazackerley	24	22	3	
HL Graham	c Matthews b Hancock	10	8	1	
TMM Newton	not out	10	6	1	
KH Brunt					
LK Ebsary					
PM Cleary					
EL King					
EJ Smith +					
	9 w	9			
6 overs:2-39	18.5 overs	4-134			

Fall: 1-24 (Daffara, 3.5), 2-24 (Matthews, 4.1), 3-69 (Joyce, 12.3), 4-86 (Pyke, 15.3), 5-99 (Hall, 16.4), 6-118 (Redmayne, 18.5), 7-130 (Fazackerley, 19.6)

Fall: 1-38 (Villani, 5.4), 2-39 (Banting, 5.6), 3-78 (Sciver, 12.4), 4-102 (Graham, 16.1)

Scorchers - bowling	O	M	R	W	wd	nb	Dots
KH Brunt	4	0	26	1	1		9
NE Bolton	2	0	19	1			3
NR Sciver	3	0	17	1			9
PM Cleary	4	0	21	1			13
EL King	3	0	13	0			8
TMM Newton	1	0	7	1	1		3
HL Graham	3	0	27	1			3

Hurricanes - bowling	O	M	R	W	wd	nb	Dots
HK Matthews	3.5	0	29	0			9
V Pyke	3	0	18	0	1		8
BL Hepburn	2	0	20	0			2
KR Fryett	3	0	20	2	3		9
NM Hancock	3	0	20	1	2		9
IMHC Joyce	3	0	20	0	1		8
EG Fazackerley	1	0	7	1	2		2

Toss: Scorchers   Award: NE Bolton (PS)   Umpires: J Hewitt, J Paterson, Ref: TA Prue
Redmayne 50: 46 balls, 7x4, Bolton 50: 57 balls, 4x4, 1x6

Match 46 – Stars v Sixers at Casey Fields, Melbourne on January 21, 2018 – Sixers won by 5 wickets

Stars			B	4	6
L Lee	c Reakes b Kapp	2	10		
KM Mack	b Garth	2	6		
M du Preez	c Healy b Garth	4	5	1	
GA Elwiss	c McGlashan b Aley	7	12		
EA Osborne	c Reakes b Kapp	39	43	2	
AJ Lanning	c Burns b Smith	18	23	1	
AM King	st Healy b van Niekerk	10	9	1	
AJ Sutherland	not out	13	12		
MA Blows					
KM Beams *					
NM Faltum +					
	9 lb, 2 w	11			
6 overs:4-23	20 overs	7-106			

Sixers			B	4	6
AJ Healy +	c Beams b Elwiss	21	16	3	
AR Reakes	b Osborne	8	9	2	
AK Gardner	c Osborne b Sutherland	4	4	1	
EA Perry *	not out	39	45	4	1
EA Burns	st Faltum b King	14	14	2	
SJ McGlashan	run out (Blows-Faltum)	9	10		
D van Niekerk	not out	9	10	2	
M Kapp					
SE Aley					
LG Smith					
KJ Garth					
	1 lb, 2 w	3			
6 overs:3-44	18 overs	5-107			

Fall: 1-2 (Mack, 1.6), 2-4 (Lee, 2.4), 3-15 (du Preez, 3.6), 4-22 (Elwiss, 5.4), 5-63 (Lanning, 13.2), 6-86 (King, 16.3), 7-106 (Osborne, 19.6)

Fall: 1-15 (Reakes, 2.3), 2-24 (Gardner, 3.3), 3-34 (Healy, 5.2), 4-62 (Burns, 10.1), 5-87 (McGlashan, 15.2)

Sixers - bowling	O	M	R	W	wd	nb	Dots
M Kapp	4	1	13	2			14
KJ Garth	3	0	15	2	1		11
SE Aley	4	0	21	1			7
AK Gardner	2	0	13	0	1		6
D van Niekerk	4	0	16	1			10
LG Smith	3	0	19	1			4

Stars - bowling	O	M	R	W	wd	nb	Dots
EA Osborne	3	0	28	1			8
AJ Sutherland	3	0	13	1			12
KM Beams	4	0	17	0			11
GA Elwiss	4	1	27	1	1		13
AM King	3	0	15	1			10
MA Blows	1	0	6	0	1		8

Toss: Stars   Award: EA Perry (SS)   Umpires: S Brne, D Ireland, Ref: DP Herft

Australian Cricket Digest, 2018-19

Match 47 – Thunder v Strikers at Robertson Oval, Wagga Wagga on January 21, 2018 - Strikers won in a Superover

Strikers			B	4	6
SW Bates *	st Priest b Carey	40	43	4	
SFM Devine	b Farrell	0	5		
TM McGrath	c Stalenberg b Gibson	22	18	3	
TT Beaumont	b Vakarewa	10	21		
BE Patterson	not out	21	16	3	
TMS Saville	b Farrell	6	9		
M Schutt	not out	8	8		
A Wellington					
AE Price					
TJ McPharlin +					
KL Pope					
	1 b, 3 lb, 3 w	7			
6 overs: 1-32	20 overs	5-114			

Thunder			B	4	6
RL Haynes	c Devine b Bates	22	27	3	
RH Priest +	c Bates b Devine	22	20	4	
AJ Blackwell *	c Devine b Wellington	21	35		
NE Stalenberg	c Bates b Wellington	29	24	2	1
NJ Carey	not out	13	11	2	
SR Taylor	not out	2	3		
RM Farrell					
SL Bates					
ML Gibson					
BW Vakarewa					
FC Wilson					
	1 nb, 1 lb, 3 w	5			
6 overs: 0-35	20 overs	4-114			

Fall: 1-2 (Devine, 1.1), 2-45 (McGrath, 7.5), 3-77 (Beaumont, 13.6), 4-81 (Bates, 14.6), 5-90 (Saville, 17.1)

Fall: 1-46 (Priest, 7.4), 2-48 (Haynes, 8.2), 3-94 (Stalenberg, 16.5), 4-110 (Blackwell, 18.6)

Thunder - bowling	O	M	R	W	wd	nb	Dots
SL Bates	4	0	19	0			14
RM Farrell	4	0	21	2	1		7
SR Taylor	3	0	20	0	1		9
NJ Carey	4	0	26	1			8
ML Gibson	2	0	12	1			6
BW Vakarewa	3	0	12	1	1		9

Strikers - bowling	O	M	R	W	wd	nb	Dots
ML Schutt	4	0	23	0	2		14
SFM Devine	3	0	12	1			12
TM McGrath	4	0	20	0			7
AE Price	1	0	10	0			2
SW Bates	4	0	26	1	1		9
AJ Wellington	4	0	21	2			9

Toss: Strikers   Award: SFM Devine (AS)   Umpires: AI Scotford, D Young, Ref: IS Thomas

Superover: Thunder 1-6 (1 over), Strikers 0-7 (1 over)

Match 48 – Thunder v Renegades at Manuka Oval, Canberra on January 24, 2018 – Thunder won by 4 wickets

Renegades			B	4	6
SG Molineux	c Priest b Vakarewa	1	2		
EJ Inglis +	c Carey b Farrell	0	4		
JE Duffin	b Farrell	12	14	2	
AE Satterthwaite	c Priest b Carey	17	19	2	
CJ Koski	lbw b Bates	1	3		
C Atapattu *	c Stalenberg b Carey	16	20	1	
MJ Brown	c Wilson b Taylor	16	15	2	
HNK Jensen	lbw b Gibson	2	5		
LM Tahuhu	c Stalenberg b Taylor	1	4		
MR Strano	b Carey	1	5		
GL Wareham	not out	1	4		
		0			
6 overs: 4-22	15.5 overs	68			

Thunder			B	4	6
RH Priest +	lbw b Strano	1	7		
RL Haynes	lbw b Jensen	37	36	3	
AJ Blackwell *	c Inglis b Tahuhu	4	8		
NE Stalenberg	c Tahuhu b Jensen	6	18		
FC Wilson	c Satterthwaite b Jensen	1	5		
SR Taylor	not out	10	17		
NJ Carey	lbw b Strano	0	4		
RM Farrell	not out	4	2	1	
ML Gibson					
SL Bates					
BW Vakarewa					
	1 lb, 1 nb, 4 w	6			
6 overs: 2-20	16 overs	6-69			

Fall: 1-1 (Inglis, 0.5), 2-1 (Molineux, 1.1), 3-17 (Duffin, 4.2), 4-22 (Koski, 5.2), 5-41 (Satterthwaite, 9.3), 6-48 (Atapattu, 11.1), 7-64 (Jensen, 12.6), 8-66 (Tahuhu, 14.1), 9-67 (Brown, 14.4), 10-68 (Strano, 15.5)

Fall: 1-1 (Priest, 1.1), 2-6 (Blackwell, 2.4), 3-37 (Stalenberg, 8.6), 4-43 (Wilson, 10.4), 5-63 (Haynes, 14.5), 6-64 (Carey, 15.4)

Thunder - bowling	O	M	R	W	wd	nb	Dots
RM Farrell	3	0	10	2			11
BW Vakarewa	2	0	12	1			7
SL Bates	2	1	7	1			8
SR Taylor	3	0	11	2			10
NJ Carey	3.5	0	10	3			14
ML Gibson	2	0	18	1			5

Renegades - bowling	O	M	R	W	wd	nb	Dots
LM Tahuhu	4	0	12	1	2		15
MR Strano	4	0	16	2			14
MJ Brown	3	0	17	0	1	1	10
SG Molineux	1	0	6	0			3
HNK Jensen	3	0	11	3			11
GL Wareham	1	0	6	0			2

Toss: Thunder   Award: NJ Carey (ST)   Umpires: AGDCJ Bandara, AR Crozier, Ref: IS Thomas

Australian Cricket Digest, 2018-19

Match 49 – Stars v Hurricanes at the MCG on January 27, 2018 – Stars won by 7 wickets

Hurricanes			B	4	6
HK Matthews	c Martin b King	34	30	5	
SG Daffara	run out (Elwiss)	13	15	1	
GP Redmayne +	run out (Elwiss)	20	23	1	
IMHC Joyce *	st Faltum b King	17	23	1	
SK Moloney	c Beams b Sutherland	4	6		
V Pyke	run out (Rafferty-Faltum)	1	4		
EG Fazackerley	not out	13	9	1	
CL Hall	st Faltum b Beams	3	6		
NM Hancock	not out	2	4		
BL Hepburn					
KR Fryett					
		0			
6 overs: 0-37	20 overs	7-107			

Stars			B	4	6
KM Mack	b Matthews	42	44	5	
AM King	c Fazackerley b Hancock	7	12		
GA Elwiss	c Redmayne b Hancock	28	34	1	
EA Osborne	not out	13	16	1	
KJ Martin	not out	2	4		
AJ Sutherland					
MA Blows					
NM Faltum +					
CL Rafferty					
KM Beams *					
AJ Lanning					
	6 lb, 2 nb, 8 w	16			
6 overs: 1-28	18 overs	3-108			

Fall: 1-45 (Daffara, 6.5), 2-55 (Matthews, 8.3), 3-81 (Joyce, 14.3), 4-86 (Moloney, 15.5), 5-89 (Pyke, 16.5), 6-90 (Redmayne, 17.1), 7-93 (Hall, 18.1 ov)

Fall: 1-22 (King, 4.5), 2-77 (Mack, 12.3), 3-104 (Elwiss, 16.5)

Stars - bowling	O	M	R	W	wd	nb	Dots
EA Osborne	4	0	21	0			11
AJ Sutherland	4	0	24	1			10
KM Beams	4	0	11	1			13
GA Elwiss	4	0	28	0			10
AM King	4	0	23	2			9

Hurricanes - bowling	O	M	R	W	wd	nb	Dots
HK Matthews	4	0	26	1	2	1	13
V Pyke	4	0	18	0			11
NM Hancock	4	0	18	2	1		12
KR Fryett	2	0	14	0	2		3
BL Hepburn	2	0	13	0		1	4
EG Fazackerley	1	0	6	0			3
IMHC Joyce	1	0	7	0			3

Toss: Stars   Award: KM Mack (MS)   Umpires: DJ Brigham, DR Close, NR Johnston (TV), Ref: K Hannam

Match 50 – Sixers v Strikers at Hurstville Oval, Sydney on January 27, 2018 – Sixers won by 7 wickets

Strikers			B	4	6
SW Bates *	st Healy b Coyte	15	19	1	
SFM Devine	c Perry b Burns	70	45	5	5
TM McGrath	not out	44	35	3	1
TT Beaumont	lbw b Garth	3	9		
BE Patterson	c Garth b Coyte	8	9	1	
M Schutt	run out (Perry)	4	5		
TJ McPharlin +					
TMS Saville					
AJ Wellington					
AE Price					
KL Pope					
	3 lb, 2 nb	5			
6 overs: 0-44	20 overs	5-149			

Sixers			B	4	6
AJ Healy +	st McPharlin b Wellington	106	66	13	3
EA Perry	b Schutt	10	12		
AK Gardner	run out (Bates)	1	2		
EA Burns	not out	25	28	2	
SJ McGlashan	not out	6	9		
AR Reakes					
SE Aley					
SJ Coyte					
LG Smith					
AE Jones					
KJ Garth					
	1 nb, 1 w	2			
6 overs: 1-34	19.2 overs	3-150			

Fall: 1-56 (Bates, 8.2), 2-100 (Devine, 12.5), 3-115 (Beaumont, 15.3), 4-132 (Patterson, 18.2), 5-149 (Schutt, 19.6)

Fall: 1-34 (Perry, 5.6), 2-55 (Gardner, 7.1), 3-141 (Healy, 16.5)

Sixers - bowling	O	M	R	W	wd	nb	Dots
AK Gardner	3	0	19	0			8
EA Perry	3	0	32	0	1		7
SE Aley	3	0	21	0			7
SJ Coyte	4	0	14	2			11
KJ Garth	4	0	24	1			10
LG Smith	1	0	19	0			0
EA Burns	2	0	17	1	1		5

Strikers - bowling	O	M	R	W	wd	nb	Dots
ML Schutt	4	0	26	1			9
SFM Devine	4	0	28	0	1		10
TM McGrath	2	0	25	0	1		3
AJ Wellington	4	0	27	1			10
SW Bates	2	0	27	0			2
KL Pope	2	0	11	0			7
AE Price	1.2	0	6	0			3

Toss: Strikers   Award: AJ Healy (SS)   Umpires: A Hobson, M Penman, Ref: TM Donahoo

Devine 50: 35 balls, 3x4 4x6. Healy 50: 34 balls, 6x4 1x6; 100: 60 balls, 12x4 3x6

Match 51 – Renegades v Scorchers at Camberwell on January 27, 2018 – Renegades won by 4 wickets

Scorchers		B	4	6	Renegades		B	4	6
EJ Villani *	c Strano b Jensen	10	16	1	SG Molineux	c Villani b Cleary	62	45	8	3
NE Bolton	c &b Strano	15	10	2	C Atapattu	b King	20	24	2
MP Banting	c Strano b Brown	0	5		AE Satterthwaite *	c Sciver b Brunt	14	16	1
HL Graham	c Koskib Tahuhu	6	8		EJ Inglis +	lbw b King	0	4	
KH Brunt	b Brown	3	6		CJ Koski	c Sciver b Graham	6	10	
LK Ebsary	not out	61	44	3	3	MJ Brown	b Graham	0	1	
NR Sciver	c &b Molineux	10	12	1	JE Duffin	not out	13	15	2
TMM Newton	st Inglis b Molineux	0	1		HNK Jensen	not out	2	2	
PM Cleary	not out	12	18		LM Tahuhu				
EJ Smith +					MR Strano				
EL King					GL Wareham				
	2 lb, 5 w	7				2 b, 1 lb, 1 nb, 4 w	8		
6 overs: 3-29	20 overs	7-124			6 overs: 0-44	19.2 overs	6-125		

Fall: 1-22 (Bolton, 3.4), 2-24 (Banting, 4.4), 3-27 (Villani, 5.3), 5-38 (Graham, 8.2), 6-64 (Sciver, 12.3), 7-64 (Newton, 12.4)

Fall: 1-85 (Molineux, 10.6), 2-85 (Atapattu, 11.2 ov), 4-33 (Brunt, 6.6), 3-85 (Inglis, 11.6), 4-106 (Koski, 15.1), 5-106 (Brown, 15.2), 6-114 (Satterthwaite, 18.1)

Renegades - bowling	O	M	R	W	wd	nb	Dots	Scorchers - bowling	O	M	R	W	wd	nb	Dots
LM Tahuhu	4	0	16	1	2		14	NE Bolton	1	0	15	0			2
MR Strano	3	0	24	1			9	KH Brunt	4	0	16	1			15
MJ Brown	4	0	18	2	2		11	PM Cleary	4	0	23	1		1	12
HNK Jensen	4	0	24	1			8	HL Graham	4	0	23	2	1		11
SG Molineux	4	0	31	2			11	TMM Newton	1	0	17	0	1		2
AE Satterthwaite	1	0	9	0			1	EL King	3	1	14	2			11
								EJ Villani	2.2	0	14	0	4		7

Toss: Renegades   Award: SG Molineux (MR)   Umpires: AR Crozier, D Ireland, Ref: DP Herft.

Ebsary 50: 40 balls, 7x4 3x6. Molineux 50: 34 balls, 6x4 3x6.

Match 52 – Heat v Thunder at the Gabba, Brisbane on January 27, 2018 – Heat won by 6 wickets

Thunder		B	4	6	Heat		B	4	6
RL Haynes	c Birkett b Kimmince	43	30	4	2	BL Mooney +	c Bates b Vakarewa	27	16	5
RH Priest +	c Mooney b Johnson	4	5	1	KLH Short *	c &b Bates	6	5	1
AJ Blackwell *	c Short b Birkett	41	37	3	GM Harris	c Vakarewa b Farrell	57	45	8	1
NE Stalenberg	c Ferling b Barsby	16	19	2	DM Kimmince	b Bates	42	33	2	1
SR Taylor	not out	24	17	3	JL Jonassen	not out	8	9	1
NJ Carey	c Short b Barsby	8	9	1	DJS Dottin	not out	0	1	
FC Wilson	not out	3	3		SJ Johnson				
RM Farrell					LM Harris				
ML Gibson					HP Birkett				
SL Bates					JL Barsby				
BW Vakarewa					HL Ferling				
	1 b, 2 lb, 3 w	6				1 lb, 1 nb, 4 w	6		
6 overs: 1-57	20 overs	5-145			6 overs: 1-46	18 overs	4-146		

Fall: 1-21 (Priest, 2.6), 2-63 (Haynes, 7.4), 3-101 (Stalenberg, 14.2), 4-113 (Blackwell, 16.2), 5-131 (Carey, 18.5)

Fall: 1-14 (Short, 1.4), 2-46 (Mooney, 6.1), 3-129 (G Harris, 15.1), 4-145 (Kimmince, 17.5)

Heat - bowling	O	M	R	W	wd	nb	Dots	Thunder - bowling	O	M	R	W	wd	nb	Dots
SJ Johnson	2	0	11	1	1		7	RM Farrell	4	0	34	1			10
JL Jonassen	3	0	30	0	1		6	SL Bates	3	0	23	2			5
GM Harris	3	0	22	0			5	BW Vakarewa	3	0	17	1	1		12
DJS Dottin	3	0	19	0			5	NJ Carey	4	0	37	0	1		7
JL Barsby	4	0	32	2	1		9	ML Gibson	2	0	17	0	1		2
DM Kimmince	3	0	16	1			7	SR Taylor	2	0	17	0			4
HP Birkett	2	0	12	1			4								

Toss: Thunder   Award: GM Harris (BH)   Umpires: MS Branch, SE Dionysius, Ref: N Findlay

G Harris 50: 41 balls, 7x4 1x6.

Match 53 – Stars v Hurricanes at the MCG on January 28, 2018 – Hurricanes won by 2 runs

Hurricanes		B	4	6
HK Matthews	c Mack b Osborne	44	44	5
SG Daffara	st Faltum b King	13	17	1
GP Rdmayne +	c Sutherland b Elwiss	40	37	1
SK Moloney	b Osborne	14	11	1
EG Fazackerley	b Osborne	0	2	
VP yke	c Martin b Elwiss	9	7	1
NM Hancock	not out	3	2	
M Phillips				
IMHC Joyce *				
C Raack				
KR Fryett				
	2 lb, 5 w	7		
6 overs: 0-37	20 overs	6-130		

Stars		B	4	6
KM Mack	c Raack b Hancock	17	17	3
KJ Martin	lbw b Matthews	15	17	1
GA Elwiss	run out (Joyce)	13	18	
EA Osborne	c Joyce b Pyke	30	29	1
AJ Lanning	run out (Moloncy)	7	7	1
AM King	c Phillips b Hancock	13	13	1
AJ Sutherland	not out	8	8	1
MA Blows	c &b Matthews	16	10	3
KM Beams *	not out	2	2	
CL Rafferty				
NM Faltum +				
	2 lb, 1 nb, 4 w	7		
6 overs: 1-36	20 overs	7-128		

Fall: 1-38 (Daffara, 6.3), 2-77 (Matthews, 13.1), 3-110 (Moloney, 17.2), 4-110 (Fazackerley, 17.4), 5-125 (Redmayne, 19.2), 6-130 (Pyke, 19.6)

Fall: 1-30 (Martin, 4.4), 2-42 (Mack, 7.1), 3-55 (Elwiss, 9.3), 4-68 (Lanning, 11.6), 5-95 (King, 15.6), 6-99 (Osborne, 16.4), 7-125 (Blows, 19.3)

Stars - bowling	O	M	R	W	wd	nb	Dots
EA Osborne	4	0	23	3	1		14
AJ Sutherland	3	0	20	0	1		7
KM Beams	4	0	33	0			6
GA Elwiss	4	0	25	2			10
AM King	4	0	21	1	1		10
MA Blows	1	0	6	0	1		3

Hurricanes - bowling	O	M	R	W	wd	nb	Dots
KR Fryett	1	0	13	0	1		1
VP yke	4	0	28	1			10
HK Matthews	4	0	19	2	1		11
NM Hancock	4	0	22	2	2	1	10
C Raack	3	0	18	0			4
IMHC Joyce	2	0	10	0			5
EG Fazackerley	1	0	8	0			2
M Phillips	1	0	8	0			1

Toss: Stars   Award: HK Matthews (HH)   Umpires: S Brne, D Ireland, Ref: K Hannam

Match 54 – Renegades v Scorchers at Camberwell on January 28, 2018 – Scorchers won by 4 wickets

Renegades		B	4	6
SG Molineux	c Cleary b Brunt	1	4	
C Atapattu	c Brunt b Cleary	10	18	2
KL Britt	b Brunt	18	22	1
AE Satterthwaite	c Brunt b Bolton	26	30	3
EJ Inglis	c Sciver b Graham	28	19	3 1
CJ Koski	b Brunt	3	8	
MJ Brown	c Villani b Cleary	2	8	
HNK Jensen	c Ebsary b Cleary	3	4	
LM Tahuhu	st Smith b Graham	0	3	
MR Strano	not out	1	2	
GL Wareham	not out	5	2	1
	7 lb, 8 w	15		
6 overs: 2-26	20 overs	9-112		

Scorchers		B	4	
EJ Villani *	lbw b Molineux	18	12	2
NE Bolton	c Atapattu b Wareham	18	19	1
MP Banting	b Wareham	6	7	1
NR Sciver	not out	39	33	4
HL Graham	c Molineux b Wareham	11	12	1
LK Ebsary	lbw b Satterthwaite	2	5	
KH Brunt	c Molineux b Brown	15	9	3
TMM Newton	not out	0	1	
PM Cleary				
EJ Smith +				
EL King				
	1 nb, 3 w	4		
6 overs: 1-44	16.1 overs	6-113		

Fall: 1-2 (Molineux, 0.5), 2-19 (Atapattu, 5.1), 3-57 (Britt, 10.4), 4-79 (Satterthwaite, 13.5), 5-99 (Koski, 16.4), 6-99 (Inglis, 17.1), 7-104 (Brown, 18.4), 8-104 (Jensen, 18.5), 9-106 (Tahuhu, 19.3)

Fall: 1-24 (Villani, 2.4), 2-44 (Banting, 6.1), 3-45 (Bolton, 6.3), 4-75 (Graham, 10.4), 5-79 (Ebsary, 12.1), 6-110 (Brunt, 15.5)

Scorchers - bowling	O	M	R	W	wd	nb	Dots
KH Brunt	4	0	11	3			17
NE Bolton	4	0	23	1	1		11
HL Graham	4	0	27	2	2		12
PM Cleary	4	0	25	3	2		13
EL King	4	0	19	0	1		11

Renegades - bowling	O	M	R	W	wd	nb	Dots
LM Tahuhu	1	0	14	0	2		2
MR Strano	2	0	12	0			3
SG Molineux	3.1	0	24	1			8
HNK Jensen	2	0	9	0			7
GL Wareham	4	0	19	3			11
MJ Brown	3	0	27	1	1	1	9
AE Satterthwaite	1	0	8	1			2

Toss: Scorchers   Award: KH Brunt (PS)   Umpires: DJ Brigham, AR Crozier, Ref: DP Herft.

Match 55 – Sixers v Strikers at Hurstville Oval, Sydney on January 28, 2018 – Sixers won by 7 wickets

Strikers			B	4	6	Sixers			B	4	6
S W Bates *	lbw b Gardner		6	11		A J Healy +	c Bates b Price		63	52	7
S FM Devine	b Garth		23	25	1 1	E A Perry *	c McGrath b Wellington		13	25	1
T M McGrath	c Smith b Coyte		12	17	1	A K Gardner	c Wellington b Schutt		9	11	1
T T Beaumont	c Reakes b Coyte		28	31	1	A E Jones	not out		16	19	2
B E Patterson	run out (Smith)		4	7		E A Burns	not out		5	2	1
A Wellington	c Garth b Aley		16	11	1 1	S J McGlashan					
M Schutt	c Gardner b Coyte		5	5		A R Reakes					
T M S Saville	run out (Healy)		6	6		S E Aley					
A E Price	run out (McGlashan)		4	6		L G Smith					
T J McPharlin +	not out		0	0		S J Coyte					
K L Pope	not out		1	1		K J Garth					
	1 lb, 5 w		6				1 lb, 5 w		6		
6 overs: 1-27	20 overs		9-111			6 overs: 0-33	18.1 overs		3-112		

Fall: 1-20 (Bates, 4.4), 2-32 (Devine, 7.1), 3-56 (McGrath, 11.2), 4-63 (Patterson, 13.1), 5-92 (Wellington, 16.4), 6-97 (Schutt, 17.3), 7-99 (Beaumont, 17.5), 8-109 (Saville, 19.3), 9-110 (Price, 19.5)

Fall: 1-53 (Perry, 8.5), 2-76 (Gardner, 12.3), 3-107 (Healy, 17.4)

Sixers - bowling	O	M	R	W	wd	nb	Dots	Strikers - bowling	O	M	R	W	wd	nb	Dots
AK Gardner	4	0	19	1			12	ML Schutt	4	0	21	1			13
EA Perry	1	0	2	0			5	SFM Devine	4	0	28	0	2		9
SE Aley	4	0	27	1			9	TM McGrath	1	0	10	0			2
SJ Coyte	4	0	18	3			10	AJ Wellington	4	0	20	1			12
KJ Garth	3	0	15	1	2		12	AE Price	2	0	16	1	1		5
AR Reakes	2	0	19	0			2	KL Pope	3	0	12	0			9
EA Burns	2	0	10	0			3	SW Bates	0.1	0	4	0			0

Toss: Strikers   Award: SJ Coyte (SS)   Umpires: TM Penman, GS Stubbings, Ref: IS Thomas. Healy 50: 38 balls, 6x4

Match 56 – Heat v Thunder at Allan Border Field, Brisbane on January 28, 2018 – Thunder won by 2 runs

Thunder			B	4	6	Heat			B	4	6
R H Priest +	c L Harris b Johnson		17	14	2 1	B L Mooney +	c Carey b Farrell		0	2	
R L Haynes	c L Harris b Dottin		6	8	1	K L H Short *	c Priest b Vakarewa		14	12	2
A J Blackwell *	b Barsby		18	23	1	G M Harris	lbw b Vakarewa		33	30	5 1
S R Taylor	c Mooney b Kimmince		12	17	2	D M Kimmince	c Carey b Vakarewa		2	8	
N J Carey	c G Harris b Johnson		26	26	2 1	J L Jonassen	c Vakarewa b Farrell		33	21	2 2
F C Wilson	c Short b Barsby		0	4		D J S Dottin	c Taylor b Carey		16	13	2
R M Farrell	c L Harris b Barsby		19	16	2 1	L M Harris	st Priest b Bates		8	6	1
L Griffith	c Short b Barsby		2	6		S J Johnson	c Blackwell b Farrell		0	1	
M L Gibson	not out		2	4		H P Birkett	c Gibson b Carey		2	3	
S L Bates	not out		5	3		J L Barsby	not out		3	5	
B W Vakarewa						H L Ferling	b Bates		3	5	
	2 b, 1 lb, 1 nb, 6 w		10				1 w		1		
6 overs: 2-37	20 overs		8-117			6 overs: 1-41	17.4 overs		115		

Fall: 1-20 (Priest, 2.6), 2-27 (Haynes, 3.6), 3-46 (Taylor, 7.4), 4-85 (Blackwell, 14.1), 5-85 (Wilson, 14.5), 6-99 (Carey, 15.4), 7-110 (Griffith, 18.3), 8-110 (Farrell, 18.5)

Fall: 1-0 (Mooney, 0.2), 2-41 (Short, 6.1), 3-43 (Kimmince, 8.1), 4-50 (G Harris, 8.5), 5-91 (Dottin, 13.4 ov), 6-100 (Jonassen, 14.4), 7-101 (Johnson, 14.6), 8-107 (L Harris, 15.4), 9-109 (Birkett, 16.1), 10-115 (Ferling, 17.4)

Heat - bowling	O	M	R	W	wd	nb	Dots	Thunder - bowling	O	M	R	W	wd	nb	Dots
SJ Johnson	3	0	29	2	1	1	11	RM Farrell	4	0	19	3			10
DJS Dottin	3	0	17	1	2		9	SL Bates	3.4	0	28	2	1		7
HL Ferling	2	0	12	0	2		5	BW Vakarewa	4	0	17	3			15
DM Kimmince	4	0	19	1	1		10	NJ Carey	3	0	32	2			6
GM Harris	2	0	12	0			6	L Griffith	1	0	1	0			5
HP Birkett	2	0	9	0			6	ML Gibson	2	0	18	0			5
JL Jonassen	2	0	14	0			7								
JL Barsby	2	0	2	4			10								

Toss: Heat   Award: BW Vakarewa (ST)   Umpires: MS Branch, SJ Farrell, Ref: N Findlay

First Semi Final – Thunder v Scorchers at Perth Stadium on February 1, 2018 – Scorchers won by 27 runs

Scorchers		B	4	6	Thunder		B	4	6
EJ Villani *	lbw b Carey	38	37	5	RH Priest +	c Sciver b Cleary	25	19	5
NE Bolton	c Stalenberg b Taylor	37	26	7	RL Haynes	lbw b Bolton	1	3	
NR Sciver	not out	38	28	4	AJ Blackwell *	c Villani b King	9	22	
HL Graham	not out	27	29	2	NE Stalenberg	st Smith b King	1	6	
PM Cleary					SR Taylor	c Newton b Graham	7	11	1
LK Ebsary					NJ Carey	b King	22	20	3
KH Brunt					FC Wilson	run out (Sciver-Smith)	46	28	8
EL King					RM Farrell	c Smith b Brunt	3	5	
TMM Newton					ML Gibson	not out	2	4	
MP Banting					SL Bates	not out	2	2	
EJ Smith +					BW Vakarewa	did not bat			
	2 lb, 6 w	8				1 lb, 2 w	3		
6 overs: 0-51	20 overs	2-148			6 overs: 2-33	20 overs	8-121		

Fall: 1-65 (Villani, 9.1), 2-86 (Bolton, 11.4)

Fall: 1-10 (Haynes, 1.2), 2-31 (Priest, 4.6), 3-35 (Stalenberg, 7.3), 4-44 (Blackwell, 9.5), 5-46 (Taylor, 10.4), 6-88 (Carey, 15.4), 7-107 (Farrell, 18.2), 8-118 (Wilson, 19.3)

Thunder - bowling	O	M	R	W	wd	nb	Dots	Scorchers - bowling	O	M	R	W	wd	nb	Dots
RM Farrell	4	0	34	0	2		7	KH Brunt	4	0	24	1	2		11
SL Bates	3	0	22	0			8	NE Bolton	4	0	22	1			14
BW Vakarewa	3	0	21	0			6	PM Cleary	4	1	24	1			11
SR Taylor	4	0	23	1			10	EL King	4	0	17	3			13
NJ Carey	2	0	16	1			6	HL Graham	4	0	33	1			8
ML Gibson	4	0	30	0			6								

Toss: Thunder Award: NE Bolton (PS) Umpires: GA Joshua, AK Wilds, SA Lightbody (TV), Ref: RL Parry

Second Semi Final – Sixers v Strikers at Adelaide Oval on February 2, 2018 – Sixers won by 17 runs

Sixers		B	4	6	Strikers		B	4	6
AJ Healy +	c Patterson b Devine	2	8		SFM Devine	c & b Garth	7	7	
EA Perry *	c McGrath b Devine	16	31		SW Bates *	c Smith b Aley	14	14	3
AK Gardner	st McPharlin b Wellington	72	45	5	6	TM McGrath	c Coyte b Aley	0	1	
EA Burns	c McPharlin b Schutt	25	17	4	TT Beaumont	lbw b Coyte	50	46	7
SJ McGlashan	not out	12	12	1	BE Patterson	c Healy b Garth	0	3	
AE Jones	lbw b Bates	3	6		A Wellington	lbw b Aley	0	2	
AR Reakes	not out	2	1		TMS Saville	lbw b Aley	0	2	
SE Aley					M Schutt	lbw b Burns	14	16	1
LG Smith					AE Price	st Healy b Coyte	19	17	2
SJ Coyte					TJ McPharlin +	not out	8	8	
KJ Garth					KL Pope	not out	7	4	1
	6 w	6				2 w	2		
6 overs: 1-33	20 overs	5-138			6 overs: 0-23	20 overs	9-121		

Fall: 1-3 (Healy, 1.4), 2-90 (Perry, 13.2), 3-104 (Gardner, 14.6), 4-131 (Burns, 18.2), 5-136 (Jones, 19.5)

Fall: 1-20 (Bates, 3.1), 2-20 (McGrath, 3.2), 3-22 (Devine, 4.3, 4-22 (Patterson, 4.6), 5-23 (Wellington, 5.4), 6-23 (Saville, 5.6), 7-71 (Schutt, 13.1), 8-95 (Beaumont, 16.3), 9-112 (Price, 18.6)

Strikers - bowling	O	M	R	W	wd	nb	Dots	Sixers - bowling	O	M	R	W	wd	nb	Dots
ML Schutt	4	0	17	1			15	AK Gardner	3	0	24	0			7
SFM Devine	4	0	21	2	2		16	EA Perry	2	0	20	0	2		3
SW Bates	3	0	29	1			6	SE Aley	4	1	18	4			4
AJ Wellington	4	0	28	1	3		10	KJ Garth	3	0	14	2			10
KL Pope	2	0	17	0	1		5	SJ Coyte	4	0	32	2			7
AE Price	2	0	17	0			2	EA Burns	4	0	13	1			11
TM McGrath	1	0	9	0			1								

Toss: Sixers Award: SE Aley (AS) Umpires: MW Graham-Smith, JD Ward, CA Polosak (TV), Ref: D Talalla
Gardner 50: 31 balls, 2x4 4x6, Beaumont 50: 45 balls, 7x4

The Final – Sydney Sixers v Perth Scorchers at Adelaide Oval on February 4, 2018 – Sixers won by 9 wickets

Scorchers		B	4	6	Sixers		B	4	6
EJ Villani*	st Healy b Coyte	16	29	3	AJ Healy+	st Smith b King	41	32	5	1
NE Bolton	lbw b Garth	5	13		EA Perry*	not out	36	42	5
NR Sciver	c Healy b Perry	2	4		AK Gardner	not out	22	16	2	1
MP Banting	c Smith b Burns	5	9		EA Burns				
TMM Newton	lbw b Coyte	12	17		SJ McGlashan				
HL Graham	b Coyte	14	16		AE Jones				
KH Brunt	c Gardner b Aley	10	13		AR Reakes				
LK Ebsary	c Healy b Burns	4	4	1	SE Aley				
PM Cleary	not out	18	14	2	LG Smith				
EL King	run out (Gardner-Burns)	2	2		SJ Coyte				
EJ Smith+	run out (Gardner-Burns)	0	0		KJ Garth				
	2 lb, 1 nb, 8 w	11				1 w	1		
6 overs: 0-22	20 overs	99			6 overs: 0-39	15 overs	1-100		

Fall: 1-23 (Villani, 6.3), 2-26 (Bolton, 7.1), 3-29 (Sciver, 8.2), 4-41 (Banting, 9.5), 5-61 (Newton, 14.1), 6-66 (Graham, 14.6), 7-71 (Ebsary, 15.6), 8-90 (Brunt, 18.6), 9-94 (King, 19.4), 10-99 (Smith, 19.6)

Sixers - bowling	O	M	R	W	wd	nb	Dots	Scorchers - bowling	O	M	R	W	wd	nb	Dots
AK Gardner	4	0	19	0			11	KH Brunt	3	0	20	0	1		10
EA Perry	2	0	9	1	2		5	NE Bolton	2	0	20	0			5
SE Aley	4	0	19	1	1		14	HL Graham	4	0	17	0			13
KJ Garth	2	0	7	1	1		9	PM Cleary	2	0	17	0			4
SJ Coyte	4	0	17	3	3		13	EL King	4	0	26	1			10
EA Burns	4	0	26	2		1	7								

Toss: Scorchers.   Umpires: GJ Davidson, JD Ward, MW Graham-Smith (TV), Ref: DJ Harper.   Award: SJ Coyte (SS)
Series Award: Amy Satterthwaite (HH) 35, Elysa Villani (PS) 28, Ellyse Perry (SS) 27, Beth Mooney (BH) 25, Suzie Bates (AS) 25

WBBL03 Stats
ADELAIDE STRIKERS

Batting & Fielding	M	Inn	NO	Runs	HS	Avge	100s	50s	6s	S/Rate	Ct	St
SW Bates	15	15	1	434	103	31.00	1	1	2	109.59	12	-
SFM Devine	15	15	1	355	70	25.35	0	1	17	117.54	5	-
TT Beaumont	15	15	0	301	50	20.06	0	1	3	90.39	2	-
BE Patterson	15	15	4	213	37	19.36	0	0	1	109.79	3	-
T Saville	15	11	5	109	31*	18.16	0	0	0	81.34	5	-
TM McGrath	15	15	1	229	44*	16.35	0	0	1	106.01	5	-
M Schutt	15	12	5	91	20*	13.00	0	0	1	118.18	2	-
A Price	13	6	0	41	19	6.83	0	0	0	97.61	5	-
A Wellington	15	8	0	52	16	6.50	0	0	2	110.63	3	-
RS Dick	3	1	0	6	6	6.00	0	0	0	60.00	1	-
TJ McPharlin	15	7	4	17	8*	5.66	0	0	0	77.27	2	10
K Pope	9	4	4	8	7*	-	0	0	0	160.00	0	-
SM Betts	5	1	1	5	5*	-	0	0	0	166.66	2	-

Bowling	M	Overs	Mdns	Runs	Wkts	Avge	Best	Econ	SR	4w	Dot %
ML Schutt	15	59	1	339	12	28.25	2-14	5.74	29.5	0	53
TM McGrath	15	41	0	251	13	19.30	3-17	6.12	18.9	0	42
A Price	13	30.5	0	190	7	27.14	2-4	6.16	26.4	0	34
SFM Devine	15	48	0	298	17	17.52	2-10	6.20	16.9	0	46
AJ Wellington	15	54.2	0	355	17	20.88	3-9	6.53	19.1	0	41
SW Bates	15	31.1	1	240	7	34.28	2-6	7.70	26.7	0	35
RS Dick	3	4	0	33	1	33.00	1-12	8.25	24.0	0	21
SM Betts	5	6.5	0	70	2	35.00	2-22	10.24	20.5	0	33

Also Bowled: K Pope (9 matches) 7-0-40-0.

BRISBANE HEAT

Batting & Fielding	M	Inn	NO	Runs	HS	Avge	100s	50s	6s	S/Rate	Ct	St
BL Mooney	14	14	3	465	86*	42.27	0	5	5	143.51	9	3
GM Harris	4	4	1	111	57	37.00	0	1	3	115.62	2	-
JL Jonassen	14	10	4	203	55*	33.83	0	1	8	120.11	6	-
KL Short	14	14	1	308	79	23.69	0	2	1	99.67	9	-
DM Kimmince	14	12	2	229	87*	22.90	0	1	7	117.43	3	-
DJS Dottin	14	13	2	171	45	15.54	0	0	2	89.06	1	-
HL Ferling	14	6	4	23	10*	11.50	0	0	0	100.00	3	-
L Harris	14	9	3	60	17	10.00	0	0	1	100.00	4	-
JL Barsby	13	5	1	30	13	7.50	0	0	0	88.23	2	-
L Wolvaardt	6	6	1	32	13	6.40	0	0	0	59.25	2	-
H Birkett	14	6	0	33	15	5.50	0	0	0	82.50	4	-
SJ Johnson	14	7	1	31	10	5.16	0	0	1	68.88	1	-
G Prestwidge	4	1	1	0	0*	-	0	0	0	-	0	-

Also played: C Hill (1 match) did not bat.

Bowling	M	Overs	Mdns	Runs	Wkts	Avge	Best	Econ	SR	4w	Dot %
DM Kimmince	14	45	1	272	11	24.72	3-23	6.04	24.5	0	40
JL Barsby	13	38	0	231	13	17.76	4-2	6.07	17.5	1	38
JL Jonassen	14	45.5	1	296	11	26.90	2-17	6.45	25.0	0	46
DJS Dottin	14	37	0	240	8	30.00	2-13	6.48	27.7	0	43
H Birkett	14	35.5	0	238	10	23.80	3-15	6.64	21.5	0	36
SJ Johnson	14	35.2	0	239	10	23.90	2-24	6.76	21.2	0	53
GM Harris	4	12	0	85	3	28.33	2-22	7.08	24.0	0	36
HL Ferling	14	18	0	128	4	32.00	1-8	7.11	27.0	0	38

Australian Cricket Digest, 2018-19

HOBART HURRICANES

Batting & Fielding	M	Inn	NO	Runs	HS	Avge	100s	50s	6s	S/Rate	Ct	St
IMHC Joyce	6	5	1	99	52*	24.75	0	1	0	96.11	-	
HK Matthews	14	14	0	297	44	21.21	0	0	0	94.28	-	
G Redmayne	14	14	0	297	53	21.21	0	1	0	86.58	2	1
V Krishnamurthy	9	9	1	144	40	18.00	0	0	1	101.40	-	
S Daffara	12	12	1	181	30	16.45	0	0	0	89.16	-	
V Pyke	14	14	4	139	35*	13.90	0	0	1	94.55	-	
SK Moloney	8	6	2	47	15*	11.75	0	0	0	117.50	-	
L Winfield	8	8	0	72	15	9.00	0	0	0	80.00	-	
C Raack	11	7	5	17	6*	8.50	0	0	0	94.44	-	
K Fryett	9	4	1	25	19	8.33	0	0	0	89.28	-	
EG Fazackerley	5	5	1	30	13*	7.50	0	0	0	120.00	-	
CL Hall	12	11	1	60	14	6.00	0	0	0	75.94	-	
E Thompson	4	4	0	22	9	5.50	0	0	0	61.11	-	
B Hepburn	12	8	2	32	11	5.33	0	0	0	84.21	-	
NM Hancock	14	11	2	33	12	3.66	0	0	0	67.34	-	
M Phillips	2	1	0	0	0	0.00	0	0	0	0.00	-	

Bowling	M	Overs	Mdns	Runs	Wkts	Avge	Best	Econ	SR	4w	Dot %
NM Hancock	14	43.2	1	281	11	25.54	2-18	6.48	23.6	0	44
IMHC Joyce	6	11	0	74	1	74.00	1-26	6.72	66.0	0	41
HK Matthews	14	52.2	0	362	6	60.33	2-29	6.91	52.3	0	42
V Pyke	14	40	0	289	6	48.16	4-17	7.22	40.0	1	41
C Raack	11	30	0	226	2	113.00	1-14	7.53	90.0	0	34
E Thompson	4	7	0	53	2	26.50	2-26	7.57	21.0	0	36
B Hepburn	12	27.3	1	219	7	31.28	3-24	7.96	23.5	0	37
EG Fazackerley	5	5	0	42	1	42.00	1-7	8.40	30.0	0	30
K Fryett	9	20	0	171	3	57.00	2-20	8.55	40.0	0	35
M Phillips	2	3	0	27	0	-	-	9.00	-	0	28
V Krishnamurthy	9	5	0	51	1	51.00	1-18	10.20	30.0	0	27

MELBOURNE RENEGADES

Batting & Fielding	M	Inn	NO	Runs	HS	Avge	100s	50s	6s	S/Rate	Ct	St
AE Satterthwaite	14	12	1	368	65	33.45	0	2	2	108.55	7	-
JE Duffin	10	9	1	238	81	29.75	0	1	4	112.26	8	-
S Molineux	14	14	2	318	62	26.50	0	2	7	116.48	9	-
EJ Inglis	14	13	2	193	42*	17.54	0	0	4	112.86	4	5
C Atapattu	14	13	2	175	42	15.90	0	0	1	81.77	3	-
HNK Jensen	13	7	3	54	19	13.50	0	0	0	80.59	5	-
CJ Koski	14	12	3	111	33*	12.33	0	0	4	113.26	3	-
KL Britt	9	8	1	68	19	9.71	0	0	0	85.00	3	-
M Brown	14	9	3	56	16*	9.33	0	0	1	103.70	4	-
M Strano	14	3	1	5	3	2.50	0	0	0	38.46	8	-
LMM Tahuhu	13	4	0	7	4	1.75	0	0	0	43.75	2	-
G Wareham	11	3	3	7	5*	-	0	0	0	100.00	0	-

Bowling	M	Overs	Mdns	Runs	Wkts	Avge	Best	Econ	SR	4w	Dot %
M Strano	14	48.1	0	291	14	20.78	3-16	6.04	20.6	0	45
HNK Jensen	13	36	0	218	15	14.53	3-11	6.05	14.4	0	43
LMM Tahuhu	13	43.5	1	278	16	17.37	3-25	6.34	16.4	0	54
G Wareham	11	23	0	146	10	14.60	3-19	6.34	13.8	0	38
M Brown	14	44.4	0	284	15	18.93	3-28	6.35	17.8	0	47
S Molineux	14	23.1	0	148	6	24.66	2-31	6.38	23.1	0	47
AE Satterthwaite	14	35	0	230	11	20.90	2-5	6.57	19.0	0	35
C Atapattu	14	11	0	86	4	21.50	2-6	7.81	16.5	0	32
CJ Koski	14	1	0	13	0	-	-	13.00	-	0	50

MELBOURNE STARS

Batting & Fielding	M	Inn	NO	Runs	HS	Avge	100s	50s	6s	S/Rate	Ct	St
L Lee	12	12	0	349	76	29.08	0	3	17	111.14	4	-
EA Osborne	14	14	6	211	39	26.37	0	0	0	92.54	8	-
M du Preez	12	12	1	269	58	24.45	0	1	1	112.08	5	-
GA Elwiss	10	10	2	184	59*	23.00	0	1	0	93.40	0	-
KM Mack	14	14	1	291	57	22.38	0	1	2	105.43	3	-
M Blows	14	2	0	19	16	19.00	0	0	0	146.15	1	-
A Lanning	14	12	2	174	35	17.40	0	0	1	83.25	2	-
KJ Martin	2	2	1	17	15	17.00	0	0	0	80.95	2	-
A King	14	10	2	112	23	14.00	0	0	3	99.11	2	-
E Kearney	10	4	1	20	11	6.66	0	0	0	105.26	0	-
N Faltum	9	1	0	0	0	0.00	0	0	0	0.00	0	6
A Sutherland	7	3	3	22	13*	-	0	0	0	104.76	3	-
KM Beams	12	2	2	2	2*	-	0	0	0	100.00	4	-
HM Brennan	1	1	1	1	1*	-	0	0	0	50.00	0	-
GL Triscari	7	1	1	0	0*	-	0	0	0	0.00	1	-

Also played: CL Rafferty (2 matches) did not bat.

Bowling	M	Overs	Mdns	Runs	Wkts	Avge	Best	Econ	SR	4w	Dot %
A Sutherland	7	21.1	0	116	9	12.88	4-20	5.48	14.1	1	36
KM Beams	12	46	0	264	4	66.00	1-7	5.73	69.0	0	39
EA Osborne	14	53.3	0	339	15	22.60	4-20	6.33	21.4	1	43
M Blows	14	17	0	112	4	28.00	1-19	6.58	25.5	0	32
A King	14	46	0	345	13	26.53	2-12	7.50	21.2	0	34
GA Elwiss	10	35.3	1	269	7	38.42	2-22	7.57	30.4	0	33
E Kearney	10	31.1	0	266	4	66.50	1-21	8.53	46.7	0	37
GL Triscari	7	11	0	116	3	38.66	1-10	10.54	22.0	0	23

Also bowled: M Du Preez (12 matches) 1-0-6-0, HM Brennan (1 match) 2 -0-36-0

PERTH SCORCHERS

Batting & Fielding	M	Inn	NO	Runs	HS	Avge	100s	50s	6s	S/Rate	Ct	St
P Cleary	15	5	4	43	18*	43.00	0	0	0	97.72	3	-
EJ Villani	16	16	3	535	84*	41.15	0	5	7	125.88	9	-
NR Sciver	16	16	6	339	84	33.90	0	2	3	118.53	13	-
NE Bolton	16	16	1	482	71	32.13	0	3	10	101.47	4	-
LK Ebsary	16	10	4	159	61*	26.50	0	1	3	116.05	6	-
KH Brunt	14	8	1	104	29	14.85	0	0	1	83.87	4	-
H Graham	15	12	2	136	27*	13.60	0	0	1	89.47	4	-
M Carmichael	6	4	1	40	22	13.33	0	0	0	95.23	2	-
TMM Newton	14	8	4	50	16	12.50	0	0	1	96.15	4	-
M Hinkley	5	2	1	11	9	11.00	0	0	0	73.33	3	-
EL King	16	3	1	9	5	4.50	0	0	0	64.28	2	-
M Banting	6	4	0	11	6	2.75	0	0	0	47.82	0	-
C Piparo	2	2	0	2	2	1.00	0	0	0	40.00	0	-
EJ Smith	16	3	1	0	0*	0.00	0	0	0	0.00	2	3

Also played: KJ Hartshorn (1 matches) & T Peschel (2 matches) both did not bat.

Bowling	M	Overs	Mdns	Runs	Wkts	Avge	Best	Econ	SR	4w	Dot %
KH Brunt	14	54	1	261	23	11.34	3-11	4.83	14.0	0	58
EL King	16	56.5	1	341	15	22.73	3-17	6.00	22.7	0	38
P Cleary	15	49	1	300	13	23.07	3-19	6.12	22.6	0	45
NE Bolton	16	36	0	228	8	28.50	2-14	6.33	27.0	0	49
H Graham	15	53.5	1	375	14	26.78	2-20	6.96	23.0	0	37
NR Sciver	16	33	0	257	4	64.25	1-7	7.78	49.5	0	41
T Peschel	2	5	0	46	1	46.00	1-19	9.20	30.0	0	13
TMM Newton	14	14.5	0	140	6	23.33	2-15	9.43	14.8	0	53

Also bowled: KJ Hartshorn (1 match) 4-0-39-0 (21 % dots), EJ Villani (1 match) 2.2-0-14-0.

SYDNEY SIXERS

Batting & Fielding	M	Inn	NO	Runs	HS	Avge	100s	50s	6s	S/Rate	Ct	St
EA Perry	16	16	4	552	91*	46.00	0	3	10	98.57	3	-
A Gardner	14	14	1	347	114	26.69	1	1	21	138.80	4	-
AJ Healy	16	16	0	421	106	26.31	1	2	5	136.68	8	6
EA Burns	16	15	4	285	54*	25.90	0	1	6	118.25	9	-
D van Niekerk	12	11	4	145	44*	20.71	0	0	4	115.07	7	-
AE Jones	4	2	1	19	16*	19.00	0	0	0	76.00	0	-
AR Reakes	15	9	5	60	13*	15.00	0	0	1	120.00	4	-
SJ McGlashan	16	13	3	145	44	14.50	0	0	1	97.97	3	-
LG Smith	16	4	2	26	13*	13.00	0	0	0	123.80	6	-
SE Aley	16	6	2	29	13*	7.25	0	0	0	116.00	0	-
M Kapp	12	7	0	50	14	7.14	0	0	0	76.92	3	-
KJ Garth	14	4	3	3	3*	3.00	0	0	0	37.50	5	-

Also played: SJ Coyte (4 matches) did not bat, 1 catch, J Hicks (5 matches) did not bat, 1 catch.

Bowling	M	Overs	Mdns	Runs	Wkts	Avge	Best	Econ	SR	4w	Dot %
M Kapp	12	48	2	227	12	18.91	2-13	4.72	24.0	0	56
SJ Coyte	4	16	0	81	10	8.10	3-17	5.06	9.6	0	43
D van Niekerk	12	42	0	234	20	11.70	4-13	5.57	12.6	2	46
KJ Garth	14	37	0	217	13	16.69	2-14	5.86	17.0	0	43
SE Aley	16	58.5	3	361	23	15.69	4-18	6.13	15.3	1	45
EA Burns	16	14	0	86	4	21.50	2-26	6.14	21.0	0	33
A Gardner	14	37	0	255	5	51.00	1-9	6.89	44.4	0	47
EA Perry	16	29	0	206	5	41.20	2-15	7.10	34.8	0	51
LG Smith	16	30	0	233	7	33.28	2-32	7.76	25.7	0	31
AR Reakes	15	3	0	30	0	-	-	10.00	-	0	11

SYDNEY THUNDER

Batting & Fielding	M	Inn	NO	Runs	HS	Avge	100s	50s	6s	S/Rate	Ct	St
AJ Blackwell	15	15	4	338	81*	30.72	0	2	1	95.48	4	-
RM Farrell	15	6	4	61	25*	30.50	0	0	1	141.86	4	-
RL Haynes	15	15	1	426	78*	30.42	0	4	7	120.67	4	-
NJ Carey	15	10	5	149	47*	29.80	0	0	2	126.27	6	-
NE Stalenberg	14	10	1	227	48	25.22	0	0	6	112.37	9	-
SR Taylor	15	14	7	168	33*	24.00	0	0	1	84.00	3	-
H Kaur	9	7	2	107	29	21.40	0	0	3	95.53	5	-
RH Priest	15	14	0	264	51	18.85	0	1	7	118.91	4	7
FC Wilson	6	4	1	50	46	16.66	0	0	0	125.00	1	-
L Griffith	6	1	0	2	2	2.00	0	0	0	33.33	3	-
S Bates	14	2	2	7	5*	-	0	0	0	140.00	3	-
ML Gibson	15	2	2	4	2*	-	0	0	0	50.00	2	-

Also played: BW Vakarewa (11 matches) did not bat, 3 catches.

Bowling	M	Overs	Mdns	Runs	Wkts	Avge	Best	Econ	SR	4w	Dot %
BW Vakarewa	11	29	0	165	11	15.00	3-17	5.68	15.8	0	56
S Bates	14	48.4	1	286	16	17.87	3-12	5.87	18.2	0	48
RM Farrell	15	58.4	1	354	17	20.82	3-19	6.03	20.7	0	45
SR Taylor	15	37.4	0	234	15	15.60	4-15	6.21	15.0	1	41
ML Gibson	15	42	0	277	9	30.77	1-12	6.59	28.0	0	37
NJ Carey	15	52.1	0	350	17	20.58	3-10	6.70	18.4	0	38
H Kaur	9	6	0	42	3	14.00	3-18	7.00	12.0	0	44
L Griffith	6	12.1	0	122	0	-	-	10.02	-	0	34
NE Stalenberg	14	1	0	14	0	-	-	14.00	-	0	33

Australian Cricket Digest, 2018-19

WBBL COMPETITION RECORDS

THE FINALS

Season	Batted first	Batted Second	Venue	Player of match
2015-16	Sydney Sixers 7-115	lost to Sydney Thunder 7-116	MCG	Erin Osborne (ST)
2016-17	Sydney Sixers 5-124	def Perth Scorchers 7-117	WACA	Sarah Aley (SS)
2016-17	Perth Scorchers 99	lost to Sydney Sixers 1-100	Adelaide Oval	Sarah Coyte (SS)

WIN/LOSS RECORD OF EACH TEAM

Team	Matches	Won	Lost	NR	Titles	R-up
Adelaide Strikers	41	17	24	0	0	0
Brisbane Heat	43	22	21	0	0	0
Hobart Hurricanes	43	17	26	0	0	0
Melbourne Renegades	42	16	26	0	0	0
Melbourne Stars	42	19	23	0	0	0
Perth Scorchers	47	25	22	0	0	2
Sydney Sixers	48	32	16	0	2	1
Sydney Thunder	44	27	17	0	1	0

LEADING RUN SCORERS

	M	Inn	NO	Runs	HS	Avge	S/Rate	100s	50s	6s
EA Perry	45	45	10	1366	91*	39.03	96.4	0	7	20
BL Mooney	43	43	9	1347	86*	39.62	119.5	0	14	9
EJ Villani	47	47	6	1303	84*	31.78	115.5	0	12	14
AJ Healy	44	44	1	1185	106	27.56	127.0	1	7	16
AJ Blackwell	44	44	14	1134	81*	37.80	101.8	0	3	7
MM Lanning	27	27	6	1062	97*	50.57	116.7	0	10	17
RL Haynes	43	43	1	1031	78*	24.55	105.8	0	5	12
NE Bolton	47	44	6	988	71	26.00	95.0	0	4	11

HUNDREDS (5)

	Balls	4s	6s		Venue	Season
AK Gardner	114	52	9	10	Sixers v Stars	North Sydney	2017-18
AJ Healy	106	66	13	3	Sixers v Strikers	Hurstville Oval	2017-18
SFM Devine	103*	48	10	8	Strikers v Hurricanes	Glenelg Oval	2016-17
GM Harris	103	55	14	4	Heat v Sixers	Aquinas Coll, Perth	2015-16
SW Bates	102	65	15	0	Strikers v Hurricanes	Glenelg Oval	2017-18

HIGHEST TEAM SCORES

Total		Venue	Season
4-242	SS v MS	Nth Syd No 1	2017-18
6-200	ST v MR	Nth Syd No 1	2017-18
3-190	BH v SS	Aquinis Coll, Perth	2015-16
6-189	MR v ST	Nth Syd No 1	2017-18

LOWEST TEAM SCORES

		Venue	Season
66	ST v MS	Syd Showg	2015-16
66	BH v MR	Docklands	2017-18
66	HH v SS	Gabba	2016-17
68	MR v ST	Manuka Oval	2017-18

RECORD PARTNERSHIPS

Wkt				for	v..	Season	venue
1	156	BL Mooney	GM Harris	Heat	Sixers	2015-16	Aquinas Coll, Perth
2	156*	MM Lanning	M du Preez	Stars	Strikers	2015-16	Junction Oval, St Kilda
3	117	SW Bates	SFM Devine	Strikers	Hurricanes	2017-18	Glenelg Oval
4	85*	SFM Devine	TM McGrath	Strikers	Hurricanes	2016-17	Glenelg Oval
5	83*	BL Mooney	DM Kimmince	Heat	Hurricanes	2015-16	Kingston Twin Ovals
6	76*	TT Beaumont	AJ Wellington	Strikers	Heat	2016-17	Gabba
7	83*	NJ Carey	RM Farrell	Thunder	Renegades	2017-18	North Sydney No 1
8	60*	LK Ebsary	PM Cleary	Scorchers	Renegades	2017-18	Camberwell
9	46	AK Gardner	SE Aley	Sixers	Scorchers	2015-16	Aquinas Coll, Perth
10	29	LK Ebsary	AJ Wellington	Strikers	Renegades	2015-16	Adelaide No 2

MILESTONE INNINGS

FASTEST 50S

	Bls		Season	Venue
AK Gardner	22	Sixers v Stars	2017-18	North Sydney Oval No 1
L Lee	22	Stars v Sixers	2017-18	North Sydney Oval No 1
SJ McGlashan	25	Sixers v Heat	2015-16	Aquinas College, Perth
SFM Devine	26	Strikers v Hurricanes	2016-17	Glenelg Oval
NR Sciver	28	Scorchers v Heat	2017-18	North Sydney Oval No 1

Australian Cricket Digest, 2018-19

FASTEST 100S

	Bls		Season	Venue
AK Gardner	47	Sixers v Stars	2017-18	North Sydney Oval No 1
SFM Devine	48	Strikers v Hurricanes	2016-17	Glenelg Oval
GM Harris	53	Heat v Sixers	2015-16	Aquinas College, Perth
AJ Healy	60	Sixers v Strikers	2017-18	Hurstville Oval, Sydney
SW Bates	64	Strikers v Hurricanes	2017-18	Glenelg Oval

LEADING WICKET TAKERS

	M	Overs	Mdns	Runs	Wkts	Avge	Best	4i	5i	Econ
SE Aley	48	165	5	990	70	14.14	4-8	3	0	6.00
RM Farrell	44	169	1	987	54	18.28	4-18	1	0	5.84
MR Strano	42	149.5	3	903	53	17.04	5-15	1	1	6.03
KH Brunt	44	168.3	5	868	49	17.71	4-17	1	0	5.15
NJ Carey	44	151.3	0	959	47	21.04	4-12	1	0	6.53
M Kapp	40	151.5	7	708	42	16.86	4-18	1	0	4.66
AE Satterthwaite	38	112.2	0	717	40	17.92	5-17	1	1	6.38
JL Jonassen	43	153.2	2	854	39	21.90	3-11	0	0	5.57

FIVE WICKETS IN AN INNINGS (3)

			Venue	Season
MR Strano	5-15	Renegades v Stars	MCG	2015-16
AE Satterthwaite	5-17	Hurricanes v Thunder	Bellerive	2016-17
HK Matthews	5-19	Hurricanes v Heat	Bellerive	2016-17

HAT-TRICKS (3)

			Venue
GL Triscari	Stars v Thunder	2015-16	Sydney Showground
AE Satterthwaite	Hurricanes v Thunder	2016-17	Bellerive Oval
D van Niekerk	Sixers v Hurricanes	2017-18	Bellerive Oval, Hobart

BEST ECONOMY IN A FOUR OVER SPELL

			Venue	Season
KM Beams	1-7	Stars v Heat	Harrup Park, Mackay	2017-18
NR Sciver	1-7	Stars v Renegades	MCG	2015-16
RM Farrell	1-8	Thunder v Sixers	Olympic Park Stadium	2015-16
AJ Wellington	2-8	Strikers v Heat	Gabba	2016-17
ML Schutt	3-8	Strikers v Hurricanes	York Park, Launceston	2015-16
M Kapp	1-8	Sixers v Stars	Drummoyne Oval	2015-16

Australian Cricket Digest, 2018-19
FEMALE UNDER 18 CHAMPIONSHIPS – THE BETTY BUTCHER SHIELD
WON BY ACT/NSW COUNTRY, RUNNER-UP NEW SOUTH WALES METRO - HELD IN CANBERRA

Round One – November 27, 2017 (Twenty20 am games)
Victoria 2-71 (11.4 overs) **v Cricket Australia - washed out no result.** Washed out no result: ACT/NSW Country v Queensland, Tasmania v South Australia and Western Australia v NSW Metro

Round Two – November 27, 2017 (Twenty20 pm games)
ACT/NSW Country 6-85 (18 overs) **lost to NSW Metro 4-89** (16.4 overs). **Western Australia 1-149** (18 overs) (C Wain 69, R West 49*) **def Tasmania 4-67** (18 overs). **South Australia 6-86 cc** (E de Broughe 36*) **lost to Victoria 7-87** (19.2 overs) (Z Griffiths 31). **Queensland 7-41** (10 overs) **lost to Cricket Australia XI 3-42** (9.4 overs)

Round Three – November 28, 2017 (Twenty20 am games)
Tasmania 6-79 cc (E Manix-Geeves 34*) **lost to NSW Metro 4-83** (12.3 overs). **South Australia 9-101** (L Awyzio 3-9) **lost Queensland 8-102** (19.4 overs) (JE Doley 32). **Victoria 2-83 cc** (A Sutherland 41*) **def Western Australia 6-81.** ACT/NSW Country 2-141 cc (R Trenaman 64*) **def Cricket Australia XI 5-120 cc**

Round Four – November 28, 2017 (Twenty20 pm games)
Tasmania 5-95 cc (C Webb 60*) **lost to Victoria 0-97** (13.3 overs) (A Sutherland 58*, N Faltum 35*). **Western Australia 41** (16 overs) (N Lynch 3-6) **lost (9.1 overs). ACT/NSW Country 6-136 cc** (T Wilson 64, R Trenaman 34) **def South Australia 102** (18 overs). **NSW Metro 7-104 cc def Cricket Australia XI 6-79 cc**

Round Five – November 30, 2017 (Twenty20 am games)
Victoria 5-90 cc **def NSW Metro 7-90 cc** (K Barry 38; E Quinn 3-16) **in a Superover.** Western Australia 7-79 cc (R West 37) **lost to ACT/NSW Country 1-81** (12.3 overs) (A Handono 42). **Tasmania 9-65 cc** (L Awyzio 4-7) **lost to Queensland 3-67** (12.4 overs). **Cricket Australia XI 8-90 cc lost to South Australia 3-93** (19.1 overs) (E de Broughe 39, R Church 34*)

Round Six – November 30, 2017 (Twenty20 pm games)
South Australia 47 (18 overs) **lost to NSW Metro 1-48** (9.1 overs). **Tasmania 9-72 cc** (A Taylor 4-13, R Trenaman 3-11) **lost to ACT/NSW Country 1-73** (12.2 overs) (T Wilson 30*). **Cricket Australia XI 6-115 cc def Western Australia 85** (19.4 overs) (J Davidson 3-5, including a hat-trick). **Queensland 9-99 cc** (G Voll 41, Z Griffiths 3-14) **lost to Victoria 1-100** (15.3 overs) (A Sutherland 57 no, N Faltum 31).

Round Seven – November 28, 2017 (Twenty 20 games)
Queensland 5-116 cc (C Sippel 45, G Voll 38) **lost to NSW Metro 3-117** (18.1 overs) (A Day 46*). **ACT/NSW Country 5-116 cc** (R Trenaman 41, M Lugg 39) **def Victoria 7-91 cc** (K Beaumont 4-6). **South Australia 6-105** (R Church 34) **def Western Australia 91** (18.3 overs) (K Rowe 3-11). **Tasmania 63** (20 overs) (C Knott 3-4) **lost to Cricket Australia XI 3-64** (11.5 overs) (S Turner 33*)

Twenty20 table: 1. ACT/NSW 11 points, NRR +1.406, 2. NSW Metro 11, +1.299, 3. Vic 11, +0.511, 4. Qld 7, +0.594, 5. CA XI 7, +0.227, 6. SA 5, -0.641, 7. WA 3, -0.714, 8. Tas 1, -0.257

Twenty20 Finals Day – December 1, 2017 (Twenty20)
Grand Final: ACT/NSW Country 3-131 cc (T Wilson 72) **lost to NSW Metro 1-100** (12.1 overs) (M Darke 41 no) **by DLS Method**
3rd v 4th: Queensland 7-121 cc (J Dooley 56) **def Victoria 9-97 cc**
5th v 6th: South Australia 5-128 cc (S Daly 42, R Church 32) **def Cricket Australia XI 7-107 cc**
7th v 8th: Tasmania 2-117 cc (C Webb 53*, E Manix-Geeves 44*) **def Western Australia 4-86** (14 overs) (C Wain 42) **by DLS Method**

Twenty 20 Final Standings: 1. NSW Metro, 2. ACT/NSW Country, 3. Queensland, 4. Victoria, 5. SA, 6. Cricket Australia XI, 7. Tasmania, 8. WA.

50 over competition

Round One – December 3, 2017
Tasmania 7-195 cc (B Davies 56, C Webb 48) **def WA 180** (46 overs) (C Wain 50, G Ireland 33; C Webb 4-24)
Matches abandoned with a ball being bowled: NSW Metro v ACT/NSW Country, SA v Queensland and CA XI v Victoria

Round Two – December 4, 2017 (All no result)
South Australia 2-46 (14 overs) **v NSW Metro, Queensland 5-31** (17.2 overs) **v ACT/NSW Country, Tasmania 2-79** (25 overs) **v Cricket Australia XI 1-19** (3.5 overs), Victoria 1-4 (2 overs) **v Western Australia**

Round Three – December 6, 2017
Tasmania 9-103 (37 overs) (E Manix-Geeves 35) **lost to Victoria 0-105** (16.4 overs) (NM Faltum 47*, A Sutherland 46*). **Queensland 88** (38.4 overs) (I Afaras 3-18) **lost to NSW Metro 5-89** (16.1 overs) (A Day 30*, R Johnston 3-15). **ACT/NSW Country 9-239 cc** (M Lugg 74, T Wilson 71; S Ferris 3-12) **def South Australia 40** (21.4 overs) (E Dalgarno-Fixter 5-13, A Taylor 3-0). **Cricket Australia XI 9-227 cc** (D Chauhan 44, L Cripps 43; E Meuleman 4-24) **def Western Australia 117** (28.3 overs) (J Allen 3-19)

Final Standings: 1. ACT/NSW Country, 2. NSW Metro, 3. Victoria, 4. Cricket Australia XI, 5. Queensland, 6. SA, 7. Tasmania, 8. WA.

Overall Stats

BATTING	M	Runs	Avge	HS	100s	50s	BOWLING	M	Wkts	Avge	Best
Annabel Sutherland (Vic)	11	340	48.57	58*	0	3	Ellie Dalgarno-Fixter				
Courtney Webb (Tas)	11	304	38.00	77	0	3	(ACT/NSW C)	9	15	8.47	5-13
Tahlia Wilson							Charlie Knott (CA)	10	14	9.21	3-4
(ACT/NSW C)	9	284	40.57	72	0	3	Stella Campbell (NSW M)	10	12	13.58	3-17
Rachel Trenaman							Ruth Johnston (Qld)	10	11	7.82	3-15
(ACT/NSW C)	9	212	35.33	64*	0	1	Abbey Taylor				
Chloe Wain (WA)	12	209	23.22	69*	0	2	(ACT/NSW C)	6	11	8.18	4-13

Australian Cricket Digest, 2018-19

UNDER 15 GIRLS IN ADELAIDE – WON BY ACT/NSW COUNTRY, Runners-up South Australia.

Round One - January 17, 2018 (40 overs per side)
ACT/NSW Country 5-214 cc (H Faux 64*, K Burton 60) **def Vic Country 60** (30.3 overs)
Vic Metro 7-198 cc (R Roberts 54, M Gardiner 3-34) **def Western Australia 27** (13 overs) (T Flintoff 4-9, E Hayward 3-2)
Queensland 170 (39.1 overs) (K Holmes 42; J Allen 5-30) **lost to NSW Metro 3-172** (33.4 overs) (H Silver-Holmes 105 off 106, 15x4 2x6)
South Australia 7-225 cc (C Wendland 50*) **def Tasmania 54** (16.3 overs) (S Beazleigh 5-6)

Round Two – January 18, 2018 (40 overs per side) Split innings due to heat, all matches were abandoned with DLS deciding games
NSW Metro 4-85 (20 overs) (A Genford 30) **def Vic Country 3-49** (20 overs) (J Allen 2-11)
Queensland 7-78 (22 overs) (D Baker 3-20) **lost to ACT/NSW Country 1-92** (20 overs) (G Dugnam 43*)
Vic Metro 1-95 (20 overs) (E Hayward 29no J Grant 28) **def Tasmania 6-55** (20 overs) (E Williams 5-28)
South Australia 3-110 (S Beazleigh 56 no) **def Western Australia 68** (18.1 overs) (T Jones 3-20)

Round Three – January 19, 2018 (morning games - 20 overs per side)
NSW Metro 7-173 cc (H Sllver-Holmes 60, A Genford 45) **def Tasmania 4-21** (5 overs) (J Allen 2-5)
Vic Metro 116 (19.5 overs) (A McGregor 4-29, J Anthony 3-25) **def Vic Country 3-39** (9 overs) (K Nainhabo 2-22)
Western Australia 5-64 cc (M Healy 27, J Cavanough 2-6, C Knott 2-8) **lost to Queensland 1-51** (9.1 overs) (E Johnston 27*)
South Australia 68 (18.3 overs) (I Greig 5-9, J Bassett 2-6, H Faux 2-9) **lost to ACT/NSW Country 1-53** (10 overs) (P Litchfield 26*)

Round Four - Afternoon games (Vic M v NSW M, Qld v SA, Tas v ACT/NSW Country and WA v Vic Country) **all abandoned due to heat**

Round Five – January 21, 2018 (20 overs per side)
Queensland 2-140 cc (G Voll 44, C Knott 33*) **def Vic Metro 9-95 cc** (K Aruirajah 30)
Tasmania 6-88 cc (A McGregor 2-16) **lost to Vic Country 3-89** (17.3 overs)
South Australia 7-99 cc (A Genford 4-3) **lost to NSW Metro 4-101** (15.3 overs) (S Vaughan 48*, H Silver-Holmes 35*, S Beazleigh 3-19)
ACT/NSW Country 5-150 cc (P Litchfield 53, H Faux 31) **def Western Australia 40** (19 overs) (H Faux 3-7, G Dignam 2-8)

Round Six – January 21, 2018 afternoon games (20 overs per side)
Tasmania 43 (15.4 overs) (M Mettam 2-19) **lost to Queensland 0-44** (4.4 overs)
Western Australia 7-92 cc (L Thompson 30; J Allen 2-18) **lost to NSW Metro 3-93** (13.1 overs)(K Peterson 36*; S Brown 2-6)
South Australia 8-114 cc (J Field 2-20, R McKenna 2-22) **def Vic Country 90** (19 overs) (T Jones 3-13, S Beazleigh 2-18)
ACT/NSW Country 8-103 cc (P Litchfield 48; K Nainhabo 3-7, E Williams 2-17) **def Vic Metro 7-71 cc** (E Hayward 25, I Greig 2-5)

Round Seven – January 22, 2018 (40 overs per side)
NSW Metro 193 (39.1 overs) (H Silver-Holmes 65, J Errington 32) **lost to ACT/NSW Country 5-194** (36.2 overs) (G Dignam 55, P Litchfield 42)
Queensland 185 (39 overs) (R Strange 45, G Voll 30; G Gall 4-22) **def Vic Country 9-141 cc** (C Mackenzie 32*; R Johnston 3-13)
Western Australia 8-187 cc (M Healy 47, L Thompson 46) **def Tasmania 139** (34.5 overs) (T Jones 3-4)
South Australia 7-138 cc (D Brown 34) **def Vic Metro 121** (35.5 overs) (D Brown 4-21, T Jones 3-25)

TABLE	W	L	Points	NRR
ACT/NSW Country	6	-	15	+2.409
South Australia	4	2	12	+1.824
NSW Metro	5	1	11	+1.091
Queensland	4	2	9	+0.937
Vic Metro	3	3	9	+0.859
Western Australia	1	5	3	-2.609
Vic Country	1	5	2	-1.745
Tasmania	-	6	0	-2.730

Finals Day – January 23, 2018 (40 overs per side)
The Final: South Australia 87 (38 overs) (H Green 6-22) **lost to ACT/NSW Country 1-88** (K Burton 36, G Dignam 30*)
3rd v 4th: Queensland 6-190 cc (G Voll 55, R Johnson 44) **lost to NSW Metro 3-191** (37 overs) (H Silver-Holmes 80*, K Peterson 59*)
5th v 6th: Vic Metro 5-268 cc (T Flintoff 89, E Hayward 84) **def Western Australia 125** (24 overs) (M Healy 40; R Roberts 3-11)
7th v 8th: Tasmania 85 (35.4 overs) (A Christie 4-11) **lost to Vic Country 3-88** (18.5 overs)

Final Standings: 1. ACT/NSW Country, 2. SA, 3. NSW Metro, 4. Qld, 5. Vic Metro, 6. WA, 7. Vic Country, 8. Tasmania

OVERALL STATS

LEADING BATTING	M	Runs	Avge	HS	100s	50s	LEADING BOWLING	M	Wkts	Avge	Best
Hayley Silver-Holmes (NSW M)	7	350	87.50	105	1	3	Tamsin Jones (SA)	7	14	8.07	3-13
Ella Hayward (Vic M)	7	197	32.83	84	0	1	Jade Allen (NSW M)	7	12	14.08	5-30
Phoebe Litchfield (ACT/N)	7	181	45.25	53	0	1	Stephanie Beazleigh (SA)	7	11	6.55	5-6
Grace Dignam (ACT/N)	7	170	42.50	55	0	1	Hannah Green (ACT/N)	7	10	7.40	6-22
Dracie Brown (SA)	7	159	22.71	34	0	0	Arnika McGregor (Vic C)	7	10	11.50	4-29

Australian Cricket Digest, 2018-19

Australian Capital Territory (Bronwyn Calver Medal): Sam Bates (30 votes), then Katie Mack 23 and Dane van Niekerk 19.
New South Wales (Belinda Clark Medal): Won by Ellyse Perry, Runner-up Rachael Haynes, third was Alyssa Healy
WNCL Award: Won by Rachael Haynes, then Ellyse Perry, Alyssa Healy, Alex Blackwell
Sydney Sixers Award: Won by Ellyse Perry, then tied for second was Dane van Niekerk and Alyssa Healy
Sydney Thunder Award: Won by Rachael Haynes, then came Rene Farrell, Nicola Carey, Alex Blackwell.
Queensland Fire Player of the Year: Sammy-Jo Johnson. Fire player of the season: Sammy-Jo Johnson
Brisbane Heat MVP: Beth Mooney
South Australia (Andrea McCauley trophy - WNCL MVP): Sophie Devine. Most Improved: Tabatha Saville.
Adelaide Strikers MVP: Sophie Devine
Tasmania Roar Player of the Year: Georgia Redmayne. Hobart Hurricanes: Hayley Matthews.
Victoria (Sharon Tredrea Medal - WNCL MVP): Kristen Beams. Renegades MVP: Amy Satterthwaite. Stars: Erin Osborne
Western Australia WNCL MVP (Zoe Goss Medalist): – Elyse Villani. Female Rising Star – Taneale Peschel.
Scorchers: Katherine Brunt

ADELAIDE A Grade Final: West Torrens 204 (50 overs) (TM McGrath 45, B Harris 73) **def Northern Districts 161** (42 overs) (SM Betts 63*; EM Falconer 3-18, B Harris 4-33)
T20 Grand Final: Kensington 65 (17.3 overs) (LK Ebsary 4-5) **def West Torrens 4-66** (15.3 overs) (LK Ebsary 4-66)
Karen Rolton Medal: Brooke Harris (West Torrens) on 25 votes, runner-up was Teghan McPharlin (Northern Districts) 24.
Team of the season: Jess Joseph (West Torrens – captain), Eliza Doddridge (Kensington), Brooke Harris (West Torrens), Stacey Oates (Sturt), Tegan McPharlin (Northern Districts), Rachel Church (Kensington), Annie O'Neil (Sturt), Dani Ransley (Sturt), Sarah Lowe (Kensington), Eliza Bartlett (Sturt – wicketkeeper), Neisha Iles (Northern Districts), Stephanie Beazleigh (Northern Districts).
BRISBANE A Grade Final: Western Suburbs 5-284 (50 overs) (JE Dooley 76, HL Ferling 97) **def Sandgate Redcliffe 110** (40.4 overs) (A Sims 4-7, M Dixon 3-19)
T20 Title: Western Suburbs 4-182 (20 overs) (GM Harris 114* - 67 balls) **def Sandgate Redcliffe 83** (18.4 overs) (A Sims 3-22)
Kath Smith Medal: Sammy-Jo Johnson (Gold Coast) 17 votes, Jemma Barsby (Sandgate-Redcliffe) 15
CANBERRA A Grade Final: Tuggeranong 154 (38.2 overs) (AE Wells 3-19, L Woods 3-25) **lost to Western Districts UC 5-155** (32 overs) (Z Cooke 98; V King 4-38). **T20 Title: Western Creek Molonglo 9-81** (20 overs) **lost to Western Districts UC 1-83** (9.2 overs) (Z Cooke 47*). **SJ Moore Medal: Zoe Cooke (Wests/UC) with 23 votes,** fourth win in a row for Cooke, runner-up was Amy Jason-Jones (Eastlake) on 21 votes, third Makayla Clark (Tuggeranong) on 17.
MELBOURNE A Grade Final: Essendon Maribyrnong Park 9-163 (50 overs) (HM Brennan 6-24) **lost to Box Hill 9-166** (49.4 overs) (M Kelly 61).
T20 Title: Melbourne 8-96 (20 overs) (T Norris 3-22) **lost to Essendon Maribyrnong Park 3-97** (13.4 overs) (J Taffs 41)
Una Paisley Medal: Anna Lanning (Box Hill). Team of the Year: Emma Inglis (Prahran, captain, keeper), Amy Vine (Melbourne), Anna Lanning (Box Hill), Jenny Taffs (Essendon Maribyrnong), Kylie Crowley (Melbourne), Annabel Sutherland (Prahran), Molly Strano (Box Hill), Zoe Griffiths (Box Hill), Anna O'Donnell (Melbourne), Hayleigh Brennan (Box Hill), Gemma Triscari (Prahran), Cassie Brock (Box Hill)
HOBART Statewide Final: North Hobart 9-183 (40 overs) (SG Daffara 58) **def South Hobart Sandy Bay 94** (31 overs)
T20 Title: Kingborough 3-128 (20 overs) (E Divin 58) **def South Hobart Sandy Bay 8-102** (20 overs) (I Joyce 50)
Kim Fazackerly Medal: Sterre Kalis (Uni of Tasmania) 18 votes
Team of the Year: Sterre Kalis (Uni), Erin Fazackerley (Clarence), Anita Silva (New Town), Emily Divin (Captain, Kingborough), Olivia McDonald (Clarence), Paris Crowe (Lindisfarne), Emma Thompson (Clarence), Emma Manix-Geeves (New Town), Lauren Hepburn (Kingborough), Johanna Jones (Kingborough), Grace Pullen (North Hobart). Coach: Mark Divin (Kingborough).
PERTH A Grade Final: Melville 8-215 (50 overs) (A Edgar 41) **def Midland Guildford 101** (27.1 overs) (M Carmichael 4-29, RK Chappell 3-18)
T20 Grand Final: Midland Guildford 61 (18.2 overs) (A Edgar 3-0, 6 run outs) **lost to Melville 2-62** (10.2 overs)
Player of the year (Karen Read Medal): Mathilda Carmichael (Melville)
Team of the year: Melissa Cameron (South Perth), Chloe Piparo (Midland Guildford), Megan Banting (Subiaco Floreat), Mathilda Carmichael (Melville), Annelies Gevers (Midland Guildford), Rhiannon Vinkovich (Midland Guildford), Meg Thompson (Melville), Renee Chappell (Melville), Siobhan Spargo (Midland Guildford), Sue Gray (Midland Guildford), Cassie Stephens (Uni), Angela McSwain (Midland Guildford)
SYDNEY First Grade Final: Universities 5-289 (50 overs) (A Day 79, G Redmayne 141*) **def St George Sutherland 152** (39.1 overs) (Q Jalil 3-5). *Georgia Redmayne faced 149 balls, hit 13x4 1x6*
T20 Grand Final: Bankstown Sports 5-118 (20 overs) (R Dick 36) **def St George Sutherland 8-95** (20 overs) (S Devlin 3-15)
Player of the year: Rhiannon Dick (Bankstown) 835, then Joanne Kelly (St George-Sutherland) 714, Laura Wright (Bankstown) 675

RECORDS SECTION
ONE DAY INTERNATIONAL RECORDS - AUSTRALIA V SOUTH AFRICA

	Matches	Australia Won	Sth Africa Won	Tied	No Result
Overall	96	47	45	3	1
In Australia	36	18	17	1	-
Adelaide	1	-	1	-	-
Brisbane	4	2	2	-	-
Canberra	1	1	-	-	-
Hobart	1	1	-	-	-
Melbourne (Docklands)	5	3	1	1	-
MCG	7	1	6	-	-
Perth	6	2	4	-	-
Sydney	11	8	3	-	-

Recent Series

Season	Result	Venue	Notes
2008-09	SA 4-1	Australia	
2008-09	SA 3-2	South Africa	
2011-12	Aus 2-1	South Africa	
2014	SA 2-1	Zimbabwe	Tri-series won by South Africa
2014-15	Aus 4-1	Australia	
2016	1-1	West Indies	Tri-series won by Australia
2016-17	SA 5-0	South Africa	

Leading Run Scorers

	Runs	ODIs	Inn	NO	HS	Avge	SR
RT Ponting (Aus)	1879	48	48	1	164	39.98	83.14
JH Kallis (SA)	1639	47	47	2	104*	36.42	73.63
JM Rhodes (SA)	1610	55	52	12	83*	40.25	77.82
SR Waugh (Aus)	1581	47	44	7	120*	42.73	72.90
WJ Cronje (SA)	1364	39	36	7	112	47.03	72.90
HH Gibbs (SA)	1324	44	44	0	175	30.09	83.64
AB de Villiers (SA)	1250	26	25	4	136*	59.52	99.05
G Kirsten (SA)	1167	39	39	2	112	63.01	63.01

Highest Team Totals

	by	Season	Venue
9-438	SA	2005-06	Wanderers
4-434	Aus	2005-06	Wanderers
6-377	Aus	2006-07	Basseterre
6-372	SA	2016-17	Durban
6-371	Aus	2016-17	Durban

Lowest Team Totals

	By	Season	Venue
69	SA	1993-94	SCG
93	Aus	2005-06	Cape Town
106	SA	2001-02	SCG
123	SA	1994-95	Wellington (Basin)
125	Aus	1997-98	MCG

Highest Scores

		BF	4s	6s	By	Season	Venue
Q de Kock	178	113	16	11	South Africa	2016-17	Centurion
HH Gibbs	175	111	21	7	South Africa	2005-06	Wanderers
DA Warner	173	136	24	-	Australia	2016-17	Cape Town
RT Ponting	164	105	13	9	Australia	2005-06	Wanderers
AB de Villiers	136*	106	11	2	South Africa	2014	Harare
RT Ponting	129	126	15	1	Australia	2001-02	Bloemfontein

Record Partnerships – for Australia v South Africa

Wkt			Season	Venue
1st	170	AC Gilchrist & ML Hayden	2001-02	Durban
2nd	136	DA Warner & UT Khawaja	2016	St Kitts
3rd	175	DM Jones & ME Waugh	1993-94	SCG
4th	222	MG Bevan & ME Waugh	2000	Melbourne (Dock)
5th	124	MG Bevan & MJ Slater	1996-97	Gauhati
6th	121	SPD Smith & MS Wade	2014-15	MCG
7th	123	MEK Hussey & B Lee	2005-06	Brisbane
8th	119	PR Reiffel & SK Warne	1993-94	Port Elizabeth
9th	71	JP Faulkner & MA Starc	2014	Harare
10th	45*	MG Bevan & AC Dale	1996-97	East London

Australian Cricket Digest, 2018-19

Record Partnerships for Australia v South Africa in Australia

Wkt			Season	Venue
1st[t]	118	AJ Finch & DA Warner	2014-15	Canberra
2nd	135	SE Marsh & RT Ponting	2008-09	Hobart
3rd	175	DM Jones & ME Waugh	1993-94	SCG
4th	222	MG Bevan & ME Waugh	2000	Melbourne (Dock)
5th	101	SR Waugh & MG Bevan	1997-98	MCG
6th	121	SPD Smith & MS Wade	2014-15	MCG
7th	123	MEK Hussey & B Lee	2005-06	Brisbane
8th	88*	DS Lehmann & B Lee	2001-02	Perth
9th	57	IJ Harvey & AJ Bichel	1997-98	Perth
10th	16	MR Marsh & JR Hazlewood	2014-15	WACA

Record Partnerships – South Africa v Australia

Wkt			Season	Venue
1st	160	GC Smith & AB de Villiers	2006-07	Basseterre
2nd	187	GC Smith & HH Gibbs	2005-06	Wanderers
3rd	206	F du Plessis & AB de Villiers	2014	Harare
4th	178	RR Rossouw & JP Duminy	2016-17	Cape Town
5th	134	WJ Cronje & JN Rhodes	1997-98	Sydney
6th	119	AB de Villiers & SM Pollock	2005-06	Port Elizabeth
7th	107*	AL Phehlukwayo & DA Miller	2016-17	Durban
8th	71	L Klusener & N Boje	2001-02	Wanderers
9th	61	SM Pollock & J Botha	2005-06	Docklands
10th	46	M Morkel & Imran Tahir	2014-15	WACA

Record Partnerships for South Africa in Australia

Wkt			Season	Versus	Venue
1st	151	KC Wessels & AC Hudson	1991-92	England	MCG
2nd	247	HM Amla & F du Plessis	2014-15	Ireland	Canberra
3rd	144*	HM Amla & AB de Villiers	2008-09	Australia	Adelaide
4th	134	RR Rossouw & AB de Villiers	2014-15	West Indies	SCG
5th	138	JN Rhodes & MV Boucher	2001-02	New Zealand	Perth
6th	97*	JN Rhodes & SM Pollock	2001-02	New Zealand	Perth
7th	56	MV Boucher & JA Morkel	2008-09	Australia	Sydney
8th	56*	SM Pollock & N Boje	2000	Australia	Melbourne (Docks)
9th	61	SM Pollock & J Botha	2005-06	Australia	Docklands
10th	40	PL Symcox & AA Donald	1997-98	Australia	Sydney

Highest Partnerships – Australia v South Africa

	Wkt		Season	Venue
222	4th	MG Bevan & SR Waugh	2000	Melbourne (Docks)
189	4th	SR Waugh & RT Ponting	2001-02	Centurion
183	4th	RT Ponting & DS Lehmann	2001-02	Port Elizabeth

Highest Partnerships – South Africa v Australia

	Wkt	Players	Season	Venue
206	3rd	F du Plessis & AB de Villiers	2014	Harare
187	2nd	GC Smith & HH Gibbs	2005-06	Wanderers
178	4th	RR Rossouw & JP Duminy	2016-17	Cape Town
160	1st	GC Smith & AB de Villiers	2006-07	Basseterre

Leading Wicket takers

Player	ODIs	Balls	Mdns	Runs	Wkts	Ave	Best	Econ	5WM
SK Warne	45	2464	23	1718	60	28.63	4-29	4.18	-
GD McGrath	41	2255	43	1380	58	23.79	4-24	3.67	-
SM Pollock	42	2230	34	1525	55	27.73	5-36	4.10	1
AA Donald	30	1606	10	1169	45	25.98	4-29	4.37	-
DW Steyn	**24**	**1305**	**9**	**1224**	**42**	**29.14**	**4-27**	**5.63**	**-**
B Lee	20	1107	14	946	40	23.65	5-22	5.13	1
M Ntini	24	1293	20	1103	38	29.03	6-22	5.12	1
PR Reiffel	31	1592	24	978	34	28.76	4-13	3.69	-
JH Kallis	47	1721	9	1561	33	47.30	3-30	5.44	-

Australian Cricket Digest, 2018-19

Best Economy Rate (qualification: 10 matches, 12 wickets)

Player	ODIs	Balls	Mdns	Runs	Wkts	Ave	Econ	Best	5WM
EO Simons	11	622	14	356	14	25.43	3.43	2-22	-
CR Matthews	11	599	12	365	24	15.21	3.66	4-10	-
GD McGrath	41	2255	43	1380	58	23.79	3.67	4-24	-
PR Reiffel	31	1592	24	978	34	28.76	3.69	4-13	-
CJ McDermott	14	767	15	478	17	28.12	3.74	3-32	-

Best Bowling

		For	Season	Venue
M Ntini	6-22	South Africa	2005-06	Cape Town
AJ Bichel	5-19	Australia	2001-02	Sydney
M Morkel	5-21	South Africa	2014-15	WACA
N Boje	5-21	South Africa	2001-02	Cape Town
B Lee	5-22	Australia	2005-06	Melbourne (Dock)
L Klusener	5-24	South Africa	1997-98	MCG
JR Hazlewood	5-31	Australia	2014-15	WACA
SM Pollock	5-36	South Africa	1999	Edgbaston
RP Snell	5-40	South Africa	1993-94	MCG
NW Bracken	5-67	Australia	2005-06	Wanderers

Best Economy Rate in a match (min 8 overs)

	Overs	Econ	For	Season	Venue
CR Matthews	4-10	8	1.25	South Africa	1993-94	Durban
TM Moody	1-10	8	1.25	Australia	1997-98	MCG
GD McGrath	2-13	10	1.30	Australia	1999-2000	Cape Town
WJ Cronje	1-14	10	1.40	South Africa	1993-94	Sydney
PR Reiffel	4-13	8	1.63	Australia	1993-94	Sydney

TWENTY 20 RECORDS - AUSTRALIA V SOUTH AFRICA

	Matches	Australia Won	South Africa Won
Overall	17	11	6
In Australia	6	5	1

Matches played in Australia

Venue	Bat first	Bat second	Result	Date	Man of match
Gabba	Aus 3-209	SA 114	Aus 95 runs	9 Jan 2006	DR Martyn (A) 96
MCG	Aus 9-182	SA 130	Aus 52 runs	11 Jan 2009	DA Warner (A) 89
Gabba	SA 5-157	Aus 4-161	Aus 6 wickets	13 Jan 2009	MEK Hussey (A) 53*
Adelaide	Aus 6-144	SA 3-145	SA 7 wkts	5 Nov 2014	RR Rossouw (SA) 78
MCG	SA 7-101	Aus 3-102	Aus 7 wkts	7 Nov 2014	CJ Boyce (A) 2-15
Olympic Stad	SA 6-145	Aus 8-146	Aus 2 wkts	9 Nov 2014	CL White (A) 41*

Highest Scores

		BF	4s	6s	By	Season	Venue
HM Amla	97	62	8	4	South Africa	2015-16	Cape Town
DR Martyn	96	56	7	5	Australia	2005-06	Gabba
GC Smith	89*	58	11	1	South Africa	2005-06	Wanderers
DA Warner	89	43	7	6	Australia	2008-09	MCG
DJ Hussey	88*	44	5	6	Australia	2008-09	Wanderers

Best Bowling

		For	Season	Venue
XJ Doherty	3-20	Australia	2012-13	Colombo RPS
D Wiese	3-21	South Africa	2014-15	Olympic Park
KJ Abbott	3-21	South Africa	2014-15	Adelaide
Imran Tahir	3-21	South Africa	2015-16	Durban

Australian Cricket Digest, 2018-19
TEST RECORDS - AUSTRALIA V INDIA

Season	Host	Matches	Won by		Season	Host	Matches	Won by	
1947-48	Aus	5	Aus	4-0	1996-97	Ind	1	Ind	1-0
1956-57	Ind	3	Aus	2-0	1997-98	Ind	3	Ind	2-1
1959-60	Ind	5	Aus	2-1	1999-00	Aus	3	Aus	3-0
1964-65	Ind	3		1-1	2000-01	Ind	3	Ind	2-1
1967-68	Aus	4	Aus	4-0	2003-04	Aus	4		1-1
1969-70	Ind	5	Aus	3-1	2004-05	Ind	4	Aus	2-1
1977-78	Aus	5	Aus	3-2	2007-08	Aus	4	Aus	2-1
1979-80	Ind	6	Ind	2-0	2008-09	Ind	4	Ind	2-0
1980-81	Aus	3		1-1	2010-11	Ind	2	Ind	2-0
1985-86	Aus	3		0-0	2011-12	Aus	4	Aus	4-0
1986-87	Ind	3		0-0	2012-13	Ind	4	Ind	4-0
1991-92	Aus	5	Aus	4-0	2014-15	Aus	4	Aus	2-0
1991-92	Aus	5	Aus	4-0	2016-17	Ind	4	Ind	2-1

BY AUSTRALIAN VENUES

Venue	Matches	Australia	India	Drawn
Adelaide	11	7	1	3
Brisbane	6	5	0	1
Melbourne	12	8	2	2
Perth	4	3	1	0
Sydney	11	5	1	5
In Australia	**44**	**28**	**5**	**11**

HIGHEST SCORES

for		Season	venue
7-705	Ind	2003-04	Sydney
674	Aus	1947-48	Adelaide
4-659	Aus	2011-12	Sydney
7-657	Ind	2000-01	Kolkata
5-633	Ind	1997-98	Kolkata
7-613	Ind	2008-09	Delhi
7-604	Aus	2011-12	Adelaide
9-603	Ind	2016-17	Ranchi
4-600	Ind	1985-86	Sydney
577	Aus	2008-09	Delhi

LOWEST SCORES

	for	Season	venue
58	Ind	1947-48	Brisbane
67	Ind	1947-48	Melbourne
83	Aus	1980-81	Melbourne
93	Aus	2004-05	Wankhede
98	Ind	1947-48	Brisbane
104	Ind	2004-05	Mumbai
105	Aus	1959-60	Kanpur
105	Ind	2016-17	Pune
107	Aus	1947-48	Sydney
107	Aus	1969-70	Delhi

HIGHEST AND LOWEST TEAM TOTALS AT EACH VENUE

Venue	Highest				Lowest			
	Aust	Series	Ind	Series	Aust	Series	Ind	Series
Adelaide	674	1947-48	526	2007-08	145	1991-92	110	1999-00
Brisbane	8-382	1947-48	409	2003-04	166	1977-78	58	1947-48
Melbourne	8-575	1947-48	465	2014-15	83	1980-81	67	1947-48
Perth	394	1977-78	402	1977-78	212	2007-08	141	1991-92
Sydney	4-659	2011-12	7-705	2003-04	107	1947-48	150	1999-00

BEST INDIVIDUAL SCORES AT EACH VENUE

Venue	Australia	Score	Season	India	Score	Season
Adelaide	RT Ponting	242	2003-04	RS Dravid	233	2003-04
Brisbane	DG Bradman	185	1947-48	SC Ganguly	144	2003-04
				M Vijay	144	2014-15
Melbourne	RT Ponting	257	2003-04	V Sehwag	195	2003-04
Perth	DA Warner	180	2011-12	SM Gavaskar	127	1977-78
Sydney	MJ Clarke	329*	2011-12	SR Tendulkar	241*	2003-04

Australian Cricket Digest, 2018-19

MOST RUNS

	for	M	Inn	NO	HS	Runs	Avge	100s	50s	0s
SR Tendulkar	Ind	39	74	8	241*	3630	55.00	11	16	4
RT Ponting	Aus	29	51	4	257	2555	54.36	8	12	4
VVS Laxman	Ind	29	54	5	281	2434	49.67	6	12	3
RS Dravid	Ind	32	60	6	233	2143	39.69	2	13	3
MJ Clarke	Aus	22	40	2	329*	2049	53.92	7	6	2
ML Hayden	Aus	18	35	3	203	1888	59.00	6	8	2
V Sehwag	Ind	22	43	1	195	1738	41.38	3	9	3
AR Border	Aus	20	35	5	163	1567	52.23	4	9	2
SM Gavaskar	Ind	20	31	1	172	1550	51.67	8	4	2
GR Viswanath	Ind	18	31	2	161*	1538	53.03	4	9	1
SPD Smith	**Aus**	**10**	**20**	**3**	**192**	**1429**	**84.06**	**7**	**3**	**0**
SC Ganguly	Ind	24	44	4	144	1403	35.08	2	7	2
V Kohli	**Ind**	**15**	**27**	**1**	**169**	**1322**	**50.85**	**6**	**3**	**2**
DB Vengsarkar	Ind	24	38	4	164*	1304	38.35	2	7	1
M Vijay	**Ind**	**13**	**24**	**0**	**167**	**1275**	**53.13**	**4**	**6**	**1**
DC Boon	Aus	11	20	3	135	1204	70.82	6	2	0

HIGHEST INDIVIDUAL SCORES

	for		Balls	Mins	4s	6s	Season	venue
MJ Clarke	Aus	329*	468	617	39	1	2011-12	Sydney
VVS Laxman	Ind	281	452	631	44	-	2000-01	Kolkata
RT Ponting	Aus	257	458	590	25	-	2003-04	Melbourne
RT Ponting	Aus	242	352	508	31	-	2003-04	Adelaide
SR Tendulkar	Ind	241*	436	613	33	-	2003-04	Sydney
RS Dravid	Ind	233	446	594	23	1	2003-04	Adelaide
MS Dhoni	Ind	224	265	365	24	6	2012-13	Chennai
JL Langer	Aus	223	355	355	30	-	1999-00	Sydney
RT Ponting	Aus	221	404	516	21	-	2011-12	Adelaide

MOST RUNS IN A SERIES

	for	Series	in	M	Inn	NO	HS	Runs	Avge	100s	50s	0s
SPD Smith	Aus	2013-14	Aus	4	8	2	192	769	128.17	4	2	0
DG Bradman	Aus	1947-48	Aus	5	6	2	201	715	178.75	4	1	0
RT Ponting	Aus	2003-04	Aus	4	8	1	257	706	100.86	2	2	1
V Kohli	Ind	2013-14	Aus	4	8	0	169	692	86.50	4	1	0
MJ Clarke	Aus	2011-12	Aus	4	6	1	329*	626	125.20	2	0	0
RS Dravid	Ind	2003-04	Aus	4	8	3	233	619	123.80	1	3	0
KJ Hughes	Aus	1979-80	Ind	6	12	2	100	594	59.40	1	5	0
DC Boon	Aus	1991-92	Aus	5	9	2	135	556	79.43	3	1	0
ML Hayden	Aus	2000-01	Ind	3	6	1	203	549	109.80	2	2	0
RT Ponting	Aus	2011-12	Aus	4	6	1	221	544	108.80	2	3	0
RB Simpson	Aus	1977-78	Aus	5	10	0	176	539	53.90	2	2	0
AR Border	Aus	1979-80	Ind	6	12	0	162	521	43.42	1	3	0
GR Viswanath	Ind	1979-80	Ind	6	8	1	161*	518	74.00	2	2	0
VVS Laxman	Ind	2000-01	Ind	3	6	0	281	503	83.83	1	3	0

CARRIED BAT IN AN INNINGS

	For	Score	Series	Venue
WM Lawry	Aus	49*	1969-70	Delhi

HUNDRED IN EACH INNINGS

	For	Score	Series	Venue
DG Bradman	Aus	132 & 127*	1947-48	MCG
VS Hazare	Ind	116 & 145	1947-48	Adelaide
DA Warner	Aus	145 & 102	2014-15	Adelaide
V Kohli	Ind	115 & 141	2014-15	Adelaide

Australian Cricket Digest, 2018-19

HIGHEST PARTNERSHIP FOR EACH WICKET

AUSTRALIA

Wkt				Season	venue
1	217	DC Boon	GR Marsh	1985-86	Sydney
2	236	SG Barnes	DG Bradman	1947-48	Adelaide
3	222	AR Border	KJ Hughes	1979-80	Chennai
4	386	RT Ponting	MJ Clarke	2011-12	Adelaide
5	334*	MJ Clarke	MEK Hussey	2011-12	Sydney
6	197	ML Hayden	AC Gilchrist	2000-01	Mumbai
7	173	A Symonds	GB Hogg	2007-08	Sydney
8	117	SM Katich	JN Gillespie	2003-04	Sydney
9	133	SR Waugh	JN Gillespie	2000-01	Kolkata
10	77	AR Border	DR Gilbert	1985-86	Melbourne

INDIA

Wkt				Season	venue
1	289	M Vijay	S Dhawan	2012-13	Mohali
2	370	M Vijay	CA Pujara	2012-13	Hyderabad
3	308	M Vijay	SR Tendulkar	2010-11	Bangalore
4	353	SR Tendulkar	VVS Laxman	2003-04	Sydney
5	376	VVS Laxman	RS Dravid	2000-01	Kolkata
6	298*	DB Vengsarkar	RJ Shastri	1986-87	Mumbai
7	132	VS Hazare	HR Adhikari	1947-48	Adelaide
8	129	SR Tendulkar	Harbhajan Singh	2007-08	Sydney
9	140	MS Dhoni	B Kumar	2012-13	Chennai
10	94	SM Gavaskar	NS Yadav	1985-86	Adelaide

HIGHEST PARTNERSHIP FOR EACH VENUE

ADELAIDE

Australia			Season	Wkt	India			Season
159	PA Jaques	ML Hayden	2007-08	1	95	SM Gavaskar	K Srikkanth	1985-86
236	SG Barnes	DG Bradman	1947-48	2	81	M Vijay	CA Pujara	2014-15
172	RB Simpson	RM Cowper	1967-68	3	185	M Vijay	V Kohli	2014-15
386	RT Ponting	MJ Clarke	2011-12	4	136	GR Viswanath	DB Vengsarkar	1977-78
239	SR Waugh	RT Ponting	1999-00	5	303	RS Dravid	VVS Laxman	2003-04
76	RM Cowper	BN Jarman	1967-68	6	188	VS Hazare	DG Phadkar	1947-48
163	SPD Smith	MJ Clarke	2014-15	7	132	VS Hazare	HR Adhikari	1947-48
83	RT Ponting	JN Gillespie	2003-04	8	107	A Kumble	Harbhajan Singh	2007-08
44	KJ Hughes	RM Hogg	1980-81	9	36	M Prabhakar	SLV Raju	1991-92
47	JR Thomson	IW Callen	1977-78	10	94	SM Gavaskar	NS Yadav	1985-86

BRISBANE

Australia			Season	Wkt	India			Season
116	WM Lawry	IR Redpath	1967-68	1	61	AS Chopra	V Sehwag	2003-04
140	ML Hayden	RT Ponting	2003-04	2	81	SM Gavaskar	M Amarnath	1977-78
106	JL Langer	DR Martyn	2003-04	3	75	DB Vengsarkar	GR Viswanath	1977-78
128*	DR Martyn	SR Waugh	2003-04	4	128	RF Surti	Nawab of Pataudi	1967-68
84	RB Simpson	PM Toohey	1977-78	5	146	SC Ganguly	VVS Laxman	2003-04
49	RB Simpson	AL Mann	1977-78	6	119	ML Jaisimha	CG Borde	1967-68
148	SPD Smith	MG Johnson	2014-15	7	58	N Kapil Dev	M Prabhakar	1991-92
46	KD Walters	JW Gleeson	1967-68	8	60	S Dhawan	UT Yadav	2014-15
56	MA Starc	NM Lyon	2014-15	9	43	SMH Kirmani	BS Bedi	1977-78
51	MA Starc	JR Hazlewood	2014-15	10	33	M Prabhakar	J Srinath	1991-92

MELBOURNE

Australia			Season	Wkt	India			Season
191	RB Simpson	WM Lawry	1967-68	1	165	SM Gavaskar	CPS Chauhan	1980-81
234	ML Hayden	RT Ponting	2003-04	2	137	V Sehwag	RS Dravid	2003-04
169	DG Bradman	AL Hassett	1947-48	3	117	RS Dravid	SR Tendulkar	2011-12
159	RN Harvey	SJE Loxton	1947-48	4	262	V Kohli	AM Rahane	2014-15
223*	AR Morris	DG Bradman	1947-48	5	93	RS Dravid	SC Ganguly	2003-04
144	RT Ponting	AC Gilchrist	1999-00	6	79	RJ Shastri	N Kapil Dev	1985-86
72	BJ Haddin	PM Siddle	2011-12	7	49	Nawab of Pataudi	S Abid Ali	1967-68
					49	GR Viswanath	SMH Kirmani	1980-81
106	SPD Smith	RJ Harris	2014-15	8	74	Nawab of Pataudi	RF Surti	1967-68
59	DW Fleming	B Lee	1999-00	9	77	KS More	SLV Raju	1991-92
77	AR Border	DR Gilbert	1985-86	10	35	KS More	J Srinath	1991-92

Australian Cricket Digest, 2018-19

PERTH

	Australia		Season	Wkt		India		Season
214	EJM Cowan	DA Warner	2011-12	1	82	K Srikkanth	NS Sidhu	1991-92
42	J Dyson	AD Ogilvie	1977-78	2	193	SM Gavaskar	M Amarnath	1977-78
139	AL Mann	AD Ogilvie	1977-78	3	139	RS Dravid	SR Tendulkar	2007-08
173	DM Jones	TM Moody	1991-92	4	39	M Amarnath	DB Vengsarkar	1977-78
101	RB Simpson	SJ Rixon	1977-78	5	84	RS Dravid	V Kohli	2011-12
102	A Symonds	AC Gilchrist	2007-08	6	76	DB Vengsarkar	SMH Kirmani	1977-78
52*	DM Jones	AR Border	1991-92	7	75	VVS Laxman	MS Dhoni	2007-08
47	RB Simpson	WM Clark	1977-78	8	64	S Venkataraghavan	S Madan Lal	1977-78
73	MG Johnson	SR Clark	2007-08	9	81	SR Tendulkar	KS More	1991-92
17	MG Johnson	SW Tait	2007-08	10	32	KS More	J Srinath	1991-92

SYDNEY

	Australia		Season	Wkt		India		Season
217	DC Boon	GR Marsh	1985-86	1	191	SM Gavaskar	K Srikkanth	1985-86
95	MA Taylor	DC Boon	1991-92	2	224	SM Gavaskar	M Amarnath	1985-86
196	SR Watson	SPD Smith	2014-15	3	141	KL Rahul	V Kohli	2014-15
288	RT Ponting	MJ Clarke	2011-12	4	353	SR Tendulkar	VVS Laxman	2003-04
334*	MJ Clarke	MEK Hussey	2011-12	5	196	RJ Shastri	SR Tendulkar	1991-92
95*	RT Ponting	AC Gilchrist	1999-00	6	101	SR Tendulkar	PA Patel	2003-04
173	A Symonds	GB Hogg	2007-08	7	81	SMH Kirmani	KD Ghavri	1977-78
117	SM Katich	JN Gillespie	2003-04	8	129	SR Tendulkar	Harbhajan Singh	2007-08
44	DC Boon	SK Warne	1991-92	9	57	SMH Kirmani	KD Ghavri	1980-81
40	KD Walters	JW Gleeson	1967-68	10	31	SR Tendulkar	I Sharma	2007-08

HIGHEST WINNING MARGINS

BY AN INNINGS

Won	By	Season	venue
Aus	Inn & 226 runs	1947-48	Brisbane
Ind	Inn & 219 runs	1997-98	Kolkata
Aus	Inn & 177 runs	1947-48	Melbourne

BY RUNS

Won	By	Season	venue
Aus	342 runs	2004-05	Nagpur
Aus	337 runs	2007-08	Melbourne
Aus	333 runs	2016-17	Pune
Ind	320 runs	2008-09	Mohali
Aus	300 runs	1991-92	Perth

NARROW WINNING MARGINS

BY RUNS

Won	By	Season	venue
Ind	13 runs	2003-04	Wankhede, Mumbai
Aust	16 runs	1977-78	Brisbane
Aust	38 runs	1991-92	Adelaide
Aust	39 runs	1967-68	Brisbane

BY WICKETS

Won	By	Season	venue
Ind	1 wicket	2010-11	Mohali
Ind	2 wickets	2000-01	Chennai
Ind	2 wickets	1964-65	Mumbai
Aus	2 wickets	1977-78	Perth

MOST WICKETS

	for	Wkts	M	Balls	Mdns	Runs	Avge	Best	5i	10m	SR	Econ
A Kumble	Ind	111	20	6516	180	3366	30.32	8-141	10	2	58.70	3.10
Harbhajan Singh	Ind	95	18	5806	172	2846	29.96	8-84	7	3	61.12	2.94
Kapil Dev	Ind	79	20	4746	198	2003	25.35	8-106	7	0	60.08	2.53
R Ashwin	Ind	71	14	4838	172	2307	32.49	7-103	5	1	68.14	2.86
NM Lyon	Aus	64	14	3664	72	2132	33.31	8-50	5	1	57.25	3.49
Zaheer Khan	Ind	61	19	3857	113	2171	35.59	5-91	3	0	63.23	3.38
EAS Prasanna	Ind	57	13	4331	173	1637	28.72	6-74	5	1	75.98	2.27
BS Bedi	Ind	56	12	4033	176	1395	24.91	7-98	5	1	72.02	2.08
NS Yadav	Ind	55	13	3995	181	1583	28.78	5-99	1	0	72.64	2.38
B Lee	Aus	53	12	3028	93	1695	31.98	5-47	2	0	57.13	3.36
R Benaud	Aus	52	8	2953	198	956	18.38	7-72	5	1	56.79	1.94
GD McGrath	Aus	51	11	2558	157	951	18.65	5-48	2	1	50.16	2.23

Australian Cricket Digest, 2018-19
BEST FIGURES

IN AN INNINGS			Season	venue		BEST FIGURES IN A MATCH			Season	venue
JM Patel	9-69	I	1959-60	Kanpur	H Singh	15-217	I	2000-01	Chennai
NM Lyon	8-50	A	2016-17	Bangaluru	JM Patel	14-124	I	1959-60	Kanpur
H Singh	8-84	I	2000-01	Chennai	A Kumble	13-181	I	2004-05	Chennai
N Kapil Dev	8-106	I	1985-86	Adelaide	H Singh	13-196	I	2000-01	Kolkata
A Kumble	8-141	I	2003-04	Sydney	SNJ O'Keefe	12-70	A	2016-17	Pune
JJ Krejza	8-215	A	2008-09	Nagpur	BS Chandrasekhar	12-104	I	1977-78	MCG
MR Whitney	7-27	A	1991-92	Perth	AK Davidson	12-124	A	1959-60	Kanpur
RR Lindwall	7-38	A	1947-48	Adelaide	BA Reid	12-126	A	1991-92	MCG
RR Lindwall	7-43	A	1956-57	Chennai	G Dymock	12-166	A	1979-80	Kanpur
A Kumble	7-48	I	2004-05	Chennai	R Ashwin	12-198	I	2012-13	Chennai
Ghulam Ahmed	7-49	I	1956-57	Kolkata	A Kumble	12-279	I	2003-04	Sydney

MOST WICKETS IN A SERIES

	for	Series	in	M	Balls	Mdns	Runs	Wkts	Avge	Best	5i	10m
Harbhajan Singh	Ind	2000-01	Ind	3	1071	44	545	32	17.03	8-84	4	2
CJ McDermott	Aus	1991-92	Aus	5	1586	75	670	31	21.61	5-54	3	1
BS Bedi	Ind	1977-78	Aus	5	1759	39	740	31	23.87	5-55	3	1
AK Davidson	Aus	1959-60	Ind	5	1469	85	431	29	14.86	7-93	2	1
R Benaud	Aus	1959-60	Ind	5	1934	146	568	29	19.59	5-43	2	0
R Ashwin	Ind	2012-13	Ind	4	1448	74	583	29	20.10	7-103	4	1
AA Mallett	Aus	1969-70	Ind	5	1792	129	535	28	19.11	6-64	3	1
Kapil Dev	Ind	1979-80	Ind	6	1339	53	625	28	22.32	5-74	2	0
WM Clark	Aus	1977-78	Aus	5	1585	27	701	28	25.04	4-46	0	0
BS Chandrasekhar	Ind	1977-78	Aus	5	1579	24	704	28	25.14	6-52	3	1

WICKET KEEPING-FIELDING
MOST DISMISSALS

KEEPERS	Total	For	M	Ct	St	Byes/Inn		FIELDERS	Total	for	M
AC Gilchrist	75	Aus	18	73	2	2.86		RS Dravid	46	Ind	32
MS Dhoni	71	Ind	19	56	15	4.94		RT Ponting	36	Aus	29
SMH Kirmani	41	Ind	17	29	12	4.00		VVS Laxman	36	Ind	29
BJ Haddin	58	Aus	13	56	2	3.73		MJ Clarke	29	Aus	22
IA Healy	26	Aus	9	26	0	3.50		ME Waugh	29	Aus	14
SJ Rixon	22	Aus	5	22	0	1.33		ML Hayden	23	Aus	18
WP Saha	**20**	**Ind**	**7**	**19**	**1**	**3.93**		SR Tendulkar	23	Ind	39
ATW Grout	20	Aus	5	18	2	6.80		V Sehwag	22	Ind	22
								RB Simpson	21	Aus	11
								MEK Hussey	20	Aus	14

MOST DISMISSALS BY A KEEPER IN A SERIES

For Australia	Total	Ct	St	Series	Venue
AC Gilchrist	25	25	0	2007-08	Australia
BJ Haddin	22	21	1	2014-15	Australia
SJ Rixon	22	22	0	1977-78	Australia
IA Healy	19	19	0	1991-92	Australia
BJ Haddin	18	18	0	2011-12	Australia
For India					
SMH Kirmani	14	11	3	1979-80	Australia
MS Dhoni	14	9	5	2012-13	India
MS Dhoni	14	13	1	2014-15	Australia
WP Saha	**14**	**13**	**1**	**2016-17**	**India**

MOST CATCHES BY A FIELDER IN A SERIES

			M	Series	Venue
RS Dravid	13	Ind	4	2004-05	India
DF Whatmore	12	Aus	5	1979-80	India
ME Waugh	10	Aus	4	1991-92	Australia
RN Harvey	10	Aus	3	1956-57	India
ED Solkar	10	Ind	4	1969-70	India
IM Chappell	10	Aus	5	1969-70	India

Australian Cricket Digest, 2018-19
ONE DAY INTERNATIONAL RECORDS - AUSTRALIA V INDIA

	Matches	Australia Won	India Won	Tied	No Result
Overall	128	73	45	-	10
In Australia	48	35	11	-	2
Adelaide	5	4	1	-	-
Brisbane	7	4	2	-	1
Canberra	1	1	0	-	
Hobart	1	1	0	-	-
MCG	14	9	5	-	-
Perth	4	3	1	-	-
Sydney	16	13	2	-	1

Leading Run Scorers

	ODIs	Inn	NO	HS	Runs	Avge	SR	100s	50s	0s
SR Tendulkar	71	70	1	175	3077	44.59	84.74	9	15	2
RT Ponting	59	59	5	140*	2164	40.07	81.38	6	9	3
AC Gilchrist	46	45	1	111	1622	36.86	99.27	1	12	2
RG Sharma	28	28	4	209	1593	66.38	97.73	6	5	1
ML Hayden	28	28	1	126	1450	53.70	86.05	3	10	2
MS Dhoni	48	41	8	139*	1355	41.06	81.68	2	7	2
DC Boon	29	29	3	111	1212	46.62	68.82	2	7	1
V Kohli	28	26	3	118	1182	51.39	94.71	5	5	2
SR Waugh	53	45	7	81	1117	29.39	72.63	0	7	1
AR Border	38	35	9	105*	1104	42.46	78.13	1	7	2

Highest Scores

	BF	4s	6s	By	Season	Venue
RG Sharma	209	158	12	16	Ind	2013-14	Bangalore
SR Tendulkar	175	141	19	4	Ind	2009-10	Hyderabad
RG Sharma	171*	163	13	7	Ind	2015-16	WACA
GJ Bailey	156	114	13	6	Aust	2013-14	Nagpur
SPD Smith	149	135	11	2	Aus	2015-16	WACA

Highest Team Totals

	by	Season	Venue
6-383	Ind	2013-14	Bangalore
1-362	Ind	2013-14	Jaipur
2-359	Aus	2002-03	Wanderers
5-359	Aus	2013-14	SCG
5-359	Aus	2013-14	Jaipur

Lowest Team Totals

	By	Season	Venue
63	Ind	1980-81	SCG
100	Ind	1999-2000	SCG
101	Aus	1991-92	WACA
125	Ind	2002-03	Centurion
129	Aus	1983	Chelmsford

Record Partnerships – Australia v India

Wkt			Season	Venue
1st	231	AJ Finch & DA Warner	2017-18	Bangalore
2nd	219	ML Hayden & RT Ponting	2000-01	Visakhapatnam
3rd	242	SPD Smith & GJ Bailey	2015-16	WACA
4th	129*	MJ Clarke & CL White	2010-11	Visakhapatnam (ADC)
5th	153	GJ Bailey & GJ Maxwell	2013-14	Ranchi
6th	103	SR Waugh & DS Lehmann	1997-98	Sharjah
7th	102*	SR Waugh & GC Dyer	1986-87	Delhi (Feroz)
8th	49	WB Phillips & RM Hogg	1984-85	MCG
9th	115	JP Faulkner & CJ McKay	2013-14	Bangalore
10th	25	NM Hauritz & BW Hilfenhaus	2009-10	Nagpur (V)

Australian Cricket Digest, 2018-19

Record Partnerships – Australia v India in Australia

Wkt			Season	Venue
1st	187	DA Warner & AJ Finch	2015-16	Canberra
2nd	182	AJ Finch & SPD Smith	2014-15	SCG
3rd	242	SPD Smith & GJ Bailey	2015-16	WACA
4th	122	AC Gilchrist & A Symonds	2003-04	Perth
5th	143	A Symonds & MJ Clarke	2003-04	MCG
6th	85	MR Marsh & MS Wade	2015-16	SCG
7th	80	GJ Maxwell & JP Faulkner	2015-16	MCG
8th	49	WB Phillips & RM Hogg	1984-85	MCG
9th	20	DT Christian & XJ Doherty	2011-12	SCG
10th	20	SR Waugh & SP Davis	1985-86	MCG

Record Partnerships – India v Australia

Wkt			Season	Venue
1st	178	RG Sharma & S Dhawan	2013-14	Nagpur (V)
2nd	212	S Dhawan & V Kohli	2015-16	Canberra
3rd	140	SR Tendulkar & RS Dravid	1998-99	Dhaka
4th	213	VVS Laxman & Yuvraj Singh	2003-04	SCG
5th	167	RG Sharma & MS Dhoni	2013-14	Bangalore
6th	123	S Ramesh & RR Singh	1999-2000	Colombo (SSC)
7th	102	HK Badani & AB Agarkar	2003-04	MCG
8th	84	Harbhajan Singh & P Kumar	2009-10	Baroda
9th	59	Z Khan & Harbhajan Singh	2000-01	Visakhapatnam
10th	41	Z Khan & RP Singh	2007-08	Baroda

Record Partnerships – India in Australia

Wkt			versus	Season	Venue
1st	130	V Sehwag & SR Tendulkar	Zimbabwe	2003-04	Bellerive
2nd	212	S Dhawan & V Kohli	Australia	2015-16	Canberra
3rd	133	VVS Laxman & Yuvraj Singh	Australia	2003-04	Gabba
4th	213	VVS Laxman & Yuvraj Singh	Australia	2003-04	SCG
5th	184*	G Gambhir & MS Dhoni	Sri Lanka	2007-08	Gabba
6th	87*	Kapil Dev & RJ Shastri	New Zealand	1965-86	Gabba
7th	102	HK Badani & AB Agarkar	Australia	2003-04	MCG
8th	53	C Sharma & RMH Binny	New Zealand	1985-86	Lanceston
9th	47	C Sharma & SMH Kirmani	Australia	1985-86	Gabba
10th	35	MM Sharma & Mohammed Shami	England	2014-15	WACA

Highest Partnerships – for Australia v India

	Wkt		Season	Venue
242	3rd	SPD Smith & GJ Bailey	2015-16	WACA
234*	3rd	RT Ponting & DR Martyn	2002-03	Wanderers
231	1st	AJ Finch & DA Warner	2017-18	Bangalore

Highest Partnerships – for India v Australia

	Wkt		Season	Venue
213	4th	VVS Laxman & Yuvraj Singh	2003-04	SCG
212	2nd	S Dhawan & V Kohli	2015-16	Canberra
207	2nd	RG Sharma & V Kohli	2015-16	WACA

Leading Wicket takers

	ODIs	Balls	Mdns	Runs	Wkts	Avge	Best	Econ	5WM
B Lee	32	1543	15	1155	55	21.00	5-27	4.49	4
Kapil Dev	41	2032	47	1246	45	27.69	5-43	3.68	1
MG Johnson	27	1323	11	1121	43	26.07	5-26	5.08	1
SR Waugh	53	1545	6	1270	43	29.53	4-40	4.93	-
AB Agarkar	21	1050	7	1023	36	28.42	6.42	5.85	1
GD McGrath	25	1236	24	910	34	26.76	4-8	4.42	-
J Srinath	29	1489	17	1214	33	36.79	4-30	4.89	-

Australian Cricket Digest, 2018-19

Best Economy Rate (qual: 8 matches, 8 wickets)

Player	ODIs	Balls	Mdns	Runs	Wkts	Avge	Econ	Best	5WM
RM Hogg	8	348	11	196	8	24.50	3.38	3-40	-
SP Davis	14	699	15	403	14	28.79	3.46	3-10	-
Kapil Dev	41	2032	47	1246	45	27.69	3.68	5-43	1
BA Reid	18	996	13	629	21	29.95	3.79	5-53	1
RJ Shastri	31	1448	13	918	27	34.00	3.80	5-15	1
CJ McDermott	22	1199	14	826	30	27.53	4.13	4-56	-

Best Bowling

	For	Season	Venue
6-27 M Kartik	Ind	2007-08	Wankhede
6-39 KH MacLeay	Aus	1983	Trent Bridge
6-42 AB Agarkar	Ind	2003-04	MCG
5-15 GS Chappell	Aus	1980-81	SCG
5-15 RJ Shastri	Ind	1991-92	WACA
5-26 MG Johnson	Aus	2007-08	Baroda

TWENTY 20 RECORDS - AUSTRALIA V INDIA

	Matches	Australia Won	India Won
Overall	15	5	10
In Australia	6	2	4

Matches played in Australia

Venue	Bat first	Bat second	Result	Date	Man of match
MCG	India 74	Aus 1-75	Aus 9 wkts	1 Feb 2008	MJ Clarke (A) 37*
Olympic Park	Aus 4-171	India 6-140	Aus 31 runs	1 Feb 2012	MS Wade (A) 72
MCG	Aus 131	India 2-135	Ind 8 wkts	3 Feb 2012	RA Jadeja (I) 1-16
Adelaide	India 3-188	Aus 151	Ind 37 runs	26 Jan 2016	V Kohli (I) 90*
MCG	India 3-184	Aus 8-157	Ind 27 runs	29 Jan 2016	V Kohli (I) 59*
SCG	Aus 5-197	Ind 3-200	Ind 7 wkts	31 Jan 2016	SR Watson (A) 124*

Highest Scores

		BF	4s	6s	By	Season	Venue
SR Watson	124*	71	10	6	Australia	2015-16	SCG
V Kohli	90	55	9	2	India	2015-16	Adelaide
AJ Finch	89	52	14	1	Australia	2013-14	Rajkot
V Kohli	82*	51	9	2	India	2015-16	Mohali

Best Bowling

	For	Season	Venue
R Ashwin	4-11	India	2013-14	Mirpur
JP Behrendorff	4-21	Aus	2017-18	Gauhati

Australian Cricket Digest, 2018-19
TEST RECORDS - AUSTRALIA V SRI LANKA

Season	Host	Matches	Won by		Season	Host	Matches	Won by	
1982-83	SL	1	Aus	1-0	2003-04	SL	3	Aus	3-0
1987-88	Aus	1	Aus	1-0	2004	Aus	2	Aus	1-0
1989-90	SL	2	Aus	1-0	2007-08	Aus	2	Aus	2-0
1992-93	SL	3	Aus	1-0	2011	SL	3	Aus	1-0
1995-96	Aus	3	Aus	3-0	2012-13	Aus	3	Aus	3-0
1999-2000	Aus	3	SL	1-0	2016	SL	3	SL	3-0

BY AUSTRALIAN VENUES

Venue	Matches	Australia	Sri Lanka	Drawn
Adelaide	1	1	0	0
Brisbane	2	1	0	1
Cairns	1	0	0	1
Darwin	1	1	0	0
Hobart	3	3	0	0
MCG	2	2	0	0
Perth	2	2	0	0
SCG	1	1	0	0
In Australia	**13**	**11**	**0**	**2**

HIGHEST TEAM SCORES

for		Season	venue
5-617	Aus	1995-96	Perth
4-551	Aus	2007-08	Brisbane
8-547	SL	1992-93	Colombo SSC
5-542	Aus	2007-08	Hobart
517	Aus	2004	Cairns
4-514	Aus	1982-83	Kandy
SL	**Best**	**in Aust**	
455	SL	2004	Cairns

LOWEST TEAM SCORES

for		Season	venue
97	SL	2004	Darwin
105	SL	2011	Galle
106	Aus	2016	Galle
117	SL	2016	Pallekele
120	Aus	2003-04	Kandy
153	SL	1987-88	WACA
Aus	**Lowest**	**in Aust**	
201	Aus	2004	Darwin

MOST RUNS

	for	M	Inn	NO	HS	Runs	Avge	100s	50s	0s
MEK Hussey	Aus	8	13	4	142	994	110.44	5	2	0
RT Ponting	Aus	14	23	2	105*	975	46.43	1	7	0
DPMD Jayawardena	SL	16	29	0	105	969	33.41	2	5	2
KC Sangakkara	SL	11	21	1	192	878	43.90	1	7	1
PA de Silva	SL	12	19	2	167	803	47.24	1	6	0
MJ Clarke	Aus	8	12	2	145*	746	74.60	3	5	0
SR Waugh	Aus	8	11	3	170	701	87.63	3	3	0

HIGHEST INDIVIDUAL SCORES

	for	Balls	Mins	4s	6s	Season	venue
MJ Slater	Aus	219	321	460	15	5	1995-96	WACA
KC Sangakkara	SL	192	282	429	27	1	2007-08	Bellerive
BKG Mendis	SL	176	254	319	21	1	2016	Pallekele
SR Waugh	Aus	170	316	421	13	-	1995-96	Adelaide
PA de Silva	SL	167	361	491	17	1	1989-90	Gabba
JL Langer	Aus	166	295	405	13	2	2003-04	Colombo SSC

MOST RUNS IN A SERIES

	for	Series	in	M	Inn	NO	HS	Runs	Avge	100s	50s	0s
MEK Hussey	Aus	2011	SL	3	5	0	142	463	92.60	2	2	0
DS Lehmann	Aus	2003-04	SL	3	6	0	153	375	62.50	2	1	0
SR Waugh	Aus	1995-96	Aus	2	3	2	170	362	362.00	2	1	0
DR Martyn	Aus	2003-04	SL	3	6	0	161	333	55.50	2	0	0
GRJ Matthews	Aus	1992-93	SL	3	6	0	96	329	54.83	0	5	0
DM de Silva	SL	2016	SL	3	6	1	129	325	65.00	1	1	0
Most by SL	**in**	**Australia**										
PA de Silva	SL	1989-90	Aus	2	3	0	167	314	104.67	1	2	0

Australian Cricket Digest, 2018-19
HIGHEST PARTNERSHIP FOR EACH WICKET
AUSTRALIA

Wkt				Season	venue
1	255	ML Hayden	JL Langer	2004	Cairns
2	246	SE Marsh	SPD Smith	2016	Colombo SCC
3	200	AC Gilchrist	DR Martyn	2003-04	Kandy
4	258	SE Marsh	MEK Hussey	2011	Pallekele
5	176	MJ Clarke	MEK Hussey	2011	Colombo SSC
6	260*	DM Jones	SR Waugh	1989-90	Bellerive
7	129	GRJ Matthews	IA Healy	1992-93	Moratuwa
8	107	RT Ponting	JN Gillespie	1999-2000	Kandy
9	47	AC Gilchrist	MS Kasprowicz	2004	Darwin
10	49	IA Healy	MR Whitney	1992-93	Colombo SSC

SRI LANKA

Wkt				Season	venue
1	134	MS Atapattu	ST Jayasuriya	2003-04	Colombo SSC
2	143	MS Atapattu	KC Sangakkara	2007-08	Bellerive
3	125	ST Jayasuriya	S Ranatunga	1995-96	Adelaide
4	230	AP Gurusinha	A Ranatunga	1992-93	Colombo SSC
5	161	TM Dilshan	AD Mathews	2012-13	Bellerive
6	211	LD Chandimal	DM de Silva	2016	Colombo SSC
7	144	PA de Silva	JR Ratnayeke	1989-90	Bellerive
8	73*	LD Chandimal	R Herath	2016	Colombo SSC
9	74	KC Sangakkara	SL Malinga	2007-08	Bellerive
10	79	C Vaas	M Muralitharan	2003-04	Kandy

MOST WICKETS

	for	M	Balls	Mdns	Runs	Wkts	Avge	Best	5i	10m	SR	Econ
R Herath	SL	11	3135	101	1494	66	22.64	7-64	6	1	47.50	2.86
SK Warne	Aus	13	3167	132	1507	59	25.54	5-43	5	2	47.58	2.86
M Muralitharan	SL	12	3789	92	1971	54	36.50	6-59	5	1	70.17	3.12
C Vaas	SL	12	2593	93	1229	38	32.34	5-31	1	-	68.24	2.84
GD McGrath	Aus	8	1828	84	1828	37	22.24	5-37	2	-	49.41	2.70
MA Starc	**Aus**	**5**	**1120**	**39**	**651**	**34**	**19.15**	**6-50**	**4**	**1**	**32.94**	**3.49**
NM Lyon	**Aus**	**9**	**2085**	**59**	**1113**	**31**	**35.90**	**5-34**	**1**	**-**	**67.26**	**3.20**

BEST BOWLING

IN AN INNINGS		Season	venue		BEST FIGURES IN A MATCH		Season	venue
MS Kasprowicz	7-39	A	2004	Darwin	R Herath	13-145	SL	2016	Colombo SSC
R Herath	7-64	SL	2016	Colombo SSC	MA Starc	11-94	A	2016	Galle
R Herath	7-157	SL	2011	Colombo SSC	Muralitharan	11-212	SL	2003-04	Galle
MA Starc	6-50	A	2016	Galle	MDK Perera	10-99	SL	2016	Galle
M Muralitharan	6-59	SL	2003-04	Galle	SK Warne	10-155	A	2003-04	Kandy
RJ Ratnayake	6-66	SL	1989-90	Bellerive	SK Warne	10-159	A	2003-04	Galle

MOST WICKETS IN A SERIES

	for	Series	in	M	Balls	Mdns	Runs	Wkts	Avge	Best	5i	10m
R Herath	SL	2016	SL	3	870	41	357	28	12.75	7-64	3	1
M Muralitharan	SL	2003-04	SL	3	1255	37	649	28	23.18	6-59	4	1
SK Warne	Aus	2003-04	SL	3	1008	37	521	26	20.04	5-43	4	2
MA Starc	Aus	2016	SL	3	620	28	364	24	15.17	6-50	3	1
GD McGrath	Aus	1995-96	Aus	3	929	35	438	21	20.86	5-40	1	-
CPH Ramanayake	SL	1992-93	SL	3	874	28	434	17	25.53	5-82	1	-

Best series bowling by a Sri Lanka in Australia

UDU Chandana	SL	2004	Aus	2	370	4	270	12	22.50	5-101	2	1
R Herath	SL	2012-13	Aus	3	808	16	407	12	33.92	5-95	1	-

WICKET KEEPING/FIELDING - MOST DISMISSALS

KEEPERS	For	M	Ct	St	Total	Byes/Inn	FIELDERS	M	Total	for
AC Gilchrist	Aus	7	32	5	37	2.79	DPMD Jayawardene	16	20	SL
IA Healy	Aus	11	32	2	34	3.32	RT Ponting	14	16	Aus
KC Sangakkara	SL	5	20	4	24	7.69	SK Warne	13	15	Aus

OBITUARIES

Cec AUSTEN died on October 29, 2017 one day short of his 99th birthday. Cec played one first-class match (2 & 2/0-77) for South Australia in 1945-46. He played Aussie rules football for Hawthorn in 1942 and later at Sturt in 1944 to 1946. Born in Kew, Melbourne, Cec played two seasons for Collingwood CC, taking 52 wickets at 16.90. Austen served as a pilot in the RAAF during World War II.

Tony BENNEWORTH died suddenly in a fishing accident in Anson's Bay on March 10, 2018, aged 68. Launceston born Benneworth was an all-rounder who played 15 first-class matches and 10 List A matches between 1971-72 and 1981-82. He also played in Tasmania's first ever Sheffield Shield match in 1977-78 but perhaps his most important contribution came when he took 3-14 off 8.2 overs in the 1978-79 Gillette Cup Final versus Western Australia, which was Tasmania's first ever domestic title. Later on he was the Federal Liberal candidate for Bass in the 2001 election and was also a Cricket Tasmania Board Director. He was also well known as an expert radio commentator for the ABC.

At the time of his death he was fondly remembered at Lancashire League club Lowerhouse, where he played in 1973 as an Amateur and in 1974 as the club's Professional, where he led the competition batting aggregate. He received the Order of Australia Medal for service to sporting organisations in 2014. Former Australian selector and Tasmanian batsman Jamie Cox was one of many who paid tribute to Benneworth at the time of his death.

Peter DAVIES died after a long battle with cancer on March 10, 2018 aged 60. Davies was a left-handed batsman who played six first-class matches for Victoria across the 1981-82 and 1982-83 seasons. He averaged 21.81 with his best score of 57 coming against South Australia at the Adelaide Oval in 1981-82. An accomplished lawyer, Davies was a prolific run getter in Victorian first grade cricket, scoring 8,088 runs at 33.84 (14 hundreds) in 21 seasons for Waverley and Richmond.

Alec DICK died on January 31, 2018 aged 95, and played once for Western Australia as a right-arm fast-medium bowler in 1948-49. He played at South Perth CC, making 4,660 runs, taking 221 wickets and was named in the clubs "Home grown" Champion team to celebrate the clubs 75th anniversary in 2004-05. His brother Ian was captain of the Australian field hockey team at Melbourne Olympics in 1956.

Dick GUY who died on May 16, 2018 aged 81, played eight first-class matches for New South Wales and was also an Australian and New South Wales selector. Starting 1960-61, he took 25 wickets with his leg-breaks, playing his last game for NSW in 1968-69. He had a magnificent 18 seasons with the Gordon club in Sydney, where he took 786 first grade wickets at 16.44 between 1957-58 and 1974-75. Guy took 50 wickets in a grade season seven times, his best season was in 1967-68, when he took 71 wickets and was named *The Daily Telegraph* First Grade player of the year.

After his playing career, Guy turned to the role of selector. He joined the NSW panel in 1972-73, was chairman from 1979-80, before finishing up in 1987-88. He was also an Australian selector for a period of time, which included the picking of little known off-spinner Peter Taylor, who took 6-78 on debut against England in the 1986-87 Ashes series.

Guy was also on the NSW Cricket board for seven years and the Australian Cricket Board for six years. He was elected Life Member of the NSW Cricket Association in 1981 and was awarded life membership at Gordon Cricket Club in 1969, also being Club President for five years.

Leon HILL who died aged 81 on January 22, 2018, represented both South Australia and Queensland in first-class cricket between 1958-59 and 1962-63. A product of the Adelaide Cricket Club, Hill played for SA between 1958-59 and 1960-61, before moving to Queensland where he played two matches in the 1962-63 season. Hill in all played 17 – first class matches, making 584 runs at 18.83 with one first-class century, an even 100 for SA versus Victoria on the Adelaide Oval in 1959-60. Hill was also a passionate golfer, as a member at the Metropolitan Golf Club in Melbourne, one death notice in *The Age* saying *"His escapades will keep the WAGs at Metropolitan Golf Club comparing notes for years to come."*

Brian ILLMAN died on August 4, 2018, played six first-class games, taking 11 wickets at 48 as a right-arm pace bowler for South Australia in the 1960-61 season. He was a life member of the Glenelg Cricket Club, where he took 291 first grade wickets at 20.13, and captained the A Grade to its 1973-74 Premiership win, filling in as skipper for Ian Chappell who was on the Australian Test tour to New Zealand at the time.

Robert George "Bob" HOLLAND died on September 17, 2017 aged 70, of brain cancer. Holland was a fine leg-spin bowler who played 11 Test matches for Australia, debuting at the age of 38 in the mid-1980s, taking 34 wickets at 39.76. He debuted in first-class cricket at the age of 32 and took 316 wickets in 95 matches at 31.19, including best figures of 9-83 for New South Wales versus South Australia at the SCG in 1984-85.

Of Holland's 11 Tests, he played a crucial part in three memorable victories for Australia. The first was against the West Indies at the SCG, when Holland took 6-54 and 4-90, as Australia won fifth Test of the series by an innings. The second was at Lord's in 1985, when he took 5-68 in the second innings, to help Australia to a four wicket win, its only victory of that series. The third came against New Zealand at the SCG in 1985-86, when he took 6-106 and 4-68, with Australia pulling off a daring run chase on the final day to win by four wickets.

Sadly after just two more Tests, Holland's Test career was over, India's Kris Srikkanth gave him a mauling on the opening day of the third Test at the SCG in January 1986, the leg-spinner taking 1-113 off 21 expensive overs.

Holland was an important member of the New South Wales side which won Sheffield Shield titles in the mid 1980's. While they were successful seasons for him with the ball, he needed to make contributions with the bat to enable the Blues to raise the trophy. In the 1984-85 final at the SCG, he scored 10 in the second innings, helping Peter Clifford add 34 for the ninth wicket as New South Wales chased down 223 with a wicket in hand. In next season's final at the SCG, he helped deny Queensland again, being unbeaten without scoring for 34 minutes to hold out Queensland for a draw.

For over 50 years he was associated with the Southern Lakes District Cricket Club on the northern coast of New South Wales. A tribute night was held by the club just a couple of days before he died, compered by former Australian skipper Mark Taylor.

Jack LAVER who died on October 3, 2017 at the age of 100, was a handy right-handed batsman and off-break bowler. It is believed he is the only Tasmanian cricketer to reach the milestone. Laver played 13 first-class matches for Tasmania and Tasmania Combined between 1946-47 and 1951-52. His highest score of 93 came on debut for Tasmania against Victoria at the TCA Ground, Hobart in 1946-47. His career best with the ball came in his second match, when he took 5-26 against MCC in the same season. He also captained West Launceston, Longford and the Northern Tasmania Cricket Association, later becoming a northern Tasmanian delegate on the Tasmanian Cricket Executive and was also a state selector. His uncle was Frank Laver, who played 15 Tests for Australia between 1899 and 1909.

Jeff KOWALICK died on February 28, 2018 aged 71. Jeff played one Sheffield Shield match for South Australia versus Western Australia in 1966-67, where Colin Milburn made 129, Kowalick bowling him, in what was his only wicket. Kowalick played 128 A grade matches for Sturt between 1968 and 1980 in Adelaide Grade cricket, taking 292 wickets at 20.46 and was later awarded life membership. He was also club coach of Adelaide University.

Keith SCHMIDT who died on October 4, 2017, aged 95, played 16 first-class matches for Tasmania and Tasmania Combined between 1949-50 and 1960-61. He made 551 runs at 19.00 with two half centuries and took 19 wickets at 44.78 with his leg-spinners. His career best of 59 came versus South Australia at Adelaide Oval in 1960-61. His best bowling of 4-34 was against Victoria at the NTCA ground in Launceston in 1950-51, one of his victims was a future Australian Test opener named Colin McDonald. Schmidt also played 217 first grade games for Kingborough, scoring 7,096 runs at 31.12 (including eight hundreds) and took 487 wickets at 16.91 being named in the club's team of the century in 2001.

John SHAW who died on August 5, 2018 aged 76, was a right-handed batsman and fine close to the wicket fielder, who played for Victoria between 1953-54 and 1960-61. In his 55 first-class matches he made 3,276 runs at 40.44 with four centuries, including a career best of 167 *(Wisden 1959 noted "Strong on the pull")*, against New South Wales at the SCG in 1957-58. In the 1959-60 season he toured New Zealand with an Australian team captained by Ian Craig, playing in all four "unofficial" Tests, making 203 runs at 29. His top score of 81 came at Christchurch, where he and Len Maddocks (49) added 106 for the sixth wicket in 2¼ hours to prevent the Australians from following-on in the second "Test" of the four played.

John was born in Geelong and played for 156 first-grade games for South Melbourne (now Casey-South Melbourne) in the VCA competition, scoring 5,434 runs at 37.47 with six hundreds between 1949-50 and 1967-68. He was a member of Premiership teams in 1952-53 and 1967-68 and topped the VCA batting averages in 1952-53 (538 runs at 59.77) and 1955-56 (458 at 76.33). As *Wisden* Obituary writer Warwick Franks passed onto me by email "He was Lindsay Hassett's nephew, looking and playing like his famous uncle. He never quite made his elegant runs at a time when he could have caught the selectors' bleary eyes and being sconed at the SCG by Pat Crawford did him no favours."

Noel SHAW died on December 10, 2017, aged 80. Noel was a right-arm pace bowler who played one Sheffield Shield game for Victoria in 1957-58 and was also named in the Collingwood (now Camberwell Magpies) team of the century. His one game was against Western Australia at the WACA, he made three and took 0-38 and 3-23, including the wicket of John Rutherford. Shaw took 244 first-grade wickets for Collingwood at 17.03, with best figures of 9-25.

Neil SMYTH who kept wicket for Victoria in three Sheffield Shield matches between 1951-52 and 1953-54, died on August 14, 2017, aged 89. Smith started his VCA cricket career with Melbourne in 1947-48, before moving to Prahran in 1951-52, where he ended up playing until 1960-61. In a 14 season club career, he took 273 dismissals (221 catches/52 stumpings) and was a member of Prahran's 1954-55 Premiership team.

Australian Cricket Digest, 2018-19
STATE SQUADS, 2018-19
NEW SOUTH WALES
Coach: Phil Jacques (replaces Trent Johnston)

	No.	DOB	Place		
Sean Abbott	77	29/2/92	Windsor, NSW	RHB	RFM
Nick Bertus		24/7/93		LHB	
Harry Conway	5	17/9/92	Darlinghurst, Sydney	RHB	RFM
Trent Copeland	9	14/3/86	Gosford, NSW	RHB	RM
Patrick Cummins *	30	5/8/93	Westmead, Sydney	RHB	RF
Ben Dwarshuis	14	23/6/94	Woronora Heights, Sydney	RHB	LFM
Mickey Edwards	15	23/12/94	Sydney, NSW	RHB	RFM
Dan Fallins	42	12/8/96	Kograrah, NSW	RHB	LEG
Ryan Gibson	93	30/12/93	Penrith, NSW	RHB	RM
Josh Hazlewood *	8	8/1/91	Tamworth, NSW	RHB	RFM
Moises Henriques	21	1/2/87	Funchal, Portugal	RHB	RFM
Liam Hatcher	7	17/9/96	Liverpool, NSW	RHB	RFM
Daniel Hughes	3	2/7/79	Bathurst, NSW	LHB	RFM
Nick Larkin	36	1/5/90	Taree, NSW	RHB	
Nathan Lyon *	67	20/11/87	Young, NSW	RHB	ROB
Arjun Nair	12	12/4/98	Canberra, ACT	RHB	ROB
Peter Nevill	20	13/10/85	Hawthorn, Melbourne	RHB	WK
Stephen O'Keefe	72	9/10/84	Malaysia	RHB	SLA
Kurtis Patterson	17	5/5/93	Hurstville, NSW	LHB	RM
Jason Sangha	23	8/9/99	Randwick, Sydney	RHB	LEG
Mitchell Starc *	56	30/1/90	Baulkham Hills, Sydney	LHB	LF
Charlie Stobo	25	8/3/95	Sydney	RHB	RFM
Henry Thornton	6	16/12/96	Kogarah, NSW	RHB	RFM
Param Uppal	10	26/10/98	Chandigrah, India	RHB	ROS
Rookies					
Jack Edwards	18	19/4/00	Allambie Heights, NSW	RHB	RFM
Jordan Gauci		27/6/98	Blackwood, NSW	RHB	SLA
Ryan Hackney		15/7/99	Faulconbridge, NSW	LHB	SLA
Ryan Hadley		17/11/98	Blacktown, NSW	RHB	RFM
Baxter Holt		21/10/99	Carlingford, NSW	RHB	WK
Chad Sammut	31	11/9/98	Fairfield, NSW	LHB	LFM

*CA Contract

In – **Mickey Edwards (Rookie), Daniel Fallins, Liam Hatcher (Rookie), Jason Sangha (Rookie), Param Uppal (Rookie).**

Off Contract list for 2018-19

Doug Bollinger	4	24/7/81	Baulkham Hills, Sydney	LHB	LFM
Ed Cowan	27	16/6/82	Paddington, Sydney	LHB	
Jay Lenton	70	10/8/90	Belmont, NSW	LHB	WK
Nic Maddinson	53	21/12/91	Nowra, NSW	LHB	SLA
Gurinder Sandhu	11	15/6/93	Blacktown, Sydney	LHB	RFM
Steven Smith	49	2/6/89	Sydney, NSW	RHB	LEG
Will Somerville	28	9/8/84	Wadestown, Wellington, NZ	RHB	ROB
David Warner	31	27/10/86	Paddington, Sydney	LHB	LEG

2017-18 Award Winners
Steve Waugh Medalist won by Daniel Hughes, 2. Trent Copeland, 3. Nic Maddinson, 4. Mitchell Starc
Sheffield Shield Award won by Trent Copeland, 2. Stephen O'Keefe, equal 3. Dan Hughes, Mitchell Starc
JLT Cup Award won by Nic Maddinson, 2. Dan Hughes, 3. Mitchell Starc, 4. Doug Bollinger

Australian Cricket Digest, 2018-19
QUEENSLAND
Coach – Wade Seccombe

	No.	DOB	Place		
Xavier Bartlett		17/12/98	Adelaide, SA	RHB	RFM
Joe Burns	15	6/9/89	Herston, Brisbane	RHB	ROS
Brendan Doggett	35	3/5/94	Rockhampton, Qld	RHB	RFM
Luke Feldman	58	1/8/84	Sunnybank, Qld	RHB	RFM
Jason Floros	52	24/11/90	Canberra	LHB	ROS
Cameron Gannon	21	23/1/89	Baulkham Hills, Sydney	RHB	RFM
Peter George	14	16/10/86	Woodville, Adelaide	RHB	RFM
Sam Heazlett	47	12/9/95	Sunnybank, Qld	LHB	SLA
Charlie Hemphrey	44	31/8/89	Doncaster, Yorkshire	RHB	ROS
Usman Khawaja *	4	18/12/86	Islamabad, Pakistan	LHB	
Marnus Labuschagne	9	22/6/94	Klerksdorp, South Africa	RHB	RM
Michael Neser	20	29/3/90	Pretoria, South Africa	RHB	RFM
Jimmy Peirson	59	13/10/92	Sydney	RHB	WK
Lachlan Pfeffer	33	8/4/91	Beaudesert, Qld	LHB	WK
Jack Prestwidge		28/2/96	Brisbane	RHB	RFM
Matthew Renshaw *	94	28/3/96	Middlesborough, UK	LHB	ROS
Billy Stanlake *	64	4/11/94	Hervey Bay, Qld	RHB	RFM
Mark Steketee	16	17/1/94	Monto, Qld	RHB	RFM
Mitch Swepson	22	4/10/93	Brisbane	RHB	LEG
Sam Truloff	25	24/3/93	Marburg, Qld	RHB	LEG
Jack Wildermuth	24	1/9/93	Toowoomba, Qld	RHB	RMF
Rookies					
Max Bryant		10/3/99	Murwillumbah, NSW	RHB	RM
Blake Edwards		26/10/99		RHB	RFM
Matthew Kuhnemann		20/9/96	Brisbane	LHB	SLA
Nathan McSweeney		8/3/99	Brisbane	RHB	ROS
Bryce Street		25/1/98	Gosford, NSW	LHB	RM
Connor Sully		24/10/00		RHB	RFM

*CA Contract

In – Xavier Bartlett and Jack Prestwidge (both upgraded from Rookie list)
New Rookies – Nathan McSweeney, Blake Edwards, Connor Sully
Off Contract list for 2018-19

James Bazley		8/4/95	Buderim, Qld	RHB	RM
Ben Cutting	31	30/1/87	Sunnybank, Brisbane	RHB	RFM
Peter Forrest	66	15/11/85	Windsor, NSW	RHB	
Harry Wood		27/12/98		RHB	

2017-18 Award Winners
Ian Healy Medalist (Bulls player of the season) – Michael Neser
Sheffield Shield players of the season – Brendan Doggett
JLT Cup player of the season – Usman Khawaja. Bulls Players' player award: Peter Forrest

SOUTH AUSTRALIA
Coach – Jamie Siddons

	No.	DOB	Place		
Tom Andrews	29	7/10/94	Darwin, NT	LHB	SLA
Alex Carey *	5	27/8/91	Loxton, SA	LHB	WK
Tom Cooper	26	26/11/86	Woollongong, NSW	RHB	ROS
John Dalton	7	9/6/96	Adelaide, SA	RHB	RM
Callum Ferguson	12	21/11/84	North Adelaide	RHB	RM
David Grant	14	24/5/97	North Adelaide	RHB	RFM
Travis Head © *	34	29/12/93	Adelaide, SA	LHB	ROS
Jake Lehmann	33	8/7/92	Adelaide, SA	LHB	SLA
Conor McInerney	39	30/3/94	Woodville South, SA	LHB	SLA
Joe Mennie	15	24/12/88	Coffs Harbour, NSW	RHB	RFM
Harry Nielsen	4	3/5/95	Adelaide, SA	LHB	WK
Elliot Opie	13	16/4/91	Melbourne, SA	RHB	RFM
Patrick Page	37	15/1/98	Wallaroo, SA	LHB	RM
Kane Richardson *	55	12/2/91	Eudunda, SA	RHB	RFM
Luke Robins	11	18/5/94	Snowtown, SA	RHB	RFM
Alex Ross	49	17/4/92	Melbourne	RHB	ROS
Chadd Sayers	27	31/8/87	Adelaide, SA	RHB	RMF
Kelvin Smith	19	5/9/94	Bow Hill, SA	LHB	ROS
Cameron Valente	3	6/9/94	Adelaide, SA	RHB	RFM
Jake Weatherald	28	4/11/94	Darwin, NT	LHB	LEG
Nick Winter	44	19/6/93	Garran, ACT	LHB	LFM
Daniel Worrall	1	10/7/91	Melbourne, Vic	RHB	RFM
Adam Zampa	63	31/3/92	Shellharbour, NSW	RHB	LEG
Rookies					
Michael Cormack	17	29/6/97	North Adelaide	RHB	ROS
Spencer Johnson	21	16/12/95	Adelaide	LHB	LFM
Ben Pengelley	2	16/2/98	Yulara, NT	LHB	LMF
Lloyd Pope	24	1/12/99	Adelaide	RHB	LEG
Jake Winter	10	2/6/97	Glenelg, Adelaide	RHB	ROS

*CA Contract

In – Connor McInerney, Elliot Opie, Luke Robins

Off Contract list for 2018-19

Nick Benton	30	29/6/91	Ashford, Adelaide	RHB	RMF
Daniel Drew	11	22/5/96	Grange, Adelaide	RHB	RM

2017-18 Award Winners
Neil Dansie (MVP) Medalist – Joe Mennie (140 votes)
Lord Hampton (Shield) Trophy: Nick Winter
JLT Cup Award: Joe Mennie
Barry Jarman award (Most improved): Nick Winter
Barry "Nuggett" Rees award: Harry Nielsen

TASMANIA
Coach: Adam Griffith

	No.	DOB	Place		
George Bailey	10	7/9/82	Launceston	RHB	
Gabe Bell	5	3/7/95	Trevallyn, Tas	RHB	RFM
Jackson Bird	22	11/12/86	Sydney	RHB	RFM
Nick Buchanan		3/4/91	Sunnybank, Qld	RHB	RFM
Alex Doolan	64	29/11/85	Launceston, Tasmania	RHB	WK
Jake Doran	2	2/10/96	Blacktown, NSW	LHB	WK
James Faulkner	25	29/4/90	Launceston, Tasmania	RHB	LFM
Caleb Jewell		21/4/97	Hobart, Tas	LHB	
Hamish Kingston	29	17/12/90	Hobart, Tas	RHB	RMF
Ben McDermott	28	12/12/94	Caboolture, Qld	RHB	RM
Riley Meredith	12	21/6/96	Bellerive, Tas	LHB	RFM
Simon Milenko	15	24/11/88	Sydney	RHB	RMF
Tim Paine *	36	8/12/84	Hobart, Tas	RHB	WK
Sam Rainbird	43	5/6/92	Hobart, Tas	RHB	LMF
Tom Rogers	6	3/3/94	Bruce, ACR	RHB	RFM
Gurinder Sandhu	11	14/6/93	Blacktown, Sydney	LHB	RFM
Jordan Silk	21	18/1/91	Penrith, NSW	RHB	
Matthew Wade	31	26/10/87	Hobart	LHB	WK
Charlie Wakim	9	9/7/91	Paddington, NSW	RHB	RM
Beau Webster	20	1/12/93	Snug, Hobart	RHB	ROB
Rookies					
Liam Devlin		21/11/98		LHB	LEG
Jarrod Freeman		15/7/00	Launceston, Tas	RHB	ROB
Aaron Summers		24/3/96		RHB	RFM
Lawrence Neil-Smith		1/6/99	NSW	RHB	RMF
Jack White		8/7/99	Hobart	LHB	SLA
Mac Wright		22/1/98	Ferntree Gully, Vic	RHB	LEG

*CA Contract. Jackson Bird and Matthew Wade went off CA contracts.
In: Hamish Kingston returns having not been on contract in 2017-18, Caleb Jewell (Rookie),
Gurinder Sandhu (NSW). New Rookies – Jarrod Freeman, Lawrence Neil-Smith (NSW), Jack White.
Off Contract list for 2018-19

Cameron Boyce	13	27/7/89	Charleville	RHB	LEG
Ben Dunk	51	11/3/87	Innisfail, Qld	LHB	WK
Andrew Fekete	17	18/5/85	Melbourne	RHB	RFM
Jake Hancock		29/11/91	Williamstown, Vic	RHB	
Corey Murfet		21/1/97		LHB	RM
Andrew Perrin		23/6/90		RHB	RFM
Cameron Stevenson	3	30/10/92		RHB	RFM

2017-18 Award Winners
Ricky Ponting Medalist –George Bailey 223 votes, Jake Doran 197, Jackson Bird 194, Jordan Silk 179
David Boon Medalist (Sheffield Shield) – Jake Doran 197 votes, Jackson Bird 185, Tom Rogers 140,
Matthew Wade 140
Jack Simmons Medalist (Matador Cup) – George Bailey 149, Cameron Boyce 103, Jordan Silk 79, Andrew
Fekete 62
Jamie Cox Young Player of the year – Beau Webster

VICTORIA
Coach: Andrew McDonald

	No.	DOB	Place	Type	
Scott Boland	24	11/4/89	Parkdale, Vic	RHB	RFM
Jackson Coleman	3	18/12/91	Black Rock, Vic	RHB	LFM
Xavier Crone		19/12/97	Strathfieldsaye, Vic	RHB	RFM
Travis Dean	29	1/2/92	Williamstown, Vic	RHB	
Aaron Finch *	5	17/11/86	Colac, Victoria	RHB	SLA
Seb Gotch	36	12/7/93	Hughesdale, Vic	RHB	WK
Sam Grimwade		16/12/97	Armadale, Vic	RHB	ROB
Peter Handscomb *	54	26/4/91	Melbourne	RHB	WK
Sam Harper	7	10/12/96	Knoxfield, Vic	RHB	WK
Marcus Harris	14	21/7/92	Scarborough, WA	LHB	
Mac Harvey		18/9/00	East St Kilda, Vic	LHB	RMF
Jon Holland	18	29/5/87	Sandringham, Vic	RHB	SLA
Glenn Maxwell *	32	14/10/88	Kew. Melbourne	RHB	ROS
Tom O'Connell		14/6/00		LHB	LEG
James Pattinson *	19	3/5/90	Melbourne	LHB	RFM
Will Pucovski	10	2/2/98	Malvern, Vic	RHB	
Jake Reed	34	28/9/90	Mildura, Vic	RHB	RFM
Matthew Short	2	8/11/95	Ballarat, Vic	RHB	RM
Peter Siddle	20	25/11/84	Traralgon, Vic	RHB	RF
Will Sutherland	12	27/10/99	East Melbourne, Vic	RHB	RFM
Chris Tremain	99	10/8/91	Dubbo, NSW	RHB	RFM
Eamonn Vines	22	17/1/94	Geelong, Vic	LHB	
Cameron White	9	18/8/83	Bairnsdale, Vic	RHB	LEG
Rookies					
Wes Agar	6	5/2/97	Malvern, Vic	RHB	RFM
Zak Evans		26/3/00		RHB	RFM
Jonathan Merlo		15/12/98	Melbourne	RHB	RMF
Edward Newman		12/3/99	East St Kilda, Vic	LHB	SLA
Mitch Perry		27/4/00		LHB	RFM
Patrick Rowe		28/1/01	Randwick, NSW	RHB	

*CA Contract

In: Sam Grimwade and Will Sutherland (upgraded Rookies), Mac Harvey. Tom O'Connell (Sturt, SA) and Eamonn Vines.

New Rookies - Wes Agar, Edward Newman, Jonathan Merlo and Patrick Rowe.

Off Contract list for 2018-19

Fawad Ahmed	80	5/2/82	Marghuz, Pakisan	RHB	LEG
Daniel Christian	45	4/5/83	Campberdown, NSW	RHB	RMF
John Hastings	11	4/11/85	Penrith, NSW	RHB	RFM
Jackson Koop		9/6/95	North Carlton, Vic	RHB	RM
James Muirhead	1	30/6/93	Altona, Vic	RHB	LEG
Tom O'Donnell		23/10/96	Kilmore, Vic	RHB	LFM
Blake Thomson		9/12/97	Ballarat, Vic	RHB	ROS
Guy Walker		12/9/95	Ruddington, UK	RHB	RM

2017-18 Award Winners
Bill Lawry Medal (Sheffield Shield): Chris Tremain
Dean Jones (JLT Cup) Medal: Peter Siddle
John Scholes Players Award: Scott Boland

WESTERN AUSTRALIA
Coach: Adam Voges replaces Justin Langer (Australia)

	No.	DOB	Place		
Ashton Agar *	18	14/10/93	Melbourne	LHB	SLA
Cameron Bancroft	4	19/11/92	Attadale, Perth	RHB	WK
Jason Behrendorff	5	23/4/81	Camden, NSW	RHB	LFM
Will Bosisto	39	8/9/93	Geraldton, WA	RHB	ROS
Hilton Cartwright	35	14/2/92	Harare, Zimbabwe	RHB	RM
Nathan Coulter-Nile	13	11/10/87	Osborne Park, WA	RHB	RFM
Cameron Green		3/6/99	Subiaco, WA	RHB	RMF
Liam Guthrie	6	3/4/97	Subiaco, WA	LHB	LFM
Josh Inglis	95	4/3/95	Leeds, Yorkshire	RHB	WK
Matt Kelly	12	7/12/94	Durban, Sth Africa	RHB	RMF
Simon Mackin	33	1/9/92	Wyalkatchem, WA	RHB	RFM
Mitchell Marsh *	10	20/10/91	Attadale, Perth	RHB	RFM
Shaun Marsh *	20	9/7/83	Narrogin, WA	LHB	SLA
David Moody	15	28/4/95	Mt Lawley, WA	RHB	RFM
Joel Paris	3	11/12/92	Subiaco, WA	LHB	LMF
Josh Philipee	27	1/6/97	Subiaco, WA	RHB	
Jhye Richardson *	2	20/9/96	Murdoch, WA	LHB	RFM
D'Arcy Short	23	9/8/90	Katherine, NT	LHB	SLC
Marcus Stoinis *	16	16/8/89	Perth, WA	RHB	RM
Ashton Turner	17	25/1/93	Perth, WA	RHB	ROS
Andrew Tye *	68	12/12/86	Perth, WA	RHB	RFM
Jonathan Wells	8	13/8/88	Hobart, Tasmania	RHB	RM
Sam Whiteman	9	19/3/92	Doncaster, Yorkshire	LHB	WK
Rookie Contracts:					
Alex Bevilaqua		29/10/96	Perth, WA	RHB	RFM
Jake Carder		11/12/95	Perth, WA	LHB	RM
Aaron Hardie		7/1/99	Bournemouth, England	RHB	RM
Clint Hinchliffe		23/10/96	Perth, WA	LHB	SLA
Lance Morris		28/3/98	Busselton, WA	RHB	RFM
Matthew Spoors		6/5/99		RHB	LEG

*CA Contract

Ins – Tim David (Claremont-Nedlands), Aaron Hardie (Willetton), Lance Morris (Scarborough).

Off Contract list for 2017-18

Michael Klinger	7	4/7/80	Kew, Vic	RHB	
Kyle Gardiner		8/12/96	Bunbury, WA	RHB	LEG
Andrew Holder		22/9/99	Glengarry, WA	RHB	RFM

2017-18 Award Winners
Lawrie Sawle Medal: Mitchell Marsh.
Four Day Player of the Year – Ashton Turner
JLT Cup Player of the Year – Shaun Marsh
Gold Cup (Best WA player across all levels): Shaun Marsh

Australian Cricket Digest, 2018-19
WNCL SQUADS
AUSTRALIAN CAPITAL TERRITORY
Coach – James Allsopp

	No.	DOB	Place	Club	Bat	Bwl/k
Sam Bates	99	17/8/92	Newcastle, NSW		R	SLA
Maitlan Brown		5/6/97	Taree, NSW		R	RM
Erin Burns	29	22/6/88	Woolongong, NSW	Glenorchy, Tas	R	ROS
Zoe Cooke		17/9/95	Bruce, ACT		R	RM
Nicola Hancock	4	8/11/95	Prahran, Vic		R	RM
Clara Iemma		31/10/98	Beverley Hills, NSW		L	ROS
Hayley Jensen	17	7/10/92	Christchurch, NZ		R	RM
Erica Kershaw	12	23/12/91	Castlemaine, Vic		L	LEG
Claire Koski	55	13/3/91	Campbelltown, NSW	Campbelltown-Camden	R	RM
Anna Lanning		25/3/94	Sydney		R	RM
Katie Mack	2	14/9/93	Melbourne	Northern Districts	R	LEG
Matilda Lugg		12/11/99		Sawtell	R	RM
Erin Osborne	67	27/6/89	Taree, NSW	Sydney	R	ROS
Angela Reakes	68	27/12/90	Byron Bay, NSW	Sydney	R	LEG

In – Matilda Lugg, Zoe Cooke, Anna Lanning (Vic). Outs: Dane van Niekerk, Marizanne Kapp, Nicole Goodwin, Emily Leys

NEW SOUTH WALES
Coach – Jo Broadbent

	No.	DOB	Place	Club	Bat	Bwl/k
Sarah Aley	3	3/6/84	Sydney	Bankstown	R	RM
Nicola Carey *	5	10/9/93	Camperdown, NSW	St George-Sutherland	L	RM
Lauren Cheatle	25	6/11/98	Bowral, NSW	Campbelltown-Camden	L	LMF
Renee Farrell	88	13/1/87	Kogarah, NSW	St George-Sutherland	R	RMF
Ash Gardner *		15/4/97	Bankstown, NSW		R	ROS
Maisy Gibson	13	14/9/96	Singleton, NSW	Universities	L	LEG
Lisa Griffith	24	28/8/92	Bathurst, NSW	Penrith	R	RMF
Rachael Haynes *	15	26/12/86	Carlton, Vic	Sydney	L	LM
Alyssa Healy *	77	24/3/90	Gold Coast, Qld	Sydney	R	WK
Mikayla Hinkley	1	1/5/88	Penrith, NSW	Penrith	R	ROS
Carly Leeson	74	9/11/98		Universities	R	RM
Saskia Horley		23/2/00		Gordon	R	ROS
Ellyse Perry *	8	3/11/90	Wahroonga, NSW	Sydney	R	RMF
Lauren Smith	2	6/10/96	Central Coast, NSW	Sydney	R	ROS
Naomi Stalenburg	10	19/4/94	Blacktown, NSW	Penrith	R	RM
Rachel Trenaman	8	18/4/01	Broken Hill, NSW	Wagga City, NSW	R	LEG
Hannah Trethewy	46	18/1/99		Campbelltown-Camden	R	RM
Belinda Vakarewa	47	22/1/00	Griffith, NSW	Campbelltown-Camden	R	RM
Tahlia Wilson		21/10/99		St George-Sutherland	R	RM

In – Ash Gardner (SA). Out – Alex Blackwell (retired)

QUEENSLAND – Coach: Peter McGiffin

	No.	DOB	Place	Club	Bat	Bwl/k
Jemma Barsby	15	4/10/95	Herston, Qld	Sandgate-Redcliffe	L	ROS
Haidee Birkett	23	1/1/97	Brisbane	Sandgate-Redcliffe	R	RM
Tess Cooper	36	27/9/96	Townsville, Qld	Sandgate-Redcliffe	R	WK
Megan Dixon		23/4/97	Townsville, Qld	Sandgate-Redcliffe	R	RM
Josie Dooley		21/1/00	Brisbane	Wests	R	WK
Jess Duffin (Cameron)		27/6/89	Williamstown, Vic		R	LEG
Holly Ferling	9	22/12/95	Kingaroy, Qld	University of Qld	R	RMF
Grace Harris	17	18/9/93	Ipswich, Qld	Wests	R	ROS
Laura Harris	4	6/8/90	Ipswich, Qld	University of Qld	R	
Sammy-Jo Johnson	58	5/11/92	Lismore, NSW	Gold Coast	R	RM
Sterre Kalis		30/8/99	Delft, Netherlands		R	RM
Jess Jonassen *	21	5/11/92	Emerald, Qld	University of Qld	L	SLA
Delissa Kimmince *	11	14/5/89	Warwick, Qld	Gold Coast	R	RM
Beth Mooney *	6	14/1/94	Shepparton, Vic	Sandgate-Redcliffe	L	WK
Georgia Prestwidge	16	17/12/97	Brisbane, Qld	Sandgate-Redcliffe	R	RMF
Kirby Short	10	3/11/86	Brisbane	Wests	R	ROS
Courtney Sippel	71	27/4/01	Ballina, NSW	Valley	L	LM

In – Jess Duffin (ex Vic), Sterre Kallis (Netherlands), Meagan Dixon, Courtney Sippel

Out - Carly Fuller, Courtney Hill, Kara Sutherland (retired)

SOUTH AUSTRALIA - Coach: Andrea McCauley

	No.	DOB	Place	Club	Bat	Bwl/k
Kelly Armstrong	11	10/11/98	Adelaide	Kensington	R	LEG
Samantha Betts	14	16/2/96	Orroroo, SA	Northern Districts	R	RM
Shae Daly	23	15/11/99	Adelaide	Kensington	R	ROS
Eliza Doddridge	16	15/2/99	Adelaide	Kensington	R	RM
Ellen Falconer	3	3/8/99	Selkirk, Scotland	West Torrens	R	RM
Brooke Harris	31	27/8/97	Adelaide	West Torrens	R	RM
Sarah Lowe	32	26/1/93	Adelaide	Kensington	R	RM
Tahlia McGrath	9	10/11/95	Adelaide	West Torrens	R	RM
Tegan McPharlin	7	7/8/88	Balaklava, SA	Northern Districts	R	WK
Annie O'Neil	5	18/2/99	Murray Bridge	Sturt	R	LEG
Bridget Patterson	21	12/4/94	Kingscote, SA	Kensington	R	ROS
Katelyn Pope	18	29/3/96	Adelaide	Kensington	R	LM
Alex Price	12	5/11/95	Adelaide	Sturt	L	ROS
Tabatha Saville	13	13/4/98	Suva, Fiji	Northern Districts	R	ROS
Megan Schutt *	27	15/1/93	Adelaide	Sturt	R	RMF
Amanda Wellington *	10	29/5/97	Adelaide	Port Adelaide	R	LEG

In – Kelly Armsrogg, Shae Daly. Out – Ash Gardner (NSW), Brittany Perry, Sophie Devine.

TASMANIA - Coach: Salliann Briggs

	No.	DOB	Place	Club	Bat	Bwl/k
Stef Daffara	7	13/6/95	Illawara, NSW		R	RM
Ashley Day		17/9/99		ex-NSW	R	LEG
Erin Fazackery	3	3/7/98	Hobart	Clarence	R	RM
Katelyn Fryett	9	28/5/92	Launceston, Tas	University	R	RM
Corinne Hall	23	12/10/87	Gosford, NSW	South Hob/Sandy Bay	R	ROS
Brooke Hepburn	12	19/4/90	Launceston, Tas	New Town/Launceston	R	RM
Emma Manix-Geeves		12/8/00		Riverside	R	RM
Sasha Moloney		14/7/92	Longford, Tas	University	R	
Meg Phillips	10	2/2/96	Evandale, Tas	Launceston/Glenorchy	R	RM
Veronica Pyke	4	4/11/81	Hobart	North Hobart	R	LM
Celeste Raack	2	18/5/94	Sydney, NSW	Lindisfarne	R	LEG
Georgia Redmayne	8	8/12/93	Lismore, NSW	Universities	L	WK
Emma Thompson	74	12/2/90	Baulkham Hills, NSW		R	RM
Courtney Webb	1	30/11/99	Launceston, Tas	South Launceston	R	RM

In – Ashley Day, Emma Manix-Geeves, Sasha Moloney. Out: Emily Divin, Isobel Joyce, Laura Wright.

Australian Cricket Digest, 2018-19
VICTORIA - Coach: David Hemp

	No.	DOB	Place	Club	Bat	Bwl/k
Kristen Beams (V/c)	26	6/11/84	Launceston, Tas	Essendon Maribyrnong	R	LEG
Makinley Blows	15	12/12/97	Broken Hill, NSW	Essendon Maribyrnong	L	RM
Elly Donald				Melbourne	R	RM
Nicole Faltum	4	17/6/00	Traralgon, Vic	Dandenong	R	WK
Emma Inglis	19	15/7/98	Fitzroy, Vic	Prahran	R	WK
Alana King	13	22/11/95	Clarinda, Vic	Prahran	R	LEG
Meg Lanning © *	7	25/3/92	Singapore	Box Hill	R	RM
Sophie Molineux *	25	17/1/98	Bairnsdale, Vic	Dandenong	L	SLA
Courtney Neale		4/7/98		Dandenong	R	RM
Rhiann O'Donnell		14/4/98	Terng, Vic	Plenty Valley	R	RM
Chloe Rafferty	37	16/6/99	Williamstown, Vic	Essendon Maribyrnong	R	RM
Molly Strano	5	5/10/92	Sunshine, Vic	Essendon Maribyrnong	R	ROS
Annabel Sutherland	3	12/10/01	East Melbourne	Prahran	R	RM
Elyse Villani *		6/10/89	Greensborough, Vic		R	RM
Amy Vine				Melbourne	R	LEG
Tayla Vlaeminck	7	27/10/98	Bendigo, Vic	Plenty Valley	R	RM
Georgia Wareham	32	26/5/99	Terang, Vic	Essendon Maribyrnong	R	RM

In – Elly Donald, Amy Vine, Courtney Neale, Elyse Villani. Out – Anna Lanning (ACT), Hayleigh Brennan, Gemma Triscari (retired)

WESTERN AUSTRALIA - Coach: Lisa Keightley

	No.	DOB	Place	Club	Bat	Bwl/k
Meg Banting	4	11/2/96	Subiaco, WA	Subiaco-Floreat	R	WK
Nicole Bolton *	12	17/1/89	Subiaco, WA	Subiaco-Floreat	L	ROS
Melissa Cameron	13	13/6/97	Mt Lawley, WA	South Perth	R	RM
Mathilda Carmichael	5	4/4/94	St Leonards, NSW	Melville	R	RM
Piepa Cleary	8	17/7/96	Subiaco, WA	South Perth	R	RM
Sheldyn Cooper		29/7/00	Swan Districts, WA	Midland-Guildford	R	RM
Bhavi Devchand	24	24/12/92	Zimbabwe	Midland-Guildford	R	RM
Amy Edgar		27/12/97	Cowra, NSW	Penrith, NSW	R	RM
Heather Graham	11	5/10/96	Subiaco, WA	Subiaco-Floreat	R	RM
Kath Hempenstall		20/9/88	Brunswick, Vic		R	RM
Ashlee King		1/9/00		Melville	R	RM
Emma King	2	25/3/92	Subiaco, WA	Subiaco-Floreat	R	ROS
Tanaele Peschel	7	29/8/94	Rockingham, WA	Midland-Guildford	R	RM
Chloe Piparo	28	5/9/94	Bunbury, WA	Midland-Guildford	R	RS
Emily Smith	33	9/1/95	Sunshine, Vic	Uni of WA	R	RM

In – Ashlee King, Kath Hempenstall (ex-Vic). Out – Katie Hartshorn, Elyse Villani, Rebecca West.

Australian Cricket Digest, 2018-19
Squads from BBL07 plus any known changes
Uncertain or yet to be confirmed players in Italics
ADELAIDE STRIKERS
Coach: Jason Gillespie

	No.	DOB	Place	Ht	Bt	Bwl/k
Wes Agar	21	5/2/97	Malvern, Vic	193	R	RFM
Alex Carey	5	27/8/91	Loxton, SA	182	L	WK
Michael Cormack	17	29/6/97	North Adelaide		R	ROS
Jono Dean	77	23/6/84	Bathurst, NSW	185	R	ROS
Daniel Drew		*22/5/96*	*Ashford, Adelaide*		*R*	*ROS*
David Grant	14	24/5/97	North Adelaide		R	RFM
Travis Head	34	29/12/83	Adelaide, SA	180	L	ROS
Colin Ingram	41	3/7/85	Port Elizabeth	173	L	LEG
Rashid Khan	19	20/9/98	Nangarhar, Afghanistan	168	R	LEG
Ben Laughlin	56	3/10/82	Box Hill, Victoria	183	R	RMF
Jake Lehmann	33	8/7/92	Adelaide, SA	181	L	SLA
Harry Nielsen	4	3/5/95	Adelaide, SA		L	WK
Michael Neser	20	29/3/90	Pretoria, South Africa	183	R	RFM
Liam O'Connor	9	20/6/93	Perth, WA		R	LEG
Matt Short	9	8/11/95	Melbourne	187	R	ROS
Peter Siddle	64	25/11/84	Traralgon, Vic	187	R	RFM
Kelvin Smith	19	5/9/94	Bow Hill, SA	179	L	ROS
Billy Stanlake	3	4/10/93	Hervey Bay, Qld	204	R	RFM
Jake Weatherald	28	4/11/94	NT	178	L	LEG
Jonathan Wells	29	13/8/88	Hobart	170	R	RM
Nick Winter	44	19/6/93	Canberra, ACT		L	LMF

BBL07 MVP – Rashid Khan. In: Matt Short (Renegades),

BRISBANE HEAT
Coach: Daniel Vettori

	No.	DOB	Place	Ht	Bt	Bwl/k
Max Bryant	1	10/3/99	Murwillumbah, NSW		R	RM
Joe Burns	15	6/9/89	Herston, Brisbane	182	R	RM
Ben Cutting	31	30/1/87	Sunnybank, Brisbane	192	R	RFM
Brendan Doggett	35	3/5/94	Rockhampton, Qld		R	RFM
Cameron Gannon	*21*	*23/1/89*	*Baulkham Hills, Sydney*	*199*	*R*	*RFM*
Sam Heazlett	47	12/9/95	Sunnybank, Qld		L	SLA
Marnus Labuschagne	9	22/6/94	Klerksdrop, Sth Africa		R	RM
Josh Lalor	2	2/11/87	Penrith, Sydney	178	R	LFM
Chris Lynn	50	10/4/90	Brisbane	180	R	SLA
Brendon McCullum	42	27/9/81	Dunedin, NZ	171	R	ROS
James Pattinson		3/5/90	Melbourne	186	L	RFM
James Peirson	59	13/10/92	Sydney		R	WK
Jack Prestwidge	14	28/2/96	Brisbane		R	RFM
Matthew Renshaw	77	28/3/96	Middlesborough, UK	186	L	ROS
Alex Ross	49	17/4/92	Melbourne	179	R	ROS
Mark Steketee	6	17/1/94	Monto, Qld	187	R	RFM
Mitch Swepson	4	4/10/93	Brisbane	187	R	RFM

BBL07 MVP – Yasir Shah. **In:** James Pattinson (Renegades).
Out: Shadab Khan, Yasir Shah (Pakistan commitments)

Australian Cricket Digest, 2018-19
HOBART HURRICANES
Coach: Gary Kirsten

	No.	DOB	Place	Ht	Bt	Bwl/k
Jofra Archer	11	1/4/95	Bridgetown, Barbados	188	R	RF
George Bailey	10	7/9/82	Launceston, Tas	178	R	RFM
James Bazley	*77*	*8/4/95*	*Buderim, Qld*		*R*	*RFM*
Alex Doolan	*14*	*29/11/85*	*Launceston, Tas*	*183*	*R*	*WK*
James Faulkner	5	29/4/90	Launceston, Tasmania	186	R	LFM
Hamish Kingston	29	17/12/90	Hobart	190	R	RMF
Ben McDermott	28	12/12/94	Caboolture, Qld	191	R	
Riley Meredith	*21*	*21/6/96*	*Hobart*		*L*	*RFM*
Simon Milenko	24	24/11/88	Sydney, NSW		R	RM
Tymal Mills	72	12/8/92	Dewsbury, West Yorks	183	R	LF
Tim Paine	*27*	*8/12/84*	*Hobart, Tas*	*180*	*R*	*WK*
Sam Rainbird	43	5/6/92	Hobart, Tas	186	R	LFM
Nathan Reardon	*36*	*8/11/84*	*Chinchilla, Qld*	*173*	*L*	*RM*
Jake Reed	*44*	*28/9/90*	*Mildura, Vic*	*190*	*L*	*RFM*
Tom Rogers	6	3/3/94	Bruce, ACT		L	RFM
Clive Rose	31	13/10/89	Dandenong, Vic		R	SLA
Darcy Short	23	9/8/90	Katherine, NT		L	SLC
Aaron Summers	35	24/3/96			R	RFM
Matthew Wade	64	26/12/84	Hobart	170	L	WK

BBL07 MVP – Darcy Short.

In: James Faulkner (Stars). Out: Cameron Boyce (Hurricanes), Daniel Christian (Hurricanes)

MELBOURNE RENEGADES
Coach: Andrew McDonald

	No.	DOB	Place	Ht	Bt	Bwl/k
Cameron Boyce		27/7/89	Charleville, Qld	178	R	LEG
Dwayne Bravo	47	7/10/83	Santa Cruz, Trinidad	175	R	RMF
Daniel Christian	54	4/5/83	Camperdown, Sydney	183	R	RMF
Tom Cooper	26	26/11/86	Woollongong, NSW	187	R	ROB
Zak Evans	2	26/3/2000			R	RMF
Aaron Finch	5	17/11/86	Colac, Victoria	176	R	SLA
Marcus Harris	21	21/7/92	Scarborough, WA	173	L	
Mac Harvey	3	18/9/00	St Kilda, Melbourne		L	RM
Brad Hogg	31	6/2/71	Narrogin, WA	183	L	SLC
Jon Holland	18	29/5/87	Sandringham, Vic	183	R	SLA
Trent Lawford	*37*	*18/4/88*	*Melbourne*	*191*	*R*	*RFM*
Tim Ludeman	15	23/6/87	Warrnambool, Vic	176	R	WK
Joe Mennie	16	24/12/88	Coffs Harbour, NSW	190	R	RFM
Mohammed Nabi	77	1/1/85	Loger, Afghanistan		R	ROS
Kieron Pollard	*00*	*12/5/87*	*Tacariqua, Trinidad*	*198*	*R*	*RM*
Kane Richardson	55	12/2/91	Eudunda, SA	190	R	RFM
Nathan Rimmington	*35*	*11/11/82*	*Redcliffe, Qld*	*183*	*R*	*RFM*
Will Sutherland		27/10/99	East Melbourne		R	RFM
Chris Tremain	34	10/8/91	Dubbo, NSW	188	R	RFM
Beau Webster	20	1/12/93	Snug, Hobart	194	R	ROS
Cameron White	7	18/8/83	Bairnsdale, Vic	187	R	LEG
Jack Wildermuth	10	1/9/93	Toowoomba, Qld		R	RFM

BBL07 MVP – Tom Cooper. Support staff: Tom Moody (director of cricket).

In: Cameron Boyce (Hurricanes), Dan Christian (Hurricanes), Zak Evans, Mac Harvey, Will Sutherland
Out: Brad Hodge (retired), Matt Short (Strikers), Guy Walker (AFL), James Pattinson (Heat)

Australian Cricket Digest, 2018-19
MELBOURNE STARS
Coach: Stephen Fleming

	No.	DOB	Place	Ht	Bt	Bwl/
Michael Beer	19	9/6/84	Malvern, Vic	187	R	SLA
Scott Boland	25	11/4/89	Parkdale, Vic	189	R	RFM
Liam Bowe	*23*	*23/3/97*			*L*	*SLC*
Jackson Coleman	9	18/12/91	Black Rock, Vic	196	R	LFM
Ben Dunk	51	11/3/87	Innisfail, Qld	184	L	WK
Dan Fallins		12/8/96			R	LEG
Seb Gotch	13	12/7/93	Hughesdale, Vic	168	R	RM
Evan Gulbis	4	26/3/86	Carlton, Vic	182	R	RFM
Peter Handscomb	54	26/4/91	Melbourne	183	R	
Sam Harper	3	10/12/96	Knoxfield, Vic	168	R	WK
Ben Hilfenhaus	20	15/3/83	Ulverstone, Tasmania	186	R	RFM
Nic Maddinson	53	21/12/91	Nowra, NSW	185	L	SLA
Glenn Maxwell	32	14/10/88	Kew, Melbourne	182	R	ROS
Marcus Stonis	16	16/8/89	Perth, WA	185	R	RM
Daniel Worrall	17	10/7/91	Melbourne, Vic	183	R	RFM
Adam Zampa	66	31/3/92	Shellharbour, NSW	175	R	RLG

BBL07 MVP – Glenn Maxwell.

In: Nic Maddinson. **Out:** James Faulkner (Hurricanes), Kevin Pietersen, Rob Quiney (retired), Luke Wright (retired),

PERTH SCORCHERS
Coach: Adam Voges (replacing Justin Langer)

	No.	DOB	Place	Ht	Bt	Bwl/k
Ashton Agar	18	14/10/93	Melbourne	187	L	SLA
Cameron Bancroft	4	19/11/82	Attadale, Perth	182	R	
Jason Behrendorff	5	23/4/81	Camden, NSW	194	R	LFM
Will Bosisto	39	8/9/93	Geraldton, WA		R	ROS
Tim Bresnan	28	28/2/85	Pontefract, Yorkshire	183	R	RFM
Hilton Cartwright	35	14/2/92	Harare, Zimbabwe	188	R	RM
Nathan Coulter-Nile	13	11/10/87	Osborne Park, WA	191	R	RFM
Tim David	16	16/3/96	Sinagpore		R	RMF
Cameron Green		3/6/99			R	RFM
Josh Inglis	95	4/3/95	Leeds, Yorkshire		R	WK
Matt Kelly	12	7/12/94	Durban, Sth Africa		R	RFM
Michael Klinger	7	4/7/80	Kew, Melbourne	179	R	
Mitchell Marsh	10	20/10/91	Attadale, Perth	193	R	RFM
Shaun Marsh	20	9/7/83	Narrogin, WA	186	L	
Haydan Morton	21	27/2/94			R	ROS
James Muirhead	67	30/6/93	Altona, Vic	183	R	LEG
Joel Paris	3	11/12/92	Subiaco, WA	191	L	LFM
Josh Philipee	27	1/6/97	Subiaco, WA		R	
Jyhe Richardson	2	20/9/96	Murdoch, WA	180	L	RFM
Ashton Turner	17	25/1/93	Perth	191	R	ROS
Andrew Tye	68	12/12/86	Perth	192	R	RMF
Cameron Valente	*38*	*6/9/94*	*Adelaide*	*180*	*R*	*RFM*
Sam Whiteman	9	19/3/92	Doncaster, Yorks	183	L	WK
David Willey	8	28/2/90	Northampton, Eng	185	L	LFM

BBL07 MVP (Simon Katich Medalist) – Ashton Agar. Out – Mitchell Johnson, Adam Voges (both retired)

Australian Cricket Digest, 2018-19
SYDNEY SIXERS
Coach: Greg Shipperd

	No.	DOB	Place	Ht	Bt	Bwl/k
Sean Abbott	77	29/2/92	Windsor, NSW	184	R	RFM
Sam Billings	*7*	*15/6/91*	*Pembury, Kent*	*178*	*R*	*WK*
Jackson Bird	*33*	*11/12/86*	*Sydney*	*195*	*R*	*RFM*
Doug Bollinger	*4*	*24/7/81*	*Baulkham Hills, Sydney*	*192*	*L*	*LFM*
Johan Botha	*65*	*2/5/82*	*Johannesburg, S.Africa*	*178*	*R*	*ROB*
Carlos Brathwaite	*26*	*18/7/88*	*Barbados*	*193*	*R*	*RMF*
Joe Denly	*24*	*16/3/86*	*Canterbury, Kent, UK*	*178*	*R*	
Ben Dwarshuis	23	23/6/94	Kareela, NSW	183	L	LFM
Mickey Edwards	78	23/12/94	Sydney	198	R	RFM
John Hastings	11	4/11/85	Penrith, NSW	196	R	RFM
Moises Henriques	21	1/2/87	Funchal, Portugal	189	R	RFM
Daniel Hughes	16	2/7/79	Bathurst, NSW	188	L	
Nick Larkin	*36*	*1/5/90*	*Taree, NSW*		*R*	
Nathan Lyon	67	20/11/87	Young, NSW	181	R	ROB
Peter Nevill	20	13/10/85	Hawthorn, Melbourne	182	R	WK
Stephen O'Keefe	72	9/10/84	Malaysia	175	R	SLA
Jason Roy	*20*	*21/7/90*	*Durban, Sth Africa*	*182*	*R*	
Jordan Silk	14	18/1/91	Penrith, Sydney	187	R	
Henry Thornton		16/12/96	Kogarah, NSW		R	RFM
Will Somerville	*28*	*9/8/84*	*Wellington, New Zealand*		*R*	*ROS*
Mitchell Starc	*56*	*30/1/90*	*Baulkham Hills, Sydney*	*197*	*L*	*LF*

BBL07 MVP – Sam Billings. In: John Hastings (Stars). **Out:** Nic Maddinson (Stars)

SYDNEY THUNDER
Coach: Shane Bond (replaces Paddy Upton)

	No.	DOB	Place	Ht	Bt	Bwl/k
Fawad Ahmed	52	5/2/82	Marghuz, Pakistan	183	R	LEG
Jos Buttler	63	8/9/90	Taunton, England	180	R	WK
Patrick Cummins	30	5/8/93	Westmead, Sydney	192	R	RF
Andrew Fekete	11	18/5/85	Melbourne		R	RFM
Callum Ferguson	12	21/11/84	North Adelaide	180	R	
Ryan Gibson	77	30/12/93	Penrith, NSW	190	R	
Chris Green	93	1/10/93	Durban, South Africa	190	R	ROS
Liam Hatcher	*19*	*17/9/96*	*Liverpool, NSW*		*R*	*RFM*
Usman Khawaja	18	18/12/86	Islamabad, Pakistan	177	L	ROS
Jay Lenton	70	10/8/90	Belmont, NSW	194	L	WK
Nathan McAndrew	*44*	*14/7/93*	*Wollongong, NSW*		*R*	
Mitch McClenaghan	81	11/6/86	Hastings, NZ	188	L	LFM
Arjun Nair	7	12/4/98	Canberra		R	ROS
Kurtis Patterson	97	5/5/93	Hurstville, NSW	192	L	
Joe Root	66	30/12/90	Sheffield, England	183	R	ROS
Daniel Sams	27	27/10/92	Milperra, NSW		R	LFM
Gurinder Sandhu	11	14/6/93	Blacktown, Sydney	194	L	RFM
Jason Sangha	3	8/9/99	Randwick, Sydney	183	R	LEG
James Vince	*14*	*14/3/91*	*Cuckfield, Sussex*	*183*	*R*	*RM*
Shane Watson	33	17/6/81	Ipswich, Queensland	183	R	RFM

BBL07 MVP – Shane Watson. In: Joe Root (England). **Out:** Aiden Blizzard, Clint McKay, Ben Rohrer (retired), Andre Russell (not retained)

Squads from WBBL03 and those know to be playing in WBBL04

ADELAIDE STRIKERS
Coach: Andrea McCauley

	No.	DOB	Place	Bat	Bwl/k
Suzie Bates (NZ)	11	16/9/87	Dunedin, NZ	R	RM
Tammy Beaumont (Eng)	2	11/3/91	Dover, Kent, UK	R	WK
Samantha Betts	14	6/2/96	Ororoo, SA	R	RM
Sophie Devine (NZ)	77	1/9/89	Wellington, NZ	R	RM
Rhiannon Dick	*22*	*21/9/90*	*Bankstown, NSW*	*L*	*SLA*
Ellie Falconer	3	3/8/99	Clare	R	RM
Tahlia McGrath	9	10/11/95	Adelaide	R	RM
Tegan McPharlin	7	7/8/98	Balaklava, SA	R	WK
Annie O'Neill	5	18/2/99			
Bridget Patterson	*21*	*12/4/94*	*Kangaroo Island*	*R*	*ROS*
Katelyn Pope	18	29/3/96	Adelaide	R	LM
Alex Price	12	5/11/95	Adelaide	L	ROS
Tabitha Saville	13	13/4/98	Suva, Fiji	R	RM
Megan Schutt	27	15/1/93	Adelaide	R	RMF
Amanda Wellington	10	29/5/97	Adelaide	R	LEG

Strikers WBBL03 MVP – Sophie Devine. **Support staff:** Luke Williams (Assistant coach)

BRISBANE HEAT
Coach: Andy Richards

	No.	DOB	Place	Bat	Bwl/k
Jemma Barsby	15	4/10/95	Brisbane	L	ROS
Haidee Birkett	23	1/1/97	Brisbane	R	RM
Tess Cooper	*36*	*27/9/96*	*Townsville, Qld*	*R*	*WK*
Grace Harris	17	18/9/93	Ipswich, Qld	R	ROS
Laura Harris	*4*	*6/8/90*	*Ipswich, Qld*	*R*	
Courtney Hill	22	9/1/87	Maryborough, Qld	R	RM
Sammy-Jo Johnson	58	5/11/92	Lismore, NSW	R	RM
Jess Jonassen	21	5/11/92	Emerald, Qld	L	SLA
Delissa Kimmince	11	14/5/89	Warwick, Qld	R	RM
Smriti Mandhana (Ind)	*18*	*18/7/96*	*Mumbai, India*	*L*	*RM*
Beth Mooney	6	14/1/94	Shepparton, Vic	L	WK
Georgia Prestwidge	16	17/12/97		R	RMF
Kirby Short	10	3/11/86	Brisbane	R	ROS
Laura Woolvardt	*14*	*26/4/99*	*Milnerton, Sth Africa*	*R*	

WBBL03 MVP – Beth Mooney. **Out – Deandra Dottin, Holly Ferling (Stars), Courtney Hill, Kara Sutherland (retired)**

HOBART HURRICANES
Coach: Salliann Briggs (new)

	No.	DOB	Place	Bat	Bwl/k
Stefanie Daffara	7	13/6/95	Illawara, NSW	R	RM
Erin Fazackery	3	3/7/98	Hobart	R	RM
Katelyn Fryett	9	28/5/92	Launceston, Tas	R	RM
Corinne Hall	27	12/10/87	Gosford, NSW	R	ROS
Nicola Hancock	44	8/11/95	Prahran, Vic		
Brooke Hepburn	12	19/4/90	Launceston, Tas	R	RM
Isobel Joyce (Ire)	*33*	*25/7/83*	*Wicklow, Ireland*	*R*	*LM*
Veda Krishnamamurthy	79	16/10/92	India	R	LEG
Hayley Matthews (WI)	50	19/3/98	Barbados	R	ROS
Sasha Moloney	99	14/7/92	Kongford, Tas	R	
Meg Phillips	10	2/2/96	Evandale, Tas	R	RM
Veronica Pyke	4	4/11/81	Hobart	R	LM
Celeste Raack	2	18/5/94	Sydney	R	LM
Georgia Redmayne	8	8/12/93	Lismore, NSW	L	WK
Emma Thompson	74	12/2/90	Baulkham Hills, NSW	R	RM
Lauren Winfield	58	16/8/90	York, England	R	WK

WBBL03 MVP – Hayley Matthews.

MELBOURNE RENEGADES
Coach: Tim Coyle

	No.	DOB	Place	Bat	Bwl/k
Maitlan Brown	77	5/6/97	Taree, NSW	R	RM
Jess Duffin (Cameron)	27	27/6/89	Williamstown, Vic	R	LEG
Emma Inglis	19	15/7/88	Fitzroy, Vic	R	WK
Erica Kershaw		23/12/91	Castlemaine, Vic	L	WK
Claire Koski	55	13/3/91	Campbelltown, NSW	R	RM
Anna Lanning		25/3/94	Sydney	R	RM
Sophie Molineux	23	17/1/98	Bairnsdale, Vic	L	SLA
Rhiann O'Donnell	*26*	*26/5/99*	*Terang, Vic*	*R*	
Amy Satterthwaite © (NZ)	17	7/10/86	Christchurch, NZ	L	RM
Molly Strano	5	5/10/92	Sunshine, Vic	R	ROS
Jenny Taffs	*9*	*18/6/95*	*Zimbabwe*	*R*	*LEG*
Lea Tahuhu (NZ)	6	23/9/90	Christchurch	R	RM
Tayla Vlaeminck	7	27/10/98	Bendigo, Vic	R	RM
Georgia Wareham	32	26/5/99	Terang, Vic	R	RM
Courtney Webb		30/11/99	Launceston, Tas	R	RM
Danni Wyatt	28	22/4/91	Stoke-on-Trent	R	ROS

WBBL03 MVP – Amy Satterthwaite

Out – Chamari Atapattu (SL – not retained), Kris Britt (retired), Hayley Jensen (NZ – not retained).

In – Danni Wyatt (England)

Australian Cricket Digest, 2018-19
MELBOURNE STARS
Coach: David Hemp

	No.	DOB	Place	Bat	Bwl/k
Kristen Beams	26	6/11/84	Launceston, Tas	R	LEG
Makinley Blows	15	12/12/97	Broken Hill, NSW	L	RM
Hayley Brennan	27	5/3/97	Dandenong, Vic	R	RM
Mignon du Preez (SA)	00	13/7/89	Pretoria, Sth Africa	R	
Georgia Elwiss (Eng)	34	31/3/91	Wolverhampton, UK	R	RM
Nicole Faltum	4	17/1/00	Traralgon, Vic	R	WK
Holly Ferling	9	22/12/95	Kingaroy, Qld	R	RMF
Emma Kearney	22	24/9/89	Hamilton, Vic	R	RM
Alana King	13	22/11/95	Clarinda, Vic	R	LEG
Lizelle Lee (SA)	67	2/4/92	Ermelo, Sth Africa	R	
Katie Mack	2	14/9/93	Melbourne	R	LEG
Katey Martin (NZ)	*21*	*7/2/85*	*Dunedin, NZ*	*R*	*WK*
Erin Osborne	76	27/6/89	Taree, NSW	R	ROS
Chloe Rafferty	7	16/6/99	Williamstown, Vic		RM
Annabel Sutherland	3	12/10/01	East Melbourne	R	RM
Gemma Triscari	8	24/1/90	Subiaco, WA	L	LM

WBBL03 MVP – Erin Osborne. In: Holly Ferling (Heat)

PERTH SCORCHERS
Coach: Lisa Keightley

	No.	DOB	Place	Bat	Bwl/k
Meg Banting	4	11/2/96	Subiaco, WA	R	WK
Nicole Bolton	12	17/1/89	Subiaco, WA	L	ROS
Katherine Brunt (Eng)	26	2/7/85	Barnsley, Eng	R	RMF
Mathilda Carmichael	5	4/4/94	St Leonards, Sydney	R	RM
Piepa Cleary	8	17/7/96	Subiaco, WA	R	RM
Lauren Ebsary	22	15/3/83	Snowtown, SA	R	RM
Heather Graham	11	10/5/96	Subiaco, WA	R	RM
Katie Hartshorn	16	20/6/94	Subiaco, WA	R	SLA
Mikayla Hinkley	1	1/5/98	Penrith, NSW	R	ROS
Emma King	2	25/3/92	Subiaco, WA	R	ROS
Meg Lanning	7	25/3/92	Singapore	R	RM
Thamsyn Newton (NZ)	79	3/6/95	Paraparaumu, NZ	R	RM
Chloe Piparo	28	5/9/94	Bunbury, WA	R	RS
Taneale Peschel	*23*	*29/8/94*	*Rockingham, WA*	*R*	*RM*
Nat Sciver	39	20/8/92	Tokyo, Japan	R	RM
Emily Smith	33	9/1/95	Sunshine, Vic	R	RM
Elyse Villani	3	6/10/89	Melbourne	R	RM

WBBL03 MVP – Katherine Brunt. In: Meg Lanning (Stars)

Australian Cricket Digest, 2018-19
SYDNEY SIXERS
Coach: Ben Sawyer

	No.	DOB	Place	Bat	Bwl/k
Sarah Aley	3	3/6/84	Sydney	R	RM
Erin Burns	29	22/6/88	Woollongong, NSW	R	RM
Lauren Cheatle	5	6/11/98	Sydney	L	LM
Sarah Coyte	14	30/3/91	Camden, NSW	R	RM
Ashleigh Gardner	6	15/4/97	Bankstown, NSW	R	ROS
Kim Garth	*34*	*25/4/96*	*Dublin, Ireland*	*R*	*RM*
Alyssa Healy	77	24/3/90	Gold Coast, Qld	R	WK
Jodie Hicks	*4*	*19/1/97*	*Hay, NSW*	*R*	*RM*
Clara Iemma	13	31/10/98	Beverley Hill, NSW	L	ROB
Marizanna Kapp (SA)	17	4/1/90	Port Elizabeth, SAF	R	RM
Amy Jones (Eng)	*40*	*12/6/93*	*Solihull, Yorks, Eng*	*R*	*WK*
Carly Leeson	74	9/11/98		R	RM
Emily Leys	9	18/2/93	Gunnedah, NSW	L	LM
Sara McGlashan	28	28/3/82	Napier, NZ	R	WK
Ellyse Perry	8	3/11/90	Wahroonga, NSW	R	RMF
Angela Reakes	*33*	*27/12/90*	*Byron Bay, NSW*	*R*	*LEG*
Lauren Smith	2	6/10/96	Central Coast, NSW	R	ROS
Dane Van Niekerk (SA)	23	14/5/93	Pretoria, Sth Africa	R	LEG

WBBL03 MVP – Ellyse Perry

SYDNEY THUNDER
Coach: Joanne Broadbent

	No.	DOB	Place	Bat	Bwl/k
Sam Bates	34	17/8/92	Newcastle, NSW	R	SLA
Alex Blackwell ©	2	31/8/83	Wagga Wagga, NSW	R	RM
Nicola Carey	5	10/9/93	Sydney	L	RM
Hannah Darlington	*25*	*25/1/01*		*R*	*RM*
Renee Farrell	*88*	*13/1/87*	*Kogarah, NSW*	*R*	*RMF*
Maisy Gibson	13	14/9/96	Singleton, NSW	L	LEG
Lisa Griffith	*54*	*28/8/92*	*Bathurst, NSW*	*R*	*RM*
Rachael Haynes	15	26/12/86	Carlton, Vic	L	LM
Harmanprett Kaur (Ind)	45	8/3/89	Moga, Punjab, India	R	RM
Rachel Priest (NZ)	3	13/6/85	New Plymouth, NZ	R	WK
Naomi Stalenburg	10	19/4/94	Blacktown, NSW	R	RM
Stafanie Taylor (WI)	24	11/6/81	Spanish Town, Jamaica	R	ROS
Rachel Trenaman	46	18/4/01		R	LEG
Hannah Trethewy		*18/1/99*		*R*	*RM*
Belinda Vakarewa	47	22/1/00	Griffith, NSW	R	RM
Fran Wilson	*35*	*7/11/91*	*Farnham, England*	*R*	*ROS*

WBBL03 MVP – Rachael Haynes

348

AUSTRALIAN CRICKET HALL OF FAME

Name	Inducted	Career	Details
Jack Blackham	1996	1877-1894	35 Tests, 800 runs at 15.69, 37 ct/24 st
Fred Spofforth	1996	1877-1887	18 Tests, 94 wickets at 18.41, Best 7-44
Victor Trumper	1996	1899-1912	48 Tests, 3163 runs at 39.05, HS 214*
Clarrie Grimmett	1996	1925-1936	37 Tests, 216 wickets at 24.22, Best 7-40
Bill Ponsford	1996	1924-1934	29 Tests, 2122 runs at 48.23, HS 266
Sir Donald Bradman	1996	1928-1948	52 Tests, 6996 runs at 99.94, HS 334
Bill O'Reilly	1996	1932-1946	27 Tests, 144 wickets at 22.59, Best 7-54
Keith Miller	1996	1946-1956	55 Tests, 2958 runs at 36.98, HS 147, 170 wkts at 22.98
Ray Lindwall	1996	1946-1960	61 Tests, 1502 runs at 21.15, HS 118, 228 wkts at 23.03
Dennis Lillee	1996	1971-1984	70 Tests, 355 wickets at 23.92, Best 7-83
Warwick Armstrong	2000	1902-1921	50 Tests, 2863 runs at 38.69, HS 159*, 87 wkts at 33.60
Neil Harvey	2000	1948-1963	79 Tests, 6149 runs at 48.42, Best 205
Allan Border	2000	1979-1994	156 Tests, 11174 runs at 50.56, Best 205
			ICC World Cup winning captain 1987
Bill Woodfull	2001	1926-1934	35 Tests, 2300 runs at 46.00, HS 161
Arthur Morris	2001	1946-1955	46 Tests, 3533 runs at 46.49, HS 206
Greg Chappell	2002	1971-1984	87 Tests, 7110 runs at 53.86, HS 247*
Stan McCabe	2002	1930-1938	39 Tests, 2748 runs at 48.21, HS 232
Ian Chappell	2003	1964-1980	75 Tests, 5345 runs at 42.42, HS 196
Lindsay Hassett	2003	1938-1953	43 Tests, 3073 runs at 46.56, HS 198*
Hugh Trumble	2004	1890-1904	32 Tests, 851 runs at 19.79, HS 70, 141 wkts at 21.79
Alan Davidson	2004	1953-1963	44 Tests, 1328 runs at 24.59, 186 wickets at 20.53
Clem Hill	2005	1896-1912	49 Tests, 3412 runs at 39.22, HS 191
Rod Marsh	2005	1970-1984	96 Tests, 3633 runs at 26.52, HS 132, 343 ct/12 st
Bob Simpson	2006	1957-1978	62 Tests, 4869 runs at 46.82, HS 311
Monty Noble	2006	1898-1909	42 Tests, 1997 runs at 30.26, HS 133, 121 wkts at 25.00
Charlie Macartney	2007	1907-1926	35 Tests, 2131 runs at 41.78, HS 170, 45 wickets at 27.56
Richie Benaud	2007	1952-1964	63 Tests, 2201 runs at 24.46, 248 wickets at 27.03
George Giffen	2008	1881-1896	31 Tests, 1238 runs at 23.35, 103 wickets at 27.09
Ian Healy	2008	1988-1999	119 Tests, 4356 runs at 30.22, HS 161* (366 ct/29 st)
Steve Waugh	2009	1985-2004	168 Tests, 10927 runs at 51.06, HS 200, 92 wickets
			ICC World Cup winning captain 1999
Bill Lawry	2010	1961-1971	67 Tests, 5234 runs at 47.15, Best 210
Graham McKenzie	2010	1961-1971	60 Tests, 246 wickets at 29.78, Best 8-71
Mark Taylor	2011	1988-1999	104 Tests, 7525 runs at 43.49, HS 334*
Doug Walters	2011	1965-1981	74 Tests, 5357 runs at 48.26, HS 250, 49 wickets at 29
Shane Warne	2012	1992-2007	145 Tests, 708 wickets at 25.41, Best 8-71
			ICC World Cup win in 1999
Glenn McGrath	2013	1993-2007	124 Tests, 563 wickets at 21.64, Best 8-24
			ICC World Cup wins in 1999, 2003 & 2007
Charlie Turner	2013	1997-1895	17 Tests, 101 wickets at 16.53, Best 7-43
Belinda Clark	2014	1990-2005	15 Tests, 919 runs at 45.95, HS 136
			ICC World Cup winning skipper in 1997
Mark Waugh	2014	1988-2004	128 Tests, 8029 runs at 41.81, HS 153*
			ICC World Cup win in 1999
Jack Ryder	2015	1912-1932	20 Tests, 1394 runs at 51.62, HS 201*
Adam Gilchrist	2015	1999-2008	96 Tests, 5570 runs at 47.60, HS 204*, 379 ct/37 st
			ICC World Cup wins in 1999, 2003 & 2007
Wally Grout	2016	1946-1966	51 Tests, 890 runs at 12.81, 163 ct, 24 st
Jeff Thomson	2016	1974-1986	51 Tests, 200 wickets at 28.00
David Boon	2017	1984-1996	107 Tests, 7422 runs at 43.56, HS 200
			ICC World Cup win 1987
Matthew Hayden	2017	1993-2009	103 Tests, 8625 runs at 50.73, HS 380
Betty Wilson	2017	1948-1958	11 Tests, 862 runs at 57.46, 68 wkts at 11.80, Best 7-7
Norman O'Neill	2018	1958-1965	42 Tests, 2779 runs at 45.55, HS 181
Ricky Ponting	2018	1995-2012	168 Tests, 13378 runs at 51.85, HS 257, 41 tons
			ICC World Cup wins in 1999, 2003 ©, 2007 ©
Karen Rolton	2018	1995-2009	14 Tests (1002 runs @ 55) 141 ODIs (4814 @ 48)
			ICC World Cup wins in 1997 & 2005

Australian Cricket Digest, 2018-19
Miscellaneous info ahead of 2018-19
CRICKET AUSTRALIA UMPIRES PANEL (Stats for on-field matches only)

	State	DOB Date of Birth	Matches Shield	umpired DOD	BBL
Gerard Abood	NSW	28-2-1972	47	38	54
Shawn Craig	VIC	23-6-1973	18	13	25
Greg Davidson	NSW	7-11-1970	16	15	23
Phillip Gillespie	VIC	23-10-1975	15	13	20
Mike Graham-Smith	TAS	5-8-1969	21	14	31
Geoff Joshua	VIC	12-3-1970	45	39	48
Simon Lightbody	NSW	26-9-1964	7	4	7
Sam Nogajski	TAS	1-1-1979	30	24	34
John Ward	VIC	27-4-1962	60	55	49
Tony Wilds	NSW	1-11-1963	10	9	9
Paul Wilson	NSW	12-1-1972	39	38	49
Elite Umpires					
Simon Fry	SA	29-7-1966	67	58	47
Bruce Oxenford	Qld	5-3-1960	52	35	14
Paul Reiffel	Vic	19-4-1966	41	39	23
Rod Tucker	NSW	28-8-1964	26	19	13
Not retained or used 2017-18 (late decision to retire)					
Mick Martell	WA	28-9-1966	42	37	32

Development Umpire Panel Members for 2018-19

	State	Date of Birth	Matches Shield	umpired DOD	BBL
Darren Close	Tas	31-3-1968	17	2	0
Nathan Johnstone	WA	8-10-1980	0	4	0
Donovan Kock	Qld	11-10-1976	0	2	0
Claire Polosak	NSW	7-4-1988	0	1	0
David Shepard	Vic	30-10-1970	0	0	0
Ben Treloar	NSW	12-7-1982	0	0	0

National Referees Panel – Steve Bernard, Daryl Harper, Peter Marshall, Bob Parry, Bob Stratford and David Talalla.

Supplementary Referees Panel: John Biddiss, Tim Donahoo, Neil Findlay, Dave Gilbert, Kent Hannam, Damian Herft, David Johnston, Terry Prue, Ian Thomas, Kepler Wessels.

Cricket Australia's umpiring panels are chosen by a selection panel consisting of Match Referees & Umpire Selection Manager Simon Taufel, former ICC Elite Panel Umpire Steve Davis, and Match Officials Manager Sean Easey.

CRICKET AUSTRALIA AWARDS 2017-18

Sheffield Shield Player of the Year: Chris Tremain (Vic) 13 votes, then Jackson Bird (Tas) and Nick Winter (SA) on 12.

Matador Cup Player of the year: Shaun Marsh (WA)

Benaud Spirit of Cricket Awards: Mens – Queensland, Womens – Victoria

ACA One-Day Interstate All*Star Team of the Year: Nic Maddinson (NSW), Daniel Hughes (NSW), Usman Khawaja (Qld), Shaun Marsh (WA), George Bailey (Captain, Tas), Peter Handscomb (Vic), Michael Neser (Qld), Sean Abbott (NSW), Jhye Richardson (WA), Joe Mennie (SA), Fawad Ahmed (Vic), Michael Klinger (WA – 12th man)

ACA Sheffield Shield All*Star Team of the Year: Joe Burns (Qld), Marcus Harris (Vic), Glenn Maxwell (Vic), Callum Ferguson (SA), Travis Head (captain, SA), Jake Doran (Tas), Matthew Wade (Tas, WK), Michael Neser (Qld), Chris Tremain (Vic), Jackson Bird (Tas), Nick Winter (SA), Tom Rogers (Tas, 12th man)

ACA Big Bash League All*Star Team of the Year: D'Arcy Short (Hurricanes), Alex Carey (Keeper, Strikers), Shane Watson (Thunder) Cameron White (Captain, Renegades), Glenn Maxwell (Stars), Tom Cooper (Renegades), Ashton Turner (Scorchers), Jofra Archer (Hurricanes), Rashid Khan (Strikers), Andrew Tye (Scorchers), Fawad Ahmed (Thunder), Dwayne Bravo (12th man - Renegades)

Lord's Taverners Indigenous Cricketer of the Year: D'Arcy Short (Western Australia and Hobart Hurricanes)

Cricket Australia Umpire Award: Paul Wilson

ACA WBBL All*Star Team of the Year: Beth Mooney (Keeper, Heat), Elyse Villani (Scorchers), Ellyse Perry (Sixers), Rachael Haynes (Thunder), Suzie Bates (Captain, Strikers), Amy Satterthwaite (Hurricanes), Sophie Devine (Strikers), Katherine Brunt (Scorchers), Marizanne Kapp (Sixers), Sarah Aley (Sixers), Rene Farrell (Thunder), Samantha Bates (Thunder – 12th)

ACA WNCL All*Star Team of the Year:

Nicole Bolton (WA), Elyse Villani (WA), Rachael Haynes (Captain, NSW), Sophie Devine (SA), Ellyse Perry (NSW), Alex Blackwell (NSW), Alyssa Healy (WK, NSW), Nicola Carey (NSW), Kate Cross (WA), Kristen Beams (Vic), Rene Farrell (NSW), Sophie Molineux (NSW)

Australian Cricket Digest, 2018-19
MCC World Cricket committee statements - Tuesday 7th August 2018

Key outcomes: Pace of play a concern and needs further scrutiny
Protection for bowlers must be considered
MCC to assist the Global Cricket Strategy and ICC Global Development Strategy
Prospect of MCC touring Zimbabwe to be explored
The MCC World Cricket committee met at Lord's on Monday 6th and Tuesday 7th August.
ICC Chief Executive David Richardson, ICC Head of Global Development William Glenwright, FICA representative Tom Moffat and ECB Chief Commercial Officer Sanjay Patel were present for certain parts of the meeting having been invited to address the committee.

Chairman Mike Gatting said, "It's been a very constructive two days, not least because the relationship between MCC and ICC has been strengthened as a result. The presentations we received, together with David Richardson's 2018 MCC Spirit of Cricket Cowdrey Lecture, emphasised the opportunities that exist for our two organisations to work together and I look forward to developing that relationship further.

"The input from FICA provided useful insights into the current perspectives of professional players globally and the committee was reassured to hear from ECB about the current plans for its new tournament.

"The meeting was also notable as it was the last for Rod Marsh, who is retiring after six years on the committee, during which time he's given us many a good steer."

The main outcomes of the meeting are as follows:

Zimbabwe

After hearing reports from ICC Chief Executive David Richardson, and Vintcent van der Bijl (MCC World Cricket committee member and a consultant to Zimbabwe Cricket), the World Cricket committee agreed that the measures put in place by ICC had created a more positive environment for Zimbabwe Cricket and that there was cause for optimism for the future. It was also noted that the World Cup qualifying tournament in Zimbabwe, which included Scotland and Ireland, was completed successfully.

MCC has observed the outcome of recent elections and has taken advice from the Foreign and Commonwealth Office (FCO) and ECB regarding the possibility of touring Zimbabwe. No objections have been received. The committee was in agreement that MCC should continue to monitor the situation and should consider sending a team to tour Zimbabwe once conditions were right. The strength of the team should be decided in consultation with Zimbabwe Cricket so as to provide the most helpful opposition to create opportunities for the appropriate level of cricketers.

Global Cricket Strategy

The World Cricket committee welcomed the opportunity to hear from ICC Chief Executive David Richardson and General Manager – Strategic Communications Claire Furlong about the Global Cricket Strategy, and to be one of the stakeholders which is invested in the progress of the plan. The committee was interested to hear some of the statistics which have emerged from ICC's recent global market research project, which indicate that 64% of cricket fans continue to be supportive of all three formats of the sport (Test, ODIs and T20). The committee particularly welcomed the news that 87% of respondents to ICC's recent survey supported cricket in the Olympics, and that it was a goal for ICC to have T20 included in the 2028 Olympic Games. The World Cricket committee has indicated its support in the past for the inclusion of cricket for both men and women in the Olympics, and will do whatever it can to assist ICC in its endeavours, especially in regards to staging compelling cricket matches and supporting the spirit of the game. The committee also noted that women's cricket hopes to be included in the programme for the 2022 Commonwealth Games in Birmingham, which it views as a very positive step.

Cricket's culture

The World Cricket committee debated the future of cricket's culture in the light of the ball tampering incident during the South Africa v Australia series in March and escalating misconduct on the field which has sparked the recent scrutiny of what is meant by the "spirit of cricket". The committee believes that a holistic approach is required, starting with international boards taking responsibility for the conduct of their teams, as well as the scheduling of touring programmes to ensure that visiting teams are adequately prepared. This extends to pitch preparation, provision of net bowlers and player socialising.

Women's cricket

The committee heard from New Zealand captain (and committee member) Suzie Bates, as well as from the ICC about the inclusion of women's cricket in the Global Cricket Strategy. The news was universally welcomed that an ICC Women's cricket committee, to be responsible for all playing conditions and cricket playing activity, would be set up. The committee recognised the need to continue to grow the base below international cricket, to prevent the widening of the gap between the nations which can afford to pay its players, and those that currently can't.

Pace of play

The World Cricket committee thanked ICC for sharing its statistical trends data, which is an invaluable tool to help, amongst other things, to track the balance between bat and ball, the volume of cricket and pace of play.

After reviewing the trends for the past twelve months, the committee expressed concern that over rates in Test and T20 formats had slowed down (Test over rates are the lowest for 11 years and T20 have fallen to their lowest ever level). The committee discussed various possible measures to improve the pace of play, including adopting a "shot clock" from the moment a bowler reached the top of his mark to the moment the over was completed as well as captains taking greater responsibility. The committee was encouraged by indications that ICC will be reviewing measures to improve the pace of play across the board and will continue to monitor the trend.

Laws of Cricket

The committee discussed feedback received about Law 41.7 concerning above waist-high full tosses. This amendment to the Laws, which was incorporated in October 2017 and which sees a bowler removed from the attack after two such deliveries, has been poorly received at various levels of the game; in many cases, it is being ignored or overwritten by playing conditions. The committee supported the recommendation from the Laws sub-committee that the Club should review this Law at the earliest opportunity.

Protection for bowlers (and all players)

The committee viewed footage of recent accidents involving bowlers who had been hit immediately after completing their delivery by powerful straight drives, especially in T20 cricket. The incidents, including one involving Nottinghamshire's Luke Fletcher last year, gave serious cause for concern. ECB and MCC have been in discussions to launch a design project for manufacturers to develop head protection for bowlers and the committee is supportive of this move. It was also felt that a review of existing protection for batsmen and fielders should be conducted to ensure that current models are providing the best possible protection.

ICC Global Development Strategy

The committee considered the insights shared by ICC Head of Global Development William Glenwright. In support of the strategy, MCC will work with ICC to identify countries that would benefit from its touring programme and other meaningful interventions such as coaching, pitch preparation and umpire tuition. The Club is also very willing to share its resources, for example its e-learning platform for umpires.

New formats

Sanjay Patel, Chief Commercial Officer and Managing Director, New Competition of ECB, addressed the committee to share the concept of The Hundred, ECB's proposed new competition which is due to launch in 2020. The committee was reassured that the new competition would still be a recognisable form of cricket and commended ECB for its desire to seek new audiences for the sport.

Thoughts from departing committee member, Rod Marsh

Rod Marsh stated that it had been an honour and a privilege to serve on the committee over the past six years and listed some of the key topics covered during that time, which include:

• Day/night Test cricket

• Corruption in cricket, which seems to be less of an issue now than it was when he first joined the committee

• Governance

• Universal adoption of DRS

• Limiting the size of bats to help the balance between bat and ball

GILLESPIE SPORTS CRICKET ACADEMY
Under 16 tour to South Africa – April 2018

At Groenkloff Ground, Pretoria on April 15, 2018 — 50 over match. Match Rained out
Africaans Hoers Seuns Skool 5-327 (A Ward 3-45) drew with Gillespie Sports 5-63
At Sinoville Oval, Pretoria, on 16th April 2018 – 40 over match. Centurion High School won by 6 wickets
Gillespie Sports 122 (J Ramage 55) lost to Centurion H.S 4-124
At Groenkloff Ground, Pretoria on April 17, 2018 - Twenty 20 match. Hoerskool Waterkloff won by 5 wickets
Gillespie Sports 5-117 (J Ramage 42, D Herriot 28) lost to Waterkloof 5-123 (J Bastian 3-24)
At Groenkloff Ground, Pretoria on April 17, 2018 - Twenty 20 match. Menlo Park HS won by 7 wickets
Gillespie Sports 6-99 (A Ward 25) lost to Menlo Park H.S. 3-100
At Groenkloff Ground, Pretoria on April 18, 2018 – 50 over match. Menlo Park HS won by 4 wickets
Gillespie Sports 6-209 (A Ward 74, J Ramage 27, J Bastian 26*) lost to Menlo Park H.S. 6-210 (H.Edey 3-21)
At Distell Oval, Stellenbosch on April 26, 2018 v Paul Roos Gymnasium Skool rained off without a ball bowled.
At Distell Oval, Stellenbosch on April 29, 2018 – 50 over match. CSA Tygerburgh RPA won by 216 runs.
CSA 258 (O Blizzard 4-34, J Bastian 3-38, H Edey 2-29) def Gillespie Sports 42

AVERAGES	M	I	NO	Runs	HS	Ave	Ct/St	O	M	R	W	Ave	Econ
Michael Arnold	6	6	3	47	14*	15.66	3	1	0	12	0		12.00
Jack Bastian	6	6	3	40	26*	13.33	1	34	2	154	9	17.10	4.52
Luca Bernardi	6	6	0	36	11	6.00	2						
Jack Billing	6	3	1	11	5*	5.50	3	15	0	111	2	55.50	7.40
Ollie Blizzard	5	1	0	0	0	0.00	1	22	0	157	5	37.40	7.13
Heath Edey	5	1	0	5	5	5.00	-	22.2	1	119	5	23.80	5.36
Darcy Herriot	6	6	0	61	28	10.16	-	13	0	64	0		4.92
Lachlan Hoy	6	6	0	53	17	8.83	-	23.4	2	110	4	27.50	4.70
Michael Parker	4	2	1	0	0*	0.00	1	15	0	138	2	69.00	9.20
Jack Ramage	6	6	0	154	55	25.66	5/1						
Adam Ward	6	6	0	107	74	17.83	3	22	0	134	4	33.50	6.09
Charlie Warner	6	2	0	1	1	0.50	1	18	0	130	1	130.00	7.22

Australian Cricket Digest, 2018-19
FIXTURES 2018-19

* Indicates some or all match under lights

AUSTRALIAN v PAKISTAN IN UAE

Oct 7-11	1st Test	Dubai
Oct 16-20	2nd Test	Dubai
Tue Oct 23 *	1st T20	Dubai
Thu Oct 25 *	2nd T20	Dubai
Sat Oct 28 *	3rd T20	Dubai

SOUTH AFRICA IN AUSTRALIA
all exclusively LIVE on FOX

Wed Oct 31 *	PM XI	Manuka Oval
Sun Nov 4 *	1st ODI	Perth Stadium
Fri Nov 9 *	2nd ODI	Adelaide Oval
Sun Nov 11 *	3rd ODI	Bellerive Oval
Sat Nov 17 *	Only T20	Cararra, Gold Coast

INDIA IN AUSTRALIA
T20s/ODIs LIVE EXCLUSIVE on FOX
Tests on FOX/Seven

Wed Nov 21 *	1st T20	Gabba
Fri Nov 23 *	2nd T20	MCG
Sun Nov 25 *	3rd T20	SCG
Nov 29-Dec 1	CA XI	SCG
Dec 6-10	1st Test	Adelaide Oval
Dec 14-18	2nd Test	Perth Stadium
Dec 26-30	3rd Test	MCG
Jan 3-7	4th Test	SCG
Sat Jan 12 *	1st ODI	SCG
Tue Jan 15 *	2nd ODI	Adelaide Oval
Fri Jan 18 *	3rd ODI	MCG

SRI LANKA IN AUSTRALIA

Jan 17-19 *	CA XI	Bellerive Oval
Jan 24-28 *	1st Test	Gabba
Feb 1-5	2nd Test	Manuka Oval

JLT CUP
* Some part floodlit, + TV via FOX SPORTS

Sun Sep 16	Qld v Vic	Townsville
Tue Sep 18 *	WA v NSW +	WACA
Wed Sep 19	Tas v Vic	Townsville
Thu Sep 20 *	SA v NSW +	WACA
Sat Sep 22	Qld v Tas	Townsville
Sat Sep 22 *	WA v SA +	WACA
Sun Sep 23	NSW v Vic +	North Sydney
Sun Sep 25	SA v Qld	Hurstville Oval
Tue Sep 25 *	NSW v Tas +	North Sydney
Wed Sep 26	Vic v WA +	Junction Oval
Thu Sep 27	SA v Tas	Bankstown Oval
Fri Sep 28	WA v Qld	Hurstville Oval
Sun Sep 30	Vic v SA +	Junction Oval
Mon Oct 1	Tas v WA	Hurstville Oval
Mon Oct 1 *	NSW v Qld +	Drummoyne Oval
Wed Oct 3 *	Playoff 3 v 6 +	North Sydney
Thu Oct 4 *	Playoff 4 v 5 +	Drummoyne Oval
Sat Oct 6 *	Semi-Final +	Drummoyne Oval
Sun Oct 7	Semi-Final +	Junction Oval
Wed Oct 10	The Final +	Junction Oval

BIG BASH LEAGUE 08 - All live on FOX SPORTS
43 Live Games on 7 Network

+ indicates 16 Exclusive Fox games +

* Indicates played as a DAY game

Wed Dec 19	Heat v Strikers	Gabba
Thu Dec 20	Renegades v Scorchers	Marvel St
Fri Dec 21	Thunder v Stars	Canberra
Sat Dec 22	Sixers v Scorchers +*	SCG
	Heat v Hurricanes +	Gabba
Sun Dec 23	Strikers v Renegades	Adel Oval
Mon Dec 24	Hurricanes v Stars +*	Bellerive
	Thunder v Sixers	Syd Show
Wed Dec 26	Scorchers v Strikers	Perth Stad
Thu Dec 27	Sixers v Stars	SCG
Fri Dec 28	Hurricanes v Thunder	Bellerive
Sat Dec 29	Renegades v Sixers +	Marvel St
Sun Dec 30	Hurricanes v Scorchers	York Park
Mon Dec 31	Strikers v Thunder	Adel Oval
Tue Jan 1	Heat v Sixers *	Gold Coast
	Stars v Renegades	MCG
Wed Jan 2	Thunder v Scorchers	Syd Show
Thu Jan 3	Renegades v Strikers	Geelong
Fri Jan 4	Hurricanes v Sixers	Bellerive
Sat Jan 5	Stars v Thunder +	MCG
	Scorchers v Heat +	Perth Stad
Sun Jan 6	Strikers v Sixers	Adel Oval
Mon Jan 7	Renegades v Hurricanes	Marvel St
Tue Jan 8	Thunder v Heat	Syd Show
Wed Jan 9	Stars v Scorchers	MCG
Thu Jan 10	Heat v Renegades	Gabba
Fri Jan 11	Strikers v Stars +	Adel Oval
Sun Jan 13	Thunder v Strikers +	Syd Show
	Renegades v Heat	Geelong
	Scorchers v Sixers	Perth Stad
Mon Jan 14	Stars v Hurricanes	MCG
Wed Jan 16	Sixers v Renegades	SCG
Thu Jan 17	Heat v Thunder	Gabba
Fri Jan 18	Scorchers v Hurricanes +	Perth Stad
Sat Jan 19	Renegades v Stars +	Marv St
Sun Jan 20	Sixers v Heat	SCG
Mon Jan 21	Strikers v Hurricanes	Adel Oval
Tue Jan 22	Thunder v Renegades	Syd Show
Wed Jan 23	Stars v Strikers *	Moe (TBC)
	Sixers v Hurricanes	SCG
Thu Jan 24	Scorchers v Thunder	Perth Stad
Sun Jan 27	Stars v Heat	MCG
Mon Jan 28	Scorchers v Renegades	Perth Stad
Tue Jan 29	Hurricanes v Heat +	Bellerive
	Sixers v Strikers +	SCG
Wed Jan 30	Renegades v Strikers +	Marvel St
Thu Jan 31	Hurricanes v Strikers	York Park
Fri Feb 1	Heat v Scorchers	Gabba
Sat Feb 2	Sixers v Thunder +	SCG
Sun Feb 3	Strikers v Heat +	Adel Oval
	Scorchers v Stars	Perth Stad
Thu Feb 7	Hurricanes v Renegades	Bellerive
Fri Feb 8	Heat v Stars	Gabba
Sat Feb 9	Strikers v Scorchers *	Alice Spr
	Thunder v Hurricanes +	TBC
Sun Feb 10	Stars v Sixers *	MCG
Thu Feb 14	First Semi Final	TBC
Fri Feb 15	Second Semi Final	TBC
Sun Feb 17	Big Final 08 *	TBC

This schedule is current as at 31 August, 2018. Cricket Australia reserves the right in its absolute discretion to change or amend the program at any time, without notice.

Australian Cricket Digest, 2018-19

SHEFFIELD SHIELD - Qld 10.00 start; all others 10.30

Oct 16-19	SA v NSW	Adelaide Oval
	Qld v Tas	Gabba
	WA v Vic	WACA
Oct 25-28	Vic v NSW	MCG
	SA v Qld	Adelaide Oval
	WA v Tas	WACA
Nov 3-6	NSW v Tas	TBC
	Vic v SA	MCG
	Qld v WA	A B Field
Nov 16-19	NSW v Qld	Manuka Oval
	SA v WA	Adelaide Oval
Nov 17-20	Tas v Vic	Bellerive Oval
Nov 27-30	Tas v SA	Bellerive Oval
	Qld v Vic	Gabba
	WA v NSW	Perth Stadium
Dec 7-10	Vic v WA	MCG
	NSW v SA	SCG
	Tas v Qld	Bellerive Oval
Feb 23-26	Vic v Qld	Junction Oval
	NSW v WA	TBC
	SA v Tas	Adelaide Oval
March 3-6	Vic v Tas	MCG
	Qld v NSW	Gabba
	WA v SA	WACA
March 11-14	NSW v Vic	TBC
	Qld v SA	Gabba
	Tas v WA	Bellerive Oval
March 20-23	Tas v NSW	Bellerive Oval
	SA v Vic	K. Rolton Oval
	WA v Qld	WACA
Mar 28-Apr 1	The Final	TBA (Fox)

WOMENS CRICKET
NEW ZEALAND IN AUSTRALIA

Sat Sep 29 *	1st T20 7	North Sydney Oval
Mon Oct 1	2nd T20 7	Allan Border Field
Fri Oct 5 *	3rd T20 7	Manuka Oval
Fri Feb 22	1st ODI 7	WACA
Sun Feb 24	2nd ODI 7	Karen Rolton Oval
Thu Feb 28	Gov Gen XI Fox	Drummoyne
Sun March 3	3rd ODI 7	Junction Oval

ICC WORLD TWENTY20 in WEST INDIES
Australian schedule – Group A (Fox Sports)

Fri Nov 9	Aust v Pakistan	Guyana
Sun Nov 11	Aust v Ireland	Guyana
Tue Nov 13	Aust v NZ	Guyana
Sat Nov 17	Aust v India	Guyana
Thu Nov 22	First Semi	North Sound
Thu Nov 22	Second Semi	North Sound
Sat Nov 24	The Final	North Sound

WNCL – 50 over competition (CA Live streamed)

Fri Sep 21	Qld v NSW	Bill Pippen Oval
	Tas v ACT	Allan Border Field
	WA v Vic	Murdoch Uni
Sat Sep 22	Vic v SA	Murdoch Uni
Sun Sep 23	Tas v NSW	Bill Pippen Oval
	Qld v ACT	Allan Border Field
	WA v SA	Murdoch Uni
Fri Nov 9	Tas v Qld	TCA Ground
	NSW v WA	Blacktown ISP #1
	ACT v Vic	Manuka
Sat Nov 10	Qld v SA	TCA Ground
Sun Nov 11	ACT v WA	Manuka Oval
	NSW v Vic	Blacktown ISP #1
	Tas v SA	TCA Ground
Fri Feb 1	Tas v WA	Casey Fields
Fri Feb 1	Vic v Qld	Junction Oval
	SA v NSW	Karen Rolton Oval
Sat Feb 2	NSW v ACT	Karen Rolton Oval
Sun Feb 3	Qld v WA	Casey Fields
	Vic v Tas	Junction Oval
	SA v ACT	Karen Rolton Oval
Sat Feb 9	The Final	TBA

WBBL04
7 = Televised by Seven Network/Fox Simulcast

Sat Dec 1	Scorchers v Hurricanes 7	Junc Oval
	Stars v Sixers 7	Junc Oval
Sun Dec 2	Strikers v Heat 7	Junc Oval
	Renegades v Thunder 7	Junc Oval
Fri Dec 7	Sixers v Scorchers * 7	Nth Syd
Sat Dec 8	Hurricanes v Stars	Burnie
	Renegades v Strikers	Junc Oval
	Heat v Scorchers 7	Nth Syd
	Sixers v Thunder 7	Nth Syd
Sun Dec 9	Hurricanes v Stars	Burnie
	Renegades v Strikers	Junc Oval
	Thunder v Heat 7	Nth Syd
Sat Dec 15	Stars v Scorchers	Junc Oval
	Strikers v Thunder 7	Bellerive
	Hurricanes v Sixers	Bellerive
Sun Dec 16	Scorchers v Stars	WACA
	Thunder v Strikers	Bellerive
	Hurricanes v Sixers * 7	Bellerive
	Renegades v Heat	TBC
Tue Dec 18	Hurricanes v Scorchers	Bellerive
Wed Dec 19	Heat v Stars	Gabba
Fri Dec 21	Thunder v Hurricanes 7	Canberra
	Stars v Strikers	TBC
Sat Dec 22	Sixers v Heat	SCG
	Scorchers v Renegades *	WACA
Sun Dec 23	Strikers v Stars 7	Adel Oval
	Sixers v Heat	Hurstville
	Scorchers v Thunder	Lilac Hill
Mon Dec 24	Thunder v Hurricanes 7	Syd Show
Wed Dec 26	Scorchers v Heat * 7	Perth Stad
Thu Dec 27	Sixers v Renegades	SCG
Fri Dec 28	Sixers v Strikers	Hurstville
Sat Dec 29	Scorchers v Thunder	Lilac Hill
	Hurricanes v Heat	York Park
	Renegades v Stars	Marvel St
Sun Dec 30	Scorchers v Thunder	Perth Stad
	Hurricanes v Heat 7	York Park
Mon Dec 31	Strikers v Sixers 7	Adel Oval
Tue Jan 1	Stars v Renegades	MCG
Wed Jan 2	Thunder v Sixers 7	Syd Show
Thu Jan 3	Renegades v Hurr'cane 7	Geelong
Sat Jan 5	Thunder v Stars	Blacktown
	Heat v Strikers *	Mackay
Sun Jan 6	Thunder v Stars	Bankstown
	Heat v Renegades	Mackay
Tue Jan 8	Thunder v Renegades 7	Syd Show
	Strikers v Hurricanes	K Rolton Ov
Wed Jan 9	Strikers v Hurricanes	K Rolton Ov
Thu Jan 10	Heat v Stars 7	Gabba
Sat Jan 12	Strikers v Scorchers	Alice Spr
	Renegades v Hurricanes	Junc Oval
	Heat v Thunder *	Cairns
Sun Jan 13	Scorchers v Strikers	Alice Spr
	Renegades v Sixers	TBC
Mon Jan 14	Stars v Sixers 7	MCG
Sat Jan 19	First Semi Final 7	TBC
	Second Semi Final 7	TBC
Sat Jan 26	WBBL Final 04	TBC

ICC WORLD CUP, 2019

Thu May 30	Eng v Sth Africa	The Oval
Fri May 31	WI v Pakistan	Trent Bridge
Sat June 1	NZ v SL	Sophia Gardens
	Afgh v Aust	Bristol
Sun June 2	Sth Africa v Ban	The Oval
Mon June 3	Eng v Pakistan	Trent Bridge
Tue Jan 4	Afgh v SL	Sophia Gardens
Wed June 5	Sth Africa v Ind	The Rose Bowl
	Ban v NZ	The Oval
Thu June 6	Aust v WI	Trent Bridge
Fri June 7	Pak v SL	Bristol
Sat June 8	Eng v Ban	Sophia Gardens
	Afgh v NZ	Taunton
Sun June 9	Aus v Ind	The Oval
Mon June 10	Sth Afr v WI	The Rose Bowl
Tue June 11	Ban v SL	Bristol
Wed June 12	Aus v Pak	Taunton
Thu June 13	India v NZ	Trent Bridge
Fri June 14	Eng v WI	The Rose Bowl
Sat June 15	Aus v SL	The Oval
	Sth Africa v Afg	Sophie Gardens
Sun June 16	India v Pak	Old Trafford
Mon June 17	WI v Ban	Taunton
Tue June 18	Eng v Afgh	Old Trafford
Wed June 19	NZ v Sth Africa	Edgbaston
Thu June 20	Aust v Ban	Trent Bridge
Fri June 21	Eng v SL	Headingley
Sat June 22	India v Afgh	The Rose Bowl
	WI v NZ	Old Trafford
Sun June 23	Pak v Sth Africa	Lord's
Mon June 24	Ban v Afgh	The Rose Bowl
Tue June 25	Eng v Aus	Lord's
Wed June 26	NZ v Pak	Edgbaston
Thu June 27	WI v India	Old Trafford
Fri June 28	SL v Sth Africa	Riverside
Sat June 29	Pak v Afgh	Headingley
	Aust v NZ	Lord's
Sun June 30	Eng v India	Edgbaston
Mon July 1	SL v WI	Riverside
Tue July 2	Ban v Ind	Edgbaston
Wed July 3	Eng v NZ	Riverside
Thu July 4	Afgh v WI	Headingley
Fri July 5	Pak v Ban	Lord's
Sat July 6	SL v India	Headingley
	Aust v Sth Africa	Old Trafford
Tue July 9	First Semi	Old Trafford
Thu July 11	Second Semi	Edgbaston
Sun July 14	The Final	Lord's

THE ASHES – 2019

Aug 1-5	1st Test	Edgbaston, Birmingham
Aug 14-18	2nd Test	Lord's, London
Aug 22-26	3rd Test	Headingley, Leeds
Sep 4-8	4th Test	Old Trafford, Manchester
Sep 12-16	5th Test	The Oval, London

ICC FUTURE TOURS PROGRAM

Feb 2019 – Away to India for 5 ODIs & 2 T20s

March 2019 – Away for 5 ODIs v Pakistan

May 30-July 14, 2019 – ICC Cricket World Cup in England

July-Sep 2019 – 5 Ashes Tests in England

Oct 2019 – Away to Bangladesh for 3 T20s

Nov 2019 – Host Sri Lanka for 3 T20s

Nov 2019 – Host Pakistan for 2 Tests & 3 T20s

Dec 2019-Jan 2020 – Host New Zealand for 3 Tests & 3 ODIs

Jan 2020 – Away to India for 3 ODIs

Feb 2020 – Away to Bangladesh for 2 Tests

Feb-Mar 2020 – Away to South Africa for 3 ODIs & 3 T20s

Mar 2020 – Away to New Zealand for 3 T20s

June 2020 – Host Zimbabwe for 3 ODIs

July 2020 – Away to England for 3 ODIs & 3 T20s

October 2020 – Host West Indies for 3 T20s

October 2020 – Host India for 3 T20s

October-November 2020 – Host World T20 in Australia

November 2020 – Host Afghanistan for one off Test

Nov 2020 – Jan 2021 – Host India for 4 Tests & 3 ODIs

January 2021 – Host New Zealand for 3 ODIs

Feb-March 2021 – Away to South Africa for 3 Tests

March 2021 – Away to New Zealand for 3 T20s

June 2021 – World Test Championship final in England

June-July 2021 – 3 ODIs & 3 T20s in West Indies

Oct-Nov 2021 – World T20 in India

Nov 2021 – Dec 2012 – Host England for 5 Ashes Tests

Jan-Feb 2022 – Host South Africa for 3 ODIs & 3 T20s

IN PREVIOUS EDITIONS OF THE AUSTRALIAN CRICKET DIGEST
(Copies still available)

Volume 1 – 2012-13 Edition (312 pages)
1972 Ashes – 40 years on with Greg Chappell
Coaching Yorkshire – Jason Gillespie about coaching the famous club
Players of the season - Michael Clarke and Ben Hilfenhaus

Volume 2 – 2013-14 Edition (312 pages)
Darren Lehmann and Michael Vaughan review the 2013 Ashes
30 years on – Wayne Phillips reflects on two special tons
Players of the season - Michael Clarke and Ryan Harris

Volume 3 – 2014-15 Edition (280 pages)
Remembering Victor Trumper by David Frith
20 years on – Greg Blewett reflects on his ton in Test debut in Adelaide
Players of the season - Mitchell Johnson and Brad Haddin

Volume 4 – 2015-16 Edition (332 pages)
2015 Ashes analysed by Jason Gillespie, Tom Moody and Damien Fleming
Philip Hughes – a life cut short
Richie Benaud by Ric Finlay
1985-86 Rebel tours remembered by Doug Ackerley
Player of the season – Steve Smith

Volume 5 – 2016-17 Edition (312 pages)
Ryan Harris talks 2013-14 Ashes and coaching
Umpires in helmets
Australia in South Africa 1966-67 by David Jenkins
Players of the season – Adam Voges and Travis Head

Volume 6 – 2017-18 Edition (304 pages)
Obituaries – Max Walker and Drew Morphett
Jason Gillespie reflects on the 1997 Ashes
11 questions with Darren Lehmann
Graham Dawson nearly 50 years in the Media
Players of the season – Josh Hazlewood and Steve Smith

THANKS AGAIN FOR SUPPORTING THE DIGEST